MODERN MACROECONOMICS

THIRD EDITION

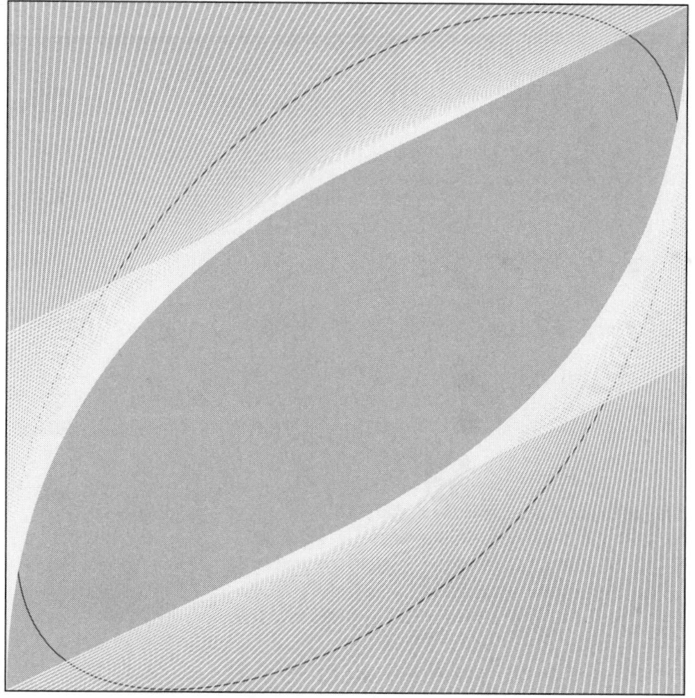

Michael Parkin
Robin Bade
UNIVERSITY OF WESTERN ONTARIO

Prentice-Hall Canada Inc., Scarborough, Ontario

Canadian Cataloguing in Publication Data
Parkin, Michael, 1939–
Modern macroeconomics

3rd ed.
Includes index.
ISBN 0-13-591140-0

1. Macroeconomics. 2. Canada—Economic conditions—1945– . I. Bade, Robin. II. Title.

HB172.5.P3 1992 339 C91-094634-5

Prentice Hall, Inc., Englewood Cliffs, New Jersey
Prentice-Hall International, Inc., London
Prentice-Hall of Australia, Pty., Ltd., Sydney
Prentice-Hall of India Pvt., Ltd., New Delhi
Prentice-Hall of Japan, Inc., Tokyo
Prentice-Hall of Southeast Asia (Pte.) Ltd., Singapore
Editora Prentice-Hall do Brasil Ltda., Rio de Janeiro
Prentice-Hall Hispanoamericana, S.A., Mexico

ISBN 0-13-591140-0

COVER ART:
GABO, Naum American, 1890–1977 (b. Russia)
Linear Construction in Space No. 1 1942–49
perspex with nylon
61.3 × 61.3 × 13.0 cm
ART GALLERY OF ONTARIO, TORONTO
Gift of the Volunteer Committee Fund, 1986

For Prentice-Hall Canada Inc.:

ACQUISITIONS EDITOR: Marjorie Walker
DEVELOPMENTAL AND PRODUCTION EDITOR: Maryrose O'Neill
PRODUCTION ASSISTANT: Anna Orodi
COVER AND INTERIOR DESIGN: Julian Cleva
TYPESETTING AND COMPOSITION: Compeer Typographic Services

Printed and bound in the USA by R.R. Donnelley & Sons Ltd.

1 2 3 4 5 RRD 96 95 94 93 92

To Richard

Contents

Table of Contents

PART II AGGREGATE DEMAND FLUCTUATIONS 87

Preface

TO MAKE THE MACROECONOMICS of the 1990s accessible to students of the 1990s. To enable today's students to understand today's macroeconomic issues and participate in the policy debate with confidence from a well-informed position. These are our goals in writing this book.

Perspective, Position, and Pedagogy

Modern Macroeconomics presents a clear and comprehensive account of the mainstream theories of economic fluctuations, inflation, unemployment, exchange rates, debts and deficits, fiscal and monetary policy, and global economic coordination and integration. It also presents a deeper look at the microeconomic foundations of these mainstream theories. Finally, it gives a guide to the new developments in macroeconomics and the current research agendas.

The dead debates of the past are not found in these pages. The live debates of the present (and future) *are* found here. But they are presented for what they are: scientific disagreements that conscientious, thoughtful, and creative scholars are attempting to resolve using normal methods of enquiry. No sides are taken—at least not consciously—and we have striven hard to suppress our own provisional guesses as to which of the competing views is likely to turn out to be right.

But this book is not a flat, featureless plain of knowledge and ideas. It is permeated with the point of view that macroeconomics is a mature social science that has made great progress in understanding its range of phenomena and that progress has been made by developing macroeconomic models—caricatures of real economies—and then confronting these models with the facts generated by real life experiments. This interplay between models, theories, and facts that has brought progress in our endeavor as macroeconomists forms the fundamental organizing principle of this book.

This third edition of *Modern Macroeconomics* is a radical revision of its predecessor. It is completely up-to-date; it is organized in a more streamlined and yet flexible way; it fully integrates the open economy and policy issues; and it has an expanded treatment of the microeconomic foundations of macroeconomics. But users of the previous edition will recognize the strengths of that edition here. We have tried to build on and consolidate those strengths.

Every chapter begins with a scene-setter—an overview of either some aspect of the real macroeconomy or a body of theory—and then proceeds to set out some facts to be explained (which we highlight as *MACROFACTS*). Following such a section, we proceed to develop and explain a relevant body of theory that explains (or purports to explain) the highlighted facts. This is followed with a return to the facts, sometimes the same facts, sometimes to new facts that "test" the theory (which we highlight as *TESTCASE*). This pattern is repeated as each chapter unfolds, sometimes several times within a single chapter.

The facts in question are those generated by our macroeconomic experience. Since this book is for students in universities and colleges in Canada, the experience of the Canadian economy dominates our selection of examples, especially when we deal with policy issues. But the globe is ever-shrinking, and we are now members of a world economy. Because of this, we have used a liberal sprinkling of examples from around the world, choosing the best example available to illustrate a particular idea or theory. (We are fortunate in having had the opportunity to live, work, and teach not only in Canada but also in the United States, Australia, Europe, and Japan, and have benefited enormously from the exposure this diversity has brought.)

The overwhelming thrust of this book is directed toward *understanding macroeconomic phenomena, not improving macroeconomic performance*. If the latter occurs as a result of this book's helping to create a better informed community of citizens and voters, we will not be disappointed. But our goal is enlightenment, not persuasion.

To Students

Uppermost in our minds in writing this book has been you, the student. We have written a book that we hope you will find not only informative, but also stimulating and interesting. To achieve this end, we have used a variety of pedagogic devices. They are

- Chapter opening scene-setter
- Chapter objectives
- Annotated and actively labeled figures
- Extended captions to figures
- Chapter summaries
- Highlighted key terms
- End of chapter key terms and concepts
- End of chapter review questions
- End of chapter problems
- Mathematical appendixes

When you begin a new chapter, read the scene-setter and objectives a couple of times and make sure you have a good sense of what the chapter contains and how it builds on what you've already studied. Then read the body of the chapter at a pace that enables you to follow the logic of what you are reading. Your aim is not to read and remember: it is to read and *understand*. Once you've understood something, you can't forget it even if you try!

This book contains a large number of figures and each figure has been designed to make your job easier. Be especially careful to "read" each figure along with the text that explains its action. And when you begin to "read" a figure pay careful attention to the labels on its axes. Some figures present facts; others explain theories. Many of those that present facts also show relationships among variables. In studying these figures, look for the patterns. The figures that present theories use color in a systematic way. Color highlights the action: the starting point is always black (or grey) and the ending point is always blue. Bold arrows, colored to match the shifting curves, emphasize the action that brought about the change. In studying these figures, keep this set of "color rules" in mind.

Most figures contain short notes or labels, highlighting key features of the figure. All the figures have an extended caption that gives a summary of the figure. When you have read the chapter twice and think you understand it, look again at each figure and read its caption. This will give you a quick review of the chapter and enable you to check your understanding.

After your first reading of a chapter, look at the end of chapter review. Check the chapter summary to see if you understand it. Check the key terms and concepts to see if you know them. Then attempt to answer the review questions. Make note of any question you can't answer and be especially on the lookout for its answer on your second reading of the chapter. When you think you're completely on top of the chapter, do the end of chapter problems.

The *Study Guide* provides you with even more insight into macroeconomics. For each chapter of the text, it contains learning objectives, summaries, multiple choice and true/false questions, worked problems, problems for you to work, and answers.

To Instructors

We've also had you, our colleagues, the teachers of macroeconomics, in mind. We know only too well that there remains a great deal of well-based and legitimate disagreement as to which aspects of macroeconomics are the most relevant and which order to unfold the complexities of this subject is best. To give you the maximum possible flexibility, we've written a book that can be used in a wide variety of orders. We've also consciously *not* presented the material in the order that most closely conforms to that in which we teach it. Instead, we have built in flexibility by placing later in the book most of the material that can be treated as optional.

Organization and Flexibility

The book contains *four main themes*. They are

- Microfoundations
- Core
- Policy
- International

The following organization and flexibility chart shows how the chapters handle these themes.

A logical sequence of core theory runs from Chapters 1 through 3 (introduction), Chapters 4 and 5 (the *IS-LM* model of aggregate demand), Chapters 8 through 10 (aggregate supply, unemployment, and growth), and Chapters 12 and 13 (inflation, deficits, and debts). But the order of the aggregate demand block together with its microfoundations, policy and international applications (Chapters 4, 5, 6, 7, 17, 18, and 19) and the aggregate supply block together with its microfoundations (Chapters 8, 9, 10, 20, and 21) may be reversed if desired.

Policy permeates the book and appears in many of the core chapters. But three chapters treat policy themes more explicitly. These can be done as a group after completing the core, or can be taken in their set order.

International examples also permeate the core chapters, but there are three complete open economy and international chapters. Again, these may be deferred until after completing the core, or can be taken in their set order.

The microfoundations of aggregate demand, Chapters 17 through 19, can be brought forward and studied immediately following Chapter 5. The microfoundations of aggregate supply (the "new macroeconomics"), Chapters 20 and 21, can be brought forward and studied immediately following Chapter 10.

Supplements are available to enhance your use of the text. They are

- *Instructor's Manual* which contains chapter outlines, chapter learning objectives, and the answers to all the questions in the text.

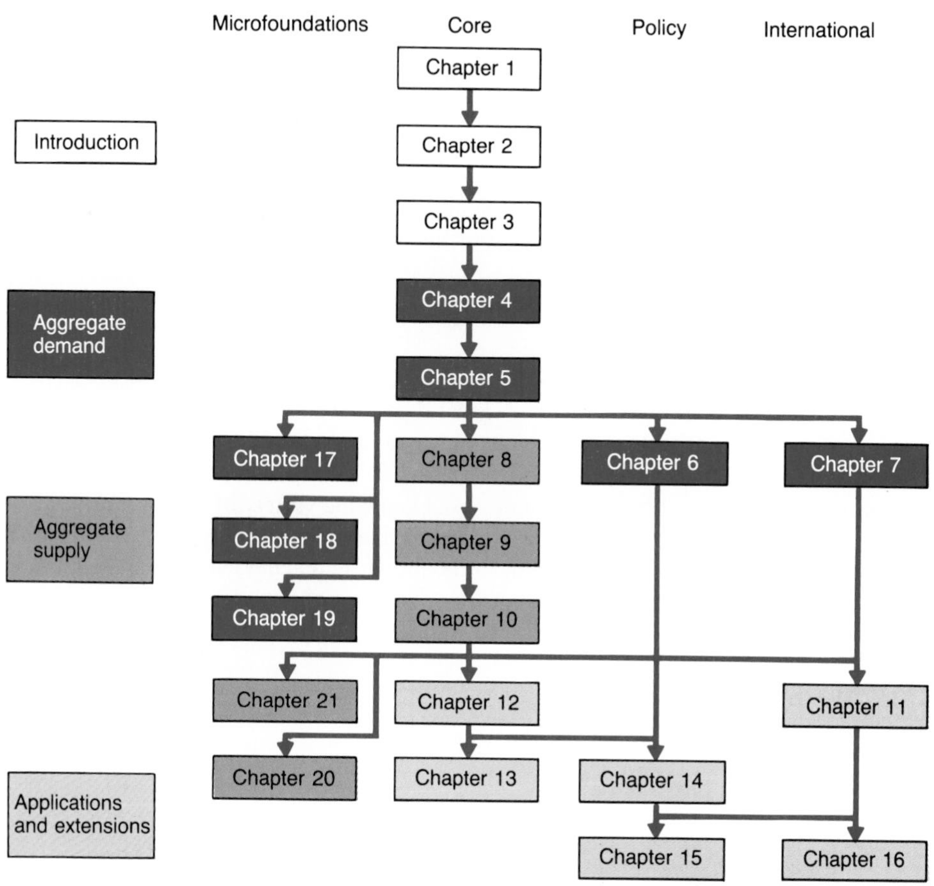

- *Test Item File*, a comprehensive bank of multiple choice, true/false, numerical problems, and short answer questions. Answers are provided, and all questions are page-referenced to the text.
- *Easytest*, a computerized version of the printed test bank. This test manager allows instructors to generate, edit, add to, and save tests. *Easytest* is available in both 5.25″and 3.5″ IBM formats.

Acknowledgments

We thank our students, the more than 4,000 undergraduates in ten universities, on four continents, to whom it has been our privilege to teach macroeconomics during the past 27 years. The instant feedback that comes from the look of puzzlement or excitement in the classroom has taught us how to teach this subject.

We have benefited from the help of a large number of colleagues who have commented on earlier drafts of this book, or the first edition from which it is an outgrowth. We are especially grateful to Valerie Bencivenga (Cornell University), Ronald Bodkin (University of Ottawa), Paul Booth (University of Alberta), Bruce Champ (University of Western Ontario), Jeremy Greenwood (University of Rochester), David Laidler (University of Western Ontario), John Lapp (North Carolina State University), Glenn MacDonald (University of Rochester), Andrea Maneschi (Vanderbilt University), Stephen Margolis (North Carolina State University), Sharon Pearson (University of Alberta),

Andrew Policano (University of Wisconsin at Madison), and Marco Terrones (Vanderbilt University). We are also indebted to the (anonymous) reviewers who read the entire manuscript.

We are grateful to our colleagues and students in the Department of Economics at the University of Western Ontario for providing us with the stimulation and opportunity to write this book.

We also thank Richard Parkin, who managed all the data and art files and whose energy and creativity contributed enormously to the clarity of the figures that appear in this diagram-intensive book; Jane McAndrew, who took the legwork out of our use of the University of Western Ontario library system; Barbara Craig, who loaded and edited and repeatedly re-edited the evolving manuscript; Marjorie Walker, an exceptional editor, who helped us fashion the book's major themes and directions; and finally, Maryrose O'Neill, our developmental and production editor, whose tireless and cheerful efforts and conscientious attention to detail have brought all the elements together to produce what you will find to be an extremely effective book.

Michael Parkin
Robin Bade
University of Western Ontario, London,
Ontario, Canada

I

Introduction

C H A P T E R

1 What Is Macroeconomics?

RIDING THE MACROECONOMIC WAVES

THE ECONOMY IS LIKE AN INCOMING TIDE. It moves in one general direction but at an ever changing pace, ebbing and flowing, rising and falling, familiar yet impossible to predict. Every day we live the life of a surfer riding this tide and on some days the surf is especially rough. One such day was October 19, 1987, when the Canadian and world stock markets crashed, wiping billions of dollars off share values. Another was August 2, 1990, when Saddam Hussein's tanks rolled into Kuwait City and world oil and stock markets gave a violent reaction. How well we ride the macroeconomic surf depends on how well we understand it.

World-class riders of the great breakers off the California and Hawaii coasts have studied the surf and know how to use it to their advantage. They can't predict any one wave movement, but they know how the waves behave, on the average. As a result, they usually get a good ride. But sometimes they fall flat on their faces.

Like world-class surfers, people who have studied the economy can use its turbulent waves to get a better economic ride. For example, people who predicted the stock market crash of Monday, October 19, and sold out on the previous Friday were able to buy shares at Monday's low prices and actually benefit from the crash. But also like the ocean surfer, no one can predict every movement in the economic waves — each major change in the economy. And like the surf rider, even experienced economic surfers sometimes fall flat on their faces!

Two such economic surfers were the Commercial and Northland Banks in Alberta. These banks knew their markets very well. Knowing a particular market is like knowing your own surfboard. You know how it behaves on a particular type of wave. But to get a good ride you must know about waves in general. You must know the environment in which you are riding your board. These two banks fell off their economic surfboards in 1986 because they didn't have a good enough understanding of the bigger picture — the macroeconomy — and how it was going to evolve.

Part of being successful at surfing is knowing how things work out on the average — recognizing the patterns of the waves. Another part is understanding the deeper forces that produce the waves in the first place. It is exactly the same with macroeconomics. Part of the subject is a study of the patterns made by the macroeconomic waves. Another part is a study of the deeper forces that create those waves. It is especially important to study the deeper forces producing the macroeconomic waves because the macroeconomic surfer wants to tame the waves! To tame the waves, it is necessary not only to learn their patterns, but to probe beneath the surface and discover the laws that govern their behavior — the wave-making mechanism. This mechanism must be modified if a smoother economic ride is to result.

From this book and your course in macroeconomics, you will gain a deeper understanding of the macroeconomic surf. You will learn about the patterns of the macroeconomic waves and learn what is currently known about the forces that produce those waves. You will *not* learn how to predict future rises and falls in the macroeconomic ocean. In the current state of knowledge, no one can do that. But you will learn how to do the best that can be done.

The rest of this chapter takes a first look at the macroeconomic ocean. After studying it, you will be able to

- Explain what macroeconomics is about
- Describe the changing pace of economic expansion and inflation in the Canadian and world economies
- Describe the problem of stabilizing the economy
- Describe the main schools of thought on how the economy works and how it might be stabilized

Let's begin with the first of these objectives — what *is* macroeconomics about?

1.1 *What Macroeconomics Is About*

Macroeconomics is the study of aggregate economic activity. **Aggregate economic activity** is the performance of the economy as a whole — the economy in the aggregate. That performance is described by the growth of people's incomes and living standards; by fluctuations in unemployment; by inflation — rising prices — and changes in the value of money. In pursuit of its task, macroeconomics tries to answer three main questions. The three big questions for macroeconomics are

- What determines the rate of growth of real GDP?
- What causes fluctuations in the rates of economic growth and of unemployment?
- What determines the average level of prices and the rate at which they rise?

Let's take a look at these questions.

Growth of real GDP

Real GDP is a measure of the quantity of the goods and services that can be bought with the income of all the individuals in the economy — a measure of living standards. The growth in real GDP is a measure of the growth of people's real incomes — the pace of improvement in living standards. Differences in growth rates of real GDP produce large differences in living standards between countries. Trying to understand the causes of real GDP growth and the reasons for persistent differences in growth rates and income levels between countries is a major part of macroeconomics. It is also the most fundamental question of economics, and the one that gave birth to the science of economics, back in 1776 when Adam Smith published *An Enquiry into the Nature and Causes of the Wealth of Nations*.[1]

[1]Although first published in 1776, this book has been reprinted many times. A good version to read is that edited by Edwin Cannan, with a new preface by George J. Stigler, published as two volumes in one by the University of Chicago Press, Chicago, 1976.

Fluctuations in economic growth and unemployment

Sometimes economic growth is rapid and at other times it is slow. There are even occasions when the economy stops growing and actually shrinks for a period. A rapidly growing economy is one in which people are enjoying rapidly rising living standards and in which good jobs are easy to find. In a slow growing or shrinking economy living standards decline and unemployment becomes a serious problem.

Unemployment is measured by the **unemployment rate**, the percentage of the labor force that is either out of work and seeking jobs or on temporary layoff. At times when the unemployment rate is high it can take a long time to find a job, especially for young people leaving school and entering the work force for the first time. Although unemployment is a permanent feature of our economic life, it sometimes becomes an extremely serious problem. One such time was the late 1920s and 1930s when, throughout Western Europe, North America, and most of the world, almost 20 percent of the labor force was unemployed. This period of persistently high unemployment gave rise, in 1936, to the birth of macroeconomics as a separate sub-discipline with the publication of John Maynard Keynes's *The General Theory of Employment, Interest, and Money.*[2]

For some time, especially in the early 1960s, many people thought that the unemployment problem had been solved. But a severe recession in 1981-1982 showed us that unemployment is not a phenomenon of the past. Also, in Canada and in Western Europe, high unemployment persisted well beyond the end of that recession, throughout the 1980s. Understanding what causes unemployment and why its rate fluctuates is a major part of the study of macroeconomics.

Price level and inflation

Inflation is a process of rising prices. Equivalently it is a process in which money steadily loses value and buys fewer and fewer goods and services. Inflation is a problem because changes in its rate are hard to forecast and have important effects on people, especially on borrowers and lenders. An unexpected upturn in the inflation rate reduces the debts of borrowers and the wealth of lenders. If inflation becomes extremely rapid, money loses its usefulness as a means of paying for goods and services.

Inflation is not a new phenomenon. It has been around since the time of the Roman Empire and perhaps even longer. But the first scientific study of the problem was not undertaken until the sixteenth century. At that time, following a period of European (particularly Spanish) colonization of the Americas, there was a huge influx of gold into Europe and prices rose quickly. It was the French philosopher Jean Bodin who first suggested a cause and effect mechanism between the influx of gold and the rising level of prices and that mechanism was first explained by the Scottish philosopher David Hume in the essay "Of Money" published in 1741.[3]

Macroeconomics attempts to understand the forces that generate inflation, leading to fluctuations in its rate and to differences in its rate from one country to another.

Other questions

In addition to the three main questions, macroeconomics tries to answer three other important questions. These are

[2]John Maynard Keynes, *The General Theory of Employment, Interest, and Money* (London: Macmillan and Co. Ltd.), 1936.

[3]David Hume, *Essays: Moral, Political and Literary*, first published in 1741 and 1742, (London: Oxford University Press), 1963.

1. What determines interest rates?
2. What determines the Canadian balance of payments with the rest of the world?
3. What determines the value of the dollar abroad?

Interest rates Interest rates have a big effect on our well-being. When they rise quickly, borrowers — people with credit card debt, homeowners, people who run small businesses, and farmers — suffer. Even the federal government with its multibillion dollar debt faces problems. Interest rates became a very big issue in the early 1980s when they reached the 20 percent zone and the economy went into a tailspin recession.

Macroeconomics attempts to understand why interest rates rise and fall; why in some times and places they are extremely high and in other times and places, low.

Balance of transactions with rest of world Every year, Canadian firms and individuals undertake massive business and financial transactions with firms and individuals in other countries. In 1990, we bought and sold internationally more than $300 billion worth of goods and services. We also invest in firms in other countries and buy their stocks and bonds. Foreigners invest in the Canadian economy and buy Canadian stocks and bonds.

In recent years, the Canadian balance of trade with the rest of the world has become an important political issue. Since the mid-1980s, our exports of goods and services have fallen short of our imports by more than $10 billion a year. Foreign investment in the Canadian economy has exceeded our investment abroad.

Macroeconomics tries to understand what determines the scale and balance of our international economic transactions — our international balance of payments. The study of these phenomena is an old one and was begun by David Hume. Hume's account of what determines the balance of a nation's trade, even today, reads as a clear-headed explanation of this phenomenon.[4]

The value of the dollar abroad The value of the dollar is constantly changing. It changes at home because of inflation — money steadily loses value and buys fewer and fewer goods. But the dollar also changes value abroad, because its value in terms of other currencies fluctuates. Between 1976 and 1986, the Canadian dollar declined in value against the U.S. dollar, the Japanese yen, and the German mark. But it increased in value against the British pound. Since 1986, the Canadian dollar has been rising in value against the U.S. dollar. Macroeconomics tries to explain and understand such fluctuations in the foreign exchange value of a currency.

All six macroeconomic questions are important for Canada at the beginning of the 1990s. At many points throughout this book, we'll be looking at facts about the Canadian economy and the world economy — the facts that give rise to each of the questions that macroeconomics tries to answer.

1.2 *Canadian Growth, Fluctuations, and Inflation*

MACROFACTS

Our first look at the facts concentrates on the three big macroeconomic issues — real GDP growth, economic fluctuations, and inflation. It examines these features of macroeconomic performance in Canada over the 64-year period from 1926 to 1990.[5]

[4]David Hume, "Of the Balance of Trade," in *Essays: Moral, Political and Literary* (London: Oxford University Press, 1963), pp. 316-333.

[5]A good source of facts about the current state of the Canadian economy is the *Bank of Canada Review*. This monthly publication contains data on all aspects of the Canadian economy.

Real GDP growth

Figure 1.1 charts the course of real GDP in Canada between 1926 and 1990. The precise meaning of "real GDP" and the way in which it is measured are described in Chapter 2. For now, just think of real GDP as the total volume of goods and services produced that could be purchased with the total of all the incomes earned in Canada in a given year.

In the 64-year period shown in Figure 1.1, the Canadian economy has expanded at an average rate of 4.2 percent a year, resulting in a 20-fold increase in income over that period. Over the same period, the population grew at an average rate of 1.6 percent a year, resulting in an increase of 2.8-fold over the 64-year period. Real GDP per person increased at an average rate of 2.6 percent a year, or 5-fold over the 64-year period.

The expansion of the Canadian economy has produced a standard of living unimaginable in 1926. If the Canadian economy continues to expand at the same rate over the next 64 years, by the year 2054 the *average* Canadian will have $133,000 to spend each year. These dollars are 1991 dollars—one 1991 dollar will buy as much in the year 2054 as one dollar bought in 1991. Clearly, economic expansion on this scale sustained over long periods of time can transform our lives in extraordinary ways.

FIGURE 1.1
Real GDP in Canada: 1926 to 1990

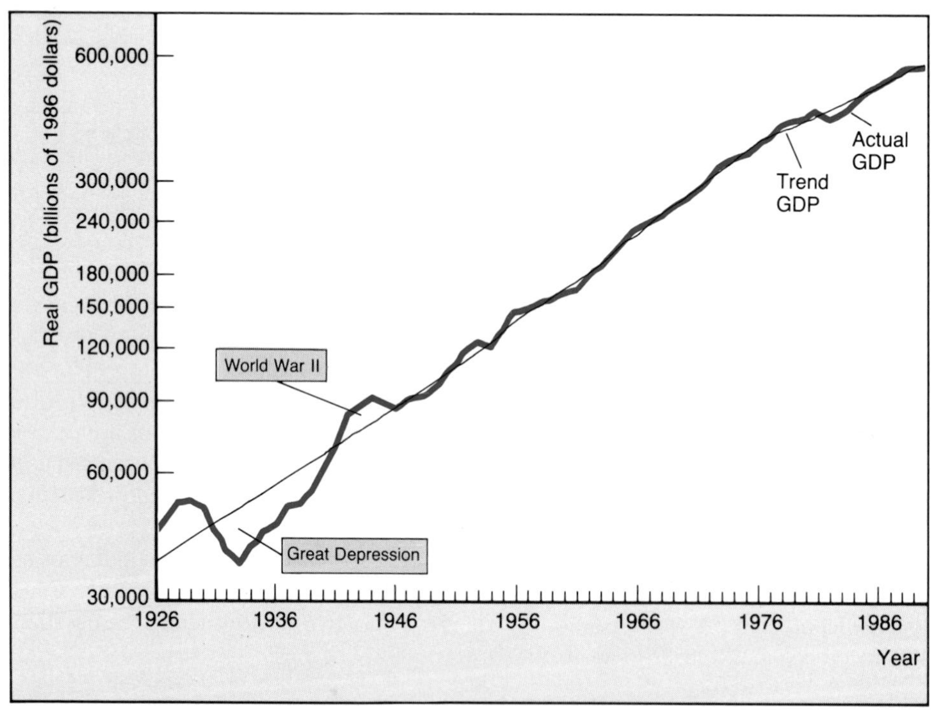

Real GDP is a measure of the value of all the goods and services that can be bought with the incomes earned in the Canadian economy in a year. The figure* shows the actual and trend values of real GDP. The trend GDP line shows the underlying pace of expansion of the economy. The economy has grown at an average rate of 4.2 percent a year. But the path of actual GDP has meandered around the trend, growing extremely quickly in some years, such as those of World War II, and declining sharply, such as it did in the Great Depression years of the early 1930s.

Sources: 1926-1977, *National Income and Expenditure Accounts*, Statistics Canada, Ottawa, 1988, Catalogue 13-531; 1978-1989, *National Income and Expenditure Accounts*, Statistics Canada, Ottawa, 1990, Catalogue 13-201; 1990, *National Income and Expenditure Accounts*, Statistics Canada, Ottawa, 1991, Catalogue 13-001.

*Notice that real GDP is measured on a *ratio scale*. On a ratio scale, the distance measured between 50 and 100 is the same as the distance measured between 100 and 200—the ratio of 100 to 50 is the same as the ratio of 200 to 100. Ratio scales are useful ones for graphing economic time series, because the steepness of the line graphed represents the rate of growth of the variable. We'll use the same type of scale later when we look at the price level.

This amazing economic expansion has not occurred at an even pace. The Canadian economy has not grown at 4.2 percent year after year. That 4.2 growth rate is the average or trend growth rate. Figure 1.1 shows this growth rate as the line labeled "Trend GDP." Actual GDP grows sometimes faster, sometimes slower than the average. So actual GDP meanders around trend GDP in Figure 1.1. Let's focus a bit more closely on the uneven pace of expansion.

Economic fluctuations

The recurring fluctuation in the pace of economic expansion is called the **business cycle**. The business cycle shows up most clearly if we graph the deviation of real GDP from its trend. We calculate the deviation of real GDP from trend as actual GDP minus trend GDP divided by trend GDP, expressed as a percentage. For example, in 1982 actual real GDP was $426 billion and trend real GDP was $444 billion, and the difference was −$18 billion. $18 billion is 4.2 percent of $444 billion, so the deviation in 1982 was −4.2 percent. Figure 1.2 graphs the deviation of real GDP from trend in each year.

Several features of the business cycle stand out in Figure 1.2. First, the fluctuations are large. The Canadian economy expanded most quickly during World War II, when it grew at a rate of 19 percent in 1942. It contracted most severely in the early years of the Great Depression—1929 to 1933. It also contracted quickly at the end of World War II, in 1945-1946.

The Great Depression and World War II produced the biggest swings that our economy has ever experienced. But it has undergone many other swings as well, some of them in recent years. Figure 1.3 looks more closely at these years, showing the business cycle in the Canadian economy since 1950, with some of the most important episodes highlighted. Notice that economic booms are usually associated with war—the Korean War in the early 1950s and the Vietnam War in the 1960s. Contractions are sometimes related to international events such as the oil price increases of the 1970s and

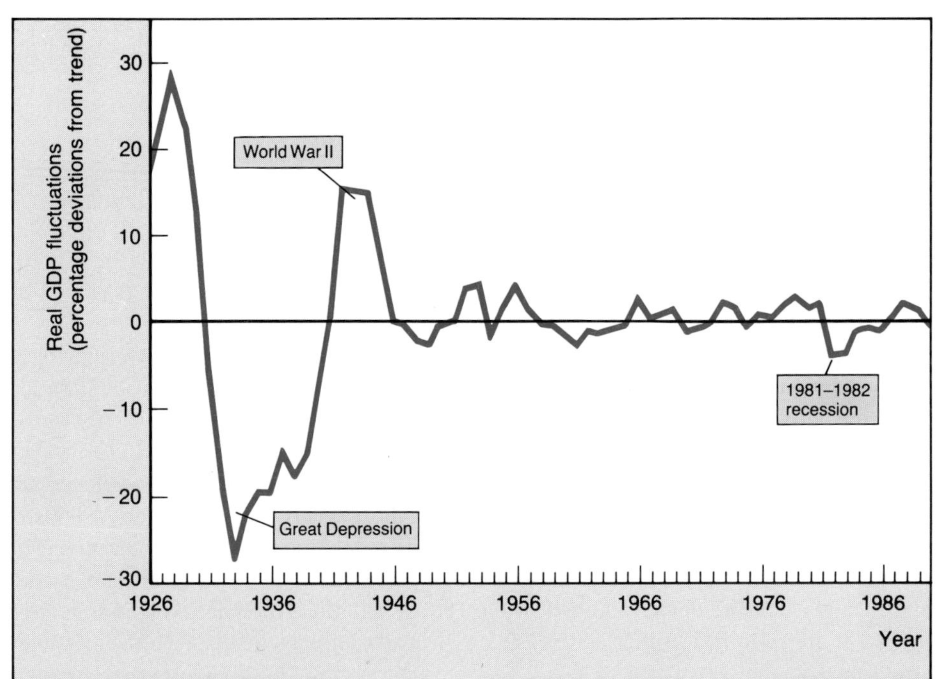

FIGURE 1.2
The Canadian Business Cycle: 1926-1990

The Canadian business cycle is illustrated by the percentage deviations of real GDP from trend. Before World War II the cycle was much more severe than it became in the post-war period. The deepest recession occurred in the 1930s and the largest boom occurred in the years of World War II.

Source: See Figure 1.1.

FIGURE 1.3
The Canadian Business Cycle: 1950 to 1990

The economy has experienced a series of expansions and contractions in the postwar years. Expansions were associated with the Korean and Vietnam wars. The most severe recession, in 1981-1982, resulted from tight monetary policies designed to reduce inflation. The 1990 recession resulted from the world-wide downturn accentuated by the Bank of Canada's "zero inflation" strategy.

Source: See Figure 1.1.

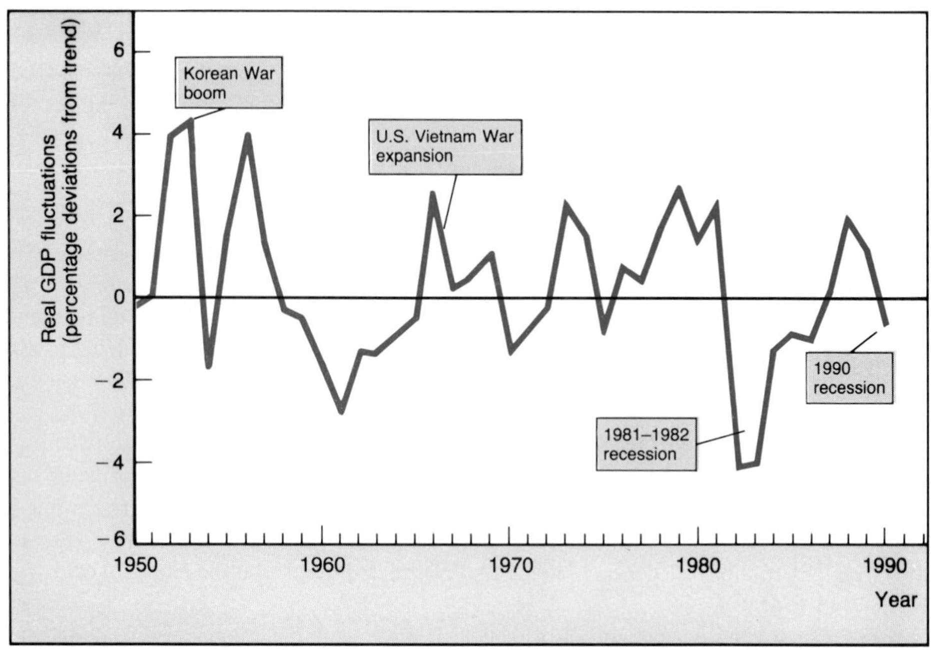

the Gulf crisis (Iraq's invasion of Kuwait) of 1990. The severe recession in 1981-1982 resulted from a policy of monetary restraint, which Gerald Bouey, governor of the Bank of Canada, implemented to reduce inflation. And finally, the 1990-1991 recession resulted from a downturn in the world economy, reinforced by severe monetary restraint implemented by John Crow, the governor of the Bank of Canada, in his effort to achieve "zero" inflation.

The Canadian economy has experienced two large and long expansions in our economy, one beginning in the early 1960s, and the other beginning in 1982 and running through the rest of the 1980s. In 1990, the economy reacted to the Gulf crisis and the "zero inflation" monetary restraint and began to turn down.

Inflation

Figure 1.4 shows what has been happening to the price level and the inflation rate in Canada since 1926. The *height* of the line in the graph tells us about the *level of prices*. Its *slope* tells us about the *rate of inflation*. When the line is rising steeply, inflation is rapid. When the line is pointing downward, there is deflation — a period of falling prices.

As you can see, prices fell during the Great Depression. Since then prices have increased every year — the line has moved persistently upward. The pace of inflation was especially fast during World War II, and it also accelerated in the late 1970s.

Figure 1.5 sharpens our focus on the years between 1950 and 1990. Until the late 1960s, inflation was steady and averaged about 3 percent a year. It trended upward during the Vietnam War — as it had done during the Korean War in the early 1950s — and took a leap in 1973, and again in 1979, when oil prices increased sharply. The inflation rate remained high until 1982, when a period of monetary restraint lowered it significantly. During the second half of the 1980s, inflation stood at less than 5 percent a year. It began to fall further as the Bank of Canada implemented its "zero inflation" strategy.

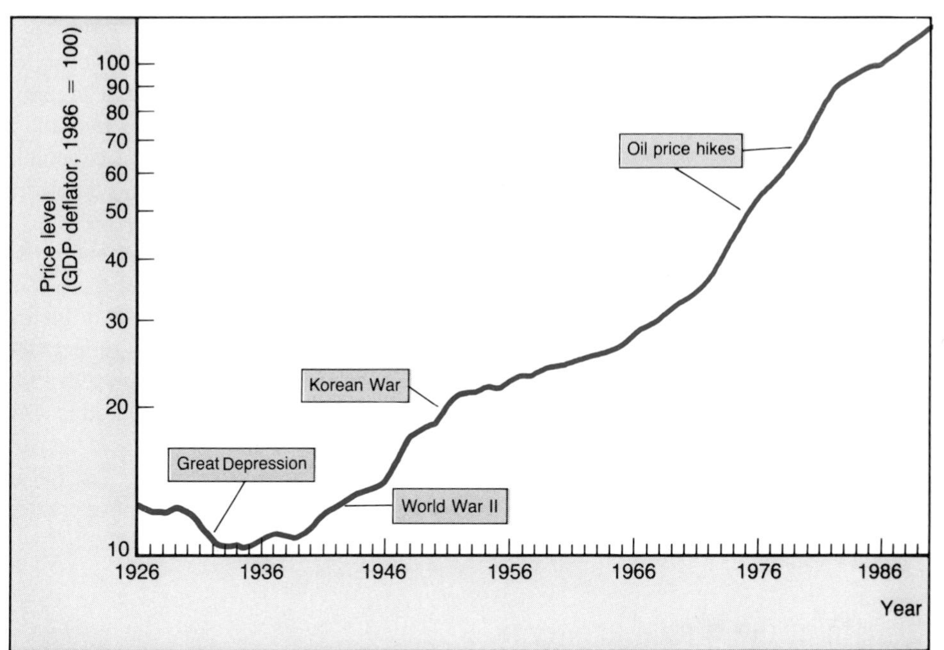

FIGURE 1.4
The Price Level in Canada: 1926 to 1990

The price level was some 10 times higher in 1990 than at its lowest level in 1933. But the pace of increase has not been uniform. Prices fell during the Great Depression years of the early 1930s and rose most sharply during World War II and again in the 1970s.

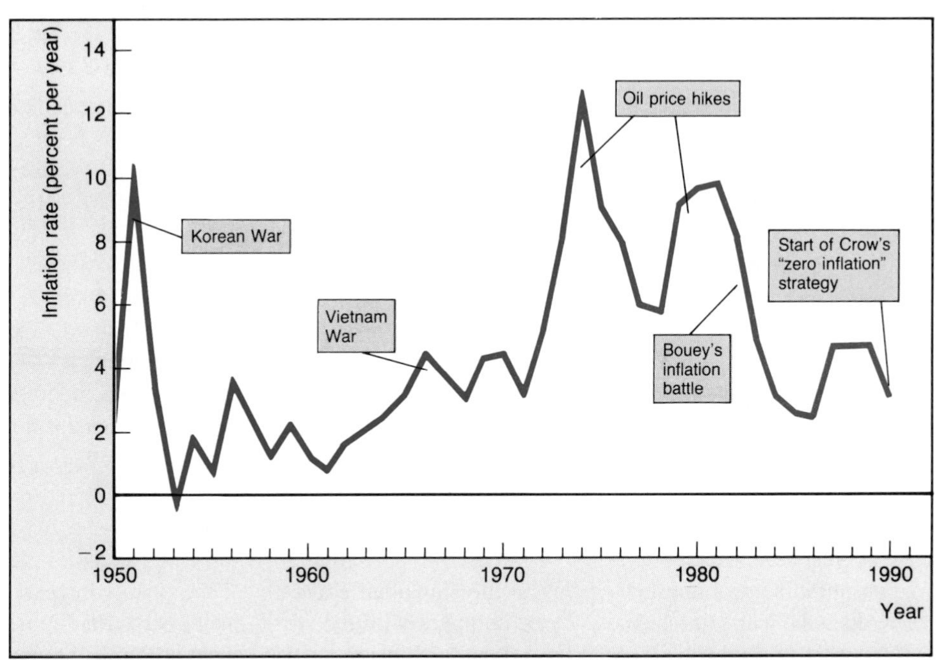

FIGURE 1.5
Inflation in Canada: 1950 to 1990

Four periods of accelerating inflation have occurred in Canada since 1950. The first two resulted from the Korean and Vietnam Wars. The next two resulted from oil price increases. The high inflation of the late 1970s was eradicated by severe disinflationary policies administered by Gerald Bouey, then governor of the Bank of Canada, in the early 1980s. In the late 1980s inflation remained below 5 percent a year, and began to fall further as the Bank of Canada implemented its "zero inflation" strategy.

Source: See Figure 1.1.

These facts about Canadian economic growth, fluctuations, and inflation generate questions and set much of the agenda for our study of macroeconomics. But they are far from the whole story. The Canadian economy does not operate in isolation. In the modern world, a global economic village has emerged, whose economic fortunes exert a strong influence on the Canadian economy. Let's look at some features of that global economy.

MACROFACTS

1.3 *Canada in the World Economy*

The world economy is made up of more than 130 national economies. In terms of population, Canada represents just a half a percent of the world economy, but in terms of the quantity of the goods and services produced, real GDP, it represents two and a half percent of the world. But we are a close neighbor of and have strong economic links with the world's largest economy, the United States. The U.S. represents 5 percent of the world's population and produces one quarter of its output.

Because of the sheer size of its economy, the United States exerts an enormous influence on the rest of the world in general and on Canada in particular. But the rest of the world exerts a big influence on the United States and Canada as well, an influence that has increased over the years. This changing balance of influence partly reflects the decreasing relative size of the United States in the world economy. Although today the United States produces 25 percent of total world output, in 1960 it produced almost 40 percent of the world's total output. Also, the influence of the rest of the world on Canada has increased because international trade has increased in the modern world. The fall in transportation costs and the dramatic fall in electronic communication costs have created a global economy.

Growth in the global economy

The growth of real income per person in Canada is shown in Figure 1.6. These data are measured in 1980 dollars (the purchasing power of the dollar in 1980). Between 1960 and 1985, income per person in Canada increased from around $7,500 to more than $12,000. Set alongside the Canadian graph are those of income per person in other countries or groups of countries.

Part (a) shows what's happened in the rich countries. As you can see, Canadian income per person has grown faster than that in the United States. But there has been an even faster growth rate of real income per person in Japan and in the ''big four'' Western European countries (France, West Germany, Italy, and the United Kingdom). Real income levels in these rich countries appear to be converging.

Part (b) takes a broader look at the world, bringing Central and South America, Africa, Asia, and other European countries into view. The line labeled the ''Rich 18'' includes the countries shown in part (a), together with Australia, New Zealand, and other rich countries of Western Europe. Real income levels in all these countries are gradually converging on that in Canada and the United States. But notice that incomes in Central and South America, Africa, and other Asian and European countries are not growing fast enough to close the gap between themselves and the rich countries.

Fluctuations in the global economy

We've noted some important cycles in the Canadian economy in the post-war years. How does the Canadian business cycle compare with the world business cycle? Figure 1.7 answers this question. It tracks the Canadian business cycle shown in Figure 1.3 but for a shorter period, starting in 1960. Alongside it is the business cycle for the rest of the world—measured in the same way as the Canadian cycle, as deviations of the value of output in the rest of the world from its trend.

There are some striking similarities between the business cycle in the rest of the world and that in Canada. The recession of the early 1960s and the strong recovery through 1965 were almost identical in Canada and the rest of the world. The other major fluctuations in the economies of the rest of the world align closely with those in Canada,

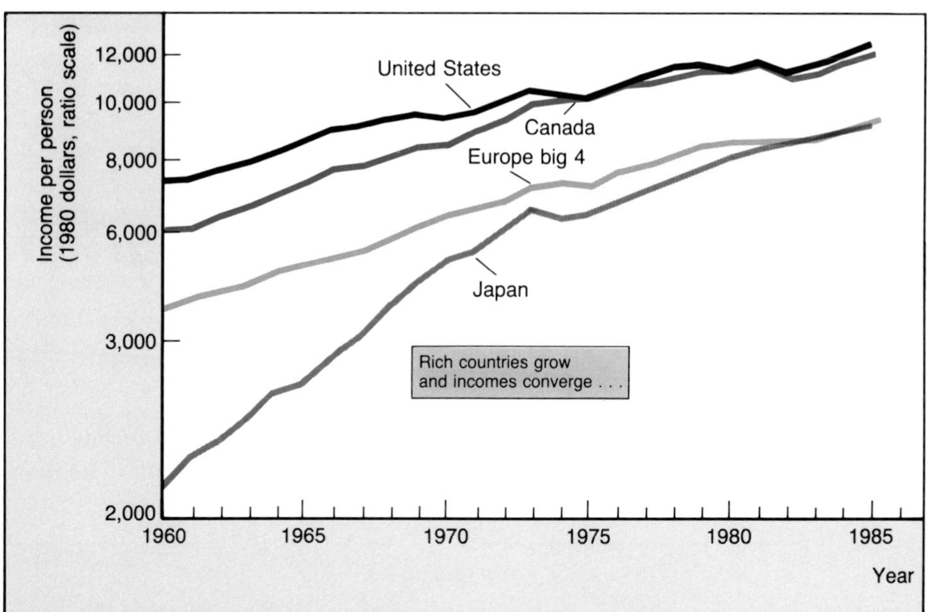

(a) The Seven Richest Countries

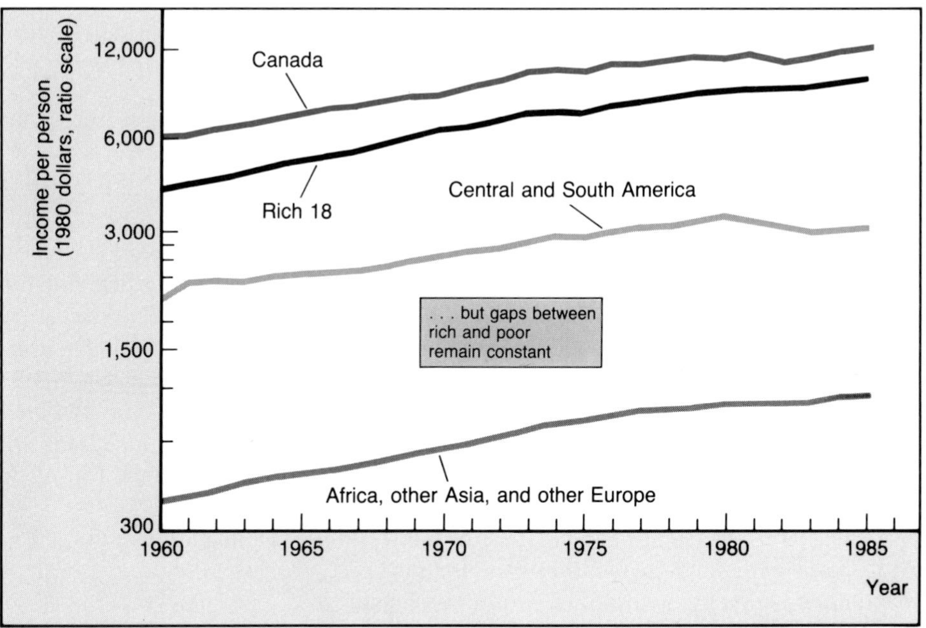

(b) The Perpetual Gaps between the Rich and the Poor

FIGURE 1.6
Real Income Per Person in Canada and the Rest of the World: 1960-1985

Part (a) shows how real income per person has increased steadily in Canada from $7,500 (measured in 1980 dollars) in 1960 to more than $12,000 in 1985. Growth rates in other rich countries, such as the United States, Europe's "big four" (France, West Germany, Italy, and the United Kingdom), and Japan have been higher and incomes in these countries are converging on that of Canada.

In part (b), real income in groups of countries is compared with Canada. The 18 richest countries—those in part (a) together with Australia, New Zealand, and the countries of Western Europe—can be seen to be converging on Canada. But the gap between real income per person in the rich countries and in the poorer countries of Central and South America, and between the rich countries and the poorest countries of all of Africa, the rest of Asia, and Europe, are virtually constant.

Source: Alan Heston and Robert Summers, appendix B of "A New Set of International Comparisons of Real Product and Price Levels; Estimates for 130 Countries, 1950-1985," *Review of Income and Wealth*, series 34, vol. 1, 1988, pp. 1-25, and *International Financial Statistics* and our calculations.

but there are some differences in terms of the strength of the recession and recovery. For example, the economy of the rest of the world dipped much more deeply into recession in the early 1970s than did the Canadian economy. But the rest of the world had a smaller recession in 1981 and also a weaker recovery in the late 1980s than did Canada.

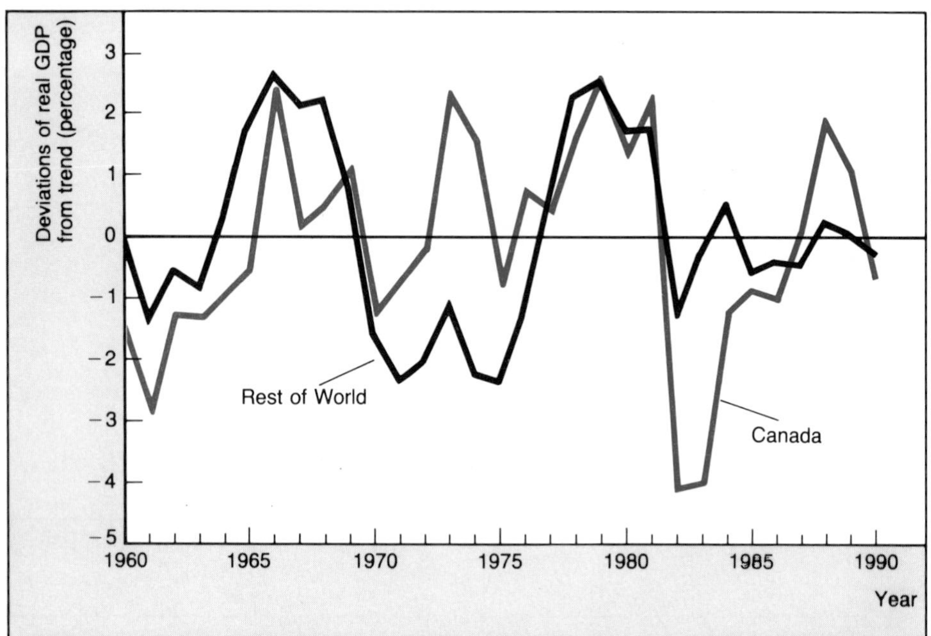

FIGURE 1.7
The Business Cycle in Canada and the Rest of the World

The business cycle in the rest of the world lines up remarkably closely with that in Canada. But there are some differences in the degree of recession and recovery. The rest of the world had a deeper recession in the early 1970s than did Canada. But Canada had a deeper recession in 1981 and a stronger recovery in the late 1980s than did the rest of the world.

Source: Canada, see Figure 1.1. Rest of world, *International Financial Statistics*, and our calculations.

Understanding the forces that cause the alignment of Canadian and rest-of-world business cycles and also the forces that enable our economy to have a different cyclical performance from that of the rest of the world is an important part of the study of macroeconomics.

Inflation

How does inflation in Canada compare with inflation in the rest of the world? You can see the answer to this question by looking at Figure 1.8, which shows Canadian inflation and average inflation in the rest of the world between 1960 and 1990. As in the case of the business cycle, there is a tendency for inflation in Canada to line up with that in the rest of the world. For example, the bursts of inflation that occurred in Canada in 1974 and 1975 and again in 1980 and 1981 also occurred in the rest of the world. But there have been inflation explosions in the rest of the world that did not occur in Canada—in 1964, 1983, and 1988. Also, between 1964 and 1969, inflation *fell* in the rest of the world while it rose in Canada.

The average inflation rate in the rest of the world is much higher than in Canada. At its peak, in the mid-1970s, Canadian inflation nearly reached 10 percent a year. At that time, inflation in the rest of the world was running at 25 percent a year.

The numbers shown in Figure 1.8 are *averages*. They hide the fact that some countries experience very rapid inflation—many hundreds of percent a year. They also hide the fact that some individual countries, such as West Germany, Switzerland, and Japan in recent years have had a lower inflation rate, on the average, than Canada.

These facts about inflation give rise to a further set of questions that macroeconomics tries to answer. Why in the late 1960s did the Canadian inflation rate increase while that of the rest of the world decreased? Why did inflation generally accelerate in the 1970s and fall off in the 1980s? Why has the rest of the world experienced higher average inflation than Canada?

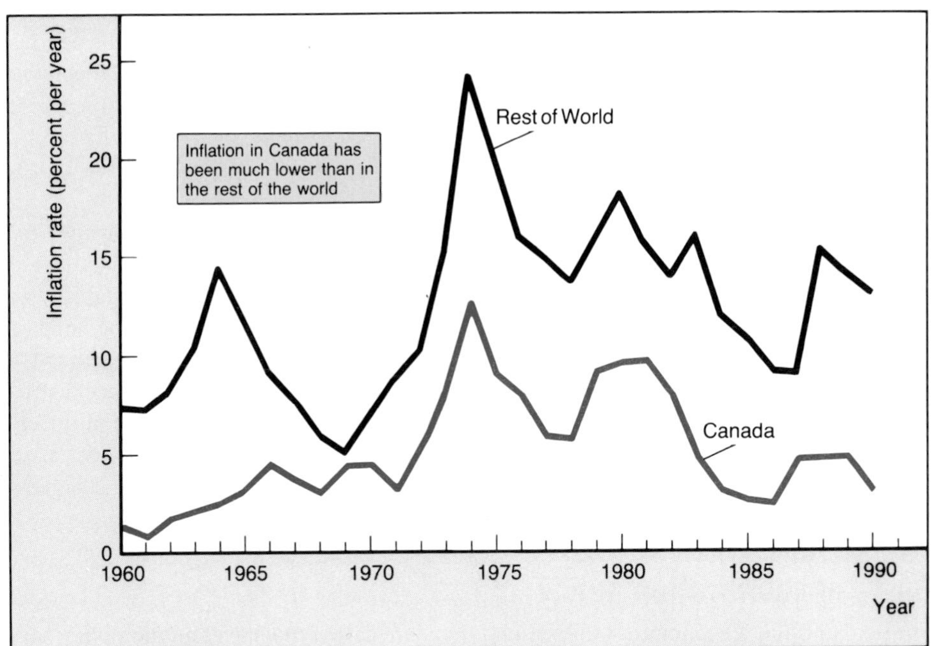

FIGURE 1.8
Inflation in Canada and World Economies: 1960 to 1990

Although Canada has experienced persistent inflation, inflation has been more severe in the rest of the world. But the cycles in inflation have been similar in Canada and the rest of the world. There have been several occasions on which inflation accelerated in the rest of the world while remaining moderate in Canada.

Sources: See Figures 1.1 and 1.6.

The facts about the Canadian economy and world economy that we have just reviewed reinforce the three big macroeconomic questions. They also give rise to a range of additional questions. Are we at the mercy of macroeconomic forces, or is it possible to influence macroeconomic performance? So we approach a topic that interests all macroeconomic surfers: stabilizing the economy.

1.4 *Stabilizing the Economy*

There are three broad questions concerning economic stabilization policy. They are

- What are the tools of stabilization policy?
- What should stabilization policy try to achieve?
- What can stabilization policy achieve?

Tools of stabilization policy

There are three sets of policy tools available for stabilizing the economy:

1. Fiscal policy
2. Monetary policy
3. Direct controls

Fiscal policy uses variations in the levels of government purchases of goods and services and taxes to influence the state of the economy. The fiscal policy instrument is wielded by the government of Canada. An example of fiscal policy is the restraints on public spending announced by then Finance Minister, Michael Wilson, in the budget of May 1991. The hope was that by keeping its spending in check, the government could reduce its deficit and improve confidence leading to recovery from the 1991 recession.

Monetary policy uses variations in the money supply and in interest rates to influence the state of the economy. The monetary policy instruments are in the hands of the Bank of Canada. One of the most dramatic examples of monetary policy was the actions of the Bank in the early 1980s when interest rates were pushed up to almost 20 percent a year in a bid to slow the economy down and stop inflation. Another is the current policy of restraining money supply growth in an attempt to achieve ''zero'' inflation by the mid-1990s. High interest rates are designed to encourage people to save more, borrow less, and spend less.

Direct controls are specific laws, rules, and regulations designed to modify the way people behave. Direct controls stem from laws passed by Parliament and implemented by a wide variety of agencies. Examples of direct controls that influence the stability of the economy are wage and price controls that have sometimes been used in the hope of keeping inflation in check.

Macroeconomists have a variety of views on the appropriate way to use these instruments of stabilization policy. Some of the differences of opinion arise because of different views about how the economy responds to the instruments. Other differences arise from disagreements about the goals of stabilization policy. Let's look at these disagreements next.

Goals of stabilization policy

The goals of macroeconomic stabilization policy are called **macroeconomic policy targets**. These targets are generally agreed to include

- A high and sustained rate of growth of real income
- A low unemployment rate
- Mild fluctuations in the growth rate of real income and of the unemployment rate
- A low inflation rate

To undertake an economic stabilization program, these general targets have to be made more precise and expressed as specific numerical targets. But faster real income growth, lower unemployment, milder economic fluctuations, and lower inflation have both benefits and costs. Therefore, cost-benefit calculations have to be undertaken to determine how fast the real income growth rate should be, how low the unemployment rate should be, how mild the fluctuations in the economy should be made, and how low its inflation rate should be set.

Benefits and costs Speeding up the growth rate of real income brings the benefit of higher consumption levels — more people can buy more goods and services. But the cost of higher consumption is a more rapid depletion of resources, increased congestion, pollution, and larger environmental problems such as acid rain, global warming, and the destruction of the earth's ozone layer. The costs of all these consequences of faster growth must be balanced against the benefits of higher consumption levels in determining the target real income growth rate.

Keeping the unemployment rate low brings the benefit of more people having jobs and spreads the gains of economic expansion. In an economy with a high unemployment rate, high costs are borne by those people who can't find jobs or who have to spend a very long time searching for a job. But the unemployment rate can also be too low. In an economy with very low unemployment, firms have a hard time finding the right kind of labor and are less able to respond to increases in demand for their products. However, a lower unemployment rate brings the cost of having a less flexible economy and also of people taking less time to be sure that they have found the job they really want. These costs must be balanced against the benefits of a low unemployment rate in setting a precise numerical goal.

Smoothing out the fluctuations in the economy brings the benefit of less severe recessions and lower peaks in the unemployment rate. But smoothing out fluctuations involves making booms less strong as well as slumps less severe. Booms are periods of rapid technological change and smoothing them out runs the risk of slowing down the pace of technological innovation. Deciding just how much to try to smooth the fluctuations requires that these costs and benefits be balanced.

Fluctuations in the inflation rate make it difficult for people to predict the future value of money and make it hard, therefore, for them to know how much to save, borrow, and lend. Money, the measuring rod of value, becomes an unreliable measure. It is like using an elastic ruler to measure length. So there are clear benefits from slowing down inflation and keeping its pace steady. But the process of slowing down inflation can, at least temporarily, slow down the pace of economic growth and increase unemployment. Again, these costs and benefits need to be balanced in setting a precise inflation goal.

Possibilities and policies

We may be able to agree on the desirability of macroeconomic goals and to set specific numerical targets. But do we have the ability to stabilize the economy? Do the tools at our disposal — fiscal policy, monetary policy, and direct controls — enable us to design policies that speed up economic growth, reduce unemployment, tame the business cycle, and contain inflation? And if the tools are adequate for the task, how do they work, and which are the best ones to use to achieve any given objective?

In contrast to the broad agreement on the goals of stabilization policy, economists disagree on the possibility, and the appropriate method, of achieving economic stability. The main reason for this disagreement is that we still lack a deep enough understanding of macroeconomic phenomena. In other words, we lack good theories; no one particular theory fits the facts so exactly that it is compelling. But this state of affairs does not mean that macroeconomics is just a matter of opinion. On the contrary, there exists a solid core of macroeconomic theory that economists support regardless of their policy positions. And even when economists disagree about the relevant theoretical approach, they often agree about how to proceed to resolve conflicts and disputes.

This book will inform you about the lack of complete agreement and the lack of a perfect correspondence between theory and fact. You will come to understand the existing theories. You will learn the facts — both the facts that the theories explain and those they do not. You will also learn something about the unexplained facts and the research agenda they generate.

1.5 *Schools of Thought*

Macroeconomists disagree about three distinct things:

- How the economy works
- What stabilization policy can achieve
- How best to research the workings of the economy

Disagreements about how the economy works

Economists hold two broad views about how the economy works. They are called

1. Classical
2. Keynesian

Classical macroeconomics is a body of macroeconomic theory based on the idea that the economy is a self-regulating mechanism, always tending in the direction of full employment. Classical macroeconomics is an outgrowth and distillation of the work of economists ranging from Adam Smith in the eighteenth century to Alfred Marshall of the University of Cambridge, England, and Irving Fisher of Yale University in the early part of this century. The intellectual leader of the modern classical school is Robert E. Lucas Jr., of the University of Chicago. Classical macroeconomists recognize that the economy exhibits fluctuations in the growth rate of real GDP and unemployment, but they regard these phenomena as the natural consequences of an ever-changing technological, political, and social environment.

Keynesian macroeconomics is a body of macroeconomic theory based on the idea that the economy does not possess a self-regulating mechanism and, left to its own devices, it can get stuck with a high and persistent level of unemployment and lost output. This view is an outgrowth of the writings of John Maynard Keynes. Modern Keynesian macroeconomists include Alan S. Blinder of Princeton University and Robert M. Solow of MIT.

Disagreements about stabilization policy

Differences in belief about how the economy works strongly influence economists' opinions about how the economy can be stabilized. And, not surprisingly, there are two broad views about this matter. That is, there are two schools of thought on macroeconomic stabilization policy issues. They are

1. Monetarists
2. Activists

The differences of view between monetarists and activists can be best described by considering their answers to two macroeconomic policy questions:

1. Should macroeconomic policy be global or detailed?
2. Should macroeconomic stabilization policy be governed by a set of rules or be discretionary?

Global vs detailed Should macroeconomic policy be global or detailed? Global policies influence the values of a small number of aggregate variables, such as the money supply, the foreign exchange rate, the overall level of government purchases of goods and services, the overall level of taxes, and the size of the government's budget deficit. Those who believe that only a small number of aggregate policy instruments should be used generally believe in the efficiency of free markets.

Detailed policies control the prices of, or other terms concerning the exchange of, a large number of specific goods and services. Some examples of detailed policies are: wage and price controls; minimum wage policies; interest rate ceilings or other regulations on banks, savings and loan institutions, and insurance companies; special regional subsidies; investment incentives; regulation of private businesses; regulation of international trade by the use of tariffs and quotas; and regulation of international capital flows. Economists who favor detailed policies generally take the view that free markets do not work efficiently and that detailed government intervention is needed to modify the outcome of the market process.

Often, the disagreement between those who advocate detailed intervention and those who argue against it is not about the existence of a problem that the free market is having trouble solving. Rather, the argument is whether the government can solve the problem better than the market can.

Rules vs discretion Policy rules place restraints on what governments can do. Such rules are rarely adopted but widely advocated. The most famous stabilization policy rule is the one advocated by Milton Friedman many years ago to keep the money supply growing at a constant rate each year.

Economists who favor rules do not unanimously agree on what the rules should be. They do agree, however, on one crucial point: controlling an economy is fundamentally different from controlling a mechanical system, such as, for example, a building's heating/cooling system. Controlling the economy involves controlling people. Unlike machines, people are able to understand that they are being controlled and are capable of learning the procedures that the controllers — the government — use. As a result, people can react by organizing their affairs to take best advantage of the situation a policy creates. A policy based on fixed rules minimizes the uncertainty that people face and thus enables a better economic performance.

Economists who favor discretion believe that rules can tie the hands of the government and the Bank of Canada, making them insufficiently flexible to react to a changing world. They argue that as new situations develop, it would be foolish not to react in the best possible way as evaluated at the time. By committing itself to a set of rules, the government ties its hands and bars itself from reacting in new and creative ways to previously unforeseen events.

We have reviewed the differences in opinion on the answers to two macroeconomic policy questions. Because there are two questions and two possible answers, macroeconomists could fall into four different groups on stabilization policy issues. In fact, they fall into the two that we identified above — monetarists and activists. The reason is that, on the whole, those who favor global policies also favor rules, while those who favor detailed policies also favor discretionary intervention. Let's now look more closely at the two policy schools.

The monetarist view Monetarists advocate that governments have policies toward a limited number of global macroeconomic variables such as money supply growth, government expenditure, taxes, and/or the government deficit. They advocate the adoption of fixed rules for the behavior of these variables. They also argue that whatever policy interventions do occur should be announced as far ahead as possible to enable people to take account of them in planning and ordering their own economic affairs.

The intellectual leader of the monetarist school is Milton Friedman, formerly of the University of Chicago and now working at the Hoover Institution at Stanford University.

The activist view Activists advocate detailed intervention to "fine tune" the economy, keeping it as close as possible to full employment with steady and low inflation. The main instruments that they would employ are those of monetary and fiscal policy. Activists would use these instruments with discretion to stimulate the economy in a recession and to hold it back in a boom, modifying the policy, as necessary, in the light of the current situation. Activists believe that policy changes are best *not* announced before they are instituted so as to deter speculation and allow the policy change to have maximum effect. As a last resort, some activists would attempt to keep inflation in check by direct controls on wages and prices and restrain aggregate demand by direct controls on the amount of credit available.

The intellectual leaders of the activist macroeconomists are Franco Modigliani of MIT and James Tobin of Yale University.

Overlapping views Despite the many areas of disagreement, the opinions of various groups of economists do overlap, as you can see in Figure 1.9. Most activists have a Keynesian view about how the economy works; most monetarists have a classical view. Monetarists favor rules; Keynesians favor discretion. But there is some overlap between the two groups on what should be done about the government budget. Some economists in each group favor stronger methods of achieving a balanced or a more nearly balanced budget.

Disagreements about the macroeconomics research program

Regardless of the school of thought concerning the working of the economy or the appropriate way to stabilize it, macroeconomists agree that we do not have the answers to all the macroeconomic questions and that some of the answers we do have are just not good enough. There is disagreement, however, on the direction research should take to expand our understanding of macroeconomic phenomena. There are three broad views on this matter. They are

1. Mainstream
2. New classical
3. New Keynesian

The mainstream view is that there exists a solid core of sensible macroeconomic theory that needs to be improved, but only at the edges. Chiseling away at the edges of an essentially complete sculpture is all that remains to be done. This view was widely held in the 1960s and early 1970s but is less fashionable today. Most younger macroeconomists do not subscribe to the mainstream position and are either new classical or new Keynesian.

FIGURE 1.9
Schools of Thought

Macroeconomists can be divided into various schools of thought, based on their views on how the economy works and how a successful stabilization policy might be implemented. Monetarists tend to be classical economists who favor rules, while activists tend to be Keynesian economists who favor discretion.

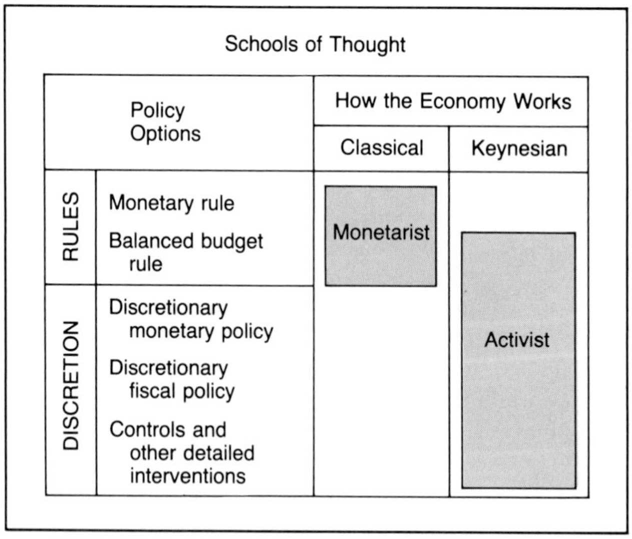

Schools of Thought

Policy Options		How the Economy Works: Classical	How the Economy Works: Keynesian
RULES	Monetary rule Balanced budget rule	Monetarist	Activist
DISCRETION	Discretionary monetary policy Discretionary fiscal policy Controls and other detailed interventions		Activist

New classical macroeconomists believe that the classical view of the economy is a fruitful one and one likely to lead to better macroeconomic theory. Their goal is to explain such macroeconomic phenomena as fluctuations in economic growth and unemployment as the "natural" consequences of a well-functioning economy in which everyone is doing the best they can for themselves and in which markets work efficiently.

New Keynesians believe that markets do not always work efficiently and that prices and wages are sticky, at least in the short run, so that the economy can get stuck a long way from full employment. Their research agenda is to explain fluctuations in economic growth and unemployment as the consequence of price and wage stickiness and other failings of the market economy.

There is one thing that all the new macroeconomists, new classical and new Keynesians, share — a commitment to finding a firm microeconomic foundation for macroeconomics.

Micro foundations

In principle, it's possible to do macroeconomics without worrying about what's going on inside the individual households and firms that make up the economy. It is possible to study the relationships among aggregates and to find patterns and regularities in their behavior. It is then, in principle, possible to devise ways of influencing the economy by manipulating aggregates.

Macroeconomics took that approach in the 1940s, 1950s, and early 1960s. But macroeconomists have always had at least one eye on the behavior of the individual households and firms that comprise the macroeconomy. From time to time, and at the present time, the belief that macroeconomics should be based on a microeconomic foundation has surfaced. Today, all macroeconomists regard the search for a micro foundation as an important one. What do we mean by a micro foundation?

A microeconomic foundation for macroeconomics is a model of the behavior of individual households, individual firms, and government enterprises and organizations, together with a detailed explanation of how these individual entities interact to produce the overall performance of the economy. The components of the micro foundations are identical to those studied in microeconomics — households make choices to maximize utility, firms make choices to maximize profit, and decisions about demand and supply made by households and firms interact in markets to produce prices and quantities traded.

We'll pay quite a lot of attention to the micro foundations as we proceed through our study of macroeconomics in the rest of this book.

■ This first chapter has introduced you to the subject matter of macroeconomics, to some facts about macroeconomic performance in Canada and the rest of the world, and to the problem of macroeconomic stabilization. It has also given you a sketch of the range of beliefs of macroeconomists about how the economy works, how it might be stabilized, and how we can learn more about the workings of the macroeconomy.

Our next task is to learn about the measurement and observation of macroeconomic activity—how a nation's macroeconomic performance is recorded. That's the subject of Chapter 2.

CHAPTER REVIEW

Summary

WHAT MACROECONOMICS IS ABOUT

Macroeconomics is the study of fluctuations in aggregate economic activity. It seeks to understand what determines

- The unemployment rate
- The level and rate of growth of real GDP
- The general level of prices and the rate of inflation
- The level of interest rates
- The balance of transactions with the rest of the world
- The value of the dollar in relation to other currencies

THE CHANGING PACE OF ECONOMIC EXPANSION AND INFLATION IN THE CANADIAN AND WORLD ECONOMIES

Real incomes per person have grown steadily in Canada and in most other countries. Real income per person in Canada is among the highest in the world, but growth rates in the rich countries (Japan, West Germany, France, Italy) are higher, on the average, than those in Canada and real income levels in the rich countries are converging. Growth rates in poorer countries are similar to those in rich countries, but the gap between the rich and the poor persists.

Income growth does not take place at an even pace. Periods of rapid expansion alternate with periods of contraction over the business cycle. The Canadian business cycle has been less severe since World War II than in the Great Depression years but remains an important feature of economic life. The world business cycle and the Canadian business cycle are strongly aligned. Inflation has been a persistent feature of economic life in Canada and throughout the world. In the 1960s, the Canadian inflation rate increased slightly while that in the rest of the world decreased. In the 1970s, there was a worldwide inflation explosion in which Canada shared. In the 1980s Canadian inflation moderated. In general, inflation in the rest of the world has been more severe than in Canada.

THE PROBLEM OF STABILIZING THE ECONOMY

The problem of stabilizing the economy is one of setting the goals to be achieved and devising arrangements that achieve those goals. There is general agreement that it is desirable to attain a high and steady rate of growth of real GDP, a low and stable level of unemployment, and a moderate or zero rate of inflation. There is less agreement on whether it is possible to achieve these goals and, if so, how best to do so.

THE MAIN SCHOOLS OF THOUGHT

Economists hold a variety of views that, in general, reflect differences about

- How the economy works
- How it might be stabilized

Classical macroeconomists believe the economy operates like a self-regulating mechanism, always tending toward full employment. Keynesian macroeconomists believe the economy has a fundamental design problem that can keep it away from full employment for long periods at a time.

On stabilization policy issues, there are also two views. Monetarists believe that a fixed rule governing the growth rate of the money supply and possibly other rules governing the size of the federal government budget deficit offer the best hope for achieving macroeconomic stability. Activists believe that discretionary changes in interest rates, taxes, and government spending are an essential component of any policy that will achieve a more stable economy.

On the macroeconomic research agenda there are also two views. New classical macroeconomists are trying to find explanations for economic fluctuations and unemployment based on the notion that the economy is an efficient self-regulating mechanism. New Keynesian macroeconomists are seeking to develop explanations based on wage and price stickiness and other sources of market failure.

Key Terms and Concepts

Aggregate economic activity The performance of the economy as a whole, that is, in the aggregate.

Business cycle The recurring fluctuation in the pace of economic expansion.

Classical macroeconomics A body of theory based on the idea that the economy is a self-regulating mechanism, always tending in the direction of full employment.

Direct controls Specific laws, rules, and regulations designed to modify the way people behave.

Fiscal policy The use of variations in the levels of government spending and taxes to influence the state of the economy.

Inflation The process of rising prices.

Keynesian macroeconomics A body of theory based on the idea that the economy does not possess a self-regulating mechanism and, left to its own devices, it can get stuck with a high and persistent level of unemployment and lost output. This view is an outgrowth of the writings of John Maynard Keynes.

Macroeconomic policy targets The goals of macroeconomic stabilization policy.

Macroeconomics The study of aggregate economic activity and, in particular, the study of real GDP growth, unemployment, and inflation.

Monetary policy The use of variations in the supply of money and interest rates to influence the state of the economy.

Real GDP A measure of the quantity of the goods and services that can be bought with the income of all the individuals in the economy in a year.

Unemployment rate The percentage of the labor force that is out of work and seeking jobs.

Review Questions

1. Explain what macroeconomics studies.
2. What is aggregate economic activity?
3. What are the six important questions for macroeconomics?
4. For the Canadian economy from 1926 to 1990, describe the main features of
   (a) real GDP growth
   (b) the business cycle
   (c) unemployment
   (d) inflation
5. Compare growth, cycles, and inflation in the Canadian economy with that in the rest-of-the-world economy since 1970.

6. What are the goals of stabilization policy? Are macroeconomists generally agreed on these goals?
7. How can the goals of macroeconomic stabilization policy be achieved? Are macroeconomists generally agreed on how to achieve macroeconomic stability?
8. Describe the main schools of thought and explain the main disagreements between them.
9. Compare and contrast classical and Keynesian macroeconomics.
10. Compare and contrast the stabilization policy recommendations of monetarists and activists.

Problems

1. Read the following statements carefully and classify each of them according to whether it (i) deals with detailed or global policy; (ii) is talking about a rule or discretion in the conduct of policy; or (iii) is a probable policy recommendation of a monetarist or activist:
   (a) A law requiring the government to balance its budget will rob the government of needed flexibility in adjusting spending and tax plans.
   (b) Almost every country has curbed its money supply in the fight against inflation.
   (c) People look to the government for a wide array of social programs: generous old-age pensions, broad medical coverage, education loans, and unemployment insurance.
   (d) The decisive political issue for the 1990s will be to get government expenditures under control.
   (e) Wage and price controls will never work because they are self-defeating.
   (f) The steady deterioration of the Western economies has put ever greater pressure on politicians to find a way to revive economic growth and reduce unemployment.
   (g) Price controls on natural gas keep its price artificially low and people consume more than they should. They waste it.
   (h) Another crucial policy issue facing all nations is the proper role of government in revitalizing industry and promoting technological progress.
   (i) The inflation cycle can be broken only if governments reduce their spending and keep their money supplies expanding at a slow pace.
   (j) Conservation of gasoline should be pushed a bit faster and further than market prices alone have done.
   (k) In Western countries, economic programs are usually based on the fundamental precept that government must respect, protect, and enhance the freedom and integrity of the individual.
   (l) For several decades, an ever-larger role for the federal government and, more recently, inflation have zapped Canada's economic vitality.
   (m) The government's commitment to regulatory reform is clear in its sale of crown corporations and in the increased competition among airlines.
   (n) The government supports a policy of gradual and less volatile reduction of the growth of the money supply.
   (o) To spur further business investment and productivity growth, a new tax law that provides faster write-offs for capital investment is needed as well as a restructuring of investment tax credits. A new tax credit is needed to encourage more research and development.

(p) Across-the-board cuts in individual income tax rates phased in over three years and the indexing of tax brackets in subsequent years will help put an end to making inflation profitable for the government.
(q) The progress in reducing inflation began during 1981 and continued in 1982.
(r) Long-term interest rates have remained high in recent years.
(s) Gasoline prices at the retail level increased during the Gulf crisis.

2. Use the data in Appendix A (at the end of this book) to compare the evolution of the economy during the 1960s and the 1980s. During which period was
(a) unemployment lower on the average?
(b) inflation lower on the average?
(c) the trend in inflation upward?
(d) real income growing the faster?
(e) the value of the dollar stronger, on the average, abroad?

3. Use the data in Appendices A and B to compare the growth of real income, inflation, and unemployment in the U.S. and Canadian economies in the 1960s and 1980s.

C H A P T E R

Monitoring Macroeconomic Activity

A DAY IN THE LIFE OF THE ECONOMY

EVERY WORKING DAY IN CANADA, an incredible volume of economic activity takes place. Some highlights:

- Consumers spend more than $1 billion on goods and services.
- Businesses buy more than $0.3 billion worth of new plant and equipment and inventories.
- Federal, provincial, and local governments spend $0.3 billion, providing us with various kinds of public goods and services, such as highways, public health, education, and defense.
- We sell almost $0.3 billion worth of goods and services to foreigners and buy a similar quantity from them.
- Firms produce goods and services worth almost $2 billion.
- Firms spend several billion dollars buying raw materials, semi-finished products, and component parts for use in later stages of production.
- Cheques worth more than $3 billion pass through our banking system.
- We supply 80 million hours of labor services, earning us $1.2 billion of income.
- The government collects $0.6 billion from us in taxes and pays back $0.3 billion in benefits, such as family allowances, pension benefits, and unemployment benefits.
- More than $40 billion of money circulates in our economy and the total volume of government debt outstanding exceeds $300 billion.
- Stocks and bonds worth many billion dollars change hands.
- Banks and trust companies make billions of dollars of new loans.
- Many millions of dollars worth of foreign exchange transactions take place, not only to pay for exports and imports of goods and services, but to buy and sell stocks and bonds in the world capital markets.

These are just some of the things that happen each day in the life of the Canadian economy. How do we keep track of all this enormously complex range and scale of economic activity so that we can begin to make sense of it all? The answer is that we use a system of aggregate economic accounts. These accounts are similar to those used by firms and households to keep track of and monitor their own economic activities. The goal of this chapter is to describe and explain the aggregate economic accounts and the concepts used in constructing them.

After studying this chapter, you will be able to

- Explain the distinction between flows and stocks
- Explain the distinction between expenditure on final goods and intermediate transactions
- Explain why aggregate income, expenditure, and product (or the value of output) are equal
- Explain the connection between the government budget deficit and the international trade deficit
- Define gross domestic product (GDP)
- Define nominal GDP and real GDP
- Explain what a balance sheet measures
- Define capital, wealth, and money
- Describe the main features of the debt explosion of the 1980s
- Explain how economic growth and inflation are measured

Let's begin by learning about the distinction between flows and stocks.

2.1 *Flows and Stocks*

An important distinction that helps us keep track of economic activity — both for the nation and for ourselves — is between a flow and a stock. A **flow** is a variable that measures a rate per unit of time. The number of airplanes taking off from Toronto's Pearson International Airport in an hour is a flow. Examples of macroeconomic flows are income and expenditure. These flows are expressed as dollars per unit of time. Another macroeconomic flow is the number of hours worked per week. Contrasting with a flow is a stock. A **stock** is a variable measured at a point in time. The number of airplanes sitting on the ground at Toronto Airport at any given point in time is a stock. Examples of macroeconomic stocks are the total amount of money in the economy or the total amount of buildings, plant, and capital equipment in operation at a given point in time.

Links between flows and stocks

Flows and stocks are linked because flows change stocks. Suppose you plug the drain of an empty bathtub and then open the faucet. Water *flows* into the tub. The water in the tub is a stock. As the water flows in, the *stock* increases. Conversely, if you turn off the faucet and take out the plug, water flows through the drain and the stock of water in the bathtub decreases. You can even imagine having the faucet open and the drain unplugged, with the flow of water into the tub exactly matching the flow out and the stock remaining constant.

Capital and investment

One of the most important macroeconomic stocks is the stock of capital. **Capital** is the stock of buildings, plant and equipment, houses, consumer durable goods, and inventories. Additions to the stock of capital are called investment. That is, **investment** is the purchase of new buildings, plant and capital, houses, consumer durable goods, or inventories. For some purposes it is useful to distinguish between investment in inventories, called **inventory investment**, and all other forms of investment, called **fixed investment**.

The opposite of investment is depreciation. **Depreciation** is the reduction in the value of capital that results from the use of the capital or from the passage of time. The capital stock increases because of investment and decreases because of depreciation. The total additions to the capital stock in a given period of time are called **gross investment**. The change in the capital stock equals gross investment minus depreciation, and is called **net investment**.

Let's illustrate the relationship between capital, investment, and depreciation with a concrete example. Imagine that on June 1, 1991, you had a 1985 car with a current market value of $4000. In the year from June 1, 1991, to June 1, 1992, the market value of the car fell to $3200. The value of the car on June 1 each year is a stock. That stock fell from $4000 in 1991 to $3200 in 1992. The decrease in the value of the car—depreciation—is a flow. That flow is $800 a year (or, equivalently, $66.67 a month). If, in May 1992, you sold your 1985 car and replaced it with a 1988 car valued at $6000, your capital stock in June of 1992 would be the same $6000. In this case you've made an investment. The value of your investment is $2800—the difference between the $6000 that your newer car is worth and the $3200 that your old car would have been worth, had you kept it. The change in your capital stock from June 1991 to June 1992 is not $2800 but $2000. This increase in your capital stock is made up of the $2800 investment in the new car—your *gross investment*—minus the $800 depreciation of the old car. The difference between your gross investment and depreciation is your *net investment*.

Think about the similarity between this example and the bathtub. You can think of the water in the bathtub as the capital stock—the value of your car; the outflow through the drain as depreciation—the fall in the value of your car; and the inflow through the faucet as gross investment—your purchase of a car. The inflow minus the outflow is net investment—the change in the value of your car.

We're going to be looking more closely at both macroeconomic flows and macroeconomic stocks in this chapter. First, let's look at flows and discover what we mean by income, expenditure, and product.

2.2 Defining Income, Expenditure, and Product

Macroeconomic flows are divided into the following categories:

- Income
- Expenditure
- Product
- Intermediate transactions

We are about to discover that, for the economy as a whole, the magnitudes of the first three of these items—income, expenditure, and product—are equal. But to establish this fact, we must be careful about how these terms are defined and measured.

Income

Income is the total payment made for the services of the factors of production employed in the economy. It is the sum of wages paid to labor, interest paid to the suppliers of capital, rent paid to the suppliers of land, and profit paid to the owners of firms. Income is important because it is a measure of the general standard of living. It is also a measure of aggregate economic activity based on the total amount paid to the factors of production that have created the goods and services produced.

Expenditure

Expenditure is the purchase of final goods and services. **Final goods and services** are goods and services bought by households—including consumer durable goods and new houses; new plant, equipment, and buildings bought by firms, and net increases in firms' inventories; goods and services bought by governments; and goods and services bought by foreigners (exports) minus the goods and services we buy from the rest of the world (imports). Expenditure is another measure of aggregate economic activity based on the value of all the final goods and services bought by households, firms, governments, and foreigners.

Product

The value of final goods and services produced is called **product**. This is a third measure of aggregate economic activity based on the value of all the final goods and services produced in the economy.

Intermediate transactions

The purchase of goods and services by firms for use in later stages of the production of final goods and services are **intermediate transactions**. Intermediate transactions *do not* measure aggregate economic activity. The same individual item can be the subject of many intermediate transactions. For example, the wood pulp in the paper on the page that you're reading was bought by the papermaker and turned into paper. It was then bought, this time in the form of paper, by the printer. Next, it was bought by the publisher, and then by the bookstore, and finally by you. Adding together all these intermediate transactions would count the value of the wood pulp many times over.

Let's take a close look at the distinctions between the four types of macroeconomic flows by studying an example.

Example: The life of a chocolate bar

Suppose that you buy a chocolate bar from the local store for $1.00. The store bought that chocolate bar from its wholesale supplier for 80¢; the wholesaler bought it from the manufacturer for 72¢; the manufacturer bought milk for 4¢, cocoa beans for 8¢, sugar for 8¢, and hydro for 12¢; it paid wages to its workers of 28¢ and made a 12¢ profit, which it paid to its stockholders. The total flow of money in the story of the chocolate bar is $1.00 + 80¢ + 72¢ + 4¢ + 8¢ + 8¢ + 12¢ + 28¢ + 12¢ = $3.24. Of this $3.24, only $1.00 is expenditure on final goods and services. The other $2.24 is a combination of payments to factors of production—income—and intermediate transactions. Table 2.1(a) shows how the total money flow divides into expenditure on final goods and services, factor incomes, and intermediate transactions.

Recall that one of the main purposes of macroeconomics is to explain fluctuations in aggregate economic activity. Aggregate economic activity can be measured by total income or total expenditure (that is, the total payments made for the services of factors of production, or the total payments made for the purchases of final goods and services). It cannot be measured by intermediate transactions. There are two reasons.

Intermediate transactions—not an aggregate First, intermediate transactions depend on the structure and organization of an industry. If that structure and organization changed, so would intermediate transactions even though there is no change in final expenditure or payments to factors of production. For example, if the chocolate manufacturer sold directly to the retailer (for the 80¢ charged by the wholesaler in the above

TABLE 2.1
Classifying Transactions

(a) Final Expenditure, Factor Incomes, and Intermediate Transactions

ITEM	FINAL EXPENDITURE	FACTOR INCOMES	INTERMEDIATE TRANSACTIONS
Price of a chocolate bar	$1.00	—	—
Wholesaler's selling price	—	—	80¢
Manufacturer's selling price	—	—	72¢
Farmer's income (milk)	—	4¢	—
Farmer's income (cocoa beans)	—	8¢	—
Farmer's income (sugar)	—	8¢	—
Hydro producer's income	—	12¢	—
Chocolate producer's wages	—	28¢	—
Chocolate producer's profit	—	12¢	—
Wholesaler's profit	—	8¢	—
Retailer's profit	—	20¢	—
Total	**$1.00**	**$1.00**	

(b) Value Added

PRODUCER	VALUE ADDED
Milk farmer	4¢
Cocoa farmer	8¢
Sugar farmer	8¢
Hydro company	12¢
Chocolate manufacturer	40¢
Wholesaler	8¢
Retailer	20¢
Total	**$1.00**

example), intermediate transactions would fall by 72¢. There would be no change in aggregate economic activity, as measured by the goods and services actually consumed or the work done by factors of production. Expenditure on final goods and services would still be $1.00. Also, factor incomes would still be $1.00. The profit of the wholesaler would have been eliminated but the profit of the manufacturer would have increased by the same amount.

Intermediate transactions ''double count'' There is a second reason why intermediate transactions do not measure aggregate economic activity. They count the same thing several times. At each stage in the evolution of the chocolate bar from the manufacturer of the ingredients, the conversion of those ingredients into a chocolate bar, and the transportation, distribution, and retail services that make it finally available in a convenient place to the consumer, the chocolate bar becomes more valuable—value is added to the emerging product. Each time a transaction takes place, transferring ownership of the evolving chocolate bar from manufacturer to wholesaler to retailer and eventually to final consumer, the amount paid reflects the total value of all the previous stages. The value of these previous stages of production gets counted in the total value of intermediate transactions several times. This phenomenon of counting the same thing more than once is called ''double counting.'' Double counting can be avoided by counting only the *final expenditure* on the good. It can also be avoided by counting only the value added at each stage in the production process, instead of the total value exchanged at each stage of the process.

Value added The increase in the value of a product when factors of production are used to transform it from one stage in the production or distribution process to the next is called **value added**. In the example of the chocolate bar, the value added by the milk farmer is 4¢, by the cocoa bean farmer is 8¢, by the sugar farmer is 8¢, and by the hydro producer is 12¢. The value added by the chocolate manufacturer is 40¢. This amount is made up of the wages paid to the workers and the profit resulting from the organization of the production process. Value added by the wholesaler is 8¢ and by the retailer is 20¢. The sum of all the value-added components is the same as the factor incomes.

We've defined income, expenditure, and product and have used the example of an individual product—a chocolate bar—to illustrate these concepts. Let's now go beyond the definitions and example and study *aggregate* income, expenditure, and product.

2.3 The Circular Flow of Income and Expenditure

To understand *aggregate* income, expenditure, and product, let's begin by considering an economy that is much simpler than the one we live in. We'll then add various features to this economy until we have a picture that corresponds quite closely to the real world.

The simplest economy

Imagine an economy that has no transactions with the rest of the world—no one exports goods and services to foreigners or imports from them, and no borrowing or lending takes place across national borders. Also imagine that there is no government. That is, no one pays taxes; all expenditures by households are voluntary; and all the goods and services that firms produce are bought by households, rather than some of them being bought by governments or their agencies.

The economy consists of just two kinds of economic agents: households and firms. Households:

1. Own the factors of production
2. Buy all final goods and services

Firms:

1. Hire factors of production from households
2. Sell goods and services to households
3. Pay any profits made to households

To see this economy, look at Figure 2.1. The circle labeled *Households* represents the households in this economy, and the circle labeled *Firms* represents the firms. Two kinds of flows take place between households and firms. First, real things flow from households to firms and from firms to households—households supply factors of production to firms, and firms supply goods and services to households. The black line represents the real flows. Second, money flows between households and firms in exchange for the real things. Firms pay income to households, and households spend their income on goods and services. The blue lines represent the money flows, which move in the opposite direction to the real flows. The flow of money into households is income; the flow of money from households is consumer expenditure. **Consumer expenditure** is the value of goods and services bought by households. We'll call the aggregate income payment to households Y and aggregate consumer expenditure C.

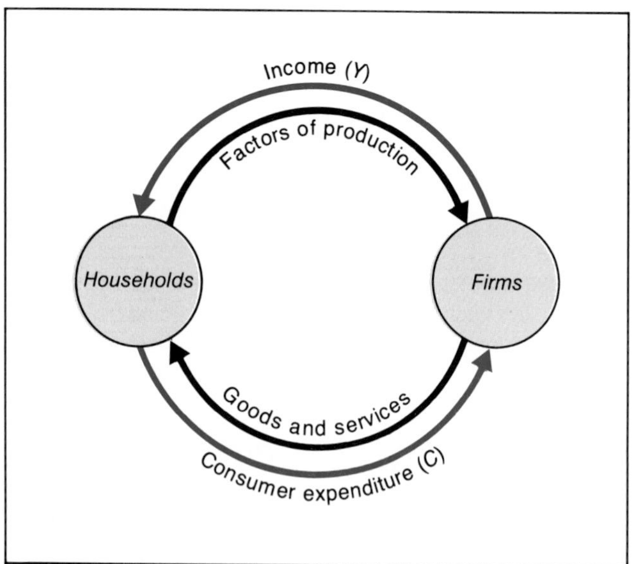

FIGURE 2.1
Real Flow and Money Flows in a Simplified Economy

The flow of factors of production from households to firms and the flow of goods and services from firms to households are matched by equivalent flows of money—firms paying income to households (Y) and households paying firms for goods and services (C).

In this economy, the income households receive from firms and the expenditure that households make on goods and services are equal. Also the value of the goods and services produced by the firms is equal to the expenditure on goods and services by the households. In other words,

$$\textit{Expenditure} = \textit{Income} = \textit{Product}.$$

By looking at this simple economy, we have established the equality of income, expenditure, and product. This equality follows from the definitions of these terms. Let's now go on to see that this equality also holds in a more complicated world.

A more realistic economy: saving and investment

Households do not spend all their income on goods and services. They save some of it. **Saving** is the difference between household income and consumer expenditure. So there is something missing from Figure 2.1. If households save some of their income, then consumer expenditure must be less than income, and, therefore, the flow of expenditure from households to firms must be smaller than the flow of income received by households from firms. Does this mean that firms are continually short of cash, paying out more than they are receiving? How does household saving affect the equality of income, expenditure, and product?

To answer these questions, look at Figure 2.2. Households receive income Y from firms and dispose of that income either by spending it on goods and services or by saving it. The flow of household expenditure goes back to firms as consumer expenditure. Household saving flows into the financial markets. Some of it winds up as money in the bank, some of it is used to buy stocks and bonds, and some of it is used to pay off loans. Saving is a leakage. A **leakage** is a flow from the circular flow of income and expenditure.

Firms' receipts are from consumer expenditure (C) and investment (I). Consumer expenditure flows from households to firms. Investment is the purchase of new capital —*fixed investment*— and net additions to inventories — *inventory investment*. To buy new capital equipment and additional inventories, firms borrow in capital markets.

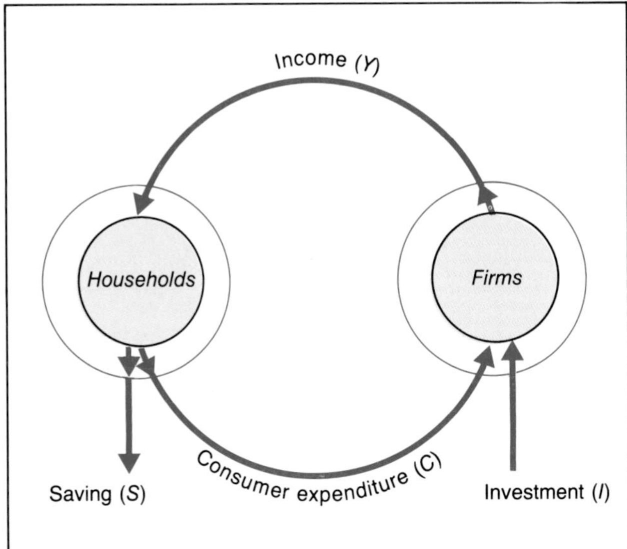

FIGURE 2.2
Money Flows in an Economy with Saving and Investment

Focus on the circles around Households and Firms that contain arrows showing the flows into and out of the two sectors. An arrow leading into a sector is a receipt, an arrow leading from a sector is a payment. Total receipts by each sector equal total payments. For households, income (Y) equals consumption expenditure (C) plus saving (S). For firms, payments for factor services (income) equals receipts from the sale of goods and services (C) plus the sale of new capital equipment (I). Because Y equals $C + S$ and Y equals $C + I$, S equals I.

Investment is an injection. An **injection** is a flow into the circular flow of income and expenditure. It is the capital markets—markets in which people borrow and lend—that link saving (a leakage) and investment (an injection).

Figure 2.2 illustrates an important relationship between saving and investment. To see this relationship, focus first of all on firms. There you see an extra blue circle around *Firms* that contains three arrows, two leading into firms and one going from firms.

Firms' receipts are equal to total expenditure, which is the sum of consumer expenditure and investment. That is,

$$\textit{Expenditure } (E) = \textit{Consumer Expenditure } (C) + \textit{Investment } (I)$$

or

$$E = C + I \tag{2.1}$$

Firms' payments are equal to total income (Y). But what firms receive they pay out to households as incomes. That is,

$$E = Y \tag{2.2}$$

Next, focus on households and on the blue circle surrounding *Households* in Figure 2.2. This circle has three arrows, one leading into households and two going from households. Since households can dispose of their income only by spending it or saving it, consumer expenditure plus saving (the outflows from households) must equal income. That is,

$$Y = C + S \tag{2.3}$$

Since expenditure equals income an implication of Equations (2.1) and (2.2) is that saving is always equal to investment in this imaginary economy. That is, the leakage from the circular flow of income and expenditure and the injection into it are always equal. Table 2.2 shows you why.

You may be saying to yourself: I can see that saving and investment are equal to each other in this model economy, but what brings that equality about? The key to understanding why saving and investment are equal lies in the behavior of inventory investment. Suppose that firms produce $1000 worth of goods and services and they

TABLE 2.2
Leakages Equal Injections: No International Trade and No Government

(a) Definitions

		SYMBOLS
1. *Income* = *Expenditure*		$Y = E$
2. *Income* = *Consumer expenditure* + *Saving*		$Y = C + S$
3. *Expenditure* = *Consumer expenditure* + *Investment*		$Y = C + I$
4. Leakages:	*Saving*	S
5. Injections:	*Investment*	I

(b) Calculations

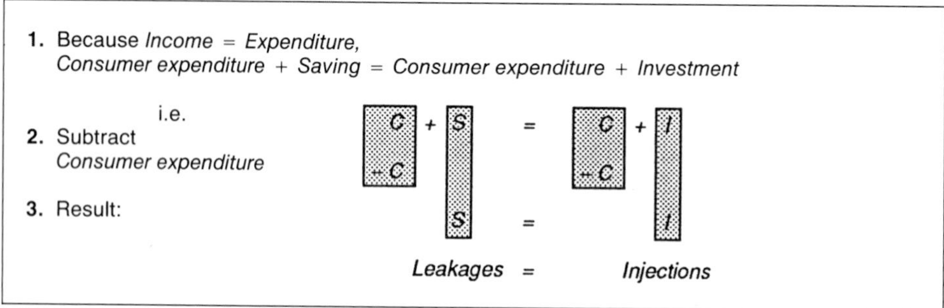

pay incomes of $1000 to households. Suppose that households buy $900 worth of goods and services and save $100. Suppose, finally, that firms do not buy any new capital equipment. The only investment is the net change in the value of inventories—inventory investment. By how much do the firms' inventories change? Answer: by $100. That is, inventories change by an amount equal to the difference between the value of the goods produced ($1000) and the value of the goods and services sold ($900). Thus saving equals investment—the leakage equals the injection.

Expenditure equals income and it is also equal to product, the value of output. To see this, all you have to do is to recognize that the value of the goods and services produced is equal to the value placed on them by the final demanders of those goods and services. That value is the value of consumer expenditure plus investment. Thus income, expenditure, and product are equal again in this more ''realistic'' representation of the world.

The economy that we have been studying has many features of the real economy but it lacks sufficient detail to be a useful model. In particular, it has no government. Let's examine how government macroeconomic activity enters the picture.

2.4 *The Government*

Governments undertake three important types of macroeconomic activity:

- Purchases of goods and services
- Collection of taxes
- Payment of benefits and subsidies

In its purchases of goods and services, the government acts in a way similar to households. **Government purchases of goods and services** is expenditure by the government on final goods and services. It buys goods and services from firms. An example of a government purchase is the purchase of a new telephone system from Northern Telecom.

Governments collect taxes from both households and firms. But the taxes paid by firms are really paid on behalf of the households that own the firms. We'll keep things clearer if we pretend that firms pay households their total income (income including taxes), and then households pay the taxes directly to the government.

Payments of benefits and subsidies by the government are called **transfer payments**. Think of transfer payments as negative taxes — they are flows of money from government to households that partially offset the taxes paid by households to government. In macroeconomics we usually take transfer payments and total taxes paid together and use the term **taxes** to mean total taxes paid minus transfer payments.

Figure 2.3 illustrates an economy with a government sector. Households receive income (Y) from firms and they dispose of it by buying goods and services (C), paying taxes (T), or saving (S). Firms receive consumer expenditure (C) as well as investment (I) (financed by various capital market operations). They also receive the government's expenditure on goods and services (G). The government receives taxes (net of the transfer payments it makes to households) and purchases goods and services.

Let's now look at income, expenditure, and product that emerge from this more complex world. Focus first of all on the arrows flowing into and out of firms. Firms pay out income (Y) and receive consumer expenditure (C), government purchases (G), and investment (I). Since everything firms receive they pay out to households as income (Y),

$$E = C + I + G \tag{2.4}$$

$$E = Y \tag{2.5}$$

Next, focus on households. They receive income (Y) and dispose of that by spending it on goods and services (C), saving (S), and paying taxes (net of transfer payments) (T). So

$$Y = C + S + T \tag{2.6}$$

In this model economy, expenditure is still equal to income, but expenditure now incorporates consumer expenditure, investment, and government purchases of goods and services. As in the two simpler economies considered above, not only are income

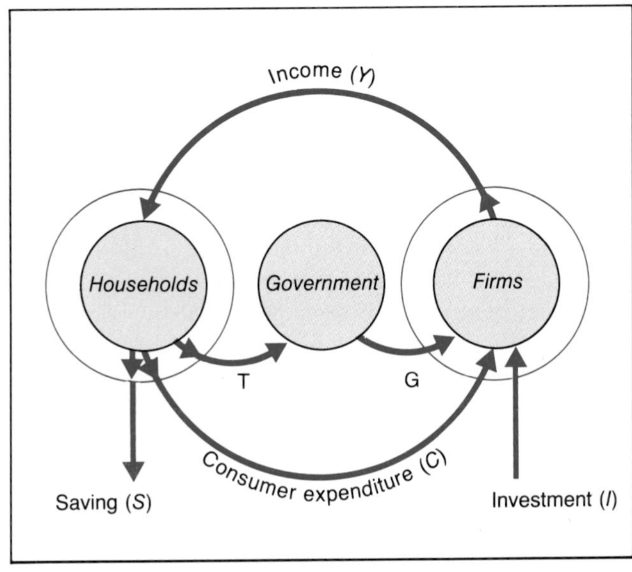

FIGURE 2.3
Money Flows in an Economy with Saving, Investment, and Government

The government buys goods and services produced by firms — government purchases of goods and services are shown by G. The government taxes households and makes transfer payments to households. The taxes collected net of the transfer payments made is shown by T. For households, income equals expenditure, so that $Y = C + I + T$. For firms, income paid out equals receipts, so that $Y = C + I + G$. There is no requirement for government purchases to equal taxes. The government may run a budget surplus ($T > G$), or a budget deficit ($T < G$).

and expenditure equal to each other, but product is also equal to income and expenditure. The value of the goods and services bought by households (C), by firms (I), and by government (G) represents the value of the goods and services produced in the economy — the output of the economy. Hence, even in this more complex economy, income, expenditure, and product are equal.

Saving and investment are no longer equal in this economy. But leakages and injections are equal. In this economy, leakages from the circular flow are saving and taxes, and injections are investment and government purchases. There is equality between saving *plus* taxes and investment *plus* government purchases of goods and services and this equality is explained in Table 2.3. Again, it is inventory investment that always ensures this equality.

TABLE 2.3
Leakages Equal Injections: No International Trade

(a) Definitions

	SYMBOLS
1. *Income* = *Expenditure*	$Y = E$
2. *Income* = *Consumer expenditure* + *Saving* + *Taxes*	$Y = C + S + T$
3. *Expenditure* = *Consumer expenditure* + *Investment* + *Government purchases*	$Y = C + I + G$
4. Leakages: *Saving* + *Taxes*	$S + T$
5. Injections: *Investment* + *Government purchases*	$I + G$

(b) Calculations

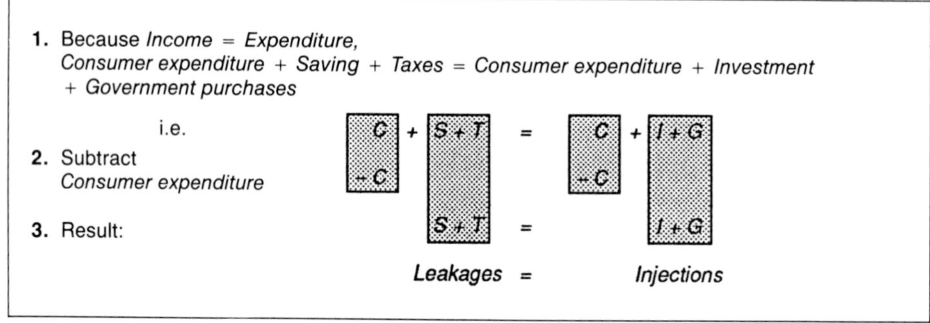

2.5 *The Rest of the World*

Let's now bring the rest of the world into our model. Figure 2.4 illustrates the economy, now made up of four agents—households, firms, government, and the rest of the world. All the flows are as before, except for some additional flows between the rest of the world and the domestic economy. The left part of Figure 2.4 is identical to Figure 2.3. The additional activities in Figure 2.4 are exports and imports of goods and services. Foreigners buy goods and services from domestic firms. **Exports** (EX) is the flow of money from the rest of the world in exchange for domestically produced goods and services. Domestic firms buy goods and services from foreigners. **Imports** (IM) is the flow of money to the rest of the world in exchange for foreign produced goods and services. **Net exports** is exports minus imports.

Let's consider income, expenditure, and product by first focusing on the flows into and out of households. Households buy goods and services, some of which now have

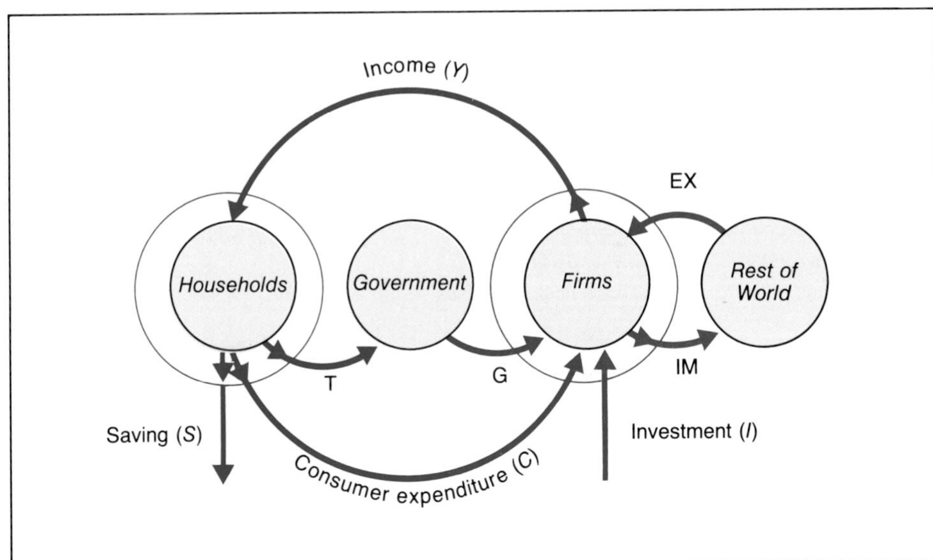

FIGURE 2.4
Money Flows in an Economy with Saving, Investment, Government Economic Activity, and Transactions with the Rest of the World

Firms export goods and services to the rest of the world, which results in a flow (*EX*). The rest of the world imports goods and services from firms, which results in a flow (*IM*) out of firms. Extending the flows to include those with the rest of the world leaves household income and expenditure unchanged. That is, $Y = C + S + T$. For firms, the income paid out to households equals their receipts from the sale of goods and services they produce, that is, $Y = C + I + G + EX - IM$. Combining these two equations gives $S + T + IM = I + G + EX$. There is no requirement for exports (*EX*) to equal imports (*IM*). There may be a trade surplus ($EX > IM$) or a trade deficit ($EX < IM$) with the rest of the world.

been imported by the firms from the rest of the world and sold to households. Expenditure on imported goods do not show up directly as a flow from the households. Their inflow of income (Y) still is equal to consumer expenditure (C), plus saving (S), plus taxes (T), as shown in Equation (2.6) above.

In Figure 2.4, we can see the imports and exports by looking at firms. There are now two arrows leading out of firms and four arrows flowing into firms. Firms pay incomes to households (Y) and pay foreigners for the value of goods and services imported from them (IM). They receive from foreigners payments for exports (EX), government purchases on goods and services (G), consumer expenditure (C), and investment (I). Thus total expenditure is now given by

$$E = C + I + G + EX - IM. \quad \textbf{(2.7)}$$

The right side of this equation is the total expenditure on domestic output.

Income is the flow of money from firms to households, and it represents the value of the factor services supplied by households to firms. Expenditure is equal to the sum of consumer expenditure (C), investment (I), government purchases of goods and services (G), and exports of goods and services (EX) minus imports of goods and services (IM). So, the equality between income and expenditure is retained in this more realistic economy. In addition, product (the value of output) is equal to income and expenditure.

An implication of the equality of income and expenditure and Equations (2.6) and (2.7) above is that leakages equal injections. Leakages are saving, taxes, and imports. Injections are investment, government purchases of goods and services, and exports. The equality of leakages and injections is shown in Table 2.4.

TABLE 2.4
Leakages Equal Injections

(a) Definitions

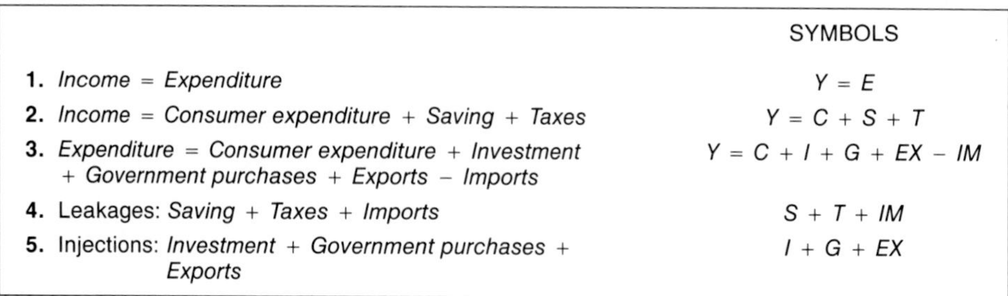

	SYMBOLS
1. *Income* = *Expenditure*	$Y = E$
2. *Income* = *Consumer expenditure* + *Saving* + *Taxes*	$Y = C + S + T$
3. *Expenditure* = *Consumer expenditure* + *Investment* + *Government purchases* + *Exports* − *Imports*	$Y = C + I + G + EX - IM$
4. Leakages: *Saving* + *Taxes* + *Imports*	$S + T + IM$
5. Injections: *Investment* + *Government purchases* + *Exports*	$I + G + EX$

(b) Calculations

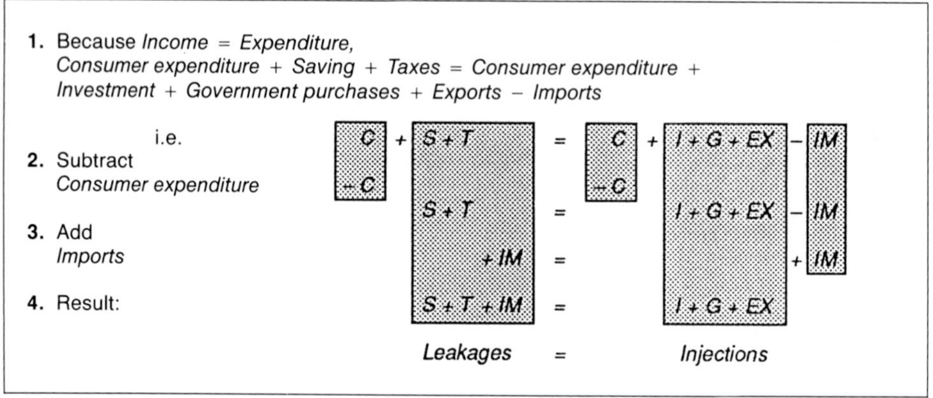

1. Because *Income* = *Expenditure*,
Consumer expenditure + *Saving* + *Taxes* = *Consumer expenditure* + *Investment* + *Government purchases* + *Exports* − *Imports*

i.e. $C + S + T = C + I + G + EX - IM$

2. Subtract *Consumer expenditure* $-C$ $\qquad S + T = I + G + EX - IM$

3. Add *Imports* $\qquad +IM = +IM$

4. Result: $\qquad S + T + IM = I + G + EX$

Leakages = *Injections*

Leakages, injections, deficits, and surpluses

The equality of leakages and injections,

$$S + T + IM = I + G + EX \tag{2.8}$$

has another interesting implication. It is that the private sector's net financial surplus plus the government's budget surplus plus the foreign sector's trade surplus with Canada always equals zero. To see this fact, first start with Equation (2.8), above. Then subtract from both sides of the equation I, G, and EX. You will then obtain

$$(S - I) + (T - G) + (IM - EX) = 0. \tag{2.9}$$

The first term in this equation $(S - I)$ is the excess of saving over investment by the private sector (by households and firms) and is the private sector's financial surplus. The second term $(T - G)$ is the government's budget surplus (when G is greater than T, the balance on the government's budget is negative—it has a deficit). The third term $(IM - EX)$ is the balance of the rest of the world's trade with Canada. This balance is the negative of the Canadian balance of trade with the rest of the world. That is, the rest of the world's surplus is our deficit, and vice versa.

Equation (2.9) says that the sum of these three sector balances is always zero. This implies that if the government spends more than it collects in taxes — it has a budget deficit—then either investment must be less than saving or there must be a trade deficit with the rest of the world—imports must exceed exports—to enable the government to make purchases of goods and services in excess of the taxes it collects.

2.6 *The Twin Deficits*

TESTCASE

We've just learned that the balances of the private sector, the government sector, and the rest of the world must add up to zero. Two of these sector balances have become especially important during the 1980s — the government sector balance and the rest of the world balance. The government sector balance has moved into a large deficit—taxes have been less than government purchases. The rest of the world has moved into a large surplus with Canada or, equivalently, Canada has moved into a large deficit with the rest of the world. The government's budget deficit and the Canadian deficit with the rest of the world are called the **twin deficits**.

You can see the twin deficits in Figure 2.5. This figure also shows the private sector balance. Notice that the bars for each year stretch above and below the zero line. Surpluses are measured above the zero line and deficits below it. Notice also that the bars above and below the zero line look like mirror images of each other. That tells us that in each year the surpluses equal the deficits. In other words, this picture agrees with Equation (2.9)—the sum of the sector balances is zero. Look, for example, at 1985. In

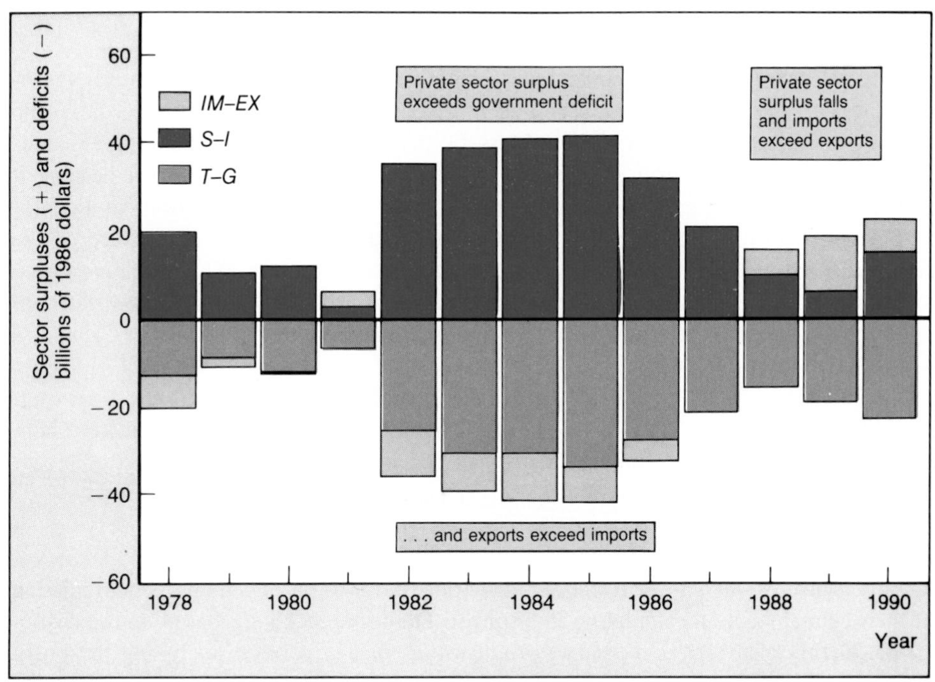

FIGURE 2.5
The Relationship Between Sector Balances

Sector balances for the private sector ($S - I$), the foreign sector ($IM - EX$), and the government sector ($T - G$) are shown. Surpluses appear above the zero line and deficits below it. Surpluses equal deficits. The surpluses and deficits are a mirror image of each other and sum to zero. Usually, there is a private sector surplus. When the government sector has a deficit, as it did throughout the 1980s, that deficit has to be matched by either a private sector surplus or a foreign sector surplus. During the mid-1980s, the private sector deficit exceeded the government deficit and the foreign sector is in deficit—Canadian exports exceed imports. In the later 1980s as the private sector surplus declined and in absolute terms became smaller than the government sector deficit, a foreign sector surplus emerged. A foreign sector surplus is the same thing as a Canadian trade deficit, and the trade deficit is financed by borrowing from the rest of the world.

Source: 1978-1989, *National Income and Expenditure Accounts*, Statistics Canada, Ottawa, 1990, Catalogue 13-201; 1990, *National Income and Expenditure Accounts*, Statistics Canada, Ottawa, 1991, Catalogue 13-001.

that year the private sector surplus of $41 billion was equal to the government sector deficit of $33 billion plus the foreign sector deficit (Canadian surplus with the rest of the world) of $8 billion.

The figure shows that the private sector had a surplus—saving exceeded investment—in all the years between 1978 and 1990. The figure also shows the swelling government sector deficit in the mid-1980s. This deficit occurred when the recession lowered tax revenue. But after 1985, the government deficit declined. The private sector surplus also declined and a deficit with the rest of the world opened up.

There are no simple mechanical rules enabling us to predict the pattern of the private sector and the foreign sector balances that result from a particular government sector deficit. Equation (2.9) tells us that the three sector balances add up to zero, so we know if the government has a budget deficit, either the private sector or the rest of the world must have a surplus and the combination of those two surpluses equals the government budget deficit. But the way in which the government budget deficit is matched by private and foreign balances is complex and changes over time.

2.7 The Measures of Aggregate Economic Activity

Aggregate economic activity can be measured in terms of aggregate expenditure, aggregate income, or aggregate product. The most common measures are gross domestic product and domestic income. **Gross domestic product (GDP)** is the the total expenditure on final goods and services in a year in Canada. GDP is a *gross* measure because it includes gross investment—firms' expenditure on new capital and additions to inventories. Depreciation of the existing capital is not deducted. GDP is a measure of the *domestic* economy—all economic activity taking place in Canada. An alternative measure of aggregate economic activity is gross *national* product (GNP). **Gross national product** is the total expenditure in a year on goods and services produced by Canadians wherever in the world that activity takes place.

Both GDP and GNP are valued at *market prices*, the prices paid by the final user. The difference between GDP and GNP is known as "net investment income from non-residents." It is not large for most countries and is small for Canada. Most countries pay more attention to GDP than to GNP for measuring aggregate economic activity.

Domestic income is the total income, including profit, paid for the services of factors of production used to produce goods and services in Canada in a year. Domestic income measures *net* aggregate economic activity because firms deduct the depreciation of their capital stock in calculating their profit. Domestic income is based on the cost of all the factors of production used to produce the good or service, including the profit made. It values domestic income at *factor cost*.

In most modern economies, including Canada, governments tax expenditure on some goods and subsidize expenditure on others. Provincial sales taxes and excise duties on liquor and tobacco are taxes on expenditure, and the sale of water from major irrigation projects at less than cost is a subsidized expenditure. Aggregate economic activity can be valued on either the market price or factor cost basis. The market price valuation includes taxes on expenditure and is net of subsidies. Factor cost valuation excludes taxes on expenditure but does not have subsidies netted out. If the government increases sales taxes and cuts income taxes by equal amounts, nothing happens to the level of aggregate economic activity. The market price valuation, however, rises, because market prices have increased as a result of the sales tax increase. The factor cost valuation does not change. Since macroeconomics is concerned with measuring the scale of economic activity, it uses the factor cost valuation. However, in practice, provided there are no large changes in indirect taxes and subsidies, the market price valuation also provides a good measure of the scale of economic activity.

Nominal GDP and Real GDP The value of goods and services produced in a year, measured in *current year prices,* is called **nominal GDP**. Nominal GDP changes either because of changes in prices or in the quantities of goods and services produced. To isolate the changes in the quantity of goods and services produced, we use the concept of real GDP. **Real GDP** is the value of the goods and services produced in a year, when output is valued at the prices prevailing in a base year. It is a measure of the quantity of goods and services *independent* of the current year's prices. So changes in *real* GDP tell us about the changes in the quantities of goods and services produced.

We'll look more closely at the distinction between nominal and real GDP later in this chapter. But next we're going to see how the various measures of aggregate economic activity that we've just reviewed are actually measured by Statistics Canada and used to produce our national income and expenditure accounts.

2.8 *National Income and Expenditure in Canada*

MACROFACTS

Gross domestic product (GDP) in Canada is measured by three alternative approaches:

- The expenditure approach
- The factor incomes approach
- The output approach

Let's look at each in turn.

The expenditure approach

To measure GDP using the expenditure approach, national income statisticians measure consumer expenditure (C), investment (I), government purchases of goods and services (G), exports (EX), and imports (IM). They then obtain a measure of GDP by using the equation

$$Y = C + I + G + EX - IM.$$

The expenditure approach values GDP at market prices. To convert this measure to the factor cost measure needed for macroeconomic analysis, it is necessary to deduct taxes on expenditure and add subsidies. National income statisticians measure investment as firms' gross investment, so the expenditure approach gives a gross measure of expenditure, income, or product.

The factor incomes approach

National income statisticians use the factor incomes approach to measure GDP by measuring domestic income. This approach adds together the incomes of all the factors of production—wages, interest, rent, and profits. This measure is automatically on a factor cost basis. But, since firms deduct the depreciation of their capital stock in calculating their profit, the factor incomes approach is a net measure of expenditure, income, or product. To convert this measure to a gross measure, it is necessary to add back the depreciation of the nation's capital stock.

The output approach

A third method of measuring national income and expenditure is to measure the value of output of each industry and then aggregate these values to arrive at an estimate of aggregate product. In addition to providing a third way of arriving at an estimate of GDP, this approach also provides estimates of the product of each major sector of the economy.

The relationship between the three approaches

Figure 2.6 illustrates the relationship between the expenditure approach, income approach, and output approach to the measurement of GDP. Each of the three columns on the left of the figure add up to GDP. The first column shows the expenditure approach to measuring GDP. The second column shows the output approach. The fourth column shows the factor incomes approach. The factor incomes approach gives us domestic income. The third column shows how GDP is divided between domestic income and the two adjustment items described above — depreciation and expenditure taxes minus subsidies.

Personal income concepts

Not all the income that makes up *domestic income* is actually paid out to households. Some of it is paid to the government in taxes, and some is retained by firms and used to finance new investment. Also, not all the income received by households comes from firms. Some comes from governments in the form of *transfer payments*. The total income actually received by households is called **personal income**. Personal income equals *national income* plus transfer payments from government minus business retained profits. *Business retained profits* are those profits not distributed to households in the form of dividends. Thus retained profits are part of income but not part of personal income. **Personal disposable income** is personal income minus personal income tax payments. Personal disposable income has an important influence on household spending and saving plans, as we'll discover in Chapter 4.

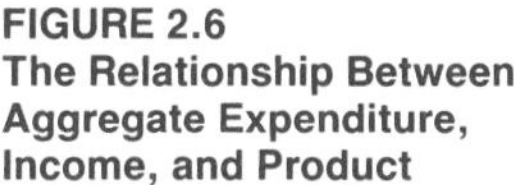

FIGURE 2.6
The Relationship Between Aggregate Expenditure, Income, and Product

The components of aggregate expenditure — consumer expenditure, investment, government purchases of goods and services, and net exports — add up to the same total as gross domestic product and to domestic income plus indirect taxes less subsidies plus depreciation. Domestic income is equal to the total of wages and other labor income, proprietors' income, profits, and interest.

Source: National Income and Expenditure Accounts, Statistics Canada, Ottawa, 1991, Catalogue 13-001.

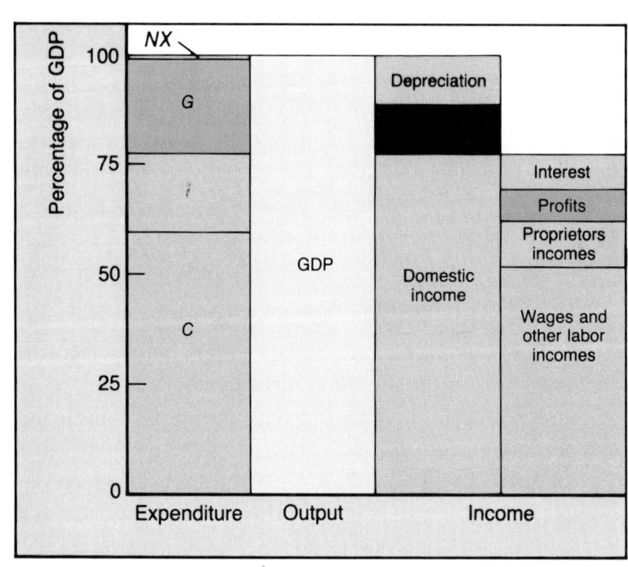

2.9 *Reading the Canadian National Income and Expenditure Accounts*

The Canadian national income accounts are assembled by Statistics Canada. The accounts are drawn up on a quarterly and annual basis and are published in the *National Income and Expenditure Accounts*.[1]

If you look at the *National Income and Expenditure Accounts* of Canada (you will find a copy in your college or university library or in the business/economics section of many public libraries), the first thing you'll notice (probably with mild alarm) is the immense detail it presents. It is hard to know where to begin. Fortunately, for the purposes of macroeconomic analysis, three tables contain most of what is needed. Table 2 gives the details of expenditure on the gross domestic product; Table 4 shows the relation between the domestic and national measures of aggregate income, and gives the information needed to calculate the factor cost, together with depreciation of the capital stock (capital consumption). Table 3 gives the real measure of gross domestic product at market prices.

The contents of these tables are brought together in Table 2.5 in a form that will enable you to see the relationships among the variables we have studied in this chapter.

TABLE 2.5
Canadian Domestic Income and Expenditure in 1990

		$ Millions
	Consumer expenditure (*C*) (personal expenditure on consumer goods and services, Table 2, line 1)	402,055
add	Investment (*I*) (gross private domestic investment, Table 2, line 6)	121,631
add	Government purchases (*G*) (government current expenditure on goods and services plus government investment, Table 2, lines 2, 3, and 4)	149,287
add	Exports (*EX*) (exports, Table 2, line 12)	168,435
deduct	Imports (*IM*) (imports, Table 2, line 15)	–165,464
deduct	Statistical discrepancy (Table 2, line 18)	1,956
equals	Gross domestic product (GDP) at market prices (gross domestic product, Table 2, line 19)	677,900
deduct	Indirect taxes less subsidies (Table 1, line 8)	–76,451
add	Statistical discrepancy (Table 2, line 18)	1,956
equals	Gross domestic product (GDP) at factor cost (*Y*) (not shown in official tables)	603,405
	Capital consumption (Table 1, line 9)	76,916
	Net investment income from non-residents (Table 4, line 2)	–24,223

Source: National Income and Expenditure Accounts, Catalogue 13-001 (Ottawa: Statistics Canada, April, 1991).

[1]Statistics Canada Catalogue 13-201 for annual data and Catalogue 13-001 for quarterly data; Statistics Canada, Ottawa, K1A 0T6.

The name (or names) of the items given in parentheses beneath each major item refers to the details contained in the national income and expenditure accounts tables. There is no need to memorize all this detail. You may, however, find it a useful reference if you want to construct your own accounts for a year or for years other than 1990, the example used here.

Looking at the major items in Table 2.5, you will see that consumer expenditure (C), *plus* investment (I), *plus* government purchases (G), *plus* exports (EX), *less* imports (IM) and a small statistical discrepancy adds up to gross domestic product (GDP) at market prices. By deducting indirect taxes less subsidies and adding the statistical discrepancy, gross domestic product (GDP) at factor cost is arrived at. The corresponding *net* domestic product, income, or expenditure is calculated by deducting capital consumption (depreciation of the capital stock).

The bottom of the table notes the amount of net investment income from non-residents. By adding net investment income from non-residents to the *domestic* figures, you will arrive at the corresponding *national* income, expenditure, or product.

How accurate is the official measure of GDP?

How good a job does Statistics Canada do in accurately measuring the value of all the goods and services produced in Canada? Some economists have suggested that the official measure *under*estimates the true value of GDP because it omits what is called the underground economy.

Underground economy The **underground economy** is that part of the economy engaged in illegal activities. It includes both criminal activity, such as drug dealing, and activities that are not themselves illegal but are concealed to avoid government regulations or taxes. This type of underground economic activity includes working while collecting unemployment benefits, working for cash and not declaring the income, or underreporting tips.

How big is the underground economy? No one knows the answer but estimates range from as little as 3 percent to as much as 30 percent of GDP.

Pollution and natural resource depletion

Some economists suggest that the official estimates of GDP *over*estimate the true value of GDP because they omit the cost of pollution and the destruction of natural resources such as the forests. These costs have not been estimated but they certainly exist. And they could be very large costs if the worst-case scenarios about global warming and ozone layer depletion turn out to be correct.

Sampling errors

In addition to these large problems of measurement, a smaller problem arises because it is just too costly for Statistics Canada to keep track of every single transaction that takes place in the economy. Instead it uses a sample and other statistical methods to infer rather than actually measure many kinds of transaction. In fact, Statistics Canada publishes several official estimates of GDP for each quarter. The first one becomes available about four weeks after a quarter ends. This is followed by a series of revisions. But don't lose sight of the fact that GDP is an *estimate*. It can never be comprehensive and fully accurate.

We began this chapter by learning the distinction between flows and stocks. But most of our attention has focused on flows. It's now time to look at the way we keep the accounts that measure the important macroeconomic stocks.

2.10 *The Nation's Balance Sheet*

A **balance sheet** is a statement about what someone owns and owes. There are balance sheets for individual households, for firms, for governments and government agencies, and for entire sectors of the economy, or for the economy as a whole. Items that are owned are called **assets**. Items that are owed are called **liabilities**. Thus a balance sheet is a list of assets and liabilities. There are two types of assets: financial and real. A **real asset** is a concrete, tangible object. Examples of real assets are the desk at which you sit and study, your Walkman and tapes, your car, skis, motorcycle, surfboard, and so on. Other examples of real assets are highways, steel mills, coal mines, power stations, and airplanes.

Financial assets are pieces of paper that represent promises to pay. That is, they define a debt relationship between two agents. Thus for each financial asset, there is a corresponding financial liability. What one person owns, another owes. One person's financial asset is another person's financial liability. Examples of financial assets (which are also someone else's financial liabilities) are your savings account at the local bank —from your point of view this is a financial asset (you *own* the deposit), whereas from the point of view of the bank, it is a liability (the bank *owes* you the deposit); or an Olympia and York bond—this is an asset to the person who owns it but a liability to the stockholders of Olympia and York.

The best way to get a feel for a balance sheet is to consider the balance sheet of a student like yourself. Table 2.6 sets out Cindy's balance sheet, which lists the things that Cindy owns (her assets) and owes (her liabilities). The assets are divided between financial items (at the top of the balance sheet) and real items (at the bottom). Cindy has $25 of bank notes and coins, a savings account of $150, and a $200 Canadian savings bond. These are Cindy's financial assets. She has two financial liabilities: a bank loan of $1000 and an outstanding balance of $200 on her Mastercard. She has $375 worth of financial assets and $1200 of financial liabilities. Cindy owes more (has bigger liabilities) than she owns (has assets).

The next items are real assets. Cindy has a car worth $1500 and a CD player and CDs worth $1000, giving total real assets of $2500. Cindy has total assets, both financial and real, of $2875 and total liabilities of $1200. Cindy has assets of $2875 and liabilities of $1200.

TABLE 2.6
Cindy's Balance Sheet

ITEM	ASSETS (DOLLARS)	LIABILITIES (DOLLARS)
Bank notes and coins	25	
Savings account	150	
Canadian savings bonds	200	
Bank loan		1000
Mastercard account		200
Total financial assets and liabilities	$375	$1200
Car	1500	
CD player and CDs	1000	
Total real assets	$2500	
Total assets and liabilities	$2875	$1200
Net worth		$1675
Totals	**$2875**	**$2875**

Wealth and net worth

Wealth is equal to the difference between total assets and total liabilities. The value of a person's wealth appears in a balance sheet as a fictitious liability called **net worth**. Net worth appears on the liability side of the balance sheet to make the balance sheet balance. You can see why, by looking again at Cindy's balance sheet. Her assets add up to $2875. Her liabilities add up to $1200, so Cindy's wealth is $1675.

The principles that lie behind Cindy's balance sheet also lie behind the balance sheet of whole sectors of the economy or the entire nation. Let's look at the nation's balance sheet. It is set out in Table 2.7. The nation's balance sheet is divided into three separate parts, one for each of the three big sectors whose flows we studied earlier in this chapter: the private sector, the government sector, and the rest of the world sector. The real assets in the economy are the capital stock — the stock of buildings, plant, equipment, and inventories. Most of these are owned by the private sector, but the government sector also owns a large amount of capital. Financial assets and liabilities are made up of such items as bank deposits and loans, government bonds, bonds issued by corporations, the stocks of corporations, foreign securities, and consumer debt on such things as credit cards. The totals of the financial assets and liabilities of each sector and of the whole economy are shown in the table. The net worth, or wealth, of each sector and the economy as a whole is found by calculating the difference between its total assets and total liabilities. The table shows these calculations. As you can see, most of the nation's wealth is held by the private sector. The government sector has approximately no net worth. Canada owes the rest of the world approximately $0.3 trillion more than the rest of the world owes Canada. The net worth of the economy as a whole is $2.3 trillion, which is divided between the private sector ($2.0 trillion) and the rest of the world ($0.3 trillion).

TABLE 2.7
National Balance Sheet as at 31 December 1990 (trillions of dollars)

	PRIVATE SECTOR		GOVERNMENT		REST OF WORLD		ECONOMY	
ITEM	*A*	*L*	*A*	*L*	*A*	*L*	*A*	*L*
Capital stock	2.0		0.3				2.3	
Financial assets	3.2		0.2		0.5		3.9	
Financial liabilities		3.2		0.5		0.2		3.9
Net worth		2.0		0.0		0.3		2.3
Totals	**5.2**	**5.2**	**0.5**	**0.5**	**0.5**	**0.5**	**6.2**	**6.2**

Source: National Balance Sheet Accounts Matrix, Statistics Canada, Ottawa, 1991

Money

There is one special financial asset and liability that plays a crucial role in our economy and in the study of macroeconomics. It is a group of assets collectively called money. **Money** is anything that is generally acceptable as a medium of exchange. A **medium of exchange** is anything that is acceptable in exchange for goods and services. Assets used as the medium of exchange have varied across societies and over time. Gold has commonly served as a medium of exchange; so has silver, and so have other metals. In some prisoner-of-war camps in World War II, cigarettes circulated as a medium of exchange.

In modern societies, money is a financial asset. It is the financial liability of either the central bank or other banks. There are four widely used alternative measures of the money supply in Canada today. One is sometimes called *narrow money*, or M1, another is referred to as *broad money*, or M3; and the third is an aggregate intermediate between these two, M2. The fourth, M2 +, is broader than M3.

Narrow money (M1) consists of currency (Bank of Canada notes and coins) in circulation, and demand deposits (chequing account balances) at chartered banks (but not counting government deposits). The components of M1 definitely pass the test of being commonly used as medium of exchange assets.

The intermediate aggregate (M2) consists of M1 plus personal savings deposits and non-personal notice deposits at chartered banks. Since people can write cheques on their personal saving deposit accounts these accounts are medium of exchange assets and properly included in the definition of money. Notice deposits may only be withdrawn (without an interest penalty) by giving the agreed amount of notice. These accounts are not, therefore, medium of exchange assets. But they can be converted into such assets easily and quickly and so are counted in this broader definition of money.

Broad money (M3) is M2 plus fixed term deposits of firms and financial institutions at chartered banks so long as those deposits are booked in Canada. Fixed term deposits are those placed for an agreed number of months (or even years). They are not usable, directly, as a medium of exchange. But they are safe assets and can be borrowed against, so are regarded as a possible indicator of total purchasing power. Some Canadian dollar fixed term deposits are booked outside Canada (in the United States, the Caribbean, and Europe) but these are excluded from M3.

M2+ consists of M2 plus deposits at trust and mortgage loan companies, and deposits and shares at caisses populaires and credit unions.

Notice that savings deposits, which are included in the M2 and M3 definitions of money but excluded from the M1 measure, are not directly transferable from one person to another by writing a cheque, and although it is customary to think of such deposits as "money in the bank," it is important to recognize that only M1 is money in the strict sense that it is a means of payment.

The M2, M3, and M2+ definitions of money include some items that are not exactly medium of exchange assets. These items are called **quasi-money**, a name that draws attention to the fact there is no sharp boundary between what is and what is not money.

Although there are some imprecise borderline cases between money and nonmoney, there is no doubt at all that money does not include credit cards, such as a Mastercard or Visa card. These cards are convenient identification tags that enable you to create two debts simultaneously. One debt is between you and the credit card company and the other is between the credit card company and the seller. These debts are settled when you pay the credit card company and the credit card company pays the seller.

Another recent innovation is harder to distinguish from "money" than is the credit card: money market mutual funds. A money market mutual fund is in many respects like a bank deposit. Individuals and firms place deposits with financial institutions, which in turn invest that money in short-term money market securities. The value of one dollar deposited in a money market mutual fund fluctuates with the market fortunes of the fund itself. In this respect, a money market mutual fund deposit is different from a bank deposit. When you deposit a dollar in the bank, no matter what happens to the market value of the investments that the bank acquires using your dollar, you continue to have a one-dollar deposit in the bank. In the case of a money market mutual fund, the value of that one-dollar deposit fluctuates in line with fluctuations in the market value of the assets of the fund. Just as in the case of a chequing deposit at the bank, it is possible to transfer a money market mutual fund deposit from one account to another by writing what is, in effect, a cheque. In this respect, money market mutual funds are like bank deposits. But there is a minimum size requirement for any cheque written on a money market mutual fund, usually so large that the fund isn't convenient to use for ordinary transactions.

National balance sheets and national income accounts Changes in net financial assets are related to flows in the national income accounts. The change in the net financial assets of the private sector is saving (S) minus investment (I) (shown in Table 2.8 as $S - I$). Why? Saving is the difference between what is earned (the private sector's income) and what is spent on consumer goods and services and paid in taxes. Some of that saving is used to buy capital goods. That is, it is invested in real assets. What is not invested (that is, not used to buy real assets) is used to buy financial assets. Therefore, the change in the net financial assets of the private sector is the same thing as saving minus investment. The change in the government's net financial assets is the difference between its tax receipts (T) and its purchases (G). Thus in Table 2.8 we show $T - G$ as the change in net financial assets of the government. The change in the net financial assets of the rest of the world is the difference between the flow of expenditures by domestic residents on foreign goods (imports, IM) and the flow of foreign expenditures on domestic goods (exports, EX). The change in net financial assets of the rest of the world is the difference between imports and exports ($IM - EX$).

If we add up net financial assets across all the sectors, we wind up with zero. That is, whatever one sector issues as a liability, another sector, or sectors, holds as an asset. If we add up the change in net financial assets across all sectors, that is, saving minus investment ($S - I$), plus taxes minus government purchases ($T - G$), plus imports minus exports ($IM - EX$), then we also always come out with zero. That is,

$$(S - I) + (T - G) + (IM - EX) = 0.$$

Let's look at some facts about one important aspect of the nation's balance sheet in the 1980s—the debt explosion.

TABLE 2.8
Change in Financial Assets and the Flows in National Income Accounts

	SECTORS		
ITEM	Private	Government	Rest of World
Change in net financial assets	$S - I$	$T - G$	$IM - EX$

MACROFACTS

2.11 *The Debt Explosion of the 1980s*

We've seen that balance sheets keep a record of debts—of those owed by and owed to different sectors of the economy. During the 1980s, there has been an enormous increase in the overall level of indebtedness, among individuals, firms, and government. Federal government debt has received the most attention, increasing at an annual average rate of almost 16 percent during the 1980s. Much of this increase has arisen simply because prices have risen. But even in real terms (measured in constant 1986 dollars) federal government debt has grown at 9 percent a year. Government debt has also increased relative to GDP. That is, government debt as a percentage of GDP has increased. You can see this fact in Figure 2.7.

There has also been growth in household debt in the 1980s. But the main components of household debt, consumer credit and mortgages, unlike government debt, have not grown at a persistently faster rate than GDP. As Figure 2.7 also shows, these items were close to 40 percent of GDP at the start of the 1980s but then declined to a little more than 30 percent of GDP as the economy went through a severe recession. They grew rapidly during the mid-1980s and by 1989 had returned to their 1980 percentages of GDP.

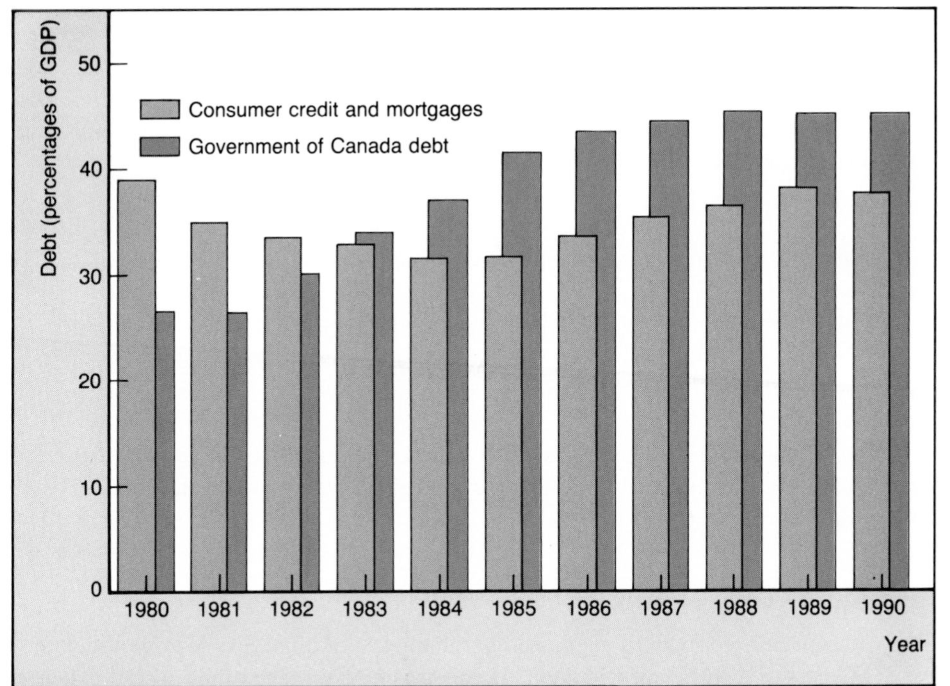

FIGURE 2.7
The Debt Explosion of the 1980s

During the 1980s, the debt of the federal government increased rapidly. In 1980 federal government debt was 27 percent of GDP; by 1988 it had increased to 45 percent of GDP. Household debt—consumer credit and mortgages—declined from almost 40 percent of GDP in the early 1980s as the economy went into a severe recession, but by 1989 it had returned to its 1980 level.

Source: Consumer credit (series B120), mortagages (series B970), Government of Canada debt (B2502), *Bank of Canada Review*, July 1991.
GDP, see Figure 1.1.

2.12 *Economic Growth and Inflation*

We've seen that *nominal* GDP is the value of the goods and services produced in the economy in a year measured using the current year's prices; and that *real* GDP is the value of goods and services produced in the economy in a year measured using the prices prevailing in a base year. The change in nominal GDP measures a combination of change in real GDP and changes in prices—inflation. Let's look more closely at how we separate real economic growth from rising prices.

Economic growth is the rate of change of real GDP from one year to the next. *Inflation* is the rate at which prices rise from one year to the next. We measure economic growth by calculating the percentage rate of change in real GDP. We measure inflation by calculating the percentage rate of change in the average level of prices. But there are several alternative ways of measuring the average level of prices. One is the GDP deflator.

The GDP deflator

The **GDP deflator** is an index number calculated as the ratio of nominal GDP to real GDP multiplied by 100. *Real GDP* is the value of the goods and services produced in the economy, when output is valued at the prices prevailing in a base year. (In Canada, the base year currently is 1986.) The GDP deflator is a measure of the price level. Let's probe the GDP deflator a bit more closely.

To calculate the GDP deflator, we first calculate *nominal GDP*, or GDP in current dollars. To do that, we take the quantity of each final good and service produced in the current year, Q_i^t, and multiply the quantity by its current price, P_i^t. The subscript i refers to the particular good or service, and the superscript t refers to the current year. We then sum the resulting values for all final goods and services in the economy. This gives nominal GDP. That is,

$$\text{Nominal GDP} = P_1^t Q_1^t + P_2^t Q_2^t + \cdots + P_n^t Q_n^t$$

Now, instead of valuing GDP at current prices, let's value aggregate product at base-year prices — for example, the prices prevailing in year 0. This calculation gives us real GDP, or GDP in constant dollars. That is,

$$\text{Real GDP} = P_1^0 Q_1^t + P_2^0 Q_2^t + \cdots + P_n^0 Q_n^t$$

Real GDP values the aggregate product in year t at the prices prevailing in the base year, year 0.

Now if we divide the nominal GDP by real GDP, we obtain the GDP deflator:

$$\text{GDP } \textit{deflator} = \frac{\textit{Nominal}\text{ GDP}}{\textit{Real}\text{ GDP}} \times 100$$

The inflation rate is calculated as the rate of change in the GDP deflator, expressed as a percentage. The inflation rate tells us the rate at which prices on the average are rising.

Consumer Price Index

The Consumer Price Index is another important measure of prices. A **price index** measures the cost of a particular ''basket'' of goods as a percentage of the cost of that same basket in a base period. The **Consumer Price Index (CPI)** measures movements in the prices of goods and services typically consumed by urban Canadian families. It is calculated and published by Statistics Canada each month.

The CPI is the weighted average of price movements of several thousand goods and services grouped into almost 500 categories. The goods and services included in the CPI and the weights attached to them are chosen to be representative of the goods and services usually bought by urban families. The basket of goods and services is based on data from a periodically conducted *Family Expenditure Survey*, and the current base year for the CPI is 1986. The CPI for 1986 equals 100. Each month, price data on more than 130,000 items are collected in 64 urban centres — built-up areas with populations of 30,000 or more inhabitants — from selected retail outlets. The CPI is calculated from all these numbers using the following formula:

$$\frac{P_1^t Q_1^0 + P_2^t Q_2^0 + \cdots + P_{490}^1 Q_{490}^0}{P_1^0 Q_1^0 + P_2^0 Q_2^0 + \cdots + P_{490}^0 Q_{490}^0} \times 100$$

Although this formula looks formidable, it is in fact quite easy to interpret. Let us take it piece by piece. The numerator

$$P_1^t Q_1^0 P_2^t Q_2^0 + \cdots + P_{490}^t Q_{490}^0$$

represents the total cost in month t at the prices ruling in month t of the bundle of commodities used to weight the prices. The term P_1^t is the price of commodity class 1 in month t, and Q_1^0 is the quantity (or number of units) of commodity class 1 in the basket of goods being valued. If we add up the total outlay on each of the 490 commodity classes in the index, then we arrive at the total cost of the basket of commodities at the prices prevailing in month t. (The dots in the middle of the expression stand for commodities 3 to 489.)

The denominator of the index number calculation

$$P_1^0 Q_1^0 + P_2^0 Q_2^0 + \cdots + P_{490}^0 Q_{490}^0$$

is the cost in the base period of the index basket of commodities valued at the prices ruling in the base period. The term P_1^0 is the price of commodity class 1 in the base period, period 0. So, $P_1^0Q_1^0$ is the outlay on items in commodity class 1 in the base period. Adding the outlays on all commodities that make up the 490 commodity classes gives the sum of money that would have had to have been spent purchasing the index bundle of commodities in the base period.

The ratio of the outlay in month t to the outlay in the base period multiplied by 100 gives the index number for the Consumer Price Index in month t. If that index number is 100, then prices have been constant. If the index is greater than 100, prices have risen; and if the index is less than 100 prices have fallen.

Various subsidiary index numbers are available for food, all items excluding food, housing, clothing, transportation, health and personal care, recreation, reading and education, and tobacco and alcohol. In addition, separate CPIs are published for 15 urban centres. A detailed description of the calculation of the Consumer Price Index is given in *The Consumer Price Index Reference Paper, Concepts and Procedures* (Ottawa: Statistics Canada, 1982).

The CPI is not, strictly speaking, a measure of the price level. It measures the prices of particular goods and services and can be used to calculate relative price changes. To measure the price level and the inflation rate and to break the growth rate of GDP into its real and inflationary components, we use the broadest of price measures — the GDP deflator.

■ In this chapter, we've learned how to use the principles of economic accounting to measure domestic product, income, and expenditure; how to measure the price level and to distinguish between the real and inflationary components of GDP; how to calculate sector financial balances for the private, government, and rest-of-world sectors; how the national balance sheet accounts keep track of the values of assets and liabilities; and how the sector balances and debt levels in our economy have changed over recent years. That is, we've learned how the complex range and scale of economic activity is observed, organized, and recorded. Our next task is to see how these systematic records of aggregate economic activity are used to build macroeconomic models — models that give us a deeper understanding of the forces creating the fluctuations in our economy.

CHAPTER REVIEW

Summary

THE DISTINCTION BETWEEN FLOWS AND STOCKS

A flow is a variable that measures a rate per unit of time. Income and expenditure are flows. The dimension of a flow is dollars per unit of time, such as an income of $50 a week. A stock is a value at a point in time. Money in the bank is a stock. Stocks are measured as dollars on a given day. Flows and stocks are linked because flows change stocks. A flow of water into a bathtub increases the stock of water in the tub. A flow of water out through the drain decreases the water in the tub.

Capital—buildings, plant and equipment, houses, consumer durable goods, and inventories—is an important macroeconomic stock. Investment—the purchase of new capital—is an important macroeconomic flow. An investment flow increases the capital stock. The capital stock decreases as a result of depreciation. A change in the capital stock is equal to net investment, which in turn equals gross investment minus depreciation.

THE DISTINCTION BETWEEN EXPENDITURE ON FINAL GOODS AND INTERMEDIATE TRANSACTIONS

Expenditure on final goods and services is the purchase of goods and services by households (including consumer durable goods and new houses) and the purchase by firms of new buildings, plant, and equipment. Also included in expenditure on final goods is the net change in the value of firms' inventories—inventory investment.

Intermediate transactions are the purchases and sales that take place as raw materials and goods at various semifinished stages pass from one firm to another to eventually reach the final consumer. Intermediate transactions do not measure aggregate economic activity. They double-count (or more accurately, count many times) the same final goods and services. To measure aggregate economic activity, we count only expenditure on final goods and services. Alternatively, we can count the value added at each stage of the production process and then sum the values added.

WHY AGGREGATE INCOME, EXPENDITURE, AND PRODUCT (OR THE VALUE OF OUTPUT) ARE EQUAL

Aggregate income is the sum of the payments to households for the supply of the services of factors of production. It includes the wages paid to labor, rent paid for the use of land, interest paid on loans, and also profit resulting from business activity. Expenditure is the sum of consumer expenditure, investment, government purchases of goods and services, and net exports (exports minus imports of goods and services). Investment includes inventory investment—the value of goods produced but not yet sold. Product (or the value of output) is the value of all the goods and services produced.

Aggregate income, expenditure, and product are equal because of the definitions of the terms. Product is the value of output. Two factors are key to understanding the equality of income, expenditure, and product:

1. When output is valued by the cost of the factors of production used to produce it, including the firms' profits, it equals income.
2. When output is valued by the total amount spent on goods and services, including inventory investment—the value of unsold production—it equals expenditure.

THE CONNECTION BETWEEN THE GOVERNMENT BUDGET DEFICIT AND THE INTERNATIONAL TRADE DEFICIT

Because income equals expenditure, leakages from the circular flow of income—saving, taxes, and imports of goods and services—equal the injections into the circular flow of income—investment, government purchases, and exports of goods and services. Because leakages equal injections, the financial balances of the private sector, government sector, and the rest of the world sum to zero. That is,

$$(S - I) + (T - G) + (IM - EX) = 0.$$

This equation means that whenever the government has a budget deficit, that deficit must be matched by either a private sector financial surplus or a surplus for the rest of the world. A surplus for the rest of the world means Canada has a balance of trade deficit and borrows from the rest of the world.

During the 1980s a large government deficit emerged. This deficit was increasingly financed by borrowing from abroad.

GROSS DOMESTIC PRODUCT AND DOMESTIC INCOME

Gross domestic product (GDP) is the total expenditure in a year on goods and services produced in the geographical domain of Canada. GDP is a *gross* measure because it does not have depreciation of the existing capital deducted. GNP is a measure of the *national* economy—all economic activity of the residents of Canada no matter where in the world it is undertaken. Gross national product (GNP) is the total expenditure in a year on goods and services by Canadian residents. Both GDP and GNP are valued at *market prices*.

Domestic income is the total income, including profit, received by residents of Canada in a year. Domestic income is a *net* measure because depreciation is deducted in calculating profits and domestic income is valued at *factor cost*.

WHAT A BALANCE SHEET MEASURES

A balance sheet is a statement of assets (what someone owns) and liabilities (what someone owes). Assets are divided into real assets—capital—and financial assets—paper assets that represent indebtedness between economic agents.

CAPITAL, WEALTH, AND MONEY

The difference between total assets and total liabilities is called net worth, and it measures wealth. The wealth of the economy as a whole is equal to its capital stock plus its net foreign assets (which may be positive or negative).

An important financial asset is money, the group of assets that serve as the medium of exchange. In our economy, these assets are notes and coins and bank deposits.

There is a connection between the national balance sheet and the national income accounts. The sector balances, saving minus investment, taxes minus government purchases, and imports minus exports, are equal to the changes in the net financial assets of the sectors of the economy.

THE DEBT EXPLOSION OF THE 1980s

During the 1980s the amount of debt in our economy has increased rapidly. Government debt increased more rapidly than inflation and more rapidly than the growth rate of nominal GDP. As a result, the amount of debt outstanding has increased steadily as a percentage of GDP. Consumer debt and mortgages, the main components of household debt, also increased but, in the early 1980s, not as quickly as GDP.

ECONOMIC GROWTH AND INFLATION

GDP changes over time. Any change in GDP can be decomposed into economic growth and inflation. Economic growth is the rate of change of real GDP from one year to the next. *Real GDP* is the value of the goods and services produced in the economy, when output is valued at the prices prevailing in a base year. (In Canada, the base year currently is 1986.)

Inflation is the rate of change of the price level—the GDP deflator. The GDP deflator is an index number calculated as the ratio of nominal GDP to real GDP multiplied by 100.

Key Terms and Concepts

Assets Items that are owned.

Balance sheet A statement about what someone owns and owes.

Capital The stock of buildings, plant and equipment, houses, consumer durable goods, and inventories.

Consumer expenditure The expenditure by households on final goods and services.

Consumer Price Index (CPI) An index that measures movements in the prices of goods and services typically consumed by urban Canadian families.

Depreciation The reduction in the value of capital that results from the use of the capital or from the passage of time.

Domestic income The total income, including profit, paid for the services of factors of production used to produce goods and services in Canada in a year.

Economic growth The rate of change of *real GDP* from one year to the next.

Expenditure The purchase of final goods and services.

Exports The flow of money from the rest of the world in exchange for domestically produced goods and services.

Final goods and services Goods and services bought by households; new plant, equipment, and buildings bought by firms, and net increases in firms' inventories; goods and services bought by governments; and goods and services bought by foreigners (exports) minus the goods and services we buy from the rest of the world (imports).

Financial assets Pieces of paper that represent promises to pay.

Fixed investment The purchase of new buildings, plant and capital, houses, and consumer durable goods.

Flow A variable that measures a rate per unit of time.

GDP deflator An index number calculated as the ratio of nominal GDP to real GDP, multiplied by 100.

Government purchases of goods and services Expenditure by the government on final goods and services.

Gross domestic product Total expenditure in a year on goods and services produced in the geographical domain of Canada.

Gross investment The total additions to the capital stock in a given period of time.

Gross national product Total expenditure on goods and services in a year by Canadian residents.

Imports The flow of money to the rest of the world in exchange for foreign produced goods and services.

Income The total payment made for the services of the factors of production employed in the economy.

Injection A flow into the circular flow of income and expenditure.

Intermediate transactions The purchase of goods and services by firms for use in later stages of the production of final goods and services.

Inventory investment Investment in inventories.

Investment The purchase of new buildings, plant and capital, houses, consumer durable goods, or inventories.

Leakage A flow from the circular flow of income and expenditure.

Liabilities Items that are owed.

Medium of exchange Anything that is acceptable in exchange for goods and services.

Money Anything that is generally acceptable as a medium of exchange.

Net exports Exports minus imports.

Net investment The change in the capital stock equal to gross investment minus depreciation.

Net worth A fictitious liability on a balance sheet representing the value of a person's wealth.

Nominal GDP The value of goods and services produced in the economy when output is valued at current year prices.

Personal disposable income *Personal income* minus personal income tax payments.

Personal income *Domestic income* plus transfer payments from government minus business retained profits.

Price index An index that measures the cost of a particular "basket" of goods and services as a percentage of the cost of that same basket in a base period.

Product The value of final goods and services produced.

Quasi-money Components of the measured money supply that are not medium of exchange assets.

Real asset A concrete, tangible object.

Real GDP The value of the goods and services produced in the economy, when output is valued at the prices prevailing in a base year.

Saving The difference between household income and consumer expenditure.

Stock A variable that is measured at a point in time.

Taxes Total taxes paid minus transfer payments.

Transfer payments Payments of benefits and subsidies by the government to households and firms.

Twin deficits The government's budget deficit and the Canadian deficit with the rest of the world.

Underground economy The part of the economy that engages in illegal activities.

Value added The increase in the value of a product when factors of production are used to transform it from one stage in the production or distribution process to the next.

Wealth The difference between total assets and total liabilities.

Review Questions

1. Distinguish between flows and stocks. Give three examples of macroeconomic flows and stocks. What is the stock that changes as a result of each of your flows? What are the flows that change each of your stocks?
2. Explain why aggregate income, expenditure, and product are always equal.
3. Explain the expenditure approach to measure GDP.
4. Explain how national income statisticians use the factor incomes approach to measure domestic income. What adjustments have to be made to domestic income to get GDP?

5. What are personal income and personal disposable income?
6. Is measured GDP an accurate measure of aggregate product? Why might measured GDP over- or underestimate aggregate production?
7. Explain what money is. What are the three commonly used measures of the money supply in Canada today?
8. What is a balance sheet? What is net worth?
9. Distinguish between financial assets, financial liabilities, and real assets. Give three examples of each.
10. What are the twin deficits? Describe what happened to these deficits between 1970 and 1990.
11. What determines the change in net financial assets of the private sector? the government sector? the rest of the world? Why is the stock of net financial assets for the economy as a whole always zero?
12. What is the debt explosion? What happened to the nominal and real debt of (a) the federal government, (b) households in the 1980s?
13. How do we measure the general level of prices?
14. What is a price index? What does the Consumer Price Index measure?
15. Explain what the inflation component of GDP is? How is the inflation component of the growth in GDP measured?
16. What is economic growth? How is it measured?

Problems

1. Look at the list of highlights of events in ***A Day in the Life of the Economy*** at the beginning of this chapter and determine for each item whether it is a
   (a) Stock
   (b) Flow
   (c) Factor income
   (d) Expenditure
   (e) Intermediate expenditure
   (f) Asset
   (g) Liability
2. The following activities took place in an imaginary economy last year:

ITEM	($)
Wages paid to labor	800,000
Consumer expenditure	650,000
Taxes paid by households	200,000
Transfer payments	50,000
Total profits made by firms	200,000
Profits retained by firms	50,000
Investment	250,000
Interest earned by households	100,000
Rent received by households	40,000
Taxes paid by firms	50,000
Government purchases of goods and services	200,000
Exports of goods and services	250,000
Imports of goods and services	150,000
Depreciation	50,000

Calculate:
(a) GDP at market prices. Which approach to measuring GDP did you use?
(b) GDP at factor cost. Which approach to measuring GDP did you use?
(c) Saving
(d) The government's budget deficit
(e) The change in net financial assets of (i) the private sector, (ii) the government sector, and (iii) the foreign sector
(g) Indirect taxes less subsidies
(h) Personal income
(i) Personal disposable income
(j) Leakages and injections. Are they equal?

3. A troupe of Russian dancers tours Canada. The dancers fly to Montreal on an Aeroflot (Soviet airline) flight at a total round trip cost of $200,000. They travel inside Canada on domestic airlines at a total cost of $185,000. Their hotel and food bills in Canada amount to $150,000. The receipts from ticket sales for performances of the troupe amount to $1,000,000. The cost of renting theatres and hiring Canadian musicians is $200,000, and advertising is $50,000. The Russian dancers' wages amounted to $75,000 for the period of the visit. The dancers bought Canadian-made souvenirs worth a total of $2,500. Any profit or loss on the visit accrued to or was borne by the Soviet government. Show where each of the economic activities described here appears in the Canadian national income accounts.

4. The following table gives data for the Canadian economy in billions of 1986 dollars:

ITEM	IN 1986	IN 1988
Taxes—Government purchases	−27.3	−15.7
Imports—Exports	−4.8	5.7

(a) For each year, calculate the change in the net financial assets of
  (i) The government
  (ii) The Canadian private sector
  (iii) The rest of the world
(b) In which year was Canadian borrowing from the rest of the world larger? What does this borrowing finance?
(c) Explain why the change in the net financial assets of the private sector are so different in these two years.

5. Each month Sticky Donuts, a donut producer, spends $1000 on eggs and flour. It pays wages of $500, interest on a bank loan of $300, and machine repair costs of $100. It also buys $400 on hydro. It sells the donuts produced to Handy Harry's, a convenience store, for $2500. Handy Harry's sells the donuts to its customers for $3000.
(a) Classify each transaction as
  (i) Expenditure on final goods and services
  (ii) Intermediate transactions
  (iii) Factor income
(b) Calculate the total value added.

6. An economy produces only three goods and services: ice cream, hot-air balloons, and balloon rides. Households buy ice cream and balloon rides but the hot-air balloons are purchased only by the firms—they sell balloon rides. The outputs produced and the market prices in 1990 and 1991 were as follows:

ITEM	1990 OUTPUT	1990 PRICE	1991 OUTPUT	1991 PRICE
Ice cream	500	$1	500	$1.50
Balloons	10	$100	15	$100
Balloon rides	150	$20	200	$25

Calculate:

(a) Consumer expenditure in 1991
(b) Investment in 1991
(c) Nominal GDP in 1991
(d) Real GDP in 1991
(e) GDP deflator in 1991
(f) What is the percentage increase in nominal GDP in 1991?
(g) What is the economic growth rate of the economy in 1991?
(h) What is the inflation rate in 1991?
(i) The CPI in 1991, if the typical urban family buys 500 units of ice cream and 150 balloon rides a year. Is the CPI or the GDP deflator a better measure of the price level? Why?

CHAPTER

Explaining Business Cycles, Growth, and Inflation

MODELS, THEORIES, AND REALITY

IN THIS CHAPTER WE ARE GOING TO STUDY a macroeconomic model. A **macroeconomic model** is a description of how households, firms, governments, and foreigners make economic decisions and how these decisions are coordinated in markets. Although an economic model is a description, it is not a *detailed* description. It is selective — it emphasizes some things and ignores others. Also, a model explains some things and takes others as given. Variables whose values are determined by a model are called **endogenous variables**. Variables whose values are determined outside a model and taken as given are called **exogenous variables**.

The purpose of the model is to improve our understanding of some aspect of reality — of the world in which we live. When we *understand* something, we have a way of *explaining* the past and *predicting* the future that works in all circumstances. Such understanding comes from developing models that closely mimic the relevant features of reality.

Models are not all equally good. Some, in fact, are utterly useless. They do not "work" — they do not enable us to explain the past or predict the future. Such models, once they are "found out," need to be assigned to the scrap heap and should be remembered only as the useless tools they turned out to be so that they are never revived. Other models have *some* value but their value is limited because they work only in certain special circumstances. The way that a model gets found out is by confronting it with the facts.

In constructing an economic model the economist begins by *assuming* that some things are important, some things are unimportant, and some things are exogenous variables. Based on these assumptions, the economist constructs a description of economic behavior capable of making "what if" predictions. That is, if the assumptions are correct and if the exogenous variables take on certain values, then the endogenous variables will have specific values. A model is tested by checking the correspondence between reality and the model's predictions. When a model predicts well it is provisionally accepted. When it works badly it is rejected.

By developing, testing, and rejecting models, economists are gradually accumulating a body of macroeconomic theory. **Macroeconomic theory** is a body of laws and generalizations about how the economy works based on macroeconomic models whose predictions have not yet been rejected.

In this chapter we are going to study the aggregate demand-aggregate supply model. In this model, real GDP and the price level are endogenous variables and the model predicts the behavior of real GDP and the price level, helping us explain economic growth and inflation. This model is a fairly general one and has evolved over more than 50 years. It is the outgrowth of two special-case models that we will also take a brief look at: a classical model and a Keynesian model. These models work in some circumstances but not always. The classical model works best in the long run, explaining broad economic trends. The Keynesian model works best in the short run, when there is severe unemployment and wages and prices are inflexible. The aggregate demand-aggregate supply model applies equally to an economy at full employment and to an economy with unemployment, helping us explain both long-term growth trends and fluctuations around those trends.

Although our main focus in this chapter is the aggregate demand-aggregate supply model, it is not our exclusive focus. We are going to begin by looking again at some facts — the facts that the aggregate demand-aggregate supply model explains. We will then study the model and also return to the facts to see how the model explains them. After studying this chapter, you will be able to

- Set out and explain the aggregate demand-aggregate supply model
- Explain what determines aggregate demand
- Explain what determines aggregate supply
- Explain how aggregate demand and aggregate supply interact to determine real GDP and the price level
- Use the aggregate demand-aggregate supply model to explain the 1982 recession and the 1980s expansion
- Explain the difference between the classical and Keynesian models of aggregate demand and aggregate supply
- Explain how the classical and Keynesian models interpret fluctuations in real GDP and the price level
- Describe the objectives of the research programs of new classical and new Keynesian macroeconomists

Let's begin by looking at the facts that the aggregate demand-aggregate supply model is designed to explain.

MACROFACTS

3.1 *Cycles, Real GDP Growth, and Inflation in the Canadian and World Economies*

Our economy usually expands, and real GDP grows, year after year. But sometimes that expansion is punctuated by recession. During the 20 years between 1970 and 1990, our economy expanded by 111 percent, as measured by real GDP growth. And the economy expanded in 15 of those 20 years. But recessions, and some serious ones, occurred in 1974-1975, 1981-1982, and 1990-1991.

Our economy also experiences continuous inflation. Prices rise every year and, between 1970 and 1990, that increase was 3.6-fold. But the 3.6-fold increase in prices did not occur at a uniform pace. Between 1974 and 1982, inflation was rapid. Before 1974 and after 1982, it was much more moderate.

A good way of looking at the expansion of real GDP and the rising price level is with a scatter diagram, as shown in Figure 3.1. Part (a) tells us about Canada and part (b) about the rest of the world. Each point in the figure shows the price level and real GDP in a particular year, the year being identified by the two-digit number. For example, the point marked "70" in part (a) tells us that in 1970, the price level in Canada was 33 and real GDP was $270 billion. Movements to the right represent real GDP growth and movements upward represent inflation.

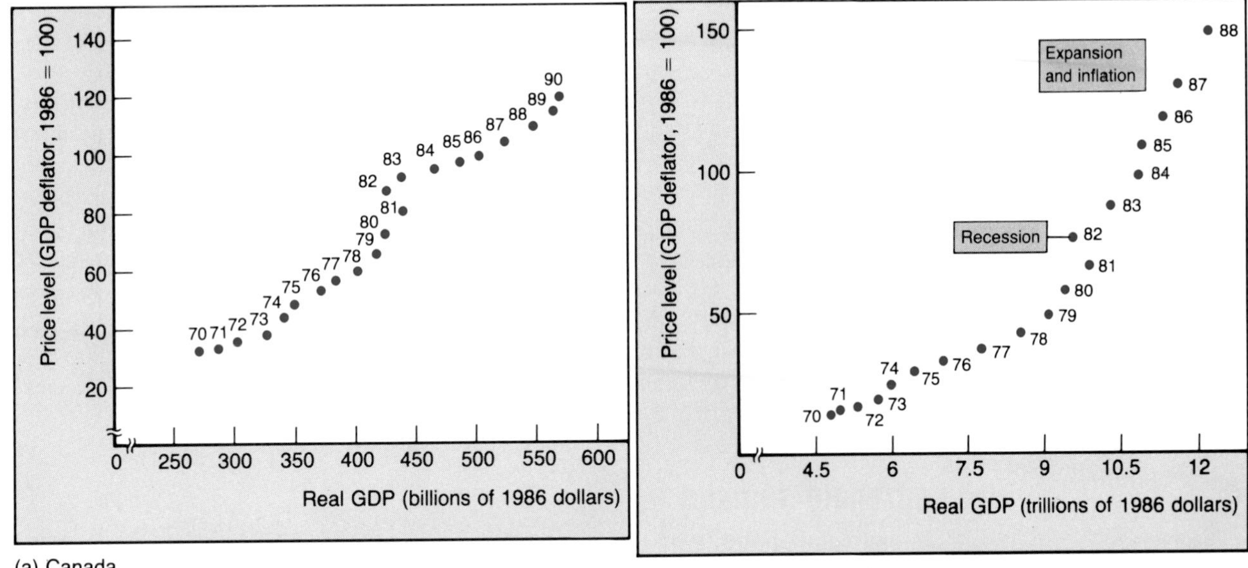

(a) Canada

(b) The Rest of the World

FIGURE 3.1
Expansion and Inflation in the Canadian and World Economies

Between 1970 and 1990, real GDP increased by 75 percent and the price level increased threefold. Growth halted in the recessions of 1975 and 1982, inflation was most rapid in the late 1970s, and expansion was most rapid in the late 1980s.

During the same 20 years, the world economy experienced growth, inflation, and cycles similar to those in Canada.

Source: Canada: *National Income and Expenditure Accounts, Statistics Canada,* Catalogue 13-001 and 13-201. Rest of world: *International Financial Statistics* and our calculations.

Part (a) shows the expansion, cycles, and rising price level in the Canadian economy between 1970 and 1990. It provides a clear picture of the ebbs and flows in the economy, the general tendency for real GDP to expand and the price level to rise, as well as the changing pace of expansion and inflation and the occasional halt to the process of expansion in years of recession.

The rest of the world (part b) shares many features of Canadian macroeconomic performance, but there are also some differences. The similarities are the tendency for real GDP to grow and prices to rise. The differences are the overall scale of expansion and rising prices, the changing pace of expansion and inflation, and the occurrence of recessions. Like Canada, the world economy went into recession in 1982. Unlike Canada, the rest of the world continued to expand through the 1970s. Also, world inflation became much more severe in the 1980s than it had been in the early 1970s, and world expansion slowed down during those years. This contrasts with the moderate inflation and rapid expansion of the Canadian economy in the second half of the 1980s.

These facts about business cycles, real GDP growth, and rising prices pose some of the central questions that macroeconomics tries to answer. Why does the economy expand, and why does the pace of expansion vary? Why do prices rise, and why does their rate of increase fluctuate?

To answer questions like these, we need a macroeconomic theory—a body of macroeconomic laws that are reliable and that enable us to explain, interpret, and predict macroeconomic events. The macroeconomic theory you're going to study in this chapter is one based on a model of aggregate demand and aggregate supply. Let's begin to explore that model.

3.2 *The Aggregate Demand-Aggregate Supply Model*

The model of aggregate demand and aggregate supply that you are about to study is designed to explain fluctuations in real GDP and the price level. The model is based on the same ideas as the demand and supply model in microeconomics. But there are some crucial differences between the *aggregate* demand and supply model and the *micro* demand and supply model. The most important difference is that the macro model is designed to explain aggregate variables—the price level and real GDP—while the micro model is designed to explain the prices and quantities of individual goods and services—the price and quantity of hamburgers and submarines.

We'll first set out the model in broad terms. Then we'll go more deeply into the forces that influence aggregate demand and aggregate supply and bring about changes in real GDP and the price level.

Aggregate demand

The **aggregate quantity of goods and services demanded**—the quantity of real GDP demanded—is the total value (measured in constant dollars) of consumer expenditure, investment, government purchases of goods and services, and net exports. The **aggregate demand schedule** lists the quantity of real GDP demanded at each price level, holding constant all other influences on the buying plans of households, firms, governments, and foreigners. The **aggregate demand curve** is a graph of the aggregate demand schedule. When we use the term **aggregate demand** we are referring to the relationship between the quantity of real GDP demanded and the price level—that is, to the entire aggregate demand schedule or aggregate demand curve.

Figure 3.2(a) shows an aggregate demand curve. The curve slopes downward, indicating that, holding everything else constant, the higher the price level, the lower is the quantity of real GDP demanded. For a given aggregate demand curve, a change in the price level brings about a change in the aggregate quantity of real GDP demanded. Anything that shifts the aggregate demand curve changes the level of aggregate demand.

Aggregate supply

The **aggregate quantity of goods and services supplied**—the quantity of real GDP supplied—is the total value (measured in constant dollars) of all the goods and services produced in the economy. An **aggregate supply schedule** lists the quantity of real GDP supplied at each price level, holding constant all other influences on firms' production plans. An **aggregate supply curve** is a graph of an aggregate supply schedule. Firms' production plans and the way they respond to the price at which they can sell their output depends on how firms' costs behave. Costs are determined by factor prices, and especially by wages. In the short run, factor prices and wages are fixed. In the long run, they vary. Thus in studying aggregate supply it is necessary to distinguish between two time-frames: the long-run and the short-run.

Long-run aggregate supply

Long-run aggregate supply is the quantity of real GDP supplied when all wages and prices have adjusted so that each firm is producing its profit-maximizing output and there is full employment. This level of aggregate supply is determined by the size of the labor force, the capital stock, the state of technology, and the natural rate of unemployment. The **natural rate of unemployment** is the percentage of the labor force that is unemployed when the only unemployment is that

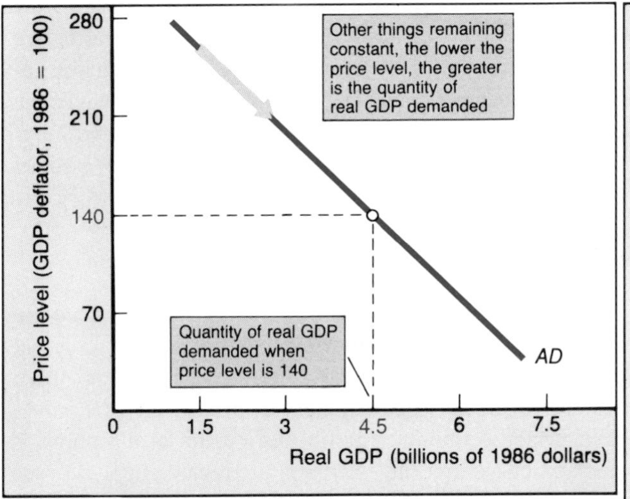

(a) The aggregate demand curve

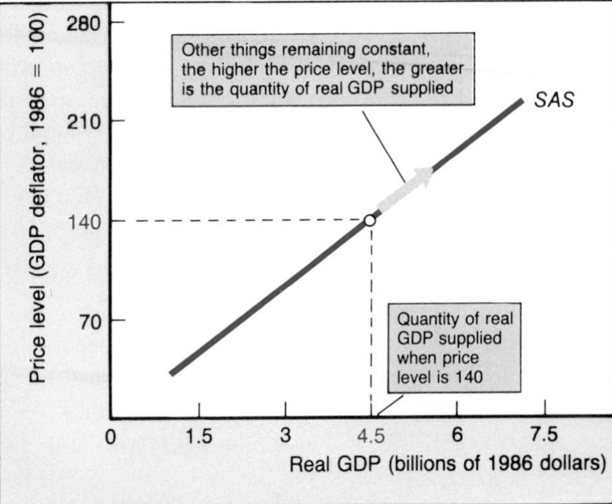

(c) The short-run aggregate supply curve

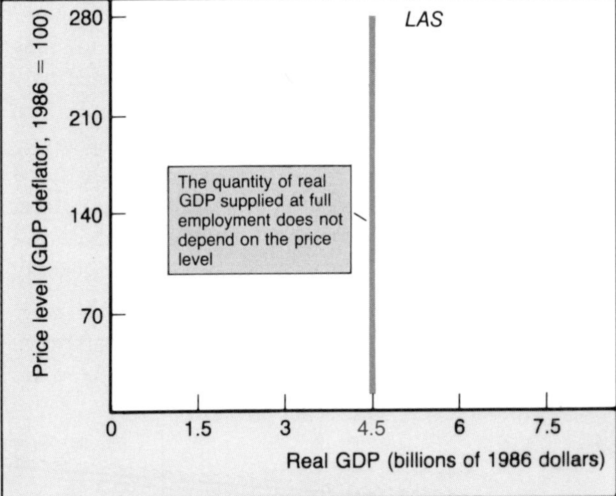

(b) The long-run aggregate supply curve

FIGURE 3.2
Aggregate Demand and Aggregate Supply Curves

The aggregate demand curve (part a) graphs the quantity of real GDP demanded against the price level, holding constant all other influences on the buying plans of households, firms, governments, and foreigners. The lower the price level, the higher is the quantity of real GDP demanded. The aggregate demand curve (*AD*) slopes downward.

The long-run aggregate supply curve (part b) graphs the level of real GDP supplied when there is full employment. This level of real GDP does not depend on the price level—the long-run aggregate supply curve (*LAS*) is vertical.

The short-run aggregate supply curve (part c) graphs the quantities of real GDP supplied at each price level, holding constant the prices of the factors of production, and in particular the wage rate. The higher the price level, the higher is the quantity of real GDP supplied. The short-run aggregate supply curve (*SAS*) slopes upward.

arising from the normal job-search activity of new entrants to the labor force and labor market turnover. The economy is at full employment when unemployment is at its natural rate. Thus long-run aggregate supply does not depend on the price level. If the price level changes, in the long run so do all prices, including the prices of factors of production, leaving the quantity of goods and services produced unchanged. Thus long-run aggregate supply is a fixed level of real GDP, and the long-run aggregate supply curve is a vertical line, such as that shown in Figure 3.2(b).

Short-run aggregate supply The **short-run aggregate supply schedule** is a list of the quantities of real GDP supplied at each price level, holding constant the prices of the factors of production and, in particular, the wage rate. The **short-run aggregate supply curve** is a graph of the short-run aggregate supply schedule. Figure 3.2(c) illustrates the short-run aggregate supply curve. Along the short-run aggregate supply curve, the higher the price level, the greater is the quantity of real GDP supplied, up to some maximum amount. That maximum is the physical limit of the economy to produce goods and services. When we use the term **aggregate supply** we are referring to the relationship between the quantity of real GDP supplied and the price level. That is, we are referring to the relationship described by the short-run and long-run aggregate supply curves. A change in the price level does not change aggregate supply. It changes the quantity of real GDP supplied and produces a movement along the short-run and long-run aggregate supply curves. Other influences on aggregate supply shift one or both of the aggregate supply curves.

Macroeconomic equilibrium

The interaction of aggregate demand and aggregate supply produces a macroeconomic equilibrium. **Macroeconomic equilibrium** is a situation in which the quantity of real GDP demanded equals the quantity of real GDP supplied. At any given moment, there is a particular level of wages and other factor prices, and these determine the economy's short-run aggregate supply curve. Macroeconomic equilibrium occurs at the point of intersection of the aggregate demand curve and the short-run aggregate supply curve. Figure 3.3 illustrates a macroeconomic equilibrium: real GDP is $4.5 billion and the price level is 140. To see why this is an equilibrium, consider what happens if the price level is 100. In this case, the aggregate quantity of real GDP demanded ($6 billion) exceeds the quantity supplied ($3.5 billion). There is a large and general shortage of goods and services. In such a situation, the prices of all goods will increase, and they continue to increase as long as the shortage lasts. The shortage will be eliminated only when the price level has increased to 140. Next, imagine that the price level is 180. In this situation, the aggregate quantity of goods and services supplied exceeds the aggregate quantity demanded. There is a general surplus of goods and services. Unable to sell all their output, firms will cut prices and continue to do so until they sell all their current output. Prices will fall until the price level has reached 140, at which point there is a balance between the aggregate quantity of goods and services demanded and the quantity supplied.

FIGURE 3.3
Macroeconomic Equilibrium

The price level and real GDP are determined at the point of intersection of the aggregate demand and short-run aggregate supply curves. Where those curves intersect, the equilibrium price level and real GDP are determined. At price levels above the equilibrium, there is an excess of the quantity of real GDP supplied over the quantity demanded and a tendency for the price level to fall. At a price level below the equilibrium, there is an excess of the quantity of real GDP demanded over the quantity supplied and a tendency for the price level to rise. Only at the equilibrium are the forces of aggregate demand and aggregate supply balanced against each other with no tendency for the price level to change.

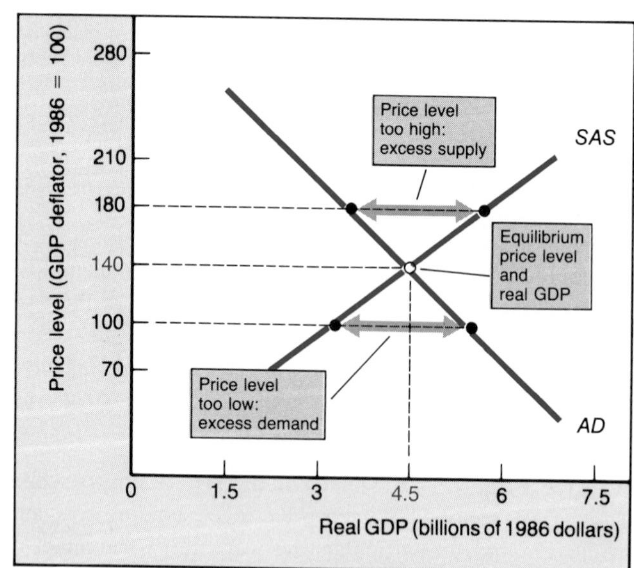

Macroeconomic equilibrium does not mean full employment

There's no guarantee that when the aggregate quantity of goods and services demanded equals the aggregate quantity supplied the economy is at full employment. **Full-employment equilibrium** is a situation in which macroeconomic equilibrium occurs at a point on the long-run aggregate supply curve. Figure 3.4(a) illustrates such a situation. But macroeconomic equilibrium can occur with unemployment or with above-full employment. An **unemployment equilibrium** is a situation in which macroeconomic equilibrium occurs at a level of real GDP below long-run aggregate supply. Figure 3.4(b) illustrates an unemployment equilibrium. **Above full-employment equilibrium** is a situation in which macroeconomic equilibrium occurs at a level of real GDP above long-run aggregate supply. Figure 3.4(c) illustrates an above full-employment equilibrium.

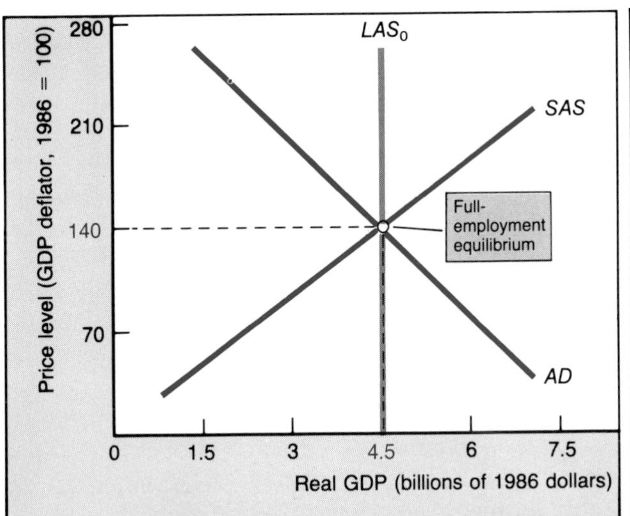

(a) Full employment

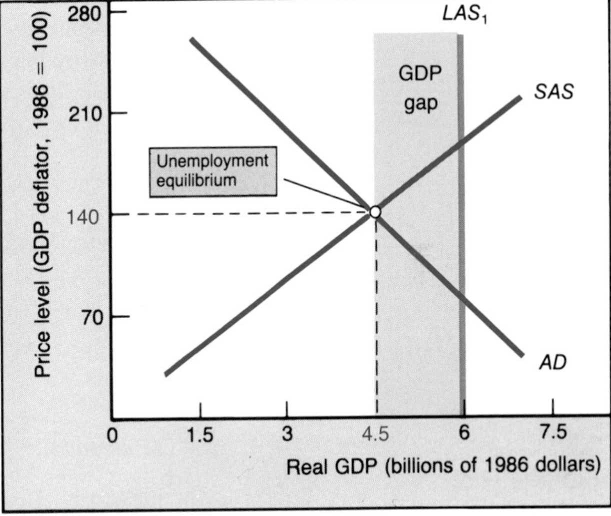

(b) Unemployment

FIGURE 3.4
Three Kinds of Macroeconomic Equilibrium

Macroeconomic equilibrium may occur at full employment (part a), below full employment (part b), or above full employment (part c). The state of employment in a macroeconomic equilibrium depends on the position of the long-run aggregate supply curve relative to the equilibrium level of real GDP. At full employment, the equilibrium occurs on the long-run aggregate supply curve. With unemployment, equilibrium occurs below the long-run aggregate supply curve, resulting in a GDP gap. At above full employment, equilibrium occurs above the long-run aggregate supply curve.

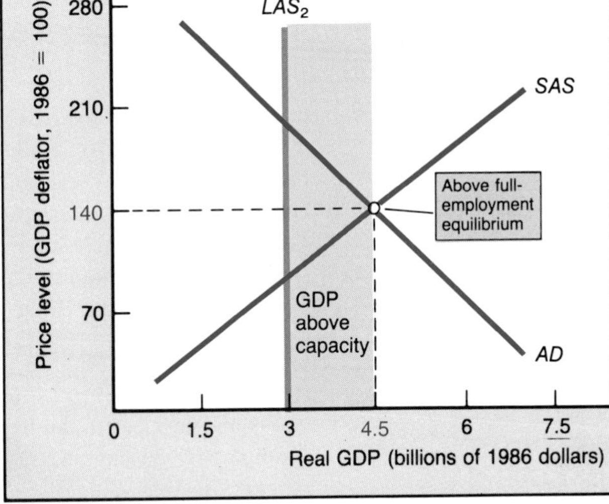

(c) Above full employment

You now have a general picture of the aggregate demand-aggregate supply model and the way in which that model determines the level of real GDP and the price level. You have also seen that in the aggregate demand-aggregate supply model it is possible to have an equilibrium with unemployment. We want to use this model to understand the forces at work in the Canadian economy, producing events such as the inflation of the 1970s, the recession of 1982, and the strong expansion of real GDP but with moderate inflation during the 1980s. To do this, however, we need to know more about the aggregate demand and aggregate supply curves. Why does the aggregate demand curve slope downward and the short-run aggregate supply curve slope upward? And what makes these curves shift? Let's now turn to these questions.

3.3 *What Determines Aggregate Demand?*

We're now going to discover why the aggregate demand curve slopes downward and what makes the aggregate demand curve shift. To understand the influences on aggregate demand, let's begin by recalling the agents whose expenditures make up aggregate demand: households, firms, governments, and the rest of the world. What influences the spending plans of each of these agents?

Households

Households contribute to aggregate demand by buying consumer goods and services, consumer durable goods, and new houses. There are four main influences on the total quantity of goods and services produced in Canada and bought by households. They are

1. Disposable income
2. Interest rates
3. Real money holdings
4. Real exchange rate

Disposable income **Disposable income** is households' income minus total taxes paid. Other things being equal households spend more on goods and services as disposable income increases. So, the higher income is, the greater is the quantity of goods and services demanded; and the higher taxes are, the lower is the quantity of goods and services demanded.

Interest rates Interest rates influence the quantity of goods and services bought because they affect households' decisions to save and to borrow. When interest rates are high, there is a greater inducement for households to save and take advantage of the higher earnings they can get from bank deposits, deposits at trust companies, stocks, and bonds. High interest rates also discourage borrowing. Conversely, when interest rates are low, households have a greater inducement to borrow and less incentive to save. Other things being equal, the higher the interest rate, the smaller is consumer expenditure and the smaller is the aggregate quantity of goods and services demanded by households.

Real money holdings **Real money** is money expressed in terms of the quantity of goods and services it can buy. It is measured as dollars divided by the price level. For example, if you have \$500 of money in the bank and the price level increases by 20 percent, the real value of your money in the bank falls by 20 percent. Having \$500 with prices 20 percent higher is like having \$400 with prices at their original lower level.

Other things being equal, consumer expenditure increases as the quantity of real money in the economy increases.

Real exchange rate The **real exchange rate** is a measure of the price of foreign goods and services relative to the price of domestic goods and services. The real exchange rate rises if foreign goods and services—such as Toyotas, Roquefort cheese, and British banking services — become more expensive relative to domestically produced goods and services — such as Chevys, Quebec cheese, and Canadian banking services. Such changes in foreign prices relative to domestic prices can occur either because the prices of the goods themselves change or because the foreign exchange value of the dollar changes. For example, a Toyota could become more expensive either because its price has increased in terms of Japanese yen or because the dollar has fallen in value against the yen so that it now costs more dollars to buy a Toyota even though the yen price has not changed.

If foreign goods and services become more expensive relative to domestically produced goods and services (the real exchange rate rises), the demand by households for imports decreases and the demand for domestically produced goods and services increases.

Firms

Firms contribute to aggregate demand through their investment in new plant and equipment and net changes in inventories. There are two main influences on firms' investment. They are

1. Interest rates
2. State of confidence

Interest rates Interest rates influence firms in much the same way that they influence households. The higher the interest rate, the more expensive it is for firms to borrow and the greater is the inducement for firms to economize on purchases of new plant and equipment. The higher the interest rate, other things being equal, the lower is investment.

Confidence The major influence on firms' investment is their state of confidence about future business prospects. At times when firms anticipate an expanding and booming economy, investment is high; and when firms anticipate a slack, depressed economy, investment is low.

Government

Government's contribution to aggregate demand comes through its purchases of goods and services. Of the many influences on government purchases of goods and services, the two most important ones are the state of the world and the state of the economy. The state of the world influences military expenditure. For example, during world wars there is a massive increase in government purchases of military supplies. In times of heightened tension, such as the Gulf crisis of 1990, there is also an increase in government purchases. Government purchases are influenced by the state of the economy when the government seeks to use its own spending to attempt to moderate fluctuations in the overall level of aggregate demand. Thus if the economy is going into a boom, the government might try to cut back its own spending to moderate the degree of the boom. If the economy is going into a recession, the government might increase its own purchases of goods and services to lessen the severity of the recession.

Rest of world

The demand by the rest of the world for goods and services produced in Canada shows up as the export component of aggregate demand. There are two main influences on exports. They are

1. The level of rest of world income
2. The real exchange rate

Rest of world income Other things being equal, the higher the income in the rest of the world, the greater is the quantity of goods and services bought by the rest of the world. Some of these goods are bought from Canada; therefore, the higher the income in the rest of the world, the greater is the rest-of-world demand for Canadian-produced goods and services.

Real exchange rate The real exchange rate influences the rest of the world's demand for Canadian-produced goods and services in a symmetric way to its influence on the Canadian demand for foreign-produced goods and services. Other things being equal, the more expensive Canadian-produced goods and services are relative to those produced in the rest of the world, the smaller is the rest-of-world demand for Canadian-produced goods and services. Higher inflation in Canada than in the rest of the world leads to an increase in Canadian prices relative to foreign prices and, other things being equal, decreases in the rest-of-the-world demand for Canadian-produced goods. A strengthening of the dollar in the foreign exchange market also makes Canadian-produced goods more expensive for foreigners, other things being equal. More yen and deutsche marks have to be used to buy a given number of dollars, weakening the inducement to convert foreign currency into dollars in order to buy Canadian-produced goods.

Position and slope of aggregate demand curve

Table 3.1 summarizes the above description of the influences on aggregate demand. It lists seven influences on aggregate demand:

- Disposable income
- Interest rates
- Business confidence
- Government
- Real money supply
- Foreign income
- Real exchange rate

TABLE 3.1
Influences on Aggregate Demand

INFLUENCE	MEASURED AS	INFLUENCES C	I	G	EX	IM
Disposable income	$Y - T$	Yes				Yes
Interest rates	r	Yes	Yes			
Business confidence	Confidence index		Yes			
Government				Yes		
Real money supply	M/P	Yes				Yes
Foreign income	Y^*				Yes	
Real exchange rate	SP^*/P				Yes	Yes

Symbols Y = GDP, T = Taxes, r = Interest rates, M = Money supply, P = Price level, S = Exchange rate (dollars per unit of foreign currency), P^* = Price level in the rest of world, Y^* = GDP in the rest of world.

Holding the price level constant, a change in any one of these influences changes aggregate demand and shifts the aggregate demand curve, as illustrated in Figure 3.5. When aggregate demand increases, the aggregate demand curve shifts to the right. The events that can produce an increase in aggregate demand are

- A decrease in taxes
- A fall in interest rates
- An increase in confidence
- An increase in government purchases
- An increase in the money supply
- An increase in income in the rest of the world
- An increase in foreign prices
- A weakening of the dollar in the foreign exchange market

If these factors change in the opposite direction, aggregate demand decreases and the aggregate demand curve shifts to the left.

There is one more important influence on aggregate demand: the size of the population. In fact, you can regard the influences set out in Table 3.1 as influences on aggregate demand per person. The larger the population, other things being equal, the larger is the level of aggregate demand.

We've seen how the position of the aggregate demand curve is influenced by the many factors that affect spending plans. But why does the aggregate demand curve slope downward? You can see the influence of the price level on the aggregate quantity of real GDP demanded in Table 3.1 in two places—in its effects on the real money supply and on the real exchange rate. Other things being equal, the higher the price level, the lower is the quantity of real money and therefore the lower is the quantity of real GDP demanded. This is the first reason the aggregate demand curve slopes downward. Second, the higher the price level, the lower is the real exchange rate and therefore the greater is the demand for foreign goods and services and the smaller is the demand for domestically produced goods and services.

There is a third reason, not directly visible in Table 3.1, why the aggregate demand curve slopes downward. It is the indirect influence of the price level on interest rates.

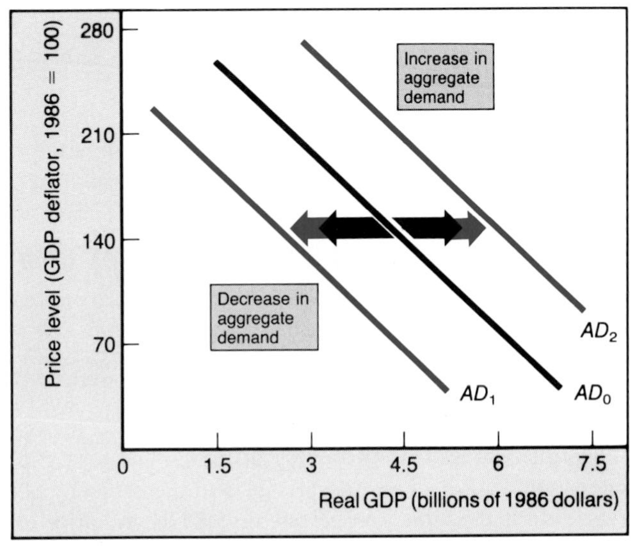

FIGURE 3.5
Changes in Aggregate Demand

When aggregate demand increases, the aggregate demand curve shifts to the right—from AD_0 to AD_2. When aggregate demand decreases, the aggregate demand curve shifts to the left—from AD_0 to AD_1. Factors that lead to an increase in aggregate demand are a decrease in taxes, a fall in interest rates, an increase in confidence, an increase in income in the rest of the world, an increase in the money supply, an increase in foreign prices, or a weakening of the dollar in the foreign exchange market. When these forces work in the opposite direction, there is a decrease in aggregate demand.

Other things being equal, the smaller the real money supply, the higher is the average level of interest rates. Thus there is an indirect influence of the price level on interest rates. A higher price level leads to a lower real money supply, a decrease in the supply of loans, an increase in the demand for loans, and an increase in interest rates.

Time lags All these influences on aggregate demand are average tendencies rather than rigid mechanical links. That is, the quantitative impact of each influence varies over time. Also, each influence operates with a time lag. Changing interest rates, foreign exchange rates, or income levels do not have a full and immediate effect on spending plans. Rather, these effects are spread out over time. For example, when interest rates fall, investment increases. But not everyone will be quick off the mark in seeking new investment opportunities. Some will have plans already worked out and be waiting for the lower interest rate. In such cases, the change in investment will be immediate. Others, seeing the lower interest rates, will begin to make an investment that may take several months and perhaps even years to implement.

Other influences In addition to the factors we have identified there are thousands of other small influences on aggregate demand. Sometimes these could be important—such as the effects of sudden very cold weather that unexpectedly increases demand for hydro—but their effects tend to be temporary and are often offset by other effects so that, in aggregate, we may safely ignore them.

3.4 *What Determines Aggregate Supply?*

Long-run aggregate supply is determined by

- The size of the labor force
- The size of the capital stock
- The state of technology
- The natural rate of unemployment

Other things being equal, the larger the labor force, the lower the natural unemployment rate, the larger the capital stock, and the more productive the available technology, the larger is long-run aggregate supply.

Short-run aggregate supply depends on

- All the influences on long-run aggregate supply
- Factor prices

Other things being equal, the higher are factor prices, such as the wage rate, the lower is the quantity of real GDP supplied in the short run.

Why the short-run aggregate supply curve slopes upward

The short-run aggregate supply curve slopes upward because when prices change wages do not. With constant wages and higher prices firms are anxious to sell more. There is an increase in the quantity of goods and services supplied. Conversely, with constant wages and lower prices firms want to sell less so the quantity of goods and services supplied decreases.

There is another interesting way of looking at things that also explains why the short-run aggregate supply curve slopes upward. It is in the behavior of the real wage rate. The **real wage rate** is the money wage rate divided by the price level—it is the real price or real cost of labor to firms. The lower that real cost—the lower the real wage rate—the larger is the quantity of labor firms hire and the larger the output they produce. The real wage rate is influenced by the price level. The higher the price level, the lower is the real wage rate. Hence, the higher the price level, the greater is the quantity of labor demanded and the larger is the quantity of real GDP supplied.

Shifts in the aggregate supply curves

The influences on aggregate supply that we have just discussed can all be illustrated in terms of the position of and shifts in the short-run and long-run aggregate supply curves.

An increase in wages, other things remaining the same, decreases short-run aggregate supply and leaves long-run aggregate supply unchanged. The short-run aggregate supply curve shifts to the left and the long-run aggregate supply curve does not move. This effect is shown in Figure 3.6(a). At any given price level, aggregate real GDP supplied decreases. A decrease in the wage rate would have the opposite effect, increasing short-run aggregate supply and shifting the short-run aggregate supply curve to the right.

An increase in the labor force, a decrease in the natural rate of unemployment, an increase in the capital stock, or technological change that increases productivity increases long-run aggregate supply. In such a case, both the long-run and short-run aggregate supply curves shift to the right as shown in Figure 3.6(b). Changes in these influences in the opposite direction bring a decrease in long-run aggregate supply and shift both aggregate supply curves to the left.

Now that we have studied the influences on aggregate demand and aggregate supply, we are ready to see how real GDP and the price level are determined and why they change.

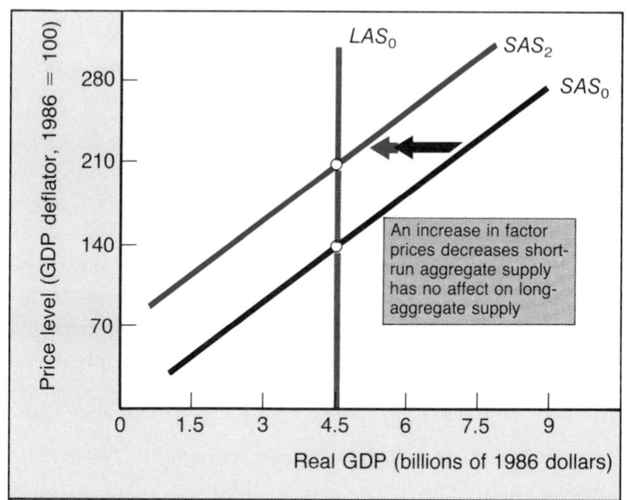

(a) An increase in factor prices

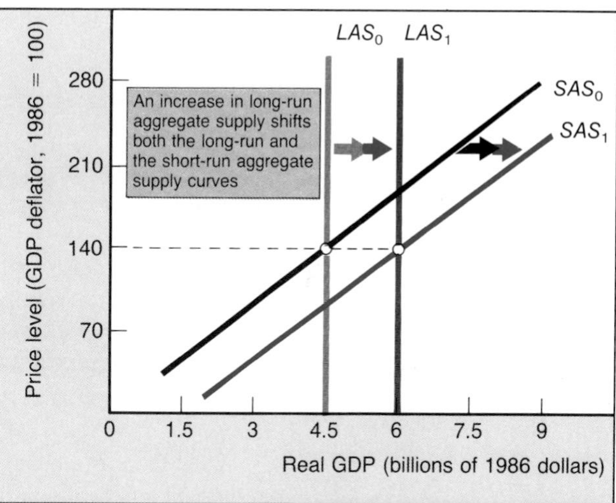

(b) An increase in long-run aggregate supply

FIGURE 3.6
Changes in Aggregate Supply

A change in the wage rate or in other factor prices, other things being equal, shifts the short-run aggregate supply curve but does not affect the long-run aggregate supply curve. For example, in part (a), an increase in wages would shift the short-run aggregate supply curve from SAS_0 to SAS_2.

An increase in the capital stock, the labor force, or an advance in technology that increases the economy's ability to produce goods and services, shifts the long-run aggregate supply curve and the short-run aggregate supply curve together. The new short-run aggregate supply curve intersects the new long-run aggregate supply curve at the same price level as the original curves intersected. The shift from LAS_0 to LAS_1, and SAS_0 to SAS_1, in part (b), illustrates such an increase in long-run aggregate supply.

3.5 *What Determines Real GDP and the Price Level?*

We'll study the influences on real GDP and the price level by considering the separate influences on

- Aggregate demand
- Short-run aggregate supply
- Long-run aggregate supply

A change in aggregate demand

An increase in government purchases of goods and services, a decrease in taxes, an increase in business confidence, an increase in the money supply, an increase in foreign income, an increase in the foreign price level, or a weakening of the dollar in the foreign exchange market leads to an increase in aggregate demand and a rightward shift in the aggregate demand curve. Figure 3.7(a) illustrates the effects of an increase in aggregate demand. The short-run aggregate supply curve is SAS_0. Initially, the aggregate demand curve is AD_0. The economy is at full-employment equilibrium, with a price level of 140, and real GDP of $4.5 billion. When any influence just listed increases aggregate demand, the aggregate demand curve shifts to the right to become the new aggregate demand curve AD_1. The effect of this change on real GDP and the price level is found by looking for the intersection of the new aggregate demand curve with the short-run aggregate supply curve. This is the new macroeconomic equilibrium. The price level rises and real GDP rises. In this example, the price level increases from 140 to 147 and real GDP increases from $4.5 billion to $4.7 billion.

Influences on short-run aggregate supply

There are many influences on short-run aggregate supply that can shift the short-run aggregate supply curve. Some of these also influence long-run aggregate supply and shift both the short-run and long-run aggregate supply curves. We'll consider those forces later.

First, let's focus on the things that change short-run aggregate supply and leave long-run aggregate supply constant. One possible factor is a change in wages. For example, the government could pass a minimum wage law increasing minimum wages. Also, labor unions could push wages higher. Another possible source of a change in short-run aggregate supply is an increase in the price of raw materials such as imported oil.

When there is a change in factor prices, the short-run aggregate supply curve shifts but there is no change in the long-run aggregate supply curve. Figure 3.7(b) illustrates. The aggregate demand curve is *AD* and initially the short-run aggregate supply curve is SAS_0. But an increase in, say, minimum wages or the price of oil shifts the short-run aggregate supply curve to SAS_1. The price level and real GDP are now determined by the intersection point of the new SAS curve and the AD curve. The price level increases and real GDP decreases. In this example, the price level increases from 140 to 148 and real GDP decreases from $4.5 billion to $4.3 billion.

Influences on long-run aggregate supply

An increase in the labor force, a decrease in the natural unemployment rate, an increase in the capital stock, or a technological advance that increases productivity shifts the

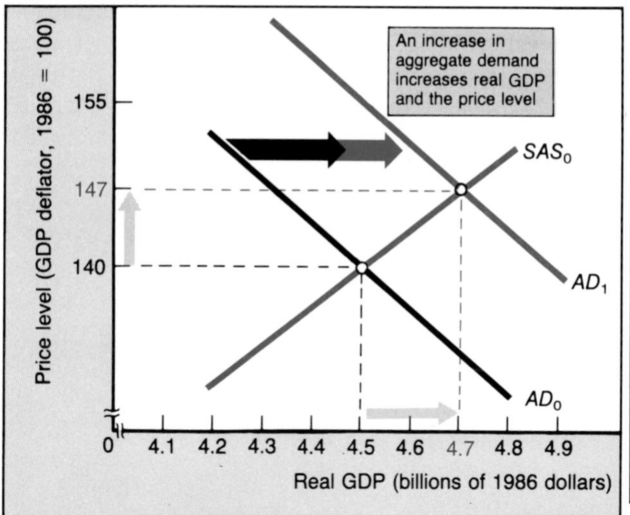

(a) An increase in aggregate demand

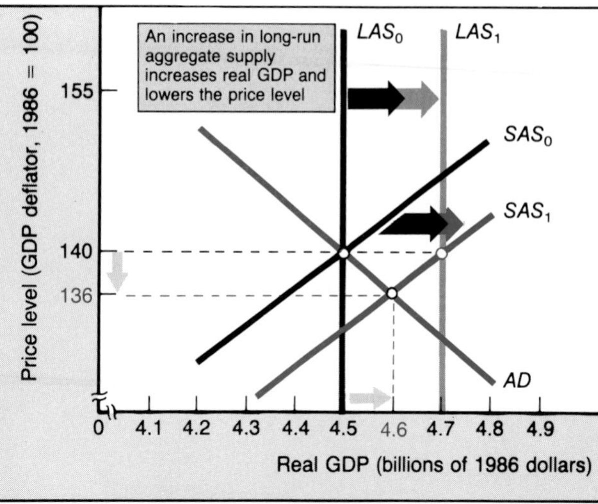

(c) An increase in long-run aggregate supply

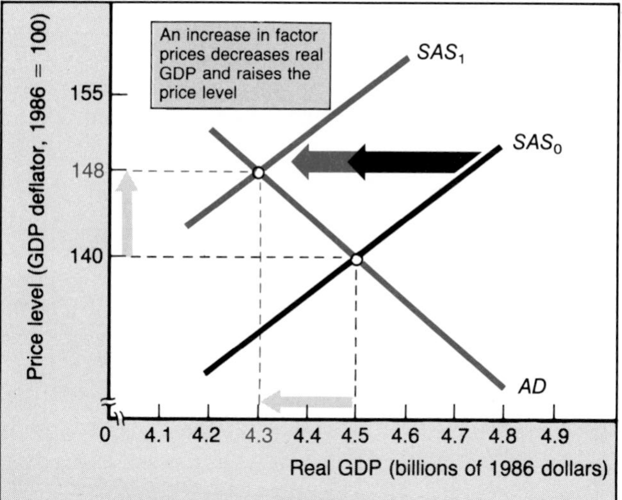

(b) A decrease in short-run aggregate supply

FIGURE 3.7
Predictions of the Aggregate Demand-Aggregate Supply Model

Other things being equal, an increase in aggregate demand leads to an increase in real GDP and a rise in the price level (part a). Other things being equal, an increase in factor prices that shifts the short-run aggregate supply curve to the left decreases real GDP and raises the price level (part b). Other things being equal, an increase in the economy's capacity to produce goods and services shifts the long-run and short-run aggregate supply curves to the right, increases real GDP and lowers the price level (part c).

long-run aggregate supply curve and the short-run aggregate supply curve to the right. Figure 3.7(c) illustrates. The aggregate demand curve is *AD*. Initially, the long-run aggregate supply curve is LAS_0 and the short-run aggregate supply curve is SAS_0. The increase in aggregate supply shifts the aggregate supply curves to the right — to LAS_1 and SAS_1. The new equilibrium is at the intersection point of the new *SAS* curve and the *AD* curve. This equilibrium occurs at a price level of 136 and a real GDP of $4.6 billion. Notice that in this situation, the economy is at less than full employment. Long-run aggregate supply has increased to $4.7 billion but real GDP has increased to only $4.6 billion. More could be produced. When real GDP is less than long-run aggregate supply a **GDP gap** exists. The GDP gap here is $0.1 billion.

Long-run adjustments In the three experiments that we have just conducted, we've seen how a change in aggregate demand, in short-run aggregate supply, and in long-run aggregate supply each brings about changes in real GDP and the price level. But suppose the economy is not at full-employment equilibrium. With no change in aggregate demand and no change in long-run aggregate supply, there will be adjustments taking place in such a situation. Suppose, for example, that an increase in aggregate demand has increased real GDP above the long-run level so that there is an above-full employment equilibrium. What happens in such a situation? Figure 3.8(a) illustrates. With real GDP at $4.7 billion, the unemployment rate is below its natural rate. Firms find it difficult to hire all the labor they want and workers find it easy to get jobs. In this situation, there is upward pressure on wage rates. As wage rates increase, the short-run aggregate supply curve shifts to the left, intersecting the aggregate demand curve *AD* at higher price levels but at lower levels of real GDP. The economy follows the arrowed path in Figure 3.8(a) until it eventually settles down on the long-run aggregate supply curve at a real GDP of $4.5 billion — the level of long-run aggregate supply — and at a price level of 155.

Alternatively, suppose the economy is at an unemployment equilibrium. Such a situation arises if aggregate demand decreases, short-run aggregate supply decreases, or

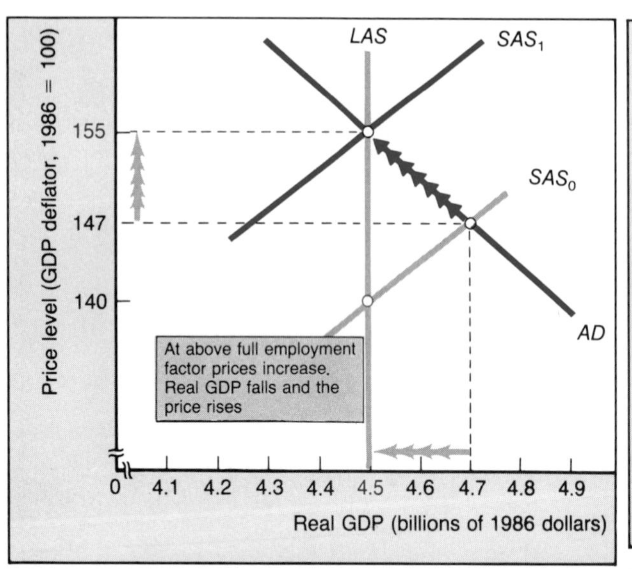

(a) Adjustment from above full employment

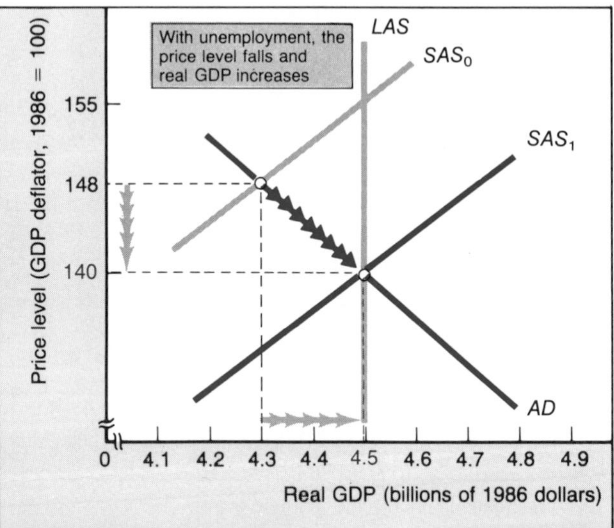

(b) Adjustment from unemployment

FIGURE 3.8
Long-run Adjustment

When the economy is at a macroeconomic equilibrium different from full employment, a dynamic adjustment process takes place. From above full employment (part a), factor prices rise, shifting the short-run aggregate supply curve to the left, from SAS_0 to SAS_1. As the short-run aggregate supply curve shifts, the price level gradually rises and real GDP gradually falls. The process comes to an end when the short-run aggregate supply curve intersects the aggregate demand curve along the long-run aggregate supply curve.

When the economy is below full employment, factor prices fall (relative to the prices of goods and services) and the short-run aggregate supply curve shifts to the right from SAS_0 to SAS_1. As the short-run aggregate supply curve shifts, it intersects the aggregate demand curve at lower and lower price levels and higher and higher levels of real GDP. The process comes to an end when the short-run aggregate supply curve, SAS_1, intersects the aggregate demand curve along the long-run aggregate supply curve (part b).

long-run aggregate supply increases. Any of these influences on the economy results in an unemployment equilibrium. How does the economy get out of such an equilibrium? Figure 3.8(b) illustrates. With unemployment in excess of the natural rate, firms find it easy to hire labor and workers find it hard to get jobs so there is downward pressure on the wage rate. Wages begin to fall. As they do so, the short-run aggregate supply curve shifts to the right, intersecting the aggregate demand curve at higher levels of real GDP and lower price levels. Such a process is illustrated in Figure 3.8(b). The price level gradually decreases to 140 and real GDP gradually increases to $4.5 billion.

But surely wages never fall Wages very rarely fall in reality. But the rate at which they rise varies and sometimes they hardly rise at all. The adjustment process that is described in Figure 3.8(b) is not one that the real world actually follows. This does not mean that the model is wrong. The model is simply holding constant something that in reality is not constant for very long—the level of aggregate demand. In reality, the level of aggregate demand is steadily increasing so that the aggregate demand curve steadily shifts toward the right. The adjustment process illustrated in Figure 3.8(b) is a tendency that is superimposed on an underlying economy that is expanding and inflating. When such a process is taking place, real GDP is increasing faster than long-run aggregate supply and prices are inflating more slowly than their trend level.

Let's summarize the various influences that we've just worked out: an increase in aggregate demand increases real GDP and raises the price level. A decrease in short-run aggregate supply decreases real GDP and increases the price level. An increase in long-run aggregate supply increases real GDP and decreases the price level. Whenever the economy is at an equilibrium other than full-employment equilibrium, a dynamic adjustment process takes place, pushing the economy toward the full-employment equilibrium. At above full-employment, wages increase, shifting the *SAS* curve to the left, increasing the price level and decreasing real GDP. When there is an unemployment equilibrium, wages decrease (other things given) and the price level falls and real GDP increases.

We've now worked out the effects of various influences on aggregate demand and aggregate supply on real GDP and the price level. Let's put our model to work by explaining a particular episode in our recent macroeconomic history—the episode that we looked at in section 3.1 of this chapter.

3.6 *Expansion and Slowdown in the 1980s*

TESTCASE

Glance back at Figure 3.1(a) and refresh your memory of the expansion that began in 1983. From 1983 to 1988 real GDP increased by 25 percent—or 4.6 percent a year. Prices also increased but at a much slower pace than before. During these years of expansion the price level increased by only 20 percent—an annual inflation rate of 3.6 percent. But after 1988, the expansion slowed. Real GDP growth dropped to an annual rate of only 2 percent. And inflation crept upward to an annual rate of 4 percent. Let's see how the aggregate demand-aggregate supply model accounts for these events.

1983-1988

In 1983, the economy was in an unemployment equilibrium. This equilibrium is illustrated in Figure 3.9(a) at the intersection of the black curves. The long-run aggregate supply curve was LAS_{83}, the short-run aggregate supply curve was SAS_{83}, and the aggregate demand curve was AD_{83}. Equilibrium real GDP was $439 billion and the price level, measured by the GDP deflator, was 92.

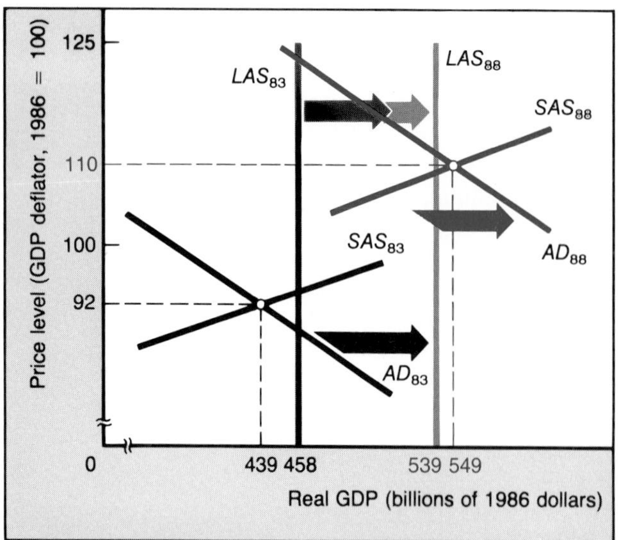

(a) 1983 to 1988

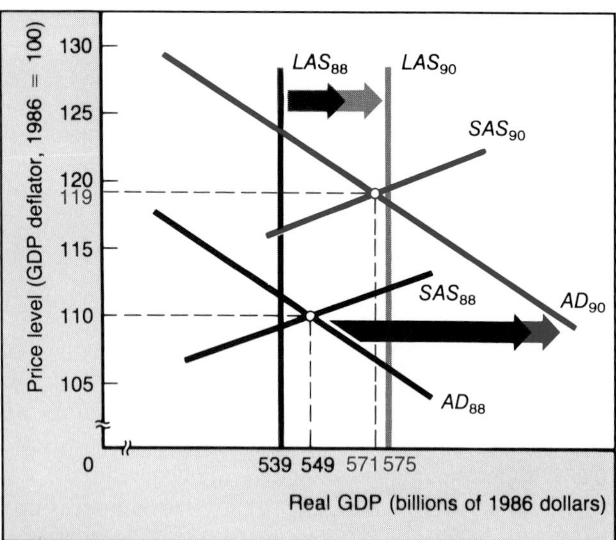

(b) 1988 to 1990

FIGURE 3.9
Expansion and Slowdown in the 1980s

In 1983 (part a), the economy was at an unemployment equilibrium on aggregate demand curve AD_{83} and short-run aggregate supply curve SAS_{83}. Equilibrium real GDP was $439 billion and the GDP deflator was 92. The long-run aggregate supply curve was LAS_{83} and there was a GDP gap of $19 billion ($458 billion *less* $439 billion). Between 1983 and 1988, labor force and capital stock growth and technological change increased long-run aggregate supply to LAS_{88}. Money supply growth, a persistent government budget deficit, and a strong expansion in the world economy increased aggregate demand to AD_{88}. Factor prices increased steadily, shifting the short-run aggregate supply curve upward to SAS_{88}. The aggregate demand curve in 1988—AD_{88}—intersected the short-run aggregate supply curve for that year—SAS_{88}—at a price level of 110 and a real GDP of $549 billion. Part of the real GDP increase was an increase in full employment real GDP, part was eliminating the 1983 GDP gap, and part was moving above full employment in 1988.

Between 1988 and 1990 (part b), the long-run aggregate supply curve shifted to LAS_{90}. Monetary policy was tightened to hold aggregate demand growth in check and the aggregate demand curve shifted to AD_{90}. Increased wages combined with growth in long-run aggregate supply shifted the short-run aggregate supply curve to SAS_{90}. By 1990, the economy was below full employment at the intersection point of AD_{90} and SAS_{90}. Real GDP was $571 billion and the GDP deflator was 119.

Between 1983 and 1988, the population and the labor force grew and so did the capital stock. Technology also advanced. The combined effect of these factors led to an increase in long-run aggregate supply. By 1988, long-run aggregate supply was $539 billion and the long-run aggregate supply curve was LAS_{88}.

Also, during these five years, aggregate demand increased. Increased aggregate demand resulted from three main forces. First, the money supply expanded quickly. Second, and probably more important in these years, taxes were held steady, government spending remained high, and a persistent government budget deficit emerged. Third, the world economy continued to expand. These forces resulted in a large increase in aggregate demand. By 1988, the aggregate demand curve had shifted to the right to AD_{88}.

If there had been no changes in factor prices, the short-run aggregate supply curve would have shifted to the right by the same amount as the shift in the long-run aggregate supply curve. But factor prices increased steadily through these years. As a consequence, the short-run aggregate supply curve shifted upward to SAS_{88}.

The combined effect of the increase in aggregate demand and the decrease in short-run aggregate supply was an increase in the price level and no change in real GDP. The aggregate demand curve in 1988 — AD_{88} — intersected the short-run aggregate supply curve for that year—SAS_{88}—at a price level of 110 and a real GDP of $549 billion. Part of that increase was an increase in full employment real GDP—the increase from $458 billion to $539 billion—and part of it was taking up the slack of the 1983 GDP gap of $19 billion. Yet another part was moving above full employment, for by 1988 the economy was in an above full-employment equilibrium. There was an inflationary gap of $10 billion. In this situation, there was a tendency for wages to rise more quickly than the rate at which prices were rising — and for the economy to be moving toward full employment.

1988-1990

The finishing point of the analysis of the 1983-1988 period is the starting point for the analysis here. Figure 3.9(b) shows the economy in 1988 at the point of intersection of the black aggregate demand and short-run aggregate supply curves, AD_{88} and SAS_{88}, with real GDP at $549 billion and the price level at 110. In 1988, the long-run aggregate supply was $539 billion and the long-run aggregate supply curve LAS_{88}.

The tendency for wages to rise relative to prices was pushing the economy from its 1988 position toward full employment—a real GDP of $539 billion. But other changes were also taking place.

Labor force growth, capital accumulation, and technological advances increased long-run aggregate supply and by 1990 the long-run aggregate supply curve had shifted to LAS_{90} at a real GDP of $575 billion.

There were also forces at work increasing aggregate demand, but they were not as strong as before. In particular, monetary policy was holding demand growth in check. The result was an increase in aggregate demand that shifted the aggregate demand curve to the right to AD_{90}.

Two sets of forces were working on the short-run aggregate supply curve. First, the increase in long-run aggregate supply moved the short-run aggregate supply curve to the right. Second, increased wages and other costs shifted the short-run aggregate supply curve to the left. The net effect of these two forces was a shift in the short-run aggregate supply curve to SAS_{90}.

By 1990, the economy was below full employment—the intersection point of AD_{90} and SAS_{90} was at a level of real GDP below the long-run aggregate supply curve, LAS_{90}. The price level had increased to 119, 8 percent higher than in 1988. Real GDP had increased to $571 billion.

These, then, are the stories of the sustained expansion from 1983 to 1988 and the slowdown in the late 1980s as told by the aggregate demand-aggregate supply model. The model interprets the historical movements in real GDP and the price level as resulting from continual changes in aggregate demand and aggregate supply. The actual real GDP and the price level are determined at the intersection point of the aggregate demand curve and the short-run aggregate supply curve. The economy's state of employment—above full employment, full employment, or unemployment—is determined by the position of the macroeconomic equilibrium relative to the position of the long-run aggregate supply curve.

3.7 *The Classical and Keynesian Models*

The aggregate demand-aggregate supply model that we have just studied is the mainstream model of modern macroeconomics. This model has evolved from two special-case models—the classical and the Keynesian.

The classical model

The classical model is based on the central assumption of classical macroeconomics that the economy operates like a self-regulating mechanism, always tending in the direction of full employment. Underlying this model is a presumption that markets function smoothly and efficiently to achieve an allocation of resources that active intervention cannot improve. At this early stage in your study of macroeconomics it isn't possible to appreciate all the fine details of classical macroeconomics. But you can begin to understand the viewpoint of classical macroeconomics in terms of the aggregate demand-aggregate supply framework you have just studied. For classical macroeconomics, that framework is too eclectic — that is, not selective enough in respect of the forces that operate to influence aggregate demand, aggregate supply, and the evolution of real GDP and the price level. Let's look at the way classical macroeconomics views aggregate demand and aggregate supply.

Aggregate demand In the classical view, of all the many possible influences on aggregate demand, only one actually operates — the money supply. Changes in the money supply generate changes in aggregate demand. None of the other potential influences operate. In particular, fiscal policy and the rest-of-world influences present in our general model are seen as having no effect on aggregate demand.

Fiscal policy—a change in government purchases of goods and services or a change in taxes — has no effect on aggregate demand because of some offsetting changes in investment. According to the classical view, an increase in government purchases or a tax cut lead to an rise in interest rates. The higher interest rates cause investment and consumer expenditure to decrease and by amounts that offset the initial increase stemming from the change in fiscal policy. Thus fiscal policy affects the composition of expenditure but not its total amount.

The classical model has a similar view of potential foreign influences on aggregate demand. A change in the foreign demand for domestic goods and services (resulting from either a change in foreign real income or the foreign price level) leads to a change in the exchange rate and that exchange rate adjustment serves to eliminate the effects of the change in the rest of the world on domestic aggregate demand.

Thus in classical macroeconomics, the aggregate demand curve looks exactly like it does in the general model that we considered above, but changes in only one factor—the money supply—lead to changes in aggregate demand.

Aggregate supply Classical macroeconomics makes no distinction between long-run aggregate supply and short-run aggregate supply. There is just one aggregate supply curve and that curve is vertical—the quantity of real GDP supplied does not depend on the price level.

Classical macroeconomics derives this proposition from its view of the way the labor market works. We saw in the general model that when unemployment is above the natural rate, there is a tendency for wages to fall (in reality, to rise less quickly than the price level is rising). We also saw that when unemployment is below the natural rate, there is a tendency for wages to increase (in reality, to increase more quickly than the price level is rising). According to classical macroeconomics, these tendencies for wages to adjust to labor market conditions are so strong and operate so quickly that unemployment is always at the natural rate.

Classical macroeconomists are aware (just as anyone is) that unemployment fluctuates. They're also aware that unemployment is high at times. They interpret such events as fluctuations in the natural rate of unemployment rather than fluctuations of unemployment around the natural rate.

It is possible to interpret the classical theory of aggregate supply in terms of the short-run and long-run aggregate supply curves of the general model, but that interpretation is not useful or interesting. For the classical macroeconomist, the short-run aggregate supply curve always moves to intersect the long-run aggregate supply curve at the same point as the aggregate demand curve intersects the long-run aggregate supply curve. Thus the position of the short-run aggregate supply curve is determined by macroeconomic equilibrium, rather than the short-run supply curve being something that determines equilibrium. The equilibrium is determined by the intersection of the aggregate demand and the long-run aggregate supply curves.

Predictions In a classical macroeconomic model, equilibrium occurs where the forces of aggregate demand and aggregate supply are balanced. Aggregate demand depends only on the money supply and aggregate supply depends on technology and is the full-employment level of real GDP. The predictions of classical macroeconomics follow directly from this equilibrium. A change in the money supply leads to a change in the price level but to no change in real GDP. Money growth causes inflation but not real GDP growth. Advances in technology and accumulation of capital as well as growth in the labor force lead to growth in real GDP. Other things being equal, these factors lead to falling prices. Prices don't actually fall because a steadily rising money supply more than offsets this tendency. Changes in taxes and government spending have no influence on real GDP and the price level. But they do influence interest rates and the composition of aggregate demand.

The classical macroeconomic model described here is a summary of the macroeconomics that preceded the Keynesian revolution of the 1930s. By the early 1950s, this revolution had developed an alternative Keynesian model. Let's now look at that model.

The Keynesian model

Like the classical macroeconomics that it replaced, Keynesian macroeconomics is complex and subtle. As we did for the classical model, here we'll look at the Keynesian model in terms of its propositions about aggregate demand, aggregate supply, and their interaction.

Aggregate demand In Keynesian macroeconomics, the most important influences on aggregate demand are fiscal policy and those stemming from the rest of the world. The potential influence of changes in the money supply is regarded as either weak or nonexistent. In the Keynesian model, a change in the money supply influences aggregate demand through its effects on investment. The effects of money on investment operate indirectly, through the interest rate: an increase in the money supply makes credit easier, lowers interest rates, and stimulates investment. According to the Keynesian model, none of these influences is strong. An increase in the money supply does not lead to a very large decrease in interest rates and interest rates themselves have only a weak influence on investment.

In contrast, changes in taxes and in government purchases of goods and services have a large effect on aggregate demand in the Keynesian model. Their large effect arises from the same mechanism that makes the effect of money weak. Keynesians agree with classical economists that an increase in government purchases or a tax cut *could* lead to increased interest rates that, in turn, choke off investment, eliminating the effect of increased government purchases or lower taxes. But they regard this interest rate mechanism as a weak one. In the Keynesian model, an increase in government purchases or a tax cut has a small effect on interest rates which, in turn, have a small effect on investment, leaving government spending and tax changes with a big effect on aggregate demand.

Aggregate supply In the Keynesian model, the short-run aggregate supply curve is horizontal — any quantity of real GDP will be supplied (over some range) at a given price level. Furthermore, the short-run aggregate supply curve shifts only slowly if the economy is away from the natural rate of unemployment. The slow-moving short-run aggregate supply curve results from slowly changing wages and prices. In the Keynesian model, even a large amount of unemployment, substantially in excess of the natural rate, will lead to very slow adjustments in wages relative to prices. Similarly, if unemployment is below the natural rate, the pressure for wages to rise more quickly is a small one.

In addition to wage stickiness, prices are also sticky in the Keynesian model. Firms set prices, for example, by printing catalogues and price lists, and change those prices infrequently. Thus at any given moment, there is an average level of prices at which firms are willing to supply whatever is demanded. The average of these prices determines the position of the short-run aggregate supply curve.

Predictions In the Keynesian model, equilibrium occurs at that quantity of real GDP demanded, read off the Keynesian aggregate demand curve, at the price level that temporarily prevails as a result of the price-setting decisions of firms. An increase in government purchases or a tax cut leads to an increase in aggregate demand and an increase in real GDP but to no change in the price level. An increase in wages, an increase in raw material prices, or an increase in foreign prices leads to a shift in the short-run aggregate supply curve, generating an increase in the price level and, other things being equal, a decrease in real GDP. Changes in the money supply have small (or perhaps no) effect on real GDP and the price level.

TESTCASE

3.8 *The 1980s Again*

No one in the 1990s (or at least very few) is a classical or a Keynesian macroeconomist in the terms described by the classical and Keynesian models that we have just set out. These models are caricatures of modern macroeconomists' views. Most macroeconomists adopt an intermediate position described by the general aggregate demand-aggregate supply model we studied earlier in this chapter. Nevertheless, the caricatures that we have just looked at do define points of view toward which many economists tend. That is, although they use the more general aggregate demand-aggregate supply model, some macroeconomists believe that the Keynesian caricature is a more nearly appropriate one, while others believe that the classical caricature more nearly fits the facts. We can see these differences by looking again at the 1980s. How do macroeconomists on the classical end of the spectrum explain the recession of the early 1980s and the expansion that followed it? How do those at the Keynesian end of the macroeconomic spectrum account for these same facts?

Classical explanation for the 1980s

According to classical macroeconomics, all the fluctuations in real GDP that we observe result from technological supply-side forces. When real GDP expands quickly, it is because capital is accumulating rapidly or technological change is proceeding at an unusually rapid pace. The strong expansion through the 1980s is seen by classical macroeconomists as arising from such forces. In particular, the widespread application of computer technology in the transportation, communications, and financial services sectors, as well as to just about every manufacturing process, was responsible for the long-sustained expansion that began in 1982. When real GDP is expanding slowly, it is because capital is accumulating slowly or there is a lull in the process of technological change.

But how do classical macroeconomists account for a fall in real GDP? Except in times of war, there has never been a period in which the capital stock has actually declined. Nor does our technological knowledge regress. How, then, can it be that sometimes real GDP falls if all the changes in real GDP result from changes in the economy's full-employment capacity to produce? Classical macroeconomists have not developed a clear answer to this question. Usually, however, they suggest that a decline in real GDP occurs because of changes in the structure and composition of output. Rapid technological change in one sector may be accompanied by slow or even no technological change in another, resulting in a reallocation of resources between the sectors. Some of those resources are labor. In effect, certain kinds of specific human capital have a high depreciation rate. The adjustment process involves a large amount of search activity for new jobs and new profit opportunities. While such a process is going on, the natural rate of unemployment is higher than normal and full-employment real GDP lower than normal.

For classical macroeconomists, the supply-side shocks most responsible for the decrease in real GDP in the early 1980s were the large changes in relative prices resulting from the increase in the price of energy and also the technological changes that increased the international competition faced by the manufacturing sector of the Canadian economy. These changes resulted in a temporary increase in the natural rate of unemployment and decrease in full-employment real GDP. Finally, for classical macroeconomists, the inflation path of the 1980s was the outcome of the growth of the money supply combined with the fluctuations in aggregate supply stemming from real forces.

The Keynesian explanation of the 1980s

The Keynesian model explains the 1980s in a manner very different from that of the classical model. According to the Keynesian model, the recession of the early 1980s arose from a sharp increase in world oil prices combined with slow growth of aggregate demand. The result was a sharp upward (vertical) shift of the horizontal short-run aggregate supply curve with the aggregate demand curve shifting to the right by an insufficient amount to allow real GDP to increase. Thus the inflation of the early 1980s and the recession, in effect, stemmed from the same source — shifts in the short-run aggregate supply curve.

The recovery of the 1980s resulted from strong aggregate demand growth and the most important influence on aggregate demand was an expansionary fiscal policy—large and persistent government deficit.

Sorting out the competing views

Discriminating between competing views about how the economy works is a major part of macroeconomics. This brief account of the 1980s seen through the eyes of the classical model and the Keynesian model is enough to put us on notice that is not easy to discriminate between competing models. We have to work hard to design tests that are sufficiently sharp and that enable us to say one model fits these facts and another does not. A good deal of what you'll be studying in the rest of this book is an account of the attempts by macroeconomists to sort out competing claims and converge upon a reliable and useful set of macroeconomic laws.

The research activity and the research programs that macroeconomists are pursuing are still heavily influenced by the old classical-Keynesian distinction. But the distinction has now taken a new turn. Here we'll take a quick look at some of the key elements in the new macroeconomics.

3.9 *New Classical and New Keynesian Extensions: A Preview*

New classical and new Keynesian macroeconomics are best viewed as research programs rather than established bodies of knowledge and points of view on how the economy works. New classical macroeconomists are pursuing a line of research designed to improve our understanding of macroeconomic phenomena by developing models that share many features of the classical macroeconomic model. New Keynesians are embarked on a parallel program that seeks to improve our understanding by developing models that share features of the Keynesian model. But there are also some strong points of agreement by all new macroeconomists. The points of agreement are these:

- A need for microfoundations
- A respect for the facts

Microfoundations

All modern macroeconomists agree that models of the aggregate economy must be consistent with models of individual household and firm behavior. But we cannot have one microeconomics and another macroeconomics. A key feature of microeconomic models is the assumption of rational maximizing households and firms. A further key feature of micro models is that households and firms interact in markets — markets for goods and services, factors of production, and financial and real assets. The new macroeconomics uses these same basic ideas of microeconomics to construct models of the aggregate economy.

Respect for the facts

All modern macroeconomists regard the facts as the final arbiters of the usefulness of their models. In fact, macroeconomics, more than any other part of our discipline, is driven by a central goal of explaining well-documented, actual historical episodes.

Although all new macroeconomists agree that macro models with micro foundations are needed and that models should stand or fall by their ability to account for the facts, they do not agree on the most promising route to progress and increased knowledge.

Differences in approach

New classical macroeconomists believe that we will be able to understand and predict macroeconomic fluctuations with models that are essentially competitive in nature and in which markets do a good job at allocating resources.

New Keynesian macroeconomists believe that we will not be able to understand aggregate fluctuations unless we develop models in which markets, in some important sense, fail in their objectives. Markets are mechanisms for coordinating the actions of individual households and firms. For new Keynesian macroeconomists, the existence of high and persistent unemployment is, in and of itself, a symptom of a failure of that coordination mechanism. They want to develop models, therefore, that describe the technology of coordination in such a way as to be able to understand why that mechanism sometimes delivers a low rate of unemployment and at other times, a high rate.

For new classical macroeconomists, the existence of high and persistent unemployment is just as real a phenomenon but one that constitutes a puzzle to be explained as arising from fully efficient markets that have no coordination difficulties.

In your study of macroeconomics, you will spend most of the time dealing with relatively noncontroversial issues, learning the general model of aggregate demand and aggregate supply and digging more deeply behind the aggregate demand and aggregate supply curves. In this process you will learn more about the markets for goods and services—real GDP—for financial assets and liabilities, and for factors of production. You will also, however, from time to time, encounter points of conflict between the classical and Keynesian approaches. At the end of your study, we'll return to these big themes and look in some greater detail at the attempts of new classical and new Keynesian macroeconomists to give form to their ideas and to develop not only a new, but a better, macroeconomics.

■ You've now studied the key facts that give rise to the questions that macroeconomics tries to answer; you've seen how we monitor macroeconomic activity and measure the key variables such as real GDP and the price level; you've studied the general model of aggregate demand-aggregate supply that explains fluctuations in real GDP and the price level; and finally, you've looked at the two leading schools of macroeconomic thought — the classical and Keynesian schools — and seen both the origins of those schools and something of the way in which macroeconomists are currently trying to advance our understanding.

Our next task is to start digging more deeply into the aggregate demand-aggregate supply model. We'll begin with aggregate demand (Chapters 4 through 7) and then go on to aggregate supply (Chapters 8 through 10). But these two blocks of chapters can be read in either order.

CHAPTER REVIEW

Summary

A GENERAL MODEL OF AGGREGATE DEMAND AND SUPPLY

Macroeconomists use a model of aggregate demand and aggregate supply to determine real GDP and the price level and to predict fluctuations in real GDP and the price level.

WHAT DETERMINES AGGREGATE DEMAND

The quantity of real GDP demanded is the sum of consumer expenditure, investment, government purchases of goods and services, and net exports. Aggregate demand is the relationship between the quantity of real GDP demanded and the price level, holding constant all other influences on the buying plans of households, firms, governments, and foreigners.

The aggregate demand curve slopes downward—a rise in the price level, other things being constant, lowers the quantity of real GDP demanded. Real GDP demanded falls because the higher price level lowers the real exchange rate and lowers the quantity of real money, which, in turn, raises interest rates.

The position of the aggregate demand curve is determined by all the influences on aggregate demand other than the price level. Aggregate demand increases (the aggregate demand curve shifts to the right) if taxes are cut, interest rates fall, business confidence improves, foreign income increases, the money supply increases, foreign prices increase, or the dollar weakens on the foreign exchange market.

WHAT DETERMINES AGGREGATE SUPPLY

Aggregate supply is the relationship between the quantity of real GDP supplied and the price level. There are two time frames for aggregate supply: the long run and the short run.

Long-run aggregate supply is the quantity of real GDP supplied when each firm is producing its profit-maximizing output and there is full employment. Long-run aggregate supply is determined by the size of the capital stock, the state of technology, and the natural rate of unemployment. The long-run aggregate supply curve is vertical.

Short-run aggregate supply is the quantity of real GDP supplied at each price level, holding factor prices constant—in particular, the wage rate. The short-run aggregate supply curve is upward sloping until the physical limit of the economy to produce goods and services is reached, when it becomes vertical. The curve slopes upward because, as the price level increases, given the money wage, the real wage decreases and firms hire more labor and increase the output of goods and services.

Aggregate supply increases if the labor force increases, the natural rate of unemployment decreases, the capital stock increases, or technological advance increases labor productivity. Such changes increase both long-run and short-run aggregate supply and shift the long-run and short-run aggregate supply curves to the right. Increases in factor prices, the wage rate in particular, decrease aggregate supply and shift the short-run aggregate supply curve to the left.

REAL GDP AND THE PRICE LEVEL

The interaction of aggregate demand and aggregate supply determines macroeconomic equilibrium—real GDP and the price level. Equilibrium real GDP and the price level are determined at the intersection point of the aggregate demand and short-run aggregate supply curves. An increase in aggregate demand shifts the aggregate demand curve to the right, increasing real GDP and the price level. An increase in aggregate supply arising from an increase in the labor force, a decrease in the natural rate of unemployment, an increase in the capital stock, or a technological advance shifts both the short-run and long-run aggregate supply curves to the right, increasing real GDP and lowering the price level. But an increase in factor prices shifts the short-run aggregate supply curve to the left and leaves the long-run aggregate supply curve unchanged, decreasing real GDP and increasing the price level.

Macroeconomic equilibrium can occur at full employment, above full employment or at unemployment. If the economy is at an unemployment equilibrium, firms find it easy to hire workers and workers find it hard to get a job. Wages begin to fall, the short-run aggregate supply shifts to the right, and the economy gradually moves toward full employment. If the economy is at an above full-employment equilibrium, firms find it hard to hire workers and workers find it easy to get jobs. Wages begin to rise, the short-run aggregate supply curve shifts to the left, and the economy gradually moves toward full employment.

EXPANSION AND SLOWDOWN IN THE 1980s

The aggregate demand-aggregate supply model explains the period of strong expansion between 1983 and 1988 as arising from growth in aggregate supply and a more rapid growth in aggregate demand. On the supply side, the labor force and the capital stock grew and technology advanced. But factor prices increased steadily so short-run aggregate supply did not increase as quickly as long-run aggregate supply. On the demand side, the money supply expanded quickly, a persistent government budget deficit prevailed, and the world economy expanded. The combined effect of these forces resulted in a 25 percent expansion in real GDP and a 20 percent rise in the price level. Part of the real GDP increase was an increase in long-run real GDP, part was taking up the slack of the 1983 GDP gap, and part was moving above full employment.

With an inflationary gap in 1988, wages increased, pushing the economy toward full employment. Monetary policy was tightened, and aggregate demand growth was held in check. These forces slowed the growth of real GDP in the late 1980s.

DISTINCTION BETWEEN THE CLASSICAL AND KEYNESIAN MODELS

The classical model assumes that the economy works like a self-regulating mechanism. Wages adjust to keep the labor market at full employment. There is only one aggregate supply curve and it is vertical. Changes in aggregate demand result mainly from changes in the money supply and produce price level changes. Real GDP remains at full employment. Fluctuations in real GDP result from changes in the natural rate of unemployment.

The Keynesian model assumes that the economy does not work like a self-regulating mechanism. Wage stickiness allows only a slow adjustment of unemployment to the natural rate. The short-run aggregate supply curve is horizontal because the prevailing price level is the result of prices set by firms that are (like wages) temporarily sticky. Changes in aggregate demand arise from changes in fiscal policy—changes in government purchases and taxes—and net exports, and produce changes in real GDP with no change in the price level. Any change in short-run aggregate supply shifts the short-run aggregate supply curve vertically and generates increases in the price level and a decrease in real GDP.

HOW THE CLASSICAL AND KEYNESIAN MODELS EXPLAIN FLUCTUATIONS IN REAL GDP AND THE PRICE LEVEL

In the classical model, the economy is always at full employment. That is, the economy is always at the natural rate of unemployment. Fluctuations in real GDP arise from uneven technological change and capital accumulation between sectors of the economy which results in a higher-than-usual labor turnover and from supply-side shocks, such as increases in factor prices. Fluctuations in the price level are the result of fluctuations in the money supply. In the Keynesian model, fluctuations in real GDP arise from fluctuations in aggregate demand which result from changes in fiscal policy and net exports. Fluctuations in the price level arise from shifts in the short-run aggregate supply curve, which occur when factor prices change.

NEW CLASSICAL AND NEW KEYNESIAN RESEARCH PROGRAMS

Most macroeconomists today agree on two things:

- Macro models should be built on the foundations of microeconomics.
- Macro models should be judged by their ability to account for the facts.

But modern macroeconomists disagree about the types of models likely to provide a better understanding of macroeconomic performance. New classical economists are attempting to show that aggregate fluctuations can be interpreted as arising from fluctuations in the timing of economic activity—intertemporal substitutions—in an economy that is essentially competitive and in which the choices of individual agents are coordinated through well-functioning markets. New Keynesian macroeconomists are attempting to show that aggregate economic fluctuations arise because markets fail in their attempt to coordinate individual choices.

Key Terms and Concepts

Above full-employment equilibrium A situation in which macroeconomic equilibrium occurs at a level of real GDP above long-run aggregate supply.

Aggregate demand The relationship between the quantity of real GDP demanded and the price level—either the aggregate demand schedule or the aggregate demand curve.

Aggregate demand curve A graph of the quantity of real GDP demanded at each price level, holding constant all other influences on the buying plans of households, firms, governments, and foreigners.

Aggregate demand schedule A list of the quantity of real GDP demanded at each price level, holding constant all other influences on the buying plans of households, firms, governments, and foreigners.

Aggregate quantity of goods and services demanded The quantity of real GDP demanded—the total value (measured in constant dollars) of consumer expenditure, investment, government purchases of goods and services, and net exports.

Aggregate quantity of goods and services supplied The quantity of real GDP supplied—the total value (measured in constant dollars) of all the goods and services produced in the economy.

Aggregate supply The relationship between the quantity of real GDP supplied and the price level—either the aggregate supply schedule or the aggregate supply curve.

Aggregate supply curve A graph of the quantity of real GDP supplied at each price level, holding constant all other influences on firms' production plans.

Aggregate supply schedule A list of the quantity of real GDP supplied at each price level, holding all other influences on firms' production plans constant.

Disposable income Households' income minus total taxes paid.

Endogenous variable A variable whose value is determined by a model.

Exogenous variable A variable whose value is determined outside the model and taken as given.

Full-employment equilibrium A situation in which macroeconomic equilibrium occurs at a point on the long-run aggregate supply curve.

GDP gap When real GDP is less than long-run aggregate supply.

Long-run aggregate supply The quantity of real GDP supplied when all wages and prices have adjusted so that each firm is producing its profit-maximizing output and there is full employment.

Macroeconomic equilibrium A situation in which the quantity of real GDP demanded equals the quantity of real GDP supplied.

Macroeconomic model A description of how households, firms, governments, and foreigners make economic decisions and how their decisions are coordinated in markets.

Macroeconomic theory A body of laws and generalizations about how the economy works based on macroeconomic models whose predictions have not yet been rejected.

Natural rate of unemployment The percentage of the labor force that is unemployed when the only unemployment is that arising from the normal job-search activity of new entrants to the labor force and labor market turnover.

Real exchange rate A measure of the price of foreign goods and services relative to domestic goods and services.

Real money Money expressed in terms of the quantity of goods and services that it can buy.

Real wage rate The money wage rate divided by the price level—it is the real price or real cost of labor to firms.

Short-run aggregate supply curve A graph of the quantity of real GDP supplied at each price level, holding constant the prices of factors of production and, in particular, the wage rate.

Short-run aggregate supply schedule A list of the quantities of real GDP supplied at each price level, holding constant the prices of the factors of production and, in particular, the wage rate.

Unemployment equilibrium A situation in which macroeconomic equilibrium occurs at a level of real GDP below long-run aggregate supply.

Review Questions

1. Explain why macroeconomists use a model of aggregate demand and aggregate supply.
2. What does the term ''aggregate demand'' mean? What are the influences on aggregate demand? How do these influences change aggregate demand?
3. What do we mean by short-run aggregate supply?
4. What do we mean by long-run aggregate supply?
5. What influences on aggregate supply change both long-run aggregate supply and short-run aggregate supply?
6. What influences on aggregate supply change only the short-run aggregate supply?
7. What is macroeconomic equilibrium? What are the three sorts of macroeconomic equilibrium that can be experienced?
8. What are the determinants of aggregate demand?
9. What are the factors that change aggregate demand? Explain how each of these factors increases aggregate demand.
10. Why is the long-run aggregate supply curve vertical?
11. Why does the short-run aggregate supply curve slope downward?

12. Explain why an increase in wages shifts the short-run aggregate supply curve to the left but leaves the long-run aggregate supply curve unchanged.
13. What is the effect of an increase in aggregate demand on real GDP and the price level?
14. What is the effect of an increase in wages on real GDP and the price level?
15. What is the effect of an increase in the rate of capital accumulation on real GDP and the price level?
16. Use the general model of aggregate demand and aggregate supply to explain the 1982 recession.
17. Use the general model of aggregate demand and aggregate supply to explain the recovery from 1982 to 1990.
18. What are the key assumptions of the classical model? What are its predictions?
19. What are the key assumptions of the Keynesian model? What are its predictions?
20. Compare the classical model's explanation and the Keynesian model's explanation of the 1980s.
21. How do the research programs for the new classical and the new Keynesian extensions of the general model of aggregate demand agree and differ?

Problems

1. You're given the following information about an economy:
   The *AD* curve is $Y^d = 600 - 50P$
   The *SAS* curve is $Y^s = 50P$
   The *LAS* curve is $Y^s = 300$
   (a) What is the equilibrium real GDP and the price level? How would you describe this macroeconomic equilibrium?
   (b) Technological advances increase aggregate supply by 30 units. What is the change in real GDP and the price level? How would you describe this macroeconomic equilibrium?
   (c) Beginning with the original aggregate supply and aggregate demand curves, what is the change in real GDP and the price level if aggregate demand increases by 60 units? How would you describe this macroeconomic equilibrium?
   (d) An increase in wages lowers the short-run aggregate supply curve by 10 units. What is the change in real GDP and the price level? How would you describe this macroeconomic equilibrium?
2. You are given the following information about an economy.
   The *AD* curve is $Y^d = 1000 - 20P$
   The *SAS* curve is $Y^s = 20P$
   The *LAS* curve is $Y^s = 500$
   (a) What is the macroeconomic equilibrium?
   (b) If aggregate demand rises by 100 units, what is the new *AD* curve?
   (c) In question (b), what is the resulting change in real GDP and the price level?
   (d) If the *AD* curve is in its initial position, and the natural rate of unemployment falls such that aggregate supply increases by five units, what is the new *SAS* curve? What is the new *LAS* curve?
   (e) In question (d), what is the change in real GDP and the price level?
   (f) If factor prices increase such that the *SAS* curve shifts to the left by 2 units, what is the equation to the new *SAS* curve?
   (g) In question (f), what is the new equilibrium real GDP and price level?

II
Aggregate Demand Fluctuations

CHAPTER

Aggregate Expenditure and Income

THE AMPLIFICATION OF SPENDING SHOCKS

ONE PERSON'S EXPENDITURE IS ANOTHER PERSON'S INCOME. When Calgary hosted the Winter Olympic Games in 1986 the development of additional winter sports facilities, and the creation of extra accommodation and transportation facilities brought a big increase in the incomes of construction companies and their workers. The spending by the large number of visitors to Calgary in hotels and restaurants, boutiques, car rentals, and airlines brought higher incomes to the owners and workers in the hospitality, retailing, and transportation sectors. When the higher incomes of Calgarians were spent, purchases at supermarkets increased and countless other businesses experienced increased sales. Extra workers were hired and orders increased to replenish falling inventories. The initial extra spending on the Olympic Games themselves was amplified and resulted in even more spending in the Alberta economy. This extra spending sent ripple effects across the whole nation's economy. How does such a process come to an end? Does spending keep rising forever or does something bring it to a natural limit?

This chapter answers questions such as this. It does so by developing a more detailed model of aggregate demand, one that determines the components of aggregate demand and the way they interact with each other. In particular, in this chapter, we're going to study the factors that influence consumer expenditure and the way in which fluctuations in investment, exports, and government purchases interact with consumer expenditure to produce fluctuations in aggregate expenditure. There's a connection between what we learned in Chapter 2 about aggregate demand and what we're about to study here. To see that connection, we need to distinguish between *aggregate demand* and *aggregate expenditure*.

Aggregate demand is the relationship between the quantity of real GDP demanded and the price level. **Aggregate expenditure** is the quantity of real GDP demanded *at a given price level.* In this chapter we'll focus on aggregate expenditure. To sharpen this focus we'll study an economy in which the price level is temporarily frozen at its current level. This will enable us to concentrate our attention on the forces that determine consumer expenditure and the equilibrium level of aggregate expenditure for a given level of investment, government purchases, and exports. We'll also ignore any effects of the variables we're studying on the interest rate, the foreign exchange rate, or any of the many other possible influences on the components of aggregate expenditure. In subsequent chapters, we'll unfreeze the price level and the other variables and study a more wide-ranging set of interactions.

After studying this chapter, you will be able to

- Describe the components of aggregate expenditure, the relative importance of each, and the extent to which each fluctuates
- Set out a simple model of consumption and saving
- Describe the relationship between consumption and income in the Canadian economy
- Explain how expenditure equilibrium is determined
- Explain how the economy converges to an expenditure equilibrium
- Define and derive the multiplier
- Define and derive the fiscal policy multipliers
- Explain the effects of changes in investment, government purchases, taxes, and exports on equilibrium aggregate expenditure

Let's begin by examining the facts about the components of aggregate expenditure.

4.1 *The Components of Spending*

MACROFACTS

Just as a matter of arithmetic, aggregate expenditure can be divided up in an infinite number of ways. It is possible to distinguish between the expenditure on beer, pretzels, steak, ketchup, power stations, highways, and so on, and for some purposes, such a detailed disaggregation of the total volume of spending in the economy is essential. But for the purpose of the questions addressed in macroeconomics such a detailed classification is unnecessary. It is useful, however, to divide aggregate expenditure into a small number of key components, the determination of each of which involves different considerations. Specifically, for the purpose of doing macroeconomic analysis, aggregate expenditure is divided into four components. They are

1. Consumer expenditure
2. Investment
3. Government purchases of goods and services
4. Net exports

We defined these components of aggregate expenditure in Chapter 2 when we studied the national income and product accounts. How important is each component's contribution to aggregate expenditure? Which components fluctuate most, generating fluctuations in aggregate economic activity?

Relative importance

Figure 4.1(a) shows the relative importance of the components of aggregate expenditure. Consumer expenditure, by far the largest single component of aggregate expenditure, comprises about 60 percent of the total. The second largest component, government purchases of goods and services, accounts for slightly more than 20 percent of total expenditure. Investment comes third, representing between 15 and 20 percent of the total. Net exports, the smallest component, fluctuates around the zero. In the early 1980s net exports were positive (we exported more than we imported), but in the later years of the 1980s net exports became negative (we imported more than we exported). Figure 4.1(b) shows the behavior of both exports and imports that produce the movements in net exports. As you can see, both have increased but imports have increased faster than exports, especially in the 1980s.

FIGURE 4.1
The Components Aggregate Expenditure

Consumer expenditure is the largest component of aggregate expenditure (about 60 percent of GDP). Government purchases of goods and services are around 20 percent of GDP and investment accounts for between 15 and 20 percent of GDP. Exports and imports are similar in magnitude but imports have grown somewhat more quickly than exports in the 1980s.

Source: National Income and Expenditure Accounts, Catalogue 13-201, Statistics Canada, December, 1990.

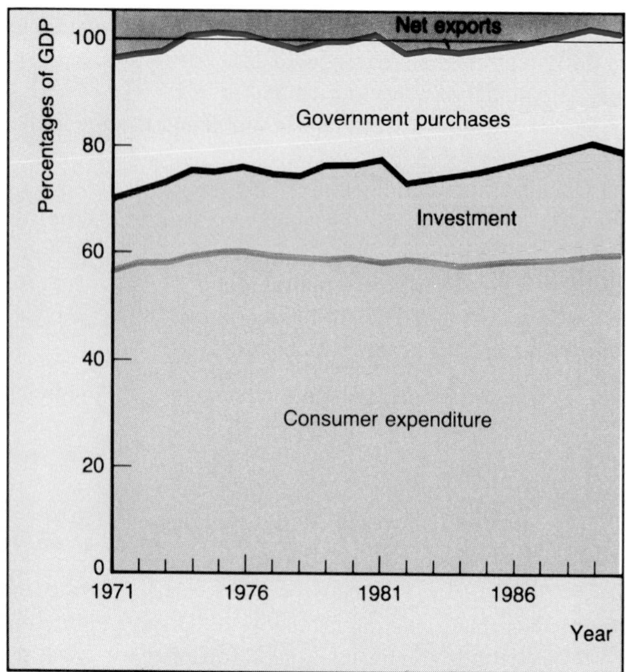

(a) Components of expenditure

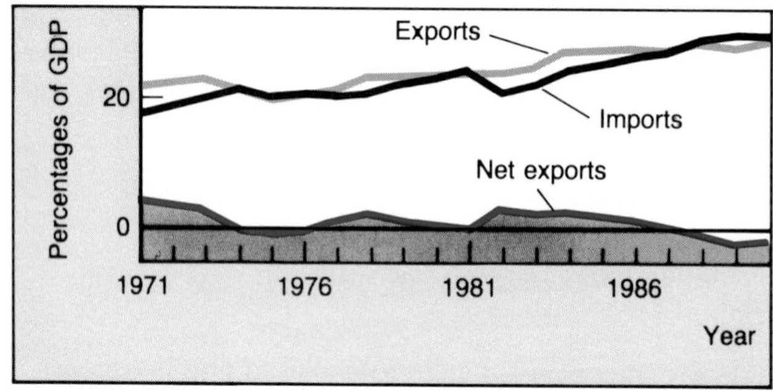

(b) Exports and imports

Relative volatility

The relative volatility of the components of aggregate expenditure is illustrated in Figure 4.2, which shows the annual percentage growth rates of various components of expenditure. Part (a) shows that investment and exports fluctuate much more strongly than consumer expenditure. In 1973 and 1984, for example, investment plus exports grew by about 15 percent while in 1975, they decreased by 5 percent and in 1982, they decreased by 15 percent. In contrast, fluctuations in consumer expenditure are small, ranging between 8 percent and −3 percent.

Figure 4.2(b) shows the relative importance of fluctuations in government purchases and investment plus exports. Here you can see that the growth rate of government purchases increased between 1972 and 1975, decreased between 1975 and 1979, and increased through the 1980s. Also, the fluctuations in the growth rate of government purchases have been small compared with the fluctuations in investment plus exports. Further, there is a tendency for government purchases to fluctuate countercyclically relative to the private components of spending. For example, when investment plus

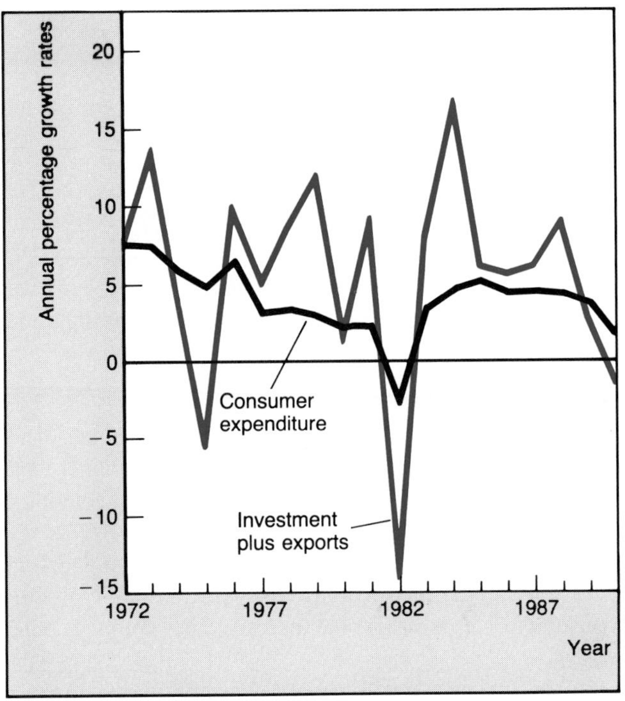

(a) Private spending

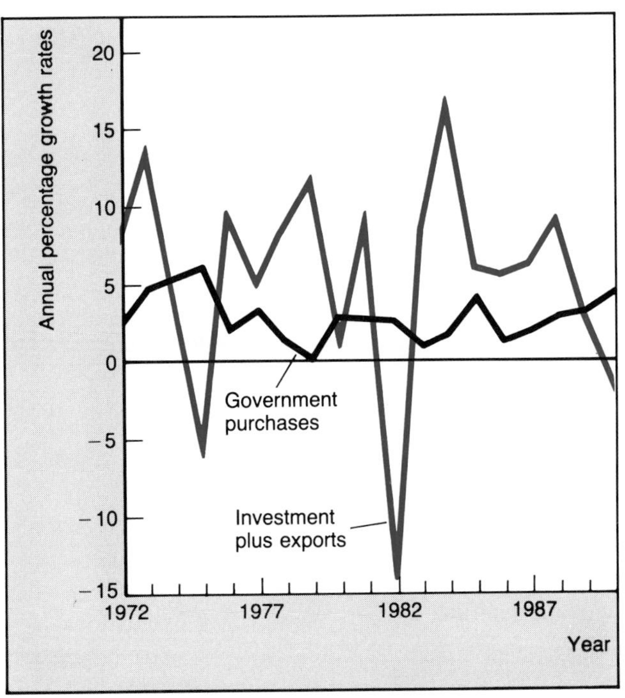

(b) Government spending and private spending

FIGURE 4.2
Fluctuations in Expenditure

The most volatile elements of aggregate expenditure are investment and exports. Fluctuations in this aggregate have a much larger amplitude than fluctuations in consumer expenditure (part a) or government purchases of goods and services (part b). There is a tendency for fluctuations in consumer expenditure and investment plus exports to move in sympathy with each other and for government purchases to move in the opposite direction to fluctuations in investment plus exports.

Source: National Income and Expenditure Accounts, Catalogue 13-201, Statistics Canada, December, 1990.

export growth was negative in 1975, the growth of government purchases was at its strongest. As investment and export growth increased after 1975, the growth of government purchases decreased.

Now that we've described the components of aggregate expenditure, let's begin to explain how they are determined, starting with a model of consumption, saving, and income.

4.2 Consumption, Saving, and Income

The model of consumption and saving that we're now going to study was first suggested by John Maynard Keynes in what he called a theory of the consumption function.

The consumption function

The **consumption function** is the relationship between consumer expenditure and disposable income. Keynes's theory of the determination of consumer expenditure rests on the premise that, of the many possible factors influencing the level of consumer expenditure, the level of real disposable income is most important. This is so, according to Keynes, because of "the fundamental psychological law upon which we are entitled to depend with great confidence: that men are disposed, as a rule and on the average, to increase their consumption as their income increases, but not by as much as the increase in their income."[1]

Table 4.1(a) gives an example of Keynes's consumption function. It lists four levels of disposable income — income, y, minus taxes, t — and the corresponding consumer expenditure, c, of a household at each income. Even with a zero disposable income, the household has some minimum consumption plans. It spends on basic food, clothing, and shelter. In this example, this consumption costs $5,000 a year. This level of consumer

TABLE 4.1
The Consumption and Saving Functions

(a) Income, consumer expenditure, and saving

	DISPOSABLE INCOME	CONSUMER EXPENDITURE	AUTONOMOUS CONSUMER EXPENDITURE	INDUCED CONSUMER EXPENDITURE	SAVING
	$y - t$	c	a	$b(y - t)$	s
	(thousands of dollars per year)				
A	0	5	5	0	−5
B	20	20	5	15	0
C	40	35	5	30	5
D	60	50	5	45	10

(b) The marginal propensities to consume and save

CHANGE IN DISPOSABLE INCOME	CHANGE IN CONSUMER EXPENDITURE	CHANGE IN SAVING	MARGINAL PROPENSITY TO CONSUME	MARGINAL PROPENSITY TO SAVE
$\Delta(y - t)$	Δc	Δs	$\frac{\Delta c}{\Delta(y - t)} = b$	$\frac{\Delta s}{\Delta(y - t)} = (1 - b)$
+20	+15	+5	0.75	0.25

[1]John Maynard Keynes, *The General Theory of Employment, Interest, and Money* (London: Macmillan and Co. Ltd., 1936), p. 96.

expenditure is called **autonomous consumer expenditure.** Autonomous consumer expenditure is constant regardless of the level of income. As disposable income increases, so does consumer expenditure. **Induced consumer expenditure** is the part of consumer expenditure that varies with disposable income. It is consumer expenditure in excess of autonomous consumer expenditure. In this example, when disposable income is $20,000, induced consumer expenditure is $15,000.

The relationship described in Table 4.1(a) is graphed in Figure 4.3(a). Here, the vertical axis measures consumer expenditure and the horizontal axis measures disposable income. Autonomous consumer expenditure, row *A* of the table, is the intercept on the vertical axis, marked *A*, at $5,000 a year. The points *B*, *C*, and *D* on the graph represent the other three rows of Table 4.1(a). The line passing through those points is the consumption function. It shows that as disposable income increases, so does consumer expenditure, but consumer expenditure increases by a smaller amount than the increase in disposable income. The larger the disposable income, the larger is consumer expenditure, but each additional dollar of disposable income does not lead to an additional dollar of consumer expenditure. In this example, for each additional dollar of income, 75 cents is spent.

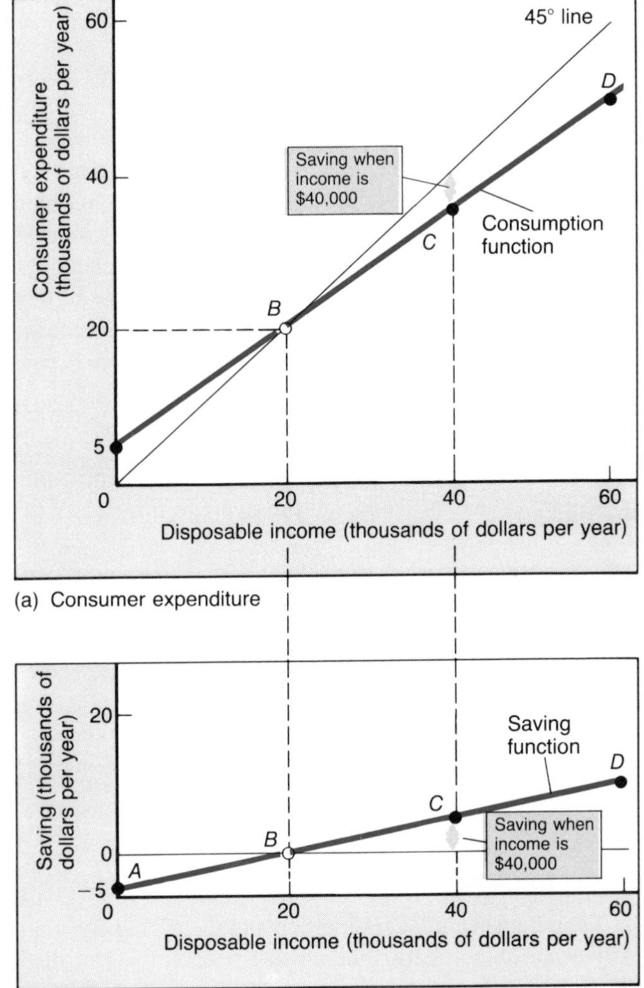

FIGURE 4.3
The Consumption and Saving Functions

The consumption function (part a) shows how consumer expenditure varies as disposable income varies. Autonomous consumer expenditure is the amount of consumer expenditure when disposable income is zero. As disposable income increases, so does consumer expenditure but by a smaller amount than the increase in disposable income. The saving function (part b) shows how saving varies as disposable income varies. When disposable income is zero, saving is negative (there is dissaving). As disposable income increases, so does saving. There is a relationship between the consumption function and saving function. At the disposable income at which the consumption function intersects the 45° line, the saving function intersects the zero line—the x-axis. In part (a), the vertical distance between the 45° line and the consumption function measures saving, which is also measured by the vertical distance between the zero line and the saving function in part (b).

The saving function

The relation between saving and disposable income is called the **saving function**. The saving function is illustrated in Table 4.1(a) and in Figure 4.3(b). The table records the saving at each level of disposable income. When disposable income is zero, consumer expenditure is $5,000, so saving is a negative $5,000. When saving is negative, it is called **dissaving**. As disposable income increases, so does saving.

The relationship between disposable income and saving shown in Table 4.1(a) is graphed in Figure 4.3(b). The points *A*, *B*, *C*, and *D* in the figure correspond to the rows in the table.

The propensities to consume and save

The relationship between consumption and disposable income and between saving and disposable income are described by the propensities to consume and save.

The propensity to consume The **average propensity to consume** is the ratio of consumer expenditure to disposable income. For example, along the consumption function in Figure 4.3(a), the average propensity to consume is 1 when disposable income is $20,000 a year. When disposable income is $40,000 a year, consumer expenditure is $35,000 so the average propensity to consume is $35,000 divided by $40,000, which equals 7/8.

The **marginal propensity to consume** is the ratio of a *change* in consumer expenditure to a *change* in disposable income. The marginal propensity to consume is constant along a linear consumption function, such as shown in Figure 4.3(a). It is calculated in Table 4.1(b). Regardless of which disposable income level we begin with, consumer expenditure increases by $15,000 when disposable income increases by $20,000. Thus the change in consumer expenditure divided by the change in disposable income is 0.75. The slope of the consumption function measures the marginal propensity to consume. You can check this by calculating the slope of the consumption function in Figure 4.3(a). It is the change in consumer expenditure divided by the change in disposable income between any two points on the consumption function. Because this consumption function is linear (has constant slope), the marginal propensity to consume is constant.

The propensity to save The **average propensity to save** is the ratio of saving to disposable income. For the saving function of Figure 4.3(b), when disposable income is $20,000 a year, the average propensity to save is zero. When disposable income is $40,000 a year, $5,000 a year is saved and the average propensity to save is $5,000 divided by $40,000, which equals 1/8.

The ratio of a *change* in saving to a *change* in disposable income is called the **marginal propensity to save**. The slope of the saving function measures the marginal propensity to save. Along the linear saving function in Figure 4.3(a), the marginal propensity to save is constant and equal to 0.25. That is, each additional dollar of disposable income generates an additional 25 cents of saving. The calculation of this marginal propensity to save is illustrated in Table 4.1(b). When disposable income increases by $20,000, saving increases by $5,000. Thus the marginal propensity to save is $5,000 divided by $20,000, which equals 0.25.

The connection between the consumption and saving functions

There is a relationship between the consumption and the saving function. That relationship can be verified in Table 4.1 by noticing that at each level of disposable income, consumer expenditure and saving sum to disposable income. Thus for example, on row

D, when disposable income is \$60,000, consumer expenditure is \$50,000 and saving is \$10,000. Verify that on each row of the table, consumer expenditure plus saving equals disposable income.

This relationship can also be seen in Figure 4.3. To see it, focus first on Figure 4.3(a) and the line labeled 45° line. This line plots points at which consumer expenditure is equal to disposable income. The vertical distance between the 45° line and the consumption function is a measure of saving. Saving is also measured in part (b) as the vertical distance between the saving function and the zero line—the x-axis. You can see that when disposable income is at \$20,000 a year, there is no saving. Consumer expenditure exactly equals disposable income. At disposable incomes below \$20,000, consumer expenditure exceeds disposable income and there is dissaving. At disposable incomes above \$20,000 a year, consumer expenditure is less than disposable income and saving. The figure highlights the amount of saving when income is \$40,000 a year.

There is also a relationship between the marginal propensity to consume and the marginal propensity to save—the slopes of the consumption and saving functions. An additional dollar of disposable income can only be spent on goods and services or saved. The fraction spent on goods and services is the marginal propensity to consume and the fraction saved is the marginal propensity to save. These fractions—the marginal propensity to consume and the marginal propensity to save—always sum to one.

The algebra of the consumption and saving functions

The consumption function can be described by an equation that links consumer expenditure (c) to disposable income ($y - t$). Such an equation is

$$c = a + b(y - t). \tag{4.1}$$

Here, a is autonomous consumer expenditure—the amount of consumer expenditure when disposable income is zero. In the example shown in Figure 4.3, a is equal to \$5,000 a year. The influence of disposable income on consumer expenditure is measured by b, which is a fraction. In the example in Figure 4.3, b equals 0.75. The parameter b is the *marginal propensity to consume*. Induced consumer expenditure is $b(y - t)$.

To see the relationship between the consumption function and the saving function, we use the fact that household income is either spent on goods and services, saved, or paid in taxes. That is,

$$y = c + s + t. \tag{4.2}$$

With consumer expenditure determined by the consumption function (Equation 4.1), a household's saving plan must be consistent with its consumer expenditure plan. To find out what saving is, substitute the consumption function (Equation 4.1) into the household's budget (Equation 4.2), and solve for saving. That solution is

$$s = -a + (1 - b)(y - t). \tag{4.3}$$

Notice that if we add together the household's consumer expenditure and saving,

$$c = a + b(y - t)$$
$$s = -a + (1 - b)(y - t)$$

then we see that

$$c + s = y - t. \tag{4.4}$$

Equation (4.4) says that households allocate their disposable income, $y - t$, between consumer expenditure and saving, according to the rules described in Equations (4.1) and (4.3).

TESTCASE

4.3 Consumption, Saving, and Income, 1929-1990

We can test the Keynesian theory of the consumption function by examining data on consumer expenditure and disposable income in the Canadian economy. Such data are presented in Figure 4.4, where each dot in the figure shows the personal disposable income and consumer expenditure in a particular year, each measured in constant 1986 dollars.

Figure 4.4(a) shows the long-run consumption function. The **long-run consumption function** is the *average* relationship between consumer expenditure and disposable income over several decades. You can see the clear, general tendency for the dots to lie along an upward-sloping line. Such a line is the long-run consumption function for the Canadian economy. The slope of the long-run consumption function is 0.85. That is, on the average over the long run, consumer expenditure equals 85 percent of personal disposable income—the marginal propensity to consume is 0.85.

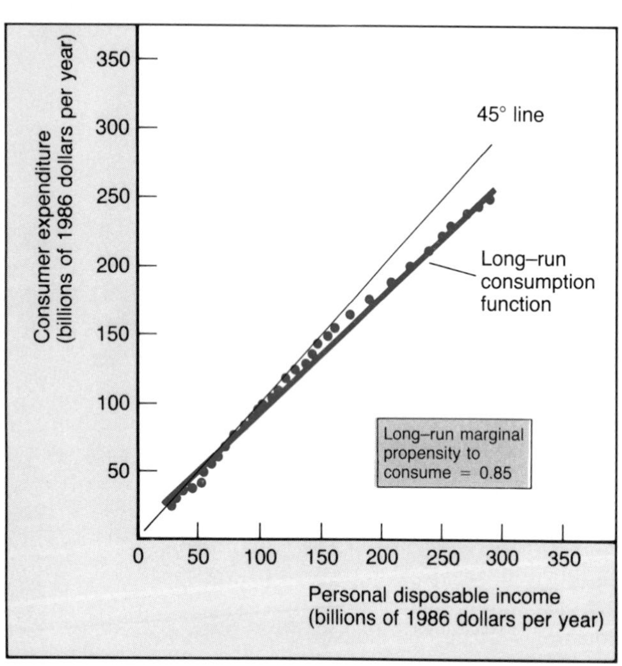

(a) Long run

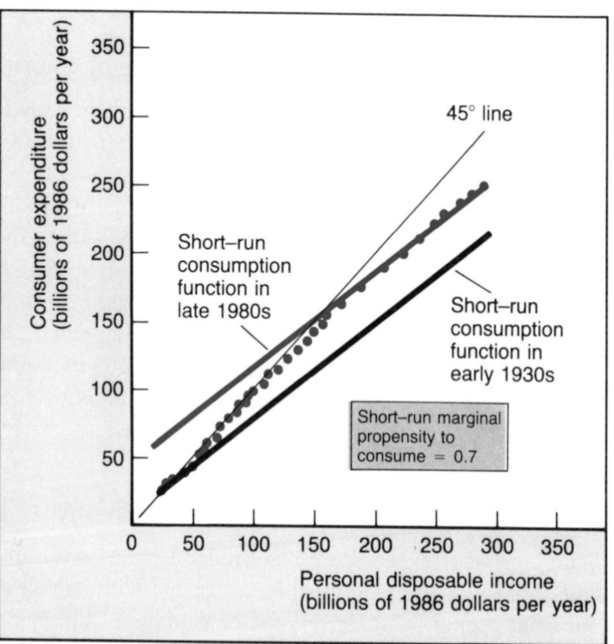

(b) Short run

FIGURE 4.4
The Canadian Consumption Function

Each point shows the level of consumer expenditure and personal disposable income in a given year between 1929 and 1990. The points lie on an upward-sloping line that represents the long-run consumption function. The long-run marginal propensity to consume is 0.85. Changes in consumer expenditure resulting from year-to-year changes in personal disposable income do not fall along the long-run consumption function. Instead, they are described by a sequence of short-run consumption functions that shift generally upward but occasionally downward. Two short-run consumption functions, one for the early 1930s and the other for the late 1980s, are shown in the figure. These short-run consumption functions have a marginal propensity to consume of 0.7, a value in the middle of the range of those estimated.

Source: National Income and Expenditure Accounts, Catalogue 13-201, Statistics Canada, December, 1990.

The long-run consumption function is not a good description of the way consumer expenditure *changes* in response to *changes* in personal disposable income from one year to the next. There is a large amount of variation in consumer expenditure around the long-run consumption function. The relationship between consumer expenditure and personal disposable income in a particular year is called the **short-run consumption function**. The short-run consumption function shifts over time. Two short-run consumption functions are shown in Figure 4.4(b), one for the early 1930s and the other for the late 1980s. The slope of this short-run consumption function measures the short-run marginal propensity to consume and, in the figure, this marginal propensity to consume is 0.7. Macroeconomists aren't in complete agreement on the exact magnitude of the short-run marginal propensity to consume, but 0.7 is in the middle of the range suggested by a large number of studies using many different methods of calculation and estimation.

The general tendency is for the short-run consumption function to shift upward over the years. For many purposes, and certainly for accurate forecasting, we need a more complete theory of consumer expenditure that explains the deviations from the simple consumption function.[2] But for now, we can use the simple Keynesian consumption function, keeping in mind that it is only approximately correct and sometimes gives a misleading forecast of consumer expenditure for a given level of disposable income.

Let's use the simple theory of consumer expenditure to explore the determination of the equilibrium level of aggregate spending.

4.4 *Expenditure Equilibrium*

We've discovered that the largest component of aggregate expenditure is consumer expenditure and that the most volatile components are investment and exports. We've also discovered that consumer expenditure varies in a systematic way with disposable income—consumer expenditure is a function of disposable income. But when we studied the national income accounts in Chapter 2, we learned that aggregate expenditure and aggregate income are different ways of measuring the same object—GDP. We're now going to discover how consumer expenditure and the other components of aggregate expenditure interact to determine the equilibrium level of aggregate expenditure and equilibrium real GDP at a given price level.

Equilibrium

Expenditure equilibrium exists when aggregate planned expenditure equals real GDP. **Aggregate planned expenditure** is the sum of planned consumer expenditure, investment, government purchases of goods and services, and net exports.

To get a really deep understanding of the concept of expenditure equilibrium, it's a good idea to begin by ignoring the complications arising from foreign economic activity. Then later in this chapter, we'll bring the rest of the world back into the picture.

Planned consumer expenditure We've just discovered that consumer expenditure varies directly with disposable income: the greater the disposable income, the greater is consumer expenditure. The consumption function is a statement of consumer expenditure plans. It tells us the amount of expenditure that households plan to undertake at each level of disposable income. Our goal is now to develop a model that determines the equilibrium level of aggregate expenditure and real GDP. To do this, we need to

[2]Theories of the consumption function that account for these deviations from the simple Keynesian consumption function are presented in Chapter 17.

determine how consumer expenditure varies as GDP varies, and not only as disposable income varies. There is, however, a simple connection between disposable income and GDP. It arises from the fact that disposable income is the difference between GDP and taxes. That is,

$$\text{Disposable income} = y - t.$$

For the moment we'll suppose that taxes are fixed, independent of income.[3] Taxes that do not vary with income are called **autonomous taxes**. Given autonomous taxes equal to t_0, and given the consumption function

$$c = a + b(y - t)$$

you can see that

$$c_p = a - bt_0 + by. \tag{4.5}$$

Here c_p is planned consumer expenditure, the term $a - bt_0$ is autonomous consumer expenditure and by is induced consumer expenditure. If we assume the following values for a, b, and t_0,

$$a = 0.505 \text{ billion 1986 dollars}$$
$$b = 0.6$$
$$t_0 = 0.8 \text{ billion 1986 dollars}$$

$$\text{then} \quad c_p = 0.505 - 0.480 + 0.6y \quad \text{billions 1986 dollars}$$

$$\text{or} \quad c_p = 0.025 + 0.6y \quad \text{billions 1986 dollars.}$$

This equation tells us that if real GDP is zero, consumers plan to spend \$0.025 billion on goods and services. For each additional dollar of GDP, they plan to spend 60 cents and to save the other 40 cents.

Planned investment Planned investment is determined by the decisions of firms who make plans to accumulate new buildings, plant, and machinery and additional inventories based on their assessment of future profit prospects and the cost of borrowing. We'll study the details of these decisions in the next chapter. Here, we'll assume that firms have made their decisions and plan to undertake a particular level of investment.

Let's suppose that firms are planning to spend \$0.775 billion on new buildings, plant and equipment, and inventories in the coming year. Calling planned investment i_p,

$$i_p = 0.775 \text{ billion 1986 dollars.} \tag{4.6}$$

Planned government purchases For now, let's take government purchases plans as fixed and suppose that the government is planning on spending \$1 billion in the coming year. Calling planned government purchases g_p,

$$g_p = 1.0 \text{ billion 1986 dollars.} \tag{4.7}$$

Aggregate expenditure plans We've defined aggregate planned expenditure as the sum of the components of planned expenditure. In this economy, those components are consumer expenditure, investment, and government purchases. Thus aggregate planned expenditure, what we'll call e_p, is found by adding together planned consumer expenditure, planned investment, and planned government purchases.

[3] We'll take the fact that taxes vary with income into account later in this chapter.

Given planned consumer expenditure, planned investment, and planned government purchases, we know that

$$c_p = 0.025 + 0.6y \text{ billion 1986 dollars} \quad \textbf{(4.5)}$$

$$i_p = 0.775 \text{ billion 1986 dollars} \quad \textbf{(4.6)}$$

$$g_p = 1.000 \text{ billion 1986 dollars} \quad \textbf{(4.7)}$$

$$\overline{e_p} = \overline{1.800 + 0.6y} \text{ billion 1986 dollars} \quad \textbf{(4.8)}$$

Equilibrium expenditure exists when aggregate planned expenditure equals real GDP. But in Equation (4.8), real GDP equals y. Thus in an expenditure equilibrium,

$$e_p = y.$$

To find the expenditure equilibrium, we need to find the level of aggregate planned expenditure and real GDP that are equal and that are consistent with the aggregate planned expenditure equation (Equation 4.8). You can find that value by substituting real GDP (y) for aggregate planned expenditure (e_p) in Equation (4.8) to obtain

$$y = 1.8 + 0.6y \text{ billion 1986 dollars.}$$

Factoring y

$$y(1 - 0.6) = 1.8 \text{ billion 1986 dollars}$$

or,

$$\begin{aligned} y &= \frac{1.8}{0.4} \text{ billion 1986 dollars} \\ &= \$4.5 \text{ billion 1986 dollars.} \end{aligned}$$

We've just worked out that the expenditure equilibrium in this example occurs when real GDP is \$4.5 billion. At this level of real GDP, people plan to spend \$4.5 billion. That is, they plan to spend \$1.8 billion plus 0.6 times \$4.5 billion, which equals \$4.5 billion. Planned investment is \$0.775 billion, planned government purchases are \$1 billion, and planned consumer expenditure is \$2.725 billion.

Equilibrium in a diagram

There is a neat diagram that summarizes the calculations that we've just done and that explains how expenditure equilibrium is determined. The diagram is seen in Figure 4.5(a). On the vertical axis we measure aggregate expenditure and on the horizontal axis real GDP, both in billions of 1986 dollars. The 45° line traces the points at which aggregate planned expenditure equals real GDP. The line labeled *AE* is the aggregate expenditure curve. The **aggregate expenditure curve** is a curve showing aggregate planned expenditure at each level of real GDP. It is a graph of Equation (4.8). When real GDP is zero, the *AE* curve touches the vertical axis at \$1.8 billion, the level of aggregate planned investment plus planned autonomous consumer expenditure. The slope of the *AE* curve is the marginal propensity to consume. In this example, the marginal propensity to consume is 0.6, so the slope of the *AE* curve is 0.6. Verify that fact by noting that slope equals rise over run and that the rise from \$1.8 billion to \$4.5 billion (\$2.7 billion) divided by the run from 0 to \$4.5 billion is equal to 0.6.

Notice that the aggregate expenditure curve is above the 45° line at income levels below \$4.5 billion and below the 45° line at income levels above \$4.5 billion. The vertical distance between the 45° line and the aggregate expenditure curve tells us about departures of aggregate planned expenditure from real GDP. When the *AE* curve is

FIGURE 4.5
Expenditure Equilibrium and Real GDP

Aggregate expenditure plans are represented by the aggregate expenditure curve in part (a). This curve graphs planned consumer expenditure plus planned investment plus planned government purchases at each level of real GDP. When real GDP is zero, the level of aggregate planned expenditure, autonomous expenditure, is $1.8 billion. Each additional dollar of real GDP induces an additional 60¢ of aggregate planned expenditure. Equilibrium expenditure occurs at the level of real GDP at which aggregate planned expenditure equals real GDP—at $4.5 billion in the figure. At real GDP above the expenditure equilibrium, real GDP exceeds aggregate planned expenditure and at real GDP below the expenditure equilibrium, aggregate planned expenditure exceeds real GDP.

Part (b) shows that at an expenditure equilibrium leakages from and injections into the circular flow of income and expenditure are equal. Saving and taxes are leakages and investment and government purchases are injections. The level of investment and government purchases is fixed at $1.775 billion. Autonomous taxes are fixed but saving increases with real GDP. Thus leakages increase as real GDP increases. At real GDP above the expenditure equilibrium, leakages exceed injections, and at real GDP below the expenditure equilibrium, injections exceed leakages.

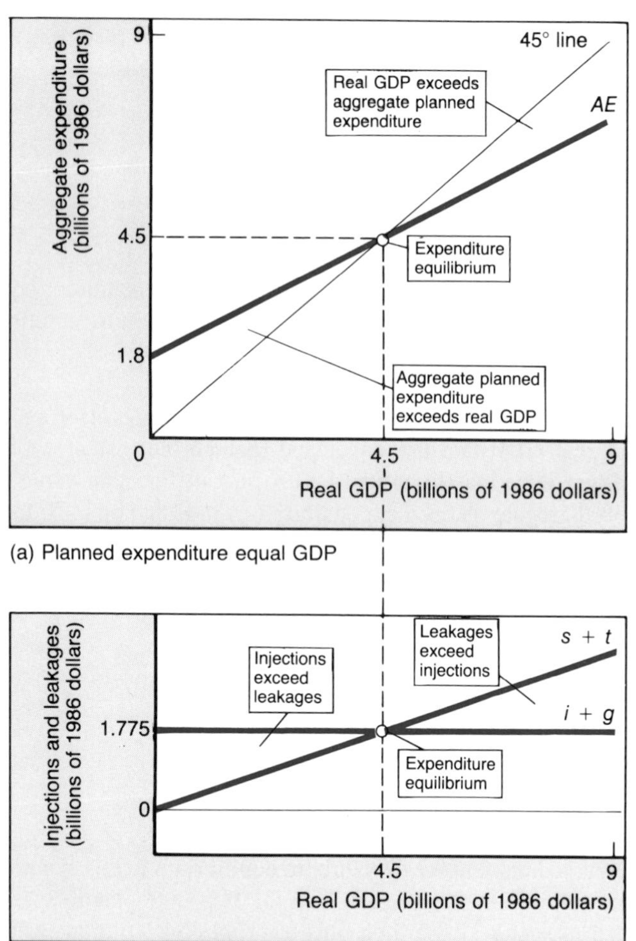

above the 45° line, aggregate planned expenditure exceeds real GDP. When the *AE* curve is below the 45° line, aggregate planned expenditure falls short of real GDP. There is one point, and only one point, at which the *AE* curve cuts the 45° line. That point is the expenditure equilibrium. It is the point at which the aggregate planned expenditure generated by a given real GDP equals the given real GDP. If real GDP is $4.5 billion, households plan to spend $4.5 billion. If they actually spend $4.5 billion, real GDP will indeed be $4.5 billion. So the level of real GDP at which there is an expenditure equilibrium is the only level of real GDP that generates expenditure plans consistent with the real GDP.

Figure 4.5(b) shows another view of the determination of expenditure equilibrium. This view approaches it from the perspective of *leakages* and *injections*. Investment plus government purchases are planned injections. The saving function plus taxes, the line labeled $s + t$ measures planned leakages. At levels of real GDP above $4.5 billion, planned leakages exceed planned injections. At levels of real GDP below $4.5 billion, planned injections exceed planned leakages. Only at a real GDP of $4.5 billion are planned leakages and planned injections equal to each other. This is the expenditure equilibrium.

Equivalence of conditions for equilibrium

Table 4.2 summarizes the conditions that exist at an expenditure equilibrium showing the equivalence between the two approaches we've just explored. Aggregate planned expenditure equals real GDP and planned leakages from the circular flow of income and expenditure equal planned injections into it. The leakages are saving plus taxes, and the injections are investment plus government purchases. A change in either investment or government purchases leads to a change in income that in turn leads to a change in saving. In equilibrium, saving changes by an amount equal to the change in spending that brought it about.

But suppose that the economy is not at an expenditure equilibrium. What happens then?

TABLE 4.2
Expenditure Equilibrium, Leakages, and Injections

ITEM	INCOME AND EXPENDITURE	LEAKAGES AND INJECTIONS
Income is allocated to consumer expenditure, saving, and taxes	$y = c + s + t$	
Leakages are saving plus taxes		$y - c = s + t$
Aggregate planned expenditure is the sum of consumer expenditure, investment, and government purchases	$e_p = c_p + i_p + g_p$	
Injections are investment plus government purchases		$e_p - c_p = i_p + g_p$
At an expenditure equilibrium, income equals aggregate planned expenditure	$y = e_p$	$y - c = i_p + g_p$
At an expenditure equilibrium, planned leakages equal planned injections		$s + t = i_p + g_p$

4.5 *Convergence to Equilibrium*

You have seen in section 4.4 that when real GDP is $4.5 billion, aggregate expenditure is also equal to $4.5 billion, and there is an expenditure equilibrium. But suppose that real GDP is *not* $4.5 billion and aggregate planned expenditure is not equal to real GDP. What then? Are there some forces that operate to move the economy toward equilibrium? Or does the economy just stay wherever it happens to be? In fact, forces are at work moving the economy toward its equilibrium. Thus expenditure equilibrium is an important position that the economy is either at or always moving toward. Let's see what those forces are and how they operate.

Inventories and unplanned spending

Planned expenditure is not necessarily equal to actual expenditure. Let's assume, however, that consumer expenditure plans, government purchases plans, and net export plans are all carried out. That is, actual consumer expenditure, government purchases, and net exports equal their planned counterparts. But investment plans are not necessarily fulfilled. That is, actual investment does not necessarily equal planned investment.

Recall that investment is divided into two components, *fixed investment* and *inventory investment*. Fixed investment plans are fulfilled but inventory investment plans are not necessarily fulfilled. Sometimes the change in inventories is planned, but at other times the change in inventories is unintended.

Suppose, for example, that your local supermarket has bought 500 tubs of ice cream, which it expects to sell during the upcoming weekend. The weekend weather turns out to be cold and wintry and ice cream sales are off, at only 300 tubs. The 200 tubs not sold remain in the supermarket's refrigerators and are unintended additions to the supermarket's ice cream inventory. Focusing only on ice cream, actual real expenditure is equal to 500 tubs of ice cream. Planned consumer expenditure equals 300 tubs and unplanned inventory investment equals 200 tubs. For the economy as a whole, unplanned inventory investment occurs when, in the aggregate, the spending plans of households, firms, and the government fall short of the current level of real GDP. Such a situation is illustrated in Figure 4.6, when real GDP is at the level marked *B*. With real GDP at *B*, planned aggregate expenditure is *B*′, which is less than real GDP. In this situation, firms have produced goods and services valued at *B* but sell goods and services valued only at *B*′. The difference is their unintended addition to inventories.

What happens when inventories begin to accumulate?

FIGURE 4.6
Convergence to Equilibrium

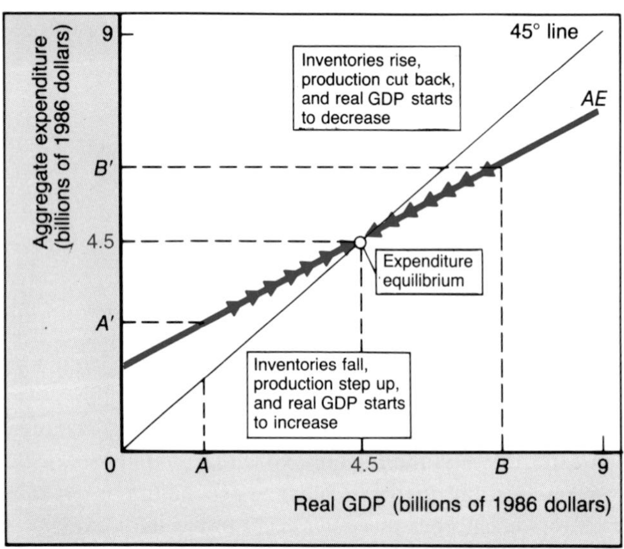

If the economy is not at its expenditure equilibrium, forces operate to bring it back to equilibrium. If real GDP is at *A*, aggregate planned expenditure is *A*′, which is greater than real GDP. In such a situation, there is an unintended decrease in inventories. Production is increased to restore inventory levels, and additional workers are hired. Real GDP increases. Higher income induces additional consumer expenditure, and the economy moves toward its expenditure equilibrium following the arrowed lines along the aggregate expenditure curve. Similarly, if the economy is at *B*, aggregate planned expenditure of *B*′, which is less than real GDP. There is an unintended increase in inventories. Firms cut back on their production and lay off workers. Falling income induces lower consumer expenditure, which leads to yet further decrease in income. Aggregate planned expenditure declines along the *AE* curve, following the arrows toward the expenditure equilibrium. Only at the expenditure equilibrium are there no unintended changes in inventories, setting up a process that changes the real GDP and aggregate planned expenditure.

When inventories pile up

To see what happens when firms' inventories begin to pile up unintendedly, let's go back to the local supermarket. What does the supermarket do when it has 200 tubs of ice cream on its hands that it had planned to sell during the previous weekend? It cuts back on its ice cream orders. The ice cream factory, faced with lower orders, cuts back on production and lays off some workers. The ice cream workers, with lower incomes, cut back on their purchases of movie tickets and popcorn. Movie theatre operators and popcorn producers cut back on their production and have smaller incomes. This process continues until there are no forces at work, leading to further cuts in orders and purchases.

For the economy as a whole, you can see such a process at work by returning to Figure 4.6. Starting with real GDP at *B* and aggregate planned expenditure at *B*′, firms' inventories are accumulating. As a result, some firms cut back on their orders and other firms cut back on their production. Workers are laid off and incomes fall. As incomes fall, the economy moves to a lower level of real GDP than *B*. Aggregate planned expenditure falls below *B*′. The economy travels along its aggregate expenditure curve (*AE*), following the arrows marked in the figure. The process continues until real GDP is \$4.5 billion. At that level of real GDP, aggregate planned expenditure equals real GDP and there are no unintended changes in inventories. With no unintended inventory changes, there are no changes in planned orders and no further changes in income.

When inventories unexpectedly fall

We've just seen what happens when the economy starts out at a real GDP level that is above expenditure equilibrium and inventories pile up unintendedly. But what happens if real GDP is below expenditure equilibrium? The answer can be found by working through a similar analysis but in reverse. Suppose that real GDP is *A* in Figure 4.6 and aggregate planned expenditure is *A*′. In this situation, planned expenditure is greater than actual expenditure, so inventory investment is unintentionally low (the supermarket sells more ice cream on the weekend that it had expected to). In such a situation, firms order the larger volume of goods to replenish their inventories. As they do so, the producers of goods and services step up the production rate and hire more labor. Income increases in the process. Higher income leads to higher planned expenditure. The economy travels upward along its *AE* curve, following the arrows marked in the figure. This process of increasing income and increasing aggregate planned expenditure continues until there are no forces at work making for further increases in orders and increases in inventories. This situation is arrived at when real GDP is \$4.5 billion, at which point aggregate planned expenditure also equals \$4.5 billion.

Definitions and equilibrium conditions

In the above description of the process of convergence to an expenditure equilibrium, we've distinguished between actual and planned expenditure. There is a corresponding distinction between *identities* — things that are equal by definition — and *equilibrium conditions* — things that are equal only in equilibrium. Actual expenditure is always equal to income *by definition*. Planned expenditure is only equal to income *in equilibrium*. Similarly, actual leakages are always equal to actual injections by definition while planned injections are equal to planned leakages only in equilibrium. Table 4.3 summarizes the identities that are always true and the conditions that hold only at an expenditure equilibrium.

TABLE 4.3
Identities and Equilibrium Conditions

	IDENTITIES: always satisfied by definition	EQUILIBRIUM CONDITIONS: hold only at an expenditure equilibrium
1.	Actual aggregate expenditure = real GDP	Planned aggregate expenditure = real GDP
2.	Unintended inventory investment = real GDP *minus* planned aggregate expenditure	Unintended inventory investment = 0

Because the economy is constantly moving toward an expenditure equilibrium, we focus most of our attention on that level of real GDP. We study the forces that determine the expenditure equilibrium and that change the expenditure equilibrium. That's what we're going to do next. We're going to study the way in which the expenditure equilibrium changes and see how underlying shocks have a larger effect—a multiplier effect—on aggregate expenditure and real GDP.

4.6 *The Multiplier*

The economy is in a constant state of change. One of the forces initiating some of that change is autonomous expenditure. **Autonomous expenditure** is the part of aggregate expenditure that does not depend on real GDP. Autonomous expenditure changes when there is a change in autonomous consumer expenditure, investment, government purchases, or exports. For example, at some times, firms are pessimistic about the future economic outlook and hold back on their investment in new plant and equipment. At other times, they are optimistic and step up their investment. Since investment is one component of aggregate expenditure, it is obvious that fluctuations in investment bring fluctuations in aggregate expenditure. But are those fluctuations in aggregate expenditure larger, smaller, or the same as the fluctuations in investment? To answer that question, we have to work out the effects of a change in investment on consumer expenditure. Does an increase in investment bring an increase in consumer expenditure, thereby magnifying its effects on aggregate expenditure? Or does an increase in investment bring a decrease in consumer expenditure, thereby moderating its influence on aggregate expenditure? These are the questions that we're now going to study.

Initial equilibrium

Let's continue to study the economy shown in Figures 4.4 and 4.5. Initially, real GDP is \$4.5 billion and aggregate planned expenditure is also \$4.5 billion. The aggregate expenditure curve is that labeled AE_0 in Figure 4.7. All the forces bringing about a convergence to that equilibrium have worked themselves out and real GDP and aggregate expenditure are steady at \$4.5 billion.

Now suppose that firms become much more optimistic about future profit prospects and step up their investment plans. There is a massive increase in orders for new buildings, plant, and equipment of all kinds. Let's suppose that the increase in investment is \$1 billion. What happens when investment increases by \$1 billion?

The immediate answer is that the aggregate expenditure curve shifts. It moves upward by \$1 billion to become the curve labeled AE_1 in Figure 4.7. At the same time, aggregate planned expenditure increases from \$4.5 billion to \$5.5 billion at point *A* in the figure.

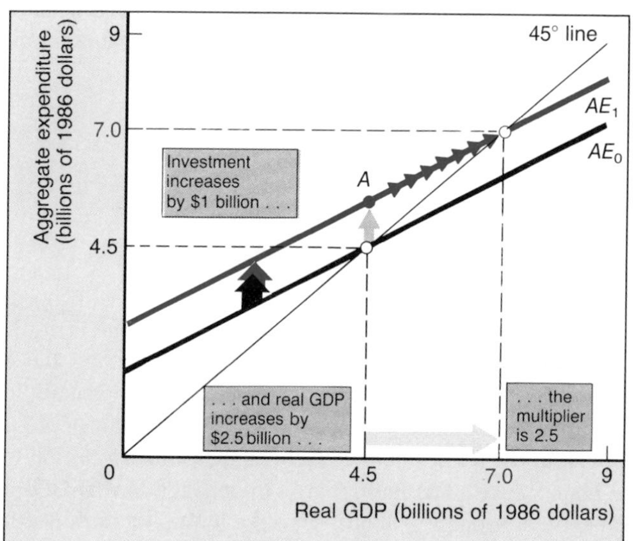

FIGURE 4.7
The Multiplier

An increase in autonomous expenditure such as an increase in investment shifts the aggregate expenditure curve upward from AE_0 to AE_1. Aggregate planned expenditure increases to *A* but actual expenditure remains at $4.5 billion. There is an unintended decrease in inventories. Firms increase production, hire more workers, and pay out additional incomes. The additional incomes induce additional consumer expenditure and the multiplier process that eventually increases real GDP to its new equilibrium level is set off. In this example, an increase of autonomous expenditure of $1 billion induces an increase in real GDP of $2.5 billion—the multiplier is 2.5.

Convergence

Point *A* is not an expenditure equilibrium. Aggregate planned expenditure exceeds real GDP, so inventories fall to levels below those desired. To replenish their inventories, firms increase production, hire more labor, and pay out higher incomes. As incomes increase, so does aggregate planned expenditure. The economy tracks along its new *AE* curve, following the arrows in the figure. This process of convergence is exactly like the one that we described in the previous section. The process continues until there are no forces producing further increases in orders and unintended changes in inventories. The process ends when the economy is at the new expenditure equilibrium where the aggregate expenditure curve AE_1 intersects the 45° line. At this new expenditure equilibrium, real GDP and aggregate expenditure are each $7 billion.

Multiplier effect

Notice that the increase in real GDP that was induced by a $1 billion increase in investment is much larger than $1 billion. In fact, it is $2.5 billion. The effect of an increase in investment on real GDP is called the investment multiplier. The **investment multiplier** is the ratio of the change in real GDP to the change in investment that caused it. In this example, the investment multiplier is 2.5. This is calculated as the change in real GDP — $2.5 billion — divided by the initial change in investment — $1 billion. Since investment is part of autonomous expenditure, the investment multiplier is identical to the multiplier associated with a change in autonomous expenditure and is often called simply the multiplier.

The size of the multiplier

The size of the multiplier is determined by the marginal propensity to consume, or, equivalently, the marginal propensity to save. The larger the marginal propensity to consume, the larger is the multiplier. The larger the marginal propensity to save, the smaller is the multiplier.

The marginal propensity to consume is b and the marginal propensity to save is $1 - b$. That is, for each additional dollar of income, fraction b is spent by households on goods and services, and one minus that fraction is saved. The multiplier, k, is given by the formula

$$k = \frac{1}{1 - b}$$

or

$$k = \frac{1}{\text{marginal propensity to save}}.$$

Figure 4.8 explains why the multiplier is equal to 1/marginal propensity to save. It uses the injections and leakages approach to calculate the change in equilibrium expenditure. Initially, autonomous expenditure is $1.775 billion along the curve $i_0 + g$. Investment increases by $1 billion, shifting the autonomous expenditure curve up to $i_1 + g$. This increase in investment is measured by the distance *AB*. The resulting increase in real GDP at the expenditure equilibrium, from $4.5 billion to $7 billion, is measured by the distance *AC*. The multiplier is the change in real GDP divided by the change in investment that brought it about. Thus the multiplier is *AC*/*AB*. But recall that the marginal propensity to save is calculated as the change in saving divided by the change in disposable income. With taxes autonomous, the change in disposable income equals the change in real GDP. That is, the marginal propensity to save, *mps*, is *AB*/*AC*. But notice that 1/*mps* is *AC*/*AB*, the value that we've just established for the multiplier.

Why does the size of the multiplier depend on the marginal propensity to save? The answer is that when investment increases, the extent to which the resulting increase in income induces additional consumer expenditure depends on how much of the additional income leaks out of the circular flow. The larger the amount that leaks out, the smaller is the increase in induced consumer expenditure and the smaller is the ultimate increase in aggregate expenditure and real GDP. Equivalently, but telling the story the opposite way around, the larger the fraction of additional income spent by households on goods and services, the larger is the amount that remains in the circular flow of income and expenditure and that generates additional income, which induces yet more expenditure.

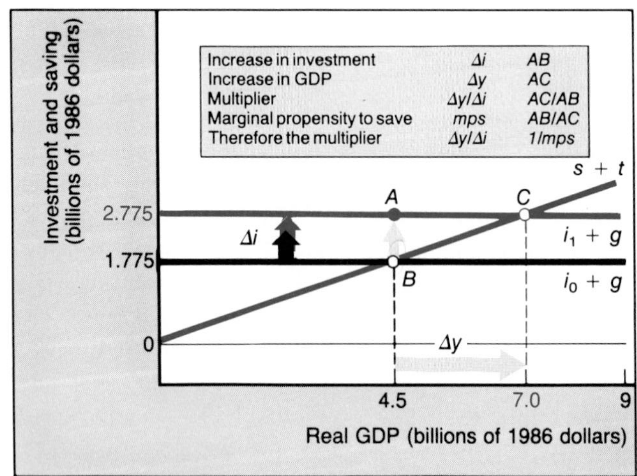

FIGURE 4.8
Injections, Leakages, and the Multiplier

Initially the expenditure equilibrium is at point *B*, where leakages ($s + t$) from the circular flow equal injections ($i_0 + g$) into the circular flow. An increase in investment increases autonomous expenditure from $1.775 billion to $2.775 billion—a $1 billion increase—and shifts the autonomous expenditure curve upward from $i_0 + g$ to $i_1 + g$. The new expenditure equilibrium occurs at point *C*. Real GDP increases by $2.5 billion. The multiplier is the increase in real GDP ($2.5 billion) divided by the increase in investment that caused it ($1 billion), which equals 2.5.

The multiplier process You can perhaps see this better by thinking of the multiplier as a process. In round 1, income increases by an amount equal to the increase in investment. In round 2, income increases by the additional consumer expenditure induced by the additional income of round 1. That additional consumer expenditure is determined by the marginal propensity to consume and is $b\Delta i$. In each subsequent round, income increases by the amount of additional consumer expenditure induced by the increase in income in the previous round. To work out the increase in round 3, recall that income increased in round 2 by $b\Delta i$. Thus in round 3, consumer expenditure increases by b multiplied by $b\Delta i$, or $b^2\Delta i$. The entire sequence of changes in income is equal to

$$\begin{aligned}\Delta y &= \Delta i + b\Delta i + b^2\Delta i + \cdots + b^n\Delta i \\ &= \Delta i[1 + b + b^2 + \cdots + b^n].\end{aligned}$$

The multiplier, k, is the change in income divided by the change in investment. That is,

$$k = \frac{\Delta y}{\Delta i} = [1 + b + b^2 + \cdots + b^n].$$

We can work out the value of k using the following neat piece of algebra. First, write down the equation for k—the multiplier—as

$$k = 1 + b + b^2 + \cdots + b^n \tag{4.9}$$

Multiply this equation by b to give

$$bk = b + b^2 + \cdots + b^n + b^{n+1} \tag{4.10}$$

Subtract Equation (4.9) from Equation (4.10) to give

$$(1 - b)k = 1 - b^{n+1}$$

Because b is a fraction, after many, many rounds, b^{n+1} will be so close to zero that we may ignore it. Thus the multiplier is

$$k = \frac{1}{1 - b}.$$

But recall that this is the formula for the multiplier we derived in Figure 4.8.

The Hibernia oil field multiplier in Newfoundland You may get a better understanding of what's going on in a multiplier process if we think of a real-world multiplier process. In the early 1990s, a multibillion dollar oil field is being developed in Newfoundland. This huge investment in scientific equipment, oil-drilling platforms, helicopters, and concrete is an injection into the circular flow of income and expenditure. It increases the incomes of all the workers and owners of firms operating in the project. Once the increased incomes are received, consumer expenditure increases. Supermarkets, movie theatres, package vacation suppliers, airlines, gas stations, and many other firms, not only in Newfoundland but around Canada, experience an increase in sales. Initially, the inventories of supermarkets and gas stations and of thousands of other firms decline. To make up for the fall in inventories orders are increased and producers step up output, hiring more workers in the process. The extra income generates additional consumer expenditure on goods and services that, in turn, induces yet a further round of expansion. The expansion of income and spending continues until an expenditure equilibrium is reached—incomes have increased to equal the increased aggregate planned expenditure.

TESTCASE

4.7 The Multiplier in the Great Depression

We've just worked out what happens when there is an increase in investment brought on by increased optimism about the future. The years 1929 through 1933 were the exact opposite of that — years when a wave of extreme pessimism brought an almost total collapse in investment. They also brought a decrease in autonomous consumer expenditure, which shifted the consumption function downward. In the Great Depression (the years between 1929 and 1933) autonomous expenditure measured in 1986 dollars decreased by $15 billion. During those same years, real GDP measured in 1986 dollars declined by $16 billion. The multiplier was 1.07. (You can calculate the multiplier as $16 billion divided by $15 billion.)

Figure 4.9 illustrates the multiplier during the Great Depression. In 1929, the aggregate expenditure curve was AE_{29} and expenditure equilibrium occurred at a real GDP of $52 billion. When autonomous expenditure declined, the aggregate expenditure curve shifted downward to AE_{33}. As it did so, unintended inventory accumulations led to decreased orders, lower production, and layoffs. The process resulted in a relentless decrease in real GDP, all the way to $36 billion by 1933. The depression bottomed out in 1933. Brighter prospects led to a gradual increase in investment in subsequent years and the economy eventually recovered.

This episode in Canadian economic history is the single most severe depression. Its severity resulted from the very large decrease in autonomous expenditure, amplified by the multiplier effect that induced yet further decreases in consumer expenditure and real GDP.

It was the Great Depression and the vast quantities of underemployed resources of that era that produced the Keynesian revolution in macroeconomics. A key ingredient in that revolution was the realization that aggregate expenditure could be manipulated consciously by government action. Let's now examine the way in which government can manipulate aggregate expenditure and exploit its fiscal policy powers to stabilize aggregate expenditure.

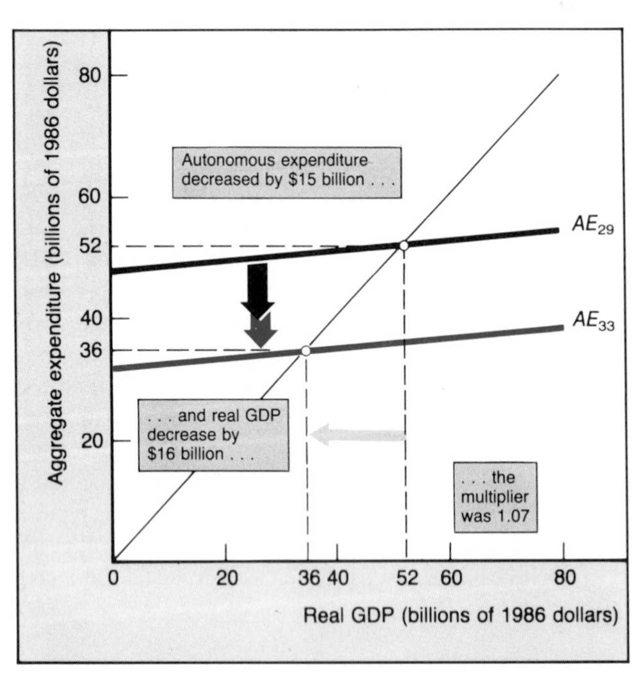

FIGURE 4.9
The Multiplier in the Great Depression

During the contraction years of the Great Depression, 1929 to 1933, autonomous expenditure decreased by $14 billion. The *AE* curve shifted downward from AE_{29} to AE_{33}. This decrease in autonomous expenditure set up a multiplier process that decreased real GDP by an even larger amount. The new equilibrium at the bottom of the depression in 1933 saw real GDP decline by $16 billion. The multiplier was 1.07.

Source: National Income and Expenditure Accounts, Statistics Canada, Ottawa, July, 1986, and our calculations and assumptions.

4.8 *Fiscal Policy Multipliers*

Government activity affects the circular flow of income and expenditure and the expenditure equilibrium for two reasons. First, government purchases of goods and services are a component of aggregate expenditure and an injection into the circular flow. Second, taxes are a withdrawal from the private sector and a leakage from the circular flow. Taxes also drive a wedge between GDP and disposable income. The higher the level of taxes, the lower is the level of disposable income for any given level of GDP. Thus taxes affect the relationship between consumer expenditure and real GDP. Let's see how government purchases of goods and services and taxes influence the expenditure equilibrium.

We know that expenditure equilibrium occurs where real GDP equals aggregate planned expenditure. Continuing to ignore the foreign sector for the moment, expenditure equilibrium occurs when

$$y = c + i + g. \qquad \textbf{(4.11)}$$

We've seen that consumer expenditure depends on disposable income:

$$c = a + b(y - t). \qquad \textbf{(4.12)}$$

Combining Equations (4.11) and (4.12) determines the expenditure equilibrium for a given level of investment, government purchases, and tax. Using the consumption function to replace consumer expenditure in Equation (4.11) gives

$$y = a + b(y - t_0) + i + g.$$

This equation can be rearranged as follows:

$$y = a - bt_0 + i + g + by.$$

In this equation, the first group of terms, $a - bt_0 + i + g$ is *autonomous* expenditure and the term by is *induced* expenditure. Expenditure equilibrium can be found by solving this equation for real GDP—y. We can obtain the solution by first collecting together the terms involving y:

$$(1 - b)y = a - bt_0 + i + g.$$

Then, dividing both sides of this equation by $(1 - b)$ gives

$$y = \frac{1}{1 - b}(a - bt_0 + i + g).$$

Let's check that we can calculate the expenditure equilibrium using this equation. Assume the following values for the parameters and the levels of autonomous taxes, investment, and government purchases:

$$\begin{aligned} a &= \$0.505 \text{ billion} \\ b &= 0.6 \\ t &= \$0.8 \text{ billion} \\ i &= \$0.775 \text{ billion} \\ g &= \$1.0 \text{ billion.} \end{aligned}$$

With these values, Equation (4.13) tells us that real GDP is equal to \$4.5 billion. That is,

$$\begin{aligned} y &= \frac{1}{1 - 0.6} \cdot (0.505 - 0.6 \times 0.8 + 0.775 + 1.0) \\ &= \frac{1}{0.4} \times 1.8 \\ &= \$4.5 \text{ billion.} \end{aligned}$$

Government purchases multiplier

The **government purchases multiplier** is the ratio of the change in real GDP to the change in government purchases that caused it. We can use Equation (4.13) to work out the government purchases multiplier, which is exactly the same value as the investment multiplier we have just been studying. You can see that from the equation. Investment and government purchases are both components of autonomous expenditure. An additional dollar of government purchases is exactly equivalent to an additional dollar of investment in terms of the extra autonomous expenditure that it generates. Thus regardless of whether autonomous expenditure increases because investment increases or government purchases increase, a multiplier effect is set up that has exactly the same effect on aggregate expenditure and equilibrium expenditure.

You can also see that an increase in government purchases and an increase in investment are equivalent in terms of their expenditure generation by returning to the example of the Hibernia oil field. Most of the funds required to develop Hibernia are coming from the government. But whether those funds are provided by the private sector or the government makes no difference to the total spending generated. The people building the platforms and pouring the concrete get an extra income which they then spend on goods and services which, in turn, generates additional incomes for others. The multiplier process that we described above is the same regardless of whether Ellis-Don, the government of Newfoundland, or the Canadian government increased spending and started the process off.

The fact that government purchases have a multiplier effect is important, for it means that the government can adjust its purchases of goods and services as a way of offsetting fluctuations in autonomous expenditure. If you turn back to Figure 4.2(b), you will see that on occasion the government does precisely that. In 1985 and again in 1989-1990, for example, when the private component of autonomous expenditure declined, government purchases increased, thereby helping to stabilize the overall level of aggregate expenditure. In 1978, when private autonomous expenditure increased sharply, government purchases declined, again helping to stabilize aggregate expenditure.

Autonomous tax multiplier

A change in autonomous taxes also has a multiplier effect. An additional dollar of autonomous taxes decreases disposable income by a dollar and decreases consumer expenditure by an amount determined by the marginal propensity to consume (b). In our example b is 0.60, so a one-dollar increase in autonomous taxes leads to a 60-cent decrease in consumer expenditure. This decrease in consumer expenditure sets up a multiplier process exactly like the ones that we have just been studying. The **autonomous tax multiplier** is the ratio of the change in real GDP to the change in autonomous taxes that caused it.

Let's calculate the autonomous tax multiplier. When autonomous taxes change, everything else remaining constant, equilibrium real GDP also changes. We can calculate the change using Equation (4.13). The change in real GDP is given by

$$\Delta y = \frac{1}{1-b} \times -b\Delta t_0.$$

Therefore, the autonomous tax multiplier is equal to

$$\frac{-b}{1-b}.$$

In our example, b is 0.6 and $1 - b$ is 0.4, therefore the autonomous tax multiplier is -1.875. That is, a one-dollar increase in autonomous taxes results in a decrease in real GDP of \$1.875. Notice that the autonomous tax multiplier is negative, whereas the investment and government purchases multipliers are positive. An increase in autonomous taxes leads to an expenditure equilibrium at a smaller real GDP. Notice also that the magnitude of the autonomous tax multiplier is smaller — fraction b — of the investment and government purchases multiplier.

Balanced budget multiplier

If the government increases its purchases of goods and services and finances the purchase by an increase in autonomous taxes, then the government budget deficit does not change. Such a fiscal policy change has a multiplier effect on real GDP, which is called the **balanced budget multiplier**. We can calculate the balanced budget multiplier by adding the government purchases multiplier, associated with the increase in government purchases, and the autonomous tax multiplier, associated with the increase in autonomous taxes. That is,

$$\begin{aligned}\text{Balanced budget multiplier} &= \frac{1}{1-b} + \frac{-b}{1-b} \\ &= \frac{1-b}{1-b} = 1.\end{aligned}$$

The balanced budget multiplier is 1, which tells us that if the government increases its purchases of goods and services by \$0.5 billion and increases autonomous taxes by \$0.5 billion to pay for the purchase, then real GDP increases by only \$0.5 billion.

So far, we've supposed that taxes are autonomous, that is, they don't vary with income. Let's now look at income taxes and their effect on expenditure equilibrium and real GDP.

Income taxes

Taxes fall into two categories: **induced taxes** — those that vary as income varies — and *autonomous taxes* — those that are independent of income. We can represent taxes paid by a tax function. The **tax function** is the relationship between taxes paid and income. If the tax function is

$$t = t_1 y + t_0, \quad \textbf{(4.14)}$$

then induced taxes are $t_1 y$ and autonomous taxes are t_0. Using the tax function in the definition of disposable income gives

$$y - t = y - t_1 y - t_0$$

or,

$$y - t = (1 - t_1)y - t_0. \quad \textbf{(4.15)}$$

We can use this relationship between taxes and GDP to determine the relationship between planned consumer expenditure and GDP. To do so, we start with the consumption function:

$$c = a + b(y - t)$$

and use the tax function to eliminate taxes. This gives

$$c = a - bt_0 + b(1 - t_1)y. \quad \textbf{(4.16)}$$

The first two terms taken together, $a - bt_0$, represent planned autonomous consumer expenditure and the second term, $b(1 - t_1)y$, is the planned consumer expenditure induced by the level of real GDP.

Let's work through a numerical example of this relationship between planned consumer expenditure and real GDP. Suppose that autonomous consumer expenditure is \$0.1 billion and that the marginal propensity to consume is 0.75. Then the consumption function is

$$c = 0.1 + 0.75(y - t) \text{ billions of 1986 dollars.}$$

If autonomous taxes are \$0.1 billion and induced taxes are 0.2 of income, the tax function is

$$t = 0.2y + 0.1 \text{ billions of 1986 dollars.}$$

Using these two equations, we can obtain the relationship between planned consumer expenditure and real GDP. Calling planned consumer expenditure c_p,

$$c_p = 0.025 + 0.6y \text{ billions of 1986 dollars.}$$

This equation tells us that if real GDP is zero, consumers plan to spend \$0.025 billion on goods and services. For each additional dollar of real GDP, households plan to spend 60 cents and to save and pay in taxes the other 40 cents. The fraction of each additional dollar of real GDP that households spend on goods and services is called the **marginal propensity to consume out of real GDP**.

Let's find the expenditure equilibrium and real GDP when taxes include not only autonomous taxes but also induced taxes. Aggregate planned expenditure is

$$e_p = c_p + i_p + g_p. \tag{4.17}$$

Using Equation (4.16), planned consumer expenditure is

$$c_p = a + bt_0 + b(1 - t_l)y.$$

At an expenditure equilibrium,

$$e_p = y. \tag{4.18}$$

Combining these three equations for a given level of planned investment and government purchases, we obtain

$$y = a + bt_0 + i + g + b(1 - t_1)y.$$

We can solve this equation for y by first collecting terms in y to give

$$[1 - b(1 - t_1)]\, y = a - bt_0 + i + g.$$

Then divide by $[1 - b(1 - t_1)]$ to give the expenditure equilibrium,

$$y = \frac{1}{1 - b(1 - t_1)} \times (a - bt_0 + i + g). \tag{4.19}$$

Now, if there is a change in investment or government purchases, real GDP changes by an amount equal to the change in autonomous expenditure multiplied by

$$\frac{1}{1 - b(1 - t_1)}. \tag{4.20}$$

In other words, the formula in (4.20) is the multiplier when there are induced taxes. Its value is determined by the marginal propensity to consume out of real GDP, $b(1 - t_1)$.

We've now seen how induced taxes affect the value of the multiplier effect of a change in autonomous expenditure. But *changes* in the marginal tax rate have a multiplier effect. Let's see what that effect is.

Marginal tax rate multiplier

The **marginal tax rate** is the fraction of an additional dollar of income paid out in taxes. Induced taxes equal the marginal tax rate multiplied by income. A change in the marginal tax rate sets up a multiplier effect on real GDP. The **marginal tax rate multiplier** is the ratio of the change in real GDP to the change in the marginal tax rate that caused it. An increase in the marginal tax rate of Δt_1 decreases disposable income by $\Delta t_1 \times y$ and decreases consumer expenditure by $b\Delta t_1 \times y$. The initial change in aggregate expenditure is $-b\Delta t_1 \times y$. This change sets up a multiplier process of decreasing incomes and decreasing aggregate expenditure. The marginal tax rate multiplier is

$$\frac{-by}{1 - b(1 - t_1)}.$$

But the change in the marginal tax rate also affects the values of all the other multipliers. The higher the marginal tax rate, the smaller is the investment multiplier, the government purchases multiplier, and the autonomous tax multiplier. You can see this by considering the effect of the marginal tax rate on the investment multiplier, $1/[1 - b(1 - t_1)]$. When the marginal tax rate is 20 percent ($t_1 = 0.2$), the multiplier is 2.5. With the same value of the marginal propensity to consume ($b = 0.75$), a marginal tax rate of 10 percent ($t_1 = 0.1$) gives a multiplier of 3.1, and a tax rate of 30 percent ($t_1 = 0.3$) gives a multiplier of 2.1.

Automatic stabilization

Income taxes act like automatic stabilizers. Because a higher marginal tax rate makes the investment multiplier smaller, the higher the marginal tax rate, the smaller is the effect of fluctuations in investment on aggregate expenditure. The reason is easy to see. A fall in investment that leads to a fall in income cuts disposable income by a smaller amount because taxes also decrease. But the extent to which taxes decrease depends on the marginal tax rate. The higher the marginal tax rate, the larger is the decrease in taxes. Thus the smaller is the effect of the initial fall in investment on aggregate expenditure.

The government budget deficit As the economy fluctuates, so does the government budget deficit. The fluctuations in the government budget deficit have an automatic stabilizing effect. Recall that the government budget deficit is government purchases of goods and services minus taxes. That is:

$$\text{government budget deficit} = g - t.$$

But we've seen that taxes are determined by income. Using the tax function

$$\text{government budget deficit} = g - t_1 y - t_0.$$

Thus as income increases, taxes increase and the government budget deficit decreases. Leakages from the circular flow of income and expenditure increase as income increases. Conversely, if income decreases, taxes decrease and the government budget deficit increases. Leakages from the circular flow of income and expenditure decline.

Also, if the government increases its purchases of goods and services, its budget deficit does not rise by as much as the increase in spending. The reason is that the higher government purchases induce additional income that also brings in additional taxes.

4.9 *International Trade and the Multiplier*

Now it's time to bring in the rest of the world. International economic transactions affect aggregate expenditure and the multiplier in two ways. First, Canadian exports of goods and services to the rest of the world are part of the injections into the circular flow of income and expenditure. An increase in exports acts in exactly the same way as an increase in investment or an increase in government purchases. It sets up a multiplier process resulting in an expenditure equilibrium at a higher real GDP. Imports into Canada have the opposite effect. They are a leakage from the circular flow of income and expenditure. But imports depend on the level of real GDP. The higher the level of real GDP, the greater is the quantity of imports into Canada. The level of imports is determined by the **import function** — the relationship between the quantity of imports and real GDP. The import function can be written as

$$im = im_0 + my.$$

In this equation, im_0 represents autonomous imports — imports that would take place even if real GDP was zero; and m is the **marginal propensity to import** — the change in imports resulting from a one-dollar increase in real GDP. Suppose that im_0 is \$0.05 billion and the marginal propensity to import is 0.1. Then

$$im = 0.05 + 0.1y \text{ billions of 1986 dollars.}$$

Introducing imports and exports into the model of expenditure equilibrium modifies the multiplier. To see how, let's calculate the multiplier again. The starting point is as before, with the definition of aggregate planned expenditure:

$$e_p = c_p + i_p + g_p + ex_p - im_p. \tag{4.21}$$

Using the consumption function from our earlier analysis, and using the import function that we have just defined, we can rewrite aggregate planned expenditure as

$$e_p = a - bt_0 + b(1 - t_1)y + i_p + g_p + ex_p + im_0 - my. \tag{4.22}$$

At an expenditure equilibrium, aggregate planned expenditure equals real GDP. Therefore,

$$y = e_p. \tag{4.23}$$

Using Equation (4.22) in Equation (4.23) gives

$$y = a - bt_0 + b(1 - t_1)y + i_p + g_p + ex_p - im_0 - my$$

and factoring the terms in y gives

$$[1 - b(1 - t_1) + m]\, y = a - bt_0 + i_p + g_p + ex_p - im_0.$$

Solving for y gives

$$y = \frac{1}{1 - b(1 - t_1) + m}(a - bt_0 + i_p + g_p + ex_p - im_0). \tag{4.24}$$

Notice the similarity between Equation (4.22) and Equation (4.18). In an open economy, the term multiplying investment, government purchases, and exports to determine the level of real GDP is $1/[1 - b(1 - t_1) + m]$. This value is the multiplier in an open economy. This multiplier is smaller than the one we calculated in the closed economy. It is smaller because imports are an additional leakage from the circular flow of income and expenditure. In our example, where the marginal propensity to consume (b)

is 0.75 and the marginal tax rate (t_1) is 0.2, the multiplier in the closed economy is 2.5. With a marginal propensity to import (m) of 0.1, the multiplier in the open economy is 2. You can check that by using these values in the above formula.

4.10 *The Declining Multiplier in the 1980s*

TESTCASE

We've seen that value of the multiplier depends on the marginal propensity to consume, the marginal tax rate, and the marginal propensity to import. Over the years, the marginal tax rate has steadily increased. In the nineteenth century tax rates were less than 10 percent and in the twentieth century they have gradually increased. In Canada today, the marginal tax rate for most people is between 25 and 35 percent, but in some countries, in particular those of Western Europe, they are as high as 40 percent.

International trade has also increased steadily over the years. In the 1960s and early 1970s only about 15 percent of Canadian GDP was traded internationally. Today, our marginal propensity to import may be as high as 0.3. Some countries, especially members of the European Community such as Germany, France, Italy, and the United Kingdom, have an even higher marginal propensity to import, perhaps as high as 0.4. Countries with a high marginal tax rate and a high marginal propensity to import have a small multiplier. The reason is that they have a larger leakage from the circular flow of income and expenditure. An additional dollar of expenditure does not generate a large addition to aggregate expenditure because much of it leaks out, either through higher taxes or higher imports. A country with a low tax rate and a low marginal propensity to import has a large multiplier. With a low tax rate and a low marginal propensity to import, an additional dollar of expenditure generates only a small amount of leakage and more and more expenditure as it flows around the circular flow of income and expenditure.

The effects of the marginal propensity to import and the marginal tax rate on the value of the multiplier are illustrated in Figure 4.10. In this figure, the marginal propen-

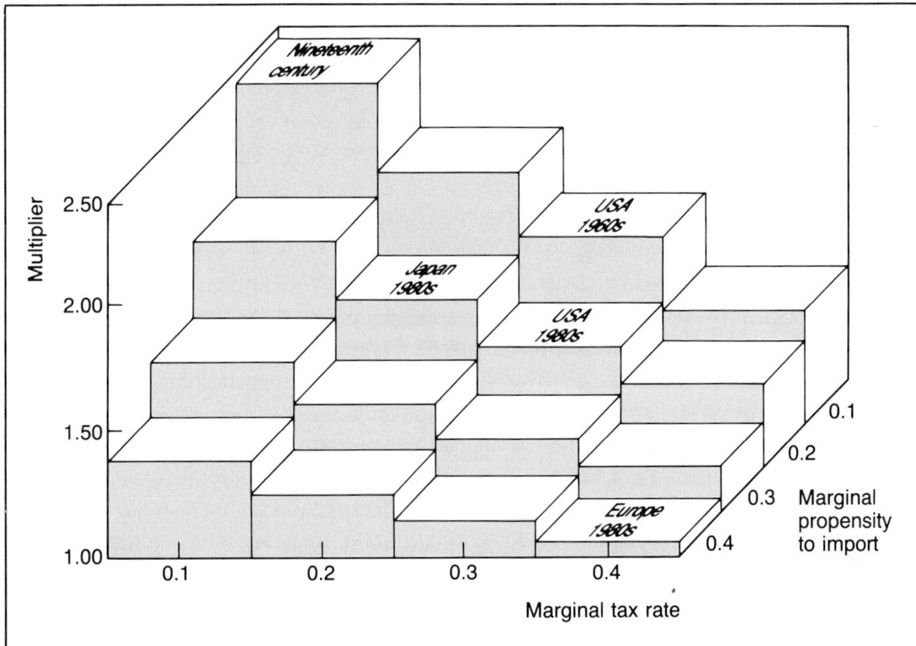

FIGURE 4.10
The Declining Multiplier

The multiplier depends on the marginal tax rate and the marginal propensity to import. In the nineteenth century, when marginal tax rate and the marginal propensity to import were low, the multiplier was around 2.5. The multiplier has gradually declined over the years. It is lowest in Western European countries, where marginal tax rates are high and where there is also a high marginal propensity to import.

sity to consume is 0.75 and the marginal propensity to import and the marginal tax rate vary between 0.1 and 0.4. In the nineteenth century, most countries were in the back corner of this figure with multipliers approaching 2.5. In Western Europe today, where marginal tax rates and the marginal propensity to import are high, the multiplier is only slightly greater than 1. The Canadian multiplier lies between these values but has been declining as a result of our increasing marginal propensity to import.

■ We've now completed our study of the determination of expenditure equilibrium. It's important to remember the conditions that prevail in the economy that we have studied: a given price level and given levels of other variables, such as interest rates and the exchange rate. This does not means that these variables are actually constant. It means that we have analyzed forces that operate at given values for them. Working out how these forces interact with interest rates, prices, and other variables involves analyzing the entire aggregate demand-aggregate supply mechanism. In the next chapter, we're going to continue to keep the price level fixed but will broaden our view of the determination of aggregate expenditure and study the way in which interest rates and money influence investment and interact with the forces that we have studied in this chapter.

CHAPTER REVIEW

Summary

THE COMPONENTS OF AGGREGATE EXPENDITURE: RELATIVE IMPORTANCE AND VOLATILITY

The components of aggregate expenditure are consumer expenditure, investment, government purchases of goods and services, and net exports (exports minus imports). Of these, the most important is consumer expenditure (about 60 percent of GDP) with government purchases next, representing around 20 percent of GDP and then investment, representing between 15 and 20 percent of GDP. The components of aggregate expenditure that fluctuate most are investment and exports. In comparison, the fluctuations in consumer expenditure and government purchases of goods and services, although important, are much less pronounced.

A SIMPLE MODEL OF CONSUMPTION AND SAVING

A simple model of consumption and saving is based on the idea that the fraction of an additional dollar of disposable income allocated to consumer expenditure and to saving is relatively stable. This idea gives rise to the theory of the consumption function and the saving function. The consumption function is the relationship between consumer expenditure and disposable income. Consumer expenditure is composed of autonomous consumer expenditure—the level of consumer expenditure at a zero disposable income level—and induced consumer expenditure. The effect of an additional dollar of disposable income on consumer expenditure is the marginal propensity to consume. Since an additional dollar of disposable income is either consumed or saved, there is also a saving function—a relationship between saving and disposable income. The effect of a change in disposable income on saving is determined by the marginal propensity to save. The marginal propensity to consume and the marginal propensity to save sum to one—each additional dollar of disposable income is either consumed or saved.

THE RELATIONSHIP BETWEEN CONSUMPTION AND INCOME IN THE CANADIAN ECONOMY

The simple theory of the consumption function is a good approximation of the data for the Canadian economy, but it is not a precise description. In the data, there appears to be a long-run consumption function relating consumer expenditure to disposable income over several decades. This consumption function has a marginal propensity to consume of around 0.85. There is also a short-run consumption function—the relationship between consumer expenditure and disposable income in a given year. The short-run consumption function has a marginal propensity to consume of around 0.7. The short-run consumption function shifts over time, generally upward, but occasionally downward. Many individual factors produce these shifts in the short-run consumption function.

HOW EXPENDITURE EQUILIBRIUM IS DETERMINED

Expenditure equilibrium is determined at the level of real GDP that makes aggregate planned expenditure equal to real GDP. The higher the level of real GDP, the higher is the level of planned consumer expenditure. Planned investment and planned government purchases of goods and services do not vary systematically with real GDP and we take them as given. The sum of planned consumer expenditure, planned investment, and planned government purchases equals aggregate planned expenditure.

If real GDP is above the expenditure equilibrium, aggregate planned expenditure is below real GDP. Actual aggregate expenditure equals real GDP because inventories increase by an unintended amount—there is positive unintended investment. If real GDP is below the expenditure equilibrium, aggregate planned expenditure exceeds real GDP. Actual aggregate expenditure equals real GDP because inventories decrease by an unintended amount—there is negative unintended investment. Only when real GDP is at an expenditure equilibrium is aggregate planned expenditure equal to actual expenditure and inventory investment is also at its planned level.

HOW THE ECONOMY CONVERGES TO AN EXPENDITURE EQUILIBRIUM

If real GDP is above the expenditure equilibrium level, aggregate planned expenditure is below GDP and unwanted inventories are piling up. In order to reduce their unwanted inventories, firms cut back their orders and producers cut back on their scale of output and employment. A decrease in employment lowers incomes. With lower incomes, people cut back their planned consumer expenditure and so aggregate planned expenditure falls. Inventories continue to pile up but at a smaller pace. Output and orders continue to be cut back but on a smaller scale. This process of falling output and employment leading to falling incomes and falling planned consumer expenditure gradually converges upon that level of real GDP at which aggregate planned expenditure equals GDP.

If real GDP is below its expenditure equilibrium level, a similar process of adjustment takes place, but in the opposite direction. In this situation, aggregate planned expenditure exceeds real GDP so inventories decline to levels considered too low. To replenish their low inventories, firms increase orders and increase production. Additional workers are hired and incomes increase. The extra income generates additional planned consumer expenditure but not by as much as the increased income itself. Nevertheless, the increased consumer expenditure continues to deplete inventories and leads to a further round of increased output and employment and yet higher incomes. This process continues until real GDP has reached the level at which aggregate planned expenditure equals GDP.

THE MULTIPLIER

The multiplier is the quantitative effect of a change in investment (or other component of autonomous expenditure) and real GDP. The multiplier is defined as the change in real GDP divided by the change in autonomous spending that caused it. In the simplest economy that has only autonomous taxes and no foreign trade, the multiplier is equal to 1 divided by the marginal propensity to save. For example, if the marginal propensity to save is 0.25, the multiplier is 4.

The process whereby real GDP converges to its expenditure equilibrium level gives rise to the multiplier. An initial increase in autonomous expenditure increases aggregate planned expenditure by the same amount. But it has no effect, the instant it occurs, on *actual* aggregate expenditure. There is an unintended decrease in inventories that offsets the planned increase in spending. But the lower inventories lead to higher production and the higher production generates higher incomes. For each additional dollar of income received, fraction b is consumed and fraction $1 - b$ is saved. The fraction that is consumed goes on to generate yet more income that, in turn, is spent in the next round so that consumer expenditure increases by b^2 times the initial dollar increase. This process continues until the new equilibrium is reached.

FISCAL POLICY MULTIPLIERS

Government purchases of goods and services are one component of autonomous expenditure. A change in government purchases has a multiplier effect exactly like a change in investment. The government can take advantage of this fact and attempt to stabilize aggregate expenditure. When there is a change in investment, or some other private component of aggregate planned expenditure, the government can attempt to change its own purchases of goods and services in the opposite direction to offset the potential multiplier effect of the change in private spending.

Taxes can also be used by the government to stabilize aggregate expenditure. A change in autonomous taxes changes disposable income and leads to a change in consumer expenditure, the magnitude of which is determined by the marginal propensity to consume. An increase in taxes brings a decrease in aggregate planned expenditure. Thus the tax multiplier is negative. Also, since the change in taxes operates indirectly by changing disposable income and therefore, changing consumer expenditure, the magnitude of the tax multiplier is smaller than that of the government purchases multiplier.

Induced taxes, such as income taxes, have important effects on the economy. First, the higher the marginal tax rate, the smaller is the autonomous expenditure multiplier. The reason is, for any given increase in autonomous expenditure, the higher the marginal tax rate, the larger is the leakage from the circular flow of income and expenditure resulting in higher tax payments and the smaller is the amount left over to induce additional consumer expenditure and an additional multiplier effect on aggregate expenditure.

THE EFFECTS OF CHANGES IN INVESTMENT, GOVERNMENT PURCHASES, TAXES, AND EXPORTS ON EQUILIBRIUM AGGREGATE EXPENDITURE

Our economy's international trading links with the rest of the world also have important effects on the multiplier. An increase in real GDP leads to an increase in imports—and an additional leakage from the circular flow of income and expenditure. The relationship between imports and real GDP is determined by the marginal propensity to import. The higher the marginal propensity to import, the greater is the leakage through imports and the smaller is the multiplier. Over the years, the multiplier has declined in magnitude, partly because of the increased importance of international trade that has increased the marginal propensity to import, and partly because an increase in the scale of government has increased the marginal tax rate.

Key Terms and Concepts

Aggregate expenditure The quantity of real GDP demanded at a given price level.

Aggregate expenditure curve A curve showing the relationship between aggregate planned expenditure and real GDP.

Aggregate planned expenditure The sum of planned consumer expenditure, investment, government purchases of goods and services, and net exports.

Autonomous consumer expenditure Consumer expenditure that is independent of the level of income.

Autonomous expenditure That part of aggregate expenditure that does not depend on real GDP.

Autonomous tax multiplier The ratio of change in real GDP to the change in autonomous taxes that caused it.

Autonomous taxes Taxes that are independent of income.

Average propensity to consume The ratio of consumer expenditure to disposable income.

Average propensity to save The ratio of saving to disposable income.

Balanced budget multiplier The ratio of the change in real GDP to the change in government purchases financed by an equal change in autonomous taxes that produced it.

Consumption function The relationship between consumer expenditure and disposable income.

Dissaving Negative saving.

Expenditure equilibrium A situation in which aggregate planned expenditure equals real GDP.

Government purchases multiplier The ratio of the change in real GDP to the change in government purchases that caused it.

Import function The relationship between the quantity of imports and real GDP.

Induced consumer expenditure Consumer expenditure that varies with disposable income.

Induced taxes Taxes that vary with income.

Investment multiplier The ratio of the change in real GDP to the change in investment that caused it.

Long-run consumption function The average relationship between consumer expenditure and personal disposable income over several decades.

Marginal propensity to consume The ratio of a *change* in consumer expenditure to a *change* in disposable income.

Marginal propensity to consume out of real GDP The fraction of each additional dollar of real GDP that households spend on goods and services.

Marginal propensity to import The change in imports resulting from a one-dollar increase in real GDP.

Marginal propensity to save The ratio of a *change* in saving to a *change* in disposable income.

Marginal tax rate The fraction of an additional dollar of income paid out in taxes.

Marginal tax rate multiplier The ratio of the change in real GDP to the change in the marginal tax rate that caused it.

Saving function The relationship between saving and disposable income.

Short-run consumption function The relationship between consumer expenditure and personal disposable income at a particular year.

Tax function The relationship between taxes paid and income.

Review Questions

1. What are the main components of aggregate expenditure that macroeconomics studies? Which components are most important? And which are most volatile?
2. Explain what a consumption function is. Who first introduced the theory of the consumption function and what is that theory?
3. Distinguish between autonomous consumer expenditure and induced consumer expenditure. Why do macroeconomists make this distinction?
4. Explain what a saving function is.
5. For a given consumption function,

$$c = a + b(y - t_0)$$

   derive the saving function.
6. Distinguish between the average propensity to save and the marginal propensity to save.
7. Explain the relationship between the marginal propensity to save and the marginal propensity to consume.
8. Is there a relationship between the average propensity to save and the average propensity to consume? If so, explain what it is.
9. Distinguish between the long-run consumption function and the short-run consumption function.
10. How can the data on Canadian consumer expenditure and Canadian disposable income be interpreted using the
    (a) long-run consumption function?
    (b) short-run consumption function?
11. During World War II, the Canadian short-run consumption function shifted downward. Explain what happened to the Canadian saving function during these years.
12. Explain the conditions that hold at an expenditure equilibrium.
13. The Canadian economy is initially at an expenditure equilibrium. Explain the process of convergence to a new expenditure equilibrium if
    (a) the Canadian government increases its purchases of goods and services
    (b) the government of Saskatchewan decreases taxes
    (c) Japan cuts its purchases of Canadian lumber
    (d) the CBC builds new recording studios, a library, and broadcast studios in Toronto
14. Explain why the multiplier is greater than 1. What parameters determine its value in a closed economy?
15. Derive the fiscal policy multipliers for a closed economy.
16. Compare the government purchases multiplier and the autonomous tax multiplier.
17. Derive the balanced budget multiplier for a closed economy.
18. Explain what an automatic stabilizer is and how it works.
19. Explain what a tax function is.
20. What determines the marginal leakage rate in a closed economy?
21. What is the marginal tax rate multiplier in a closed economy?
22. Explain how an increase in the marginal tax rate reduces the size of the multiplier.
23. Explain what an import function is.
24. Is the multiplier in an open economy larger or smaller than in a closed economy? Why?
25. Explain how and why the size of the multiplier changed over the 1980s.

Problems

1. On Daydream Island, the marginal propensity to consume is 0.8 and at zero disposable income consumer expenditure is 1.2 billion in 1986 dollars.
   (a) What is the consumption function?
   (b) What is induced consumption expenditure?
   (c) What is autonomous consumer expenditure?
   (d) What is the saving function?
   (e) What is the marginal propensity to save?
   (f) Which is steeper, the consumption function or the saving function?
   (g) Over what income range is there dissaving?
2. In Magic Land, the consumption function is

$$c = 10 + 0.9\,(y - t) \text{ billions of 1990 dollars.}$$

   (a) What is the slope of the consumption function?
   (b) What is its intercept on the vertical axis?
   (c) If autonomous consumer expenditure increases by $1 billion, how does the consumption function change?
   (d) If Magic Land goes to war and the marginal propensity to consume falls to 0.8, how does the consumption function change?
3. On Sun Island, a closed economy, the consumption function is

$$c = 1 + 0.75\,(y - t) \text{ billions of 1990 dollars.}$$

   The government of Sun Island levies taxes of $1 billion a year and buys goods and services worth $1 billion a year. Investment on Sun Island is $0.5 billion a year.
   (a) Calculate real GDP at expenditure equilibrium.
   (b) Calculate total leakages from the circular flow of income and expenditure.
   (c) Calculate total injections into the circular flow of income and expenditure. Do injections equal leakages?
   (d) Calculate the multiplier.
   (e) If investment increases by $0.25 billion a year, what is the change in real GDP?
   (f) Go back to the initial expenditure equilibrium. The government plans to increase its purchases of goods and services by $0.25 billion a year. What are the resulting changes in consumption and saving?
   (g) Explain the adjustment process to the new equilibrium.
   (h) How does the government's purchase of $0.25 billion worth of goods and services get financed?
   (i) In problem (f), show that leakages from the circular flow equal injections into it.
   (j) Go back to the initial expenditure equilibrium. The government plans to increase its purchases of goods and services by $0.25 billion and to finance that purchase by an increase in autonomous taxes. What is the new expenditure equilibrium?
   (k) Compare the multipliers at work in problems (f) and (j). Which is larger?
4. In a closed economy, the consumption function is

$$c = 1.15 + 0.75(y - t) \text{ billions of 1990 dollars.}$$

   The tax function is

$$t = 0.1y + 0.1 \text{ billions of 1990 dollars.}$$

Planned investment is \$1 billion and planned government purchases are \$1.5 billion.

Calculate:

(a) Real GDP at the expenditure equilibrium
(b) Consumer expenditure
(c) Saving
(d) The investment multiplier
(e) The government budget deficit
(f) The leakages from and injections into the circular flow of income and expenditure. Do leakages equal injections?

5. In Happy Land, the consumption, tax, and import functions are as follows:

$c = 1.7 + 0.8(y - t)$	billions of 1990 dollars
$t = 0.1y + 0.2$	billions of 1990 dollars
$im = 0.06 + 0.1y$	billions of 1990 dollars

Planned investment is \$2 billion, planned government purchases is \$1 billion, and planned exports are \$1 billion.

Calculate:

(a) Real GDP at expenditure equilibrium
(b) The marginal leakage rate
(c) The investment multiplier
(d) The autonomous tax multiplier
(e) The marginal tax rate multiplier
(f) The government budget deficit
(g) The balance of trade
(h) The change in real GDP resulting from a \$1 billion rise in government purchases

(i) In problem (h), the changes in saving, consumer expenditure, and the government budget deficit

6. In problem 5, the government of Happy Land is planning to change taxes to balance its budget.

(a) If the government adjusts only autonomous taxes, by how much do they change?
(b) If the government adjusts only the marginal tax rate, by how much does it change?
(c) Compare the effect of the tax changes in (a) and (b) on real GDP. Which plan would you recommend the government adopt? Why?

APPENDIX

The Algebra of the Multipliers

EXPENDITURE EQUILIBRIUM

An expenditure equilibrium occurs when aggregate planned expenditure equals real GDP. Aggregate planned expenditure, e_p, is the sum of consumer expenditure, investment, and government purchases of goods and services. That is,

$$e_p = c + i + g \tag{4A.1}$$

Consumer expenditure is determined by the consumption function, which is

$$c = a + b(y - t), a > 0, 0 < b < 1 \tag{4A.2}$$

This equation tells us that consumer expenditure (c) is equal to the autonomous component of the consumer expenditure a plus the induced component $b(y - t)$, where b is the marginal propensity to consume and $(y - t)$ is disposable income. In terms of a graph, a is the intercept of the consumption function on the vertical axis and b is its slope.

Investment and government purchases are exogenous. That is,

$$i = i_0 \tag{4A.3}$$

$$g = g_0 \tag{4A.4}$$

We will assume initially that taxes are constant, independent of income. That is,

$$t = t_0 \tag{4A.5}$$

Substituting Equations (4A.2), (4A.3), (4A.4), and (4A.5) into Equation (4A.1) gives aggregate planned expenditure

$$e_p = a + b(y - t_0) + i_0 + g_0 \tag{4A.6}$$

Expenditure equilibrium prevails when aggregate planned expenditure equals real GDP. That is,

$$e_p = y \tag{4A.7}$$

Substituting Equation (4A.6) into Equation (4A.7) gives

$$y = a + b(y - t_0) + i_0 + g_0 \tag{4A.8}$$

Collecting terms in y, this equation may be rearranged as

$$(1 - b)y = a - bt_0 + i_0 + g_0 \tag{4A.9}$$

Solving this equation for real GDP gives

$$y = \frac{1}{1 - b}(a + i_0 + g_0 - bt_0) \tag{4A.10}$$

Equation (4A.10) tells us the level of real GDP at which an expenditure equilibrium occurs—the level of real GDP that makes aggregate planned expenditure equal to real GDP, given investment i_0, government purchases g_0, and taxes t_0. The real GDP at which an expenditure equilibrium occurs depends on investment i_0, government purchases g_0, and taxes t_0. An increase in investment or government purchases increases equilibrium real GDP and an increase in taxes decreases equilibrium real GDP. Let's see what determines the size of the change in equilibrium real GDP.

INVESTMENT MULTIPLIER

If investment increases to $i + \Delta i$, equilibrium real GDP increases to $y + \Delta y$. Substituting these quantities into Equation (4A.10) gives

$$y + \Delta y = \frac{1}{1-b}(a + i_0 + \Delta i + g_0 - bt_0) \tag{4A.11}$$

Subtracting Equation (4A.01) from Equation (4A.11) gives

$$\Delta y = \frac{1}{1-b}\Delta i \tag{4A.12}$$

That is, a \$1 billion increase in investment increases real GDP by \$1/(1 − b) billion. The investment multiplier is equal to the number by which the increase in investment is multiplied to get the increase in real GDP. That is, the investment multiplier is equal to $\Delta y/\Delta i$, which is

$$\text{Investment multiplier} = \frac{1}{1-b} \tag{4A.13}$$

The investment multiplier is larger, the larger the marginal propensity to consume.

GOVERNMENT PURCHASES MULTIPLIER

If government purchases increase to $g_0 + \Delta g$, equilibrium real GDP increases to $y + \Delta y$. Substituting these quantities into Equation (4A.10) gives

$$y + \Delta y = \frac{1}{1-b}(a + i_0 + g_0 + \Delta g - bt_0) \tag{4A.14}$$

Subtracting Equation (4A.10) from Equation (4A.14) gives

$$\Delta y = \frac{1}{1-b}\Delta g \tag{4A.15}$$

That is, a \$1 billion increase in government purchases increases real GDP by \$1/(1 − b) billion. The government purchases multiplier is the number by which the increase in government purchases is multiplied to get the increase in real GDP. That is, the government purchases multiplier is equal to y/g, which is

$$\text{Government purchases multiplier} = \frac{1}{1-b} \tag{4A.16}$$

The government purchases multiplier is the same as the investment multiplier, and is larger, the larger the marginal propensity to consume.

AUTONOMOUS TAX MULTIPLIER

If the government increases autonomous taxes from t_0 to $t_0 + \Delta t$, equilibrium real GDP increases to $y + \Delta y$. Substituting these quantities into Equation (4A.10) gives

$$y + \Delta y = \frac{1}{1-b}(a + i_0 + g_0 - bt_0 + b\Delta t) \tag{4A.17}$$

Subtracting Equation (4A.10) from Equation (4A.17) gives

$$\Delta y = \frac{-b}{1-b}\Delta t \tag{4A.18}$$

That is, a \$1 billion increase in autonomous taxes increases real GDP by $\$ - b/(1 - b)$ billion. The autonomous tax multiplier is the number by which the increase in autonomous taxes is multiplied to get the increase in real GDP. Notice that the autonomous tax multiplier is negative. That is, a \$1 billion *increase* in autonomous taxes *lowers* real GDP by $\$b/(1 - b)$ billion. The autonomous tax multiplier is equal to $\Delta y/\Delta t$, which is

$$\text{Autonomous tax multiplier} = \frac{-b}{1 - b} \qquad \textbf{(4A.19)}$$

The size of the autonomous tax multiplier is smaller than the government purchases multiplier—only b times the government purchases multiplier.

So far we've assumed that taxes are independent of income—taxes are autonomous. What is the autonomous tax multiplier if taxes also increase with income. Let's assume that taxes are

$$t = t_0 + t_1 y \qquad \textbf{(4A.20)}$$

Autonomous taxes are t_0 and the marginal tax rate is t_1. Equilibrium real GDP is no longer given by Equation (4A.10). Using Equation (4A.20) instead of Equation (4A.5) to calculate equilibrium real GDP gives

$$y = \frac{1}{1 - b(1 - t_1)}(a + i_0 + g_0 - bt_0) \qquad \textbf{(4A.21)}$$

If the government increases autonomous taxes to $t_0 + \Delta t$, equilibrium real GDP increases to $y + \Delta y$. Substituting these quantities into Equation (4A.21) gives

$$y + \Delta y = \frac{1}{1 - b(1 - t_1)}(a + i_0 + g_0 - bt_0 + b\Delta t) \qquad \textbf{(4A.22)}$$

Subtracting Equation (4A.21) from Equation (4A.22) gives

$$\Delta y = \frac{-b}{1 - b(1 - t_1)}\Delta t \qquad \textbf{(4A.23)}$$

That is, a \$1 billion increase in autonomous taxes increases real GDP by $\$ - b/[1 - b(1 - t_1)]$ billion. Again the autonomous tax multiplier is negative, but now its size is smaller than in the case when all taxes are autonomous $-b/(1 - b)$. This arises because the increase in autonomous taxes reduces real GDP and as a result the induced taxes (those that depend on income) decrease as real GDP decreases. That is, the increase in autonomous taxes is offset to some degree by a decrease in induced taxes. For a given increase in autonomous taxes real GDP decreases by a smaller amount.

But not only is the size of the autonomous tax multiplier smaller when taxes are a function of income, so too are the investment and government purchases multipliers smaller. They are each equal to

$$\frac{1}{1 - b(1 - t_1)} \qquad \textbf{(4A.24)}$$

BALANCED BUDGET MULTIPLIER

If the government increases government purchases by Δg and at the same time increases taxes so the government's budget balance does not change, by how much does real GDP now increase? The ratio of the increase in real GDP to the increase in government purchases is called the balanced budget multiplier. Let's assume that the government increases autonomous taxes. Because taxes are increased at the same time as government purchases, the balanced budget multiplier is the sum of the government purchases multiplier and the autonomous tax multiplier. If all taxes are autonomous, the balanced budget multiplier is

$$\text{Balanced budget multiplier} = \frac{1}{1-b} + \frac{-b}{1-b} = 1 \tag{4A.25}$$

If taxes do not increase with income, then the balanced budget multiplier is 1. A \$1 billion increase in government purchases paid for by autonomous taxes increases real GDP by \$1 billion.

If some taxes increase with income, the balanced budget multiplier is

$$\text{Balanced budget multiplier} = \frac{1}{1-b(1-t_1)} + \frac{-b}{1-b(1-t_1)} = \frac{1-b}{1-b(1-t_1)} \tag{4A.26}$$

When taxes are a function of income the balanced budget multiplier is less than 1. That is, a \$1 billion increase in government purchases paid for by an increase in autonomous taxes increases real GDP by less than \$1 billion.

MARGINAL TAX MULTIPLIER

So far we have consider the multipliers for a given marginal tax rate. Let's now see what the marginal tax multiplier is. Equation (4A.21) gives the equilibrium value of real GDP when autonomous taxes are t_0 and the marginal tax rate is t_1. Namely,

$$y = \frac{1}{1-b(1-t_1)}(a + i_0 + g_0 - bt_0) \tag{4A.21}$$

We can rearrange this equation by multiplying both sides by $[1 - b(1 - t_1)]$ to give

$$[1 - b(1 - t_1)]\, y = (a + i_0 + g_0 - bt_0) \tag{4A.27}$$

If the government increases the marginal tax rate from t_1 to $t_1 + \Delta t$, real GDP increases from y to $y + \Delta y$. Substituting the amounts into Equation (4A.28) gives

$$[1 - b(1 - t_1 + \Delta t)](y + \Delta y) = (a + i_0 + g_0 - bt_0) \tag{4A.28}$$

Rearranging this equation gives

$$[1 - b(1 - t_1)]\,(y + \Delta y) + b\Delta t(y + \Delta y) = (a + i_0 + g_0 - bt_0) \tag{4A.29}$$

Subtracting Equation (4A.27) from Equation (4A.29) gives

$$[1 - b(1 - t_1)]\Delta y + b\Delta t(y + \Delta y) = 0 \tag{4A.30}$$

If Δt is small, Δt multiplied by Δy will approach zero. Substituting zero for $\Delta t \Delta y$ and rearranging this equation gives

$$\Delta y = \frac{-by}{1-b(1-t_1)}\Delta t \tag{4A.31}$$

That is, an *increase* in the marginal tax rate of Δt *lowers* real GDP by $by/[1 - b(1 - t_1)]$ times Δt. The increase in the marginal tax rate immediately increases taxes by Δty. This has a multiplier effect just like an increase in autonomous taxes of the same magnitude. We have already seen that the autonomous tax multiplier is $-b/[1 - b(1 - t_1)]$, so that real GDP decreases by $b/[1 - b(1 - t_1)]$ times Δty. The marginal tax multiplier is the number by which the increase in the marginal tax rate is multiplied to give the increase in real GDP. That is,

$$\text{Marginal tax multiplier} = \frac{-by}{1 - b(1 - t_1)} \qquad \textbf{(4A.32)}$$

INTERNATIONAL MULTIPLIERS

Let's now bring in the rest of the world. International economic transactions affect aggregate expenditure and the multiplier in two ways. First, Canadian exports (ex) of goods and services to the rest of the world are exogenous. Imports into Canada are determined by the import function, which can be written as

$$im = im_0 + my \qquad \textbf{(4A.33)}$$

In this equation, im_0 represents autonomous imports and my is induced imports, where m is the marginal propensity to import. Introducing imports and exports into the model of expenditure equilibrium modifies the multiplier. To see how, let's calculate the multiplier again. Aggregate planned expenditure is

$$e_p = c + i + g + ex - im \qquad \textbf{(4A.34)}$$

Substituting the consumption function and the import function into Equation (4A.34) gives

$$e_p = a - bt_0 + b(1 - t_1)y + i + g + ex - im_0 - my \qquad \textbf{(4A.35)}$$

Using the same procedure as above to solve for real GDP, it is

$$y = \frac{1}{1 - b(1 - t_1) + m}(a - bt_0 + i + g + ex - im_0) \qquad \textbf{(4A.36)}$$

Notice the similarity between Equation (4A.36) and Equation (4A.10). In an open economy, the term multiplying investment, government purchases, and exports to determine real GDP is $1/[1 - b(1 - t_1) + m]$. This value is the multiplier in an open economy. This multiplier is smaller than the closed economy one. So too are the magnitudes of the tax multipliers and the balanced budget multiplier. The multipliers are smaller because imports are an additional leakage from the circular flow of income and expenditure.

CHAPTER

5 Aggregate Expenditure, Interest Rates, and Money

PUTTING MONEY IN THE PICTURE

IN CHAPTER 4, WE DISCOVERED HOW CHANGES in investment or other components of autonomous expenditure are amplified through the *multiplier* to produce even bigger fluctuations to aggregate expenditure. We used the aggregate expenditure model to work out those effects. But the model of Chapter 4 has two important limitations. First, it takes investment as exogenous — that is, fluctuations in investment are not explained but are taken as given. In Chapter 5 we explain how investment is determined and discover the crucial role interest rates play. Second, money has no role in the aggregate expenditure model presented in Chapter 4. In this model people decide how much to save and spend but they do not decide what to do with their saving — whether to stuff money into a mattress, put it in a bank or a trust company, or use it to buy stocks and bonds. Nor do the amount of money people hold or interest rates have any effect on saving and spending decisions. In Chapter 5 we study the factors that determine the amount of money people plan to hold and the influence of interest rates on this decision.

You're going to discover that interest rates affect investment, which in turn influences real GDP. You're also going to discover that real GDP affects the amount of money that people want to hold, which in turn influences interest rates. This sounds circular: interest rates determine investment, which determines real GDP, which determines the amount of money people want to hold, which determines interest rates . . . . But, as you'll discover, there is no circularity. Interest rates and real GDP are *simultaneously* determined to achieve expenditure equilibrium and equilibrium in the markets for money and financial assets.

But as you'll also discover, there isn't a unique combination of the interest rate and real GDP. There is one for each price level. Indeed, it is by varying the price level, while holding everything else constant, that we generate the aggregate demand curve. In a nutshell, this chapter is about the theory of aggregate demand. It sets out the model of aggregate demand used by forecasters and policymakers to predict and control the level of aggregate demand and its components.

But even this model does not look at everything! It focuses on a closed economy. You can think of the model as applying, therefore, to the world as a whole, or to a country that has limited international trade and capital links with the rest of the world. Of course, international factors do influence aggregate demand and these are brought into the picture in Chapter 7.

After studying this chapter, you will be able to

- Describe the fluctuations in Canadian investment and interest rates in the 1970s and 1980s
- Explain what determines investment
- Explain the distinction between the nominal interest rate and the real interest rate
- Define and derive the investment function
- Describe the shifts in the Canadian investment function in the 1970s and 1980s
- Define and derive the *IS* curve
- Describe the fluctuations in Canadian money supply and interest rates in the 1970s and 1980s
- Explain what determines the demand for money
- Describe the shifts in the Canadian demand for money function in the 1970s and 1980s
- Define and derive the *LM* curve
- Determine the equilibrium interest rate and real GDP
- Derive the aggregate demand curve

5.1 *Canadian Investment and Interest Rates in the 1970s and 1980s*

MACROFACTS

As you've seen, investment fluctuates a great deal. In fact, fluctuations in investment, which get magnified through the multiplier effect, generate most of the fluctuations in aggregate expenditure. But what determines investment? That's one of the main questions this chapter answers. We'll discover that one of the key influences on investment is the cost of borrowing—interest rates. Let's look at the behavior of Canadian investment and interest rates during the 1970s and 1980s.

Figure 5.1(a) shows investment. Gross investment—purchases of new plant, equipment and buildings and the replacement of those worn out—grew steadily in the 1970s and 1980s; by 1990 it was more than $100 billion. But gross investment fluctuated, and during the recession of 1981-1982 it fell sharply. It also fell in 1990 as the economy teetered on the brink of recession. The figure also shows that most fluctuations in gross investment result from fluctuations in net investment—the purchase of *new* buildings, plant, machinery, and equipment. Replacement investment—gross investment minus net investment—was relatively constant by comparison.

What happened to interest rates during the 1970s and 1980s? Figure 5.1(b) answers this question. Through the 1970s they fluctuated between 7 and 9 percent. Then, at the beginning of the 1980s, they climbed to unprecedented heights. The rate shown here is the interest rate at which the government of Canada can borrow on a long-term basis. That interest rate peaked at 15 percent in 1981 and has declined in two waves through the 1980s.

Interest rates tend to be high when the inflation rate is high. In fact, when money is losing its value, one of the ways lenders are compensated for this loss in value is by higher interest rates. To emphasize the idea that interest includes an inflation component, we call the market interest rate the **nominal interest rate**. This is the interest rate actually paid in dollar terms. The nominal interest rate minus the inflation rate is called the **real interest rate**. This is the interest rate that is *really* paid and received after taking inflation into account. Figure 5.1(b) shows that the real interest rate fell dramatically in the mid-1970s and actually became negative for a while. It then began a period of

FIGURE 5.1
Investment and Interest Rates

Gross investment (part a) fluctuates but steadily increases over time. Most of gross investment is replacement investment, which does not fluctuate much. Most of the fluctuations in investment are in net investment which, in recession years such as 1981-1982, declines very sharply.

Interest rates (part b) increased steadily throughout the 1970s and increased sharply in 1981 but have declined through the 1980s. Real interest rates (the nominal interest rate minus the inflation rate) became negative in the early 1970s but then increased through 1978. After a dip in 1979 they climbed for five years. After 1984 they declined steadily for the rest of the decade.

There is a loose relationship between net investment and the real interest rate (part c). When interest rates decrease sharply, as they did in the early 1970s, net investment increases and when they increase sharply, as they did in the early 1980s, there is a tendency for net investment to decrease. But there are many other influences on investment so the relationship is not a strong one. For example, in the second half of the 1980s, when real interest rates were quite high, net investment was also high.

Sources: National Income and Expenditure Accounts, Statistics Canada, catalogue 13-531 for 1970-1986 and catalogue 13-001 for 1987-1990, and *Bank of Canada Review*, June 1983 and June 1991.

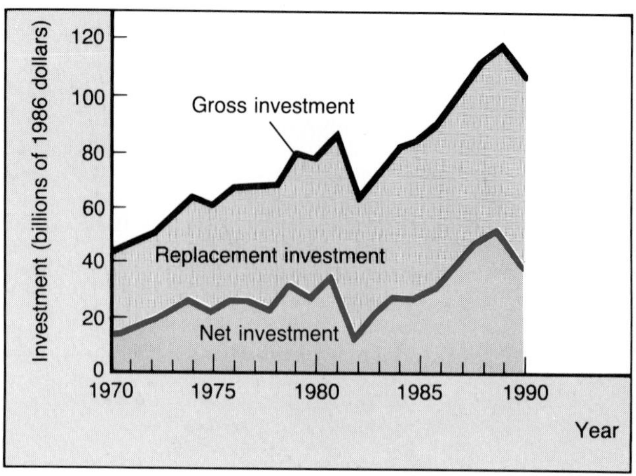

(a) Gross and net investment

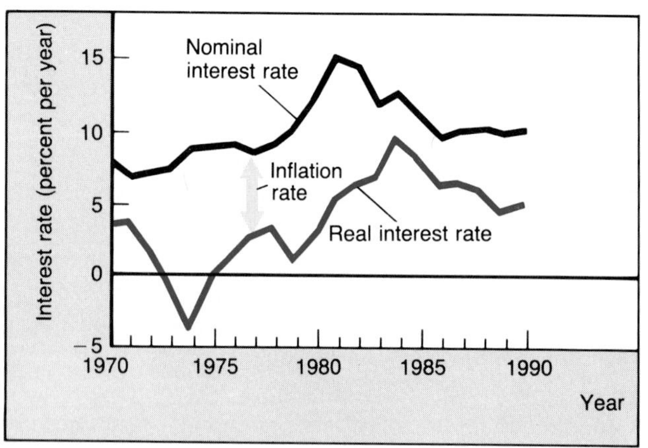

(b) Nominal and real interest rates

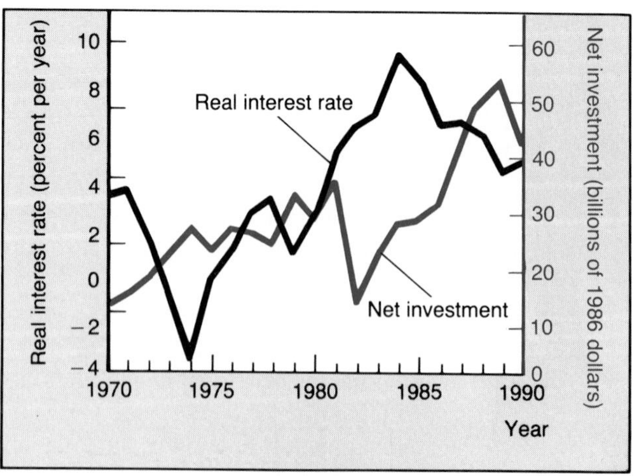

(c) Net investment and the real interest rate

massive increase, interrupted briefly in 1979, reaching a peak of 8 percent in 1984. In the second half of the 1980s the real rate declined.

How do fluctuations in investment and interest rates line up with each other? Figure 5.1(c) shows the answer to this question. Here, net investment is measured on the right axis and the real interest rate is measured on the left axis. As you can see, sometimes there is a tendency for these two variables to move in opposite directions: as the real interest rate increases (the cost of borrowing becomes higher), net investment declines. An example of this pattern occurs in 1981-1982 when real interest rates climbed and investment collapsed. But at other times, such as 1982-1984, the real interest rate and net investment moved in the same direction. This chapter explores the reasons for these movements in interest rates and investment in the Canadian economy.

5.2 *Investment Demand*

Investment demand is the planned rate of purchase of new capital — the planned rate of investment.[1] There are two main determinants of investment:

- The interest rate
- The rate of return on capital

The interest rate

Other things being equal, the higher the interest rate, the smaller is the planned rate of investment. It is obvious why the interest rate affects investment financed by borrowed funds. The higher the interest rate, the greater amount that has to be paid for the borrowed funds and so, other things being equal, the smaller the amount of borrowing and investment that will be undertaken.

But the interest rate also influences investment financed with a firm's or household's own funds. For these funds could be lent to someone else at the going interest rate. Thus the interest rate is the *opportunity cost* of a household or firm using its own financial resources to buy capital goods.

Regardless then of whether a firm borrows to finance its investment or uses its own funds (the profits it has made from previous activities), the higher the interest rate, the smaller is the level of planned investment.

The rate of return on capital

The **rate of return** on a piece of capital equipment is equal to the net income received from using the equipment expressed as a percentage of the equipment's price. In calculating the net income received, we do not count the interest charged on loans used to finance the purchase. To determine whether a particular investment is worthwhile, we compare its rate of return with the interest rate. Investment projects with a rate of return greater than the interest rate are undertaken. Those with a rate of return below the interest rate are not. Investment projects are undertaken up to the point at which the rate of return equals the interest rate.

This principle works both for investment projects financed with borrowed money and those financed with the investor's own resources. If money is going to be borrowed, it pays to invest in capital equipment only if the rate of return on that capital is greater than or equal to the cost of borrowing. If the owner's own financial resources are going

[1]The development of the theory of investment presented in this chapter is based very closely on Dale W. Jorgensen, "Capital Theory and Investment Behaviour," *American Economic Review Papers and Proceedings*, vol. 53 (1963), pp. 247-59.

to be used, it pays to invest in a piece of capital equipment only if the rate of return obtained is at least as high as the rate of interest that could be earned on stocks, bonds, or other financial assets.

Let's illustrate these principles with an example.

A property developer's investment problem

Suppose that you are a property developer trying to figure out how many apartments to build in a particular neighbourhood. For the number of apartments you're thinking about, the cost of building an apartment is constant at \$100,000. Your capital investment is the cost of the apartments you build. For example, if you build 200 apartments your capital investment will be \$20 million (200 × \$100,000).

As apartments get older, they lose value relative to new apartments—they depreciate. Let's suppose that apartments depreciate at the rate of 2 percent a year. That is, you face a cost of \$2,000 a year in the first year on each apartment. You can think of this as the cost of maintaining the apartment in mint condition. Another important factor works counter to depreciation: because of inflation, apartment prices increase year after year. The increase in the value of your apartments resulting from this source is part of your return. Let's suppose that inflation is running at 5 percent a year and that apartment prices, along with the prices of all other goods and services, are increasing at that rate. Thus you make a return on each apartment of \$5,000 a year because of inflation. The final component of your return is the rent that you get. You know that the more apartments you build, the lower is the rent you'll get. If you build 200, you expect that you can rent them for \$10,000 a year each; 300 apartments would rent for \$7,000 a year each; and 400 would rent for \$4,000 a year each.

What is your rate of return on 200, 300, and 400 apartments? Table 5.1 sets out the relevant numbers. As you can see there, the rate of return decreases as the number of apartments increases. Two hundred apartments yield a return of 13 percent, while 400 yield a return of 7 percent.

Figure 5.2 illustrates the information presented in Table 5.1. Part (a) shows the demand for rental apartments. Here, the quantity of apartments demanded is plotted against the annual rent. Points, *A*, *B*, and *C* correspond to the rows in Table 5.1. Figure 5.2(b) plots the capital invested in apartments against the rate of return. It also shows the interest rate—in this example, 10 percent a year. If you invest less than \$30 million in apartments (that is, if you build fewer than 300 apartments), the rate of return is higher than the interest rate. If you invest more than \$30 million in apartments (build more than 300 apartments), the rate of return is lower than the interest rate. It will pay you to invest in whatever number of apartments makes the rate of return equal to the interest rate. In this example, you will build 300 apartments, investing \$30 million in apartments.

TABLE 5.1
The Developer's Decision Problem

CASE	NUMBER OF APARTMENTS	CAPITAL INVESTMENT (\$ million)	ANNUAL RENT PER APARTMENT (dollars)	CAPITAL GAIN PER APARTMENT (dollars)	DEPRECIATION PER YEAR (dollars)	GROSS INCOME PER APARTMENT (dollars)	RATE OF RETURN (percent per year)
A	200	20	10,000	5,000	2,000	13,000	13
B	300	30	7,000	5,000	2,000	10,000	10
C	400	40	4,000	5,000	2,000	7,000	7

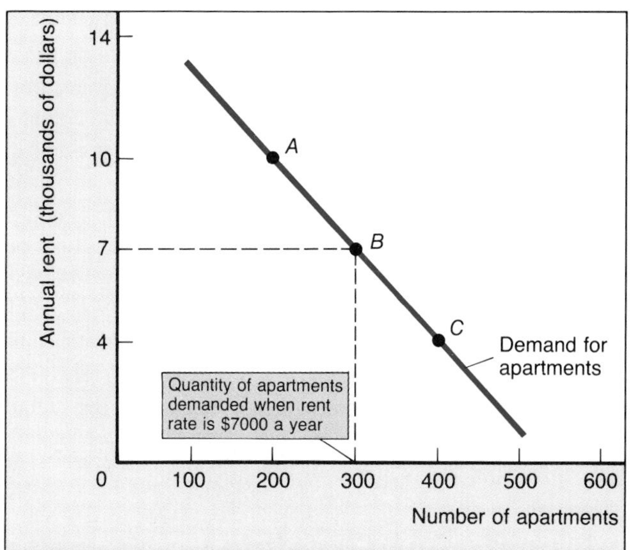

(a) The demand for apartments to rent

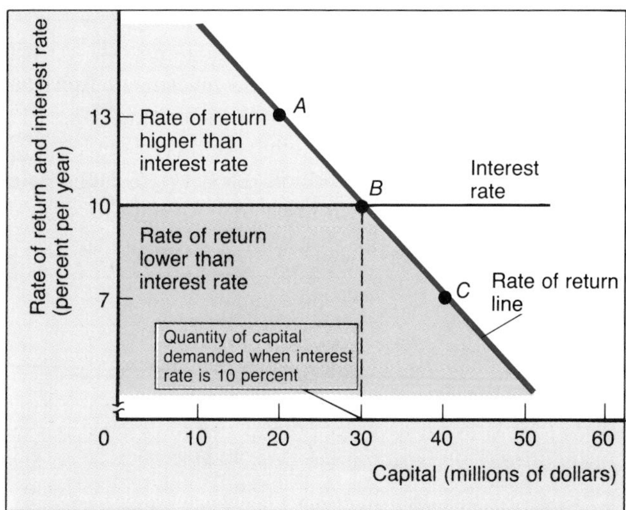

(b) The demand for capital

FIGURE 5.2
Rates of Return and the Demand for Capital

Other things being equal, the quantity of apartments demanded for rent depends on the level of rent. The higher the rent, the smaller is the quantity demanded for rent (part a).

The rate of return on rented apartments is equal to the net income received expressed as a percentage of the price of the apartment. Apartments and other capital assets are demanded provided the rate of return on them is greater than or equal to the interest rate. Other things being equal, the lower the interest rate, the greater is the quantity of capital demanded (part b).

The economy as a whole

The investment problem for an individual property developer that we've just considered illustrates principles that apply to all sectors of the economy. What is true for the property developer is true for everyone. The higher the rate of return on Boeing 747s, the greater is Canadian Airlines International's planned rate of investment in these pieces of capital equipment. The higher the rate of return on robotic auto assembly lines, the greater is the quantity of these types of capital bought by Ford and General Motors.

For the economy as a whole, the higher the rate of return on capital and the lower the interest rate, the greater is the level of planned investment.

5.3 *Real and Nominal Interest Rates*

We've discovered that the planned rate of investment depends on the rate of return on capital and the interest rate. A neat alternative way of describing the determinants of investment distinguishes between the *nominal interest rate*—the actual interest rate paid and received—and the *real interest rate*—the nominal interest rate minus the inflation rate.

The rate of return on capital depends in part on the rate at which prices are rising. In fact, there is a one-to-one relationship between the rate of return on capital and the inflation rate. If the inflation rate increases by 1 percentage point, so does the rate of return on capital. The rate of return on capital minus the inflation rate is called the **real rate of return on capital**. Comparing the real rate of return on capital with the real interest rate is exactly the same as comparing the (nominal) rate of return on capital with the nominal interest rate. Thus other things being equal, the higher the real rate of return on capital and the lower the real interest rate, the faster is the pace of planned investment.

5.4 *The Investment Function*

The **investment function** is the relationship between investment and the interest rate, holding all other influences on investment constant. We've seen that the rate of investment depends on the rate of return on capital and the interest rate. Anything that changes the interest rate results in a *movement along* the investment function. Anything that changes the rate of return on capital *shifts* the investment function.

Figure 5.3 illustrates an investment function. In this example, at an interest rate of 5 percent, planned investment is \$0.775 billion. Each 1 percentage point increase in the interest rate leads to a \$0.1125 billion cut in planned investment.

We can describe an investment function with an equation, such as

$$i = i_0 - hr \quad i_0, h > 0. \tag{5.1}$$

FIGURE 5.3
The Investment Function

Other things being equal, the higher the rate of return on capital and the lower the interest rate, the higher is planned investment. Changes in the interest rate lead to a movement along the investment function. Changes in the expected rate of return on capital lead to a shift in the investment function.

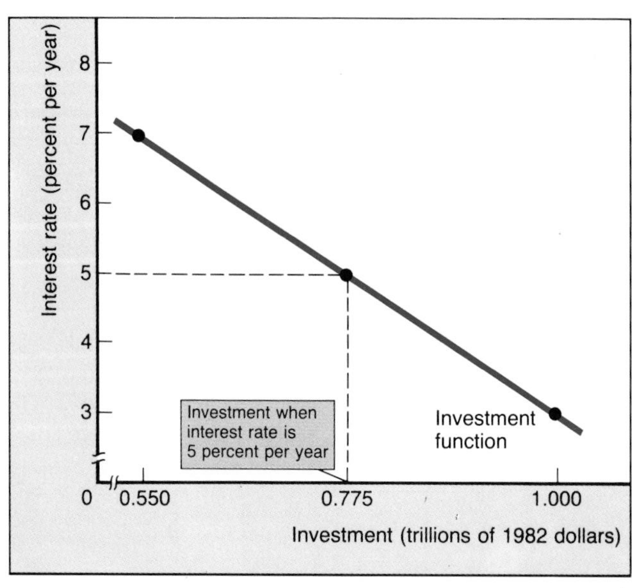

In this equation, i_0 represents the planned investment that would occur at an interest rate of zero, the parameter h measures the sensitivity of planned investment to the interest rate, and r is the interest rate. A 1 percentage point increase in the interest rate lowers investment by $\$h$. The slope of the investment function is $-1/h$. The volatility of investment is reflected in shifts in the investment function, or equivalently, in exogenous changes in the intercept of the investment function, i_0. These exogenous changes arise from many factors such as changes in taxes, technology, population size and composition, entrepreneurial perceptions of profit opportunities, and the (slowly evolving) capital stock itself.[2]

The investment function shown in Figure 5.3 is a particular example of Equation (5.1). Its parameters are

$$i_0 = 1.3375 \text{ billion dollars}$$
$$h = 0.1125 \text{ billion dollars.}$$

In this case, the investment demand function is

$$i = 1.3375 - 0.1125r.$$

We've seen that changes in the interest rate lead to a movement along the investment function and changes in the rate of return lead to a shift in the investment function. Factors that change the rate of return change the value of the parameter i_0. The bigger the rate of return, the higher is the value of i_0 and the farther to the right is the investment function.

Now that we've reviewed the theory of the investment function, let's look at the investment function in the Canadian economy.

5.5 *The Canadian Investment Function*

TESTCASE

Let us now turn from the theory of investment to an examination of the facts about investment in Canada. Does investment in Canada vary inversely with the real interest rate as predicted by the theory of investment? Is investment volatile? That is, are there massive fluctuations in investment that are independent of movements in the interest rate? Another way of asking this same question is: does the intercept of the investment function, i_0, fluctuate as the theory of investment predicts?

To answer these questions we need to examine the facts about investment and the real interest rate. Between 1970 and 1990 the real interest rate fluctuated between a low of -4 percent a year in 1974 and a high of almost $+10$ percent a year in 1984. For most of the 1970s, the real interest rate fluctuated between zero and 5 percent a year and in the 1980s, it hovered around 7 percent a year, on the average.

The investment function in the Canadian economy is constantly shifting as a result of changes in expectations about the rate of return on capital. These expectations are driven mainly by waves of optimism and pessimism about future profit prospects as the economy ebbs and flows over the business cycle. It is also constantly shifting to the right as replacement investment increases. We can see the fluctuations in investment more clearly if we remove replacement investment from the picture and look only at *net investment*.

[2]As in the case of the consumption function, the theory of investment presented here is highly condensed and selective. A superb treatment of the subject at a more advanced level, however, may be found in Frank Brechling, *Investment and Employment Decisions* (Manchester: Manchester University Press, 1975). A good, up-to-date, though again fairly demanding survey is Andrew B. Abel, "Empirical Investment Equations: An Integrative Framework," in Karl Brunner and Allan H. Meltzer (eds.), *On the State of Macroeconomics*, Carnegie-Rochester Conference Series, vol. 12 (spring 1980), pp. 39-91.

Figure 5.4 does this. It illustrates the relationship between net investment and the real interest rate in Canada between 1970 and 1990. Each dot in that figure represents a year identified by its label. Thus for example, the point marked 1989 tells us that in that year, the real interest rate was almost 5 percent a year and net investment was about $53 billion.

We can interpret the data on real interest rates and net investment using the theory of investment that we've just been studying. In the early 1970s, the investment function was ID_0. Fluctuations in the real interest rate between 1970 and 1975 resulted in movements along that investment function—as indicated by the arrows along ID_0. Then, after the OPEC oil shock of 1974 and when the economy had recovered from its recession, future profit expectations became optimistic and net investment increased. The investment function shifted to the right to ID_1. Fluctuations in the real interest rate between 1976 and 1980 brought movements along that new investment function (ID_1) (although the curve shifted again to the right in 1979—not illustrated in the figure).

By 1981, the investment demand curve had shifted all the way to ID_2 but it stayed there very briefly. In 1982, the economy went into a recession and expectations about future profit were pessimistic. The investment function shifted back all the way to ID_0. By 1984, the economic outlook was extremely bright and future profit prospects were high. As a result, the investment function shifted sharply to the right, passing through ID_1 in 1983 to ID_2 in 1984. It stayed there through 1986 and then shifted again to ID_3 in 1987 and ID_4 by 1988 and 1989. Then at the end of the decade, with the onset of pessimism associated with the emerging recession of 1990, expectations were again less optimistic, and the investment function moved back again to ID_3.

The equation that describes the investment function in Figure 5.4 is

$$i = i_0 - 2.5r.$$

The intercept on the horizontal axis, i_0, fluctuates and takes on the following values: $30 billion for ID_0, $40 billion for ID_1, $50 billion for ID_2, $60 billion for ID_3, and $70

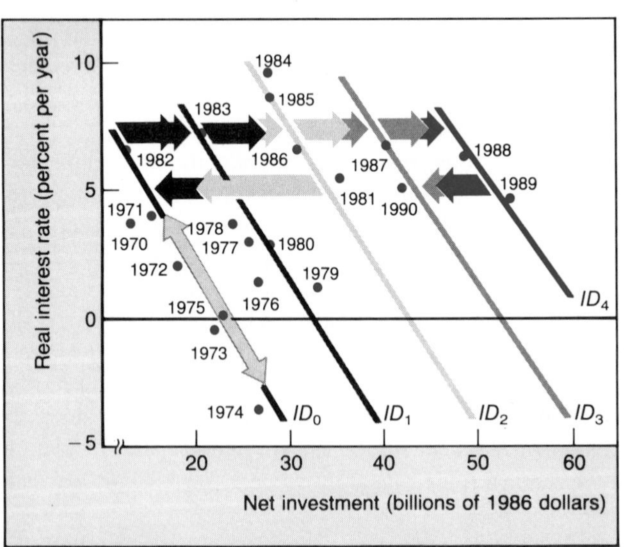

FIGURE 5.4
The Canadian Investment Function in the 1970s and 1980s

The vertical axis shows the real interest rate and the horizontal axis net investment (in billions of 1986 dollars). These data can be interpreted as having been generated by an investment function, *ID*, that has shifted over time from ID_0 in the early 1970s all the way to ID_4 in the late 1980s. The investment function shifts to the right when the economy is expanding and rate of return expectations are high, and to the left when the economy is contracting and rate of return expectations are low. The (net) investment function is $i = i_0 - 2.5r$. That is, other things being equal, a 1 percentage point increase in the real interest rate brings a $2.5 billion decrease in net investment.

Source: See Figure 5.1.

billion for ID_4. At the average value of the interest rate and net investment, the elasticity of net investment with respect to the real interest rate is about $-1/3$.

The particular investment function shown in Figure 5.4 — its assumed slope and shifts — are not the only possible rationalization of these data. The slope of the investment function is not known with certainty. But the slope assumed here is both reasonable and consistent with the data.

Given this interpretation of Canada's investment function, you can see that both sources of variation in investment have been important in the 20 years from 1970 to 1990. Fluctuations in the real interest rate have brought large and important movements in investment along a given investment function. But there have also been large shifts in the investment function, to the right in times of economic expansion and optimism and to the left in times of economic contraction and pessimism.

Investment, as we've seen, is the sum of net investment and replacement investment. The capital stock is constantly increasing, and so is replacement investment. Thus there is a general tendency for the investment function to drift rightward over time. Fluctuations in the pace of that rightward drift are determined by fluctuations in net investment, which in turn depend on future profit prospects. Thus even if there is a severe recession in the 1990s, it is unlikely that the investment function will shift as far to the left as it was in the early 1980s.

We've now seen how investment is influenced by the interest rate. Our next task is to work out how interest rates influence aggregate expenditure.

5.6 *The IS Curve*

The ***IS* curve** is the relationship between real GDP and the interest rate such that aggregate planned expenditure — planned consumer expenditure plus investment plus government purchases — is equal to real GDP. Since consumer expenditure depends on real GDP, different levels of real GDP will bring forth different levels of consumer expenditure. Investment depends on the interest rate, and different interest rates will bring forth different amounts of investment. At a particular real GDP and interest rate, the addition of government purchases to consumer expenditure and investment results in a particular level of aggregate planned expenditure. The *IS* curve traces the relationship between real GDP and the interest rate such that the level of aggregate planned expenditure generated is equal to real GDP.

The *IS* curve does not describe the plans of any single agent or group of agents. Rather, it is an equilibrium locus. It shows the combinations of real GDP and the interest rate at which aggregate planned expenditure equals real GDP. You can think of the *IS* curve as a kind of aggregate demand curve. The *aggregate demand curve* defined in Chapter 3 is the relationship between the aggregate quantity of goods and services demanded and the price level. The *IS* curve tells us the aggregate quantity of goods and services demanded as we vary the interest rate, holding everything else constant. Let's derive the *IS* curve.

Deriving the *IS* curve

Along an *IS* curve, aggregate planned expenditure equals real GDP. But we have met this condition before: it is an expenditure equilibrium — that is, the same as the equality of planned injections in the circular flow and planned leakages from it. Thus the *IS* curve is the relationship between real GDP and the interest rate such that planned investment plus government purchases equals planned saving plus taxes. The *IS* curve is derived in Figure 5.5. That figure looks more difficult than it is, so don't be put off

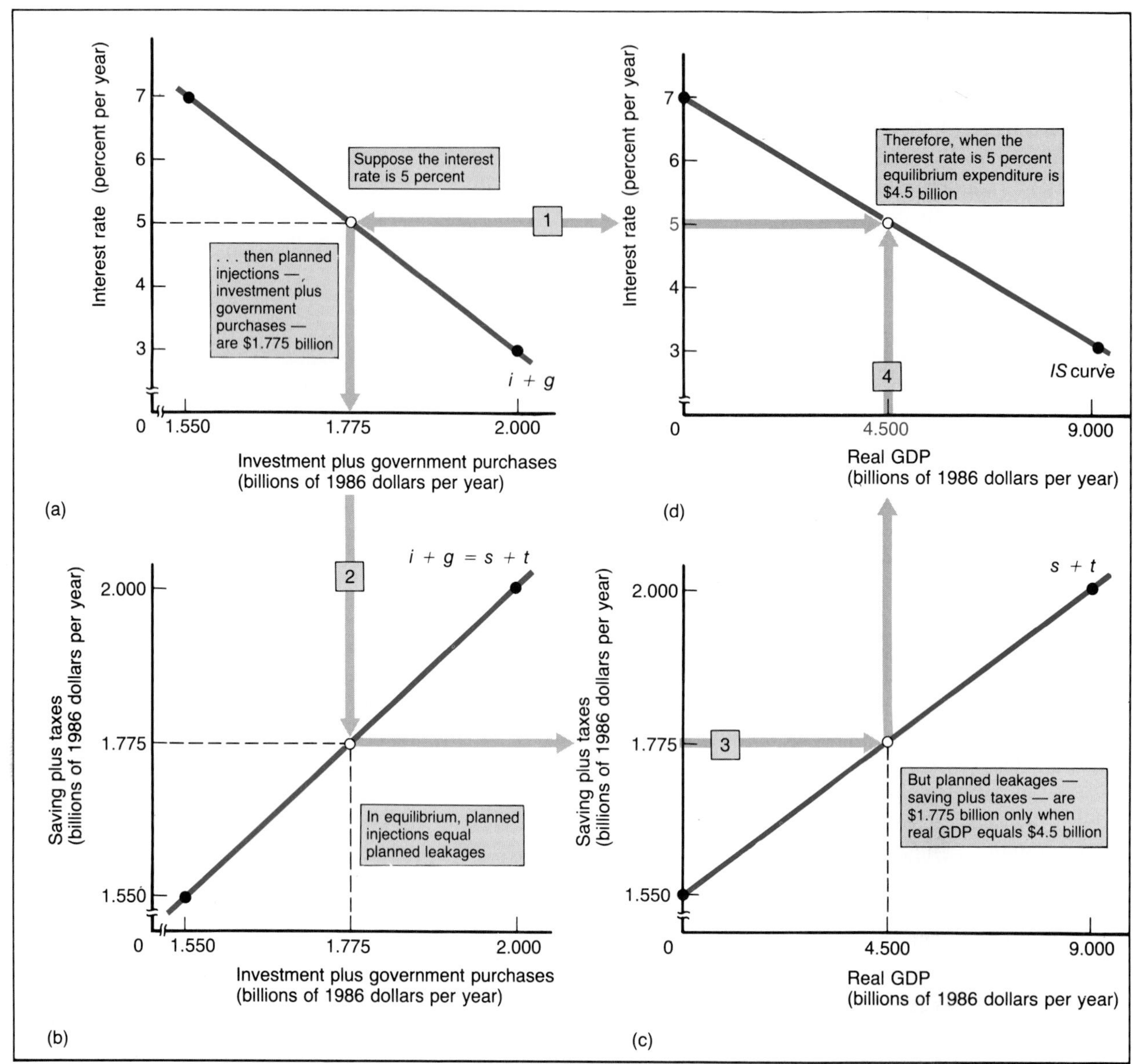

FIGURE 5.5
Deriving the *IS* Curve

The *IS* curve traces the relationship between the interest rate and real GDP that makes aggregate planned expenditure equal to real GDP. Equivalently, it is the relationship between the interest rate and real GDP when planned leakages equal planned injections. To derive a point on the *IS* curve, start in part (a) with an interest rate of 5 percent. Planned injections are $1.775 billion. In equilibrium, planned injections equal planned leakages (part b) and if planned leakages are to be $1.775 billion, real GDP must be $4.5 billion (part c). Thus a real interest rate of 5 percent and a level of real GDP of $4.5 billion achieves equilibrium between planned leakages and planned injections and is a point on the *IS* curve (part d). Using the same logic but starting at a different interest rate generates other points on the *IS* curve.

by your first glance at it. Just follow the text carefully as it leads you through the derivation.

Part (a) graphs investment plus government purchases of goods and services against the interest rate. Investment depends on the interest rate, increasing as the interest rate decreases, but government purchases do not depend on the interest rate or on real GDP. We're treating them as constant. Adding the constant level of government purchases to the investment at each interest rate and graphing the result gives the $i + g$ curve. For example, at an interest rate of 5 percent, investment plus government purchases is $1.775 billion.

Part (b) shows the equilibrium condition — the equality of planned injections and planned leakages. Injections are investment plus government purchases and leakages are saving plus taxes. The line in part (b) is a 45° line indicating equality between the value on the horizontal axis, $i + g$, and the value on the vertical axis, $s + t$.

Part (c) shows saving plus taxes as a function of real GDP. Saving increases as real GDP increases. Adding a constant level of taxes to the saving at each level of real GDP gives the line labeled $s + t$. Thus for example, when real GDP is $4.5 billion, saving plus taxes are $1.775 billion. The *IS* curve is illustrated in part (d). It shows the relationship between the interest rate and real GDP such that planned injections equal planned leakages.

To derive the *IS* curve, begin at point 1 in the figure by supposing that the interest rate is 5 percent. At that interest rate, planned injections — investment plus government purchases — are $1.775 billion. Follow the blue arrow to position 2 in the figure. Here, we discover that if there is to be an expenditure equilibrium, planned leakages must equal that same $1.775 billion of planned injections. Follow the blue arrow to position 3, and there discover that for planned leakages to equal $1.775 billion, real GDP must be $4.5 billion. Finally, follow the blue arrow to position 4 and to the conclusion that at an interest rate of 5 percent and a real GDP of $4.5 billion, planned injections equal planned leakages. We have derived one point on the *IS* curve.

Check that you can derive other points on the *IS* curve. For example, if you begin with an interest rate of 3 percent in part (a), you will wind up at the point on the *IS* curve where the interest rate is 3 percent and real GDP is $9 billion. If you begin with an interest rate of 7 percent in part (a), you will find the point on the *IS* curve at which the interest rate is 7 percent and real GDP is zero. Try to find other points on the *IS* curve in the figure.

The interest rate and aggregate expenditure

You already know that the *IS* curve slopes downward — you can see this from Figure 5.5(d). Because the *IS* curve slopes downward, a decrease in the interest rate brings about an increase in real GDP to keep the economy at an expenditure equilibrium. But how big an increase? Let's use Figure 5.6 to work out the answer.

Suppose that the interest rate falls from 5 percent to 4 percent. Then investment increases by Δi, (part a) and real GDP increases by Δy (part d). What is the relationship between the change in real GDP and the change in investment when the interest rate decreases by 1 percentage point? Real GDP changes such that the economy remains at an expenditure equilibrium — the condition that holds along the *IS* curve. Since injections have increased by Δi, leakages (Δs) must increase by an equal amount, as shown in part (b). The blue triangle in part (c) shows the increase in saving that results from the increase in real GDP in part (d). Since taxes are constant, the slope of the $s + t$ curve is equal to $1 - b$, the marginal propensity to save. The increase in saving is

$$\Delta s = (1 - b)\Delta y. \qquad \textbf{(5.2)}$$

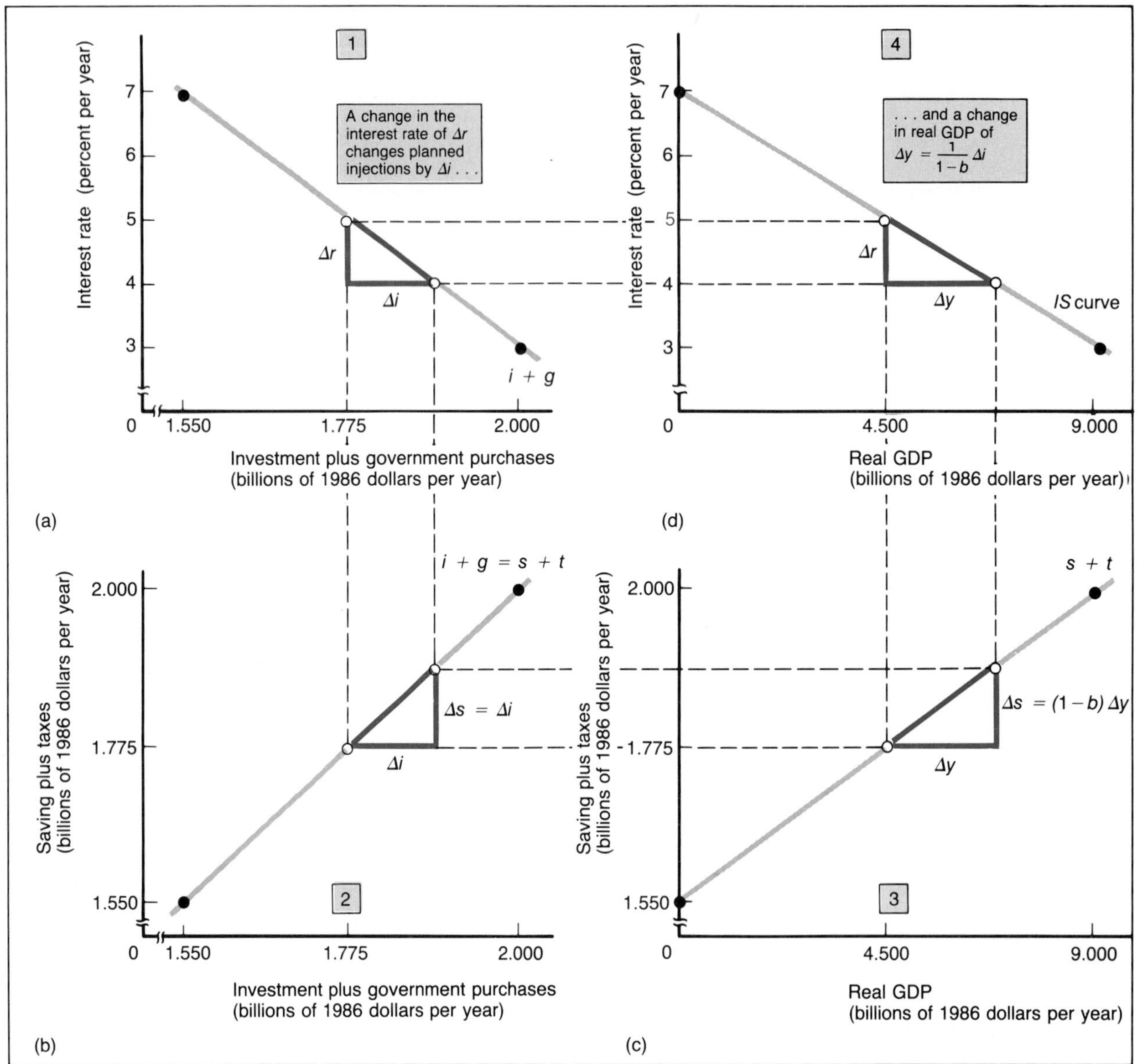

FIGURE 5.6
The Response of Real GDP to the Interest Rate

The *IS* curve slopes downward. That is, the lower the interest rate, the higher is equilibrium aggregate planned expenditure and real GDP. For a change in the interest rate that changes investment by Δi, equilibrium aggregate planned expenditure and real GDP (Δy) increase. The increase is equal to $[1/(1 - b)]\Delta i$.

But from part (b) Δs also equals Δi. Therefore

$$(1 - b)\Delta y = \Delta i \qquad \textbf{(5.3)}$$

Dividing both sides of Equation (5.3) by the marginal propensity to save $(1 - b)$ gives

$$\Delta y = \frac{1}{1 - \mathrm{b}}\Delta(i) \qquad \textbf{(5.4)}$$

This is the famous multiplier that you have already met in Chapter 4. It says that the change in real GDP is $1/(1 - b)$ times the change in investment. Clearly, since b is a fraction, $1 - b$ is also a fraction, and $1/(1 - b)$ is a number bigger than one, a multiple giving rise to the name "multiplier."

Shifts in the *IS* curve

The *IS* curve shifts if government purchases, taxes, or any other component of autonomous expenditure changes. This implies that the *IS* curve will shift as a result of a change in any component of aggregate expenditure that is not itself induced by a change in either real GDP or the interest rate. We'll focus on changes in government purchases here.

Figure 5.7 illustrates the analysis. The pale blue curves reproduce the curves already used in Figures 5.5 and 5.6. Now suppose that government purchases increase by the amount Δg. Since planned injections increase by Δg, the curve labeled $i + g$ in Figure 5.7(a) shifts to the right by an amount equal to the increase in government purchases. The magnitude of this shift is shown by the thin horizontal line labeled Δg. What are the implications of the shift in the $i + g$ curve for the *IS* curve? You can answer this question by using the new $i + g + \Delta g$ curve in part (a) to derive the new *IS* curve. Applying the method that you have learned in Figure 5.5 you will discover that the new *IS* curve is IS_2 in part (d).

What is the effect of the increase in government purchases on the *IS* curve? The *IS* curve shifts to the right, and by more than the increase in government purchases (Δg). By how far does the *IS* curve shift?

The *IS* curve shifts by $1/(1 - b)$ times the change in government purchases. Let's see why. The increase in government purchases increases injections into the circular flow of income and expenditure. For expenditure equilibrium, leakages (Δs) must increase by Δg, as shown in part (b). But for saving to increase, real GDP must increase. Part (c) shows the relationship between the increase in saving and income. Namely,

$$\Delta s = (1 - b)\Delta y. \tag{5.5}$$

But Δs also equals Δg. Therefore

$$(1 - b)\Delta y = \Delta g. \tag{5.6}$$

Dividing both sides of Equation (5.6) by the marginal propensity to save $(1 - b)$ gives

$$\Delta y = \frac{1}{1 - \mathrm{b}}(\Delta g). \tag{5.7}$$

This equation tells us that the increase in real GDP at a given interest rate—the shift in the *IS* curve—induced by an increase in government purchases is equal to the increase in government purchases (Δg) multiplied by $1/(1 - b)$.

You have now discovered that an increase in government purchases shifts the *IS* curve by an amount equal to the increase in government purchases multiplied by the autonomous multiplier. Any change in autonomous expenditure shifts the IS curve, and the amount by which the *IS* curve shifts is determined by the multiplier that we discovered in Chapter 4. An increase in investment resulting from a shift in the investment function or an increase in autonomous consumer expenditure has identical effects to those of an increase in government purchases. A decrease in taxes also shifts the *IS* curve to the right, and by an amount determined by the autonomous tax multiplier. Calling the change in taxes Δt, the shift in the *IS* curve is equal to

$$\Delta y = \frac{-b}{1 - b}\Delta t. \tag{5.8}$$

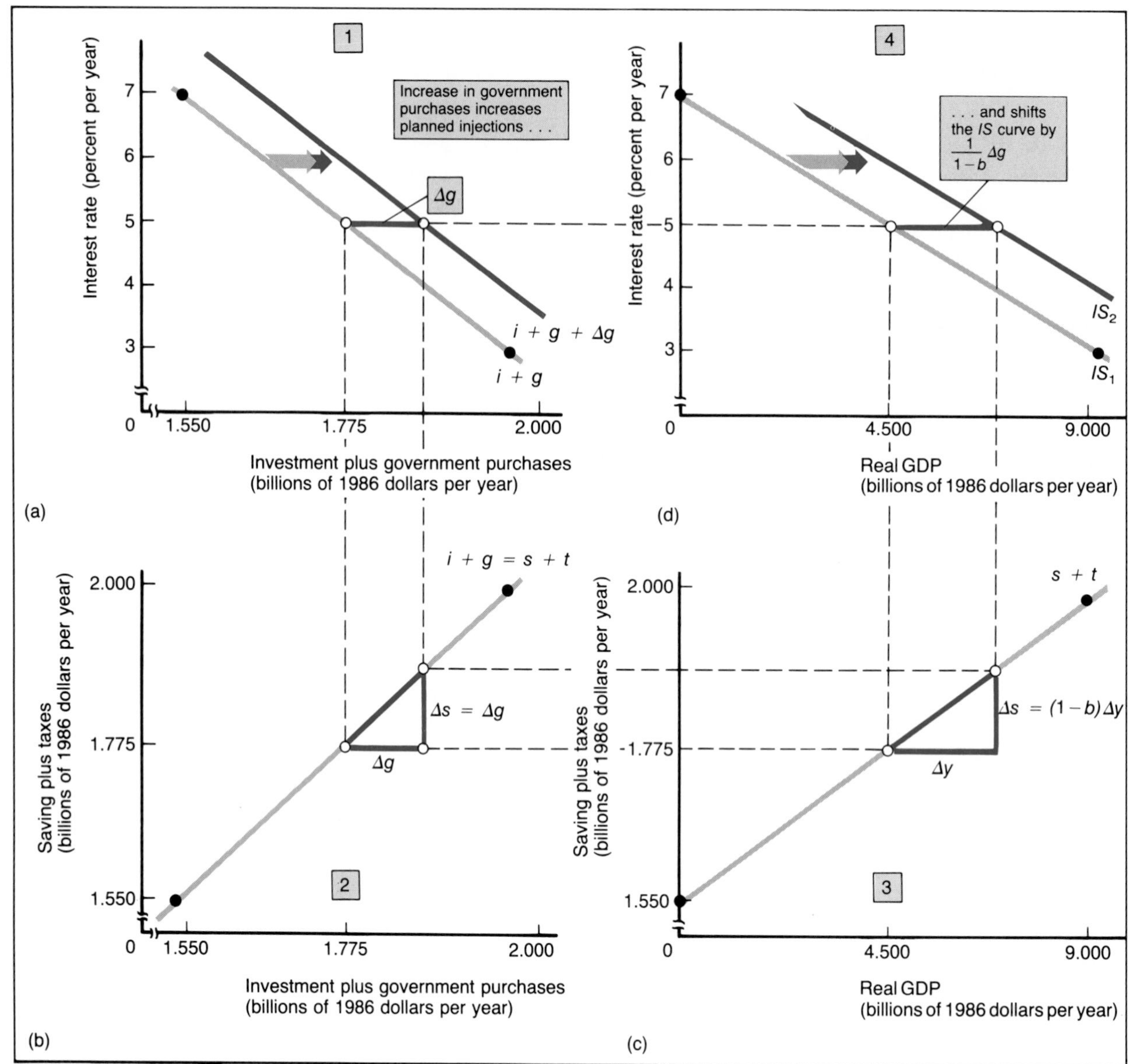

FIGURE 5.7
A Change in Government Purchases Shifts the *IS* Curve

A rise in government purchases of Δg shifts the $i + g$ curve to the right by the amount Δg (part a). That is, at a constant interest rate, planned injections increase. To restore the expenditure equilibrium, planned leakages (Δs) must rise (part b). But planned leakages increase only if real GDP (Δy) rises (part c). As a result the *IS* curve shifts to the right and by an amount equal to $[1/(1 - b)]\Delta g$.

5.7 *Canadian Money Supply and Interest Rates in the 1970s and 1980s*

MACROFACTS

Some key facts about money and interest rates in Canada during the 1970s and 1980s are shown in Figure 5.8. Part (a) shows the growth rate of the money supply. The particular money aggregate shown here is M2. The **M2** measure of money includes currency in circulation, demand deposits, personal savings deposits, and nonpersonal notice deposits.[3]

Interest rates are shown in part (b). Here, the short-term rate is that on 3-month treasury bills, and the long-term interest rate is that on government bonds over 10 years.

Four separate episodes are especially interesting:

- 1970-1980
- 1981-1984
- 1985-1987
- 1988-1990

1970-1980

During the 1970s two major oil price shocks hit the economy, one in 1974 and the other in 1979-1980. Each of these shocks took inflation to new heights. And each was accommodated by a strong burst of money supply growth. You can see these bursts in Figure 5.8(a). Through this same period, the Bank of Canada was keeping interest rates as steady as it could but, as shown in Figure 5.8(b), they could not prevent rates from steadily rising. The rising interest rates were a direct consequence of rising inflation. As money lost value more quickly, capital markets compensated lenders and charged borrowers with higher interest rates.

1981-1984

At the start of the 1980s, Canada was experiencing a serious burst of inflation triggered by large increases in world oil prices and accommodated by the Bank of Canada's previous policy of permitting rapid money supply growth. In 1980-1981, the Bank of Canada decided to apply a severe dose of monetary discipline: the money supply growth rate was not permitted to keep up with rapidly rising prices. As a result, interest rates increased sharply in 1981. For the next three years, money supply growth was lowered and interest rates were permitted to decline only slowly. By the mid-1980s, the double-digit inflation of 1980 was well and truly beaten.

1985-1987

Through these two years, interest rates were lowered and the money supply growth rate was increased to keep the economy expanding. But inflation started to increase again and the Bank of Canada started to pay more attention to the fear of inflation than to the fear of recession.

1988-1990

In 1988, the Bank of Canada started to worry more about rekindling inflation than keeping the recovery alive and tightened its monetary policy, raising interest rates and slowing money supply growth. By 1990, the Bank's zero inflation strategy was beginning to take shape. The money supply growth rate was lowered and interest rates increased yet again. By this time many people believed that the Bank of Canada had tightened its grip too far, pushing the economy over the edge into recession.

---

[3]The M2 definition of money is described more fully in Chapter 15.

FIGURE 5.8
Money Supply Growth and Interest Rates

During the 1970s, the M2 money supply growth rate (shown in part a) was high and fluctuated to accommodate large oil price increases. Inflation increased and so did interest rates (shown in part b). Between 1981 and 1984 money supply growth decreased and, at first, interest rates increased sharply. As inflation fell, so did interest rates. In the second half of the 1980s, money supply growth increased to keep the economy growing quickly and again interest rates moved upward as inflation began to increase again. By 1990, monetary policy was tightened and M2 money supply growth rate was held steady at between 9 and 10 percent in 1991 (part a). But rapid inflation increased the demand for money and pushed interest rates up (part b). Fluctuations in short-term and long-term interest rates have moved in sympathy with each other but short rates have fluctuated more than long rates.

Source: Bank of Canada Review, June 1983 and June 1991.

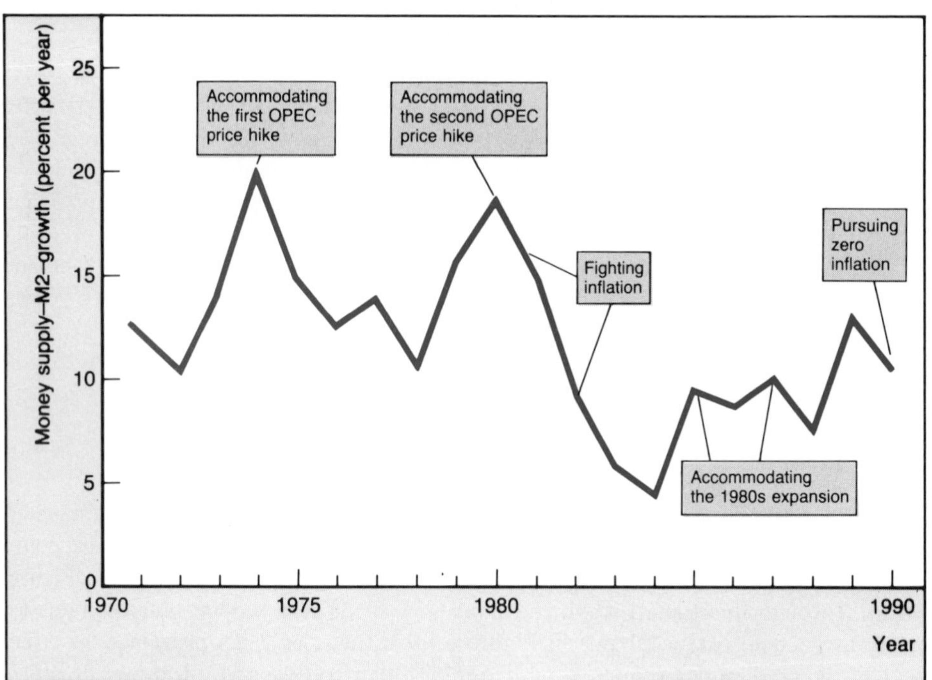

(a) Money supply growth rate

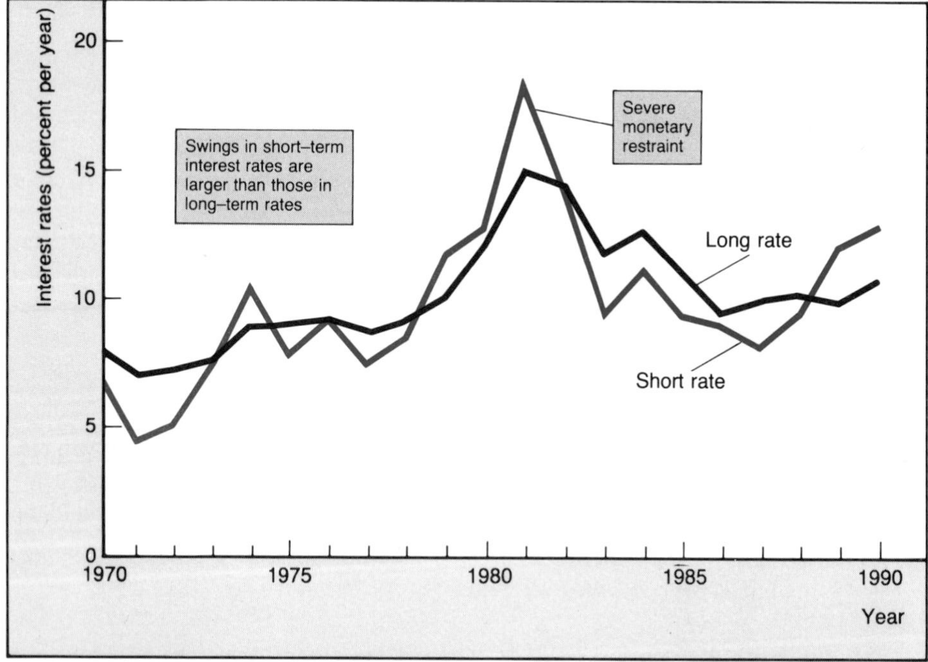

(b) Interest rates

We've seen how interest rates have fluctuated and also seen that fluctuations in interest rates influence investment. We're now going to discover how fluctuations in interest rates are themselves determined and how they are influenced by fluctuations in the money supply growth rate. The first step in this process is a study of the influences on the demand for and the supply of money.

5.8 *The Demand for Money*

The **quantity of money demanded** is the amount of money that people plan to hold on a given day in given circumstances. For a given individual, this amount will be highest on payday and lowest just before the next payday. But the fluctuations in individuals' money holding from one day to the next disappear in the aggregate. Your money holding is high just after you've been paid and low just before the next payday, but your employer's money holding is low just after she's paid you and high before the next payday.

What determines the amount of money that people plan to hold?

Determinants of planned money holding

The quantity of money demanded depends on three things:

- The price level
- Real income
- The interest rate

The price level The value of money depends on the level of prices. Imagine two economies that are identical in every way except that in one, prices and all incomes are twice as high as in the other. In the high-price, high-income economy, people will plan to hold twice as much money as in the other. **Real money** is the quantity of money divided by the price level. The amount of real money held in the two economies will be the same. The quantity of money demanded is proportional to the price level. The quantity of real money demanded is independent of the price level and depends on the two other influences on planned money holdings—real income and the interest rate.

Real income The higher the level of real income, the larger is the quantity of money demanded. To see why, compare the planned money holding of a student who earns $200 a week delivering pizza with a new economics graduate who earns $20,000 a year working as a junior executive. The student's average money holding will be much lower than the junior executive's. People simply find it convenient to hold a larger amount of money, on the average, the larger their income and expenditure.

The interest rate The higher the rate of interest, the smaller is the quantity of money people plan to hold. The reason is that the interest rate is the *opportunity cost* of holding money. If you have a wallet stuffed with cash, you're making no interest on it. If you buy some savings bonds, you earn interest. The higher the interest rate on savings bonds, the more you lose by holding cash in your pocket. It's true that if you put money into an interest-bearing account at the bank, you will also make interest on that part of your money holding. But the higher the interest rate on savings bonds, treasury bills and bonds, and other ways of holding your wealth, other things equal, the greater the opportunity cost of holding money even if it's earning interest at the bank.

The demand for money function

The **demand for money function** is the relationship between the quantity of real money demanded and the factors on which it depends, real income and the interest rate. The **demand curve for real money** shows the quantity of real money demanded at a given real income as the interest rate varies. Such a demand curve is shown in Figure 5.9(a). In this figure, when the interest rate is 5 percent, the quantity of real money demanded

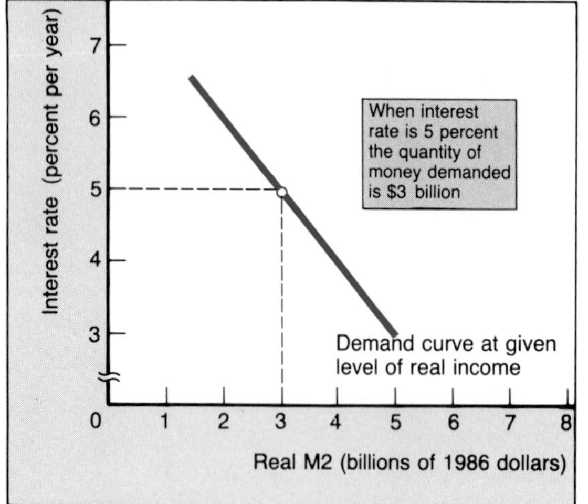

(a) Demand for money curve

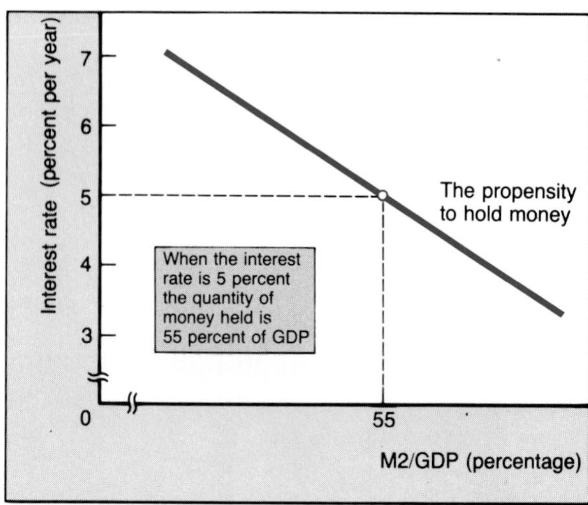

(b) The propensity to hold money

FIGURE 5.9
The Demand for Money Function

The demand for money function is the relationship between the quantity of real money demanded and real income and the interest rate. The demand for money function can be shown either as the demand curve for money (part a) or as the propensity to hold money (part b). The demand curve for money shows the quantity of real money demanded at a given level of real income (real GDP) as the interest rate varies. The propensity to hold money shows the quantity of money held as a percentage of GDP as the interest rate varies.

is $3 billion. The level of real income is held constant along that demand curve. If real income increases, the demand curve shifts to the right; if real income decreases, the demand curve shifts to the left.

The propensity to hold money

An alternative way to graph the relationship between the quantity of real money demanded and the interest rate is to graph the propensity to hold money. The **propensity to hold money** is the ratio of the quantity of real money demanded to real income. Let's call the propensity to hold money k, then

$$k = \frac{M^d}{Py}. \tag{5.9}$$

In this equation, M^d is the quantity of money demanded. The d is there to remind you that it is the quantity *demanded*. P is the price level and y is real income. For the economy as a whole, y is real GDP and Py is nominal GDP. Thus the ratio of real money to real income is the same as the ratio of nominal money to nominal income.

Figure 5.9(b) graphs the demand for money as the propensity to hold money against the interest rate. In this example, when the interest rate is 5 percent, the ratio of money holding to GDP is 55 percent. The higher the interest rate, the smaller is the amount of money held, expressed as a percentage of GDP.

We've now examined the theory of the demand for money. Let's turn again to the facts and study the Canadian demand for money function.

5.9 The Canadian Demand for Money Function

TESTCASE

What does the Canadian demand for money function look like? Is the theoretical formulation of the propensity to hold money shown in Figure 5.9 a good representation of the facts about the propensity to hold money in Canada?

Figure 5.10 contains the answer. In that figure, we have plotted the short-term interest rate on the vertical axis and two measures of k on the horizontal axis. Recall that $k = M^d/Py$, where Py is nominal GDP. The amount of money held, expressed as a proportion of GDP, is the propensity to hold money. This is the variable plotted on the horizontal axis of Figure 5.10. One measure of k (in part a) is based on the M1 definition of money. **M1** is the sum of currency in circulation plus demand deposits. The other measure of k (in part b) is based on the M2 definition of money — M1 plus personal saving deposits and nonpersonal notice deposits. The data shown cover the period between 1970 and 1990, and each point represents a year.

As you can see, there is a large degree of variability in the propensity to hold money in Canada. The propensity to hold M1 (in part a) has ranged between 0.06 (6 percent of GDP) and 0.11 (11 percent of GDP) and the marginal propensity to hold M2 has ranged between 0.28 (28 percent of GDP) and 0.38 (38 percent of GDP).

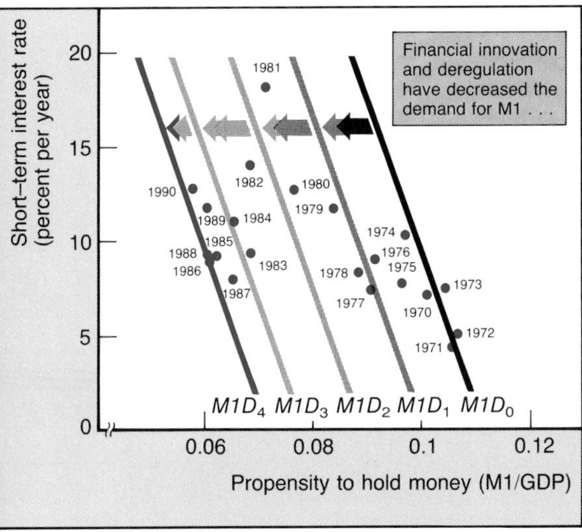

(a) The demand for M1

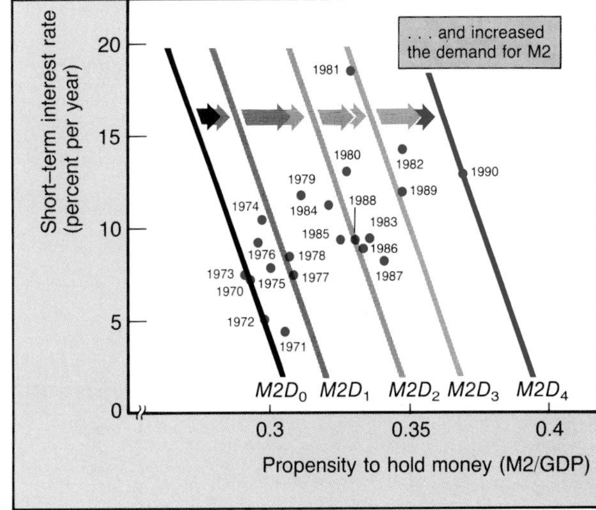

(b) The demand for M2

FIGURE 5.10
Canadian Demand for Money: 1970-1990

Part (a) shows the demand for M1 and part (b) shows the demand for M2, each measured as proportions of GDP. Each point shows the short-term interest rate and the propensity to hold money in a particular year. The years are identified. For example, the point labeled 1981 shows that in 1981 the interest rate was almost 20 percent and the propensity to hold M1 was slightly more than 0.07 and the propensity to hold M2 was about 0.34. The relationship between the short-term interest rate and the propensity to hold money in Canada is similar to the theoretical relationship between these two variables shown in Figure 5.9, provided we allow for the fact that the demand for money shifted during the 1970s and 1980s. The introduction of new types of savings accounts and technological change in the financial sector decreased the demand for M1 in part (a)—decreasing the propensity to hold M1 at each interest rate—and increased the demand for M2 in part (b)—increasing the propensity to hold M2 at each interest rate.

Source: Money supply and interest rate, See Figure 5.8. GDP, *National Income and Expenditure Accounts*, Statistics Canada, catalogue 13-531 for 1970-1986 and catalogue 13-001 for 1987-1990.

It is possible to interpret these data as being generated by demand for money functions of the type that we've seen above, but which have shifted over the years. Let's look at such an interpretation starting with M1 in part (a).

The M1 data can be interpreted as being generated by a demand for money curve that has shifted from $M1D_0$ in the early 1970s to $M1D_4$ in the late 1980s and 1990. Fluctuations in interest rates brought movements along that curve. Changes in other factors that influence the amount of money held shifted the curve. The most important of these other influences were two types of financial innovation. First, new kinds of savings accounts, not included in M1, were introduced. These gave chequing accounts and currency tougher competition as people held less of their money in the form of currency and chequing deposits and more in the form of other types of bank accounts. Second, there were technological changes. One of the most dramatic of these was the spread of the automatic teller machine. With such machines, we can obtain cash at an instant's notice and at any time of the day or night. Our demand for currency, in such a situation, decreases. Since we can use automatic teller machines to access our savings accounts, we do not need to keep chequing account balances to meet our sudden needs for cash. These factors were likely responsible for the important shift in the demand function for M1 during the 1970s and more strongly during the 1980s.

Next let's look at M2 in Figure 5.10(b). The same factors that shifted the demand curve for M1 in part (a) also shifted the demand curve for M2 in part (b). But the M2 demand curve shifted in the opposite direction. The new types of savings accounts that decreased the demand for M1 are part of M2 and, when people switched out of M1 chequing deposits and currency and into other types of bank accounts, they were switching into M2.

Once the factors that change the demand for money are allowed for, it is clear that the theory of the demand for money provides a good rationalization of the facts about the relationship between short-term market interest rates and the propensity to hold money.

5.10 *The* LM *Curve*

The ***LM* curve** is a relationship between the interest rate and real GDP such that the quantity of money demanded equals the quantity supplied.[4] The *LM* curve is like the *IS* curve in that it is an equilibrium locus. Let's derive the *LM* curve.

Deriving the *LM* curve

Figure 5.11 shows the derivation of the *LM* curve. Part (a) shows the money market. The money supply is determined by the actions of the Bank of Canada. It is an exogenous variable and is taken as given at any point in time. In this model, the price level is also an exogenous variable. Thus the real money supply is exogenous. Assuming the real money supply to be \$3 billion, it is shown in the figure as the vertical line labeled "Money supply."

[4]You may be wondering why the *LM* curve is so called. The name was first used by Sir John Hicks who invented the *IS-LM* analysis. The letter *L* stands for "Liquidity Preference," the name that Keynes gave to the demand for money (what we are calling M^d). The letter *M* stands for the supply of money. Thus the label *LM* reminds us that this curve depicts values of the interest rate and income at which the demand for money (*L*) equals the supply of money (*M*).

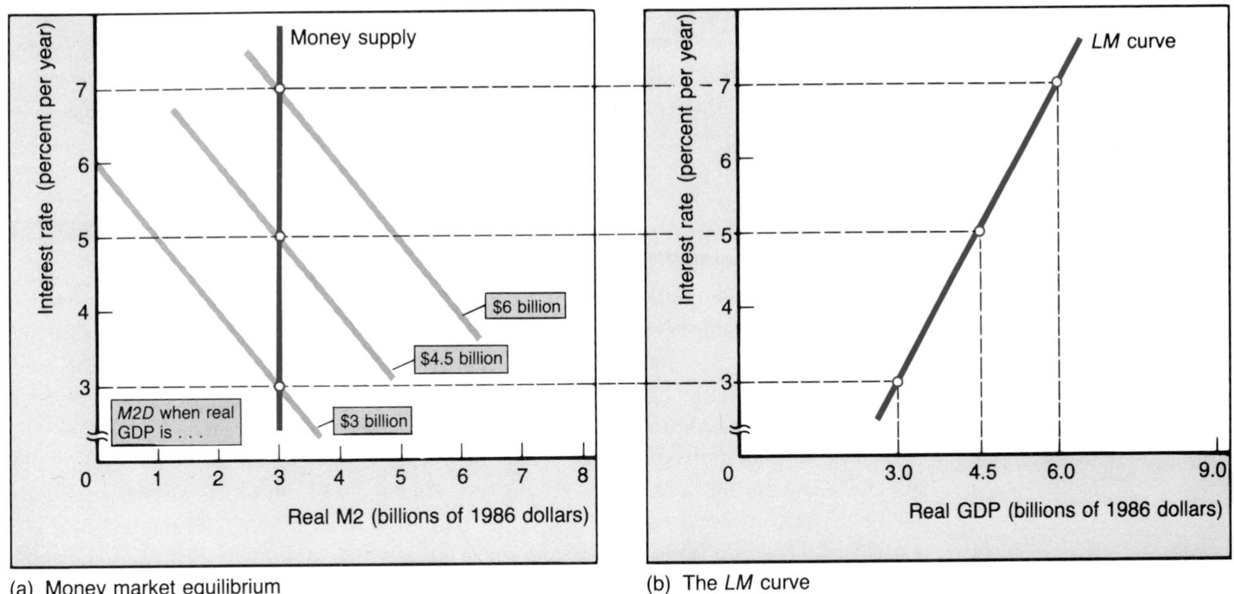

(a) Money market equilibrium

(b) The *LM* curve

FIGURE 5.11
Deriving the *LM* Curve

The *LM* curve traces the relationship between the interest rate and the level of real GDP that makes the quantity of money demanded equal the quantity supplied. The demand curve for money (part a) depends on real GDP. The higher the level of real GDP, the further to the right is the demand curve for money. With a given money supply, the higher the level of real GDP, the higher the equilibrium interest rate. This relationship traces the *LM* curve shown in part (b).

Figure 5.11(a) also shows the demand for money. We'll assume that the demand for money function is *linear*.[5] Its position depends on real GDP: the higher the real GDP, the greater is the demand for money. Thus the higher the real GDP, the farther to the right is the demand for money curve. The figure shows three curves, those for real GDP of $3 billion, $4.5 billion, and $6 billion.

Interest rates adjust to bring the quantity of money demanded into equality with the quantity supplied. If people want to hold more money than is available, they will try to obtain it by selling financial assets. The process of selling financial assets lowers their prices and increases their yields — interest rates. Let's convince ourselves that interest rates do indeed fall when bond prices rise.

Bond prices and interest rates Suppose a bond pays $5 a year in interest in perpetuity and its current market price is $50. The interest rate is 10 percent — $5 divided by $50 expressed as a percent. Now suppose that the bond's price is $25. The interest payment is still $5 a year, but now the interest rate is 20 percent ($5 divided by $25). Further, suppose that the bond's price is $100 instead of $50. In this case, with an interest payment of $5 a year, the interest rate is 5 percent ($5 divided by $100). You see, then, that the interest rate on a bond (the nominal interest rate in the economy) is inversely related to its price.

[5]The functional form of the demand for money that best fits the data is a logarithmic function: the logarithm of the quantity of real money demanded is a linear function of the logarithm of real GDP and the level (not logarithm) of the interest rate.

Continuing now with the story: if people are holding more money than they want, they will attempt to get rid of some of it by buying financial assets. This process increases the price of financial assets and lowers the interest rates. Thus when people want to hold less money than is available, interest rates decrease; when they want to hold more money than is available, interest rates increase. But when interest rates change, so does the quantity of money demanded: as interest rates increase, the quantity of money demanded decreases; and when interest rates decrease, the quantity of money demanded increases.

At any given moment, real GDP determines the demand for real money and, with the given supply of real money, the interest rate is such that the quantity of money demanded equals the quantity supplied.

For a given quantity of real money, the equilibrium interest rate depends on the level of real GDP. You can see this fact clearly in Figure 5.11(a). The higher the level of real GDP, the higher is the interest rate at which the quantity of money demanded equals the quantity supplied.

These combinations of real GDP and the interest rate at which the quantity of money demanded equals the quantity supplied trace out the *LM* curve, as shown in Figure 5.11(b). You can see in part (a) that when real GDP is $3 billion, the interest rate is 3 percent. This is one point on the *LM* curve in part (b). Again, in part (a), when real GDP is $4.5 billion, the interest rate is 5 percent — another point on the *LM* curve. Finally, in part (a), when real GDP is $6 billion, the interest rate is 7 percent — a third point on the *LM* curve.

Shifts in the *LM* curve

Two things shift the *LM* curve:

1. A shift in the demand for money arising from any source other than a change in real GDP or a change in the interest rate
2. A change in the real money supply

An *increase* in the demand for money has the same effect on the *LM* curve as an equal *decrease* in the supply of money. Thus we can analyze the effects of these two influences on the *LM* curve by focusing on just one of them. In the following discussion, we'll talk about the effects of changes in the supply of money. Keep in mind, however, that changes in the opposite direction in the demand for money have the same effects.

Recall that the real money supply is the nominal money supply divided by the price level. Since the position of the *LM* curve depends on the real money supply, anything that changes the real money supply shifts the *LM* curve. But regardless of the source of the change in the real money supply, the effect on the *LM* curve is the same. That is, a 1 percent increase in the nominal money supply with a given price level has the same effect as a 1 percent decrease in the price level with a given nominal money supply. Let's work out how the *LM* curve shifts in response to a change in the real money supply.

Figure 5.12 illustrates the effects on the *LM* curve of an increase in the money supply. The money supply initially is M and increases to $M + \Delta M$, as shown in Figure 5.12(a). For a given real GDP, there is a given demand curve for real money and when the money supply increases, the interest rate decreases. For example, if real GDP is $6 billion, the interest rate is 7 percent when the money supply is M but the interest rate falls to 6 percent when the money supply increases to $M + \Delta M$. Similarly, when real GDP is $4.5 billion, the interest rate is 5 percent if the money supply is M and 4 percent if the money supply is $M + \Delta M$.

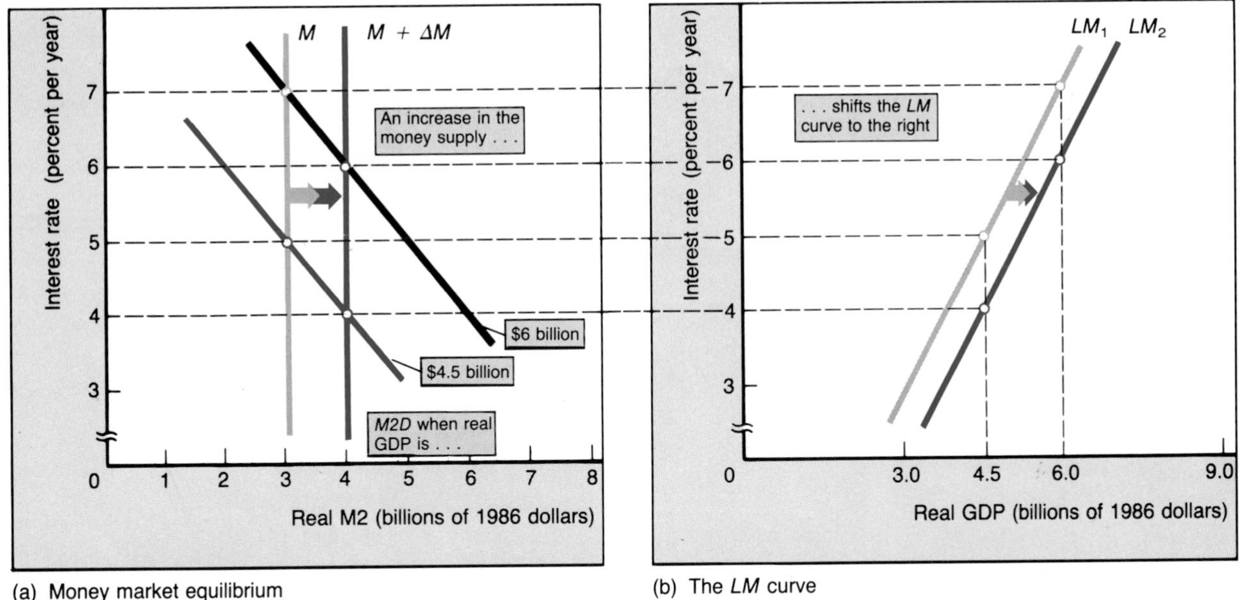

(a) Money market equilibrium

(b) The *LM* curve

FIGURE 5.12
A Change in the Money Supply Shifts the *LM* Curve

A change in the money supply shifts the *LM* curve. An increase in the money supply from *M* to *M* + Δ*M* (part a) shifts the *LM* curve from LM_1 to LM_2 (part b).

An increase in the money supply lowers the interest rate at each real income level, so the *LM* curve moves to the right of the original *LM* curve. That is, the *LM* curve shifts from LM_1 to LM_2 in part (b). Alternatively, a decrease in the money supply raises interest rates and shifts the *LM* curve to the left.

A change in the price level changes the real money supply and shifts the *LM* curve. A decrease in the price level increases the real money supply and shifts the *LM* curve to the right. An increase in the price level decreases the real money supply and shifts the *LM* curve to the left. If both the price level and the money supply increase by the same percentage, the real money supply is constant and the *LM* curve does not move.

5.11 IS-LM *Equilibrium*

We've now discovered two relationships between the interest rate and real GDP. Along the *IS* curve, planned leakages equal planned injections. Along the *LM* curve, the quantity of money demanded equals the quantity of money supplied. These are two equilibrium conditions. When they are both satisfied, people are spending what they plan to spend and are holding the amount of money that they plan to hold. Such an equilibrium occurs where the *IS* and *LM* curves intersect, as shown in Figure 5.13. Here, when the interest rate is 5 percent and real GDP is $4.5 billion, planned leakages equal planned injections and the quantity of money demanded equals the quantity supplied. But what are the forces that bring about such an equilibrium?

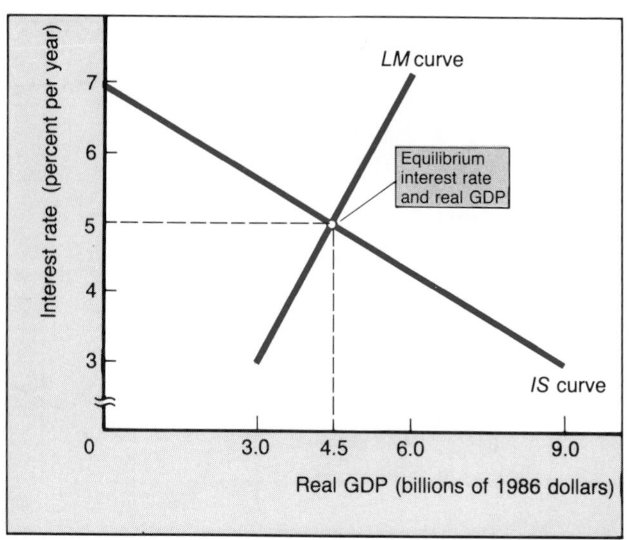

FIGURE 5.13
***IS-LM* Equilibrium**

When planned injections equal planned leakages, the economy is on its *IS* curve and when the quantity of money demanded equals the quantity of money supplied, the economy is on its *LM* curve. When the economy is on both of these curves, it is in *IS-LM* equilibrium. Such an equilibrium is shown at a level of real GDP of $4.5 billion with an interest rate of 5 percent.

Convergence to equilibrium

To study how the economy converges to equilibrium, we have to work out what is happening away from equilibrium. That is, we have to examine the forces that operate when the economy is "off" both the *IS* and *LM* curves. Let's begin with the *IS* curve.

Off the *IS* curve, real GDP adjusts Suppose the economy is off the *IS* curve. Figure 5.14(a) illustrates the following discussion. If the economy was to the right of the *IS* curve, investment plus government purchases would be less than saving plus taxes. That is, you could view the interest rate as being too high, thereby depressing investment to too low a level; or income is too high, raising saving to too high a level. Either way, saving plus taxes would exceed investment plus government purchases. If the economy was to the left of the *IS* curve, the reverse inequality would hold. The interest rate is too low, stimulating too much investment, or income is too low, generating too little saving. Either way, investment plus government spending exceeds saving plus taxes.

Suppose the economy is in this second situation, with too much investment plus government purchases relative to the amount of saving plus taxes. What happens to real GDP? The answer is, it rises because aggregate planned expenditure exceeds real GDP. To see this, recall that consumer expenditure equals GDP minus saving minus taxes. This means that if saving plus taxes is less than investment plus government purchases, the sum of consumer expenditure, investment, and government purchases is larger than GDP. Inventories start to fall, so firms step up the production rate to replenish those inventories. The multiplier process is under way. The process comes to an end only when aggregate planned expenditure equals real GDP. But this happens when the economy reaches a point on its *IS* curve.

Consider the reverse situation. Suppose the economy is to the right of the *IS* curve, with saving plus taxes bigger than investment plus government purchases. In this case, aggregate planned expenditure is less than GDP. Inventories increase, so firms cut back production. Income falls until aggregate planned expenditure and income are equal, again at a point on the *IS* curve.

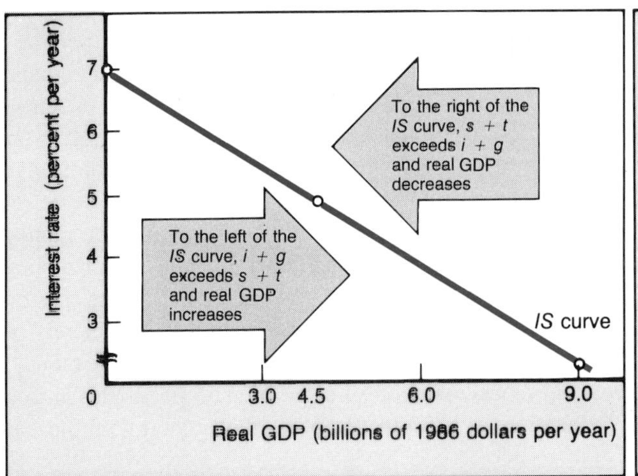

(a) Income adjustments

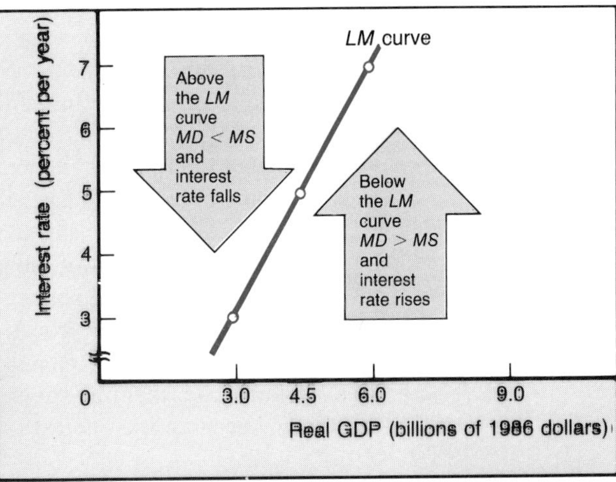

(b) Interest rate adjustments

FIGURE 5.14
Equilibrating Forces

If aggregate planned expenditure does not equal real GDP, the economy is off its *IS* curve (part a). Equivalently, aggregate planned leakages do not equal planned injections. If $i + g$ exceeds $s + t$, real GDP rises, and if $i + g$ is less than $s + t$, real GDP falls. The movement in real GDP takes the economy to a point on its *IS* curve.

If the demand for money is not equal to the supply of money, the economy is "off" its *LM* curve (part b). If *MD* is less than *MS*, the interest rate falls, and if *MD* exceeds *MS*, the interest rate rises. The movement in the interest rate takes the economy to a point on its *LM* curve.

These equilibrating forces operating together move the economy to the point of intersection of the *IS* and *LM* curves as shown in part (c).

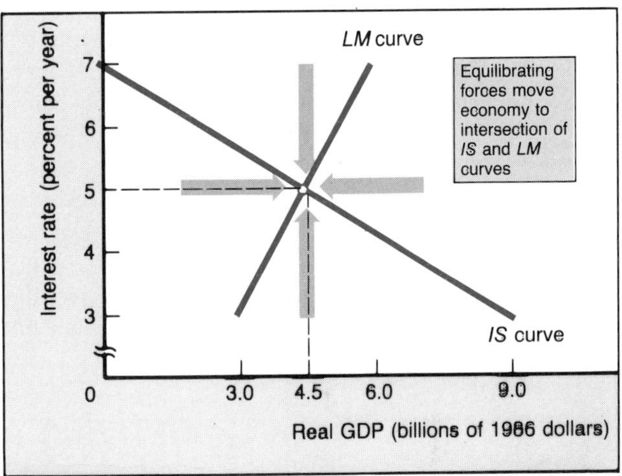

(c) Equilibrium

We've now seen that one part of the equilibrating force is a change in real GDP that brings aggregate planned expenditure into equality with real GDP. Equivalently, it brings planned investment plus government purchases into equality with planned saving plus taxes.

Off the *LM* curve, the interest rate adjusts Next, consider what happens if the economy is off the *LM* curve. These situations are shown in Figure 5.14(b). Below the *LM* curve, the demand for money exceeds the supply of money. The interest rate is too low or real GDP is too high, generating a larger amount of money demanded than the amount available. Above the *LM* curve, the demand for money is less than the supply of money. The interest rate is too high and/or real GDP is too low, making the amount of money demanded fall short of the amount available to be held.

What happens if the economy is in one of these situations? Let's start out above the *LM* curve, where the demand for money is less than the supply of money. People are actually holding more money than they want, so they try to get rid of their excess money holdings by buying bonds and other kinds of financial assets. Each individual can get rid of unwanted excess money holdings by buying bonds, but in the aggregate the economy cannot do so. One person's decreased money holding is another person's increased money holding. Nonetheless, as people try to get rid of money and buy bonds, there is an increase in the demand for bonds. Their price rises and their rate of return decreases. Interest rates fall. This process continues until the interest rate has fallen far enough to eliminate the excess supply of money — that is, until people are holding an amount of money equal to the amount they want to hold.

The same mechanism works in the opposite direction. If the demand for money exceeds the amount of money in existence, individuals will seek to add to their money balances by selling bonds. The price of bonds will then fall, and the interest rate on them will rise. This process will continue until the interest rate has risen sufficiently to make the amount of money in existence enough to satisfy people's demand for money. Either way, then, an excess demand or excess supply in the money market leads to a movement in the interest rate by an amount sufficient to place the economy on the *LM* curve.

Simultaneous adjustment of real GDP and interest rate Now bring these two stories together. If the economy is off the *IS* curve, income adjusts to bring about an equality between saving plus taxes and investment plus government purchases. If the economy is off the *LM* curve, the interest rate adjusts to bring about an equality between the quantity of money demanded and the quantity supplied. These two forces, operating simultaneously, bring changes in both real GDP and the interest rate as shown in Figure 5.14(c). Interest rate adjustments take place rapidly so that the economy is probably almost always on the *LM* curve. The income adjustment process, however, takes longer.

You have now seen how aggregate planned expenditure, real GDP, and the interest rate are determined at a given price level. But what's true at one price level is true at any. Therefore, the relationships we've just worked with determine real GDP at each price level. That is, they enable us to derive the aggregate demand curve.

5.12 *Deriving the Aggregate Demand Curve*

The *aggregate demand curve* is the relationship between aggregate planned expenditure in a given period of time and the price level. Figure 5.15 explains how the aggregate demand curve is derived. Begin in part (a), which shows the *IS-LM* equilibrium and concentrate on the *LM* curve when the price level is 140. The relevant *LM* curve is the one labeled "140." With this *LM* curve, the equilibrium interest rate is 5 percent and equilibrium real GDP is $4.5 billion. Since at the point of intersection of the *IS* and *LM* curves there is an expenditure equilibrium, equilibrium real GDP is equal to aggregate planned expenditure. That is, when the price level is 140, aggregate planned expenditure equals $4.5 billion. We've just found a point on the aggregate demand curve. It is the point labeled *A* in Figure 5.15(b). Let's generate two other points on the aggregate demand curve.

Suppose that the price level is 200. In this case, the real money supply is less than before and the *LM* curve lies to the left of the *LM* curve when the price level is 140. Part (a) shows this *LM* curve — it is labeled "200." With this *LM* curve, the equilibrium interest rate is r_1 and real GDP is $3 billion. Thus when the price level is 200, equilibrium real GDP and aggregate planned expenditure equal $3 billion. This is a second point on the aggregate demand curve of part (b) labeled *B* in the figure.

Next, suppose that the price level is lower than 140, say 80. In this case, the real money supply is higher than when the price level is 140 and the *LM* curve lies farther to

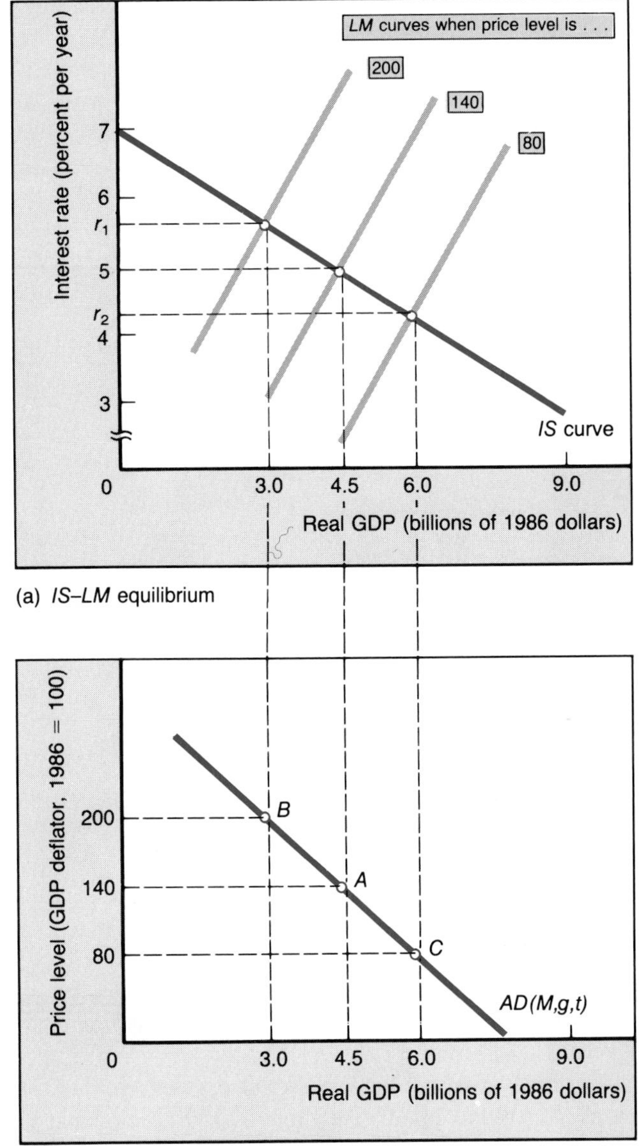

FIGURE 5.15
Deriving the Aggregate Demand Curve

By varying the price level between 80 and 200, the *LM* curve shifts (part a), generating different equilibrium interest rate and real GDP levels. Each equilibrium level of real GDP is the level of aggregate planned expenditure at a given price level. The combinations of the price level and the level of real GDP generate points *A*, *B*, and *C* on the aggregate demand curve in part (b). The position of the aggregate demand curve depends on the money supply (*M*), government purchases (*g*), and taxes (*t*).

the right—it's the one labeled "80." With this *LM* curve, the equilibrium interest rate is r_2 and equilibrium real GDP is \$6 billion. That is, when the price level is 80, equilibrium real GDP and aggregate planned expenditure are \$6 billion. This is a third point on the aggregate demand curve and is labeled *C* in part (b). By joining up the points *B*, *A*, and *C*, we trace out the aggregate demand curve.

In conducting the *IS-LM* analysis, we discovered the factors that shift either the *IS* curve or *LM* curve at a *given* price level. These factors include the money supply, government purchases of goods and services, and taxes. A change in *any* of these factors changes equilibrium real GDP. This analysis tells us how a point on the aggregate demand curve, such as point *A*, travels *horizontally* when influences on aggregate demand such as the money supply, government purchases of goods and services, and taxes change. That is, the *IS-LM* analysis tells us about the factors that cause horizontal shifts in the aggregate demand curve. But anything that shifts point *A* will also shift points *B* and *C* in the same horizontal direction. Thus an increase in government purchase of goods and services or a tax cut or an increase in the money supply will shift the aggregate demand curve to the right. To remind us of this, the aggregate demand curve in Figure 5.15(b) is labeled $AD(M, g, t)$.

■ In this chapter, we've discovered what determines investment and the demand for money and how interest rates and real GDP are determined in an *IS-LM* equilibrium. We've seen how, by varying the price level, we can generate a sequence of different *IS-LM* equilibria and generate the economy's aggregate demand curve.

Our next task, in Chapter 6, is to see how variations in the money supply, government purchases of goods and services, and taxes can be used to manipulate aggregate demand and to influence investment and aggregate expenditure, as well as real GDP and the price level.

CHAPTER REVIEW

Summary

FLUCTUATIONS IN CANADIAN INVESTMENT AND INTEREST RATES IN THE 1970s AND 1980s

There have been large fluctuations in net investment with a steep decline in 1982 and a strong recovery through 1984. Net investment was steady between 1985 and 1990. Replacement investment has grown steadily and not fluctuated much.

Interest rates increased steadily through the 1970s and reached record high levels in 1981. They then gradually declined until 1986 when they started to rise gently. Real interest rates became negative in the mid-1970s but then increased to a peak in 1984, after which they declined steadily.

There is no simple relationship between net investment and interest rates. In the early 1970s net investment increased as real interest rates declined and in the early 1980s net investment declined as real interest rates increased. But in the later 1980s, real interest rates and net investment tended to move in the same direction.

WHAT DETERMINES INVESTMENT?

Investment is determined by the rate of return on capital and the interest rate. Investment projects are undertaken if their rate of return exceeds or is equal to the interest rate. Other things being equal, the higher the rate of return and the lower the interest rate, the larger is the investment rate.

NOMINAL AND REAL INTEREST RATE

The nominal interest rate is the interest rate that is actually paid and received. The real interest rate equals the nominal interest rate minus the inflation rate. It measures the interest *really* paid and received. The real rate of return on an investment project equals the rate of return minus the inflation rate. Investment projects are undertaken if their real rate of return exceeds the real interest rate.

THE INVESTMENT FUNCTION

The investment function is the relationship between the rate of investment and the interest rate. A change in the interest rate produces a movement along the investment function. A change in the expected rate of return on capital shifts the investment function.

CANADIAN INVESTMENT FUNCTION

The Canadian investment function shifts because of changes in the expected rate of return on capital. During the early 1970s, the economy moved along its investment function as net investment increased in response to falling interest rates. In 1975, the investment function shifted to the right as the economy recovered from the OPEC oil shock. In 1982, as the economy went into recession, the investment function shifted to the left. After 1984, the investment function shifted to the right as the economy recovered, but by 1990 it shifted again to the left as the economy went into recession.

THE *IS* CURVE

The *IS* curve is the relationship between the interest rate and real GDP such that aggregate planned expenditure equals real GDP. Equivalently, the *IS* curve is the relationship between the interest rate and real GDP such that planned injections equal planned leakages. The lower the interest rate, the higher is planned investment and, hence, planned injections. The higher the level of real GDP, the higher is planned saving and, hence, planned leakages. Since planned injections increase as the interest rate falls and planned leakages increase as real GDP rises, the *IS* curve slopes downward; a decrease in the interest rate requires an increase in real GDP to maintain equality between planned injections and planned leakages.

CANADIAN MONEY SUPPLY AND INTEREST RATES IN THE 1970s AND 1980s

In the 1970s Canadian monetary policy accommodated two massive waves of inflation initiated by world oil price increases. Interest rates steadily increased. In 1981 the Bank of Canada embarked on a tough anti-inflation program tightening the money supply and increasing interest rates sharply. By the mid-1980s this policy had reduced inflation substantially. In 1985-1987 the money supply growth rate was increased to keep the recovery going but inflation and interest rates began to edge upward. Starting in 1988 the Bank of Canada began to pay more attention to inflation and tightened its policy again. The money supply growth rate was cut back and interest rates increased.

THE DEMAND FOR MONEY

The quantity of money demanded is the amount of money that people plan to hold on a given day and in given circumstances. There are three main influences on this quantity: the price level, real income, and the interest rate. The amount of money that people plan to hold is proportional to the price level. The real quantity of money is the ratio of the quantity of money to the price level. The amount of real money that people plan to hold depends on real income and the interest rate. Other things being equal, the higher the level of income, the greater is the quantity of money demanded; and the higher the interest rate, the smaller is the quantity of money demanded. The demand for money function describes this relationship between the amount of real money that people plan to hold and real income and the interest rate.

CANADIAN DEMAND FOR MONEY FUNCTION IN THE 1970s AND 1980s

Throughout the 1970s and 1980s, the introduction of new types of bank deposits steadily shifted the Canadian money function. The demand for M1 has steadily decreased and the demand for M2 has steadily increased. Once these shifts are taken into account, there is a clear, systematic inverse relationship between the amount of real money held, measured as a percentage of GDP, and the interest rate.

THE *LM* CURVE

The *LM* curve is the relationship between the interest rate and real GDP along which the quantity of money demanded equals the quantity supplied. With a given money supply determined by the actions of the Bank of Canada and a given price level, there is a given amount of real money in the economy. The higher the level of real GDP, the greater is the amount of real money demanded. To keep the quantity demanded equal to the quantity supplied, a higher level of real GDP requires a higher interest rate. Thus the *LM* curve slopes upward.

EQUILIBRIUM INTEREST RATE AND REAL GDP

The point of intersection of the *IS* and *LM* curves determines the equilibrium interest rate and real GDP. To the right of the *IS* curve, real GDP exceeds aggregate planned expenditure or, equivalently, planned leakages exceed planned injections. If the economy is to the right of the *IS* curve, inventories decline and real GDP falls. To the left of the *IS* curve, aggregate planned expenditure exceeds real GDP or, equivalently, planned injections exceed planned leakages. If the economy is to the left of the *IS* curve, inventories decline and production increases, so real GDP rises. Below the *LM* curve, the quantity of money demanded exceeds the quantity supplied. If the economy is below the *LM* curve, people try to increase their money holdings but in doing so interest rates will increase. Above the *LM* curve, the quantity of money is less than the quantity supplied. If the economy is above the *LM* curve, people attempt to decrease their money holdings but in doing so interest rates will fall. The equilibrating forces on real GDP and the interest rate move the economy to the *IS-LM* equilibrium—the point of intersection of the *IS* and *LM* curves.

AGGREGATE DEMAND CURVE

The aggregate demand curve traces the relationship between aggregate planned expenditure and the price level. In equilibrium, aggregate planned expenditure equals real GDP. The aggregate demand curve can be derived from the *IS-LM* equilibrium. At each price level, there is a different *LM* curve and, therefore, a different equilibrium real GDP and aggregate planned expenditure. By varying the price level and shifting the *LM* curve, we can generate a sequence of points on an aggregate demand curve. The position of the aggregate demand curve depends on the money supply (which determines the position of the *LM* curve) and on government purchases of goods and services and taxes (which determine the position of the *IS* curve).

Key Terms and Concepts

Demand curve for real money A curve that shows the quantity of real money demanded at a given real income as the interest rate varies.

Demand for money function The relationship between the quantity of real money demanded and the two factors on which it depends, real income and the interest rate.

Investment demand The planned rate of purchase of new capital—the planned rate of investment.

Investment function The relationship between investment and the interest rate, holding all other influences on investment constant.

***IS* curve** The relationship between real GDP and the interest rate such that aggregate planned expenditure equals real GDP.

***LM* curve** The relationship between the interest rate and real GDP such that the quantity of money demanded equals the quantity supplied.

M2 A measure of money including currency, demand deposits, other chequable deposits, and savings deposits.

Nominal interest rate The interest rate actually paid and received.

Propensity to hold money The ratio of the quantity of real money demanded to real income.

Quantity of money demanded The amount of money that people plan to hold on a given day in given circumstances.

Rate of return The net income received from using a piece of capital equipment expressed as a percentage of the equipment's price.

Real interest rate The nominal interest rate minus the inflation rate.

Real money The quantity of money divided by the price level.

Real rate of return on capital The rate of return on capital minus the inflation rate.

Review Questions

1. Explain the distinction between investment and the capital stock.
2. What determines the rate of investment?
3. What is an investment function? What is exogenous, and what varies as we move along the investment function?
4. Explain why the investment function slopes downward.
5. What causes the investment function to shift?
6. What is an *IS* curve?
7. Explain why an *IS* curve is an equilibrium locus.
8. Why does the *IS* curve slope downward?
9. What happens to the *IS* curve if government purchases of goods and services increase by $1 million?
10. What happens to the *IS* curve if government transfers to individuals in the form of pensions and unemployment benefits increase by $1 million?
11. What happens to the *IS* curve if the government cuts pensions by $1 million and raises defense spending by $1 million?
12. What is the *LM* curve?
13. Which markets are in equilibrium along the *LM* curve?
14. Why does the *LM* curve slope upward?
15. What happens to the *LM* curve if the money supply rises?
16. What happens to the *LM* curve if the price level rises?
17. What happens to the *LM* curve if the money supply and the price level both increase by the same percentage?
18. What markets are in equilibrium at the intersection of the *IS* and *LM* curves?
19. How do equilibrium real GDP and the interest rate change in response to
    (a) an increase in the money supply?
    (b) an increase in government purchases?
    (c) an increase in taxes?
    (d) an increase in the government budget deficit?
20. Explain how to derive the aggregate demand curve.
21. What factors shift the aggregate demand curve? Draw a diagram showing how each of these factors shifts the aggregate demand curve.

Problems

1. A car that you are thinking of buying costs $6,000 and will, after one year, have a resale value of $5,000. The rate of interest on the bank loan that you would take if you did buy the car is 15 percent. A friend who already owns an identical car offers to lease you that car for one year for $1,800 (you buy the gas and pay for maintenance). Will you accept the offer from your friend or will you buy the car?
2. You are given the following information about an economy:
   $c = 100 + 0.8(y - t)$
   $i = 500 - 50r$
   $g = 400$
   $t = 400$
   (c = consumption; i = investment; g = government purchases of goods and services; t = taxes; r = interest rate)
   (a) What is the equation for the *IS* curve?
   (b) At a 5 percent interest rate, what is equilibrium aggregate expenditure?
   (c) If the interest rate falls from 5 percent to 4 percent, what is the change in investment and the change in equilibrium aggregate expenditure?
   (d) In question (c), compare the changes in investment and equilibrium aggregate expenditure.
   (e) Compare the slopes of the *IS* curve and the investment function.
   (f) Calculate the shift of the *IS* curve resulting from an increase in government purchases of goods and services of 100.
   (g) Show that an increase in taxes shifts the *IS* curve to the left by four times the tax increase.
   (h) How far does the *IS* curve shift if government purchases and taxes both increase by 100?
3. The *LM* curve of an economy is given by
   $y = 3000 + 50r$
   (a) Draw a graph of the *LM* curve.
   (b) Calculate the slope of the *LM* curve.
   (c) If real income is 3250, what is the interest rate?
   (d) If the interest rate falls from 5 percent to 4 percent, what is the change in the quantity of money demanded as the economy moves along the *LM* curve?
   (e) Explain the shift of the *LM* curve resulting from an increase in the money supply.
   (f) Explain the shift of the *LM* curve resulting from an increase in the price level.
   (g) Explain the shift of the *LM* curve resulting from an equal percentage increase in the money supply and the price level.
4. An economy has the following *IS* and *LM* curves when the price level is 100:
   $y = 2800 - 100r$
   $y = 2000 + 50r$
   (a) What is equilibrium real GDP?
   (b) What is the equilibrium interest rate?
   (c) What is one point on the aggregate demand curve?

APPENDIX

The Algebra of the IS-LM Model

This appendix takes you through the algebra of the determination of the equilibrium levels of real GDP and the rate of interest in a closed economy when the price level is fixed at P_0.

IS CURVE

The *IS curve* shows the relationship between real GDP and the interest rate such that aggregate planned expenditure equals real GDP. Aggregate planned expenditure, e_p, is the sum of consumer expenditure, investment, and government purchases of goods and services. That is,

$$e_p = c + i + g \tag{5A.1}$$

Consumer expenditure is determined by the consumption function, which is

$$c = a + b(y - t), \qquad a > 0, 0 < b < 1 \tag{5A.2}$$

Investment is determined by the investment function, which is

$$i = i_0 - hr, \qquad i_0, h > 0 \tag{5A.3}$$

Expenditure equilibrium prevails when aggregate planned expenditure equals real GDP. That is,

$$e_p = y \tag{5A.4}$$

The above four equations taken together constitute the equation for the *IS* curve. That equation may be derived by using Equations (5A.1), (5A.2), (5A.3), and (5A.4) to give

$$y = a + b(y - t) + i_0 - hr + g \tag{5A.5}$$

This may be rearranged or "solved" for real GDP as

$$y = \frac{1}{1 - b}(a + i_0 + g - bt - hr) \tag{5A.6}$$

Equation (5A.6) is the equation for the *IS* curve. It tells us the level of real GDP at each interest rate that makes aggregate planned expenditure equal to real GDP, given government purchases, g, and taxes, t. A 1 percentage point increase in the interest rate lowers the level of real GDP at the expenditure equilibrium by $\$h/(1 - b)$. That is,

$$\text{Slope of the } IS \text{ curve} = \frac{1 - b}{h} \tag{5A.7}$$

The slope of the *IS* curve is equal to the inverse of the coefficient on the interest rate, r, in Equation (5A.6).

The position of the *IS* curve depends on government purchases and taxes. An increase in government purchases of \$1 billion at a given interest rate increases the real GDP at which equilibrium expenditure occurs by $\$1/(1 - b)$ billion. That is, an increase in government purchases shifts the *IS* curve to the right by $1/(1 - b)$ times the increase in government purchases. Notice that $1/(1 - b)$ is the coefficient on g in Equation (5A.6). Similarly, an increase in taxes shifts the *IS* curve to the right by $-b/(1 - b)$ times the increase in taxes. Again, notice that $-b/(1 - b)$ is the coefficient on t in Equation (5A.6).

LM CURVE

The *LM curve* is a relationship between the interest rate and real GDP such that the quantity of money demanded equals the quantity supplied. The demand for money function, M^d, is given by

$$\frac{M^d}{P_0} = m_0 + ky - \ell r, \qquad k > 0, \ell > 0 \tag{5A.8}$$

Equilibrium occurs at the intersection point of the demand for money and the supply of money. That is,

$$M^d = M \tag{5A.9}$$

Substituting Equation (5A.8) into Equation (5A.9) yields and solving for real GDP gives

$$y = \frac{1}{k}\left[\frac{M}{P_0} - m_0 + \ell\, r\right] \tag{5A.10}$$

This is the equation for the *LM* curve. It tells us the level of real GDP at each interest rate that makes the quantity of money demanded equal to the quantity supplied, given the money supply and the price level. A 1 percentage point increase in the interest rate increases the level of real GDP at which money market equilibrium occurs by $\$\ell/k$. That is,

$$\text{Slope of the } LM \text{ curve} = \frac{\ell}{k} \tag{5A.11}$$

The slope of the *LM* curve, k/ℓ, is equal to the inverse of the coefficient on the interest rate, r, in Equation (5A.10).

The position of the *LM* curve depends on the real money supply, M/P_0. An increase in real money supply of \$1 billion at a given interest rate, increases the real GDP at which money market equilibrium occurs by $\$1/k$ billion. That is, an increase in the real money supply shifts the *LM* curve to the right by $1/k$ times the increase in the real money supply. Notice that $1/k$ is the coefficient on M/P_0 in Equation (5A.6). An increase in the real money supply can occur because the money supply, M, is increased or the price level, P, decreases.

IS-LM EQUILIBRIUM

Equations (5A.6) and (5A.10), the equations for the *IS* and *LM* curves, contain two unknowns—real GDP and the interest rate. Setting the real GDP in Equation (5A.6) equal to the real GDP in Equation (5A.10) and solving for the interest rate gives

$$r = \frac{1}{1 - b + kh/\ell}\left[\frac{k}{\ell}(a + i_0 + g - bt) - \frac{1-b}{\ell}\left(\frac{M}{P_0} - m_0\right)\right] \tag{5A.12}$$

Equation (5A.12) is an algebraic expression for the equilibrium value of the interest rate in the *IS-LM* analysis. By substituting Equation (5A.12) back into Equation (5A.10) to eliminate the interest rate, you obtain an expression for real GDP:

$$y = \frac{1}{1 - b + kh/\ell}\left[(a + i_0 + g - bt) + \frac{h}{\ell}\left(\frac{M}{P_0} - m_0\right)\right] \tag{5A.13}$$

Equation (5A.13) is the solution of the *IS-LM* analysis for equilibrium real GDP.

AGGREGATE DEMAND CURVE

The *aggregate demand curve* is the relationship between real GDP demanded in a given period of time and the price level. The *IS-LM* equilibrium determines the level of real GDP at a given price level. At the price level P_0, real GDP is given by Equation (5A.13). Namely,

$$y = \frac{1}{1 - b + kh/\ell}\left[(a + i_0 + g - bt) + \frac{h}{\ell}\left(\frac{M}{P_0} - m_0\right)\right] \qquad \textbf{(5A.13)}$$

To find the equation to the aggregate demand curve allow the price level to vary and work out the relationship between the price level and real GDP. In Equation (5A.13) replace the fixed price level P_0 with the variable price level P. Then the relationship between real GDP demanded and the price level is

$$y = \frac{1}{1 - b + kh/\ell}\left[(a + i_0 + g - bt) + \frac{h}{\ell}\left(\frac{M}{P} - m_0\right)\right] \qquad \textbf{(5A.14)}$$

Because we usually plot the price level on the vertical axis, we can rearrange this equation as follows:

$$P = \frac{(h/\ell)M}{(1 - b + kh/\ell) - (a + i_0 + g - bt) + m_0} \qquad \textbf{(5A.15)}$$

CHAPTER

Monetary and Fiscal Policy Influences on Aggregate Demand

MANIPULATING AGGREGATE DEMAND

KEEPING AGGREGATE DEMAND GROWING at a steady pace is a major goal of macroeconomic policy. If aggregate demand grows faster than trend real GDP, we get inflation. If it grows more slowly, we get unemployment and recession. Since almost everyone agrees that these outcomes are undesirable, people generally conclude that keeping aggregate demand growing at a steady pace close to the growth rate of trend real GDP is a desirable objective. But macroeconomists and policymakers disagree on exactly how best to achieve this goal. Everyone *does* agree, however, on one other matter: namely, the need to understand the ways that available policy instruments influence aggregate demand.

The *IS-LM* model of aggregate demand you studied in Chapter 5 provides a useful foundation for that understanding. Equilibrium in the *IS-LM* model determines the interest rate and real GDP as well as the components of aggregate expenditure at a given price level. By varying the price level, at each price level the new *IS-LM* equilibrium generates an aggregate demand curve. That aggregate demand curve, interacting with the short-run aggregate supply curve (of Chapter 3), determines real GDP and the price level. The position of the aggregate demand curve depends on the settings of the instruments of monetary and fiscal policy—the money supply, government purchases of goods and services, and taxes.

By manipulating the levels of these policy instruments, the Bank of Canada and the government are able to manipulate aggregate demand and modify the course of real GDP and the price level. For example, in the early 1980s, the Bank of Canada stepped on the monetary brake, keeping money supply growth in check and increasing interest rates. The result was a decrease in real GDP and a slowdown in inflation—a lower price level than otherwise would have occurred. Later in the 1980s, tax cuts stimulated investment and consumer expenditure, increasing real GDP.

Working out how policies such as these influence aggregate demand and, in turn, affect real GDP and the price level is the major goal of this chapter. After studying this chapter, you will be able to

- Describe the fluctuations in money supply growth, government purchases, and taxes in Canada in recent years
- Explain how a change in the money supply influences interest rates, real GDP, and the price level
- Describe how monetary policy has been used to slow down the Canadian economy

- Explain how changes in government purchases influence interest rates, real GDP, and the price level
- Explain how changes in taxes influence interest rates, real GDP, and the price level

Let's begin by looking at how the instruments of monetary and fiscal policy have behaved in Canada.

6.1 *Fluctuations in Money, Government Purchases, and Taxes*

MACROFACTS

Both monetary and fiscal policy exert important influences on our economic fortunes. But it is monetary policy that has fluctuated most in our history. Let's begin by looking at some of the main patterns in monetary policy in the period between 1960 and 1990.

Monetary policy

During the 1960s, the world operated on a **gold exchange standard**, a monetary arrangement in which each country kept its monetary policy in close harmony with the policies of other countries in a system of fixed exchange rates. At first, Canada did not play by the rules of this fixed exchange rate game and the Canadian dollar fluctuated in value against other currencies. But in April 1962 the value of the Canadian dollar was fixed at 92.5 U.S. cents, a value it maintained until May 1970. The value of the U.S. dollar was also fixed, but in terms of gold. Thirty-five U.S. dollars bought one fine ounce of gold. Thus the Canadian dollar was also fixed in terms of gold. During this period, the growth rate of our money supply fluctuated around a low average value.

In 1971, the world monetary order that had prevailed since World War II collapsed. Countries allowed the values of their currencies to fluctuate against each other, and the United States abandoned its commitment to maintain the value of the U.S. dollar in terms of gold. The international gold exchange ended. The main reason the international gold exchange standard ended was that 20 years of creeping inflation had gradually made 35 U.S. dollars an ounce an unrealistic price for gold. Gold was trading in the free market at a much higher price. And the main reason fixed exchange rates were abandoned was that differences in inflation rates among the major countries had made the previously agreed exchange rates unrealistic.[1]

During the 1970s, money supply growth rates fluctuated dramatically, climbing to double digits and occasionally crashing to rates similar to those of the 1960s. In the second half of the 1970s most central banks, including the Bank of Canada, committed themselves to **monetary targetting**, a policy of announcing a target growth rate for the money supply and then attempting to deliver a growth rate inside the announced target range.

In Canada, the particular monetary aggregate chosen for targetting was M1 and, for the most part, the Bank of Canada hit its M1 growth targets. But through these years, M2 growth mushroomed and inflation did not subside. Many (probably most) people believed that inflation would remain at around 10 percent a year forever.

By 1980, Gerald Bouey, the governor of the Bank of Canada, was convinced that a tougher war against inflation must be fought if the economy was ever to be able to shake off that problem and resume a period of sustained expansion. And he knew that to do so, interest rates would have to be driven up to very high levels. For the next two years

[1]The matters touched on here are explained in greater detail in Chapters 7, 11, and 16.

M1 growth was lowered to almost zero and for the next four years the growth rate of M2 declined. Interest rates increased sharply but only for about one year—1981—after which they began to fall. By mid-decade, it was clear that the fight against inflation had been successful, the double-digit inflation having been replaced with a much more agreeable 3 to 4 percent range. At this time, it was seen as more important to keep the expansion of real GDP going ahead than lowering inflation any farther. Through the

FIGURE 6.1
Monetary Policy: 1970-1990

Money supply growth rates (part a) were high during the early 1970s but in 1975 a period of monetary targetting—targetting the growth rate of M1—began. M1 growth targets were achieved but M2 growth increased. In the early 1980s, both M1 and M2 growth rates were cut back and the real money supply (part b) almost stopped growing.

Source: Bank of Canada Review, June 1983 and June 1991.

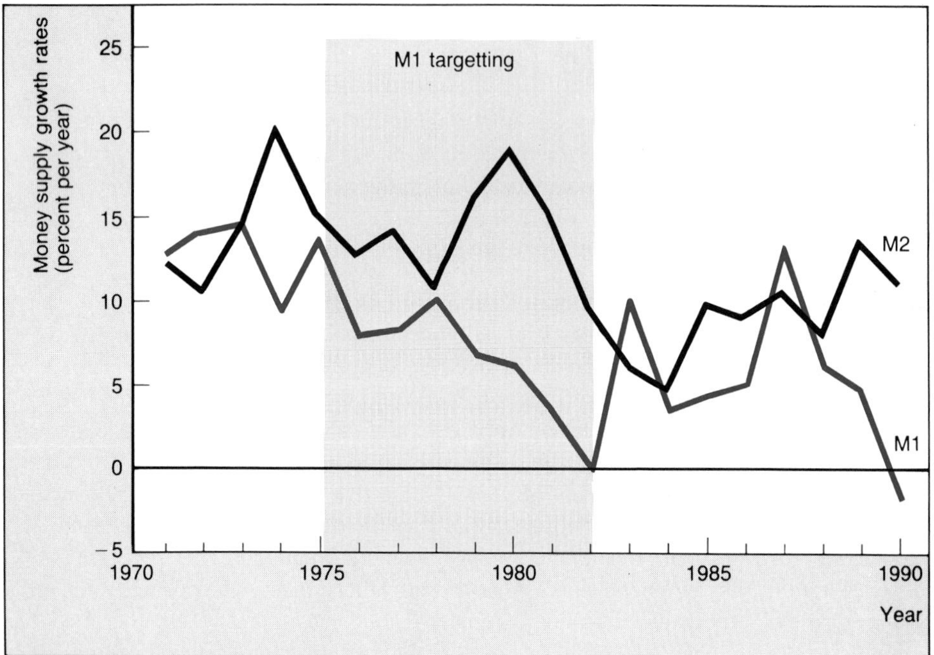

(a) Money supply growth

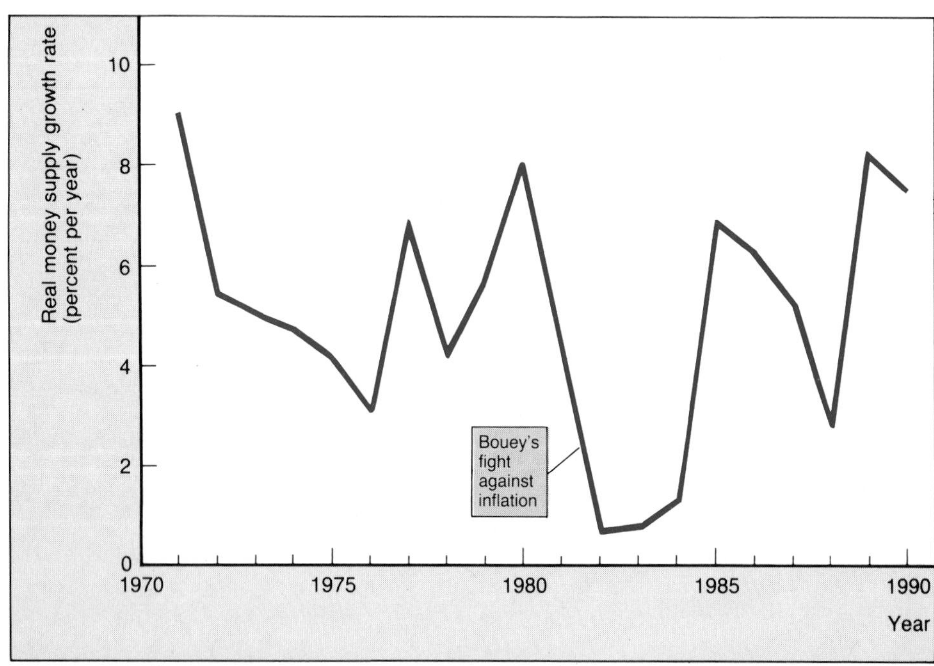

(b) Real money supply growth

balance of the 1980s, the Bank of Canada tried to do just this, yet at the same time, not rekindle the inflation flame. It kept its eye on several intermediate targets, such as the growth rate of money, interest rates, and the exchange rate.

Through the years between 1985 and 1989, the money supply growth rate increased slightly, helping to sustain the long economic recovery. But by 1990, the Bank of Canada was again turning its attention with greater concern to inflation and began to formulate its "zero-inflation" strategy. Money supply growth was again tightened and interest rates increased and so severely that it helped push the economy into its 1991 recession.

The history of Canadian monetary policy between 1970 and 1990 is summarized in Figure 6.1. Part (a) shows the growth rates of M1 and M2 and highlights the period of monetary targetting. Part (b) shows what happened to the real money supply. Recall from your study of the *IS-LM* model in Chapter 5 that the real money supply influences the position of the *LM* curve and, therefore, affects equilibrium interest rates and real GDP.

Before studying the effects of monetary policy further, let's next look at some of the key facts about fiscal policy during this same period, 1960 to 1990.

Fiscal policy

The most obvious and dramatic feature of Canadian fiscal policy is the deficit that emerged between government spending and tax revenue in 1975 and that has persisted since that time. This feature is so important that we devote a separate study to it in Chapter 13. But there are other important aspects of fiscal policy that influence aggregate demand.

Some of these are illustrated in Figure 6.2. This figure shows the scale of government spending and tax revenue as percentages of GDP. As you can see, in the first half of the 1960s, both government spending and tax revenue declined as a percentage of GDP. But over the entire period between 1965 and 1985, government spending was on

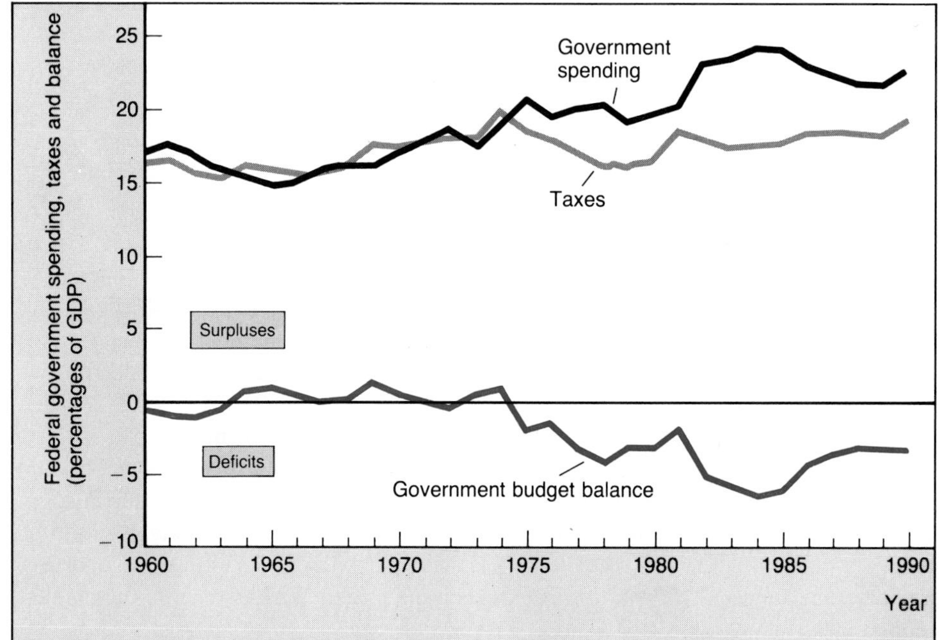

FIGURE 6.2
Fiscal Policy: 1960-1990

Between 1960 and 1965 and again between 1985 and 1990, government spending (as a percentage of GDP) declined, but between 1965 and 1985 it increased steadily. Until 1975, taxes (as a percentage of GDP) fluctuated in step with spending and there was an alternation of small deficits and surpluses. After 1975, taxes at first decreased and then held steady and a persistent deficit has emerged.

Source: Bank of Canada Review, June 1983 and June 1991.

an upward trend relative to GDP. After 1985, government spending again declined as a percentage of GDP. Through 1974, you can see there was a tendency for taxes and government spending to fluctuate in step with each other. But in 1975 that pattern was broken. In that year, there was a temporary burst of government spending and lower taxes. This was a consequence of the first OPEC oil price hike. Notice that the deficit increased quickly in that year. Government spending continued to trend upward through 1985 but taxes broadly remained steady and actually declined for a few years in the late 1970s. These were the years in which the deficit became gradually larger. But the deficit really took off in the early 1980s when another burst of spending was accompanied by slightly falling taxes.

The final episode in our fiscal policy history began in the mid-1980s when the government started to wrestle with the deficit by holding the lid on its spending and increasing revenue slightly. But these moves did not eliminate the deficit.

With this broad-brush picture of the evolution of monetary and fiscal policy in Canada in the 30 years to 1990, let's now turn to an analysis of how these policy instruments influence the economy. We'll start with monetary policy.

6.2 *Monetary Policy in the* IS-LM *Model*

If the economy is operating with unemployment above the natural rate, one possible policy is to try to stimulate the economy by increasing the money supply. But if the economy is operating with low unemployment and climbing inflation, one possible policy to bring the inflation under control is to slow the growth rate of the money supply. How does the economy react to a change in the money supply growth rate? Let's answer this question by looking at a situation where the economy seems to need some stimulation.

Stimulating aggregate demand

We're going to study the effects of an increase in the money supply designed to stimulate aggregate demand and bring the economy to full employment. We'll keep track of the analysis in Figure 6.3. It shows what's happening in terms of the *IS* and *LM* curves (part a) and in terms of the aggregate demand and aggregate supply curves (part b).

Suppose that at full employment, real GDP is y_1 (identified on the horizontal axis of each part of Figure 6.3) but that initially real GDP is \$4.5 billion, which is below y_1. The interest rate is 5 percent and the price level is 140. The economy is at the intersection point of the *IS* curve and the black *LM* curve, LM_0 (in part a), and at the intersection point of the black aggregate demand curve, AD_0, and the short-run aggregate supply curve, *SAS* (in part b).

Now suppose that the Bank of Canada increases the money supply by enough to shift the *LM* curve right to *LM*′. Let's temporarily freeze the price level at 140. With no change in the price level, we can work out what happens to the aggregate demand curve. It too shifts right (shown in part b), to the curve AD_1. This aggregate demand curve passes through the point where the price level is 140 and real GDP is \$6 billion — the same real GDP at which the new *LM* curve, *LM*′, intersects the *IS* curve.

But the *LM* curve will not remain at *LM*′ because the price level will not remain constant at 140. If it did, there would be a shortage of goods and services: the quantity demanded is \$6 billion and the quantity supplied is \$4.5 billion. This shortage will force prices upward, and they will continue to rise as long as there is a shortage of goods and services. The shortage will be eliminated when the price level has risen to the point at

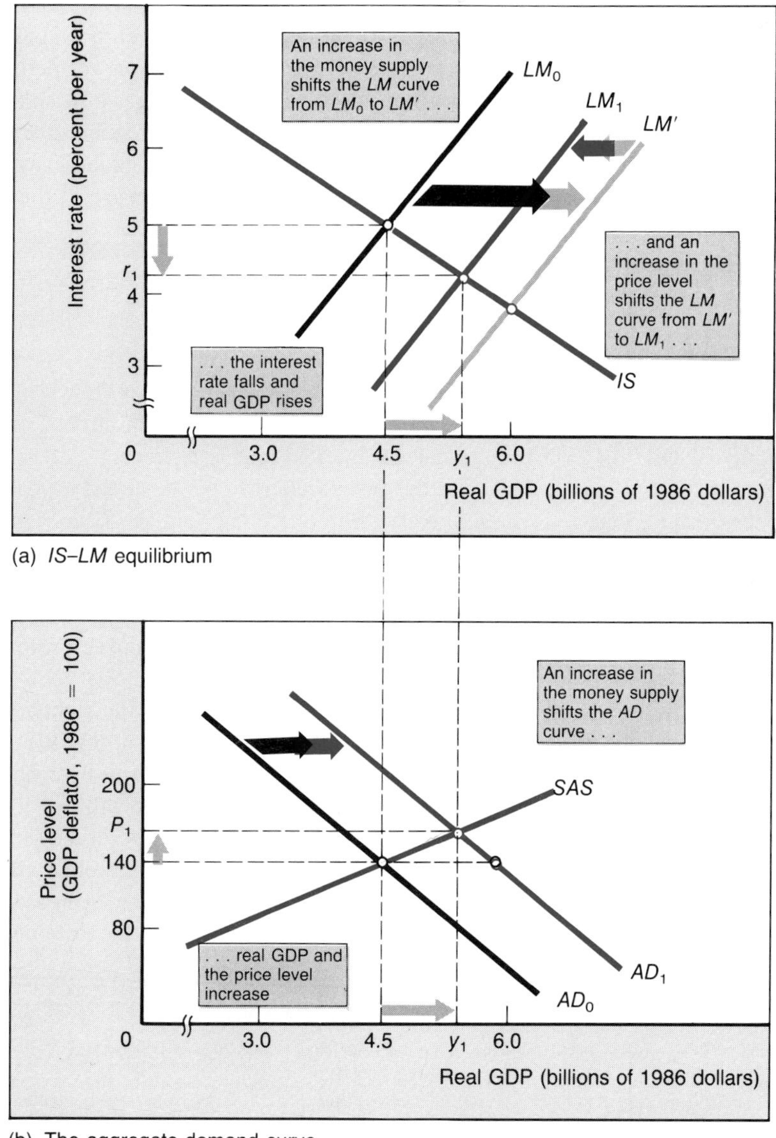

FIGURE 6.3
The Effects of Monetary Policy

Initially, the economy is at the point of intersection of the *IS* curve and the *LM* curve, LM_0, in part (a), with real GDP at $4.5 billion and the interest rate at 5 percent. In part (b), the equilibrium is at the intersection of the aggregate demand curve, AD_0, and the short-run aggregate supply curve, *SAS*. The price level is 140. An increase in the money supply shifts the *LM* curve right to *LM′* in part (a). The aggregate demand curve shifts right to AD_1 in part (b). The higher level of aggregate demand increases real GDP to y_1 and the price level to P_1. The higher price level decreases the real money supply and shifts the *LM* curve back from *LM′* to LM_1. The interest rate falls from 5 percent to r_1, the price level rises to P_1, and real GDP increases to y_1.

which the aggregate demand curve, AD_1, intersects the short-run aggregate supply curve, *SAS*. This occurs at a price level of P_1 and an income level of y_1. The increase in the price level shifts the *LM* curve. With a higher price level and a given quantity of money, the real money supply falls so the *LM* curve shifts from *LM′* to LM_1. This *LM* curve intersects the *IS* curve at a real GDP of y_1 and determines the interest rate at r_1.

The economy is now at full employment by assumption — we *assumed* that at full employment real GDP was y_1 — and full employment has been achieved by an increase in the money supply. In the process of getting to this equilibrium, the price level increased and the interest rate decreased. With a lower interest rate, investment has increased but with a higher income, consumer expenditure has also increased. Thus the two main components of aggregate expenditure have increased.

How much stimulation is needed?

We have just increased the money supply by exactly the amount needed to get the economy from a real GDP of \$4.5 billion to its full-employment level of real GDP, y_1. But what determines the degree of stimulation needed? Part of the answer depends on the slope of the short-run aggregate supply curve, because it determines how an increase in aggregate demand breaks down between an increase in real GDP and an increase in the price level. The flatter the *SAS* curve, the smaller is the shift needed in the aggregate demand curve to produce a given change in real GDP. But an increase in the money supply shifts the aggregate demand curve. How far it shifts depends on

- The slope of the *IS* curve
- The slope of the *LM* curve

The slope of the *IS* curve To see how the slope of the *IS* curve affects the potency of a change in the money supply, consider two cases: one *IS* curve as shown in Figure 6.3 and another that is much flatter. Figure 6.4 shows these two *IS* curves. Initially, equilibrium real GDP is \$4.5 billion and the interest rate is 5 percent — the point of intersection of the *LM* curve, LM_0, and the two *IS* curves. We've already worked out what happens if the *IS* curve is the relatively steep one, identified as IS_A in Figure 6.4. With no change in the price level, real GDP increases to \$6 billion. That is, the aggregate demand curve shifts to the right by \$1.5 billion. But if the *IS* curve is flatter — the curve IS_B — the same increase in the money supply increases real GDP to y_2, at a constant price level — a level higher than \$6 billion. The aggregate demand curve, in this case, shifts to the right by more than \$1.5 billion.

We've just discovered that the flatter the *IS* curve, the larger is the rightward shift in the aggregate demand curve for any given increase in the money supply. Why does a flatter *IS* curve produce a bigger effect on aggregate demand? The answer has to do with the extent to which lower interest rates stimulate investment. Recall that the slope of the *IS* curve depends partly on the investment multiplier and partly on the sensitivity of investment to interest rates. The more sensitive investment is to interest rates, the flatter is the *IS* curve. The bigger the increase in investment resulting from a decrease in interest rates, the more potent is monetary policy and the smaller the dose needed to achieve a given objective.

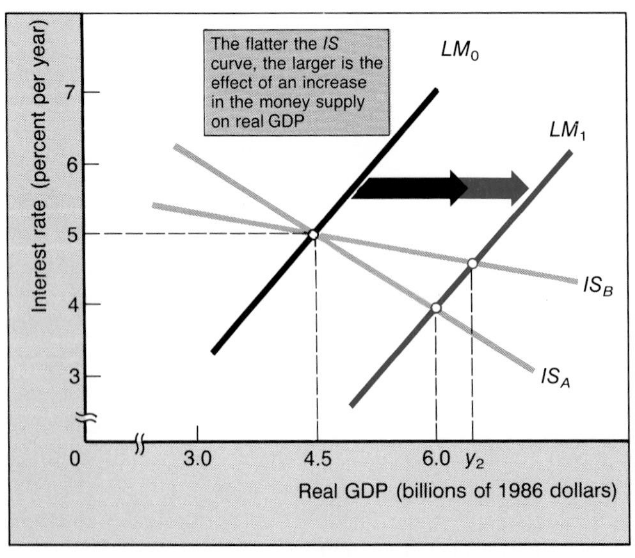

FIGURE 6.4
Monetary Policy and the *IS* Curve Slope

The flatter the *IS* curve, the larger is the effect of a change in the money supply on equilibrium real GDP. Here, an increase in the money supply that shifts the *LM* curve from LM_0 to LM_1 increases real GDP to \$6 billion if the *IS* curve is IS_A and increases it to y_2 if the *IS* curve is IS_B.

***LM* curve slope** The potency of monetary policy is also influenced by the slope of the *LM* curve. The steeper the *LM* curve, the larger is the effect of a change in the money supply on aggregate demand. To see this, look at Figure 6.5. It shows two alternative *LM* curves—LM_A is the same as that in Figure 6.3 and LM_B is less steep.

Initially, the economy is at an interest rate of 5 percent and a real GDP of $4.5 billion. An increase in the money supply shifts the *LM* curve to the right, from the black to the blue curve. For the economy with the relatively steep *LM* curve, LM_A, the equilibrium real GDP (at a constant price level) increases to $6 billion. The aggregate demand curve shifts to the right by $1.5 billion. For the economy with the relatively flat *LM* curve, LM_B, equilibrium real GDP is y_1, which is below $6 billion. Thus the aggregate demand curve shifts to the right but in this case by a smaller amount than $1.5 billion.

Why does a flatter *LM* curve make monetary policy less potent— make it have a smaller effect on aggregate demand? The reason is that the flatter the *LM* curve, the more sensitive to interest rates is the demand for money. When the money supply increases, interest rates fall, but how far they fall depends on the demand for money function. If the demand for money is highly responsive to interest rate changes, then a large increase in the money supply brings only a small fall in interest rates. The smaller the interest rate fall, the smaller the increase in investment and, therefore, the smaller the increase in aggregate demand.

Keeping demand in check

We've just worked out how monetary policy operates when the goal is to increase aggregate demand. Monetary policy can also be used to keep demand in check and avoid inflation. The analysis we've just done applies equally well to that objective. Instead of increasing the money supply, a decrease in it shifts the *LM* curve to the left. In so doing, it lowers aggregate demand and shifts the aggregate demand curve to the left. Real GDP falls and so does the price level. We'll examine some real-world episodes of this case.

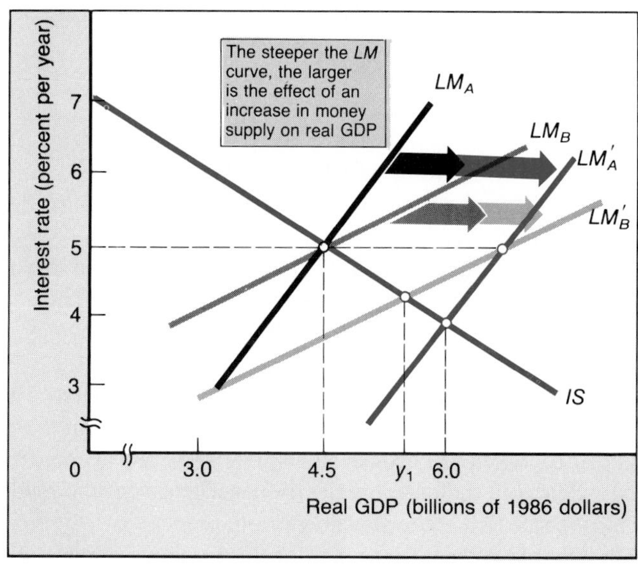

FIGURE 6.5
Monetary Policy and the *LM* Curve Slope

The steeper the *LM* curve, the larger is the effect of a change in the money supply on equilibrium real GDP. In this example, if the *LM* curve is LM_A, an increase in the money supply that shifts the *LM* curve to LM'_A increases real GDP to $6 billion. If the *LM* curve is LM_B, the same increase in the money supply shifts the *LM* curve from LM_B to LM'_B, increasing real GDP to y_1, a level below $6 billion.

TESTCASE

6.3 *Monetary Slowdown in Three Canadian Contractions*

Since 1970, the real money supply — real M2 — in Canada has never actually declined. But as we saw in Chapter 5, the demand for M2 has been steadily increasing so periods of very slow real M2 growth can be regarded as ones in which money might have been exerting a negative influence on real GDP. There are three periods of unusually slow real M2 growth:

1. 1976-1978
2. 1980-1982
3. 1987-1988

1976-1978 In 1976, the economy was still reeling from the first major oil price hike of the Organization of Petroleum Exporting Countries (OPEC). Trying to hold down inflation, the Bank of Canada kept a tight rein on the growth rate of the money supply. It was targetting M1 growth but as we saw in Chapter 5, the demand for M1 was falling so M1 targetting probably did little more than slow M1 *supply* growth in line with M1 *demand* growth. More significantly, in 1976 the real M2 growth rate fell to barely 3 percent. The following year, the M2 growth rate increased but only briefly for it was back at only 4 percent by 1978.

1980-1982 In 1980, the economy was reeling from the second OPEC oil shock and fears were setting in that the double-digit inflation would not end. For the next two years, monetary policy was very tight and the real M2 supply growth rate dropped to almost zero.

1987-1988 Between 1984 and 1987, the Bank of Canada permitted the money supply growth rate to increase to encourage a strong and sustained expansion of real GDP. But in 1988, the Bank was worrying about inflation again, slowing money supply growth and pushing interest rates upward.

What were the effects of these slow downs in the real money supply growth rate? Did they have the effects predicted by the *IS-LM* and *AD-AS* models? We'll answer this question in two ways. First, we'll look at the raw data to see how real GDP responded to changes in the real money supply. Second, we'll go back to the *IS-LM* model and see how it explains these events.

The raw data

Figure 6.6 shows the growth rate of real M2 and the behavior of real GDP between 1971 and 1990. Here, the growth rate of real M2 is measured against the left axis and deviations of real GDP from trend on the right axis.

The overall message of Figure 6.6 is striking. When the real money supply growth rate fell in 1980-1982, the economy experienced a severe contraction starting one year later than the slowdown in money supply growth. When the real money supply growth rate slowed down in 1976 there was a mild slowdown in real GDP in 1977. When real M2 growth slowed in 1988, again real GDP slackened off a year later. There is unevenness in the strength of the response of real GDP to a slow down in the growth rate of M2 but in each episode, when M2 growth slows, real GDP slows about a year later.

These broad patterns in the data are clearly consistent with the model we've been studying. It would be surprising if a slowdown in the money supply growth rate made real GDP growth slow down immediately. Monetary policy operates with a time lag.

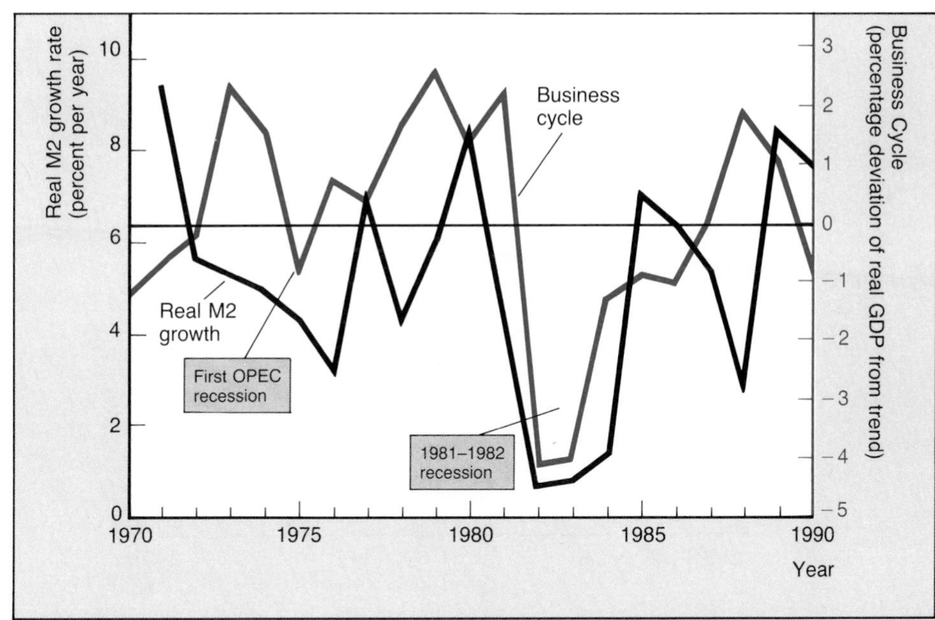

FIGURE 6.6
Three Money Growth Slowdowns

The real money supply growth rate was unusually low during three episodes: 1976-1978, 1980-1982, and 1987-1988. On each occasion, real GDP growth slowed down in the subsequent year. But there is a great deal of variation in the timing and strength of the response of real GDP to a change in the real money supply.

Source: Bank of Canada Review, June 1983 and June 1991.

When the money supply growth rate is cut back, interest rates rise fairly quickly. Higher interest rates gradually bring cutbacks in investment plans and, through the multiplier process, a fall in investment gradually brings declines in the other components of aggregate expenditure. Let's pay more attention to this detailed timing of events by looking at how the *IS-LM* model explains the effects of a cut in the real money supply.

A real money supply cut in the *IS-LM* model

Figure 6.7 shows the effect of a decrease in the money supply on real GDP and interest rates. The economy starts out at a real GDP of y_1 and an interest rate of r_1 — the intersection point of the *IS* curve and the black *LM* curve LM_0 in Figure 6.7(a). In part (b), the price level is P_1 and real GDP y_1 — the intersection point of the black aggregate demand curve AD_0 and the short-run aggregate supply curve, *SAS*.

Now the Bank of Canada slows down the growth rate of the money supply, causing the real money supply to grow less quickly than the demand for money. The result is a shift in the *LM* curve. The *LM* curve shifts to the left, from LM_0 to LM'. The immediate effect of the cut in the real money supply is an increase in interest rates. Real GDP stays at y_1 and the price level at P_1. The economy is now on its *LM* curve but off its *IS* curve. It is to the right of the *IS* curve, so aggregate planned leakages exceed aggregate planned injections. Planned investment has decreased and this cuts planned injections. A multiplier process ensues in which real GDP declines.

The shift in the *LM* curve to the left lowers aggregate demand and shifts the aggregate demand curve from AD_0 to AD_1. Thus it has created a gap between the quantity of real goods and services supplied and the quantity demanded at the price level P_1. This gap puts downward pressure on the price level. As the price level falls along the AD_1 curve, the real money supply begins to increase, shifting the *LM* curve slightly back to the right. Interest rates start to fall. Eventually, the economy settles down on the new *LM* curve, LM_1, and the new aggregate demand curve, AD_2 — real GDP is \$4.5 billion, the price level is 140, and the interest rate is 5 percent.

FIGURE 6.7
How Monetary Slowdown Brings Recession

When the growth rate of the money supply is less than the inflation rate, the real money supply falls. The *LM* curve shifts to the right, such as from LM_0 to LM'. The aggregate demand curve shifts to the left, from AD_0 to AD_1. Real GDP and the price level both fall. (In practice, the growth rate of real GDP and the inflation rate both slow down.) With a lower price level, the initial decrease in the real money supply is to some extent reversed and the *LM* curve shifts slightly to the right, to LM_1. The interest rate increases.

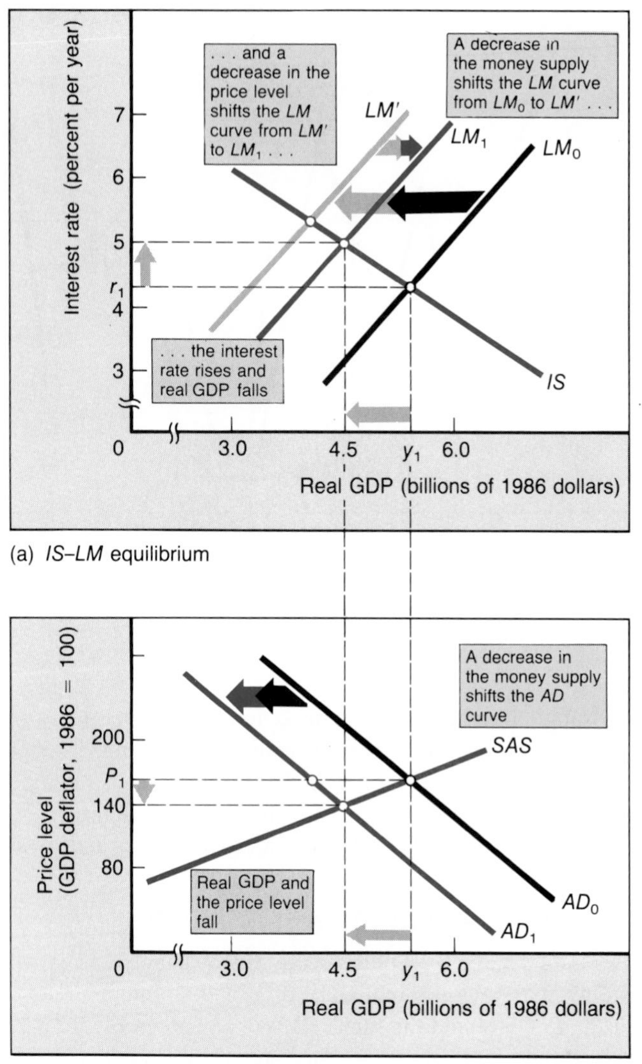

Let's summarize the detailed timing of events. When the money supply growth rate is cut back, interest rates rise immediately but nothing else happens. After that, real GDP begins to fall, and then the price level. Falling prices mean that the inflation rate begins to ease. Eventually, interest rates begin to slacken off slightly.

Does this sequence of events happen in reality? To answer this question, look at Figure 6.8. Part (a) shows interest rates and part (b) shows investment during the three episodes of monetary slowdown. If the theory is correct, interest rates increase and investment subsequently falls. Does this happen? Apparently it does. In each of these episodes, the real interest rate increased and investment, as a percentage of GDP, declined.

We've seen that the *IS-LM* model of aggregate demand gives a useful account of what happens when the Bank of Canada slows down the growth rate of the money supply. Let's now look at fiscal policy, the other main tool for managing aggregate demand.

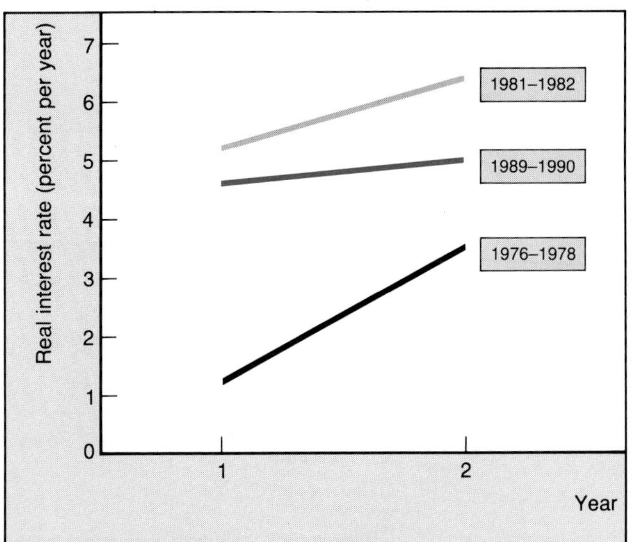

(a) Real interest rate

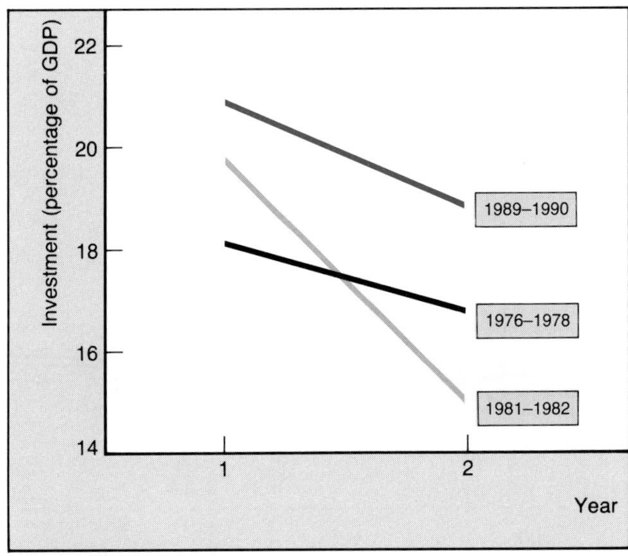

(b) Investment

FIGURE 6.8
Real Interest Rates and Investment in Three Contractions

The mechanism whereby a slowdown in money growth leads to a slowdown in the economy is through an increase in interest rates and a decrease in investment. This mechanism did operate in the three investment slowdowns shown here.

Source: See Figure 6.1.

6.4 *Government Purchases in the* IS-LM *Model*

We've seen that government purchases have steadily increased as a percentage of GDP and that, on occasion, the increase in government purchases has not been matched by an increase in taxes. Let's look at the effects of such a change.

Stimulating demand

What happens if the government increases its purchases of goods and services while holding taxes and the money supply constant? To answer this question, let's study Figure 6.9. Suppose that initially real GDP is $4.5 billion, the interest rate is 5 percent, and the price level is 140. That is, the economy is at the intersection point of the black *LM*

FIGURE 6.9
Fiscal Policy: A Change in Government Purchases

An increase in government purchases of goods and services shifts the *IS* curve to the right, from IS_0 to IS_1 (part a). It also shifts the aggregate demand curve to the right, from AD_0 to AD_1 (part b). With a high level of aggregate demand, real GDP increases to y_1 and the price level increases to P_1. The higher price level decreases the real money supply, shifting the *LM* curve to the left, from LM_0 to LM_1. The interest rate increases to r_1.

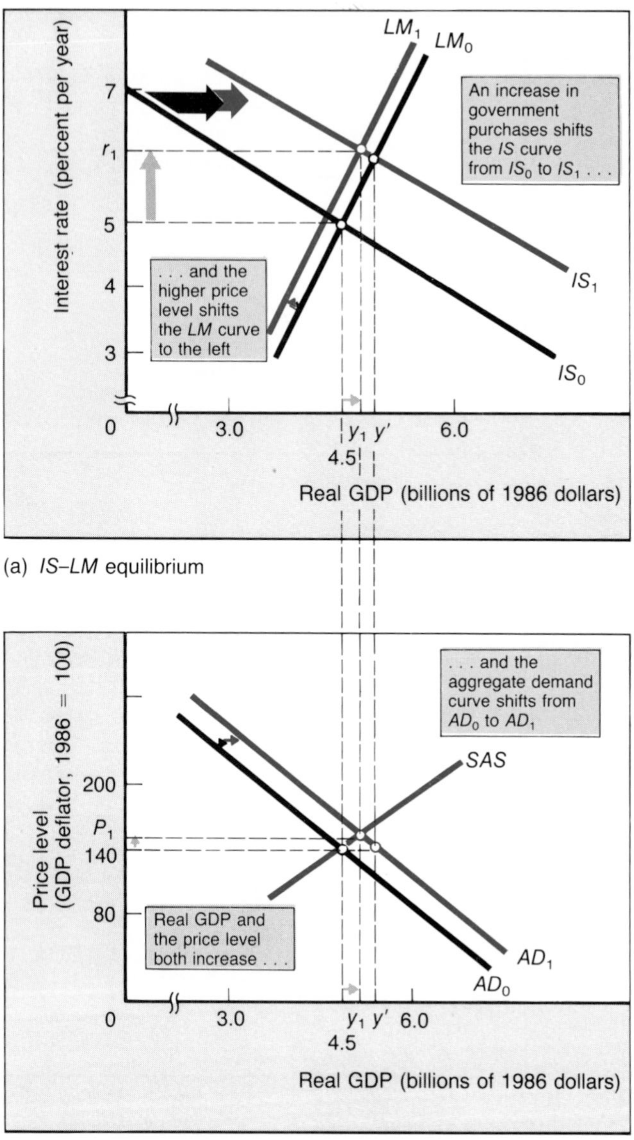

curve, LM_0, and the black *IS* curve, IS_0, in part (a) and the black aggregate demand curve, AD_0, and the short-run aggregate supply curve, *SAS*, in part (b).

Now suppose that with everything else held constant, government purchases of goods and services increase. We worked out in Chapter 5 what that does to the *IS* curve: it shifts it to the right. Suppose that the new *IS* curve in Figure 6.9(a) is IS_1. With no change in the money supply and no change in the price level, the new equilibrium of real GDP will be y'. That is the value of real GDP where the new *IS* curve, IS_1, intersects the original *LM* curve, LM_0. This level of real GDP tells us where the new aggregate demand curve is in part (b). It shifts to the right so that, when the price level takes on its initial value of 140, real GDP is y'. Thus the blue curve AD_1 is the new aggregate demand curve.

To find the new equilibrium, we need to establish where the new *AD* curve intersects the short-run aggregate supply curve. This point of intersection is at the price level P_1 and real *GDP* y_1. The increase in the price level from 140 to P_1 decreases the real money supply and causes the *LM* curve to shift slightly to the left, from LM_0 to LM_1. To find the equilibrium interest rate, we look for the point of intersection of LM_1 and IS_1. The equilibrium interest rate is r_1.

You can now summarize the effects of an increase in government purchases of goods and services. They are

- The *IS* curve shifts to the right
- The aggregate demand curve shifts to the right
- Equilibrium real GDP increases
- The equilibrium price level increases
- The higher price level shifts the *LM* curve to the left

The combination of the rightward shift of the *IS* curve and the leftward shift of the *LM* curve increases the interest rate.

How much bang per buck?

We've seen that an increase in government purchases increases real GDP, the price level, and the interest rate. But by how much? How big an increase in government purchases is required to achieve a given objective?

First, the slope of the short-run aggregate supply curve plays a crucial role in determining how the change in aggregate demand gets divided between a change in the price level and a change in real GDP. The flatter that supply curve, the larger is the effect on real GDP and the smaller the effect on the price level. In long-run equilibrium along the vertical long-run aggregate supply curve, the entire effect is on the price level; none of it is on real GDP. We'll look more closely at that case in the next section. Here, let's focus on the effects of the change in government spending on the shift in the aggregate demand curve itself. By how much does a given change in government purchases shift the aggregate demand curve? The answer is that the shift in the aggregate demand curve depends on

- The slope of the *LM* curve
- The slope of the *IS* curve

The slope of the *LM* curve To see how the slope of the *LM* curve influences the effect of government purchases, look at Figure 6.10. There are two different *LM* curves, the one we used in Figure 6.9, here labeled LM_A, and a less steep *LM* curve labeled LM_B. You can see that the shift in the *IS* curve from IS_0 to IS_1 has a smaller effect on real GDP and a larger effect on the interest rate, the steeper the *LM* curve. Why? When increased government purchases increase aggregate expenditure and real GDP, the demand for money increases too. People want to hold more money to finance their higher spending. But there is a given amount of money in the economy. As individuals try to increase the amount of money held, they sell bonds and other financial assets. This act of selling financial assets lowers their price and increases their interest rate. The higher interest rate causes people to slide along their demand for money curve, becoming more willing to hold a smaller quantity of money as the interest rate rises. The less sensitive the quantity of money demand to a change in the interest rate, the larger is the change in the interest rate needed to restore equilibrium in money holdings. With a higher increase in the interest rate, a smaller amount of investment takes place. The decrease in investment to some extent cancels out the initial effect of an increase in government purchases and so reduces the overall effect of the increased government purchases on real GDP.

FIGURE 6.10
Fiscal Policy and the Slope of the *LM* Curve

The flatter the *LM* curve, the larger is the effect of a change in government purchases on real GDP. If the *LM* curve is LM_A, an increase in government purchases shifts the *IS* curve from IS_0 to IS_1 and increases real GDP to y_1. If the *LM* curve is LM_B, the same change in government purchases and shift in the *IS* curve increases real GDP to \$6 billion, a level much higher than y_1.

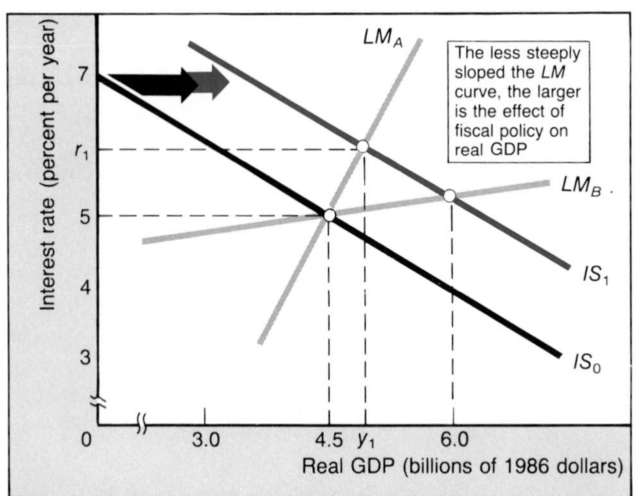

The slope of the *IS* curve To see how the slope of the *IS* curve affects the potency of a change in government purchases, look at Figure 6.11. Here, we consider two slopes to the *IS* curve, the original one from Figure 6.9, now identified as IS_A, and a new *IS* curve that has a steeper slope, IS_B. You can see here that when there is an increase in government purchases that shifts the *IS* curve, the steeper *IS* curve results in a larger increase in both real GDP and the interest rate. That is, the steeper the *IS* curve, the larger is the effect of a change in government purchases on real GDP and on the interest rate.

Why? The slope of the *IS* curve depends on the sensitivity of investment to the interest rate. The less sensitive investment is to a change in the interest rate, the steeper the *IS* curve. An increase in government purchases shifts the *IS* curve to the right and increases interest rates. But with a steeper *IS* curve, the higher interest rate has a smaller negative effect on investment and so a smaller offsetting effect on the initial increase in government purchases.

FIGURE 6.11
Fiscal Policy and the *IS* Curve Slope

The steeper the *IS* curve, the larger is the effect of a change in government purchases on equilibrium real GDP. If the *IS* curve is IS_A, an increase in government purchases that shifts the *IS* curve to $IS_{A'}$ increases real GDP to y_1. If the *IS* curve is IS_B, the same increase in government purchases shifts the *IS* curve to $IS_{B'}$ and increases real GDP to y_2, a higher level than y_1.

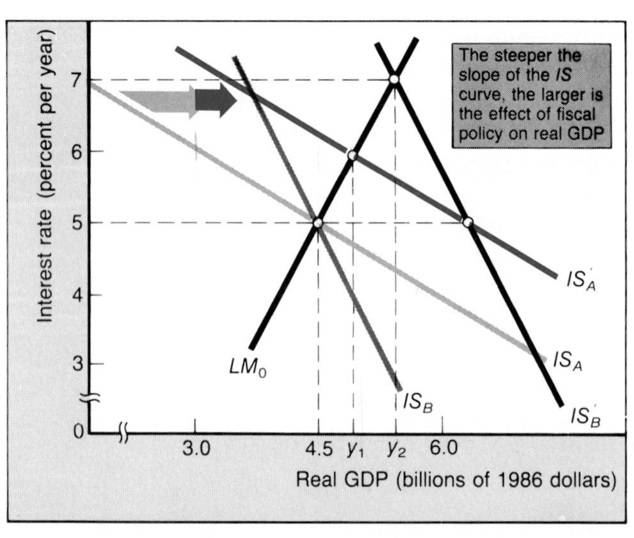

6.5 *Do Government Purchases Crowd Out Investment?*

Crowding out is the name for the effect of an increase in government purchases on investment. In all the exercises we've just conducted, partial crowding out occurs. In the discussion of the sensitivity of real GDP to a change in government purchases, we've discovered that the slopes of the *IS* and *LM* curves play a crucial role. We've also seen that they play a crucial role in determining the effects of a change in government purchases on interest rates and, therefore, on investment. In these exercises, an increase in government purchases always brings about some decrease in investment. Is this outcome inevitable? Are there some cases in which an increase in government purchases leads to an increase in investment? And what about the opposite extreme? Is it possible for an increase in government purchases to lead to a decrease in investment that equals the original increase in government purchases? Can complete crowding out occur?

Crowding out at full employment

At full employment, an increase in government purchases can occur only if some other component of aggregate expenditure decreases. In the *IS-LM* model, the component that decreases is investment. To see this, look at Figure 6.12. Part (a) tracks what is happening to investment and government purchases, and in part (b) we work out the *IS-LM*

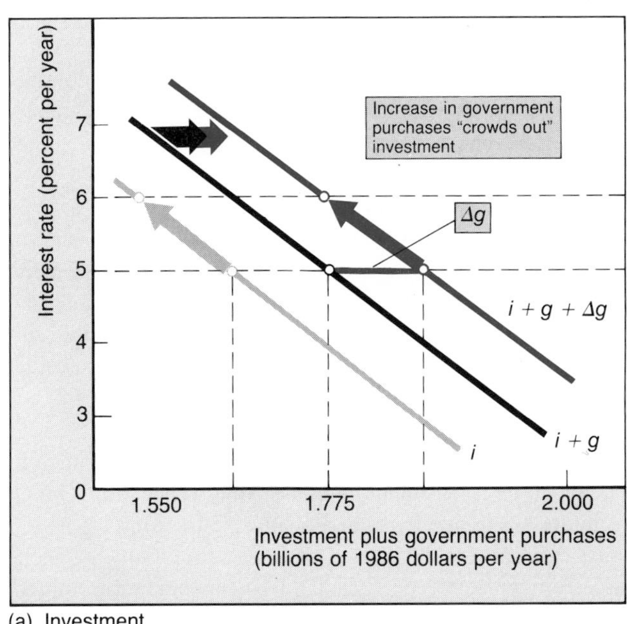

(a) Investment

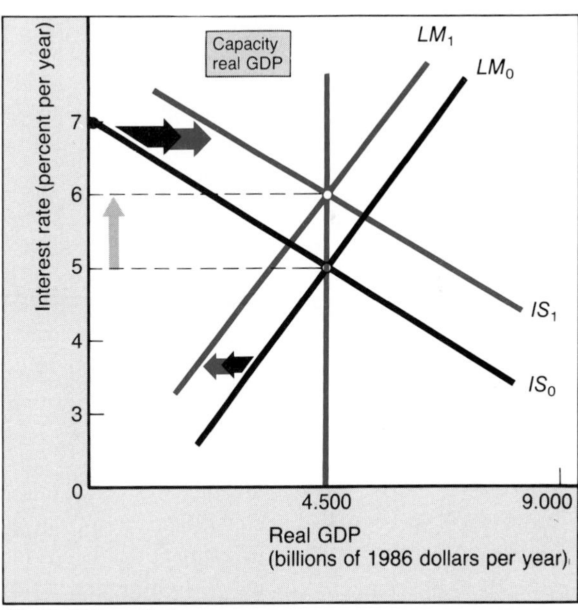

(b) *IS–LM* equilibrium

FIGURE 6.12
Crowding Out at Full Employment

An increase in government purchases of goods and services at full employment shifts the $i + g$ curve to $i + g + \Delta g$ (part a) and shifts the *IS* curve from IS_0 to IS_1 (part b). Aggregate demand increases and the price level begins to rise. Factor prices also begin to rise, shifting the short-run aggregate supply curve (not shown) upward until full employment is restored. At this point, the price level has increased such that the *LM* curve has shifted to the left, from LM_0 to LM_1. The interest rate has increased from 5 percent to 6 percent. Investment has decreased (part a) by an amount exactly equal to the initial increase in government purchases. The increase in government purchases has crowded out investment.

equilibrium. To orient yourself, find the vertical line where real GDP is \$4.5 billion (part b). This line represents full-employment real GDP—the level of real GDP along the long-run aggregate supply curve. Suppose the economy is at full employment and the government increases its purchases of goods and services. In part (a), the $i + g$ curve shifts to $i + g + \Delta g$. In part (b), the *IS* curve shifts to the right from IS_0 to IS_1.

The shift in the *IS* curve increases aggregate demand and shifts the aggregate demand curve to the right. The higher level of aggregate demand intersects a short-run aggregate supply curve (not shown) at a higher price level and higher level of real GDP. Also, with the economy above full employment, factor prices begin to increase. As they do so, the short-run aggregate supply curve shifts upward. That curve continues to shift upward as long as real GDP is above its full-employment level. Eventually, it reaches the point at which real GDP has declined to its full-employment level and is again at \$4.5 billion. In this position, the price level has increased but real GDP has remained constant. The higher price level shifts the *LM* curve to the left, from LM_0 to LM_1. In the new equilibrium, the *LM* curve intersects the *IS* curve IS_1 along the full-employment real GDP line. The interest rate increases to 6 percent.

Back in part (a), with the interest rate at 6 percent, investment declines. The decrease in investment exactly equals the initial increase in government purchases. Complete crowding out has occurred.

Partial crowding out at less than full employment

If real GDP is below its full-employment level, an increase in government purchases need not completely crowd out investment. You saw that in the examples we worked through in the previous section. An increase in government purchases led to an increase in real GDP. The higher real GDP brought about a higher level of consumer expenditure. (Recall that consumer expenditure increases with disposable income, so the higher is real GDP for a given level of taxes, the higher are disposable income and consumer expenditure.)

Complete crowding out occurs at less than full employment if the *LM* curve is vertical or the *IS* curve is horizontal. But in reality, neither of these extremes occurs. A vertical *LM* curve means that the propensity to hold money does not depend on the interest rate — in other words, it does not depend on the opportunity cost of holding money. With a given money supply, only one level of real GDP is compatible with equilibrium, and the interest rate has to adjust to bring aggregate expenditure into line with that level of real GDP. In this case, higher government purchases lead to higher interest rates and lower investment but no change in real GDP.

A horizontal *IS* curve occurs when investment is infinitely sensitive to a change in the interest rate. In this case, a change in government purchases that, other things being equal, leads to a change in the interest rate generates an equal and offsetting change in investment that keeps the interest rate constant. All other cases—with an upward-sloping *LM* curve and a downward-sloping *IS* curve — result in partial but not complete crowding out.

Can government purchases stimulate investment?

There are several channels, not present in the *IS-LM* model that we've been studying, whereby a change in government purchases could stimulate investment. The major channel is its possible effect on the state of expectations. When studying the determinants of investment, we saw that the investment function swings from side to side as waves of optimism and pessimism pass through the economy. At times of recession and heavy unemployment, the business outlook is bleak and the investment demand curve shifts to the left. At times of rapid growth and optimistic profit expectations, the investment function shifts to the right.

If the economy is depressed and the government increases its purchases of goods and services, expectations of rapid economic growth following such government pump-priming may lead to increasingly optimistic profit prospects and a rightward shift of the investment demand curve. If this happens, investment and government purchases will increase along with consumer expenditure to fill the gap between the current depressed level of output and the economy's long-run capacity to produce.

But such direct stimulation of investment by increased government purchases cannot be a long-run phenomenon. As the economy approaches full employment, if government purchases have increased and the investment function has shifted to the right, there will be upward pressure on interest rates, which will to some degree choke off additional investment.

Another possible channel is the international one. We'll explore this channel more thoroughly in Chapter 7. But here's how it works. Increased government purchases could initially result in increased Canadian imports. Our imports are someone else's exports — an injection into the circular flow of income in other countries. Increased exports could stimulate the world economy, leading to a higher demand for Canadian goods and services. Improved profit prospects in the world economy could lead to a rightward shift of the investment function and so stimulate investment.

6.6 *Taxes in the* IS-LM *Model*

Taxes work in the *IS-LM* model in a similar manner to government purchases, except that their effect is absolutely smaller and their direction opposite. Taxes have a smaller effect than government purchases because they work indirectly through their influence on disposable income. A one-dollar change in taxes changes disposable income by one dollar but changes aggregate expenditure by a fraction of a dollar — a fraction equal to the marginal propensity to consume. This initial injection is then blown up by the multiplier effect the way an additional dollar of any other injection is. Taxes work in the opposite direction to government purchases because a tax cut — a decrease in taxes — increases disposable income and aggregate demand.

You can work through the effects of a tax cut on the *IS* curve, the aggregate demand curve, real GDP, the price level, and the interest rate, by studying Figure 6.9 again and reinterpreting the initial shift in the *IS* curve as resulting from a decrease in taxes rather than an increase in government purchases.

Because taxes work in a similar way to government purchases in the *IS-LM* model, they too can crowd out investment. By cutting taxes and stimulating consumer expenditure, interest rates increase and investment declines. But for all the reasons we discussed above, crowding out may not actually occur because of mechanisms at work in the real world that are not present in the *IS-LM* model.

Tax changes have other effects because of their influence on wages and interest rates. People make decisions about how much labor to supply based on the after-tax wage rate. Firms make investment decisions based on their assessment of the after-tax rate of return on capital. Because changes in tax rates influence after-tax wages and after-tax rates of return, they also influence the quantity of labor supplied and the amount of investment. Lowering taxes increases after-tax wages and increases the level of employment. It also increases after-tax rates of return, increasing investment. It is these incentive effects of taxes that lie at the heart of so-called supply-side policies.

So, in reality, tax cuts might have little effect on incentives and crowd out investment. Or tax cuts might have a strong effect on incentives (or have other positive effects on optimism and the investment outlook) and stimulate investment. But here again, things could go either way. A tax cut might stimulate aggregate expenditure and lead to increased optimism. But a tax cut that creates a deficit might create uncertainty about the future, leading to greater pessimism. Thus there's no simple way to predict how investment will respond to tax changes.

■ In this chapter, we've studied the effects of monetary and fiscal policy on real GDP, the price level, and interest rates. We've also studied their effects on the components of aggregate expenditure and, in particular, on investment. We've seen how changes in government purchases and taxes, as well as changes in the money supply, can stimulate or hold back the level of aggregate demand and how, in the process, they affect the rest of the economy. Throughout this analysis, we've concentrated on things that are happening inside the Canadian economy, for the most part ignoring influences in the rest of the world and interactions between the Canadian and world economies. In the next chapter, we'll broaden our view and study these international factors.

CHAPTER REVIEW

Summary

CANADIAN MONEY SUPPLY GROWTH, GOVERNMENT PURCHASES, AND TAXES IN RECENT YEARS

During the 1960s the major countries, including (after 1962) Canada, were members of an international gold exchange standard with fixed exchange rates. The growth rate of the money supply fluctuated but had a low average. In the 1970s, the fixed exchange rate system collapsed and was replaced by monetary targetting. Canada's monetary targets were hit but the target, M1 growth, was becoming less and less relevant and M2 growth continued at a rapid pace. In 1980, the Bank of Canada paid less attention to its M1 target and pushed interest rates up to record levels. In 1982, the Bank of Canada formally abandoned M1 targetting and broadened the range of its policy targets, paying more attention to the exchange rate and interest rates. But it continued to keep money supply growth in check.

Government purchases (as a percentage of GDP) declined between 1960 and 1965 and again between 1985 and 1990 but steadily increased between 1965 and 1985. Tax revenue moved in line with spending until 1975 but spending outstripped taxes and a deficit emerged in that year.

HOW THE MONEY SUPPLY INFLUENCES INTEREST RATES, REAL GDP, AND THE PRICE LEVEL

An increase in the money supply may be used to stimulate the economy, bringing it from recession to full employment. A higher money supply lowers interest rates, which in turn stimulate investment. Higher investment, through a multiplier, brings higher consumer expenditure and higher aggregate planned expenditure. An increase in aggregate demand brings an increase in both real GDP and the price level. The higher price level decreases the real money supply, to some extent offsetting the initial increase resulting from the increase in the money supply. But this force only dampens, and does not reverse, the initial impact of lower interest rates and increased aggregate expenditure. The final outcome from an increase in the money supply is an increase in real GDP, a higher price level, and lower interest rates.

The potency of monetary policy depends on the responsiveness of investment to interest rate changes and the responsiveness of the demand for money to the interest rate. The more responsive is investment and the less responsive is the demand for money, the larger the effect of a given change in the money supply on real GDP and the price level.

How a change in aggregate demand divides between a change in real GDP and a change in the price level depends on the slope of the short-run aggregate supply curve. The steeper that curve, the larger is the change in the price level and the smaller the change in real GDP.

At full employment, with a vertical long-run aggregate supply curve, the entire effect of a change in the money supply is on the price level, with no change in real GDP and no change in the interest rate.

MONETARY POLICY IN THREE ECONOMIC SLOWDOWNS

The real money supply (M2) has not fallen but its growth rate has slowed during three episodes between 1970 and 1990: in 1976-1978, 1981-1982, and 1987-1988. On each occasion, this event was followed by an economic slowdown, although the strength and the timing of the response was variable. Such a response is consistent with the mechanisms at work in the *IS-LM* model. A decrease in the real money supply (relative to the demand for real money) increases interest rates. The higher interest rate brings a decrease in investment, which lowers aggregate planned expenditure. The aggregate demand curve shifts to the left and real GDP growth and inflation slow down. Such movements in interest rates and investment occurred in all three episodes.

HOW GOVERNMENT PURCHASES INFLUENCE INTEREST RATES, REAL GDP, AND THE PRICE LEVEL

An increase in government purchases may be undertaken to stimulate the economy, bringing it from below full employment to full employment. But more often than not, changes in government purchases occur for reasons other than the government's desire to stabilize the economy. They are driven by a broader set of political and international factors. Regardless of the reason for an increase in government purchases, it affects interest rates, real GDP, and the price level in the following way.

An increase in government purchases is an injection into the circular flow of expenditure and income and increases aggregate planned expenditure. The multiplier effect induces additional increases in consumer expenditure. Higher expenditure brings an increase in the demand for money and puts upward pressure on interest rates. Higher interest rates bring a cutback in investment that partially (and possibly completely) offsets the initial increase in government purchases. If the offsetting decrease in investment is smaller than the initial increase in government purchases, the aggregate demand curve shifts to the right and real GDP and the price level both rise.

The higher price level decreases the real money supply, putting even more upward pressure on interest rates and more downward pressure on investment.

The final outcome of an increase in government purchases that does not completely crowd out investment is that real GDP, the price level, and interest rates all increase.

The potency of a change in government purchases depends on the responsiveness of the demand for money to interest rates and of investment to interest rates. The effect of government purchases is larger, the smaller the interest sensitivity of investment and the higher the interest sensitivity of the demand for money.

The way that a change in government purchases divides between a change in real GDP and a change in the price level depends on the slope of the short-run aggregate supply curve. In the long run, when the aggregate supply curve is vertical, the entire effect comes out on the price level, so that the real money supply declines, the interest rate increases, and investment declines to exactly offset the initial increase in government purchases. There is complete crowding out.

Complete crowding out does not occur at less than full employment and might not occur even at full employment because of international considerations. Higher government purchases may lead to additional imports, turning net exports negative.

HOW TAXES INFLUENCE INTEREST RATES, REAL GDP, AND THE PRICE LEVEL

Taxes operate in the opposite direction to government purchases. A tax decrease has a similar effect to an increase in government purchases. However, the magnitude of the effect of a tax change is smaller than that of a change in government purchases. Taxes change disposable income, which changes consumer expenditure by an amount determined by the marginal propensity to consume.

Key Terms and Concepts

Bank rate The interest rate at which banks borrow from one another.

Crowding out The effect of an increase in government purchases on investment.

Gold exchange standard A monetary arrangement in which Canada kept its monetary policy in close harmony with the policies of other countries in a system of fixed exchange rates.

Monetary targetting A policy of announcing a target growth rate for the money supply and then attempting to deliver a growth rate inside the announced target range.

Review Questions

1. Show the effects in the *IS-LM* analysis of an increase in government spending on real GDP and the interest rate. What conditions would lead to only the interest rate changing? What conditions would lead to only real GDP changing?
2. Suppose the government's budget deficit increases (g increases relative to t). What does the *IS-LM* analysis predict will happen to the rate of interest?
3. Show the effect in the *IS-LM* analysis of an increase in the money supply on the rate of interest and real GDP. What conditions would lead to only interest rates changing?
4. Which markets are in equilibrium along that aggregate demand curve? What is held constant along the aggregate demand curve? Why does the aggregate demand curve slope downward?

Problems

You are given the following information about an economy:

$c = 100 + 0.8(y - t)$
$i = 500 - 50r$
$g = 400$
$t = 400$
$M^d/P = 0.2y + 500 - 25r$

The price level is fixed at 1.
The money supply is 520.
(c = consumption; i = investment; g = government purchases; t = taxes; r = interest rate; M^d = demand for money; P = price level; y = real GDP)

1. Calculate equilibrium real GDP and the interest rate.
2. Calculate consumer expenditure.
3. Calculate investment.
4. The central bank increases the money supply by one unit.
   (a) Calculate the change in aggregate expenditure.
   (b) How far does the aggregate curve shift?
   (c) What is the change in interest rates and investment?
   (d) What is the change in consumer expenditure?
   (e) What is the change in the government budget?
5. The government increases its purchases of goods and services by one unit.
   (a) Calculate the change in aggregate expenditure.
   (b) How far does the aggregate demand curve shift?
   (c) What is the change in interest rates and investment?
   (d) Does investment get crowded out?
6. The government increases taxes by one unit.
   (a) Calculate the shift of the *IS* curve.
   (b) What is the change in the level of aggregate demand?
   (c) What is the change in interest rates and investment?
   (d) What is the change in disposable income and consumer expenditure?
   (e) What is the change in the government's budget balance?

APPENDIX

The Algebra of Monetary and Fiscal Policy in the IS-LM Model

This appendix takes you through the algebra of the effect of monetary and fiscal policy on the equilibrium levels of real GDP and the rate of interest when the price level is fixed at P_0.

We derived the equations to the *IS* and *LM* curves in the Appendix to Chapter 5. The equation to the *IS* curve is

$$y = \frac{1}{1-b}(a + i_0 + g - bt - hr) \qquad \textbf{(6A.1)}$$

The equation to the *LM* curve is

$$y = \frac{1}{k}\left[\frac{M}{P_0} - (m_0 + \ell r)\right] \qquad \textbf{(6A.2)}$$

Equations (6A.1) and (6A.2), the equations to the *IS* and *LM* curves, contain two unknowns — real GDP and the interest rate. Setting the real GDP in Equation (6A.1) equal to the real GDP in Equation (6A.2) and solving for the interest rate gives

$$r = \frac{1}{1 - b + kh/\ell}\left[\frac{k}{\ell}(a + i_0 + g - bt) - \frac{1-b}{\ell}\left(\frac{M}{P_0} - m_0\right)\right] \qquad \textbf{(6A.3)}$$

Equation (6A.3) is an algebraic expression for the equilibrium value of the interest rate in the *IS-LM* analysis. By substituting Equation (6A.3) back into Equation (6A.2) to eliminate the interest rate, you obtain an expression for real GDP:

$$y = \frac{1}{1 - b + kh/\ell}\left[(a + i_0 + g - bt) + \frac{h}{\ell}\left(\frac{M}{P_0} - m_0\right)\right] \qquad \textbf{(6A.4)}$$

Equation (6A.4) is the solution of the *IS-LM* analysis for equilibrium real GDP.

To better understand what those equations are saying, let's examine Equations (6A.3) and (6A.4) to see how the interest rate and real GDP vary as we vary the three policy instruments — government purchases, taxes, and the money supply. Imagine that each of those three policy variables takes on a different value from g, t, and M. Specifically, suppose that g increases to g', t to t', and M to M'. In this case, we know that the solutions for the interest rate and real GDP can be expressed as

$$r' = \frac{1}{1 - b + kh/\ell}\left[\frac{k}{\ell}(a + i_0 + g' - bt') - \frac{1-b}{\ell}\left(\frac{M'}{P_0} - m_0\right)\right] \qquad \textbf{(6A.5)}$$

$$y' = \frac{1}{1 - b + kh/\ell}\left[(a + i_0 + g' - bt') + \frac{h}{\ell}\left(\frac{M'}{P_0} - m_0\right)\right] \qquad \textbf{(6A.6)}$$

Equations (6A.5) and (6A.6) are identical to Equations (6A.3) and (6A.4) except that the value of the variables (r and y on the left side and g, t, and M on the right side) have all changed from their original values to their new (primed) values.

Now subtract Equation (6A.3) from Equation (6A.5) to obtain Equation (6A.7). Also subtract Equation (6A.4) from Equation (6A.6) to obtain Equation (6A.8). Notice that in Equations (6A.7) and (6A.8) the terms a, i_0, and m_0 have disappeared because they are common to both the original solutions and the new solutions for y and r. Thus

$$r' - r = \frac{1}{1 - b + kh/\ell}\left[\frac{k}{\ell}(g' - g) - \frac{bk}{\ell}(t' - t) - \frac{1-b}{\ell}\left(\frac{M'}{P_0} - \frac{M}{P_0}\right)\right] \quad \textbf{(6A.7)}$$

and

$$y' - y = \frac{1}{1 - b + kh/\ell}\left[(g' - g) - b(t' - t) + \frac{h}{\ell}\left(\frac{M'}{P_0} - \frac{M}{P_0}\right)\right] \quad \textbf{(6A.8)}$$

Now call the gap between y' and y the change in y and label it Δy. Similarly, call the gap between r' and r, Δr, and likewise for the policy variables. That is, $g' - g$ is Δg, $t' - t$ is Δt, and $M' - M$ is ΔM. Using this convention, you can write Equations (6A.7) and (6A.8) slightly more compactly as Equations (6A.9) and (6A.10):

$$\Delta r = \frac{1}{1 - b + kh/\ell}\left[\frac{k}{\ell}\Delta g - \frac{bk}{\ell}\Delta t - \frac{1-b}{\ell P_0}\Delta M\right] \quad \textbf{(6A.9)}$$

$$\Delta y = \frac{1}{1 - b + kh/\ell}\left[\Delta g - b\Delta g + \frac{h}{\ell P_0}\Delta M\right] \quad \textbf{(6A.10)}$$

You can now interpret Equations (6A.9) and (6A.10) directly. Notice that the expression

$$\frac{1}{1 - b + kh/\ell}$$

is a positive coefficient relating the changes in the policy variables to the changes in the rate of interest and the level of real GDP. (You know that this expression will be positive since b is a positive fraction, $1 - b$ is also a positive fraction, and k, h, and ℓ are all positive parameters.) You can see that, in general, Equation (6A.9) says a rise in g will raise the interest rate, whereas a rise in t and a rise in M will cut the interest rate. From Equation (6A.10) you can see that in general, a rise in g or a rise in M will raise real GDP, but a rise in t will cut real GDP. Equations (6A.9) and (6A.10) are nothing other than algebraic expressions for the equivalent propositions obtained in Chapter 6.

The relationship between an endogenous variable such as real GDP or the interest rate and an exogenous variable such as government expenditure, taxes, or the money supply is called a multiplier. It is the number that multiplies a change in an exogenous variable in order to provide the magnitude of the change in the endogenous variable. The multipliers can be read off from Equations (6A.9) and (6A.10). For example, the government expenditure multiplier on the interest rate is the coefficient on Δg in the equation that determines Δr, Equation (6A.9). This is

$$\frac{k/\ell}{1 - b + hk/\ell}$$

In this chapter we looked at how the potency of policy changes is affected by the slopes of the *IS* and *LM* curves. We can now do this more precisely with the algebraic solutions in Equations (6A.9) and (6A.10). Let's look at some extreme cases.

SOME SPECIAL CASES

First, suppose that the parameter h became infinitely big. An infinitely big h means that the investment function and, hence, the *IS* curve is horizontal; it also means that the interest rate remains constant. What are the changes in the interest rate and real GDP when h is infinitely big? By inspecting Equations (6A.9) and (6A.10), you can establish that the changes are as follows:

$$\Delta r = 0 \tag{6A.11}$$

$$\Delta y = \frac{1}{kP_0}\Delta M \tag{6A.12}$$

What this says is that the aggregate demand curve will shift (y will change by Δy) only as a result of a change in the money supply. The shift will be equal to $1/kP_0$ times the change in the money supply. Changes in government purchases and taxes will have no effect on aggregate demand in this special case.

The next special case is that in which $\ell = 0$. In this case, the demand for money is completely insensitive to interest rates. You can think of this situation as arising when money is such a unique asset that it is completely nonsubstitutable for any other asset. In this case, you will discover from Equations (6A.9) and (6A.10) that the changes in the interest rate and real GDP become

$$\Delta r = \frac{1}{h}\left(\Delta g - b\Delta t - \frac{1-b}{kP_0}\Delta M\right) \tag{6A.13}$$

and

$$\Delta y = \frac{1}{kP_0}\Delta M \tag{6A.14}$$

In this case, the interest rate changes when government purchases, taxes, or the money supply changes. It will rise with an increase in government purchases, and it will fall with an increase in taxes or the money supply. The change in real GDP will be exactly the same as in the previous special case.

Now consider the special case opposite to the first one, where instead of h being infinitely big, it becomes infinitely small, specifically, zero. This would be the case where firms' investment plans were completely unresponsive to interest rates. In this case, the changes in the interest rate and in the real GDP are given by

$$\Delta r = \frac{1}{1-b}\left(\frac{k}{\ell}\Delta g - \frac{kb}{\ell}\Delta t - \frac{(1-b)}{\ell P_0}\Delta M\right) \tag{6A.15}$$

$$\Delta y = \frac{1}{1-b}(\Delta g - b\Delta t) \tag{6A.16}$$

This tells you that, in this case, an increase in government purchases will raise the interest rate, and an increase in taxes or the money supply will cut the interest rate. Unlike the two previous special cases, an increase in government purchases or a cut in taxes will raise real GDP, but a change in the money supply will leave real GDP unaffected. Equation (6A.16) says that in the special case of $h = 0$, aggregate demand shifts only as a result of changes in fiscal policy variables and will remain unchanged when the money supply changes.

Now consider the special case opposite to the second one, in which we let the parameter ℓ become infinitely big. In this case, money is a perfect substitute for other nonmoney assets. Substituting an infinite value for ℓ in Equations (6A.9) and (6A.10) gives the solutions

$$\Delta r = 0 \tag{6A.17}$$

$$\Delta y = \frac{1}{1-b}(\Delta g - b\Delta t) \tag{6A.18}$$

This time the interest rate is entirely unaffected by changes in any of the variables. Real GDP changes, however, as a result of changing government purchases or taxes (rises when government purchases increase and falls when taxes increase) but is unaffected by a change in the money supply.

Notice that Equations (6A.16) and (6A.18) are identical, as are Equations (6A.12) and (6A.14). Equations (6A.12) and (6A.14) say that only the money supply affects aggregate demand, whereas Equations (6A.16) and (6A.18) say that only fiscal policy affects aggregate demand.

These two sets of results are the two extreme cases that arise as the parameter values ℓ and h are allowed to vary. The effect of a change in government purchases, taxes, and the money supply on real GDP actually depends only on the ratio of h to ℓ. As this ratio goes from zero to infinity, so the value of the government purchases multipliers falls from $1/(1 - b)$ to 0, and that of the money multipliers, normalizing the price level equal to 1, rises from 0 to $1/k$.

CHAPTER

World Influences on Aggregate Demand

IN THE GLOBAL VILLAGE

IT USED TO BE SAID THAT "when America sneezes, Europe catches cold." Today, when any big country sneezes, the whole world catches cold. And the economic viruses travel around the globe at the speed of light. A ceaseless hum of international economic activity. Boeing 747s move people and parcels around the globe, delivering overnight to almost anywhere. Telephones connected with geosynchronous satellites bounce messages about stock and commodity prices from computers in Tokyo to computers in Frankfurt, New York, and Toronto. The whole world is linked in a global village economy. In such a world, it is no longer possible to make sense of what is happening in one country without paying attention to events going on in others. Canada is influenced by events in the United States, Japan, Western Europe, and other regions.

The model of aggregate demand we studied in Chapters 5 and 6, the *IS-LM* model, is a **closed economy model** — a model that excludes international considerations. Such a model is useful for studying macroeconomic developments in the world as a whole, for the world economy is a closed economy. It sheds a great deal of light on the behavior of the Canadian economy, but many questions cannot be answered with a closed economy model. They require an **open economy model** — a model that takes into account linkages between the domestic economy and the rest of the world.

There are three broad areas in which an open economy model can improve our understanding of the performance of the Canadian economy. First, it gives us more accurate predictions about the effects of monetary and fiscal policy, taking into account their effects not only on aggregate expenditure and interest rates but also on net exports, international borrowing and lending, and the value of the dollar on the foreign exchange markets. Second, it enables us to understand how developments in the rest of the world — for example, monetary policy in the United States, Japan, or Western Europe — influence the Canadian economy. Third, it enables us to understand the forces that determine our balance of payments and exchange rate. After studying the chapter, you will be able to

- Describe the trends in Canadian international trade, deficit, and indebtedness
- Describe the balance of payments accounts
- Explain how net exports are determined
- Explain the behavior of net exports in the 1980s
- Explain how foreign exchange markets work and how the foreign currency value of the Canadian dollar is determined
- Describe the behavior of interest rates around the world in the 1980s

- Explain why interest rates vary from one country to another and why they are really equal
- Explain the open economy *IS-LM* model
- Explain how fiscal policy operates with a fixed exchange rate
- Explain how fiscal and monetary policy operate with a flexible exchange rate

Let's begin by looking at some facts about world trade, deficits, and debt.

7.1 Growing Canadian Trade, Deficits, and Debt

MACROFACTS

In 1970, only 21 percent of Canadian production was exported and 18 percent of Canadian spending was on goods and services made abroad. By 1990, we were sending 28 percent of our production abroad and more than 30 percent of our spending was on foreign-produced goods and services. International trade has become increasingly important for Canada in the past 20 years.

International trade has grown and it has also fluctuated. After declining in the first half of the 1970s, exports as a percentage of GDP grew very quickly after 1975. Imports grew quickly in the first half of the 1970s but then stabilized until the early 1980s when they surged again. They fell in 1981-1982 and after that grew rapidly. These two forces together produced large swings in net exports. A series of cycles alternating between surpluses and deficits occurred throughout the 1970s and 1980s. The deficit was largest in 1988. Figure 7.1 gives a snapshot picture of these developments in imports, exports, and net exports.

(a) Exports and imports

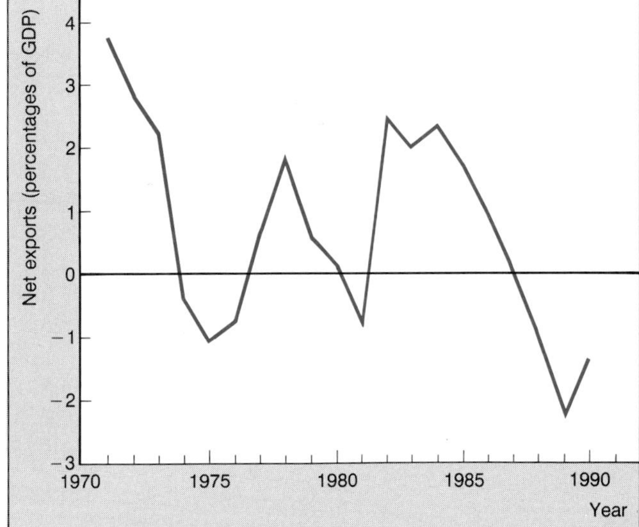

(b) Net exports

FIGURE 7.1
Canadian Exports, Imports, and Net Exports: 1970-1990

International trade has become increasingly important in the Canadian economy, with exports and imports increasing from an average of 20 percent to almost 30 percent of real GDP in a 20-year period. Imports grew more quickly than exports during the 1980s, when net exports became severely negative.

Source: Figure 3.1.

When net exports are positive — when exports exceed imports — a country earns more in the rest of the world than it spends there. How do foreigners cope in such a situation? How do they buy goods in excess of the goods that they're selling? The answer is they borrow from the rest of the world. A country with positive net exports lends to the rest of the world — it buys foreign assets. When net exports are negative — imports exceed exports — a country earns less in the rest of the world than it spends there and the rest of the world lends to it. Canada is a net borrower from the rest of the world. Foreigners are accumulating more assets in Canada than Canada is accumulating in the rest of the world.

Why is Canada a net borrower? Why have our net exports been so hugely negative during the 1980s? This chapter answers these questions and more. But first, it's important to understand how a nation keeps track of its international transactions — its balance of payments accounts.

7.2 *The Balance of Payments Accounts*

The balance of payments accounts used to keep track of a nation's international transactions are

- Current account
- Capital account
- Official settlements account

Current account

The **current account** records the values of

1. Net exports
2. Net income from foreign investments
3. Unilateral transfers

Net exports is the value of exports of goods and services minus the value of imports of goods and services. We have seen that this item appears in the National Income and Expenditure Accounts and is part of aggregate expenditure. Transactions in this category are the purchase of lumber by a Japanese paper producer (an export from Canada to Japan) and a Canadian's purchase of a Honda Civic (a Canadian import from Japan). **Net foreign investment income** is the earnings of Canadian residents on assets held in the rest of the world minus the earnings of foreigners on assets held in Canada. This category includes such items as the profits earned by the Bank of Montreal on its branches in the Caribbean (investment income to Canada) and the profits that Elders makes from its investment in Molsons (investment income from Canada to Australia). **Unilateral transfers** are gifts from Canadians to people in the rest of the world minus gifts to Canadians from people in other countries. The most important component of this item is funds brought into Canada by new immigrants.

Capital account

The **capital account** records new investments by Canadian residents in the rest of the world and foreign investments in Canada. For example, when a British insurance company buys Bell Canada stock, Canada receives capital from the rest of the world. When Conrad Black's company Hollinger Inc. buys a stake in an Australian newspaper company, Fairfax, a payment is recorded in the Canadian capital account as money flows from Canada to Australia. New investments flowing into Canada from the rest of the world are called **capital imports** and investments by Canadian residents in the rest of the world are called **capital exports**. Capital imports minus capital exports is a country's capital account balance.

Official settlements account

The **official settlements account** records the net receipts and payments of gold and foreign currency resulting from all transactions recorded in the current and capital accounts. The balance on the official settlements account, known simply as the **official settlements balance**, is the change in the country's foreign exchange reserves less the change in its official borrowing. It is, if everything is accurately measured, exactly equal to the sum of the current account balance and the capital account balance. (By accounting convention, the official settlements balance is defined as the negative of the sum of the current account and capital account balance so that when the balances on all three accounts are added together the resulting sum is always zero.)

Your own balance of payments accounts

Think of your own balance of payments accounts. Your current account records your income from work minus your expenditure on goods and services. Your income minus expenditure is your net exports. The current account also keeps track of any income you have from investments—the interest that you receive from money in the bank, stocks, or bonds. Finally, your current account contains a record of any gifts you give or receive.

Your capital account keeps track of loans made and repaid. If you run up some debt on your credit card, that's a payment from the credit card company to you—your capital import. When you pay off the credit card, you make a capital export.

The balance on your current account plus the balance on your capital account equals the balance on your settlements account. That's simply the change in the amount of money you have in your purse and at the bank.

If you earn more than you spend, you have a current account surplus. If you lend your surplus, you have a capital account deficit. Your money in the bank stays constant. If you don't lend your surplus, your money in the bank increases and you have a settlements account surplus. Conversely, if you spend more than you earn, you have a current account deficit. If you borrow to cover that deficit, you have a capital account surplus and a constant amount of money in the bank. If you don't borrow to cover your deficit, you have to use your own money and the amount of money you have at the bank decreases. You have a settlements account deficit.

The most important component of a nation's balance of payments accounts is its net exports of goods and services. This is the biggest single item in a nation's current account and the dominant influence on the amount of international borrowing and lending it undertakes—on its capital account. What determines a nation's net exports?

7.3 *What Determines Net Exports?*

Since *net exports* are *exports* of goods and services minus *imports* of goods and services, whatever determines exports and imports also determines net exports. The main influences on exports are

1. The real exchange rate
2. Income of the rest of the world

The main influences on imports are

1. The real exchange rate
2. Canadian real GDP

The real exchange rate

The **real exchange rate** is the price of domestic goods and services relative to the price of foreign goods and services. It is a relative price or *opportunity cost*. It measures the number of units of a foreign good that can be obtained for one unit of a domestic good.

Let's calculate a real exchange rate—the real exchange rate between Japanese and Canadian automobiles. The calculations are summarized in Table 7.1. Suppose this Japanese car, a Honda, can be bought for ¥1,200,000. Suppose that GM in Oshawa makes a Pontiac similar to the Honda in all the relevant respects that consumers value, that can be bought for $10,000. To calculate the real exchange rate, we first need to know the nominal exchange rate. The **nominal exchange rate** (*ER*) is the number of units of a foreign currency that can be obtained with one unit of domestic currency. The exchange rate *ER* is the inverse of the number of units of domestic currency per unit of foreign currency, S.[1] In this example, the exchange rate is the number of yen per dollar. Suppose this exchange rate is 120. We can now calculate the real exchange rate—the relative price of Canadian and Japanese cars. Table 7.1 gives the formula for this calculation. The Canadian real exchange rate, *RER*, is equal to the nominal exchange rate multiplied by the price of a Canadian car divided by the price of a Japanese car. Using the numbers in row *A* of the table, the real exchange rate equals 1.00. That is,

$$RER = 120 \times 10{,}000 \div 1{,}200{,}000 = 1.00.$$

Check carefully that you can see why the units of measurement of the real exchange rate are Japanese cars per Canadian car. The reasoning is set out in Table 7.1. The price of a Canadian car is measured as dollars per Canadian car. When we multiply this price by the exchange rate, we convert it to yen per Canadian car. Dividing this number by yen

TABLE 7.1
Real Exchange Rate Calculations

CASE	PRICE OF JAPANESE CAR (¥)	PRICE OF CANADIAN CAR ($)	EXCHANGE RATE (¥ PER $)	REAL EXCHANGE RATE (JAPANESE CARS PER CANADIAN CAR)
A	1,200,000	10,000	120	1.00
B	1,200,000	12,000	120	1.20
C	1,000,000	10,000	120	1.20
D	1,200,000	10,000	144	1.20

Why real exchange rate is measured in units of Japanese cars per Canadian car.

Price of Japanese car (P_J) is measured in yen per Japanese car.

Price of Canadian car (P_C) is measured in dollars per Canadian car.

Exchange rate (*ER*) is measured in yen per dollar.

$$\text{Real exchange rate} = \frac{ER \times P_C}{P_J}$$

$$\text{Its units of measure are } \frac{\text{yen per dollar x dollars per Canadian car}}{\text{yen per Japanese car}} \text{ or}$$

Japanese cars per Canadian car

per Japanese car gives us the real exchange rate. It is measured in Japanese cars per Canadian car.

The real exchange rate we've just calculated is made up of three separate bits of information: the foreign price (expressed in foreign currency), the domestic price (expressed in domestic currency) and the exchange rate (foreign currency per unit of domestic currency). A change in any one of these changes the real exchange rate. Table 7.1 illustrates a change in each source that increases the real exchange rate from 1 to 1.2: in row *B*, the Canadian price of a car increases by 20 percent, from $10,000 to $12,000; in row *C*, the price of a Japanese car decreases by 20 percent, from ¥1.2 million to ¥1 million; in row *D*, the nominal exchange rate changes — the number of yen per dollar increases by 20 percent.

Notice that when the real exchange rate rises, the number of units of a foreign good per unit of domestic good increases. For example, in Table 7.1, more Japanese cars can be bought per Canadian car. Foreign goods become cheaper relative to domestic goods.

In the above example, we calculate the real exchange rate between two cars. In macroeconomics, the study of economic aggregates, we measure the real exchange rate in terms of price indexes of a wide range of goods and services. Also, since Canada trades with many countries and each has its own currency and exchange rate, we calculate the nominal exchange rate as the average of all these exchange rates.

Net exports and the real exchange rate

Other things being equal, the higher the Canadian real exchange rate, the smaller is the value of Canadian exports and the greater is the value of Canadian imports. A higher real exchange rate leads to smaller net exports (or greater net imports).

This response of exports and imports to a change in the real exchange rate comes about because people are constantly looking for the best possible deal, substituting away from goods that become relatively more expensive toward goods that become relatively less expensive. If the Canadian real exchange rate increases, Canadian goods become more expensive relative to foreign-produced goods. As a result, foreigners will be less inclined to buy Canadian goods and more inclined to buy foreign-produced goods. Canadian exports decline. Also, Canadians, looking for the best available deal, will be more inclined to substitute an imported good for a domestically produced good. Canadian imports increase. Thus when a country's real exchange rate rises, its exports decrease and its imports increase.

To see how this works out, suppose that Hondas are selling for ¥1,200,000 and Pontiacs for $10,000. If the exchange rate is ¥120 yen per dollar, the Canadian real exchange rate is 1 and these two cars are selling for exactly the same price. Now suppose that the yen falls in value so that $1 buys ¥144. Ten thousand dollars will now buy ¥1,440,000. You could buy a Honda for ¥1,200,000 and have ¥240,000 in change. In other words, you can now buy the Honda for less than the price of the Pontiac. Of course, people for whom the price difference isn't enough to make them switch will stick with the Pontiac. But for others the price difference is sufficiently attractive to make them switch from the Pontiac to the Honda. When the people substituting Hondas for Pontiacs are Canadians, Canadian imports increase. When the people making that substitution are foreigners, Canadian exports decrease.

Income and net exports

Canadian exports are foreigners' imports. And foreigners make decisions about how much to import in exactly the same way that Canadians do. One influence on imports is price — the real exchange rate, which we've just considered. Another is income. The higher the income in the rest of the world, the larger is the quantity of Canadian goods and services imported by the rest of the world and the greater are Canadian exports. Income in the rest of the world is the total gross domestic product of the rest of the world. Canadian imports are determined by incomes in Canada—real GDP. The higher the real GDP in Canada, the greater are Canadian imports.

Net export function

The **net export function** is the relationship between net exports and the variables that influence it—real GDP, income in the rest of the world, and the real exchange rate.

We illustrate the net export function with the net export curve shown in Figure 7.2(a). The **net export curve** is the relationship between net exports and real GDP, holding the real exchange rate constant. From a nation's point of view, income in the rest of the world is exogenous and is therefore constant. When real GDP changes, there is a movement along the net export curve. In this example, when real GDP is \$4 billion, net exports are zero; when real GDP is below \$4 billion, net exports are positive; and when real GDP is above \$4 billion, net exports are negative. The negative relationship arises from the influence of real GDP on imports. A higher level of real GDP increases imports but has no effect on exports, so net exports decrease.

The net export curve shifts when the real exchange rate changes. A decrease in the real exchange rate increases net exports and shifts the net export curve to the right, from NX_0 to NX_1 in Figure 7.2(b). An increase in the real exchange rate decreases net exports and shifts the net export curve to the left, from NX_0 to NX_2 in Figure 7.2(b).

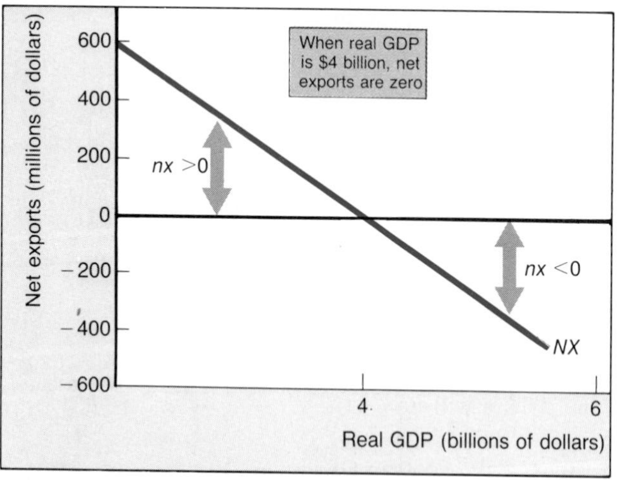

(a) The net exports curve

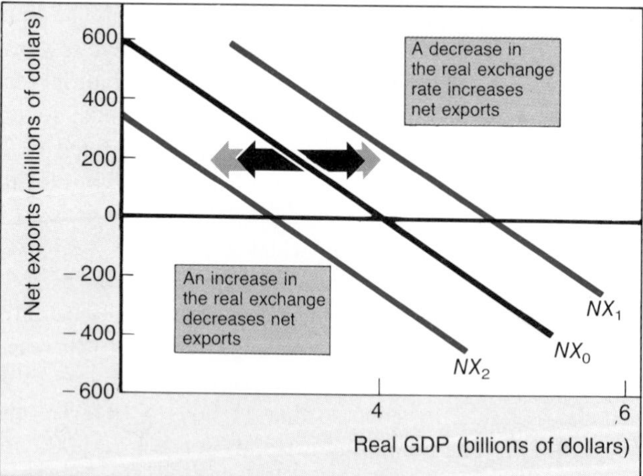

(b) Shift in the net exports curve

FIGURE 7.2
The Net Exports Curve

The net exports curve (part a) shows the relationship between net exports and real GDP, holding constant all other influences on net exports. The higher the level of real GDP, the lower the level of net exports. In this example, when real GDP exceeds \$4 billion, net exports are negative.

The net exports curve shifts when any other influence on net exports changes (part b). A decrease in the real exchange rate shifts the net exports curve to the right, from NX_0 to NX_1. An increase in the real exchange rate shifts the net exports curve left, to NX_2.

7.4 *Net Exports in the 1980s*

TESTCASE

We looked at the behavior of net exports in Canada in the first part of this chapter. There, we discovered that net exports increased and were positive in the early 1980s and then decreased after 1983. By 1986, net exports had become negative. They bottomed out in 1988 and then, while remaining negative, began to increase. Does the theory of net exports that we have just reviewed account for the performance of Canadian net exports during the 1980s?

The answer is, it does in part; the evidence is summarized in Figure 7.3. Part (a) graphs imports against real GDP. There, you can see the clear tendency for imports to increase as real GDP increases. That is, other things being equal, the higher is the real GDP, the higher the level of imports. You can also see that imports are not a constant fraction of real GDP; the blue dots do not lie on one straight line. Imports change independent of changes in real GDP. These fluctuations in imports, as well as in exports, are driven mainly by the behavior of the real exchange rate.

Figure 7.3(b) shows the relationship between the real exchange rate and net imports (the negative value of net exports). The real exchange rate is graphed on the left scale and net imports on the right scale. First, look at the real exchange rate (the black line). By definition, its value in 1985 is 100. In 1980, the real exchange rate was 93 percent of its 1985 value. From 1980 to 1983 the real exchange rate increased steadily. Between 1983 and 1986, it fell back to a level slightly below its 1980 level. After 1986, the real exchange rate began to increase rapidly. Recall that when the real exchange rate

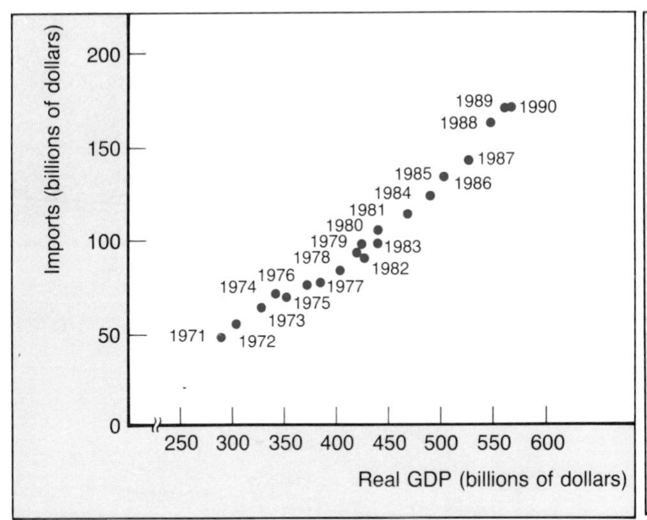

(a) Import function

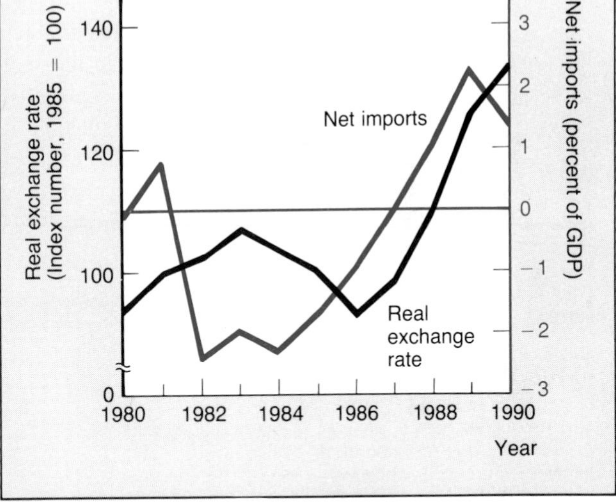

(b) Net imports and the real exchange rate

FIGURE 7.3
Canadian Imports, Exports, and Real Exchange Rate

There's a strong relationship between imports and real GDP, the import function (part a). There is also a relationship between net imports (the negative of net exports) and the real exchange rate (part b). Other things being equal, when the real exchange rate increases, so do net imports. In six of the years, you can see this response in part (b). But in four of the years net imports move in the opposite direction to the real exchange rate. These are years in which the change in real GDP has the dominant effect on net imports.

Source: Figure 3.1 and *International Financial Statistics Yearbook*, 1990.

increases, Canadian goods become more expensive relative to foreign-produced goods —equivalently, foreign-produced goods become cheaper relative to Canadian goods. As the real exchange rate increases, other things remaining the same, imports increase and exports decrease. That is, net exports decline and net imports increase. Do the Canadian data correspond with these predictions?

In some years they do and in others they don't. Years in which the real exchange rate and net exports move in the same direction (as predicted) are 1981, 1983, 1984, and 1987-1989 and years in which they move in opposite directions are 1982, 1985-1986, and 1990. In the years in which net exports and the real exchange rate move in opposite directions, there are large changes in Canadian real GDP and the effect of real GDP on imports (and on the percentage of GDP imported) swamps the effect of the change in the real exchange rate. Net exports fell in 1982 and 1990 despite the rise in the real exchange rate because real GDP growth slowed. It became negative in 1982 and close to zero in 1990. Net imports increased when the real exchange rate fell in 1985 and 1986 because real GDP grew very quickly, increasing imports sharply.

It is clear from Figure 7.3 that changes in the real exchange rate influence net imports (and net exports). But what produces the change in the real exchange rate? We've seen that there are three possible sources — a change in the domestic price, a change in the foreign price, and a change in the nominal exchange rate. Which variable is responsible for the movements in the Canadian real exchange rate? The answer is that the cycle in the real exchange rate has been associated with a cycle in the nominal exchange rate, but the trend in the real exchange rate is associated with the difference between the inflation rates in Canada and the rest of the world. You can see this in Figure 7.4, which plots the real exchange rate and the nominal exchange rate, each measured as an index number (or average) across all the currencies and countries with which Canada has international transactions. The cycles in the real exchange rate and the nominal exchange rate are very similar. But the nominal exchange rate has no trend, while the trend in the real exchange rate is steadily upward. The increase in the real exchange rate is especially strong after 1986.

If the real exchange rate influences net exports, and if the nominal exchange rate influences the real exchange rate, what produces movements in the nominal exchange rate? That is our next question.

FIGURE 7.4
Real and Nominal Exchange Rates

Cycles in the real exchange rate are associated with cycles in the nominal exchange rate. But the real exchange rate has an upward trend resulting from inflation differences, while the nominal exchange rate does not have a trend.

Source: International Financial Statistics Yearbook, 1991.

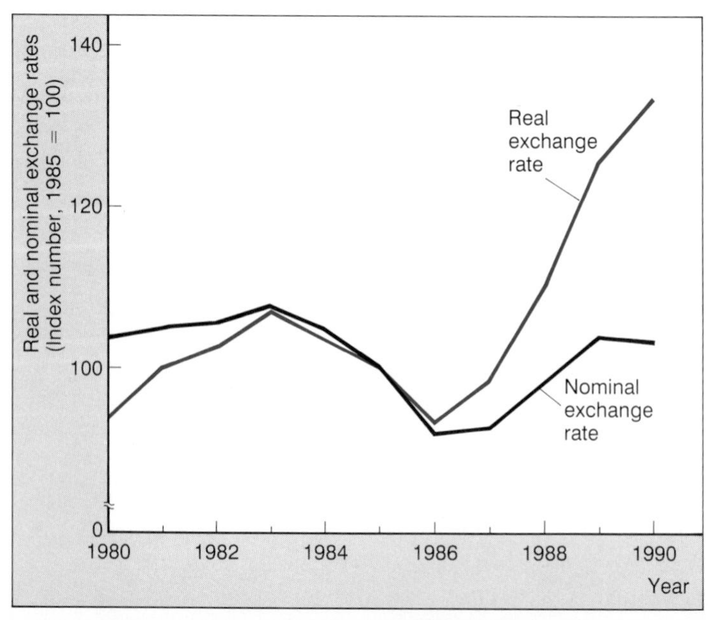

7.5 *The Foreign Exchange Rate*

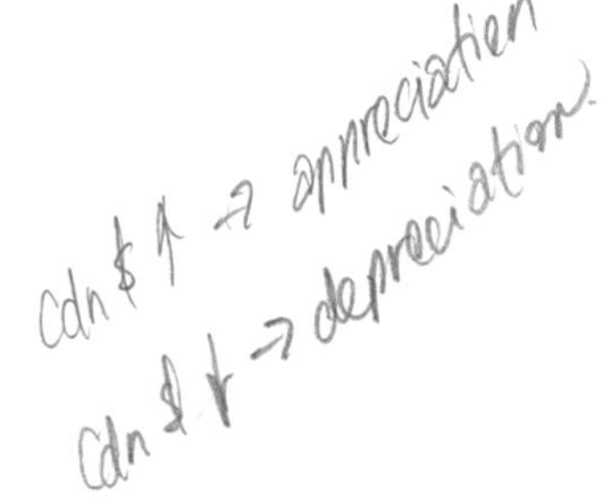

A **foreign exchange rate** is the number of units of foreign money that one dollar will buy. For example, in January 1991, one Canadian dollar would buy 115 Japanese yen. This is the exchange rate between the Canadian dollar and the yen. A rise in the value of the dollar is called **appreciation of the dollar**. When the dollar appreciates, it buys more units of foreign money. If, for example, the number of yen you can get for a dollar increases from 115 to 126.5, the dollar has appreciated by 10 percent. Conversely a fall in the number of units of foreign money that a dollar will buy is a **depreciation of the dollar**.

Effective exchange rate

There is not, of course, just one foreign exchange rate. There are as many as there are foreign currencies. For the Canadian economy, the most important exchange rates are those between the Canadian dollar and the U.S. dollar, the Japanese yen, the British pound, the French franc, and the German mark. So that we can measure the value of the Canadian dollar in relation to all other currencies, we use the concept of the effective exchange rate.

The **effective exchange rate** of the Canadian dollar is an index number calculated as a weighted average of the value of the Canadian dollar in terms of all other currencies, where the weight on each currency is the proportion of Canadian international trade undertaken in that currency. The International Monetary Fund calculates the effective exchange rate for the Canadian dollar (and for other currencies as well). It is the average nominal exchange rate whose behavior we examined in Figure 7.4. When the effective exchange rate increases, the dollar appreciates on the average against all other currencies. When the effective exchange rate decreases, the dollar depreciates on the average against all other currencies. Recall that the dollar appreciated between 1980 and 1983 and then depreciated through 1986. It then appreciated through 1989 and depreciated slightly in 1990.

Exchange rate regimes

Since 1971, exchange rates have fluctuated and, as we have seen, some of the fluctuations have been large. But this has not always been the case because the behavior of the exchange rate depends in an important way on the international monetary system. There are three possible international monetary arrangements. They are

- Fixed exchange rate
- Flexible exchange rate
- Managed floating exchange rate

Fixed exchange rate Under a **fixed exchange rate regime**, the central bank declares a central or par value for the exchange rate, which it will act to maintain. Usually it also declares an intervention band — a small range of value over which the exchange rate may move without intervention from the central bank. That is, in declaring a fixed exchange rate, a country announces that if the exchange rate rises above or falls below the par value by more than a certain percentage amount, its central bank will intervene in the foreign exchange market to prevent the rate from moving any further away from the par value. In order to maintain a fixed exchange rate, the central bank stands ready to use its stock of foreign exchange reserves to raise or lower the quantity of money outstanding so as to maintain a constant relative price with some other money.

From 1945 to 1971 the Western world operated a fixed exchange rate system, called the Bretton Woods system. Its name comes from Bretton Woods, New Hampshire, where the plan for the world monetary system was negotiated. Under the Bretton Woods system, the United States declared that one ounce of gold was worth US$35. Each country then fixed the exchange rate between its currency and the U.S. dollar. Thus the world's money was pegged to gold. Under the Bretton Woods system, the United States took no responsibility for maintaining the exchange rates between the U.S. dollar and other currencies. Its job was to maintain the price of gold at US$35 per ounce. Each country was then left to maintain its own exchange rate against the U.S. dollar. Thus for example, if the pound sterling began to fall toward the lower limit or rise toward the upper limit of the intervention band, the Bank of England (the central bank of the United Kingdom) would intervene in the foreign exchange market, exchanging U.S. dollars from its foreign exchange reserves for pounds, or exchanging pounds for U.S. dollars, in order to keep the value of the pound inside the intervention band.

Flexible exchange rate A **flexible exchange rate**—sometimes also called a **floating exchange rate**—is one whose value is determined by market forces. The central bank does not declare a target value for the exchange rate and has no direct interest in the value of the exchange rate. The central bank does not intervene in the foreign exchange market to manipulate the relative price of its currency.

Managed floating exchange rate A **managed floating exchange rate** is one that the central bank manipulates but does not necessarily hold constant. Usually, in a managed floating regime, the central bank announces that it is floating, but does not tell the market what course it would like to see the exchange rate follow. The Western world has operated this type of exchange rate regime since the collapse of the Bretton Woods system in the early 1970s.

What determines the exchange rate when it is freely floating and how can its value be manipulated in a managed float?

Exchange rate determination

There are two theories of the exchange rate, one that explains its long-run movements and the other its short-run day-to-day movements. Let's begin with the long run.

The long run: purchasing power parity **Purchasing power parity (PPP)** is a condition that exists when the value of money in one country is the same as its value in another country. The purchasing power parity theory of the exchange rate says that, in the long run, the exchange rate between two currencies will be such that purchasing power parity prevails. For example, suppose that a Pontiac compact car sells in Canada for $10,000 and that an identical Japanese car sells in Japan for ¥1,200,000. Purchasing power parity exists if the exchange rate is ¥120 per dollar. In this situation, $10,000 will buy either the Pontiac or ¥1,200,000, which will buy the Japanese car.

The purchasing power parity theory predicts that the exchange rate between two national moneys will be such that they have equal purchasing power—purchasing power parity prevails. That is, it predicts that in the long run, the real exchange rate will be 1. Purchasing power itself is determined by the price level.

We already have a theory of the price level. It is determined by the interaction of aggregate demand and aggregate supply. Since the purchasing power parity theory is a long-run theory of the exchange rate, we need to use the aggregate demand-aggregate supply model as a long-run theory of the price level. In the long run, the aggregate supply curve is vertical because all prices, including factor prices, are flexible. Thus in the long run, the price level in each country is determined by the level of aggregate demand. This in turn is determined mainly by the nation's money supply. Other things being equal, the higher the money supply, the higher is the level of aggregate demand and the price level and the lower is the foreign exchange value of a nation's money.

The purchasing power parity theory implies that, in the long run, a nation's currency will change in value (appreciate or depreciate) at a rate equal to the difference between the two countries' inflation rates. If Canada has an inflation rate of 5 percent a year and Japan an inflation rate of 2 percent a year, the Canadian dollar will depreciate against the Japanese yen at a 3 percent annual rate and the yen will appreciate against the dollar at the same 3 percent annual rate.

The short run: asset market equilibrium The purchasing power parity theory of the exchange rate explains long-run tendencies, not day-to-day fluctuations in the exchange rate. On any given day, the exchange rate, like any other price, is determined by supply and demand. The value of the dollar on the foreign exchange market is determined by the supply of dollar assets and the demand for dollar assets. **Dollar assets** are securities such as bonds, stocks, treasury bills, bank deposits and loans denominated in Canadian dollars. They are promises to pay (and receive) a certain number of Canadian dollars on a certain date.

Of the many factors that influence the demand for and the supply of dollar assets, the most important is the expected rate of return on dollar assets compared with the expected rate of return on assets denominated in other currencies. Other things being equal, the higher the expected rate of return on dollar assets, the greater is the demand for dollars. The higher the demand for dollars, the higher is the value of the dollar—that is, the higher is the exchange rate. In the short run, the exchange rate adjusts minute by minute to keep the quantity of dollar assets demanded equal to the quantity supplied.

By manipulating Canadian interest rates, the Bank of Canada can manipulate the rate of return and expected rate of return on dollar assets and influence the foreign exchange value of the Canadian dollar. Other things being equal, on a given day, the higher the Canadian interest rate relative to interest rates in other countries, the higher is the value of the Canadian dollar.

To understand more fully how the value of the dollar and interest rates are determined, we need to broaden our view and look more closely at interest rates and their relationship to the value of the dollar. Let's start with some facts about interest rates.

7.6 *Interest Rates Around the World*

MACROFACTS

We've seen, at various points in our study, that Canadian interest rates have fluctuated a great deal in recent years. In the early 1980s, they stood at between 15 and 20 percent a year. In recent years, they have been around 12 percent a year. Are Canadian interest rates typical? Do all countries have interest rates that behave like those in Canada?

The answer is, they do not. In some countries, interest rates are much higher than Canadian interest rates, and in others they are lower. Figure 7.5 shows short-term interest rates in Canada, the United States, Japan and Italy since 1980. Japan and Italy are representative of countries with low and high interest rates. Interest rates in Japan behave much as they do in Germany and Switzerland. Italy's interest rates are similar to those in the United Kingdom and Australia. As you can see, the Canadian and U.S. interest rates lie in the center of the band. Most other countries' interest rates also lie inside the range of those of Italy and Japan.

However, interest rates in a few countries, mostly in Latin America, are stratospheric compared with these. At times in their recent history, Brazil, Bolivia, Argentina, and Chile have had interest rates of several hundred percent a year, as has Israel. Only

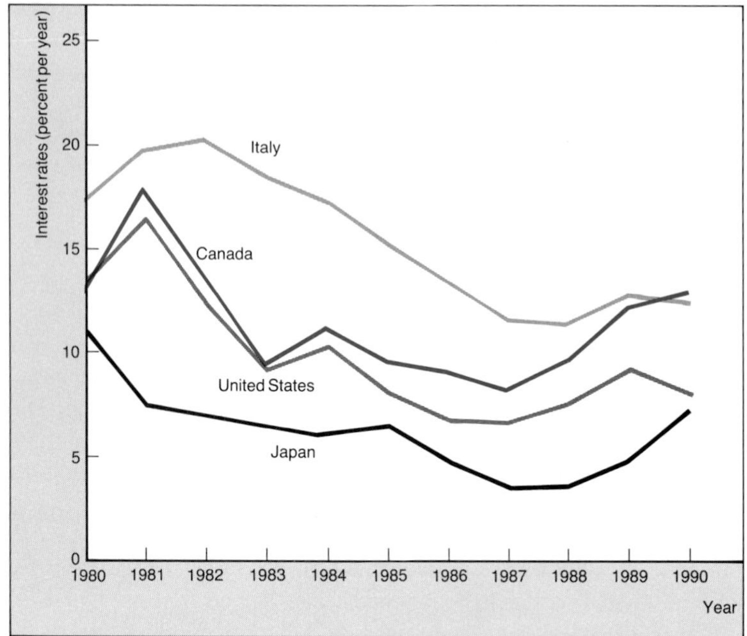

FIGURE 7.5
Interest Rates Around the World

Interest rates vary from one country to another. They have been persistently higher in Italy and lower in Japan than in Canada and the United States.

Source: International Financial Statistics Yearbook, 1991.

in countries that are experiencing very severe inflation do interest rates rise to these extraordinary magnitudes so that borrowers compensate lenders for the falling value of money. But the same principle applies to other countries with low interest rates. Persistent differences in interest rates reflect the fact that some countries have higher inflation rates than others. Japan is a low inflation country, Italy is a relatively high inflation country, and Canada and the United States lie in between.

But how can interest rate differences between countries persist year after year? Why don't people borrow in countries with low interest rates and lend in countries with high interest rates, thereby making a profit? And as a result, why don't countries with high interest rates have ever-appreciating currencies as people put more and more money into those countries? To answer these questions, we need first to establish that although interest rates may differ from country to country they are not *really* different. Let's see why.

7.7 Interest Rate Parity

Interest rate parity (IRP) prevails when investors make the same rate of return regardless of the currency in which they borrow and lend. The interest rate parity theory predicts that rates of return on assets denominated in different currencies are equal once the expected rate of currency depreciation or appreciation is taken into account. The theory also predicts that the exchange rate will adjust from hour to hour and day to day to ensure that interest rate parity prevails.

Let's work through an example. Suppose that interest rates in Canada are 20 percent a year and in the United States 10 percent a year. Today, the exchange rate between the two currencies is C$1 equals 85.3¢ US and one year from today, the exchange rate is expected to be C$1 equals 76.3¢ US. You're considering making a loan and trying to decide whether to make a Canadian dollar loan or a U.S. dollar loan. Table 7.2 shows what happens for each Canadian dollar you lend. If you make a Canadian dollar loan, you lend a dollar and a year later you will receive $1.20. Your rate of return is 20 percent a year. If you're going to make a U.S. dollar loan, first you have to buy U.S.

dollars. You get 83.3¢ US for C$1 and lend the 83.3¢ at an interest rate of 10 percent a year. At the end of the year, you will have a 91.6¢ (the original 83.3¢ plus 9.3¢ interest). But you're interested in buying goods in Canada so at the end of the year you will have to sell your U.S. dollars to get Canadian dollars. You expect the exchange rate then to be 76.3¢ US per C$1. Converting 91.6¢ US into Canadian dollars you will expect to get C$1.20. Your expected rate of return is 20 percent a year, exactly the same as if you'd lent Canadian dollars.

TABLE 7.2
Interest Rate Parity: An Example

You are considering lending 1 Canadian dollar for one year. You can make the loan in Canada in Canadian dollars or in the United States in U.S. dollars.	
Canadian Dollar Loan	
Interest rate in United States	20% per year
You lend $1.00 for one year.	
At year end, you receive $1.20 (principal plus interest).	
Rate of return	20% per year
U.S. Dollar Loan	
Interest rate in the United States	10% per year
Spot exchange rate	83.3¢ US per C$
Forward exchange rate	76.3¢ US per C$1
To make a U.S. dollar loan, you need U.S. dollars.	
C$1 buys 83.3¢ US which you lend for one year.	
At year end, you receive 91.6¢ US (principal plus interest).	
You sell the 91.6¢ US at 76.3¢ US per C$1 to receive C$1.20.	
Rate of return	20% per year

Interest rate parity theory is based on the idea that investors try to do the best they can and seek the highest rate of return available. Suppose that you expect the Canadian dollar to be worth less than 76.3¢ US at the end of the year. In this case, you will expect a higher rate of return from a U.S. dollar loan than a Canadian dollar loan. In such a situation, you will buy U.S. dollars. And so will lots of other people. The process of buying U.S. dollars will make the U.S. dollar appreciate today, wiping out the expected profit opportunity. Conversely, if you expect the Canadian dollar to depreciate less in the coming year, you will expect a higher rate of return from a Canadian dollar loan than a U.S. dollar loan. So would everyone else. The Canadian dollar will be bought, making it appreciate. The Canadian dollar will continue to appreciate against the U.S. dollar until the expected rates of return from loans in the two currencies are equal.

Interest rate parity theory does not actually explain whether the interest rate or the exchange rate does the adjusting to make the expected rates of return equal. All it tells us is that the relationship between today's exchange rate, next year's expected exchange rate, and the interest rates in two countries will be lined up such that there is no expected profit from lending in one currency rather than another.

Does the interest rate parity theory work in practice? Let's see.

TESTCASE

7.8 *The Eurocurrency Markets*

In the 1950s, the Soviet Union accumulated a sizable amount of foreign currency, most of which was held as U.S. dollars in banks in the United States. With the Cold War at its height, the Soviets were afraid that the United States might freeze these assets. But they regarded the U.S. dollar as the safest currency in which to keep their funds. They didn't want to take their money out of U.S. dollars and put it into British pounds or French francs. They did, however, want the security of having their money in a bank in Europe. So was born the idea of Eurodollars. **Eurodollars** are U.S. dollars deposited in foreign banks outside the United States or foreign branches of U.S. banks. From this modest beginning has grown a huge business called the Eurocurrency market. In the Eurocurrency market, it is possible to borrow and lend through banks located in Europe in any currency the borrower or lender chooses.

This is a particularly good market for studying interest rate parity because all the transactions are taking place not just in a single country but often in a single bank. One bank has deposits and loans denominated in U.S. dollars, Japanese yen, French francs, British pounds, German marks, and so on. A single investor can borrow in one currency and lend in another. Let's look at this market on December 31, 1990. On that day, banks were accepting three-month deposits in British pounds at an interest rate of 14.03 percent a year. They were also lending British pounds at an interest rate of 15 percent a year. Thus as you would expect, you can't borrow pounds from a bank and lend them pounds and make money. It's banks that make money on that kind of deal!

But banks were lending in Japanese yen at an interest rate of 8 percent a year. Doesn't this mean that you could borrow some Japanese yen at 8 percent, convert them into pounds and deposit them, and earn 14.03 percent, thereby making a profit of 6.03 percent?

In fact, you couldn't. The reason is that the exchange rate between the British pound and the Japanese yen was not going to be constant over the three-month period. The pound was going to depreciate against the yen. Table 7.3 sets out the information and the calculations of the return on this transaction. On December 31, 1990, one British pound bought ¥260.838. Thus if you borrowed that number of yen you could buy £1. Investing the pound in a three-month bank deposit with an interest rate of 14.03 percent a year would give you £1.033367 at the end of three months.

But at the end of three months, you're going to owe the bank ¥260.838 plus three months' interest at 8 percent a year—a total of ¥265.905. To avoid taking a risk at the time you borrow the yen, you'd better enter into a forward contract to buy some yen three months in the future. A **forward contract** is a contract entered into today to buy or sell an agreed quantity at an agreed future date and at an agreed price. The forward contract price — the price at which one currency is traded for another is called the **forward exchange rate**. To contrast it with the forward exchange rate, the exchange rate between two currencies for immediate delivery is called the **spot exchange rate**.

On December 31, 1990, the forward exchange rate between the yen and the pound — the price for which yen and pounds traded for three months future delivery — was ¥257.216 per pound. That is, the pound was expected to depreciate against the yen and that expectation was reflected in the price at which yen and pounds were traded for delivery three months in the future. Since you knew that you would have £1.033367 in three months' time to convert into yen, you could sell that quantity of pounds, buying ¥265.798 for delivery in three months. At the end of three months, you're going to have to pay the bank ¥265.905 yen. You've made a loss of ¥0.107. It's not a big loss but it is a loss nonetheless.

This example illustrates that you cannot make a profit by borrowing at low interest

TABLE 7.3
The Eurocurrency Market

On December 31, 1990:	
Interest rate on 3-month deposit in British pounds	14.03 percent per year
Bank's prime lending rate on British pounds	15.00 percent per year
Bank's prime lending rate on Japanese yen	8.00 percent per year
Why you can't make a profit by borrowing Japanese yen and lending British pounds	
On December 31, 1990:	
Spot exchange rate	260.838 yen per pound
Three-month forward exchange rate	257.216 yen per pound
Borrow	260.838 yen
Sell ¥260.838 yen at spot exchange rate and buy	1 pound
Take out forward contract, at the forward exchange rate, to buy	265.798 yen
On March 31, 1991:	
Loan in pounds earns (principal and interest)	1.033367 pounds
Repay yen loan + interest	265.095 yen
Profit	−0.107 yen
Profit rate	0 percent

rates in one currency and lending at higher interest rates in another currency. Expected changes in exchange rates wipe out any expected profit. Interest rate parity prevails.

The example we've just worked out is one of what is known as covered interest parity. **Covered interest parity** is the equality of rates of return when no risk is taken and when the investor covers the transaction by taking out a forward contract. In contrast, **uncovered interest parity** refers to the equality of rates of return where the investor takes a risk and does not cover the transaction by taking out a forward contract. Uncovered interest rate parity holds in the sense that investors' expectations of the future exchange rate are equal to the forward exchange rate. If an individual trader's expectation was not equal to the forward rate, this trader will attempt to profit by speculating in the forward market, buying and selling currencies for forward delivery without actually ever taking delivery.

We've seen that interest rate parity works almost exactly in the Eurocurrency markets. But it also holds on the average in all international asset markets. Figure 7.6 illustrates how taking account of changes in the exchange rate closes the gap between different interest rates. Recall Figure 7.5, showing persistent and systematic differences in the interest rates on three-month loans in Canada, the United States, Japan, and Italy through the 1980s. If we take account of the fluctuations in the Canadian dollar, the depreciation of the Italian lire, and the appreciation of the Japanese yen against the U.S. dollar, we discover that those systematic differences in rates of return are eliminated. It is true that the interest rates fluctuate and are not exactly equal, but there are no systematic and persistent differences between the interest rates in the three countries once we look at the rate of return from the point of view of someone investing U.S. dollars.

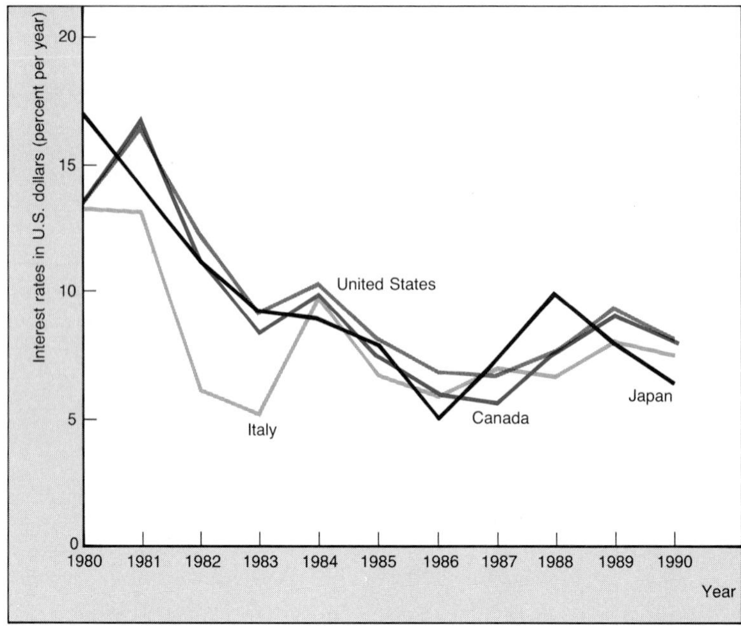

FIGURE 7.6
Interest Rates Adjusted for Exchange Rate Changes

Taking into account the appreciation of the Japanese yen, depreciation of the Italian lira, and fluctuations in the Canadian dollar against the U.S. dollar, there are no persistent divergences between interest rates in Japan, Italy, Canada, and the United States.

Source: International Financial Statistics Yearbook, 1991.

We've now discovered that interest rates, exchange rates, and expected future exchange rates are linked by interest rate parity. But how is the exchange rate determined and how do fiscal policy and monetary policy affect the exchange rate and influence real GDP, the price level, and the balance of international trade? These are the next questions that we tackle.

7.9 *The Open Economy* IS-LM *Model*

The *IS-LM* model of the open economy determines equilibrium real GDP, aggregate planned expenditure and its components, the interest rate, and the exchange rate, taking as exogenous the price level, the instruments of monetary and fiscal policy—the money supply, government purchases of goods and services and taxes—as well as economic conditions in the rest of the world such as income and interest rates. In the case of the closed economy, the open economy *IS-LM* model is a model of aggregate demand. That is, it is possible to find an equilibrium real GDP at each price level, thereby generating an aggregate demand curve.

Let's begin our study of the open economy *IS-LM* model by looking at the *IS* curve in the open economy.

The *IS* curve in an open economy

The definition of the *IS* curve in an open economy is exactly the same as in the closed economy. It is the relationship between the interest rate and real GDP such that aggregate planned expenditure equals real GDP. Equivalently, it is the relationship between the interest rate and real GDP such that aggregate planned injections equal aggregate planned leakages.

The key difference stems from the differences in leakages and injections in the two economies. In the closed economy, injections are investment and government purchases and leakages are saving and taxes. The open economy has an additional injection, exports, and an additional leakage, imports.

We've seen that net exports—the difference between exports and imports—depend on three factors: real GDP in the rest of the world, Canadian real GDP, and the real exchange rate. Real GDP in the rest of the world is exogenous. It affects the level of net exports and the position of the *IS* curve. An increase in real GDP in the rest of the world shifts the open economy *IS* curve to the right. Canadian real GDP is an endogenous variable. Its value varies along the *IS* curve. Whether the real exchange rate is an endogenous variable depends on the exchange rate regime. In a fixed exchange rate regime, the real exchange rate is exogenous, changing only when either the foreign price level, the Canadian price level, or the exchange rate changes. In a flexible exchange rate regime, the real exchange rate is an endogenous variable. Its endogeneity arises from interest rate parity: the domestic interest rate minus the foreign interest rate equals the expected rate of depreciation of the domestic currency. For a given foreign interest rate and a given expected future exchange rate, the higher the domestic interest rate, the higher is the foreign exchange rate and the higher is the real exchange rate.

The open economy *IS* curve in a fixed exchange rate regime, illustrated in Figure 7.7.(a), is steeper than the closed economy *IS* curve. The reason is that a change in Canadian real GDP induces a change in imports, making the multiplier effect of a change in autonomous expenditure smaller than in the closed economy. For example, if the interest rate increases, investment decreases and via a multiplier effect aggregate planned expenditure and real GDP decrease. But the multiplier effect is smaller in the open economy because some of the additional expenditure leaks out through imports into the rest of the world. For this reason, equilibrium real GDP is less sensitive to a change in the interest rate in an open economy with a fixed exchange rate than in a closed economy.

The *IS* curve in an open economy with a flexible exchange rate, illustrated in Figure 7.7(b), is much flatter than the open economy *IS* curve in a fixed exchange rate regime because a change in the interest rate also changes the real exchange rate. As the interest

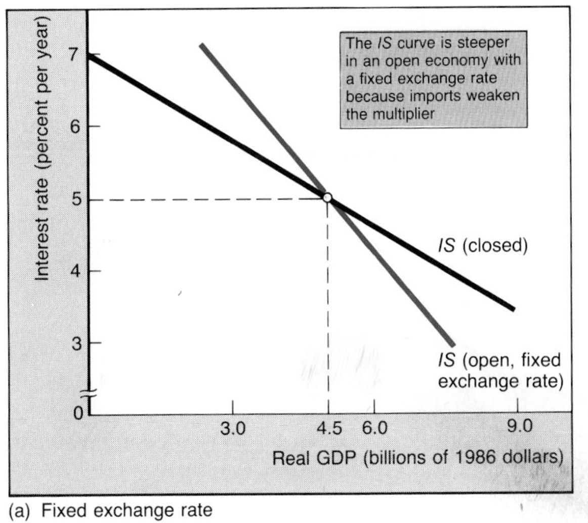

(a) Fixed exchange rate

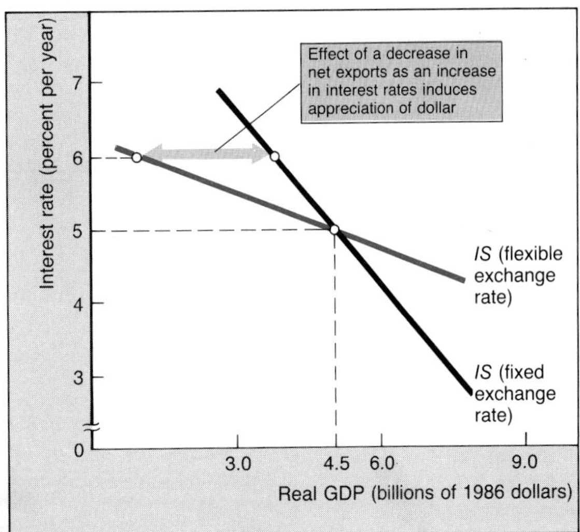

(b) Fixed and flexible exchange rates

FIGURE 7.7
The *IS* Curve in the Open and Closed Economies

With a fixed exchange rate (part a), the *IS* curve is steeper in the open economy than in the closed economy. The reason is that imports, a leakage, weaken the multiplier effect of a change in investment resulting from an interest rate change.

Under flexible exchange rates, the *IS* curve is flatter than under fixed exchange rates (part b). The reason is that an increase in the interest rate not only decreases investment but increases the real exchange rate, decreasing net exports.

rate increases, the dollar appreciates, reducing exports and increasing imports. Net exports decrease. Therefore the higher interest rate decreases net exports as well as investment, so the initial fall in autonomous expenditure is larger than in the open economy with a fixed exchange rate. Thus via the multiplier effect, there is a much larger decrease in aggregate planned expenditure resulting from a given increase in the interest rate when the exchange rate is flexible.

In Figure 7.7(b), the horizontal gap between the open economy *IS* curves for fixed and flexible exchange rate economies measures the effect of the induced decrease in net exports resulting from the appreciation of the dollar.

Shifts in the open economy *IS* curve

The position of the open economy *IS* curve depends on

1. Government purchases of goods and services
2. Taxes
3. Real income in the rest of the world
4. Interest rates in the rest of the world
5. The price level

Changes in government purchases and taxes shift the *IS* curve in the open economy in a similar manner to their effects in the closed economy. An increase in government purchases or a cut in taxes shifts the *IS* curve to the right. The magnitude of this shift depends on the autonomous expenditure multiplier. For the open economy, this multiplier is smaller than for the closed economy because of the import leakage.

A change in real income or interest rates in the rest of the world shifts the *IS* curve. An increase in real income or interest rates in the rest of the world shifts the open economy *IS* curve to the right. A change in real income in the rest of the world operates through its effect on Canadian exports and rest-of-world imports. A change in interest rates works through its effects on the exchange rate: an increase in interest rates in the rest of the world, other things being equal, depreciates the Canadian dollar, which leads to a decrease in Canadian imports and an increase in Canadian exports — net exports increase.

The price level does not affect the position of the *IS* curve in a closed economy but it does in the open economy. The effect operates through the real exchange rate. The higher the price level, other things being equal, the higher is the real exchange rate. (Recall that the real exchange rate changes when either the nominal exchange rate, the domestic price level, or the rest of the world price level changes.) An increase in the real exchange rate reduces Canadian exports and increases Canadian imports — net exports decline—and the *IS* curve shifts to the left.

The *LM* curve in an open economy

The *LM* curve in the open economy is similar to that in the closed economy. It is the relationship between the interest rate and real GDP along which the quantity of money demanded equals the quantity supplied. However, two features of the *LM* curve can differ in the open economy:

1. The response of the quantity of money demanded to the interest rate
2. The endogeneity or exogeneity of the money supply

Response of money to interest rates In an open economy, people can choose whether to hold their wealth in the form of money or other financial assets. And if they choose to hold money, they can choose domestic or foreign money. Because there is an extra way of holding wealth, people may switch from domestic money to foreign money if they believe that the opportunity cost of holding foreign money is lower than that of holding domestic money. This extra dimension of choice may make the quantity of money demanded — domestic money demanded — more sensitive to interest rates in the open economy than in the closed economy. Although this theoretical possibility exists, no one has come up with strong evidence to suggest that it is important in practice. For this reason, we'll continue to suppose that the demand for money function is fairly insensitive to interest rate changes and will not change the slope of the *LM* curve in the open economy compared with that in the closed economy.

Exogeneity or endogeneity of money supply In the closed economy, the money supply is determined by the actions of the Bank of Canada. The Bank of Canada decides whether to increase or decrease the money supply and then takes the appropriate actions to achieve its objective. As far as the *IS-LM* model is concerned, the money supply is exogenous.

The same is true for an open economy with a flexible exchange rate. But for a fixed exchange rate economy, the money supply is endogenous — the Bank of Canada does not have ultimate control of it.

The reason is this. In a fixed exchange rate system, the value of the Canadian dollar is pegged in terms of the value of other currencies, and the Bank of Canada is committed to maintaining the foreign exchange value of the Canadian dollar. The quantity of Canadian dollars in existence depends on the demand for Canadian dollars. If people can get a better return on Canadian dollars than on other currencies such as U.S. dollars, yen or pounds, they will move their wealth into Canadian dollars and the quantity of Canadian dollars will increase. Conversely, if a higher rate of return can be obtained on U.S. dollars, yen or pounds than on Canadian dollars, people will move their money out of Canadian dollars into these other currencies and the quantity of Canadian dollars will decrease. Thus with a fixed exchange rate the Bank of Canada loses control of the quantity of Canadian dollars in existence.

This loss of control of the money supply under a fixed exchange rate is not a problem under flexible exchange rates. With flexible exchange rates, the Bank of Canada fixes the quantity of Canadian dollars and the foreign exchange market determines the price at which Canadian dollars exchange for other currencies — the foreign exchange rate.

Interest rate parity

In the open economy, there are three equilibrium conditions involving the interest rate:

1. The *IS* curve
2. The *LM* curve
3. Interest rate parity

We've just considered the *IS* and *LM* curves; let's now examine interest rate parity. You've already discovered that interest rate parity is the equality of the rates of return obtainable from lending in either domestic or foreign currency. It implies the following equation:

$$\text{Domestic interest rate} = \text{foreign interest rate} + \begin{array}{l}\text{expected rate of depreciation of}\\ \text{domestic currency}\end{array}$$

Call the domestic interest rate r, the foreign interest rate r^f, the exchange rate ER, and the expected exchange rate one year in the future ER^e. Then, the above interest rate parity condition is

$$r = r^f + \left(\frac{ER}{ER^e} - 1\right) \qquad \textbf{(7.1)}$$

The role played by the interest rate parity condition depends on the exchange rate regime. With fixed exchange rates, the actual exchange rate, *ER*, equals the expected future exchange rate, ER^e. In this case, Equation (7.1) becomes:

$$r = r^f \qquad \textbf{(7.2)}$$

In an open economy with a fixed exchange rate, the interest rate equals the foreign interest rate. The foreign interest rate is determined by a closed economy (world economy) *IS-LM* equilibrium, and from the point of view of a single country, the foreign interest rate is exogenous. That is, interest rate parity implies that under fixed exchange rates, the domestic interest rate is equal to the given foreign interest rate.

With flexible exchange rates, the expected future exchange rate does not necessarily equal the current exchange rate. That expectation is the currently best available forecast of what the future exchange rate will be. Taking that forecast as given, Equation (7.1) tells us that, given the foreign interest rate, the higher the domestic interest rate, the higher is the current value of the exchange rate. But this is precisely the relationship we used in deriving the *IS* curve for an open economy with a flexible exchange rate. That is, in determining how equilibrium aggregate expenditure changes as the interest rate changes, we took into account the fact that when the domestic interest rate rises, so does the exchange rate. Thus the interest rate parity condition is built into the shape of the *IS* curve in the open economy with a flexible exchange rate. Along this *IS* curve, interest rate parity prevails.

This means that the *IS* curve for the flexible exchange rate economy is a slightly more complicated relationship. It is the relationship between the interest rate and real GDP when two equilibrium conditions are satisfied:

1. Aggregate planned expenditure equals real GDP.
2. Interest rate parity prevails.

Let's now look at equilibrium in the open economy.

Equilibrium

To find the equilibrium interest rate and real GDP in the open economy *IS-LM* model, we need to know whether the economy we're dealing with has a fixed exchange rate or flexible exchange rate.

Fixed exchange rate With a fixed exchange rate, the *IS* curve is steeper than in a closed economy (as shown in Figure 7.7a). The *LM* curve has the same slope as in the closed economy, but, because the money supply is endogenous, so is the position of the *LM* curve. That is, we don't know where the *LM* curve is until we know the money supply and the money supply is not determined by the Bank of Canada but by the actions of private individuals making choices about the currency in which to hold their wealth. But interest rate parity with a fixed exchange rate requires that the domestic interest rate is equal to the foreign interest rate. That is, Figure 7.8(a) shows interest rate parity as the horizontal line (*IRP*) at the foreign interest rate (assumed to be 5 percent a year) that bolts down the domestic interest rate. Equilibrium occurs where the *IS* curve intersects the *IRP* line. That equilibrium determines real GDP—\$4.5 billion in Figure 7.8(a). The quantity of money compatible with this equilibrium determines the position of the *LM* curve as the light blue *LM* curve in the figure.

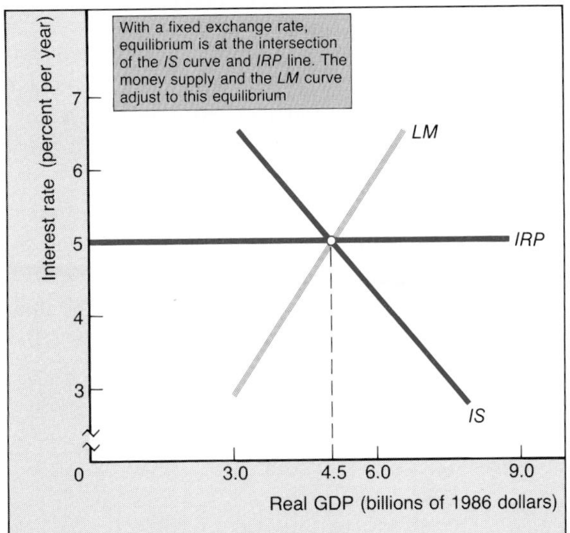

(a) Equilibrium with a fixed exchange rate

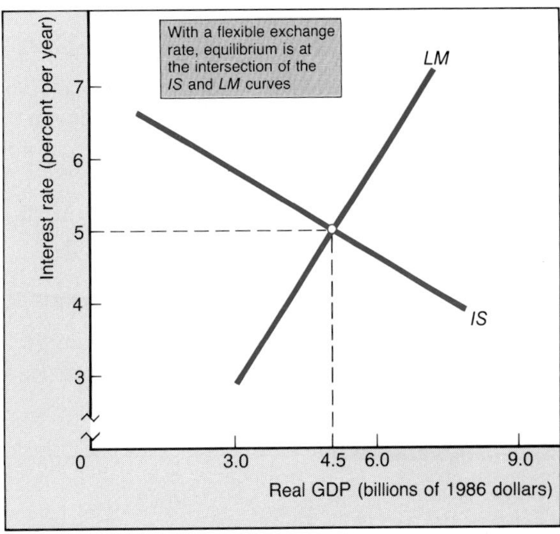

(b) Equilibrium with a flexible exchange rate

FIGURE 7.8
Equilibrium in the Open Economy

With a fixed exchange rate (part a), equilibrium is determined where the *IS* curve and *IRP* line intersect. The *IRP* line bolts down the interest rate and, given the interest rate, the *IS* curve determines real GDP. The money supply is endogenous—it adjusts through the balance of payments—to determine the position of the *LM* curve.

With a flexible exchange rate, equilibrium is determined at the intersection of the *IS* and *LM* curves. At all points along the *IS* curve, interest rate parity prevails.

Notice what happens if the money supply is "too large." The *LM* curve will lie to the right of the curve shown in Figure 7.8(a) and will intersect the *IS* curve at an interest rate below the foreign interest rate. With a domestic interest rate below the foreign interest rate, money will flow from Canada to the rest of the world and the *LM* curve will shift to the left. The *LM* curve will keep shifting so long as there is an interest rate differential. That differential is wiped out only when the *LM* curve lies in the position shown in Figure 7.8(a) with a domestic interest rate of 5 percent a year.

Conversely, suppose that the domestic money supply is "too low" so that the *LM* curve is to the left of that shown in Figure 7.8(a). Now, the *LM* curve will intersect the *IS* curve at an interest rate above the foreign interest rate, and money will flow into Canada seeking this higher rate of return. As it does so, the money supply will increase and the *LM* curve will shift to the right, and keep on doing so until the interest rate differential is wiped out. That is, the domestic interest rate will equal the foreign interest rate, 5 percent a year in the figure.

Flexible exchange rate With a flexible exchange rate, the money supply is exogenous so the *LM* curve, the blue curve shown in Figure 7.8(b), is bolted down by the actions of the Bank of Canada. The *IS* curve in Figure 7.8(b) incorporates the interest rate parity condition between the interest rate and the exchange rate. Notice that the *IS* curve with a flexible exchange rate is flatter than the *IS* curve with a fixed exchange rate in Figure 7.8(a). Equilibrium occurs where the *IS* curve intersects the *LM* curve. At that point, interest rate parity is satisfied, since it is satisfied at all points along the *IS* curve.

Let's now use the open economy *IS-LM* model to discover how fiscal and monetary policy operate in an open economy.

7.10 *Fiscal Policy with a Fixed Exchange Rate*

Between the end of World War II in 1945 and the early 1970s, the major countries of the world operated a fixed exchange rate system. Under such a system, each country's money supply is endogenous and so there can be no independent monetary policy. But there is a role for fiscal policy. How does fiscal policy operate with a fixed exchange rate?

To answer this question, let's examine the effects of an increase in government purchases of goods and services or a tax cut on equilibrium real GDP, the interest rate, and net exports. Figure 7.9 summarizes the analysis.

First, suppose that the economy starts out at the equilibrium shown at the intersection of the black *IS* curve, IS_0, and the IRP line. The *LM* curve is the grey LM_0. Net exports, shown in part (b), are zero.

FIGURE 7.9
Fiscal Policy with Fixed Exchange Rate

The economy starts out with real GDP at \$4.5 billion, the interest rate at 5 percent a year, and net exports zero at the intersection of IS_0 and LM_0 (part a) and on net export curve *NX* (part b). Expansionary fiscal policy shifts the *IS* curve to IS_1. The interest rate rises to 6 percent a year and real GDP to y_1. Higher interest rates than in the rest of the world bring money into the domestic economy, shifting the *LM* curve to LM_1. The interest rate falls, but real GDP rises further to \$6 billion. Higher real GDP brings additional imports and net exports become negative.

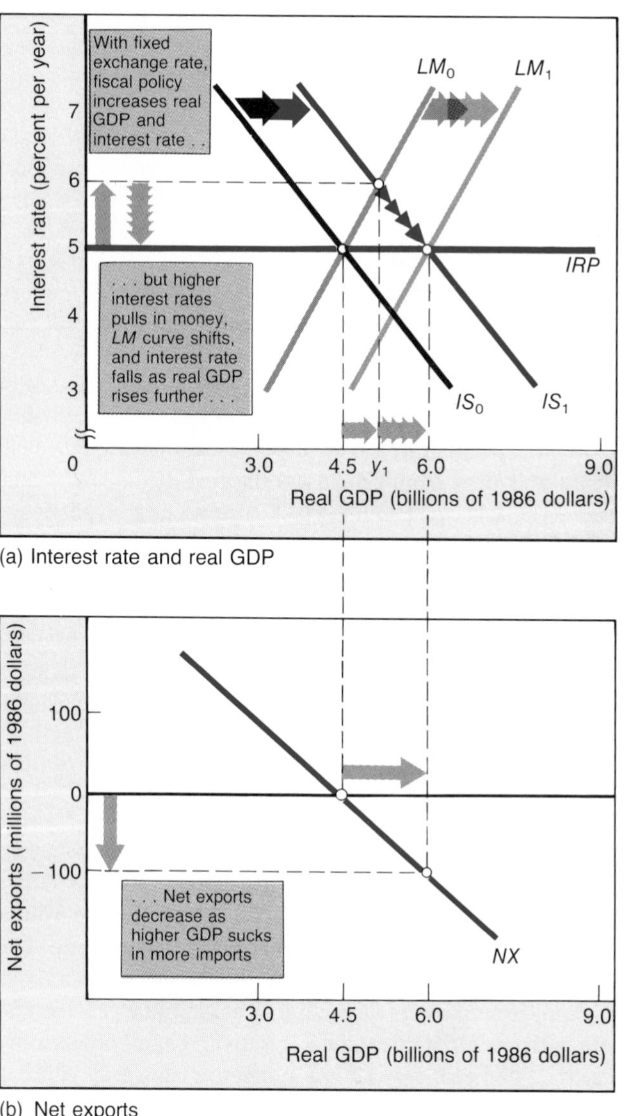

Now expansionary fiscal policy—an increase in government purchases or a tax cut—shifts the *IS* curve to the right, to IS_1. Initially, this action brings about an equilibrium where the new *IS* curve, IS_1, intersects the *LM* curve, LM_0. The interest rate increases to 6 percent a year and real GDP increases to y_1.

But this equilibrium does not prevail for long. With an interest rate of 6 percent in Canada and 5 percent in the rest of the world, money flows into Canada where it earns a higher rate of return. As it does so, the *LM* curve starts to shift to the right, moving toward LM_1. As the *LM* curve shifts, it intersects the *IS* curve, IS_1, at successively lower interest rates and higher real GDP. Money keeps flowing into Canada until the interest rate is 5 percent, at which point real GDP is $6 billion.

Net exports, in part (b), have decreased along the net export curve, *NX*. In this example, net exports decrease to –$100 million.

The potency of fiscal policy

Fiscal policy has a big effect on aggregate demand in an economy with a fixed exchange rate. Its effect stems exclusively from the increase in government purchases or the initial increase in consumption from a tax cut magnified by the autonomous expenditure multiplier. That is, aggregate demand increases by the entire rightward shift of the *IS* curve. The slopes of the *IS* curve and the *LM* curve have no effect on the magnitude of the aggregate demand shift. Because interest rate parity links the domestic interest rate to the world interest rate, there is no crowding out of investment when government purchases increase. Instead, foreign goods are sucked into the economy—imports increase.

Large economy A large open economy such as the United States will respond differently from the one we've just worked out. If a large country undertakes an expansion of government purchases, not only does the country's *IS* curve shift to the right, but so does the world *IS* curve. If the world *IS* curve shifts, the foreign interest rate increases. In Figure 7.9(a), the *IRP* line shifts upward. To the extent that the economy exerts an influence on interest rates in other countries by its own actions, some partial crowding out of investment occurs and the effect of the fiscal expansion depends on the slopes of the world *IS* and world *LM* curves in exactly the way that we analyzed in Chapter 6.

At full employment The fiscal policy experiment that we have just analyzed is one that takes place when the price level is fixed. We know that expansionary fiscal policy shifts the aggregate demand curve. What happens to equilibrium real GDP and the price level depends on aggregate supply conditions. Imagine, for the moment, that the short-run aggregate supply curve is horizontal—the price level is fixed. In this case, there is no change in the price level and real GDP changes by the amount shown in Figure 7.9. But consider the opposite extreme. Suppose there is full employment so that the aggregate supply curve is vertical. Now an increase in aggregate demand increases the price level and real GDP remains unchanged. The entire effect of the increase in aggregate demand is on the price level. How can this occur and how can this result be consistent with Figure 7.9? To answer this question, you need to recall the role of the price level in the *LM* and *IS* curves. The higher the price level the lower is the quantity of real money and the further to the left is the *LM* curve. In the open economy, the *IS* curve also depends on the price level. This effect arises because of the influence of the price level, other things being equal, on the real exchange rate. The higher the price level, the lower are net exports and the further to the left is the *IS* curve.

If the fiscal policy expansion we've just analyzed takes place at full employment, the aggregate demand curve will shift to the right and the price level will increase. The higher price level will shift the *LM* curve and the *IS* curve back to their original positions, leaving equilibrium real GDP at $4.5 billion.

But net exports will not be zero in this new situation. With a fixed exchange rate and higher price level, the net export curve (in Figure 7.9b) will shift to the left, so that net exports are lower even when real GDP is back at its full-employment level.

Intermediate case We've just considered two extreme cases — one in which the price level is fixed and the entire effect of a change in aggregate demand is on real GDP, and the other in which the aggregate supply curve is vertical so that the entire effect of the change in aggregate demand is on the price level. In general, the outcome of an expansionary fiscal policy lies between these two extremes, since the short-run aggregate supply curve is upward sloping. That is, expansionary fiscal policy increases aggregate demand, increasing both the price level and real GDP. The higher price level will shift the *IS* and *LM* curves to the left of IS_1 and LM_1 in Figure 7.9(a), but not so far as to return them to IS_0 and LM_0.

7.11 *Fiscal and Monetary Policy with a Flexible Exchange Rate*

Since the early 1970s, the major countries of the world have operated with a flexible exchange rate. Let's see how fiscal and monetary policy influence an economy with a flexible exchange rate. We'll begin with fiscal policy.

Fiscal policy

Figure 7.10 illustrates the economy's initial situation. Real GDP is $4.5 billion, the interest rate is 5 percent a year, and net exports are zero. The economy is at the point of intersection of the *IS* curve, IS_0, and *LM* curve, LM_0, in part (a) and is on the net export curve, NX_0, in part (b).

Expansionary fiscal policy — an increase in government purchases or a tax cut — shifts the *IS* curve to the right, from IS_0 to IS_1. In part (a), the interest rate increases to r_1 and real GDP increases to y_1.

But recall that along the *IS* curve the exchange rate changes to preserve domestic interest rate parity — a higher interest rate increases the exchange rate (the currency appreciates). Thus when the interest rate rises from 5 percent to r_1, the exchange rate increases and since the world price level and domestic price level are fixed, the real exchange rate increases.

The rise in the real exchange rate shifts the net export curve from NX_0 to NX_1 in part (b). That is, net exports decline at each level of real GDP. In the new equilibrium, net exports have fallen from zero to −$100 million. That decline in net exports has two sources: the higher real GDP brings in more imports and the higher exchange rate brings in more imports and decreases exports. These two separate effects are shown in part (b).

Crowding out in the open economy

We noticed that in a closed economy expansionary fiscal policy increases interest rates and, to some degree, crowds out investment. Crowding out also occurs in the open economy, but it takes two forms. First, the higher interest rate crowds out investment just as it does in a closed economy. Second, the higher interest rate induces a higher exchange rate, which decreases exports. The expansionary fiscal policy also crowds out exports.

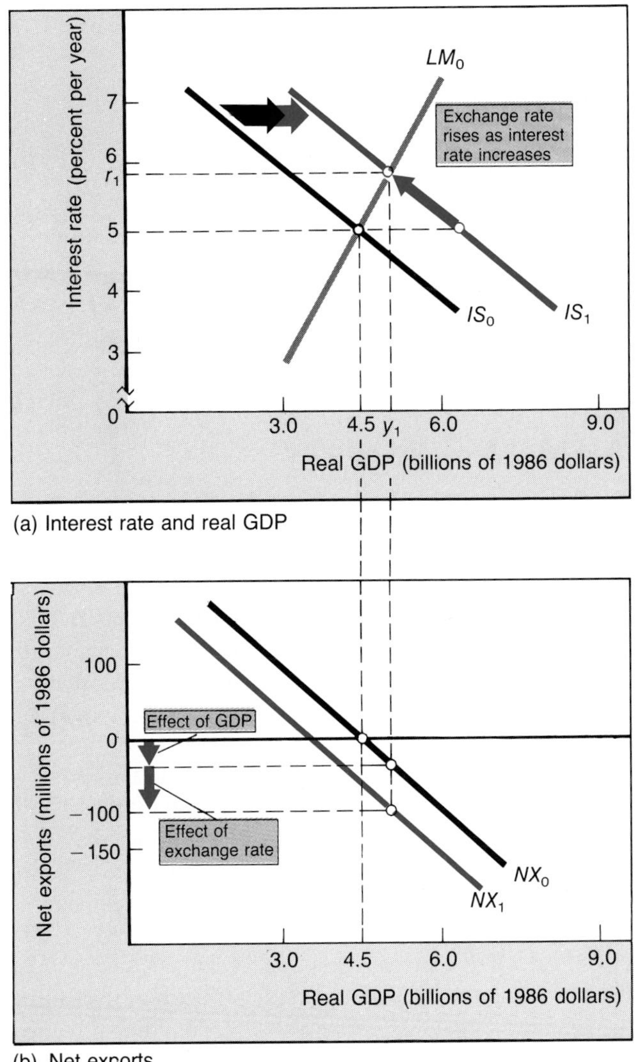

FIGURE 7.10
Fiscal Policy with Flexible Exchange Rate

Under flexible exchange rates, an expansionary fiscal policy shifts the IS curve from IS_0 to IS_1. Real GDP increases to y_1 and the interest rate to r_1. The higher interest rate increases the real exchange rate, shifting the net export curve to the left. Net exports decrease because higher real GDP brings in more imports and a higher real exchange rate brings in more imports and decreases exports.

"Twin deficits"

Two deficits became important in Canada in the 1980s—the government budget deficit and the Canadian deficit with the rest of the world. Figure 7.10 shows the connection between these deficits. Suppose that the shift in the *IS* curve occurred when the government budget was balanced. That is, initially the government budget was balanced and net exports were zero. Let's also suppose that the government increases its purchases of goods and services but does not increase taxes. Thus a government budget deficit arises. The *IS* curve shifts to the right and, following through the exercise of Figure 7.10, net exports become negative. The government budget deficit has generated a Canadian deficit with the rest of the world.

Aggregate supply and demand

We've worked out the effects of an expansionary fiscal policy in an open economy with a flexible exchange rate on real GDP, holding the price level constant. That is, we've worked out the effect of expansionary fiscal policy on the position of the aggregate demand curve. If the aggregate supply curve is horizontal, the effects shown in Figure 7.10 are the end of the matter. But if the aggregate supply curve slopes upward, there are some further adjustments to take into account. The increase in aggregate demand increases the price level and shifts the *IS* and *LM* curves and the net export curve. The higher the price level, the farther to the left are all these curves, other things being equal. A higher price level shifts the *LM* curve to the left because it decreases the real money supply. It shifts the *IS* curve to the left because it increases the real exchange rate, decreasing net exports. It shifts the net exports curve to the left for the same reason. The directions of change of real GDP, the interest rate, and net exports are still the same as those in Figure 7.10, but the magnitudes of the changes are modified by the induced price level effects.

Next, let's look at monetary policy.

Monetary policy

Figure 7.11 shows the effects of an increase in the money supply in an open economy with a flexible exchange rate. Initially, the economy is at the intersection of the *LM* curve, LM_0, and the *IS* curve in part (a), with real GDP at $4.5 billion and an interest rate of 5 percent a year. In part (b), the economy is on the net export curve NX_0, with net exports equal to zero.

An increase in the money supply shifts the *LM* curve to the right, to LM_1. In part (a), the interest rate falls to r_1 and real GDP increases to $6 billion.

But recall that as the economy moves along its *IS* curve, the exchange rate changes. In this case, the interest rate falls and so does the exchange rate. The lower exchange rate with a constant price level lowers the real exchange rate and shifts the net export curve to the right to NX_1 (in part b). Net exports change, but the full effect is ambiguous. The higher level of real GDP increases imports and decreases net exports. But the exchange rate effect works in the opposite direction—the lower exchange rate increases net exports. In the figure, the real GDP effect is larger, but in reality the exchange rate effect could be larger. That is, the net export curve could shift to the right by more than that shown here, resulting in an increase rather than a decrease in net exports.

Price level effects

We've just worked out the effects of a change in the money supply when the price level is given. But we know that when aggregate demand increases, both the price level and real income increase along the short-run aggregate supply curve. To see how this increase in the price level modifies the above results, let's consider what happens at full employment, when the aggregate supply curve is vertical. In this case, the increase in aggregate demand results in an increase in the price level and no change in real GDP.

Because real GDP does not change, we know that in the new equilibrium, real GDP is going to be $4.5 billion. But if real GDP is going to remain at $4.5 billion, the *LM* curve needs to go back to LM_0 and the *IS* curve needs to stay put. How does this come about? The answer is that the price level increases by the same percentage as the increase in the money supply so that the real money supply remains constant. This takes the *LM* curve back to LM_0. Also, the exchange rate falls by the same percentage as the price

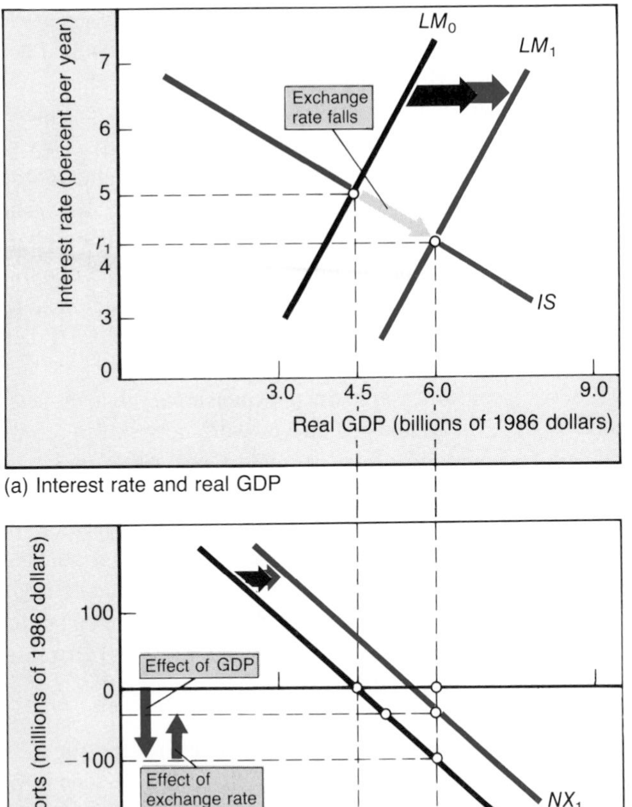

FIGURE 7.11
Monetary Policy with Flexible Exchange Rate

An increase in the money supply shifts the *LM* curve from LM_0 to LM_1. Real GDP increases to \$6 billion and the interest rate falls to r_1. The lower interest rate decreases the real exchange rate, shifting the net export curve to the right (in part b). The change in net exports is ambiguous. Higher real GDP decreases net exports (increases imports) but the lower real exchange rate increases net exports (decreases imports and increases exports).

level rises, keeping the real exchange rate constant. Because there is no change in the real exchange rate, there is no shift in the net export curve. Thus the equilibrium that results from an increase in the money supply at full employment is exactly the same, in real terms, as the initial equilibrium. Real GDP is \$4.5 billion, the interest rate is 5 percent a year, and net exports are zero. The only effect of the higher money supply is an increased price level and a lower exchange rate.

These full-employment effects are one extreme. The effects shown in Figure 7.11 are the other extreme when the price level is fixed and real GDP changes. Along an upward-sloping short-run aggregate supply curve, the outcome is intermediate between these two extremes: real GDP, the interest rate, and net exports all change but by a smaller amount than shown in the figure.

TESTCASE

7.12 *Another Look at the 1980s*

We can use the open economy *IS-LM* model with a flexible exchange rate to make sense of Canadian macroeconomic performance during the 1980s.

In the early 1980s, government purchases of goods and services increased and taxes decreased as a percentage of GDP. The government deficit grew. This was a period of expansionary fiscal policy. The *IS* curve was shifting to the right. It was also a period of tight monetary policy. The *LM* curve was shifting to the left. The interest rate increased sharply but real GDP did not grow much. The Canadian dollar weakened but Canada's inflation rate exceeded that in other countries and the combination of these facts led to an increase in the real exchange rate. The higher real exchange rate reduced net exports (increased net imports), but the low growth of real GDP kept imports low so net exports remained positive.

In the mid-1980s, fiscal policy remained expansionary but monetary policy also became expansionary. Both the *IS* and *LM* curves were now shifting to the right but the *LM* curve was shifting faster. Interest rates decreased, real GDP grew more rapidly, and the real exchange rate began to decrease. The more rapid growth of real GDP brought in more imports and net exports, although remaining positive, began to decline.

In the late 1980s, fiscal policy was tightened and so was monetary policy. The rightward shifts in the *IS* and *LM* curves now slowed down. Interest rates in the United States fell steadily but in Canada they remained steady and even began to increase. The Canadian dollar strengthened and the real exchange rate also increased. Real GDP growth slowed but did not stop and net exports turned negative.

■ In this chapter, we've extended our view of the forces influencing aggregate demand to bring international economic linkages into the picture. We've seen how monetary and fiscal policy influence not only real GDP and the interest rate but also the exchange rate and net exports.

In our discussion, we've focused most attention on aggregate demand effects—the effects of policy changes on the level of aggregate demand at a given price level. But, at each stage, we've examined how the price level and real GDP react by taking into account aggregate demand and aggregate supply.

It is now time to pay more attention to aggregate supply. In the next three chapters, we're going to focus on the supply side of the economy, studying why the economy deviates from full employment, the determinants of the slope of the short-run aggregate supply curve, and the forces that shift the long-run aggregate supply curve over time, producing economic growth and expansion.

CHAPTER REVIEW

Summary

TRENDS IN CANADIAN INTERNATIONAL TRADE, DEFICIT, AND INDEBTEDNESS

International trade—imports and exports—have become an increasingly important feature of the Canadian economy, rising from an average of 20 percent of GDP in 1970 to almost 30 percent of GDP in 1990. But during the 1980s, imports increased more quickly than exports and an international trade deficit emerged. This deficit peaked in 1985. The deficit of the 1980s brought increased foreign investments in Canada and lower Canadian investments in other countries. Canada is a net borrower from the rest of the world.

THE BALANCE OF PAYMENTS ACCOUNTS

The balance of payments accounts are the

- Current account
- Capital account
- Official settlements account

The current account records the values of net exports, net income from foreign investments, and unilateral transfers. The capital account records the difference between Canadian investments in the rest of the world and foreign investments in Canada. The official settlements account records the net receipts and payments of gold and foreign currency resulting from the transactions in the current and capital accounts.

HOW NET EXPORTS ARE DETERMINED

Net exports are determined by the real exchange rate, income in the rest of the world, and Canadian real GDP. The higher the real exchange rate—the price of domestic goods and services relative to the price of foreign goods and services—the greater are imports and the smaller are exports. The higher the income in the rest of the world, the greater are exports. The higher is Canadian real GDP, the greater are imports.

The net export function is the relationship between net exports and the three variables that influence it. The net export curve is the relationship between net exports and real GDP, holding constant income in the rest of the world and the real exchange rate. The net export curve shifts when the real exchange rate changes and income in the rest of the world changes.

CANADIAN NET EXPORTS IN THE 1980s

There is a strong relationship between imports and Canadian real GDP, and increasing real GDP brought in more imports through the 1980s. Another influence on net exports is the real exchange rate. When the real exchange rate increases—as the price of domestic goods increases relative to the price of foreign goods—net exports decrease. The only exceptions to this pattern have occurred in years in which changes in real GDP produced changes in imports that offset the effect of the real exchange rate.

FOREIGN EXCHANGE MARKETS AND THE FOREIGN EXCHANGE RATE

The money of one country is exchanged for the money of another country in the foreign exchange market. The price at which these exchanges take place is the foreign exchange rate—the number of units of foreign money that one unit of domestic money will buy. The average of the exchange rates between the Canadian dollar and all other currencies, weighted by the importance of these other currencies in Canadian international trade, is the effective exchange rate.

There are three possible foreign exchange market arrangements—a fixed exchange rate regime, a flexible exchange rate regime, and a managed floating exchange rate regime. After World War II and until the early 1970s, the world operated a fixed exchange rate system. Through the 1970s and 1980s a floating exchange rate system has been in place with various degrees of management and intervention in the market.

In the long run, the value of one currency in relation to another is determined by purchasing power parity—the money of one country has the same purchasing power as the money of another country. But in the short run, asset market equilibrium determines the exchange rate.

INTEREST RATES AROUND THE WORLD IN THE 1980s

Interest rates vary considerably from one country to another. Even major industrial countries, such as Canada, the United States, Japan, and the countries of Western Europe such as Italy have widely differing interest rates. During the 1980s, Japanese interest rates were systematically lower than those in Canada and the United States, which in turn were systematically lower than those in Italy. Interest rates in some countries were spectacularly high, especially those in Latin American countries and, for a time, Israel.

INTEREST RATE PARITY

Interest rate parity is the equality of rates of return on assets denominated in different currencies, once the expected rate of depreciation or appreciation of each currency is taken into account. For interest rate parity to prevail, a country with a low interest rate is one whose currency is expected to appreciate against other currencies. A country with a high interest rate is one whose currency is expected to depreciate.

Interest rate parity holds exactly for short-term investments covered by forward exchange transactions. That is, a loan denominated in one currency taken to finance the purchase of an asset denominated in another currency where the proceeds from the sale of the asset are sold in the forward exchange market yields a rate of return of zero. The operation of interest rate parity links exchange rates and interest rates together but does not, on its own, determine the level of either.

THE OPEN ECONOMY *IS-LM* MODEL

The open economy *IS-LM* model determines a country's interest rate, exchange rate, net exports, and real GDP (and the other components of aggregate planned expenditure).

The *IS* curve in an open economy depends on the exchange rate regime. With a fixed exchange rate, it is steeper than in a closed economy. The reason is that a change in the interest rate induces a change in investment that in turn induces a change in aggregate planned expenditure. But part of the increased spending is a leakage into the rest of the world, imports, so the multiplier effect of the change in investment is smaller than in a closed economy.

With a flexible exchange rate, the *IS* curve is flatter than with a fixed exchange rate. The reason is that a higher interest rate induces currency appreciation and an increase in the real exchange rate. A higher real exchange rate decreases net exports, lowering aggregate planned expenditure by more than in the fixed exchange rate case.

The *IS* curve in the open economy shifts for the same reasons the closed economy *IS* curve does, but in addition it shifts because of changes in income in the rest of the world. The higher is income in the rest of the world, the farther to the right is the *IS* curve. Also, in a flexible exchange rate economy, other things being equal, a change in the price level shifts the *IS* curve because it affects the real exchange rate.

The *LM* curve in the open economy is the same as in the closed economy except that, with a fixed exchange rate, the money supply is endogenous so the *LM* curve is also endogenous—its position is determined within the model. An additional ingredient of the open economy *IS-LM* model is interest rate parity. This relationship bolts down the domestic interest rate under fixed exchange rates and links the interest rate and the real exchange rate, influencing the slope of the *IS* curve under flexible exchange rates.

Equilibrium is determined for the fixed exchange rates at the point of intersection of the *IS* curve and the interest rate parity condition. Equilibrium occurs on the *IS* curve at that interest rate determined in the rest of the world. The *LM* curve passes through this intersection point because the money supply adjusts through a balance of payments surplus or deficit. With a flexible exchange rate, equilibrium occurs at the intersection point of the *IS* and *LM* curves. Along the *IS* curve, the interest rate parity condition is satisfied.

FISCAL POLICY WITH A FIXED EXCHANGE RATE

An increase in government purchases or a tax cut shifts the *IS* curve to the right. But because of interest rate parity, there is no decrease in the interest rate. Instead, real GDP increases by an amount determined by the autonomous expenditure multiplier. Imports grow and exports don't change, so net exports become negative. But with higher real GDP and no change in the money supply interest rates increase and a higher rate of return brings in money from the rest of the world. The increased money supply shifts the *LM* curve to the right, keeping the domestic interest rate equal to the interest rate in the rest of the world.

The potency of fiscal policy with a fixed exchange rate depends only on the size of the autonomous expenditure multiplier. It does not depend on the slopes of the *IS* and *LM* curves.

FISCAL AND MONETARY POLICY WITH A FLEXIBLE EXCHANGE RATE

An expansionary fiscal policy—an increase in government purchases or a tax cut—shifts the *IS* curve to the right, increasing real GDP and the interest rate. The higher interest rate induces a currency appreciation and an increase in the real exchange rate. The higher real exchange rate shifts the net export curve to the left. Net exports decrease because the higher real GDP brings in more imports and a higher real exchange rate reinforces that effect on imports but decreases exports.

An expansionary monetary policy—an increase in the money supply—shifts the *LM* curve to the right, increasing real GDP and decreasing the interest rate. The lower interest rate lowers the real exchange rate and shifts the net export curve to the right. The change in net exports is ambiguous. Higher real GDP brings in more imports but a lower real exchange rate decreases imports and increases exports.

CANADIAN FISCAL AND MONETARY POLICY DURING THE 1980s

The early 1980s was a period of expansionary fiscal policy and tight monetary policy. The *IS* curve was shifting rapidly to the right and the *LM* curve was shifting to the left. The interest rate increased and real GDP stagnated. The real exchange rate increased but low real GDP growth kept net exports positive.

In the mid-1980s, fiscal policy remained expansionary and monetary policy also became expansionary. The *LM* curve was shifting to the right even faster than the *IS* curve and interest rates decreased, real GDP grew rapidly, the real exchange rate fell, and net exports began to decline.

In the late 1980s, both fiscal and monetary policy were tightened and the rightward shifts in the *IS* and *LM* curves slowed down. Interest rates remained steady and then began to increase. In the United States interest rates were falling and the Canadian dollar strengthened. The real exchange rate increased, and net exports turned negative.

Key Terms and Concepts

Appreciation of the dollar An increase in the number of units of foreign money that a dollar will buy.

Capital account An account that records the receipts from nonresidents and payments made to nonresidents arising from the issuing of new debt or the repayment of old debt.

Capital exports Investments by residents of the domestic economy in the rest of the world.

Capital imports New investments flowing into the domestic economy from the rest of the world.

Closed economy model A model in which there are no international transactions between the domestic economy and the rest of the world.

Covered interest parity The equality of rates of return when no risk is taken—the investor covers the transaction by buying or selling currencies on the forward market.

Current account An account that records the flows of goods and services and other current receipts and payments between residents of the domestic economy and residents of the rest of the world.

Depreciation of the dollar A decrease in the number of units of foreign money that one dollar can buy.

Dollar assets Securities such as bonds, stocks, treasury bills, bank deposits, and loans denominated in Canadian dollars.

Effective exchange rate An exchange rate index that is a weighted average of the value of a unit of domestic money in terms of all other foreign currencies, where the weight on each foreign currency is equal to the proportion of the economy's international trade undertaken in that currency.

Eurodollars U.S. dollars deposited in foreign banks outside the United States (or foreign branches of U.S. banks).

Fixed exchange rate regime A regime in which the central bank declares a central or par value for the exchange rate which it will act to maintain.

Flexible exchange rate A foreign exchange rate whose value is determined by market forces.

Floating exchange rate A foreign exchange rate whose value is determined by market forces.

Foreign exchange rate The number of units of foreign money that one unit of domestic money will buy.

Forward contract A contract entered into today to buy or sell an agreed quantity at an agreed future date and at an agreed price.

Forward exchange rate The price at which one currency is traded for another for delivery at a specified future date.

Interest rate parity The equality of rate of return on assets, independent of the currency in which they are denominated.

Managed floating exchange rate An exchange rate that is manipulated by the central bank, but not necessarily held constant.

Net export curve The relationship between net exports and real GDP, holding the real exchange rate constant.

Net export function The relationship between net exports, real GDP, income in the rest of the world, and the real exchange rate.

Net foreign investment income The earnings of residents of the domestic economy on assets held in the rest of the world minus the earnings of foreigners on assets held in the domestic economy.

Nominal exchange rate The number of units of a foreign currency that one unit of domestic currency will buy.

Official settlements account An account that records the net receipts and payments of gold and foreign currency resulting from current account and capital account transactions.

Official settlements balance The change in a country's foreign exchange reserves less the change in its official borrowing.

Open economy model A model that takes into account linkages between the domestic economy and the rest of the world.

Purchasing power parity The equality of the value of money in all countries.

Real exchange rate The price of domestic goods and services relative to the price of foreign goods and services.

Spot exchange rate The exchange rate between two currencies for immediate delivery.

Uncovered interest parity The equality of rates of return where the investor takes the risk—does not cover the transaction by taking out a forward contract.

Unilateral transfers Gifts made by residents of the domestic economy to foreigners minus gifts received from foreigners.

Review Questions

1. What are the balance of payments accounts? Explain the types of transactions that are recorded in each account. Give some examples of transactions in each of the Canadian balance of payments accounts.
2. What are foreign exchange reserves?
3. What is the net export function? What shifts it? What produces a movement along it?
4. Is Canada a net borrower or a net lender? Explain your answer.
5. What is a foreign exchange rate? Give some examples.
6. Explain what is meant by (a) depreciation of a currency and (b) appreciation of a currency. When has the Canadian dollar depreciated and appreciated against the U.S. dollar? What were the foreign exchange rate changes?
7. What is an effective exchange rate? What are its units of measurement? How has the effective exchange rate of the Canadian dollar changed since 1970?
8. What is a real exchange rate? Explain why a real exchange rate is an opportunity cost.
9. Explain why the real exchange rate changes.
10. If Canada fixes the exchange rate between the Canadian dollar and the British pound at 1.50 pounds per dollar, explain how the Bank of Canada would keep the

exchange rate fixed. Would the Bank of Canada ever allow the Canadian dollar to become worth more or less than 1.50 pounds? Explain your answer.

11. Suppose there are foreign exchange market forces in question 10 that will lead to a fall in the exchange rate to 1.00 pound per Canadian dollar. What actions will the Bank of Canada take to eliminate these forces?
12. If Canada adopts a flexible exchange rate, what is the role for the Bank of Canada in the foreign exchange market?
13. Distinguish between a flexible exchange rate and a managed floating exchange rate.
14. What is the forward exchange market? What is a forward exchange rate?
15. Explain why the Bank of Canada has no control of the money supply if Canada adopts a fixed exchange rate.
16. What is the purchasing power parity theory? What are its predictions?
17. What is the interest rate parity theory?
18. Explain why the *IS* curve in an open economy with a fixed exchange rate is steeper than the *IS* curve in a closed economy.
19. Explain why under a flexible exchange rate regime the *IS* curve is flatter than the *IS* curve under a fixed exchange rate regime.
20. Under a fixed exchange rate regime, what shifts the *LM* curve?

Problems

1. Divide the following items into four categories: those items that belong in (i) the current account, (ii) the capital account, (iii) the official settlements account, and (iv) none of the balance of payments accounts:
   (a) Your summer vacation expenses in Europe
   (b) The purchase of the government of Quebec's bonds by Canadian residents
   (c) The Royal Bank's purchase of Travelers' Checks from American Express in New York
   (d) The transfer of 1,000 ounces of gold by the Bank of England to the Bank of Canada
   (e) Canadian imports of Japanese cars
   (f) Canadian exports of wheat
   (g) The takeover of a Canadian corporation by a Japanese corporation
   (h) The payment of interest on Canadian government bonds
   (i) The money brought into Canada by new immigrants
   (j) Canadian aid to poor countries
2. Using the following items and numbers, construct the balance of payments accounts of the hypothetical economy:

ITEM	$m
Capital imports	2,000
Interest received from abroad	800
Exports of goods and services	1,000
Capital exports	1,800
Gifts made to foreigners	100
Imports of goods and services	1,100
Interest paid abroad	700

   (a) What is the current account balance?
   (b) What is the capital account balance?
   (c) What is the official settlements account balance?
   (d) What is the balance of payments?

3. Explain why the Bretton Woods system is an international gold exchange standard.
4. What will be the price of broccoli in Canada if the U.S. price is $5.00 per kilogram and the exchange rate is C$1.25 per U.S. dollar? If after one year, broccoli still costs $5.00 per kilogram in the United States and the exchange rate is C$1.20 per U.S. dollar,
   (a) What is the percentage change in the Canadian price?
   (b) What is the percentage change in the exchange rate?
   (c) What is the change in the U.S. real exchange rate?
5. You have $10,000 to invest for one year. A Canadian government bond will give you a sure return of 13 percent after one year. If you convert your $10,000 into U.S. dollars, you will do so at an exchange rate of 83.3¢ US per Canadian dollar. You can buy a U.S. government bond that will give a sure return after one year of 10 percent.
   (a) What will the one-year forward exchange rate between Canadian and U.S. dollars have to be for it to be just worth buying the Canadian bond?
   (b) If you firmly expect the Canadian dollar to be cheaper than your answer to part (a), will you buy the Canadian bond or the U.S. bond?
   (c) If people generally share your expectation, what will happen?
6. In question 5(b), for covered interest rate parity to hold, what transactions will you undertake?
7. In question 5(b), what risk will you take if your transaction is not covered?
8. The United States is a major importer of natural gas from Canada. If the price of natural gas in Canada increases by 10 percent and at the same time the Canadian dollar depreciates against the Canadian dollar by 5 percent, what is the increase in the price of natural gas in the United States?
9. At the *IS-LM* equilibrium in an open economy,
   (a) Which markets are in equilibrium?
   (b) Does interest rate parity hold?
   (c) Does purchasing power parity hold?
10. Do your answers to question 9 depend on the exchange rate regime? If so, why? If not, why not?
11. Work out the effects of the following on an economy with the exchange rate fixed:
   (a) An increase in government purchases of goods and services
   (b) An increase in taxes
   (c) An increase in the money supply
   (d) A rise in income in the rest of the world
   (e) A rise in interest rates in the rest of the world
12. Suppose that the economy in question 11 switched to a flexible exchange rate. What are the effects on the economy now?
13. Explain how a government deficit leads to an international deficit.
14. Explain why the Japanese yen appreciated against the Canadian dollar in the 1980s, despite the fact that interest rates in Japan are so much lower than in Canada.
15. If real incomes in Eastern Europe, China, and India rise dramatically, what will be the effect on the following?
   (a) Canadian net exports
   (b) Canadian real income
   (c) Canadian interest rates
16. If inflation in the rest of the world increases, what will be the effect on the following?
   (a) Canadian inflation
   (b) The effective exchange rate of the Canadian dollar

APPENDIX

The Algebra of the Open Economy IS-LM Model

OPEN ECONOMY *IS* CURVE

The *IS* curve shows the relationship between real GDP and the interest rate such that aggregate planned expenditure equals real GDP. Aggregate planned expenditure is the sum of consumer expenditure (c), investment (i), government purchases (g), and net exports (nx). That is

$$e_p = c + i + g + nx \qquad \textbf{(7A.1)}$$

Consumer expenditure is determined by the consumption function:

$$c = a + b(y - t), \quad a > 0, 0 < b < 1 \qquad \textbf{(7A.2)}$$

Investment is determined by the investment function:

$$i = i_0 - hr, \quad i_0, h > 0 \qquad \textbf{(7A.3)}$$

Net exports is equal to exports minus imports. Exports are determined by the export function—exports depend on income in the rest of the world and the real exchange rate:

$$ex = ex_0 + ex_1 y_f - ex_2 \frac{ER \times P}{P_f}, \quad ex_0, ex_1, ex_2 > 0 \qquad \textbf{(7A.4)}$$

where ex_0 is autonomous exports, ex_1 tells us how exports respond to a change in income in the rest of the world, and ex_2 tells us how exports respond to a change in the real exchange rate. The real exchange rate is defined as the relative price of domestically-produced goods and services on world markets, $ER \times P/P_f$. It is equal to the price of domestic goods and services ($ER \times P$) divided by the price of foreign goods and services (P_f), all expressed in units of foreign currency. As the real exchange rate increases, domestically-produced goods and services become relatively more expensive, so exports decline.

Imports are determined by the import function—imports depend on domestic income and the real exchange rate :

$$im = im_0 + im_1 y + im_2 \frac{ER \times P}{P_f}, \quad im_0, im_1, im_2 > 0 \qquad \textbf{(7A.5)}$$

where im_0 is autonomous exports, im_1, the marginal propensity to import, tells us how imports increase with domestic real GDP, and im_2 tells us how imports respond to a change in the real exchange rate, $ER \times P/P_f$. As real GDP increases, imports increase. As the real exchange rate increases, domestically-produced goods and services become relatively more expensive, so imports increase.

Net exports (nx) can be found by subtracting Equation (7A.5) from Equation (7A.4). That is

$$nx = \left(ex_0 + ex_1 y_f - ex_2 \frac{ER \times P}{P_f}\right) - \left(im_0 + im_1 y + im_2 \frac{ER \times P}{P_f}\right) \qquad \textbf{(7A.6)}$$

Rearranging Equation (7A.6) gives

$$nx = ex_0 - im_0 + ex_1 y_f - im_1 y - (ex_2 + im_2) \frac{ER \times P}{P_f} \qquad \textbf{(7A.7)}$$

$$nx = nx_0 + ex_1 y_f - im_1 y - nx_2 \frac{ER \times P}{P_f}, \quad nx_2 > 0 \qquad \textbf{(7A.8)}$$

where nx_0, autonomous net exports, equals $ex_0 - im_0$ and nx_2, which equals $ex_2 + im_2$, tells us how net exports respond to a change in the real exchange rate. Since an increase in the real exchange rate decreases exports and increases imports, net exports decrease.

We can now find aggregate planned expenditure by substituting Equations (7A.2), (7A.3), and (7A.8) into Equation (7A.1):

$$e_p = a + b(y - t) + i_0 - hr + g + nx_0 + ex_1 y_f - im_1 y - nx_2 \frac{ER \times P}{P_f} \quad \textbf{(7A.9)}$$

Goods market equilibrium prevails when aggregate planned expenditure equals real GDP. That is,

$$e_p = y \quad \textbf{(7A.10)}$$

and the equation to the *IS* curve is

$$y = a + b(y - t) + i_0 - hr + g + nx_0 + ex_1 y_f - im_1 y - nx_2 \frac{ER \times P}{P_f} \quad \textbf{(7A.11)}$$

Rearranging Equation (7A.11) gives us the equation to the open economy *IS* curve:

$$y = \frac{1}{(1 - b + im_1)} \left(a + i_0 + g - bt + nx_0 + ex_1 y_f - nx_2 \frac{ER \times P}{P_f} - hr\right) \quad \textbf{(7A.12)}$$

We saw in Figure 7.7 that the open economy *IS* curve is not the same under fixed exchange rates and flexible exchange rates. Let's take a closer look at the *IS* curves in these two cases, beginning with the fixed exchange rate case.

UNDER FIXED EXCHANGE RATES

In a fixed exchange rate regime, the real exchange rate is exogenous, changing only when the exchange rate (*ER*), the domestic price level (*P*), or the foreign price level (P_f) changes.

Slope *IS* curve In this case, the slope of the *IS* curve equals the inverse of the coefficient on r in Equation (7A.12). That is,

$$\text{Slope of } IS \text{ curve} = -\frac{(1 - b + im_1)}{h} \quad \textbf{(7A.13)}$$

Since im_1, the marginal propensity to import, is a positive fraction, the magnitude of the slope of the *IS* curve in an open economy with a fixed exchange rate is larger than the magnitude of the slope of the closed economy *IS* curve, $(1 - b)/h$. That is, the *IS* curve under a fixed exchange rate regime is steeper than the closed economy *IS* curve.

Shifts of *IS* curve The *IS* curve under a fixed exchange rate regime shifts as a result of a change in four variables:

1. Government purchases
2. Taxes
3. Real income in the rest of the world
4. Real exchange rate

We can see how the *IS* curve shifts by looking at the coefficients on these variables in Equation (7A.12).

An increase in government purchases (g) shifts the *IS* curve to the right, just as it does in a closed economy. But in an open economy with a fixed exchange rate the shift of the *IS* curve equals $1/(1 - b + im_1)$ times the change in government purchases.

An increase in taxes (t) shifts the *IS* curve to the left, just as in a closed economy. But the *IS* curve in the open economy shifts by $-b/(1 - b + im_1)$ times the change in taxes.

An increase in income in the rest of the world, y_f, increases exports and shifts the *IS* curve to the right. The shift of the *IS* curve is equal to $1/(1 - b + im_1)$ times the resulting change in exports.

The real exchange rate increases if the domestic price level rises, the foreign price level decreases, or the domestic currency is devalued on foreign currency markets. An increase in the real exchange rate decreases net exports and shifts the *IS* curve to the left. The shift of the *IS* curve is equal to $-1/(1 - b + im_1)$ times the resulting change in net exports.

UNDER FLEXIBLE EXCHANGE RATES

Under flexible exchange rates, interest rate changes change the nominal exchange rate so as to maintain interest rate parity.

Interest rate parity The nominal exchange rate (ER) adjusts to keep the return on domestic assets equal to the expected return on foreign assets. The return on domestic assets is the interest rate (r). The expected return on foreign assets is the foreign interest rate (r_f) plus the expected rate of depreciation of domestic currency on foreign exchange markets. We have defined the exchange rate as the number of units of foreign currency per unit of domestic currency. To calculate the rate of depreciation, we need to express the exchange rate in units of domestic currency per unit of foreign currency. That is, as $1/ER$. Then the expected rate of depreciation of domestic currency is equal to

$$\frac{\frac{1}{ER^e} - \frac{1}{ER}}{\frac{1}{ER}}$$

which is equal to $\left(\frac{ER}{ER^e} - 1\right)$.

The interest rate parity condition can be written as

$$r = r_f + \left(\frac{ER}{ER^e} - 1\right) \qquad \textbf{(7A.14)}$$

For a given r_f and ER^e, an increase in the domestic interest rate r increases ER. The spot exchange rate (ER) increases, so that given the expected exchange rate (ER^e), the expected rate of depreciation of the domestic currency increases. Because the spot exchange increases, so too does the real exchange rate. Thus under flexible exchange rates the real exchange rate is not exogenous. We highlight the influence of the domestic interest rate on the real exchange rate as follows:

$$\frac{ER \times P}{P_f} = \beta_0 + \beta_1 r, \quad \beta_0, \beta_1 > 0 \qquad \textbf{(7A.15)}$$

where β_1 tells us how the real exchange rate responds to changes in the domestic interest rate and β_0 shows the ffect on the real exchange rate of changes in exogenous variables, such as the foreign interest rate.

Slope of *IS* curve Because the real exchange rate is endogenous under flexible exchange rates, the *IS* curve under flexible exchange rates is flatter than the *IS* curve under fixed exchange rates. To see why, recall the equation to the open economy *IS* curve:

$$y = \frac{1}{(1 - b + im_1)}\left(a + i_0 + g - bt + nx_0 + ex_1 y_f - nx_2 \frac{ER \times P}{P_f} - hr\right) \qquad \textbf{(7A.12)}$$

Substituting Equation (7A.15) into Equation (7A.12), and collecting the terms in r, gives us the equation to the *IS* curve under flexible exchange rates. That is,

$$y = \frac{1}{(1 - b + im_1)}(a + i_0 + g - bt + nx_0 + ex_1 y_f - nx_2 \beta_0) - \frac{(h + nx_2 \beta_1)}{(1 - b + im_1)} r \qquad \textbf{(7A.16)}$$

The slope of *IS* curve under flexible exchange rates equals the inverse of the coefficient on r in Equation (7A.16). That is,

$$\text{Slope of } IS \text{ curve} = -\frac{(1 - b + im_1)}{(h + nx_2\beta_1)} \quad \textbf{(7A.17)}$$

Since nx_2 and β_1 are positive numbers, the magnitude of the slope of the *IS* curve under a flexible exchange rates is less than the magnitude of the slope of the *IS* curve under fixed exchange rates. The *IS* curve under flexible exchange rates is flatter than the *IS* curve under fixed exchange rates.

Shifts of *IS* curve The *IS* curve under a flexible exchange rate regime shifts as a result of a change in six variables:

1. Government purchases
2. Taxes
3. Real income in the rest of the world
4. Interest rates in the rest of the world
5. The price level
6. The price level in the rest of the world

We can see how the *IS* curve shifts by looking at the coefficients on these variables in Equation (7A.16).

An increase in government purchases shifts the *IS* curve to the right, an increase in taxes shifts the *IS* curve to the left, and an increase in income in the rest of the world shifts the *IS* curve to the right, just as in a fixed exchange rate regime.

An increase in interest rates in the rest of the world depreciates the domestic currency and decreases the nominal exchange rate and the real exchange rate. It decreases β_0, and net exports increase. The *IS* curve shifts to the right. The shift of the *IS* curve is equal to $1/(1 - b + im_1)$ times the resulting increase in net exports.

An increase in the domestic price level increases the real exchange rate. That is, β_0 increases and net exports decreases. The *IS* curve shifts to the left. The shift of the *IS* curve is equal to $1/(1 - b + im_1)$ times the resulting decrease in net exports. An increase in the price level in the rest of the world shifts the *IS* curve in the opposite direction. The real exchange rate decreases, net exports increase, and the *IS* curve shifts to the right. It shifts by $1/(1 - b + im_1)$ times the resulting increase in net exports.

LM CURVE

The *LM* curve is the relationship between the interest rate and real GDP such that the quantity of money demanded equals the quantity supplied. The demand for money function, M^d, is given by

$$\frac{M^d}{P} = m_0 + ky - \ell r, \quad k > 0, \ell > 0 \quad \textbf{(7A.18)}$$

Money market equilibrium occurs when the quantity of money demanded equals the quantity of money supplied. That is,

$$M^d = M \quad \textbf{(7A.19)}$$

Substituting Equation (7A.18) into Equation (7A.19) and solving for real GDP gives

$$y = \frac{1}{k}\left[\frac{M}{P} - m_0 + \ell r\right] \quad \textbf{(7A.20)}$$

This is the equation for the *LM* curve in an open economy. The slope of the *LM* curve is the inverse of the coefficient on r in the Equation (7A.20). That is,

$$\text{Slope of the } LM \text{ curve} = \frac{k}{\ell} \tag{7A.21}$$

The equation to the *LM* curve and its slope are the same in an open economy and a closed economy. In a closed economy, the money supply is determined by the central bank and is exogenous. In an open economy, whether the money supply is exogenous depends on the exchange rate regime.

UNDER FIXED EXCHANGE RATES

In a fixed exchange rate regime, the central bank conducts monetary policy so as to maintain the fixed value of the exchange rate. In this case, the money supply is endogenous—determined within the model. The central bank cannot choose the size of the money supply, but rather it is determined by the model. Thus under fixed exchange rates the position of the *LM* curve is also determined by the model.

UNDER FLEXIBLE EXCHANGE RATES

In a flexible exchange rate regime, the central bank does not intervene in foreign exchange markets in an effort to adjust the value of the exchange rate. The central bank can choose the size of the money supply, in exactly the same way as it can in a closed economy. The money supply is exogenous, and so too is the position of the *LM* curve. The *LM* curve in an open economy with a flexible exchange rate is identical to the *LM* curve in a closed economy. An increase in the money supply shifts the *LM* curve to the right, and an increase in the domestic price level shift the *LM* curve to the left.

IS-LM EQUILIBRIUM

Because the *LM* curve is endogenous under fixed exchange rates and exogenous under flexible exchange rates, equilibrium in the *IS-LM* model is not independent of the exchange rate regime.

UNDER FIXED EXCHANGE RATES

Since under fixed exchange rates the position of the *LM* curve is endogenous, equilibrium is not determined by the intersection of the *IS* and *LM* curves. It is determined by the *IS* curve and interest rate parity. Let's take a closer look at the condition for interest rate parity.

Interest rate parity Interest rate parity is given by

$$r = r_f + \left[\frac{ER}{ER^e} - 1\right] \tag{7A.22}$$

Under fixed exchange rates ER^e equals ER, so Equation (7A.22) tells us the domestic interest rate equals the interest rate in the rest of the world. That is,

$$r = r_f \tag{7A.23}$$

That is, the equilibrium domestic interest rate is equal to r_f and equilibrium real GDP (y^*) is determined by the *IS* curve at the domestic interest rate that equals the interest rate in the rest of the world. The *IS* curve is

$$y = \frac{1}{(1 - b + im_1)}\left(a + i_0 + g - bt + nx_0 + ex_1 y_f - nx_2 \frac{ER \times P}{P_f} - hr\right) \tag{7A.12}$$

Substituting r_f for r gives equilibrium real GDP (y^*)

$$y^* = \frac{1}{(1 - b + im_1)}\left(a + i_0 + g - bt + nx_0 + ex_1 y_f - nx_2 \frac{ER \times P}{P_f} - hr_f\right) \tag{7A.24}$$

Equation (7A.24) tells us that fiscal policy—the level of g and t—influences equilibrium real GDP, but that monetary policy does not. A change in the real exchange rate ($ER \times P/P_f$) changes real GDP. This results from the *IS* curve shifting as net exports respond to the change in the real exchange rate. The real exchange rate changes if the nominal exchange rate is adjusted, or the domestic or foreign price level changes. For example, a devaluation decreases the number of units of foreign currency per unit of domestic currency (*ER*), shifts the *IS* curve to the right, and increases real GDP.

UNDER FLEXIBLE EXCHANGE RATE

In a flexible exchange rate regime, the money supply is exogenous. Equilibrium occurs at the intersection of the *IS* and *LM* curves. The equation of the *IS* curve is

$$y = \frac{1}{(1 - b + im_1)}(a + i_0 + g - bt + nx_0 + ex_1 y_f - nx_2 \beta_0) - \frac{(h + nx_1 \beta_2)}{(1 - b + im_1)} r \quad \textbf{(7A.16)}$$

The equation to the *LM* curve is

$$y = \frac{1}{k}\left[\frac{M}{P} - m_0 + \ell r\right] \quad \textbf{(7A.20)}$$

We can find the *IS-LM* equilibrium by solving Equation (7A.16) and (7A.20) for r and y:

$$y^* = \frac{1}{(1 - b + im_1) + (h + nx_2)k/\ell}\left[(a + i_0 + g - bt + nx_0 + ex_1 y_f - nx_2 \beta_0) + \frac{(h + nx_2 \beta_1)}{\ell}\left(\frac{M}{P} - m_0\right)\right] \quad \textbf{(7A.25)}$$

$$r^* = \frac{k/\ell}{(1 - b + im_1) + (h + nx_2)k/\ell}\left[(a + i_0 + g - bt + nx_0 + ex_1 y_f - nx_2 \beta_0) - \frac{(1 - b + im_1)}{k}\left(\frac{M}{P} - m_0\right)\right] \quad \textbf{(7A.26)}$$

Equations (7A.25) and (7A.26) tells us that fiscal policy—the level of g and t—and monetary policy—the level of M—influence both equilibrium real GDP (y^*) and the interest rate (r^*). Expansionary fiscal policy increases both real GDP and the interest rate. Expansionary monetary policy increases real GDP and decreases domestic interest rates. But what is the effect of expansionary fiscal and monetary policy on the spot exchange rate?

Exchange rate In a flexible exchange rate regime, the exchange rate adjusts to maintain interest rate parity. Interest rate parity is given by

$$r = r_f + \left(\frac{ER}{ER^e} - 1\right) \quad \textbf{(7A.14)}$$

When the domestic interest rate (r) increases, the spot exchange rate (*ER*) adjusts, given the foreign interest rate (r_f) to make the expected rate of depreciation of the exchange rate ($ER/ER^e - 1$) maintain interest rate parity, Equation (7A.14). Expansionary fiscal policy increases the interest rate and appreciates the currency. Expansionary monetary policy decreases the interest rate and depreciates the currency.

Real exchange rate As the spot exchange rate adjusts to maintain interest rate parity, what happens to the real exchange rate and net exports? Equation (7A.15) shows the relationship between the interest rate and the real exchange rate:

$$\frac{ER \times P}{P_f} = \beta_0 + \beta_1 r, \quad \beta_0, \beta_1 > 0 \tag{7A.15}$$

The real exchange rate is the left side of the equation. You can see that a policy that increases the domestic interest rate also increases the real exchange rate. Expansionary fiscal policy increases the interest rate and increases the real exchange rate. Expansionary monetary policy decreases the interest rate and decreases the real exchange rate.

Net exports We can see the effect of a policy change on net exports from Equation (7A.8):

$$nx = nx_0 + ex_1 y_f - im_1 y - nx_2 \frac{ER \times P}{P_f}, \quad nx_2 > 0 \tag{7A.8}$$

Expansionary fiscal policy increases real GDP (y) and increases the real exchange rate. The increase in real GDP increases imports, which by itself decreases net exports, but the increase in the real exchange rate reduces net exports further. For two reasons expansionary fiscal policy decreases net exports. Expansionary monetary policy increases real GDP and decreases the real exchange rate. The increase in real GDP increases imports, which decreases net exports, but the decrease in the real exchange rate increases net exports. In this case, it is not possible to say whether net exports increase or not.

Rest of world shocks The domestic economy is sometimes hit by foreign shocks, such as a change in income in the rest of the world. If income in the rest of the world increases, exports increase, and both real GDP and the interest rate increase. The higher interest rate leads to an appreciation of the spot exchange rate and an increase in the real exchange rate. What happens to net exports? It is not possible to say. The increase in world income increases exports, but the increase in real GDP increases imports and the increase in the real exchange rate decreases net exports.

Capital mobility internationally In the above analysis, capital is assumed to be mobile internationally, but not perfectly mobile. If capital is perfectly mobile, what is the influence of fiscal and monetary policy? If capital is perfectly mobile, the domestic interest rate won't stray from the foreign interest rate. The spot exchange rate adjusts to keep r equal to r_f. This makes the *IS* curve horizontal at r equal to r_f. Let's take a closer look the model. The *IS* curve is

$$r = r_f \tag{7A.27}$$

The *LM* curve is

$$y = \frac{1}{k}\left[\frac{M}{P} - m_0 + \ell r\right] \tag{7A.20}$$

The *IS-LM* equilibrium occurs at

$$r^* = r_f \tag{7A.28}$$

$$y^* = \frac{1}{k}\left[\frac{M}{P} - m_0 + \ell r_f\right] \tag{7A.29}$$

Expansionary monetary policy increases real GDP and the exchange rate decreases (domestic currency depreciates) to keep the interest rate equal to r_f. Fiscal policy has no effect on real GPD. But expansionary fiscal policy puts pressure on interest rates to rise, and the exchange rate decreases (domestic currency appreciates) to keep r equal to r_f. Foreign shocks also may have no effect on real GDP; the shock changes only the exchange rate. For example, an increase in income in the rest of the world puts pressure on interest rates to rise and the domestic currency appreciates.

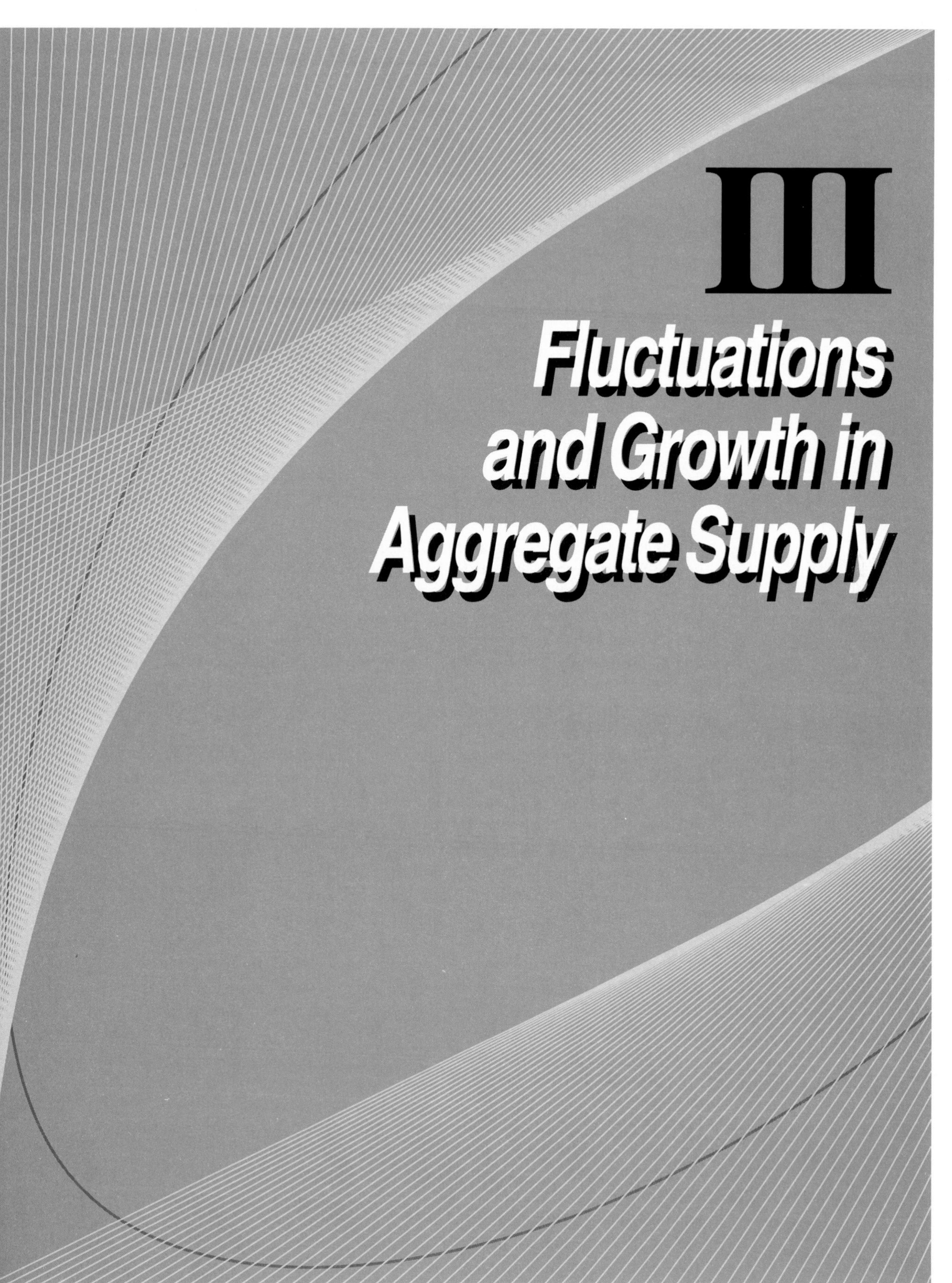

III

Fluctuations and Growth in Aggregate Supply

C H A P T E R

The Labor Market and Aggregate Supply

THE CORE OF CONTROVERSY

HAVE YOU EVER WANTED A JOB but been unable to get one? Have you ever thought of offering your services for a lower wage than the going one? Have you ever found yourself on the other side of the labor market, trying to get a job done, but unable to find someone suitable to do it? Would you think of offering someone a higher wage to get them to work for you?

Questions such as these are at the core of the controversy in macroeconomics. The key disagreement arises from the question, Do wages adjust quickly enough to keep the quantity of labor demanded equal to the quantity of labor supplied? In other words, does the labor market, like the stock market, achieve continuous price adjustments to maintain equilibrium?

Most non-economists — and most economists for that matter — think the question is silly and the answer obvious. Most people's wages do not change from day to day, or even from week to week or month to month. They change at annual or even less frequent intervals. So how can the labor market behave like the stock market? It can't and it doesn't, most people believe. Fluctuations in demand and supply do occur in the labor market, but those fluctuations don't bring wage changes — at least not quickly and continuously. Instead, they bring fluctuations in the number of people with jobs, the number of people unemployed, and the number of job vacancies.

A growing and increasingly influential minority of macroeconomists is challenging this conventional view. They are developing models of labor markets that have flexible wages and that maintain a continuous balance between the quantity of labor demanded and the quantity supplied. These models give rise to fluctuations in employment and unemployment and wages that are consistent with our observations of the facts in real world labor markets.

The way labor markets work has an important influence on aggregate supply. The slope and position of the short-run aggregate supply curve and the speed with which it shifts in response to wage changes are all influenced by the working of the labor market.

In this chapter and the next, we're going to study the labor market and its influence on the short-run aggregate supply curve. In Chapter 10, we'll move our focus to the long run and study the forces that promote long-term economic growth and expansion and make the long-run aggregate supply curve shift.

But first we examine the labor market and the core of controversy of macroeconomics. After studying this chapter, you'll be able to

- Describe the behavior of cycles in real GDP, unemployment, and real wages
- Explain how labor productivity influences the demand for labor
- Compare the changes in labor productivity and the demand for labor in Canada and Japan
- Explain how labor supply decisions are made
- Derive the long-run aggregate supply curve
- Derive the short-run aggregate supply curve
- Explain the main competing theories of wage determination
- Explain the behavior of wages over the business cycle

Let's begin by looking at some facts about the business cycle, unemployment, and wages.

8.1 *Canadian Real GDP, Unemployment, and Real Wages*

MACROFACTS

The *business cycle* is the ebb and flow of aggregate economic activity, measured by fluctuations in real GDP and other aggregates. One of those other aggregates is the *unemployment rate*—the percentage of the labor force without work. In fact, fluctuations in real GDP around its trend and in unemployment are so similar they describe virtually the same cycle.

Unemployment and the business cycle

Figure 8.1 shows the Canadian business cycle—the black line. It graphs the percentage deviations of real GDP from trend from 1970 to 1990. There, you can see in the mid-1970s the dip in real GDP relative to trend that resulted from the first OPEC oil shock, in the early 1980s the recession that resulted from the world economic slowdown rein-

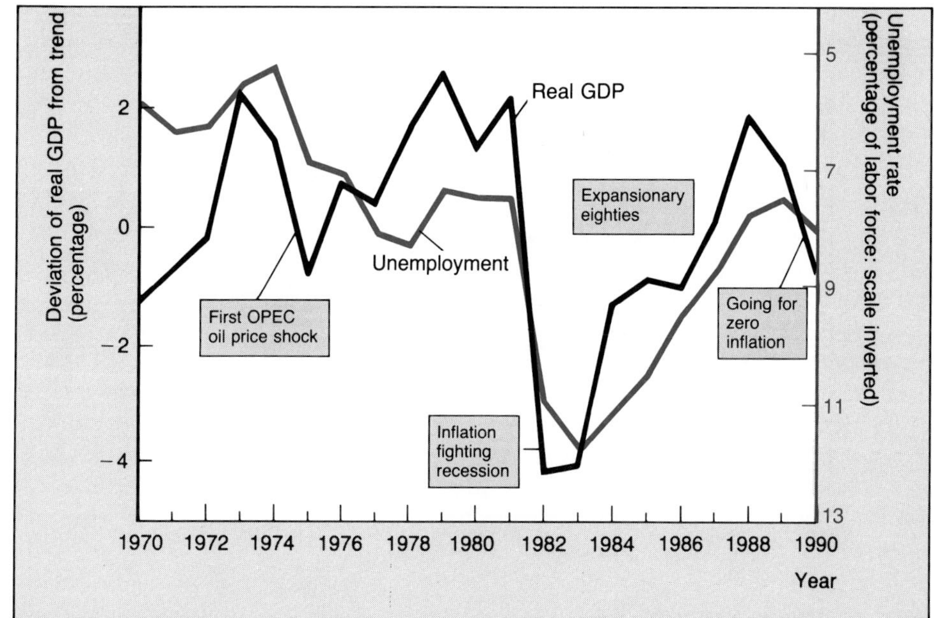

FIGURE 8.1
Unemployment and the Business Cycle

Fluctuations in real GDP, measured as deviations of real GDP from trend (left-hand scale) and unemployment measured as the percentage of the labor force (right-hand scale, inverted) trace an almost identical business cycle.

Source: National Income and Expenditure Accounts, Statistics Canada, Catalogue 13-201, and *Historical Labour Force Statistics*, Statistics Canada, Catalogue 71-201.

forced by the Bank of Canada's disinflationary monetary policies, and the slowdown of 1990. You can also see the strong expansion in real GDP that occurred between 1983 and 1988.

The graph also measures the unemployment rate. To emphasize the relationship between unemployment and the business cycle, we've measured the unemployment rate on the right-hand scale and inverted it. That is, the highest unemployment rates are shown at the bottom of the figure. The blue line tracks the unemployment rate. Notice how closely these two lines move together. Discrepancies exist but the overwhelming fact illustrated here is that when real GDP moves above trend the unemployment rate falls, and when real GDP moves below trend the unemployment rate rises.

It's clear that understanding what causes the business cycle must include an explanation of why fluctuations in unemployment so closely match those of the deviation of real GDP from trend.

Real wages and the business cycle

The wage rate — the price of labor — is expressed as dollars per hour. One of the several reasons why wage rates fluctuate is that the value of money continuously changes. In an economy that experiences ongoing inflation, money loses value. The **real wage rate** is the price of labor measured in constant purchasing power — in terms of the purchasing power of dollars in a given year. The real wage rate is the opportunity cost of labor. How does the real wage rate behave over the business cycle? Does it rise in a boom as the unemployment rate falls and fall in a recession as the unemployment rate rises?

In Figure 8.1 we saw that real GDP and unemployment move together. Do real wages and real GDP also move together? If they do, real wages rise most quickly when unemployment is low and most slowly, or even fall, when unemployment is high. The facts about real wages and real GDP are shown in Figure 8.2, where their growth rates

FIGURE 8.2
Real Wages and the Business Cycle

Real wages — the goods and services one hour of work buys — grow at a fluctuating rate. Sometimes their growth is procyclical — it moves in sympathy with the fluctuations in real GDP and at other times it is countercyclical — it grows in opposition to fluctuations in real GDP. In the rapid expansion of the mid-1980s, real wages were procyclical; in the slow down of 1990, countercyclical.

Source: National Income and Expenditure Accounts, Statistics Canada, Catalogue 13-201, and *Historical Labour Force Statistics*, Statistics Canada, Catalogue 71-201 and our calculations.

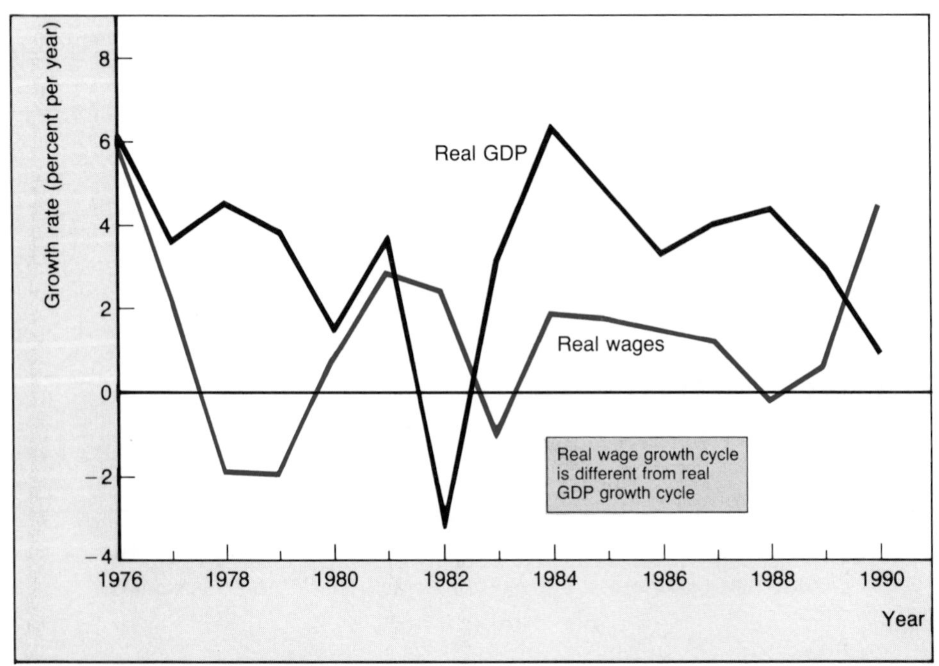

are plotted for the years 1975 to 1990. Most striking in this figure is the general lack of any clear, simple relationship between real wage growth and real GDP growth. It is certainly not like the relationship in Figure 8.1, where the two series line up almost exactly. There are periods such as the 1982 recession and the 1990 slow down when real wages are countercyclical. A variable is **countercyclical** when its fluctuations are opposite to the fluctuations in real GDP. When the economy is weak—when real GDP growth is low—real wage growth is high. But that countercyclical pattern breaks down in the expansion of the 1980s when, to the extent that there is any relationship at all, it is procyclical. A variable is **procyclical** when its fluctuations are in line with the fluctuations in real GDP. When the economy is strong—when real GDP growth is high—real wage growth is high, and when the economy is weak with low real GDP growth, real wage growth is low.

A theory of the business cycle must account for these movements in real wages. Why are real wages sometimes countercyclical, sometimes procyclical? Why aren't real wages always procyclical?

To answer these questions about unemployment and real wages, we need to explore the behavior of the labor market. We're going to begin by studying the demand for labor and the effect of labor productivity on that demand.

8.2 Labor Productivity and the Demand for Labor

At any given moment, the economy has a stock of capital equipment, a labor force, and a body of knowledge—a state of technology. To vary output, firms vary the quantity of labor employed and the degree of utilization of the stock of capital equipment, given the state of technology. Changes in output resulting from changes in employment with a given capital stock and state of technology are determined by the short-run production function.

Short-run production function

The **short-run production function** is the relationship between real GDP and the level of employment, holding constant the capital stock and the state of technology. Figure 8.3(a) illustrates a short-run production function measuring employment (in millions of hours a year) on the horizontal axis and real GDP (in billions of 1986 dollars a year) on the vertical axis.

Notice the shape of the short-run production function. It slopes upward — an increase in employment brings an increase in real GDP. But the slope is not constant. It starts out steep and gets flatter and flatter as employment increases. The slope of the short-run production function measures the marginal product of labor. The **marginal product of labor** is the increase in output produced as a result of employing one additional unit of labor. The marginal product of labor declines as more labor is employed.

To measure the marginal product of labor, we measure the slope of the short-run production function at a given point. For example, the slope when employment is 225 million hours a year is equal to the slope of the tangent (black line) at this employment level. It is equal to the slope of the hypotenuse of the triangle drawn in the figure. The base of the triangle, the change in employment, Δn, is 100 million hours; the height, the change in real GDP, Δy, is $1 billion ($1,000 million). Dividing the change in real GDP by the change in employment ($1,000 million divided by 100 million hours) gives a slope of $10 an hour. That is, the marginal product of labor is $10 an hour.

FIGURE 8.3
Production Function and Demand for Labor

The short-run production function (part a) shows how the level of real GDP varies as the level of employment varies, other things held constant. Lying behind the short-run production function are a given capital stock and state of technology. The slope of the short-run production function measures the marginal product of labor—the increase in output resulting from a one-unit increase in labor input.

Firms hire the quantity of labor such that the marginal product of labor equals the real wage rate. The lower the real wage rate, the greater is the quantity of labor hired. Thus the demand for labor curve slopes downward (part b).

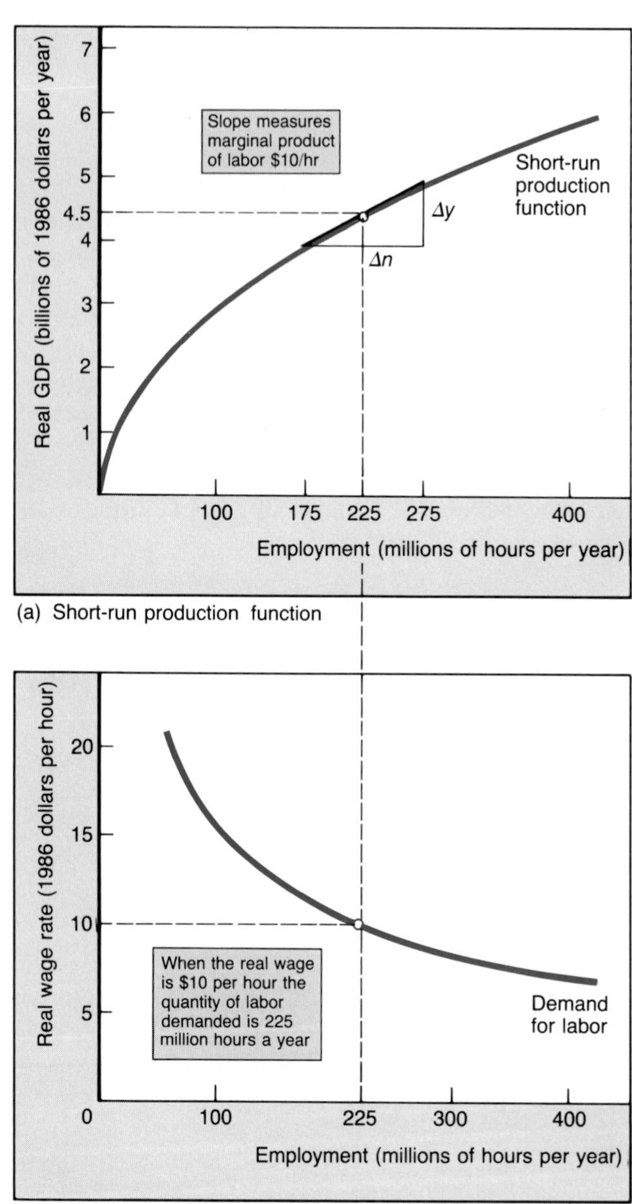

The demand for labor

The **demand for labor**—the relationship between the quantity of labor employed and the real wage rate—is determined by the marginal product of labor. Firms hire labor to produce the goods and services they seek to sell for a profit. Their objective is to maximize profit. To do so, firms hire the quantity of labor at which the cost of the last hour of labor employed brings in an equal amount of revenue. The cost of the last hour of labor employed is the wage rate per hour. The revenue brought in depends on the marginal product of the last hour of labor and the price for which the output is sold. That is, the revenue brought in is the marginal product of labor multiplied by the price for which the output is sold. To maximize profit, firms hire labor up to the point at which the wage rate (W) equals the marginal product of labor (MP) times the price of the output (P). That is,

$$W = MP \times P. \tag{8.1}$$

Dividing both sides of this equation by P gives

$$\frac{W}{P} = MP. \tag{8.2}$$

That is, firms maximize profit by employing the quantity of labor such that the marginal product of labor equals the real wage rate. If the marginal product of labor is greater than the real wage rate, it pays firms to hire more labor. If the marginal product of labor is less than the wage rate, firms cut back employment.

The lower the real wage rate, the greater is the quantity of labor employed. Figure 8.3(b) illustrates this relationship — the demand for labor. The position of the demand for labor curve depends entirely on the short-run production function. Anything that shifts the short-run production function also shifts the demand for labor curve.

Shifts in the production function and demand for labor

The production function and the demand for labor curve shift over time as a result of capital accumulation and technological change. With more capital per worker and with more advanced technologies, a given amount of labor can produce a larger real GDP. For example, if an automobile plant in the eastern part of Germany (the former East Germany) had as much capital per worker as an automobile plant in the former West Germany, car production in the east would be much higher. As the car factories in the eastern part of Germany are gradually upgraded to the standards of the factories in the western part of the country, so output per worker in the eastern part of Germany will increase.

Because of capital accumulation and technological change, the short-run production function shifts upward over time. At the same time, it gets steeper — that is, at any level of employment the marginal product of labor is higher. Thus the demand for labor curve shifts to the right.

Occasionally, forces operate to shift the short-run production function downward. When this happens, the marginal product of labor falls and the demand for labor curve shifts to the left. Massive disruption to the world supply of oil during the mid-1970s produced such a shift in the short-run production function and demand for labor curve. The sharp increase in the price of oil in the late 1970s caused the short-run production function to shift downward as firms economized on their use of high-cost energy and reduced the rate of utilization of capital.

8.3 *Canada and Japan*

TESTCASE

Let's look at two short-run production functions and demand for labor curves in the real world — those of Canada and Japan. How have the Canadian and Japanese short-run production function and demand for labor changed over time, and how do they compare with each other? The answers to these questions can be found by studying the relationship between real GDP and the level of employment and between real wages and the level of employment. Figure 8.4 illustrates the situation in Canada in 1975 and 1990 (part a) and Japan in 1970 and 1988 (part b). Parts (a) and (b) each consist of two graphs: (i) the short-run production function and (ii) the demand for labor curve.

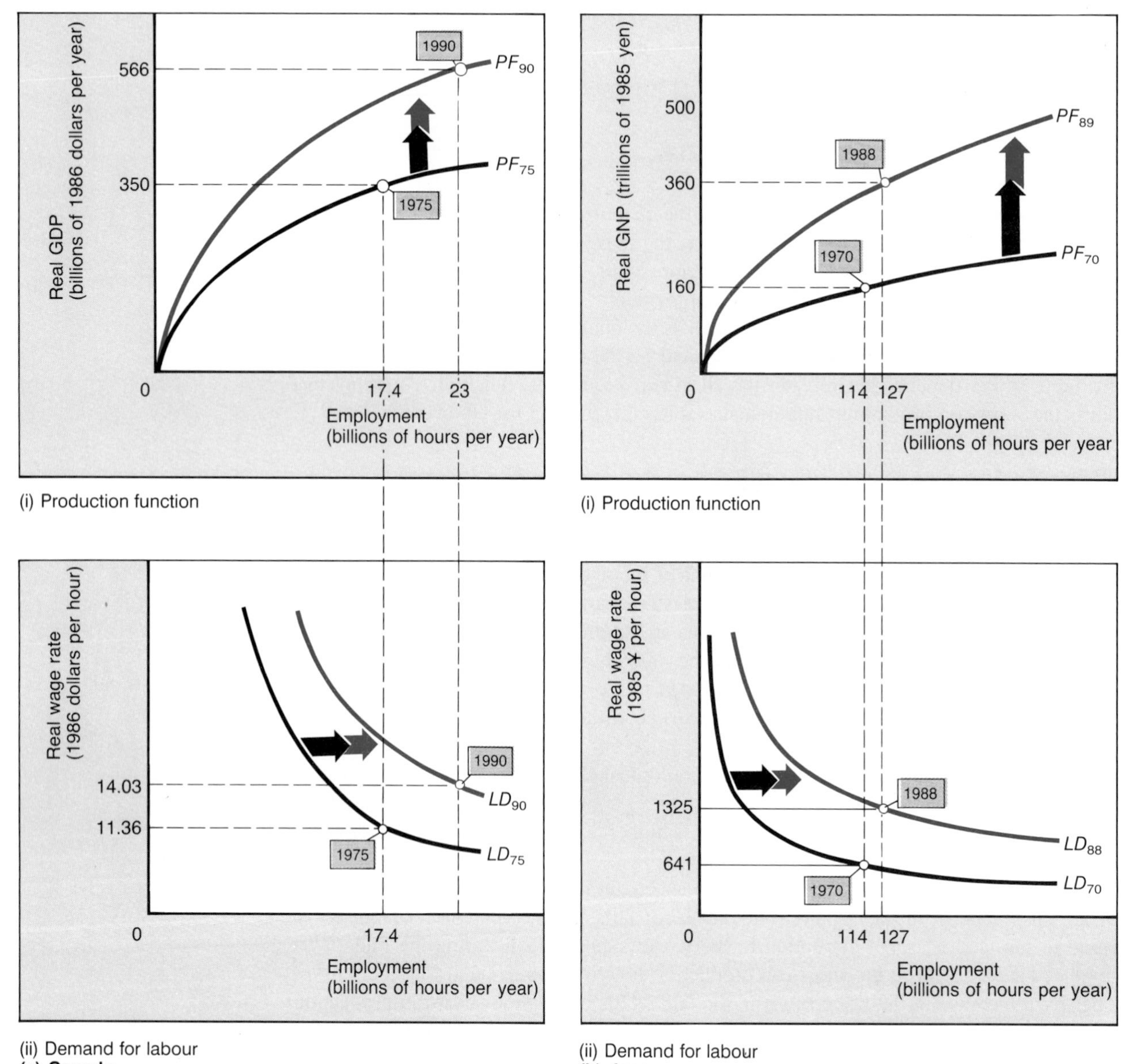

(i) Production function

(ii) Demand for labour
(a) Canada

(i) Production function

(ii) Demand for labour
(b) Japan

FIGURE 8.4
Short-Run Production Function and Demand for Labor in Canada and Japan

The short-run production function and demand curve for labor are shown for Canada in 1975 and 1990 (part a) and Japan in 1970 and 1988 (part b). Capital accumulation and technological change have shifted the short-run production function upward and have increased the demand for labor. Capital accumulation was much stronger in Japan, so its production function and the demand for labor curve shifted more than those of Canada. Real wages increased more in Japan than in Canada, partly because the demand curve for labor shifted farther to the right and partly because employment did not increase as much in Japan as in Canada.

Sources: Canada *National Income and Expenditure Accounts*, Statistics Canada, Catalogue 13-201, and *Historical Labour Force Statistics*, Statistics Canada, Catalogue 71-201 and our calculations; Japan, *Economic Statistics Annual*, Research and Statistics Department, Bank of Japan, 1977-1982, 1989.

First, let's look at Canada: in 1975, its short-run production function was the black curve in part a(i). The economy was at the point labeled 1975—employment was 17.4 billion hours and real GDP $350 billion. In the labor market, part a(ii), the demand for labor curve was LD_{75} and the economy was at the point labeled 1975 — 17.4 billion hours of labor employed at a real wage rate of $11.36 an hour. Between 1975 and 1990, capital accumulation and technological change increased the economy's production potential. The short-run production function shifted upward, to PF_{90} in part a(i), and the economy was at the point labeled 1990—23 billion hours of labor employed, producing a real GDP of $566 billion. In part (b), the increased productivity of labor shifted the demand for labor curve right to LD_{90}. The economy was operating at the point labeled 1990—23 billion hours of labor were employed at a real wage rate of $14.03.

Canadian labor productivity increased by approximately 40 percent between 1975 and 1990. That is, at any given level of employment, 40 percent more goods and services were produced in 1990 than in 1975. But real wages did not increase by anything like 40 percent. In fact, they increased by little more than half that amount. Why? The reason is, the level of employment increased. If employment had remained constant, real wages would have increased to more than $16 an hour, an increase similar to the 40 percent increase in labor productivity. But remember that the marginal product of labor diminishes — the higher the level of employment, other things being equal, the smaller is the marginal product of labor — and therefore the real wage rate. Between 1975 and 1990, increased labor productivity shifted the demand for labor curve to the right, increasing the real wage rate. But the increase in employment resulted in a movement along the new demand for labor curve so that the increase in the real wage rate was much smaller than the increase in productivity at a given employment level.

Next, look at Japan. In 1970, Japan was on the black short-run production function and demand for labor curves in part (b). It was operating at the points on those curves labeled 1970. By 1988, Japan's short-run production function and demand for labor curves shifted upward to the blue curves in part (b). The magnitude of the shift in Japan's production function and demand for labor curve was much larger than that in Canada. At any given employment level, the Japanese economy's capacity to produce goods more than doubled. Similarly, at any given employment level, the marginal product of labor and real wage rate more than doubled. This massive upward shift in Japan's short-run production function and demand for labor curve arose mainly from the pace of capital accumulation in that economy, more rapid than the pace in Canada. We'll see in Chapter 10 exactly how capital accumulation rates differed across countries and how those differences contributed to the more rapid growth of Japan's economy.

Notice also that not only did the demand for labor increase more in Japan than in Canada, but so did real wages. In Canada, real wage growth was checked by a large increase in employment, resulting in a movement along (and down) the 1988 demand curve for labor. Also, in Japan, employment did not increase by as much as in Canada. The average length of a work week declined in Japan much more than in Canada and the number of people working grew in Canada at a much more rapid pace than in Japan. As a consequence, in Japan the decrease in real wages resulting from the increase in employment was much smaller than in Canada.

We've seen how Canadian and Japanese short-run production functions have changed over time and how those changes have led to changes in the demand for labor. In examining the changes that have occurred in employment and real wages, we've noticed that employment increased a great deal in Canada but much less in Japan. But we've not yet *explained* this behavior of real wages and employment. Why does employment increase as real wages increase? To answer this question, we need to study the supply of labor.

8.4 *The Supply of Labor*

Labor supply decisions are made by households, who allocate their time between

- Work
- Other activities

"Other activities" include leisure, job search, and work in the home. Work and job search are called **market activity**. Work in the home and leisure are called **nonmarket activity**. The **quantity of labor supplied** is the amount of time allocated to work.

In deciding how much labor to supply, a household considers two margins:

- Work versus other activities
- Work today versus work later

In making its choices, a household has to work out the opportunity costs involved. Let's examine these.

Work versus other activities

In order to decide to spend an extra hour on nonwork activities and an hour less at work, a household has to figure out the opportunity cost of the extra hour of other activities. This opportunity cost is the real wage rate—the goods and services foregone by giving up the wage that an hour of work earns. The real wage rate is the dollars that could have been earned from working divided by the price level.

The real wage rate has two effects on the quantity of labor supplied—an income effect and a substitution effect. The substitution effect encourages more work, the higher the real wage rate. The income effect is ambiguous. At low income levels, an increase in the real wage rate will likely induce an increase in the quantity of labor supplied. But at a high enough income level, a higher real wage rate will likely induce a decrease in the quantity of labor supplied.

Taking account only of the choice between work and other activities, the individual supply of labor curve is backward bending. Up to some real wage rate, the higher the real wage rate, the greater is the quantity of labor supplied. Above that wage rate, the higher the real wage rate, the smaller is the quantity of labor supplied.

Work today versus work later

A household's second margin of choice involves the substitution of nonwork activities today for nonwork activities in the future or, equivalently, work in the future for work today. Holding total nonwork activities constant, what is the opportunity cost of more nonwork activities today and less tomorrow? That opportunity cost is equal to

$$\frac{\text{Today's real wage rate} \times (1 + \text{real interest rate})}{\text{Tomorrow's real wage rate}}$$

To see why this formula gives the opportunity cost of an extra hour of nonwork activities today versus an hour tomorrow, we need to consider the effect of this substitution on the amount of goods and services the household can buy. An hour less of work today costs today's real wage rate. An extra hour of work tomorrow earns tomorrow's real wage rate. But how does today's real wage rate compare with tomorrow's real wage rate? The earlier an income is received, the more it is worth because it can earn interest. Thus a wage earned by working one hour today will accumulate to the wage plus the interest earned on it tomorrow—today's wage rate multiplied by (1 + real interest rate). This is the amount that has to be compared with tomorrow's wage rate.

The effect of a change in the real wage rate on the timing of work depends on whether the change in the wage rate is temporary or permanent. If the increase in today's real wage rate is permanent, then tomorrow's real wage rate increases by the same amount as today's and the opportunity cost of the retiming of work does not change. But an increase in today's real wage rate with no expected increase in tomorrow's—a temporary increase in the today's real wage rate—increases the incentive to work today and take more time off from work in the future.

The labor supply curve

The **labor supply curve** is the relationship between the quantity of labor supplied and the real wage rate. There are two labor supply curves: one shows the response of the quantity of labor supplied to a permanent change in the real wage and the other to a temporary change. These labor supply curves are shown in Figure 8.5(a). Because of the intertemporal substitution—the retiming of work and other activities—the quantity

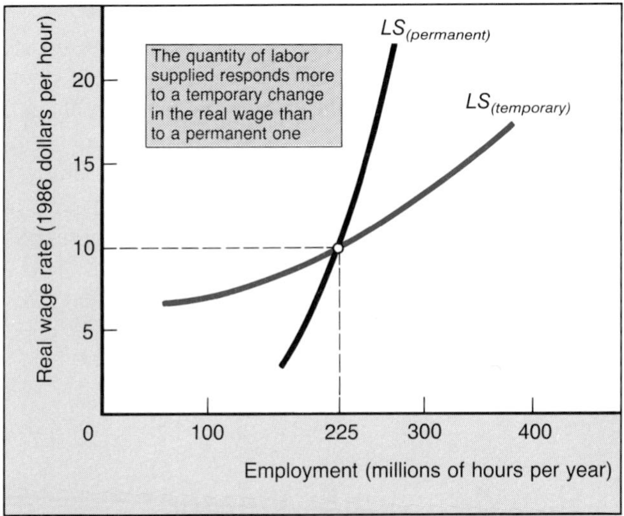

(a) The labor supply curves

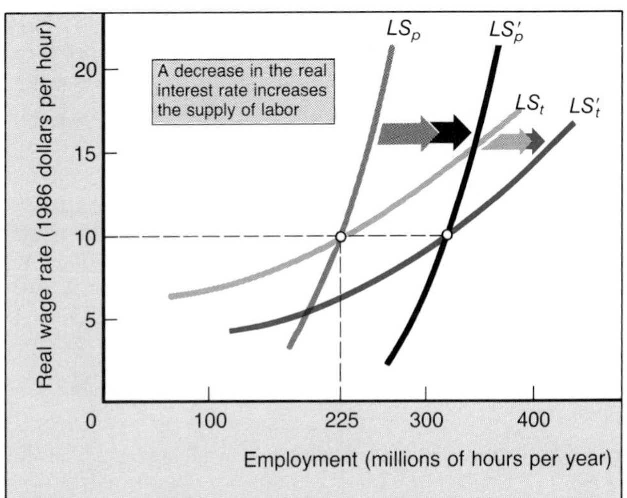

(b) The interest rate and the supply of labor

FIGURE 8.5
The Supply of Labor

The higher the real wage rate, the greater is the quantity of labor supplied. A temporary change in the real wage rate has a larger effect on employment than a permanent change because of intertemporal substitution. With a temporarily higher real wage rate, it pays to work more hours today and fewer tomorrow, when the real wage rate will have fallen again. Intertemporal substitution is also influenced by the real interest rate. The higher the real interest rate, the more it pays to work today, bringing in an income that can earn a high interest rate. This effect shifts the supply of labor curve, as shown in part (b).

of labor supplied responds more to a temporary change in the real wage rate than to a permanent one. So the labor supply curve describing that response is much flatter than the one describing the response to a permanent change in the real wage rate.

Changes in the supply of labor

A change in the real wage rate induces a change in the quantity of labor supplied and the movement along the labor supply curve. Which labor supply curve the economy moves along depends on whether the wage change is permanent or temporary.

Any factor other than a change in the real wage rate changes the supply of labor and shifts the labor supply curve. The more important influences on the supply of labor are

1. Population
2. Real interest rate

Changes in the population influence the supply of labor in a natural way. The larger the number of working-age people in the population, the greater is the supply of labor and the farther to the right are the labor supply curves.

The real interest rate affects the supply of labor because it affects intertemporal substitution. The higher the real interest rate, the greater is the tendency to work today and take more time for other activities in the future. The reason is an extra dollar earned today can earn interest at a higher rate and so is worth more than a dollar earned from future work. Hence the substitution away from working in the future toward working today. The higher the real interest rate, the farther to the right are the labor supply curves. Figure 8.5(b) shows shifts in the labor supply curves resulting from an increase in the real interest rate.

Now we're ready to bring the forces that influence the demand for labor and the supply of labor together to see how labor market equilibrium determines aggregate supply in both the long and the short run.

8.5 *Long-Run Aggregate Supply*

The *long-run aggregate supply curve* shows the relationship between the quantity of real GDP supplied and the price level when wages and other factor prices are flexible and have adjusted to achieve full employment and when firms are producing their profit-maximizing output. To derive the long-run aggregate supply curve, we need to examine the labor market and the short-run production function.

Labor market equilibrium

The labor market achieves a full-employment equilibrium at a real wage rate such that the quantity of labor demanded equals the quantity supplied. Figure 8.6(a) illustrates such an equilibrium at the intersection of the demand for labor curve, *LD*, and the supply of labor curve, *LS*. This supply curve is the one along which the quantity of labor responds to a change in the real wage, holding everything else, including the future real wage and the future real interest rate, constant. In this example, the real wage rate is \$10 an hour, and 225 billion hours of labor are supplied each year.

Labor market equilibrium determines the real wage rate and the level of employment but not the level of real GDP. For that, we need to go to the short-run production function.

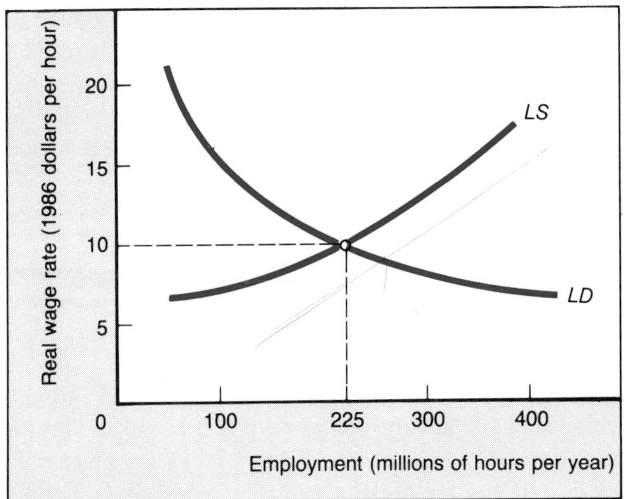

(a) Labor market

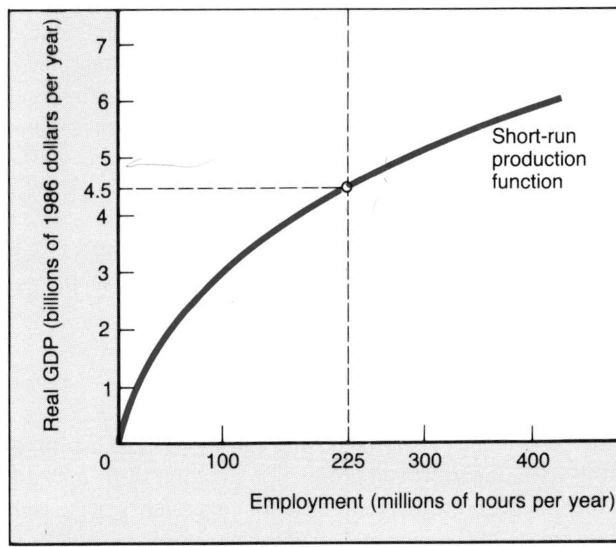

(b) Short-run production function

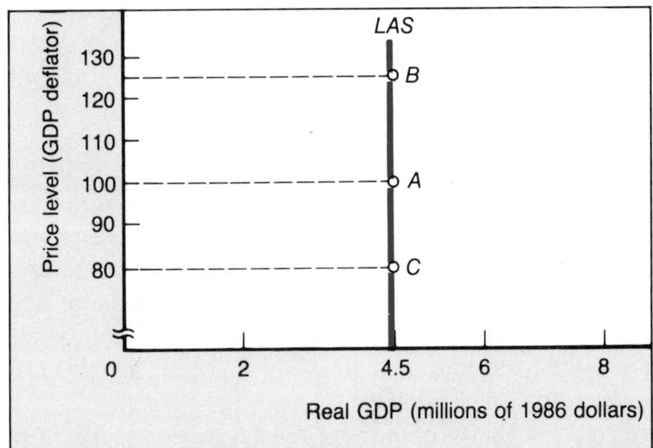

(c) Long-run aggregate supply curve

FIGURE 8.6
The Long-Run Aggregate Supply Curve

Labor market equilibrium (part a) determines the real wage rate and the employment level. The short-run production function (part b) determines the level of real GDP. This equilibrium real wage, employment, and real GDP level is independent of the price level. Any price level is consistent with this equilibrium level of GDP (part c) because the money wage rate changes in proportion to changes in the price level along the *LAS* curve.

The short-run production function

The short-run production function traces the relationship between the level of employment and real GDP for a given capital stock and given state of technology. Since the labor market equilibrium determines the equilibrium level of employment, we can use the short-run production function to determine equilibrium real GDP, as Figure 8.6(b) illustrates. When employment is at its equilibrium level (225 million hours a year), real GDP is $4.5 billion.

Long-run aggregate supply curve

To derive the long-run aggregate supply curve, we have to ask what happens to equilibrium real GDP as the price level changes. The answer is, nothing. To understand why, recall the meaning of the real wage rate. The real wage rate is the dollar wage rate divided by the price level. The equilibrium real wage rate of $10 an hour can arise because the price level is 100 and the dollar wage rate is $10 an hour. In this case, the economy will be at point *A* in Figure 8.6(c). But the real wage rate is also $10 an hour if the price level is 120 and the dollar wage rate is $12 an hour, in which case the economy will be at point *B* in Figure 8.6(c). Or the price level is 80 and the dollar wage rate is $8 an hour, in which case the economy will be at point *C* in Figure 8.6(c). The points *C*, *A*, and *B* lie on the economy's long-run aggregate supply curve.

The long-run aggregate supply curve is vertical because any change in the price level changes the money wage rate by the same percentage so as to preserve the equilibrium real wage rate. There is only one equilibrium employment level, and this determines a unique level of real GDP.

Shifts in the long-run aggregate supply curve

Long-run aggregate supply changes and the long-run aggregate supply curve shifts when

1. The short-run production function changes
2. The supply of labor changes

Short-run production function An increase in the capital stock or a technological advance increases the amount of real GDP that can be produced from a given level of employment. In this case, the short-run production function shifts upward. The marginal product of labor increases, so the demand for labor curve shifts to the right. Other things being equal, this increase in the demand for labor increases the real wage rate and the equilibrium level of employment and real GDP. Long-run aggregate supply increases, so the long-run aggregate supply curve shifts to the right. If the capital stock increase and technological change are permanent, permanently increasing the real wage rate, the relevant labor supply curve for determining the new equilibrium is LS_p, the steeper of the two labor supply curves that we studied earlier (Figure 8.5a).

Labor supply An increase in the working age population or in the real interest rate increases the quantity of labor supplied at each real wage rate and shifts the labor supply curve to the right. Other things being equal, such a change decreases the real wage rate, increases the equilibrium level of employment, and as a result increases long-run aggregate supply. Over time, population growth, capital accumulation, and technological change shift the long-run aggregate supply curve to the right. But because these forces operate at variable paces, sometimes the long-run aggregate supply curve moves rightward quickly, at other times more slowly.

On occasion, rightward shifts of the long-run aggregate supply curve are halted and it shifts to the left. In recent times, shocks to the world's energy supply have been the most important source of such shifts. An oil embargo and the quadrupling of the price of oil in 1974 and a further steep increase in the price of oil in the late 1970s and 1980 caused firms to find more efficient ways of using energy. These shocks led to a large, temporary downward shift of the short-run production function and to a decrease in the demand for labor. Other things being equal, a shock of this type decreases the real wage rate and the equilibrium level of employment and lowers long-run aggregate supply.

8.6 *Aggregate Supply in the Short Run*

The *short-run aggregate supply curve* shows the relationship between the quantity of real GDP supplied and the price level when the wage rate (and other factor prices) is fixed. Along the short-run aggregate supply curve, firms are producing their profit-maximizing output. As the prices for which they sell their output vary and the wage rate paid to labor stays constant, firms maximize their profit by adjusting their output.

Firms maximize profit at each point on the demand for labor curve. (Recall that the demand for labor is the relationship between the quantity of labor demanded and the real wage rate such that firms are maximizing profit.) But for a given money wage rate, different price levels produce different real wage rates and so different equilibrium levels of employment. This effect of the price level on the real wage rate makes the short-run aggregate supply curve slope upward, unlike the long-run aggregate supply curve.

Let's derive a short-run aggregate supply curve. Suppose that the money wage rate is \$10 an hour. If the price level is 100, the real wage rate is also \$10 an hour. The economy is at point *A* in Figure 8.7(a), with 225 million hours of labor employed. That amount of labor produces \$4.5 billion of real GDP (at point *A* on the short-run production function in Figure 8.7b). Thus at a price level of 100, equilibrium real GDP supplied is \$4.5 billion. We've found one point on the short-run aggregate supply curve, point *A* in Figure 8.7(c).

Now, with the money wage rate fixed at \$10 an hour, suppose that the price level is lower than 100—for example, 80. With a price level of 80 and a money wage rate of \$10 an hour, the real wage rate is \$12.50 an hour (\$10 × 100 ÷ 80 = \$12.5). When the real wage is \$12.5, the quantity of labor demanded is 144 million hours (point *B* on the demand for labor curve in Figure 8.7a). This quantity of labor produces \$3.6 billion of real GDP (point *B* in Figure 8.7b). We've now found a second point on the short-run aggregate supply curve—point *B* in Figure 8.7(c), where the price level is 80 and the equilibrium real GDP supplied \$3.6 billion.

Finally, suppose that the price level is higher than 100—for example, 125. With a money wage rate of \$10 an hour and a price level of 125, the real wage rate is \$8 an hour (\$10 × 100 ÷ 125 = \$8). With this real wage rate, the quantity of labor demanded is 352 million hours—point *C* on the demand for labor curve in Figure 8.7(a). This level of employment produces \$5.6 billion of real GDP, point *C* in Figure 8.7(b). We've now found a third point on the short-run aggregate supply curve—point *C* in Figure 8.7(c), where the price level is 125 and equilibrium real GDP supplied is \$5.6 billion.

The short-run aggregate supply curve is found by repeating this exercise for every possible price level. The short-run aggregate supply curve passes through the points *B*, *A*, and *C*. It is an upward-sloping curve—as the price level increases with a fixed money wage rate, the real wage rate falls, employment increases, and real GDP supplied increases.

Shifts in the short-run aggregate supply curve

The short-run aggregate supply curve shifts when

FIGURE 8.7
The Short-Run Aggregate Supply Curve

The money wage rate is fixed, in this example at $10 an hour. If the price level is 100, real wages are also $10 an hour and firms demand 225 million hours at point *A* on the demand for labor curve in part (a). Output is determined at point *A* on the short-run production function (in part b). Thus at a price level of 100, real GDP supplied is $4.5 billion, point *A* in part (c). If the price level increases to 125, the real wage rate decreases to $8 an hour and firms hire labor at point *C* on the labor demand curve (part a). Output increases to $5.6 billion, as determined at point *C* in part (b) on the short-run production function. Thus when the price level is 125, the economy produces $5.6 billion of real GDP—point *C* in part (c). If the price level is 80, real wages are $12.50, and firms operate at point *B* in part (a). Real GDP is determined at point *B* on the short-run production function in part (b). Thus when the price level is 80, real GDP supplied is $3.6 billion—point *B* in part (c). The points *B*, *A*, and *C* in part (c) trace the economy's short-run aggregate supply curve.

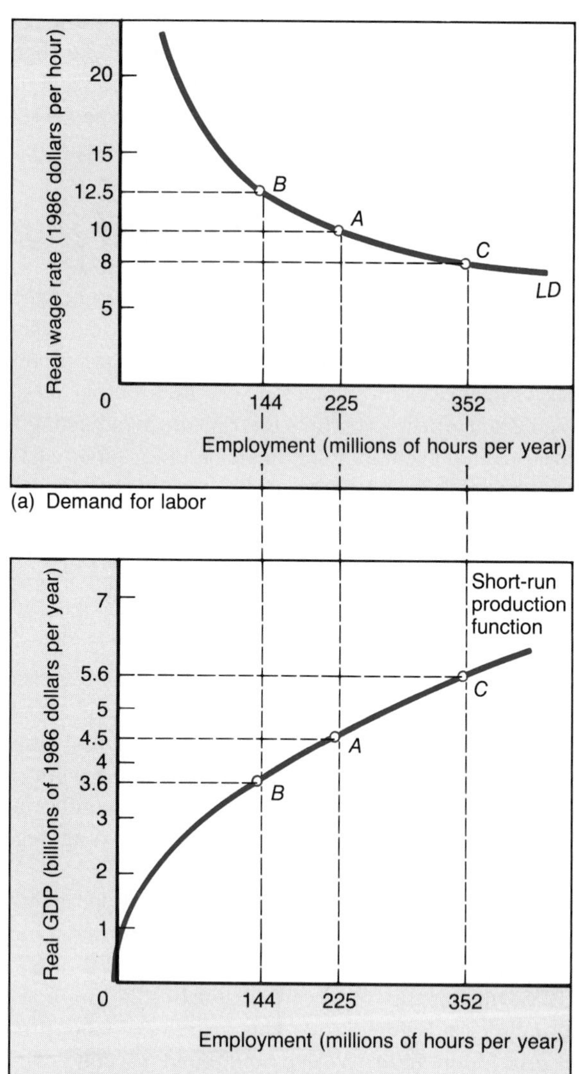

(a) Demand for labor

(b) Short-run production function

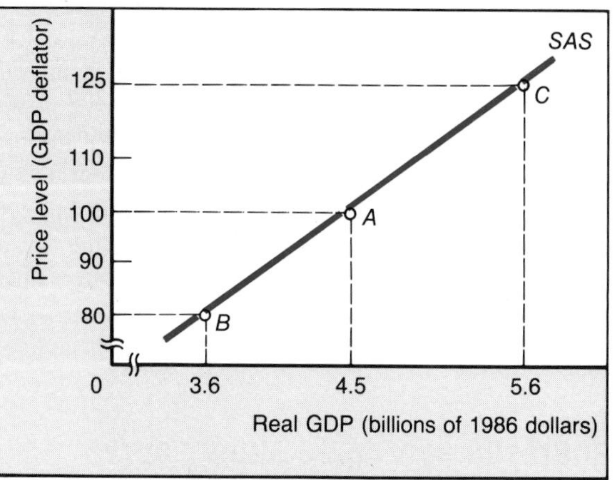

(c) Short-run aggregate supply curve

1. The money wage rate changes
2. Long-run aggregate supply changes

Money wage rate An increase in the money wage rate decreases short-run aggregate supply. That is, for any given price level, an increase in the money wage rate decreases the quantity of real GDP supplied. Figure 8.8 illustrates how the short-run aggregate supply curve shifts if the money wage rate increases from \$10 an hour to \$12.50. We've seen that when the real wage rate is \$10 an hour, the quantity of labor employed produces a real GDP of \$4.5 billion. This is the real GDP supplied when the money wage rate is \$10 an hour and the price level is 100—point *A*. But this quantity of real GDP is also supplied if the money wage rate is \$12.50 an hour and the price level is 125—the real wage rate is \$10 (\$12.50 × 100 ÷ 125 = \$10). Thus the short-run aggregate supply curve shifts to the left when the money wage rate increases. The distance it shifts can be measured most accurately in the vertical direction. The price level at which a given quantity of real GDP is supplied increases by the same percentage as the increase in the money wage rate. When the money wage rate increases from \$10 to \$12.50 an hour (a 25 percent increase), the price level at which any given quantity of real GDP is supplied increases by 25 percent.

Changes in long-run aggregate supply Changes in long-run aggregate supply also change short-run aggregate supply. The short-run aggregate supply curve intersects the long-run aggregate supply curve at the price level that delivers, for a fixed money wage rate, a real wage rate equal to the equilibrium. The short-run aggregate supply curve lies to the right of the long-run aggregate supply curve at higher price levels, because the real wage rate is below the equilibrium. It lies to the left of the long-run aggregate supply curve at lower price levels, because the real wage rate is higher than the equilibrium.

The relationship between the short-run aggregate supply curve and the long-run aggregate supply curve is maintained when long-run aggregate supply changes. As we've seen, an increase in the capital stock or an advance in technology shifts the long-run aggregate supply curve to the right. It also shifts the short-run aggregate supply curve by the same amount, so that the short-run aggregate supply curve continues to intersect the long-run aggregate supply curve at the same price level.

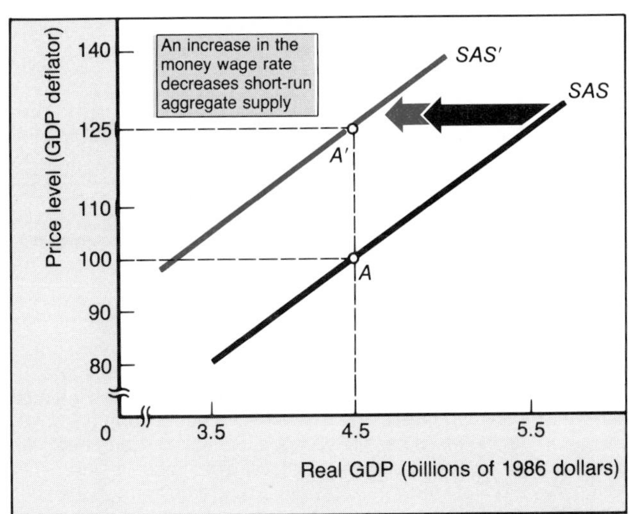

FIGURE 8.8
Changes in Short-Run Aggregate Supply

An increase in the money wage rate shifts the short-run aggregate supply curve upward. A higher price level is required to bring forth any given quantity of real GDP.

8.7 *Wage Determination*

The forces determining the money wage rate play a crucial role in determining the position and the speed at which the short-run aggregate supply curve shifts. There are two theories of wage determination:

- Labor market clearing
- Gradual adjustment

Labor market clearing

The **labor market clearing theory of wages** is that the money wage rate adjusts continuously to keep the real wage rate at the level that makes the quantity of labor demanded equal to the quantity of labor supplied. If the real wage rate is below the equilibrium level, there is an excess demand for labor—the quantity of labor demanded exceeds the quantity supplied. Figure 8.9 shows an excess demand for labor at a real wage rate of $8 an hour. In such a situation, firms are not able to hire all the labor they want, putting upward pressure on the real wage rate. The money wage rate rises so that the real wage rate increases to $10 an hour. If the economy is experiencing inflation, the real wage rate will increase only if the money wage rate increases at a rate faster than the inflation rate.

If the real wage rate is above the equilibrium level, there is an excess supply of labor — the quantity of labor demanded is less than the quantity supplied — an excess supply of labor. Figure 8.7 shows an excess supply of labor at a real wage rate of $12.50 an hour. In this case, there is downward pressure on the real wage rate. The money

FIGURE 8.9
Wage Determination

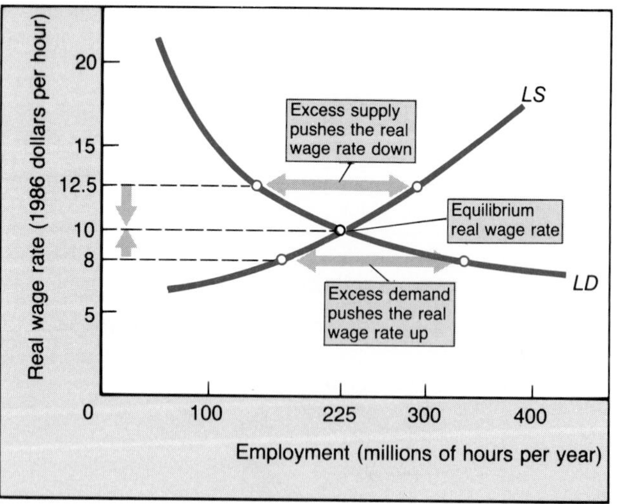

At a real wage rate of $12.50, there is an excess supply of labor and downward pressure on the real wage rate. At a real wage rate of $8 an hour, there is excess demand for labor and upward pressure on the real wage rate. At $10 an hour, the quantity of labor demanded equals the quantity supplied, and there is no pressure to change the real wage rate—it is the equilibrium real wage rate. The market clearing theory of wages is that the pressures on the wage rate are so strong that the economy always operates at the equilibrium real wage and employment level. The gradual adjustment theory of wages is that the pressures on the wage rate are weak and take a long time to move the economy to the equilibrium real wage rate and employment level.

wage rate adjusts so as to lower the real wage rate to $10 an hour. If the economy is experiencing inflation, the real wage rate will decrease only if the money wage increases at a rate slower than the inflation rate.

Only when the real wage rate is at its equilibrium level — where the quantity of labor demanded equals the quantity of labor supplied — is there no pressure for the real wage rate to change. If the economy is experiencing inflation, this means that the money wage rate increases at the same rate as the inflation rate, keeping the real wage rate steady at its equilibrium level.

The main implication of the labor market clearing theory of wages is that the labor market is always operating at the point of intersection of the demand for labor and supply of labor curves, so there is always full employment. The short-run aggregate supply curve shifts every time there is a change in the price level so the only relevant supply curve is the long-run aggregate supply curve. Aggregate economic fluctuations arise only as a result of fluctuations in the long-run aggregate supply curve.

Gradual wage adjustment

The **gradual adjustment theory of wages** is that the money wage rate responds to excess demand and supply of labor, gradually adjusting toward its labor market clearing level. That is, if the real wage rate is below its equilibrium level and there is an excess demand for labor, the money wage rate increases more quickly than the price level, bringing an increase in the real wage rate. But the real wage rate increases only slowly, taking a long time to get to the equilibrium level. Similarly, if the real wage rate is too high so that there is an excess supply of labor, money wages increase more slowly than the price level, lowering the real wage rate. But again, this process takes a long time for the real wage rate to get to the equilibrium level.

Even if the real wage rate is at its equilibrium level, an increase or decrease in the price level that moves it away from the equilibrium sets up a process of slow return to the equilibrium.

The main implication of the gradual adjustment theory of wages is that the short-run aggregate supply curve moves only slowly. When real GDP is above its long-run aggregate supply level, the short-run aggregate supply curve moves upward slowly; and when real GDP is below the long-run equilibrium level, the short-run aggregate supply moves downward slowly.

Another implication of the gradual adjustment theory is that unemployment fluctuates around its natural rate. When the real wage rate is too high, there is an excess supply of labor and unemployment is above its natural rate. When the real wage rate is too low, there is an excess demand for labor and unemployment is below its natural rate.

The gradual adjustment theory supposes that when the real wage rate is not at its equilibrium, the level of employment is determined by the demand for labor. That is, firms are always able to employ the quantity of labor they want. It is easy to see how they can do that when the real wage rate is too high — there is unemployment. But how do they do so when the real wage rate is too low? How do they persuade households to supply more labor than the quantity determined by their supply curves? According to the gradual wage adjustment theory, they do so by offering workers long-term contracts: in exchange for long-term security, households are willing to work longer hours in the short term than they would really like to.

At the beginning of this chapter, we looked at some facts about real wages and the business cycle. One of the key facts was that in the 1970s the pattern of real wages over the business cycle was different from that in the 1980s. Having studied the labor market and the determination of wages, employment, and aggregate supply, we can now explain those patterns.

TESTCASE

8.8 Canadian Wages Over the Business Cycle

We began this chapter by observing that sometimes real wages are procyclical and sometimes they are countercyclical. They were procyclical in the mid-1980s as the economy was recovering from recession and they were countercyclical in the 1981-1982 recession and in the 1990 slow down. We're now able to explain these real wage movements using the analysis of the labor market, the short-run production function, and aggregate supply that we've studied in this chapter.

The key reason real wages are sometimes procyclical and at other times countercyclical has to do with the sources of the shocks generating the business cycle. No single shock generates the business cycle: sometimes it's one thing and sometimes it's another. But it's useful to group such shocks into two categories:

- Shocks to aggregate supply
- Shocks to aggregate demand

Shocks to aggregate supply: the 1980s recovery

The rapid burst of economic expansion that began in 1983 surged ahead extremely strongly in 1984 mainly because of positive shocks to the supply side of the economy. Capital accumulation had speeded up a year earlier and new capital embodying the latest computer related technologies was creating unusually rapid productivity gains. The macroeconomic consequences of this positive supply shock can be analyzed by using the model of the aggregate labor market. Figure 8.10 shows you how.

In 1983, the economy was on the supply of labor curve, *LS*, and on the demand curve, LD_{83}. The real wage rate (in 1986 dollars) was $12.53 an hour and 19.2 billion hours of labor were worked that year. Unemployment was 11.8 percent.

The consequence of the rapid productivity growth was to increase the marginal product of labor, shifting the demand for labor curve right to LD_{84}. Real wages increased to $12.77 and employment increased to 19.6 billion hours. Unemployment decreased to 11.2 percent.

Because the main source of the strong growth in real GDP in 1984 was a positive shock to aggregate supply that shifted the short-run production function, thus increasing the demand for labor, both employment and the real wage rate increased. Real GDP also increased so real wages were procyclical.

Next, let's look at an aggregate demand shock.

FIGURE 8.10
Procyclical Real Wages

Procyclical movements in real wages occur when the shocks generating the business cycle are on the supply side of the economy. A large productivity increase shifts the demand for labor curve right. At the original real wage rate, there is an excess demand for labor and real wages rise. Real GDP and employment also increase — a procyclical real wage change.

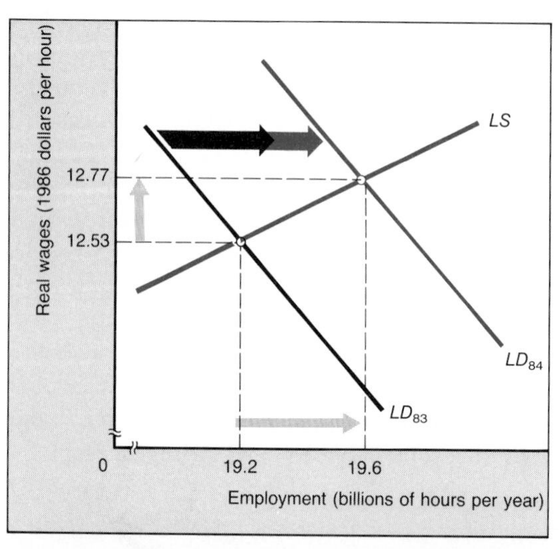

Aggregate demand shock: the 1989-1990 slow down

Figure 8.11 illustrates the economy in 1989 and 1990. In 1989 the real wage rate was \$13.43 with 23.2 billion hours of labor employed — at the point of intersection of the demand curve, *LD*, and the supply curve, *LS*. At this time inflation was running at close to 5 percent a year and most people expected inflation to continue at that pace. But the Bank of Canada did not want to see inflation remaining this high and began to take steps to slow the growth of aggregate demand by keeping money tight and pushing interest rates upward. Also, the government was keeping the lid on its own expenditure so fiscal policy was also reducing aggregate demand.

Money wages increased quickly in 1990 in line with expectations of inflation continuing at around 5 percent and with expectations of continuing strong productivity growth. But in 1990 inflation slowed and so did productivity growth. The real wage increased to \$14.03 and there was virtually no increase in the demand for labor — no shift in the demand for labor curve. With higher real wages firms slid up their demand for labor curves, hiring less labor, and the economy slid up its demand for labor curve. An excess supply of labor emerged, taking the unemployment rate from 7.5 percent in 1989 to 8.1 percent in 1990.

In this slow down, wages moved countercyclically. As real GDP growth slowed and employment decreased, real wages increased.

In general, fluctuations in the aggregate economy, triggered by fluctuations in the short-run production function, produce procyclical wage movements. Those produced by fluctuations in aggregate demand generate countercyclical wage movements. Bombarded as it is both by aggregate demand and aggregate supply shocks, the economy shows no one simple pattern in the relationship between real wages and the business cycle. When aggregate supply shocks dominate, a procyclical relationship shows up. When aggregate demand shocks dominate, a countercyclical relationship shows up. And sometimes the shocks come from both sides with sufficiently even measure. Then there is no clear cyclical behavior in the real wage rate.

■ We've now studied a model of the labor market and seen how we can determine the real wage rate and level of employment as well as the aggregate supply — the short-run and long-run aggregate supply curves. So far, in our analysis of the labor market, unemployment has been mentioned only in passing. But unemployment is one of the central problems of macroeconomics and it is the subject of the next chapter.

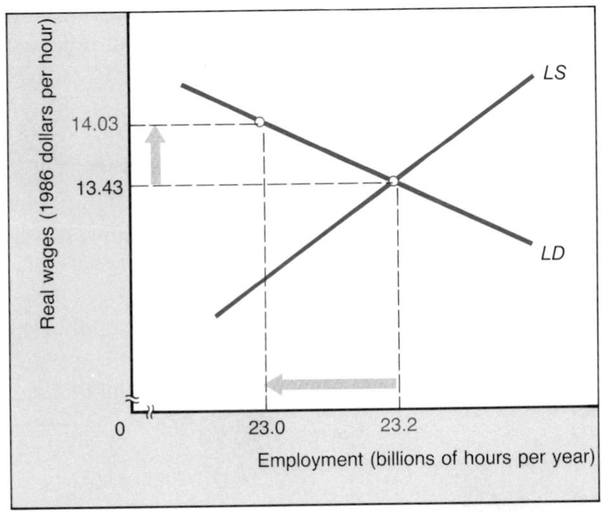

FIGURE 8.11
Countercyclical Real Wages

Real wages are countercyclical when the business cycle results from an aggregate demand disturbance. A decrease in aggregate demand does not affect the demand for labor curve, but it decreases the price level and increases the real wage rate. Real GDP and employment decrease as the real wage rate increases — a countercyclical real wage movement.

CHAPTER REVIEW

Summary

CYCLES IN REAL GDP, UNEMPLOYMENT, AND REAL WAGES

A close relationship exists between fluctuations in real GDP and unemployment over the business cycle. The further real GDP is below trend, the higher the unemployment rate.

A more complicated relationship exists between real wages and the business cycle. At some times, such as the mid-1980s, the relationship is procyclical—real wages and real GDP move together. At other times, such as the 1981-1982 recession and the 1990 slow down, the relationship is countercyclical—real wages and real GDP move in opposite directions.

LABOR PRODUCTIVITY AND THE DEMAND FOR LABOR

When the employment level changes, so does real GDP. The increase in real GDP resulting from a one-unit increase in labor input is the marginal product of labor. Firms hire the quantity of labor such that marginal product of labor equals the real wage rate. Other things being equal, the lower the real wage rate, the greater is the quantity of labor employed.

Capital accumulation and technological change shift the short-run production function—the relationship between employment and real GDP—and shift the demand for labor curve. Over time, production possibilities at each employment level expand and the demand for labor curve shifts to the right.

PRODUCTIVITY AND THE DEMAND FOR LABOR IN CANADA AND JAPAN

The Canadian short-run production function shifted upward by more than 40 percent between 1975 and 1990. The demand for labor curve shifted by a similar percentage amount, but real wages increased by about half that amount. The reason is that the level of employment has increased, which, other things being equal, lowered the marginal product of labor. Capital accumulation and technological advance increased the marginal product of labor, but the increase in employment has somewhat offset this increase.

In contrast, the Japanese short-run production function and demand for labor have increased by more than 100 percent between 1970 and 1988. Real wages have almost doubled in Japan as well. But because its increase in employment has been much smaller than that in Canada, the tendency for Japan's marginal product of labor to decrease has been much smaller.

HOW LABOR SUPPLY DECISIONS ARE MADE

Households allocate their time between work and other activities. The opportunity cost of other activities is the real wage rate. Other things being equal, the higher the real wage, the higher is the quantity of labor supplied, but up to some maximum. Once that maximum has been reached, if the real wage rate continues to increase, the quantity of labor supplied decreases.

Households can also determine the timing of their labor supply. The opportunity cost of time today in exchange for work tomorrow is determined by today's real wage rate relative to tomorrow's real wage rate but including the fact that the interest rate makes wages earned today more valuable tomorrow than wages earned tomorrow. Other things being equal, the higher today's real wage rate relative to tomorrow's and the higher the real interest rate, the greater is the quantity of labor supplied today.

The labor supply curve traces the quantity of labor supplied as the real wage rate changes, other things being equal. The slope of the labor supply curve depends on whether the wage change being considered is temporary or permanent. A permanent change in the wage rate does not produce an intertemporal substitution effect; a temporary one does. Thus a temporary wage change produces a bigger response in the quantity of labor supplied than a permanent change does.

LONG-RUN AGGREGATE SUPPLY CURVE

The long-run aggregate supply curve shows the relationship between the quantity of real GDP supplied and the price level when wages and all prices are flexible and have adjusted to achieve full employment and when firms are producing the profit-maximizing output. The long-run aggregate supply curve is vertical—there is a unique level of real GDP regardless of the price level. The reason is that there is only one equilibrium level of employment—where the real wage rate is such that the quantity of labor demanded equals the quantity supplied. Any price level with an appropriate money wage rate can deliver that equilibrium real wage rate. Given the equilibrium real wage rate and the employment level, the short-run production function determines the level of long-run aggregate supply.

SHORT-RUN AGGREGATE SUPPLY

The short-run aggregate supply curve shows the relationship between the quantity of real GDP supplied and the price level when wages are fixed. With a fixed money wage rate, changes in the price level change the real wage rate. The higher the price level, the lower is the real wage rate and the greater is the quantity of labor demanded. The quantity of labor employed is the same as the quantity demanded. Hence, the lower the real wage rate, the greater is the level of output. Since lower real wages come from higher prices, the higher the price level, the greater is the quantity of real GDP supplied.

THEORIES OF WAGE DETERMINATION

There are two theories of wage determination, labor market clearing and gradual adjustment. The labor market clearing theory is that real wages rise when there is an excess demand for labor and fall when there is an excess supply of labor so as to make the quantity of labor demanded equal to the quantity supplied. For given labor demand and supply curves, a change in the price level changes the money wage rate, keeping the real wage rate at its equilibrium level. An implication of the labor market clearing theory is that the short-run aggregate supply curve always shifts whenever there is a change in the price level so that the only relevant aggregate supply curve is the long-run one.

The gradual adjustment theory is that real wages rise when there is excess demand and fall when there is excess supply; but the speed of adjustment is slow, so for long periods of time the labor market may remain away from its market clearing position. Changes in the price level change the equilibrium real wage rate but that change sets up a slow gradual movement in the money wage rate toward its new equilibrium level.

An implication of the gradual wage adjustment theory is that the short-run aggregate supply curve shifts whenever the economy is away from full employment, but it shifts slowly.

EXPLAINING THE BEHAVIOR OF WAGES AND THE BUSINESS CYCLE

During the strong expansion of 1984, real wages were procyclical because the major impulse generating the expansion was on the supply side. A large increase in investment in 1983 and the rapid technological advances brought about by computers increased the productivity of labor at a rapid rate. The short-run production function shifted to the right and increased the demand for labor. With a higher demand for labor, equilibrium resulted at a higher real wage, higher employment, and higher real GDP.

During the 1990 slow down, real wages were countercyclical because the major impulse generating the slow down was on the demand side. The slow down resulted from a tightening of monetary policy by the Bank of Canada and of fiscal policy by the government of Canada. Wages grew quickly in anticipation of inflation and productivity growth continuing at their previous levels. But both slowed down so real wages increased and the quantity of labor demanded decreased.

Key Terms and Concepts

Countercyclical A variable is countercyclical when its fluctuations are in the opposite direction to the fluctuations in real GDP.

Demand for labor The relationship between the quantity of labor employed and the real wage rate.

Gradual adjustment theory of wages The theory that money wages adjust slowly in response to excess demand and excess supply of labor.

Labor market clearing theory of wages The theory that the money wage rate adjusts continuously to keep the real wage rate at the level that makes the quantity of labor demanded equal to the quantity of labor supplied.

Labor supply curve The relationship between the quantity of labor supplied and the real wage rate.

Marginal product of labor The increase in output produced as a result of employing one additional unit of labor.

Market activity Work and job search.

Nonmarket activity Work performed at home and leisure.

Procyclical A variable is procyclical when its fluctuations match the fluctuations in real GDP.

Quantity of labor supplied The amount of time that households allocate to work.

Real wage rate The price of labor measured in constant purchasing power—the purchasing power of dollars in a given year.

Short-run production function The relationship between real GDP and the level of employment, holding constant the capital stock and the state of technology.

Review Questions

1. What is the main source of disagreement among macroeconomists?
2. Describe the relationship between Canadian real GDP fluctuations and unemployment.
3. Describe the relationship between Canadian real GDP fluctuations and those in real wages.
4. What is the connection between the marginal product of labor and the short-run production function?

5. Explain what produces a movement along the short-run production function and what makes it shift up and down.
6. Explain why the demand for labor curve slopes downward. What conditions increase the demand for labor?
7. Explain why the supply of labor curve slopes upward. What factors shift the labor supply curve?
8. Explain the market clearing theory of wages.
9. Explain the gradual adjustment theory of wages.
10. What is meant by long-run aggregate supply? Why is it independent of the price level?
11. Explain why short-run aggregate supply slopes upward. What factors shift the short-run aggregate supply curve to the left?
12. What factors shift both the long-run and short-run aggregate supply? Explain the process that shifts these curves.
13. Which aggregate supply curve is derived from the market-clearing theory of wages? Explain your answer.
14. Which aggregate supply curve is derived from the gradual adjustment theory of wages? Explain your answer.
15. Describe the behavior of Canadian wages over the business cycle.
16. Explain what happens to labor productivity and real GDP when the economy experiences an aggregate demand shock.
17. Explain what happens to labor productivity and real GDP when the economy experiences an aggregate supply shock.

Problems

1. An economy has the following short-run production function:

$$y = 20n - 0.1n^2$$

where y is real GDP and n is the quantity of labor employed.

(a) What is the marginal product of labor when 100 million hours of labor are employed?

(b) What is the marginal product of labor when 50 million hours of labor are employed?

(c) What is the demand for labor?

2. An economy's short-run production function, demand for labor, and supply of labor are

$$y = 100n - 0.2n^2$$
$$n^d = 250 - 2.5(W/P)$$
$$n^s = 100 + 2.5(W/P)$$

where y is real GDP, n is the quantity of labor, W is the money wage rate, and P is the price level.

(a) What is the equilibrium level of employment?

(b) What is long-run aggregate supply?

(c) If the money wage rate is \$30 an hour, what is the quantity of real GDP supplied?

(d) If the money wage rate is \$30 an hour and the price level is 96, what is the level of employment?

(e) In question (d), what is the quantity of real GDP supplied?

(f) If the money wage rate is $30 an hour, what is the short-run aggregate supply?
(g) If the money wage rate increases by 10 percent, what is the change in short-run aggregate supply?

3. Aggregate demand and aggregate supply in an economy, when the money wage is $10 an hour, is
Aggregate demand $y^d = 1000 - 5P$
Long-run aggregate supply $y^s = 500$
Short-run aggregate supply $y^s = 5P$
where y is real GDP and P is the price level.
(a) What is macroeconomic equilibrium?
(b) What is the change in real GDP and the real wage rate if the economy experiences an aggregate demand shock that increases aggregate demand by 100 units. Is the real wage procyclical or countercyclical?
(c) What is the change in real GDP and the real wage rate if the economy experiences an aggregate supply shock that increases aggregate supply by 50 units? Is the real wage rate procyclical or countercyclical?

CHAPTER

Unemployment

THE GREATEST MARKET FAILURE?

IN THE 1930s, UNEMPLOYMENT SOARED to 20 percent of the labor force of most industrial countries. The costs of this high unemployment were enormous. Real GDP fell by 25 percent. Goods and services that could have been produced weren't. Many families could not even feed their children. And for some, especially older workers, the experience left wounds that never healed. Skills became rusty, and those unemployed longest found it hardest to get work when the depression ended.

Unemployment in the early 1930s was extreme but not unique. Recently, the decade of the 1980s saw unemployment rates climbing to more than 10 percent and staying there for several years, especially in Western Europe and Canada.

Are the presence and persistence of unemployment, sometimes on a large scale, symptoms of a fundamental flaw in the design of the market economy? Many economists thought so, especially during the 1930s. But that is not the conventional wisdom today.

Much unemployment is, in fact, a natural consequence of a well-functioning market economy. Automobiles, hotel rooms, airplane seats, and many other objects are routinely "unemployed" in the sense that there is excess supply waiting for sudden bursts of demand to take it up. Sometimes people are unemployed because a change in the pattern of demand has created a shortage of some skills and a surplus of others, and it takes time for people to tool up and acquire new skills. Also, some people classified as "unemployed" have just entered or re-entered the labor force and are taking time to find the best available job. But at times, unemployment is higher than can be accounted for by either of these explanations. And its rate does fluctuate and fluctuate very closely with the business cycle.

The objective of this chapter is to help you better understand the causes of unemployment and the sources of fluctuations in its rate. After studying this chapter, you will be able to

- Describe the patterns in unemployment in Canada and Europe during the 1980s
- Describe Okun's Law
- Explain exactly what unemployment is and how it is measured
- Describe how employment, unemployment, and average work hours fluctuate over the business cycle
- Explain why average work hours fluctuate much less than employment and unemployment
- Explain the meaning of the natural rate of employment and the reasons it fluctuates
- Describe the variations in the natural rate of unemployment during the 1970s and 1980s

- Explain why unemployment fluctuates and sometimes rises above its natural rate
- Explain the unemployment during the recession of the early 1980s

Let's begin with some facts about unemployment in Canada and Europe in recent years.

MACROFACTS

9.1 *Unemployment in Canada and Europe in the 1980s*

Unemployment was a serious problem in Canada during the 1980s. We've seen in Chapter 8 that more than 11 percent of the labor force was unemployed for three years at the depths of the recession in the early 1980s. But unemployment fell gradually from 1984 to the end of the decade. It began to increase again in 1990-1991.

International comparison of unemployment

How does the Canadian experience with unemployment compare with other countries'? Is Canada typical or does it differ in an important way from the rest of the world? These questions are answered in Figure 9.1. Part (a) compares unemployment in Canada with that in its closest neighbor, the United States, and in the other giant and successful industrial economy, Japan.

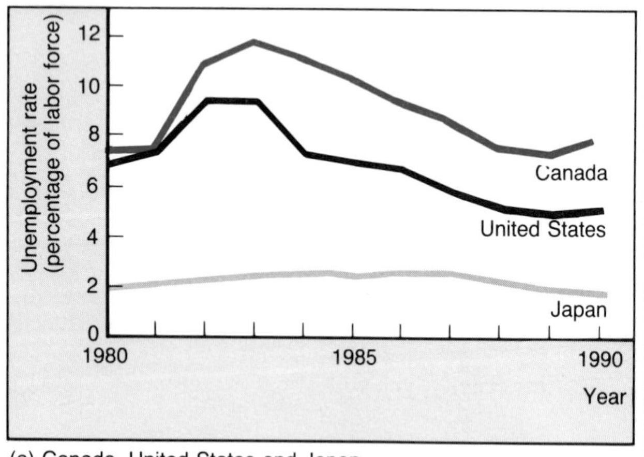

(a) Canada, United States and Japan

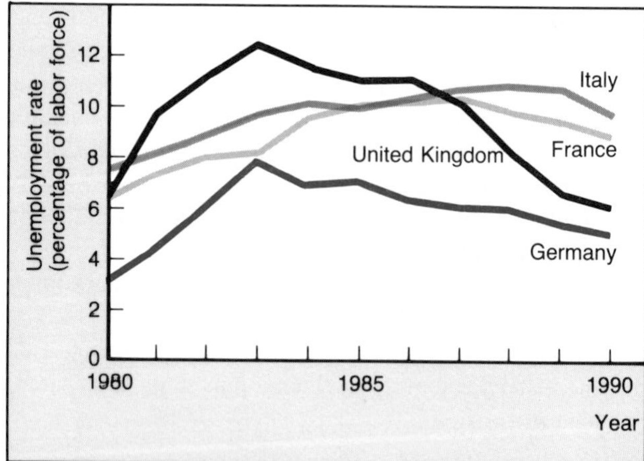

(b) Western Europe

FIGURE 9.1
Unemployment Around the World

Unemployment experiences vary across countries. Japan has had the lowest unemployment rate and Canada and the United Kingdom the highest during the 1980s. High unemployment persisted for longer in Canada and the United Kingdom than in the United States. In France and Italy, unemployment steadily increased through most of the 1980s. Of the big European countries, Germany has the lowest unemployment rate and is most similar to the United States.

Source: Main Economic Indicators, Organization for Economic Co-operation and Development (monthly). The data are standardized according to the OECD's international definitions.

Unemployment in Canada and the United States fluctuates in a similar way but Canadian unemployment became significantly higher than U.S. unemployment during the 1980s. Japan, in contrast, has an unemployment rate that barely fluctuates, starting the decade at 2 percent, rising gently to a peak of 2.8 percent in 1987, and then falling again to end the decade at just 2.2 percent.

The other major industrial economy is Western Europe's and the four most important countries making up that economy are France, Germany[1], Italy, and the United Kingdom. Figure 9.1(b) shows their unemployment experience in the 1980s. Two interesting divergent patterns are at work here. The fluctuations in unemployment in two countries, Germany and the United Kingdom, are similar to those in North America. Unemployment climbs to a peak in 1983 and then falls during the rest of the decade. But the unemployment rates themselves are very different in these two economies. Germany, for the most part, has an unemployment rate lower than that of Canada, while in the United Kingdom the unemployment rate climbed to more than 12 percent at its peak in 1983. In contrast to these cyclical patterns of unemployment, in France and Italy unemployment tended to increase relentlessly throughout the decade of the 1980s.

Why did the Canadian unemployment rate increase so sharply in the early 1980s and then persistently decline for the rest of that decade? Why do the unemployment rates of the United States, Germany, and the United Kingdom share these patterns of change? Why has the unemployment rate steadily increased in Italy and France, and why is it so steady and so low in Japan? These are some of the questions that this chapter answers.

Demographic differences in unemployment

Unemployment rates differ from one country to another, and they also differ from one demographic group to another within a country. In Canada in April 1991, for example, with the average unemployment rate 8.1 percent, 6.2 percent of persons described as "family heads" (the group with the lowest unemployment rate) were unemployed and 15.4 percent of 15 to 19 year old males (the group with the highest unemployment rate) were unemployed. Figure 9.2(a) shows in greater detail how the unemployment rates of various demographic groups differ.

Duration and origins of unemployment

Unemployment is a serious problem for the unemployed but most unemployed persons do not remain so for very long. Figure 9.2(b) illustrates some features of the anatomy of unemployment. The duration of unemployment is less than 4 weeks for almost a quarter of the people unemployed and between 5 and 13 weeks for another quarter. Yet another quarter of those unemployed remain in that state for between 14 weeks and 26 weeks. Only 7 percent of the unemployed remain so for more than a year. The figure also shows that about two thirds of the people classified as unemployed had lost their jobs and about one third were those entering or re-entering the labor force.

These facts suggest that unemployment is a phenomenon involving ongoing dynamic change. Unemployment always exists, but a constantly changing group of people are experiencing it. Any explanation of unemployment has to account for these facts.

[1]Although Germany is now united, here we are referring to the former West Germany only. Unemployment in the former East Germany was extremely high following reunification.

FIGURE 9.2
The Anatomy of Canadian Unemployment

Young men (between 15 and 19) have the highest unemployment rate in Canada. Household heads have the lowest rate. The patterns shown in part (a) for 1991 have been a persistent feature of Canadian unemployment.

In 1991, about a quarter of the unemployed stayed unemployed for less than 4 weeks, a further quarter for between 5 and 13 weeks and yet a further quarter for 14 to 26 weeks. About two thirds of all the unemployed have lost a job. The other one third are entering or re-entering the labor force (part b).

Source: The Labour Force, Statistics Canada, Catalogue 71-001, April 1991.

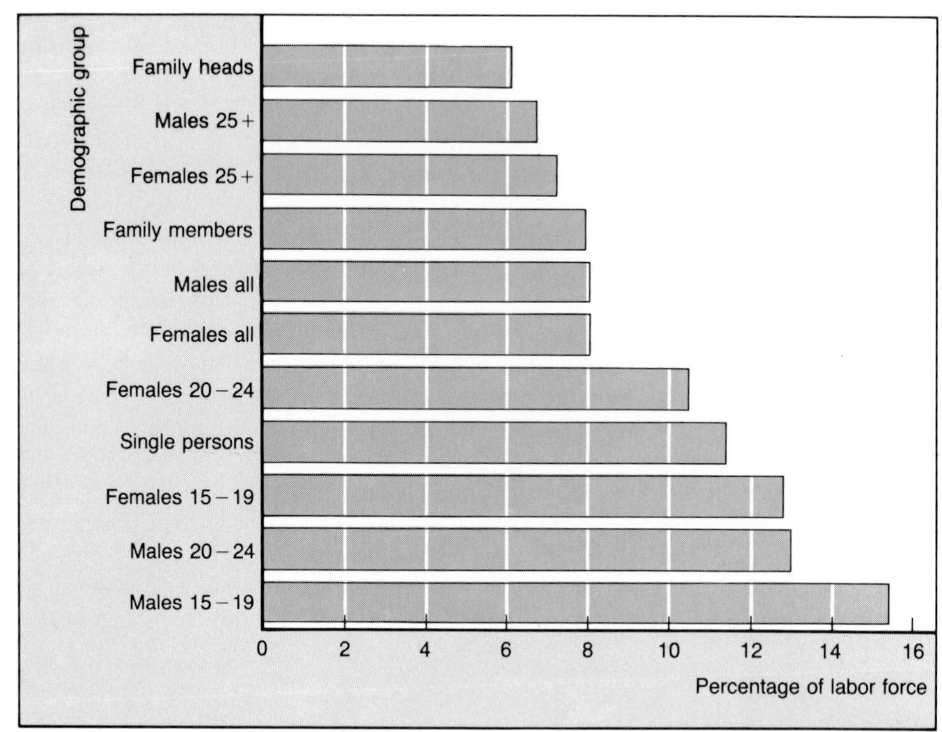

(a) Demographic characteristics of unemployed

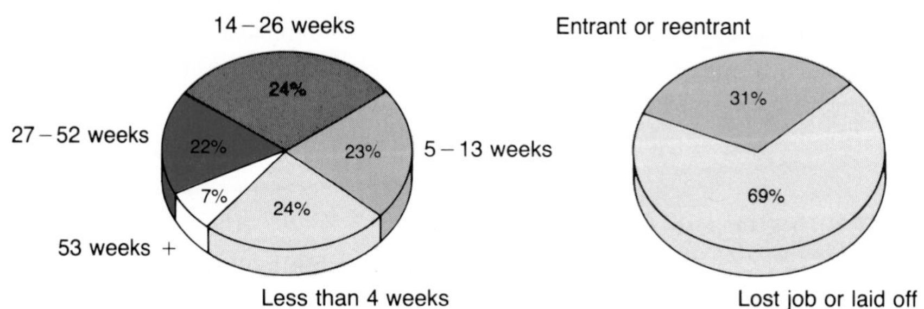

(b) Duration and origin in 1991

MACROFACTS

9.2 *Okun's Law*

Okun's Law, a proposition about the relationship between the unemployment rate and the level of real GDP relative to its long-run, or capacity, level states

> The higher the level of real GDP as a percentage of capacity real GDP, the lower is the unemployment rate.

Figure 9.3 illustrates Okun's Law. Each dot in the figure represents the unemployment rate and the level of real GDP as a percentage of capacity real GDP for a particular year. The grey and black lines illustrate Okun's Law—the negative relationship between real GDP as a percentage of capacity real GDP and the unemployment rate. To see

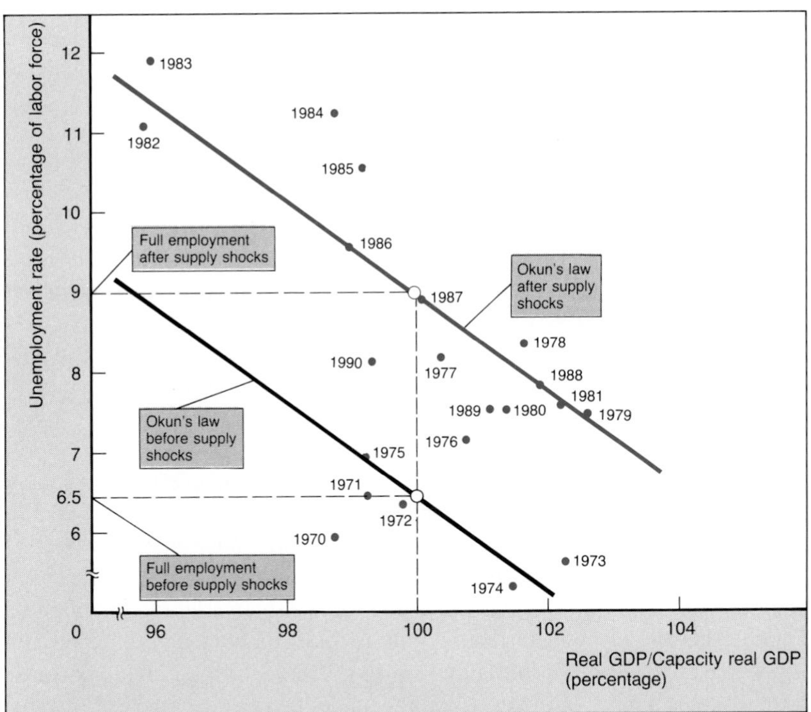

FIGURE 9.3
Okun's Law

Okun's Law—the proposition that when real GDP falls below its capacity level, unemployment increases and when real GDP is above capacity, unemployment decreases—is present in Canadian data, but only when allowance is made for a shift in the Okun relationship in the second half of the 1970s.

Source: National Income and Expenditure Accounts, Statistics Canada, Catalogue 13-201, and *Historical Labour Force Statistics*, Statistics Canada, Catalogue 71-201 and our calculations.

Okun's Law in the Canadian data it is necessary to interpret the Okun relationship as having shifted upward during the second half of the 1970s following the shocks to productivity and aggregate supply resulting mainly from world oil price increases. Once this shift is taken into account, there is a clear tendency for unemployment and real GDP relative to full-employment real GDP to be negatively related to each other.

This chapter answers the questions posed above about unemployment in Canada and other countries and the relationship between unemployment and fluctuations of real GDP. Let's begin by establishing exactly what unemployment is and how it is measured.

9.3 *What Exactly Is Unemployment and How Is It Measured?*

A person is **unemployed** when he or she is able and willing to work and is available for work but does not have work. The number of people unemployed in an economy is the number of people who fit that description. The **unemployment rate** is the number of people unemployed expressed as a percentage of the labor force. The **labor force** is the number of people employed plus the number of people unemployed.

Measuring unemployment in Canada

Unemployment figures are calculated by Statistics Canada and published each month in *The Labour Force*. A lot of detail about the anatomy of unemployment is provided by Statistics Canada. Unemployment is classified by province, sex, age, industry and occupation, duration of unemployment, type of work sort, activity prior to looking for work, job search methods used, reason for leaving last job, and whether the worker is looking for work.

Unemployment data are based on information generated from a sample survey of households called the Labour Force Survey. Each month about 56,000 households across

Canada are interviewed. The actual households surveyed change each month as new households are added and some old households are rotated out. The Labour Force Survey began in November 1945 and has from time to time been upgraded and improved. A detailed account of the existing methods employed in the Labour Force Survey is published in *Methodology of the Canadian Labour Force Survey 1976*, Catalogue 71-526 (Ottawa: Statistics Canada, October 1977).

Statistics Canada defines the following people as being unemployed:

> Those who did not work during a specific week (called the reference week), made specific efforts to find a job within the 4 previous weeks, and were available for work during the reference week. Also counted as unemployed are the people who did not work at all during the reference week, were available for work, and were waiting either to be called back to a job from which they had been laid off for 26 weeks or less or to report to a new job within 4 weeks.

Although the Labour Force Survey counts the number of people without jobs who are able and willing to work and who are available for work, it does not ask those surveyed whether they are willing to work at the going wage rate. What macroeconomists really want to know is the number of people who are able and willing to work and who are available for work *on the terms and conditions currently available*. Although there is a presumption that the respondents are willing to work on currently available terms and conditions, the lack of such information is a shortcoming of the Labour Force Survey.

Another shortcoming of the measured unemployment rate is that discouraged workers and part-time workers who want full-time employment are excluded from those counted as unemployed. **Discouraged workers** are people who have no jobs, are willing to work, and are available for work but have stopped searching for work because of their discouraging experience. The number of discouraged workers is likely to be greatest when the measured unemployment rate is high and has been high for some time. Also, part-time workers who want full-time employment may be considered partly unemployed. But the measured unemployment rate misses this type of employment. A broader measure of the unemployment rate that includes discouraged workers and partly employed part-time workers will be higher than the one measured by Statistics Canada.

Measuring unemployment in other countries

From the *MACROFACTS* in Section 9.1, we know there is substantial variation in unemployment rates across countries — from Japan, where unemployment barely exceeds 2 percent, to the United Kingdom, where in the early 1980s it exceeded 12 percent. Do other countries measure unemployment the way it is measured in Canada? Or are some of the apparent differences in unemployment rates across countries due simply to the fact that countries measure different things?

The answer is, all countries seek to measure the same concept of unemployment. There are differences in the detailed definitions and measures recorded in the various countries. But there is a standardized international definition of unemployment, and the Organization for Economic Cooperation and Development (OECD) publishes standardized unemployment rates for the major countries. These OECD standardized measures of unemployment were used to construct Figure 9.1. Although national definitions and measurements of unemployment do differ, these differences are not responsible for the cross-country variation Figure 9.1 shows. That variation arises from genuine differences in the percentage of the labor force able and willing to work and available for work but without work, at least as far as anyone can tell.

9.4 *Employment, Unemployment, and Hours*

MACROFACTS

We've seen that unemployment varies a great deal over the business cycle. This means that variations in the total number of person hours worked varies, at least in part because the number of people employed varies. But what happens to average work hours over the business cycle? Do they fluctuate and as much as employment does? That is, do the people who have jobs work shorter hours in a recession and longer hours when the economy is in a recovery or boom? Or are work hours for those with jobs more or less independent of the state of the economy?

Trends in hours

The work week has declined over the years, most dramatically over the past 100 years — from a work week of more than 70 hours in the mid-nineteenth century to around 35 hours today. The work week continued to decline steadily even in the 1970s and 1980s. As Figure 9.4(a) shows, average work hours declined from about 36 hours a week in 1975 to 34.5 hours in the mid-1980s. But the average work week increased slightly again in the late 1980s.

Cycles in hours

Although the trend has been a shorter work week, the rate at which average work hours have changed has fluctuated. These fluctuations are shown as the black line in Figure 9.4(b). Also shown are the fluctuations in the growth rates of real GDP and employment. You can see from this figure that the growth rates of employment and average weekly hours fluctuate in sympathy with fluctuations in real GDP, but that the fluctuations in hours are smaller and less strongly related to the cycle in real GDP growth than the fluctuations in employment.

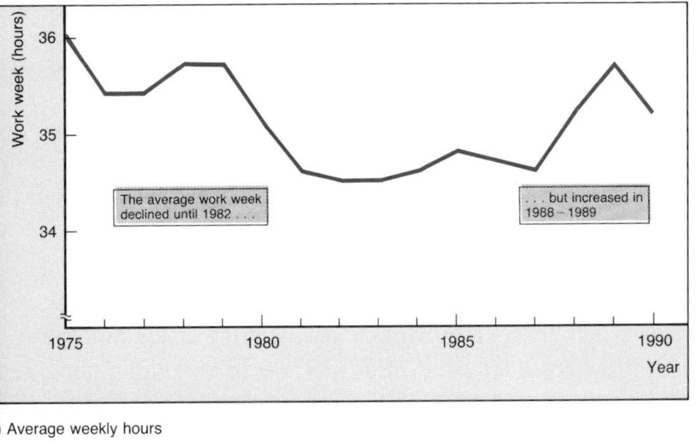

) Average weekly hours

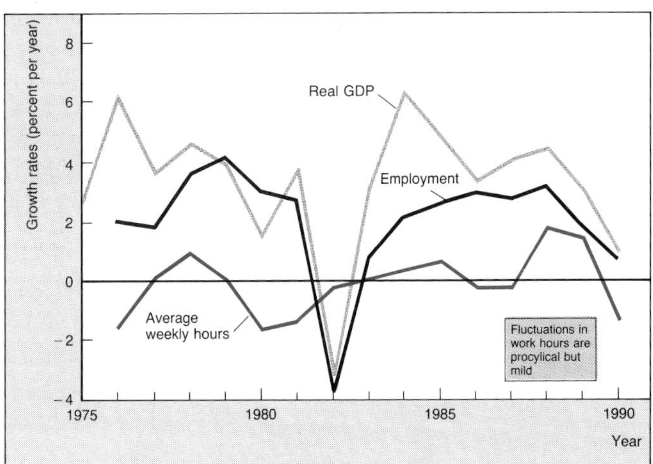

(b) Employment, hours, and real GDP growth

FIGURE 9.4
Work Hours and Employment

The average work week declined up to the mid-1980s but increased again in 1988-1989 (part a). Fluctuations in hours (shown as the black line in part b) are smaller and their relationship to fluctuations in real GDP weaker than fluctuations in the number of persons employed.

Source: National Income and Expenditure Accounts, Statistics Canada, Catalogue 13-201, and *Historical Labour Force Statistics*, Statistics Canada, Catalogue 71-201 and our calculations.

The conclusion from Figure 9.4(b) is that when employment varies over the business cycle, both the number of persons employed and the average hours they work fluctuate together. Further, the fluctuations in average hours are small and make only a tiny contribution to the fluctuations in total hours worked. Fluctuations in the number of people employed account for most of the fluctuations in total hours worked.

Why do work hours fluctuate so little over the business cycle? Why is most of the fluctuation in total hours worked the result of changes in the number of people with jobs?

9.5 *Why Does Employment Fluctuate More Than Work Hours?*

Why do work hours fluctuate so little and employment so much? The full answer to the second question takes the rest of this chapter. This section answers the first question.

Fluctuations in average work hours are small because stability is in the best interests both of households who supply labor and firms who demand labor.

Households

Why do households in general prefer stable hours? Stable work hours enable a household to

- Use time efficiently
- Reduce income uncertainty
- Minimize startup costs

Time allocation People allocate their time, a scarce resource, to get the most out of it. People enjoy leisure activities, but these have an opportunity cost—the wage foregone. People allocate their time between work and leisure so that the benefit (or utility) derived from the last hour of leisure equals the real wage rate that the hour of leisure costs (the goods and services foregone by not working). As a result, for any real wage rate, there is a given allocation of a person's time between work and leisure.

Uncertainty Fluctuations in work hours bring fluctuations in income. Most people prefer more certainty to less certainty. This is the second reason why households prefer stable work hours—they bring more stable and predictable incomes.

Startup costs Startup costs are the costs associated with beginning an activity. The startup costs of working include the costs of both time and transportation to and from work. These costs have to be borne whether a person works for one hour or ten hours a day. For many people, it's true that these costs are small. But for most urban commuters, the time, effort, and expense of getting to work become too costly when the work day is too short. There's a limit to how short a work day makes it worthwhile incurring these startup costs.

Firms

Like households, firms also prefer stable hours of work for each employee. With stable hours, firms are able to

- Obtain optimal work effort
- Organize team production more efficiently

Work effort In most jobs, an employee takes some time to warm up and get into the job, so as to do the work at the most efficient pace. Also, people who work for too many hours tire and become less efficient. There's an optimal number of hours that balances these two factors. This number of hours achieves maximum output from each employee's work effort. If work hours fluctuated and became too short, too big a fraction of the hours paid for would be warm-up hours, and if work hours became too long, too big a fraction of them would be hours of low productivity resulting from fatigue.

Team production Many production processes involve teamwork, where it is important for members of the team to work at the same time. With variable work hours, extra costs have to be incurred to enable team members to communicate with each other and coordinate their actions. With fixed work hours, team production can be organized efficiently.

Market interaction

The interactions of households and firms in the labor market determine not only the level of employment and the wage rate — the quantity and price in the labor market — but also an equilibrium work week. Firms offer jobs with a fixed work week because that optimizes the effort they get from their workers and better enables them to organize team production. Households, in general preferring a fixed work week to a variable one, accept a lower average hourly wage for a fixed work week than for the more inconvenient variable work week.

Now you know the main reasons why the average work week does not vary much over the business cycle. But why do the levels of employment and unemployment vary?

9.6 *Fluctuations in Employment and Unemployment: The Natural Rate*

Unemployment is divided into three kinds:

1. Frictional
2. Structural
3. Cyclical

Frictional unemployment is the number of people who are searching for a job. These people are new entrants into the labor force and those who have re-entered the labor force or voluntarily quit their jobs to search for a better one. **Structural unemployment** is the number of people who are in the wrong location and have the wrong skills for the available jobs. **Cyclical unemployment** is unemployment in excess of frictional plus structural unemployment. The **natural rate of unemployment** is the percentage of the labor force that is frictionally and structurally unemployed. The *cyclical unemployment rate* is the actual unemployment rate minus its natural rate.

Labor market flows

All unemployment arises from the fact that the labor market is a dynamic mechanism — it undergoes constant change. As people leave school and start work, they search for their first job. Finding a job — at least a good job — is a difficult business, so even someone who has a job may leave it to look for a better one. Many female workers temporarily leave the labor force for a period of child-rearing, often to job-search again when they re-enter the labor force. Finally, people who reach retirement age leave the labor force, creating vacancies for others to move into.

Firms, too, undergo constant change. Every day new firms are born and old ones die. When a firm dies, its workers are thrown into the jobless pool and they begin the search for a new job. When a new firm is born, it looks for people to fill its available jobs.

Figure 9.5 illustrates this ever-changing labor market. In this figure, you can see three groups: the population, the employed, and the unemployed. The employed and unemployed constitute the labor force. The labor market coordinates the decisions of the suppliers of labor (the labor force) and the demanders of labor (firms).

Four flows determine the number unemployed, as shown in Figure 9.5. They are

1. New entrants
2. Job losers
3. Job finders
4. Discouraged workers

New entrants and job losers swell the ranks of the unemployed; job finders and discouraged workers lower the number of the unemployed.

Three flows influence the number employed:

1. Job losers
2. Retirees
3. Job finders

Job losers and retirees decrease the number employed; job finders increase the number employed. Job changers are people switching jobs without first becoming unemployed.

How are the flows between employment and unemployment determined and what determines the percentage of the labor force unemployed?

Labor market flows and unemployment rate

Although Figure 9.5 illustrates all the flows the labor market experiences, the most important ones determining unemployment are those between the employed group and the unemployed. We'll suppose that the flows into and out of the labor force — new entrants, discouraged workers, and retirements — all balance out so that the size of the labor force is constant. (This is not a description of reality but an assumption that allows us to concentrate on the flows in the labor market that are most important for understanding unemployment.)

FIGURE 9.5
Labor Market Flows

Employment and unemployment are dynamic states through which individuals pass. Unemployment increases when people become new entrants or lose jobs and decreases when people find jobs or become discouraged workers. Employment decreases when people lose jobs or retire and increases when people find jobs. The rate at which these flows take place determines the stocks of employment and unemployment.

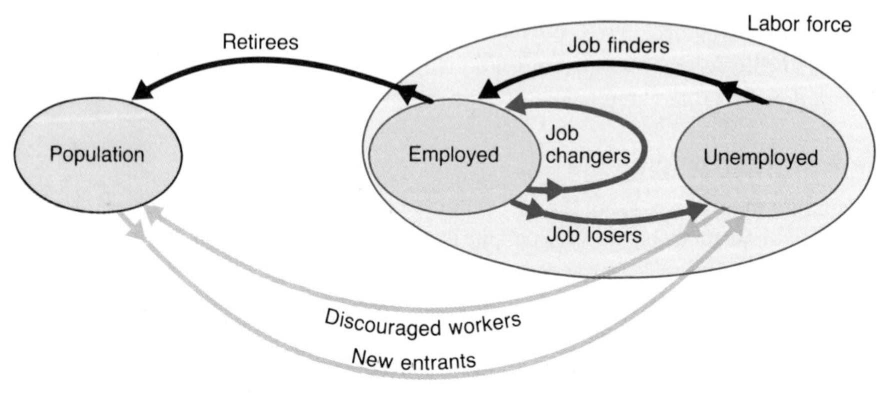

In any period of time, some proportion of the unemployed find a job. Let's call that proportion f and the number unemployed U. Thus the number of people who find a job is fU. In the same period, some proportion of the people employed lose their job. Let's call that proportion ℓ and the number employed E. Then the number of people who lose their job is ℓE.

The change in unemployment is the number of people who lose jobs minus the number who find jobs. The change in unemployment (ΔU) is given by

$$\Delta U = \ell E - fU \tag{9.1}$$

Recall that the labor force is the number of people employed plus the number unemployed. Equivalently, the number employed is equal to the labor force minus the number unemployed. If we call the labor force L, the number employed is

$$E = L - U. \tag{9.2}$$

Using Equation (9.2) in Equation (9.1), you can see that

$$\Delta U = \ell(L - U) - fU$$

or

$$\Delta U = \ell L - (\ell + f)U. \tag{9.3}$$

Equation (9.3) describes the dynamics of unemployment — how unemployment changes. Figure 9.6, which shows the effect of job losses and job finds on unemployment, illustrates this equation. Unemployment is measured on the horizontal axis from left to right and employment from right to left. The labor force here is 12.5 million and the number of people who find jobs is proportion f of the number of people unemployed. Thus for any number of unemployed, the number of job finders is shown by the blue, upward-sloping curve—its slope is f. The larger the proportion of the unemployed that find a job, the larger is the number of job finders and the steeper is the curve. The number of job losers is proportional to the number employed. For each additional person unemployed, there is one fewer person employed. Thus the black curve showing the number of job losses slopes downward, and the magnitude of its slope is equal to ℓ. That is, for each additional person unemployed, there is one fewer person employed and the number of job losses falls by proportion ℓ of the fall in employment.

When the number of job losses equals the number of job finds, unemployment is constant. This occurs, in this example, when 0.5 million people are unemployed. In this situation, 0.48 million jobs are found and lost every period.

What happens if fewer than 0.5 million people are unemployed? The number of job losers exceeds the number of job finders, and unemployment increases. If more than 0.5 million people are unemployed, the number of job finders exceeds the number of job losers and unemployment decreases. Dynamic forces at work in the labor market keep the number unemployed moving toward 0.5 million—the number that balances the number of job finders against the number of job losers.

In this example, the labor force is 12.5 million, 0.5 million are unemployed, so the unemployment rate is 4 percent. That is, the labor market keeps the unemployment rate moving toward 4 percent. This unemployment rate is equal to the natural rate of unemployment. But what determines this unemployment rate?

The natural rate of unemployment is such that the unemployment rate is constant. That is, the number of people unemployed is not changing, ΔU is equal to zero. From Equation (9.3), this means that

$$\ell L = (\ell + f)U. \tag{9.4}$$

FIGURE 9.6
Equilibrium Employment and Unemployment

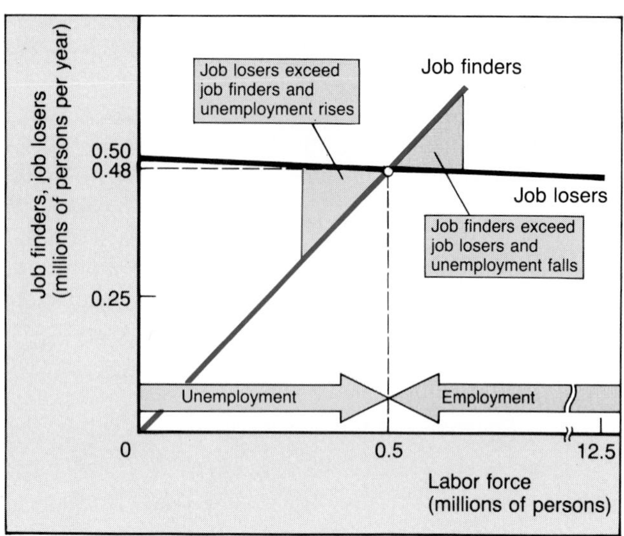

The horizontal axis measures the labor force. Unemployment is measured from left to right and employment from right to left. Unemployed people look for jobs, and the larger the number of people looking for jobs—the larger the number of people unemployed—the larger is the number of jobs found. The job finder's curve (blue) shows how the number of job finders increases with the number of people unemployed. Some proportion of the people with jobs lose them each period. The higher the level of employment and the lower the level of unemployment, the higher is the number of job losses. The job loser's curve is shown as the black line. In this example, the labor force is 12.5 million. When fewer than 0.5 million persons are unemployed (in this example) the number of job losses exceeds the number of job finds and unemployment increases. When more than 0.5 million people are unemployed (fewer than 12 million employed) the number of job finders exceeds the number of job losers and unemployment decreases. When 0.5 million persons are unemployed, the number of job losers is balanced by the number of job finders and unemployment is steady. This is the equilibrium level of unemployment. The equilibrium unemployment rate is 4 percent—(0.5/12.5) x 100.

The unemployment rate is the number unemployed divided by the labor force, or U/L. Solving Equation (9.4) for the unemployment rate gives

$$\frac{U}{L} = \frac{\ell}{\ell + f}. \tag{9.5}$$

That is, the natural rate of unemployment is equal to the rate at which people lose jobs divided by the sum of the rates at which people lose and find jobs.

We've seen that the natural rate of unemployment depends on the rate of job loss and the rate at which unemployed workers find jobs. But what determines these rates?

The rate of job loss

The rate of job loss is influenced by four main factors:

1. Technological change
2. Changes in international competitiveness
3. Regional effects
4. The phase of the business cycle

Technological change Technological change decreases the demand for some skills and increases the demand for others. The development of new plastics, for example, has decreased the demand for steel workers in Hamilton, Ontario, but increased the demand for petrochemical workers in Sarnia, 200 kilometres to the west.

International competitiveness Through the 1980s, newly industrializing countries, such as South Korea, Taiwan, Hong Kong, and Singapore, have brought a massive increase in the availability of many consumer goods, such as textiles, electronic products, and automobiles. Canadian producers of these goods experience great competitive pressure. Almost every television set and VCR sold in Canada and a large percentage of the clothing is now manufactured in Asia. This competitive pressure has decreased the demand for unskilled labor in Canada but increased the demand for labor in international shipping, transportation, insurance, finance, wholesaling, retailing, and the servicing of imported goods.

Changes in regional effects Technological change and changes in international competition have big regional effects. Often industries are concentrated in one part of the country. This makes the boom in one industry concentrated in one region while the decline in another is concentrated somewhere else. For example, the growth of the financial and other service sectors in Toronto is not matched by the decline of industries in that city. Instead, the declining industries have been in the West and the Maritimes.

Business cycle As the economy moves from recession through recovery to boom, the demand for labor of all types increases, and as the economy moves from boom to recession, the demand for labor across all types of jobs and skills decreases.

Effects on job loss rate All four factors we've reviewed influence the job loss rate. The faster the pace of technological change, the tougher the international competition, the bigger the regional effect, and the lower the overall level of economic activity through the business cycle, the larger is the rate of job loss.

Job-finding rate

The job-finding rate is determined by each unemployed worker's decision to stop looking for a better job and accept the best job currently available. Unemployment and job search can be viewed as an investment an unemployed person makes. This investment has a cost and an expected return. The cost of job search is the loss of wages while unemployed minus any unemployment benefit received. The benefit from job search is the expected higher wage that might be obtained from looking longer and harder for a better job than what's currently available. Three main factors influence the outcome of job search and determine the rate at which unemployed workers find jobs. They are

1. The scale of unemployment benefits
2. The minimum wage
3. The degree of structural mismatch between the unemployed and jobs available

Unemployment benefits Unemployment benefits provide unemployed workers with an income. The scale of unemployment benefit divided by the wage rate a worker can earn is called the **replacement ratio.** The higher the replacement ratio, the lower is the opportunity cost of job search and unemployment. The lower the cost of unemployment, the longer it pays a person to remain unemployed, searching for the best available job. Other things being equal, the higher the replacement ratio, the lower is the rate of finding a job.

Minimum wage Minimum wages in Canada are legislated by each of the provinces. There is also a minimum wage for federal employees. These minimum wages influence the rate at which unemployed workers can find jobs by decreasing the total number of jobs available. Firms hire labor such that the marginal product of labor equals the real wage rate. The minimum wage increases the real wage rate and so increases the marginal product of the last workers hired. It decreases the number of workers it pays a firm to hire.

Degree of mismatch People have incredible diversities of talent and skill, and jobs require an equally diverse array of talents. A good match between worker and job is one to which both workers and firms devote considerable resources and time. But technological change alters the composition of skills demanded. It may also alter the geographical location of jobs demanding particular skills. At times when there is a good match between the skills available, the skills demanded, and their geographical locations, unemployed people find work quickly. At other times, when massive technological change has brought a steep decline in the demand for particular types of labor in particular regions, such as textile workers in Quebec or fish processing workers in Atlantic Canada, then unemployed workers may take a long time to find a job and may have to move to another part of the country before doing so.

Unemployment and labor supply

In Chapter 8, we ignored unemployment when we studied the labor market and the determination of employment and wages by the interaction of the demand for and supply of labor. We've now examined the labor market in greater detail, seeing that unemployment is a central feature of that market. How can we now include unemployment in our analysis of the determination of employment and wages?

We've seen that fluctuations in total hours employed arise mainly from fluctuations in the number of persons employed. Because of this fact, we'll measure the quantity of labor in numbers of persons employed rather than in total hours. Also, we'll think of the wage rate as the average weekly wage rather than the hourly wage.

We've already distinguished between the *labor force* and the level of *employment*. It's useful to maintain that distinction in thinking about the supply of labor. Figure 9.7(a) shows two curves, the labor force curve, *LF*, and the labor supply curve, *LS*. The labor force curve describes how the labor force varies as the real wage rate varies. It tells us the number of persons who are working or seeking work at each real wage rate. The labor supply curve describes how the number of people working varies as the real wage rate varies. It tells us the number of persons ready to take a job and work, here and now, at each real wage rate. At a given real wage rate, the horizontal distance between these two curves measures the amount of frictional and structural—''natural''—unemployment. Thus for example, at a real wage rate of \$300 a week, the distance *AB* measures the number unemployed.

The vertical distances *AC* and *DB* are important and interesting economic magnitudes. When the real wage rate is \$300, 12 million people are employed. The last person to take a job—the 12 millionth person—just finds it worthwhile working at that real wage rate. But that person would stay in the labor force and keep looking for a job even if the real wage rate fell all the way to \$240 a week. The distance *AC*, \$60 a week in this example, is the value that this person places on job search.

The distance *DB* has a similar interpretation. At a real wage rate of \$300, 12.6 million people are in the labor force. The last person in the labor force, the 12.6 millionth person, does not have a job but is looking for one. That person would take a job at a real wage rate of \$360 a week. Thus the value placed on job search by this person is the distance *DB* or, in this example, \$60 a week.

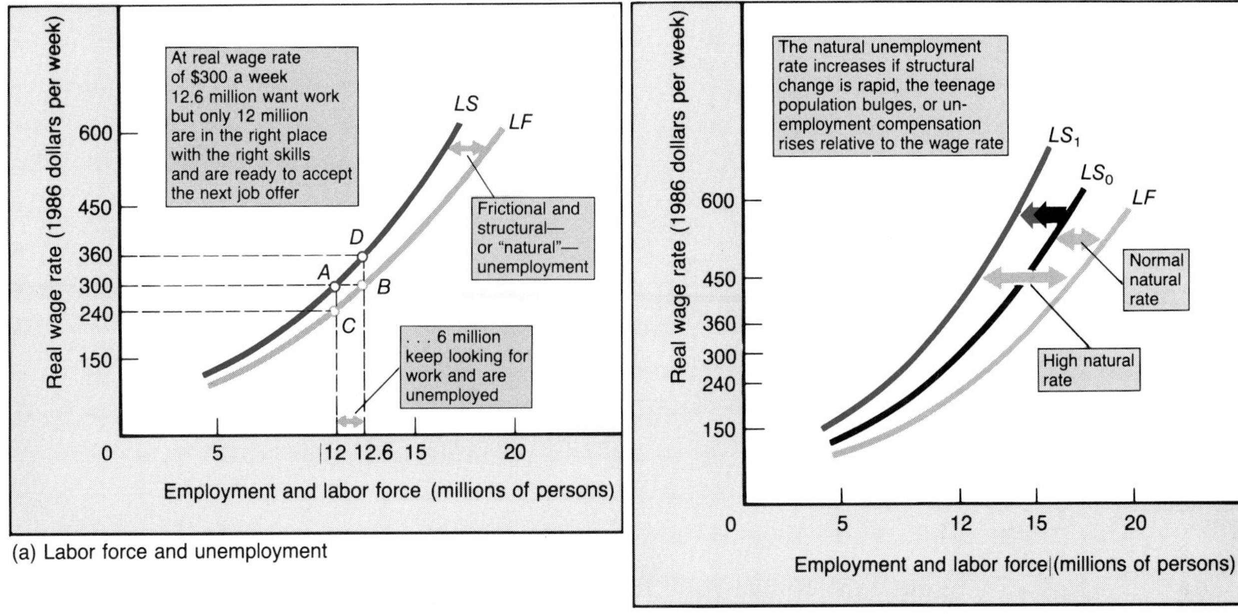

(a) Labor force and unemployment

(b) Changes in the natural unemployment rate

FIGURE 9.7
Unemployment, the Labor Force, and the Supply of Labor

The labor force curve, *LF*, shows the number of people offering themselves for work at each level of real wages. The higher the real wage rate, the larger is the number of people offering to work. Because there is variety in people and jobs, it takes time for people to find the best available job. The labor supply curve, *LS*, shows the number of people who've found the best job available and are ready to start work at each real wage rate. The horizontal distance between these two curves measures frictional and structural—natural—unemployment. The distance *AB* measures unemployment when the real wage is $300 a week. The distance *DB* measures the value that the last person looking for a job places on continued job search.

An increase in the rate of job loss caused by rapid structural change and a decrease in the rate of job finding caused by increased unemployment compensation increases the natural rate of unemployment and shifts the *LS* curve to the left from LS_0 to LS_1 in part (b).

It's important to emphasize that the labor market shown in Figure 9.7(a) is dynamic. At any real wage rate, a given number of people are employed and another number unemployed, but the actual people employed and unemployed is continuously changing. That is, lying behind these curves is the dynamic process of labor turnover that we analyzed earlier. Some people are losing jobs and becoming unemployed, others are finding jobs; first-time job seekers are entering the labor market, others are leaving it. At any real wage rate, the flows into and out of the labor force are balanced. So too are the flows into and out of employment and into and out of unemployment. But the individuals involved are changing continuously.

Any of the factors described above that influence the rates at which jobs are found and lost and, therefore, influence the natural rate of unemployment affect the positions of the *LS* and *LF* curves. Anything that increases the natural unemployment rate shifts the *LS* curve to the left, increasing the natural unemployment rate at any given real wage rate. Such a shift is shown in Figure 9.7(b).

Now that we've distinguished between the labor force and the supply of labor, let's determine equilibrium in the labor market. Figure 9.8 shows that equilibrium occurs

FIGURE 9.8
Labor Market Equilibrium

Labor market equilibrium is determined where the demand for labor curve, *LD*, intersects the labor supply curve, *LS*. Here, equilibrium occurs at a real wage rate of $300 a week; 12 million persons are employed and 0.6 million are unemployed.

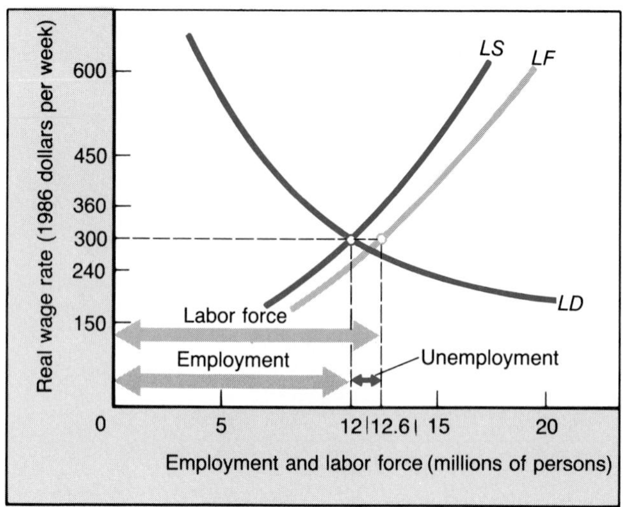

where the demand curve *LD* intersects the supply curve *LS* — 12 million people are employed at $300 a week. The number of people in the labor force is read from the *LF* curve at the equilibrium real wage rate. The labor force is 12.6 million. Of the 12.6 million in the labor force, 12 million are employed and 0.6 million are unemployed.

You may be wondering why equilibrium doesn't occur where the *LF* curve intersects the *LD* curve. That is, why don't wages fall below $300 a week? The answer is that firms would not then be able to hire the labor they wanted. The quantity of labor demanded is read from the curve *LD*, and the quantity available for work here and now is read from the curve *LS*. Firms would not be able to hire the labor they demand so the wage rate would begin to increase. It would keep doing so until it reached $300. At this real wage rate, there is an equilibrium in the sense that the quantity of labor demanded equals the quantity of labor available for work here and now, and there is no pressure for the real wage to change.

TESTCASE

9.7 The Canadian Natural Unemployment Rate in the 1970s and 1980s

We've now examined the forces that influence the natural rate of unemployment and that might cause it to vary. What has happened to the natural rate of unemployment in Canada since 1970?

Unfortunately, macroeconomists are not yet able to answer this question. Some believe that the natural rate of unemployment has fluctuated very little and that most of the fluctuations in actual unemployment have been fluctuations in cyclical unemployment — fluctuations around the natural rate. This view is illustrated by the blue line shown in Figure 9.9. The black line in the figure illustrates the opposite extreme view, that all the fluctuations in unemployment are fluctuations in the natural rate. An intermediate view is that most of the fluctuations in unemployment are deviations from the natural rate but that the natural rate has increased in the 1980s compared with the early 1970s. This view is illustrated by the light blue line in Figure 9.9.

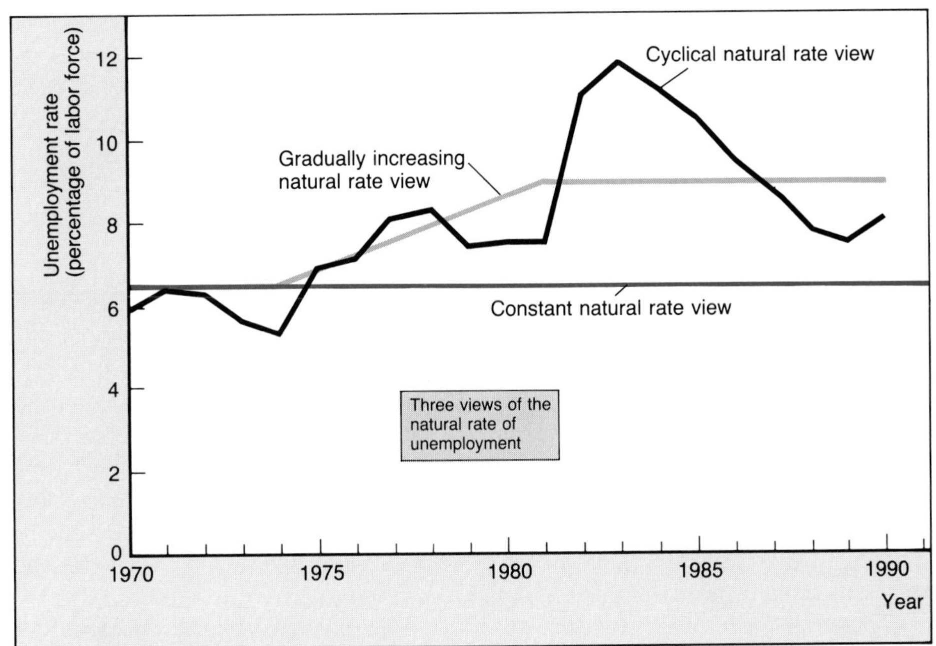

FIGURE 9.9
The Natural Rate of Unemployment

Economists disagree about how the actual unemployment rate should be separated into natural unemployment and cyclical unemployment. Some see the natural unemployment rate as being constant, some see all the fluctuations in unemployment as being fluctuations in the natural rate, and some see the natural rate as having increased but not as being cyclical.

Currently, there is no agreement on which line in Figure 9.9 shows the Canadian natural rate of unemployment. There are good theoretical reasons, reviewed above, for believing that the natural rate fluctuates. But theoretical reasons don't answer questions about numerical magnitudes. And macroeconomists have to do further work to find the acid test that enables them to figure out which line in Figure 9.9 represents the Canadian natural rate of unemployment (or, more likely, which comes closest to representing it).

If macroeconomists are not sure how fluctuations in unemployment are decomposed between fluctuations in the natural rate and fluctuations due to demand, they do agree on one broad set of facts: unemployment and the business cycle move up and down together.

We've seen that the unemployment rate fluctuates in sympathy with the business cycle. We've also seen, though, that there is no sure way of knowing whether the fluctuations in unemployment are fluctuations in its natural rate or in cyclical unemployment — around the natural rate. We have not, however, examined how fluctuations in cyclical unemployment occur. That's our next task.

9.8 *Aggregate Demand Fluctuations and Unemployment*

If money wages are flexible enough to preserve labor-market equilibrium in the face of price level changes, changes in aggregate demand have no effect on any real variables. They only change nominal variables. But if money wages adjust only gradually to achieve labor-market equilibrium, aggregate demand changes have real effects. Let's work out the effect of a decrease in aggregate demand on unemployment.

Aggregate demand decrease

If aggregate demand decreases and if money wages are sticky, the decrease in aggregate demand shifts the aggregate demand curve to the left, lowers real GDP, and lowers the price level. With sticky money wages, the lower price level increases the real wage rate. Figure 9.10 illustrates what happens in the labor market.

Suppose that the economy starts out at a full-employment equilibrium. That is, the unemployment is only frictional and structural. The economy is at the intersection of the curves *LS* and *LD*, employing 12 million persons with an average weekly wage of \$300. Suppose that the decrease in aggregate demand lowers the price level such that the real wage increases to \$360 a week. The quantity of labor demanded at this real wage rate is determined by the demand curve for labor — 11.5 million people. This is also the quantity of labor employed. Also at this higher real wage rate, the quantity of labor supplied and the labor force are larger. The labor force is 13.5 million, with 11.5 million employed and 2 million unemployed. But there are two components to unemployment: natural unemployment — the horizontal distance between the curves *LS* and *LF* — and cyclical unemployment — the horizontal distance between the labor demand and labor supply curves. Natural unemployment is 0.5 million and cyclical unemployment is 1.5 million. Thus a decrease in aggregate demand lowers real GDP, lowers the price level, increases the real wage rate, decreases the level of employment, and increases unemployment.

This response of unemployment is similar to that predicted by Okun's Law. Real GDP has fallen relative to trend, and unemployment has increased above its natural rate.

Does the behavior of the Canadian economy correspond to this working of the labor market and Okun's Law, or are variations in the unemployment rate variations in the natural rate, as some macroeconomists have suggested? To shed more light on this question, let's look at one recent episode in Canadian macroeconomic history: a severe cutback in aggregate demand and a sharp rise in unemployment.

FIGURE 9.10
Cyclical and Natural Unemployment

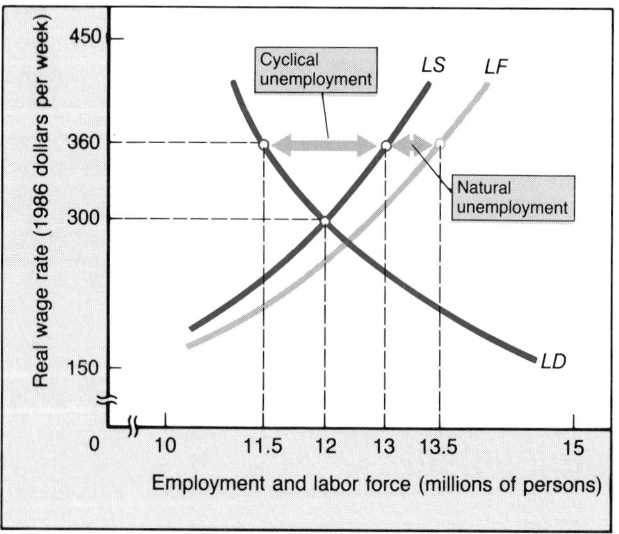

Full employment occurs at a real wage rate of \$300 a week with 12 million persons employed. If a decrease in aggregate demand lowers the price level and if wages are sticky so that the money wage rate stays constant and real wages increase, cyclical unemployment arises. In this example, at a real wage rate of \$360 a week, 2 million persons are unemployed. Natural unemployment is 0.5 million persons and cyclical unemployment 1.5 million.

9.9 Unemployment in Recession

TESTCASE

Between 1981 and 1982 the Canadian economy contracted severely. Two forces were at work in the contraction: first, a massive supply shock in the form of an oil price increase and, second, a restrictive monetary policy. In 1981, the unemployment rate was 7.4 percent. By 1982, it had increased to 11 percent. The labor market in 1981 is illustrated in Figure 9.11. The demand curve for labor was LD_0, the labor force curve was LF, and the supply of labor was LS_0. The real wage was W_0, employment was E_0, and the labor force was L_0. This equilibrium can be seen in both parts of Figure 9.11. What happened over the next three years? There are two possible interpretations, and they both begin with a decrease in the demand for labor. The oil price shocks of the late 1970s severely affected labor productivity, especially in the more energy-intensive parts of the economy. The demand for labor curve shifted left, to LD_1.

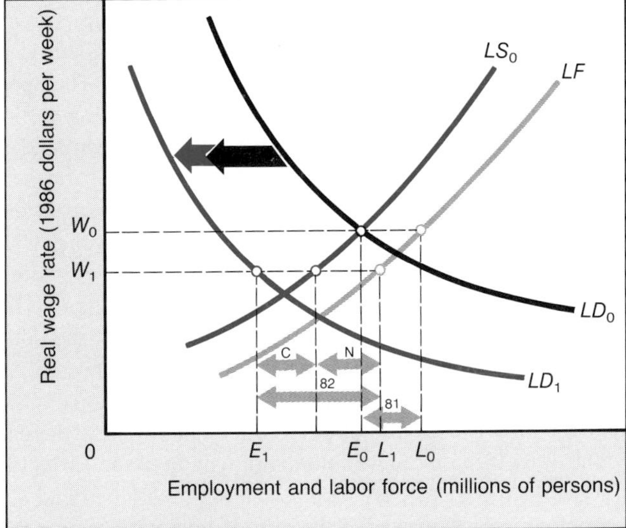

(a) Gradual wage adjustment?

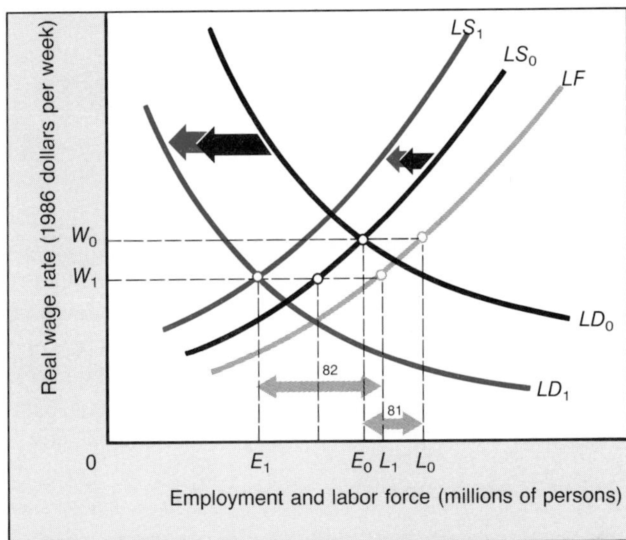

(b) Market clearing

FIGURE 9.11
Two Views of the 1982 Recession

In the early 1980s, oil price shocks and other supply disturbances lowered the productivity of labor and shifted the demand for labor curve from LD_0 to LD_1 (parts a and b). The Bank of Canada slowed down the growth rate of the money supply and the growth of aggregate demand. Real wages decreased and unemployment increased. In both parts (a) and (b), the money wage rate fell from W_0 to W_1 and unemployment increased from the amount indicated with the arrow marked 81 to the amount marked 82.

Part (a) interprets this movement in the gradual wage adjustment model. The real wage rate fell but not by enough to achieve labor-market equilibrium. The natural unemployment, *N* in part (a), did not change and the increased unemployment was cyclical (marked *C*).

Part (b) interprets the same events with labor market clearing. The shocks that lower the productivity of labor increase the rate of job loss and decrease the rate of job finding, so the labor supply curve shifts to the left from LS_0 to LS_1. The money wage rate W_1 is determined at the intersection of LS_1 and LD_1.

The tight monetary policy slowed the growth of aggregate demand and slowed down the inflation rate. Prices rose less quickly than they otherwise would have done. But wage growth also slowed down, and real wages decreased. Was the decrease in real wages enough to keep the economy at full employment? Figure 9.11(a) says no and part (b) says yes.

Part (a) shows the equilibrium for 1982 at the real wage rate W_1. This generates an employment level of E_1 from the demand curve for labor. The supply curve remains at LS_0, and actual unemployment exceeds the natural rate of unemployment. This description of the 1982 recession pictures the natural rate of unemployment as remaining constant and the rise in the actual unemployment rate being entirely cyclical and due to demand forces.

How does the story in Figure 9.11(b) differ from this? It shows the labor supply curve shifting left, to LS_1. For a given labor force, the labor supply curve shifts left when the natural rate of unemployment increases. Why might the natural rate have increased in the early 1980s? The answer is contained in the factors influencing the rates at which employed people lose jobs and unemployed workers find them. The big change in oil prices was a contributory factor. It changed the relative competitiveness of different sectors of the economy. Oil-intensive sectors became less competitive and the industries producing oil-saving, energy-efficient equipment expanded. The need to reallocate the labor force away from energy-consuming toward energy-saving activities created a temporary increase in the mismatch between available jobs and available skills, increasing the natural rate of unemployment.

With a decrease in the supply of labor to LS_1, the new labor supply curve intersects the new labor demand curve at wage rate W_1 and employment level E_1. Thus in the two figures, the employment level and real wage rate are identical. They represent the actual values of those variables in 1982. Unemployment is the same in the two figures as well. But the decomposition of that unemployment differs. In part (b), the entire increase in unemployment is an increase in the natural rate of unemployment.

Figure 9.11 contains two explanations of the 1980s recession. Which is correct? The answer to this question is vital to not only understanding how the economy works but also how to control it. If the increase in unemployment in the early 1980s did result from the forces at work in part (a), an increase in aggregate demand could bring the economy to full employment. However, if part (b) is correct, an increase in aggregate demand would merely raise the price level.

TESTCASE

9.10 *Unemployment Around the World*

At the beginning of this chapter we discovered that unemployment fluctuates over time and differs markedly across countries. Can the cross-country variations in unemployment help us distinguish between the two competing theories about fluctuations in unemployment? They can certainly help but they cannot settle the question. Everyone agrees that differences in unemployment rates across countries are not due to differences in the level of aggregate demand and cyclical unemployment. No one believes that Japan keeps its unemployment rate at 2 percent by running an overheated economy with a high level of demand. Why, then, is the Japanese unemployment rate so low and European rates so high, and why have the Italian and French unemployment rates grown so much? Do the answers to these questions help us settle disagreements about how labor markets work?

It is relatively easy to account for these cross-country differences with the theory of the labor market that you studied in this chapter. In low-unemployment countries and situations, the rate of job loss is low and the rate at which unemployed workers find jobs is high. At times and in countries with a high unemployment rate, the rate of job loss is high and the rate at which unemployed workers find jobs is low. The reasons for these differences are specific cases of the general reasons for variations in the natural rate of unemployment that we reviewed.

For example, in the case of Japan, the rate of job loss is low because of the Japanese institutional arrangement of lifetime attachments between workers and firms. In Western Europe, the job loss rate has been high and the job-finding rate low because of the massive structural changes taking place in the European economy as it approaches complete economic and monetary union in the early 1990s. In Britain, especially in the early- to mid-1980s, the job-loss rate was high and the job-finding rate low because of structural change associated with Margaret Thatcher's policies of deregulating and privatizing large parts of the British economy. Such structural changes bring a temporary, but occasionally prolonged, increase in the natural rate of unemployment.

■ In the last two chapters, we've studied the working of the labor market and seen how, with sticky wages, variations in aggregate demand can bring variations in output and employment. We've also seen that output, employment, and unemployment can vary even when wages are flexible. But we've ignored the forces that produce long-term economic growth and expansion. We've been studying markets with a given capital stock and state of technology. Even so, we saw that an increase in capital stock and advancing technology shifts the short-run production function upward. We'll study the forces of economic growth and expansion more systematically in Chapter 10.

CHAPTER REVIEW

Summary

PATTERNS IN UNEMPLOYMENT IN CANADA AND EUROPE

In the industrial world, Japan has had the lowest unemployment rate in the 1980s (around 2 percent), Canada and the United Kingdom have had the highest (around 12 percent), and the United States has been in the middle of this range. European unemployment, especially in Italy and France, was persistently high through the 1980s; and in all European countries and Canada, unemployment fell more slowly than in the United States after the 1982 recession.

There is an enormous range of unemployment across demographic groups in the United States: Young Canadian men, those under 19 years, experience more than twice as much unemployment as the average and more than twice as much as adults.

Most unemployed persons find a job within a few weeks and three quarters within six months. About two thirds of the unemployed are people who lost jobs and the other third have entered or re-entered the labor force.

OKUN'S LAW

Okun's Law is that the higher the level of real GDP as a percentage of capacity real GDP, the lower is the unemployment rate. Okun's relationship in Canada has shifted in the late 1970s. Before the supply shocks of the mid-1970s, on the average, when real GDP equalled capacity real GDP, unemployment was 6.5 percent. By the 1980s, that unemployment rate had increased to 9 percent.

HOW UNEMPLOYMENT IS MEASURED

Unemployment is measured in Canada by surveying 56,000 households. To be unemployed, a person must have made specific efforts to find a job within the previous four weeks and must have been available for work during the week of the survey. The unemployed also include people who did not work during the week of the survey and who are waiting either to be called back to a job from which they've been laid off for 26 weeks or less or to report to a new job within 4 weeks.

Measured unemployment does not include discouraged workers—people who've withdrawn from active job search because of repeated failure to find a suitable job. Nor does it include those part-time workers who want full-time employment.

EMPLOYMENT, UNEMPLOYMENT, AND AVERAGE WORK HOURS

Average work hours have declined over the years. Fluctuations around the declining trend have been mild. Most of the fluctuations in employment over the business cycle are fluctuations in the number of persons employed, not fluctuations in the average hours per person.

WHY WORK HOURS FLUCTUATE LESS THAN EMPLOYMENT AND UNEMPLOYMENT

Both households and firms prefer stable work hours to highly variable work hours. Stable hours enable households to use their time efficiently, reduce income uncertainty, and optimize travel to work and other startup costs.

Stable hours enable firms to optimize employees' work effort and more efficiently organize team production.

THE NATURAL RATE OF UNEMPLOYMENT

There are three kinds of unemployment: frictional, structural, and cyclical. The natural rate of unemployment is the percentage of the labor force that is frictionally and structurally unemployed. The cyclical unemployment rate is the actual unemployment rate minus the natural rate.

Unemployment arises from the fact that the labor market is a dynamic mechanism. New workers continually enter the labor force; people with jobs continually lose them; unemployed people continually find jobs. The rate at which these flows occur determines the natural rate of unemployment. Some proportion of those employed lose jobs each period and some proportion of those unemployed find jobs in each period. The change in unemployment is the difference between these two groups. The natural rate of unemployment equals the proportion of the employed losing jobs divided by the sum of the proportion of employed losing jobs and the proportion of unemployed finding jobs. The rate of job loss (and therefore the natural rate of unemployment) is influenced by the pace of technological change, changes in international competitiveness and regional effects, and the phase of the business cycle. The rate at which people find jobs is influenced by the scale of unemployment benefits, the minimum wage, and the degree of structural mismatch between the unemployed and the jobs available.

Because of unemployment, there is a gap between the number of persons offering themselves for work and the number of persons available for work at any given moment. The higher the real wage rate, the higher is the number of persons in the labor force (employed and looking for work) and the higher is the number of persons ready to accept the best job found. The labor force curve describes the relationship between the real wage rate and the number of persons in the labor force; the labor supply curve describes the relationship between the real wage rate and the number of persons ready to accept the best job currently found. Equilibrium in the labor market occurs where the demand for labor curve intersects the labor supply curve. At this real wage rate, the labor force exceeds the quantity of labor employed by the amount of natural unemployment.

THE NATURAL UNEMPLOYMENT RATE IN CANADA

There is disagreement about how fluctuations in the actual unemployment rate decompose into fluctuations in the natural unemployment rate and fluctuations in cyclical unemployment. Some economists believe that the natural unemployment rate is almost constant so that all the fluctuations in unemployment are fluctuations in cyclical unemployment. Others believe that the natural rate of unemployment itself has a large cyclical component.

WHY UNEMPLOYMENT FLUCTUATES AND SOMETIMES RISES ABOVE ITS NATURAL RATE

Unemployment can fluctuate either because of a change in the natural unemployment rate or because of a change in cyclical unemployment. An increase in the rate of job loss or a decrease in the rate of job finding shifts the labor supply curve to the left, increasing the natural unemployment rate.

A decrease in aggregate demand that decreases the price level increases real wages. If money wages adjust only gradually, the real wage exceeds the market-clearing real wage. The quantity of labor demanded is less than the quantity of labor supplied, and unemployment increases above the natural rate.

UNEMPLOYMENT DURING THE RECESSION OF THE EARLY 1980s

Between 1981 and 1982 the Canadian economy moved into a deep recession. Real wages fell slightly and unemployment increased sharply.

There are two interpretations of these facts. Both begin with a decrease in the demand for labor resulting from supply-side shocks, such as the energy price increases at the beginning of the 1980s. This decrease in the demand for labor brought a decrease in the real wage rate. The gradual wage adjustment theory emphasizes that money wages adjust gradually and do not move immediately to their market-clearing level. In this interpretation, although the real wage rate fell in the early 1980s, it did not fall to its market-clearing level, and some of the resulting unemployment was cyclical—the quantity of labor demanded was less than the quantity supplied.

The labor market clearing interpretation emphasizes the effects of productivity disturbances on the rate of job loss and a consequential temporary increase in the natural rate of unemployment. Not only did the demand for labor curve shift to the left, but so did the labor supply curve, according to this theory. The entire increase in unemployment was accounted for by a temporary increase in the natural rate of unemployment.

Key Terms and Concepts

Cyclical unemployment Unemployment in excess of frictional plus structural unemployment.

Discouraged workers People who have no jobs, are willing to work, and are available for work but have stopped searching for work because of their discouraging experience.

Frictional unemployment The number of unemployed people who are searching for a job.

Labor force The number of people employed plus the number of people unemployed.

Natural rate of unemployment The percentage of the labor force that is frictionally and structurally unemployed.

Replacement ratio The scale of unemployment benefits divided by the wage rate that a worker can earn.

Structural unemployment The number of people who are in the wrong location and have the wrong skills for the available jobs.

Unemployed person A person who is able and willing to work and is available for work but does not have work.

Unemployment rate The number of unemployed people expressed as a percentage of the labor force.

Review Questions

1. How does Canadian unemployment compare with U.S., Japanese, and Western European unemployment?
2. How does Canadian unemployment differ across demographic groups?
3. Describe the duration and origins of unemployment in Canada.
4. What is Okun's Law? Does it explain fluctuations in Canadian unemployment?
5. How do macroeconomists define unemployment?
6. How does Statistics Canada measure unemployment? What are the main problems with measured unemployment?
7. Describe the trend and cycles in average hours worked each week in Canada.
8. Explain why hours of work are more stable than the number of people employed.
9. Describe the various kinds of unemployment. How does each arise?
10. Describe the natural rate of unemployment.
11. Describe the main flows into and out of the labor market, the pool of unemployed, and the employed.
12. What determines the rates at which the unemployed find jobs and the employed lose jobs?
13. Define the unemployment rate. Explain what determines its magnitude.
14. How do technological change, international competitiveness, and regional competitiveness influence the unemployment rate?
15. How do unemployment benefits, minimum wages, and mismatch of skills and location influence the unemployment rate?
16. Describe the change in the Canadian natural rate of unemployment since 1975.
17. Explain the effect of a decrease in aggregate demand on employment, unemployment, and the labor force.
18. In question 17, how does the change in unemployment break down into the various types of unemployment?

19. Explain why unemployment increased during the 1981-1982 recession.
20. Explain why unemployment rates are low in Japan and sometimes low in Canada and high in Western Europe and sometimes high in Canada.

Problems

1. The labor market is described by
   The demand for labor $n^d = 100 - 5(W/P)$
   The supply of labor $n^s = 5(W/P)$
   The labor force $L = 7(W/P)$
   where n^d is the quantity of labor demanded, n^s is the quantity of labor supplied, (W/P) is the real wage rate, and L is the size of the labor force.
   Calculate:
   (a) The equilibrium real wage rate and the level of employment
   (b) The size of the labor force
   (c) The natural rate of unemployment
   (d) The value placed on job search by the last person employed
   (e) The value placed on job search by the last person to join the labor force
2. The labor market of an economy is described by the following schedule:

Real wage rate	1	2	3	4	5	6	7	8	9	10
Labor supplied	10	20	30	40	50	60	70	80	90	100

   The economy has 10 identical firms each with the following short-run production function:

Employment	1	2	3	4	5	6	7	8	9	10
Real GDP	20	37	44	50	55	59	62	64	65	64

Calculate:
   (a) The equilibrium real wage rate and the level of employment
   (b) The size of the labor force
   (c) The level of unemployment
   (d) The natural rate of unemployment
3. In problem 1, if the government introduces a minimum wage that has the effect of increasing the economy's average real wage rate by 20 percent, calculate:
   (a) The equilibrium real wage rate and the level of employment
   (b) The size of the labor force
   (c) The unemployment rate
   (d) The natural rate of unemployment
   (e) Cyclical unemployment
   (f) The value placed on job search by the last person in the labor force
4. In problem 1, a decrease in aggregate demand lowers the price level by 10 percent. What is the effect of the fall in the price level on
   (a) The demand for labor
   (b) The supply of labor
   (c) The level of employment
   (d) The natural rate of unemployment
   (e) Cyclical unemployment
5. In problem 4, does Okun's Law describe the movements in unemployment and real GDP? Explain your answer.

C H A P T E R

10 Capital, Technology, and Economic Growth

BRIGHTENING THE FACE OF THE DISMAL SCIENCE

THE MODERN INDUSTRIAL WORLD ORIGINATED in the small, smoky, grimy towns of Northern England in the mid-eighteenth century. There, the development of steam power for transportation and production and the emergence of factories producing textiles and machines set the world on an unimaginable course.

During the first hundred years of industrial life, incomes increased hugely. Larger incomes brought sanitation and housing improvements, and the infant mortality rate collapsed. Because people continued to have as many children as before, and because people lived longer, the population exploded.

This population explosion led Thomas Robert Malthus, an English clergyman-economist, to predict disaster in his great work *Essay on Population*. Industrialization had removed constraints on population growth and put the population on an exponential growth path. Malthus thought that the world's food supply could not possibly grow fast enough to keep up with the exponential growth of population, so he predicted food shortages that would act as miserable checks on population growth. Malthus and the economists who agreed with him painted such a bleak picture that Thomas Carlyle, a nineteenth-century writer and historian, branded economics "the dismal science."

Throughout the nineteenth and early twentieth centuries, controversy raged as to whether market economies, such as those of Western Europe and North America, could function effectively and avoid disaster. Malthus's prediction seemed refuted as technological advances in the use of land and fertilizers and advances in seeds and animal husbandry enabled food production to easily keep up with population growth. But other worries emerged, especially during the 1920s and 1930s. Could the market economy keep spending high enough to absorb all the goods and services it could produce? These fears gave rise to the Keynesian revolution and the birth of macroeconomics.

Running through the entire debate about how well a market economy could function was a deeply divisive political disagreement. Those inspired by the writings of the nineteenth-century historian and philosopher Karl Marx favored a centrally planned—socialist—economy. In opposition, others believed that a market—capitalist—economy could indeed deliver steadily increasing prosperity.

As we approach the middle of the third century of the industrial age, the pace of economic expansion doesn't appear to be slackening off. Productivity growth has slowed down since the mid-1970s, but such slowdowns have occurred before, and the trend rate of real GDP growth continues unabated.

This chapter studies the forces producing economic growth. It examines the uneven pace of expansion in the Canadian economy since the mid-nineteenth century and then goes on to study the sources of economic growth and the economic mechanism generating it. After studying this chapter, you will be able to

- Describe the main features of the expansion of Canadian output from 1926 to 1990
- Describe the sources of economic growth
- Explain the neoclassical model of economic growth
- Explain how the saving rate influences the rate of economic growth
- Explain how technological change influences economic growth
- Describe the importance of the contribution of technological change to Canadian economic growth
- Describe the Canadian productivity slowdown of the 1970s and explain its origins

Let's begin by looking at the facts about the uneven pace of Canadian economic expansion since 1926.

10.1 *The Uneven Pace of Canadian Economic Expansion: 1926-1990*

MACROFACTS

In the 64 years of Canadian economic history from 1926 to 1990, real gross national product has grown at an average rate of 4.1 percent a year. But the population has also grown over this period, at an average rate of 1.6 percent a year. As a result, real GDP per person has grown at an average rate of 2.5 percent a year, which means that real GDP per person has doubled every 28 years.

The Canadian economy has expanded over time, but the pace of expansion has not been smooth. Figure 10.1 shows the expansion of real GDP per person from 1926 to 1990. The path of expansion is persistent but fluctuations have occurred, especially big ones in the Great Depression and World War II.

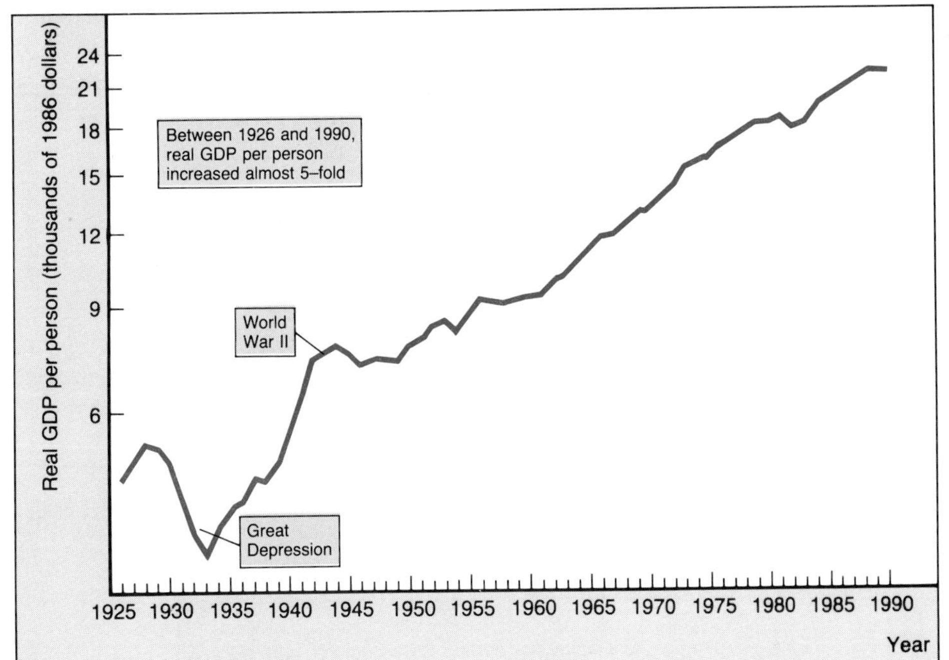

FIGURE 10.1
Real GDP per Person: 1926-1990

Between 1926 and 1990, real GDP per person in Canada grew at an average rate of 2.5 percent a year. But the pace of growth has been uneven. The economy contracted severely in the Great Depression and expanded most rapidly through World War II. These are the extremes. Usually, the pace of expansion has ebbed and flowed. The most recent slowdown in growth occurred in the 1980s.

Source: Real GDP, 1929-1990, *National Income and Product Accounts of Canada*; Population, Statistics Canada, CANSIM series D1.

This chapter focuses on the forces that have brought about the persistent expansion of real GDP. So far, we have concentrated on understanding the fluctuations in real GDP — fluctuations associated with the business cycle. In this chapter, we'll discover that some of the factors making our economy expand also contribute to fluctuations in the pace of expansion. Let's begin by examining the sources of economic growth.

10.2 *The Sources of Economic Growth*

There are two sources of economic growth:

- Capital accumulation
- Technological change

Capital accumulation

The quantity of goods and services that can be produced depends on the quantities of the factors of production available to produce them. One of the most important factors of production whose quantity we can control is capital. By consuming less than we produce, we accumulate capital. In its great variety, capital includes buildings, plant and equipment, civil engineering projects (such as highways and dams), and human capital — the skills acquired through education, training, and experience. Other things being equal, the more capital a person has, the greater is the output produced and the greater is the person's income.

The connection between a person's output and capital is shown by the *per capita* production function. The **per capita production function** is the relationship between output per person and capital per person. Output per person is equal to income per person, and we measure these two equivalent concepts as real GDP per person. Figure 10.2 illustrates a per capita production function. Notice its shape. An increase in capital per person brings an increase in real GDP per person. The increase in real GDP per person resulting from a one-unit increase in capital per person is the **marginal product**

FIGURE 10.2
The Per Capita Production Function

The per capita production function shows how real GDP per person varies as capital per person varies, holding all other influences constant. Its slope measures the marginal product of capital. The marginal product of capital diminishes as capital per person increases.

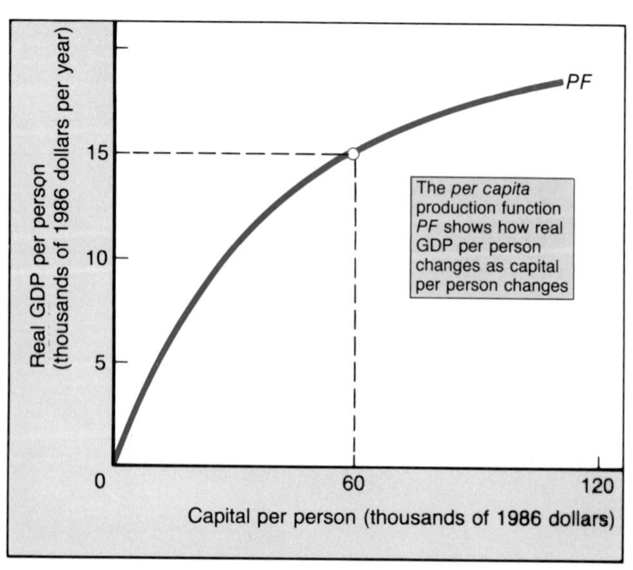

of capital. The marginal product of capital diminishes as capital per person increases. That is, an additional unit of capital brings more real GDP per person, but the extra real GDP per person resulting from an extra unit of capital gets smaller as the capital stock rises.

Because the marginal product of capital diminishes, capital accumulation alone cannot bring sustained growth in real GDP per person. The other major source of growth is technological change.

Technological change

Technological change makes it possible to produce more output from given inputs. Over the past two centuries, technological change has been steady and, in total, dramatic. From the first application of steam power in the mid-eighteenth century to the invention of the silicone chip and the manipulation of genetic material in the last quarter of the twentieth century, technological change has transformed our productive potentials beyond the wildest imaginations of those living in the mid-eighteenth century.

Technological change shifts the per capita production function upward, as shown in Figure 10.3. Notice that, unlike the case of capital accumulation, technological change doesn't lead to diminishing marginal product of capital.

But technological change itself has costs. To achieve it, resources are devoted to research and development and learning how to use new technologies. Thus even this activity has diminishing returns. But by continuously devoting resources to advancing technology, the per capita production function can be kept moving upward and ongoing economic growth can be sustained.

To explain how rapidly an economy actually grows, we need to understand the forces that determine the rate of capital accumulation and the pace of technological change. A great deal of work has been done on the first of these issues but not much on the second. Until recently, technological change was taken to be exogenous and capital accumulation endogenous. We're going to study the model of economic growth that makes those assumptions.

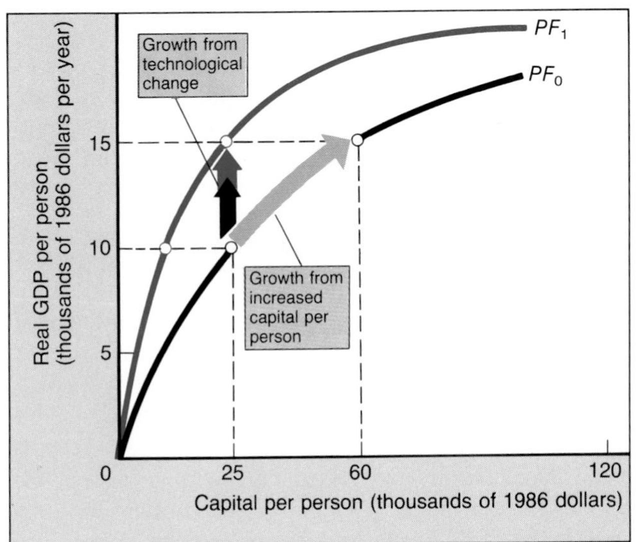

FIGURE 10.3
The Two Sources of Economic Growth

Economic growth can arise from increased capital per person or from technological change. Capital accumulation leads to economic growth by moving the economy along the per capita production function PF_0. Technological change leads to economic growth by shifting the per capita production function from PF_0 to PF_1.

10.3 *The Neoclassical Growth Model*

The **neoclassical growth model** determines real GDP per person, consumption and saving per person, capital per person, and the economic growth rate. We'll examine the simplest neoclassical growth model with no technological change—technology is given.

The first ingredient in the neoclassical growth model is the per capita production function you saw in Figure 10.2. This production function tells us how real GDP per person varies as capital per person changes, but it does not tell us what capital per person is. To determine that, we need to know how fast the capital stock is growing and how fast the population is changing.

Capital and population growth

Capital per person increases if investment per person exceeds the population growth rate and decreases if investment per person is less than the population growth rate. Capital per person is constant if investment per person equals the population growth rate. When capital per person is constant, the economy is said to be in a **steady state**—a situation in which the relevant variables are constant over time. The relevant variables for our present analysis are real GDP per person, capital per person, and consumption, saving, and investment per person.

To determine what steady-state investment per person is, we need to work out the investment that maintains a constant stock of capital, k, per person. Investment is the change in the capital stock, Δk. If the population is n, then

$$\text{Investment per person} = \Delta k/n. \qquad \textbf{(10.1)}$$

Let's multiply and divide the right side of Equation (10.1) by the capital stock. Doing this, we can write investment per person as

$$\frac{\Delta k}{n} = \frac{\Delta k}{k}\left(\frac{k}{n}\right). \qquad \textbf{(10.2)}$$

This equation is still just a definition, telling us that investment per person equals the growth rate of capital ($\Delta k/k$) multiplied by capital per person (k/n).

In a steady state, capital per person (k/n) is constant. This can occur only if the capital stock increases at the same rate as the population. That is,

$$\frac{\Delta k}{k} = \frac{\Delta n}{n}. \qquad \textbf{(10.3)}$$

The population growth rate is exogenous. So replacing the growth rate of the capital stock (an endogenous variable) with the growth rate of the population (an exogenous variable) in Equation (10.2) gives

$$\frac{\Delta k}{n} = \frac{\Delta n}{n}\left(\frac{k}{n}\right). \qquad \textbf{(10.4)}$$

This equation tells us that the capital stock per person will be constant if investment per person equals the growth rate of the population multiplied by capital per person. Figure 10.4 illustrates this equation—the curve *SS* is the steady-state investment line. The slope of the line is equal to the growth rate of the population. The greater the population growth rate, the steeper is this line. That is, for any given stock of capital per person, the faster the population grows, the greater must investment be to keep the capital stock per person constant. Also, the greater the capital stock per person, the greater must investment be to maintain this capital stock per person constant for a given population growth rate. At points above the line *SS*, investment per person exceeds the population

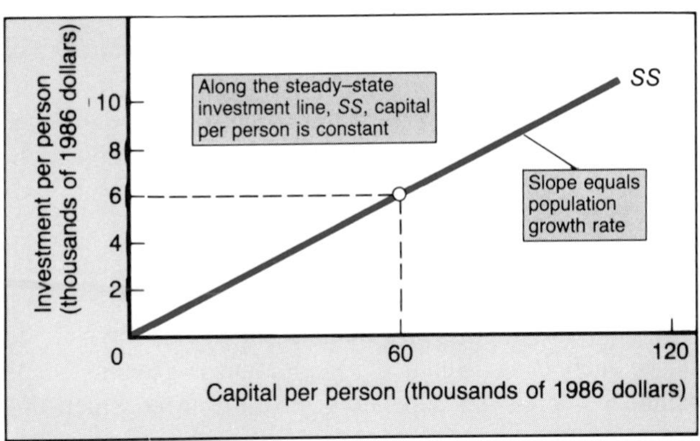

FIGURE 10.4
Steady-State Investment

The steady-state investment line, *SS*, shows the relationship between capital per person and investment per person but maintains a constant level of capital per person. Its slope equals the population growth rate. In this figure, the population growth rate is 10 percent a year. For example, if the capital stock per person is $60,000 and investment per person is $6,000, investment is 10 percent of the capital stock. Thus the capital stock grows at 10 percent a year, the same rate as the population grows, and capital per person is constant.

growth rate, so capital per person increases. At points below the line *SS* investment per person is less than the population growth rate, so capital per person decreases.

We've now worked out the investment per person needed to achieve a steady state. We know that investment equals saving. Let's now see what determines saving per person.

Per capita real GDP and saving

We have studied the influences on consumption and saving in Chapter 4, and will do a more rigorous analysis in Chapter 17. For now, we'll continue to use the proposition developed in Chapter 4 that both consumption and saving increase as income increases. We'll also suppose the fraction of income consumed is a constant, b, so that the fraction of income saved, $1 - b$, is also a constant.

We can represent saving per person in the same diagram as the per capita production function. Figure 10.5 shows two curves: the curve *S* is similar to the per capita production function, *PF*, but lies below it. At each level of capital per person, the per capita production function shows us real GDP per person, and the curve *S* shows the amount

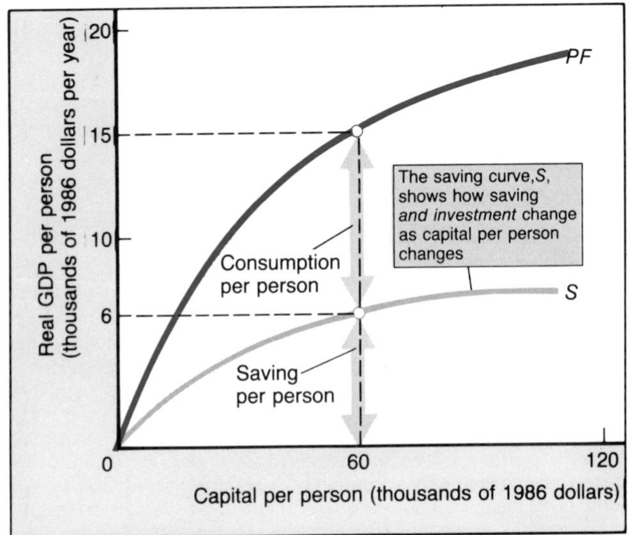

FIGURE 10.5
Income and Saving

The saving curve, *S*, shows the fraction of real GDP saved per person at each level of capital per person. Saving results in investment and capital accumulation, so the saving curve also shows investment per person as capital per person varies.

of real GDP saved per person—the fraction $(1-b)$ of real GDP per person. Figure 10.5 shows the amounts of real GDP per person and saving per person at each possible level of capital per person. It also shows consumption per person at each level of capital per person.

Figure 10.5 has an interesting and important feature you've not met before in this book. It is that one of the variables measured on the vertical axis—in this case, saving per person—is the amount by which the variable on the horizontal axis—capital per person—is changing. That is, at a particular capital per person, say \$60,000 per person, the economy produces a real GDP per person of \$15,000 a year and saving per person of \$6,000 a year. Since investment equals saving, the capital stock is growing by the \$6,000 a year that's being saved by each person. If the population were constant, capital per person would be increasing. But if the population is growing, capital per person might be increasing or decreasing depending on the rate at which the population is growing. To determine whether capital per person is increasing, decreasing, or constant, we need to bring together the two tools that we have now developed—the steady-state investment line and the saving curve.

The steady state

We've defined the steady state as a situation in which capital per person and real GDP per person are constant. To work out a steady state, we need to find the level of capital per person at which the stock of capital grows at the same rate as the population. Figure 10.6 shows how to work out the steady state.

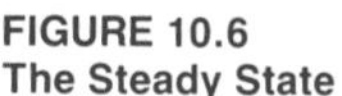

FIGURE 10.6
The Steady State

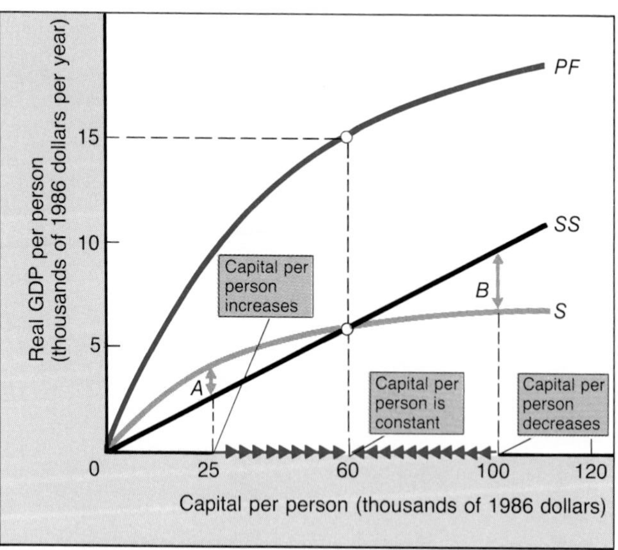

The per capita production and saving functions are combined with the steady-state investment line to determine the steady-state capital per person and real GDP per person. If capital per person is \$25,000, investment exceeds the amount required to maintain the capital per person constant by the amount *A*. Capital per person increases. If capital per person is \$100,000, saving and investment are less than the amount required to maintain the capital per person constant by the amount *B*. In this case, capital per person decreases. There is a convergence from any point below or above \$60,000 of capital per person to that level. When capital per person is \$60,000, saving and investment per person equal the amount required to maintain a constant level of capital per person. This is the economy's steady state.

First, check that you recognize the curves in Figure 10.6: the per capita production function (*PF*) you met in Figure 10.2; the steady-state investment line (*SS*) you met in Figure 10.4; and the saving curve (*S*) you met in Figure 10.5. Suppose that capital per person is $25,000. At this level of capital per person, saving per person exceeds the amount of capital accumulation needed to keep capital per person constant. The economy is not in a steady state. Arrow *A* shows the amount by which saving exceeds the amount of capital accumulation required to keep capital per person constant. In this situation, capital per person increases. The economy follows the blue arrows moving right along the horizontal axis, increasing the amount of capital per person, increasing real GDP per person, and increasing consumption and saving per person.

Next, consider what happens if capital per person is $100,000. In this case, saving per person is less than the amount required to keep the capital stock per person constant. Again, the economy is not in a steady state. Arrow *B* indicates the shortfall in saving per person. In this situation, capital per person falls. The economy follows the blue arrows moving left.

Finally, consider what happens when capital per person is $60,000. In this situation, saving per person leads to capital being accumulated at exactly the same rate as the population is growing. At this capital stock per person, the economy is in a steady state — real GDP per person is constant. Starting from any other capital stock per person, a process is set up converging the economy to its steady-state position.

The effect of the saving rate on growth rate

We've just seen that in a steady state, real GDP per person and capital per person are constant. This means that real GDP grows at the population growth rate. The capital stock also grows at this same rate, keeping capital per person constant.

How does a change in the saving rate influence the growth rate? The answer is that it has no effect on the steady-state growth rate but it does affect the level of capital per person and real GDP per person. To see why, let's see what happens if the saving rate increases. Figure 10.7 shows the effects on real GDP per person and capital per person.

Suppose that initially the economy's capital per person is $60,000 and real GDP per person is $15,000. The economy is in a steady state because at this capital per person the saving curve, S_0, intersects the steady-state investment line, *SS*.

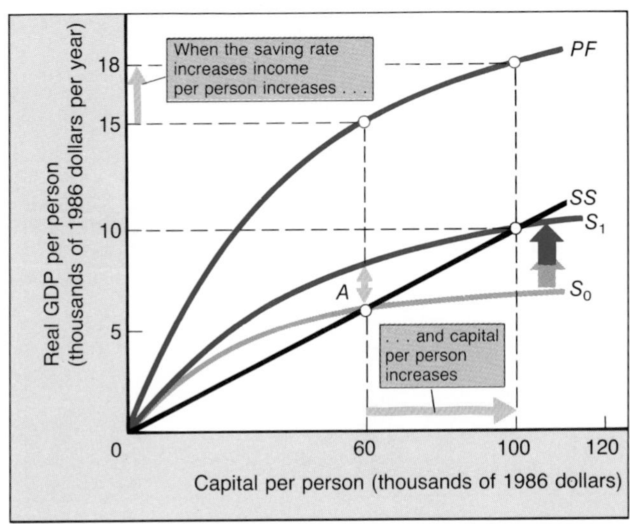

FIGURE 10.7
Effect of a Change in the Saving Rate

An increase in the saving rate shifts the saving curve up from S_0 to S_1. At the initial level of capital per person, $60,000, saving and investment per person exceeds, by the amount *A*, the amount required to keep capital per person constant. Capital per person increases. The economy converges on its new steady state, where capital per person is $100,000 and real GDP per person is $18,000.

Now suppose that the saving rate $(1 - b)$ increases (the consumption rate b decreases). The saving curve shifts upward from S_0 to S_1. With capital per person at \$60,000, the saving rate and rate of capital accumulation now exceed the population growth rate. Arrow A measures the excess. As a consequence, capital per person increases and, as it does, real GDP per person increases. This process of increasing capital and increasing real GDP per person continues as long as the rate of capital accumulation exceeds the population growth rate. A steady state is again achieved when capital per person has grown to \$100,000 and real GDP per person has increased to \$18,000.

In the new steady state, capital per person, consumption and saving per person, and real GDP per person are all higher than before. But the growth rate of real GDP is equal to the population growth rate. Thus the growth rate does not depend on the saving rate. However, the increase in the saving rate temporarily increased the growth rate. That is, in the process of moving from the initial steady state to the new steady state, the growth rate of real GDP and the capital stock exceeded the population growth rate.

We've seen that an increase in the saving rate increases capital per person and real GDP per person, but in the steady state it leaves the growth rate of GDP unchanged. Next, let's work out what happens when the population growth rate changes.

Change in population growth rate

How does the population growth rate affect the growth rate and level of real GDP and capital per person? We'll use Figure 10.8 to answer this question. Suppose that the economy is initially at a steady state at a capital per person of \$60,000 and a real GDP per person of \$15,000. That is, the economy is at the point of intersection of the steady-state investment line SS_0 and the saving curve, S.

The population growth rate decreases. As a consequence, the steady-state investment line shifts downward to SS_1. With capital per person at \$60,000 and no change in saving per person, capital is now being accumulated at a rate faster than the population growth rate. Capital per person is increasing. As it does so, real GDP per person and saving per person also increase. But eventually, when capital per person has increased

FIGURE 10.8
The Effect of a Change in the Population Growth Rate

If the population growth rate decreases, the steady-state investment rate shifts downward, from SS_0 to SS_1. At the initial level of capital per person, \$60,000, saving per person (and investment per person) now exceeds the amount required to maintain the capital per person constant by the amount A. Capital per person and real GDP per person both increase until the new steady state is reached. In this example, steady-state capital per person is \$100,000, with real GDP per person of \$18,000.

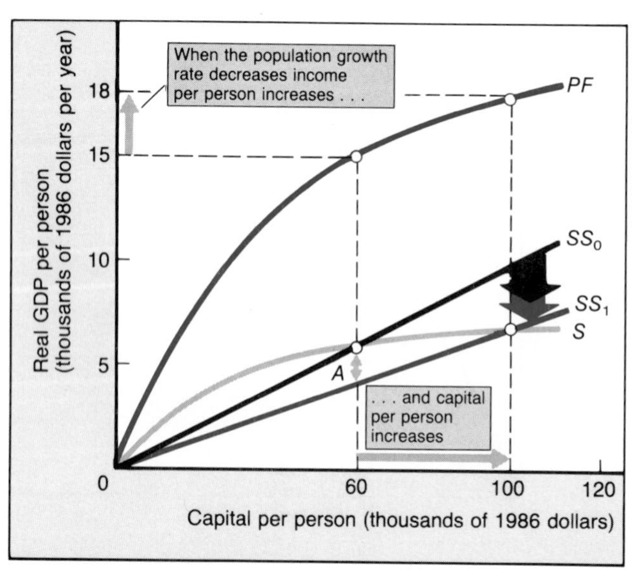

to $100,000, the saving rate — and rate at which capital is being accumulated — equals the population growth rate and a new steady state is achieved. You can see that a decrease in the population growth rate has produced an increase in the steady-state capital per person and real GDP per person. But it brings a decrease in the growth rate of real GDP in the new steady state. That is, real GDP grows at the same rate as the population in the new steady state.

The golden rule

We've seen how real GDP, consumption, and saving are determined and how, in the steady state, GDP per person is constant. Does that constant level of real GDP give people the maximum possible consumption per person? Not necessarily. Steady-state consumption per person is determined by the difference between real GDP per person and steady-state investment per person. Visually, it is determined by the gap (vertical distance) between the per capita production function (*PF*) and the steady-state investment line (*SS*) shown in Figure 10.9. Consumption per person is maximized where that gap is widest. This occurs when the slope of the per capita production function — the marginal product of capital — equals the slope of the steady-state investment line — the population growth rate. The situation in which consumption per person is maximized in the steady state is called the **golden rule**. To achieve the golden rule, the saving curve must intersect the *SS* line at that level of capital per person at which the marginal product of capital equals the population growth rate. There is nothing that guarantees this outcome, although the example of the steady state that we first calculated in Figure 10.6 is a golden rule steady state. A higher saving rate results in higher real GDP per person but lower consumption per person. A lower saving rate results in lower GDP and lower consumption per person.

We've now seen how the neoclassical growth model generates a steady state. We've also seen that the growth rate does not depend on the saving rate, although changes in the growth rate do occur, temporarily, when the saving rate changes. Now the question is, how do the predictions of the neoclassical model compare with reality?

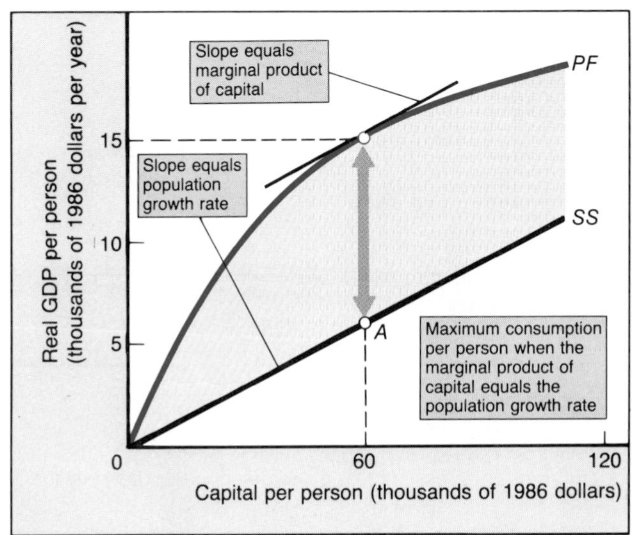

FIGURE 10.9
The Golden Rule

Possible steady-state values of consumption per person are shown by the shaded part of the figure. The actual level of consumption per person depends on the fraction of income saved. Consumption per person is maximized when the slope of the production function — the marginal product of capital — equals the slope of the steady-state investment line — the population growth rate. This is the golden rule. If the saving curve passes through point *A*, the economy has achieved maximum consumption per person — the golden rule. Saving may be either too great or too small to achieve the golden rule.

TESTCASE

10.4 *Comparisons of Growth Rates and Saving Rates Around the World*

Saving rates vary enormously across countries. Japan has the highest rate at 35 percent of GDP. The developing countries of the South Pacific, Africa, and Asia have the lowest saving rates at around 15 percent of GDP. Developed industrial countries, such as Canada, the United States, and Western Europe, as well as the countries of South America, have intermediate saving rates of between 20 and 25 percent of GDP.

Countries also differ in their growth rates of real income per person. Does a country's growth rate of real income per person relate to its saving rate? Or, as predicted by the neoclassical model, is the growth rate independent of the saving rate?

These questions are answered in Figure 10.10, which shows the growth rates of real GDP per person and the saving rates for individual countries, such as Japan, and for groups of countries, such as Asia. As you can see from that figure, countries with a high saving rate tend to have a high growth rate of real GDP per person as well. The relationship is not a precise one. But Japan, the country with the highest saving rate also has the highest growth rate. Oceania, a group of poor countries of the South Pacific, has the lowest saving rate and the lowest growth rate. Countries with intermediate saving rates, such as Canada and the United States, have an intermediate growth rate. There are some exceptions to the general rule. Australia and New Zealand have a high saving rate but a relatively low growth rate, while "other Europe"—Turkey, Portugal, and the smaller European countries—have an average saving rate but a high growth rate.

How can we explain the relationship between growth rates and saving rates? Can the neoclassical growth model account for these facts?

FIGURE 10.10
Growth Rates and Saving Rates Around the World

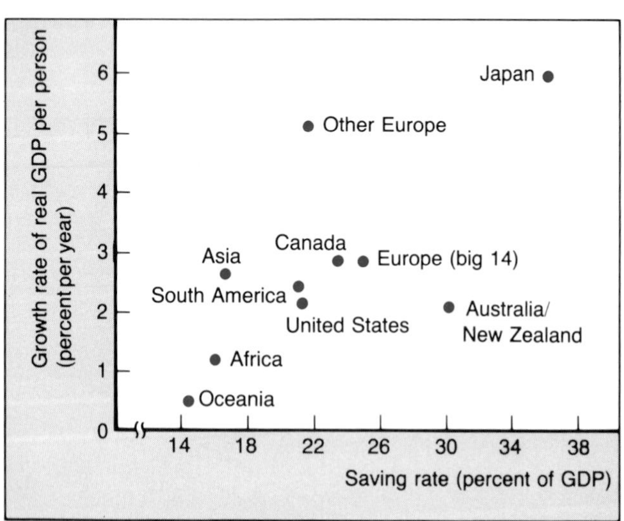

The average growth rate from 1960 to 1985 and the average saving rate for those same years is shown for 10 countries (or groups of countries). There is a positive correlation between the growth rate and saving rate.

Source: Alan Heston and Robert Summers, "A New Set of International Comparisons of Real Product and Price Levels; Estimates for 130 Countries, 1950-1985," *Review of Income and Wealth*, Series 34, vol. 1, 1988, pp. 1-25.

10.5 *Technological Change and Economic Growth*

The most important source of ongoing increases in real GDP per person is technological change. Advances have taken place on the farms, in the coal mines, in automobile production lines, steel mills, chemical plants, and factories producing just about every different type of good that we consume.

A great deal of research has been, and continues to be, undertaken to probe and deepen our understanding of the forces at work producing technological change. Despite all the effort, we still know relatively little about this process. But two things we do know. First, technological change is not a free gift of nature—it results from enormous human effort and the application of vast human and capital resources to the task of discovery. Second, there are "lucky breaks" in the quest for new knowledge. The two main approaches to understanding technological change emphasize one or the other of these facts. One approach, emphasizing the "lucky breaks," treats technological change as *exogenous*. It just happens and our ability to produce improves at an *exogenously determined rate*. The other approach emphasizes that the pace of technological change, while random, is influenced by the choices people make. In the rest of this section we'll think of technological change as an exogenous process.

When technological change takes place, the *per capita production function* shifts upward. Such a shift is shown in Figure 10.11. But this is not all that happens. Technological change brings additional capital accumulation. Advances in technology enable us to produce more output per person, giving us bigger incomes per person. And bigger incomes bring bigger saving that results in a larger stock of capital. Thus technological change increases income per person for two reasons. First, with the new technology we can produce more output from given inputs, and second, with more real income we save more and therefore accumulate more capital.

You can see these effects in Figure 10.11. The economy initially is on the per capita production function PF_0 and capital per person is \$60,000. A technological advance shifts the production function upward to PF_1. The saving curve also shifts upward, from

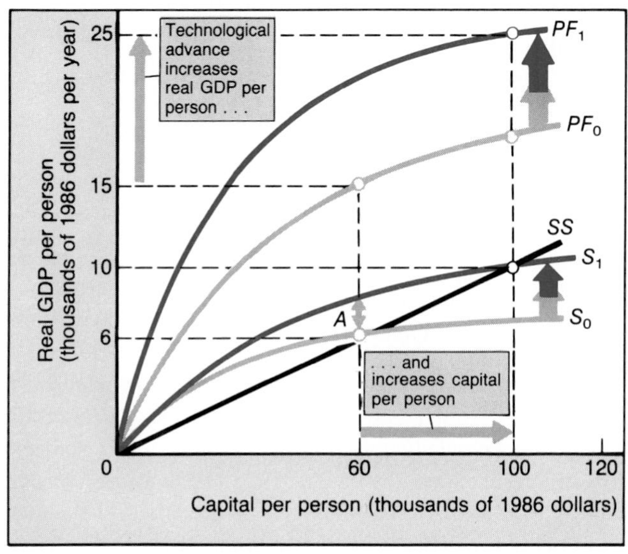

FIGURE 10.11
Technological Change and Economic Growth

A technological advance shifts the per capita production function up, from PF_0 to PF_1. The saving curve also shifts up from S_0 to S_1. With no change in capital per person, output increases and so do saving and investment. Investment now exceeds the amount needed to maintain a constant level of capital per person. Capital increases, increasing output further. A new steady state is eventually reached at which capital per person is \$100,000 and real GDP per person is \$25,000.

S_0 to S_1. At the initial capital per person, saving now results in a rate of capital accumulation that exceeds the population growth rate. Capital per person increases and so does real GDP per person. The economy converges to a new steady state where capital per person is $100,000.

Capital accumulation and the pace of technological change

We've seen that technological change leads to more capital accumulation. But technological change and capital accumulation interact in another way that runs in the opposite direction. An economy with a high rate of capital accumulation (a high investment rate) can also enjoy more rapid technological advance because most technological change takes the form of introducing new and more advanced types of capital. If the investment rate is low, new technology is adopted slowly. When the investment rate is high, new technology is adopted more rapidly. Thus the pace of technological innovation depends on the rate of capital accumulation. Economies that accumulate capital innovate quickly and enjoy the fruits of technological change earlier than others. They grow faster. This is one of the reasons we see a correlation between saving rates and growth rates in Figure 10.10. But it is not the only reason. The other is that technological change is not exogenous.

10.6 *Endogenous Technological Change and Increasing Returns*

It is obvious that the pace of technological change is influenced by people's choices. Every year in Canada and the other major industrial countries, close to 3 percent of GDP is spent on research and development—approaching $300 billion in 1990 in North America, Western Europe, and Japan. We do not have to spend this much on gaining new knowledge, and we could spend more. What determines the amount spent on finding new technologies? And how do these choices influence the rate of economic growth? Let's look at a model proposed by Paul Romer in the mid-1980s that tackles these questions.

The Romer endogenous technology model

Romer's model of the economy has a large number of competitive firms. Each firm is small relative to the size of the economy and produces output using four factors of production:

1. Labor
2. Capital
3. Its own technological knowledge
4. Economywide (aggregate) technological knowledge

The first two factors are the ones in the neoclassical model that we've just studied. The last two are new and need some explanation.

Firm's own knowledge Each firm can accumulate knowledge, just as it can accumulate capital. The more knowledge it accumulates, the greater is its output, other things being equal. But knowledge, like capital and labor, is subject to diminishing returns. **Diminishing returns** are the decreases in the *marginal product of a factor of production* as more of the factor is employed, other inputs held constant. So firms choose the amount of "knowledge" to employ in the same way they choose how much labor and capital to employ. When the marginal product of a factor equals the factor's marginal cost, profit is maximized.

Each firm's own knowledge is like a type of capital. Savings are devoted both to the accumulation of conventional capital—plant, equipment, and buildings—and to the accumulation of knowledge. The amount devoted to accumulating knowledge determines the rate of growth of income, consumption, saving, and capital accumulation per person. The per capita growth rate is endogenous.

Aggregate knowledge Economywide, or aggregate, knowledge is the sum of what every firm and worker knows. In Romer's model, the output of each firm depends on this aggregate stock of knowledge. Simply because there are other knowledgeable firms and workers around, an individual firm can produce more. For example, McDonald's can produce more hamburgers and fries in Toronto with a given labor force and stock of equipment than it can in Moscow because it can hire labor and other inputs from suppliers who have a greater stock of knowledge than their Soviet counterparts. Northern Telecom can produce communication control software more efficiently in Ontario, where the labor force and other suppliers have a large stock of knowledge about electronic communication technology, than it could in the Caribbean.

When a firm decides how much knowledge to accumulate, it evaluates the effects of its decision on its own profits. It does not take account of the fact that its own accumulation of knowledge will bring benefits to other firms. Economywide knowledge is an **externality**, a cost or benefit experienced by one economic agent that results from the actions of another agent or agents. Because economywide knowledge is an externality, when one firm invests resources in advancing its own knowledge, it is at the same time expanding the production possibilities of all the other firms in the economy as well. And for the whole economy, there are increasing returns to knowledge. **Increasing returns** occur when the marginal product of a factor of production *increases* as the quantity of the factor employed increases, other inputs held constant.

The presence of externalities and increasing returns to knowledge make it possible for a large and rich economy to grow indefinitely at a faster pace than a small and poor economy. They also make it possible for an economy to grow at an increasing pace as it becomes larger and richer. To see why, consider the following real-world example.

One of the major technological advances of the late 1970s and 1980s has been the development of low-cost, high-speed computing power. In the rich developed countries, vast numbers of people have easy access to this computing power. There are also large numbers of well trained people able to use their enhanced computing power not only to produce goods and services at lower cost but also to develop even newer technologies. Computers are used to design computers. As a matter of fact, the state-of-the-art microchip, the Intel 486, could not have been designed and manufactured without the previous developments and refinements of earlier generations of microprocessors.

The opportunities that exist in rich countries with a large and highly skilled labor force working with advanced technologies to advance technologies further are not so widely or readily available in poorer countries. In such countries, a much smaller proportion of the work force has the skills necessary to take advantage of new technologies.

In a nutshell, technological change expands production possibilities, enabling people to devote more resources to all activities, including sustaining or even accelerating the pace of technological change itself. The ability to exploit this potential increases as economies become richer.

Are Romer's ideas about the ability of increasing returns in economywide knowledge to accelerate the growth rates of richer nations important in reality? That's not yet settled. For now, let's look at some of the evidence on technological change and economic growth.

TESTCASE

10.7 *Growth Rates and Technological Change*

We've seen that real income per person can increase for two reasons — increases in capital per person or technological change. We've also seen that because technological change is influenced by people's choices and because there are externalities and possibly increasing returns in knowledge, growth rates may differ between large, rich countries and small, poor ones. How important are the two sources of economic growth? Have most increases in real income resulted from capital accumulation or from technological change? And do rich countries get even richer while the poor grow at a slower pace?

The Solow "residual" estimate of technological change

Robert Solow has suggested an interesting method for decomposing the income growth into two parts, one resulting from capital accumulation and the other from technological change. This method involves calculating the **Solow residual**, an estimate of the contribution of technological change to the change in output. To calculate the Solow residual, we start with the per capita production function, which we can write as Equation (10.5):

$$\left(\frac{y}{n}\right) = A\left(\frac{k}{n}\right)^a. \tag{10.5}$$

Here, y is real GDP, n is the population, and k is the capital stock. Thus y/n is GDP per person and k/n is the capital stock per person. The coefficient a is a constant (fraction) equal to the share of GDP accounted for by income from capital. The coefficient tells us that when capital per person increases, so does output per person, but a 1 percent increase in capital per person brings an a percent increase in real GDP per person. Using data on output, the capital stock, and population, we can calculate GDP per person and capital per person. We can also calculate the coefficient A. The coefficient A changes when technology changes. It is the Solow residual estimate of the influence of technological change.

We've estimated the Solow residual for Canada for the period from 1975 to 1990; the result is shown in Figure 10.12. Here, the black line shows the growth of real GDP per person. The light blue line shows what real GDP per person would have been in the absence of any further changes in technology after 1954 but with capital accumulation at the same pace that actually occurred. The blue line shows the Solow residual estimate of the effects on economic growth of technological change.

Two things stand out in Figure 10.12. First, most *fluctuations* in the growth rate of real GDP per person come from fluctuations in the Solow residual. By comparison, fluctuations arising from fluctuations in the pace of capital accumulation are very small. Second, capital accumulation has accounted for the ongoing, steady upward drift in real GDP per person.

But the Solow residual is an ambiguous measure of the contribution of technological change. In some ways it *underestimates* its importance and in other ways it *overestimates* it.

Underestimates The Solow residual underestimates the contribution of technological change to economic growth because it does not recognize the fact that the pace of capital accumulation is faster with technological change than without it. That is, technological change brings higher incomes, some part of which is saved and accumulated as additional capital, which raises income even more.

Overestimates The Solow residual overestimates the importance of technological change because it combines many separate influences, each of which is hard to measure separately. It includes at least the following:

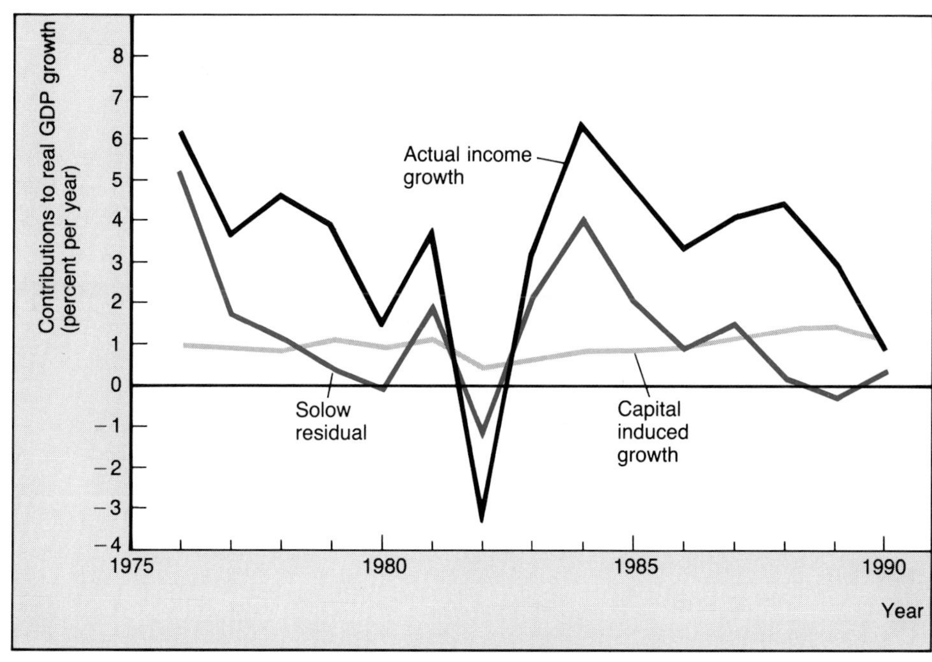

FIGURE 10.12
Real GDP Growth, Capital Accumulation, and Technological Change

Most of the *fluctuations* in real GDP growth (black line) are accounted for by fluctuations in the Solow residual (blue line). Fluctuations in the growth rate of capital are small in comparison.

Source: National Income and Product Accounts of Canada and our calculations.

- Technological advances
- The accumulation of human capital
- Changes in the composition of the labor force
- Changes in the composition of output
- Variations in the capacity utilization rate

The Solow residual attempts to isolate the effects of technological change, but it is difficult to separately identify it from the other influences just listed. It is particularly difficult to separate the effects of changes in the compositions of output and labor force and the effects of human capital accumulation.

Is growth accelerating?

We've seen that with endogenous technical change and increasing returns to economy-wide knowledge, it is possible for large, rich economies to have an advantage over small, poorer economies and to grow even faster. Are the rich getting richer at a faster pace?

The evidence is hard to read and is mixed. We saw in Chapter 1 that the gap between the rich and the poor countries is not getting any narrower. Nor is it getting wider in percentage terms, but it *is* getting wider in absolute terms. This evidence tells us that per person growth rates are similar across countries and there is no tendency for *levels* of income to converge as predicted by the neoclassical growth model.

But rich countries, with one or two important exceptions, do not seem to have gotten richer at a faster pace. Figure 10.13, which shows the facts about Canadian growth over 7 decades, reveals no clear tendency for the growth rate to accelerate. The 1940s was the decade of fastest growth and the 1930s the decade of slowest growth. During the 1960s and 1970s, growth was steady and exceeded three percent a year. But in the 1980s, growth slowed and was lower than in any other decade except for the 1930s. In fact, the slowdown during the 1980s had many people wondering whether rapid growth was ending for good. Probably not, as we'll discover in the final section of this chapter.

FIGURE 10.13
Canadian Real GDP per Person over the Decades

Decade average growth rates show that there is no systematic tendency for growth to get faster as an economy gets richer. In fact, in the 1980s, growth slowed. The fastest growth decade was the 1940s (World War II).

Source: See Figure 10.1.

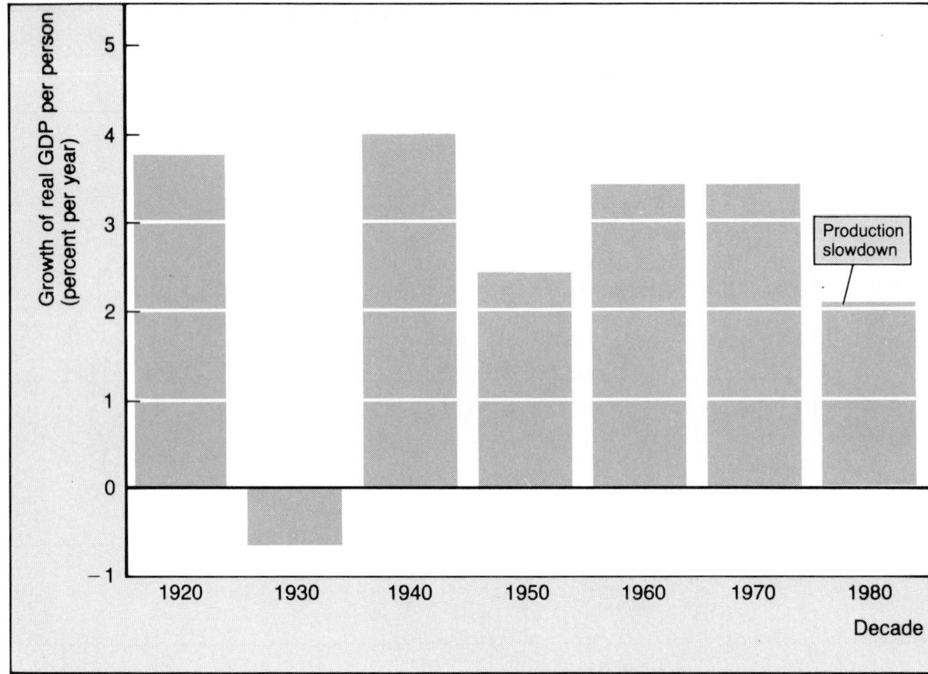

TESTCASE

10.8 *The Canadian Productivity Slowdown of the 1980s*

We saw in Figure 10.13 that real GDP per person grew at a slower pace in the 1980s than it had done in the years of strong growth of the 1960s and 1970s. In fact, real GDP grew by 3.4 percent a year on the average between 1960 and 1980 and then fell to a bare 2 percent a year in the 1980s.

What accounted for this decrease of more than 1 percent a year in the growth rate of real GDP? Although carefully scrutinized, this question still has no definitive answer. Also, the best answer currently available is not very dramatic. There is no smoking gun. Many separate factors that are hard to identify and quantify were at work. Among the more important ones so far identified are

- Energy price shocks
- Inflation
- Work force composition
- Composition of output

Energy price shocks

Energy prices and other raw material prices increased dramatically during the 1970s. First, the price of oil quadrupled in 1973-1974. As producers switched to other types of fuels, the prices of coal, natural gas, and other energy sources increased. Oil prices increased sharply again in the late 1970s and early 1980s. Higher energy prices encouraged the search for energy-saving technologies and the pace of scrapping energy-intensive capital equipment, such as gas guzzlers and inefficient airplanes and heating systems. With higher energy prices, the productivity of capital and labor declined as firms sought to economize on ever-more expensive fuels.

Because Canada is a major producer of oil and natural gas, the effects of these price increases were mixed. In Alberta, the major producing region, the economy and productivity boomed. In other regions of the country, adjustments had to be made and their economies faltered. But in the aggregate, Canada did not suffer a major economic setback in the 1970s as most other countries did.

The 1980s brought *falling* and highly volatile energy prices. As a result, the previously booming Western energy producing region suffered as income growth flagged and unemployment increased.

Inflation

We've seen that inflation became a serious problem in the mid-1970s. The possibility that it brought a slowdown in productivity growth arises because higher inflation brings higher interest rates and higher interest rates bring higher taxes on interest income. But the taxes are levied on the nominal interest income, not the real interest income. Thus with higher inflation, after-tax real interest rates become negative. This dampens the incentive to save, and the lower saving rate leads to a lower rate of capital accumulation and slower productivity growth. If the inflation effect was important, it operated by lowering the rate at which firms accumulated capital — the extent to which profits were retained and ploughed back into new capital.

Composition of the work force

The labor force increased rapidly during the late 1970s and early 1980s, mainly from an increase in the participation rate of females in the labor force. Women are paid, on the average, about 65 percent of men's wages. The value of output is measured by the costs of the factors of production employed in producing that output. Thus an increase in output resulting from an increase in female employment gets measured as less than (around 60 percent of) the increase in output resulting from an increase in male employment. This is a further reason for the apparent slowdown in productivity in the 1980s.

Composition of output

Productivity growth rates vary across sectors of the economy. In the 1980s, the most rapid growth rates occurred in the computer and electronics industries, and the slowest growth rates occurred in the farming and construction sectors. The overall productivity growth rate depends on the relative size of the different sectors and on the speed with which resources are reallocated from one sector to another. The 1970s and 1980s saw a slowdown in the movement from the farm sector to the small-business sector. This factor contributed to the slowdown in overall productivity growth.

■ We've now completed our study of aggregate supply and of the factors that make it fluctuate and grow. In Chapters 8 and 9, we focused on fluctuations in aggregate supply and how labor markets work. In this chapter, we've studied long-term supply-side issues and have seen how capital accumulation and technological change lead to sustained economic growth and expansion.

Our task in the next three chapters on inflation, deficits, and debts is to bring the aggregate demand side of the economy back into the picture. We'll study the process of inflation, the interaction of inflation with the business cycle, and the interaction between deficits, debts, and inflation.

CHAPTER REVIEW

Summary

EXPANSION OF CANADIAN OUTPUT SINCE 1926

Real GDP has grown at an average rate of 4.1 percent a year; the population has grown at an average rate of 1.6 percent a year; real GDP per person has grown at an average rate of 2.5 percent a year. At this rate of growth, real GDP per person doubles every 28 years.

The pace of expansion has been variable. During the 1930s expansion stopped; during the 1940s, the years of World War II, it was at its highest ever rate. Post-World War II growth was rapid, especially in the 1960s and 1970s. Growth slowed down in the 1980s.

THE SOURCES OF ECONOMIC GROWTH

The two main sources of economic growth are capital accumulation and technological change.

THE NEOCLASSICAL MODEL OF ECONOMIC GROWTH

The neoclassical model of economic growth determines the level and growth rate of real GDP, consumption, saving, investment, and capital per person. In the neoclassical model, population growth and technological change are exogenous.

The neoclassical model predicts a steady-state growth rate of real GDP per person equal to the population growth rate plus the rate of technological change. The growth rate does not depend on the saving rate. The higher the saving rate, the higher is the *level* of real GDP per person and capital per person but not the growth rate. An increase in the saving rate temporarily increases the growth rate. A decrease in the population growth rate temporarily increases the growth rate of real GDP per person but does not affect its steady-state growth rate.

In the neoclassical model, consumption per person is maximized—the so-called golden rule is achieved—if the marginal product of capital equals the population growth rate.

SAVING RATE AND ECONOMIC GROWTH

Contrary to the predictions of the neoclassical growth model, there is a relationship between the saving rate and the rate of economic growth. There is a clear tendency, but not a perfect correlation, for countries that have a high saving rate to also have a high rate of growth of real GDP per person.

TECHNOLOGICAL CHANGE AND ECONOMIC GROWTH

The faster the pace of technological change, the faster is the rate of growth of real GDP per person. But technological change also affects the pace of capital accumulation. More rapid technological change leads to more rapid capital accumulation. Also, countries with a high saving rate and, therefore, a high rate of capital accumulation are able to exploit newly developed technologies at a more rapid pace.

Technological change can influence a firm's ability to produce in two ways. First, advances in the firm's own knowledge increase its production potential; second, advances in the economywide stock of knowledge place each firm in a more productive environment. The economy as a whole may enjoy increasing returns in the economywide stock of knowledge. If this is the case, lucky breaks in the search for new technologies not only expand the level of production possibilities but also increase the rate at which they subsequently expand.

TECHNOLOGICAL CHANGE AND CANADIAN ECONOMIC GROWTH

It is difficult to isolate the effects of technological change on economic growth. One measure is the Solow residual. This measure suggests that most of the *fluctuations* in the growth rate of real GDP are associated with fluctuations in the pace of technological change and not with fluctuations in the growth of capital per person.

CANADIAN PRODUCTIVITY SLOWDOWN OF THE 1980s

Productivity growth in the Canadian economy slowed in the 1980s by more than 1 percent a year compared with its level of the 1960s and 1970s. Many factors contributed to this slowdown. The more important ones are energy price shocks, inflation, changes in the composition of the work force, and changes in the composition of output.

Key Terms and Concepts

Diminishing returns The decreases in the marginal product of a factor of production as more of the factor is employed, other inputs held constant.

Externality A cost or benefit experienced by one economic agent that results from the actions of another agent or agents.

Golden rule The situation in which consumption per person is maximized in the steady state.

Increasing returns A situation in which the marginal product of a factor of production increases as the quantity of the factor employed increases, other inputs held constant.

Marginal product of capital The increase in real GDP per person resulting from a one-unit increase in capital per person.

Neoclassical growth model A model that determines real GDP per person, consumption and saving per person, capital per person, and the economic growth rate.

Per capita production function The relationship between output per person and capital per person.

Solow residual An estimate of the contribution of technological change to the change in output.

Steady state A situation in which the relevant variables are constant over time.

Review Questions

1. Describe the growth rate of real GDP per person in Canada from 1926 to 1990. When was Canadian growth fastest and slowest? How would you describe the Canadian growth rate over the 1980s?
2. What are the two sources of economic growth? Explain how each factor increases real GDP per person.
3. Describe the neoclassical growth model. What does this model determine?
4. If the saving rate increases, does the neoclassical growth model predict a change in economic growth? Explain your answer.
5. If technology advances, does the neoclassical growth model predict an increase in economic growth? Explain your answer.
6. If the population growth rate rises by 10 percent a year, what is the predicted change in economic growth?

7. Explain the golden rule. Draw a figure to show that it works.
8. In the real world, is economic growth independent of the saving rate, as predicted by the neoclassical growth model? Explain your answer.
9. What are the main features of Romer's model?
10. Do the predictions of Romer's model match those of the neoclassical growth model? Explain you answer.
11. What are increasing returns to knowledge? How do they come about?
12. What is an externality? Explain why economywide knowledge is an externality.
13. What is Solow's residual? Is it a good estimate?
14. Explain why large rich countries grow faster than small poor countries.
15. Can the neoclassical growth model explain the Canadian productivity slowdown of the 1970s? If so, how; if not, why not?

Problems

1. An economy's per capita production function is

$$(y/n) = (k/n) - 0.2(k/n)^2.$$

The marginal propensity to consume is 0.9 and the population growth rate is 5 percent a year.
(a) What is the saving curve?
(b) What is the steady-state investment line?
(c) Which curve shows capital accumulation?
(d) What is steady-state capital per person?
(e) If capital per person is 1, explain why capital per person increases.
(f) If capital per person is 3, explain why capital per person decreases.

2. In problem 1, technological change increases the output that any inputs can produce by 10 percent.
(a) What is the new per capita production function?
(b) What is the new saving curve?
(c) What is the change in the steady-state growth rate?

3. In problem 1, the saving rate doubles.
(a) What is the new saving curve?
(b) What is the change in the steady-state growth rate?
(c) What is the new steady-state real GDP per person?
(d) What is the new steady-state consumption per person?
(e) What is the new steady-state investment per person?

4. An economy's per capita production function is

$$(y/n) = (k/n) - 0.25(k/n)^2.$$

The marginal propensity to consume is 0.9, and the population growth rate is 4 percent a year. Calculate:
(a) The steady-state investment line
(b) The saving curve
(c) Steady-state capital per person
(d) Steady-state real GDP per person
(e) Steady-state consumption per person
(f) Steady-state saving per person
(g) Steady-state investment per person
(h) The steady-state economic growth rate

5. In problem 4, the marginal propensity to consume falls to 0.8 and the population growth rate increases to 5 percent a year. What are your answers now?

IV

Inflation, Deficits, and Debts

CHAPTER

11 Inflation, Interest Rates, and the Exchange Rate

IT'S ONLY MONEY

BETWEEN 1970 AND 1990, PRICES, on the average, increased by 360 percent in Canada. The annual average inflation rate was 6.6 percent. A Big Mac that today costs $2.20 cost only 55¢ in 1970; a first-class letter that today needs a 40¢ stamp cost only 7¢ to mail in 1970; a $145,000 house in 1990 cost only $40,000 in 1970.

As prices have increased, so have wages and other incomes. Average hourly earnings in 1970 were less than $4. By 1990, they were approaching $20.

We're paying more money for the goods and services we buy and we're receiving more money for the work we perform. There's more money flowing around our economy. Our wallets are stuffed with more dollars and our bank accounts are larger. In 1970, the average Canadian held $200 in currency. By 1990, that amount had increased to $750. Balances in chequing accounts and savings accounts increased from $2,000 in 1970 to $8,500 by 1990.

Does it matter that prices, wages, and the amount of money flowing around our economy keep on rising year after year? What causes this ongoing inflation? And what are its consequences? What has to be done to cure it? And is curing it costly? If it is, is it worth the cost?

This and the next two chapters tackle various aspects of these questions. In this chapter, we study trends in inflation. Our focus is on why inflation rates vary from one country to another and from one time period to another. We'll also examine the effects of inflation on interest rates and the foreign exchange value of the dollar. In the next chapter, we study short-term fluctuations in inflation and the relationship between inflation and the business cycle. Then, in Chapter 13, we study the relationship between deficits, debts, and inflation.

After studying this chapter, you will be able to

- Describe the diversity of inflation, interest rates, and money growth around the world in the 1980s
- Explain the effects of an anticipated increase in the growth rate of the money supply on inflation and real GDP
- Illustrate the effects of anticipated inflation with Israel's experience in the 1980s
- Explain the effects of inflation on interest rates
- Illustrate the effects of inflation on interest rates with Switzerland's and Brazil's experiences in the 1980s
- Explain how inflation is determined in an open economy with a fixed exchange rate

- Illustrate inflation in a fixed exchange rate economy with the experiences of the major countries in the 1960s and the countries of the European Monetary System (EMS) in the 1980s
- Explain how inflation is determined in an open economy with a flexible exchange rate
  - Illustrate inflation in a flexible exchange rate economy with the world inflationary experience of the 1980s

Let's begin by looking at some facts about inflation, interest rates, and money growth around the world.

11.1 *Inflation, Money Supply Growth, and Interest Rates Around the World*

MACROFACTS

Inflation is a process of rising prices and the *inflation rate* is measured as the percentage change in a *price index*, such as the *Consumer Price Index* or *GDP deflator*.

Inflation has been a persistent feature of economic life in Canada since the 1930s but, as we saw in Chapter 3, its rate has varied. We've just seen that in the 20 years between 1970 and 1990, inflation averaged 6.6 percent a year. But at its peak in 1975 and again in 1981, it reached rates of 10 percent a year or more.

Canadian inflation has been mild compared with that of several other countries. And the range of inflation experienced is enormous. For example, on the average, during the five years between 1979 and 1984, when Canadian inflation averaged a little over 10 percent a year, Japan had virtually no inflation—just 2 percent a year—while Bolivia galloped along at an inflation rate of 200 percent a year. And even Bolivia's 200 percent is not a record. By 1985, that country's inflation had soared to 12,000 percent a year. Nicaragua notched up a 10,000 percent inflation in 1988 and Peru a 3,400 percent inflation in 1989. And big inflations are not exclusive to the Latin American world. Israel's inflation hit close to 400 percent a year in 1984.

Figure 11.1 illustrates some of the range and diversity of world inflation experience. Here, the average inflation rate for the five years 1979 to 1984 is shown for 62 countries. The figure plots the average inflation rate of each country against its money supply growth rate over the same period. The blue 45° line is a reference indicating equality between the inflation rate and the money supply growth rate; as you can see, the dots cluster around it. High-inflation countries have high money supply growth rates. Identify Bolivia, Israel, Zaire, Iceland, Peru, and Mexico, all countries with inflation rates and money supply growth rates in excess of 50 percent a year.

Most countries have low inflation rates and, in Figure 11.1(a), they are almost invisible. Figure 11.1(b) zooms in on the dots representing these countries so that we can see them more clearly. Canada is identified in this figure but the other countries are not individually named.

Notice in both parts of Figure 11.1 the clear tendency for inflation rates and money supply growth rates to be positively correlated. Correlation, especially strong for the high inflation countries, is present for all countries.

Next, let's look at interest rates and inflation between 1979 and 1984. Reliable data on interest rates are available for only a small set of the countries featured in Figure 11.1. Interest rates in these countries and their inflation rates are graphed in Figure 11.2. In this figure, the 45° line identifies points where the real interest rate is zero. At points above this line real interest rates are positive and at points below it real interest rates are negative. As you can see, the real interest rate is positive in most countries.

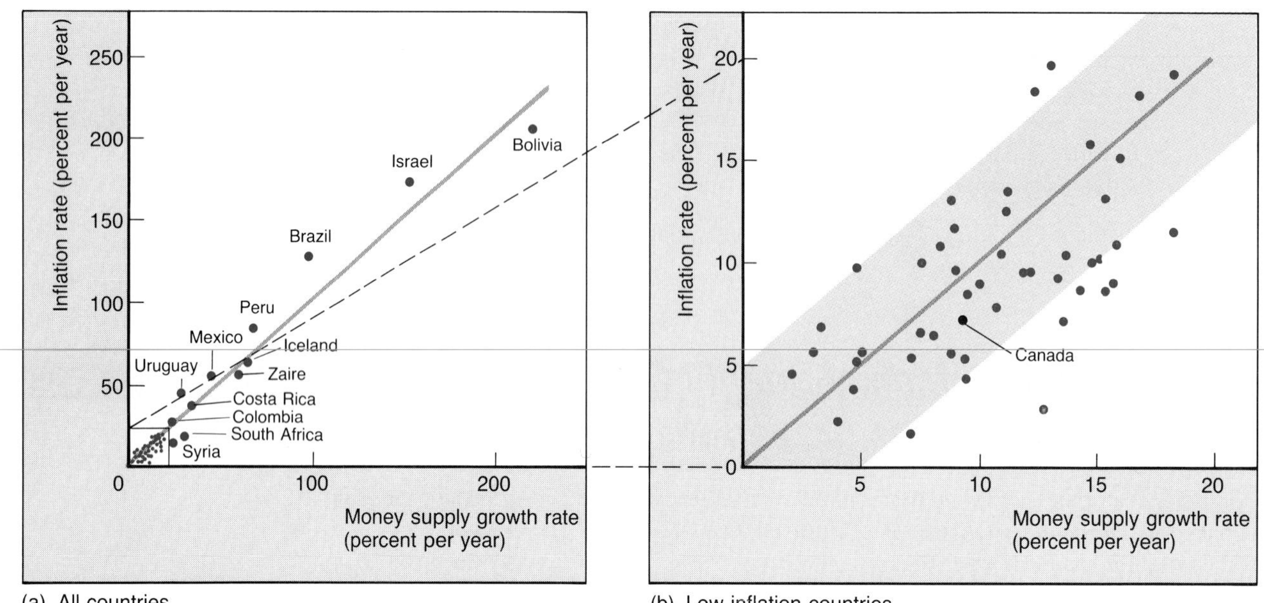

(a) All countries

(b) Low inflation countries

FIGURE 11.1
Inflation and Money Supply Growth Around the World

A strong positive correlation exists between money supply growth rates and inflation rates. The correlation is strongest across high inflation countries (highlighted in part a) but still visible for low-inflation countries (the enlargement shown in part b).

Source: Federal Reserve Bank of St. Louis, *Review*, May-June, 1988, p. 15.

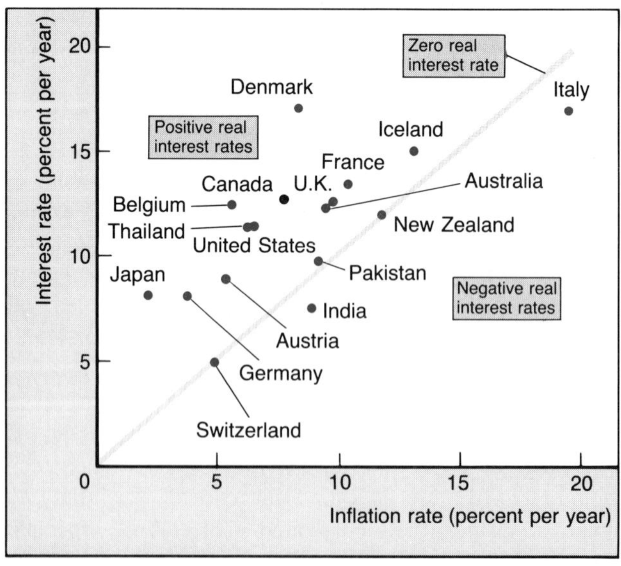

FIGURE 11.2
Interest Rates and Inflation

There is a positive correlation between interest rates and inflation. Most countries have positive real interest rates (interest rates exceed inflation); a few countries have had negative real interest rates (interest rates less than inflation).

Source: International Financial Statistics Yearbook, 1991.

The exceptions shown here are India and Italy. You can also see, however, a clear tendency for interest rates to be higher, the higher the inflation rate. The relationship is not perfect. There are variations in real interest rates from one country to another, but the correlation between interest rates and inflation is strong.

Why are money supply growth rates and inflation rates correlated? And why are inflation rates and interest rates correlated? What are the economic mechanisms generating these correlations? These are the questions this chapter answers.

Let's begin by studying the relationship between money supply growth and inflation.

11.2 *Inflation and Money Growth*

Inflation, the process of rising prices, is measured as the percentage rate of change in the price level. You already know that the aggregate demand–aggregate supply model determines the price level. We can use this model to study inflation, understanding the forces that generate ongoing changes in aggregate demand and aggregate supply. These forces lead to persistent shifts in the aggregate demand and aggregate supply curves and persistent changes in the price level. That is, we want to understand the forces generating persistent shifts in the aggregate demand and aggregate supply curves and the process of inflation. We also want to establish the quantitative relationship between the change in the money supply and the resulting change in the price level. To achieve this, we're going to study three things:

- Money growth and aggregate demand
- Wages and aggregate supply
- Equilibrium inflation

Money growth and aggregate demand

What are the precise effects of a change in the money supply on the aggregate demand curve? That is, by how much does the aggregate demand curve shift when the money supply changes by a given percentage amount? We can answer this question most clearly by recalling the connection between the aggregate demand curve and the *IS-LM* model of aggregate demand. Figure 11.3 illustrates the analysis (and provides a quick refresher).

In part (a), the point of intersection of the *IS* and *LM* curves determines the equilibrium interest rate and equilibrium level of real GDP at a given price level. Recall that for a given money supply, the price level determines the position of the *LM* curve. Therefore the *IS-LM* intersection determines a point on the aggregate demand curve. Suppose that initially the price level is 100 and the aggregate demand curve is AD_0 in part (b). Keeping the money supply constant and varying the price level, the *LM* curve in part (a) shifts, generating points along the aggregate demand curve.

But now suppose that the money supply increases by 10 percent, say from $2 billion to $2.2 billion. By how much does that increase in the money supply shift the aggregate demand curve? We answered this question in Chapter 6. But there our emphasis was on the magnitude of the horizontal shift in the aggregate demand curve. In other words, we were concerned with the change in real GDP at a given price level. Here let's concentrate on the vertical distance by which the aggregate demand curve moves. That is, let's establish the amount by which the price level increases at a given level of real GDP.

We know that if the price level increases by the same percentage as the increase in the money supply, the *LM* curve does not shift. Thus the *LM* curve in part (a) is the

FIGURE 11.3
Money Supply Growth and the Aggregate Demand Curve

The intersection of the *IS* and *LM* curves determines the equilibrium interest rate and level of real GDP at a given price level. The position of the *LM* curve depends on the price level and the money supply. But the same *LM* curve can arise from a variety of combinations of money supply and price level. An equal percentage increase in the money supply and the price level leaves the *LM* curve undisturbed and determines the same equilibrium level of real GDP. Thus an increase in the money supply shifts the aggregate demand curve (part b), and the percentage vertical displacement of the aggregate demand curve equals the percentage increase in the money supply.

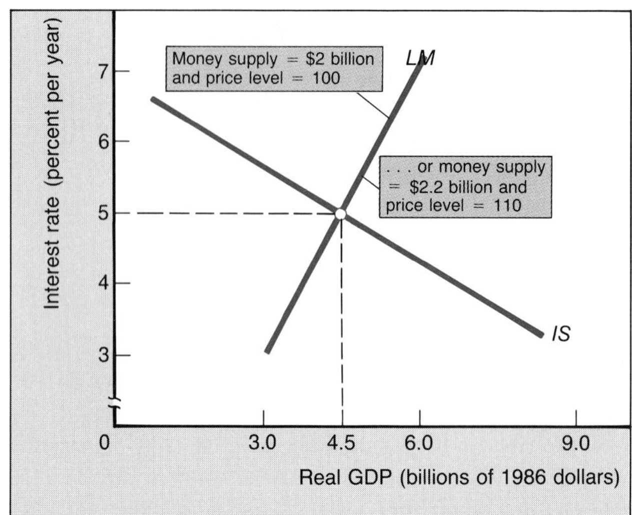

(a) *IS–LM* Equilibrium

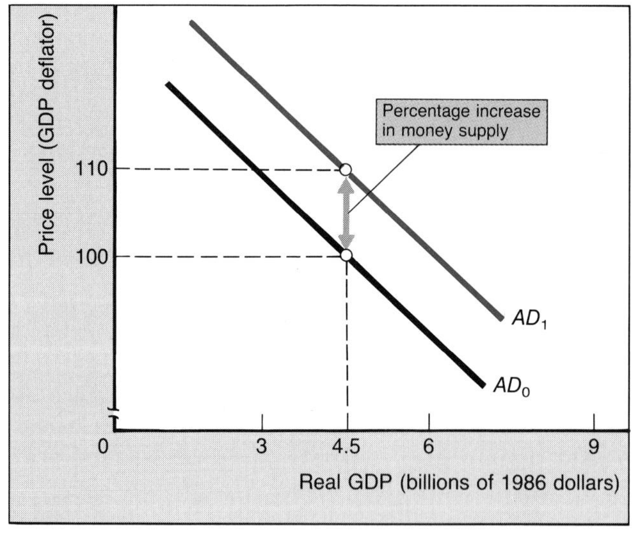

(b) *AD* curve

same when the money supply is $2.2 billion and the price level is 110 as the *LM* curve for a money supply of $2 billion and a price level of 100. In other words, the equilibrium level of real GDP is the same when the price level is higher by the same percentage as the increase in the money supply. Therefore we know that a new aggregate demand curve, AD_1, lies above (and to the right of) AD_0 and that the vertical distance between the two aggregate demand curves is such that the percentage increase in the price level equals the percentage increase in the money supply. That is, a 10 percent increase in the money supply shifts the aggregate demand curve upward by 10 percent.

This is an important result that we'll use after we've studied wages and aggregate supply.

Wages and aggregate supply

The position of the short-run aggregate supply curve is influenced by all the forces that affect long-run aggregate supply as well as by the level of money wages. Changes in long-run aggregate supply are going on in the background; but because our focus in this chapter is on the price level and inflation, we'll ignore them.

With other things held constant, the higher the money wage rate, the lower is the real GDP supplied at any given price level. In other words, the higher the money wage rate, the farther to the left is the short-run aggregate supply curve.

We can measure the shift in the short-run aggregate supply curve in two ways: how far the curve shifts to the left at a given price level and how far the curve shifts upward at a given level of real GDP. Because here we're interested in the price level and inflation, we'll find the magnitude of the shift upward at a given level of real GDP.

Any given percentage change in the money wage rate shifts the short-run aggregate supply curve vertically such that the change in the price level at a given level of real GDP equals the percentage change in the money wage rate. Figure 11.4 illustrates such a shift. Initially, the short-run aggregate supply curve is SAS_0. If the price level is 100, the quantity of goods and services supplied is \$4.5 billion. If the money wage rate increases by 10 percent, the price level at which the quantity of real GDP supplied is \$4.5 billion will be 10 percent higher. The reason is clear. For firms' profit-maximizing output to be unaffected by an increase in wages, they must be able to sell their output for a price that increases by the same percentage as the increase in wages, keeping real wages—real costs—constant.

Wage determination The short-run aggregate supply curve shifts to the left (upward) when money wages increase. But what determines the rate at which wages increase? Let's answer this question by reviewing the things we discovered when we studied the labor market in Chapter 8.

The *equilibrium real wage rate* is the real wage rate at which the quantity of labor demanded equals the quantity of labor supplied. Equivalently, it is the real wage rate when the unemployment rate equals the natural rate of unemployment. If the quantity of labor demanded exceeds the quantity of labor supplied, the real wage rate increases. If the quantity of labor demanded is less than the quantity of labor supplied, the real wage

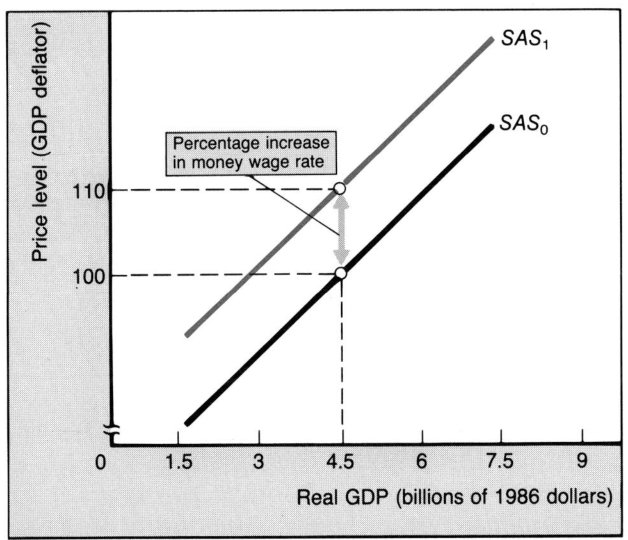

FIGURE 11.4
Wage Increases and the Short-Run Aggregate Supply Curve

The position of the short-run aggregate supply curve depends on the money wage rate. An increase in the money wage rate shifts the short-run aggregate supply curve to the left. The percentage vertical gap between the original and new short-run aggregate supply curve measures the percentage increase in the money wage rate.

rate decreases. Most economists believe that these movements in real wages are gradual rather than sudden and cause the labor market to move toward its equilibrium relatively slowly. Nevertheless, real wages do change in response to labor market conditions, increasing when there is excess demand and decreasing when there is excess supply.

The *money wage rate* is the *real wage rate* multiplied by the *price level*. Although the equilibrating forces in the labor market move the real wage rate, it is actually the money wage rate that is determined in labor market contracts. To maintain constant real wages, the money wage rate must change at the same rate as prices are changing — at the inflation rate. If money wages increase more quickly than prices, the real wage rate increases. If money wages increase less quickly than prices, the real wage rate decreases.

You can put these propositions about money wages together with what you know about the forces moving the labor market toward equilibrium. If there is an excess demand for labor, real wages increase and, to do so, money wages increase at a higher rate than inflation. If there is an excess supply of labor, real wages decrease and, to do so, money wages increase at a slower pace than the rate of inflation. With labor market equilibrium and a constant real wage, money wages increase at the same rate as prices — the rate of wage change equals the rate of inflation.

Most labor contracts involve a wage rate agreed to for a fairly long period into the future. (Labor contracts most commonly run for one to three years.) In agreeing to a money wage rate for a future period, firms and workers are taking a position on what the inflation rate will be. Even though they cannot know what that inflation rate is actually going to be, they agree on the basis of expectations. Thus the *expected inflation rate* plays an important role in determining the rate of wage increase, and wage increases influence the *actual inflation rate*. Therefore to determine the actual inflation rate, we need to know how the expected inflation rate is determined.

Inflation expectations The **expected inflation rate** is the forecasted inflation rate for some future period. To make their forecasts, people use all the information available to them about the forces that generate inflation and forecast the strength of those forces in the most efficient way possible. Such forecasts are called rational expectations. Specifically, a **rational expectation** is a forecast about the future value of an economic variable made using all available information. A rational expectation has two important properties. First, it is unbiased. The expected forecast error is zero. There is as much chance of being wrong on the upside as on the downside, and by an equal amount. Second, the forecast has the minimum possible range of error. This does not mean that it might not be wildly wrong, but there is no way to reduce the range of error in the forecast.

Once people have made the best forecast they can of future inflation, they're able to agree on the amount to increase wages for the upcoming period. Money wages will increase by an amount equal to the expected inflation rate, plus or minus an adjustment for the state of demand pressure in the labor market. With excess demand, wages will increase by more than the expected inflation rate; with excess supply, wages will increase by less than the expected inflation rate; and in labor market equilibrium, wages will increase at a rate equal to the expected inflation rate.

Equilibrium inflation

We've discovered that an increase in the money supply increases aggregate demand and shifts the aggregate demand curve (vertically) upward by the same percentage amount as the percentage increase in the money supply. We've also discovered that an increase in wages decreases aggregate supply, shifting the short-run aggregate supply curve to the left such that the vertical shift equals the percentage increase in wages. Finally, we've discovered that wages increase at a rate determined by the *expected* rate of inflation.

Equilibrium inflation is the outcome of the mix of these three forces. To determine that inflation rate, we need to distinguish between anticipated and unanticipated inflation.

Anticipated and unanticipated inflation **Anticipated inflation** is a process in which prices are increasing at the rates forecasted by all economic actors. In an anticipated inflation, the actual inflation rate equals the expected inflation rate. An **unanticipated inflation** is a process in which prices increase at a pace that has been incorrectly forecast to some degree. That is, in an unanticipated inflation, the actual inflation rate is not equal to the expected inflation rate.

Here, and for the rest of this chapter, we're going to focus on anticipated inflation. In Chapter 12, we'll redirect that focus to the more common situation of unanticipated inflation.

Equilibrium We can now work out the equilibrium inflation rate when inflation is anticipated, using Figure 11.5. Initially, the aggregate demand curve is at AD_0 and the short-run aggregate supply curve is SAS_0. Real GDP is $4.5 billion and the price level is 100. Suppose that the money supply is anticipated to increase by 10 percent. This shifts the aggregate demand curve to AD_1—a vertical shift of 10 percent, the increase in the money supply.

With inflation anticipated, money wages increased by 10 percent, shifting the short-run aggregate supply curve from SAS_0 to SAS_1. The short-run aggregate supply curve shifts vertically by 10 percent, the increase in money wages. The new equilibrium occurs where AD_1 intersects SAS_1 at a price level of 110 and at the same level of real GDP as before. A 10 percent inflation has occurred. This 10 percent inflation has resulted from a 10 percent increase in the money supply and a corresponding 10 percent increase in money wages. If the money supply continues to increase at 10 percent a year, year after year, and if the increase continues to be fully anticipated, then the process illustrated in Figure 11.5 simply repeats itself. Prices, wages, and the money supply all rise by the same percentage each year.

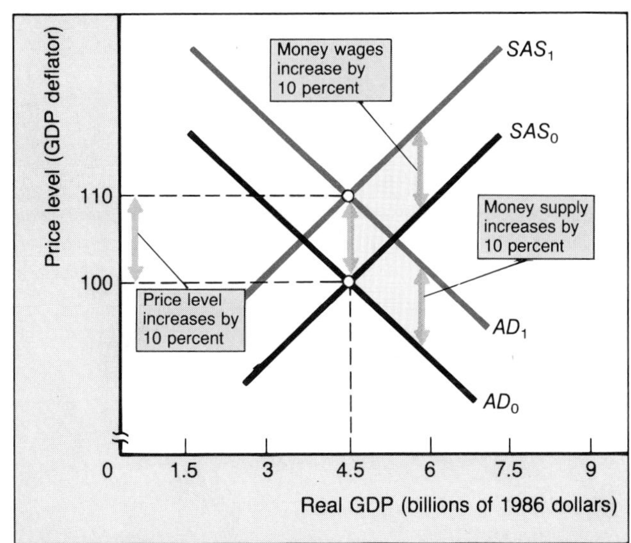

FIGURE 11.5
Anticipated Inflation

A 10 percent increase in the money supply shifts the aggregate demand curve upward by 10 percent. Because inflation is anticipated, wages also increase by 10 percent, shifting the short-run aggregate supply curve upward by that same percentage amount. The price level also increases by 10 percent, but real GDP is undisturbed.

If the money supply growth rate increases and if that increase is anticipated so that its effects are built into wage contracts, the inflation rate will also increase by the same amount as the increase in the money supply growth rate. In the opposite direction, if the money supply growth rate decreases and if the decrease is anticipated and built into wage contracts, the inflation rate will decrease. In this case, we will observe the money supply growth rate and the inflation rate fluctuating from one year to the next such that inflation and money supply growth rates line up with each other very closely.

The quantity theory of money The **quantity theory of money** is the proposition that a change in the growth rate of the money supply brings an equal percentage change in the inflation rate. The result that we have just generated is a modification of the quantity theory. We've found that an *anticipated* change in the growth rate of the money supply brings an equal percentage change in the inflation rate. It is interesting to relate these results to the quantity theory of money.

The quantity theory is an old one that was developed over two centuries and had its most refined statement in the early twentieth century in the work of Irving Fisher. The quantity theory is based on the equation of exchange. The **equation of exchange** states that the quantity of money multiplied by the velocity of circulation equals total expenditure. The equation of exchange is set out (together with some definitions and notation) in Table 11.1. The equation of exchange is just an identity. It's a definition of the velocity of circulation. The equation is always true because the velocity of circulation is the number necessary to make it true.

TABLE 11.1
The Quantity Theory of Money

Definitions:

Money supply	M;	money supply growth rate	μ
Velocity of circulation	V;	velocity growth rate	Δv
Price level	P;	inflation rate	π
Real GDP	Y;	real GDP growth rate	ρ

The equation of exchange:

$$MV = PY$$

Growth rates*:

$$\mu + \Delta v = \pi + \rho$$

The quantity theory:

Velocity is constant, so $\Delta v = 0$

Real GDP growth is independent of money supply growth

Inflation equals money growth minus real GDP growth:

$$\pi = \mu - \rho$$

***Calculations**

Start with (a)

$$MV = PY \quad \text{(a)}$$

Changes

$$\Delta M \cdot V + M\Delta V = \Delta PY + P\Delta Y \quad \text{(b)}$$

Divide (b) by (a)

$$\frac{\Delta MV}{MV} + \frac{M\Delta V}{MV} = \frac{\Delta PY}{PY} + \frac{P\Delta Y}{PY}$$

Cancel common terms

$$\frac{\Delta M \not{V}}{M \not{V}} + \frac{\not{M} \Delta V}{\not{M} V} = \frac{\Delta P \not{Y}}{P \not{Y}} + \frac{\not{P} \Delta Y}{\not{P} Y}$$

To give

$$\frac{\Delta M}{M} + \frac{\Delta V}{V} = \frac{\Delta P}{P} + \frac{\Delta Y}{Y}$$

or

$$\mu + \Delta v = \pi + \rho$$

There is a dynamic version of the equation of exchange that describes the relationship between growth rates. The growth rate of the money supply plus the growth rate of its velocity of circulation equals the growth rate of expenditure.

But what is expenditure? It is simply the price level multiplied by real GDP. So the growth rate of expenditure is the inflation rate plus the growth rate of real GDP. Thus *by definition*, the growth rate of the money supply plus the growth rate of the velocity of circulation equal the inflation rate plus the growth rate of real GDP.

The definition becomes a theory by adding some assumptions. Two key assumptions turn the equation of exchange into the quantity theory of money:

1. Velocity is constant.
2. Real GDP growth is independent of money supply growth.

If these two assumptions are correct, then inflation equals the money supply growth rate minus the growth rate of real GDP and changes in the growth rate of the money supply bring equal percentage changes in the inflation rate. These propositions are summarized in Table 11.1.

The quantity theory of money agrees with the aggregate demand–aggregate supply model of inflation that we have worked through in this section, provided we re-interpret the quantity theory of money as a theory of *anticipated* inflation. Do the propositions of the quantity theory and the *AD-AS* theory about anticipated inflation have anything to say about the real world? As a matter of fact, they do. Let's look at one such case.

11.3 *Inflation in Israel in the 1980s*

TESTCASE

Israel in the 1980s provides an interesting example of largely anticipated fluctuations in inflation. From 1980 through 1983, inflation in Israel had been remarkably steady but high. The average inflation rate in those years was around 130 percent a year. In 1984, there was an enormous burst of money supply growth and inflation. The money supply growth rate shot up to more than 400 percent a year and inflation increased to almost the same rate. Real GDP growth changed hardly at all, continuing to grow at a rate very close to its long-run average growth rate. (See Figure 11.6.)

Then, in 1985 and more dramatically in 1986, the money supply growth rate decreased. In 1985, it decreased from more than 400 percent to around 325 percent a year. The inflation rate fell by a similar amount. Again, real GDP growth stayed remarkably constant. In 1986, the money supply growth rate was cut back to 50 percent a year. The inflation rate also fell to about that same level. Again, real GDP growth stayed close to its long-run average level.

This episode of increasing inflation between 1983 and 1984 and then decreasing inflation from 1984 through 1986 with fairly steady real GDP growth can be interpreted using the aggregate demand–aggregate supply model as the effects of a fully (or almost fully) anticipated inflation. When the money supply growth rate increased in 1984, the anticipated inflation was built into wage contracts so wages also increased by a similar percentage. The economy stayed at full employment and continued to produce its long-run level of output. The decrease in the money supply growth rate in 1985 and 1986 was also anticipated, so that wages increased at a slower pace in line with the slower money supply growth. Thus the slowdown in inflation occurred because both the *AD* curve and *SAS* curve shifted upward but at a much slower pace than before.

The Israeli experience in the 1980s illustrates the possibility of an almost fully anticipated inflation and shows that when such changes occur, dramatic changes in money supply growth and inflation can occur that line up with each other and, at the same time, have little or no effect on economic growth.

FIGURE 11.6
Anticipated Inflation in Israel

Between 1983 and 1986, Israel experienced an explosion and then a contraction in inflation. These changes in inflation, caused by changes in the money supply growth rate (part a), were largely anticipated. As a result, real GDP was undisturbed by these monetary and inflationary developments (part b).

Source: International Financial Statistics Yearbook, 1991.

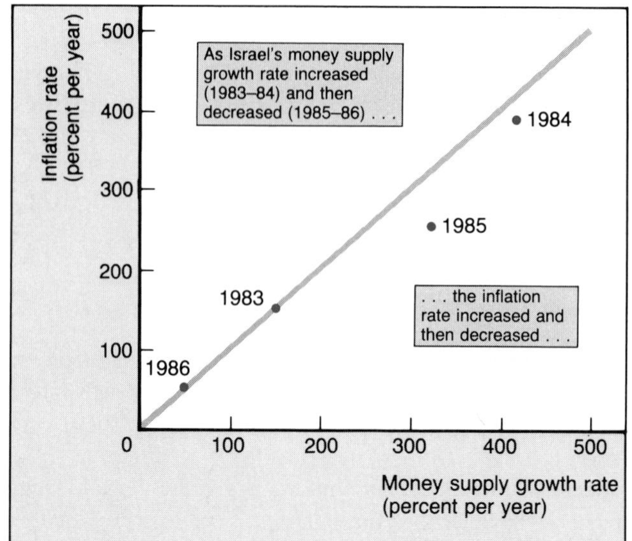

(a) Money supply and inflation

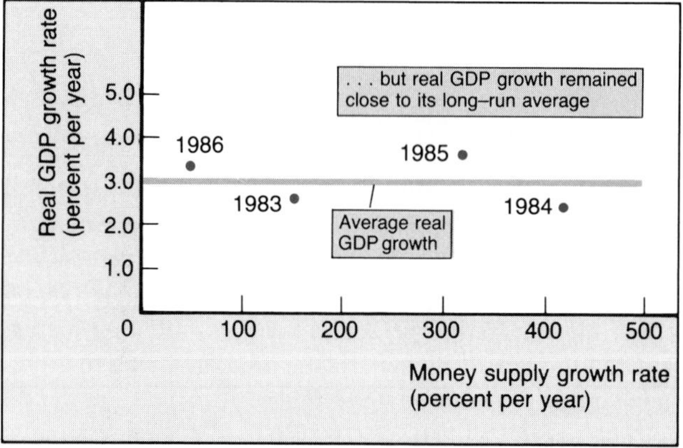

(b) Money supply and real GDP

In Chapter 12, we'll study cases in which this purely inflationary response to a change in the money supply growth rate does *not* occur. For now, however, let's continue to study anticipated inflation and look at another of its effects — that on interest rates.

11.4 *Inflation and Interest Rates*

What are the effects of anticipated change in the money supply growth rate on interest rates? We've already seen that an increase in the money supply growth rate increases the inflation rate by the same percentage. We also know that anticipated inflation affects interest rates. To work out the effects on interest rates, we need to go back to the *IS-LM* model of aggregate demand, which determines the interest rate. First, we'll study the effects of anticipated inflation on the components of the *IS-LM* model — the *IS* and *LM* curves — and then we'll work out the effects on interest rates.

Inflation and the *IS* curve

Recall that the *IS* curve traces the relationship between the interest rate and real GDP such that planned injections equal planned leakages. The *IS* curve slopes downward because one of the planned injections—investment—depends on the interest rate. Other things being equal, the higher the interest rate, the lower is the level of planned investment.

But planned investment depends not only on the interest rate. It also depends on the anticipated inflation rate. Other things being equal, the higher the anticipated inflation rate, the higher is the cutoff interest rate for any given investment project. Suppose an investment project is just profitable at an interest rate of 5 percent a year, when expected inflation is zero. That same project will just break even at an interest rate of 10 percent a year if prices are expected to rise by 5 percent a year. In other words, investment depends on the *real* interest rate, rather than on the nominal interest rate. This means that the positions of the investment function and the *IS* curve change when the expected inflation rate changes. Specifically, expected inflation shifts both these curves to the right. The size of the shift, measured in the vertical direction, equals the anticipated inflation rate.

Figure 11.7 illustrates the effects of expected inflation on the *IS* curve. Suppose that with no inflation expected the *IS* curve is IS_0. When the economy is producing its full-employment real GDP, the equilibrium interest rate is 5 percent a year. (We'll work out how such an interest rate comes about after we've studied the effects of inflation on the *LM* curve and equilibrium.) With inflation expected to be running at 5 percent a year, the *IS* curve shifts upward, from IS_0 to IS_1. Now, if real GDP is at its full-employment level, the interest rate is 10 percent a year.

It's important to emphasize that, in *real* terms, both situations illustrated in Figure 11.7 are the same. If real GDP is $4.5 billion, the real interest rate is 5 percent a year in both situations. The same is true at any level of real GDP. That is, for a given level of real GDP, the interest rate on IS_1 is 5 percentage points higher than the interest rate on IS_0.

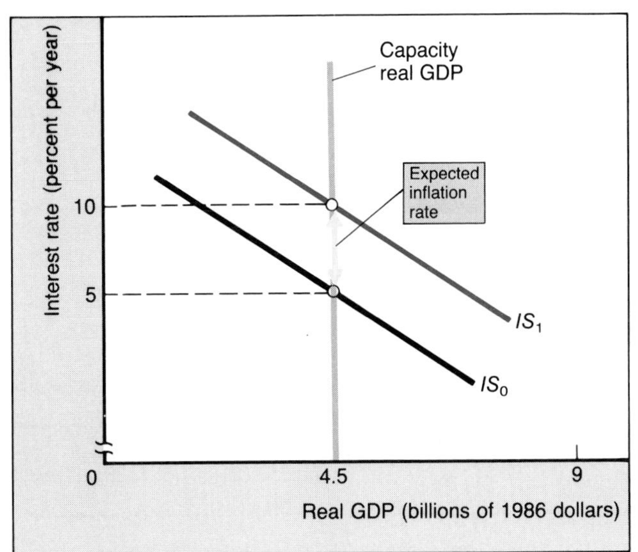

FIGURE 11.7
Inflation and the *IS* Curve

An ongoing expected inflation increases a firm's willingness to invest at each given interest rate. Because of expected inflation, returns from capital projects are expected to grow at a rate equal to the inflation rate. The interest rate at which a project becomes profitable increases by the same amount as the inflation rate. As a result, the investment demand curve and the *IS* curve shift, and the vertical distance between the original curve, IS_0, and the new curve, IS_1, measures the expected inflation rate.

The *LM* curve

How does expected inflation affect the *LM* curve? The answer is, it has no direct effect. Recall that the *LM* curve traces the relationship between the interest rate and real GDP such that the quantity of real money demanded equals the quantity of real money supplied. The real money supply depends on the nominal money supply — which is determined by the actions of the Fed — and the price level. For any given real money supply, there is a given *LM* curve.

But in an economy experiencing inflation, the price level and the money supply are both increasing. We've seen that with anticipated inflation, both the money supply and the price level increase at the same rate. This fact means that the real money supply is constant. Thus with anticipated inflation the *LM* curve stays put.

But the *LM* curve does not stay put if the expected inflation rate *changes*. We'll see why by studying the *IS-LM* equilibrium and the way in which it changes when the money supply growth rate changes.

Equilibrium

Let's work out how the equilibrium interest rate is determined in an economy experiencing inflation and how that equilibrium changes when the inflation rate changes. We'll start with an economy that has no inflation and then see what happens when an anticipated inflation begins. Figure 11.8 illustrates the analysis. Suppose the economy initially is on the *IS* curve IS_0 and *LM* curve LM_0. The interest rate is 5 percent a year, and real GDP is at its full-employment level of $4.5 billion. With no inflation, the real interest rate as well as the nominal interest rate is 5 percent a year.

Now suppose that the money supply growth rate increases by 5 percent a year and that this change is fully anticipated. What are its effects on the economy?

First, anticipating higher inflation, firms are now willing to invest at higher interest rates than before. The investment function shifts, and so does the *IS* curve. The new *IS* curve is IS_1 — exactly the same one we worked out in Figure 11.7. Since the money supply growth rate has increased by 5 percent, the *LM* curve will start shifting to the right, if there is no inflation. Other things being equal, the faster the money supply

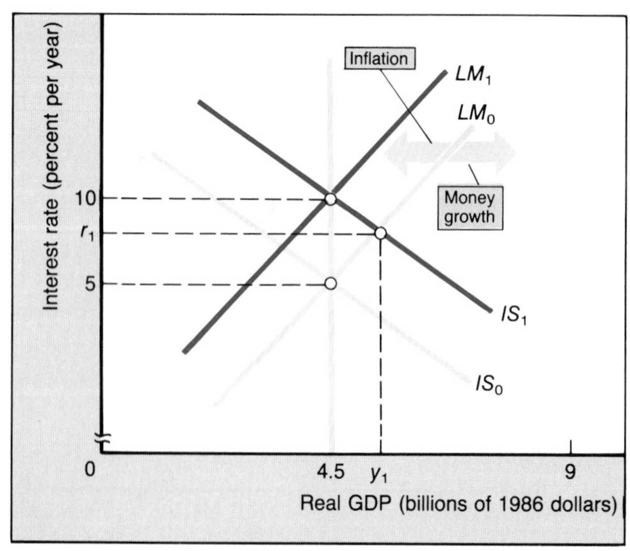

FIGURE 11.8
Interest Rate and Inflation

Initially there is no inflation. The economy is on IS_0 and LM_0 with an interest rate of 5 percent and real GDP of $4.5 billion. The money supply growth rate starts increasing by 5 percent a year. If the growth rate is anticipated and expected to continue into the indefinite future, the *IS* curve shifts upward by 5 percent, to IS_1. Inflation also increases. But initially the inflation rate is faster than the money supply growth rate. With faster inflation than money growth, the *LM* curve shifts to the left, eventually reaching LM_1. Here, interest rates have risen by an amount equal to the increase in inflation. Real interest rates are unaffected.

grows, the faster the *LM* curve shifts to the right. Second, because the increase in the money supply growth rate is anticipated, the aggregate demand curve and the short-run aggregate supply curve both start to shift upward. As they do, prices start to rise—inflation begins. The higher the inflation rate, the more quickly the *LM* curve moves to the left.

Thus if the money supply growth rate exceeds the inflation rate, the *LM* curve is shifting to the right. If the inflation rate exceeds the money supply growth rate, the *LM* curve is shifting to the left. And if the inflation rate equals the money supply growth rate, the *LM* curve is stationary.

Adjustment process

What is the adjustment process from one inflation rate to another? To answer this question, we have to keep in mind what is happening in the markets for labor and goods and services following the increase in the money supply growth rate. Suppose that initially, when the money supply growth rate increases, the *IS* curve shifts to IS_1 but the *LM* curve stays at LM_0. (This could happen at the split second at which the money supply growth rate increases.) Then, the equilibrium interest rate moves to r_1 and real GDP to y_1. The economy is now operating at above full employment. In such a situation, there is excess demand for labor and real wages begin to increase. But real wages can increase only if money wages increase at a faster pace than the inflation rate. That's what happens. Money wages begin to increase faster than inflation and the short-run aggregate supply curve starts to shift upward, *increasing* the inflation rate.

With the short-run aggregate supply curve shifting upward more quickly when prices are rising, the actual inflation rate and the rate of wage increase exceed the growth rate of the money supply. Inflation *overshoots* the growth rate of the money supply.

Overshooting How—and how much—the inflation rate overshoots the money supply growth rate depends on how quickly inflation expectations adjust. The more quickly expectations adjust, the more quickly wages and prices actually change. If expectations increase gradually, the inflation rate will increase gradually and eventually overshoot the money supply growth rate. Such a process is illustrated in Figure 11.9(a). But if the change in money supply growth rate is fully anticipated, wage growth and inflation will rise instantaneously and, at the moment of increase in the money supply growth rate, to a level higher than the money supply growth rate. Immediately thereafter, they settle down to the new growth rate of the money supply, as shown in Figure 11.9(b).

Once the inflation rate has overshot the money supply growth rate, the real money supply decreases. A decrease in the real money supply shifts the *LM* curve to the left. Such a shift continues until the *LM* curve has settled down at LM_1 (see Figure 11.8). When expectations adjust gradually, this process takes time. When expectations adjust instantaneously, the *LM* curve jumps immediately to LM_1.

Once the *LM* curve is at LM_1, the economy is in a new equilibrium, in which inflation is fully anticipated. There is an equilibrium between planned injections and planned leakages, for the economy is on its *IS* curve. There is also an equilibrium in the money market—the quantity of money supplied equals the quantity demanded—for the economy is on its *LM* curve. The inflation rate equals the growth rate of the money supply, and the interest rate has increased by the same percentage amount as the common increase in the money growth rate and the inflation rate. Also, the aggregate demand and short-run aggregate supply curves intersect on the long-run aggregate supply curve. There is no pressure to change the pace of inflation, wages, and prices.

FIGURE 11.9
Overshooting

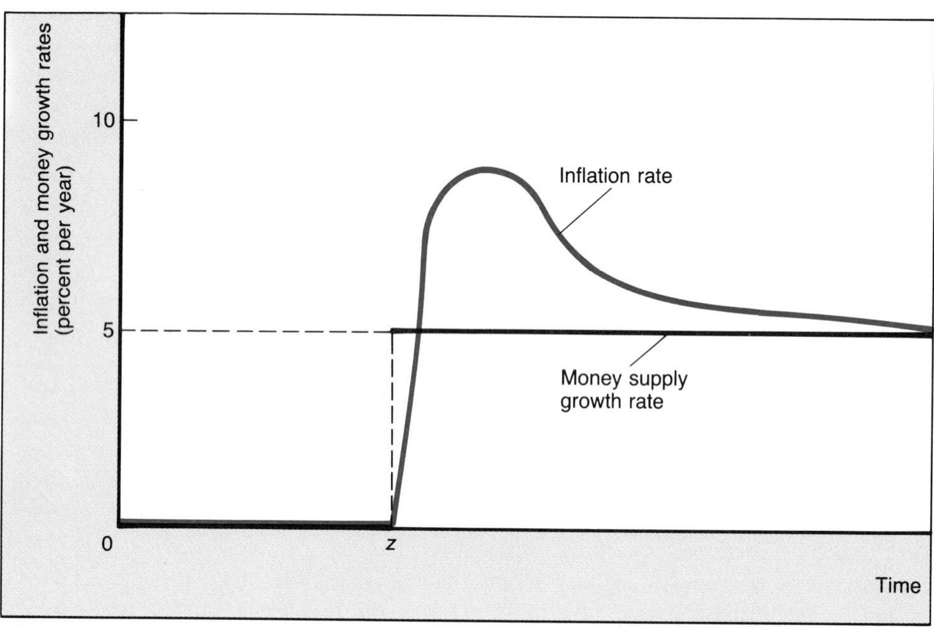

(a) Expectations gradually change

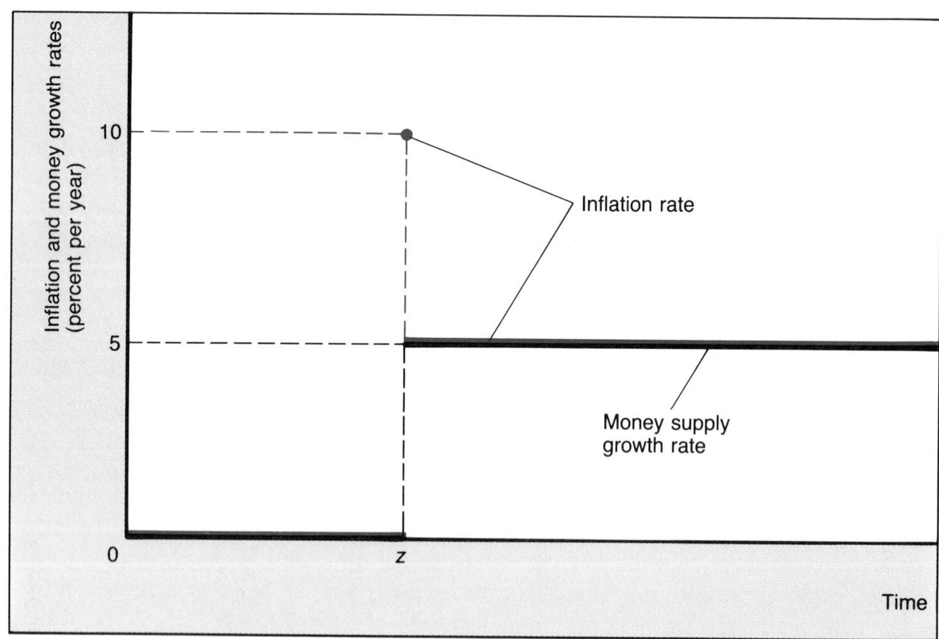

(b) Expectations instantly change

The way that inflation overshoots money supply growth when the money supply growth rate increases depends on how quickly expectations adjust. If expectations of inflation lag behind the increased money supply growth rate, the actual inflation rate will increase gradually, eventually overshoot the money supply growth rate, and then converge onto its new rate. If, when the money supply growth rate changes, the change is correctly foreseen, the inflation rate will jump at that instant, decreasing real money balances and shifting the *LM* curve to the left. Thereafter, the inflation rate and money supply growth rates will be equal again, at the new higher level.

Decrease in inflation

A fully anticipated decrease in the inflation rate works through the same mechanism we've just described, but in the opposite direction. That is, if the economy starts out with a fully anticipated inflation of 5 percent and then the money supply growth rate is cut (and is anticipated to be cut) by 5 percentage points, the interest rate will fall by 5 percentage points. It will do so because the *IS* curve shifts downward and wage inflation falls. En route to the new low (zero) inflation equilibrium, the inflation rate will fall below the growth rate of the money supply so that the real money supply increases in the new equilibrium.

Real balances and inflation

In equilibrium, the quantity of real money *is* affected by the expected inflation rate. The higher the expected inflation rate, the lower is the equilibrium quantity of real money balances. The reason is natural. Inflation is a tax on money. By holding money in an inflationary economy, people are, in effect, making a gift to the government each year equal to the inflation rate multiplied by the amount of money they hold. People will naturally try to avoid this tax. Therefore the higher the inflation rate — the higher the inflation tax — the smaller is the quantity of real money balances people will hold. But there is nothing special about inflation in influencing real money holdings. It is just the consequence of the fact that the demand for real money depends on the nominal interest rate, the opportunity cost of holding money. And inflation affects that opportunity cost.

We've seen that inflation influences interest rates and that when the inflation is fully anticipated the interest rate is affected one for one. Do interest rates in the real world behave like this?

11.5 *Interest Rates in Switzerland and Brazil*

TESTCASE

You've already seen in the *MACROFACTS* at the beginning of this chapter that interest rates and inflation are correlated across countries. Low-inflation countries tend to have low interest rates and high-inflation countries high interest rates. But we also saw a good deal of variation in real interest rates across countries.

Here, we'll look at the behavior of interest rates over time in a low-inflation country, Switzerland, and a high-inflation country, Brazil. We'll study their interest rates and inflation rates over the decade of the 1980s.

Figure 11.10 sets out the basic facts. Inflation in Switzerland (part a) has ranged between 2 and 8 percent a year. Interest rates in that country have ranged between 3 and 8 percent a year. Most of the movements in Swiss interest rates are associated with changes in the inflation rate. This is particularly noteworthy in the early 1980s, when inflation and interest rates both increased sharply (in 1981). Interest rates fell in 1982, even though there was no significant fall in the inflation rate. But in 1983-1984, both interest rates and inflation rates fell by about the same percentage amount. In the second half of the 1980s, interest rates fluctuated much more than inflation.

In summary, although Swiss interest rates and inflation rates fluctuate together — are positively correlated — there are quite a few variations in interest rates in Switzerland not associated with fluctuations in the inflation rate. In other words, Swiss real interest rates fluctuate quite a bit.

Contrast Switzerland's situation with that in Brazil, where inflation ranged between 50 percent and almost 700 percent a year in the 1980s. In that same period, interest rates fluctuated between about 50 percent and almost 500 percent a year. With the

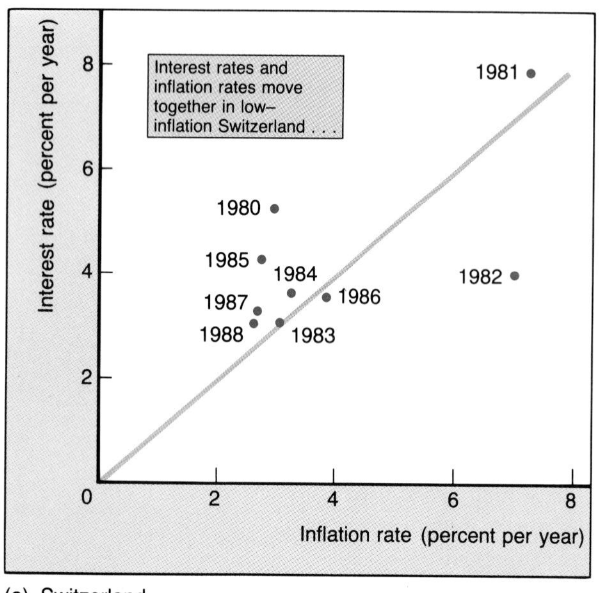

(a) Switzerland

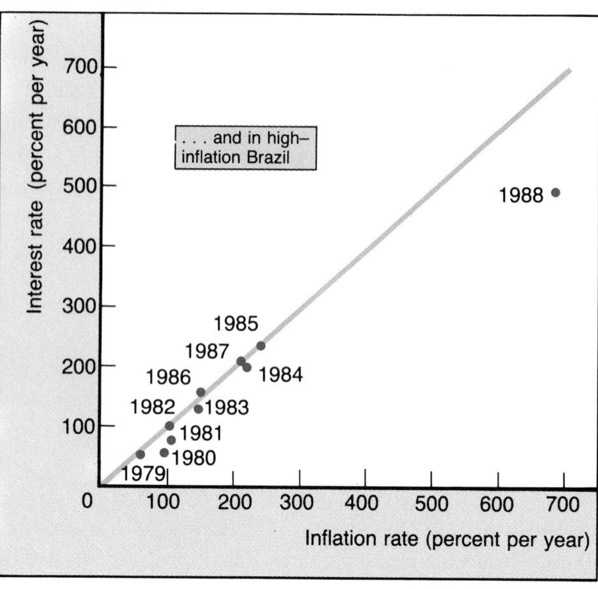

(b) Brazil

FIGURE 11.10
Interest Rates and Inflation in Switzerland and Brazil

Interest rates rise and fall with inflation rates in both low-inflation countries such as Switzerland (part a) and high-inflation countries such as Brazil (part b). There is a stronger tendency for inflation and interest rates to move together when inflation is high and its rate highly variable, because then the inflationary effects on interest rates dominate other real effects.

Source: International Financial Statistics Yearbook, 1991.

exception of 1988, interest rates and inflation in Brazil moved almost in a one-for-one manner.

Why are inflation and interest rates more highly correlated in Brazil than in Switzerland? The answer is, Brazil's inflation has been more variable. All countries have variations in their real interest rate. When inflation is low, the fluctuations in real interest rates are quite visible and may even be the dominant source of fluctuations in interest rates. When inflation is high and, more important, highly variable, fluctuations in interest rates mainly reflect fluctuations in inflation expectations. In such a situation, fluctuations in the real interest rate are much less visible. Even in the Brazilian case, however, we see a massive change in the real interest rate in 1988—much larger than anything Switzerland experienced.

From the facts illustrated in Figure 11.10, the broad conclusion is that inflation and interest rates do indeed move together but there are substantial fluctuations in interest rates not arising from fluctuations in the inflation rate. These need to be explained, but the explanation is not hard to find. Interest rates are determined at the point of intersection of the *IS* and *LM* curves. Many factors other than changes in the expected inflation rate cause the *IS* curve to shift. These factors produce fluctuations in the real interest rate that are independent of fluctuations in the inflation rate. These real factors together with inflation expectations produce the positive but less than perfect correlation between interest rates and inflation you can see both in Figure 11.2 at the beginning of this chapter and here in Figure 11.10.

11.6 *Inflation in an Open Economy*

In an open economy, there are additional influences on inflation that so far we have not taken into account. They arise from the domestic economy's interactions with the rest of the world, and these interactions depend crucially on the exchange rate regime. The inflation mechanism in an open economy is fundamentally different depending on whether the exchange rate is fixed or flexible. Let's examine inflation in the open economy by looking at the two exchange rate regimes.

Fixed exchange rate

A country with a fixed exchange rate uses its monetary policy to peg the value of its money in terms of foreign money. It does not control the money supply directly.

You can think of a country as being a bit like a monopoly. A monopoly faces a downward-sloping demand curve for its product. It can choose its price but must then produce the quantity that the market demands at that price. Alternatively, it can choose how much to produce. It must then accept the price at which the market is willing to buy that quantity of output. It is the same with a country's money. A country can decide how much money to create. If it does that, it must accept the price — the foreign exchange rate—at which that quantity of money is willingly held. Alternatively, a country can choose the foreign exchange value of its money. In that case, is must be willing to make available the quantity of money demanded at that price.

If a fixed exchange rate country does not control its money supply, it is not very interesting to know that the country's inflation rate equals its money supply growth rate. Inflation and money growth are correlated, but causation runs from inflation to money growth. This is sometimes called reverse causation. In a fixed exchange rate economy, it remains true that inflation and interest rates are correlated and that inflation and money supply growth are correlated. But what determines the value of these three variables?

Purchasing power parity The fundamental relationship that influences inflation in a fixed exchange rate economy is purchasing power parity. Internationally tradeable goods can be bought and sold in the domestic economy or in the rest of the world. The price at which they trade can be expressed either in terms of domestic currency or foreign currency. With a fixed exchange rate, it doesn't matter which currency we use to express their prices.

If goods are cheaper in one country than in another, it will pay people to buy in the country where they're cheap and sell in the country where they're more expensive, a process called **arbitrage**. Arbitrage will occur until there are no profit opportunities left from buying low and selling high. At that point, the price of an internationally tradeable good will be the same in all countries. (There may be some differences due to tariffs, local taxes, and transportation charges but we'll ignore them.)

If all goods are internationally tradeable, the price level in one country will be the same as the price level in all other countries against which a fixed exchange rate is being maintained. Inflation in all countries will be the same. In practice, not all goods are internationally tradeable; for example, many services are traded only locally. Also, changes in relative prices arising from many dozens of individual forces break the perfect link between the price level in one country and that in another. Even so, with a fixed exchange rate, the inflation rate in one country will equal the inflation rate in the other countries in the fixed exchange rate regime, other things being equal. In the short run, inflation rates may diverge, but they will tend to converge in the long run as the forces of arbitrage bring about purchasing power parity.

World money supply growth The forces of arbitrage bring inflation rates into equality in countries with a fixed exchange rate, but what determines the common inflation rate of all the countries in the fixed exchange rate system? The answer is, their combined money supply growth rate. You can think of the group of countries in a fixed exchange rates regime as a single, closed economy; its inflation rate is determined in the same way as the inflation rate in a closed economy. Changes in the anticipated growth rate of the total money supply of the countries will change the anticipated inflation rate in a way exactly equivalent to that described earlier in this chapter. This fact has been the source of problems with fixed exchange rate systems in the real world.

During the 1960s, the world was a fixed exchange rate system. No one individual country controlled the world money supply growth rate and it gradually increased, mainly as a result of increased U.S. monetary growth in the second half of the 1960s. At that time, increased U.S. government purchases not matched by U.S. tax increases were paid for partly by creating additional money. The world money supply growth rate increased, and so did the world average inflation rate. We'll look at this period more closely later in the chapter.

TABLE 11.2
Inflation and the Exchange Rate

Variables:			
Domestic price level	P;	domestic inflation rate	π
Foreign price level	P_f;	foreign inflation rate	π_f
Exchange rate (units of domestic currency per unit of foreign currency)	E;	rate of depreciation of exchange rate	$\Delta\epsilon$
Purchasing power parity:			
Price *levels* are linked by:	$P = EP_f$		
Price *changes* are linked by:	$\Delta P = E \cdot \Delta P_f + P_f \cdot \Delta E$		
Inflation rates* are linked by:	$\pi = \pi_f + \Delta\epsilon$		
Fixed exchange rate regime			
Since E is fixed, $\Delta\epsilon = 0$ and	$\pi = \pi_f$		
Flexible exchange rate regime			
The rate of depreciation of exchange rate is	$\Delta\epsilon = \pi - \pi_f$		

***Calculation**

Price *changes*: $\Delta P = E\Delta P_f + P_f\Delta E$ (a)

Price *levels* $P = EP_f$ (b)

Divide (a) by (b)
$$\frac{\Delta P}{P} = \frac{E\Delta P_f}{EP_f} + \frac{P_f \Delta E}{EP_f}$$

Cancel common terms
$$\frac{\Delta P}{P} = \frac{\cancel{E}\Delta P_f}{\cancel{E}P_f} + \frac{\cancel{P_f} \Delta E}{E\cancel{P_f}}$$

So that
$$\frac{\Delta P}{P} = \frac{\Delta P_f}{P_f} + \frac{\Delta E}{E}$$

or
$$\pi = \pi_f + \Delta\epsilon$$

Flexible exchange rates

A country with a flexible exchange rate is able to control its money supply growth rate. As far as anticipated inflation is concerned, such a country behaves in the same way as a closed economy. Its flexible exchange rate insulates it from the rest of the world. Other things being equal, an increase in the money supply growth rate increases the inflation rate and also increases the rate of depreciation of the country's currency. Recall the example of Brazil and Switzerland we examined above. Switzerland's inflation rate averaged less than 5 percent a year, while Brazil's was commonly 200 percent a year. Quite a lot of international trade and other economic activity takes place between Switzerland and Brazil. Such trade can only take place if Brazil's money (the Brazilian cruzeiro) falls in value against Swiss money (the Swiss franc) at a rate equal to the difference between the inflation rates in the two countries.

Purchasing power parity still prevails in the long run between two countries that have flexible exchange rates precisely because the change in the value of one currency in terms of the other equals the difference between the two countries' inflation rates.

Table 11.2 gives a summary of the relationship between domestic and foreign inflation and the exchange rate in the two exchange rate regimes.

We've seen that the theory of inflation in an open economy predicts radically different inflationary effects depending on whether the exchange rate is fixed or flexible. What happens in reality?

11.7 *Inflation with Fixed and Flexible Exchange Rates*

TESTCASE

To study the effects of the exchange rate regime on inflation, we need to identify episodes in which exchange rates were fixed and those in which they were flexible. We'll look at two interesting episodes of fixed exchange rates. The first is the world economy of the 1960s, and the second is the countries of the European Monetary System in the 1980s. For an example of flexible exchange rates, we'll look at the world economy of the late 1970s and early 1980s.

The world economy in the 1960s

From 1945 to the early 1970s, the entire world economy operated a fixed exchange rate system. Until the early 1960s, international trade and capital restrictions prevented that system from operating in the way predicted by the theory we've just considered. But through the 1960s, the system became more and more like the ''textbook model'' we've just considered. You can see this by looking at Figure 11.11, which shows the inflation rates of five major countries through the 1960s. As you can see, at the beginning of the decade their inflation rates differed quite markedly. By the end of the decade, they were very similar. Also, through the decade, inflation rates tended to increase.

This steady increase in inflation during the 1960s resulted from a steady increase in the *world* money supply growth rate during that period. The convergence occurred because the increasingly integrated world economy operated on a fixed exchange rate.

FIGURE 11.11
Inflation under Fixed Exchange Rates

Countries' inflation rates converge on a common inflation rate when exchange rates are fixed. The world's major countries were on such an exchange rate arrangement during the 1960s and inflation rates did indeed converge.

Source: International Financial Statistics Yearbook, 1991.

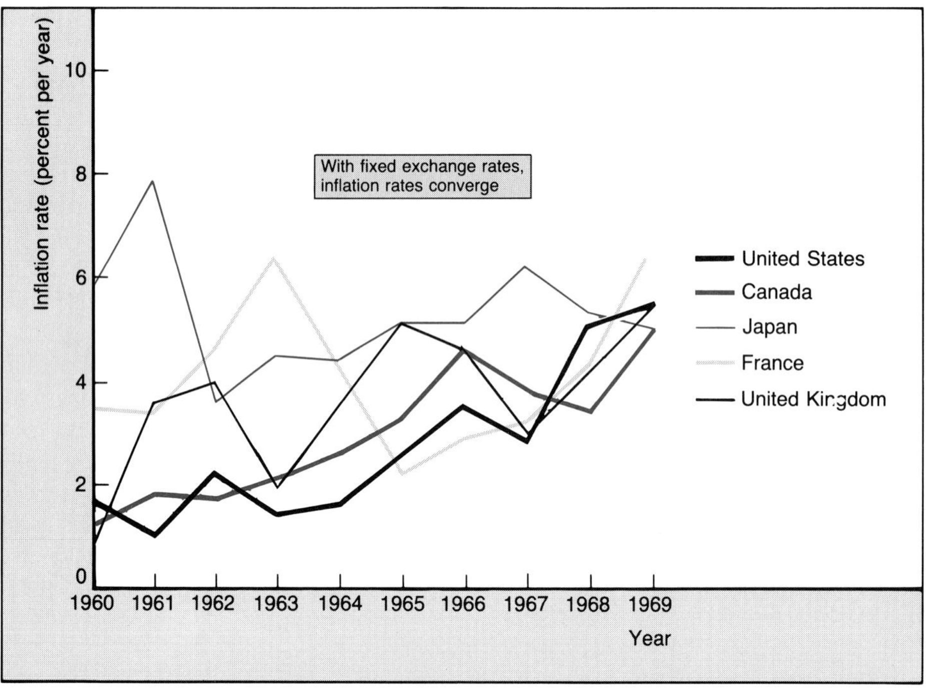

The European Monetary System

Another fixed exchange rate system has emerged in recent years — the European Monetary System. The **European Monetary System** (EMS) is a system of fixed exchange rates between some of the members of the European Community (EC). The main members of the European Monetary System are France, Germany, and Belgium, the Netherlands, and Luxembourg (Benelux). These countries' inflation rates since 1986 are shown in Figure 11.12. The European Monetary System became increasingly operational through those years. As you can see, inflation rates in its member countries have converged to almost the same rate. Inflation in Germany and the Benelux countries has increased to approach that of France.

One major country of the EC, the United Kingdom, has remained outside the European Monetary System. You can see that the predictions of the flexible exchange rate theory explain very well the divergence of inflation in the United Kingdom from that of the other European countries belonging to the EMS. More rapid money growth in the United Kingdom has produced more rapid inflation in that country and a depreciation of the British pound against the currencies of the other members of the EC.

Flexible exchange rates and the Plaza Agreement

The world fixed exchange rate system broke down in the early 1970s and by the mid-1970s had completely collapsed. Through the 1970s and early 1980s, most major countries operated a flexible exchange rate system. Figure 11.13 shows the inflation experience of all major countries from 1975 through the early 1980s. Inflation rates were highly divergent: inflation in the United Kingdom often exceeded 20 percent a year and was much higher than in most other countries, while inflation in Japan was much lower than in most other countries.

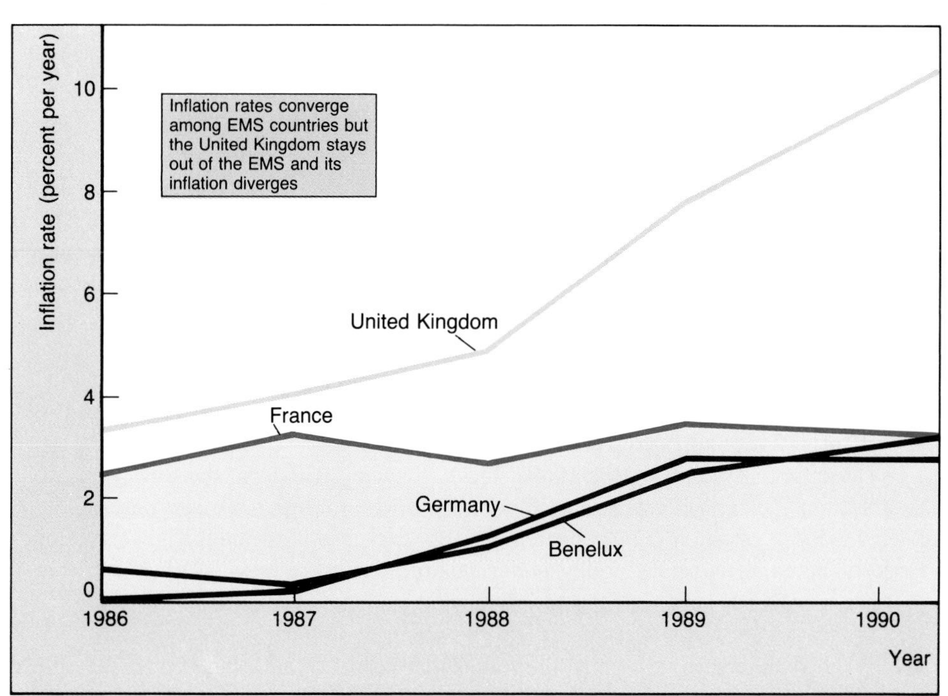

FIGURE 11.12
The European Monetary System

In the late 1980s, the major countries of the European Community formed the European Monetary System (EMS). The main members of the system are France, Germany, and the Benelux countries—Belgium, the Netherlands, and Luxembourg. The inflation rates of these countries rates of these countries converged after joining the EMS. The United Kingdom stayed outside the EMS and its inflation rate diverged.

Source: International Financial Statistics Yearbook, 1991.

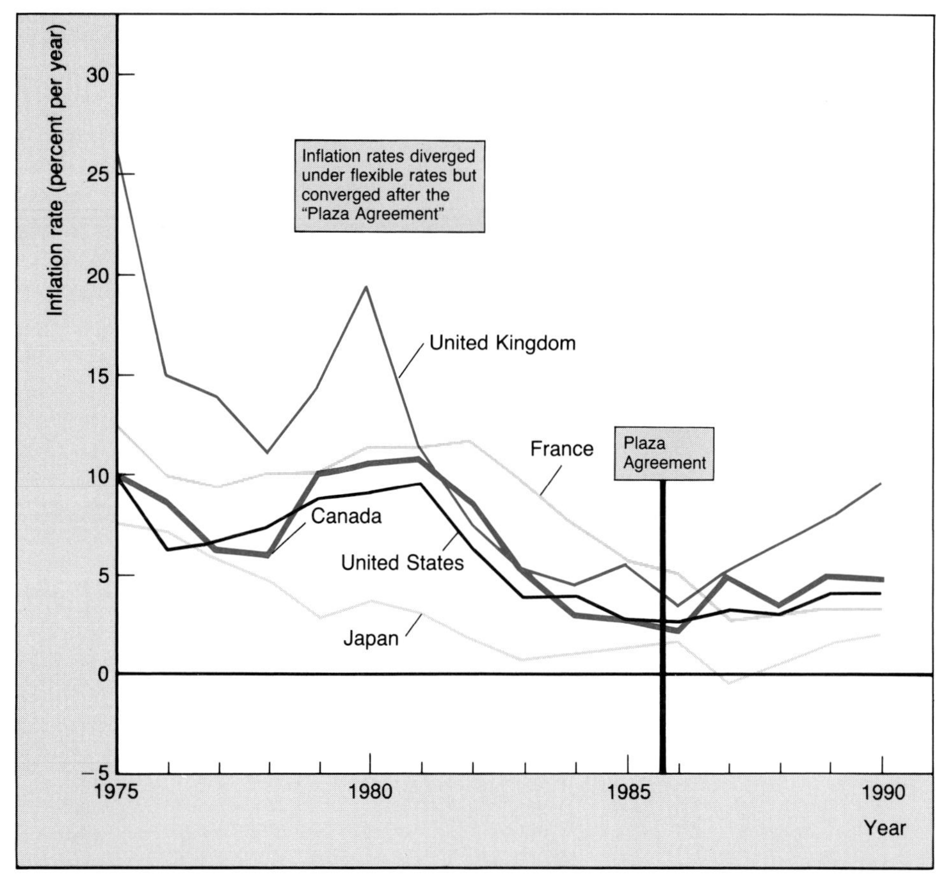

FIGURE 11.13
Inflation with Flexible Exchange Rates

With flexible exchange rates, there is no necessary tendency for inflation rates to converge. During the 1970s and early 1980s, inflation rates were highly divergent. But in the 1980s, and especially in the late 1980s, after the Plaza Agreement, inflation rates converged. The Plaza Agreement was an attempt to coordinate national monetary policies to keep exchange rates from fluctuating too wildly.

Source: International Financial Statistics Yearbook, 1991.

This diverse inflation experience illustrates the theory of inflation in a world economy with flexible exchange rates. In such a case, national inflation rates are determined by national monetary policies and foreign exchange rates adjust to permit the inflation divergence to prevail.

During the 1980s, countries became increasingly concerned about exchange rate volatility and an attempt was made to achieve a greater degree of coordination of national monetary policies. A meeting of the so-called Big Five (United States, Japan, France, United Kingdom, and Germany) at the Plaza Hotel in New York City led to the so-called Plaza Agreement. The **Plaza Agreement** was an agreement to bring national monetary policies into closer coordination with each other, thereby lowering the degree of exchange rate volatility. In effect, the Plaza Agreement was a commitment to move toward managed floating exchange rates. As countries brought their exchange rates into closer alignment with each other, they also necessarily had to align their monetary policies more closely. As money supply growth rates were brought more closely into alignment, inflation rates converged.

These three examples — the 1960s, the 1970s and 1980s, and the European Monetary System — clearly illustrate the importance of the foreign exchange rate regime on the behavior of inflation in open economies. But they also illustrate the powerful importance of national monetary policy under flexible exchange rates and world monetary policy under fixed exchange rates to influence the course of inflation.

■ In this chapter, we've studied the forces that influence anticipated inflation. We've looked at trends in inflation — inflation at full employment. While much of the variation in inflation, both over time and across countries, can be understood in terms of these models of anticipated inflation, a great deal cannot. Much of our inflationary experience is associated with fluctuations in the inflation rate around its anticipated rate and with corresponding fluctuations in the rest of the economy. In the next chapter we'll investigate the fluctuations in inflation and its relationship with the business cycle.

CHAPTER REVIEW

Summary

INFLATION, INTEREST RATES, AND MONEY GROWTH IN THE 1980s

There have been huge variations in countries' inflation rates during the 1980s. Canadian inflation has been mild compared with world average inflation, but it has not been the lowest inflation rate.

A strong positive correlation exists between inflation rates and money supply growth rates around the world. Interest rates and inflation rates are also positively correlated.

ANTICIPATED INFLATION

An anticipated increase in the money supply growth rate increases both the inflation rate and the nominal interest rate by the same percentage as the increase in the money supply growth rate. It leaves real GDP and the real interest rate undisturbed.

The mechanism producing an anticipated inflation is as follows: the aggregate demand shifts upward at a rate equal to the growth rate of the money supply; the short-run aggregate supply curve shifts upward at a rate equal to the rate of wage increase; wages increase at the expected inflation rate.

ANTICIPATED INFLATION IN ISRAEL IN THE 1980s

An anticipated inflation took place in Israel during the 1980s. From 1983 to 1986, inflation accelerated and after 1986, the inflation rate was brought under control. Both the increase and decrease in inflation were anticipated and strongly correlated with the change in the money supply growth rate. Real GDP growth was virtually unaffected by these changes in inflation.

THE EFFECTS OF INFLATION ON INTEREST RATES

The *IS* curve shifts upward by an amount equal to the expected inflation rate. The *LM* curve intersects the *IS* curve at the full-employment level of real GDP. With inflation proceeding at the same rate as the money supply growth rate, the real money supply is constant and the *LM* curve stays put.

An anticipated change in the money supply growth rate *changes* the inflation rate and interest rate, each by the same percentage amount as the change in the money supply growth rate. En route to the new inflation rate, inflation overshoots the money supply growth rate, changing the real money supply to its new equilibrium level.

INFLATION AND INTEREST RATES IN SWITZERLAND AND BRAZIL

The predicted effects of inflation on interest rates are found in the data for both low-inflation countries such as Switzerland and high-inflation countries such as Brazil. The effects are more clear and strong in high-inflation countries because there, the inflationary effects dominate other real influences on interest rates.

INFLATION WITH A FIXED EXCHANGE RATE

When a country has a fixed exchange rate, its inflation is determined by world inflation and its money supply growth rate adjusts to accommodate that inflation. Causation is reversed with a fixed exchange rate from inflation to money supply growth, not the other way around.

The mechanism bringing inflation rates into alignment among fixed exchange rate countries is international arbitrage in markets for internationally traded goods and services.

INFLATION IN THE 1960s AND IN THE EMS

When the world had fixed exchange rates during the 1960s, inflation rates converged as predicted by theory. Also, the countries of the European Monetary System that joined a fixed exchange rate arrangement in the late 1980s have experienced strong and close convergence of their inflation rates.

INFLATION WITH A FLEXIBLE EXCHANGE RATE

With a flexible exchange rate, a country is free to determine its monetary policy and inflation rate. International arbitrage forces operate as they do with a fixed exchange rate, but they do not equalize inflation rates. They work to make the country's currency depreciate at a rate equal to its inflation rate minus inflation in the rest of the world. A flexible exchange rate enables a country to pursue a divergent inflation path if it so chooses.

INFLATION IN THE 1980s

During the 1980s, most of the world's major countries operated a flexible exchange rate. In the early part of that decade, their inflation rates were highly divergent. As the decade progressed, and especially after 1985, when the Plaza Agreement, limiting movements in exchange rates, was entered into, inflation rates began to converge.

Key Terms and Concepts

Anticipated inflation A process in which prices are increasing at rates forecasted by all the economic actors.

Arbitrage Buying low and selling high.

Equation of exchange The quantity of money multiplied by the velocity of circulation equals total expenditure.

European Monetary System A system of fixed exchange rates between some of the members of the European Community (EC).

Expected inflation rate The forecasted inflation rate for some future period.

Plaza Agreement An agreement among five major nations (United States, Japan, United Kingdom, France, and Germany) to bring national monetary policies into closer harmony with each other, thereby lowering the degree of exchange rate volatility.

Quantity theory of money The proposition that an increase in the growth rate of the money supply brings an equal percentage increase in the inflation rate.

Rational expectation A forecast about the future value of an economic variable made using all available information.

Unanticipated inflation A process in which prices increase at a pace that has been incorrectly forecast to some degree.

Review Questions

1. Compare inflation in Canada since 1970 with inflation in other developed countries and with inflation in the Third World.

2. Describe the relationship between interest rates and inflation in Canada. How does the Canadian experience compare with that of other countries?
3. Explain why an increase in the money supply increases aggregate demand.
4. Explain why a 10 percent increase in the money supply shifts the aggregate demand curve upward by 10 percent.
5. Explain the relationship between the money wage rate and aggregate supply. Why does an increase in the money wage lower aggregate supply in the short run?
6. Distinguish between expected inflation, anticipated inflation, and unanticipated inflation.
7. Explain why an anticipated increase in the money supply growth rate of 10 percent produces a 10 percent increase in the inflation rate.
8. How does the aggregate demand–aggregate supply model interpret Israeli inflation of the 1980s?
9. Explain why and how anticipated inflation affects the *IS* and *LM* curves.
10. Explain the effects of an anticipated increase in the money supply growth rate on interest rates.
11. Explain why interest rates and inflation each fall by 5 percentage points as a result of an anticipated decrease in the money supply growth rate of 5 percentage points.
12. Describe the path of inflation in question 7. Does the inflation rate increase by more than 10 percent at any time? Explain why or why not.
13. In question 11, does the inflation rate gradually fall by 5 percentage points? Explain why or why not.
14. Explain why some countries have low interest rates and others high interest rates. Explain why interest rates are more variable in some countries than in others.
15. What is purchasing power parity? What are the implications of purchasing power parity in (a) a fixed exchange rate regime and (b) a flexible exchange rate regime?
16. What is "reverse causation"? Under what circumstances is there reverse causation in the correlation of inflation and money growth?
17. What determines the world inflation rate in a fixed exchange rate regime?
18. What is the European Monetary System? When did it begin and what is its purpose?
19. What is the Plaza Agreement? When and where did it take place and what was its purpose?
20. Does a flexible or a fixed exchange rate regime isolate an individual country from excessive world monetary growth? Explain your answer.

Problems

1. An economy has the following short-run aggregate supply and aggregate demand:

$$y^s = -1500 + 25P$$
$$y^d = 2000 - 25P$$

   (a) If the economy is at a full-employment equilibrium, what is real GDP?
   (b) If the money supply increases by 10 percent and this increase is expected, what is the price level and real GDP?
   (c) By how much have wages changed? Why did wages change by this amount?
   (d) What is short-run aggregate supply? Why has it changed?
2. The money supply growth rate increases from 4 percent a year to 6 percent a year and this change is anticipated.
   (a) Describe its effects on the *LM* and *IS* curves.

(b) What is the change in the inflation rate?

(c) What is the change in interest rates?

3. If the GDP deflator in Canada is 140 and the Japanese GDP deflator is 120, what is the exchange rate between the Canadian dollar and the Japanese yen if purchasing power parity holds?

4. Consider an economy with a flexible exchange rate and an inflation rate of 10 percent a year. If the foreign inflation rate is 12 percent a year, what is the rate of depreciation of the domestic currency on the foreign exchange market?

5. Imagine a fixed exchange rate world in which domestic inflation is 5 percent a year. The world money supply growth rate increases by 5 percentage points.

(a) What is the rate of depreciation of the domestic currency on foreign exchange markets?

(b) What is the change in domestic inflation?

6. Imagine a flexible exchange rate world in which the domestic inflation rate of 5 percent a year equals that in the rest of the world. The growth rate of the domestic money supply increases and is expected to increase by 2 percentage points.

(a) What is the domestic inflation rate?

(b) What is the inflation rate in the rest of the world?

(c) What is the rate of depreciation of the domestic currency on the foreign exchange market?

CHAPTER

Inflation and the Business Cycle

12

IS INFLATION THE PRICE OF FULL EMPLOYMENT?

PRICES ARE CONSTANTLY CHANGING, AND A FEW — those of personal computers, CD players, and Walkmans, for example — are constantly falling. But the last time the price level — the average of all prices — fell was 1933! Every year since then, we've had inflation — rising prices. In some years, inflation has been rapid; in others, moderate.

During the 1930s, the work of John Maynard Keynes (*The General Theory of Employment, Interest and Money*) gave birth to the science of macroeconomics. By the end of World War II, most governments — including the Canadian government — had embraced Keynesian ideas and were introducing policies designed to manage their economies maintaining full employment. Is the emergence of unending inflation and the adoption of full-employment policies a coincidence, or are cause and effect at work? Is inflation the price we're paying for the achievement of full employment? Could we beat inflation if only we were willing to put up with more unemployment? These are the main questions this chapter addresses. It also studies the way inflation fluctuates over the business cycle. Do we have more inflation in boom years and less in slump years? And, indeed, is recession the only way to lower inflation?

In the last chapter, our focus was on anticipated inflation. In this chapter, it is on unanticipated inflation. We'll also look at mixed cases, where inflation is to some degree anticipated and to some degree not.

After you have studied this chapter, you will be able to

- Describe the main features of inflation over the business cycle
- Explain the effects of unanticipated changes in aggregate demand on inflation
- Describe how an unanticipated decrease in aggregate demand brought inflation under control in the early 1980s but also brought recession
- Explain the effects of supply shocks on inflation
- Explain how oil price shocks influenced inflation in the 1970s
- Define the Phillips curve and explain Phillips curve theory
- Describe the shifts in the Canadian Phillips curve since 1960

MACROFACTS

12.1 *Canadian Inflation and the Business Cycle, 1960-1990*

There are some interesting facts about inflation and the business cycle and Figure 12.1 illustrates them. In it you can see the business cycle—GDP fluctuations—and inflation—the annual percentage change in the GDP deflator. The figure also has some shading to guide your eye. In the shaded periods, GDP was above trend and in the unshaded periods, GDP was below trend.

What do you see as the relationship between inflation and the business cycle in Figure 12.1? We suspect that your first answer is that there just is no strong, clear relationship or correlation between these two variables. They both go up and down but there doesn't seem to be any distinct pattern in the co-movements of the variables—the way they move together.

But look closer. There is an interesting relationship. The largest increases in inflation have taken place when GDP was above trend (the shaded periods). This tendency is clearest in 1973-1974 and 1978-1981. The largest decreases in inflation have taken place when GDP was below trend (the unshaded periods). This tendency is clearest in 1982-1986. In other periods, there is no clear pattern in the relationship between inflation and the cycle. For example, inflation increased in the early 1960s when real GDP was below trend and it stabilized in the late 1960s when real GDP was above trend.

Why does inflation fluctuate over the business cycle? Why are there times when the relationship between inflation and the business cycle is a strong one and other times when the relationship is weak?

We're going to discover that the cyclical pattern in inflation has two possible sources: one arising from changes in aggregate demand and the other from changes in aggregate supply. We'll also discover that there is an alternative way of viewing inflation over the business cycle—a view that involves using what is called the Phillips curve.

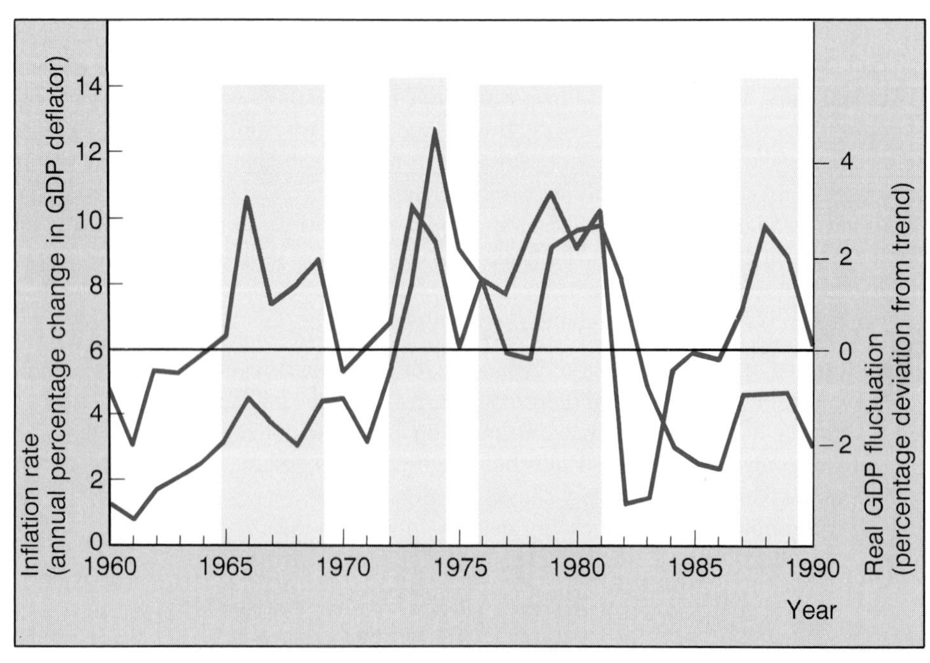

FIGURE 12.1
Inflation over the Business Cycle

Inflation increases most when real GDP is above trend—as highlighted by the shaded years. Inflation decreases fastest when real GDP is below trend—as in the unshaded years. But inflation is not perfectly correlated with the business cycle. There are several episodes in which inflation increases with real GDP below trend and decreases with real GDP above trend.

Source: National Income and Expenditure Accounts, Statistics Canada, Catalogue 13-201.

12.2 The Effects of an Unanticipated Change in Aggregate Demand

We discovered in Chapter 11 that an *anticipated* increase in aggregate demand increases inflation by the same percentage amount as the increase in aggregate demand. It also results in no change in real GDP. It is clear, from that result, that anticipated changes in aggregate demand cannot be responsible for the business cycle or for the fact that inflation tends to increase when GDP is above its long-run level. But *unanticipated* changes in aggregate demand can produce such effects.

Increase in inflation

When an increase in aggregate demand is not anticipated, wages do not rise in anticipation of rising prices. Aggregate demand increases but there is no change in short-run aggregate supply. The result is an increase in inflation *and* an increase in real GDP.

Let's use Figure 12.2 to see how this works out. The diagram shows the economy's aggregate demand, short-run aggregate supply, and long-run aggregate supply curves. Initially, the aggregate demand curve is AD_0 and the short-run aggregate supply curve is SAS_0. Equilibrium occurs at a real GDP of $4.5 billion and a price level of 100. This equilibrium is a full-employment equilibrium as it lies on the economy's long-run aggregate supply curve, *LAS*. Real GDP is $4.5 billion. The price level is constant. There is no inflation.

Now imagine an unanticipated 5 percent increase in the money supply. We saw in Chapter 11 how a change in the money supply affects the aggregate demand curve. Regardless of whether the change in the money supply is anticipated (as in Chapter 11) or unanticipated (as here), the aggregate demand curve shifts to the right, and the magnitude of the shift, measured in the vertical direction, is equal to the percentage increase in the money supply. Thus the new aggregate demand curve, AD_1, lies to the right of AD_0 and the vertical distance between these two aggregate demand curves is 5 percent—the amount of the unanticipated increase in the money supply.

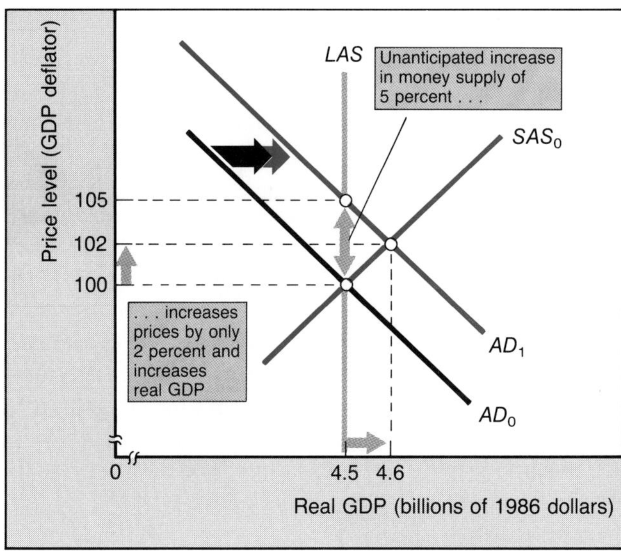

FIGURE 12.2
An Unanticipated Increase in Aggregate Demand

An unanticipated 5 percent increase in the money supply shifts the aggregate demand curve from AD_0 to AD_1. Being unanticipated, wages do not change, so the short-run aggregate supply curve stays at SAS_0. The price level increases but by less than 5 percent and real GDP increases. The economy experiences rising inflation with real GDP above trend.

Since the increase in aggregate demand is unanticipated, labor market contracts do not take account of this new situation. Wages were set at levels judged appropriate before the money supply change occurred. Thus the short-run aggregate supply curve incorporating the given level of wages is not affected by the unanticipated increase in aggregate demand. The *SAS* curve remains at SAS_0.

The new equilibrium occurs where the aggregate demand curve AD_1 intersects the short-run aggregate supply curve SAS_0. The price level increases by 2 percent, to 102, and real GDP increases to $4.6 billion. This economy now experiences inflation. The inflation rate has *increased* from 0 to 2 percent. Real GDP has gone from its full-employment level to above full employment. This economy is in exactly the same situation as the economy in the shaded periods in Figure 12.1.

Decrease in inflation

The experiment we have just conducted can also be run in the opposite direction. Suppose, instead of increasing, the money supply decreases. We can follow the analysis using Figure 12.2, but you may want to draw a diagram to keep track of the discussion. An unanticipated decrease in the money supply decreases aggregate demand and shifts the aggregate demand curve to the left of AD_0. The new aggregate demand curve lies below AD_0, such that the vertical distance between them equals the percentage change in the money supply. Since wages do not react to unanticipated changes, the short-run aggregate supply curve remains at SAS_0. Real GDP falls below its long-run aggregate supply level and the price level falls below 100. This economy experiences falling prices and unemployment.

Such a situation has not occurred in the Canadian economy since the 1930s. The experience shown in Figure 12.1 has the inflation rate decreasing when real GDP goes below its long-run aggregate supply level. It does not have the price level *falling*— negative inflation.

We can easily modify the foregoing analysis to make it agree exactly with the Canadian experience. You can imagine an economy experiencing ongoing inflation at some positive rate as a consequence of anticipated increases in aggregate demand. That is, you can imagine an economy having a trend inflation rate generated by the process we studied in Chapter 11. An unanticipated slowdown in the growth of the money supply brings an unanticipated slowdown in the growth of aggregate demand. Aggregate demand does not fall, but it increases by less than was expected. As a result, the aggregate demand curve shifts upward, but by a smaller amount than the increased wages shift the short-run aggregate supply curve upward. The result is recession combined with a fall in the inflation rate.

But do things really work out like that? Let's check by looking at a specific episode —the recession of the early 1980s.

TESTCASE

12.3 *The 1981-1982 Recession*

In 1981, inflation was raging at around 10 percent a year and the prospect of it falling below that level looked alarmingly remote. The term ''double-digit inflation'' seemed to have found a permanent place in our vocabulary. But for Gerald Bouey, governor of the Bank of Canada, the prospect of permanent double-digit inflation was unacceptable. He reasoned that economic growth and prosperity could not return until inflation was beaten. So he embarked on a relentless war on inflation.

In 1982 the stubborn inflation was broken. Its rate fell to 8 percent a year and the economy went into a deep recession. How was inflation reduced? The major part of the answer is the unexpected slowdown in the growth of aggregate demand. Figure 12.3 illustrates the events. In 1981, the economy was on its aggregate demand curve AD_{81} and short-run aggregate supply curve SAS_{81}. Real GDP was \$440 billion and the GDP deflator was 81.

Inflation was expected to continue at a similar pace to that of 1981. The pace of wage increases slowed from 1981 but only to 11 percent and the *SAS* curve in 1982 shifted upward to SAS_{82}.

But aggregate demand growth slowed severely in 1982: the aggregate demand curve shifted only to AD_{82}. The slowdown in the growth of aggregate demand resulted partly from a slowdown in money supply growth but mainly from a collapse in investment—much higher interest rates brought a large decrease in investment. With aggregate demand growing more slowly than anticipated in 1982, the economy moved to the point of intersection of the aggregate demand curve AD_{82} and short-run aggregate supply curve SAS_{82}. The GDP deflator increased to 88 and real GDP decreased to \$426 billion. The inflation rate fell below that expected (and what it had been in 1981) and the economy went into recession.

After 1982, the economy began to recover, but it remained below full employment for several years. During those years, as we saw in Figure 12.1, the inflation rate continued to decrease. This decreasing pace of inflation resulted from the maintenance of slow aggregate demand growth. At first, the slow aggregate demand growth rate was not anticipated. But the more permanent it became, the more widely was it expected and gradually the slower aggregate demand growth came to be anticipated. The economy gradually returned to full employment with inflation held in check.

We've now seen how fluctuations in aggregate demand produce fluctuations in inflation and real GDP similar to those observed in the Canadian economy. We've also seen these forces at work in a particular and important episode in our recent macroeconomic history. But demand fluctuations are not the only source of fluctuations in inflation and real GDP. Supply-side fluctuations are also at work. Let's see how these operate.

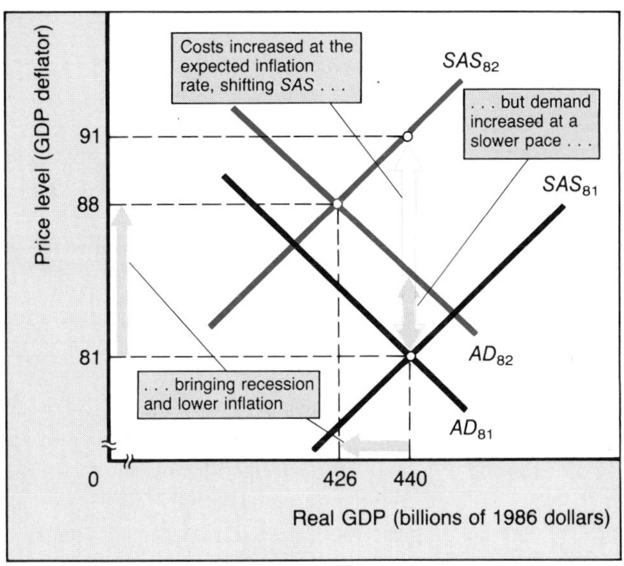

FIGURE 12.3
The 1981-1982 Recession

In the early 1980s, expectations of continuing 10 percent inflation were widespread. The short-run aggregate supply curve shifted to the left (and upward), from SAS_{81} to SAS_{82}. Aggregate demand growth slowed down so that aggregate demand increased from AD_{81} to AD_{82}. Inflation slowed as the economy went into recession.

12.4 *The Effects of a Change in Aggregate Supply*

There are many potential sources of disturbance to aggregate supply. Capital accumulation and technological change increase aggregate supply, but their pace is variable. When it is rapid, aggregate supply increases quickly; when it slows down, aggregate supply grows more slowly.

Technological change itself can bring a temporary decrease in aggregate supply when it has a strong sectoral bias. For example, the development of low-cost personal computers made typewriters and mechanical calculating machines and cash registers redundant. The capital equipment and skilled labor force used to produce these items depreciated. The physical capital — plant, machinery, and buildings used to produce typewriters and mechanical cash registers — were simply scrapped and the skilled labor force became redundant and had to be retrained and largely relocated before it could again become productive. This kind of technological change is accompanied by a temporary (but possibly prolonged) decrease in aggregate supply.

Another important type of supply disturbance is international in origin. Disruptions to the supply of key raw materials from the rest of the world or large increases in the world price of such materials have a negative impact on aggregate supply. For example, the disruption of world oil supplies in the 1970s and the successive massive increases in oil prices between 1973 and 1981 delivered large negative supply shocks to the Canadian economy.

Supply shocks, inflation, and recession

Let's see how aggregate supply shocks can increase inflation and put the economy into recession, creating **stagflation** — a process of rising prices and falling real GDP. We'll analyze the effects of supply shocks in two stages. First, we'll study the effects of such shocks on the labor market, the short-run production function, and the aggregate supply curves. Then we'll work out how the changed aggregate supply conditions interact with aggregate demand to determine the course of inflation and real GDP.

How a supply shock affects the aggregate supply curves

We derived the long-run and short-run aggregate supply curves in Chapter 8. We can use a similar analysis to work out the effects of an aggregate supply shock on the economy's aggregate supply curves, as is done in Figure 12.4. Part (a) shows the labor market, part (b) the production function, and part (c) the aggregate supply curves.

Let's begin by identifying the situation before the supply shock: the production function is PF_0, the labor demand curve is LD_0, and the supply of labor curve is LS. Equilibrium occurs where the demand for labor curve intersects the supply of labor curve, at the real wage rate W_0/P_0, and employment is n_0^*. This level of employment produces output y_0^*, as determined from the production function FP_0 in part (b). This output, y_0^*, is the level of real GDP at which the long-run aggregate supply curve LAS_0 is located (part c). With the price level at P_0, the economy is at point A on the long-run aggregate supply curve LAS_0. Point A in each part of Figure 12.4 is connected to the other points A. That is, at point A, the labor market is in equilibrium and the economy is on its production function PF_0 and on its long-run and short-run aggregate supply curves, LAS_0 and SAS_0. The short-run aggregate supply curve, SAS_0, is derived by varying the price level but keeping the money wage rate constant at W_0.

Now let's see what happens when aggregate supply decreases. Suppose an oil-price shock occurs, increasing the price of oil. This shock decreases the profit-maximizing

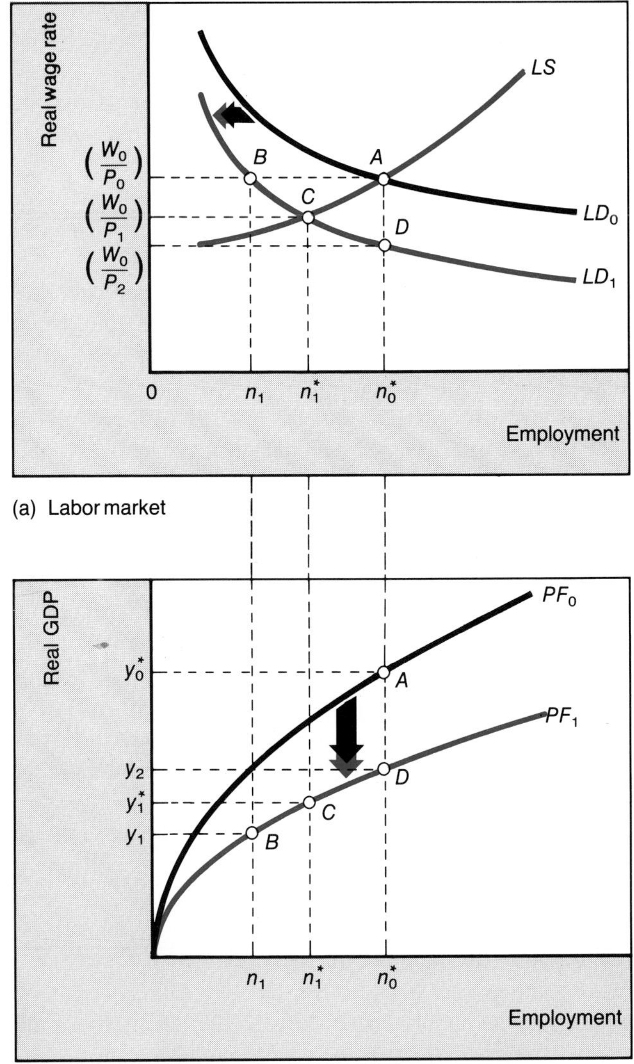

(a) Labor market

(b) Production function

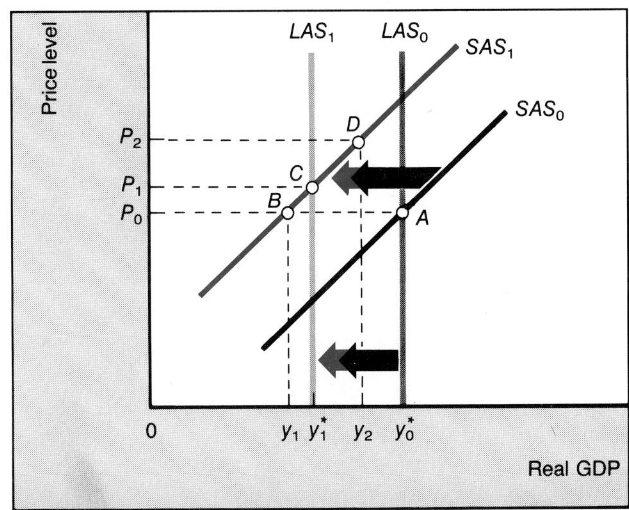

FIGURE 12.4
An Aggregate Supply Shock

Initially, the short-run aggregate supply curve is SAS_0 and the long-run aggregate supply curve LAS_0. Full employment is at point *A* (in all parts of the figure). An oil price increase or other aggregate supply shock decreases the marginal product of labor, shifting the demand for labor curve to the left from LD_0 to LD_1 (part a). This same shock shifts the short-run production function downward from PF_0 to PF_1 (part b). After the supply shock, if there is no change in the money wage rate, the economy jumps to point *B* (in all three parts). Employment decreases to n_1, real GDP falls to y_1, and the price level remains at P_0. Point *B* is on the new short-run aggregate supply curve SAS_1. If the price level increases to P_1, real wages fall to W_0/P_1 and full employment is restored. The economy is at point *C* (in all three parts) and on its new long-run aggregate supply curve, LAS_1. To return to the original employment level, the price level has to increase to P_2. The economy then moves to point *D* with above-full employment. Real GDP is y_2.

amount of energy used in all the economy's production processes. With less energy to use, labor becomes less productive. The short-run production function shifts downward, to PF_1. The marginal product of labor also declines, so the demand for labor curve shifts to the left, to LD_1.

If this is the only shock that occurs, and, in particular, if the money wage rate doesn't change, the economy moves to point B. At point B, the real wage rate is W_0/P_0 and the quantity of employment is n_1. This level of employment produces an output of y_1 (part b). Thus with the price level unchanged at P_0, the aggregate quantity of goods and services supplied is y_1, as shown in part (c). That is, the short-run aggregate supply curve has shifted to pass through point B; it is SAS_1.

But if the price level increases to P_1, so that the real wage decreases to W_0/P_1, the economy moves to point C. In part (a) the labor market is in equilibrium. There is full employment. The level of employment is n_1^*. This level of employment produces an output of y_1^*—point C on the production function PF_1 in part (b). In part (c), point C is another point on the short-run aggregate supply curve SAS_1. It is also a point on the new long-run aggregate supply curve. That is, when the price level is P_1 and the money wage rate is W_0, the real wage, W_0/P_1, is such that the labor market is in equilibrium. This employment level determines the economy's full-employment level of real GDP, y_1^*, and thus the position of its new long-run aggregate supply curve, LAS_1.

If the price level increases yet further, to P_2, the real wage decreases to W_0/P_2 and employment is at its original level of n_0^*. You can identify this point as D on the demand for labor curve LD_1 in part (a). At this employment level, the new production function PF_1 delivers an output of y_2 in part (b). That is, at the price level P_2 and real GDP of y_2, point D is on the short-run aggregate supply curve SAS_1 in part (c).

Notice, in part (c), that the aggregate supply curves shift to the left when the supply shock occurs, but the short-run aggregate supply curve shifts by more than the long-run aggregate supply curve.

The long-run aggregate supply curve shifts to the left because the production function shifts down, reducing the marginal product of labor and shifting the demand for labor curve to the left. The amount by which the long-run aggregate supply curve shifts depends partly on the magnitudes of the shifts of the production function and demand for labor curve and partly on the slope of the supply of labor curve. The flatter the supply of labor curve, the greater is the shift in the long-run aggregate supply curve.

The short-run aggregate supply curve shifts to the left by more than the long-run aggregate supply curve because of wage rigidity. The money wage rate is the same along the short-run aggregate supply curves SAS_0 and SAS_1. With no change in wages and prices, this supply shock moves the economy from point A to point B—from the economy's original long-run level of real GDP to a point below the new long-run level.

Where does the economy operate?

Where the economy operates after the supply shock depends on the response of aggregate demand and money wages. To isolate the effects of the supply shock, let's suppose that there is no change in aggregate demand and no adjustment in money wages. And to make things as clear as possible, let's suppose that before the shock the economy is experiencing no inflation and that there is full employment. Figure 12.5 illustrates this situation—the aggregate demand curve is AD_0, the short-run aggregate supply curve is SAS_0, real GDP is \$4.5 billion, and the price level is 100.

Now suppose that an aggregate supply shock, say an increase in world energy prices, occurs. Let's suppose that the effect of this supply shock is to increase costs by 10 percent at each level of real GDP. That is, the short-run aggregate supply curve shifts

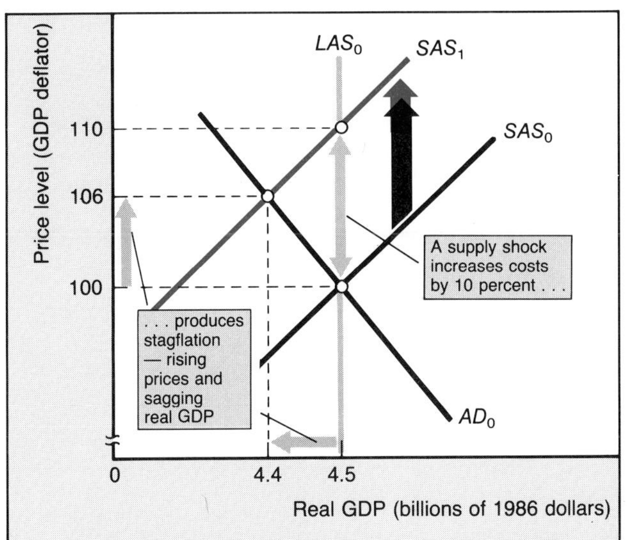

FIGURE 12.5
Supply Shock Inflation

A supply shock shifts the short-run aggregate supply curve from SAS_0 to SAS_1, increasing costs by 10 percent at each level of real GDP. Aggregate demand does not change. In the new equilibrium the price level has increased, but real GDP has decreased. The economy experiences stagflation.

from SAS_0 to SAS_1, such that the vertical distance between the two supply curves equals the 10-percent cost increase.

The economy moves to a new equilibrium where the new short-run aggregate supply curve, SAS_1, intersects the aggregate demand curve, AD_0. The price level increases to 106 and real GDP falls to $4.4 billion. This economy is now experiencing inflation and recession—stagflation.

How does the response of the economy in Figure 12.5 correspond to the performance of real economies? The answer is, the opposite usually occurs. In the real world, most of the increases in inflation occur when real GDP is above trend. But there are important exceptions. One such exception was the response of the world economy to the oil price supply shock of the mid-1970s. Let's look more closely at that episode.

12.5 *The World-wide OPEC Recession of 1975*

TESTCASE

In 1973, oil imported from Saudi Arabia was $2.70 a barrel. By 1975, that same oil cost $10.72 a barrel, with most of the increase occurring in 1974. The quadrupling of the price of one of the most vital raw materials in the world economy delivered a devastating supply shock and had widespread repercussions. Canada was cushioned from the effects of this shock by a policy of lowering taxes on energy and stabilizing its domestic price. Also, the energy-exporting sector benefitted from the higher world price. But most countries suffered a devastating blow. One such country was the United States.

There, energy-intensive activities such as transportation, steel production, heavy engineering, and chemical processing experienced larger than average cost increases. The prices of substitute fuels like coal and natural gas also increased rapidly, as did wages in the energy sector. Through this process, aggregate demand growth was moderate. The clash of massive increases in costs with moderate increases in aggregate demand led to rising prices and falling output—stagflation.

Figure 12.6 illustrates what happened in the United States (typical of the response in Japan and European countries as well) between 1973 and 1975. In 1973, U.S. real GDP was $2.8 trillion and the GDP deflator was 50. The economy was at the point of

FIGURE 12.6
The OPEC Price Shock in the United States

Between 1973 and 1975, massive oil price increases shifted the U.S. short-run aggregate supply curve from SAS_{73} to SAS_{75}. Aggregate demand growth in the United States did not match this shift in aggregate supply, and the aggregate demand curve shifted from AD_{73} to AD_{75}. Prices increased by 20 percent over the two-year period, and real GDP declined.

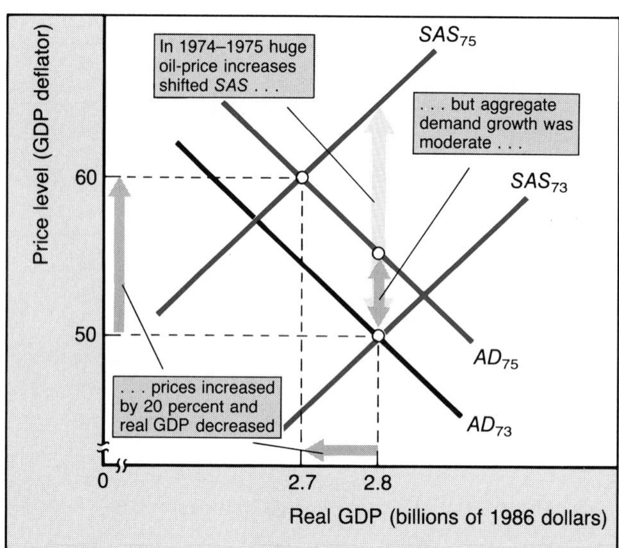

intersection of AD_{73} and SAS_{73}. Over the next two years, 1974 and 1975, the huge oil price increase along with the other cost increases it caused, shifted the short-run aggregate supply curve to SAS_{75}. Aggregate demand increased, but at a more moderate pace —in fact, a pace similar to that in previous years. During 1974 and 1975, the aggregate demand curve shifted upward to AD_{75}. By 1975, real GDP was $2.7 trillion, and the GDP deflator had increased to 60. The economy had experienced a 20 percent increase in prices (almost 10 percent a year), and real GDP declined.

In 1975, the economy was in a deep recession and inflation was falling. By 1976, costs increased at a slower pace, shifting the *SAS* curve by a smaller amount and moderating inflation. The economy moved closer to full employment.

We've used the aggregate demand-aggregate supply model to study the effects of aggregate demand changes on inflation. Another model tells the same basic story, while giving additional insights into the inflation process and the links between inflation and the business cycle. Let's have a look at this alternative approach.

12.6 *The Phillips Curve*

The **Phillips curve** is a relationship between the inflation rate and the unemployment rate, holding constant the natural rate of unemployment and the expected inflation rate. The Phillips curve provides another way of looking at the relationship between inflation and the business cycle. Let's begin by reviewing the original Phillips curve. Then we'll study the modern Phillips curve and establish the relationship between the Phillips curve and the aggregate demand-aggregate supply model.

The original Phillips curve

The Phillips curve was first proposed by A. W. (Bill) Phillips, after studying the relationship between unemployment and the rate of change of wages in the United Kingdom for the 100 years between the 1860s and 1960s. Phillips plotted the rate of change of money wages against the unemployment rate in each year and discovered that the higher the unemployment rate, the lower was the rate of wage change. With a high correlation

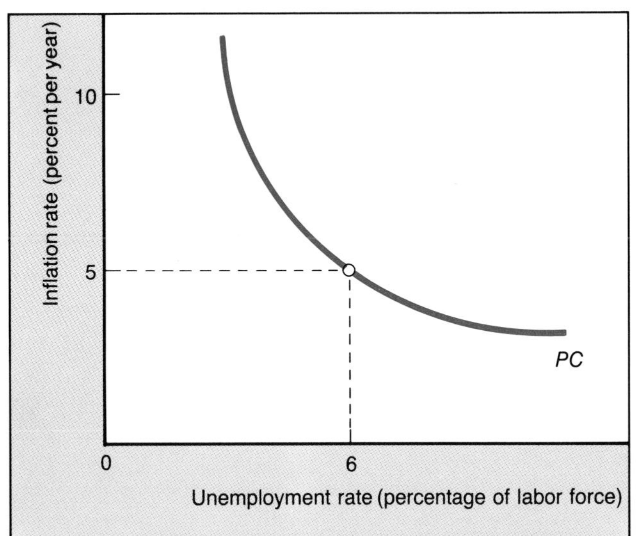

FIGURE 12.7
A Phillips Curve

A Phillips curve shows the relationship between the inflation rate and the unemployment rate, holding constant the expected inflation rate and the natural rate of unemployment. Other things being equal, the higher the unemployment rate, the lower is the inflation rate.

between wage change and inflation, the Phillips curve evolved from the relationship between wage change and unemployment to one between inflation and unemployment. Figure 12.7 shows such a Phillips curve.

Following Phillips's original work, a flood of research discovered Phillips curves in the data for Canada, the United States, and most other countries. It seemed as if every country had a Phillips curve, especially in the 1960s. The proponents of the Phillips curve thought they had found a permanent and stable relationship between inflation and unemployment. But some skeptics believed that the Phillips curve was a temporary phenomenon that many factors could cause to shift. They believed too that some of these factors were so important that they would dominate the Phillips curve itself. Most important of these factors is the expected inflation rate.

The expectations-augmented Phillips curve

The **expectations-augmented Phillips curve** is a short-run Phillips curve the position of which depends on the expected inflation rate. A **short-run Phillips curve** is a Phillips curve drawn for a particular, given, expected inflation rate. It contrasts with a **long-run Phillips curve**, the relationship between inflation and the unemployment rate when inflation is fully anticipated. The long-run Phillips curve is vertical at the natural rate of unemployment. The short-run Phillips curve intersects the long-run Phillips curve at the expected inflation rate.

These propositions about the effects of inflation expectations on the Phillips curve and the link between the short-run and long-run Phillips curves were first suggested by Milton Friedman and Edmund Phelps, both writing in the mid-1960s, at a time when there appeared to be a stable Phillips curve. They reasoned that when unemployment is at its natural rate there is neither excess demand for nor excess supply of labor, and real wages will be constant. With constant real wages, both prices and wages will rise at the same rate, but wages will also be increasing at the expected inflation rate. Thus with unemployment at its natural rate, actual and expected inflation are equal — inflation is anticipated. Any inflation rate is possible at the natural rate of unemployment as long as it is anticipated. Thus, reasoned Friedman and Phelps, the long-run Phillips curve, *LPC*, is vertical at the natural rate of unemployment. Figure 12.8 illustrates such a curve.

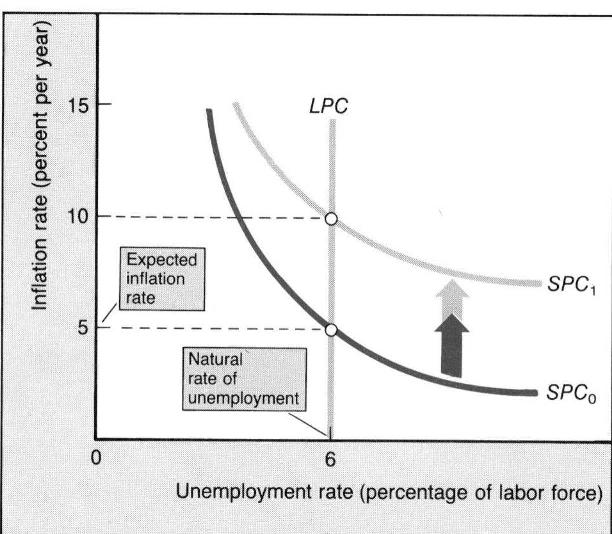

FIGURE 12.8
Expected Inflation and the Phillips Curve

Anticipated increases in aggregate demand bring anticipated inflation at full employment. Any inflation rate is possible, provided it is anticipated. The long-run Phillips curve, *LPC*, shows the relationship between anticipated inflation and unemployment. Unemployment is at its natural rate and any inflation rate is possible. The *LPC* is vertical. The short-run Phillips curve, *SPC*, depends on the expected inflation rate. It intersects the long-run Phillips curve at the expected inflation rate. When expected inflation is 5 percent, the short-run Phillips curve is SPC_0; when expected inflation is 10 percent, the short-run Phillips curve is SPC_1.

For a given expected inflation rate, for example, 5 percent a year, there is a short-run Phillips curve, SPC_0. The short-run Phillips curve intersects the long-run Phillips curve at the expected inflation rate. If unemployment is above the natural rate, there is excess supply in the labor market and real wages decrease. The actual inflation rate is less than the expected inflation rate. At all points on the short-run curve SPC_0, the expected inflation rate is 5 percent; but if unemployment goes above 6 percent, actual inflation falls below 5 percent a year. Alternatively, if unemployment is below its natural rate, there is excess demand in the labor market and real wages increase. The actual inflation rate exceeds the expected inflation rate.

A change in the expected inflation rate shifts the short-run Phillips curve. For example, if the expected inflation rate increased from 5 percent to 10 percent a year, the short-run Phillips curve would shift upward, from SPC_0 to SPC_1 in Figure 12.8.

Phillips curves and the aggregate demand-aggregate supply model

The Phillips curve is not a theory of inflation different from the one based on the aggregate demand–aggregate supply model. Both are based on the same *ideas*, but packaged differently. Figure 12.9 shows the different packaging and the relationship between the two.

Here's what's going on in Figure 12.9. Part (a) contains the aggregate demand-aggregate supply analysis. Part (b) contains Okun's Law — the relationship between unemployment and real GDP we studied in Chapter 9. Part (c) is just a device for linking parts (b) and (d); it measures the unemployment rate on each axis and contains a 45° line. Part (d) shows the Phillips curve analysis. First, let's establish the full-employment point in this economy. The long-run aggregate supply curve is *LAS*; thus long-run, or capacity, real GDP is $4.5 billion. Given Okun's Law, the natural rate of unemployment is 6 percent at this level of real GDP. The long-run Phillips curve, *LPC*, is vertical at that natural rate of unemployment.

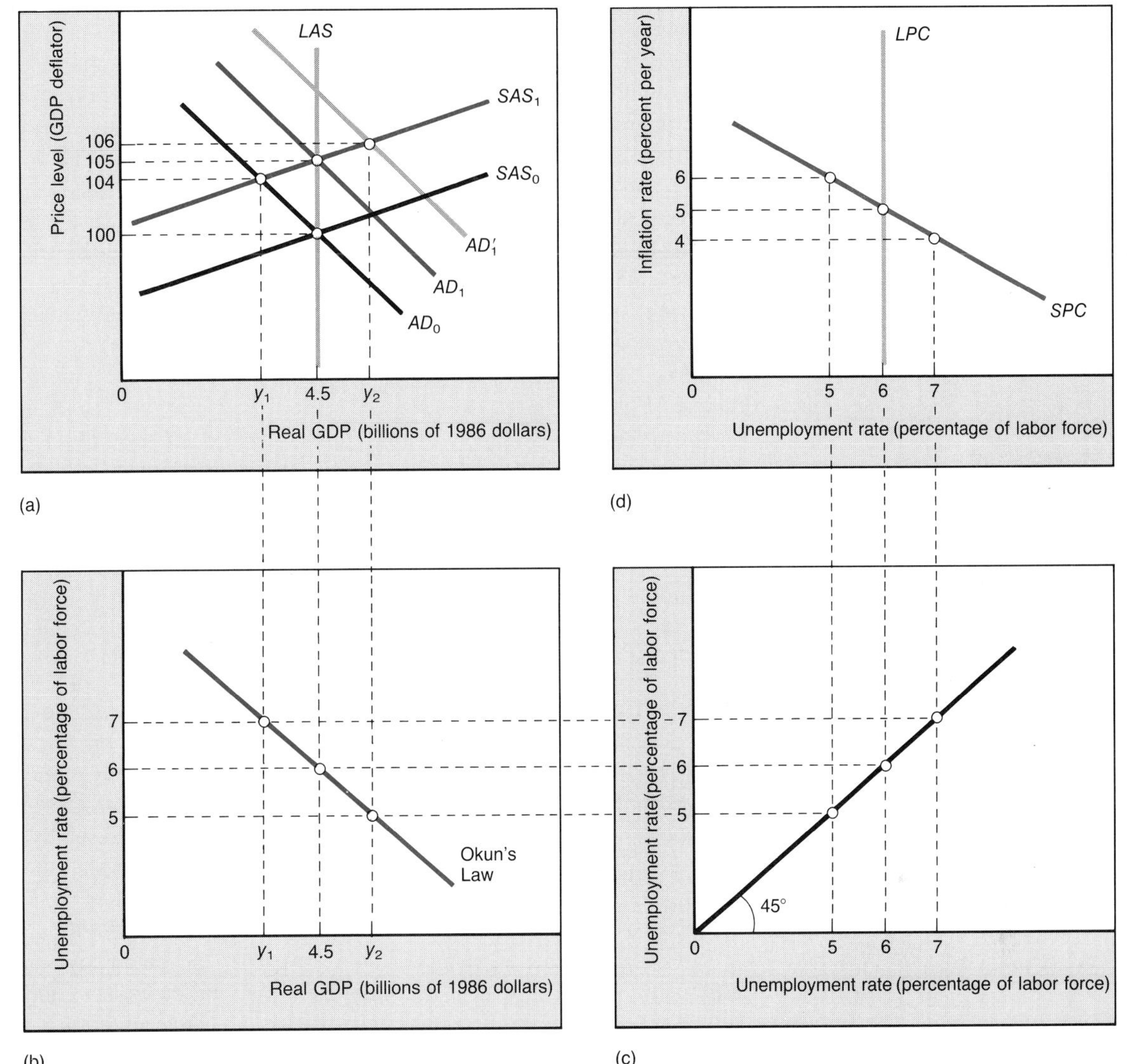

FIGURE 12.9
The Phillips Curve and the Aggregate Demand-Aggregate Supply Model

The aggregate demand-aggregate supply model and the Phillips curve are two ways of looking at the same phenomenon. Part (a) shows the aggregate demand and aggregate supply curves. Starting out with AD_0 and SAS_0, an anticipated increase in aggregate demand shifts the AD curve to AD_1. Being anticipated, wages also increase, shifting the short-run aggregate supply curve to SAS_1. The economy experiences 5 percent inflation—the price level increases from 100 to 105. Real GDP stays at its long-run level of $4.5 billion.

Part (b) illustrates Okun's Law, the relationship between the unemployment rate and real GDP. Part (c) links parts (b) and (d). Part (d) shows the Phillips curve. The long-run Phillips curve, *LPC*, is at the natural rate of unemployment—6 percent. The short-run Phillips curve, *SPC*, intersects the long-run Phillips curve at the expected inflation rate—5 percent a year. If aggregate demand is expected to increase to AD_1 but actually increases to AD'_1, real GDP increases to y_2 and price level to 106. There is a 6 percent inflation (part a). Okun's Law (part b) tells us that real GDP is y_2 and the unemployment rate is 5 percent. This is shown as a movement along the short-run Phillips curve in part (d) with unemployment falling to 5 percent as inflation increases to 6 percent.

If aggregate demand is expected to increase to AD_1 but actually remains constant at AD_0, real GDP falls to y_1 and inflation falls to 4 percent (the price level increasing to 104) in part (a). Unemployment increases to 7 percent and there is a movement along the short-run Phillips curve *SPC* in part (d) with inflation falling to 4 percent a year.

Steady-state inflation Suppose the economy is experiencing a 5 percent anticipated inflation. The expected inflation rate is 5 percent and the short-run Phillips curve, *SPC*, intersects the long-run Phillips curve, *LPC*, at that inflation rate. In the aggregate demand-aggregate supply analysis (part a), the anticipated inflation arises from a process in which the aggregate demand and short-run aggregate supply curves are constantly shifting upward at a rate of 5 percent a year. The aggregate demand curve shifts up from AD_0 to AD_1 and the short-run aggregate supply curve from SAS_0 to SAS_1. Prices increase by 5 percent a year and real GDP stays at its long-run level. In the Phillips curve analysis (part d), the economy stays at the point of intersection of the short-run Phillips curve (*SPC*) and the long-run Phillips curve (*LPC*).

If in the next year, a 5 percent inflation occurs again, the aggregate demand and short-run aggregate supply curves shift up again (not shown in the figure), to 5 percent above AD_1 and SAS_1. But again, in part (d), the economy remains at the point of intersection of *SPC* and *LPC*.

You can begin to see the advantage of the Phillips curve over the *AD-AS* model. Anticipated inflation in the *AD-AS* model shifts the aggregate demand and short-run supply curves upward each year. After two or three years, the diagram becomes very messy, with more and more *AD* and *SAS* curves, each 5 percent higher than the preceding year's, intersecting at higher and higher price levels along the vertical *LAS* curve. In contrast, the Phillips curve diagram has just one short-run Phillips curve for a given expected inflation rate. Part (d) illustrates the economy experiencing a 5 percent anticipated inflation with a single short-run Phillips curve.

Unanticipated inflation Let's continue to analyze an economy that has an expected inflation rate of 5 percent. That is, the short-run Phillips curve remains in the position shown in Figure 12.9(d). But suppose aggregate demand increases by an unanticipated amount. First, suppose that aggregate demand doesn't increase at all. It remains at AD_0, but expected inflation increases wages and shifts the short-run aggregate supply curve upward to SAS_1. According to the aggregate demand-aggregate supply model, the equilibrium now occurs at a price level of 104 and a real GDP of y_1. Inflation is 4 percent a year, not 5 percent as expected. The same outcome is illustrated by the Phillips curve. When real GDP is y_1 you can see, using Okun's Law, that the unemployment rate increases to 7 percent. With a 7 percent unemployment rate and an expected inflation rate of 5 percent, the short-run Phillips curve tells us that the actual inflation rate is 4 percent a year.

Similarly, if aggregate demand increases more than expected, we travel in the opposite direction along the short-run Phillips curve. Suppose that aggregate demand increased to AD_1'. In this case, according to the aggregate demand-aggregate supply model in part (a), the price level increases to 106 and real GDP increases to y_2. The economy experiences 6 percent inflation.

The same result is shown in the Phillips curve diagram in Figure 12.9(d). With real GDP at y_2, we can see, from Okun's Law in Figure 12.9(b), that unemployment falls to 5 percent. With 5 percent unemployment and 5 percent expected inflation, the short-run Phillips curve tells us that the inflation rate is 6 percent a year.

Strength of *AD-AS* model We've just seen that the Phillips curve way of looking at inflation has an advantage over the *AD-AS* model because we can keep track of an inflating economy without using curves that constantly shift as the price level increases. In contrast, to keep track of ongoing inflation in the *AD-AS* model, we have to keep shifting the *AD* and *SAS* curves. It seems, therefore, that the Phillips curve is a much handier tool than the *AD-AS* model. But the *AD-AS* model does have a strength: it shows us the deeper underlying sources of both inflation and unemployment. The price level and real GDP—as well as the inflation rate and unemployment—are determined by the pace at which aggregate demand and short-run aggregate supply are changing. The *AD-AS* model emphasizes that fact and shows us the consequences of these underlying forces.

The Phillips curve, in contrast, summarizes what is happening to both inflation and unemployment at a given expected inflation rate but does not give us any information about where on the short-run Phillips curve the economy is located. Thus to interpret what is happening in a Phillips curve diagram, it's always necessary to go back to the *AD-AS* model to discover the disturbances moving the economy.

Changes in the natural rate of unemployment

We've seen that a change in the expected inflation rate shifts the short-run Phillips curve. A change in the natural rate of unemployment also shifts the short-run Phillips curve. In Chapter 9, we saw that the natural rate of unemployment fluctuates over time. And when it does, the position of the long-run Phillips curve changes with it. For example, if the natural rate of unemployment increases from 6 percent to 8 percent, the long-run Phillips curve shifts from LPC_0 to LPC_1 in Figure 12.10. The short-run Phillips curve shifts with it—from SPC_0 to SPC_1. How do we know that the short-run Phillips curve shifts? Recall that the short-run Phillips curve tells us the relationship between inflation and unemployment at a given expected inflation rate. When unemployment equals its natural rate, actual and expected inflation are equal. Thus the short-run Phillips curve always intersects the long-run Phillips curve at the expected inflation rate. Therefore if the long-run Phillips curve shifts, so does the short-run Phillips curve, to intersect the new long-run Phillips curve at the given expected inflation rate.

We've seen that the Phillips curve is a useful theoretical device for keeping track of the economy's inflation rate and the relationship between expected and actual inflation. But what is the Phillips curve like in reality? Is it a practically useful device? Let's take a look.

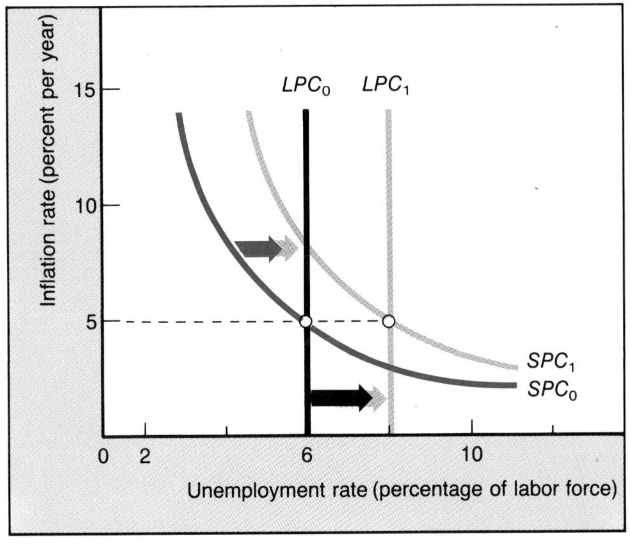

FIGURE 12.10
The Phillips Curve and the Natural Unemployment Rate

An increase in the natural rate of unemployment shifts the long-run Phillips curve to the right from LPC_0 to LPC_1. It also shifts the short-run Phillips curve to the right by the same amount so that the new short-run Phillips curve, SPC_1, intersects the new long-run Phillips curve, LPC_1, at the same expected inflation rate as the initial short-run Phillips curve, SPC_0, intersected the initial long-run Phillips curve, LPC_0.

TESTCASE

12.7 *The Canadian Phillips Curve since 1960*

In studying the Phillips curve in the Canadian economy, we'll begin by reviewing the raw data on inflation and unemployment. Then we'll see how we can interpret that data using Phillips curve theory.

The raw data

Canadian inflation and unemployment are graphed in Figure 12.11(a). Each point represents the combination of the inflation rate and unemployment rate for the identified year. You met these data in earlier chapters, but here the information is presented in an interesting and novel way. It shows you that during the early 1960s, inflation was moderate. As the 1960s evolved, unemployment decreased and inflation increased.

FIGURE 12.11
The Phillips Curve in Reality

Part (a) shows the data for Canadian inflation and unemployment between 1960 and 1990. There is no obvious Phillips curve. Instead, there is a tendency for inflation and unemployment to follow the pattern of a broken coilspring.

Part (b) interprets the data in terms of a sequence of short-run Phillips curves. In the 1960s, the Phillips curve was SPC_0. It shifted to SPC_1 in 1970 and then to SPC_2 by 1974. It kept shifting outward through 1980, when it reached SPC_3. It then shifted back, and by 1990 it was SPC_1. The Phillips curve shifted out as a result of increasing inflation expectations and an increasing natural rate of unemployment and then back as a result of decreasing inflation expectations and a decreasing natural rate of unemployment.

Source: National Income and Expenditure Accounts, Statistics Canada, Catalogue 13-201, and *Historical Labour Force Statistics*, Statistics Canada, Catalogue 71-201.

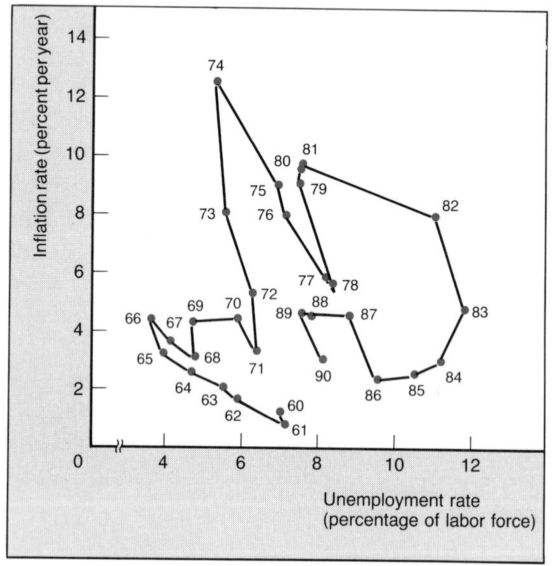

(a) The time sequence

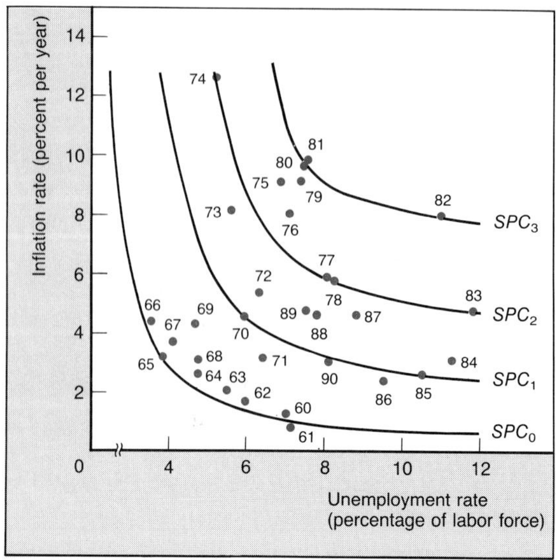

(b) Phillips curves

Between 1966 and 1971, inflation was relatively steady but unemployment increased. Then, in 1972, inflation began to increase, reaching a peak in 1974. There followed a period of falling inflation and mildly increasing unemployment up to 1978 and then another burst of inflation up to 1981. Beginning in 1982, inflation began to decline but at the cost of a steep rise in unemployment through 1983. After 1983, both inflation and unemployment began to fall. After 1986, unemployment continued to fall but inflation started to rise again.

It's not easy to see a Phillips curve in Figure 12.11(a). The general shape formed by the points looks more like a circle than a curve. On closer inspection, it's like a series of unfolding loops—something like a misshapen coil spring. But closer inspection tells us that we can indeed interpret these data as having been generated by a sequence of short-run Phillips curves.

The shifting Phillips curve

Transport yourself back to the beginning of 1970, when the only data in Figure 12.11(a) are those for 1960 through 1969. What do you see? A Phillips curve! The Phillips curve in question is SPC_0 in Figure 12.11(b). This is *the* Phillips curve discovered by John Vanderkamp when he first studied the Canadian Phillips curve data in the late 1960s.

But toward the end of the 1960s, inflation and expected inflation both began to increase. With an increase in the expected inflation rate, the short-run Phillips curve began to shift upward to SPC_1.

A combination of higher inflation expectations and a supply shock that increased the natural rate of unemployment shifted the Phillips curve to SPC_2 by 1975. The natural rate of unemployment increased again in the late 1970s, shifting the short-run Phillips curve to SPC_3. The curve remained there for a couple of years until falling inflation expectations shifted it back to the left, through SPC_2 and eventually to SPC_1. The short-run Phillips curve at the beginning of the 1990s is likely still the curve SPC_1, with a natural rate of unemployment of around 7 percent and an expected inflation rate of around 4 percent a year.

Is inflation the price of full employment?

We opened this chapter with the question, "Is inflation the price of full employment?" With what you have learned in this chapter, you can now answer this question. You have discovered that inflation is *not* the price of full employment. At full employment, the economy is on its long-run Phillips curve and any anticipated inflation rate is possible. But pushing the unemployment rate below the natural rate involves accelerating inflation. Pushing the unemployment rate above its natural rate involves falling inflation.

Do these facts mean that the only way of reducing inflation is to accept unemployment above its natural rate? This question has no simple answer. If there are widely held expectations of ongoing growth in the money supply and aggregate demand, and if these expectations are rational based on the past and best-forecasted future behavior of the Bank of Canada, then lowering inflation almost certainly does require some temporary increase in unemployment above the natural rate. For only by doing the unexpected—by lowering the growth rate of aggregate demand — can inflation be brought under control.

If, on the other hand, it is possible to slow the growth rate of aggregate demand in line with people's expectations of such a slowdown, then, in principle at least, it is possible to lower inflation without increasing unemployment above its natural rate. We saw an example of such a slowdown in inflation in the experience of Israel in the 1980s.

We have not, however, seen such an example in the recent macroeconomic history of Canada. In this economy, at least on the basis of our experience to date, it appears that slowing inflation does involve making aggregate demand grow *unexpectedly* slowly, thereby creating excess capacity and unemployment above the natural rate.

■ In this chapter, we've studied the forces that influence inflation over the business cycle and discovered the main reasons for the correlations between inflation and the business cycle that we observe in the Canadian data. Our next task is to study one of the possible sources of inflationary pressures in an economy — government deficits and debts. But we'll study deficits and debts more broadly, looking at both private as well as public deficits and borrowing.

CHAPTER REVIEW

Summary

INFLATION OVER THE BUSINESS CYCLE

No strong, simple correlation exists between inflation and the business cycle, but there is an important pattern: inflation tends to increase when real GDP is above trend and decrease when real GDP is below trend. But the turning points in inflation don't coincide with the points at which real GDP switches from being on one side of trend to the other. Inflation tends to keep on increasing for a while after real GDP falls below trend and begins to increase again before real GDP gets back above trend.

EFFECTS OF UNANTICIPATED CHANGES IN AGGREGATE DEMAND

An unanticipated increase in aggregate demand shifts the aggregate demand curve upward. But being unanticipated, wages do not increase, so the short-run aggregate supply curve does not shift upward. The combination of increased aggregate demand with no change in short-run aggregate supply increases the price level and real GDP. Real GDP moves above its full-employment level and inflation accelerates.

An unanticipated decrease in aggregate demand (or an unanticipated slowdown in the rate at which aggregate demand is growing) has the opposite effect. Real GDP dips below its full-employment level and inflation slows.

THE 1981-1982 RECESSION

In the early 1980s, the economy experienced an unanticipated slowdown in the growth of aggregate demand. Wages and other costs increased, shifting the short-run aggregate supply curve to the left (and upward) at a faster pace than the growth of aggregate demand. The result was stagflation. Real GDP declined, falling below its full-employment level, and inflation slowed.

SUPPLY SHOCKS AND INFLATION

Supply shocks produce stagflation. A supply shock shifts the production function downward, decreases the marginal product of labor, and shifts the demand for labor curve to the left. The combined effect is to decrease long-run aggregate supply and short-run aggregate supply. The short-run aggregate supply curve at a given money wage rate shifts farther to the left than the long-run aggregate supply curve. With a decrease in aggregate supply but no change in aggregate demand, real GDP falls and the price level rises.

OIL PRICE SHOCKS AND THE WORLD ECONOMY IN THE 1970s

Between 1973 and 1975, massive oil price increases shifted the short-run aggregate supply curve and long-run aggregate supply curve of most countries to the left. Aggregate demand increased, but at a much slower pace than the rising costs associated with the supply shocks. The result was a decrease in real GDP and an increase in inflation.

THE PHILLIPS CURVE

Phillips curve theory is an alternative tool for studying inflation over the business cycle. The Phillips curve is a relationship between inflation and unemployment. Phillips curve theory states that for a given natural rate of unemployment and a given expected inflation rate, the higher the unemployment rate, the lower is the inflation rate.

But the Phillips curve is a short-run relationship. There is also a long-run Phillips curve—a vertical line at the natural unemployment rate. The long-run Phillips curve states that any fully anticipated inflation rate is possible at the natural rate of unemployment. A change in the expected inflation rate shifts the short-run Phillips curve upward or downward by the same percentage amount as the change in the expected inflation. The point at which the short-run Phillips curve intersects the long-run Phillips curve is the expected inflation rate.

A change in the natural rate of unemployment shifts both the short-run and long-run Phillips curves. An increase in the natural rate shifts the Phillips curves to the right; a decrease in the natural rate shifts the Phillips curves to the left. The horizontal shift of both the short-run and the long-run Phillips curves is the same, the short-run Phillips curve always intersecting the long-run Phillips curve at the expected inflation rate.

THE PHILLIPS CURVE IN CANADA SINCE 1960

In the thirty years between 1960 and 1990, Canadian inflation and unemployment followed an unwinding spiral pattern similar to a misshapen coil. But the data can be interpreted as lying on a sequence of Phillips curves. During the 1960s, the Phillips curve was stable. In the 1970s, it started to shift upward as a result of expectations of higher inflation and a rising natural rate of unemployment. By 1980, the Phillips curve was farthest from its position of the 1960s. Through the 1980s, inflation expectations and the natural rate of unemployment gradually decreased and the short-run Phillips curve shifted back toward its 1960s level, though did not get back to that initial position by 1990.

Key Terms and Concepts

Expectations-augmented Phillips curve A short-run Phillips curve the position of which depends on the expected inflation rate.

Long-run Phillips curve The relationship between inflation and the unemployment rate when inflation is fully anticipated.

Phillips curve A relationship between the inflation rate and the unemployment rate, holding constant the natural rate of unemployment and the expected inflation rate.

Short-run Phillips curve A Phillips curve drawn for a particular, given, expected inflation rate.

Stagflation A process of rising prices and falling real GDP.

Review Questions

1. Describe the relationship between inflation and the business cycle in Canada since 1970.
2. Explain the effects of an unanticipated rise in aggregate demand growth on inflation and real GDP.
3. Explain the effects of an unanticipated fall in aggregate demand growth on inflation and real GDP.
4. How does the *AD-AS* model explain the relationship between inflation and the business cycle?
5. What was the 1981-1982 recession? When and why did it occur?
6. What is a supply shock? Give some examples of supply shocks to the world economy since 1960.
7. What is stagflation? Has the world economy experienced stagflation since 1970? If so, when?
8. Explain how a supply shock produces stagflation.
9. When did the OPEC recession occur in the United States and other major countries? How does the *AD-AS* model explain the OPEC recession?
10. Why did Canada avoid the worst of the OPEC recession? Explain using the *AD-AS* model.
11. What is the Phillips curve? What is the expectations-augmented Phillips curve? Is the short-run Phillips curve stable? Explain your answer.
12. Distinguish between the short-run and long-run Phillips curves. What is the relationship between them? Why do they shift?
13. Compare the Phillips curve analysis of inflation with that of the *AD-AS* model. What are the strengths of each approach?
14. Is the cost of lower unemployment higher inflation? Explain why or why not.

Problems

1. An economy that is experiencing no inflation has the following aggregate demand and short-run aggregate supply:

$$y^d = 750/P$$
$$y^s = 1000 - (250/P^2).$$

   (a) If aggregate demand unexpectedly increases by 1/3, what is the change in the price level and real GDP?
   (b) What is the approximate inflation rate in this economy if aggregate demand continues to grow unexpectedly by 1/3 each year?
   (c) If in problem (a) aggregate demand unexpectedly falls by 1/3, what will be the change in the price level and real GDP?
   (d) What is the approximate inflation rate in this economy if aggregate demand continues to be cut unexpectedly by 1/3 each year?
2. Find the short-run Phillips curve for the economy in problem 1.
3. In problem 1(a), if the increase in aggregate demand had been expected, would the economy have moved
   (a) along its short-run Phillips curve?
   (b) along its long-run Phillips curve?
   (c) to a new short-run Phillips curve?

4. Use problem 1 to explain why an unexpected change in aggregate demand by itself does not cause stagflation.

5. Consider an economy described by the following:

Production function	$y = 100n - 0.2n^2$
Demand for labor	$n^d = 250 - 2.5(W_0/P)$
Supply of labor	$n^s = 100 + 2.5(W_0/P)$

where W_0 is the fixed money wage, P the price level, and n the level of employment.

Calculate:

(a) Full-employment output
(b) Full-employment real wage
(c) The equation to the *LAS* curve
(d) The equation to the *SAS* curve

6. The economy in problem 5 experiences a supply shock that shifts the production function to

$$y = 50n - 0.1n^2$$

and the demand for labor to

$$n^d = 250 - 5(W_0/P).$$

(a) Find three points on the new *SAS* curve.
(b) Find a point on the new *LAS* curve.
(c) Compare the price levels at the intersection points of the *LAS* and *SAS* curves before and after the supply shock.

7. An economy experiences price stability and has the following aggregate demand and short-run aggregate supply:

$$y^d = 900/P$$
$$y^s = 1000 - 300/P^2.$$

A supply shock lowers short-run aggregate supply by 250.

(a) What is the change in the price level and real GDP?
(b) How would you describe the co-movement in the price level and real GDP?
(c) Does the economy move along its short-run Phillips curve? Explain why or why not.

APPENDIX

The Algebra of Rational Expectations Equilibrium

This appendix sets out the algebra of a rational expectations equilibrium model. It presents the simplest example of a rational expectations equilibrium. The starting point is the *IS-LM* theory of aggregate demand. The Appendix to Chapter 5 derives the equation to the aggregate demand curve. The level of real income at each price level (P) is the level of aggregate demand (y^d). To emphasize this, Equation (5A.14) is modified as follows:

$$y^d = \frac{a + i_0 + g - bt + \frac{h}{\ell}\left(\frac{M}{P} - m_0\right)}{1 - b + kh/\ell} \qquad \textbf{(12A.1)}$$

Equation (12A.1) tells us the level of aggregate demand (y^d) at each price level (P), given government purchases, taxes, and the money supply.

We can rewrite Equation (12A.1) with a different emphasis as

$$y^d = \left[\frac{a + i_0 + g - bt - \frac{h}{\ell}m_0}{1 - b + kh/\ell}\right] + \left[\frac{\frac{h}{\ell}}{1 - b + kh/\ell}\right]\left(\frac{M}{P}\right) \qquad \textbf{(12A.2)}$$

Calling m the logarithm of M, and p the logarithm of P, we may write an approximation to the above as

$$y_t^d = \alpha_t + \beta(m_t - p_t),\ \beta > 0 \qquad \textbf{(12A.3)}$$

In Equation (12A.3), α represents the first term in brackets in Equation (12A.2), and $\beta(m_t - p_t)$ is a logarithmic approximation to the second term. The subscript t is added to each variable in Equation (12A.3) to remind us that these magnitudes vary over time. Thus the subscript t represents a given point in time. Evidently, α stands for all the things that cause aggregate demand to vary, other than the real money supply. It incorporates, therefore, government expenditure, taxes, and any shifts in the investment function or the demand for money function. The money supply (m) and the price level (p) are expressed as logarithms, so that $m-p$ is the same as log M/P. (This formulation, which is linear in the logarithm of real money balances rather than the level of real money balances, makes the explicit calculation of expectations more straightforward.) The parameter β is the multiplier effect of a change in the logarithm of real money balances on the level of aggregate demand.

We can represent the short-run aggregate supply curve in equation form as

$$y_t^s = y^* + \gamma(p_t - p_t^e), \gamma > 0 \qquad \textbf{(12A.4)}$$

where y^* represents full employment output and p and p^e are the logarithms of the actual and expected price level, respectively. This is just a convenient translation into equation form of what you already know. To convince yourself of this, notice first that if the price level was equal to its expected value ($p = p^e$), then aggregate supply would be equal to full-employment aggregate supply y^*. As the actual price level exceeds the expected price level, so output rises above y^*. The positive parameter γ captures this.

Next, equilibrium prevails, in the sense that aggregate supply equals aggregate demand, and actual output y is also equal to the level of aggregate demand and aggregate supply. We can write this as two equations. That is

$$y_t = y_t^d = y_t^s \tag{12A.5}$$

The first step in finding the rational expectations equilibrium of this model is to calculate the expected values of output and the price level, given the expected values of α and m. (A full treatment would also have an explicit theory for the determination of α and m. We will not make that extension here.) Calculating the expected values of y and p, given the expected values of α and m, simply involves taking the expectations of Equations (12A.3) and (12A.4) and using the fact that actual output is the same as the level of aggregate demand and aggregate supply. Letting the superscript e stand for the expected value of a variable, you can immediately see that this implies

$$y_t^e = \alpha_t^e + \beta(m_t^e - p_t^e) \tag{12A.6}$$

and

$$y_t^e = y^* \tag{12A.7}$$

Equation (12A.6) follows directly from Equation (12A.3). If Equation (12A.3) describes what determines the actual level of aggregate output demanded and if aggregate demand equals actual output, then expected output must be equal to the expected value of α plus β times the expected value of real balances. That is all that Equation (12A.6) says. Equation (12A.7) follows directly from Equation (12A.4). It says what you already know, namely, that expected output will be equal to full-employment output since the expected price level is the rational expectation. That is, p_t^e is the same thing as the expectation of p_t, and so the second term in Equation (12A.4) is expected to be zero.

You can now solve Equation (12A.7) for the expected price level. Substitute Equation (12A.7) into Equation (12A.6) and rearrange it to give

$$p_t^e = m_t^e - \frac{1}{\beta}(y^* - \alpha_t^e) \tag{12A.8}$$

Recall that p and m are logarithms, so that this says that the expected price level is proportional to the expected money supply.

To calculate the actual levels of output and the price level, first of all, substitute Equation (12A.7) into Equation (12A.6) and subtract this equation from Equation (12A.3). Also subtract y^* from both sides of Equation (12A.4). The results are

$$y_t^d - y^* = (\alpha_t - \alpha_t^e) + \beta(m_t - m_t^e) - \beta(p_t - p_t^e) \tag{12A.9}$$

$$y_t^s - y^* = \gamma(p_t - p_t^e) \tag{12A.10}$$

Equation (12A.9) says that output will deviate from its full-employment level by the amount that α deviates from its expected level, plus the parameter β times the amount that the money stock deviates from its expected level minus the amount by which the price level deviates from its expected level, multiplied by the same parameter β. It is, in terms of the concepts discussed in the chapter, the unexpected component of aggregate demand. Equation (12A.10), says that deviations of aggregate supply from its full-employment level will be proportional to deviations of the price level from its expectation.

We may now solve these two Equations (12A.9) and (12A.10) for the *actual* levels of output and the price level. Using Equations (12A.9) and (12A.10) with (12A.5), these solutions are

$$y_t = y^* + \frac{\gamma}{\gamma + \beta}\alpha_t - \alpha_t^e + \beta(m_t - m_t^e) \qquad \textbf{(12A.11)}$$

and

$$p_t = m_t^e - \frac{1}{\beta}(y^* - \alpha_t^e) + \frac{1}{\gamma + \beta}\alpha_t - \alpha_t^e + \beta(m_t - m_t^e) \qquad \textbf{(12A.12)}$$

The output equation says that output will deviate from its full-employment level by an amount that depends on the unexpected components of α and the money supply. The price level deviates from its expected level—the first two terms in Equation (12A.12)—by an amount that depends on the deviations of α and the money supply from their expected levels.

Thus you can see that it is only unanticipated shifts in aggregate demand that affect output, and it is both the anticipated and unanticipated shifts in aggregate demand that affect the price level. The multipliers of the *IS-LM* analysis tell us about the distance of the horizontal shift of the aggregate demand curve. Equations (12A.11) and (12A.12) tell us that to the extent that this horizontal shift is anticipated, it will do nothing but raise the price level. To the extent that it is unanticipated, it will raise both output and the price level and will distribute its effects between output and the price level in accordance with the slope parameter γ, the slope of the *SAS* curve. You can see, as a matter of interest, that if γ was infinitely big, the effect of an unanticipated shift in aggregate demand would be exactly the same as the *IS-LM* model says, and it would have no effect on the price level. You can see this immediately for the price level in Equation (12A.12). For output, rearrange $\gamma/(\gamma + \beta)$ by γ to give $1/[1 + (\beta/\gamma)]$. You now see that as γ approaches ∞, so $1/[1 + (\beta/\gamma)]$ approaches 1, so that Equation (12A.11) becomes the level of real income in the *IS-LM* analysis.

CHAPTER 13

Public and Private Deficits and Debts

AN ECONOMIC BLACK HOLE?

A BLACK HOLE IS A POSTULATED OBJECT of such concentrated mass that not even light can escape its gravitational attraction. It sucks in everything within a critical distance of its center, becoming ever more and more dense and inescapable. People often talk about debt as if it were a kind of economic black hole. Debt is seen as the source of economic hardship and ever greater debt. The indebted family, firm, government, or nation is pictured as struggling to meet its interest burden, borrowing even more to pay the interest on last year's debt, and getting into a deeper and deeper debt hole every year.

Are deficits and debt a kind of economic black hole? Or are they much more ordinary objects that perhaps even play a beneficial role in economic life? This chapter studies deficits and debts (and their opposite surpluses and the accumulation of assets) of people, of firms, of governments and nations.

After studying this chapter, you will be able to

- Describe Canadian deficits and debts and place them in their historical and international context
- Explain the relationships between stocks and flows, receipts and payments, and borrowing and lending
- Describe the main sources of Canadian government deficits in the 1980s
- Explain how inflation distorts the deficit
- Explain the limits to the amount that can be borrowed
- Explain how deficits can lead to inflation
- Compare the deficits in Canada, Bolivia, and Israel in the 1980s
- Explain the burden debt places on future generations

Let's begin by looking at some facts that will help us place Canadian deficits and debts in perspective.

13.1 *Historical and International Perspective on Deficits and Debts*

MACROFACTS

We'll start our review of the historical and international facts about debts and deficits with the debt of the Canadian federal government.

Federal government debt

From the end of World War II through 1974, the debt of the Canadian federal government as a percentage of GDP steadily declined. By 1974, it was less than 20 percent of GDP. The federal government has had a deficit since the mid-1970s and its debt has steadily increased, exceeding 40 percent of GDP in the late 1980s. Is the behavior of Canadian federal government debt in the 1980s unusual? Is it cause for concern? It's easy to answer the first question. All we have to do is look at the broader set of facts on Canada's debt history and international experience. The second question is harder and takes most of this chapter to answer.

Canadian federal government debt in the 1980s is not unusual in some respects; in others, it is. To see why, let's look at the Canadian **debt-GDP ratio**—the value of debt outstanding expressed as a percentage of GDP.

Figure 13.1 illustrates the debt-GDP ratio of the federal government over the 64 years between 1926 and 1990. As you can see, the debt-GDP ratio was much higher at the end of World War II than in 1988. In fact, the debt-GDP ratio of the 1980s is unusually *low*. But it was also unusual for the debt/GDP ratio to be rising in peace time. The only other major peace time increase in the ratio took place in the Great Depression years of the early 1930s.

International perspective

International experience with government deficits makes the Canadian government deficit of the 1980s look relatively common and not at all extreme, as Figure 13.2 reveals. The figure shows government expenditures and receipts in Canada (part a) and in the world as a whole (part b). Expenditures exceed receipts not only in Canada but also in the world economy. The excess of expenditures over receipts is the government deficit. You can see that the Canadian government deficit increased sharply in the 1982 recession and then declined through the rest of the 1980s. The deficit of the world economy

FIGURE 13.1
Canadian Federal Government Debt-GDP Ratio

The Canadian federal government debt-GDP ratio increased in World War II and in the Great Depression and decreased in the postwar years until the mid-1970s. Only in the 1930s and the 1980s has the debt-GDP ratio increased in peacetime.

Source: M. C. Urquhart and K. A. H. Buckley (eds), *Historical Statistics of Canada* (Toronto: The Macmillan Company of Canada, 1965), *National Income and Expenditure*, Statistics Canada, Catalogue 13-201, and our calculations.

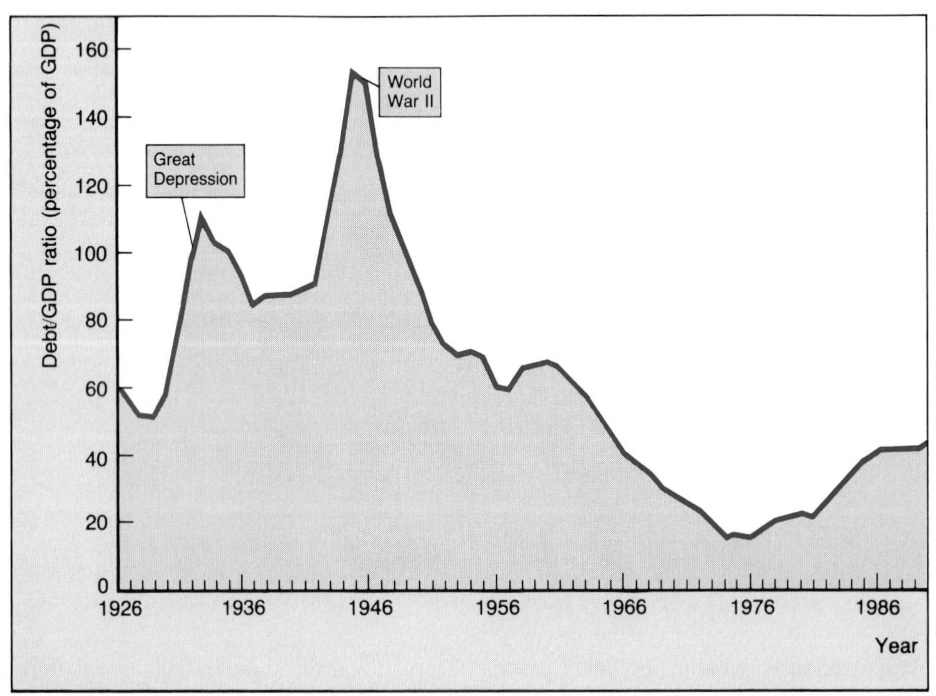

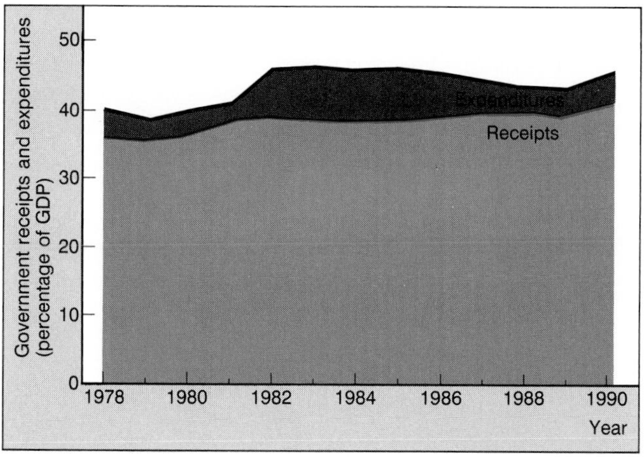

(a) Canada

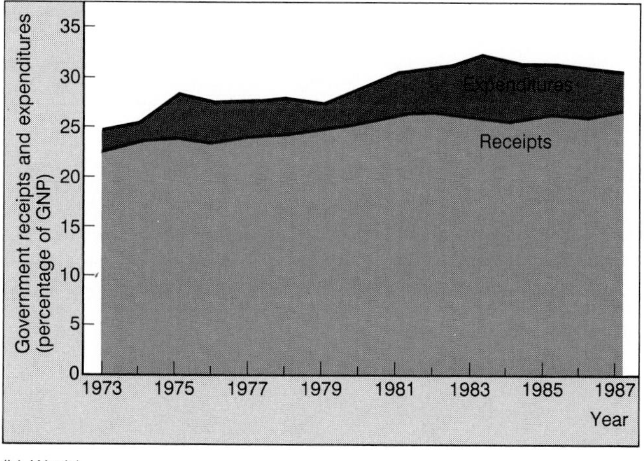

(b) World

FIGURE 13.2
Government Receipts and Expenditures in the Canadian and World Economies

Government expenditures have fluctuated more and increased more quickly than government sector receipts, in both the Canadian (part a) and world (part b) economies. The deficits that emerged have been similar in magnitude in the rest of the world and in Canada.

Source: National Income and Expenditure Accounts, Statistics Canada, Catalogue 13-201, and *International Financial Statistics Yearbook*, 1991.

behaved in a similar way, and on a similar scale, although the levels of government expenditure and taxes in the world as a whole are lower than in Canada.

External debts

External debt is the debt owed by the private and government sectors of the economy to the rest of the world. Some countries are extremely large debtors but Canada is not one of them. For the most part, the deeply indebted countries are the developing nations whose external debt-GDP ratios exploded during the 1980s. You can see this fact by looking at Figure 13.3. This figure shows the average external public debt-GDP ratios for three groups of developing countries, ranging from those with the lowest incomes to those with the highest. As you can see, the external debt-GDP ratio of these countries was below 20 percent in 1970. By 1988, the debt-GDP ratios had increased to more than 60 percent for low income countries, more than 40 percent for the lower middle-income group, and around 30 percent for the upper middle-income countries.

What are the sources of debts and deficits? What are their economic purposes? And what are their consequences? We'll answer these questions in the rest of the chapter. Let's begin by looking at the relationship between debts and deficits, and also at the relationship between debts and deficits of the public and private sectors and of the domestic and world economies.

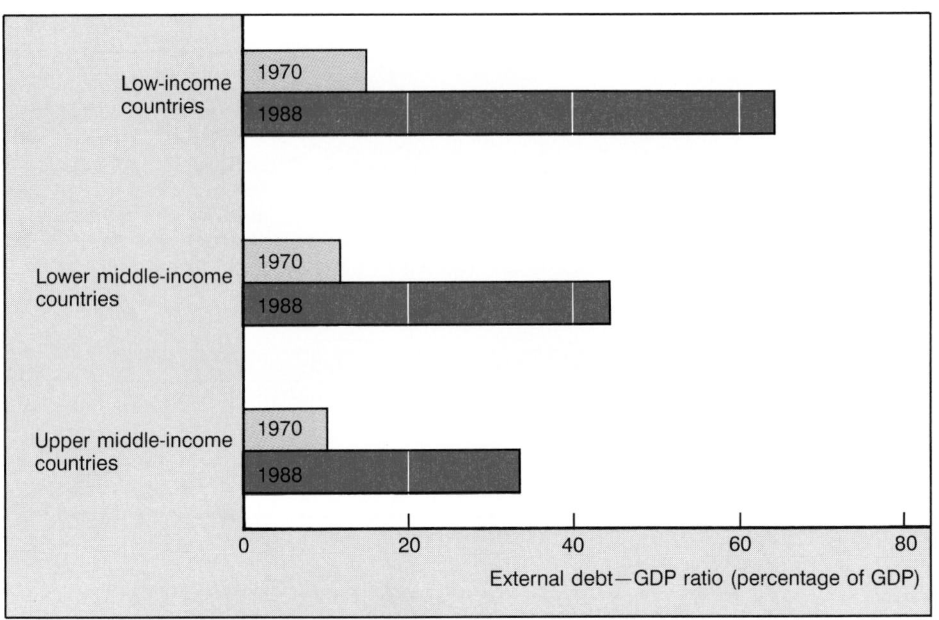

FIGURE 13.3
External Debts of Developing Countries

The 1980s was not only a decade of government deficits, it was a decade of growing external deficits and debts, especially in developing countries.

Source: World Development Report, 1990, Oxford University Press, New York, for the World Bank.

13.2 *Flows and Stocks, Budget Constraints, Borrowing, and Lending*

Let's begin our study of deficits and debts by establishing the linkages between deficits and debts and explaining their economic role.

Flows and stocks

A deficit is a flow, measured in dollars per unit of time. For example, if the Canadian government has a deficit of $24 billion in a year, this deficit is running at a rate of $2 billion a month, $6 billion a quarter, or $24 billion a year.

A debt is a stock, measured as dollars at a point in time. For example, we measure the amount owed by the Canadian government on a given date, such as December 31 of each year.

Deficits are the flows that add to the stock of debt. For example, during 1990, the Canadian government had a deficit of $20 billion, which increased its outstanding debt at the end of 1990 by that amount. The opposite of a deficit is a surplus and the opposite of a debt is an asset. When someone has a deficit, their debt increases or their assets decrease. When someone has a surplus, their debt decreases or their assets increase.

Figure 13.4 illustrates the connection between the stocks of debt and the flows of receipts and expenditures for a borrower whose debt grows (part a) and whose debt declines (part b). Debt increases if receipts are not sufficient to cover expenditure and interest on the previous outstanding debt. If receipts are larger than expenditure and debt interest, outstanding debt decreases.

Macroeconomic sectors

In studying debts and deficits and their effects on the macroeconomy, we distinguish three sectors:

- Government
- Private
- Rest of world

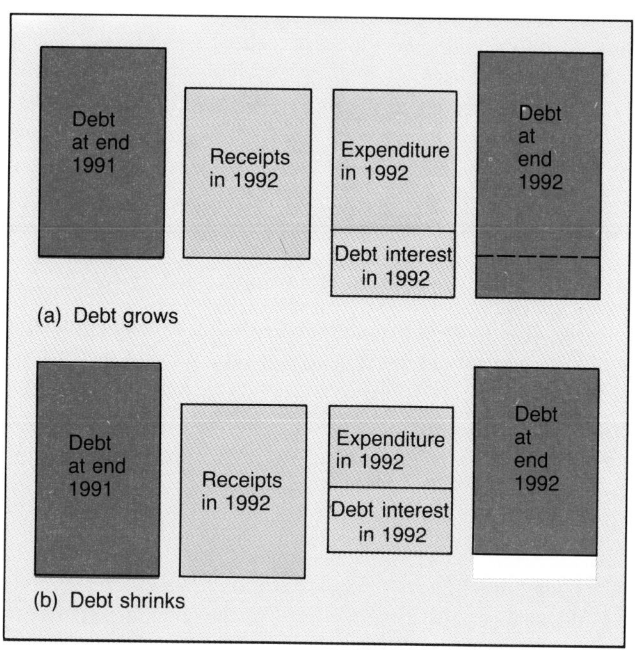

FIGURE 13.4
Stocks and Flows, Deficits and Debts

Debts are stocks measured at a point in time and deficits—the difference between receipts and expenditures—are flows measured over a given time period. When expenditures plus debt interest exceed receipts, debts grow (part a). When expenditures plus debt interest are less than receipts, debt shrinks (part b).

Government The balance of the government's budget is equal to its receipts minus its expenditures. Government receipts are personal income taxes, corporation taxes, and indirect taxes—such as customs and excise duties and sales taxes—and interest income on government investments and public enterprises. Government expenditures are the purchases of goods and services, transfer payments, and debt interest.

In terms of the national income accounts (studied in Chapter 2), the government budget balance is defined as

$$\text{Government budget balance} = T - G$$

where G equals government purchases of goods and services and T equals taxes plus government interest income minus transfer payments minus debt interest paid by the government. If T exceeds G, the government budget balance is positive and the government has a surplus. If G exceeds T, the government budget balance is negative and the government has a deficit.

The government debt record we examined at the beginning of this chapter is the Canadian *federal* government's. The government sector in the national income and expenditure accounts is broader. It includes the federal government together with *provincial and local* governments. It is important, when examining government deficits to be clear about the way "government" is being defined. To avoid confusion, we define two deficits: the **federal deficit**, the deficit of the federal government, and the **total government deficit**, the combined deficits of federal, provincial, and local governments.

Private sector The private sector has two parts, households and businesses.

Households Households' budget balance equals household saving minus household investment. Household saving is personal disposable income minus consumer expenditure. Household investment is the purchase by households of new houses and apartments.

Businesses Businesses' budget balance equals business saving minus business investment. Business saving is equal to business profits minus taxes minus dividend and interest payments to households. Business investment is the purchase of new plant, equipment, and buildings by firms, as well as net changes in inventories.

Households and businesses taken together constitute the private sector. The sum of household and business saving is aggregate saving, and the sum of household and business investment is aggregate investment. Thus in terms of the national income and product accounts of Chapter 2, the private sector budget balance equals saving minus investment. That is,

$$\text{Private sector budget balance} = S - I$$

where S equals saving and I equals investment. If saving exceeds investment, the private sector has a surplus. If investment exceeds saving, the private sector has a deficit.

Rest of world The balance on the rest of the world's transactions with Canada (viewed from the perspective of residents of the rest of the world) is equal to Canadian imports of goods and services minus Canadian exports of goods and services. That is,

$$\text{Rest of world balance} = IM - EX$$

where IM equals Canadian imports of goods and services and EX equals Canadian exports of goods and services. If Canadian imports exceed Canadian exports, the rest of the world has a surplus with Canada (and Canada has a deficit with the rest of the world).

The economy as a whole For the economy as a whole, there is a type of financial law of conservation — every deficit has a surplus and every debt has a corresponding asset. Sector balances sum to zero. That is, if one sector or group of sectors has a deficit, some other sector or group of sectors must have a surplus. In terms of the national income and product accounts of Chapter 2,

$$(T - G) + (S - I) + (IM - EX) = 0. \qquad \textbf{(13.1)}$$

That is, the sum of the government balance, the private sector balance, and the rest of world balance equals zero. Equivalently, the sum of the government and private sector balances equals our balance with the rest of the world. That is,

$$(T - G) + (S - I) = (EX - IM). \qquad \textbf{(13.2)}$$

You can see the connections between the surpluses and deficits of the government sector, the private sector, and foreign sector in Figure 13.2. When the government and private sectors have a surplus, as they did the 1950s and 1960s, the rest of the world has a deficit with Canada (Canada has a surplus with the rest of the world) and the three sector balances sum to zero. In the 1970s, the government sector deficit was small, the private sector surplus was large, and the rest of the world had a deficit with Canada (Canada had a surplus with the rest of the world). In the 1980s, the government sector budget deficit became so large that it exceeded the private sector surplus, so the rest of the world had a surplus with Canada (Canada had a deficit with the rest of the world).

Debts Debts result from ongoing deficits and assets result from ongoing surpluses. Just as deficits and surpluses balance each other, so do debts and assets. Government-sector debt plus private sector debt plus the rest of the world sector debt equals zero. Equivalently, government sector debt plus private sector debt equals net foreign investment in Canada. That is,

$$\text{Government debt} + \text{private debt} = \text{net foreign assets in Canada.}$$

Why do debts exist? Why does the government sometimes spend more than its revenue? Why does an entire nation—government and private sector—sometimes spend more than it earns, incurring deficits with the rest of the world and debts to foreigners? Let's explore these questions.

Budget constraints, borrowing, and lending

A **budget constraint** defines the limits of expenditure—the maximum that can be spent given the resources available to finance that spending. Without borrowing and lending, the maximum that a person, business, or government can spend in any given time period is its income. Government expenditure cannot exceed tax revenue; business investment cannot exceed after-tax profit; household spending cannot exceed after-tax income.

Borrowing and lending make it possible to expand the budget constraint at a given point in time. But they create an intertemporal budget constraint. An **intertemporal budget constraint** states the limits of expenditure at each point in time and the links between spending, borrowing, and lending. An intertemporal budget constraint can be written in the following way:

$$E_t + A_{t+1} = (1 + r_t) A_t + Y_t. \qquad \textbf{(13.3)}$$

In this equation, E stands for expenditure, A for assets, r for the interest rate and Y for income. The subscripts t and $t + 1$ denote a point in time: t represents a given year and $t + 1$ represents the following year. Assets (A) can be positive or negative. If A is positive, total past incomes have exceeded total past expenditures — there have been surpluses. If A is negative, there is a debt outstanding and total past expenditures have exceeded total past incomes.

You can see the connection between deficits and debts more clearly if we rearrange the intertemporal budget constraint in the following way:

$$(A_{t+1} - A_t) = Y_t - E_t + r_t A_t. \qquad \textbf{(13.4)}$$

This equation says that the change in assets from one year to the next equals income minus expenditure plus interest income. If A is negative—that is, if the institution whose intertemporal budget constraint we're considering has outstanding debt — then $r_t A_t$ is negative. That is, $r_t A_t$ is an interest payment, not an interest receipt. Debt grows by an amount equal to income minus expenditure minus debt interest.

This intertemporal budget constraint applies to all sectors: private, governments, and the rest of world. For example, the government has outstanding debt, so we can write its intertemporal budget constraint to highlight the increase in its debt. Because we've switching from assets to debts, we'll change the signs on the terms on the right side of this equation. The government's intertemporal budget constraint is

$$(D_{t+1} - D_t) = G_t + r_t D_t - T_t. \qquad \textbf{(13.5)}$$

Government debt increases by an amount equal to the sum of its purchases of goods and services and its debt interest minus its net tax revenues.

The intertemporal budget constraint explains how borrowing and lending can break the link between current expenditure and current income. It defines the constraints on expenditure when institutions borrow and lend. But it doesn't explain *why* institutions want to borrow and lend. That is, it does not explain the motive for borrowing and lending. What are these motives? There are two:

- Expenditure smoothing
- Consumption growth

Expenditure smoothing Incomes fluctuate for all kinds of reasons; and without the possibility of borrowing and lending, expenditure would have to fluctuate the way income fluctuates. But as a rule, people dislike expenditure to fluctuate. They prefer to smooth their expenditure over time. (We study the reasons for this in Chapter 17.) People can smooth their expenditure by borrowing when incomes are low and repaying the loans when incomes are high or by lending when incomes are high and borrowing when incomes are low.

Figure 13.5 illustrates how debt makes it possible to smooth expenditure. Suppose that a household's income fluctuates, as shown by the blue line in part (a). To keep expenditure constant at $20,000, the household has a deficit in period 2. By borrowing to finance the deficit, the household incurs a debt (part b). Then, in period 3 when income increases, the household has a surplus and repays its debt.

Governments face fluctuating tax revenues over the business cycle and smooth their spending by borrowing more in recessions and less in booms. Households experience fluctuations in income over the business cycle and smooth their expenditure (consumption) by saving less in recessions and more in booms.

FIGURE 13.5
Borrowing to Smooth Expenditure

Fluctuations in income (part a) can be accommodated without fluctuations in expenditure provided a deficit is incurred when income is low and a surplus is achieved when income is high. Debt increases in the deficit year and decreases in the surplus year (part b).

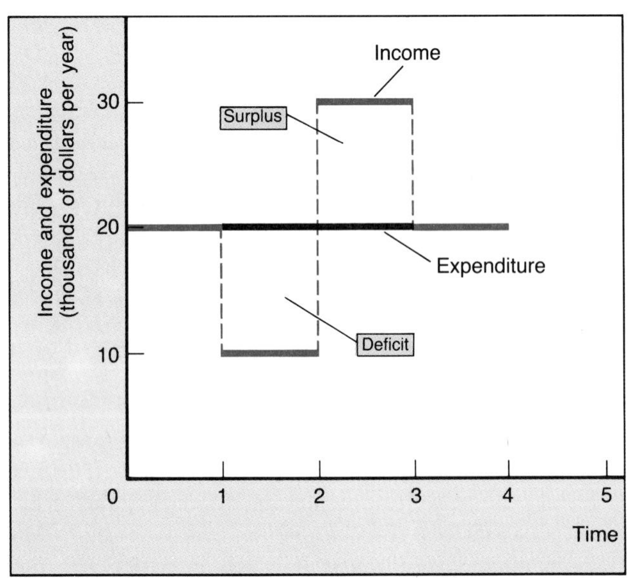

(a) Income and expenditure

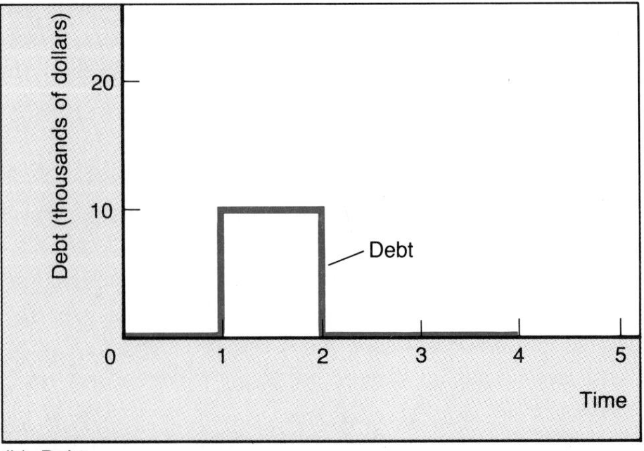

(b) Debt

Expenditure growth Another reason for decoupling expenditure from income is to enable expenditure to grow. For expenditure to grow over time, it must be less than income initially, so that interest-earning assets can be accumulated. For example, suppose that a household's income is constant at $30,000 a year. If the household spends all its income every year, its expenditure will be constant at $30,000.

But suppose the household decides to save some of its income initially. This enables the household to accumulate interest-earning assets. Figure 13.6 shows two possibilities. In the first, the household saves $10,000 in its first year, cutting back its expenditure to $20,000. As a result, it earns interest on its saving and can increase its expenditure in the following year. Expenditure grows over the household's lifetime. The smaller the initial expenditure, the more quickly a household's expenditure can grow.

For the economy as a whole, it is possible for consumer expenditure to grow only if capital is accumulated. That is, not only must households save but someone—typically businesses—must invest in physical capital that brings real returns. Thus just as households might save to experience rising consumer expenditure, so businesses borrow in order to invest in physical capital.

Borrowing to invest Households, businesses, and governments borrow to invest. Households borrow, usually on consumer credit or on mortgages to buy a house or apartment. Governments borrow to finance major public works — highways, dams, defense equipment, education, health facilities, and the like. Businesses borrow to finance the acquisition of plant and machinery, buildings, and inventories. Borrowing to invest incurs a debt on which interest has to be paid and results in acquiring an asset that earns a rate of return. If the rate of return on the assets bought exceeds the interest rate on the debt, then the loan can be repaid, over time, from the difference between the return on the assets and the debt interest. But if a bad investment is made, the assets acquired yield a return lower than the interest burden, and not only can't the debt be paid off but it grows over time as more is borrowed to pay the interest on it. Thus borrowing to buy assets is not foolproof. It requires good judgment and the acquisition of assets whose rate of return is at least equal to the interest rate on the debt incurred.

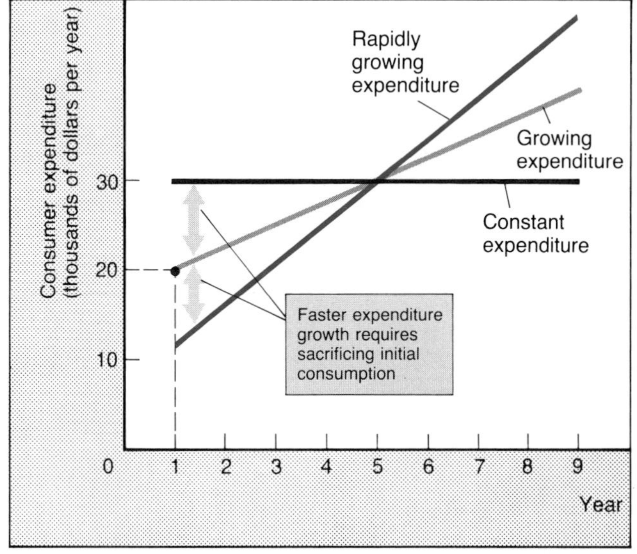

FIGURE 13.6
Borrowing and Lending for Growth

For expenditure to grow, an institution (such as a household) must cut expenditure below income and place the difference in interest-earning assets. Faster expenditure growth requires a greater sacrifice of initial consumption.

We've seen how borrowing loosens the budget constraint at a given point in time and confronts decision-makers with an intertemporal budget constraint. We've also seen how borrowing and debt can be used to smooth expenditure and achieve growth in consumer expenditure. Does either of these reasons for deficits and debt account for Canadian government deficits and debt in the 1980s? Let's find out.

MACROFACTS

13.3 *Sources of Deficits in the 1980s*

What are the sources of the government sector budget deficit incurred in Canada in the 1980s? Have deficits been incurred by all levels of government, or is the deficit mainly a federal deficit? Has the deficit arisen because spending has grown or because taxes have been cut or for a combination of these reasons? And which components of spending and taxes have changed most?

Federal and provincial and local deficits

In Canada, the bulk of the government sector deficit is a federal government deficit. Provincial and local governments have also had deficits since 1979, but much smaller ones than the federal government's. You can see these deficits for provincial and local governments and the federal government in Figure 13.7. You can also see the total government deficit in that figure.

FIGURE 13.7
Canadian Federal Deficit and Provincial and Local Surpluses

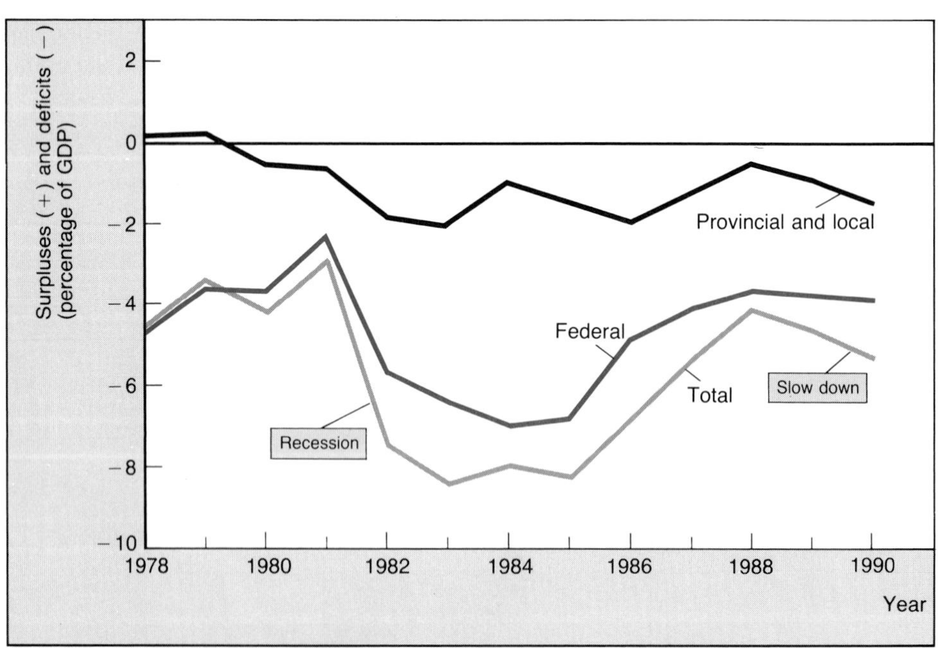

Throughout the 1980s, all levels of government in Canada have had deficits. But the federal government deficit accounts for the bulk of the total government deficit. Deficits have been largest in times of recession.

Source: National Income and Expenditure Accounts, Statistics Canada, Catalogue 13-201, and *International Financial Statistics Yearbook*, 1991.

Expenditure increases or tax cuts?

Most of the 1980s' persistent deficit has arisen from increases in expenditure, especially increases in transfer payments and subsidies and debt interest. Taxes have also increased as a percentage of GDP, although not by as much as the increase in expenditure. You can see these effects in Figure 13.8 for the total government sector.

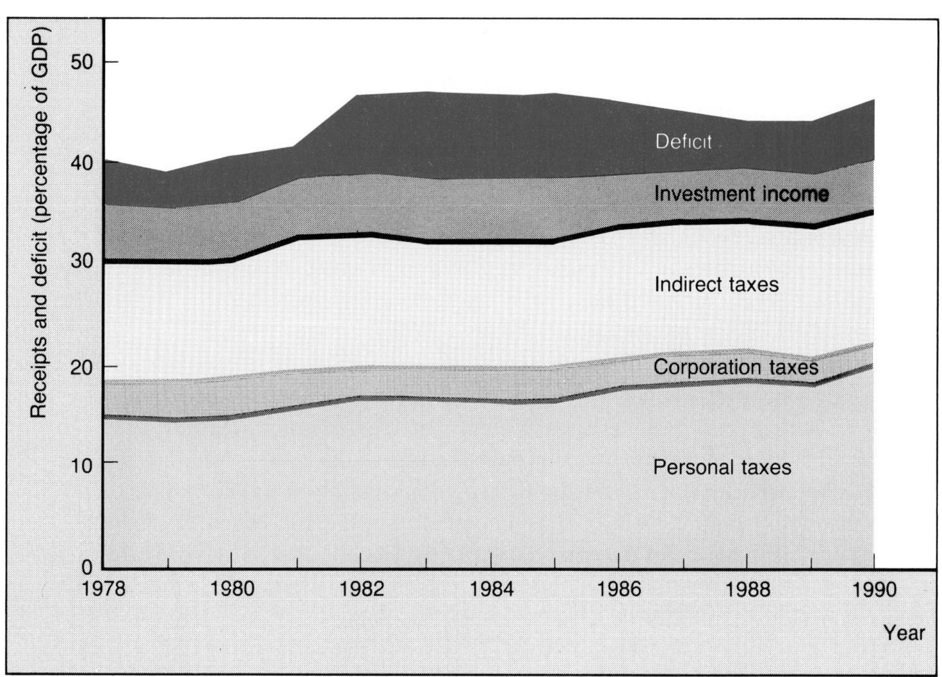

(a) Receipts and deficit

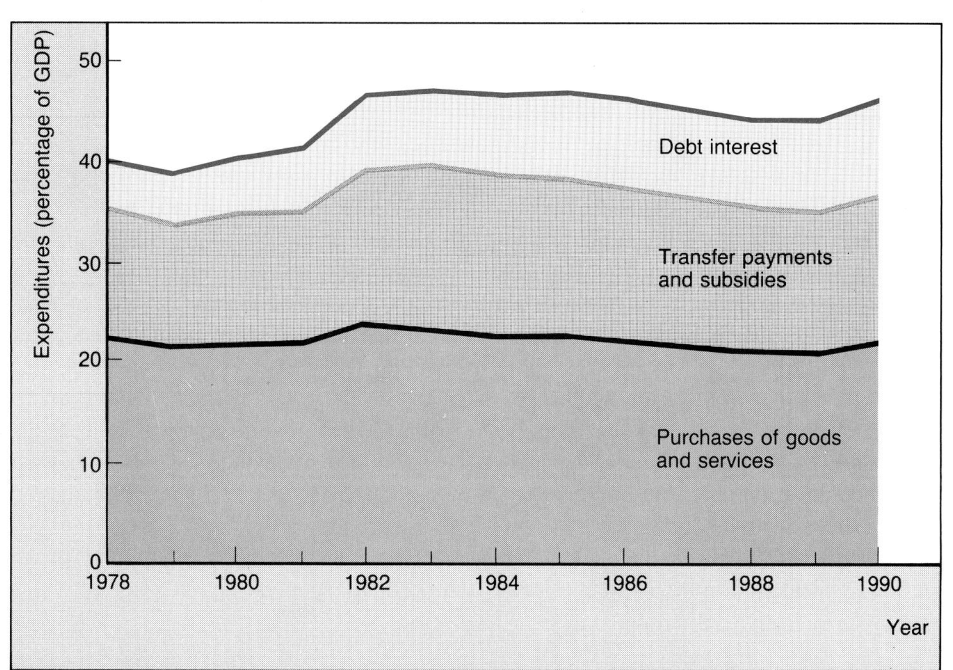

(b) Expenditures

FIGURE 13.8
Canadian Government Sector Receipts, Expenditures, and Deficits

The Canadian government sector budget deficit (part a) fluctuated between a small deficit in the early 1980s and larger deficits in the mid-1980s. The deficit also increased again in 1990. Government sector receipts (also seen in part a) which include personal taxes, corporation taxes, and indirect taxes increased slightly through the 1980s; but personal income taxes increased fastest. Expenditures (part b) have fluctuated more than receipts. Most of the fluctuations have arisen from transfer payments and subsidies that fluctuate with the business cycle. Purchases of goods and services have gradually decreased as a percentage of GDP, but transfer payments and net interest have increased.

Source: National Income and Expenditure Accounts, Statistics Canada, Catalogue 13-201, and *International Financial Statistics Yearbook*, 1991.

To what extent has the government sector deficit arisen from a desire to smooth expenditure in the face of fluctuating income? And to what extent has the deficit arisen from capital accumulation designed to increase revenue in the future?

Expenditure smoothing

Fluctuations in the government sector budget balance arise in part from the government's reaction to economic fluctuations. In an economic boom, tax revenues increase and transfer payments, especially unemployment benefits and other payments to the poor, decrease. Thus the government budget deficit decreases (or surplus increases).

The opposite occurs in a recession. When real GDP sags as the economy goes into recession, tax receipts decline. Also, the government spends more on social and unemployment programs. The combination of decreasing tax revenue and increasing transfer payments increases the government budget deficit (or decreases a surplus).

Over and above these considerations, the government may try to stimulate the economy in a recession and to dampen down demand in a boom. Cutting tax rates or increasing expenditures in a recession increases aggregate demand but also increases the deficit (decreases a surplus). Increasing taxes or cutting spending in a boom decreases aggregate demand but also decreases the deficit (or increases a surplus).

Has the Canadian government sector budget deficit increased in recession and decreased in booms? The answer is yes. You can see this pattern in Figure 13.8. The deficit shown in part (a) increases strongly in the recession year of 1982. It then decreases as the economy recovers through the rest of the 1980s. And the change in the deficit resulting from fluctuations in income comes mainly from the response of expenditure (shown in Figure 13.8b). Thus smoothing out the consequences of the business cycle is one clear source of the emergence of government deficits and their fluctuations. But it is not the whole story. For as you can also see in Figure 13.8, the deficit of the 1980s persisted despite the fact that the economy underwent one of the strongest and most prolonged periods of economic expansion in its history. Why did this deficit persist through the 1980s?

Deficit financed growth?

One possibility is that the deficit of the 1980s resulted from the government's policy of keeping both tax increases and spending cuts moderate in the hope of stimulating economic growth. Its hope was that higher incomes would eventually bring higher tax revenues, and that these would be on a scale sufficient to cover government expenditure.

But with a deficit persisting, debt interest began to grow as the debt-GDP ratio increased. Thus the deficit of the 1980s resulted from a reluctance on the part of governments, mainly the federal government, to increase taxes or cut spending and the resulting ongoing deficit fuelling itself with increased debt interest payments.

The federal budget of 1991 was designed to close the deficit gap over the succeeding five years, partly by keeping spending in check and partly by increasing taxes. But coming as it did at the time of yet another recession, income-smoothing considerations led the then Finance Minister, Michael Wilson, to go very gently with any deficit reduction in 1991-1992. Also, at the same time as the federal government was holding its deficit steady the government of Ontario, the largest of the provinces, again concerned with income smoothing, but also concerned with pursuing its political agenda, budgeted a large increase in its deficit.

The Canadian government sector budget deficit that we have been studying is the deficit as measured in the national income and product accounts. Is that a correct measure of the deficit? Let's now address that question.

13.4 How Inflation Distorts the Deficits

Debts are incurred in dollar terms. If you borrow to buy a car, you agree to pay back so many dollars over the next three years. But the value of those dollars depends on what happens to the price level. When the price level increases, the real value of an outstanding debt decreases. Borrowers gain and lenders lose.

The government is no exception. When the government has a deficit, it finances that deficit by selling treasury bills and treasury bonds. These bills and bonds are promises to pay at some future date. The shortest period over which the government borrows is 90 days (three months); the longest period is 20 years. In a three-month period, even with inflation rates as high as they were in the late 1970s, the price level does not increase by much. Anticipations of inflation can easily be incorporated into the three-month interest rate so that the amount the government repays after three months reflects expectations about rising prices.

But when the government borrows for 20 years, the real amount it repays at the end of the loan depends on the amount by which prices have increased over that 20-year period. Some of the debts incurred by the Canadian federal government in the late 1960s and early 1970s are being repaid in the early 1990s. Over that 20-year period, the dollar has fallen in value—by the early 1990s $4 is needed to buy the goods and services that $1 bought in the 1960s. As a consequence, when the government repays in the early 1990s debts incurred in the 1960s, it is using dollars that are worth only 25¢ relative to the dollars that it borrowed.

Real deficit

We've seen that deficits increase the amount of outstanding debt. In fact, the change in the value of outstanding debt equals the current period's deficit. This fact gives us the definition of the **real deficit**—the change in the real value of outstanding government debt. The deficit as measured in the national income and expenditure accounts is the change in the dollar value of outstanding government debt. Let's call it the *nominal* deficit for emphasis. Thus,

$$\text{Nominal deficit} = D_t - D_{t-1}$$

and in contrast,

$$\text{Real deficit} = (D_t/P_t) - (D_{t-1}/P_{t-1}).$$

Table 13.1 sets out the connection between the nominal deficit and the real deficit. Let's work through that table. Part (a) defines the variables and the symbols we'll use and gives some numbers for a numerical example that will help you keep track of what's going on. Part (b) sets out the calculation of the nominal deficit and the real deficit. The nominal deficit is the change in outstanding debt, $D_2 - D_1$, and it equals government expenditure, G, plus debt interest, rD_1, minus government receipts, T.

In the numerical example, government expenditures are $150, receipts are $250, and debt interest is $150 (15 percent of $1000), so the nominal deficit equals $50. Debt increases from $1000 in year 1 to $1050 in year 2. The real deficit is the change in the real value of outstanding government debt. In this example, as the price level rises by 10 percent there is a real surplus of $45, and the real value of outstanding debt decreases.

Part (c) shows the connection between the nominal deficit and the real deficit. It begins with the definition of the real deficit and shows how that definition can be rewritten as the change in the nominal deficit, $D_2 - D_1$, divided by the price level, P_2, minus the inflation rate, π, multiplied by the real debt, D_1/P_2. The next two lines show

the connection between the real deficit and the government's expenditure and receipts. The real deficit, the change in the real value of outstanding government debt, equals real government expenditures plus real interest payments on real outstanding debt minus real government receipts.

TABLE 13.1
Nominal and Real Debts and Deficits

	SYMBOLS	NUMERICAL EXAMPLE
(a) Definitions		
Debt in year 1	D_1	\$1000
Debt in year 2	D_2	
Government expenditure	G	\$150
Government receipts	T	\$250
Interest rate	r	0.15 (15%)
Price level in year 1	P_1	1.0 (100)
Price level in year 2	P_2	1.1 (110)
Inflation rate	$\pi = (P_2 - P_1)/P_1$	0.1 (10%)
(b) Calculations		
Nominal deficit	$D_2 - D_1 = G + rD_1 - T$	$= 150 + 0.15 \times 1000 - 250$ $= 50$
Debt in year 2	$D_2 = D_1 + \text{Deficit}$	$= 1000 + 50$ $= 1050$
Real deficit	$\frac{D_2}{P_2} - \frac{D_1}{P_1}$	$= \frac{1050}{1.1} - \frac{1000}{1.0}$ $= -45$
(c) Connection between nominal deficit and real deficit		
Real deficit	$\frac{D_2}{P_2} - \frac{D_1}{P_1}$	$\frac{1050}{1.1} - \frac{1000}{1.0}$
can be written as	$\frac{D_2}{P_2} - \frac{D_1}{P_2} \times \frac{P_2}{P_1}$	
but	$\frac{P_2}{P_1} = 1 + \pi$	$\frac{1.1}{1.0} = 1 + 0.1$
Therefore the real deficit is	$\frac{D_2 - D_1}{P_2} - \pi\frac{D_1}{P_2}$	$\frac{1050 - 1000}{1.1} - \frac{0.1 \times 1000}{1.1}$
but the nominal deficit is	$D_2 - D_1 = G + rD_1 - T$ $\frac{D_2 - D_1}{P_2} - \pi\frac{D_1}{P_2} = \frac{G}{P_2} + (r - \pi)\frac{D_1}{P_2} - \frac{T}{P_2}$	$= \frac{150}{1.1} + 0.05 \times \frac{1000}{1.1} - \frac{250}{1.1}$ $= -45$
(d) In words		

The real deficit, the change in the *real* value of outstanding government debt $\left(\frac{D_2}{P_2}\right) - \left(\frac{D_1}{P_1}\right)$, equals real government expenditure $\frac{G}{P_2}$ *plus* real interest payments $(r - \pi)$ on real debt $\frac{D_1}{P_2}$ *minus* real government receipts $\left(\frac{T}{P_2}\right)$.

Canadian real deficit

Canada has experienced a good deal of inflation through the 1970s and 1980s. As a consequence, the real government deficit has been smaller than the nominal deficit. Figure 13.9 shows how much smaller. As you can see, before the 1981-1982 recession when there was a nominal deficit, in real terms, the budget was basically balanced. In the recession of 1981-1982, a real deficit arose and, by 1985, it had became quite large. After 1985, the real deficit declined and then, as the deficit of 1990-1991 began, the real deficit increased again.

Inflation tax

Another way of looking at the distinction between the real deficit and the nominal deficit is in terms of the inflation tax. The **inflation tax** is the tax that people implicitly pay when the real value of money and the government debt they hold declines because of rising prices. This tax is not legislated by Parliament but people pay it nonetheless. Because people pay the inflation tax, the government receives an inflation tax revenue. When the inflation tax revenue is added to the government's other receipts, we obtain the government's real deficit.

Despite the fact that inflation distorts the deficit, making it appear larger than it *really* is, we've seen that Canada does have a real deficit and has had one for the entire period since 1982. This fact gives rise to a series of other questions about deficits. The first is, how big can a deficit become?

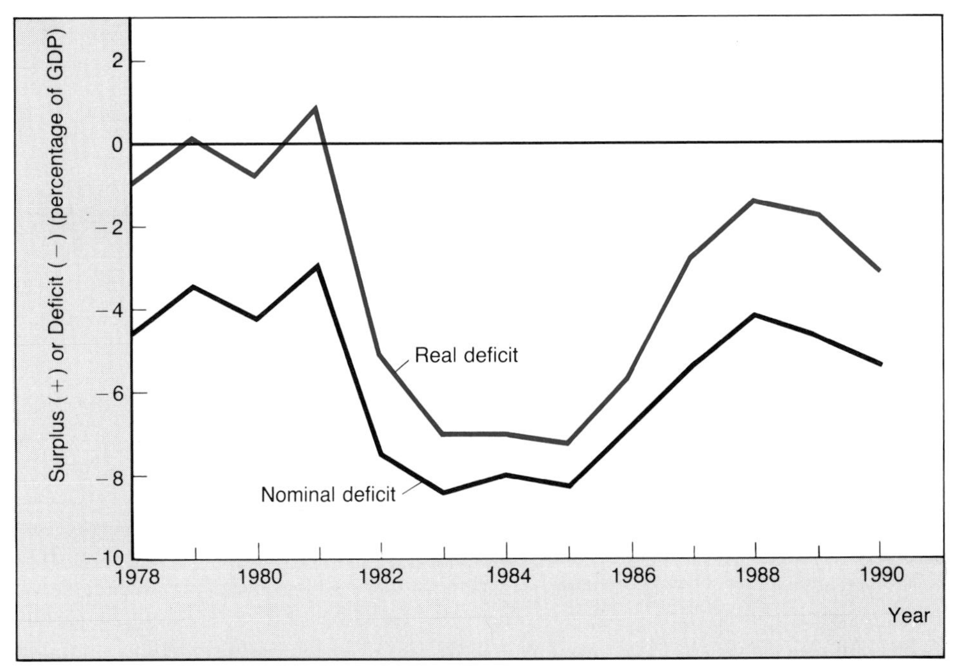

FIGURE 13.9 Canadian Federal Government Real and Nominal Deficits

The nominal deficit of the Canadian federal government overstates the true real deficit because of inflation. The real deficit is the change in the real value of government debt held by the public. Some of this real value declines each year because of inflation and the real deficit is less than the nominal deficit.

Source: National Income and Expenditure Accounts, Statistics Canada, Catalogue 13-201, and *International Financial Statistics Yearbook*, 1991, and our calculations.

13.5 *How Big Can the Deficit Be?*

A government, a country, or an individual business or household that has a deficit has growing debt. Growing debt means paying more debt interest, which, other things being equal, adds further to the deficit. So, ongoing deficits that remain unchecked create even larger deficits. But, over time, incomes grow, and as a result, so do consumer expenditure and the ability to pay debt interest. Does economic growth make it possible to have a permanent deficit? And if it does, how big a permanent deficit does it permit?

To answer these questions, we need to study the dynamics of deficits and debts—the way deficits feed on themselves. To keep our focus sharp, we'll abstract from inflation. The debts, deficits, and interest rates are all *real*.

Deficit-debt dynamics

In studying the dynamic process of deficit and debt creation, let's focus on the government sector. The government sector's **basic deficit** is its budget deficit excluding debt interest. Its total deficit equals its basic deficit plus debt interest. The question we're going to try to answer is, how big can the *basic deficit* be? To answer the question, we have to do some arithmetic, which Table 13.2 sets out. Let's work our way through that table.

Part (a) defines the symbols used and gives a numerical example. We'll assume a fairly large basic deficit of 5 percent of GDP ($z = 0.05$); the interest rate is 3 percent a year ($r = 0.03$); government debt at the beginning of year t is \$1,000; GDP in year t is \$2,000 and grows each year at 4 percent ($g = 0.04$). Given these assumptions, the debt-GDP ratio in year t is 50 percent ($d_t = 0.5$).

Let's now calculate the debt-GDP ratio after one year. This is shown in part (b) of the table. The deficit in year t is equal to the debt interest in that year (rD_t) plus the basic deficit (zY_t). For example, in year t, interest payments are \$30 and the basic deficit is \$100, so the total deficit is \$130. Debt at the beginning of year $t + 1$ is given by the next equation in the table: it equals the initial debt outstanding plus the interest payments on that debt plus the basic deficit. For our example, this debt is \$1,130. Over the year, GDP has grown by 4 percent so that at the beginning of year $t + 1$, real GDP has increased to \$2,080. Thus the debt-GDP ratio in year $t + 1$ is the new level of debt (\$1,130) divided by the new level of GDP (\$2,080), which equals 54 percent ($d_{t+1} = 0.54$).

In this example, the debt-GDP ratio has increased from 50 percent to 54 percent in one year. Does the debt-GDP ratio increase every year? And if it does, is such a process sustainable? If it is, then the government can run a deficit indefinitely. If it's not, then the government cannot and, at some point, must run a surplus to bring the debt-GDP ratio under control.

Let's work out what happens to the debt-GDP ratio over time. To do so we must find a formula for the evolution of the debt-GDP ratio. We've already worked out how debt evolves from one year to the next (the equation for debt). We also know how GDP evolves from one year to the next (the equation for GDP). Let's divide the debt equation by the GDP equation. This gives us the next row of Table 13.2, which tells us that the debt-GDP ratio in year $t + 1$ (d_{t+1}) equals its value in year t (d_t) multiplied by a number equal to $(1 + r)/(1 + g)$ plus another number $z/(1 + g)$. In our example, r is 0.03 and g is 0.04, so $(1 + r)/(1 + g)$ is approximately 0.99 and z is 0.05, so $z/(1 + g)$ is approximately 0.048. Thus the debt-GDP ratio evolves over time to equal 99 percent of its previous value plus 0.048.

What happens to the debt-GDP ratio over time depends critically on the coefficient $(1 + r)/(1 + g)$. In our example, r is less than g and that coefficient is less than 1. This

TABLE 13.2
Deficit-Debt Dynamics

	SYMBOLS	NUMERICAL EXAMPLE
(a) Definitions		
Basic deficit as proportion of GDP	z	0.05 (5%)
Interest rate	r	0.03 (3%)
Debt at beginning of year *t*	D_t	\$1000
GDP in year *t*	Y_t	\$2000
GDP growth rate	g	0.04 (4%)
Debt-GDP ratio in year *t*	$d_t = D_t/Y_t$	0.5 (50%)
(b) Calculations		
Deficit	$D_{t+1} - D_t = rD_t + z_tY_t$	$= 0.03 \times 1000 + 0.05 \times 2000$ $= 130$
Debt	$D_{t+1} = (1 + r)D_t + z_tY_t$	$= 1.03 \times 1000 + 0.05 \times 2000$ $= 1130$
GDP	$Y_{t+1} = (1 + g)Y_t$	$= 1.04 \times 2000$ $= 2080$
Debt-GDP ratio in year *t* + 1	$d_{t+1} = D_{t+1}/Y_{t+1}$	$= 1130/2080$ $= 0.54$ (54%)
But	$\frac{D_{t+1}}{Y_{t+1}} = \frac{(1+r)}{(1+g)}\frac{D_t}{Y_t} + \frac{z}{(1+g)}$	
or	$d_{t+1} = \frac{(1+r)}{(1+g)}d_t + \frac{z}{1+g}$	$= 0.99d_t + 0.048$
(c) In the steady state		
Steady-state debt-GDP ratio	$d^* = \frac{(1+r)}{(1+g)}d^* + \frac{z}{1+g}$	
or	$d^* = z/(g - r)$	$= 5$ (500%)
Deficit	$D_{t+1} - D_t = r \times 5Y_t + zY_t$	$= 0.2\ Y_t$ $= 52$

means that eventually the debt-GDP ratio converges to a steady state-constant value. But if $(1 + r)/(1 + g)$ is greater than 1, the debt-GDP ratio will increase and increase without limit. Let's work out the steady-state value of the debt-GDP ratio for our example, as set out in part (c) of Table 13.2. We'll call the steady-state value of the debt-GDP ratio d^*. Then, its steady-state value is given by

$$d^* = [(1 + r)/(1 + g)]d^* + z/(1 + g). \tag{13.6}$$

Multiplying through by $(1 + g)$ and rearranging the equation gives the steady-state value of the debt-GDP ratio:

$$d^* = z/(g - r).$$

This equation tells us that the steady-state debt-GDP ratio equals the basic deficit divided by the growth rate of GDP minus the interest rate. In our example, z is equal to 0.05 and the difference between the growth rate and the interest rate 0.01, so the steady-state debt-GDP ratio is 5. That is, in the steady state, debt is 5 times as large as GDP, or equal to 500 percent of GDP. In the steady state, the deficit is 20 percent of GDP. Interest payments are 15 percent of GDP and the basic deficit is 5 percent. Why is 15 percent of GDP paid in interest? Debt is 5 times GDP and the interest rate is 3 percent (5 times 3 percent = 15 percent of GDP paid in interest).

Figure 13.10 illustrates the evolution of the debt-GDP ratio. Part (a) shows the process when the interest rate equals the growth rate. In this case, $(1 + r)/(1 + g)$ equals 1 and the debt in any year equals the debt in the previous year plus a constant, $z/(1 + g)$. On the vertical axis, we plot the debt-GDP ratio next year and on the horizontal axis the debt-GDP ratio in the current year. The dynamic debt line (the blue line) shows the relationship between the debt-GDP ratio in the current year and its value next year. For example, for a given value of z and a given initial debt-GDP ratio (d_0), the debt-GDP ratio in the next year will be d_1. But when we get to the next year the *current* debt-GDP ratio is d_1. It, in turn, generates a debt-GDP ratio the following year of d_2. When we get to that year, that becomes the current year's debt-GDP ratio and it, in turn, generates a higher debt-GDP ratio in the following year. The debt-GDP ratio increases without limit. The debt process is unstable. The only basic deficit that's possible in this economy is a zero deficit. An interest rate bigger than the growth rate makes matters worse—the debt-GDP ratio explodes even more quickly.

Part (b) shows what happens when the interest rate is less than the growth rate, the case we worked out in Table 13.2. Here, a debt-GDP ratio of d_0 and a basic deficit of z in the current year generates the debt-GDP ratio of d_1 in the following year. When we get to the next year, d_1 is the current debt-GDP ratio, and it generates a new debt-GDP ratio of d_2 in the following year, and d_2 generates a yet higher debt-GDP ratio in the following year. But the increments in the debt-GDP ratio are getting smaller with the debt-GDP ratio and converging on d^*, a constant debt-GDP ratio.

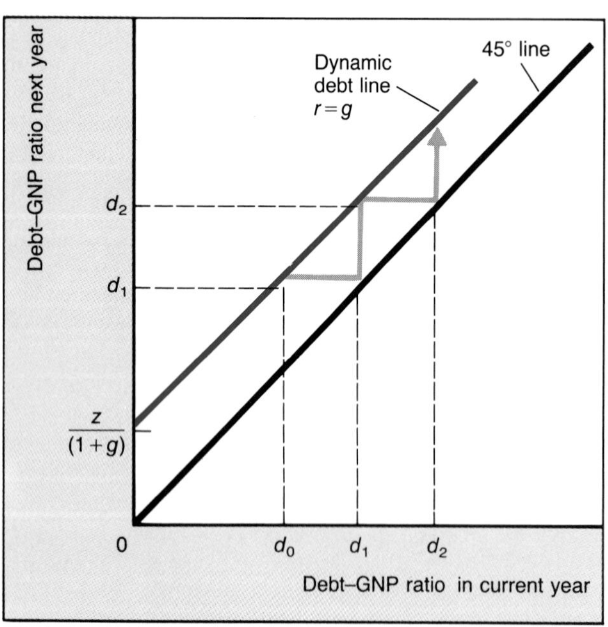

(a) Long-run deficit impossible

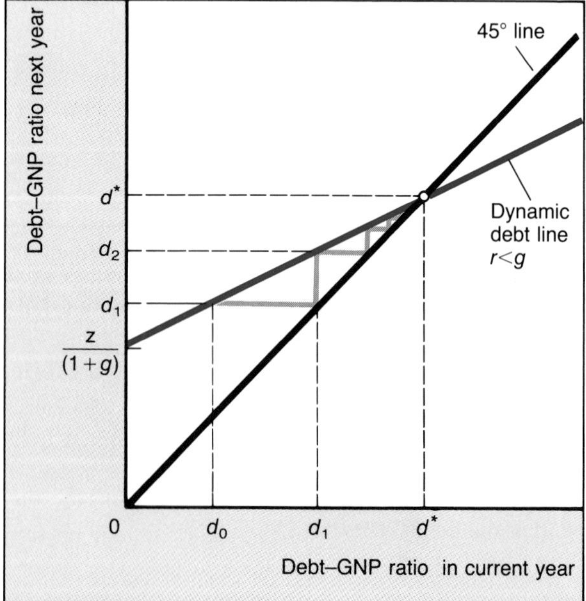

(b) Long-run deficit possible

FIGURE 13.10
Deficit-Debt Dynamics

If the interest rate equals the growth rate of the economy (part a), it is not possible for there to be a permanent deficit. If there was a deficit and the initial debt-GDP ratio was, say, d_0, then the debt-GDP ratio the following year would grow to d_1. The year after that, it would grow to d_2 and so on, exploding forever.

If the growth rate of GDP exceeds the interest rate, it is possible to have a permanent deficit. The debt-GDP ratio will increase but eventually stabilize at d^*.

Interest rate and growth rate

The critical factor determining whether a deficit can persist is the relative magnitudes of the growth rate of GDP and the interest rate. This conclusion has a natural interpretation: for a deficit to be sustained indefinitely, the growth in debt resulting from the ongoing deficit must be smaller than the growth in income that pays the debt interest. Only in such a case will the debt-GDP ratio eventually settle down at a constant value. If the interest rate exceeds the growth rate, debt grows faster than income and the debt-GDP ratio just explodes.

But we've seen that even in the case where the debt-GDP ratio eventually becomes constant, it becomes very large (5 times GDP) for a quite small initial basic deficit (5 percent of GDP). The steady-state debt-GDP ratio (d^*) equals the basic deficit z divided by the difference between the growth rate of GDP and the interest rate ($g - r$). Even if the growth rate of GDP exceeds the interest rate, it is unlikely to exceed it by much. Thus the growth rate of GDP minus the interest rate is likely to be a very small number, even if it is positive. For the steady-state debt-GDP ratio to be small, the basic deficit must also be a small percentage of GDP. For example, suppose that the growth rate of GDP is 1 percent a year higher than the interest rate (a rather optimistic assumption). For the steady-state debt-GDP ratio to be 0.5, the basic deficit can only be 5 thousandths of GDP (1 percent of 0.5 is 0.005, or 5 thousandths)!

In Canada today, a deficit of this magnitude would be about $3 billion. If the growth rate of GDP exceeds the real interest rate by only half a percent, then a basic deficit of one half this magnitude is the most that's sustainable.

Temporary deficits

So far, we've focused on deficits that persist forever. We've seen that permanent deficits are severely constrained by the logic of the dynamics of the relationship between deficits and debt. But what about temporary deficits? Does anything constrain these?

It's much less easy to say anything definite about temporary deficits. In everyday life, we see individuals taking on enormous temporary debt and running large temporary deficits. Consider, for example, a young household with a family income of $50,000. Such a household might borrow $200,000 to buy a house, some furniture, and a car. In the year in which the household runs that deficit, the deficit is four times the size of the household's income. But the household runs the deficit and at the same time commits itself irrevocably to a payments schedule that requires the household to have a surplus in each of the next several (perhaps as many as twenty) years while the debt is being repaid. The experience of ordinary households (and this experience also extends to private businesses) tells us that very large temporary deficits can be incurred. But incurring them means committing contractually to repay the debt and run a surplus over a succeeding period of years.

Governments differ from households in this respect. First, governments cannot bind their successors. Second, there are no political contracts between citizens and their governments requiring specific government action in the future. Thus when a government runs a deficit, there is no sure way of knowing whether that deficit is going to be temporary or permanent. The political decision-making process and the inherent constraints of that process determine the scale and evolution of the deficit.

History has seen some large deficits. But almost always, when large deficits occur, there is at least a lip-service commitment to reducing the deficit and eventually achieving budget discipline. Without a commitment and the expectation that the deficit will be brought under control, the deficit gets financed not by borrowing but by levying an inflation tax.

To see this, let's look at the connection between deficits and inflation.

13.6 *Is a Deficit Inflationary?*

In our study of debt-deficit dynamics, we abstracted from inflation and examined the behavior of real debt and deficits. Earlier in this chapter, we studied the way in which inflation distorts our measurement of the deficit. Now let's look at the connection between deficits and inflation in the other direction. Do deficits *cause* inflation?

Money and government debt

In Chapter 11 we discovered that an ongoing anticipated inflation results from an ongoing anticipated increase in the quantity of money. Money is created by the Bank of Canada and the banking system (we study the detailed processes involved in Chapter 15). To create money, the Bank of Canada buys government debt. Thus the Bank of Canada holds part of the quantity of government debt outstanding and when the government pays interest on its outstanding debt, some of that interest goes to the Bank of Canada. But the government owns the Bank of Canada. That is, the Bank of Canada's income is paid to the treasury and becomes part of government income. Thus in effect, the government pays no interest on its debt held by the Bank of Canada. It pays interest only on its debt held by the public. But for every dollar of government debt the Bank of Canada owns, there is a dollar of money in circulation that the Bank of Canada has created. Thus the total quantity of public debt equals the debt held by the public plus the money created by the Bank of Canada. In other words,

$$D_t = B_t + M_t \tag{13.7}$$

where D is total government debt, B is government debt in the hands of the public, and M is money (equivalently, government debt in the hands of the Bank of Canada). The government debt changes each year by an amount equal to the interest paid on the debt held by the public plus the basic deficit plus . That is,

$$D_{t+1} - D_t = rB_t + zY_t. \tag{13.8}$$

But the change in government debt equals the change in debt held by the public plus the change in debt held by the Bank of Canada. Equivalently, it is equal to the change in debt held by the public plus the change in the quantity of money issued by the Bank of Canada:

$$D_{t+1} - D_t = (B_{t+1} - B_t) + (M_{t+1} - M_t) \tag{13.9}$$

Combining Equations (13.8) and (13.9) gives the growth of debt held by the public as

$$B_{t+1} - B_t = rB_t + zY_t - (M_{t+1} - M_t). \tag{13.10}$$

It is the growth of government debt held by the public (B_t) that poses a potential problem for the government. If B_t grows too quickly relative to income, the debt burden increases and the debt-creation process potentially becomes unstable. As you can see from the above equation, creating money—and thereby creating inflation—provides a potential way of keeping interest-bearing debt under control. No matter how big the basic deficit (zY_t), by creating new money each year on a large enough scale, interest-bearing debt can be kept constant (or made to grow at the same rate as GDP, thereby keeping the debt-GDP ratio constant). The bigger the basic deficit, the bigger the need to offset some of that deficit by money creation and the greater the temptation for the government to do so.

But suppose that the government tries to resist money creation and inflation when it has a deficit. What happens?

Unpleasant arithmetic

If the government has a basic deficit that is expected to be temporary, then, as we saw above, there is no easy way of saying whether such a deficit will create a problem. There is also no reason why a temporary deficit, even if it is large, should result in inflation. But suppose the government has a permanent deficit. And further, suppose that it attempts to avoid creating money. Will the deficit, nonetheless, be inflationary? The following line of reasoning suggests that it would.[1]

Suppose that with a permanent deficit in place, the government does not create money. You can see from Equation (13.9) that, in this case, outstanding government debt held by the public increases by a larger amount than it otherwise would. Indeed, for each dollar of money *not* created, an additional dollar of interest-bearing debt *is* created. The longer the government resists money financing of the deficit, the larger will be the stock of interest-bearing government debt held by the public and the higher will be the interest burden of that debt. Rational people, viewing this process, will see that the government is storing up more and more trouble for the future. One day, it will have such a huge debt burden that it will have no choice but to finance its deficit by creating money. When that happens, inflation will take off.

But here is the unpleasant piece of the arithmetic. If people can foresee such a day in the future, they will not want to be left holding money at the time when the inflation rate does take off. They'll plan on decreasing their money holdings before inflation takes off. But decreasing money holdings, for the economy as a whole, means increasing spending, which in turn means inflation. If everyone reasons this way and reasons correctly, they will realize that the only time to get rid of unwanted money that's going to become worth less through inflation is here and now. People will reduce their holding of money, demand more goods and services, and prices will start to rise, here and now, in anticipation of future deficit-financing.

If the government follows through the same logic as the private citizens, everyone comes to the same conclusion. The unpleasant arithmetic relentlessly leads to the conclusion that a deficit expected to be permanent is likely to be financed here and now, to a large degree by money creation and, therefore, inflation.

Have deficits historically been inflationary? Let's find out.

13.7 *Deficits and Inflation in the 1980s*

TESTCASE

We'll look at the experience with deficits and inflation in three countries in the 1980s: Canada, Bolivia, and Israel.

Canada

Although a government deficit has persisted in Canada through the period since 1982, that deficit has not yet been inflationary. The worst inflation years for Canada were in the late 1970s and early 1980s, before the *real* deficit of the 1980s set in. In fact, the decade of the deficit was dominated, in the first half at least, by falling inflation. Inflation did increase in the later 1980s, but by a relatively modest amount. Thus it appears that a deficit of the magnitude of that in Canada, coupled with a general perception that the political process could not tolerate the deficit as a permanent feature of life, does not inevitably lead to inflation.

But some other countries' experiences show that deficits can indeed be inflationary if they become sufficiently large.

[1]The suggestion was made by Thomas J. Sargent of the University of Chicago and the Hoover Institution at Stanford University and Neil Wallace of the University of Minnesota.

Bolivia and Israel

The experiences of Bolivia and Israel with deficits and inflation have been dramatic. In Bolivia, the government deficit rose to a peak of 50 percent of GDP in 1985. In that year, the inflation rate accelerated to 12,807 percent a year. The relationship between the deficit and inflation in Bolivia is shown in Figure 13.11(a). You can see that as the deficit increased through 1985, so did inflation. As the deficit was brought under control after 1985, so was inflation.

The Bolivian story shows not only that deficits can be spectacularly inflationary but also that bringing the deficit under control can have a dramatic effect on inflation. For, as you can see, when the deficit was brought down from 50 percent to 15 percent to 3.5 percent of GDP, the inflation rate collapsed from almost 13,000 percent a year to less than 10 percent in two years.

Bolivia achieved this by fiscal policy reforms. In 1986, a newly forged alliance between two right-wing political groups commanded 70 percent of the votes in the Bolivian Congress. The alliance was able to implement a package of fiscal reforms that resulted in a quadrupling of government revenue and a 30 percent cut in government expenditures in that year. In the following year, revenue increased by a further 22 percent, more than twice the increase in expenditures. Thus a clear and visible fiscal policy reform that brings in more revenue and cuts expenditure brings the deficit under control and reduces inflation.

The case of Israel is not quite as spectacular as Bolivia, but still interesting. A small nation in a hostile environment, Israel spends an unusually large proportion of its GDP on national defense. See Figure 13.11(b). During the 1980s, its public finances ran into serious trouble and a deficit of 94 percent of GDP emerged by 1984. Israel's inflation increased threefold, from a little more than 100 percent in 1980 to almost 400 percent in 1984. Then, as in Bolivia, public finances were brought under control. Revenue increased and spending was kept in check, and the deficit was completely eliminated by 1986. The inflation rate followed the declining deficit, although not as spectacularly as in Bolivia.

There are many other examples of inflationary deficits. Some of the most amazing ones occurred in the 1920s in Germany, Poland, and Hungary, where deficits led to **hyperinflations** — inflation rates in excess of 50 percent a month. (The Bolivian inflation rate of 12,807 percent a year was just below the hyperinflation threshold.)

Clearly, deficits can be inflationary. What other effects might they have? In particular, do they impose a cost on future generations?

13.8 *Do Deficits Burden Future Generations?*

Some people say that the government deficit is immoral because it amounts to borrowing from our children without asking their permission. Is the deficit a burden on future generations?

It's useful, in discussing this question, to distinguish between external debts and deficits and internal debts and deficits. Let's look first at the case of external debts.

External debts

If Canada as a whole spends more than it earns, the difference has to be made up by borrowing from the rest of the world. Such borrowing has gone on during the 1980s and, as a result, Canadian citizens have incurred additional interest obligations to foreigners. Canadians will be able to consume less than their income because part of their income is being paid to the rest of the world as debt interest. With no further changes,

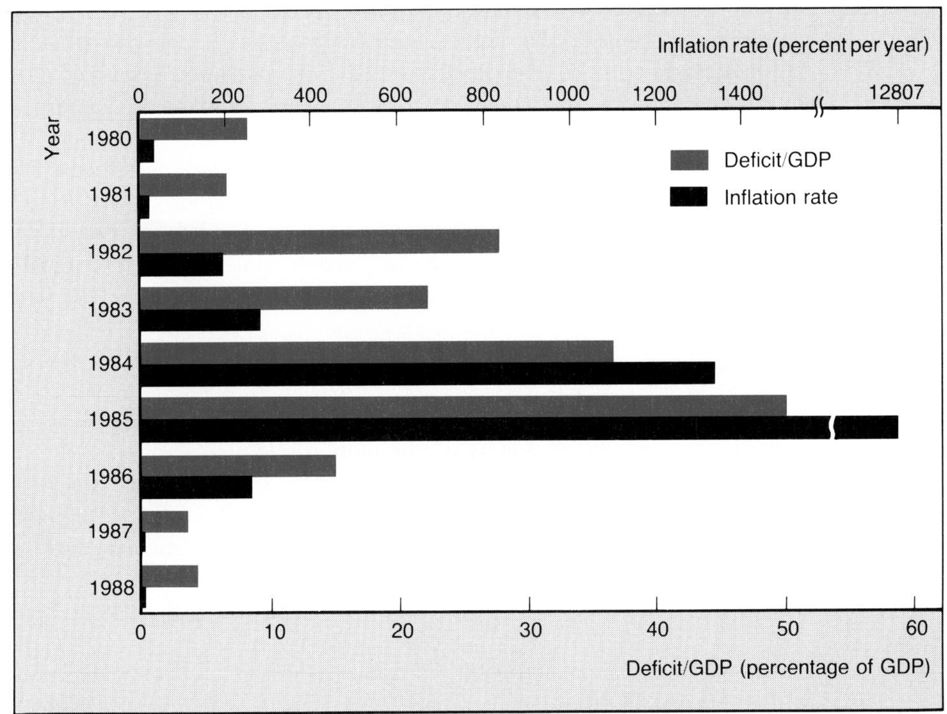

(a) Bolivia

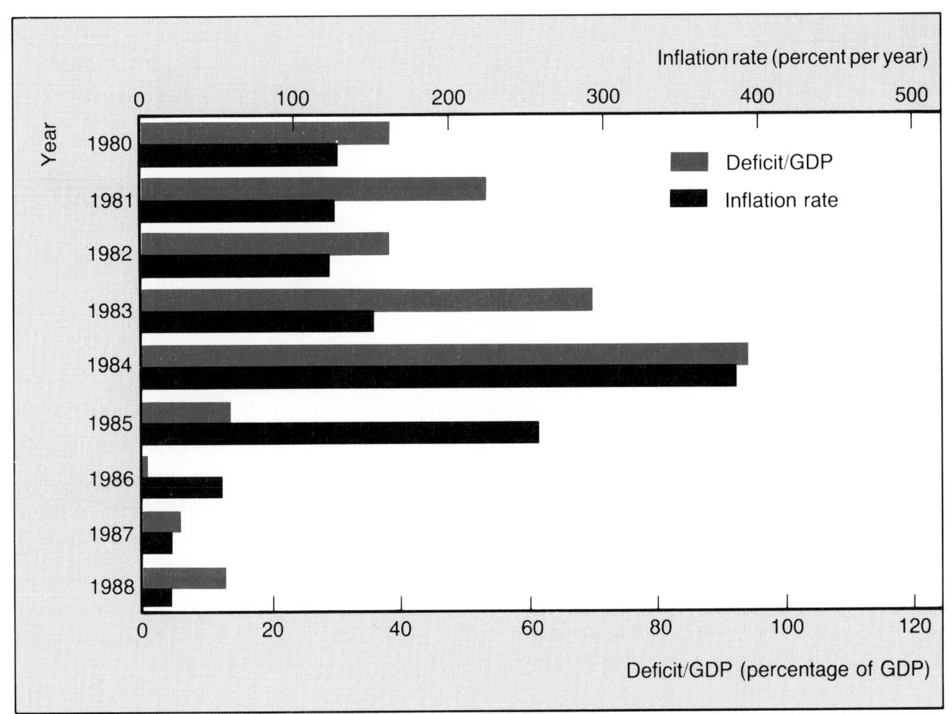

(b) Israel

FIGURE 13.11
Deficits and Inflation in Bolivia and Israel

Bolivia's government sector deficit increased to almost 50 percent of GDP by 1985. Through those same years, its inflation rate exploded, reaching 12,807 percent a year in 1985. Reforms of the tax system and government spending brought the deficit under control in 1986 and 1987, and the inflation rate collapsed.

Israel's government sector deficit increased to more than 90 percent of GDP by 1984 (part b) and that country's inflation rate also exploded. The deficit was brought under control in 1985 and 1986 and eventually inflation fell.

Source: International Financial Statistics Yearbook, 1991.

this interest burden continues into the indefinite future with future generations continuing to pay the interest on the debts that the current generation has incurred. Thus incurring external debt does impose a burden that continues into the future.

But whether it imposes a *net* burden depends on what the borrowed resources are used for. If they're used for consumption purposes, then indeed a net burden is imposed on future generations. But suppose the borrowed resources are used to invest in capital equipment and further, suppose that that equipment generates returns at least equal to the interest payments on the debt. In that case, there is no net burden. There is an interest burden, but there is also an income to offset that interest burden. Whether external debt imposes a burden on future generations depends on the rate of return and the rate of economic growth achieved with the borrowed resources.

Government debt

Similar considerations apply in assessing whether government debt imposes a burden on future generations. In this case, the reasoning is a bit more subtle.

At first thought, internal government debt doesn't appear to be a burden since it only involves a redistribution of income and wealth. Taxes have to be collected to pay interest on the debt but the interest is paid to the holders of the debt. In future generations, those who pay the taxes are burdened, but those who hold the government debt receive a benefit in the form of interest income. The two wash out, so there is no net burden.

But this line of reasoning is too simplistic. For two reasons, government debt may indeed impose a net burden on future generations. The first is that the taxes necessary to generate the interest payments on the debt can be a source of disincentive to both work effort and capital accumulation and, therefore, can result in a lower level of real GDP than would otherwise prevail.

Second, it is possible that the presence of a government deficit decreases overall saving and increases interest rates. Higher interest rates would crowd out investment, making economic growth slower and leaving future generations with a lower income than they otherwise would have.

Whether such crowding out occurs is controversial. One proposition, known as the **Ricardian equivalence theorem**, is that government debt and taxes are equivalent to each other and have no effect on interest rates. The reasoning behind the Ricardian equivalence theorem is that a decrease in taxes and an increase in the deficit and debt are matched by an equal increase in the willingness to save, and thus interest rates do not change. People recognize the future tax liability that the issues of government debt entails, so the reasoning goes, and increase their saving in anticipation.

The main source of disagreement about the validity of Ricardian equivalence turns on the extent to which people take account of future tax liabilities that will be borne not by themselves but by their children and grandchildren. For Ricardian equivalence to operate in practice, the current generation, faced with a deficit, must increase its saving and increase its bequests to the subsequent generation, leaving that generation exactly as well off as it would have been before. Whatever the deficit, an appropriate offsetting change in bequests takes place, so the burden is not passed on to the next generation.

There have been no acid tests of Ricardian equivalence and, therefore, we don't know for sure whether the deficit is a burden on future generations.

■ In this chapter, we've studied the connections between deficits and debts and seen how unchecked deficits can indeed feed on themselves and grow explosively. We've also seen how inflation distorts our view of the magnitude of the deficit. At the same time, we've seen that deficits can actually cause inflation. Finally, we've seen that whether deficits impose a burden on future generations is ambiguous, depending on what the borrowed resources are used for and whether current generations make bequests sufficient to offset the effects of the deficit on future generations.

This completes our study of inflation, deficits, and debts. We're now ready to begin an investigation of macroeconomic policy and of our efforts to stabilize economy activity, taming the business cycle, containing inflation, and achieving global macroeconomic stability.

CHAPTER REVIEW

Summary

DEFICITS AND DEBTS IN HISTORICAL AND INTERNATIONAL CONTEXT

The debt of the federal government increased throughout the 1980s. The only other peacetime period of increasing federal government debt was the Great Depression of the 1930s. The other occasion on which federal government debt increased was World War II.

Compared with the rest of the world, the Canadian government deficit of the 1980s was not unusual.

STOCKS AND FLOWS, RECEIPTS AND PAYMENTS, BORROWING AND LENDING

Deficits and surpluses are flows measured in dollars per unit of time. Debts are stocks measured in dollars at a point in time. The opposite of a debt is an asset. It is also a stock measured in dollars at a point in time. Deficits are flows that increase the stock of debt. Surpluses are flows that decrease the stock of debt or increase the stock of assets.

There are three main sectors in the macroeconomy: government, private, and rest of world. Each sector has a budget balance related to items in the national income and product accounts. The government budget balance equals tax receipts minus government expenditures. The private sector budget balance equals saving minus investment. The rest of world budget balance equals Canadian imports minus Canadian exports. For the economy as a whole, these three sector balances sum to zero.

Debts arise from intertemporal smoothing of expenditures or from the attempt to make expenditure grow by investing in assets that yield a rate of return larger than the interest rate.

SOURCES OF GOVERNMENT DEFICITS IN THE 1980s

The Canadian government sector deficit increased in the recession of 1981-1982 as the federal and provincial governments attempted to smooth private sector disposable income. But the deficit persisted after the recession and during the period of rapid economic expansion through the rest of the 1980s. The source of this deficit was an unwillingness on the part of the governments to slow the expansion of the 1980s by increasing taxes or decreasing expenditure. The hope was that economic growth would bring higher incomes and higher tax revenue. The deficit began to increase again in the late 1980s as the 1990-1991 recession approached.

HOW INFLATION DISTORTS THE DEFICITS

The deficit is the change in the value of government debt held by the public. When there is inflation, other things being equal, the real value of government debt outstanding decreases. The real deficit is the change in the real value of government debt held by the public. The higher the inflation rate, other things being equal, the more rapidly the real value of outstanding government debt falls and the smaller is the real deficit. In the 1980s, the real deficit in Canada was smaller than the nominal deficit. But the difference was not large enough to remove the deficit.

THE LIMITS TO BORROWING

The basic deficit is the deficit excluding debt interest. If a government (or any other institution) has a basic deficit, its debt increases and the amount of interest it has to pay on that debt also increases. If the interest rate exceeds the growth rate of the economy, it is not possible to have a permanent deficit. Temporary deficits are possible but, on the average, they must equal zero.

But if the growth rate of GDP exceeds the interest rate (both measured in real terms) it is possible for a permanent basic deficit to exist. However, even a small basic deficit pursued indefinitely will produce a large debt-GDP ratio.

IS A DEFICIT INFLATIONARY?

A temporary deficit need not be inflationary, but a large deficit or a permanent deficit may be. The larger the deficit, the greater is the incentive to generate inflation. The incentive arises from the fact that the government does not have to pay interest on the debt held by the central bank, the Bank of Canada in Canada. But when the Bank of Canada buys Canadian government debt, it increases the money supply.

With a large deficit, there is a temptation for the government to sell a large part of its debt to the central bank, thereby financing the deficit with money creation and inflation. No matter how large the basic deficit, the government can limit the amount of government debt held by the public by financing part of the deficit with money creation.

DEFICITS AND INFLATION IN CANADA, BOLIVIA, AND ISRAEL

During the 1980s, the Canadian deficit was not inflationary. On the contrary, the inflation rate decreased at a time when the deficit was large.

But deficits in Bolivia and Israel have been inflationary. Bolivia had a spectacular inflation explosion in the mid-1980s, resulting from an equally spectacular deficit. Israel had a similar (but much smaller) inflation explosion in the 1980s, when its deficit became large. Both these countries brought their deficits under control in the second half of the 1980s and brought inflation under control at the same time.

DO DEFICITS BURDEN GENERATIONS?

Deficits financed externally—either by borrowing from abroad or selling assets held abroad—leave future generations with a smaller income than they otherwise would have. Government deficits, however, create a debt and an asset. Some people hold government debt and so receive an income from it, while others pay taxes to pay that interest. Whether the net result imposes a burden on future generations depends on the bequests of the current generation. The Ricardian equivalence theorem—a proposition that government debt and taxes are equivalent—is based on the idea that the current generation changes its saving and the amount that it bequeaths to the next generation to exactly offset any debt created by the government sector. If Ricardian equivalence is wrong, bequests are not adjusted and the future generation is burdened by deficits.

Key Terms and Concepts

Basic deficit The budget deficit excluding debt interest.
Budget constraint The limits to expenditure.
Debt-GDP ratio The value of debt outstanding expressed as a percentage of GDP.
External debt The debt owed by the private and government sectors of the economy to the rest of the world.
Federal deficit The deficit of the federal government.
Hyperinflation An inflation rate in excess of 50 percent a month.
Inflation tax The tax that people implicitly pay when rising prices reduce the real value of money and the government debt they hold.
Intertemporal budget constraint The limits of expenditure at each point in time and the links between spending, borrowing, and lending.
Real deficit The change in the real value of outstanding government debt.
Ricardian equivalence theorem The proposition that government debt and taxes are equivalent to each other and have no effect on interest rates.
Total government deficit The deficit of the government sector—federal, state, and local.

Review Questions

1. Describe the history of the Canadian federal government deficit and debt since the end of World War II.
2. What is a debt-GDP ratio? Describe how the Canadian federal government debt-GDP ratio has changed over the last 64 years. When was it highest? When did it increase? When did it decrease?
3. Compare the Canadian private, public, and international deficits in the 1950s, 1960s, 1970s, and 1980s.
4. Compare the growth of Canadian government expenditures and receipts in the 1970s and 1980s. When did the Canadian government deficit appear in the 1970s and how has the deficit grown since?
5. What is a country's external debt? How did the Canadian external debt change during the 1980s? Explain why it changed.
6. Explain why deficits increase the stock of outstanding debt and surpluses decrease it.
7. Explain why a country's balance with the rest of the world is equal to the sum of the balances of the country's private and government sectors.
8. Distinguish between a budget constraint and an intertemporal budget constraint. Explain how an institution can be outside its budget constraint but never outside its intertemporal budget constraint.
9. All sorts of institutions borrow and lend. Explain why.
10. What is the relationship between a country's deficit over the business cycle and its attempts at smoothing expenditure?
11. Explain how inflation distorts the deficit.
12. How is the real deficit measured? Compare the real and nominal deficits in Canada in the 1980s.
13. What is a basic deficit? For a given basic deficit, what determines the steady-state debt-GDP ratio?
14. Under what circumstances is it possible to have a permanent deficit? Describe what happens under alternative circumstances.

15. Explain why a deficit can be inflationary. Compare the relationship between deficits and inflation in Canada, Bolivia, and Israel in the 1980s.
16. Do deficits burden future generations? Explain. Does the Ricardian equivalence theorem shed any light on this issue? Explain.

Problems

1. You are given the following information about a country called Happy Isle.

GDP	$170 billion
Consumer expenditure	$90 billion
Government purchases of goods and services	$30 billion
Government transfer payments and subsidies	$10 billion
Total taxes paid	$45 billion
Exports to the rest of the world	$60 billion
Imports from the rest of the world	$70 billion

(a) Calculate the government sector balance.
(b) Calculate the private sector balance. Is it a deficit or a surplus?
(c) Calculate the rest of the world's balance with Happy Isle.
(d) Is Happy Isle a net lender to or borrower from the rest of the world?
(e) If the interest rate at which Happy Isle can borrow or lend is 10 percent a year, how does the government sector balance change over time?

2. Deficits and the GDP deflator in Magic Empire in 1990 and 1991 were

YEAR	NOMINAL DEFICIT	GDP DEFLATOR
1990	$100 billion	100
1991	$110 billion	105

(a) Calculate Magic Empire's real deficit in 1991.
(b) Explain the change in real deficit from 1990 to 1991.
(c) Calculate the change in Magic Empire's nominal deficit necessary to keep its real deficit in 1992 equal to its 1991 value when inflation is expected to be 10 percent a year.

3. Desert Kingdom has no inflation and its current debt is $1 billion. Its current GDP is $10 billion and it introduces a basic deficit that is 10 percent of GDP. If it can borrow at an interest rate of 4 percent a year and its growth rate is 5 percent a year, calculate its
(a) current debt-GDP ratio
(b) debt-GDP ratio at the end of one year
(c) steady-state debt-GDP ratio
(d) steady-state deficit
4. In problem 3, if Desert Kingdom's growth rate falls to 3 percent a year what will be its steady-state deficit? Explain your answer.
5. In problem 3, if Desert Kingdom halved its basic deficit in the current year, what are your answers to problems 3 and 4?

V

Macroeconomic Policy

C H A P T E R

14 Why Macroeconomists Disagree About Policy

TAMING THE WAVES

BEFORE AND DURING THE GREAT DEPRESSION, business fluctuations were seen as an inevitable force of nature. Like earthquakes and hurricanes, they were events to be feared but endured.

In 1936, with the worst of the Great Depression behind us, the infant science of macroeconomics—based on the work of Keynes—was struggling to learn how to crawl. By the end of World War II, the science was a toddler and ready to set forth on its first stabilization policy adventures. Its initial steps were cautious and tentative. Also, it didn't stray far from home. The first country to attempt macroeconomic stabilization based on the new science was the United Kingdom, the place of its birth. But Canada was also an early devotee of Keynesian policies.

By the early 1960s, the science was an adolescent — full of hope, ambition, and confidence. And by the mid-1960s, macroeconomics had come of age. It had bought its first computer and equipped itself with large-scale **econometric models** — statistical descriptions of the economy that could be used to study the effects of alternative policies before they were implemented.

Stabilizing the business cycle was new, but taming inflation was not. Since the eighteenth century, it has been understood that inflation is a monetary phenomenon resulting from excessive growth in the money supply and one subject to government influence and control. Some macroeconomists temporarily lost sight of this important fact. They were so excited by the potential power of their new tools — Keynesian macroeconomic theory embedded in econometric models — that they believed they could solve *all* macroeconomic problems. But other macroeconomists were more cautious and concerned about possible inflation effects of business-cycle stabilization policies. They were also concerned that the business cycle couldn't actually be stabilized and that attempts to do so would destabilize the price level.

And so the modern macroeconomic policy debate was born, a debate that still smoulders even though many of the sources of disagreement have been resolved. In this chapter, we're going to study the macroeconomic policy debate, contrasting the policy advice of activists, who seek to actively intervene in the economy to achieve macroeconomic stability, and monetarists, who seek to pursue more passive stabilization policies, couched in terms of rules, in the belief that the economy will behave better under such circumstances than if it is actively manipulated.

After studying this chapter, you will be able to

- Describe the conflicting policy advice given by macroeconomists and others
- Distinguish among targets, instruments, and indicators of macroeconomic policy
- Distinguish between rules and discretion
- Explain the content and consequences of monetarist policy advice
- Describe Japan's experience with monetarist policies since 1978
- Explain the content and consequences of activist policies
- Describe the consequences of pursing activist policies in the 1960s
- Explain why monetarists and activists offer conflicting advice
- Explain the consensus policy of targetting nominal GDP

14.1 *Conflicting Policy Advice*

MACROFACTS

Although economics is the science of scarcity, there is no scarcity of economic policy advice. Just about everyone is ready to sound off at the slightest provocation on the economic policies that the government should follow. Advice is offered by callers to call-in programs and TV current affairs programs, by journalists, by economic think-tank crews, by academic economists, and by those whose advice the government buys — its senior economic advisers.

Much of the advice is self-serving. But the counsel of the government's professional advisers — the think-tank specialists and the academic economists on whose studies they draw — is a serious effort at economic engineering. Real engineers — people who build highways, bridges, and airplanes — have the solid sciences of physics and chemistry on which to draw. Economic engineers don't have such a well-founded scientific basis. Economic science at its best is less precise than the physical sciences. So even when a reasonable degree of understanding and agreement exists, there is scope for disagreement on just how strong the dose of a particular policy measure needs to be to achieve a given objective.

But many aspects of macroeconomic policymaking go beyond what the science of macroeconomics is capable of supporting in the present state of knowledge. In this respect, macroeconomic policymakers are like physicians trying to help patients who suffer from diseases that have no known cure. Business cycles and inflation, like AIDS and cancer, are facts of life that demand the best answer possible, even though the *right* answer is not known. Thus professional policy advisers find themselves giving conflicting advice.

There are some conflicts within the policymaking machine itself. That machine has two elements:

- The federal government
- The Bank of Canada

In recent years, the federal government has advocated and attempted to pursue fiscal discipline (higher taxes and curbs on public spending).

The Bank of Canada traditionally supports the government's desire for greater fiscal restraint. But there has been tension between the Bank of Canada and the federal government, the Bank paying more attention to potential inflation and less to the possibility of recession than the government would sometimes wish.

Outside the official advising circle, there are also conflicting views. The conflicting advice boils down to disagreements over three related issues:

- Policy objectives
- The current state and direction of the economy
- The effectiveness of alternative policy tools

We're going to try to make sense of the conflicting policy advice that governments receive. We'll start by learning about the targets, instruments, and indicators of macroeconomic policy.

14.2 *Targets, Instruments, and Indicators*

The **macroeconomic policy targets** are the objectives that macroeconomic policy seeks to achieve. The four main **target variables** are

- Unemployment
- Real GDP
- The current account balance
- Inflation

Macroeconomic indicators are variables that provide information, on a frequent basis, about the current state and direction of the economy. The main daily indicators are interest rates, stock prices, and exchange rates. These variables are determined minute by minute on markets that can be constantly monitored. Monthly indicators include the money supply, unemployment, consumer prices, industrial production, new housing starts, retail sales, and a host of other variables.

By monitoring the daily and monthly indicators of macroeconomic performance, the current state and trends in the economy are assessed.

Macroeconomic policy instruments are variables manipulated by the federal government or the Bank of Canada to influence macroeconomic policy targets. These instruments fall into two groups, *fiscal policy* instruments and *monetary policy* instruments. Fiscal policy instruments are government purchases of goods and services, transfer payments, and taxes. Monetary policy instruments are the monetary base, bank rate, and short-term interest rates. We'll study the details of these instruments more closely in Chapter 15.

The targets, indicators, and instruments of macroeconomic policy are summarized in Figure 14.1. The figure also shows the links between them. Let's take a closer look.

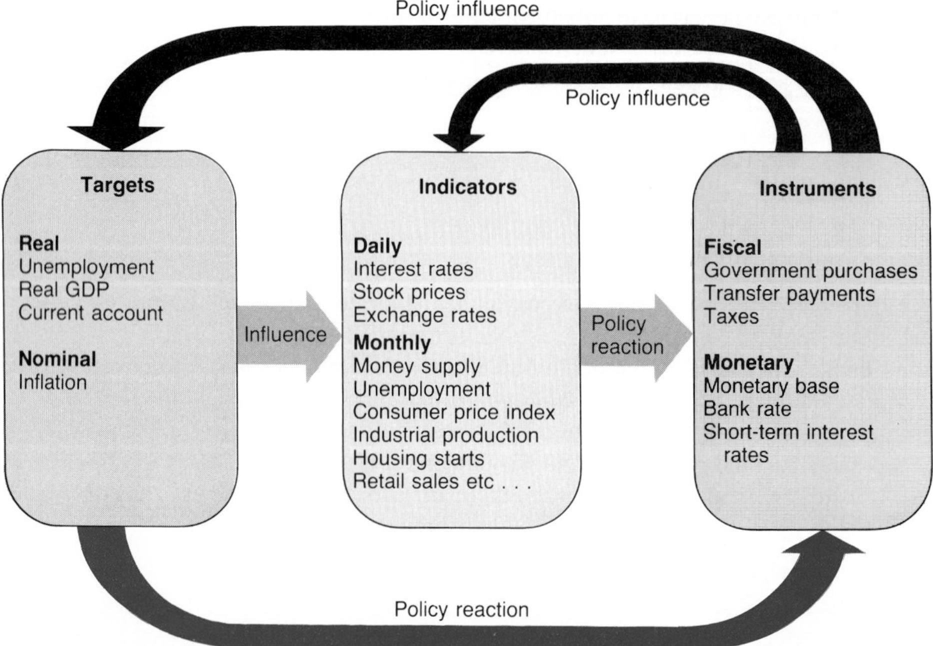

FIGURE 14.1
Macroeconomic Policy

Macroeconomic policy targets the unemployment rate, real GDP, the current account balance, and inflation. To assess where the economy is daily and monthly, indicators of economic performance are assessed. The targets influence the indicators and the targets and the indicators together lead to policy reactions—to changes in the setting of monetary and fiscal policy instruments that in turn influence both the targets and the indicators.

Macroeconomic stabilization policy involves three steps:

1. Formulating the objectives as the values of the policy target variables
2. Undertaking research to discover stable policy-invariant relationships among the variables
3. Choosing the setting and the rules governing changes in the policy instruments

The first part of the process, setting the targets, is a political matter. Each of us individually has views about the importance of unemployment, real GDP growth, inflation, and the nation's balance of payments with the rest of the world. We express those views in a variety of ways, including the votes we cast at elections. The government filters those opinions and arrives at an operational set of policy objectives. These objectives are rarely explicit. They are not usually written down as concrete precise goals. Furthermore, the target settings are not constant. They are adjusted as situations evolve. For example, during the early 1960s, an unemployment rate above 7 percent would have been regarded as utterly unacceptable, as would an inflation rate above 5 percent a year. But as the world changed in the 1970s and 1980s, inflation rates and unemployment rates in these ranges were transformed from the unacceptable to the commonplace.

The second part of the process, undertaking research, is a scientific matter. It involves specifying, testing, and often rejecting macroeconomic models. The outcome of this process is the gradual accumulation of a body of macroeconomic theory—reliable generalizations that can be used to guide policy. A further aspect of this scientific part of the policy process is reading the indicators. This involves assessing, on the basis of frequently and rapidly available data, the current state and likely trends in the policy targets.

The third part of the process—choosing the setting in the policy instruments—is a blend of the political and the scientific, and involves judgments. Some of these are objective judgments about the state of the economy and the way it responds to different types of policies. But some are value judgments based on what is desirable.

There are many different possible policies but they all fall into two broad groups—those based on rules and those based on discretion.

14.3 *Rules versus Discretion*

In ordinary speech, the word *rule* conjures up restriction and obedience, and the word *discretion* conjures up freedom of choice. This is how macroeconomics uses these words, too. A **macroeconomic policy rule**—also called a **fixed rule**—is a macroeconomic policy that does not react to changing economic conditions. It prescribes a specific policy action no matter what the circumstances. "Keep to the right" and "stop at a red traffic signal" are examples of fixed rules. The rule is not "keep to the right except when you're on a country lane and you think there's nothing coming in the opposite direction." It is "in any circumstances, keep to the right." Examples of fixed rules for macroeconomic policy are "balance the budget," "keep the exchange rate fixed," and "keep the money supply growing at a constant rate."

A **discretionary macroeconomic policy**—also called a **feedback policy**—is a policy that reacts to the current state of the economy. A good example of discretion is the actions of a judge who listens to the evidence and then decides the case as best he or she can. This example also illustrates that using discretion does not mean abandoning rules. The judge uses rules—the law—to reach a judgment. A cyclist changing to a low gear when going up a hill and to a high gear when going down a hill is also using a feedback policy. Feedback mechanisms are also embedded into many electrical and mechanical control instruments. For example, air conditioning and heating systems have feedback mechanisms built into them. The amount of heat pumped out by the furnace depends on the temperature sensed by the thermostat. An example of a macroeconomic feedback policy is cutting taxes in a recession. Another is increasing interest rates in a boom when inflation is increasing.

We can characterize *monetarists* and *activists,* whom you encountered in Chapter 1, by their adherence to different types of policies. Monetarists advocate the use of fixed rules, especially for the growth rate of the money supply. They generally place greater weight on achieving price stability than on achieving the real targets of full employment and steady real GDP growth. They also believe that the time lags involved in the operation of policy are too long for active stabilization policy to be effective. Further, they believe that the economy is a self-regulating mechanism that will return to full employment unaided, given sufficient time.

Activists advocate the use of feedback policies. They usually pay more attention to real targets of macroeconomic policy, such as unemployment and real GDP fluctuations, than they do to price level stability. They agree with monetarists that policy operates with a time lag, but they believe that the time lags are not so long as to make active stabilization policy unworkable. They also believe that the economy is not self-regulating and that, in the absence of active intervention, it may remain away from full employment for prolonged periods.

If policymakers pursue the fixed rules advocated by monetarists, households and firms will expect policy to be unresponsive to the state of the economy. If feedback policies are used, as advocated by activists, people will take these feedback policies into account when forming their expectations about the economic environment. We'll study the importance of the interactions of the rules followed by policymakers and the expectations formed by private economic decisionmakers as we examine the consequences of pursuing monetarist and activist policy advice.

14.4 *Monetarist Policy Advice and Its Consequences*

Monetarists give the following policy advice:

- Set government purchases, transfer payments, and taxes at levels that achieve an efficient allocation of resources and a fair distribution of income and wealth. (Fairness, an ethical concept, has to be determined in the political and social arena and cannot be objectively determined by an economic analyst.)
- Let the foreign exchange rate be flexible and pay no attention to the current account balance.
- Make the money supply grow at a constant rate.

The main instrument of macroeconomic policy for the monetarist (and hence the term *monetarist*) is the money supply. Monetarists advocate setting the growth rate of a monetary aggregate (either the monetary base or one of the broader monetary aggregates such as M1 or M2) so that, on the average, the inflation rate will be zero. This money supply growth rate can be computed as the growth rate of real GDP multiplied by the income elasticity of the demand for money minus the long-term growth in the velocity of circulation of money. Once calculated, monetarists advocate, the chosen monetary aggregate should be made to grow at the predetermined rate with no deviation from it, regardless of the state of the economy, the state of the government's budget, or any other economic factor.

It is easier to work out the consequences of pursuing monetarist advice if we imagine an economy that has no growth. In this case we'll be studying the movement of real GDP and employment around some constant full-employment level. This does not mean that the analysis cannot work for a growing economy. It's just easier to see what's happening if we abstract from that feature of the real world. Also, in studying the consequences of following monetarist policy advice, we'll study the effects of demand shocks and supply shocks separately, even though in practice they often occur together. We'll start by describing how demand and supply shocks affect aggregate demand and aggregate supply.

Aggregate demand shocks and the aggregate demand curve

The *IS-LM* analysis of aggregate demand, developed in Chapter 6 for the closed economy and Chapter 7 for the open economy, did not explicitly contain aggregate demand shocks. It was presented as if the level of aggregate demand is determined *exactly* once the value of the money supply and the fiscal policy variables are set. This was an oversimplification that we will now relax.

The theory of aggregate demand is based on theories of consumption, investment, the demand for money, and international trade and capital flows. Holding the money supply, fiscal policy variables, and international influences constant, the position of the aggregate demand curve is fixed and fully predictable only if the consumption function, investment function, demand for money function, and the international flows of goods and capital are also fixed and predictable. If a large enough group of individuals decides in one particular year that they can manage with a smaller ratio of money balances to income than normal, then in that particular year there will be a surge of expenditures. This will happen as these individuals put into action their decisions to lower their money balances below their normal level in relation to their incomes. Conversely, if a large enough group of individuals decides in a particular year that they want a higher ratio of money balances to income than normal, they will cut back on their expenditures as they put their decisions into effect.

There are many factors that lead individuals to vary their consumption, investment, demand for money, and international transactions over time. On the average, such factors cancel out and are not very important when aggregated over all the individuals in the economy. But from time to time, such factors can be important and might move the economy significantly away from its normal equilibrium position.

Some examples will be helpful. Suppose it is widely believed that a severe drought is going to occur. People might very well stockpile food and lower their average money holdings for a period. While this stockpiling is going on, the level of aggregate demand will increase as people attempt to fulfill their increased expenditure plans. Or, suppose it is widely believed that a major technical innovation in cars is about to make the current year's model obsolete. The sales of cars in the current year will be unusually low, as people hold on to their money balances to be ready for an increase in future expenditures. In this case, as people retime their expenditures, sales in one year will be unusually low and sales in some subsequent year will be unusually high.

These are simply examples; you can probably think of many more. Most of the examples you will think of will turn out to involve randomness in the timing of people's expenditures on durable goods, capital goods, or other goods to store. Random fluctuations in the composition of people's assets — money holdings and real assets — lead to random fluctuations in aggregate demand.

You can think of the aggregate demand curve that we worked with earlier in this book as being the position of the aggregate demand curve *on the average*. This curve is shown in Figure 14.2 as the blue line labeled $AD(M_0)$. It is labeled in this way to remind

FIGURE 14.2
Aggregate Demand Shocks

Fluctuations in consumption, investment, net exports, and the demand for money summarize the shock *e*, which shifts the aggregate demand curve around its average position, even though monetary and fiscal policy variables are fixed. On the average, the shocks are zero but range between +*e* and −*e*. The aggregate demand curve fluctuates between these limits.

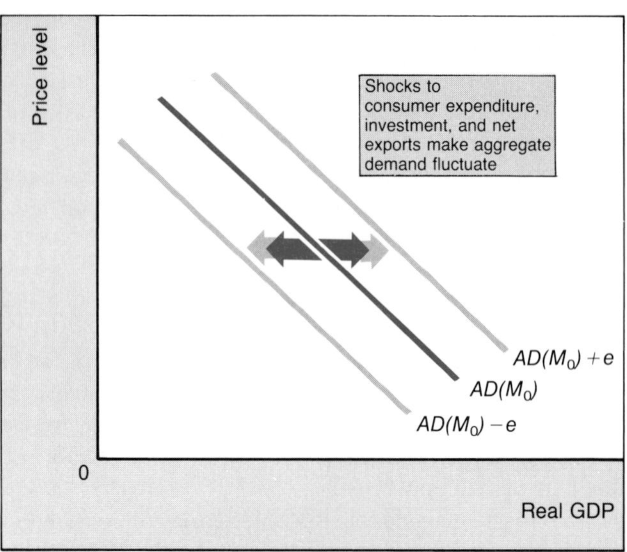

you that the position of the *AD* curve depends on, among other things, the money supply, *M*. The subscript on *M* denotes the initial value of the money supply, M_0. Later we'll analyze what happens when we change *M*, holding everything else constant.

Random shocks arising from considerations like the ones just described affect the position of the aggregate demand curve. Sometimes aggregate demand will be higher than its average value and sometimes lower than its average value. We can capture such random shocks as an addition to or subtraction from the average position of the aggregate demand curve. Let's call random shock to aggregate demand *e*. On the average, *e* is equal to zero, but it can take on large positive or negative values. If *e* is positive, the aggregate demand curve moves to the right, as shown by the light blue line $AD(M_0) + e$. If there is a negative shock, *minus e*, the aggregate demand curve moves to the left, as shown by the light blue line $AD(M_0) - e$. At any particular point in time the aggregate demand curve might lie anywhere inside the range of the two curves $AD(M_0) + e$ and $AD(M_0) - e$. On the average, the aggregate demand curve is in the middle of this range, at $AD(M_0)$.

Thus for any given level of the money supply, there is a whole set of possible aggregate demand curves. The *actual* position of the aggregate demand curve depends on the size of the random shock (*e*) and on the money supply.

Consequences of monetarist policy

What happens if an aggregate demand shock occurs when the monetary policy pursued follows the advice of monetarists? Figure 14.3 illustrates the analysis. Recall that monetarist advice involves making the money supply follow a fixed rule under all circumstances. Here we'll assume that the actual money supply is held constant at M_0. Knowing that monetarist advice is being followed, the anticipated money supply is also M_0. That is, the actual money supply will equal the anticipated money supply, and there will be no unanticipated change in the money supply.

Since, on the average, the aggregate demand shock is zero, it is rational to expect a zero aggregate demand shock. The expected aggregate demand curve is $AD(M_0)$. It is the expected aggregate demand curve in the double sense that it is drawn for expected

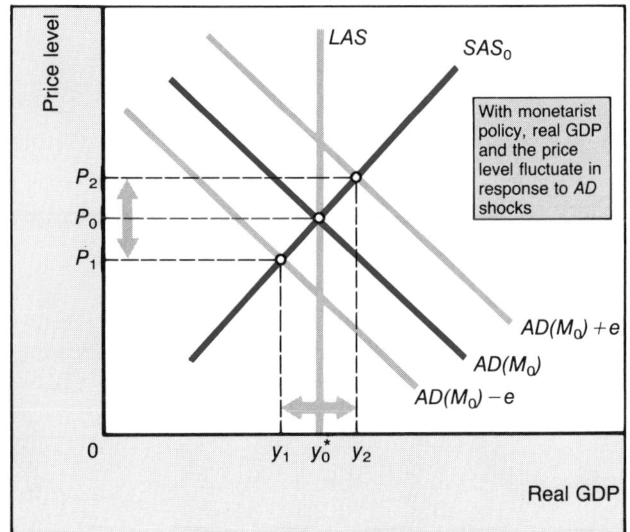

FIGURE 14.3
The Consequences of Monetarist Policy: An Aggregate Demand Shock

Monetarist policy holds the money supply constant at M_0. The expected level of aggregate demand is $AD(M_0)$. The best forecast is that the price level will be P_0 and wages are determined accordingly, so the short-run aggregate supply curve is SAS_0. Actual fluctuations in aggregate demand generate fluctuations in real GDP with procyclical fluctuations in the price level.

values of the aggregate demand shock (zero) and the money supply (M_0). The rational expectation of the price level is P_0—at the intersection of the expected aggregate demand curve $AD(M_0)$ and the long-run aggregate supply curve, *LAS*. Passing through this intersection point is the short-run aggregate supply curve, SAS_0, drawn for the money wage rate based on the expected price level, P_0.

Suppose that an aggregate demand shock increases aggregate demand so that the aggregate demand curve *actually* moves rightward to $AD(M) + e$. With monetarist policy advice being followed, the money supply is held constant at M_0, and the shock to aggregate demand increases the price level to P_1 and output to y_1.

What happens if there is a negative shock to aggregate demand? Actual aggregate demand falls, and the aggregate demand curve shifts leftward to $AD(M_0) - e$. Again, following the monetarist policy advice, the actual money supply is held steady at M_0, and the price level decreases to P_2 and output to y_2.

You can now see the consequences of following monetarist policy advice when the economy is hit by aggregate demand shocks: real GDP deviates from its long-run level and the price level from its expected level. Employment, unemployment, and the real wage also fluctuate. These fluctuations occur because the aggregate demand shocks are not offset by changes in the money supply.

Aggregate supply shocks

We studied the effects of aggregate supply shocks on the production function, the labor market, and the aggregate supply curves in Chapter 11. Let's refresh our memory by focusing on the effects on the aggregate supply curves. Figure 14.4 illustrates.

To keep things simple, let's look only at a negative supply shock. Initially, the long-run aggregate supply curve is LAS_0 and the short-run aggregate supply curve SAS_0. An aggregate supply shock shifts the production function downward and lowers the marginal product of labor. The long-run aggregate supply curve shifts to LAS_1. The short-run aggregate supply curve, based on the initial money wage rate and the new long-run aggregate supply conditions, is SAS_1. Recall that the short-run aggregate supply curve shifts to the left by more than the shift in the long-run aggregate supply curve because the money wage rate is above its full-employment level at the price level P_0. Only if the

FIGURE 14.4
Aggregate Supply Shock and Aggregate Supply Curves

A negative aggregate supply shock shifts the long-run aggregate supply curve to the left from LAS_0 to LAS_1. With a given wage rate, the short-run aggregate supply curve shifts from SAS_0 to SAS_2. The short-run aggregate supply curve shifts by more than the long-run aggregate supply curve.

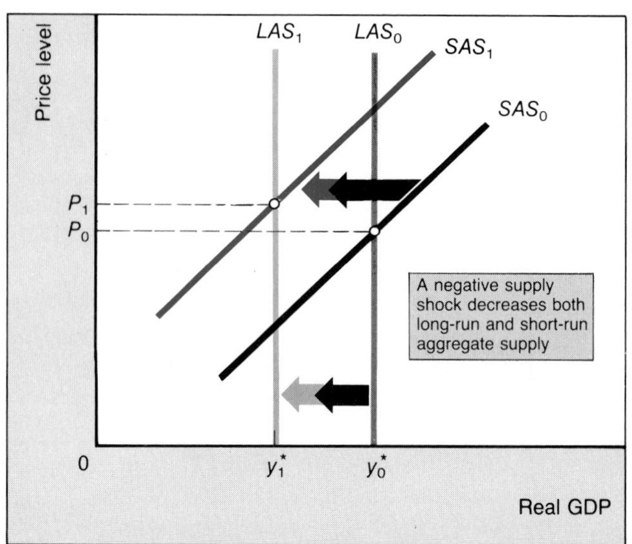

price level increased to P_1, decreasing the real wage rate, would the economy be at the full-employment point—the intersection of LAS_1 and SAS_1. Let's see how the economy reacts to such an aggregate supply shock in the face of a monetarist policy. Figure 14.5 illustrates.

Aggregate supply decreases from LAS_0 to LAS_1 (long-run) and SAS_0 to SAS_1 (short-run). Because a monetarist policy rule fixes the money stock at M_0, the aggregate demand curve remains at AD_0. Before the shock, the equilibrium level of real GDP was y_0^* and the price level was P_0. Following the supply shock, with a constant money supply leaving aggregate demand unchanged, the price level increases to P_1 and real GDP decreases to y_1. But this is not the end of the story. This response occurs only if the money wage rate remains constant.

FIGURE 14.5
Monetarist Policy with a Supply Shock

The economy is initially at full employment with real GDP y_0^* and the price level P_0. A supply shock shifts the short-run and long-run aggregate supply curves left to LAS_1 and SAS_1. In the new equilibrium, real GDP falls to y_1 and the price level increases to P_1. The economy experiences stagflation. If the shock is permanent and the monetarist policy maintained, real GDP eventually falls to y_1^* and the price level increases to P_2. If the shock is temporary, the economy returns to P_0 and y_0^*.

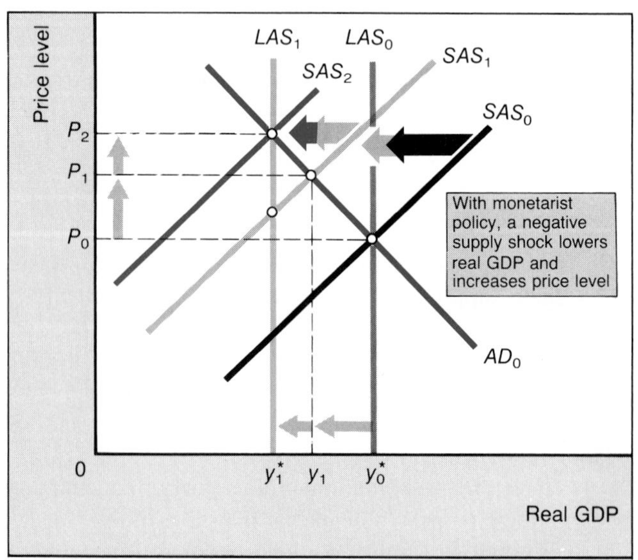

But at the price level P_1 and real GDP y_1, despite the fact that real GDP and employment have fallen, the economy is operating at a level of real GDP above its full-employment level. Unemployment, even if it has increased, is below its new natural rate. Demand pressure in the labor market moves the money wage rate upward. As it does so, the short-run aggregate supply curve shifts further to the left from SAS_1 to SAS_2. In this process, real GDP falls further, to y_1^*, and the price level increases to P_2.

Thus, following monetarist policy advice in the face of an aggregate supply shock leads to movements in real GDP and the price level in opposite directions. We have just seen that a negative aggregate supply shock decreases real GDP and increases the price level. The economy experiences *stagflation*. That is, the economy stagnates and inflates at the same time. It is to avoid stagflation in the face of an aggregate supply shock that some economists advocate adjusting the money supply to accommodate the supply shock. We'll examine such a policy later in this chapter. First, let's look a case in which monetarist policies have actually been pursued and see how they work in practice.

14.5 *Monetarist Policy in Japan, 1978-1990*

TESTCASE

Many governments and central banks have been accused of being monetarist. The most famous is the government of Margaret Thatcher during her period as prime minister of the United Kingdom in the 1980s. The Bank of Canada was also labeled ''monetarist'' during the late 1970s and early 1980s when the then governor Gerald Bouey pursued a policy of disinflation by targetting the growth rate of the money supply.

Despite the label, neither Margaret Thatcher nor Gerald Bouey pursued monetarism, at least as it is defined by macroeconomists. Monetarism is keeping the money supply growing at a steady and predictable pace, not decreasing the growth rate of the money supply so savagely as to lead the economy into recession.

There is, in fact, only one example of monetarist policies being pursued: Japan in the period since 1978. And, perhaps not surprisingly in view of the political stigma attaching to the term, the Bank of Japan does not regard itself as being monetarist! The senior officials of the Bank of Japan see themselves as pursuing pragmatic discretionary policies. The fact remains that they have come closer than any other central bank to pursuing monetarist policies for more than a decade.

Japanese-style monetarism

Since 1978, the Bank of Japan has pursued a monetarist policy of targetting the growth rate of a monetary aggregate and keeping its actual growth rate close to the target. The particular monetary aggregate targetted is a broad one—M2 plus certificates of deposit (CDs). In Japan, M2 is defined in a similar way to its definition in Canada. It is a broad monetary aggregate that includes currency, chequing accounts, and savings accounts. CDs are large-denomination time deposits easily convertible to cash because they can be resold in a secondary market.

The Bank of Japan began announcing a target growth rate for M2 plus CDs in 1978. It also declared that a target of its monetary policy was zero inflation. It announced that it would gradually slow down the growth rate of this monetary aggregate as long as prices were rising. Targetted money supply growth rates gradually decreased through 1984 and the actual money supply growth rate remained very close to target. Since 1984, targetted money supply growth rates have increased somewhat and so have actual money supply growth rates.

Policy before 1978

Prior to the adoption of monetarism in 1978, the Bank of Japan permitted the growth rate of the money supply to fluctuate within extremely wide ranges. In the early 1970s, the money supply growth rate accelerated to more than 25 percent by 1972. Then, through 1974, the money supply growth rate was severely cut back. The Bank of Japan sought to use monetary policy actively either to stimulate or dampen aggregate demand.

Economic performance before and after

The economic performance of Japan before and after adopting monetary targetting in 1978 suggests that monetary policy can indeed have a dramatic effect upon the economy. Figure 14.6 illustrates Japan's monetary policy and some key aspects of its macroeconomic performance. You can see that the period of rapid monetary expansion in the early 1970s was followed some two years later by an explosion of inflation. Then followed a period of savage monetary contraction — the money supply growth rate was cut back from more than 25 percent to about 11 percent in two years — and the economy went into a deep recession. You can see that in the period after 1978, with money supply growth rates fluctuating only mildly, the inflation rate declined — to zero by 1987 — and real GDP growth fluctuated only mildly.

There is a particularly informative comparison between the first and second oil shocks. When the first oil shock hit Japan in 1973-1974, the Japanese economy was still experiencing the effects of rapid monetary growth two years earlier. The oil shock, an aggregate supply shock, hit the economy and simultaneously, to counter the inflationary consequences, the Bank of Japan further tightened its monetary policy. The mixture of a negative aggregate supply shock and a negative aggregate demand shock sent the Japanese economy into severe recession.

When the second oil shock hit the economy in 1979-1980, the monetarist policy was in place and aggregate demand was held steady. Despite a negative aggregate supply shock, inflation did not increase and real GDP growth did not decrease.

FIGURE 14.6
Monetarism in Japan

Before 1978, Japan permitted its money supply to fluctuate (blue line in figure). Inflation and real GDP growth also fluctuated over a wide range. After 1978, the Bank of Japan adopted a monetarist policy of steadying and gradually slowing the growth rate of a broad monetary aggregate. The inflation rate gradually declined and real GDP growth stabilized. When the second oil shock hit in 1979-1980, it was barely noticeable.

Source: Economic Statistics Annual (various years), Research and Statistics Department, Bank of Japan, Tokyo.

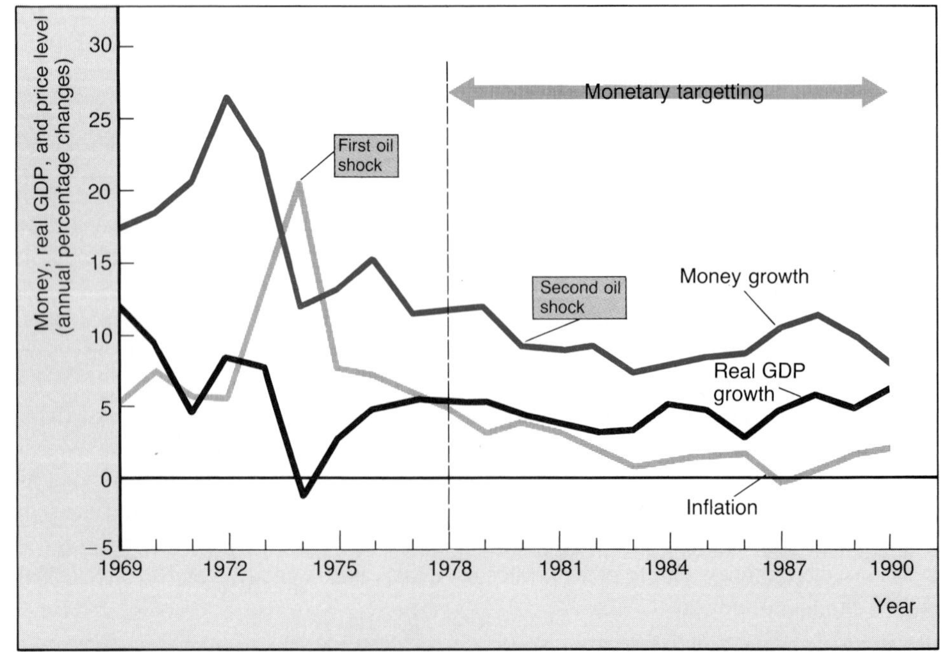

Late 1980s

In the late 1980s, Japanese monetary growth accelerated somewhat and, after 1987, so did its inflation rate. Does this mean that Japan has abandoned monetarism? To some degree, it does, and for an interesting reason. It is not that Japan has found its earlier monetary policy unsuccessful. On the contrary, it has been dramatically successful. In fact, it has been so successful that other major countries, notably the United States and those of Western Europe, have been pressing Japan to pursue more expansionary policies—policies that weaken the yen in the foreign exchange markets and strengthen the U.S. dollar and the European currencies. Under international pressure, the Bank of Japan has gradually expanded its money supply growth rate, permitting the Japanese inflation rate to increase so as to not put such severe pressure on the currencies of the United States and Western Europe to depreciate on foreign exchange markets.

We've now studied the consequences of following monetarist policy advice both in theory and in practice by looking at the only available real-world laboratory experiment with monetarism. Let's now turn to an analysis of activist policy.

14.6 *Activist Policy Advice and Its Consequences*

Activists give the following advice:

- If real GDP is (or is forecasted to be) below its full-employment equilibrium level, increase aggregate demand by increasing the money supply, increasing government purchases of goods and services, or cutting taxes.
- If real GDP is (or is forecasted to be) above its full-employment level, decrease aggregate demand by decreasing the money supply, decreasing government purchases of goods and services, or increasing taxes.

The precise amounts by which the money supply, government purchases, or taxes should be moved in order to achieve the desired change in aggregate demand is a technically complex matter, but one that activists believe can be handled with the help of econometric models.

In studying the consequences of pursuing activist policies, we'll follow exactly the same setup we adopted when studying monetarist policies. We'll begin by studying aggregate demand shocks.

Aggregate demand shocks

Figure 14.7 uses exactly the same setup that we used in Figure 14.3. The anticipated aggregate demand curve drawn for an expected zero aggregate demand shock is the curve AD_0. (For the moment, ignore the other labels on AD_0 in Figure 14.7.) With the money wage rate at its full employment level, the short-run aggregate supply curve is SAS_0.

Suppose the economy experiences a positive aggregate demand shock (e) that shifts the aggregate demand curve right to $AD_0 + e$. Activist policy advice in the face of such a shock is to decrease aggregate demand by decreasing government purchases or the money supply or increasing taxes. If aggregate demand is decreased by exactly the right amount, it is possible to offset the positive aggregate demand shock and keep the actual aggregate demand curve stationary at AD_0. Suppose the aggregate demand curve that incorporates the aggregate demand shock (e) and the changed fiscal policy and money supply is the same as AD_0. To remind you that the same aggregate demand curve can arise from a different combination of fiscal and monetary policy and aggregate demand

FIGURE 14.7
The Consequences of Activist Policy: Demand Shock

Aggregate demand shocks are offset by changes in government purchases, taxes, or the money supply to stabilize aggregate demand, real GDP, and the price level.

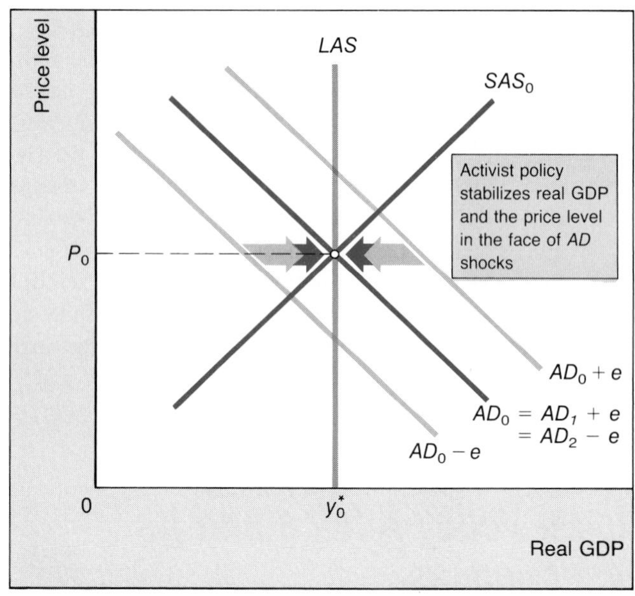

shock, we have given this aggregate demand curve a second label, $AD_1 + e$. Following activist policy advice of offsetting the aggregate demand shock keeps real GDP constant at y_0^* and the price level at its anticipated level P_0.

The same conclusion arises in the case of a negative aggregate demand shock. If aggregate demand falls by a random amount, e, with unchanged government purchases, taxes, and money supply the aggregate demand curve will shift left to $AD_0 - e$. But if activist policy advice is followed, this random shock is offset to keep the aggregate demand curve at its original level. The aggregate demand curve remains stationary at AD_0. We have labeled this aggregate demand curve $AD_2 - e$ to remind you that with a negative aggregate demand shock, it is possible to keep the aggregate demand curve in the same place by increasing government purchases, cutting taxes, or increasing the money supply by the right amount to offset the random shock to aggregate demand.

Again, following activist policy advice, the price level remains at P_0 and real GDP at y_0^*. You now know that the consequences of activist stabilization policy are to remove all the fluctuations from output and to keep the price level at its anticipated level.

Aggregate supply shocks

Figure 14.8 illustrates the consequences of following activist policy advice in the wake of aggregate supply shocks. Suppose initially the aggregate demand curve is AD_0 and the long-run and short-run aggregate supply curves are LAS_0 and SAS_0. The price level is P_0 and real GDP is y_0^*. Suppose that the economy experiences an aggregate supply shock that moves the long-run aggregate supply curve to LAS_1 and the short-run aggregate supply curve to SAS_1. Activist policy advice is to increase aggregate *demand* to offset this decrease in aggregate supply. The activist response is to shift the aggregate demand curve to AD_1 — an increase in aggregate demand just sufficient for the new equilibrium at the intersection of AD_1 and SAS_1 to occur at the original level of real GDP (y_0^*). But at this equilibrium, the price level is higher, at P_1.

What happens next depends on whether the aggregate supply shock is temporary or permanent. The case of a temporary shock is illustrated in Figure 14.8(a). In the next

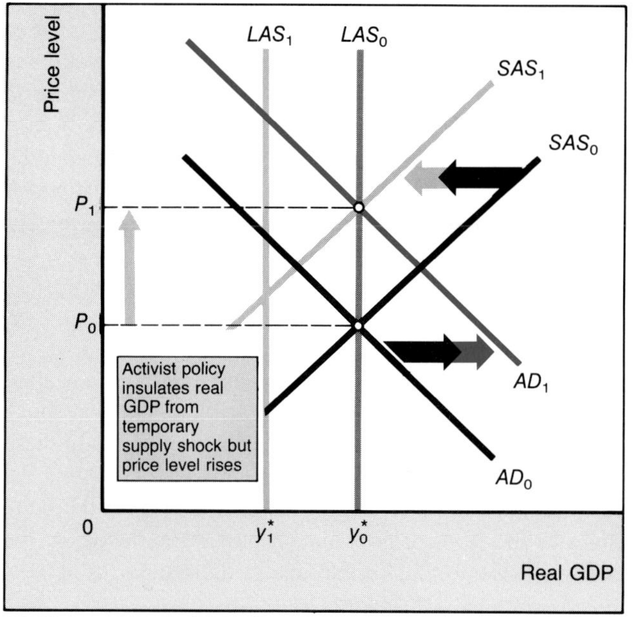

(a) Temporary supply shock

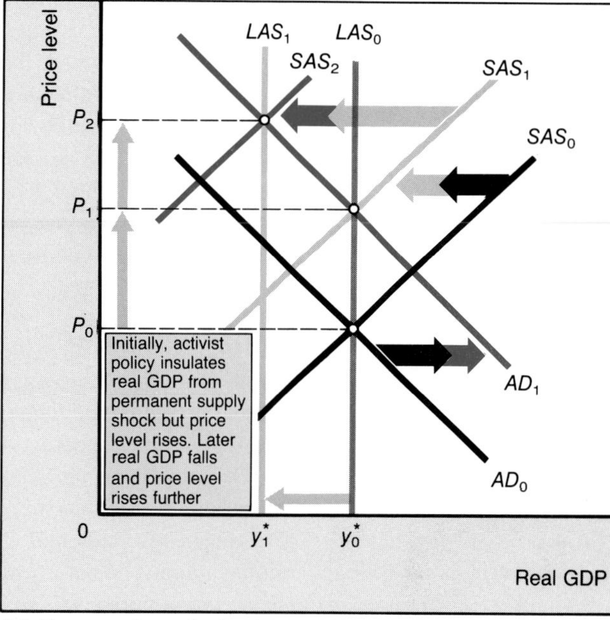

(b) Permanent supply shock

FIGURE 14.8
Activist Policy with a Supply Shock—Avoiding Stagflation

The economy initially has a real GDP of y_0^*, and a price level of P_0. An aggregate supply shock shifts the long-run aggregate supply curve to LAS_1 and the short-run aggregate supply curve to SAS_1. An activist policy increases aggregate demand from AD_0 to AD_1. The price level increases to P_1 but real GDP remains at y_0^* (both parts of the figure). If the shock is temporary (part a), real GDP returns to y_0^*, but the price level does not return to P_0—it remains at P_1. If the shock is permanent (part b), real GDP eventually falls to y_1^* and the price level increases further to P_2.

* Refer to ERRATA sheet.

period the long-run aggregate supply curve shifts back to LAS_0. What happens to the short-run aggregate supply curve depends on what happens to wages. The most likely response is a wage increase, keeping the short-run aggregate supply curve at SAS_1. Anticipating this wage response, the activist policy advice is to hold aggregate demand steady at AD_1. Real GDP returns to its original level (y_0^*) but the price level remains at P_1, above its original level.

Figure 14.8(b) illustrates what happens if the supply shock is permanent. In this case, real GDP cannot remain at y_0^* indefinitely. This level of real GDP is above the new full-employment level (y_1^*). There is excess demand for labor, and wages will increase to restore equilibrium in the labor market. As they do so, the short-run aggregate supply curve shifts to the left. If the activist policy continues to increase aggregate demand in an attempt to maintain real GDP at y_0^*, the aggregate demand curve shifts to the right by the same rate as the rising wages shift the short-run aggregate supply curve to the left. A process of never-ending accelerating inflation ensues.

If, once it is realized that the aggregate supply shock is permanent, the policy of attempting to keep real GDP at y_0^* is abandoned and y_1^* is accepted as the target, the inflation process can be brought to an end. The figure illustrates the quickest end possible—one in which aggregate demand is maintained at AD_1. In this case, real GDP falls to y_1^*, its new long-run equilibrium level, and the price level increases to P_2.

We may now summarize the consequences of following an activist policy in the face of an aggregate supply shock: initially, policy leads to inflation but no decrease in real GDP or employment. Subsequently, if the shock is temporary, the economy returns to its initial equilibrium. If the shock is permanent, prices rise further. At some point, once the permanence of the shock is recognized, real GDP will be permitted to decrease to its new long-run equilibrium level, but at a higher price level.

Notice that the activist policy of changing aggregate *demand* to accommodate an aggregate *supply* shock avoids the initial decrease in real GDP that the monetarist policy creates. But the activist policy brings a higher price level — and a temporarily higher inflation rate — as a consequence.

Policy time lags

In our analysis of activist policy, we've assumed that policymakers can react instantaneously to aggregate demand or aggregate supply shocks *at the same time as* the shock is affecting the economy. In practice, time lags occur in this process. (We study these lags in some detail in Chapter 15.) When a shock hits the economy, real GDP and the price level respond to that shock and then, at a later stage, the government or the Bank of Canada responds with changes in the level of government purchases, taxes, or the money supply. What are the consequences of such time lags in the pursuit of activist stabilization policies?

To make things as clear as possible, let's suppose that everyone knows that an activist policy is being pursued but that policymakers react with a one-period time lag. In the *current period*, they change aggregate demand in response to *last period's* aggregate demand and aggregate supply shocks. Let's work out what happens as a result of such a lag in the policy response, first when there is an aggregate demand shock and second an aggregate supply shock.

Aggregate demand shock with policy lag

Figure 14.9 illustrates the analysis. Initially, the aggregate demand curve is AD_0 and the short-run aggregate supply curve is SAS_0. The price level is P_0 and real GDP is y_0^*. A negative aggregate demand shock of e hits the economy, shifting the aggregate demand curve to $AD_0 - e$. No one has predicted this shock ahead of time. Real GDP moves from y_0^* to y_1 and the price level falls from P_0 to P_1. The economy experiences deflation and a slump in output, taking it below its long-run equilibrium level of real GDP.

Now roll the clock forward one period. The aggregate demand shock has hit and the economy is in a recession. Policymakers react to this aggregate demand shock by increasing government purchases, cutting taxes, or increasing the money supply in the next period. Assuming that there are no new aggregate demand shocks in the next period (an assumption that keeps the experiment that we are conducting clean), the new aggregate demand curve lies to the right of the original curve, AD_0.

Households, firms, and unions, observing the economy in a recession in the current period, rationally expect policy to shift the aggregate demand curve to AD_2. If they react on this expectation, the money wage rate will increase to preserve a real wage rate equal to its full-employment equilibrium level. The short-run aggregate supply curve shifts to SAS_1, the price level rises to P_2, and real GDP returns to y_0^*.

You can see that under an activist policy rule with a one-period time lag in the adjustment of aggregate demand, real GDP behaves exactly as it does under a monetarist policy. But the price level is more variable with the activist policy. When the aggregate demand shock occurs, the economy goes into recession and the price level falls (with an ongoing inflation, the inflation rate would slow rather than the price level fall). In the

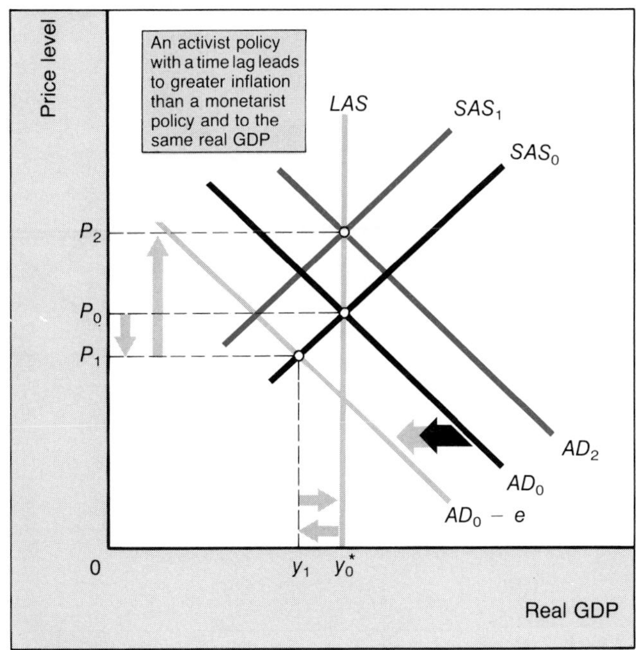

FIGURE 14.9
Activist Policy with a Time Lag: Aggregate Demand Shock

The economy starts out with a real GDP of y_0^* and a price level of P_0. A negative aggregate demand shock (*e*) shifts the aggregate demand curve to the left. Real GDP falls to y_1 and the price level falls to P_1. This is the same response as with a monetarist policy. In the next period aggregate demand is increased and the aggregate demand curve shifts to AD_2. Since this policy is expected, the expected price level is P_2 and wages change in anticipation of the higher price level, so the short-run aggregate supply curve shifts to SAS_1. The price level increases to P_2 and real GDP returns to y_0^*.

following period, full employment is restored but the price level rises above its initial level with an activist policy and returns to its initial level with a monetarist policy.

Next, let's look at an activist policy with a time lag when the economy experiences an aggregate supply shock.

Aggregate supply shock and policy lag

Suppose that everyone knows the policy reaction rule—to adopt an activist policy with a one-period reaction lag. Figure 14.10 illustrates the analysis. Initially, the economy is on the aggregate demand curve AD_0 and short-run aggregate supply curve SAS_0. Real GDP is y_0^* and the price level is P_0. An aggregate supply shock shifts the long-run aggregate supply curve to LAS_1 and the short-run aggregate supply curve to SAS_1. This is exactly the same aggregate supply shock that we analyzed earlier with no policy reaction lag. Because the policymakers cannot foresee this shock, the economy cannot react to it instantaneously. It moves to the point of intersection of the new short-run aggregate supply curve SAS_1, and the original aggregate demand curve AD_0. The price level increases to P_1 and real GDP decreases to y_1. Seeing the economy in a depressed state, policymakers react by increasing aggregate demand by enough to offset the supply shock—returning real GDP to y_0^*. They move the aggregate demand curve to AD_1. What happens to real GDP and the price level depends on whether the supply shock is temporary or permanent and whether it was anticipated to be temporary or permanent.

A temporary shock, expected to be temporary Figure 14.10(a) illustrates this case. The long-run aggregate supply curve returns to its original position (LAS_0). But with aggregate demand at AD_1, wages increase in the anticipation that the price level will be P_1'. The price level rises from P_1 to P_1' and real GDP returns to y_0^*.

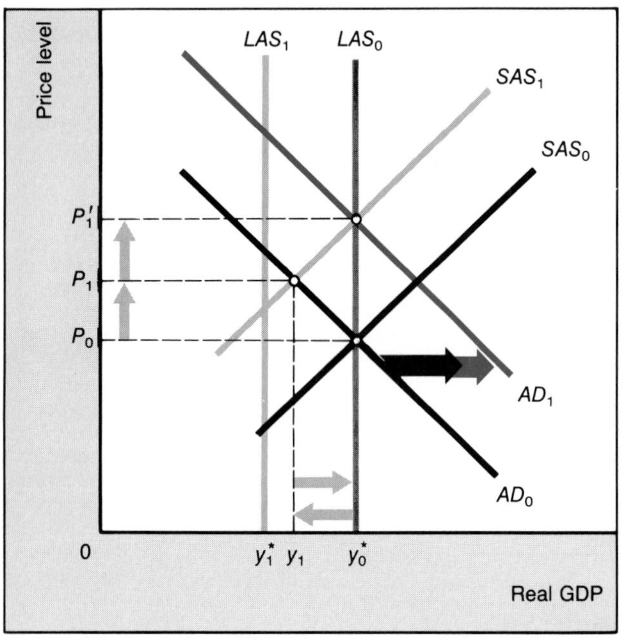

(a) Temporary supply shock

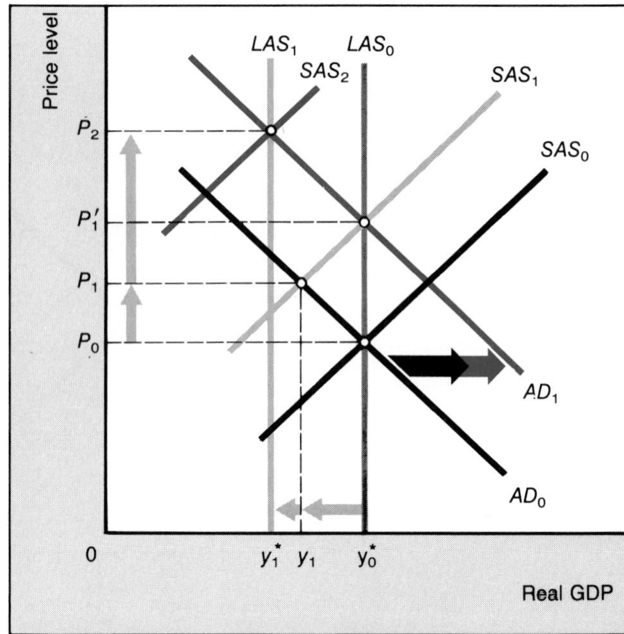

(b) Permanent supply shock

FIGURE 14.10
Activist Policy with Supply Shock and Time Lag

Starting out at real GDP of y_0^* with a price level of P_0, an aggregate supply shock shifts the long-run aggregate supply curve to LAS_1 and the short-run aggregate supply curve to SAS_1. Real GDP falls to y_1 and the price level increases to P_1 (both parts of the figure). In the next period, aggregate demand is increased to restore the previous level of output, so the aggregate demand curve shifts to AD_1. If the supply shock is—and is expected to be—temporary (part a), the expected price level in the next period is P_1'. The short-run aggregate supply curve remains at SAS_1 and in the next period the price level is P_0' and real GDP is y_0^*. If the shock is—and is expected to be—permanent, upward pressure on wages will shift the short-run aggregate supply curve to SAS_2, decreasing real GDP to y_1^* and increasing the price level to P_2.

A permanent shock, expected to be permanent Figure 14.10(b) illustrates this case. The long-run aggregate supply curve remains at its new position (LAS_1) and the aggregate demand curve remains at its new position (AD_1). The price level is expected to increase to P_2 and wages increase in anticipation of that price increase. As a consequence, the short-run aggregate supply curve shifts to SAS_2. The economy moves to its new long-run equilibrium level of real GDP, y_1^*, and the price level P_2.

A permanent shock, expected to be temporary If people expect the aggregate supply shock to be temporary but, in fact, it turns out to be permanent, the initial reaction is the same as if the shock is temporary and is expected to be temporary. The short-run aggregate supply curve remains at SAS_1 and the economy moves to real GDP of y_0^* and a price level of P_1'. But this is not the end. There will be no policy reaction in the next period because the economy is expected to be at full employment. But there will be excess demand for labor and wages will increase, shifting the short-run aggregate supply curve to the left of SAS_1. As the short-run aggregate supply curve shifts, real GDP falls below y_0^*, generating a policy reaction (not shown in the figure) that shifts the aggregate demand curve farther to the right than AD_1. Inflation ensues.

A temporary shock, expected to be permanent If the aggregate supply shock is temporary but it is perceived to be permanent, people will expect the price level to increase to P_2. Wages will increase, shifting the short-run aggregate supply curve to SAS_2. Real GDP falls to y_1^* and the price level increases to P_2. Faced with a further period of recession, the Bank of Canada will increase the money supply again (or the government will increase expenditure or cut taxes), shifting the aggregate demand curve to the right of AD_1 (not shown in the figure), increasing the price level farther and increasing real GDP again the next period. As long as policymakers react as if the shock is permanent when in fact it's temporary, ever-accelerating inflation will ensue. Only when the government and the Bank of Canada recognize that the shock is temporary and stop increasing aggregate demand will the accelerating inflation process come to an end.

Now that we've studied the theory of activist policy, let's look at an example of such a policy in action.

14.7 *Activism in the United States—The Kennedy Years*

TESTCASE

During the early 1960s, there was a much applauded textbook case of activism in the United States. Following the election of John F. Kennedy as president in 1960, a group of the most distinguished macroeconomists of the day were assembled in Washington to run the new president's Council of Economic Advisors. Chairman of the group was Walter W. Heller, a Keynesian from the University of Minnesota. Also on the council was James Tobin of Yale (subsequently a Nobel Laureate). Joining the group slightly later was Gardner Ackley, the author of one of the leading macroeconomics textbooks of the 1950s. This team of most distinguished economists, supported by the strongest team of junior researchers ever assembled, embarked on a program of applying the latest ideas about economic stabilization to the problems of the U.S. economy.

Let President Kennedy speak:

> As I took office 24 months ago, the Nation was in the grip of its third recession in seven years; the average unemployment rate was nearing seven percent; $50 billion of potential output was running to waste in idle manpower and machinery.
>
> In these last two years, the administration and the Congress have taken a series of important steps to promote recovery and strengthen the economy:
>
> 1. Early in 1961, vigorous antirecession measures helped get recovery off to a fast start and gave needed assistance to those hardest hit by the recession.
> 2. In 1961 and 1962, new measures were enacted to redevelop chronically depressed areas; . . . retrain the unemployed . . . ; . . . enlarge social security benefits . . . ; (and) . . . provide special tax incentives to boost business capital spending. . . .
> 3. Budgetary policy was designed to facilitate the expansion of private demand. . . .
> 4. Monetary conditions were also adjusted to aid recovery within the constraints imposed by balance of payments considerations. . . .
>
> These policies facilitated rapid recovery from recession in 1961 and continuing expansion in 1962—an advance that carried total economic activity onto new high ground.[1]

[1] *Economic Report of the President*, 1963, pp. x-xi.

This is President Kennedy's own review and assessment of the economic record of his first two years in office, 1961 and 1962. Despite being able to report progress, the president did not regard the job as complete. Therefore in 1963 he formulated a budget incorporating tax reductions and reforms designed to stimulate consumer expenditure and investment.

The U.S. economy performed well during the 1960s. Real GDP expanded, unemployment declined, and inflation remained remarkably low. The performance of the U.S. macroeconomy during these years gave rise to great hope for active stabilization policy—what was called "fine-tuning" the economy.

But in the second half of the 1960s, confidence began to ebb. Although the Johnson administration pursued policies similar to those of its predecessor, fiscal expansion was more vigorous; and as real GDP grew and unemployment fell, inflation began to accelerate. By the end of the 1960s, inflation was more than 5 percent a year and was still accelerating at the time of the supply shocks of the 1970s.

In retrospect, it is clear that during the Kennedy years the economy was bombarded with small aggregate demand shocks and skillful aggregate demand policy minimized the effects of those shocks. Aggregate supply shocks were mild. Only when confronted with severe supply shocks did activist policies come into disrepute.

We've now looked at monetarist and activist policies both in theory and in action. Let's return to a comparison of these two policies and examine the sources of the conflicting policy advice.

14.8 *Why Monetarists and Activists Offer Conflicting Advice*

The essence of the dispute between activists and monetarists turns on the question of information and the use that may be made of new information. The monetarist asserts that the Bank of Canada has no information advantage over private agents and that it can do nothing that private agents will not do for themselves. Any attempt by the Bank of Canada to fine-tune or stabilize the economy by making the money supply react to previous shocks everybody knows about will not keep real GDP any closer to its full-employment level and will make the price level more variable.

Activists assert that the Bank of Canada has an effective informational advantage. They agree that individuals form their expectations rationally, using all the information available to them. But they also assert that individuals get locked into contracts based on expectations of the price level that, after an aggregate demand shock, turn out to be wrong. The Bank of Canada can act after private agents have tied themselves into contractual arrangements based on a wrong price level expectation to compensate for and offset the effects of those random shocks. Figure 14.3 can be reinterpreted as showing what happens if the private sector is tied into contracts based on an expected price level that turns out to be wrong. If private agents are tied into contracts based on the expected price level P_0, *and if* the Bank of Canada can change the money supply quickly enough, then the activist policy outcome shown in Figure 14.3 can be achieved.

Thus the essence of the debate concerns the flexibility of private sector responses vis-à-vis the flexibility of the Bank of Canada's responses to random shocks to the economy. If everyone can act as quickly and as effortlessly as everyone else, there is no advantage from pursuing activist policy, only the disadvantages of the price level being more variable. If, however, the Bank of Canada can act more quickly than the private sector, pursuing activist policy may bring a gain in the form of reduced variability of both real GDP and the price level.

Exactly the same considerations are relevant in judging the appropriateness of activist and monetarist policy response to an aggregate supply shock. However, there is an additional reason for suspecting that an activist policy will be difficult to carry out. In Chapter 13 you saw that activist policy requires a great deal of information. To offset aggregate demand shocks, the Bank of Canada requires information about their magnitude. To pursue appropriate aggregate supply corrections, the Bank of Canada requires good information about aggregate supply shocks as well. But if *both* these shocks occur simultaneously, the Bank of Canada will have to be able to disentangle the separate shocks affecting the economy in order to offset each in the appropriate way, and with greater speed than the private sector can react to them.

Further, if the private sector learns that the public sector plans to react to aggregate supply shocks and if the private sector has as much information as the Bank of Canada concerning those shocks, then the Bank of Canada's reaction will always be built into the private sector's expectations and the Bank's actions themselves will result only in price level variability.

Thus, monetarists' objections to activist policy is that it does not improve the performance of the economy regarding the behavior of real GDP, and it unambiguously makes the price level less stable and less predictable than would a monetarist policy.

An unsettled scientific question

There is no easy way of deciding which of these two views better describes the world. Further scientific research is required before the matter will be settled. One thing that can be said, however, is that because it is difficult to know exactly what random shocks are hitting the economy, attempts to pursue activist policy will make the money supply more random and less predictable than would monetarist policy. You have seen (Chapter 12) that an unpredictable monetary policy gives rise to cycles in economic activity arising from the money supply movements themselves. Thus activist policy will impart some cyclical movements into the economy as a consequence of the fact that the money supply itself is less predictable. Monetarist policy will (as far as possible) remove any fluctuations from aggregate demand (or aggregate supply) shocks. The Bank of Canada will not impart any random shocks into the economy.

Whether random shocks that arise from the private sector are the dominant shocks is another matter of dispute. Here, however, there seems to be less room for disagreement. It is fairly well established that one of the major sources of fluctuations in economic activity in modern industrial economies is instability in monetary policy itself. Unanticipated variations in the money supply seem to account for much of the variation we observe in the level of economic activity. However, they certainly do not account for all the observed fluctuations. To take an extreme, the Great Depression of 1929 through 1934 has not yet been satisfactorily explained by *any* theory. We must therefore remain cautious and display a certain amount of humility. This stance, however, works against the activist policy position, which, in order that it may improve matters, must be based upon the presumption that we know rather a lot about the way the economy works.

The bottom-line defense of the monetarist is that we are too ignorant about the workings of the economy to be able to do any better than to remove at least those sources of fluctuation in economic activity that we *can* control, namely, those arising from instability in the money supply. If such fluctuations are removed, the economy will behave in a more stable manner than it has in the past. Of course, it will not work perfectly; perfection requires a great deal more information than we currently have available to us.

14.9 *Nominal GDP Targetting*

In recent years, opinion has converged on the nature of a desirable and possible macroeconomic stabilization policy. It is **nominal GDP targetting** — a policy that targets nominal GDP growth. Nominal GDP targetting is based on the presumption that it is possible to make aggregate demand more stable than it would be in the absence of active policy. It is an activist policy as far as its control of aggregate demand is concerned, but it does not seek to target real variables such as real GDP or the unemployment rate. The emergence of recession is not, in and of itself, a signal for activist demand stimulation where nominal GDP is the target.

To undertake nominal GDP targetting, the best available forecast of the direction of change of nominal GDP is made, and policies are implemented to keep nominal GDP as close to target as possible. The effects of such policies on real GDP and the price level are interesting. Let's see what they are.

Nominal GDP, real GDP, and the price level

Targetting nominal GDP does not impose a target either on real GDP or the price level. It does, however, impose some discipline on the relationship between those two variables. The discipline arises from the fact that nominal GDP equals real GDP multiplied by the price level. Once a nominal GDP target is set, that effectively sets a desired target for the relationship between real GDP and the price level. Suppose, for example, the nominal GDP target is \$5.5 billion (roughly its 1990 level). That level of nominal GDP is consistent with a real GDP of \$4.2 billion and a price level of 131 (again, their approximate 1990 values). But a \$5.5 billion nominal GDP target is consistent with other values of real GDP and the price level. For example, a level of real GDP of \$4.1 billion and a price level of 134 also gives a nominal GDP of \$5.5 billion. So does real GDP of \$4.3 billion and a price level of 128.

Figure 14.11 illustrates a nominal GDP target. It shows that for a given nominal

FIGURE 14.11
Nominal GDP Targetting

A nominal GDP target seeks to achieve a given value for nominal GDP — \$5.5 billion in the figure. Because nominal GDP equals the price level multiplied by real GDP, a nominal GDP target can be shown as a relationship between the price level and real GDP. The target is shown as a band indicating that there is some range around the target.

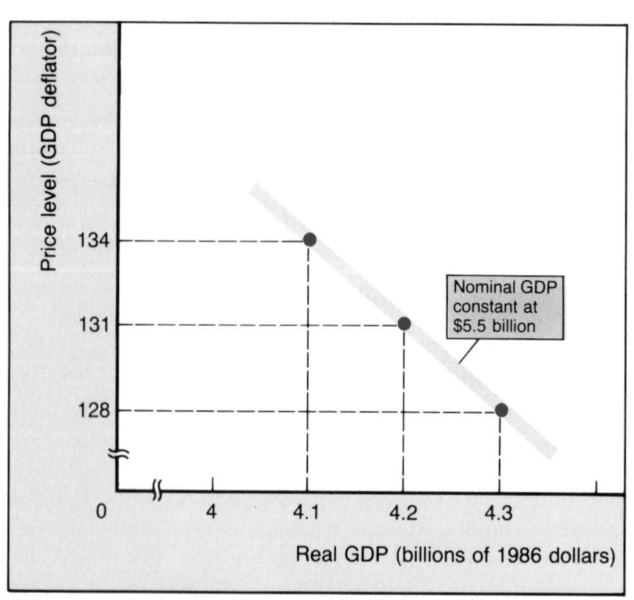

GDP target, \$5.5 billion in this case, any combinations of real GDP and the price level that satisfy that target are possible.

To see why nominal GDP targetting is an interesting idea, we need to work out what happens with such a target when the economy is bombarded with shocks to aggregate demand and supply.

Aggregate demand shocks

Figure 14.12 illustrates the effects of nominal GDP targetting in the face of demand shocks. The long-run aggregate supply curve is *LAS*. The nominal GDP target is illustrated by the shaded band in the figure. It's illustrated this way to draw your attention to the idea that a nominal GDP target is not a precise point but a range. The mid-point of the shaded band is the *expected* nominal GDP.

If the target is well announced, well understood, and credible, people will expect that the nominal GDP target is indeed going to be achieved. They will base their expectations of the price level on their best forecast of long-run aggregate supply and the nominal GDP target. Wages will be set in accordance with that expected price level. The resulting short-run aggregate supply curve will be *SAS*. This short-run aggregate supply curve intersects the long-run aggregate supply curve in the middle of the target range for nominal GDP.

When aggregate demand shocks bombard the economy, shifting the aggregate demand curve to the left or to the right, policy measures are undertaken to keep the aggregate demand curve as close as possible to the middle point of the nominal GDP target range. If that can be done perfectly, then real GDP stays at its full employment level, y^*, and the price level at its expected level, P_0.

To the extent that nominal GDP targetting is imperfect, actual aggregate demand fluctuates, and so will real GDP and the price level. If activist policy can stabilize aggregate demand more effectively than a passive policy such as monetarism can, then nominal GDP targetting will decrease the variability both of real GDP and the price level in the face of aggregate demand shocks.

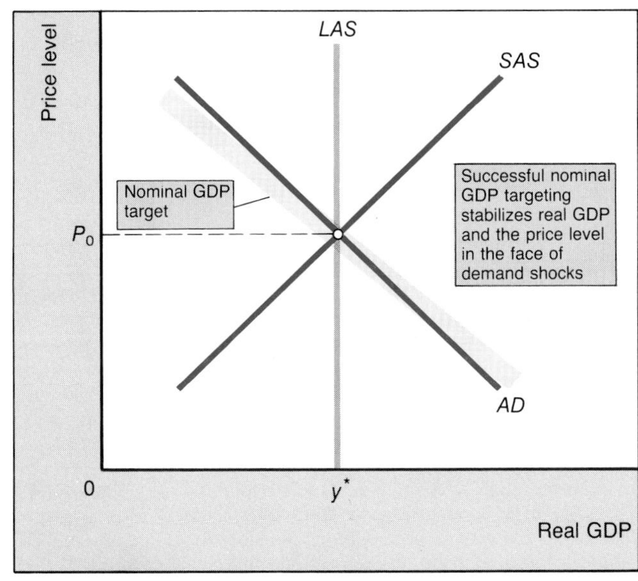

FIGURE 14.12
An Aggregate Demand Shock with Nominal GDP Targetting

With a nominal GDP target in place, the expected price level is determined at the point of intersection of the nominal GDP target and the long-run aggregate supply curve. This price level is P_0. Wages are set on the basis of that expectation, so the short-run aggregate supply curve is *SAS*. As shocks to aggregate demand occur, they are offset by activist policies designed to keep nominal GDP on target. If successful, they keep real GDP close to y^* and the price level close to P_0.

Aggregate supply shocks

Nominal GDP targetting is most useful for coping with aggregate supply shocks because it imposes discipline on the capacity of the economy to respond without an unending burst of inflation.

We saw that with activist policy such inflation is a real danger. If, faced with a permanent decrease in aggregate supply, stabilization policy continues to target the previous level of full-employment real GDP, an unending inflation spiral emerges. With nominal GDP targetting, the response to a supply shock is much less severe. Figure 14.13 illustrates.

Suppose that an aggregate supply shock shifts the long-run aggregate supply curve from LAS_0 to LAS_1 and the short-run aggregate supply curve from SAS_0 to SAS_1. Initially, the aggregate demand curve is AD_0. When the supply shock hits, if nothing is done to change aggregate demand, nominal GDP rises slightly above its target — the economy moves to the intersection point of AD_0 and SAS_1. Thus the money supply is cut only slightly to reduce aggregate demand to allow the nominal GDP targets to be achieved. The price level increases to P_1 and real GDP decreases to y_1.

This is not the end of the story. What happens next will depend on whether the aggregate supply shock is permanent or temporary and whether it is anticipated to be permanent or temporary. If the shock is permanent and anticipated to be permanent, the short-run aggregate supply will shift farther to the left, to SAS_2. Real GDP will fall to y_1^* and the price level will rise to P_2. The price level of P_2 and the real GDP level of y_1^*

FIGURE 14.13
Nominal GDP Targetting and Aggregate Supply Shocks

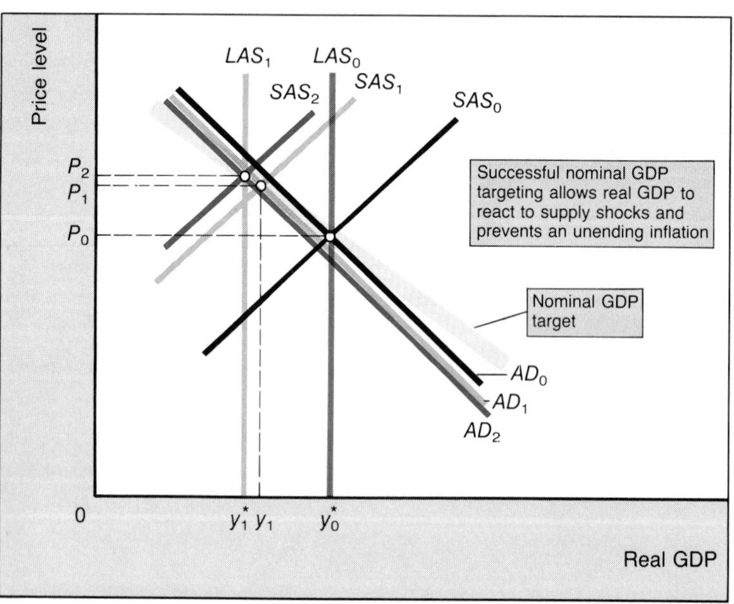

The economy initially has a real GDP of y_0^* and a price level of P_0. A nominal GDP target is in place that is well understood and that everyone expects will be achieved. A negative supply shock shifts the long-run aggregate supply curve to LAS_1 and the short-run aggregate supply curve to SAS_1. With no change in aggregate demand, there is an increase in the price level and a decrease in real GDP determined at the point of intersection of the black aggregate demand curve and the light blue short-run aggregate supply curve. This equilibrium is outside the target range for nominal GDP. Activist policy decreases aggregate demand to AD_1, achieving an equilibrium at a price level of P_1 and a real GDP of y_1. If the aggregate supply shock is temporary, the economy returns to its initial equilibrium. If the aggregate supply shock is permanent, real GDP falls to y_1^* and the price level increases to P_2. Activist policy moves the aggregate demand curve to AD_2 to keep nominal GDP on target.

are consistent with the nominal GDP target—having the same level of nominal GDP as the original price level, P_0, and real GDP, y_0^*.

If the shock is temporary and is perceived to be temporary, the aggregate supply curves will shift back to their original position and real GDP and the price level will return to their original values.

If the shock is permanent but is perceived to be temporary, the economy will gradually move from y_1 to y_1^* and the price level will gradually increase from P_1 to P_2. If the supply shock is temporary but is perceived to be permanent, the economy will move to y_1^* and the price level to P_2 as price expectations and wages increase in response to the expected permanence of the supply shock. As it becomes apparent that the supply shock is temporary, price level expectations and wages will gradually decline, and the economy will track back along its nominal GDP target path to the original position of y_0^*.

So what's wrong with nominal GDP targetting?

The remaining disputes about nominal GDP targetting center on our ability to forecast movements in nominal GDP far enough ahead to be able to implement policies that can decrease the variability of nominal GDP relative to what it would be in the absence of active intervention. The lead time necessary for forecasting nominal GDP depends on the time lags involved in the operation of policy. If policy actions spread through the economy quickly, then a short forecast horizon is adequate. But if policy actions take several months and perhaps even a year or more, then forecasts of a year or more ahead are required in order to be able to set policy instruments at the right levels to stabilize nominal GDP.

Calculations with statistical models of the Canadian economy suggest that nominal GDP targetting could indeed be used to decrease the variability of real GDP and inflation, keeping the economy closer to its full-employment level and avoiding excesses of inflation and deflation.

■ We've now studied the main elements in the macroeconomic policy debate. We've compared and contrasted macroeconomic performance under both demand and supply shocks when monetarist and activist policies are pursued. We've also studied the consequences of nominal GDP targetting. We've seen that this policy approach blends some of the anti-inflation aspects of monetarism when the economy has a negative supply shock with some of the real GDP stabilizing qualities of activist policies under both demand and supply shocks. But we've seen that the possibility of effective nominal GDP targetting depends on how successfully policymakers can forecast the future course of the economy and put activist policies in place to keep nominal GDP at its target level.

In the next chapter, we're going to study the policy process in Canada more closely, paying special attention to the alternative operating procedures available and to the time lags involved in the formulation and conduct of policy.

CHAPTER REVIEW

Summary

CONFLICTING ADVICE AND OPINION

There is a wide range of opinion about macroeconomic policy. The politically sensitive government usually favors expansion and high employment and pays some attention to inflation, while the Bank of Canada attaches more importance to inflation and less to the possibility of recession.

TARGETS, INSTRUMENTS, AND INDICATORS

The four macroeconomic policy targets—unemployment, real GDP, the current account balance, and inflation—together with macroeconomic indicators, are examined to assess the current state of the economy. Macroeconomic policy instruments are divided into two groups, fiscal policy and monetary policy. These instruments are used in an attempt to achieve a desirable macroeconomic performance.

Formulating macroeconomic policy involves three steps: formulating objectives, discovering stable policy-invariant relationships, and choosing instrument settings or rules governing instrument settings. Macroeconomic policy is a blend of the political and the scientific: setting targets is political; establishing how the economy behaves is scientific. Formulating policy is a blend of the two.

Economists offer conflicting advice, partly because they disagree about objectives and partly because they disagree about how the economy works. Monetarists place greater weight on price stability and less weight on stabilizing real GDP and unemployment than activists. Monetarists believe the economy is largely self-regulating, while activists believe there are impediments in the economy's self-regulating mechanisms.

RULES AND DISCRETION

A macroeconomic policy rule operates according to a prescribed formula. A discretionary macroeconomic policy is based on the policymaker's best judgments in given circumstances. Rules may be fixed or feedback. A feedback rule is not very different from discretion. When discretionary policies are based on careful study and assessment, they come close to being feedback rules.

Monetarists advocate fixed rules for the money supply and fiscal policy. Activists advocate feedback rules for macroeconomic stabilization policy instruments.

CONTENT AND CONSEQUENCES OF MONETARIST ADVICE

Monetarist advice is to set government purchases, transfer payments, and taxes at levels designed to give an efficient allocation of resources; to balance the budget over the business cycle; to allow the foreign exchange rate to be flexible; and to make the money supply grow at a constant rate.

With a monetarist policy, aggregate demand shocks lead to fluctuations in real GDP and the price level. A positive shock to aggregate demand increases both real GDP and the price level and a negative aggregate demand shock decreases both real GDP and the price level.

A monetarist policy in the face of a negative aggregate supply shock results in stagflation—a decrease in real GDP and an increase in the price level.

MONETARISM IN ACTION: JAPAN SINCE 1978

Monetarist policies have rarely been used in practice. The closest to a monetarist policy is that of Japan in the period since 1978. The Bank of Japan targetted the growth rate of a broad monetary aggregate, bringing its growth rate steadily down. Japan's macroeconomic performance under monetarist policies was much more stable than it had been earlier under activist policies. The difference is spectacular in the oil shock years of 1973-1974 and 1979-1980.

But Japan's real GDP growth rate did slow down in the 1980s. Also, under pressure from the international community to prevent the yen from continuing to strengthen, the Bank of Japan began to increase the money supply growth rate in the late 1980s.

CONTENT AND CONSEQUENCES OF ACTIVIST POLICIES

Activists recommend increasing aggregate demand when the economy is below full employment, and decreasing it when the economy is above full employment.

If an activist policy can be pursued with precision and foresight, shocks to aggregate demand can be offset, leaving real GDP and the price level unaffected. But shocks to aggregate supply cannot be offset. The attempt to stabilize real GDP in the face of an aggregate supply shock results in an increase in the price level; if the supply shock is permanent, real GDP eventually has to fall with prices rising further.

If an activist policy is pursued with a time lag from the shock to the implementation of the policy, the responses are more complicated. For an aggregate demand shock, the initial response of real GDP is the same as that with a monetarist policy, but the activist policy produces larger price level fluctuations. With a supply shock, real GDP and the price level initially behave the same as with a monetarist policy, but price level changes are larger under an activist policy.

ACTIVIST POLICIES IN THE 1960s

During the early 1960s, activist policies were pursued with great success in the United States. Fiscal and monetary policies were adjusted to stimulate aggregate demand to bring the economy out of a recession and keep it growing at a steady and noninflationary pace. The policy worked until the mid-1960s, by which time aggregate demand pressures were so strong and unemployment so low that inflation began to take off.

WHY MONETARIST AND ACTIVISTS OFFER CONFLICTING ADVICE

The essence of the disagreements between monetarists and activists turns on how quickly the private sector of the economy can react to new information and how it reacts to the policy environment itself.

Activists point to the fact that contracts, especially in the labor market, run for a year or more and as a consequence wages are relatively inflexible. Thus when aggregate demand changes there is not a concurrent change in short-run aggregate supply so that the adjustment of aggregate demand can influence the economy. Monetarists believe there is enough flexibility in labor markets for wages to adjust to anticipated changes in aggregate demand so that any anticipated policy changes have no effect on output and affect only the price level.

NOMINAL GDP TARGETTING

Nominal GDP targetting, a relatively new policy, combines monetarist and activist ideas. By setting a target for nominal GDP growth, the inflationary potential of business cycle stabilization policy is removed. But to achieve a nominal GDP target, activist monetary and fiscal policies need to be employed and we need the skill to foresee the movements in the economy so that such targets may be achieved.

Key Terms and Concepts

Discretionary macroeconomic policy A policy that reacts to the current state of the economy.

Econometric models Statistical descriptions of the economy that could be used to study the effects of alternative policies before they were implemented.

Feedback policy A policy that reacts to the current state of the economy.

Fixed rule A prescription of behavior that is the same regardless of the circumstances.

Macroeconomic indicators Variables that provide information, on a frequent basis, about the current state and direction of the economy.

Macroeconomic policy instruments Variables manipulated by the government or the Bank of Canada to influence the macroeconomic policy targets.

Macroeconomic policy rule A macroeconomic policy that operates according to a fixed formula.

Macroeconomic policy targets The objectives that macroeconomic policy seeks to achieve.

Nominal GDP targetting A policy of targetting a pre-determined growth path for nominal GDP.

Target variables Variables that macroeconomic policy seeks to influence.

Review Questions

1. Explain what policy targets, instruments, and indicators are. What are the main targets, instruments, and indicators?
2. Explain activist policy advice.
3. Distinguish between fixed rules and feedback rules. Give examples of such macroeconomic policy rules. Explain why discretionary macroeconomic policy can be formulated as a feedback rule.
4. Explain the consequences of following activist policy advice in the face of a positive aggregate supply shock.
5. Explain the consequences of following activist policy advice in the face of a negative aggregate supply shock.
6. Explain monetarist policy advice. Compare the contents of activist and monetarist policy advice.
7. Describe Japan's monetary policy and its consequences since 1978.
8. Explain why, since 1978, Japan's policy is monetarist rather than activist.
9. Explain why Japan's real GDP growth declined in the 1980s.
10. Explain why policy lags exist. How do policy lags modify the effects of aggregate demand and aggregate supply shocks?
11. Compare the effects of a positive aggregate demand shock following activist and monetarist policy advice, when a policy lag exists.
12. Describe macroeconomic stabilization policy in the United States during the Kennedy years of the early 1960s. Why was it more successful in the early 1960s than in the late 1960s?
13. What is the essence of the dispute between monetarists and activists? How can this dispute be settled?
14. What is nominal GDP targetting and how does it work? Can nominal GDP targetting be described as activist or monetarist? Explain why.

15. Explain the effects of nominal GDP targetting on the variability of real GDP and the price level resulting from aggregate demand and aggregate supply shocks.
16. Compare the effectiveness of nominal GDP targetting and monetarist policy to stabilize real GDP and the price level.

Problems

1. Consider the country Zapland, in which
   Long-run aggregate supply is

   $$y = 187.5$$

   Short-run aggregate supply is

   $$y^s = 250 - 250/P^2$$

   Aggregate demand is

   $$y^d = M/P$$

   A temporary demand shock hits the economy and increases aggregate demand by 10 percent.
   (a) If there is no policy lag and activist policy advice is followed, what is the path of real GDP and the price level?
   (b) If there is no policy lag and monetarist policy advice is followed, what is the path of real GDP and the price level?
   (c) Compare the paths in (a) and (b). Which policy advice delivers the smallest fluctuations in real GDP and which the smallest fluctuations in the price level?
   (d) If there is a one-period lag in implementing a policy change, what now are your answers to (a), (b), and (c)?
2. Consider the country Zonkland:
   Long-run aggregate supply is

   $$y = 750$$

   Short-run aggregate supply is

   $$y^s = 1000 - 1000/P^2$$

   Aggregate demand is

   $$y^d = M/P$$

   A temporary demand shock hits the economy and decreases aggregate demand by 10 percent.
   (a) If there is no policy lag and activist policy advice is followed, what is the path of real GDP and the price level?
   (b) If there is no policy lag and monetarist policy advice is followed, what is the path of real GDP and the price level?
   (c) Compare the paths in (a) and (b). Which policy advice delivers the smallest fluctuations in real GDP and which the smallest fluctuations in the price level?
   (d) If there is a one-period lag in implementing a policy change, what now are your answers to (a), (b), and (c)?
3. If the shock to Zapland in problem 1 is permanent, what now are your answers to problem 1?

4. If the shock to Zonkland in problem 2 is permanent, what now are your answers to problem 2?
5. The figure illustrates a temporary aggregate supply shock to an economy that, before the shock, has a real GDP of $1000 billion and a price level of 100.

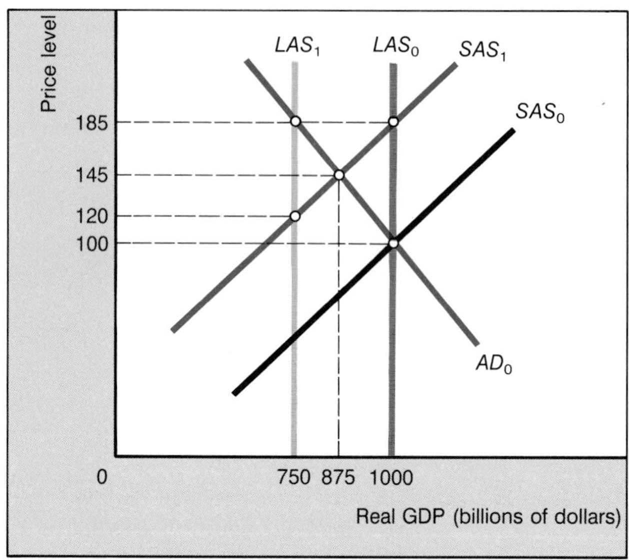

   (a) If there is no policy lag and activist policy advice is followed, what is the path of real GDP and the price level?
   (b) If there is no policy lag and monetarist policy advice is followed, what is the path of real GDP and the price level?
   (c) Compare the paths in (a) and (b). Which policy advice delivers the smallest fluctuations in real GDP and which the smallest fluctuations in the price level?
   (d) If there is a one-period lag in implementing a policy change, what now are your answers to (a), (b), and (c)?
6. Imagine in problem 5 that the economy was at a real GDP of $750 billion and a price level of 140 before the shock. The positive aggregate supply shock then hits the economy and shifts the short-run aggregate supply curve to SAS_1.
   (a) If there is no policy lag and activist policy advice is followed, what is the path of real GDP and the price level?
   (b) If there is no policy lag and monetarist policy advice is followed, what is the path of real GDP and the price level?
   (c) Compare the paths in (a) and (b). Which policy advice delivers the smallest fluctuations in real GDP and which the smallest fluctuations in the price level?
   (d) If there is a one-period lag in implementing a policy change, what now are your answers to (a), (b), and (c)?
7. If the shock in problem 5 is permanent rather than temporary, what now are your answers to problem 5?
8. If the shock in problem 6 is permanent rather than temporary, what now are your answers to problem 6?
9. In problem 5, if the monetary authorities adopt a nominal GDP target, what is the path of real GDP and the price level? Does nominal GDP targetting lead to larger or smaller fluctuations in real GDP and the price level?
10. In problems 1 to 9, explain when the policy adopted is a
   (a) fixed rule
   (b) feedback rule

CHAPTER

Stabilizing the Canadian Economy

15

POLITICAL AND ECONOMIC REALITIES

VOTERS WANT THE GOVERNMENT to do many things. Among them is achieving macroeconomic stability — full employment, low inflation, sustained economic expansion, and steady growth. Politicians want to deliver macroeconomic stability. They even promise to do so — on the campaign trail, in parliamentary speeches, and on television and radio. The governor of the Bank of Canada also wants to deliver macroeconomic stability. In speeches around the country and before parliamentary committees, he assures MPs that the Bank is doing everything possible to achieve a strong macroeconomic performance.

Yet despite the good intentions and the endless painting of rosy scenarios, macroeconomic performance stubbornly refuses to fall into line with the desires of the people and their political representatives. The fact is that when political reality confronts economic reality, economic reality always wins.

This chapter studies the macroeconomic stabilization problem in Canada today. It applies the lessons of the previous chapter and the more detailed *IS-LM* model to study the stabilization problems confronting the Bank of Canada and the federal government in the 1980s and the 1990s. It also examines how stabilization policy has evolved over recent years.

After studying this chapter, you'll be able to

- Describe the balance sheets of the Bank of Canada and chartered banks and define various monetary aggregates
- Describe the policy instruments available to the Bank of Canada
- Explain how open market operations influence the money supply and interest rates
- Explain the difference between money supply targetting and interest rate targetting
- Explain the lags in the operation of the Bank of Canada's monetary policy
- Describe the Bank of Canada's evolving policies between 1962 and 1991

MACROFACTS

15.1 *Policy Pronouncements and Performance*

There has always been a gap between macroeconomic policy pronouncements and macroeconomic performance. Governments and their economic agencies are inherently optimistic institutions. Examples abound.

In the early 1960s, political leaders in Canada and around the world foresaw a new era of full employment, economic expansion, and price stability. For a few years, macroeconomic performance was on that track, but by the mid-1960s an overheating economy was becoming inflationary. The world economy and the Canadian economy of the 1960s were heavily influenced by events in the U.S. economy. By 1967 the United States was prosecuting an unpopular war in Vietnam, which for political reasons, American voters were *not* being asked to pay with increased taxes. Aggregate demand increased in the United States and in Canada and Europe and inflation edged upwards. The political rhetoric of the day promised reduced inflation and continued full employment, but the performance defied that rhetoric. Inflation continued to accelerate through the end of the decade.

By 1971, another event in Washington changed the world macroeconomic environment irrevocably. In that year the last vestiges of a link between the value of money and the value of gold were broken and the world embarked on an era of floating exchange rates. Inflation moderated briefly but then took off again. The scene was set for the inflation explosion of the 1970s. In the mid-1970s, Pierre Trudeau promised full employment and price stability and introduced direct controls on wages and prices in an attempt to achieve these goals. For two years inflation was held in check but unemployment continued to rise. Then, in 1979-1980, inflation exploded again. Optimism returned only after the painful recession of 1981-1982 had brought inflation down.

Prime ministers and politicians are not the only macroeconomic optimists. The governor of the Bank of Canada — currently John Crow — although more cautious than the politicians, generally leans in the same direction. When recession is on the horizon, the Bank of Canada is reluctant to recognize it. When recovery might be around the corner, it is seen as being there with great clarity.

The discrepancy between macroeconomic policy pronouncements and performance is not confined only to the targets of macroeconomic policy — unemployment, inflation, and economic growth — but also applies to the instruments of policy. Repeatedly and systematically, the Bank of Canada has made pronouncements about the future growth rate of the money supply or future interest rates — the central instruments and indicators of monetary policy — that events have proved wrong. And the government has repeatedly and systematically made pronouncements about the future course of its own expenditure, revenue, and the deficit that have stayed far wide of the mark.

Macroeconomic policy actions have an important impact on the economy and on the well-being of every household and firm that makes up the economy. In making decisions about consumer expenditure, investment, labor supply, demand for labor, wages, borrowing, and lending, households and firms must form expectations about where the economy is heading — expectations about inflation, real economic growth, and real rates of return on capital. In forming their expectations, they must look at actual policy — not promised policy — and form the best forecast they can of the likely future actions of the government and the Bank of Canada and the likely future course of the economy.

It is the facts about policy and performance, and not wishes and hopes, that drive these expectations and actual policy. In the rest of this chapter, we're going to study policy as it is actually conducted, paying attention to what the Bank of Canada and the federal government do and not to what they promise they're going to do.

15.2 *The Bank of Canada, the Chartered Banks, and the Money Supply*

In the *IS-LM* model of aggregate demand we studied in Chapters 5 and 7 and in our study of the macroeconomic policy debate in Chapter 14, we took the money supply as given, determined by the actions of the Bank of Canada. It is now time to study those actions and see how the Bank of Canada influences the money supply.

The Bank of Canada

The Bank of Canada is Canada's **central bank**, a national institution that formulates and conducts monetary policy within the legal framework that established it. The Bank was established in 1935 and is currently governed by the provisions of the Bank of Canada Act of 1967.

The Bank of Canada is a publicly owned institution and its board of directors and governor are appointed by the federal government. Under the provisions of the 1967 Act, the governor of the Bank and the minister of finance are required to hold regular consultations and to reach a common position of the direction of monetary policy. In the event that the governor and minister of finance disagree, if the disagreement is mild, the governor's views carry the day and determine monetary policy. But if there is a serious disagreement, after further consultation, the government may direct the Bank to follow a specific policy course. Serious disagreement has not, so far, arisen.

The Bank of Canada's main job, conducting the nation's monetary policy, requires it to determine the money supply and interest rates. To achieve its money supply and interest rate objectives, the Bank conducts operations in financial markets that influence its own balance sheet. Let's take a look at the Bank of Canada's balance sheet. It is shown in Figure 15.1.

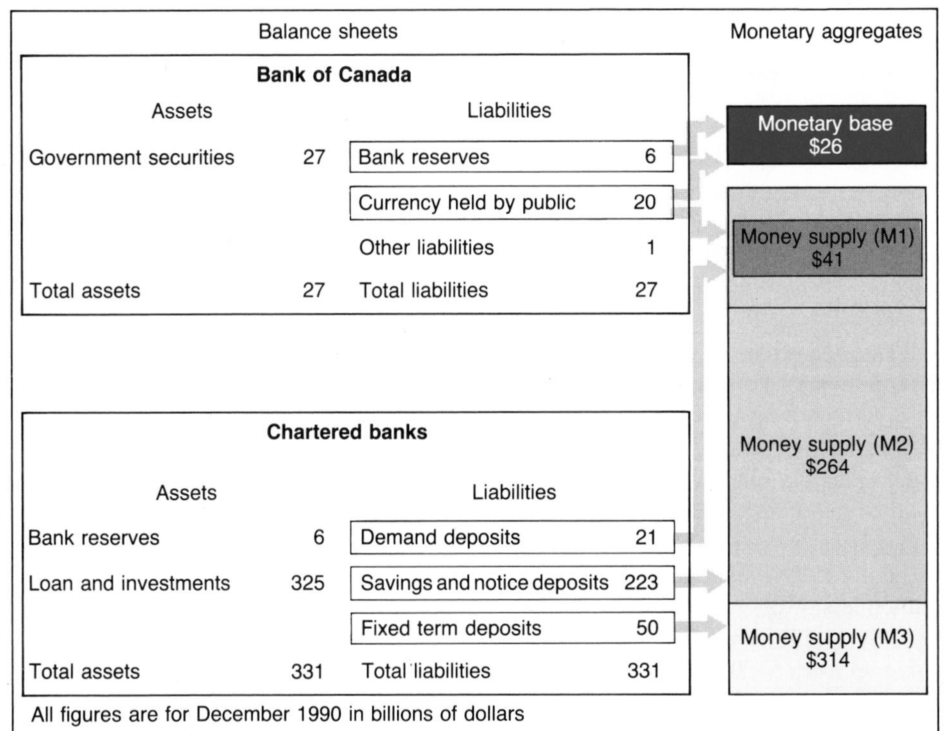

FIGURE 15.1
Balance Sheets and Monetary Aggregates

The assets of the Bank of Canada are government securities. Its liabilities are bank reserves and currency held by the public, the sum of which constitutes the monetary base.

The assets of chartered banks are bank reserves (the liability of the Bank of Canada), together with loans and investments. The liabilities of chartered banks and other depository institutions are demand deposits and other deposits. The M1 definition of the money supply consists of currency held by the public and demand deposits at chartered banks. The M2 definition of the money supply is M1 plus savings and notice deposits. The M3 definition of the money supply is M2 plus fixed term deposits.

Source: The Bank of Canada Review, February, 1991

Most of the Bank of Canada's assets are government securities—debt issued by the federal government and bought by the Bank of Canada. It's the part of the government's debt not bought by the public. We discussed these securities briefly in Chapter 13, when we studied the inflationary potential of a government deficit.

The Bank of Canada's liabilities consist of bank reserves and currency held by the public (together with some miscellaneous items). **Bank reserves** are deposits held by chartered banks at the Bank of Canada, together with currency held in the vaults and tills of chartered banks. **Currency held by the public** is the notes and coins in general circulation, held by households and firms.

The sum of bank reserves and currency held by the public is the **monetary base**. The nation's money supply consists of currency held by the public and various types of chartered bank deposits. The narrow definition of the money supply, **M1**, is currency held by the public plus demand deposits. The broad money supply, **M2**, is equal to M1 plus savings deposits and notice deposits. These deposits are the liabilities of chartered banks. A yet broader definition of the money supply, **M3**, consists of M2 plus fixed term deposits at chartered banks. Figure 15.1 also illustrates the balance sheet of the chartered banks and the relationship between it and the balance sheet of the Bank of Canada, together with the various definitions of the money supply.

Because the money supply (either M1, M2, or M3) consists of currency and bank deposits, the size of the money supply depends partly on the actions of the Bank of Canada, and partly on the response of the chartered banks, as well as the general public.

Let's see how the Bank of Canada attempts to influence the money supply.

15.3 *The Bank of Canada's Instruments of Control*

The Bank of Canada has three main instruments for influencing the money supply:

- Open market operations
- Bank rate
- Reserve requirements

Open market operations

An **open market operation** is the purchase or sale of government securities by the Bank of Canada in order to change the monetary base. How can an open market operation—a purchase or sale of government securities by the Bank of Canada—change the monetary base?

Suppose the Bank of Canada decides that it wants to increase the monetary base by $100 million. To do so, bond dealers working in the Bank of Canada place orders to buy $100 million of government securities. Suppose the Bank of Canada buys $100 million of government securities from Eaton-Bay Trust. To complete the transaction, the Bank of Canada writes a cheque payable to Eaton-Bay Trust for $100 million. Eaton-Bay Trust takes the cheque to a chartered bank, say the TD bank, where the cheque is credited to Eaton-Bay Trust's account. The TD bank presents the cheque to the Bank of Canada, which credits the $100 million to the TD bank's account at the Bank of Canada.

Let's review what happened in these transactions. Eaton-Bay Trust now has $100 million less of government securities but $100 million in the bank. The TD bank has an extra $100 million worth of liabilities—a demand deposit that it owes Eaton-Bay Trust—but an extra $100 million of reserves. The Bank of Canada is holding an extra $100 million of government securities and, on the liabilities side of its balance sheet, an extra

$100 million in bank reserves. The Bank of Canada has created additional monetary base at the stroke of a pen (or in fact, in the modern world, in the twinkle of a silicon chip).

Although the story doesn't end here—in fact, it's only just beginning—we'll pause before continuing with the events that follow an increase in the monetary base and study those events alongside the effects of the Bank of Canada's other policy instruments.

Bank rate

The Bank of Canada's second policy instrument is the bank rate. The **bank rate** is the interest rate paid by chartered banks when they borrow from the Bank of Canada. If a chartered bank borrows from the Bank of Canada, the monetary base increases by the amount borrowed. Thus the size of the monetary base depends on the amount of borrowed reserves. By manipulating the bank rate, the Bank of Canada can make borrowing additional reserves from it attractive or unattractive, thereby influencing the amount of borrowing.

You can see that bank rate is an alternative instrument to open market operations for influencing the magnitude of the monetary base. The Bank of Canada can increase the monetary base by an open market purchase of securities or by lowering bank rate, thereby encouraging banks to borrow additional reserves. In practice, the Bank of Canada does not use bank rate as an active instrument. Instead it moves bank rate by a formula that keeps it linked to the rate on treasury bills. But it could, if it wished, vary bank rate in a more active way.

Reserve requirements

The Bank of Canada has a third instrument for influencing the total amount of money created for a given monetary base. It can change reserve requirements. **Reserve requirements** are rules stating the minimum percentages of bank deposits that banks must keep as reserves (as deposits at the Bank of Canada or as currency in its vault). By stiffening reserve requirements, the Bank of Canada creates a shortage of bank reserves. By decreasing reserve requirements, it creates a surplus of bank reserves. Again, in practice, the Bank does not use this instrument on a regular basis for influencing the money supply.

The Bank of Canada's three instruments operate either by changing the supply of monetary base or changing the demand for monetary base. Let's see how these changes influence the money supply.

15.4 *How the Money Supply Is Determined*

In the story about what happens when the Bank of Canada undertakes an open market operation, we paused after Eaton-Bay Trust had taken its $100 million cheque to the TD bank and the TD bank had put the proceeds of the cheque into its reserves at the Bank of Canada. Let's pick up the story at that point.

Suppose that before this transaction took place, the TD bank's reserves equaled its reserve requirement of 2 percent of total deposits[1]. When Eaton-Bay Trust's deposit at the TD bank increases by $100 million, the TD bank needs an extra $2 million of reserves (2 percent of $100 million). But it actually has an extra $100 million of reserves, $98 million more than it needs.

[1]Reserve requirements vary depending on the types of deposits and the total size of a bank's deposits. We're using 2 percent (the required reserve ratio on notice and term deposits up to $500 million) for illustration purposes only.

The TD bank is in business to make a profit, which it does by making loans and charging an interest rate on its loans higher than the rate it has to pay on deposits. The bank makes nothing on its reserves at the Bank of Canada. So reserves in excess of required reserves are simply not earning their keep. The TD bank doesn't need the $98 million of excess reserves, so it lends this money out. When it does so, some other corporation's bank deposit increases by the amount of that loan. Suppose that the TD bank lends $98 million to Eaton's. At the instant the loan is made, Eaton's now has an extra $98 million and spends it on a variety of projects, new shops and some additional fittings, fixtures, and inventories. The $98 million now spreads across the nation, but banks across the nation each take in extra deposits and extra reserves that they too can lend at a profit. But not all the money stays in the bank. As bank deposits increase, currency holdings also increase. In fact, people tend to keep currency on hand in a proportion roughly constant to their holdings of deposits. Thus for each extra dollar of bank deposits, there's an extra fraction of a dollar held in the form of currency. As banks lend their excessive reserves, creating additional loans and additional deposits, they also stimulate a demand for currency to be held by the public. This process of lending and money creation comes to an end only when the total quantity of bank deposits has increased so that the extra demand for reserves by the banks and the extra demand for currency by the general public equals the additional $100 million of monetary base created.

The amount of money this process creates can be worked out quite easily. Table 15.1 shows the calculations. Part (a) defines symbols for the monetary base, currency

TABLE 15.1
Control of Money Supply

	SYMBOLS	NUMERICAL EXAMPLE
(a) Definition		
Monetary base	MB	$300
Currency held by public	CP	$240
Bank reserves	BR	$60
Money supply	M	
Bank deposits	D	
(b) Behavior		
Public's demand for currency	$CP = aD$	$a = 0.18$
Bank demand for reserves	$BR = bD$	$b = 0.02$
(c) Calculations		
Monetary base demanded *equals* monetary base supplied	$aD + bD = (a + b)D$ $= MB$	$0.2D$
Divide by $(a + b)$	$D = \frac{1}{(a + b)} MB$	$D = 5MB$
Money supply	$M = CP + D$ $= (1 + a)D$	$M = 1.18D$
but we've determined D, so	$M = \frac{(1 + a)}{(a + b)} MB$	$M = \frac{1 + 0.18}{0.18 + 0.02} \cdot MB$

held by the public, and bank reserves. We'll do the calculations with symbols and with a numerical example. The money supply, M, and bank deposits, D, are the magnitudes that we want to calculate.

Part (b) of the table describes the behavior of the public and of banks. The public's demand for currency is a constant proportion, a, of total deposits. We'll assume that proportion to be 0.18, or 18 percent. The banks' demand for reserves is some fixed proportion, b, of total deposits. We'll assume this to be 0.02, or 2 percent, as in our earlier discussion.

In part (c), we calculate the amount of bank deposits and money that a given amount of monetary base makes possible. The demand for monetary base equals the demand for currency by the public (aD) plus the demand for reserves by the banks (bD). For our numerical example, this is $0.2D$. The demand for monetary base must equal the supply of monetary base. Thus

$$(a + b)D = MB.$$

If we divide this equation by $(a + b)$, we get

$$D = \frac{1}{(a + b)} MB.$$

For our example, deposits equal 5 times the monetary base.

The money supply is equal to currency in the hands of the public plus bank deposits. We know that the public holds proportion a of its deposits as currency. Therefore the money supply equals $(1 + a)D$. In terms of our numerical example, the money supply is equal to 1.18 times bank deposits. Combining the equations linking the money supply and bank deposits and bank deposits and the money base, we get the relationship between the money supply and the money base:

$$M = \frac{(1 + a)}{(a + b)} MB.$$

In our numerical example, a is 0.18 and b is 0.02, so the money supply is 5.9 times the money base.

This relationship gives us the **money multiplier**, the change in the money supply per one-dollar change in the monetary base. In our example, a one-dollar increase in the monetary base increases the money supply by 5.9 dollars, so the money multiplier is 5.9.

The market for monetary base

We've just seen that the money supply is determined in the market for monetary base. When the supply of monetary base (MB) equals the demand for monetary base ($BR + CP$) the market for monetary base is in equilibrium. The main variable that adjusts to achieve this equilibrium is the total money supply.

The Bank of Canada can influence the money supply by influencing the supply of monetary base or the demand for monetary base. It influences the supply of monetary base by its open market operations or by changing the discount rate. It influences the demand for monetary base by adjusting reserve requirements.

We can illustrate the determination of the money supply and the way the Bank of Canada influences the money supply by studying a diagram of the market for monetary base — Figure 15.2. On the vertical axis we measure the monetary base and on the horizontal axis, the money supply. In part (a), the supply of monetary base is $300 billion. It is independent of the money supply and is shown as the horizontal line labeled

FIGURE 15.2
Controlling the Money Supply

The money supply is determined by equilibrium in the market for monetary base. The Bank of Canada determines the supply of monetary base, *SMB*, part (a). The quantity of monetary base demanded increases as the money supply increases. The demand for monetary base is shown as the curve *DMB*. Given the supply of monetary base, equilibrium in the market for monetary base determines the money supply. In part (a) this equilibrium occurs at a money supply of $1,770 billion.

To increase the money supply the Bank of Canada can increase the monetary base (using an open market purchase of securities). The supply of monetary base increases from SMB_0 to SMB_1. The money supply increases as a result. The example in part (b) increases from $1,770 to $2,360 billion.

The Bank of Canada can also increase the money supply by decreasing the demand for monetary base. By reducing the reserves that banks are required to hold, the demand for monetary base decreases from DMB_0 to DMB_1 and with a given supply of monetary base, the money supply increases.

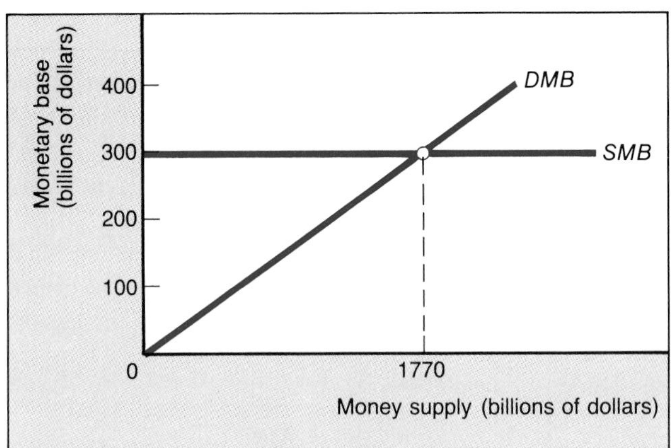

(a) Equilibrium in the market for monetary base

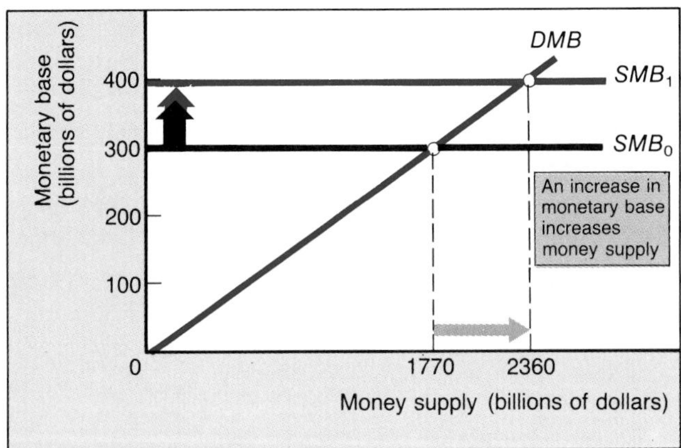

(b) An increase in monetary base

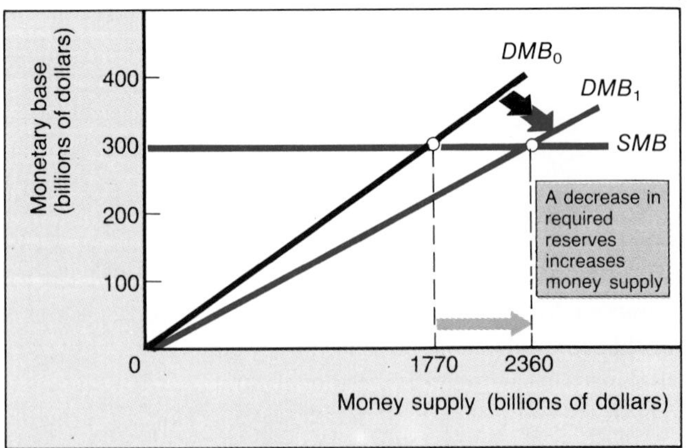

(c) A decrease in demand for monetary base

SMB. The demand for monetary base depends on the money supply. We've just seen that the money supply equals $(1 + a)D$ or equivalently,

$$D = \frac{1}{(1 + a)} M.$$

Banks' demand for reserves is given by bD and the demand for currency for by the public by aD. Adding these two together, the total quantity of monetary base demanded is $(a + b)D$, or

$$\text{Monetary base demanded} = \frac{(a + b)}{(1 + a)} M.$$

This equation tells us that the demand for monetary base increases as the money supply increases. This is illustrated in Figure 15.2(a) as the upward-sloping line *DMB*.

The demand for monetary base, *DMB*, is equal to the supply of monetary base, *SMB*, at a money supply of $1,770. This figure has been constructed using the numerical example of Table 15.1. The money multiplier is 5.9, so the money supply sustained by a monetary base of $300 billion equals 5.9 times $300 billion, which equals $1,770 billion.

Figure 15.2(b) illustrates what happens when the supply of monetary base increases. If the Bank of Canada undertakes an open market operation or decreases the discount rate, encouraging the banks to demand additional reserves, the supply of monetary base increases. In this example, we increase the monetary base by an unrealistically large amount — $100 billion. The supply of monetary base curve shifts from SMB_0 to SMB_1. A process of lending and money creation ensues, and the money supply increases until the demand for monetary base equals the new higher supply of monetary base. The equilibrium is at a money supply of $2,360 billion, an increase in the money supply of $590 billion — $100 billion of increased reserves multiplied by 5.9, the money multiplier.

Part (c) shows what happens when the Bank of Canada decreases required reserves. A decrease in required reserves decreases the demand for monetary base at each level of the money supply. Thus the demand curve for monetary base shifts downward, from DMB_0 to DMB_1. The banks lend excess reserves, creating loans and creating deposits. The money supply increases. In this example, we've picked a magnitude for the decrease in the demand for monetary base from DMB_0 to DMB_1 to be such that the money supply increases by the same amount as in part (b). It doesn't matter to the banks whether they have excessive reserves because the Bank of Canada has created new reserves or because it has told them they don't need to hold as much in reserve as before. In either case the money supply increases.

Money supply and interest rates

We've now seen how the Bank of Canada influences the money supply either by open market operations and discount rate changes that change the supply of monetary base or by reserve requirement changes that change the demand for monetary base. What do changes in the money supply, brought about by the Bank of Canada's actions, do to interest rates? You can answer this question by going back to the *IS-LM* model of Chapters 5 and 7 (for the closed and open economies, respectively). On a given day, the day on which the money supply is to be increased, there is a given level of aggregate expenditure and real GDP. The increase in the money supply shifts the *LM* curve to the right. It has no effect on the position of the *IS* curve. To achieve money market equilibrium, the interest rate decreases. The economy temporarily moves below its *IS* curve but it is on its *LM* curve. With lower interest rates, spending increases and a multiplier process ensues that increases real GDP and the interest rate. When the process comes to an end, the economy is again at the point of intersection of the *IS* and *LM* curves. The interest rate is lower and real GDP is higher than before the open market operation took place.

The sequence of events just described takes place if the price level does not change. Thus there is yet more adjusting to be done before equilibrium is restored. To work out what happens next, we must know whether the economy was at full employment or below full employment when the increase in the money supply took place. If the economy was at full employment, the increase in the money supply takes it above the full-employment level of real GDP. In such a situation, the price level increases and keeps on doing so until real GDP declines to its full-employment level. At that point, the price level will have increased and the real money supply decreased to its original level. The interest rate will be back to its original level, and so will real GDP. Thus the effect of an open market operation at full employment is to initially decrease the interest rate and increase real GDP but subsequently to increase the interest rate, decrease real GDP, and increase the price level. In the new equilibrium, only the price level has changed.

If the money supply was increased when the economy was below its full-employment position, the increase in aggregate demand moves the economy toward full employment. As it does so, the price level and real GDP increase as the economy slides up its short-run aggregate supply curve. In this case, the increase in the money supply decreases the interest rate initially, increases real GDP, and increases the price level, and in the process increases the interest rate, but not as high as initially.

Although the Bank of Canada can influence the money supply, it can also, as we've just seen, influence interest rates. As a matter of fact, the Bank of Canada has to make a choice about whether to pay more attention to interest rates or the money supply in determining the posture of its monetary policy. We'll now study this crucial choice, one on which the Bank of Canada has been of two minds.

15.5 *Money versus Interest Rate Targetting*

The monetary aggregate that the Bank of Canada can control is the *nominal* money supply. The demand for nominal money is influenced by many factors. Among the more important of these are the interest rate, real GDP, and the price level. The demand for money is also influenced by such technological factors as the availability of credit cards and other money substitutes.

The money market

We can represent the demand for nominal money as a demand curve plotted against the interest rate. When the interest rate changes, there is a movement along the demand curve for nominal money. When real income, the price level, or any of the technological influences on the demand for money changes, there is a shift in the demand curve for money.

Figure 15.3 illustrates a demand for money curve, $MD_{0,}$ and shifts of that demand curve to the right (by $+e$) and to the left (by $-e$). An increase in real GDP or the price level shifts the curve to the right and a decrease in GDP, a decrease in the price level, or a technological change reducing the amount of money that people plan to hold at a given level of real GDP, and the price level shifts the demand curve to the left. Over time, real economic growth and a rising price level shift the demand curve to the right, but technological change shifts it to the left.

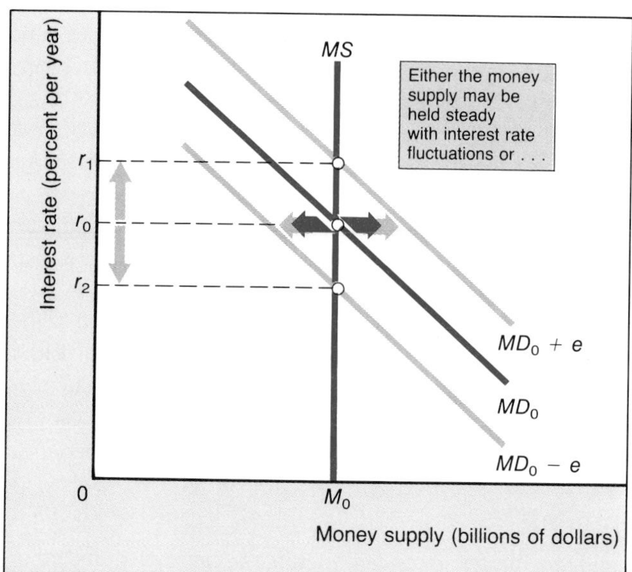

(a) Money supply targeting

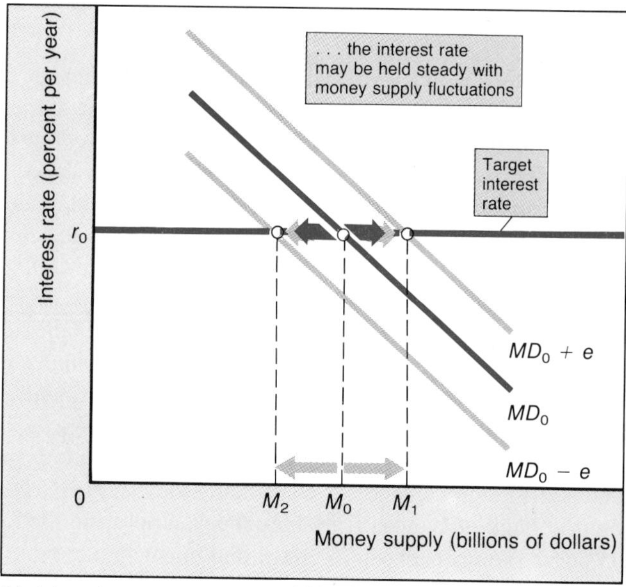

(b) Interest rate targeting

FIGURE 15.3
Money Supply versus Interest Rate Targetting: The Money Market

In part (a) the Bank of Canada fixed the money supply at M_0. Random fluctuations in the demand for money shift the demand for money between $MD_0 - e$ and $MD_0 + e$. The result is that the interest rate fluctuates between r_1 and r_2. Alternatively, in part (b), the Bank of Canada pegs the interest rate at r_0. When the demand for money fluctuates, the money supply fluctuates between M_1 and M_2.

Over any given period (a day, week, month, quarter, or year) the demand for money curve is bouncing around and may be thought of as fluctuating within the range of $MD_0 - e$ and $MD_0 + e$. What happens to the amount of money in existence and to interest rates depends on the Bank of Canada's policy actions. One possibility is that the Bank of Canada might fix the money supply, as in part (a). Here, with the money supply fixed at M_0, the interest rate changes, as the demand for money curve shifts. In this example, interest rates fluctuate between r_1 and r_2.

Alternatively, the Bank of Canada could monitor interest rates, decreasing the money supply whenever the interest rate tends to fall and increasing the money supply whenever the interest rate tends to rise. If the Bank of Canada were able to smooth out the effects of fluctuations in the demand for money on interest rates perfectly, it would peg the interest rate at r_0 (in part b), causing the money supply to fluctuate between M_2 and M_1.

To achieve either of these objectives, the Bank of Canada uses its policy instruments, which we described in the previous section. With money supply targetting, it controls the monetary base to achieve a particular level of the money supply. With interest rate targetting, it changes the monetary base in order to change the money supply and keep the interest rate steady.

The consequences of money supply targetting are not confined to the money market itself. The effects of the choice in that market are very simple. Either interest rates fluctuate with the money supply constant or the money supply fluctuates with interest rates constant. But what happens in the wider economy? And do these more far-reaching effects feed back to influence events in the money market itself?

The *IS-LM* model

Aggregate demand and interest rates can fluctuate because of shifts either in the *IS* curve or in the *LM* curve. A comparison of macroeconomic performance with interest rate targetting and with money supply targetting depends crucially on which of these two possible sources of economic fluctuation is important. Let's look first at the case of *IS* curve shocks.

Shocks to the *IS* curve We've seen that fluctuations in investment are some of the most important sources of fluctuations in aggregate demand. Some of the fluctuations in investment arise from fluctuations in interest rates. These are represented as movements along the investment demand curve and movements along the *IS* curve. But the major source of variation in investment comes from changes in expectations about rates of return that cause the investment demand curve to shift and also the *IS* curve to shift. How such fluctuations in investment and the *IS* curve influence real GDP and the interest rate depend on the Bank of Canada's monetary policy.

Figure 15.4 illustrates two cases. The Bank of Canada targets the money supply in part (a) and the interest rate in part (b). Let's look at money supply targetting first. (Actually, this is the case that we've already studied in Chapters 5 and 7, in a different context.) Suppose the *IS* curve fluctuates between $IS_0 + e$ and $IS_0 - e$ as a result of fluctuations in investment (and also possibly as a result of fluctuations in net exports—in foreign income and foreign demand for Canadian goods and services). With money supply targetting, the Bank of Canada fixes the money supply and the *LM* curve in the figure. As the *IS* curve swings between its lower and upper limits, real GDP fluctuates between y_2 and y_1 and the interest rate fluctuates between r_2 and r_1.

With interest rate targetting, the Bank of Canada does not fix the money supply. Instead, it fixes the interest rate, permitting the money supply to adjust *endogenously* to variation in the demand for money. In effect, the *LM* curve becomes the horizontal line labeled target interest rate in part (b). When the *IS* curve shifts right to $IS_0 + e$, the money supply increases and real GDP rises to y_1. When the *IS* curve shifts to the left, there is an accompanying decrease in the money supply and real GDP falls to y_2. You can think of what's happening in Figure 15.4(b) as a simultaneous shift in both the *IS* and *LM* curves, so that they intersect at a constant interest rate. You can see that when the Bank of Canada targets the interest rate, the fluctuations in real GDP are much larger than when the target is the money supply. Interest rate fluctuations are damped off (to the point of disappearing, in this example) but real GDP fluctuations increase.

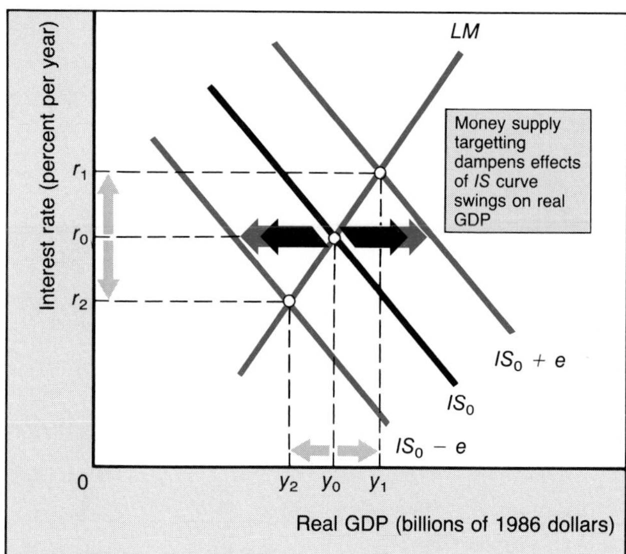

(a) Money supply targetting

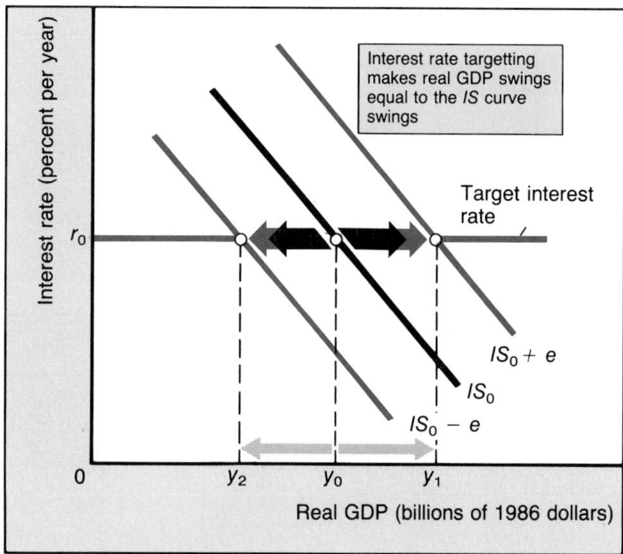

(b) Interest rate targetting

FIGURE 15.4
Money Supply versus Interest Rate Targetting: *IS* Curve Fluctuations

Random fluctuations in the *IS* curve, resulting from fluctuations in investment and other components of aggregate expenditure shift the *IS* curve between $IS_0 - e$ and $IS_0 + e$. With a fixed money supply, the *LM* curve is fixed. Real GDP fluctuates between y_1 and y_2 and the interest rate between r_1 and r_2.

With interest rate targetting, in part (b), the interest rate remains constant and fluctuations in the *IS* curve result in equal fluctuations in real GDP. Comparing the effects of *IS* curve fluctuations under a policy of monetary targetting (part a) with that of interest rate targetting (part b) shows that real GDP fluctuations are larger under interest rate targetting.

Shocks to the *LM* curve In the exercise we have just conducted, the only source of fluctuations in aggregate demand are fluctuations in the *IS* curve. There are no *LM* curve disturbances leading to aggregate demand fluctuations. Let's now examine what happens in the opposite case. Suppose that the *IS* curve is fixed at IS_0 and does not fluctuate much. But suppose there are large fluctuations in the *LM* curve resulting from fluctuations in the demand for money. A change in the price level or a change in the technological factors influencing the demand for money causes the demand for money to shift and results in the *LM* curve swinging between $LM_1 - e$ and $LM_0 + e$ in Figure 15.5(a). With money supply targetting, the *LM* curve actually shifts as shown in the figure. Interest rates swing between r_1 and r_2 and real GDP fluctuates between y_1 and y_2.

FIGURE 15.5
Money Supply versus Interest Rate Targetting: Shifts in Demand for Money

Fluctuations in the demand for money shift the *LM* curve with a given money supply. Thus with money supply targetting the *LM* curve shifts between $LM_0 - e$ and $LM_0 + e$. The interest rate fluctuates between r_1 and r_2 and real GDP between y_1 and y_2. With interest rate targetting, each time there is a random shift in the demand for money curve it brings an accommodating change in the money supply. As a result, the *LM* curve remains in a fixed position. The random shock would shift the curve to $LM \pm e$, but an offsetting change in the money supply keeps the *LM* curve at LM_0. The interest rate stays at r_0 and real GDP at y_0.

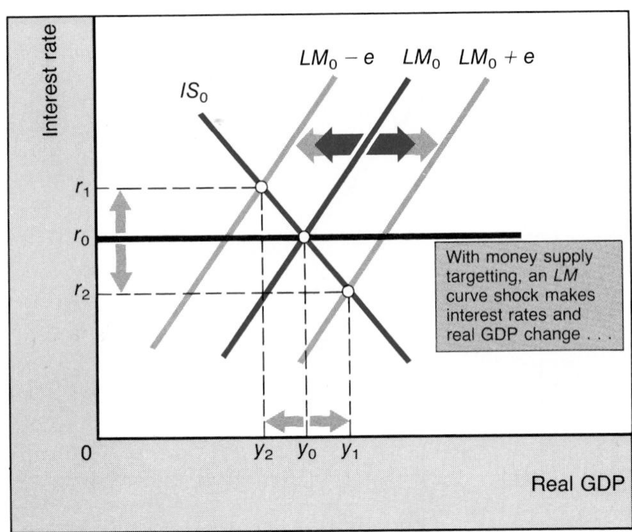

(a) Money supply targetting

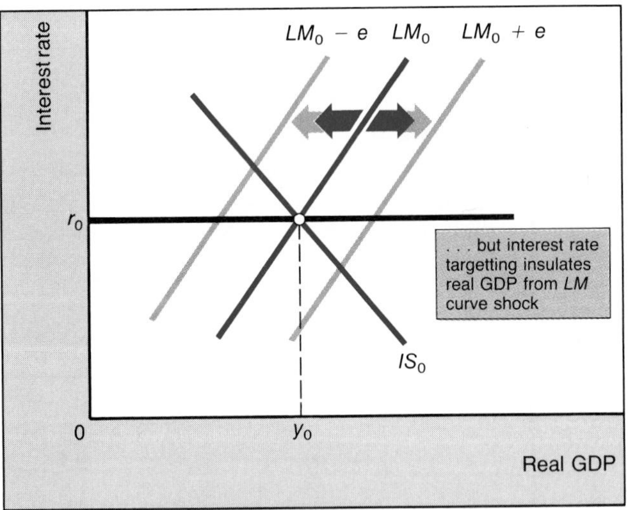

(b) Interest rate targetting

Figure 15.5(b) shows what happens with interest rate targetting. The *LM* curve remains at LM_0. When a change in the demand for money occurs that would have shifted the *LM* curve, an offsetting change in the supply of money keeps the *LM* curve in place. Thus real GDP stays at y_0 and the interest rate at r_0.

Shocks in reality You can see from these analyses that the choice of interest rate versus money supply targetting is not straightforward. If most of the fluctuations in aggregate demand result from fluctuations in investment or other components of aggregate expenditure and shifts in the *IS* curve, then interest rate targetting results in larger fluctuations in aggregate demand than does money supply targetting. But if most of the fluctuations in aggregate demand result from fluctuations in the demand for money and shifts in the *LM* curve, then money supply targetting results in *larger* fluctuations in aggregate demand, real GDP, *and* in interest rates than does interest rate targetting.

Which of these two cases is the more important one in reality? They both appear to have been important at different times. Most of the time, *IS* curve fluctuations are probably larger than *LM* curve fluctuations. Thus, except in special circumstances, money supply targetting probably results in smaller fluctuations in aggregate demand than interest rate targetting. But the exceptions are too important to be ignored. They occurred in Canada in the 1970s and 1980s and resulted from technological change and deregulation leading to financial innovation and large shifts in the demand for money function. Holding the money supply steady at such times would produce huge fluctuations in interest rates and in aggregate demand.

Thus, regardless of which of the two targets the Bank of Canada pursues, it has to constantly monitor the economy and attempt to judge the sources of instability to work out how best to react to them.

We've now seen how money supply targetting and interest rate targetting differ in the *IS-LM* model of aggregate demand. What are the implications of the two alternative monetary policy targets for the behavior of real GDP and the price level? To answer this question, we need to broaden our view yet further and see what happens in the aggregate demand–aggregate supply model.

Interest rate targetting in the *AD-AS* model

When the Bank of Canada fixes the money supply, the aggregate demand curve slopes downward and a change in the money supply shifts the aggregate demand curve. What is the slope of the aggregate demand curve when the Bank of Canada targets the interest rate?

Aggregate demand curve with interest rate targetting With interest rate targetting, the aggregate demand curve is vertical. No matter what the price level, there is a given level of aggregate demand. To see why, look at Figure 15.6. In part (a), there is an *IS* curve and an interest rate target. That interest rate target, together with the *IS* curve, determines a level of aggregate expenditure and real GDP. If the interest rate target is r_0, then real GDP is y_0. This is the level of aggregate demand at the interest rate target, regardless of the price level. A higher price level would bring forth a greater quantity of money in order to maintain the interest rate at its target (r_0). The aggregate demand curve with a target interest rate of r_0 is $AD(r_0)$ in Figure 15.6(b).

If the interest rate target is lowered from r_0 to r_1, equilibrium real GDP rises to y_1 in part (a) and the aggregate demand curve shifts to $AD(r_1)$ in part (b).

Equilibrium Equilibrium real GDP and the price level are determined at the point of intersection of the aggregate demand curve and the short-run aggregate supply curve. Figure 15.7 illustrates two possibilities. First, in part (a) the aggregate demand curve is $AD(r_0)$. It intersects the short-run aggregate supply curve SAS_0 at a price level of P_0 and real GDP of y_0. There is something special about this equilibrium. It is at full employment. The long-run aggregate supply curve is *LAS*. The *LAS* curve and the *AD* curve are in the same place. But suppose that the Bank of Canada tries to keep the interest rate below r_0, in particular, at r_1. In this case, the aggregate demand curve is $AD(r_1)$ in Figure 15.7(b). Now the equilibrium is at a real GDP of y_1 and a price level of P_1. The economy is above full employment.

In this situation, the economy is on an unstable inflationary path. Above full employment, wages begin to increase more quickly and, as they do so, the short-run aggregate supply curve begins to shift. If the Bank of Canada continues to attempt to

FIGURE 15.6
The Aggregate Demand Curve with Interest Rate Targetting

If the interest rate is set at r_0 and, given the *IS* curve, the level of real GDP demanded is y_0. This level of aggregate demand is independent of the price level. A change in the price level simply produces a change in the money supply to accommodate the change in the price level and keep the interest rate fixed. The aggregate demand curve is inelastic at $AD(r_0)$ (part b). A lowering of the interest rate target from r_0 to r_1 increases the level of aggregate demand to y_1 (part a). The aggregate demand curve remains vertical but shifts to the right (part b).

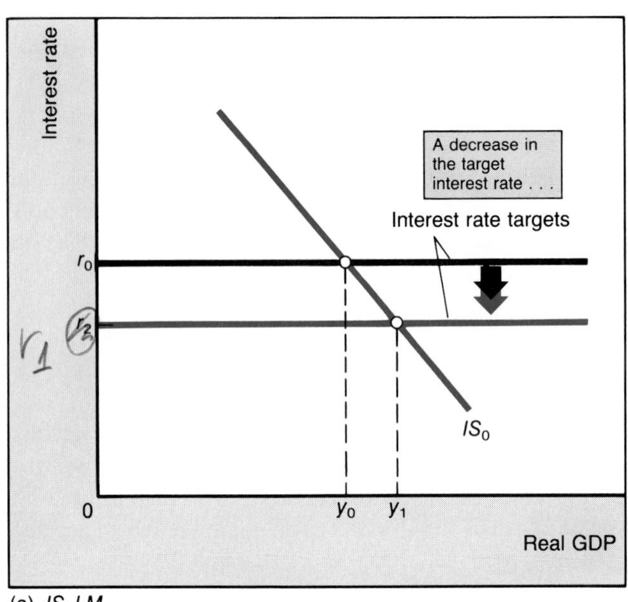

(a) *IS–LM*

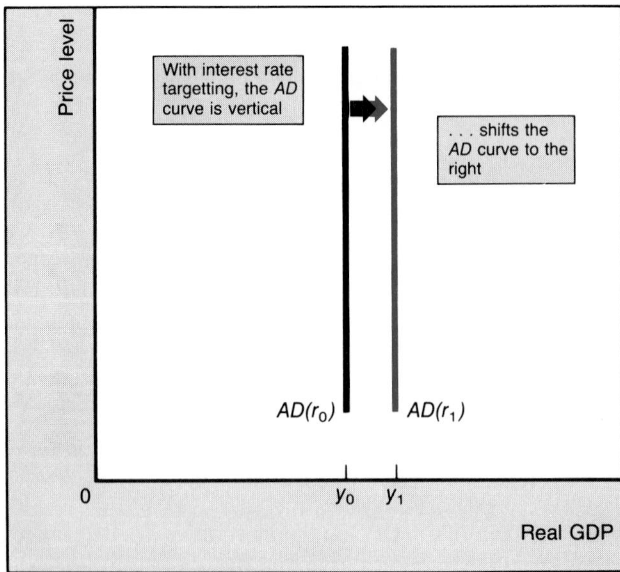

(b) Aggregate demand

peg the interest rate at r_1, the aggregate demand curve remains $AD(r_1)$. Real GDP stays constant but the price level increases. The higher price level induces yet higher wages, which feed on themselves to produce yet higher prices. An unending wage-price inflation spiral is unleashed for as long as the Bank of Canada pegs the interest rate below r_0.

Increasing equilibrium interest rate But things are worse than this. With prices now rising, the *IS* curve starts shifting to the right. Recall that the position of the *IS* curve depends in part on the expected inflation rate. The expected inflation rate influ-

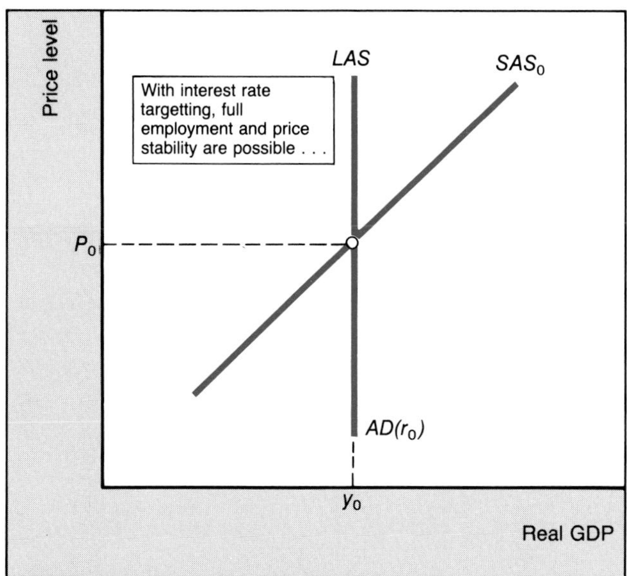

(a) Aggregate demand equals capacity real GDP

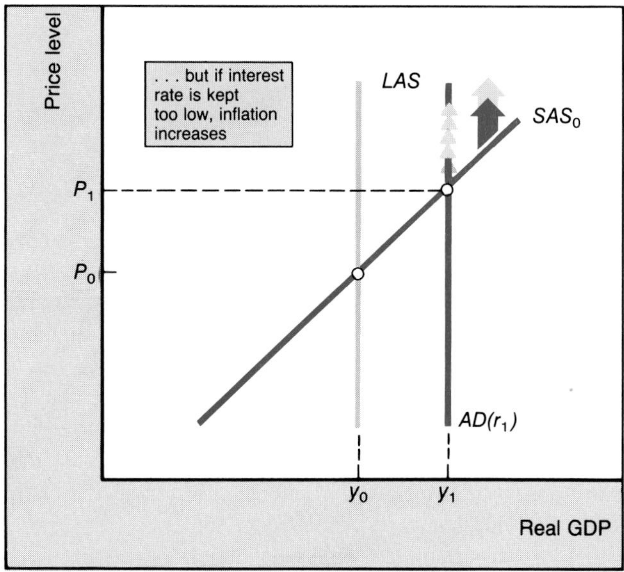

(b) Aggregate demand exceeds capacity real GDP

FIGURE 15.7
Inflation and Real GDP with Interest Rate Targetting

With interest rate targetting, the aggregate demand curve is $AD(r_0)$. It coincides with the long-run aggregate supply curve, *LAS*. The price level is determined where the short-run aggregate supply curve SAS_0 intersects the aggregate demand curve (part a). But if the interest rate is set too low and the aggregate demand curve is $AD(r_1)$, the price level is P_1 and real GDP is y_1, higher than its long-run level y_0 (part b). In this situation the economy is above full employment and wages increase. Rising wages shift the short-run aggregate supply curve upward and the price level increases. If the interest rate is not adjusted, an inflation process that has no natural limit begins. Only if interest rates are increased to shift the aggregate demand curve back to $AD(r_0)$ can the inflation process be brought to an end.

ences the *IS* curve because of its effect on expected rates of return on capital. Higher rates of return bring an increase in investment and a rightward shift in the *IS* curve. Thus as the *IS* curve starts shifting to the right, so the interest rate required for full-employment equilibrium keeps on increasing. The Bank of Canada finds itself under increasing pressure to raise interest rates to keep aggregate demand growth in check and to bring inflation under control. But unless it raises rates all the way to the point at which aggregate expenditure equals full-employment real GDP, inflationary pressures will remain.

Reaction function

Regardless of whether the Bank of Canada targets the money supply or interest rates, it does not set its target in concrete. Instead, the Bank of Canada adjusts either the money supply growth rate or interest rates in response to the evolving economy. If it sees inflation accelerating, it attempts to take measures that will slow down the growth of aggregate demand and moderate the inflation. If it sees inflation around the corner, it attempts to move in the opposite direction, speeding up the growth rate of aggregate demand and reducing the severity of the recession. Thus the aggregate demand curve is constantly being moved by the Bank of Canada's actions in an effort to achieve the smoothest available macroeconomic performance.

The Bank of Canada's ability to smooth out aggregate demand fluctuations is, however, severely limited. The most important limitations are our imperfect forecasting ability and the fact that monetary policy takes time to have its effects. Let's look at these limitations and the time lags in the operation of monetary policy.

15.6 *Monetary Policy Time Lags*

There are many time lags in the operation of monetary policy. Among the more important ones are

- Observation lags
- Interpretation lags
- Decision lags
- Implementation lags
- Effectiveness lags

Observation lags

The time lag between an economic event and observing that event is an observation lag. In a thunderstorm, you observe the flash of lightning almost as the electrical event takes place, but you hear the clap of thunder with a time lag because sound travels slower than light. Observing the economy is a bit like observing a thunderstorm (but much more complicated). Some things, like the flash of lightning, are seen almost instantly. These are foreign exchange rates, interest rates, and stock prices that flash across video monitors second by second. Some features of the economy are observed with a time lag of a week or so. These are variables such as new jobless claims and the money supply. Some variables are observed at monthly frequencies—such as the unemployment rate. Yet others are observed only quarterly—such as GDP.

Because of these observation lags, policymakers are never sure at any point in time about the current state of the economy. For example, in the late summer and early fall of 1990, the question exercising the policymakers was: "Has a recession begun?" From mid-1990, monthly indicators were pointing in that direction but not until the real data for the fourth quarter of 1990 became available did we know that real GDP had actually declined.

Interpretation lag

The interpretation lag is the time lapse between observing the economy and being able to decide how much information the observation provides. Most monthly observations fluctuate widely, and apparently randomly, from month to month. Figuring out whether a particular change in unemployment is a random perturbation or part of a new trend requires the passage of at least two and, more likely, three or four months before policymakers can be reasonably confident of the direction in which the economy is moving.

Decision lags

The time that elapses between observing and interpreting economic conditions to making decisions about policy is a decision lag. For monetary policy, those decision lags are short. The Bank of Canada's senior officials and economists meet daily and meet with their finance ministry counterparts very frequently.

Implementation lags

Implementation lags are the time lapses between a decision and a policy action. In the case of monetary policy, once the governor has determined a new policy direction, that decision is almost instantly implemented. Therefore the implementation lag in monetary policy is short.

Effectiveness lags

Effectiveness lags are the time lapses from the implementation of a policy action to its effects on the target variables. We distinguish two stages in the effectiveness lags:

- Impact effects
- Dynamic effects

Impact effects The instantaneous effects of policy actions on indicators or targets are the **impact effects**. In some cases, the impact effect is zero. For example, the moment an open market operation is undertaken, there is an impact effect on the monetary base and on short-term interest rates. But the impact effects on all other variables are either zero or negligible. There is no immediate change in aggregate expenditure, employment and unemployment, prices, or the balance of payments. There may be an impact effect, however, on the exchange rate.

Dynamic effects The drawn-out effects that take place as household and firms respond to policy actions are the **dynamic effects**. Assessing these effects is difficult and controversial. It appears, however, that some of these lags are "long and variable," especially the time lag from an open market operation to a change in real GDP or the price level.[2] Let's explore the "long and variable" lag a bit more closely.

Long and variable lag

To understand the elements in the long and variable lag, let's consider what happens starting from the day on which the Bank of Canada conducts an open market purchase that increases the monetary base. The immediate effect, which occurs that same afternoon, is a decrease in short-term interest rates and a decrease in the foreign exchange value of the dollar. Shortly thereafter, with lower short-term interest rates, people make some changes in their portfolios. They sell short-term securities and buy long-term ones.

---

[2]This conclusion, and the catchphrase "long and variable," have been most authoritatively established in Milton Friedman and Anna Schwartz, *A Monetary History of the United States, 1867-1960*, National Bureau of Economic Research (Princeton, New Jersey: Princeton University Press), 1963.

Selling short and buying long increases the prices of long-term securities, lowering their interest rates, and decreases the prices of short-term securities, increasing their interest rates. The net effect is that all interest rates have now declined following the open market operation but short-term rates have declined by more than long-term rates. Shortly after these events, people will review their expenditure plans.

With lower long-term interest rates, firms review their investment plans and consumers review their plans for purchases of consumer durable goods. Also, because the exchange rate has changed, so have international relative prices. With a lower value for the dollar, Canadian-produced goods are now relatively less expensive than foreign-produced goods. Foreigners and domestic households and firms review their import and export plans. These reviewed expenditure and international trading plans result in an increase in investment and expenditure on consumer durables and an increase in net exports.

But these increases are spread out over time. Not everyone makes a decision on the same date and many individual factors feed into decisions by each household and firm in the domestic and world economies. The total result of these spending changes is an increase in autonomous expenditure, itself spread out over time. Higher autonomous expenditure has a multiplier effect that results in subsequent increases in consumer expenditure. The combined increase in autonomous expenditure and consumer expenditure increases real GDP.

The process we've just described generates an increase in aggregate demand but with the aggregate demand curve shifting to the right gradually over a period of at least several months and, more likely, a year or more. As the aggregate demand curve shifts to the right, not only does real GDP increase, but so does the price level. If the increasing price level gives rise to increases in wages, then the short-run aggregate supply curve starts to shift.

The process just described is summarized in Figure 15.8. In that process, we're looking at the effects of an open market purchase without paying attention to feedback effects that occur en route. There are many such feedback effects. For example, with wages rising, the shift of the short-run aggregate supply curve tends to offset the initial effect of the increase in aggregate demand. Increased spending puts upward pressure on interest rates that moderates the effects of the open market operation. These feedback factors interact with the initial open market operation, complicating the dynamic response of the economy and leading to longer and more variable time lags.

Changing time lags

The time lags in the operation of monetary policy are not only long but also *variable*. Their variability arises from many sources, two of which have been especially important in the last decade or so:

- Financial innovation
- International financial system

Financial innovation The development of new financial products such as credit cards, interest bearing chequing accounts, and money market funds is called **financial innovation**. Such innovation has shifted the demand for money function in the 1980s and changed the relationship between the monetary base and interest rates. This process of financial innovation has introduced additional variations in the time lags in the response of real GDP to monetary policy.

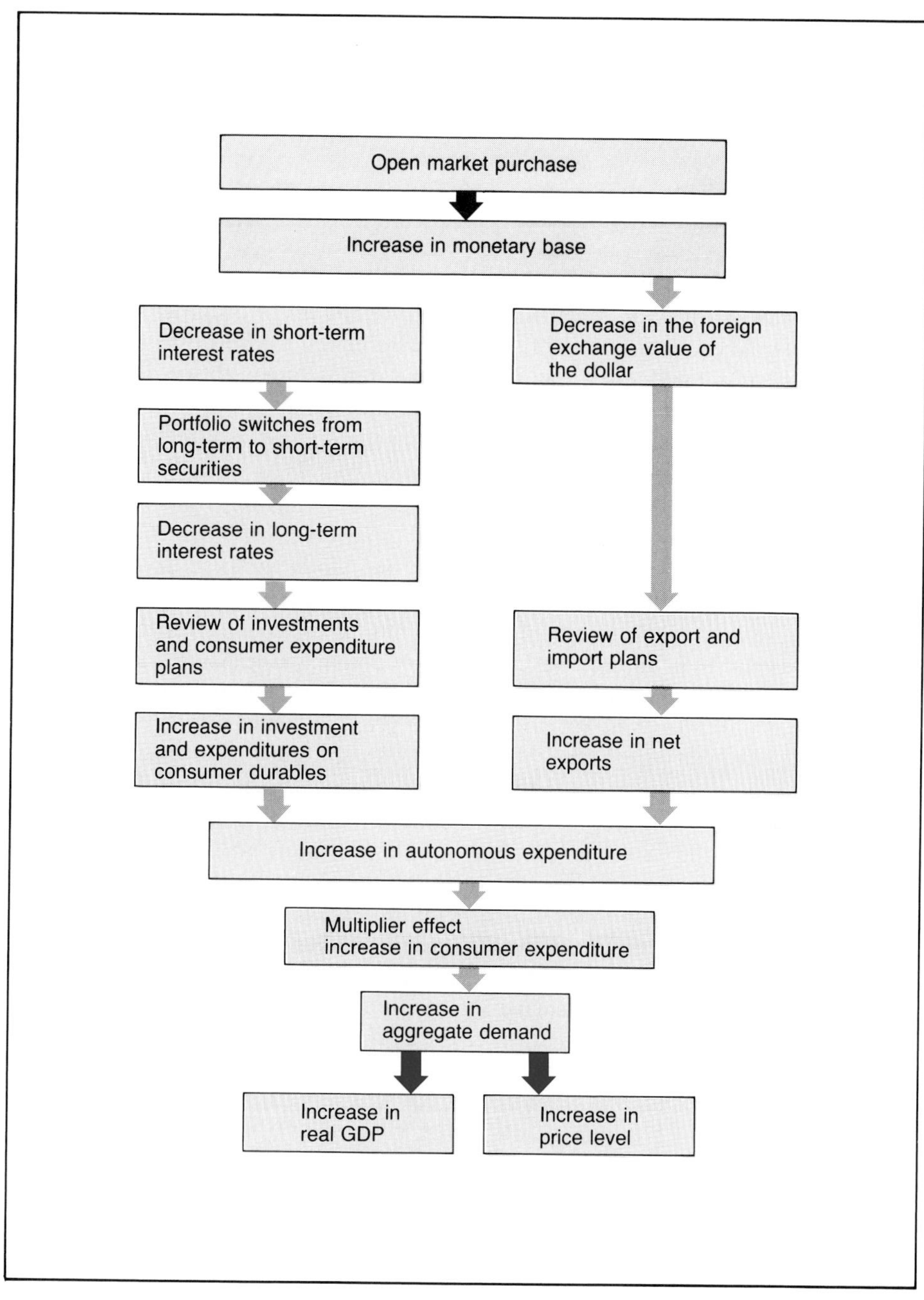

FIGURE 15.8
Lags in the Response to an Open Market Operation

The effects of an open market operation are spread out over time. The main steps in the process are shown here. Important feedback effects are not shown. However, these feedback effects complicate the process and make the time lags more unpredictable.

International financial system We saw, in Chapter 7, how aggregate demand in the open economy depends on the foreign exchange rate regime. With flexible exchange rates, aggregate spending is more responsive to a change in the interest rate than with fixed exchange rates. That additional responsiveness is a reflection of the fact that the exchange rate changes along with the interest rate, thereby inducing changes in net exports. This additional loop in the operation of the effects of monetary policy adds to the time lags involved. When all the effects are domestic, the transmission is likely to be quicker than when they involve global transmission and interactions.

TESTCASE

15.7 *Monetary Policy in Canada, 1962-1991*

Several distinct changes of regime in Canadian monetary policy occurred during the period from 1962 to 1990. Most important are two major subperiods arising from important developments in the world economy:

- 1962-1970, the Diefenbaker dollar standard
- 1971-1991, flexible exchange rates

1962-1970: The Diefenbaker dollar standard

From the end of World War II until the end of 1971 the major countries of the world operated on a gold exchange standard. This standard placed an overriding constraint on their monetary policies. At first, Canada opted out of this system, but in 1962 opted in when it adopted a fixed exchange rate for the Canadian dollar at U.S.92.5¢. The prime minister responsible for this decision, John Diefenbaker, is immortalized with his name being attached to this devalued dollar—the Diefenbaker dollar.

Overriding constraint on monetary policy Under the world monetary system in place during the era of the Diefenbaker dollar, the world was operating on a gold exchange standard. A **gold exchange standard** is a monetary system in which national currencies are exchangeable into gold. At the centre of the gold exchange standard of the 1960s was the U.S. dollar. The United States committed itself to maintaining the value of the U.S. dollar in terms of gold. One fine ounce of gold was defined as being worth $35 U.S. dollars. Using its huge stocks of gold the United States stood ready to buy or sell gold at that price. Each other country set the value of its own currency in terms of the United States dollar. Thus the currencies of the entire world (with a few exceptions) were linked to gold through the U.S. dollar value of gold. With its value fixed at U.S.92.5¢, the Canadian dollar was also fixed in value in terms of gold.

The commitment to maintaining the value of the U.S. dollar in terms of gold provided the nominal anchor to the world economy in the immediate postwar era through to 1971. And the commitment to fixing the Canadian dollar provided a nominal anchor to the Canadian economy. Under such a system, the *relative price* of gold is determined by microeconomic factors—by demand and supply in markets for gold and other individual goods and services. With the relative price of gold determined by microeconomic factors and the dollar price of gold determined by policy, the dollar prices of all other goods are linked to the price of gold. Changes in demand and supply change individual prices but the *price level* is, within limits, fixed.

If the link between the Canadian dollar and gold was firmly believed to be permanent and if some mechanism was in place to ensure the permanence of that link, there could be no persistent inflation in Canada. Prices might rise or fall as does the price of gold relative to a general basket of goods and services, but there will be no trend in the Canadian inflation rate. Such was our actual experience during the international gold exchange standard of the nineteenth and early twentieth centuries. But if there is an expectation that the link between the dollar and gold is going to be broken at some time, then inflation can take place in anticipation of that break. The pursuit of a monetary policy that reinforces the fixed price of gold reinforces the belief in the permanence of the link and stabilizes the price level. Pursuit of a monetary policy that increases the money supply increases the likelihood that the fixed price of gold will be abandoned and sets the economy out on a potentially inflationary course that will eventually guarantee the abandoning of the link between the dollar and gold.

Such was the background to Canadian monetary policy in the 1960s.

Bank of Canada operations in the 1960s During the 1960s the Bank of Canada operated a monetary policy that ultimately turned out to be inconsistent with the commitment to maintaining the fixed exchange rate. Toward the end of the 1960s, massive inflows of capital into Canada lead to the abandonment of the Diefenbaker dollar and the dollar increased in value to parity with the U.S. dollar. During the 1960s, monetary policy targetted short-term interest rates, increasing them when capital inflows were too low (or outflows too high) and lowering them when capital inflows were too high (or outflows too low).

This policy enabled the Bank of Canada to hold the fixed exchange rate for the dollar. But it possibly destabilized the domestic economy.

Destabilizing?

Was monetary policy in the 1960s destabilizing? It appears that at times it was and the evidence is presented in Figure 15.9. The figure shows the level of the *real* short-term interest rate and the growth rate of real GDP through the 1960s. The Bank controlled the *nominal* short-term interest rate but it is the *real* rate that influences aggregate demand. Higher real interest rates slow the GDP growth rate and lower interest rates speed it up. As you can see, the increases in real interest rates in 1962 and 1968 occurred at times when real GDP growth was flagging. The decreases in real interest rates in 1963 and 1967 occurred at times when real GDP growth was increasing. These reactions suggest that monetary policy was procyclical, contributing to the cycles in real GDP growth through these years.

Not only was monetary policy procyclical in the 1960s, it was also inflationary. The average growth rate of the money supply increased steadily through the decade, likely because nobody was paying attention to the money supply growth rate itself. But most of the inflation pressure was emanating from the United States. Canada had kept its own inflation under firmer control, with the result that when the fixed exchange was finally abandoned in 1970 the dollar floated upward at first.

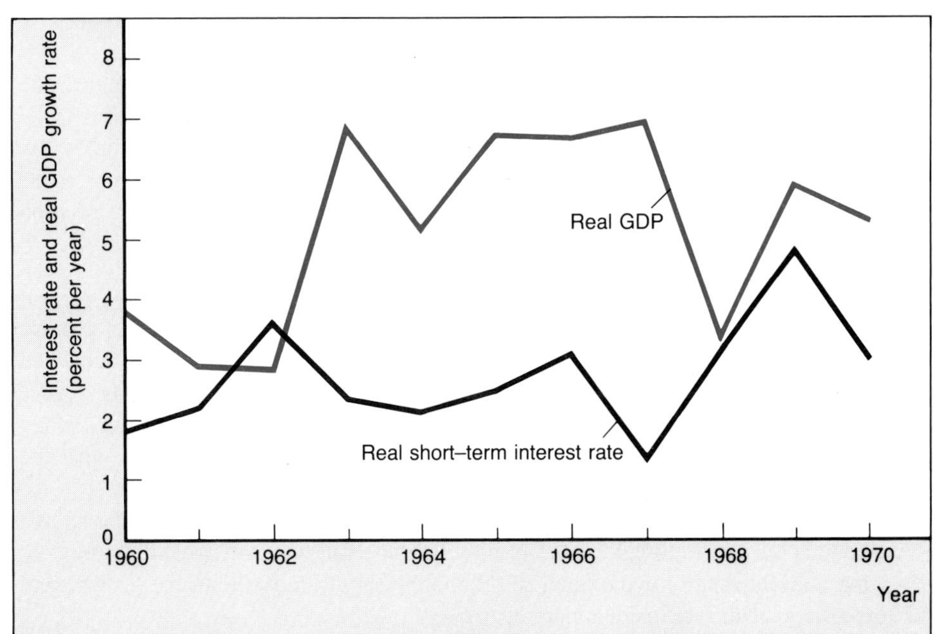

FIGURE 15.9
Interest Rates and the Business Cycle in the 1960s

In the 1960s monetary policy, measured by its effects on *real* short-term interest rates, was procyclical.

Sources: National Income and Expenditure Accounts, Statistics Canada, Catalogue 13-201, and *The Bank of Canada Review* (various issues).

1971-1991: Flexible exchange rates

The period since the adoption of flexible exchange rates in the early 1970s itself falls into three distinct subperiods:

- 1971-1974: accommodating inflation
- 1975-1981: monetary targetting
- 1982-1988: the checklist approach
- 1989- : zero inflation targetting

Accommodating inflation In 1971 Canada's inflation was running at 3 percent a year, a high rate compared with a decade earlier. The rate almost doubled in 1972 and doubled again by 1974. The era of ''double digit'' inflation had arrived. At first, the Bank of Canada continued to adjust short-term interest rates to keep the markets for domestic bonds and foreign exchange functioning smoothly and paid no attention to how much money it was permitting to be created, or to the inflationary potential of massive increases in aggregate demand. But with inflation at close to 11 percent a year in both 1974 and 1975, the Bank implemented a dramatic change in policy. It adopted targets for the growth of the money supply.

Monetary targetting With inflation running at 11 percent, policymakers became much more concerned about inflation and relatively less concerned about the business cycle and unemployment than they had been a decade earlier. The fear was that we were embarking on an ever accelerating inflation spiral. As a result, in 1975, the Bank of Canada embraced the concept of monetary targetting. The idea was to announce about a year ahead of time the target path for the growth rate of M1, and then to adjust policy in the course of the year to make the actual money supply growth rate fall somewhere inside the preannounced target range.

By announcing the monetary policy targets ahead of time, it was hoped to influence the expectations of the key decision makers in financial and labor markets. If those decisions were based on the rational expectation of falling inflation, then actual inflation might be brought down more easily and with less pain. Wages would not increase so quickly and any given degree of aggregate demand restraint would produce a larger decrease in the inflation rate and a smaller decrease in real GDP than would otherwise occur.

To understand this line of reasoning think about the aggregate demand–aggregate supply model. The short-run aggregate supply curve shifts when wages increase. If the rate of wage increase can be slowed down, the *SAS* curve shifts upward less quickly. By slowing down the money supply growth rate, the aggregate demand curve can be made to shift to the right less quickly. If both these changes can be harmonized, then inflation might be slowed down without triggering a recession.

How did the Bank of Canada implement its monetary targetting?

Cones, ranges, and drift Starting from a given money supply, the Bank of Canada announced its target growth range for a future period. This growth range was translated into a cone within which the money supply could move during the following year. Figure 15.10 illustrates such cones (the blue shaded areas in the figure). The actual money supply then evolved, if on target, somewhere inside the cone. At the end of the year the money supply was defined as the base for a new cone in the next target period.

In 1977, the Bank replaced the target cone with a target band. Such a band is shown alongside the cones in Figure 15.10. Defining the target in terms of a band amounts to specifying a target range for the level of the money supply rather than the growth rate and keeps the growth rate inside a narrower range.

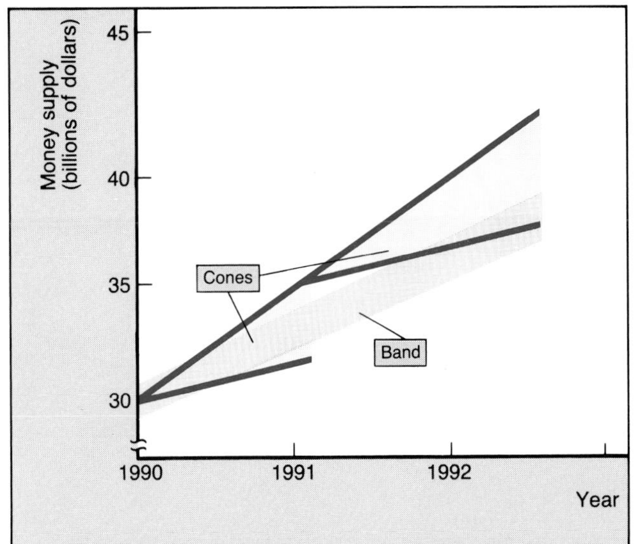

FIGURE 15.10
Target Cones and Ranges

The Bank of Canada set target growth rates for the money supply by specifying the upper and lower limit to the growth rate over a given period. In effect it set a cone for the money supply. Later, it replaced the cones with bands.

The record The Bank of Canada's record in targetting M1 growth is illustrated in Figure 15.11(a). As you can see, both the actual and target range for the money supply growth rate declined. The actual money supply growth rate was, for most of the time, either inside or even *below* its target. Thus throughout this period, the M1 growth targets were overriding objectives of Bank of Canada policy. But after a brief dip in 1976-1977, high inflation continued, remaining at double-digit levels into the early 1980s. Why?

The wrong definition of money?

During the 1970s, financial innovation was proceeding at a rapid pace and new kinds of bank deposits were being offered. As a result, people substituted out of demand deposits — part of M1 — into the new deposits — part of M2. The result was a rapid growth of M2 at the same time that M1 growth was being targetted and its growth rate lowered. You can see this M2 growth explosion in Figure 15.11(b). What seemed like tight anti-inflationary monetary policy was in fact accommodating inflation.

The overriding consideration, at least in the mind of Gerald Bouey, chairman of the Bank of Canada at this time, was to get rid of inflation. Hitting the economy hard with high interest rates seemed to be a necessary part of the cure for the inflation problem. But this would require making M1 grow at a very slow pace and possibly even fall. To gain the freedom to do this, the Bank had to abandon its M1 target. Inflation was the number one enemy, and it became the direct target of policy.

1982-1988: The checklist approach

As the economy emerged from its recession of 1981-82 with much lower inflation, monetary policy changed gear yet again. The Bank of Canada returned to its earlier practice of smoothing interest rates and paying less attention to deviations of the money supply growth rate from target. It adopted what came to be called the "check list" approach to monetary policy. The name signifies the idea that there is a list of factors to be looked to in order to judge the appropriateness of monetary policy, and they need to be checked off, one by one.

FIGURE 15.11
Target and Actual Money Supply Growth

Targetted M1 growth (part a) was lowered as targetted, but untargetted M2 growth (part b) increased and inflation persisted.

Source: The Bank of Canada Review (various issues).

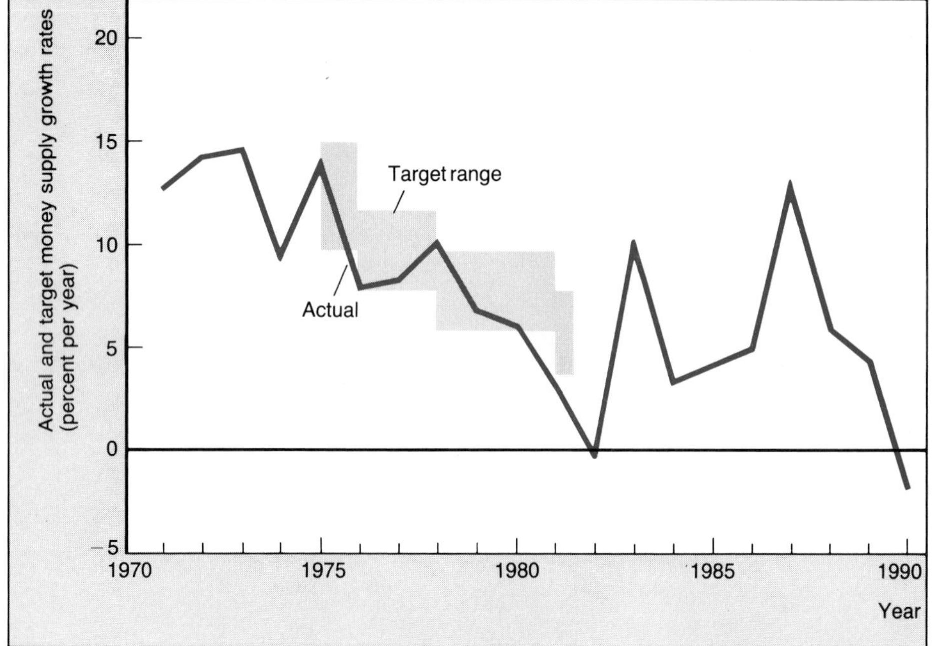

(a) M1

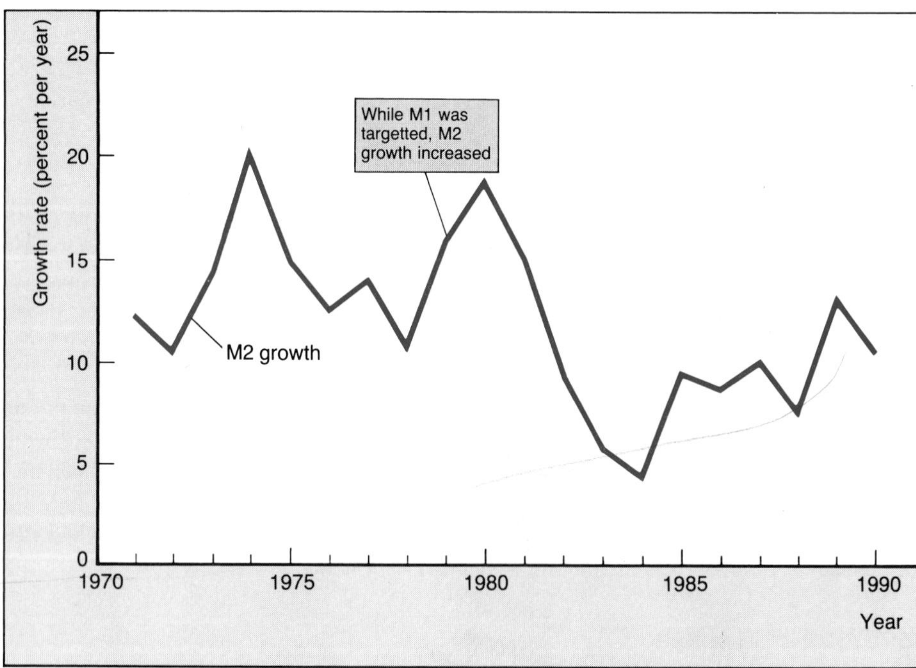

(b) M2

The Bank of Canada's check list included monetary aggregates but also, and with more weight attached to it, the exchange rate. With flexible exchange rates there are two distinct channels of transmission of monetary policy—the interest rate channel that influences domestic spending on capital goods and services and the exchange rate channel that influences domestic spending on foreign goods and services and rest of world spending on domestic goods and services. Increasingly the Bank of Canada watched all these balls in the air simultaneously. The Bank of Canada adopted the role of a circus acrobat, walking the tight rope between inflation and recession, and juggling the interest rate, the exchange rate, and the money supply simultaneously.

Throughout the 1980s, the Bank of Canada's monetary policy has been undertaken against the backdrop of a persistent federal budget deficit. This fact has placed a strain on monetary policy. It has lead to higher interest rates and made it more difficult for the Bank of Canada to keep monetary growth and inflation in check.

1989- : Zero inflation targetting

Since 1989, the Bank of Canada has again turned its attention to inflation and to the possibility of squeezing inflation out completely. In 1989, this policy simply took the form of a return to the high interest rate policies of the early 1980s. By forcing interest rates and the dollar up, the Bank aims to lower aggregate demand and eventually bring inflation under control.

In 1991, the zero inflation strategy was broadened to include fiscal policy and public sector wage cost targets that are consistent with the zero inflation goal. It also was broadened to include a formal declaration of the path for inflation, taking it down, in stages, to a 2 percent annual rate by the end of 1995. The targets, along with the actual inflation record since 1981, are shown in Figure 15.12. To achieve these targets, the Bank of Canada plans to keep money supply growth in check, making aggregate demand grow at a similar rate to the growth of long-run aggregate supply. So far, this innovative policy is working and the Bank of Canada is gaining greater credibility. Whether it will be able to stick to its targets is impossible to predict but what we learn from the present policy will be valuable whether or not it succeeds.

■ We've now studied the problems of stabilizing the Canadian economy. We have studied the Bank of Canada and its policy instruments and looked at the way in which the Bank of Canada has used those instruments to influence targets such as interest rates and the money supply and how these, in turn, have influenced the economy.

In the next chapter we broaden our view and examine the problem of stabilizing the global economy.

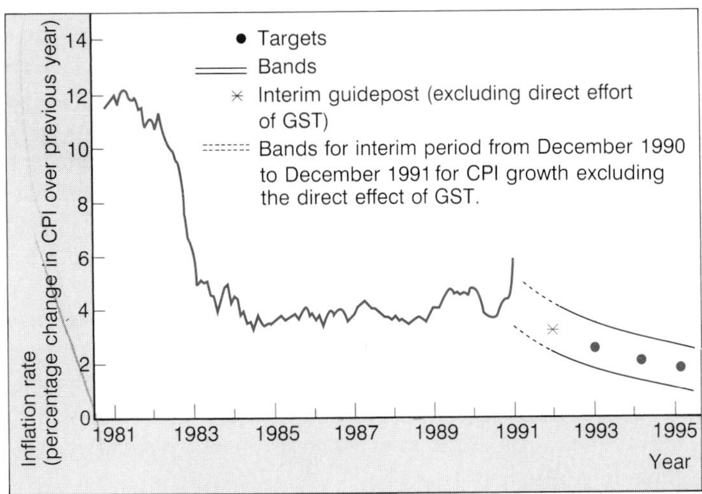

FIGURE 15.12
Actual Inflation and the Target Path to Zero Inflation

The Bank of Canada is aiming to lower the inflation rate, measured by the Consumer Price Index, to 2 percent per year by the end of 1995. The target band for the period up to 1995 is shown here, together with the actual inflation rate since 1981.

Source: Bank of Canada Press Release: Targets for reducing inflation, *Bank of Canada* 26 February, 1991.

CHAPTER REVIEW

Summary

BALANCE SHEETS AND MONETARY AGGREGATES

The balance sheets of the Bank of Canada and the chartered banks show their assets and liabilities. The assets of the Bank of Canada are government securities. Its liabilities are bank reserves and currency held by the public. The sum of these two items is the monetary base.

Chartered banks hold, as assets, reserves (the liability of the Bank of Canada) and loans. Their liabilities are demand deposits and other bank deposits. Currency held by the public plus demand deposits are M1; M1 plus savings and notice deposits are M2; M2 plus fixed term deposits are M3.

BANK OF CANADA'S INSTRUMENTS OF MONETARY CONTROL

The three main instruments of monetary control are open market operations, bank rate, and reserve requirements. Of these, open market operations are the most important and most frequently used. By purchasing or selling government securities, the Bank of Canada is able to change the monetary base. All the instruments operate by either changing the supply of or demand for monetary base. Changing bank rate changes the amount of monetary base that banks are willing to borrow and changing reserve requirements changes the demand for monetary base.

CONTROLLING THE MONEY SUPPLY

The money supply is controlled by the Bank of Canada's actions in the market for monetary base. To increase the money supply, the Bank of Canada undertakes an open market purchase of securities paying for those securities with injections into the monetary base. To decrease the monetary base, it undertakes an open market sale of securities, which banks and others pay for by using their reserves thereby decreasing monetary base. An increase in the discount rate decreases the demand for reserves and therefore the monetary base. An increase in required reserves increases the demand for monetary base and decreases the total money supply that can be supported by a given monetary base.

MONEY SUPPLY VERSUS INTEREST RATE TARGETTING

In conducting its monetary policy, the Bank of Canada may target either the interest rate or the money supply. When it targets the money supply, random fluctuations in the demand for money produce random fluctuations in interest rates. When it targets the interest rate, random fluctuations in the demand for money result in fluctuations in the quantity of money itself. If random fluctuations in the *IS* curve are the main problem, interest rate targetting results in larger fluctuations in aggregate demand than does money supply targetting. If random fluctuations in the *LM* curve are the main problem, interest rate targetting minimizes fluctuations in aggregate demand *and* in interest rates.

With money stock targetting, the aggregate demand curve slopes downward. With interest rate targetting, the aggregate demand curve is vertical. This fact means that if the Bank of Canada keeps the aggregate demand curve to the right of the long-run aggregate supply curve, inflation will accelerate. The Bank of Canada will have to continually pump in additional money to maintain its interest rate target, thereby fueling the accelerating inflation.

TIME LAGS IN MONETARY POLICY

There are five main time lags in monetary policy: observation lags, interpretation lags, decision lags, implementation lags, and effectiveness lags. There are two stages in the effectiveness lags—impact effects and dynamic adjustment effects. The lags can add up to many months and even a year or more. Also, the lags are not constant and have changed as a result of financial innovation and changes in the international financial system with the adoption of flexible exchange rates.

BANK OF CANADA POLICY: 1962-1991

There have been two distinct phases of monetary policy in Canada since 1962. First was the period 1962 to 1970, when the world operated on a fixed exchange rate system and the U.S. dollar was pegged to gold and the Canadian dollar was fixed against the U.S. dollar. Second was the period 1971 to 1991, when Canada and most of the world's major countries operated on a flexible exchange rate.

With fixed exchange rates, there were limits to what the Bank of Canada could do. Its focus in that period was adjusting interest rates to maintain the fixed exchange rate. This procedure was probably destabilizing, producing procyclical movements in interest rates and the money supply.

In the early 1970s monetary policy accommodated inflation. In 1975, monetary targetting was adopted and M1 targets were taken seriously and achieved. But M2 grew quickly and inflation persisted. In 1981 M1 targets were abandoned and very tight money brought double-digit inflation under control. From 1982 to 1988, the Bank of Canada returned to paying a great deal of attention to interest rates but had a longer "check list" that included the exchange rate and monetary aggregates. In effect, the Bank of Canada kept its eye on many intermediate targets during this period. In 1988 the Bank began to pursue "zero inflation" and by 1991 this policy was being pursued with an explicit commitment to a time path to the zero zone.

Key Terms and Concepts

Bank rate The interest rate paid by chartered banks when they borrow from the Bank of Canada.

Bank reserves Deposits held by chartered banks at Bank of Canada, together with currency held in the vaults and tills of chartered banks.

Central bank A national institution that formulates and conducts monetary policy within the legal framework that established it.

Currency held by the public The notes and coins in general circulation, held by households and firms.

Dynamic effects The drawn-out effects that take place as households and firms respond to policy actions.

Financial innovation The development of new financial products such as credit cards, interest bearing checking accounts, and money market funds.

Free reserves The reserves held by banks in excess of their required reserves and reserves borrowed from the Bank of Canada.

Gold exchange standard A monetary system in which national currencies are exchangeable into gold.

Impact effects The instantaneous effects of policy on indicators or targets.

Increasing equilibrium interest rate With prices now rising, the *IS* curve starts shifting to the right.

M1 Currency held by the public plus demand deposits at chartered banks.

M2 M1 plus savings deposits and notice deposits.

M3 M2 plus fixed term deposits.

Monetary base The sum of bank reserves and currency held by the public.

Money multiplier The change in the money supply per one-dollar change in the monetary base.

Open market operation The purchase or sale of government securities by the Bank of Canada in order to change the money base.

Reserve requirements Rules stating the minimum percentages of bank deposits that banks must keep as reserves (as deposits at the Bank of Canada or as currency in its vault).

Review Questions

1. What are some recent policy announcements that you have heard on the radio or TV or read in the newspaper?
2. What are the Bank of Canada's instruments of monetary control? Describe each of them.
3. What determines the magnitude of the money supply?
4. If the Bank of Canada decides to increase the money supply, what actions can it take to achieve that goal? Explain how the money supply actually increases.
5. What is the "market for monetary base"? What is determined in this market?
6. What is an open market operation? Explain how it works.
7. What does targetting the money supply mean? How does it work?
8. What is interest rate targetting? How does it work?
9. Under what circumstances does money targetting stabilize the economy better than interest rate targetting?
10. Under what circumstances is money targetting less inflationary than interest rate targetting?
11. What are the time lags in the operation of monetary policy? Explain how each lag works.
12. Explain how Canadian monetary policy worked in the 1960s.
13. Explain how Canadian monetary policy worked in the 1970s.
14. Explain how the Bank of Canada conducted its monetary policy in the 1980s.

Problems

1. Draw diagrams to show that
   (a) A decrease in the supply of monetary base decreases the money supply
   (b) An increase in required reserves decreases the money supply
2. Draw diagrams to show the effects of fluctuations in the demand for money on investment, when the Bank of Canada targets
   (a) The money supply
   (b) Interest rates
3. Draw diagrams to show whether money targetting or interest rate targetting is better at stabilizing real GDP when the economy experiences shocks to
   (a) The *IS* curve
   (b) The *LM* curve
4. Draw a diagram to show, in problem 3, the resulting fluctuations in interest rates.
5. Use the *AS-AD* model to explain the inflationary effects of
   (a) Money targetting
   (b) Interest rate targetting

CHAPTER

Stabilizing the World Economy

16

THE SEARCH FOR GLOBAL ORDER

FROM 1870 TO 1914, GLOBAL MACROECONOMIC ORDER PREVAILED, based on the international gold standard. An **international gold standard** is a monetary system in which most major countries fix the value of their currency in terms of gold and permit gold to freely enter and leave the country.

After World War I, the international gold standard gradually unravelled. Inflations and massive gold movements put the system under severe strain. By the time of the Great Depression, exchange rates were fluctuating widely (but not freely).

As World War II was winding down, the United States and Britain, the global leaders of the day, began planning for a new postwar world order. They created what came to be known as the Bretton Woods system — an international monetary system based on the U.S. dollar being linked to gold and all other currencies' values being fixed in terms of the U.S. dollar. This system operated until the early 1970s and was in its heyday as the world economy expanded through the 1960s. The Bretton Woods system, like the gold standard of the nineteenth century, eventually collapsed. Its demise came in the early 1970s as the world economy was bombarded by inflation and supply-side shocks. Since the early 1970s, various *ad hoc* arrangements to limit exchange rate fluctuations and coordinate monetary policies have been attempted, but no new initiatives have been tried to create a truly global financial system. But during the 1980s, regional financial systems did emerge, especially the exchange rate mechanism and monetary system of the European Community.

The absence of institutional evolution and change in international monetary affairs does not mean that governments or economists are entirely satisfied with the flexible exchange rate and current international monetary arrangements. The debate between the advocates of fixed and of flexible exchange rates has continued. Some people even favor a return to a rigid exchange rate arrangement, possibly with a renewed link to gold.

This chapter examines the problem of achieving macroeconomic stability in the global economy. It draws on much of what you have studied before in this book. In particular, we studied world influences on aggregate demand (in Chapter 7) and we looked at the interaction of the domestic and world economies in the determination of inflation and interest rates. But the whole of your study of macroeconomics needs to be brought to bear in understanding the global macroeconomy. For in a sense, the global economy is a single, integrated, closed economy. The key difference between the global economy and a national economy is that there is no single monetary or fiscal policy authority that stabilizes the global economy. Instead, more than 100 relatively independent national monetary and fiscal authorities, each pursuing policies that seem best from their own perspectives, interact to create world monetary and fiscal impulses that influence the world economy. We'll study these global impulses as well as the international linkages among national economies.

After studying this chapter, you will be able to

- Describe the main trends in the global economy
- Describe the main features of the international monetary system
- Explain how exchange rates are determined
- Explain some of the major movements in foreign exchange rates
- Explain how the balance of payments is determined
- Explain the main sources of balance of payments deficits and surpluses in recent years
- Explain the global business cycle and its international transmission

MACROFACTS

16.1 *The Global Macroeconomy*

The global macroeconomy consists of some five billion people living in 150 countries, producing some $15 trillion worth of goods and services each year, and exchanging $5 trillion worth of those goods and services across national borders. As a consequence of the electronic revolution of the 1980s, communication in this global economy is instantaneous. Markets for foreign exchange, stocks and bonds, and commodities operate on a global scale. The growth of this global economy can be seen in Figure 16.1. In the 30-year period shown in the figure, world exports expanded six-fold. The figure shows exports of the United States and Japan, the two leading nations in the global economy, as well as exports of two groups of countries—the developing countries and the industrial countries. As you can see, exports from Japan have grown steadily throughout the

FIGURE 16.1
World Exports: 1960-1990

World exports expanded rapidly during the 1970s but fell sharply through the mid-1980s before rising again. Exports from the developing countries contributed most to the decline in world exports in the 1980s. Japanese and U.S. exports grew steadily through this period, with Japan's exports almost reaching the same level as those of the United States by 1986.

Source: International Financial Statistics Yearbook, 1991.

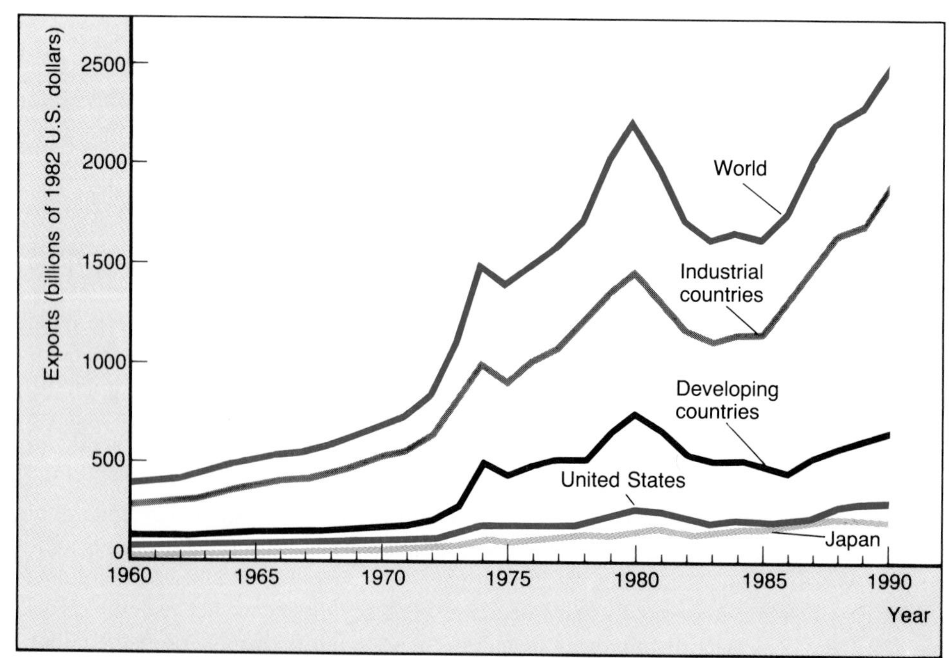

period and, by 1986, were almost as high as U.S. exports. Exports from developing countries have fluctuated a great deal, rising steeply in the second half of the 1970s but then declining between 1980 and 1986. The steady growth of world exports has resulted mainly from the steady growth of the world economy. But why have world exports fluctuated so much? And why, in particular, did the strong upward trend in exports from developing countries reverse in the early 1980s? We'll answer this question later in the chapter.

As exports have grown and fluctuated, so have imports. The difference between exports and imports — net exports — is measured by the current account of the balance of payments. If all the records are kept accurately, the world's current account balance will be zero. But individual nations and groups of nations will have current account balances, some of which were positive (surpluses) and some negative (deficits). Figure 16.2 shows the main trends in the current account balances of the United States, Japan, and the two groups of countries whose exports we looked at in Figure 16.1. This figure shows that, during the 1970s, current account balances were quite small and appear to have fluctuated largely at random. But during the 1980s, the Japanese current account balance moved into a strong surplus while that of the United States moved in the opposite direction. The developing countries also went into deficit in the 1980s, but after 1982 that deficit tended to fall, moving close to a zero balance by 1987. Industrial countries in total remained in deficit through the 1980s. But a large element of this deficit is the U.S. deficit.

International deficits are financed by international borrowing and lending. Thus capital account balances of similar magnitude but opposite sign correspond to the current account balances shown in Figure 16.2. For example, countries with a current account deficit have a capital account surplus — they borrow from the rest of the world.

International trade and capital flows are financed using foreign exchange. We've already studied the foreign exchange rate and some of its effects in Chapters 7 and 11. Later in this chapter, we'll study the forces that determine the foreign exchange rate.

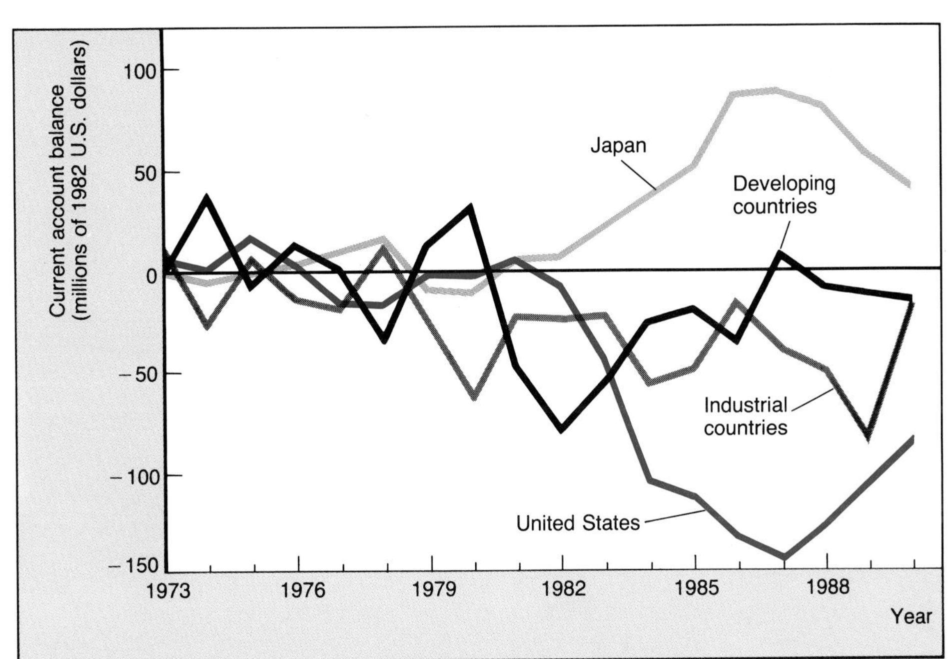

FIGURE 16.2
Current Account Balances: 1973-1990

Current account balances were small during the 1970s but exploded in the 1980s. Both developing and industrial countries moved into deficits in the 1980s. The U.S. current account deficit was especially large and mirrored an equally large Japanese current account surplus.

Source: International Financial Statistics Yearbook, 1991.

Figure 16.3(a) shows the movements in the foreign exchange rates of the Canadian dollar and three of the most important currencies: the U.S. dollar, the British pound, and the Japanese yen. It shows the values of these currencies in terms of a basket of other exchange rates. As you can see, there are both trends and cycles in the movements of these exchange rates. The Canadian depreciated steadily through 1986 and then appreciated. The Japanese yen trends upward while the British pound trends downward. The U.S. dollar has no obvious trend, but there is an important cycle in the value of the

FIGURE 16.3
Exchange Rates: 1975-1990

The Canadian dollar depreciated steadily from 1975 to 1986, and then appreciated (part a). The British pound trended downward and the Japanese yen upward. The U.S. dollar appreciated against other currencies from 1980 to 1985. It then depreciated through 1988 after which it stabilized.

Real exchange rates—exchange rates in terms of the purchasing power—of different currencies are shown in part (b). From 1975 until 1986 the Canadian dollar cycled, but after 1986 the real value of the Canadian dollar increased strongly. In the 1970s, the British pound appreciated, the U.S. dollar remained fairly constant, and the Japanese yen rose and then fell. In the 1980s, the British pound declined, the U.S. dollar increased in value, and the Japanese yen stayed steady until 1985. Since 1985, the Japanese yen has appreciated, the U.S. dollar depreciated, and the British pound declined slightly.

Source: International Financial Statistics Yearbook, 1991.

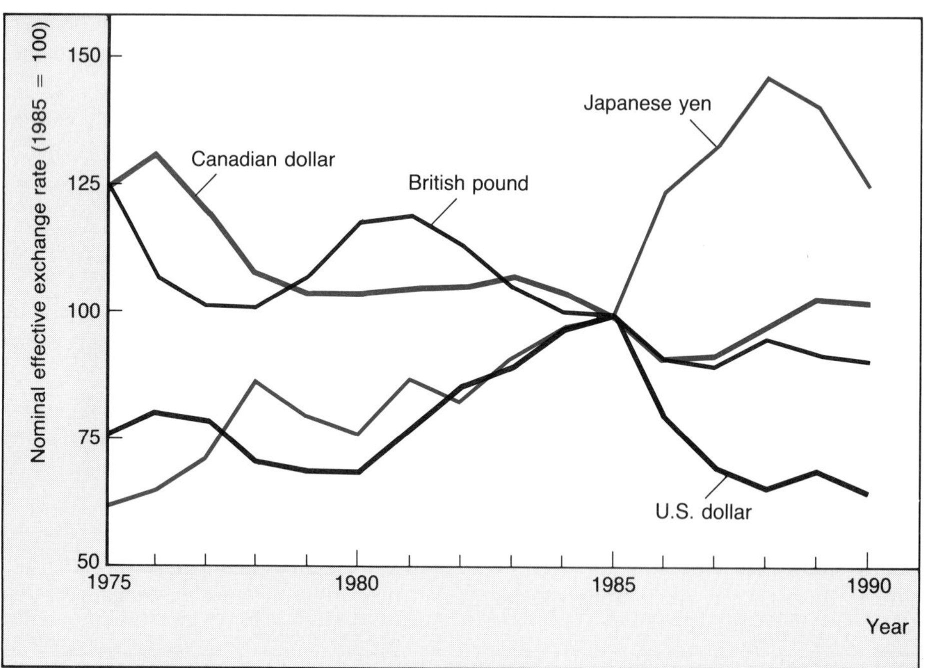

(a) Nominal exchange rate for Canadian dollar

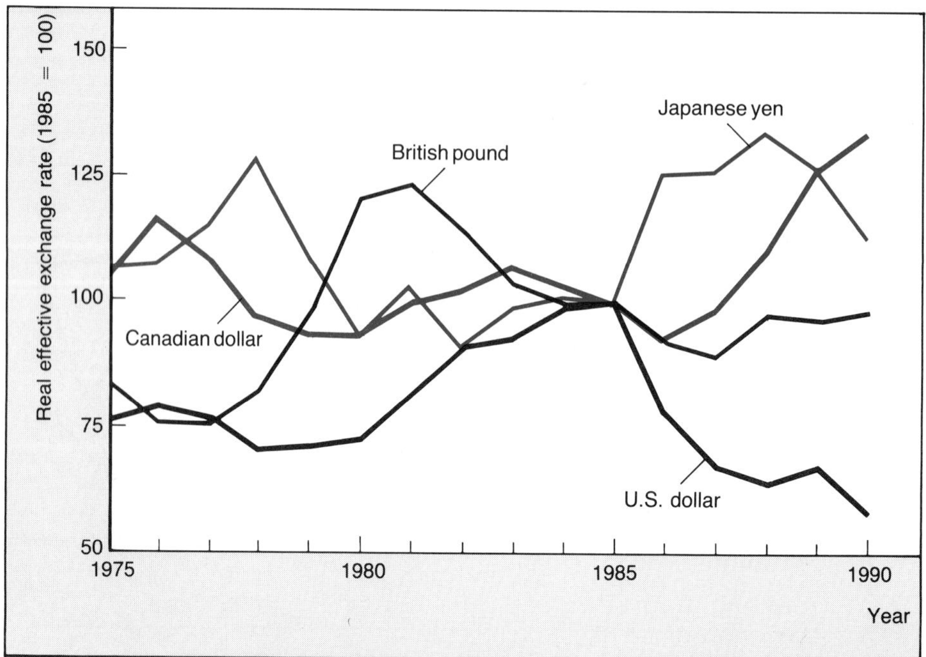

(b) Real exchange rate for Canadian dollar

U.S. dollar. It moved steadily upward from 1980 to 1985 and then downward through 1988 after which it stabilized.

The exchange rate indexes shown in Figure 16.3(a) tell us the value of one national currency against a basket of other national currencies. But they don't tell us what those national currencies bought. To discover that, we need to know what has happened to the real exchange rates. A real exchange rate is the value of a national currency in terms of the foreign goods and services that it will buy. Figure 16.3(b) shows the real exchange rate for these same four currencies. As you can see, there are no trends in the real exchange rates—just cycles. The cycle in the Canadian dollar from 1975 to 1986 is smaller than in the other currencies, but after 1986 the real value of the Canadian dollar increased strongly. The cycle in the real value of the U.S. dollar is very similar to the cycle in its nominal value. The cycle in the Japanese yen is almost a mirror image of that in the U.S. dollar, and especially so in the second half of the 1980s. The real exchange rate of the British pound behaves in a quite different way from the other three currencies. It appreciated strongly in the second half of the 1970s and then declined persistently throughout the 1980s.

What has produced these movements in the nominal and real exchange rates of these three major currencies? This is another question that this chapter is designed to answer.

In the rest of this chapter, we're going to study the forces that influence the global economy—the cycles in world economic activity, the fluctuations in world exports and payments balances, and the fluctuations in nominal and real exchange rates. Our first step in that process is to describe the international monetary system.

16.2 *The International Monetary System*

An **international monetary system** is a set of arrangements and institutions for governing the financial relations among countries. The most important aspect of an international monetary system is its rules governing the determination of exchange rates. You've already encountered (in Chapter 7) the three possibilities: *fixed exchange rates*, *flexible exchange rates*, and *managed-floating exchange rates*.

The international monetary system of the 1990s is a managed-floating system. Each major country pursues its own independent monetary policy but these independent policies are loosely coordinated through a variety of international institutions. The most important of these are the *International Monetary Fund* and the *World Bank*.

These institutions were established at the end of World War II to administer a fixed exchange rate international monetary system. Their key operational role was to enable countries to pursue their domestic goals of economic expansion and at the same time to maintain their commitments to fixed exchange rates.

To keep an exchange rate fixed, a country must stand ready to supply foreign currency in exchange for its own money. To do so, it must hold reserves of foreign exchange. But countries may have a shortage of foreign exchange—either a temporary shortage or a permanent and chronic shortage. Countries with a temporary shortage are those having temporary balance of payments deficits. Countries with a chronic shortage of foreign currency typically are poorer countries whose demand for capital outstrips their domestic saving potential. The two institutions of the world monetary system were set up to overcome these problems. The International Monetary Fund stepped in when there was a short-term problem, making credit available to a country so that it could maintain its fixed exchange rate. The World Bank was established to deal with long-term financing problems. These two institutions facilitated the flow of funds from industrial countries to the developing countries and, in some cases, on a short-term basis, back to the industrial countries themselves.

Figure 16.4 illustrates these international linkages. Industrial countries provide initial credits to the International Monetary Fund and World Bank. Industrial and developing countries draw on IMF credits on a short-term basis when they need additional reserves to maintain their exchange rate. Developing countries draw on the World Bank's resources for longer-term financing of development projects.

Under the Bretton Woods system, with a small number of exceptions, exchange rates were held steady for 20 years. But the exceptions were important. First, there were some devaluations and revaluations. A **devaluation** is the decrease in the fixed exchange rate of a currency. A **revaluation** is the increase in the fixed exchange rate of a currency. The most important devaluations were of the British pound in 1949 and again in 1967. The most important revaluations were of the German mark. Second, the Canadian dollar remained outside the fixed exchange rate system during the 1950s and its rate fluctuated, although within relatively narrow bands.

Although designed to enable a fixed exchange rate system to function, the International Monetary Fund and the World Bank continue to play an important role in the managed floating system of the 1990s. The role of the World Bank has remained the same — assisting in long-term financing of capital needs for developing countries. The International Monetary Fund has gradually redefined its role, paying more attention to the international coordination of monetary policies and to the achievement of smoother (less volatile) exchange rate movements.

A further important feature of the world monetary arrangements is the emergence of regional monetary blocs. The most important of these is the European Monetary System, which eventually will lead to the creation of a single European money. Outside Europe, although the major currencies fluctuate against each other, the currencies of many smaller countries are pegged to those of the larger countries. The choice of the currency against which to peg is determined mainly by international trade flows.

How are exchange rates determined?

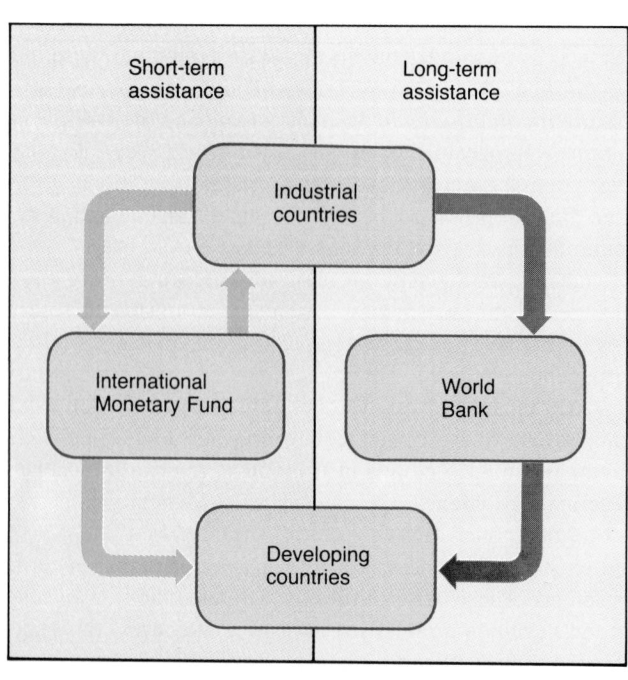

FIGURE 16.4
International Financial Institutions

The International Monetary Fund addresses short-term balance of payments problems, funneling funds between industrial countries and from industrial countries to developing countries. The World Bank handles long-term financial assistance to developing countries.

16.3 *Exchange Rate Determination*

Exchange rates are determined in foreign exchange markets by the forces of supply and demand. But what exactly are the "demand for foreign exchange" and the "supply of foreign exchange"?

To answer these questions and to study the forces that determine exchange rates, we'll study the demand for and supply of financial assets denominated in Canadian dollars. We'll call them simply dollar assets. Thus dollar assets are "foreign exchange." We'll measure the value of the Canadian dollars in terms of Japanese yen. That is, we'll study the determination of the yen price of a dollar. The smaller the number of yen that have to be given up to get one dollar, the higher is the value of the yen and the lower is the value of the dollar. When the number of yen per dollar decreases, the yen *appreciates* and the dollar *depreciates*.

The demand for foreign exchange

The **quantity of dollar assets demanded** is the quantity of net financial assets denominated in Canadian dollars that people plan to hold at a given point in time. What exactly are Canadian dollar-denominated financial assets? They are simply promises to pay so many Canadian dollars under given circumstances on a given date. Examples of such assets include Bank of Canada notes, the monetary base, M1, M2, and M3, and Canadian government debt held by the public. It is the fact that they are promises to pay a given number of Canadian dollars that makes these assets *dollar-denominated* financial assets. The dollar is the unit of account in which the assets are defined. Examples of financial assets that are not dollar-denominated assets are yen bank notes issued by the Bank of Japan, chequing and savings accounts in Japanese banks, and the debt issued by the Japanese government and Japanese corporations that is denominated in yen.

Stocks and flows The quantity of dollar assets demanded is a stock—a quantity at a given point in time. People who are holding too small a stock of dollar assets place orders to buy. These orders result in a flow demand for dollar assets in the foreign exchange market. People who are holding too many dollar assets place orders to sell. These orders result in a flow supply of dollar assets in the foreign exchange market. Because the action of buying and selling results in flows in the foreign exchange market, it seems as though these flows move the foreign exchange rate up and down. But underlying these decisions to buy and sell are decisions about the quantity of dollar assets to hold. Decisions about stocks — the stock of dollar assets to hold — determines the demand for dollar assets. What determines this demand?

People hold dollar assets (or any currency assets) either to use them in transactions or to make a return on them. Similarly, people hold yen assets either to use them in transactions or to make a return on them. The quantity of dollar assets (and, let's say, yen assets) held for transactions depends on the opportunity cost of holding dollar assets (yen assets). The higher the opportunity cost of holding assets in a particular currency, the lower is the quantity demanded of those assets. The higher the expected return from holding assets in a particular currency, the greater is the quantity demanded of assets in that currency. But the rate of return on assets in one currency is the opportunity cost of holding assets in another. Thus the higher the rate of return on assets in one currency, the lower is its opportunity cost and the greater is the quantity of assets in that currency demanded.

Let's look at the example set out in Table 16.1. By holding dollar assets, you can make a return of r^d. As an example, suppose that r^d is 0.1 (or 10 percent). At the same time, the interest rate on yen assets is r^y. Suppose that this rate is 0.05 (or 5 percent). The exchange rate between the yen and the dollar—the number of yen per dollar—is E.

TABLE 16.1
Holding Dollars vs. Holding Yen

DESCRIPTION	SYMBOLS	NUMERICAL EXAMPLE
Interest rate on dollar assets	r^d	0.10 (10 percent)
Interest rate on yen assets	r^y	0.05 (5 percent)
Exchange rate (¥/$)	E_t	130 yen per dollar
Exchange rate (¥/$) one year later	E_{t+1}	120 yen per dollar
Hold dollars One hundred dollars held in dollar yields	$\$100(1 + r^d)$	$\$100 \times 1.10 = \$110$
Hold yen One hundred dollars held in yen yields	$\$100(1 + r^y)\dfrac{E_t}{E_{t+1}}$	$\$100 \times 1.05 \times \dfrac{130}{120} = \$113.75$
Relative return on dollars $\dfrac{\text{Return on dollars}}{\text{Return on yen}}$	$\dfrac{(1 + r^d)E_{t+1}}{(1 + r^y)E_t}$	$\dfrac{\$110.00}{\$113.75} = 0.97$

We'll denote the value of the exchange rate here and now as E_t. In our example, we'll let that exchange rate be 130 yen per dollar. One year from now, the exchange rate will be E_{t+1} and let's suppose that the exchange rate is going to be 120 yen per dollar.

Now suppose that you have $100 and you have to make a choice between holding dollar assets and yen assets. One hundred dollars held in dollar assets will yield a return at the end of one year equal to $110. That's simply the initial $100 plus a 10 percent interest income. Holding $100 worth of yen assets for a year gives a return based on the interest rate on yen-dominated assets, but it also has to take account of the fact that the number of yen you get for your dollar here and now is larger than the number you will be able to get a year later. In our example, you can buy yen cheaper now (130 per dollar) than you'll be able to sell them for a year from now (120 per dollar). Thus your yield from holding yen is the sum of the $100 converted into yen at the exchange rate of 130 yen per dollar (that's $100 times E_t) and the interest that you're going to make, divided by the price for which you'll be able to buy dollars one year from now E_{t+1}. Working through the arithmetic, you'll see that if you invest $100 in yen assets now you will have $113.75 at the end of one year.

The relative return on dollar assets is the return on dollar assets expressed as a ratio of the return on yen assets. In this example, the relative return on dollar assets is less than one. That is, you'll make more by holding yen assets than dollar assets. The relative return on dollar assets is

$$\frac{(1 + r^d)E_{t+1}}{(1 + r^y)E_t}. \qquad (16.1)$$

The higher the relative return on dollar assets, the greater is the quantity of dollar assets people want to hold.

The demand curve for dollar assets The demand curve for dollar assets shows how the quantity of dollar-denominated financial assets varies as the exchange rate varies, holding everything else constant. We've just seen that the greater the return on dollar assets, the larger quantity of dollar assets that people want to hold. How does that return vary as the exchange rate varies, other things held constant? The answer is that the higher the exchange rate, the lower is the relative return on dollar assets. Thus the quantity of dollar-denominated assets demanded increases as the exchange rate decreases, other things held constant. Such a demand curve is illustrated in Figure 16.5(a). When a dollar costs 160 yen, Q_1 is the quantity of dollar assets demanded; when the dollar depreciates to 140 yen per dollar, Q_2 is the quantity of dollar assets demanded, and when the dollar depreciates further to 120 yen per dollar, Q_3 is the quantity of dollar assets demanded. All other influences on the quantity of dollar assets that people plan to hold influence the demand for dollar assets and shift the demand curve for dollar assets. What are these factors? The main ones are the three other factors that influence the relative return on dollar assets:

- The dollar interest rate
- The yen interest rate
- The future exchange rate

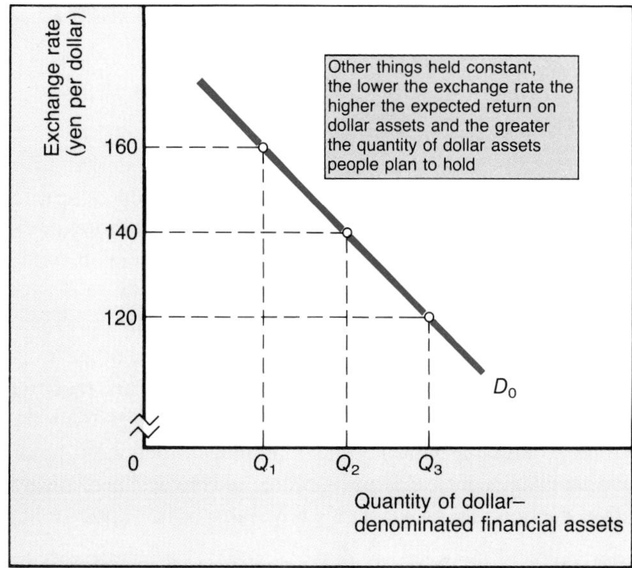

(a) Demand curve

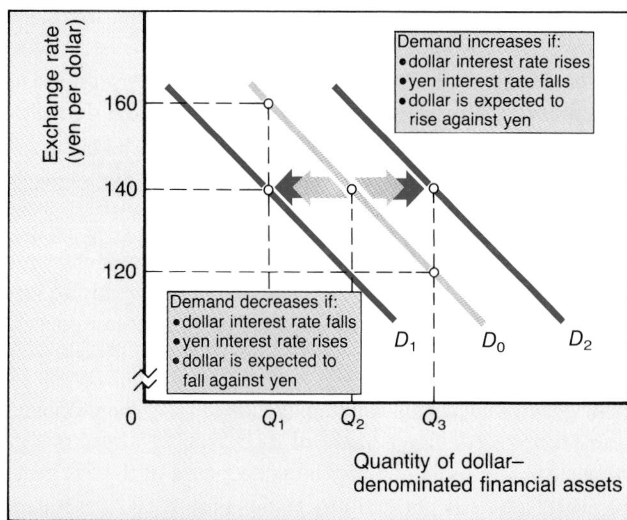

(b) Shifts in demand curve

FIGURE 16.5
The Demand for Dollar-Denominated Assets

The quantity of dollar-denominated financial assets demanded varies with the exchange rate, other things being equal. The lower the exchange rate, the higher is the expected rate of return on dollar assets and the greater is the quantity of dollar assets that people plan to hold (part a). Changes in other factors shift the demand curve for dollar-denominated assets. The most important of these are changes in interest rates and the expected future exchange rate (part b).

Other things remaining constant, the higher the interest rate on dollar assets, the greater is the demand for dollar assets; the higher the interest rate on yen assets, the smaller is the demand for dollar assets; the higher is the future exchange rate, the greater is the demand for dollar assets. Figure 16.5(b) illustrates such an increase in the demand for dollar assets by the rightward shift of the demand curve, from D_0 to D_2. A decrease in the interest rate on dollar assets, an increase in the interest rate on yen assets, or an expected fall in the dollar against the yen results in a decrease in the demand for dollar assets. Figure 16.5(b) illustrates such a decrease by a shift in the demand curve for dollar-denominated assets to the left, from D_0 to D_1 .

Other influences on demand for dollar assets The influences on the demand for dollar assets we have just studied are the most important sources of fluctuation in the demand for dollar assets. However, one other major factor results in a trend increase in the demand for dollar assets (and the demand for assets in all currencies for that matter): the scale of transactions. Other things being equal, the greater the volume of transactions undertaken using dollars, the greater is the demand for dollar assets. Growth in Canadian real GDP and growth in world trade financed by Canadian dollars lead to a trend increase in the demand for Canadian dollars.

Expected future exchange rate

We've seen that one of the most important influences on the demand for dollar assets is the expected future exchange rate. How is that expectation determined? It is likely influenced by many factors, the most important of which is the expected *future supply* of dollar assets. People making decisions about the currency in which to hold their wealth understand the laws of demand and supply and know that when the supply of something increases, its price usually decreases. Thus if the supply of dollar assets is expected to increase relative to the supply of yen assets, then, other things held constant, the price of dollar assets will be expected to decrease. This fact makes the foreign exchange market more complicated to analyze and interpret than ordinary markets. Supply in the foreign exchange market has a double influence on price. It has a direct influence through changes in the supply curve and an indirect influence through its potential effect on the demand curve. Let's now turn to the supply side of the market.

The supply of foreign exchange

The **quantity of dollar assets supplied** is the quantity of net financial assets denominated in Canadian dollars available to be held at a point in time. The supply of dollars assets is the relationship between the quantity of dollar assets supplied and the exchange rate. We've seen that the demand for foreign exchange is the demand for a stock — a certain quantity of dollar assets to hold. The supply of foreign exchange is the supply of a stock — a certain quantity of dollar available to be held. The supply of dollar assets depends on the exchange rate regime.

Fixed exchange rate Under a fixed exchange rate, the monetary authority pegs the foreign currency price of the domestic currency and stands ready to buy or sell foreign assets in exchange for domestic assets. In such a situation, the supply of dollar assets is perfectly elastic at the pegged exchange rate. Figure 16.6(a) illustrates such a case.

Flexible exchange rate With a flexible exchange rate, the monetary authority pays no attention to the foreign exchange value of its currency. There is a given quantity of dollar assets in existence and this quantity is independent of the exchange rate. Thus the supply curve of dollar assets is perfectly inelastic. Figure 16.6(b) illustrates this case.

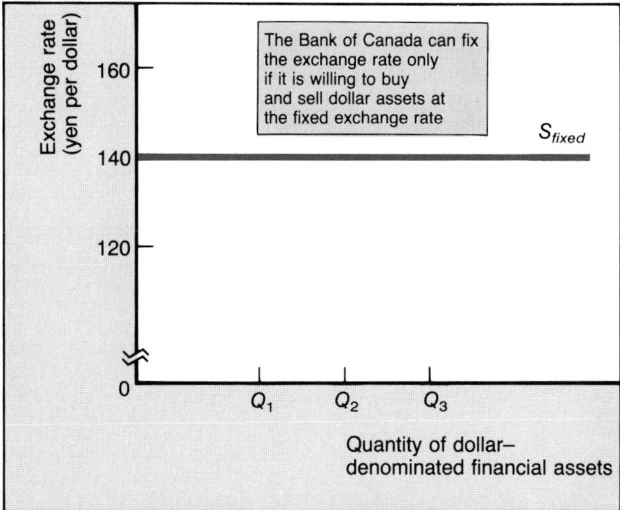

(a) Fixed exchange rate

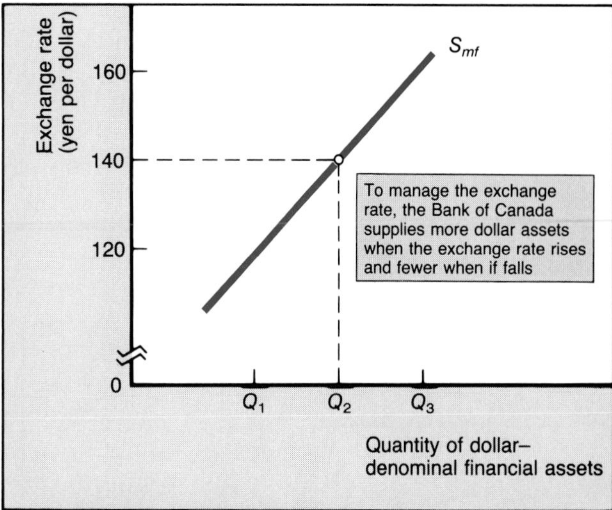

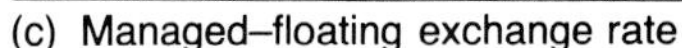

(c) Managed–floating exchange rate

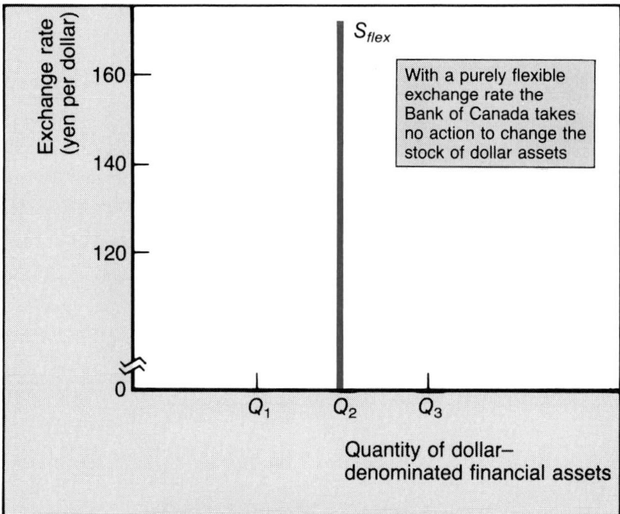

(b) Flexible exchange rate

FIGURE 16.6
The Supply of Dollar-Denominated Assets

The supply of dollar-denominated assets depends on the exchange rate regime. With a fixed exchange rate, the supply curve is perfectly elastic (part a). The monetary authority stands ready to trade dollar assets for foreign assets at the fixed exchange rate. Under flexible exchange rates the monetary authority takes no action to influence the exchange rate and the supply of dollar assets is fixed at a given point in time and inelastic (part b). Under a managed-floating rate system, the monetary authority adjusts the quantity of dollar-denominated assets outstanding in response to exchange rate changes, increasing them when the exchange rate rises and decreasing them when the exchange rate falls (part c).

Managed-floating exchange rate Under a managed-floating exchange rate, the monetary authority pays attention to the foreign exchange market and attempts to smooth out fluctuations in the exchange rate. To do this, it increases the quantity of dollar assets supplied when the dollar appreciates and decreases the quantity supplied when the dollar depreciates. Thus with a managed-floating exchange rate, the supply curve for dollar assets is upward sloping, as illustrated in Figure 16.6(c).

Equilibrium in the foreign exchange market

Equilibrium occurs at the exchange rate that makes the quantity of dollar assets demanded equal to the quantity supplied. Let's study this equilibrium and how it is disturbed when there are fluctuations in the demand for dollar assets. First, suppose that the demand for dollar assets is shown by the demand curve D_0 in Figure 16.7. Part (a) shows what happens with a fixed exchange rate and a managed-floating exchange rate and part (b) shows the case for a managed float and a flexible exchange rate. We have chosen the supply curves for fixed exchange rates, S_{fix}, for a managed-floating exchange rate, S_{mf}, and for a flexible exchange rate, S_{flex}, so that the equilibrium is the same in each case — the quantity of dollar assets in existence is Q_2 and the exchange rate is 140 yen per dollar.

FIGURE 16.7
Equilibrium in the Foreign Exchange Market

The exchange rate is determined at the intersection point of the demand curve and supply curve for foreign exchange. Under a fixed exchange rate, fluctuations in the demand for dollar assets lead to fluctuations in the quantity of dollar assets outstanding but no change in the exchange rate (part a). In contrast, under a managed-floating exchange rate, the fluctuations in the quantity of dollar assets outstanding is smaller than under a fixed exchange rate and the exchange rate also fluctuates. Under a flexible exchange rate, fluctuations in the demand for dollar assets lead to fluctuations in the exchange rate but no change in the quantity of assets outstanding (part b). In contrast, under a managed-floating exchange rate, fluctuations in the exchange rate are smaller than under a flexible exchange rate and the quantity of dollar assets outstanding fluctuates.

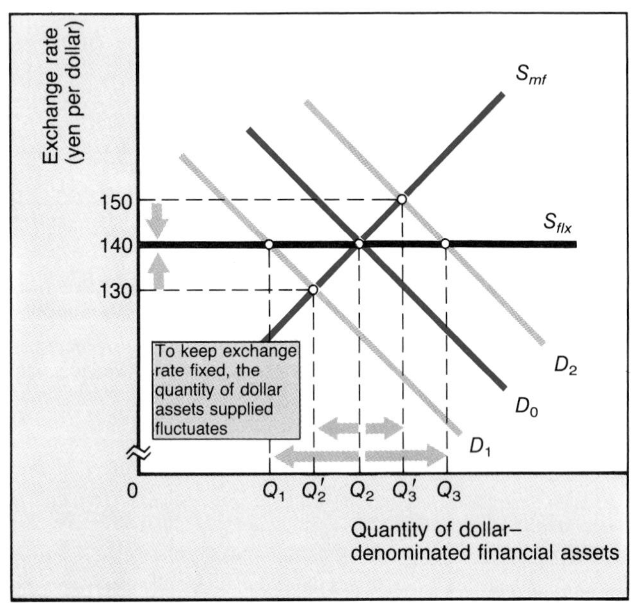

(a) Fixed rate vs. Managed float

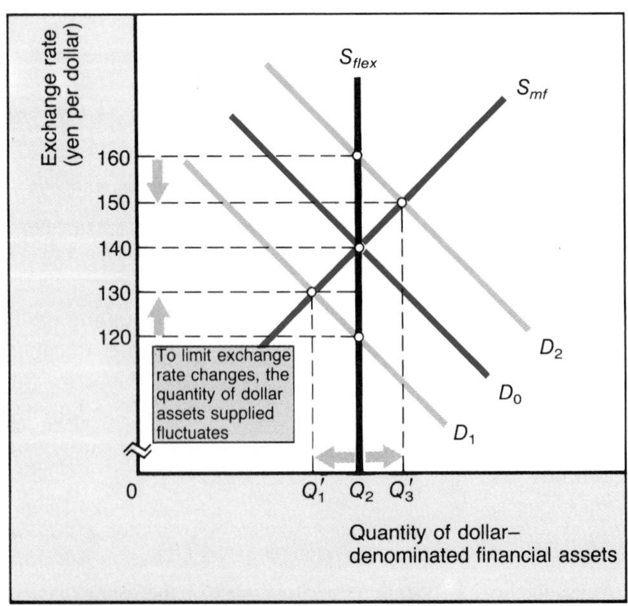

(b) Managed float vs. flexible rate

Demand fluctuations—fixed versus managed float

Suppose that the demand for dollar assets fluctuates randomly between D_1 and D_2, but on the average it is D_0. What happens to the exchange rate? The answer depends on the exchange rate regime. With a fixed exchange rate, the quantity of dollar assets in existence is adjusted to keep the exchange rate at 140 yen per dollar. The quantity of dollar assets fluctuates between Q_1 and Q_3. With a managed float, the exchange rate fluctuates between 130 and 150 yen per dollar and the quantity of dollar assets fluctuates between Q_1' and Q_3'.

Demand fluctuations: managed float versus flexible

With a flexible exchange rate, illustrated in Figure 16.7(b), there are no fluctuations in the quantity of dollar assets in existence. They remain fixed, at Q_2. As the demand for dollar assets fluctuates, the exchange rate fluctuates between 120 and 160 yen per dollar.

You can see that random fluctuations in the demand for dollar assets lead to random fluctuations in the exchange rate and/or in the quantity of dollar assets in existence. How do these fluctuations in the exchange rate and the quantity of dollar assets in existence compare under different exchange rate regimes? With fixed exchange rates, the exchange rate remains constant but fluctuations in the quantity of dollar assets in existence are greatest. With flexible exchange rates, the quantity of dollar assets in existence is fixed and fluctuations in the exchange rate are greatest. With managed-floating exchange rates, the fluctuations in the exchange rate are smaller than under a flexible exchange rate, and the fluctuations in the quantity of dollar assets are smaller than in the case of a fixed exchange rate. By determining the slope of the managed-floating supply curve, S_{mf}, the monetary authority can decide how to distribute the effects of demand fluctuations between the exchange rate and the quantity of dollar assets outstanding.

Changes in supply

How do changes in the supply of foreign exchange affect exchange rates? To answer this question, we need to consider the three exchange rate regimes separately. Let's start with fixed exchange rates.

Fixed exchange rate A change in supply is represented by a shift in the supply curve. The supply curve under fixed exchange rates is horizontal at the chosen value for the exchange rate. Thus a change in supply under fixed exchange rates means a change in the value at which the exchange rate is pegged. An increase in the foreign exchange value of its currency under fixed exchange rates is called a *revaluation* and the supply curve shifts upward. A decrease in the foreign exchange value of a currency under fixed exchange rates is called a *devaluation* and the supply curve shifts downward.

We've seen that to peg the value of the exchange rate, a country has to stand ready to buy or sell financial assets denominated in its own currency at the chosen exchange rate. Equivalently, the country must be willing to exchange foreign-currency denominated assets for domestic-currency denominated assets at the chosen rate.

Credible revaluation For a country to make a credible revaluation of its currency it must have a large enough stock of foreign exchange reserves to convince people that it can maintain the new higher value for its currency. If it does have a sufficiently large stock of reserves (or if its reserves were tending to increase at a rate that it regarded as too rapid), then it is possible to make a credible revaluation. Figure 16.8(a) illustrates such a revaluation. (For variety, we'll use the British pound as the domestic currency

FIGURE 16.8
Exchange Rate Dynamics with Fixed Rates

With a fixed exchange rate, the behavior of the exchange rate depends on the credibility of the monetary authority's policy. If the exchange rate is pegged at a credible value, the exchange rate can be maintained at its fixed value (part a). To achieve this, the monetary authority requires adequate foreign exchange reserves. If the exchange rate is pegged at a value too high to be supported by the available reserves, expectations of a future devaluation lead to a decrease in the demand for the currency and cause yet further reserve losses that increase the probability of a devaluation (part b). Such a pegged exchange rate is unsustainable and breaks down, possibly leading to larger exchange rate fluctuations than would occur under a flexible exchange rate.

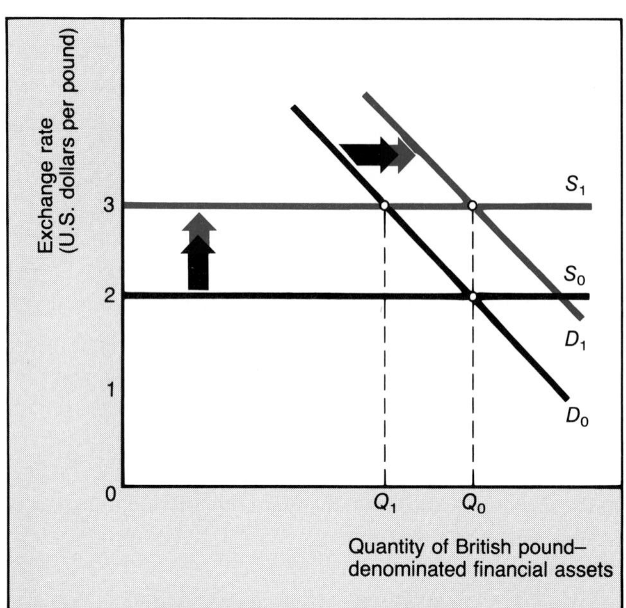

(a) Credible revaluation

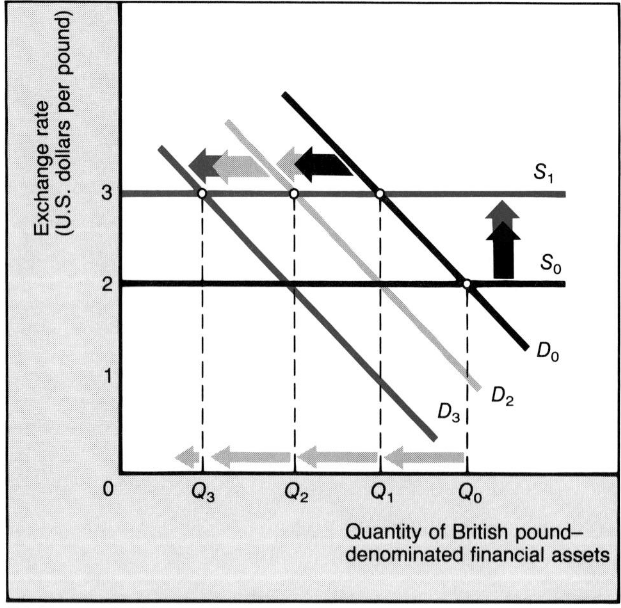

(b) Unsustainable revaluation

and the U.S. dollar as the foreign currency: thus the exchange rate is U.S. dollars per British pound.) Here the demand curve for financial assets denominated in pounds is D_0 and the Bank of England is pegging the exchange rate at \$2 per pound, so the supply curve of financial assets denominated in pounds is S_0.

Suppose the Bank of England, flush with reserves of dollar-denominated assets, decides to revalue the pound to \$3 per pound. The supply curve shifts upward from S_0 to S_1. Suppose initially that the demand for pounds is unchanged at D_0. The new exchange rate of \$3 per pound requires the Bank of England to take pound assets off the market. It does this by supplying dollar assets from its foreign exchange reserves in exchange for them. The quantity of pound-denominated assets decreases, from Q_0 to Q_1.

But suppose that the Bank of England's reserves of dollar assets remain sufficiently large to convince everyone that the new exchange rate is going to be maintained indefinitely. In this situation, the expected future exchange rate has also increased from \$2 to \$3 per pound. With an increase in both the current exchange rate and its expected future value, there is no change in the rate of return on financial assets denominated in British pounds. With no change in the expected return on holding assets denominated in pounds, there is no change in the quantity of pound assets demanded. The amount Q_0 is the quantity demanded at a fixed exchange rate of \$2 per pound when that exchange rate is also the expected future exchange rate. But Q_0 is also the quantity demanded at a fixed exchange rate of \$3 per pound when that exchange rate is the expected future exchange rate. Thus the demand curve for pound assets shifts from D_0 to D_1. The Bank of England regains the foreign reserves that it lost in maintaining the new exchange rate of \$3 per pound, and the pound now trades at \$3 a pound for the indefinite future.

There will be other implications of the change in the fixed exchange rate, such as those for exports, imports, the balance of payments, and aggregate economic activity. Later in this chapter, we're going to study these consequences and the possibility that they will have further effects on the exchange rate.

Unsustainable revaluation It is not always possible to make a revaluation stick. Suppose that the Bank of England has relatively limited stocks of dollar assets and other foreign exchange reserves but still, for some domestic reason (perhaps to reverse an increase in prices), wants to revalue the pound. Figure 16.8(b) illustrates this case. The initial situation is the same as before: the demand curve for pound assets is D_0 and the supply curve is S_0. When the Bank of England increases the exchange rate, the supply curve shifts from S_0 to S_1. The quantity of pound assets demanded decreases from Q_0 to Q_1. There is a movement along the demand curve D_0. In the process of pegging the exchange rate at its new higher value of \$3 per pound, the Bank of England has decreased the quantity of pound assets outstanding and exchanged some of its dollar reserves for pound assets. If the loss of foreign reserves by the Bank of England leads to an expectation that it will not be possible to maintain the new exchange rate, people will expect a lower return from holding pound assets than from holding dollar assets. The demand for pound assets will decrease. The demand curve for pound assets will shift to the left, to D_2.

The magnitude of the shift is arbitrary but the direction is clear. With a lower demand for pound assets, the Bank of England loses yet more foreign reserves as the quantity of pound assets outstanding decreases from Q_2 and the Bank exchanges more of its dollar reserves for pound assets. With even lower foreign reserves now, it becomes even less credible that the Bank of England can make the new exchange rate stick, and more and more people expect the foreign exchange value of the pound to fall. The expected return from holding pound assets is even lower than before, and the demand for them falls yet further. As the demand curve shifts to D_3, the Bank of England loses yet more foreign reserves in its attempt to make the new exchange rate stick. This process cannot go on forever. At some point, the Bank of England has to recognize the inevitable and abandon the fixed exchange rate of \$3 per pound. The exchange rate eventually will fall, and probably to a level even lower than the \$2 from which it started, since the Bank has lost such a large quantity of its foreign exchange reserves in the attempt to hold the exchange rate at \$3 per pound.

A disastrous example It's unusual, but not unknown, for a country to revalue its currency under fixed exchange rates to a level that proves unsustainable. The British, in fact, did that in 1926 when they restored the pre-World War I value of the pound. This move had disastrous consequences, not only in the foreign exchange market but for the entire British economy.

It is quite common, however, for countries to attempt to hold a fixed exchange rate in a situation in which they do not have enough foreign exchange reserves to make the rate stick. When they do that, a one-way bet situation arises exactly like that we've just described using Figure 16.8(b). Everyone knows that the currency is going to be devalued at some future date so they place bets on that expectation, switching their financial assets from the overvalued currency, putting that currency under yet further pressure as the country loses foreign reserves in the process.

Because of the possible unsustainability of a fixed exchange rate, a fixed exchange rate does not necessarily fluctuate less than a floating exchange rate. Fluctuations in the demand for assets in a particular currency arise from fluctuations in expectations about rates of return. When a currency is expected to be revalued or devalued, there is not much doubt about the direction in which the change is going to take place. Large expected changes in the rate of return can occur, bringing large shifts in the demand for assets denominated in the currency and, ultimately, when the fixed exchange rate peg has to be abandoned or changed, bringing large fluctuations in the exchange rate.

Flexible exchange rate With a flexible exchange rate, the quantity of dollar assets supplied is fixed at any given point in time. But that quantity is not independent of the actions of the Bank of Canada. One of the main components of the quantity of dollar-denominated assets is the Canadian money supply. Every time the Bank of Canada conducts an open market operation that changes the money supply, it changes the quantity of dollar-denominated assets in existence, leading to repercussions in the foreign exchange market. How does a change in the Canadian money supply influence the foreign exchange rate?

We'll answer this question first in the simplest possible setting. Imagine that the money supply is fixed and that the quantity of dollar-denominated assets is fixed and expected to remain fixed indefinitely. A given exchange rate and price level prevail in the Canadian economy. We'll suppose that the exchange rate and the price level are also expected to remain at their present levels indefinitely. (This setting, although unrealistic, makes as clear as possible what happens with a change in the money supply. Later we'll discuss a situation in which there is an ongoing process of inflation and money creation.)

Figure 16.9 illustrates the economy. Initially, the demand for dollar assets is D_0 and the supply S_0. The exchange rate is 132 yen per dollar, and Q_0 is the quantity of dollar assets in existence. The exchange rate is expected to remain at 132 in the following period and each period after that. The price level is expected to remain constant and we'll call the index value of the price level 100. To remind you of these facts, the demand curve has been labeled $D_0(E_{t+1} = 132, P_t = 100)$. Now suppose that an increase in the Canadian money supply increases the quantity of dollar-denominated assets from Q_0 to Q_1. The supply curve shifts from S_0 to S_1. Further, suppose that this is a one-shot change and is expected to be so. Initially, nothing happens to the price level, which remains fixed at 100. With the larger supply of dollar assets, the exchange rate falls. But how far does it fall? Does it go to the point of intersection of the demand curve D_0 and the new supply curve S_1? The answer is no. We know that because the demand curve D_0 is based on an expectation that next year the exchange rate will equal 132, but that is not going to be the case. Everyone now recognizes that the supply of dollar assets has been increased, so the equilibrium exchange rate is going to be lower. People know that the lower exchange rate is also going to bring a higher price level. Let's suppose that the demand curve D_0 is also the demand curve when the expected exchange rate is 120 (a 10 percent depreciation) and when the price level is 110 (a 10 percent inflation).

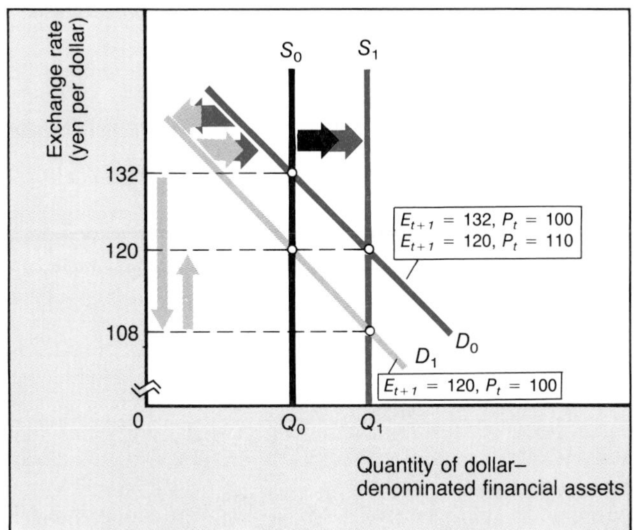

FIGURE 16.9
Flexible Exchange Rate Dynamics

Initially, the supply of dollar-denominated assets is S_0 and the demand is D_0. The actual exchange rate is 132 yen per dollar and the expected future exchange rate is also 132 yen per dollar. The price level is 100. If there is now a one-shot increase in the supply of dollar assets to S_1, the exchange rate falls, but so does the expected future exchange rate. As a result, the demand curve for dollar assets shifts. In this example, the demand curve shifts to D_1 which is the demand curve when the expected future exchange rate is 120 yen per dollar and the price level is 100. The actual exchange rate falls to 108 yen per dollar. In the following period, the price level increases, shifting the demand curve back to D_0, which is the demand curve for an expected exchange rate of 120 yen per dollar and a price level of 110. In this period, the exchange rate rises to 120 yen per dollar. As the exchange rate adjusts, it overshoots its long-run equilibrium value.

If people expect the price level to increase to 110 next period and expect the exchange rate to be 120 next period, then D_0 will be the demand curve for dollar assets next period. But it is not this period's demand curve. In this period, the price level is still 100, but the price level next period is expected to be 120. Therefore this period's demand curve is D_1. This demand curve lies below D_0 by an amount such that at a quantity Q_0, the actual exchange rate would be 120.

You can now figure out what happens when the supply of dollar assets increases to S_1. The demand curve shifts from D_0 to D_1 and the exchange rate falls from 132 to 108. Next period, the price level increases to 110, the demand curve shifts back to its original position, and the exchange rate rises from 108 to 120.

The movement of the exchange rate in this adjustment process *overshoots* its eventual equilibrium level. This overshooting of the exchange rate is illustrated with the time sequence shown in Figure 16.10. Period 1 is the initial equilibrium. In period 2 the supply of dollar assets has increased from Q_0 to Q_1 (part a), the exchange rate drops to 108 (part b), but nothing happens to the price level (part c). In period 3, the quantity of dollar assets remains constant, the price level rises, and the exchange rate rises to its new long-run equilibrium level. Figure 16.10 also shows what has happened to the real exchange rate (part d). Initially and eventually, the real exchange rate is 100. But in the process of adjustment from the initial to the new quantity of dollar assets, the real exchange rate falls.

Ongoing inflation process In the exercise that we've just conducted, we disturbed one static equilibrium position to reach another. In reality, the economy is undergoing

FIGURE 16.10
Exchange Rate Overshooting—A Time Sequence

The change in the quantity of dollar-denominated assets is shown in part (a) and the overshooting of the exchange rate in part (b). The path of the price level is shown in part (c) and the real exchange rate in part (d). The initial equilibrium occurs in period 1. At the end of period 1, the quantity of dollar-denominated assets increases and is then held at its new level. In period 2, the exchange rate falls and the price level stays constant, so the real exchange rate falls. In period 3, the price level rises, the exchange rate moves to its long-run value, and the real exchange rate returns to its initial value. In adjusting to its new equilibrium value in period 3, the exchange rate overshoots in period 2.

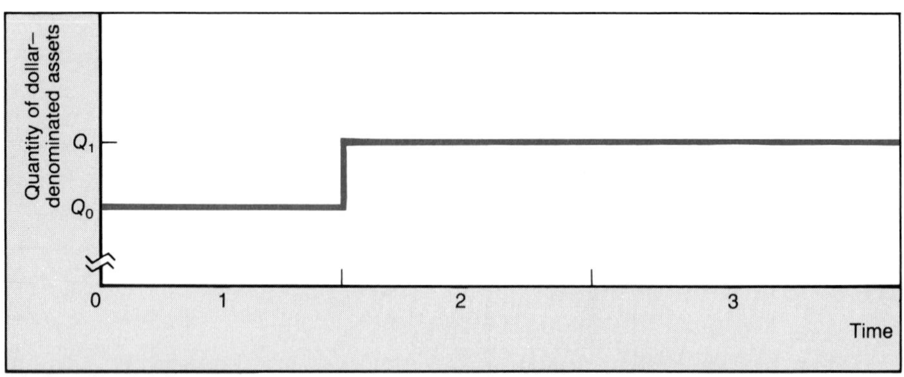

(a) Quantity of dollar assets

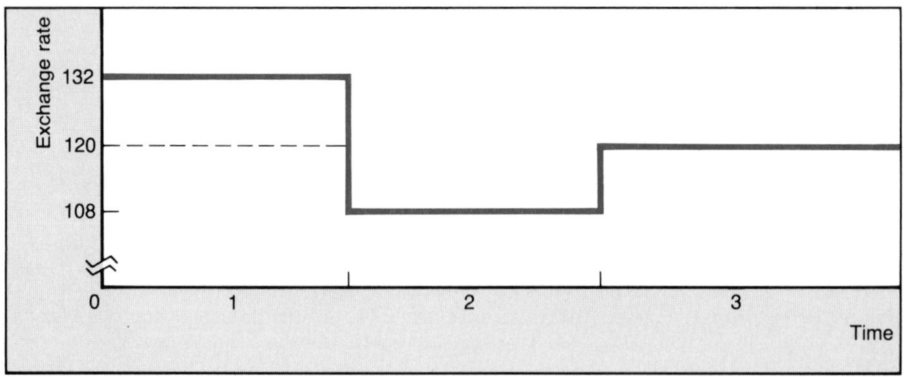

(b) Exchange rate

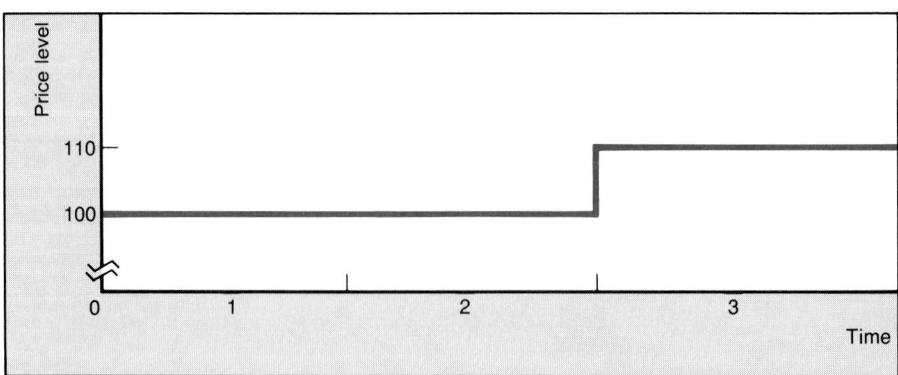

(c) Price level

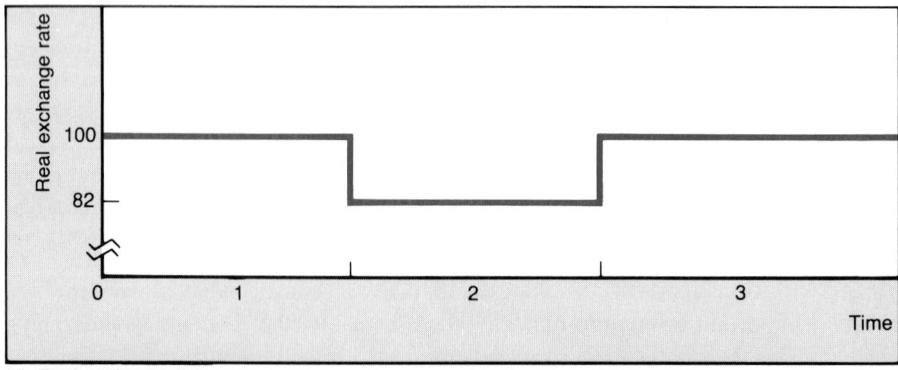

(d) Real exchange rate

constant change, with the quantity of dollar assets supplied increasing over time, the dollar exchange rate fluctuating, and prices steadily increasing. The analysis that we've just conducted applies with equal force to the more complicated real world. A change in the growth rate of the money supply leads to a depreciation of the currency that overshoots its long-run value and a gradual increase in the inflation rate. The real exchange rate depreciates temporarily. A slowdown in the growth rate of the money supply brings an overshooting of the exchange rate in the opposite direction—an appreciation—a slowdown in the inflation rate, and an increase in the real exchange rate.

Because of the sensitivity of the foreign exchange market to fluctuations in the growth rate of the money supply, monetary authorities around the world take actions to limit fluctuations in the exchange rate, seeking to manage the float. Let's now study that case.

Managed-floating exchange rate To understand how changes in the supply of dollar assets influence the exchange rate under managed floating, we have to combine the two analyses we've just conducted—the fixed exchange rate and flexible exchange rate analyses. To some degree, a managed float is similar to a fixed exchange rate, but in other ways, it is similar to a flexible exchange rate.

Under a managed float, speeding up and slowing down the growth rate of the money supply sets up the same dynamic overshooting adjustments as they do under flexible exchange rates. But by direct operations in the foreign exchange market, the monetary authority seeks to smooth the effects of those fluctuations on the exchange rate itself, permitting some change in the stock of foreign exchange reserves and in the quantity of dollar-denominated assets outstanding. Provided the monetary authority sets a path for the exchange rate that is sustainable—can be credibly achieved given its stock of foreign exchange reserves — then a managed-floating exchange rate can be made to function much like a fixed exchange rate where the targetted value for the currency is gradually gliding along a smoothly adjusting path.

But if the monetary authority has a target path for the exchange rate that cannot be sustained by its stock of foreign exchange reserves, then the managed float will, at some point, have to be abandoned. Just as in the case of a fixed rate, it will become obvious that the exchange rate has to move further, and the direction of that move will also be obvious. People will be able to place a one-way bet on the currency, forcing the monetary authority to lose reserves ever more quickly and to abandon its managed float. Under such circumstances, when a managed float breaks down, the exchange rate may fluctuate more than under a flexible exchange rate.

We've now seen that the foreign exchange market is an extremely sensitive market and one in which dynamic adjustments driven by expectations are a dominant source of exchange rate movements. Let's take a look at the foreign exchange market in action by studying one of the most important and sensitive exchange rates in the world today— that between the U.S. dollar and the Japanese yen.

16.4 *The U.S. Dollar-Yen Exchange Rate in the 1980s*

TESTCASE

There were some impressive swings in the exchange rate between the U.S. dollar and the Japanese yen during the 1980s. When the decade opened, the dollar was worth about 240 yen. By the end of 1980, it had fallen to barely 200 yen. It then climbed, not at a uniform pace, but generally upward until the end of 1984, when it stood at more than 250 yen per dollar—even higher than its 1980 level. Then followed a period of spectacular decline. By the end of 1987, the dollar was worth less than half its 1984 peak value in terms of the yen. From that low point, the value of the dollar in yen gradually increased again through the end of the decade. Can we explain these movements in the yen-dollar exchange rate using the theory of exchange rate determination that we have just studied?

In fact, a fairly convincing explanation for the movements in the yen-dollar exchange rate can be given based on the theory. The starting point is to study the main policy influences on the exchange rate. We studied the exchange rate from the U.S. point of view, looking at the market for dollar-denominated assets and expressing their price in terms of yen. Anything that increases the supply of dollar-denominated assets puts downward pressure on the exchange rate. Anything that increases the demand for dollar-denominated assets puts upward pressure on the exchange rate. Thus an increase in the U.S. money supply, other things being equal, decreases the dollar-yen exchange rate, and an increase in the demand for U.S. money increases the dollar-yen exchange rate. We discovered, when we studied the demand for money in Chapter 5, that the main influences on the demand for money are real income, the price level, and interest rates. Focus on the first two variables: the price level and real GDP. Their product is simply GDP. Thus faster GDP growth brings faster growth in the demand for dollar assets and, other things equal, increases the exchange rate.

But symmetric forces operate in Japan. Other things being equal, anything that increases the supply of yen assets decreases the value of the yen in terms of the dollar — appreciates the dollar. Anything that increases the demand for yen assets increases the value of the yen relative to the dollar — depreciates the dollar. Thus an increase in the Japanese money supply puts upward pressure on the dollar, and an increase in Japanese GDP puts downward pressure on the dollar.

To study the influence of monetary policy on the yen-dollar exchange rate, we need to take account of the *difference* between U.S. and Japanese monetary policy. A convenient way of doing this is to define the *monetary policy difference* between Japan and the United States as

(*Japanese money growth — Japanese GDP growth*)
— (*U.S. money growth — U.S. GDP growth*).

Other things being equal, the higher the monetary policy difference, the greater is the tendency for the dollar to appreciate against the yen.

Figure 16.11(a) illustrates this monetary policy difference, which ranges between about −6 percent (in 1983) and +8 percent (in 1981). It also swings about wildly, especially in the first half of the decade. After 1985, the differential moves steadily upward.

Before we look at the connection between this variable and the exchange rate, let's think about what the monetary policy difference might do to interest rates. If there is a temporary burst of money creation in Japan, Japanese interest rates will fall. If there is a temporary period of monetary tightness in the United States, U.S. interest rates will rise. A temporary increase in the monetary policy difference between Japan and the United States will make interest rates in the two countries move in the opposite direction: U.S. interest rates will rise relative to Japanese interest rates. We show this interest rate difference alongside the monetary policy difference in Figure 16.11(a). You can see that when Japanese monetary policy is expansionary relative to the United States, U.S. interest rates rise relative to Japanese interest rates. Similarly, when Japanese monetary policy tightens relative to U.S. monetary policy, U.S. interest rates fall relative to Japanese interest rates. These movements are particularly clear in the period 1980 through 1984.

If Japanese monetary policy becomes permanently more inflationary, two influences are at work on interest rates. A higher amount of money may temporarily lower interest

FIGURE 16.11
The U.S. Dollar-Yen Exchange Rate in the 1980s

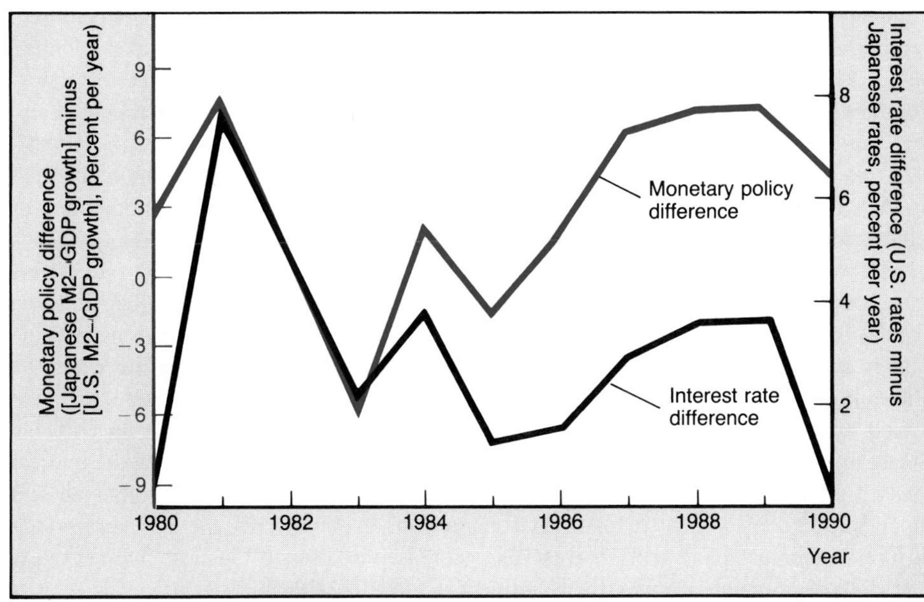

(a) Monetary policy and interest rates

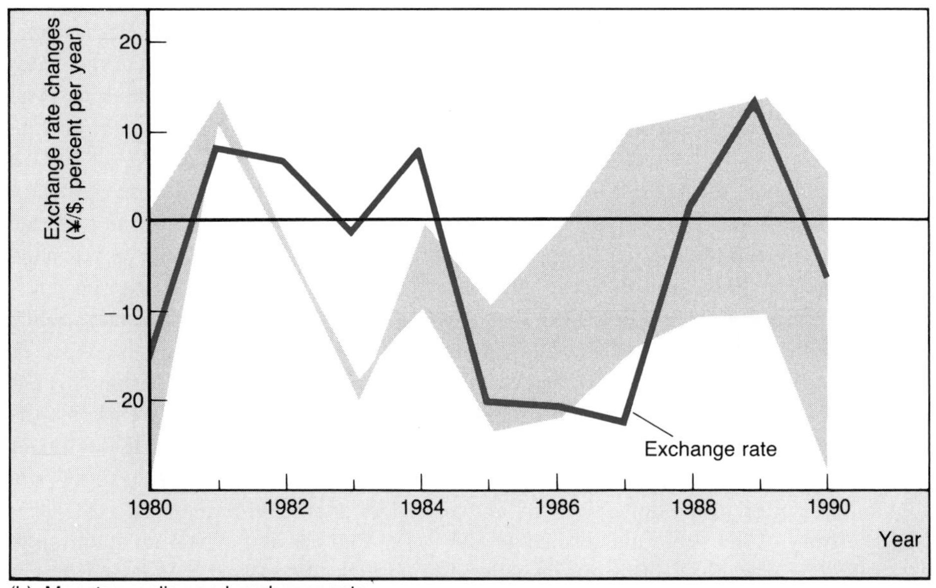

(b) Monetary policy and exchange rate

A major influence on the U.S. dollar-yen exchange rate is the difference in monetary policy between the United States and Japan. Monetary policy difference is measured as the difference between money growth minus GDP growth in the United States and in Japan. Interest rate difference also influences the exchange rate. These variables are shown in part (a). So that you can see their relationship with the exchange rate (shown in part b) we've reproduced a shadow of the pattern they form in part (b). In the first half of the 1980s, movements in the exchange rate match movements in monetary policy and interest rate differences. In 1986-1987, the dollar continued to depreciate, even though monetary policy and interest rate differences were exerting the opposite influence on the exchange rate. By 1988 and 1989, the dollar appreciated very strongly and in line with these underlying movements in monetary policy and interest rates. In 1990, the dollar depreciated, again in line with the underlying changes in monetary policy.

Source: International Financial Statistics Yearbook, 1991, and our calculations.

rates in Japan, but the expectation that money growth will persistently increase creates expectations of ongoing inflation and increases Japanese interest rates. Thus when there is a period of persistent additional inflationary pressure in Japan relative to the United States, U.S. interest rates do not rise significantly relative to Japanese interest rates. You can see this phenomenon in the second half of the 1980s. When inflationary pressure increases in Japan, especially in 1987 through 1989, the interest rate difference—U.S. interest rates minus Japanese interest rates—does not increase to the levels that prevailed in the early 1980s. The interest rate difference remains low in anticipation of a narrowing of the monetary policy difference between the two countries.

How do movements in the monetary policy difference and the interest rate difference line up with and account for movements in the exchange rate? You can find the answer to this question in Figure 16.11(b). Here, the blue line shows the percentage change in the yen-dollar exchange rate each year. The dollar is appreciating when the blue line is above zero and depreciating when it's below zero. You can see that in the period between 1980 and 1985 the fluctuations in the exchange rate line up with the fluctuations in the monetary policy difference in the two countries (and with the interest rate difference) as well. In 1981, U.S. monetary policy was severely tightened and Japanese monetary policy was held on a steady course. As a result, the monetary policy difference increased and U.S. interest rates increased relative to Japanese interest rates. The dollar appreciated under these influences. In 1982-1983, U.S. monetary policy became highly expansionary while Japanese monetary policy continued to be stable. Through these years, the monetary policy difference decreased and the interest rate difference narrowed. The dollar fell against the yen. In 1984, there was a brief reversal of this movement. The monetary policy difference increased and U.S. interest rates increased relative to those in Japan. The dollar appreciated. There was a quick reversal in 1985 when monetary policy tightened and interest rates and the exchange rate decreased.

Developments after 1985 are especially interesting. In 1986, Japanese monetary policy became more inflationary relative to U.S. monetary policy. The interest rate difference between the United States and Japan remained low. The dollar depreciated that year and in 1987, and by large amounts. These large depreciations can be interpreted as arising from expectations that Japan's more inflationary monetary policy would be temporary and, with the interest rate difference remaining low, the expected return on dollar assets was low. However, by 1988, the third year of persistently more expansionary monetary policy in Japan, expectations changed. People now expected the monetary policy difference between Japan and the United States to decline in the longer term. This change in expectations shifted the demand for dollar assets, leading to a slight appreciation of the dollar in 1988 and a stronger appreciation in 1989.

The story of the yen-dollar exchange rate we've told has so far paid no attention to exchange rate smoothing. But during several important episodes, the Federal Reserve (the U.S. central bank) and the Bank of Japan and other monetary authorities, such as the Bank of England, the Bank of Canada, and the Bundesbank (the German central bank), intervened in foreign exchange markets to smooth exchange rate movements. These interventions had important effects in the short term but were almost certainly incapable of influencing the year-to-year changes in the exchange rate that we've studied here. Intervention in the foreign exchange market can also result in changes in the domestic money supply and interest rates. To the extent that they do, we have taken them into account in the above story.

We've seen how exchange rates are determined and also examined an important episode in the history of one of the world's most important exchange rates. Let's now go on to study some of the effects of the exchange rate, in particular, its effects on the balance of payments.

16.5 *Balance of Payments*

We've seen that current account balances have fluctuated a great deal, especially in the 1980s. We've also seen large exchange rate fluctuations. Is there a connection between a country's balance of payments and its exchange rate? In fact, there is a two-way relationship between the exchange rate and the balance of payments:

- The exchange rate influences the balance of payments.
- The balance of payments influences the exchange rate.

Exchange rate influences on the balance of payments

The exchange rate influences the balance of payments through its effects on international relative prices — real exchange rates. Recall that a real exchange rate is the value of a currency in terms of the goods it will buy in the rest of the world. The real exchange rate (*RER*) measures the price of domestic goods and services relative to foreign goods and services:

$$RER = EP/P^f. \quad \textbf{(16.2)}$$

The real exchange rate influences the demand by Canadian residents for foreign goods and services. Other things being equal, the higher the real exchange rate, the less expensive foreign goods and services are relative to Canadian-made goods and services. As a result, other things being equal, the higher the real exchange rate, the larger is the volume of Canadian imports.

The real exchange rate also measures the price foreigners have to pay for Canadian-made goods and services. A higher real exchange rate means that Canadian-made goods and services cost foreigners more than their own domestic alternatives. This means that, other things being equal, the higher the real value of the dollar, the smaller is the quantity of Canadian exports. Since a higher Canadian real exchange rate increases Canadian imports and decreases Canadian exports, Canadian net exports fall, resulting in a smaller current account surplus or a larger current account deficit.

Although it is the *real* exchange rate that influences the current account, the *nominal* exchange rate is the most important short-run influence on the real exchange rate. Prices adjust much more smoothly than the exchange rate itself. Most importantly, we've seen that with flexible exchange rates the nominal exchange rate can overshoot the underlying changes in money supply and prices.

For example, a speed-up in Canadian money supply growth will make the Canadian dollar depreciate, causing the real exchange rate to fall. This, in turn, will bring an increase in the current account surplus (or a decrease in the current account deficit). In the opposite direction, a slowdown in Canadian money supply growth will bring an appreciation of the Canadian dollar, increasing the real exchange rate and cutting the current account surplus (or increasing the current account deficit).

These effects of changes in the money supply growth rate have further repercussions on aggregate demand, real GDP, employment, and unemployment. The changes in net exports resulting from the change in the real exchange rate change the injections into the circular flow of income and expenditure. These changes reinforce the other domestic effects of monetary policy on interest rates and investment. Thus with a flexible exchange rate, monetary policy has a more powerful influence on aggregate demand and the fluctuations in real domestic economic activity.

But these effects also spill over to the rest of the world. If Canada pursues an expansionary monetary policy, increasing the Canadian money supply growth rate, the resulting depreciation of the Canadian dollar lowers the real exchange rate and increases the demand for Canadian-made goods and services. The Canadian economy goes into a period of strong expansion. Rising Canadian incomes increase the Canadian demand for goods and services from the rest of the world, bringing economic expansion throughout the global economy.

But the global expansion is not uniform. Because the Canadian real exchange rate has fallen, there is a switch of expenditure from foreign goods and services to Canadian-made goods and services. This switch dampens the effects of the Canadian boom on the rest of the world and reinforces its effects within Canada.

The same pattern occurs, but in the opposite direction, when Canada pursues a contractionary monetary policy. If the Bank of Canada slows down the money supply growth rate, as it did in the early 1980s, Canadian interest rates increase and the dollar strengthens. A higher dollar increases the real exchange rate and decreases the demand for Canadian-made goods and services. Declining income in Canada lowers the Canadian demand for goods and services from the rest of the world and results in a slowdown of the world economy. But there is an asymmetry. Because the Canadian real exchange rate has increased, there is a larger decline in the demand for Canadian-made goods and services than for goods and services produced in the rest of the world, so the rest of the world is spared some of the consequences of the Canadian recession.

Balance of payments influences on exchange rate

We've now looked at the effects of the exchange rate on the balance of payments. But there are two important effects that go in the opposite direction:

- Expectations
- Intervention

Expectations A current account deficit can arise for a variety of reasons. One possibility is that aggregate demand is too high. In this case, it is likely that monetary and fiscal policy actions will be taken to decrease aggregate demand. The most likely and most effective of such policies is fiscal policy. A tightening of monetary policy to decrease aggregate demand will increase interest rates, increase the exchange rate, and make the current account even worse. A tightening of fiscal policy, on the other hand, will decrease interest rates, lower the exchange rate, and contribute to an improvement in the current account balance, both from its dampening effects on aggregate demand and by causing expenditure switching from foreign-made to domestic-made goods and services as the real exchange rate falls. If a current account deficit leads to an expectation of a tight fiscal policy, it may also lead to a depreciation of the currency in anticipation of that policy change.

A second source of a current account deficit is that the real exchange rate is too high. We've just seen how the real exchange rate affects both imports and exports and, therefore, the current account balance. If it is believed that the current account deficit arises from such a source, the expectation of a decrease in the exchange rate will automatically arise. This expectation will shift the demand curve for dollar assets downward and bring about the very change in the exchange rate that is expected.

Intervention The official settlements account of the balance of payments records the transactions by the monetary authority in the foreign exchange market. That is, it records the net intervention by the monetary authority in the foreign exchange market. By its intervention, the monetary authority influences the balance of payments. A decision to use foreign reserves to buy dollar assets worsens the balance of payments.

A decision to use dollar assets to buy foreign reserves improves the balance of payments. Thus intervention by the monetary authorities can create or prevent a balance of payments deficit or surplus but its actions directly influence the exchange rate. A decision to use foreign exchange reserves to buy dollar assets decreases the supply of dollar assets and, other things being equal, increases the exchange rate. A decision to use dollar assets to buy foreign exchange reserves improves the balance of payments, increases the supply of dollar assets, and, other things being equal, decreases the exchange rate.

16.6 *Payments Imbalances in the 1980s*

TESTCASE

During the 1980s, large international trade deficits and surpluses emerged. The most important deficit, globally, was that of the United States. The United States started the decade with a net export surplus of close to $60 billion. By 1982 the surplus had disappeared, and by 1986 a deficit of $130 billion (1982 dollars) had emerged. After this year, the deficit steadily declined, but by 1990 net exports remained negative.

Why did U.S. net exports behave in this way? Part of the answer is the behavior of the U.S. dollar exchange rate. We've seen that net exports depend on the real exchange rate and that the real exchange rate is strongly influenced by the nominal exchange rate. The nominal exchange rate, in turn, is affected by U.S. monetary policy relative to monetary policy in the rest of the world. During the early 1980s, U.S. monetary policy was extremely tight relative to that in the rest of the world, and the dollar strengthened. The real exchange rate climbed. It reached a peak in 1985, after which it steadily declined. The decline in the real exchange rate brought about a reduction in the net export deficit, but it did not bring net exports back to zero. You can see this relationship between the real exchange rate and net exports in Figure 16.12(a). In this figure, the real exchange rate is measured on the right axis, with its scale inverted so that you can see how the real exchange rate and net exports line up. As the real exchange rate increases, net exports move into deficit; and as the real exchange rate decreases, the net export deficit declines. But changes in net exports lag behind exchange rate movements. Even after the foreign exchange value of the dollar fell drastically in 1986, the net export deficit continued to increase. Why do net exports lag behind the real exchange rate and why, in particular at a time such as 1986 when there is an enormous decrease in the real exchange rate, do net exports decrease?

The answer lies in a phenomenon called the *J*-curve. The **J-curve** is the time path followed by net exports following a major change in the exchange rate. At first, a depreciation leads to a deterioration of net exports. Only after a period do net exports begin to move back toward zero. The reason has to do with the distinction between short-run and long-run responses to relative price changes. In the short run, U.S. demand for foreign goods and services is relatively unresponsive. A large decrease in the real exchange rate that makes foreign goods and services more expensive for Americans does not bring a large initial decrease in the quantity of such goods and services bought. Rather, the quantity bought remains similar to its previous level, but the price paid increases, so net exports actually deteriorate. But after a while, as people find cheaper domestic substitutes for the foreign goods and services that they have been buying, the response of imports to the change in the real exchange rate is larger and net exports deficit begins to decline. A similar effect works on the export side. When the dollar falls in value, foreigners buy more U.S.-made goods and services, but at first

FIGURE 16.12
Exchange Rates and the Balance of Payments

United States net exports declined steadily from 1980 to 1986 and after that began to increase. The decline through 1985 was matched by a rise in the real exchange rate. After 1985, the real exchange rate fell, but net exports became even more negative for one more year. These movements are shown in part (a). The failure of net exports to increase when the real exchange rate decreases is called the *J*-curve effect. The *J*-curve is illustrated in part (b). It arises from slow short-run adjustments in the quantity demanded in response to price changes.

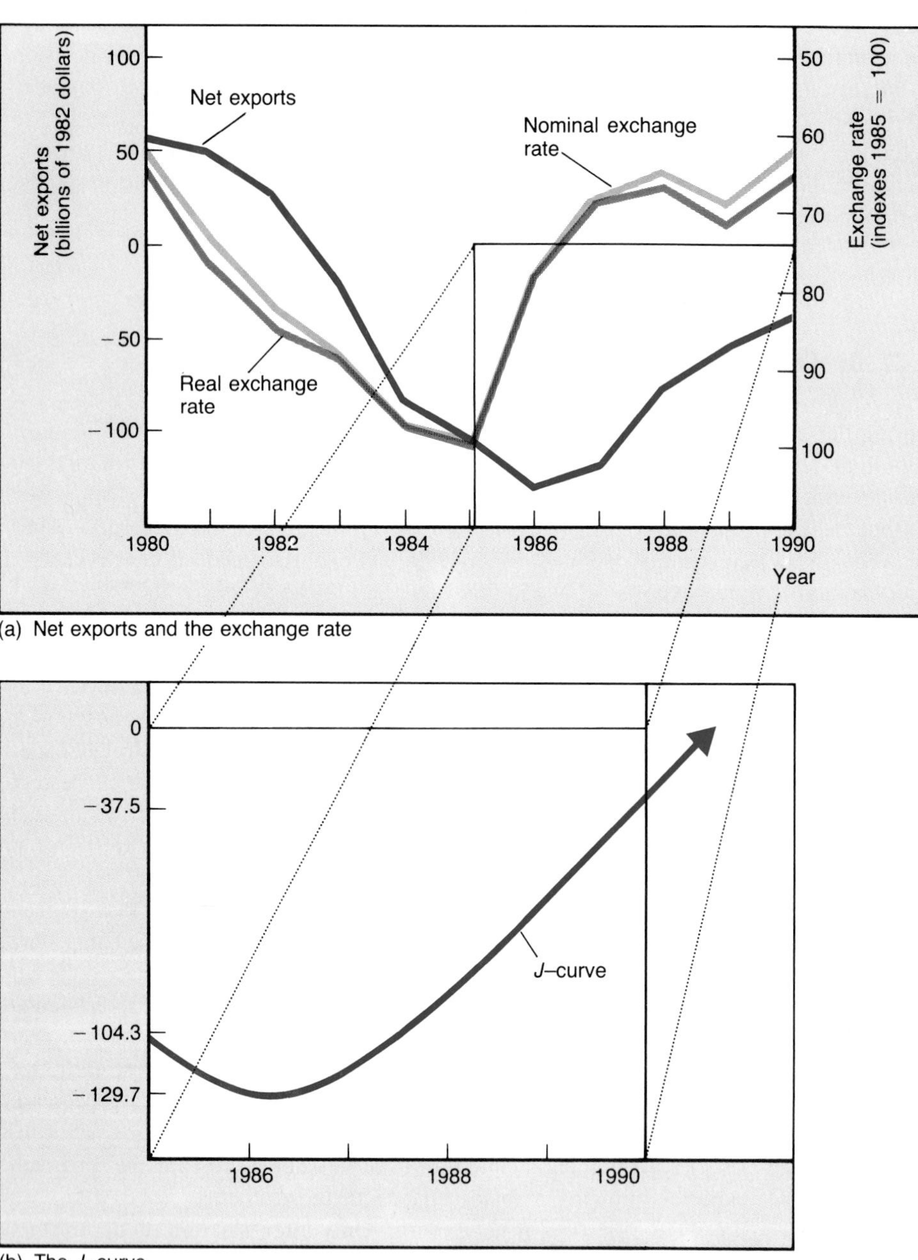

(a) Net exports and the exchange rate

(b) The *J*–curve

their response is small. They buy a similar quantity of goods and services but at a lower price. So U.S. exports fall. Eventually, as foreigners realize that U.S. goods and services are now cheaper, they start substituting more U.S. goods and services for those they have been buying and so eventually U.S. exports increase. You can see this *J*-curve response in U.S. net exports after 1985. It is highlighted in Figure 16.12(b). Eventually, if the adjustment process continues along the *J*-curve, net exports will return to zero in the early 1990s.

16.7 *The International Transmission of Disturbances*

So far in this chapter we've concentrated on the foreign exchange market and the balance of payments. Let's now examine how international disturbances are transmitted from one country to another and how they affect domestic output, interest rates, and prices. Since our focus here is on the search for global order, we'll concentrate on studying the influence of the choice of an exchange rate system on the international transmission of disturbances. Do flexible exchange rates enable countries to insulate themselves from international forces? Or do they bring additional problems and disturbances? Let's begin with fixed exchange rates.

International transmission under fixed exchange rates

A change in real GDP in one country influences economic activity in other countries initially through its effects on net exports. Let's see how such effects work out under fixed exchange rates. Suppose that Canada is in the situation described in Figure 16.13(a) on the black *IS* and *LM* curves. The world interest rate is 5 percent per year and interest rate parity[1] keeps the domestic rate at that level. Now suppose that there is a massive contraction in world economic activity that results in a decrease in Canadian exports. The *IS* curve shifts to the left, from IS_0 to IS_1. This immediately lowers Canadian interest rates to r_1 and real GDP to y_1. But, with a fixed exchange rate, that is not the end of the story. If the Canadian interest rate is below the world interest rate, capital will leave Canada. The foreign exchange reserves will be lost and the Canadian money supply will decrease. As it does so, the *LM* curve shifts from LM_0 to LM_1. In the process, the interest rate gradually increases but real GDP continues to fall further. The process comes to an end when real GDP has fallen to $3 billion and interest rates are back at 5 percent per year.

What would the same international shock have done to Canada under a flexible exchange rate regime?

International transmission with flexible exchange rates

This question is answered in Figure 16.13(b). Here, initial equilibrium is the same as in Figure 16.13(a) and it is disturbed by the same shock to the *IS* curve. But the *IS* curve under flexible exchange rates is less steep than under fixed exchange rates. The reason is that a decrease in the interest rate lowers the exchange rate, lowering the real exchange rate and increasing net exports. Thus there are two changes in net injections as we move down the *IS* curve. A lower interest rate increases investment, and a lower interest rate brings a lower exchange rate and increases net exports. When the *IS* curve shifts (by the same horizontal distance as in the previous case), the new *IS* curve intersects the *LM* curve at a lower interest rate and lower real GDP. But the fall in real GDP from $4.5 billion to y_1' is smaller than the initial decrease in real GDP under a fixed exchange rate. It is smaller because of the induced change in net exports resulting from the lower exchange rate. Furthermore, the decrease in real GDP to y_1' is the end of the process. With a flexible exchange rate, the monetary authority does not step in to defend the dollar, so the Canadian money supply does not decline. The *LM* curve remains at LM_0.

By comparing the two parts of Figure 16.13 you can see that a flexible exchange rate provides considerable immunity from fluctuations in net exports resulting from a

[1]See Chapter 7.

FIGURE 16.13
International Transmission of Disturbances

Under fixed exchange rates (part a), a world recession decreases net exports and shifts the *IS* curve to the left, from IS_0 to IS_1. Interest rates fall to r_1 and real GDP to y_1. Lower interest rates bring a capital outflow and a decrease in the money supply, shifting the *LM* curve to LM_1. Interest rates increase back to their world level and real GDP continues to fall to $3 billion.

Under flexible exchange rates (part b), the *IS* curve is more elastic than under fixed rates. A world recession shifts the *IS* curve to the left, real GDP falls, and the interest rate falls but the exchange rate also falls, lowering the real exchange rate and increasing net exports. The money supply is held constant, so the *LM* curve does not shift. The net effect on the domestic economy is smaller than under fixed exchange rates.

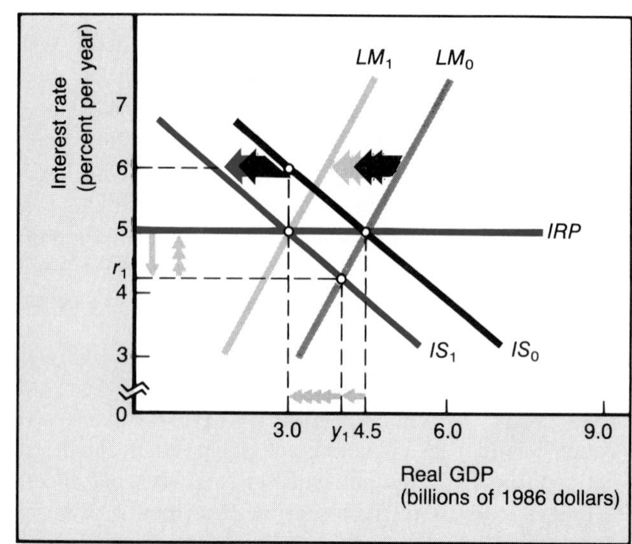

(a) Fixed exchange rate

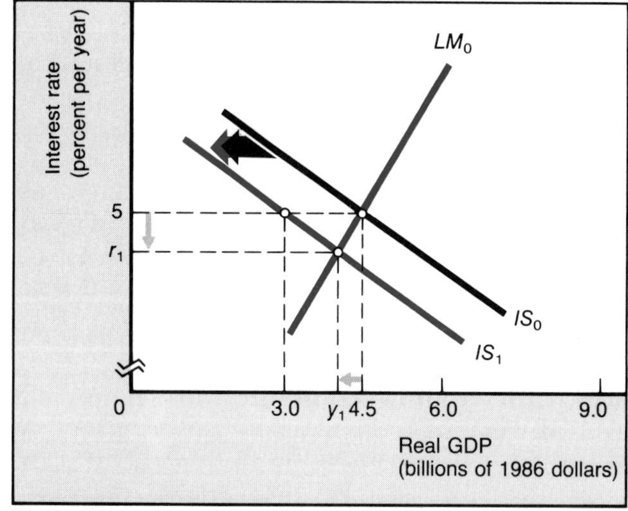

(b) Flexible exchange rate

business cycle contraction in the rest of the world. Does this mean that international transmission is less under flexible exchange rates and that there is only a world business cycle phenomenon under fixed exchange rates? The answer is no, for two reasons:

- Supply disturbances
- Exchange rate volatility

Supply disturbances

Disturbances to aggregate supply can have common effects by rippling around the world independently of the exchange rate regime. For example, an oil embargo that is imposed on all countries will influence real GDP in every country, regardless of whether the country has a flexible exchange rate. Flexible exchange rates insulate against aggregate demand disturbances only.

Exchange rate volatility

We've seen that under flexible exchange rates the exchange rate can overshoot changes in the price level, resulting in changes in the real exchange rate. Such changes in the real exchange rate bring fluctuations in net exports. These fluctuations, in turn, disturb real economic activity. This source of macroeconomic disturbance is absent in a fixed exchange rate world. Therefore it is possible that the world economy will be less stable under flexible exchange rates than under fixed exchange rates.

16.8 *The International Business Cycle—1960-1990*

TESTCASE

World macroeconomic history in the 30 years from 1960 to 1990 provides a useful laboratory in which to examine international transmission of economic disturbances under alternative exchange rate regimes. The 1960s was a decade of fixed exchange rates with aggregate demand disturbances. The 1970s was a decade of flexible exchange rates with aggregate supply shocks. The 1980s was a decade that opened with flexible exchange rates but that ended with greater exchange rate harmony.

Business cycles in the world's largest industrial economies over these three decades reveal some interesting patterns, as shown in Figure 16.14. Part (a) deals with the 1960s. As you can see, growth rates in this decade were highly divergent. Japan grew much more quickly than the other major countries. Also in this decade it is difficult to see any clear international business cycle. Real GDP growth rates fluctuated, but the fluctuations in one country did not line up with those in other countries. Perhaps this arose because, although in the 1960s exchange rates were fixed, for most of the decade there was some degree of international capital controls.

The 1970s, shown in part (b), was a decade in which there is a clear international business cycle. But the dominant feature of that cycle was the worldwide recession of 1974-1975 brought on by OPEC oil price shocks—supply shocks.

In the 1980s, shown in part (c), the international business cycle is not visible in the early 1980s. In the middle of the decade, however, after a greater measure of international policy coordination had been achieved, business fluctuations in the major countries did appear to line up with each other. But in 1989 and 1990, growth rates diverged again.

This quick tour of growth rates in the seven leading industrial countries suggests that the international business cycle is a complex phenomenon most visible when there are strong supply shocks and increasingly visible in the mid-1980s when monetary policy coordination was closer and the world economy became more highly integrated.

■ We've now studied the problems of stabilizing the world economy and the search for a global economic order. We have studied the interactions among economies under alternative exchange rate regimes and looked at the international transmission of economic disturbances. The global economy will continue to provide a rich research agenda, and the broadening of the world economy to include the Soviet Union and the former socialist countries of Eastern Europe will generate new and exciting challenges for macroeconomists. Their success in meeting those challenges will depend on the firmness of the microeconomic foundations on which macroeconomics is built. It is the study of these microfoundations that we turn to next in the final two parts of this book.

FIGURE 16.14
World Business Cycles: 1960-1990

Business cycle fluctuations were unsynchronized in the 1960s but became highly synchronized in the 1970s and late 1980s. The 1960s were dominated by aggregate demand shocks and exchange rates were fixed, but international capital controls and other impediments slowed the transmission of the business cycle. The 1970s recession was an aggregate supply shock common to all countries. The early 1980s was a period of flexible exchange rates with little coordination across countries of the business cycle, but the mid-1980s saw greater policy coordination and more perfect integration of the world economy, bringing closer harmony to the fluctuations in real GDP growth in the major countries. By the end of the 1980s and 1990, growth rates were diverging again.

Source: International Financial Statistics Yearbook, 1991.

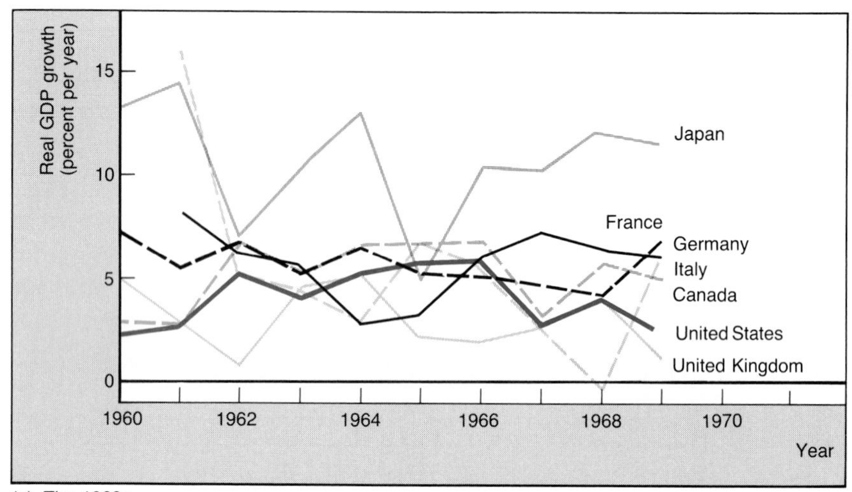

(a) The 1960s

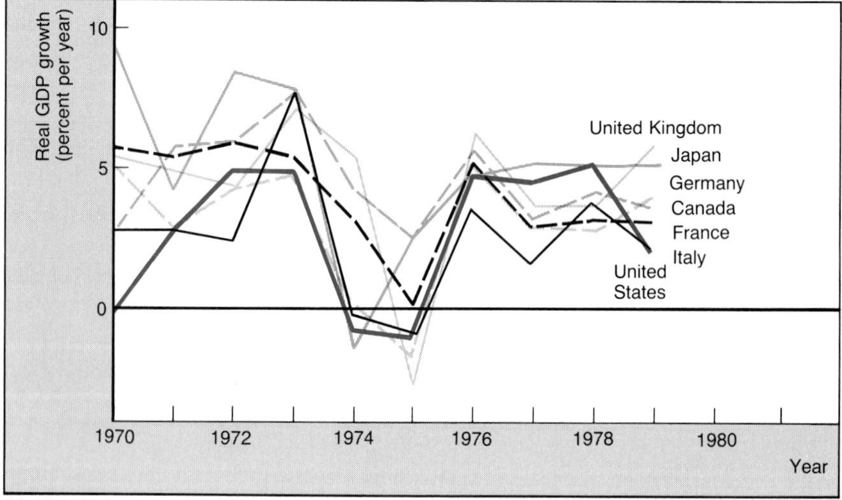

(b) The 1970s

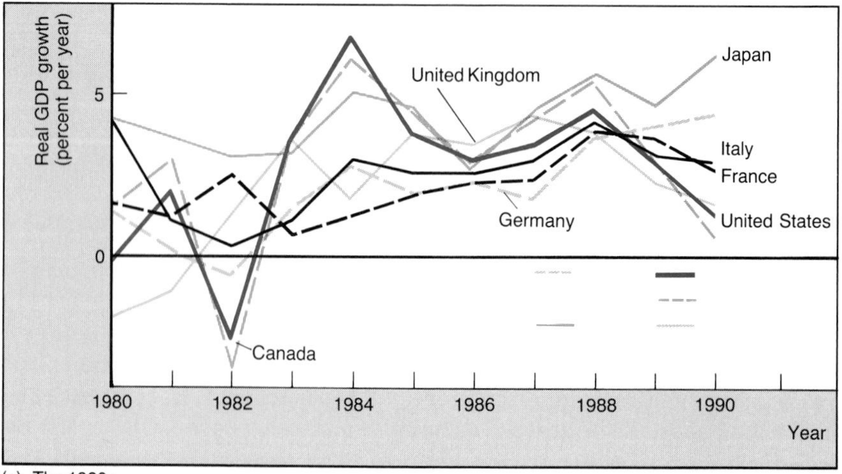

(c) The 1980s

CHAPTER REVIEW

Summary

MAIN TRENDS IN THE GLOBAL ECONOMY

The global economy has become more integrated over the years. Exports have increased steadily and current account imbalances, some of them large, have emerged. Exchange rates and real exchange rates have experienced large fluctuations, especially in the 1980s.

MAIN FEATURES OF THE INTERNATIONAL MONETARY SYSTEM

The international monetary system is one of managed-floating exchange rates with a limited measure of international policy coordination. The two main international institutions of the world monetary system are the International Monetary Fund and the World Bank. The International Monetary Fund provides assistance to countries with short-term balance of payments problems and the World Bank provides long-term financing to developing countries with chronic shortages of foreign exchange.

Important regional arrangements are emerging in the world monetary system, and the most important of these is the emergence of the European Monetary System.

EXCHANGE RATE DETERMINATION

Exchange rates are determined by equilibrium in the foreign exchange market. The quantity of dollar assets demanded depends on the exchange rate, the expected future exchange rate, and interest rates. The supply of dollar assets depends on the exchange rate regime in place. With a fixed exchange rate, the supply is perfectly elastic; with a flexible exchange rate, the supply is perfectly inelastic; with a managed-floating exchange rate, the supply is upward sloping. Fluctuations in the demand for dollar assets bring fluctuations in the exchange rate, fluctuations in the quantity of dollar assets in existence, or both, depending on the exchange rate regime. Fixed exchange rates are not necessarily less volatile than flexible exchange rates. They are if they're pegged at credible levels but not otherwise. A change in the supply of dollar assets changes the exchange rate and the exchange rate overshoots its long-run equilibrium value, bringing changes in the real exchange rate en route.

THE U.S. DOLLAR-YEN EXCHANGE RATE IN THE 1980s

Movements in the U.S. dollar-yen exchange rate in the 1980s are determined mainly by differences in monetary policy in the United States and Japan. Other things being equal, an increase in the money supply growth rate in the United States tends to depreciate the U.S. dollar while an increase in the money supply growth rate in Japan tends to bring an appreciation of the U.S. dollar. Higher interest rates in the United States relative to Japan tend to bring an appreciation (or slow the depreciation) of the U.S. dollar. Movements in the U.S. dollar-yen exchange rate quite closely match movements in monetary policy differences and interest rate differences in the first half of the 1980s but less strongly in the second half of the decade.

BALANCE OF PAYMENTS

Net exports are strongly influenced by the real exchange rate. A change in the real exchange rate changes the relative price of exports and imports. The higher the real exchange rate, the larger is the Canadian demand for foreign goods and services and the smaller is the world demand for Canadian-made goods and services. In other words, the higher the real exchange rate, the lower are net exports. A change in the exchange rate does not bring an immediate change in net exports. In the short run, the quantities of goods and services purchased change by a smaller amount than do prices, so net exports move in the direction opposite to the exchange rate, giving rise to the so-called *J*-curve effect. The current account of the balance of payments can influence exchange rates through expectations of future exchange rate changes.

PAYMENTS IMBALANCES IN THE 1980s

The emergence of a large net export deficit in the United States in the 1980s is well accounted for by the steady strengthening of the U.S. dollar in the first half of that decade. The continued increase in the net export deficit in 1986 after the dollar began to depreciate is part of the *J*-curve phenomenon.

GLOBAL BUSINESS CYCLE AND INTERNATIONAL TRANSMISSION

A change in aggregate demand in one country transmits itself to other countries through its effects on net exports. Under fixed exchange rates, the international transmission is much stronger than under flexible exchange rates. However, supply shocks influence all economies, regardless of the exchange rate regime. In the world economy, there was no clear world business cycle in the 1960s, even though exchange rates were fixed. The likely reason is that international capital controls and trade restrictions reduced the strength of the international transmission effects. In the 1970s, the world business cycle was dominated by the supply shock of the mid-1970s. In the 1980s, there was little sign of a worldwide business cycle in the early part of the decade when exchange rates were flexible, but in the second half of the decade, as monetary policies became more closely coordinated and exchange rates more closely managed, a world business cycle appears to have emerged.

Key Terms and Concepts

Devaluation A decrease in the value of a fixed exchange rate.

International gold standard A monetary system in which most major countries fix the value of their currency in terms of gold and permit gold to freely enter and leave the country.

International monetary system A set of arrangements and institutions for governing the financial relations among countries.

***J*-curve** The time path followed by net exports following a major change in the exchange rate.

Quantity of dollar assets demanded The quantity of net financial assets denominated in Canadian dollars that people plan to hold at a given point in time.

Quantity of dollar assets supplied The quantity of net financial assets denominated in Canadian dollars available to be held at a point in time.

Revaluation An increase in the value of a fixed exchange rate.

Review Questions

1. What is a fixed exchange rate system? Describe the Bretton Woods system, including when it existed and why it came to an end.
2. Explain why the International Monetary Fund and the World Bank were established.

3. What is a managed-floating exchange rate system?
4. What is the role of the International Monetary Fund and the World Bank in the managed-floating exchange rate system of the 1990s?
5. Describe the European Monetary System. Compare the European Monetary System with the Bretton Woods System.
6. Describe the market in which the exchange rate between the French franc and the Canadian dollar is determined. Draw a diagram to illustrate.
7. In question 6, explain why the demand curve slopes downward.
8. In question 6, explain what determines the slope of the supply curve.
9. In question 6, which variables influence demand? And which variables influence supply?
10. What is a revaluation? How does it differ from an appreciation? Use your diagram in question 6 to contrast a revaluation and an appreciation of the franc.
11. Draw a diagram of the foreign exchange market and use it to show the effect of a revaluation on the quantity of assets denominated in domestic currency in existence.
12. In a flexible exchange rate, explain how the Bank of Canada's monetary policy affects the value of the Canadian dollar on foreign exchange markets.
13. Explain what is meant by exchange rate overshooting. When does the exchange rate overshoot? What does it overshoot? Draw a diagram to illustrate.
14. Under a managed-floating exchange rate, explain why the Bank of Canada's monetary policy affects the value of the Canadian dollar on foreign exchange markets.
15. Describe the movements of the yen-U.S. dollar exchange rate during the 1980s. Is it possible to explain why this foreign exchange rate changed so much in this period?
16. What is a real exchange rate? What does it measure?
17. Explain the effects of exchange rate changes on the balance of payments.
18. Explain the effects of the balance of payments on the exchange rate.
19. What is a *J*-curve? What does it illustrate?
20. Explain how the international transmission of disturbances takes place. How does the degree of transmission relate to the exchange rate regime?

Problems

1. Explain the role of the United States Federal Reserve under the Bretton Woods system. Explain how the Bank of England operated under the Bretton Woods system to maintain the British pound-U.S. dollar exchange rate that it chose.
2. How does the Bank of Canada manage the foreign exchange value of the Canadian dollar under the managed-floating exchange rate regime?
3. Under which exchange rate regime do fluctuations in the demand for assets denominated in British pounds create the largest fluctuations in the pound-U.S. dollar exchange rate, expressed as U.S. dollars per pound? Explain your answer.
4. Under what conditions would a revaluation be credible? Explain your answer.
5. What is a devaluation? Under what conditions would a devaluation be unsustainable?
6. Explain why the exchange rate overshoots. What triggers exchange rate overshooting? What happens to the price level and real exchange rate as the exchange rate overshoots?

7. Which exchange rate regime insulates the domestic economy most from international shocks? Explain how this insulation occurs.
8. In a fixed exchange rate regime, can the central bank in South Korea lessen the immediate effect of major recession in the rest of the world on the South Korean economy? Explain your answer.
9. In the late 1960s, expansionary monetary policy in the United States put pressure on Germany to revalue its currency on foreign exchange markets. Explain why this pressure to revalue emerged. Germany resisted the pressure to revalue its currency. Why might Germany have chosen not to revalue?
10. In recent years, an international business cycle appears to have emerged. What do you think explains its appearance?

VI

Microfoundations of Aggregate Demand

C H A P T E R

17 Consumption and Saving

SPREADING THE PAIN AND GAIN

PEOPLE TEND TO BE IMPATIENT, preferring good things to happen sooner rather than later and preferring bad things to happen later rather than sooner. But people also tend to be realists. They recognize that they can't live on a permanent high and forever put off until tomorrow the costs and evils they would like to avoid. The day of reckoning always arrives. Because of this recognition of reality—actually, a recognition of the pervasiveness of scarcity—people have to choose *when* to enjoy the good things of life and when to pay for them. They also have to take into account the opportunity cost of consuming good things early and putting off bad things until later. In making their choices, people balance the desire to consume early and pay later against the higher opportunity cost of such an action. It turns out to be efficient for people to smooth their consumption and work activities, preferring a smooth or steady path of consumption and work effort to a highly variable one.

These facts have important implications for macroeconomic behavior. Individuals' decisions about the timing of consumption, saving, and work have important implications for fluctuations in aggregate demand and aggregate supply and, therefore, in aggregate economic activity. In this chapter we'll study these decisions, probing the choices of individual households and the timing problems they have to solve concerning when to consume, save, and work. We'll also examine the macroeconomic implications of these microeconomic decisions.

This is the first of three chapters that probe the microeconomic foundations of the theory of aggregate demand. These microfoundations provide a richer and deeper understanding of the forces at work creating business cycles and an uneven pace of macroeconomic expansion.

After studying this chapter, you will be able to

- Describe the main facts about consumption, saving, and income, both over time and across income groups
- Describe a household's intertemporal and lifetime budget constraints
- Explain how consumption and saving decisions are made
- Define permanent income and explain the permanent income hypothesis
- Explain the life-cycle hypothesis
- Explain the behavior of consumption and saving in Canada and other countries in the 1980s
- Explain the effects of taxes on consumption and saving
- Explain the effects of money and credit on consumption and saving

17.1 Consumption and Saving in Canada

MACROFACTS

We've already met some facts about Canadian consumption and saving in Chapter 4, where we studied the consumption function. We'll look at them again here. But we'll also look at some additional facts and place those earlier facts in a broader context, posing some questions about Canadian consumption and saving that this chapter will answer.

In studying the facts about consumption and saving, we distinguish between two kinds of data:

- Time-series data
- Cross-section data

Time-series data

Time-series data record the values of variables over time—from one quarter or year to the next. Time-series data can be used to calculate a consumption function—a relationship between personal consumer expenditure and personal disposable income. Figure 17.1(a) shows the raw data on the relationship between these two variables for each year between 1926 and 1990. Each year is identified with a dot, and some of the years have

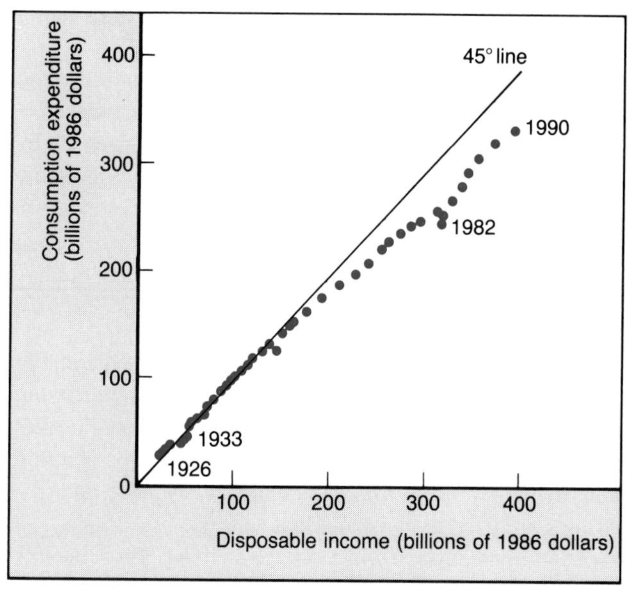

(a) Consumption expenditure and disposable income

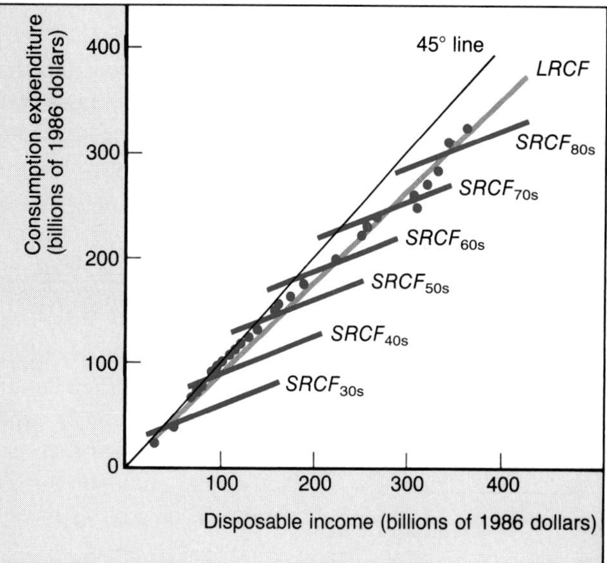

(b) Long–run and short–run consumption functions

FIGURE 17.1
Time-Series Consumption Functions

The time-series data on consumer expenditure and personal disposable income are shown in part (a). Each point represents consumer expenditure and personal disposable income in a given year. (Some years are identified.) These points lie on a long-run consumption function (*LRCF*), shown in part (b). The slope of *LRCF* is 0.85, indicating a marginal propensity to consume of 0.85. Over shorter periods, there is a sequence of short-run consumption functions (*SRCF*), six of which are illustrated in the figure.

Source: National Income and Expenditure Accounts, Statistics Canada, Catalogue 13-201, and our calculations.

been identified in the figure. As we saw in Chapter 4, these data do not describe a simple, single consumption function. In fact, it is useful to distinguish between two consumption functions in the time-series data:

- The long-run consumption function
- The short-run consumption function

Long-run consumption function The long-run consumption function is the average relationship between real personal consumer expenditure and real personal disposable income over a long period of time. This consumption function is illustrated in Figure 17.1(b). The long-run consumption function starts out at the origin and has a slope of 0.85. That is, in the long run, the marginal propensity to consume is 0.85. In other words, on the average, 85 percent of real personal disposable income is spent on consumption goods and services. The other 15 percent is saved.

Short-run consumption function The long-run consumption function shown in Figure 17.1(b) is not a good description of the relationship between real personal consumer expenditure and real personal disposable income over shorter periods. The year-to-year changes in these two variables are better described by a short-run consumption function. Figure 17.1(b) illustrates six of these short-run consumption functions, one for each decade since the 1930s. The short-run consumption function is flatter than the long-run consumption function; it has a marginal propensity to consume of about 0.7. Furthermore, the short-run consumption function shifts upward over time as autonomous personal consumer expenditure—that part of consumer expenditure that does not vary with income—increases over time.

The facts about the time-series relationships between consumer expenditure and disposable income raise two main questions. First, why is the short-run marginal propensity to consume less than the long-run marginal propensity to consume? Second, why does the short-run consumption function shift upward over time? We'll look at some answers to these questions later in the chapter. Next, let's consider the cross-section facts.

Cross-section data

Cross-section data record the level of consumer expenditure at each level of income at a point in time. When families with different income levels are studied, the relationship between the consumer expenditure and disposable income of these different families gives rise to a cross-section consumption function. Figure 17.2 shows the cross-section consumption function for Canada, using data for 1982. Consumer expenditure and disposable income of six income groups are used to construct that figure.

Two features of the cross-section consumption function are striking. First, at low income levels families consume more than their disposable income. At a disposable income of a little more than $10,000 a year, consumer expenditure equals income. Second, the consumption function is not a straight line. It becomes flatter as disposable income increases. This fact implies that the marginal propensity to consume declines as income increases. The marginal propensity to consume is 0.84 between the lowest and second-lowest income levels but only 0.51 between the second-highest and highest income levels. The declining magnitude of the marginal propensity to consume is shown in the figure.

These facts about the cross-section relationship between consumer expenditure and income raise two further questions. First, why does the marginal propensity to consume decrease as disposable income increases? Second, what is the relationship between the

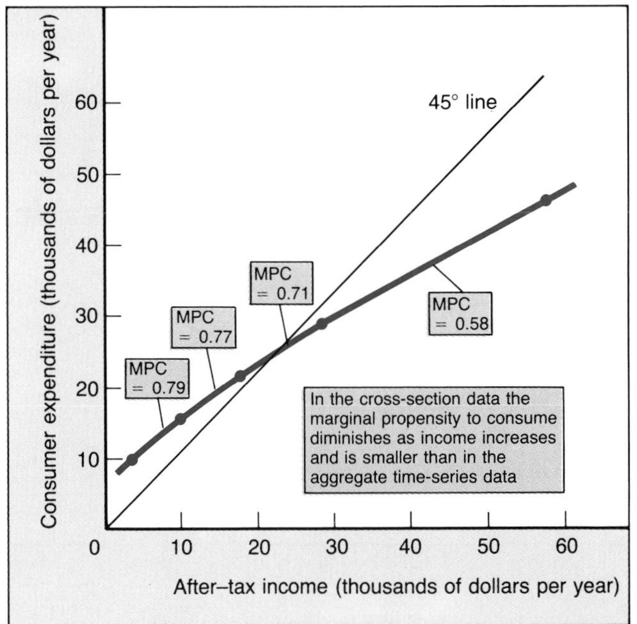

FIGURE 17.2
The Cross-Section Consumption Function

The average income of six income groups, together with the consumer expenditure of these income groups, is shown in the figure. The relationship plots the cross-section consumption function *CSCF*. In the cross-section data, the marginal propensity to consume decreases as disposable income increases.

Source: Family Expenditure in Canada, Statistics Canada.

cross-section consumption function and the time-series consumption function? In particular, how is it possible for the long-run marginal propensity to consume to be 0.85 when the short-run marginal propensity to consume is only 0.7 and the cross-section marginal propensity to consume is even lower than that. We'll look at some answers to these questions later in the chapter.

Saving So far we've looked at the relationship between consumer expenditure and income. But this relationship implies another relationship — one between saving and income. Saving is defined as disposable income minus consumer expenditure. Thus we can examine the relationship between saving and disposable income — the saving function — in much the same way as we looked at the consumption function in Figures 17.1 and 17.2. However, there is no additional information in looking at the saving function. As you saw in Figure 4.3, a given consumption function implies a particular saving function.

But some important and interesting facts about saving do not immediately stand out from what we've already looked at. These facts concern the percentage of personal income saved in Canada. In recent years this percentage has become quite low, as Figure 17.3 illustrates. As you can see, the percentage of personal disposable income saved increased between 1960 and 1982 from about 4 percent to almost 18 percent. But since 1982 the saving rate has fallen, bottoming out at 9 percent of personal disposable income in 1987.

Personal saving is not total saving. It is, however, an important component of total saving. It's important to understand, therefore, why the personal saving rate declined so steeply between 1982 and 1987. We'll also examine this question later in this chapter.

Keep these facts about consumption, income, and saving in mind as you study the micro foundations of consumption and saving choices in the rest of this chapter.

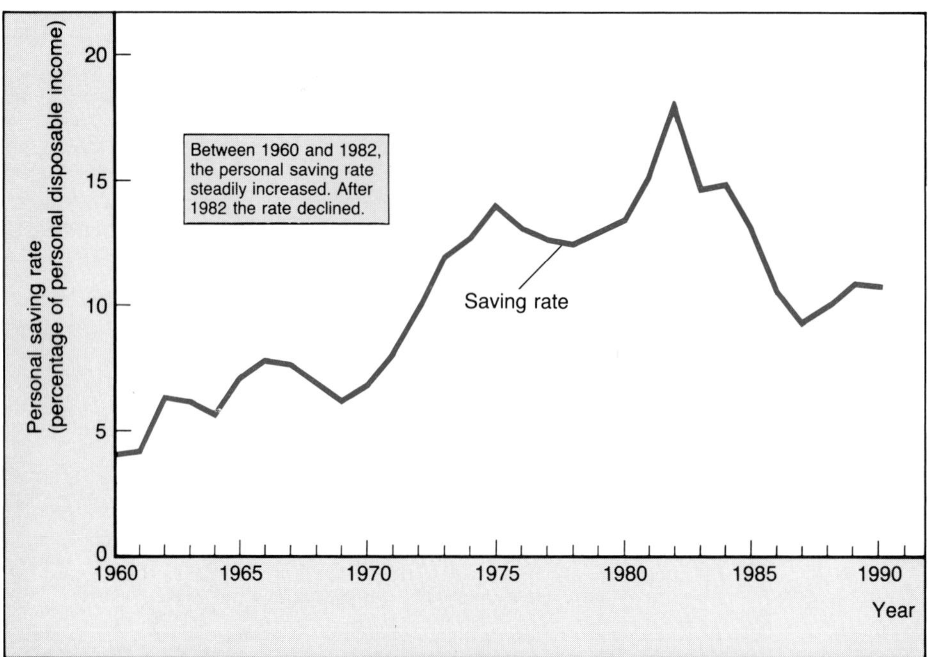

FIGURE 17.3
The Declining Rate of Personal Saving

Personal saving in Canada was on an upward trend between 1960 and 1982. Since then, it has been on a downward trend.

Source: National Income and Expenditure Accounts, Statistics Canada, Catalogue 13-201.

17.2 *The Household's Intertemporal and Lifetime Budget Constraints*

You first met the idea of the *intertemporal budget constraint* in Chapter 13, where we studied government deficits. Here we're going to apply the same intertemporal budget constraint to the choices of households. For any household, its consumer expenditure plus its assets at the end of the year cannot exceed the assets with which it started the year, the interest it earned on those assets, and the labor income it earned during the year. Let's call consumer expenditure C, assets A, labor income YL, and the interest rate r, and denote the year by the subscript t and the following year by the subscript $t + 1$. Then the intertemporal budget constraint is

$$C_t + A_{t+1} \leq YL_t + (1 + r)A_t. \quad \textbf{(17.1)}$$

Income and expenditure accounts The household's intertemporal budget constraint is closely connected with its income and expenditure account (that you studied in Chapter 2). There we call the household income Y, consumption (as here) C, and saving S. The household's income and expenditure account (ignoring taxes) is summarized in the proposition that income equals consumption plus saving. That is,

$$Y_t = C_t + S_t. \quad \textbf{(17.2)}$$

In the household's intertemporal budget constraint, its income is its labor income (YL_t) and its income from assets (rA_t). Thus the household's total income is

$$Y_t = YL_t + r_t A_t. \quad \textbf{(17.3)}$$

The household's saving is the change in the value of its assets. That is,

$$S_t = A_{t+1} - A_t. \tag{17.4}$$

Substitute the household's income ($YL_t + r_t A_t$) plus saving ($A_{t+1} - A_t$) into its income and expenditure account ($Y_t = C_t + S_t$) and you get the intertemporal budget constraint.

The household's intertemporal budget constraint is just one of a sequence of identical constraints that apply to each year. But the sequence of intertemporal budget constraints is linked by the fact that assets carried forward from year t to year $t + 1$ are the assets that earn interest in $t + 1$. Thus decisions made in the current year affect the total income earned in the following year (or years) and therefore the consumer expenditure that can be sustained.

It is easiest to work out the implications of the linkages between the sequence of intertemporal budget constraints by studying a household that lives for just two periods. This case is not "realistic" but it contains all the elements of the real-world situation.

A household with a two-period life

Our goal is to work out the household's **lifetime budget constraint** — the limits to a household's consumption over its lifetime. We'll establish the household's lifetime budget constraint by examining its sequence of intertemporal budget constraints, each describing the limits on a household's choices in any given period. To make the ideas as clear as possible, we'll work through an actual numerical example. Table 17.1 sets out the example, together with the general case using symbols. Part (a) defines the variables that feature in an intertemporal budget constraint — the household's initial assets, its labor income in the two years, the interest rate it can earn on its assets, its consumption choices in the two years, and its assets at the end of the first year. The household is assumed to have no control over the interest rate and over its labor income in each year.

TABLE 17.1
The Intertemporal and Lifetime Budget Constraints

ITEM	SYMBOLS AND EQUATIONS	NUMERICAL EXAMPLE
(a) Definitions		
Initial assets	A_0	0
Labor income in year 1	YL_1	\$50,000
Labor income in year 2	YL_2	\$55,000
Interest rate	r	0.10 (10 percent)
Consumer expenditure in year 1	C_1	Household's choice
Consumer expenditure in year 2	C_2	Household's choice
Assets at end of year 1	A_1	Household's choice
(b) Year 1 constraint	$C_1 + A_1 \leq YL_1 + (1 + r) A_0$	$C_1 + A_1 \leq \$50{,}000$
(c) Year 2 constraint	$C_2 \leq YL_2 + (1 + r) A_1$	$C_2 \leq \$55{,}000 + (1 + r) A_1$
(d) Lifetime constraint		
Assets at end of year 1	$A_1 = YL_1 - C_1$	$A_1 = \$50{,}000 - C_1$
Substitute into year 2 constraint to give	$C_2 \leq YL_2 + (1 + r)(YL_1 - C_1)$	
Maximum possible consumer expenditure in year 2	$C_2 = YL_2 + (1 + r) YL_1$	$C_2 = \$55{,}000 + (1 + 0.10) \$50{,}000 = \$110{,}000$
Change in C_2 resulting from an increase in C_1	$\Delta C_2 = -(1 + r) \Delta C_1$	$\Delta C_2 = -1.1 \Delta C_1$

It is possible to relax the assumption of no control over labor income by letting the household make an intertemporal choice about how much work to do and when to do it. But here we'll ignore that choice and focus just on its consumption and saving decisions, given its labor income each year. Thus the household chooses its consumer expenditure each year and the assets to hold at the end of year 1.

Part (b) of the table sets out the household's intertemporal budget constraint in year 1. In our example, the household begins year 1 with no assets and earns a labor income of \$50,000 in the year. Thus the maximum amount of consumer expenditure C_1 and assets bought A_1 in year 1 is \$50,000. Part (c) of the table shows the household's budget constraint in year 2. In that year, the maximum amount of consumer expenditure C_2 equals its labor income that year (\$55,000) plus the assets that it carried forward from year 1 and the interest earned on those assets.

Part (d) of the table works out the lifetime budget constraint. It starts by noting that the assets available to the household at the end of year 1 are equal to its labor income that year minus its consumer expenditure that year. Using this fact to substitute for assets in year 1 in the budget constraint in year 2 gives the next line of the table — consumer expenditure in year 2 cannot exceed labor income in year 2 plus the interest earned on assets bought in year 1. The assets bought in year 1 equals saving in that year (labor income minus consumer expenditure, $YL_1 - C_1$). This equation describes the limits to the household's lifetime consumption. Its lifetime consumption — consumption in years 1 and 2—is limited by its labor income in years 1 and 2 and the interest rate.

We can calculate the household's maximum possible consumer expenditure in year 2 by setting its consumer expenditure in year 1 equal to zero. Maximum consumer expenditure in year 2 equals the household's labor income in year 2 plus its labor income in year 1 and the interest on that income. For each additional unit of consumer expenditure in year 1, the household must decrease its consumer expenditure in year 2. You can work out by how much by using the lifetime budget constraint. A one-dollar increase in consumer expenditure in year 1 results in a $(1 + r)$-dollar decrease in consumer expenditure in year 2. Thus extra consumer expenditure in the present results in a larger decrease in consumer expenditure in the future. The reason is that anything not consumed in the first year earns interest, and so the amount not consumed plus the interest on it can be consumed in the second year. Allocating one extra dollar to consumer expenditure in the present reduces future consumer expenditure by the dollar plus the interest that could have been earned on that dollar. Thus one plus the interest rate is the opportunity cost of future consumption. It is the intertemporal relative price of consumption.

The lifetime budget line We can illustrate the lifetime budget constraint by a lifetime budget line such as shown in Figure 17.4. Point E shows the household's **endowment**, the labor income the household will receive each period of its life. If the household's consumer expenditure each year equals its entire labor income in that year — consumer expenditure in year 1 is \$50,000 and in year 2 it is \$55,000, then point E is a point on its lifetime budget line. By decreasing consumer expenditure in year 1, the household can increase its consumer expenditure in year 2. If it decreases its consumer expenditure in year 1 to zero, consumer expenditure in year 2 will be \$110,000, point A in the figure. By decreasing future consumption, the household can increase current consumption. But there is a maximum to what can be consumed in year 1. In our example, the maximum is \$100,000, labor income of \$50,000 year 1, plus \$50,000 that can be borrowed against next year's labor income. \$50,000 is the maximum that can be borrowed against next year's labor income because, at an interest rate of 10 percent a year, the household will have to pay back \$55,000, which equals the household's labor income in year 2. The line AB is the household's lifetime budget constraint.

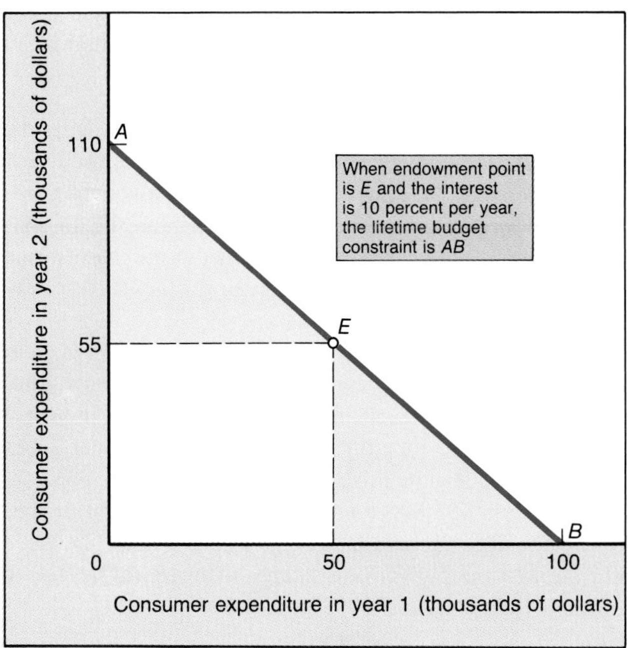

FIGURE 17.4
Lifetime Budget Constraint

A household receives a labor income of $50,000 in year 1 and $55,000 in year 2. Its endowment point is *E*. With a 10 percent interest rate, the household could consume zero in year 1, receive $5,000 of interest on its saving, and consume $110,000 in year 2 (point *A*). Alternatively, the household could borrow $50,000 against its labor income in year 2, committing itself to repaying the $50,000 plus $5,000 interest. In this case, it could consume $100,000 in year 1 at point *B*. The household can choose to consume at any point along the line *AB*, its lifetime budget constraint. A household's lifetime budget constraint passes through its endowment point and its slope is determined by the interest rate.

Wealth We defined *wealth* in Chapter 2 as the difference between total assets and total liabilities. Another way of defining wealth is the maximum amount that can be consumed in the current period if nothing is consumed in later periods. The two definitions are equivalent. The difference between a household's total assets and total liabilities is its maximum amount of consumer expenditure in the present if it consumes nothing in the future. But the second (new) definition is interesting because we can illustrate it in Figure 17.4. The wealth of this household is *B*, the point on the horizontal axis hit by the lifetime budget line. Point *B* indicates the maximum amount of consumer expenditure that can be undertaken in year 1 if no consumer expenditure takes place in year 2.

In Figure 17.4, the household's wealth is determined by the formula

$$\text{Wealth} = YL_1 + \frac{YL_2}{(1 + r)}. \qquad \textbf{(17.5)}$$

This formula emphasizes that wealth is the present value of current and future labor income. The **present value** of a future sum of money is the amount that, if invested now at the interest rate r, would accumulate to the future sum over a given number of years.

Another name for the present value of current and future labor income is **human capital**. That is, human capital is valued as the sum of money that, if invested today at the going interest rate, would yield an income stream permitting the household to consume along exactly the same path that is possible from its future stream of labor income.

Other components of wealth The household illustrated in Figure 17.4 has only one type of wealth—human capital. It begins its life with no other assets. If the household did have other assets, they would be part of its wealth. Wealth consists of human capital and of other types of assets, both financial and real. If the household has such other assets, its lifetime budget line will lie farther to the right than the one shown in Figure 17.4.

Changing constraints

The lifetime budget constraint is influenced by two things: the interest rate and labor income. Let's see how a change in either of these variables changes the lifetime budget constraint and shifts the lifetime budget line.

A change in the interest rate A change in the interest rate twists the lifetime budget line on the endowment point. It's obvious that the interest rate makes no difference to the maximum that can be consumed if the household neither borrows nor accumulates assets. Thus if the household is at its endowment point, the interest rate does not influence its consumer expenditure in each year. This tells us that as the interest rate changes the lifetime budget rotates on the endowment point. The lower the interest rate, the flatter is the lifetime budget line.

Figure 17.5(a) illustrates a decrease in the interest rate where, to make things clear and simple, the interest rate falls from 10 percent a year to zero. At a zero interest rate, even if the household consumes nothing in year 1, its maximum consumption in year 2 will be its labor income of $55,000 in year 2 plus the $50,000 it saved in year 1 — a total of $105,000. But the household can consume this same amount in year 1, using its labor income of $50,000 in year 1 plus a $55,000 loan at the zero interest rate. Thus with a zero interest rate, the lifetime budget line is *A′B′*. A higher interest rate, between 0 and 10 percent a year, makes the lifetime budget line steeper than *AB* and rotate on the endowment point, *E*. It will lie between *AB* and *A′B′*.

Change in labor income With a constant interest rate, a change in labor income shifts the lifetime budget line parallel to itself. Figure 17.5(b) illustrates the effects of a 10 percent increase in each year's labor income. Labor income increases to $60,000 in year 1 and $66,000 in year 2, so the endowment point moves to *E′*. Maximum consump-

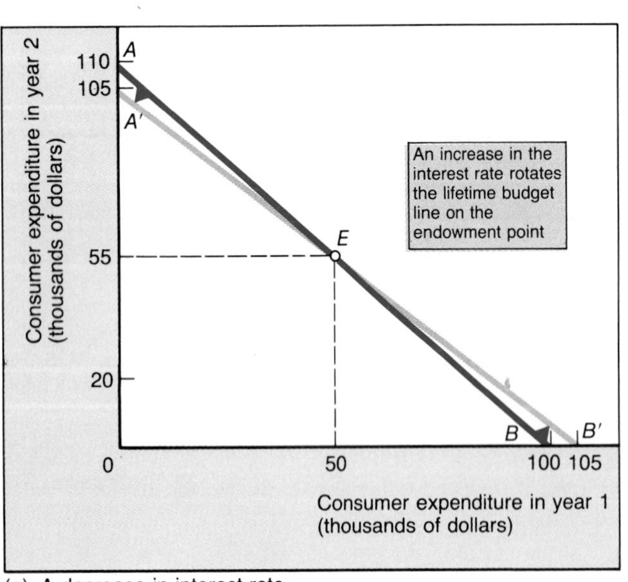

(a) A decrease in interest rate

(b) An increase in income

FIGURE 17.5
Changes in the Lifetime Budget Constraint

A change in the interest rate (part a) rotates the lifetime budget line on the endowment point. The lower the interest rate, the flatter is the lifetime budget line. An increase in income (part b) in either or both years shifts the budget line outward but leaves its slope unchanged.

tion in year 2 with no consumption in year 1 is $132,000, and maximum consumption in year 1 with no consumption in year 2 is $120,000. An increase in labor income shifts the lifetime budget line out to the right. Alternatively, a decrease in labor income shifts the lifetime budget line inward.

17.3 *Consumption and Saving Choice*

To decide how much of its current income to consume and how much to save, the household must evaluate the alternative possibilities and pick the best one. The household's lifetime budget line describes the possibilities. The evaluation of the alternatives is based on the household's preferences. *Preferences* are represented by indifference curves in the same way as indifference curves are used in microeconomics to describe a household's preferences for apples and oranges. Here, the household's preferences are for consumption in year 1 versus consumption in year 2. Consumption in any year is a good and, other things being equal, the household prefers more goods to fewer goods in any year. An indifference curve such as I_1 in Figure 17.6(a) shows the combinations of consumption in year 1 and consumption in year 2 among which the household is indifferent. Combinations lying above that indifference curve are preferred to all combinations on that indifference curve. Combinations lying below that indifference curve, such

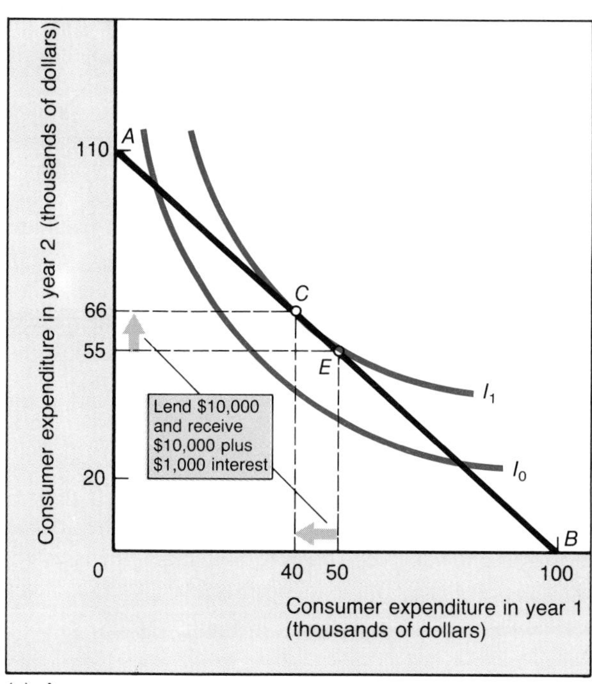

(a) A saver

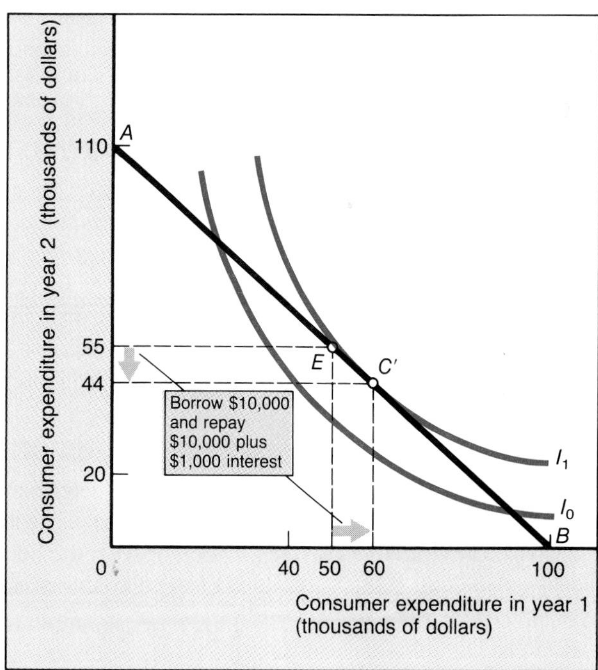

(b) A dissaver

FIGURE 17.6
Consumption and Saving Decisions

Consumption and saving decisions are determined by preferences summarized in indifference curves such as those shown here. In part (a), the household is a saver. Its best affordable consumption point is *C* on indifference curve I_1. The household consumes $40,000 in year 1 and saves $10,000. In year 2, it consumes its $55,000 income plus its saving of $10,000 and the interest received of $1,000.

In part (b), the household is a dissaver. It consumes at point *C′* on indifference curve I_1. In year 1, the household borrows $10,000 and in year 2, it repays that loan together with $1,000 of interest. In year 2, its consumption is $11,000 less than its income at $44,000.

as those along the curve I_0, are regarded by the household as less desirable than those along I_1.

The slope of the household's indifference curve equals the household's **marginal rate of intertemporal substitution** — the amount of future consumption the household is willing to give up in order to have one additional unit of current consumption. Indifference curves bow toward the origin, indicating that the marginal rate of intertemporal substitution diminishes. The more current consumption a household has, other things being equal, the smaller the amount of future consumption it is willing to give up in order to increase its present consumption.

To characterize a household's choice of consumption and saving we need to distinguish between two possible cases:

- Saver/lender
- Dissaver/borrower

Saver/lender

Figure 17.6(a) illustrates a household that saves some of its current income and lends it to others. The household's endowment point is E and its lifetime budget is AB. The household chooses its most preferred combination of consumption in year 1 and in year 2, given its lifetime budget constraint. The most preferred combination is at point C. The household spends \$40,000 out of its \$50,000 income in year 1 on consumption and lends \$10,000. In year 2, its consumer expenditure is \$66,000 — the \$55,000 labor income in year 2 plus a \$10,000 loan that is repaid plus the \$1,000 interest earned on the loan. Over the household's lifetime, no other allocation of its income dominates this particular one.

Dissaver/borrower

Figure 17.6(b) illustrates a household that dissaves and borrows. This household has the same endowment as in part (a), point E, but its preferences — indifference curves — are different. This household's most preferred combination of consumption in year 1 and in year 2 is point C'. In year 1, the household borrows \$10,000 and so its consumer expenditure is \$60,000. Then in year 2, it repays the \$10,000 borrowed and the \$1,000 of interest and spends \$44,000 on consumption. Given the household's preferences, the combination of consumption in year 1 and year 2 shown by C' is the best possible.

Fundamental determinants of choice

The fundamental determinants of the household's intertemporal choices are its preferences and lifetime budget line. The household's preferences are given. They are a description of what the household is trying to achieve. The lifetime budget line is determined by economic forces. Two key variables determine its position:

- Endowment
- Interest rate

Endowment A household's endowment is the sequence of labor income payments it will receive over its lifetime. In our example there are just two such payments, labor income in year 1 and labor income in year 2. In general, a household will have an income stream over each year in its life. It may also have some assets at the beginning of its life (in our example, we assumed these to be zero). The lifetime budget line passes through the household's endowment point. So the household's endowment determines how far from the origin its lifetime budget line is. The larger its endowment, the farther to the right is its lifetime budget line.

Interest rate The second determinant of the lifetime budget line is the interest rate. The higher the interest rate, the steeper is the budget line. But the line always passes through the endowment point.

Changes in the interest rate and changes in endowment lead to changes in the household's consumption and saving choices. Let's see how.

The effect of interest rates on household choices

The effect of interest rate changes on consumption choices has two components:

- A substitution effect
- A wealth effect

Substitution effect The *substitution effect* is the change in current consumption resulting from a change in the interest rate when there is a compensating change in wealth that leaves the household indifferent between the initial situation and the new situation. To isolate the substitution effect of an interest rate change, we give the household a (hypothetical) change in endowments at the same time so that its initial and final consumption points are on the same indifference curve. The easiest way to *see* the power of the substitution effect is to study a household whose best consumption point at the current interest rate is its endowment point, although doing so does not precisely isolate the substitution effect. Such a household is neither a borrower nor a lender and, regardless of the change in the interest rate—rise or fall—this household is able to move to a higher indifference curve than before. Also, the direction of the change in its current consumption is unambiguous. You can see this by studying Figure 17.7.

In this figure, the household's endowment point, E, is determined by its labor income Y_1 in year 1 and Y_2 in year 2. Initially, the household's lifetime budget line is the grey line passing through point E. The household's most preferred attainable consumption point is its endowment point on indifference curve I_0. Now suppose that the interest rate decreases, rotating the budget line to become the black line in the figure. The household's best consumption point is now at C_1 on indifference curve I_1. The household increases its consumption in year 1, borrowing to consume more than its current labor income. The lower interest rate has induced an increase in current consumption and some borrowing.

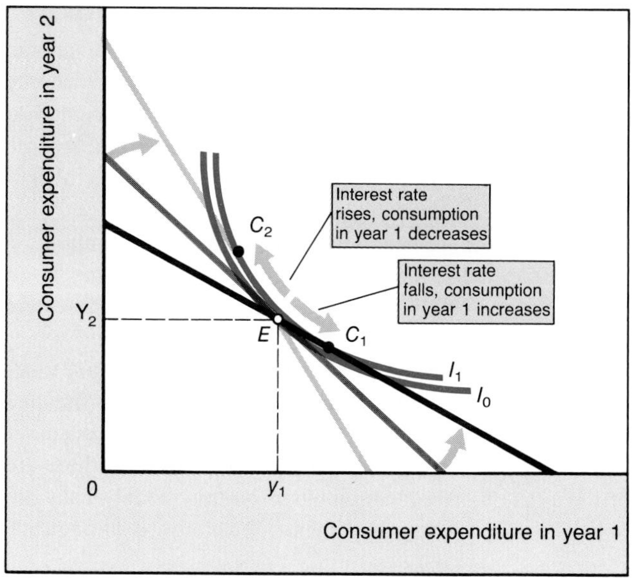

FIGURE 17.7
A Change in the Interest Rate

A change in the interest rate rotates the lifetime budget line on the endowment point, *E*. Initially, the household is consuming at point *E* (is neither a saver nor a dissaver). If the interest rate falls, the lifetime budget line becomes the black line and the household moves to C_1, increasing current consumer expenditure. If the interest rate increases, the lifetime budget line becomes the light blue line, and the household moves to C_2, decreasing current consumer expenditure.

Next, consider what happens when the interest rate increases. Suppose that the interest rate increases, rotating the budget line so that it becomes the pink line in the figure. Now the household's most preferred attainable consumption point is C_2. Consumption in year 1 is less than the household's current labor income. Thus an increase in the interest rate induces a decrease in current consumption and induces the household to lend part of its current income.

In the experiments we've just conducted, there is a substitution effect and a wealth effect. The household moves to a higher indifference curve. But it is not much higher, so in each case the substitution effect dominates and we can see it in the direction of change of consumer expenditure in year 1.

Wealth effect The *wealth effect* is the change in current consumption resulting from a change in the wealth of the household. We've seen that wealth depends on the interest rate. Other things being equal, the higher the interest rate, the lower the wealth of a household. But having lower wealth does not necessarily mean the household will decrease its consumption. The direction of the wealth effect of a change in the interest rate depends on whether the household is a borrower or a lender. If a household is a borrower, a change in the interest rate reinforces the effects we've just discovered. A higher interest rate makes a borrower worse off than before because it lowers the borrower's wealth. Being worse off, the borrower cuts back on current consumption. Thus the higher interest rate induces a lower level of current consumption.

But for a lender, things go the other way. A higher interest rate increases a lender's wealth and makes the lender better off. Being better off, the lender tends to increase current consumption. But this wealth effect works in the direction opposite to the substitution effect of the higher interest rate. There's no clear-cut outcome. Whether current consumption increases or decreases in response to a change in the interest rate depends on whether the substitution effect or the wealth effect is dominant.

For the economy as a whole, the private sector is a net lender and the government sector is a net borrower. Thus a decrease in the interest rate has a substitution effect that tends to increase current consumer expenditure but a wealth effect that tends to decrease it. It is generally reckoned that these two effects are approximately equal in magnitude, so that the interest rate effect on aggregate consumption is negligible.

Change in endowment

The most important influence on consumption and saving is income. A change in income changes the endowment point and shifts the lifetime budget line. An increase in income in the year 1, other things being equal, shifts the lifetime budget line to the right and increases consumer expenditure in year 1 and in year 2. Similarly, an increase in income in year 2, other things being equal, shifts the lifetime budget line to the right and increases consumer expenditure in both year 1 and year 2.

The implication of this model of household behavior is that current consumption is uniquely determined, given the lifetime budget line. But the lifetime budget line is not uniquely determined by current labor income. It depends on current labor income, the path of that income in the future, and the interest rate.

Thus this model of consumer behavior does not predict a simple consumption function—a relationship between consumer expenditure and disposable income in the current period. It does, however, explain and rationalize the actual data on consumer expenditure and disposable income we studied earlier in this chapter. In fact, there are two key alternative theories of the consumption function based on this model. They are the permanent income hypothesis and the life-cycle hypothesis. We'll now examine each of these theories.

17.4 The Permanent Income Hypothesis

The **permanent income hypothesis** is the proposition that consumer expenditure is proportional to permanent income. **Permanent income** is the average income the household expects to receive over the rest of its life. This hypothesis was first proposed by Milton Friedman in the mid-1950s.[1]

Friedman's key idea is very simple, and, once stated, seems obvious. A change in a household's income may be temporary or permanent. How a household's consumption responds to a change in its income depends crucially on how permanent that income change is. A temporary change will likely have a very small effect. (Friedman assumed that the effect of a temporary change in income would be zero.) A permanent change in income will have a much larger effect.

The permanent income hypothesis can be stated very clearly in terms of the intertemporal model of consumption and saving choice we've just studied. A change in current income that simply moves the household along its lifetime budget line will have no effect on its consumption plan. But a change in income that shifts the lifetime budget line will change the household's intertemporal consumption choice. If income changes and the change is expected in every future year, the lifetime budget line will shift even farther. Since the consumption choice depends on the position of the lifetime budget line, a change in permanent income that shifts the budget line outward will change the household's consumption choice, while a change in income that represents a movement along the budget line will leave consumption unaffected.

Determining permanent income

To give the permanent income hypothesis empirical content, it is necessary to specify how permanent income changes and how it reacts to current income. Friedman proposed that permanent income gradually adjusts to changes in current income. In particular, permanent income changes by some fixed proportion of the difference between current income and permanent income.

To appreciate the implications of the permanent income hypothesis and the gradual adjustment of permanent income to current income, we need to do a little algebra. This algebra is summarized in Table 17.2.

Part (a) of the table defines consumer expenditure, current income, permanent income, the propensity to consume, and the speed of adjustment of permanent income. Part (b) sets out the basic hypothesis that consumer expenditure is proportional to permanent income. Part (c) sets out the hypothesis about the gradual adjustment of permanent income. The change in permanent income is some proportion, h, of the gap between current income and permanent income. The time-series consumption function implied by the hypotheses about permanent income and its gradual adjustment is set out in part (d). It is obtained by substituting the equation in part (c)—the gradual adjustment of permanent income—into the equation in part (b)—the permanent income hypothesis.

Notice there are two ways in which we can state the time-series consumption function for the permanent income hypothesis. The first row in part (d) tells us that current consumer expenditure is proportional to the previous period's permanent income plus an amount determined by the difference between the current period's actual income and the previous period's permanent income. This difference, $Y_t - Y^P_{t-1}$, is called **transitory income.** Thus current consumer expenditure is a function of permanent income in the previous period and transitory income in the current period. Alternatively, we can

[1]Milton Friedman, *A Theory of the Consumption Function*, (Princeton, N.J.: Princeton University Press), 1957.

TABLE 17.2
The Permanent Income Hypothesis

ITEM	SYMBOLS AND EQUATIONS	NUMERICAL EXAMPLE
(a) Definitions		
Consumer expenditure in year 1	C_1	
Current income	Y_1	
Permanent income in year 1	Y_1^P	
Marginal and average propensity to consume out of permanent income	k	0.9
Speed of adjustment of permanent income	h	0.3
(b) Basic hypothesis		
Consumer expenditure is proportional to permanent income	$C_t = kY_t^P$	$C_t = 0.9\ Y_t^P$
(c) Generation of permanent Income		
Permanent income changes by a fraction of the difference between current income and permanent income	$Y_t^P - Y_{t-1}^P = h(Y_t - Y_{t-1}^P)$	$Y_t^P - Y_{t-1}^P = 0.3(Y_t - Y_{t-1}^P)$
(d) Time-series consumption function		
Consumption function	$C_t = kY_{t-1}^P + kh(Y_t - Y_{t-1}^P)$	$C_t = 0.9Y_{t-1}^P + 0.27(Y_t - Y_{t-1}^P)$
Which may be rearranged as:	$C_t = khY_t + k(1 - h)\ Y_{t-1}^P$	$C_1 = 0.27\ Y_t + 0.63Y_{t-1}^P$
Short-run marginal propensity to consume	kh	0.27
Long-run marginal propensity to consume	k	0.9

rearrange the equation as shown in the second line of part (d) of the table. This tells us that current consumer expenditure is some proportion of current income plus another proportion of the previous period's permanent income. The proportion of current income consumed is the short-run marginal propensity to consume. It is the marginal propensity to consume out of permanent income, k, multiplied by the speed of adjustment of permanent income, h. In our example, the short-run marginal propensity to consume is 0.9 multiplied by 0.3, which equals 0.27. The long-run marginal propensity to consume is interpreted as the marginal propensity to consume out of current income when current income is equal to permanent income. In this case,

$$Y_t = Y_{t-1}^P$$

and

$$C_t = kY_t.$$

Thus the long-run marginal propensity to consume is k, or, in our example, 0.9.

Interpreting the time-series data

We can use Friedman's permanent income hypothesis to interpret the time-series consumption functions we examined earlier in the chapter. Figure 17.8 illustrates. Suppose

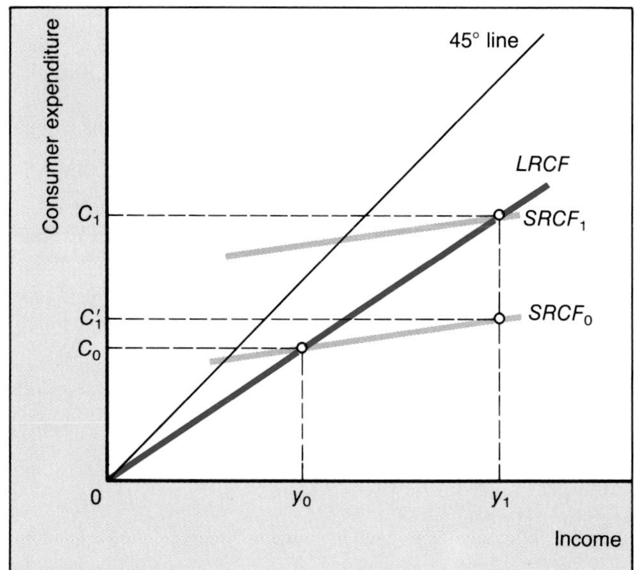

FIGURE 17.8
Consumption Functions and the Permanent Income Hypothesis

According to the permanent income hypothesis, consumer expenditure responds to permanent income. In the long run, consumer expenditure is proportional to income because permanent income and actual income are equal on the average. Curve *LRCF* is the long-run consumption function. In the short run, variations in actual income occur that are independent of permanent income. Such changes in actual income do not lead to a proportional change in consumer expenditure. The economy travels along its short-run consumption function. For example, variations in income when the permanent income is Y_0 move the economy along the short-run consumption function $SRCF_0$. Over time, as permanent income increases, the short-run consumption function shifts upward. For example, when the permanent income increases from Y_0 to Y_1, the short-run consumption function shifts upward, to $SRCF_1$. When permanent income is Y_0 and actual income is Y_1, consumer expenditure is C_1'. But when both actual and permanent income are Y_1, consumer expenditure is C_1.

that in a given year, actual and permanent income are equal, at Y_0. In that year, consumer expenditure is C_0. Purely temporary variations in actual income around Y_0 lead to fluctuations in consumer expenditure along the short-run consumption function, $SRCF_0$. For example, if income increased to Y_1 (but with permanent income remaining at Y_0), consumer expenditure would increase to C_1'. If there is no economic growth, average income remains at Y_0, and if all income fluctuations are random around that average, all we will observe in the time-series data is the short-run consumption function $SRCF_0$.

But in fact our economy grows over time. As it grows, actual income increases and so does permanent income. But permanent income increases more smoothly than does actual income—only proportion h of the change in actual income gets built into permanent income in any given year. Nonetheless, as income steadily grows over time, permanent income increases and consumer expenditure increases. The average path traced by consumer expenditure and income falls along the long-run consumption function, *LRCF*. The short-run consumption function shifts upward over time. Thus, for example, by the time permanent income has increased to Y_1, the short-run consumption function has shifted upward, to $SRCF_1$. Now, actual income of Y_1 is also the level of permanent income, so consumer expenditure is C_1.

Explaining the cross-section data

We saw in the cross-section data that the marginal propensity to consume out of income is much smaller than that in the time-series data. It also decreases as income increases.

These observations can be accounted for by the permanent income hypothesis. In any given year, there is a distribution of household income around the average income. Household fortunes vary, some households being extremely lucky in a given year and having an unusually high income, and other households being unlucky and having an unusually low income. If we divide the population into several groups ranging from low to high income groups, the lowest income groups will have a larger proportion of households whose incomes are temporarily low and the high income groups will have a large proportion of households whose incomes are temporarily high. We've seen that consumer expenditure responds much less to temporary changes in income than to permanent changes. Thus we would expect to find in the high-income groups higher consumer expenditure, but much less than proportionately higher. Similarly, in low-income groups, we would predict lower consumer expenditure, but much less than proportionately lower. Across households, just as over time, if consumer expenditure responds to permanent income, the relationship between consumer expenditure and current income will be represented by a consumption function that is much flatter than the consumption function based on permanent income.

Thus with one neat and simple proposition, Milton Friedman was able to reconcile the short-run and long-run time-series consumption functions and the cross-section consumption function.

17.5 *The Life-Cycle Hypothesis*

The **life-cycle hypothesis** is the proposition that households smooth their consumption over their lifetimes. The life-cycle hypothesis was developed by Franco Modigliani (with two collaborators) at almost the same time as Friedman's permanent income hypothesis.[2]

The life-cycle hypothesis is closely related to the permanent income hypothesis and, like it, directly derivable from the basic model of intertemporal consumption choice we studied earlier in this chapter. It emphasizes, however, the importance of the current value of a household's assets on its current and future consumption.

Let's study the life-cycle hypothesis by working through an example. Table 17.3 sets out the assumptions about the household and the economy and also summarizes the propositions about the life-cycle hypothesis.

We'll consider a household with a life that runs from age 20 to age 80 and with no uncertainty about the lifetime. Furthermore, the householder is going to retire at age 65. During the working years, income is \$40,000 each year. The interest rate is zero, so a dollar saved today is simply a dollar transferred to future consumption.

Let's suppose that the household's preferences, summarized in its indifference curves, deliver constant consumption over the entire lifetime as the best consumption plan. How much will the household consume? The answer is worked out in part (c) of the table. The household's lifetime budget constraint is the first equation. It tells us that consumption during the remaining years of life equals the initial assets plus the income that will be earned in the remaining working years. For example, at age 20, the household has 60 years of life. Thus consumption per year multiplied by 60 years is total lifetime consumption. This number cannot exceed the household's initial assets

[2]Franco Modigliani and Richard Brumberg, "Utility Analysis and the Consumption Function," in Kenneth Kurihara (ed.), *Post-Keynesian Economics* (New Brunswick: Rutgers University Press), 1954, and Albert Ando and Franco Modigliani, "The 'Life Cycle' Hypothesis of Saving: Aggregate Implications and Tests," *American Economic Review*, Vol. 53 (March 1963), pp. 55-84.

TABLE 17.3
The Life-Cycle Hypothesis

ITEM	SYMBOLS AND EQUATIONS	NUMERICAL EXAMPLE
(a) Facts about household		
Current age	t	20
Consumer expenditure per year	C	Household's choice
Labor income per year	YL	$40,000
Assets of the beginning of adult life	A_0	$0
Assets of age *t*	A_t	Household's choice
Age at retirement	R	65
Age at death	L	80
(b) Facts about the economy		
Interest rate	r	0
(c) Consumption and assets		
Lifetime consumption constraint	$C(L - t) = A_t + (R - t)YL$	$C(80 - t) = A_t + (65 - t)YL$
Assets	$A_t = A_0 + (YL - C)(t - 20)$	$A_t = (YL - C)(t - 20)$

(assumed to be 0 at age 20) plus the labor income that it will earn over its life. Since the household will earn $40,000 a year from age 20 to age 65 — 45 years — lifetime consumption cannot exceed $1,800,000. The household's annual consumption will be $30,000. This amount of consumption per year amounts to $1,800,000 over the remaining 60 years of the household's life. The household's assets will grow from their initial level by an amount equal to annual saving. Annual saving is equal to labor income minus consumption. Thus the assets of the household will grow and reach a peak in the household's retirement year.

The lifetime pattern of income, consumption, saving, and assets is set out in Figure 17.9. In part (a), you can see the household's constant annual consumption of $30,000. During its working years, from age 20 to age 65, it earns $40,000 a year and saves $10,000 a year. After retirement, the household continues to consume $30,000 a year but it has no labor income. It now dissaves $30,000 a year. Dissaving at this rate for 15 years exhausts the savings built up during 45 years of work. Part (b) shows the household's assets, which grow at the rate of $10,000 a year to retirement and then decline at the rate of $30,000 a year for the rest of the household's life.

The propensities to consume out of assets and income

We can write the consumption function of a household as

$$C = a_t A_t + b_t YL. \qquad \textbf{(17.6)}$$

Here, a_t is the marginal propensity to consume out of assets and b_t is the marginal propensity to consume out of labor income. That is, a_t tells us the amount by which consumption increases in each remaining year of the household's life if its assets increase in value by one dollar, and b_t tells us the amount by which consumption increases in each remaining year of the household's life if its labor income increases by one dollar. Notice which of the elements in this equation have a time subscript and

FIGURE 17.9
The Life-Cycle Hypothesis

According to the life-cycle hypothesis, a household consumes at a steady rate throughout its life (shown in part a). During its working years, its labor income exceeds its consumption, so the household saves. In its retirement years, the household dissaves. The household's assets (part b) reflect the household's labor income and its consumption and saving choices. During its working years, assets grow; during its retirement years, assets decline.

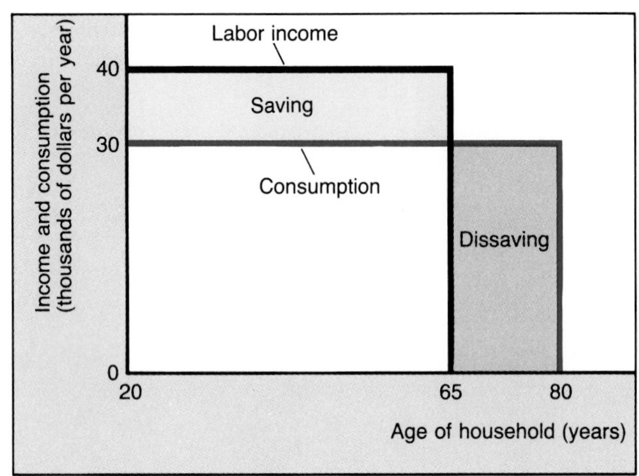

(a) Consumption and income

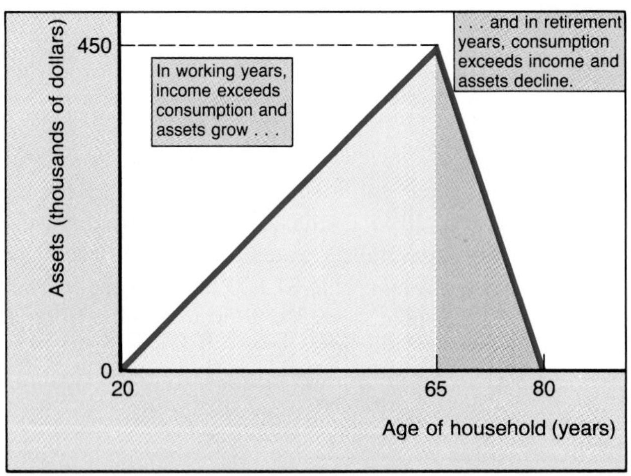

(b) Assets

which do not. Consumption, C, is a constant—the household plans to consume the same amount each year for the rest of its life. Labor income (YL) is also constant—but this is just a convenient simplifying assumption. Assets *and* the marginal propensities to consume out of assets and out of labor income vary over the household's lifetime. To see why, recall that the household's lifetime consumption constraint is

$$C(L - t) = A_t + (R - t)YL. \tag{17.7}$$

Divide both sides of this equation by the number of years of life the household has remaining $(L - t)$. The result is

$$C = \frac{1}{(L - t)}A_t + \frac{(R - t)}{(L - t)}YL. \tag{17.8}$$

Comparing Equations (17.6) and (17.8), you can see that

$$a_t = \frac{1}{L - t} \tag{17.9}$$

and

$$b_t = \frac{R - t}{L - t}. \qquad \textbf{(17.10)}$$

An important implication of these equations is that the marginal propensities to consume out of assets and out of labor income depend on the age of the household (t). The older the household, the larger is the marginal propensity to consume out of assets and the smaller is the marginal propensity to consume out of labor income. These propensities at various ages from 20 through 75 are set out in Table 17.4. As you can see, the marginal propensity to consume out of income declines steadily until, at and after retirement, it is zero. The intuition on why the marginal propensity to consume out of labor income declines is that the closer a household gets to retirement, the fewer the years remaining for it to earn an income but that income still has to be spread over a fixed number of retirement years. Thus an extra dollar of labor income generates a smaller increase in consumption, the closer the household is to retirement.

Assets work in the opposite direction. The older the household, the fewer are the remaining years for consuming and so the larger the amount that can be allocated to consumption in each remaining year. Thus an extra dollar of assets generates a larger increase in consumption, the closer the household is to retirement.

TABLE 17.4
Marginal Propensity to Consume out of Assets and Labor Income at Various Ages

ITEM	SYMBOLS AND EQUATIONS	NUMERICAL EXAMPLE
Consumption function	$C = a_t A_t + b_t YL$	
Lifetime budget constraint	$C(L - t) = A_t + (R - t)YL$	$C(80 - t) = A_t + (65 - t)YL$
Divide both sides by $(L - t)$	$C = \frac{1}{(L-t)} A_t + \frac{(R-t)}{(L-t)} YL$	$C = \frac{1}{(80-t)} A_t + \frac{(65-t)}{(80-t)} YL$

	MARGINAL PROPENSITIES TO CONSUME OUT OF:	
AGE(t)	ASSETS(a_t)	INCOME(b_t)
20	0.017	0.750
40	0.025	0.625
60	0.050	0.250
65	0.067	0
75	0.200	0

Changes in assets and labor income

What happens to a household's consumption if the value of its assets changes or if its labor income changes? We can answer these questions directly from the household's consumption function we've just explored. Suppose that the household's assets change because, for example, a stock market boom permanently adds to the value of its assets. The household is now wealthier than it had expected to be. As a result, the household increases its consumption for the rest of its life. The amount by which its consumption increases is determined by a_t, which depends on the age of the household and is larger the older the household. Older households have a shorter time to the end of their life and therefore can spread the extra wealth over a smaller number of years. A stock market crash that permanently wipes out some of the assets' value makes the household less wealthy than it had previously anticipated and results in a decrease in consumption that is maintained for the rest of the household's life. Again, the magnitude of the change in consumption is determined by the parameter a_t.

Another possibility is a change in the labor market conditions that increases the household's labor income for the rest of its life. Such a change will make the household wealthier than it previously anticipated and will increase its consumption. The amount by which consumption increases depends on the age of the household and is determined by the parameter b_t.

Explaining the data

How does the life-cycle hypothesis account for the facts about consumption and disposable income in the time-series and the cross-section data?

Time-series data To see how the life-cycle hypothesis rationalizes the time-series data, start with the life-cycle consumption function for the economy as a whole. This consumption function is

$$C_t = aA_t + bYL_t. \tag{17.11}$$

Although the marginal propensities to consume out of wealth and labor income vary for individual households depending on their age, for the economy as a whole, there is a given age distribution that in any particular year is constant. Thus aggregate consumption depends on aggregate assets and aggregate labor income with constant marginal propensities to consume, a and b.

Now divide this equation on both sides by disposable income, YD, to give

$$\frac{C_t}{YD_t} = a\frac{A_t}{YD_t} + b\frac{YL_t}{YD_t}. \tag{17.12}$$

The ratio of consumption to disposable income, C_t/YD_t, is the average propensity to consume. In the long run, this average propensity is constant at about 0.9. In the short run, it varies — decreasing during booms and increasing during recessions. The life-cycle hypothesis rationalizes these facts in the following way. First, in the long run, assets and disposable income grow at the same rate. So do labor income and disposable income. Thus in the long run, the ratios of assets to disposable income and labor income to disposable income are fairly constant. This fact gives rise to constant long-run average propensity to consume.

In the short run, fluctuations in labor income and fluctuations in disposable income keep in step with each other but assets do not fluctuate as much as disposable income. Thus in a boom, the ratio of assets to disposable income falls, reducing the average propensity to consume. In a recession, the ratio of assets to disposable income increases, increasing the average propensity to consume.

Cross-section data In the cross-section data, the average propensity to consume decreases as disposable income increases. This pattern is rationalized by the life-cycle hypothesis as a consequence of lifetime fluctuations in income and lifetime consumption smoothing. Incomes are low for both young and old people and high for people in the middle-age groups. With consumption relatively steady throughout the lifetime, the average propensity to consume is high for young and old people and low for people in the middle-age groups.

17.6 *Saving in Canada and Around the World in the 1980s*

TESTCASE

We saw at the beginning of this chapter that the percentage of personal disposable income saved in Canada declined during the 1980s. Let's see if we can explain the behavior of Canadian saving with the theory of consumption and saving we studied in this chapter.

We'll look at three different aspects of saving: first, personal saving and the saving of other sectors in the Canadian economy; second, Canadian saving in a global context, comparing our saving with that in the countries with the highest saving rates; and third, the evolution of the Canadian saving rate over the 1980s, seeing how its fluctuations might be explained.

Personal saving and total saving

It is important when studying saving to pay careful attention not only to the personal sector but also to businesses and governments. Total saving is the sum of personal saving, business saving, and government saving. The magnitudes of these three components of saving in the 1980s are shown in Figure 17.10. You can see there the decline of the personal saving rate. You can also see that the total saving rate has declined and that government saving is negative—government dissaving.

There are some important interactions between personal saving, business saving, and government saving arising from the fact that households are the ultimate owners of firms and bear the ultimate responsibility for government debt.

Business saving and personal saving Because firms are owned by households, any saving done by a firm results in a change in the value of the firm, which in turn affects the value of households' assets. Thus a household may not appear to be saving a very large percentage of its disposable income when in fact it really is, because capital

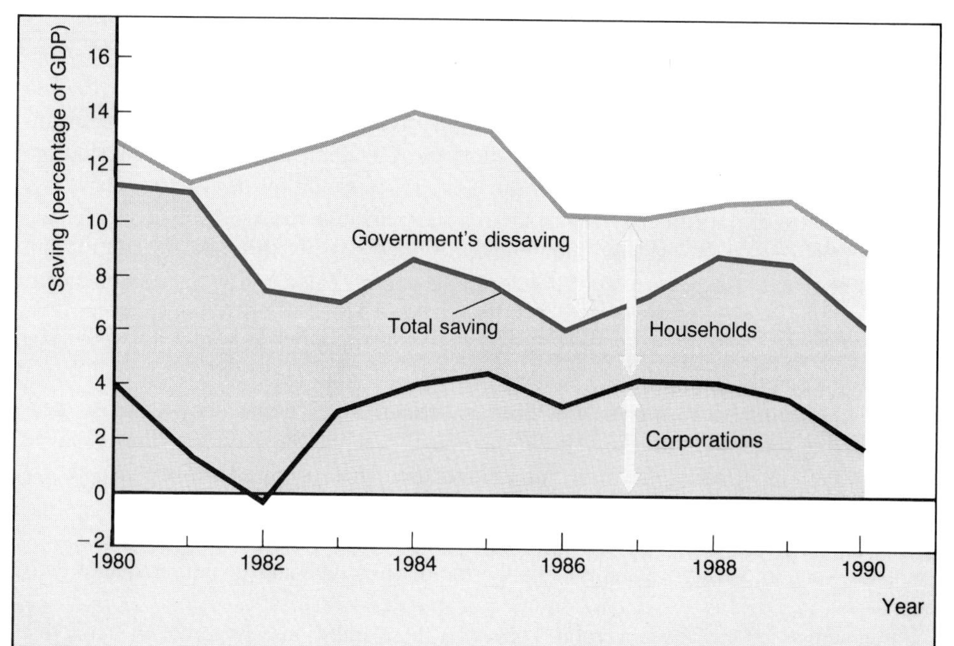

FIGURE 17.10
The Components of Saving in Canada in the 1980s

Personal saving gradually declined as a percentage of GDP. Business saving fluctuated, becoming negative in 1982, rising to a peak in 1985, and declining through the rest of the 1980s. The government sector saved a negative amount (dissaving), reflecting the fact that it had a deficit. Despite the decrease in the government sector deficit through the 1980s, total saving trended downward.

Source: National Income and Expenditure Accounts, Statistics Canada, Catalogue 13-201.

gains are increasing the stock market value of its assets. Conversely, there may be times when households appear to be saving a great deal but are really saving a small percentage of disposable income because falling stock prices are reducing the stock market value of its assets.

If households make their intertemporal choices in the way indicated by the model we've studied in this chapter, and if they take proper account of the stock market value of the firms they own and proper account of the tax liabilities on the government's debt, their saving choices will, to some degree, be a reflection of changes taking place in the business and government sectors. Other things being equal, an additional dollar retained by a firm and used to invest in new capital equipment is equivalent to a dollar distributed to households in profit, saved by the household, and invested by the household in some asset that earns an equivalent rate of return. Thus there's an important sense in which business saving and personal saving are substitutes for each other. Other things being equal, households owing shares in firms are predicted to change their saving one for one to offset business saving.

Government saving and personal saving There's a similar important interaction between the personal sector and the government. If the government increases its deficit by one dollar, that action creates a liability for households to pay interest on that dollar in perpetuity. The value of the liability created is equivalent to the dollar the government has spent. Thus again, other things being equal, a one-dollar increase in the government deficit is predicted to increase household saving by one dollar.

Total saving Viewed from the broader perspective we've just sketched, personal saving is not a very important aggregate. What matters is the nation's total saving and not the way in which total saving is allocated across households, businesses, and governments. Has total saving behaved in the same way as personal saving during the 1980s? Figure 17.10 answers this question. It shows that total saving has decreased similarly to the decrease in personal saving. The decrease has occurred because business saving has declined. The amount of government dissaving decreased between 1986 and 1989.

Canadian saving in international perspective

We've seen that the Canadian saving rate has declined from about 13 percent in 1980 to about 6 percent by the end of the decade. Is this saving rate low by international standards? The answer is yes. Figure 17.11 plots the Canadian saving rate alongside the saving rate for the world as a whole, for the United States, and for three countries whose saving rates are extraordinarily high. You can see that for the world as a whole, the saving rate is remarkably steady, although it declined slightly through the 1980s from about 24 percent at the beginning of the decade to about 22 percent by the decade's end. The Canadian saving rate is the lowest of those shown here. While lower than the U.S. and world average saving rates, the Canadian rate has trended downward in a way very similar to those two saving rates.

But a few countries have gone against that trend. Three countries with most spectacular saving rates, both in terms of their average level and the way they have behaved over the 1980s, are Japan, Germany, and Singapore. These saving rates are also shown in Figure 17.11.

Why is the Canadian saving rate less than the world average? And why do some countries, such as Singapore, Japan, and Germany, save such a large percentage of their incomes?

Economists do not have a good answer to these questions. In terms of economic models, the answer lies in preferences. The intertemporal indifference curves for different

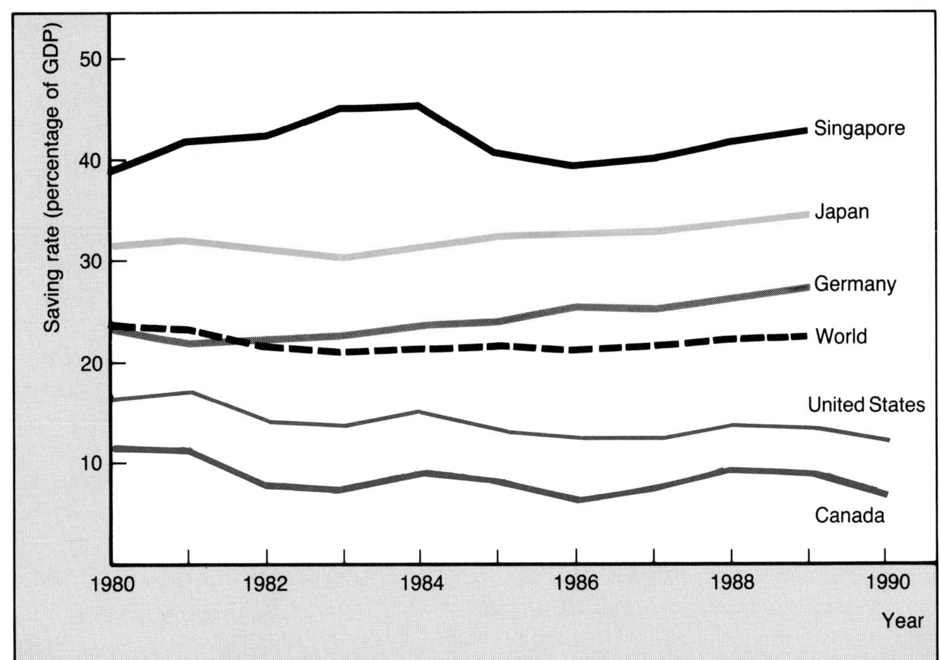

FIGURE 17.11
Saving Rates Around the World

The Canadian saving rate is lower than the world average and the decline in the Canadian saving rate is not matched by similar declines in other countries, except for the United States. The world saving rate remained fairly steady throughout the 1980s and saving rates in Germany and Japan actually increased. The most spectacular saving rate is that of Singapore.

Source: National Income and Expenditure Accounts, Statistics Canada, Catalogue 13-201 and *International Financial Statistics Yearbook*, 1991.

groups of people lie in different places, resulting in a different best affordable intertemporal allocation of consumption. Countries with very high saving rates place a high weight on future consumption and a lower weight on current consumption relative to countries that save a small proportion of their income, such as Canada. But this "answer" leaves more questions unanswered. Why are some countries more patient than others, placing greater weight on future consumption? This is a research question for the future. If we can't explain why the saving rates differ across countries, can we explain why they fluctuate over time?

Fluctuations in saving rates

Why do saving rates fluctuate over time and why, in particular, has the Canadian saving rate declined during the 1980s?

A predicted source of fluctuations in saving rates is fluctuations in income. We've seen, from the theory of intertemporal choice, that periods of unusually high income are periods of high saving. Periods of unusually low income are periods in which there is a low saving rate. But, contrary to this prediction, the Canadian saving rate *fell* when incomes were growing quickly in the middle 1980s.

A promising explanation for the behavior of savings in the 1980s is that the decline in the saving rate is an illusion that arises from mismeasuring saving. Saving, as measured in the National Income and Expenditure Accounts, even when it is measured in constant dollars, does not take into account changes in the real value of the assets that people own. Changes in the value of assets are a component of real saving. To see why, consider the saving of a family that has a disposable income of $50,000 a year and spends $50,000 on consumer goods and services. Suppose the family also has stocks valued at $100,000. According to the National Income and Expenditure Accounts, this family has a zero saving rate. If stock prices are constant, the family also really has a zero saving rate. But suppose that stock prices increase in real terms by 10 percent in the year. That is, the stock price index rises at a rate faster than the inflation rate so that the buying power of the family's stocks has gone up by 10 percent. This 10 percent increase in the value of the family's assets is really part of the family's income. It is also the family's saving. This family has a real income of $60,000 a year and is saving $10,000 a year.

The theory of consumption and saving is a theory about what households really do, not about what national income accountants measure them doing. Thus if a household's assets have increased, it may well decrease its saving out of current disposable income, so that the national income accounts will record a lower saving rate. The implication then is that when the stock market is booming, the measured saving rate declines.

17.7 *Taxes, Consumption, and Saving*

When we first studied consumption and saving behavior in Chapter 4, we emphasized the role of disposable income as the major influence on consumer expenditure and saving. A change in taxes changes disposable income and, according to the simple consumption function theory of Chapter 4, changes both consumer expenditure and saving. The amount by which consumer expenditure is influenced depends on the marginal propensity to consume, and the amount by which saving is influenced depends on the marginal propensity to save. These two marginal propensities add to 1, so the total tax change is allocated across a change in consumer spending and saving.

The theories of consumer expenditure and saving that we've studied in this chapter emphasize the importance of intertemporal substitution and the role of permanent income (in the permanent income hypothesis) or lifetime average income (in the life-cycle hypothesis). Thus according to these theories, consumption is a function of permanent or lifetime average disposable income. These theories of the consumption function have important implications for the influence of fiscal policy on consumer expenditure and saving. They imply that a tax change will have a different influence on consumption and saving depending on whether it is permanent or temporary.

A permanent tax change influences permanent disposable income and has a large effect on consumer expenditure. A temporary tax change that is going to be reversed in the future has no effect on permanent income and no effect on consumer expenditure. The entire effect of the tax change results in a change in saving.

The Ricardo-Barro hypothesis

There is a special implication of the permanent income hypothesis first suggested in the nineteenth century by David Ricardo and rigorously worked out more recently by Robert Barro of Harvard University.[3]

The Ricardo-Barro hypothesis is as follows. Suppose the government budget starts out balanced and the government cuts taxes. It borrows to cover the deficit. But at some time in the future the debt plus the interest on it has to be repaid. Rational households recognize this fact and realize that the tax cut has not changed their permanent income. It has simply changed the timing of their tax payments and the timing of their net-of-tax income receipts, but it has not changed their permanent income or shifted their lifetime budget constraint.

As a result, there is no change in consumption, but saving changes to accommodate the changed timing of tax payments.

[3] Robert J. Barro, "Are Government Bonds Net Wealth?" *Journal of Political Economy*, Vol. 82 (November/December 1974), pp. 1095-1117.

17.8 Money, Liquidity, and Consumer Expenditure

The intertemporal theories of consumption and saving recognize only one constraint on the household's consumption choice—its lifetime budget constraint. Subject only to that constraint the household could, if it chose, consume its entire wealth—the present value of its entire future labor income stream — in the present period. Have you ever tried going to a bank or other lending institution to get a loan secured by your human capital? Sure, you can borrow something, but not nearly as much as the million or so dollars you're going to earn in the 40-odd years of your working life.

The maximum amount that a household can borrow to finance current consumption out of future labor income is an additional constraint on consumption, known as a **liquidity constraint**.

The presence of a liquidity constraint means that there are two important influences on consumer expenditure other than the interest rate and the household's endowment:

- Disposable income
- Available credit

Disposable income

For a household that is on its liquidity constraint, a change in consumer expenditure can be undertaken only if there is a change in disposable income. Thus households that are constrained in this way behave in the way described by the simple theory of the consumption function. They consume a certain proportion of their disposable income and save the other proportion of it. They are not able to undertake intertemporal consumption smoothing if such smoothing requires bringing consumption forward in time. They can only postpone consumption. But since they're liquidity-constrained, they don't want to.

Because some people are liquidity-constrained and change their consumer expenditure when their disposable income changes, the aggregate consumption function is a kind of average of the simple consumption function and the permanent income/life-cycle consumption function.

Availability of credit

The amount of credit available to a household depends partly on factors relating to the individual household, such as its likely future income and its ability to repay its loans. But availability of credit also depends on economywide conditions. Sometimes, the banks themselves are short of resources and tighten up their lending rules. At other times, flush with funds, they're willing to relax those rules and lend larger amounts.

Monetary policy has an important influence, therefore, on consumer expenditure. By loosening the monetary reins, the Bank of Canada can encourage banks to increase their lending, thereby loosening the liquidity constraints on some households and stimulating consumer expenditure. This is an important potential channel of policy influence on aggregate demand.

Interest rates

Another potential channel for monetary policy to influence consumer expenditure is interest rate changes. We've seen how interest rates rotate the lifetime budget line.

We've also seen how higher interest rates induce lower current consumption for borrowers and possibly induce lower current consumption for lenders, provided the wealth effect does not dominate. Thus to the extent that monetary policy can change interest rates, it can change consumer expenditure.

But it is *real* interest rates, not nominal interest rates, that consumer expenditure responds to. You can see this fact just by thinking about the lifetime budget constraint and asking how it would be influenced if interest rates increased and the inflation rate increased by the same amount. Let's look at the intertemporal and lifetime budget constraints again, but taking inflation into account. If prices are rising, we need to keep track of the price level in each period in the lifetime budget constraint. Call C real consumption and YL real labor income. The lifetime budget constraint, taking prices into account, is

$$P_{t+1}C_{t+1} \leq P_{t+1}\,YL_{t+1} + (1 + r)P_tYL_t - (1 + r)P_tC_t. \qquad \textbf{(17.13)}$$

This is the nominal lifetime budget constraint. That is, it's the lifetime budget constraint expressed in terms of dollars. Now divide both sides of the constraint by the price level in the next period. This gives

$$C_{t+1} \leq YL_{t+1} + (1 + r)\frac{P_t}{P_{t+1}}(YL_t - C_t). \qquad \textbf{(17.14)}$$

This is the real lifetime budget constraint, and it tells us that consumption in the next period cannot exceed labor income in the next period plus real saving in the current period ($YL_t - C_t$) multiplied by the real interest rate on that saving. The real interest rate on that saving is $(1 + r)P_t/P_{t+1}$. You'll see more clearly that this is a real interest rate if you use the fact that

$$P_{t+1} = (1 + \pi)P_t \qquad \textbf{(17.15)}$$

or,

$$\frac{P_t}{P_{t+1}} = \frac{1}{1 + \pi}. \qquad \textbf{(17.16)}$$

Using this in the real lifetime budget constraint gives

$$C_{t+1} \leq YL_{t+1} + \frac{(1 + r)}{(1 + \pi)}(YL_t - C_t). \qquad \textbf{(17.17)}$$

The term $(1 + r)/(1 + \pi)$ is the real interest rate. (For low inflation rates and low interest rates, it is approximately equal to $r - \pi$.)

A change in monetary policy that changes the nominal interest rate and leaves the expected inflation rate unchanged changes the real interest rate. What kind of monetary policy would do such a thing? The answer is, an unanticipated or expected temporary change in the money supply or its growth rate. Temporary changes in the money supply change the nominal interest rate but do not change the expected inflation rate. The resulting change in the real interest rate influences current consumption and saving.

Although the interest rate does influence consumer expenditure, studies have found that its effect on aggregate consumer expenditure is not large. Nonetheless, the effect is present.

Consumption and saving: a summing up

Taking into account all the factors that we have reviewed in this chapter, aggregate consumer expenditure depends on

- Permanent income (or lifetime average income)
- The interest rate
- Current disposable income
- Available credit

Policy influences on consumer expenditure arise from tax changes and changes in monetary policy, but permanent tax changes have a much larger effect on consumer expenditure than temporary tax changes. Interest rate effects, although they are present, are thought to be small.

■ In this chapter, we've studied the microeconomic foundations of consumption and saving. You now have a deeper and richer understanding of the forces determining consumption and saving and the factors that shift the consumption function over time. These shifts in the consumption function are one source of the fluctuations in aggregate demand and aggregate economic activity. But they are not the most important source. The most volatile element of aggregate spending is investment. Our next task is to study the microfoundations of investment decisions.

CHAPTER REVIEW

Summary

TIME-SERIES AND CROSS-SECTION FACTS

There is no single simple relationship between consumer expenditure and disposable income. In the aggregate, over long periods of time, consumer expenditure is proportional to disposable income. The marginal propensity to consume and the average propensity to consume are equal at about 0.9. Over shorter time intervals, the marginal propensity to consume is lower than the average propensity to consume and the short-run consumption function drifts upward over time.

The cross-section relationship between consumer expenditure and disposable income is nonlinear. The marginal propensity to consume is less than the average propensity to consume, and the marginal propensity to consume declines as disposable income increases.

Any satisfactory theory of consumption must account for these facts.

Another interesting fact to be explained is the steady decline in the Canadian saving rate in the 1980s. During the 1980s, Canadian personal saving, household saving, and total saving, measured as a percentage of income, declined. But this decline was not matched by the world economy as a whole. Also, in Canada the percentage of GDP saved is much lower than in some other countries.

The saving rate measured in the National Income and Expenditure Accounts does not allow for changes in the value of assets. But the theory of consumption and saving emphasizes the importance of the value of assets. If the value of a household's assets is increasing, then the household is saving. It doesn't matter whether the increased assets come from decreased consumption or from increased asset prices—from rising stock market prices. In fact, the stock market value of assets increased dramatically through the 1980s. This fact possibly explains the apparent decline in the Canadian saving rate in the 1980s.

THE HOUSEHOLD'S INTERTEMPORAL AND LIFETIME BUDGET CONSTRAINTS

An intertemporal budget constraint describes the limits to consumption and asset accumulation. Current consumption and end of current period assets cannot exceed initial assets plus the interest earned on them plus other income received in the current period. There is a sequence of budget constraints since the assets carried forward at the end of the current period become the assets inherited at the beginning of the following period. The sequence of intertemporal budget constraints gives a lifetime budget constraint.

A household's lifetime budget constraint depends on its endowment—the labor income streams it will receive through its life—and on the interest rate. The household's lifetime budget line always passes through its endowment point but a change in the interest rate rotates the lifetime budget line. The higher the interest rate, the steeper is the budget line and the smaller the maximum amount that can be consumed in the current period.

HOW CONSUMPTION AND SAVING DECISIONS ARE MADE

Households have preferences, represented by indifference curves, that describe their attitude toward the timing of consumption. The slope of such indifference curves measures the household's *marginal rate of intertemporal substitution*. In each period, the household chooses its current consumer expenditure and the amount to save and lend or dissave and borrow in order to attain the highest possible indifference curve.

Given the household's preferences, the fundamental determinants of this choice are the household's endowment and the interest rate. Other things being equal, the higher the endowment, the higher is the household's consumer expenditure. A change in the interest rate has an ambiguous effect on the household's choice. If the household is a net borrower, its current consumer expenditure decreases as the interest rate increases. The reason is that the higher interest rate lowers current consumer expenditure via a substitution effect and lowers the household's wealth, lowering current consumer expenditure (a wealth effect).

A household that is a net lender may either increase or decrease its consumer expenditure in response to an increase in the interest rate. The substitution effect works in the same direction as for a net borrower, but the wealth effect works in the opposite direction.

The basic model of intertemporal choice forms the basis of the two key alternative theories of the consumption function.

THE PERMANENT INCOME HYPOTHESIS

According to the permanent income hypothesis, consumer expenditure is proportional to permanent income—to the average income the household expects to receive over the rest of its life. Permanent income changes when actual income changes, but only gradually. Transitory income, the difference between permanent income and actual income, has a small (and perhaps zero) effect on consumer expenditure.

The permanent income hypothesis interprets the facts about consumer expenditure and disposable income in the following way: in the long run, actual income and permanent income are equal, so consumer expenditure is proportional to actual income. In the short run, there are transitory changes in income that do not affect consumer expenditure, so the marginal propensity to consume in the short run is smaller than in the long run. In the cross-section data, higher actual incomes are a combination of higher permanent incomes and higher transitory incomes. It is only the permanent component of the higher income that leads to higher consumer expenditure. Hence, consumer expenditure is not proportional to actual income in the cross-section data.

THE LIFE-CYCLE HYPOTHESIS

According to the life-cycle hypothesis, households smooth their consumption over their lifetimes, accumulating assets while they're working and consuming out of assets in their retirement years. An implication of the life-cycle hypothesis is that the marginal propensity to consume out of labor income decreases as the household becomes older and the marginal propensity to consume out of the household's assets increases as the household becomes older.

The life-cycle hypothesis rationalizes the data in the following way: consumption depends both on assets and labor income. In the long run, the ratio of assets to disposable income and of labor income to disposable income are constant. As a result, the ratio of consumption to disposable income is also constant in the long run. In the short run, labor income fluctuates in line with disposable income, but assets do not. An increase in disposable income does not bring a proportionate increase in assets. Hence, it does not bring a proportionate increase in consumption. These same considerations apply to the cross-section data.

EXPLAINING CONSUMPTION AND SAVING IN CANADA AND OTHER COUNTRIES IN THE 1980s

A potential test of the life-cycle hypothesis uses data on consumption and income for different age groups. The hypothesis implies that the average propensity to consume is largest for the youngest and oldest groups and smallest for the middle-age groups. This implication is broadly consistent with the facts that the oldest groups consume less than implied by the theory. This suggests that households do not only smooth consumption over the lifetime but also across the generations. It is also possible that the oldest age groups consume less because of the fear of age-related chronic illnesses requiring expensive care.

TAXES, CONSUMPTION, AND SAVING

A permanent tax change influences permanent income (or lifetime average income) and has a larger effect on consumer expenditure than a temporary tax change. When a tax change is temporary, savings change by a large amount and consumer expenditure by a small amount.

MONEY, CREDIT, AND CONSUMPTION

Some households are *liquidity-constrained*—they have borrowed as much as anyone is willing to lend to them. Such households cannot increase current consumption unless their current disposable income increases. For these households (and because of them, for the economy as a whole), changes in disposable income have a larger effect on consumer expenditure than implied by the permanent income and life-cycle theories.

Changes in the availability of credit resulting from changes in the tightness or ease of monetary policy also can influence consumer expenditure. Interest rate changes can also influence consumer expenditure but these effects are regarded as small.

Key Terms and Concepts

Endowment The income that a household has to spend over its lifetime.

Human capital The present value of current and future labor income.

Life-cycle hypothesis The proposition that households smooth their consumption over their lifetimes.

Lifetime budget constraint The limits to a household's consumption over its lifetime.

Liquidity constraint The maximum amount of current consumption that can be financed by borrowing against future labor income.

Marginal rate of intertemporal substitution The amount of future consumption the household is willing to give up in order to have one additional unit of current consumption.

Permanent income The average income the household expects to receive from the present over the rest of its life.

Permanent income hypothesis The proposition that consumer expenditure is proportional to permanent income.

Present value The amount of a sum of money that, if invested in the present, at the interest rate r, would accumulate to the future sum over a given number of years.

Transitory income The difference between the current period's actual income and the previous period's permanent income.

Review Questions

1. Describe the nature of time-series data and cross-section data on consumer expenditure.
2. What is a time-series consumption function? Explain the relationship between the short-run consumption function and the long-run consumption function.
3. What does the slope of a time-series consumption function measure? Explain why the short-run consumption function is flatter than the long-run consumption function.
4. Using Canadian time-series data plotted in Figure 17.1, what is the marginal propensity to consume in Canada in the short run? and the long run?
5. What is a cross-section consumption function? What does its slope measure? What is the slope in Canadian cross-section consumption function? Is it constant?
6. Describe how the saving rate in Canada has evolved since 1960.
7. What is an intertemporal budget constraint? Explain the relationship between a household's intertemporal budget constraints in 1990 and 1991.
8. What is a household's lifetime budget constraint?
9. Is the household's lifetime budget constraint fixed throughout its life? If so, what keeps it fixed? If not, what makes it shift and how will it shift?
10. Explain the marginal rate of intertemporal substitution. For a household, is it a constant or does it vary? If it varies, explain how.
11. Some households choose to save and others choose to dissave. Explain the conditions that will lead a household to save. To dissave.
12. What is a household's wealth? How is it measured?
13. What conditions encourage a household to substitute current consumption for future consumption?
14. Explain whether your answer to question 13 involves a substitution effect and/or a wealth effect.

15. What is permanent income? The permanent income hypothesis? Who proposed the permanent income hypothesis? When?
16. Explain the effect of an increase in permanent income on the time-series consumption function and current consumer expenditure.
17. Explain the effect of an increase in transitory income on the time-series consumption function and current consumer expenditure.
18. Can the permanent income hypothesis explain the variation in the marginal propensity to consume in cross-section data for Canada?
19. What is a life cycle? The life-cycle hypothesis? Who proposed it? When?
20. Explain why the marginal propensities to spend out of assets and out of labor income are not constant over a household's life.
21. Explain the effect of a permanent increase in the value of a household's assets on consumption and saving over the household's life.
22. How does the life-cycle hypothesis explain the constant average long-run propensity to consume and the variable short-run average propensity to consume?
23. Can the life-cycle hypothesis explain why, in cross-section data, the average propensity to consume falls as disposable income increases? If not, why not? If so, why?
24. Describe the composition of saving in Canada and how these components evolved in the 1980s.
25. Compare the saving rates in Japan, Germany, Singapore, and Canada. Which of these saving rates exceed the world average and which one has increased most in the 1980s?
26. Why is a permanent tax change predicted to have a larger effect on consumer expenditure than a temporary tax change?
27. How might monetary policy influence consumer expenditure and saving?

Problems

1. Paradise Island has only 3 families. Their disposable income and consumer expenditure are as follows:

	DISPOSABLE INCOME		CONSUMER EXPENDITURE	
	in Year 1	in Year 2	in Year 1	in Year 2
Family A	10,000	12,000	5,000	6,000
Family B	16,000	16,000	10,000	10,000
Family C	20,000	22,000	15,000	16,500

   (a) Draw a diagram to show the cross-section consumption function in Paradise Island in year 1.
   (b) Draw a diagram to show the time-series consumption function in Paradise Island.

2. Use the data in problem 1.
   (a) If the increase in disposable income in year 2 is temporary, calculate Family A's short-run consumption function. What is its marginal propensity to consume in the short run?
   (b) If the increase in disposable income in the economy of Paradise Island in year 2 is temporary, calculate the economy's short-run consumption function and its marginal propensity to consume and save in the short run.

(c) If in year 1 each family's income is equal to its permanent income, calculate the long-run consumption function for Paradise Island.
(d) If the government of Paradise Island levies a temporary 1 percent tax on each family's income, what is the effect of the tax on Paradise Island's
  (i) Short-run consumption function
  (ii) Long-run consumption function
  (iii) Cross-section consumption function
(e) If the tax levied in problem (d) is permanent, what now are your answers to that problem?

3. Happy Harry has no inherited assets. He plans to take a job that pays $20,000 a year and work for 40 years. He then plans to enjoy 10 years of retirement. Harry wants to keep his consumption constant over the 50 years and can buy assets that pay an annual interest rate of 10 percent.
(a) Calculate Harry's human capital.
(b) Calculate Harry's wealth on the day he takes the job.
(c) Calculate Harry's consumption each year if he plans to make no bequests.
(d) Is Harry a saver or dissaver in his first 10 years and in his last 10 years?
(e) In which year does Harry own the most assets? What is their value?
(f) Calculate Harry's marginal propensity to consume out of assets 5 years before he retires and 5 years after he retires.
(g) Calculate Harry's marginal propensity to consume out of labor income 5 years before he retires and 5 years after he retires.
(h) If after 20 years of work, Harry's assets double in value, calculate the permanent change in Harry's consumption per year.
(i) If the government introduces a permanent tax of $1,000 a year, what now are your answers to (c) and (e)?

CHAPTER

Investment

18

GETTING THE TIMING RIGHT

RUPERT MURDOCH, THE AUSTRALIAN-BORN FINANCIER, hit hard times in 1990. His multinational giant, News Corp Limited, which owns TV stations, magazines (such as *TV Guide*), and satellite and cable TV companies around the world, had invested $1 billion on new printing plants, revamping movie studios, and developing cable and satellite TV facilities. But Murdoch did not count on the 1990 economic slowdown and 1991 recession. He was reported in *Newsweek* (October 29, 1990, p. 58) to have said "If we'd thought all these things were going to happen at once, . . . we might have postponed our capital development."

Rupert Murdoch is a big-time investor. But every year, millions of ordinary Canadians make an important investment decision — the decision to buy a new home. Buy when the price is at a peak and a family can suffer a huge capital loss. Buy at a time when prices are low and the capital gain of a lifetime can be made.

In Chapter 17, we discovered that households try to smooth their consumption in the face of fluctuating incomes. If all components of expenditure behaved like consumption and if everyone smoothed expenditure, there would be no fluctuations in spending or in income and output. But aggregate economic activity does fluctuate, and it fluctuates because not all components of expenditure are consumer expenditure. Households buy houses and apartments and consumer durable goods. Corporations undertake massive investments in plant, buildings, and equipment, as well as inventories. The behavior of these components of expenditure generates volatility and instability in aggregate expenditure and aggregate demand.

Timing is of the essence in making investment decisions. In this chapter, we're going to study the microeconomics of these decisions. We'll examine how firms and households make decisions about purchases of plant, equipment, buildings, and inventories.

After studying this chapter, you will be able to

- Describe the volatility of investment in Canada and other countries
- Explain the accelerator theory of investment
- Explain how the rental rate of capital is determined
- Explain why investment responds to interest rates
- Explain how monetary policy affects investment
- Explain how taxes affect investment
- Explain why there are alternating waves of optimism and pessimism
- Explain how fluctuations in investment bring fluctuating output and interest rates

MACROFACTS

18.1 Volatility in Investment in Canada and Around the World

Investment is the most volatile component of aggregate demand. Let's examine its volatility both in Canada and other economies.

Investment in Canada

Figure 18.1 shows the behavior of real gross private domestic investment in the Canadian economy between 1970 and 1990. Investment has three components:

- Change in inventories
- Residential fixed investment
- Nonresidential fixed investment

Change in inventories Inventory changes are the smallest component of gross private domestic investment, but they do fluctuate quite a lot and line up almost exactly with the business cycle. Most of the inventory fluctuations that you can see in Figure 18.1 arise from changes in *planned* inventories. When real GDP and sales are increasing quickly, firms add to their inventories so they can meet the higher demand for their products. When the economy sags, firms cut back on inventories because their sales are down. But some inventory changes are unintended. These occur as part of the mechanism of dynamic adjustment of real GDP. When aggregate planned expenditure falls below real GDP, unintended inventories accumulate and signal to firms the need to cut back production, thereby decreasing real GDP. When aggregate planned expenditure exceeds real GDP, an unintended decrease in inventories signals to firms the need to step up production, thereby increasing real GDP.

FIGURE 18.1
Gross Investment and Its Components: 1970-1990

Gross investment is divided into inventory changes, residential investment, and nonresidential investment. All three components fluctuate a great deal, bringing large fluctuations in aggregate gross private domestic investment. In a recession year such as 1982, inventories decline and the other components of investment dip sharply as well.

Source: National Income and Expenditure Accounts, Statistics Canada, Catalogue 13-201.

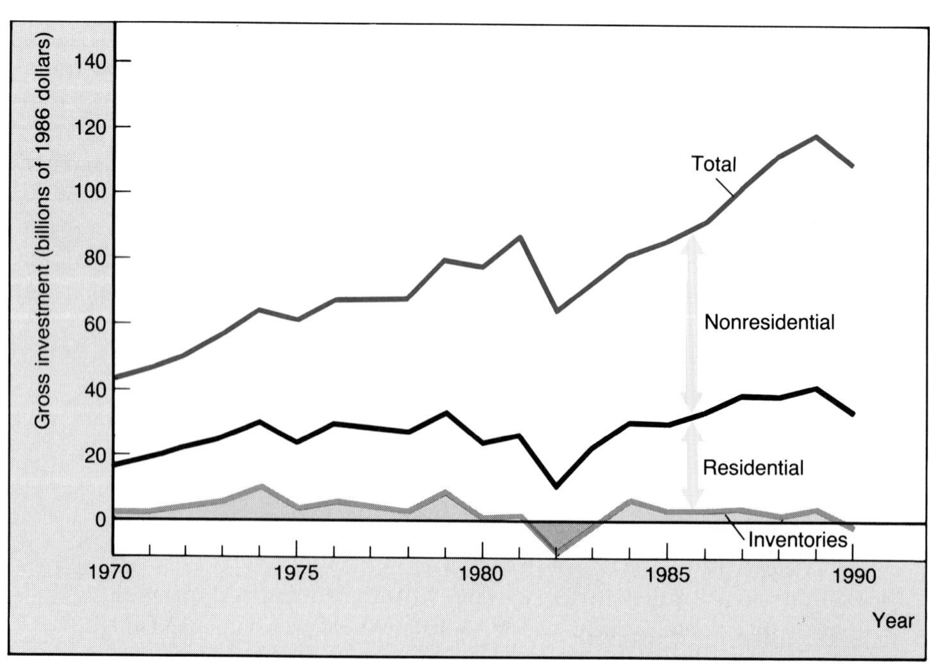

Residential fixed investment Expenditure on new houses and apartment buildings — **residential fixed investment** — is the second largest component of gross private domestic investment. It fluctuates a great deal and its fluctuations closely match the business cycle. Notice especially the declines in residential fixed investment in the mid-1970s and early 1980s at the times of the two most severe recessions of those decades.

Nonresidential fixed investment Expenditure by firms on new plant, buildings, and equipment — **nonresidential fixed investment** — is the largest component of gross private domestic investment. Fluctuations in nonresidential fixed investment lag behind those in residential fixed investment and match the business cycle.

Investment around the world

Not only Canada experiences volatile investment expenditure. The world economy has similar experiences, as you can see by looking at gross investment for the world as a whole in Figure 18.2. This figure also shows how world aggregate investment is divided between investment in developing countries, in the United States, and in other industrial countries. You can see that investment in other industrial countries and in the world as a whole fluctuates in a way very similar to the fluctuations in gross investment in Canada shown in Figure 18.1. Investment in the developing countries, however, although volatile, does not have the same timing as investment in the rest of the world. In fact, throughout the 1980s when the industrial countries were experiencing strong investment growth, investment in the developing countries declined.

This picture of investment in the world economy gives even greater importance to the questions we're going to study in this chapter. For not only does investment fluctuate a great deal, but when investment turns down in the poorest of countries, as it did in the 1980s, they get locked into persistent poverty.

The principles we'll study in this chapter apply to all countries and to all types of investment. But in studying investment, we'll focus on fixed investment — corporations' purchases of new capital equipment — since this component of investment is largest.

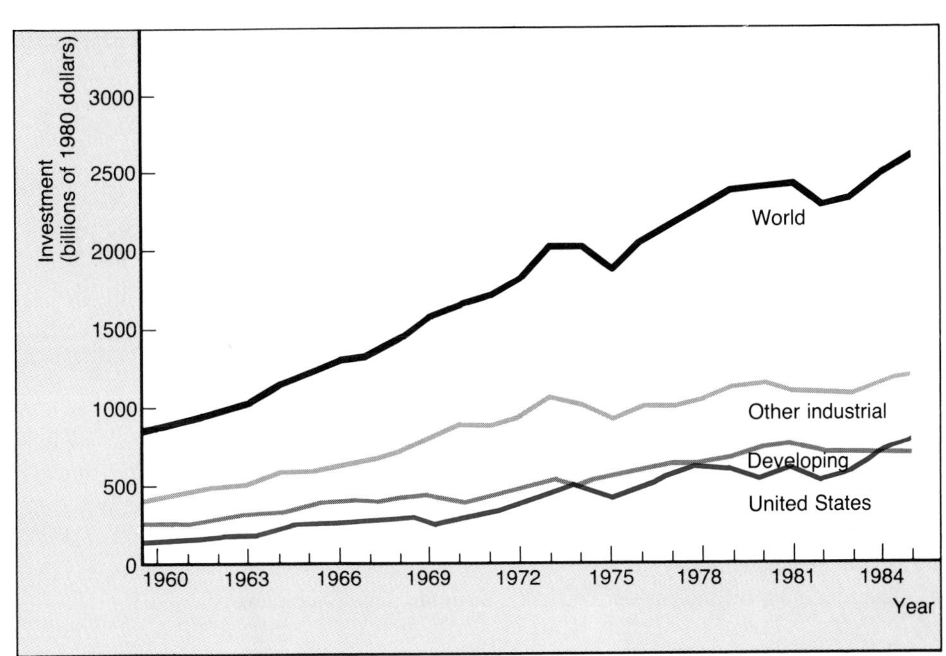

FIGURE 18.2
Investment Around the World: 1960-1985

Fluctuations in investment in Canada are similar to those in the United States, other industrial countries, and to the world as a whole. Investment in developing countries fluctuates less than in the industrial countries but declined steadily after 1981.

Source: Robert Summers and Alan Heston, "A New Set of International Comparisons of Real Product and Price Levels: Estimates for 130 Countries, 1950-1985," *Review of Income and Wealth*, Series 34, Vol. 1 (March 1988), pp. 1-25.

18.2 *Capital, Investment, and the Accelerator Theory*

To understand the sources of volatility in investment, we need to begin by recalling the concepts of stocks and flows and capital and investment. (We first studied these concepts in Chapter 2.)

Stock-flow relationships

Capital is a stock. It is measured as so many units of machines, buildings, or other pieces of equipment at a point in time. Investment is a flow. It is measured as the rate of purchase of new plant, buildings, and equipment over a particular period of time. There is a connection between the stock of capital and the flow of investment. To see the connection, we divide investment into two parts:

1. Net investment
2. Replacement investment

Net investment (I^N) is equal to the change in the capital stock (K). That is,

$$I_t^N = K_t - K_{t-1}. \tag{18.1}$$

Replacement investment (I^R) is the purchase of new plant, equipment, and buildings to replace worn-out items. In the national income and product accounts, replacement investment is called *capital consumption allowances*. In the books of firms, it is measured as *depreciation*. In any given period, some proportion (δ) of the capital stock wears out and is replaced. That is,

$$I_t^R = \delta K_{t-1}. \tag{18.2}$$

Gross and net investment in Canada You can see the distinction between gross and net investment in Canada by looking at Figure 18.3. Net investment is the component that fluctuates. In expansion years such as 1973-1974, 1978-1979, and 1983-1984, net investment expands quickly. In a deep recession such as 1982, it almost disappears.

Despite the fact that net investment fluctuates a great deal, it is such a small proportion of the capital stock that the capital stock itself grows at a relatively steady pace. This fact leads to a steady growth with virtually no fluctuations in replacement investment.

Since net investment changes the capital stock and since replacement investment is some proportion of the capital stock, the capital stock itself plays a critical role in determining investment. The amount of capital that firms have in place is the major influence on depreciation and replacement investment and the amount of capital that firms desire to have determines net investment.

Desired capital stock

One of the most important decisions a firm has to make is to figure out how much capital to use. With too little capital, firms may find themselves unable to produce enough output to meet their customers' demands and as a result lose sales and profits. With too much capital, firms may find themselves carrying too much debt interest and other costs and having unused capacity.

The two main influences on the firm's desired capital stock are

1. Expected sales
2. The cost of capital relative to the cost of labor

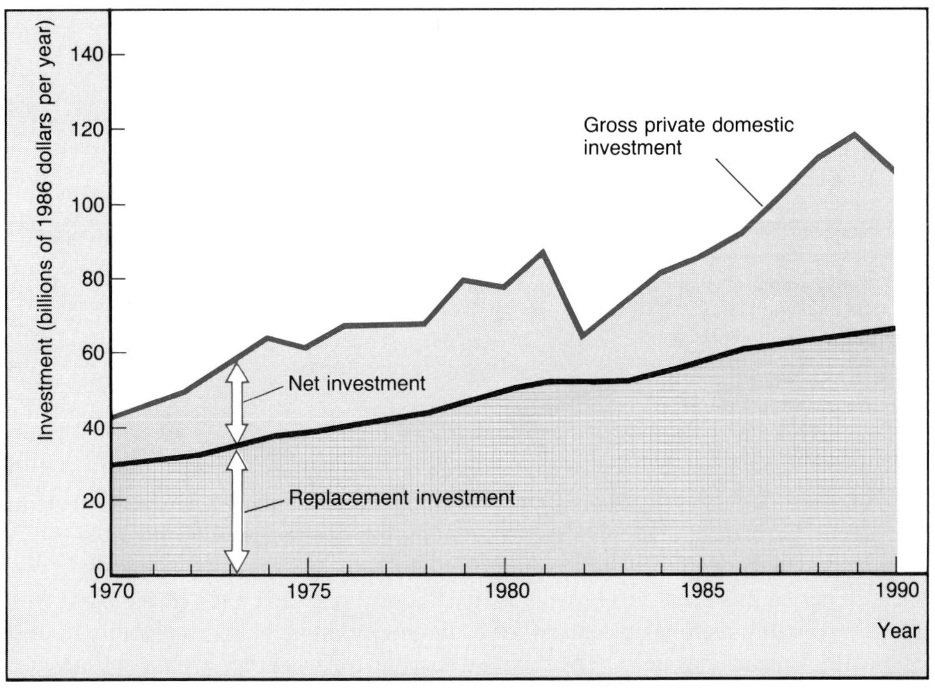

FIGURE 18.3
Gross and Net Investment

Gross investment is divided into two components—net investment and replacement investment. Replacement investment replaces worn-out capital. It grows steadily, since the capital stock and the amount of capital worn out each period also grow steadily. Net investment is the addition to the capital stock each year. This is the component of an investment that fluctuates.

Source: National Income and Expenditure Accounts, Statistics Canada, Catalogue 13-201.

Other things being equal, the higher a firm's expected sales, the larger is its desired stock of capital. Also, other things being equal, the greater the cost of capital relative to the cost of labor, the smaller is the desired stock of capital. For the rest of this section, we're going to concentrate on the first of these two influences on the desired capital stock. In Section 18.4, we'll consider the influence of relative factor costs on the desired capital stock and investment.

Accelerator mechanism

The **accelerator mechanism** is the mechanism linking the *level* of net investment to the *change* in output. The mechanism arises from the fact that firms desire to maintain a particular relationship between the *level* of their sales and the *level* of their capital stock. Because the *change* in the capital stock is net investment, a *change* in sales leads to a *temporary* increase in net investment.

To understand the accelerator mechanism, let's look at an example. The year is 2020 and the greenhouse effect has made the prairies a dustbowl. But Saskatchewan has completely solved its water problem. The massive Greening of Saskatchewan Water Company operates 40 giant desalting plants[1] off the coast of British Columbia and pumps the water across the Rockies. These plants produce billions of gallons of water a day, and each plant generates a revenue of $200 million a year. They have a life of 10 years, so 10 percent of them are replaced each year. Table 18.1 summarizes the data, and the numbers for period 1 refer to the situation we've just described. Because each plant produces an annual sales revenue of $200 million, the water company's desired ratio of capital to annual sales is 5 plants per $1 billion of sales. This is the actual ratio of capital to sales, so no net investment takes place. Gross investment equals replacement investment. Since there are 40 plants, 4 are replaced each year.

[1]Desalting plants have been used for many years in the dry, desert countries of the Middle East to produce drinking water.

TABLE 18.1
The Greening of Saskatchewan Water Company: The Simplest Accelerator Mechanism

VARIABLE	HOW DETERMINED	TIME PERIOD 1	2	3
Actual sales	Y_t is exogenous	8	10	10
Expected sales	$Y_t^e = Y_t$	8	10	10
Desired stock of desalination plants	$K_t^* = 5Y_t^e$	40	50	50
Net investment in desalination plants	$I_t^N = K_t^* - K_{t-1}$	0	10	0
Replacement of worn out desalination plants	$I_t^R = 0.1\,K_{t-1}$	4	4	5
Gross investment	$I_t = I_t^N + I_t^R$	4	14	5

Suppose that sales increase from $8 billion to $10 billion a year and that this increase is permanent and correctly forecasted. The desired stock of desalting plants now increases from 40 to 50. The water company buys 10 new plants. Its gross investment in period 2 is equal to 14 plants — 10 additional ones and 4 to replace those worn out. By period 3, there is no demand for additional desalting plants, but with a stock of 50 plants, 5 plants now need to be replaced each year. Thus gross investment increases to 5 plants per year.

In this example, a one-time but permanent increase in sales brought an enormous but temporary burst of investment. In real situations things are unlikely to work out as simply as in this example, which nevertheless gives you the sharpest possible focus on the accelerator mechanism at work.

Gradual capital-stock adjustment In real-world situations, it is more likely that firms will adjust their capital stock gradually to its new level rather than in a one-shot burst of investment as in the case we've just studied. Capital-stock adjustment is more likely to be gradual for two reasons:

1. Sales expectations lag behind actual sales
2. Capital stock deliveries lag behind orders

Both these sources of gradual capital-stock adjustment operate in the real world. Here we'll focus on one of them so that we can use a specific numerical example and calculation to illustrate the process. The example in Table 18.2 focuses on expected sales lagging behind actual sales. Suppose that the initial situation, in period 1, is exactly the same as it was in the previous example. In period 2, sales increase from $8 billion to $10 billion, but the water company does not believe this increase will be permanent so it does not increase its capital stock to a level required by such a permanent level of sales. Its expectation of future sales is that they will equal one half of their current level plus one half of their previously expected level. If the previously expected level was $8 billion and the current level is $10 billion, expected permanent sales are $9 billion. With this level of sales and a desired capital-sales ratio of 5 plants per $1 billion of sales, the water company's desired capital stock is 45 desalting plants. If there are no delays in filling orders for desalting plants, a net investment of 5 plants occurs in period 2. The capital stock increases to its desired level of 45 plants. Replacement investment remains at 4 plants since there were only 40 plants in place in the previous period. Gross investment increases to 9 plants.

TABLE 18.2
The Greening of Saskatchewan Water Company: Gradual Capital Stock Adjustment

VARIABLE	HOW DETERMINED	TIME PERIOD 1	2	3	4	5	...	∞
Actual sales	Y_t is exogenous	8	10	10.0	10.00	10.000	...	10
Expected sales	$Y_t^e = 0.5Y_{t-1}^e + 0.5Y_t$	8	9	9.5	9.75	9.875	...	10
Desired stock of desalination plants	$K_t^* = 5Y_t^e$	40	45	47.5	48.75	49.375	...	50
Net investment in desalination plants	$I_t^N = K_t^* - K_{t-1}$	0	5	2.5	1.25	0.625	...	0
Replacement of worn out desalination plants	$I_t^R = 0.1 K_{t-1}$	4	4	4.5	4.75	4.875	...	5
Gross investment	$I_t = I_t^N + I_t^R$	4	9	7.0	6.00	5.500	...	5

If sales remain at \$10 billion, expected sales gradually increase, closing the gap between expected and actual sales. The desired capital stock gradually increases, but by smaller absolute amounts. Thus net investment gradually declines. Replacement investment gradually increases, but not by as much as the decrease in net investment. Thus gross investment also gradually declines.

Figure 18.4 illustrates the accelerator mechanism. Part (a) shows the change in actual sales and also the change in expected sales when expected sales adjust gradually. Part (b) shows the response of investment if there are no lags — when expected and actual sales are equal. Part (c) shows the response of investment when there is a lag resulting from gradual adjustment of expected sales.

How well does the accelerator mechanism explain actual investment fluctuations?

18.3 *Investment in Canada and the United States in the 1980s*

TESTCASE

To see how useful the accelerator mechanism is in accounting for fluctuations in investment, let's look at the experience of Canada and the United States during the 1980s.

The Canadian accelerator

Our discussion of the accelerator mechanism in the previous section focused on the investment decision of an individual firm. Here, we want to consider the economy as a whole. How does net investment in the Canadian economy respond to *changes* in aggregate sales? To answer this question, we first need a measure of aggregate sales. The most natural measure is aggregate expenditure or real GDP. Let's look at the relationship between net investment and the change in real GDP.

You can see this relationship in Figure 18.5. In part (a), net fixed investment is measured on the left-hand scale and the change in real GDP on the right-hand scale. In part (b), inventory investment is measured on the left-hand scale. All the variables are measured in constant 1986 dollars.

The first thing that strikes the eye is the remarkably similar pattern formed by the time series of net investment and the change in real GDP. The relationship is especially strong in the case of inventory investment. When real GDP increased in 1981, so did

FIGURE 18.4
The Accelerator Mechanism

An increase in actual sales occurs in period 1 and is then maintained (part a). If the higher level is expected to be permanent, investment increases for one period (part b) and then decreases to its long-run level. If the permanence of the new higher sales level is only gradually expected (the blue line in part a), investment increases (part c) by a smaller amount in period 1 and then gradually approaches its steady-state level. The expected *change* in sales produces the change in the *level* of investment. This is the accelerator mechanism.

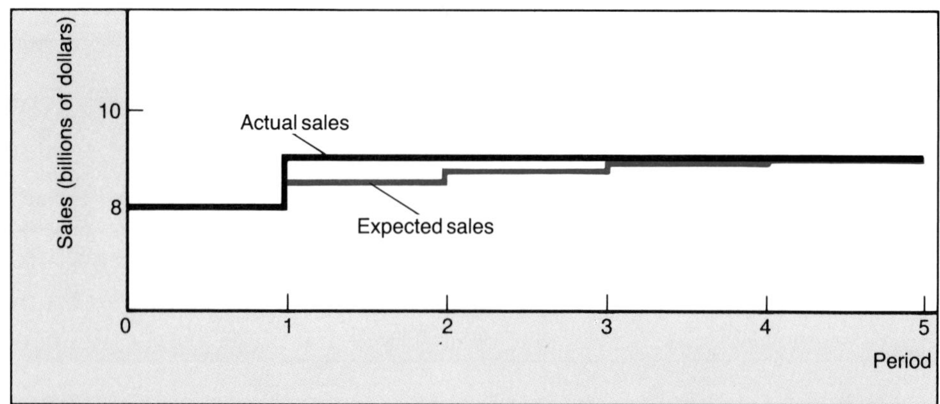

(a) Actual sales and expected sales

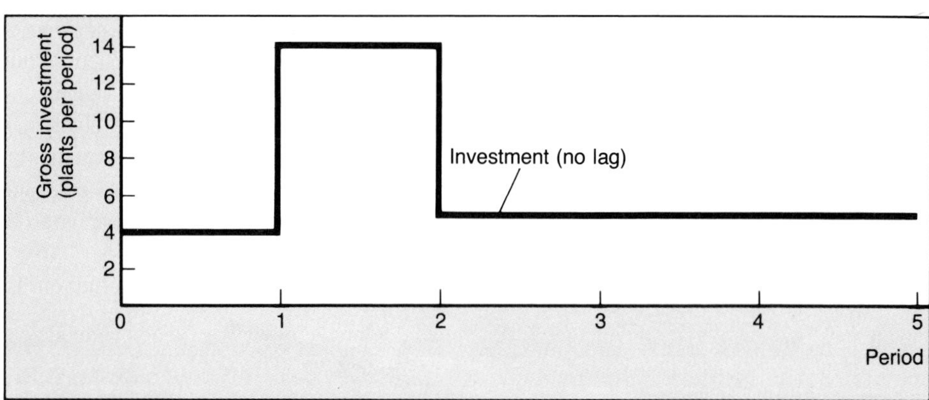

(b) Gross investment with no lag in expected sales

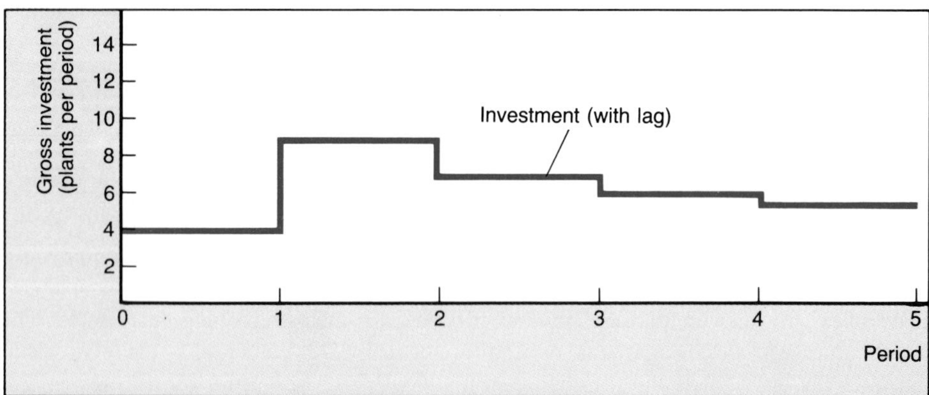

(c) Gross investment with lag in expected sales

net fixed investment and inventory investment. When real GDP crashed in 1982, net investment crashed with it. But when the recovery began in 1983, inventory investment increased but net fixed investment did not recover until two years later. Nevertheless, with a time lag, net investment did follow the path of the change in real GDP. The slow down of 1990 is also reflected in both the components of net investment.

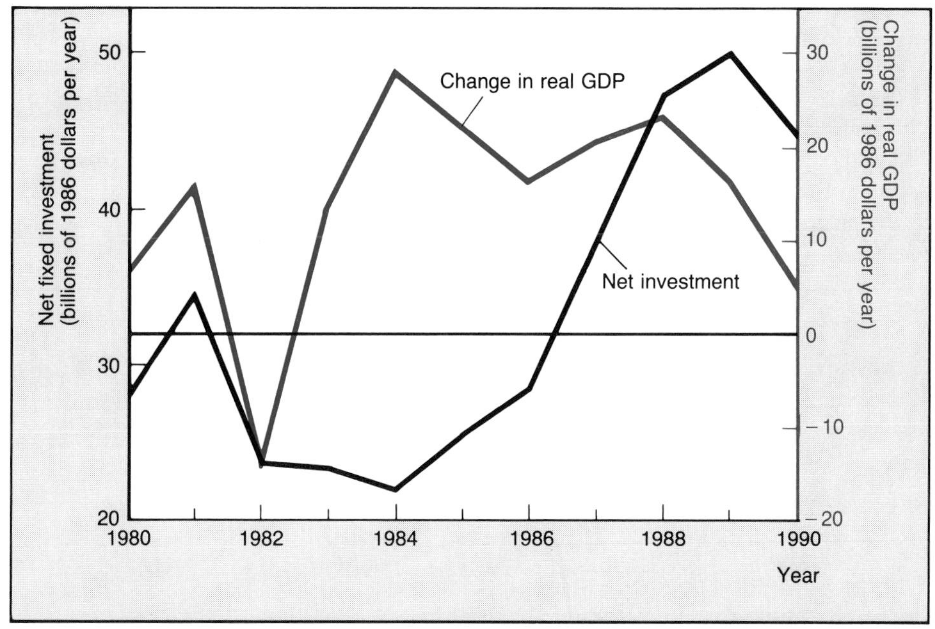

(a) Net fixed investment

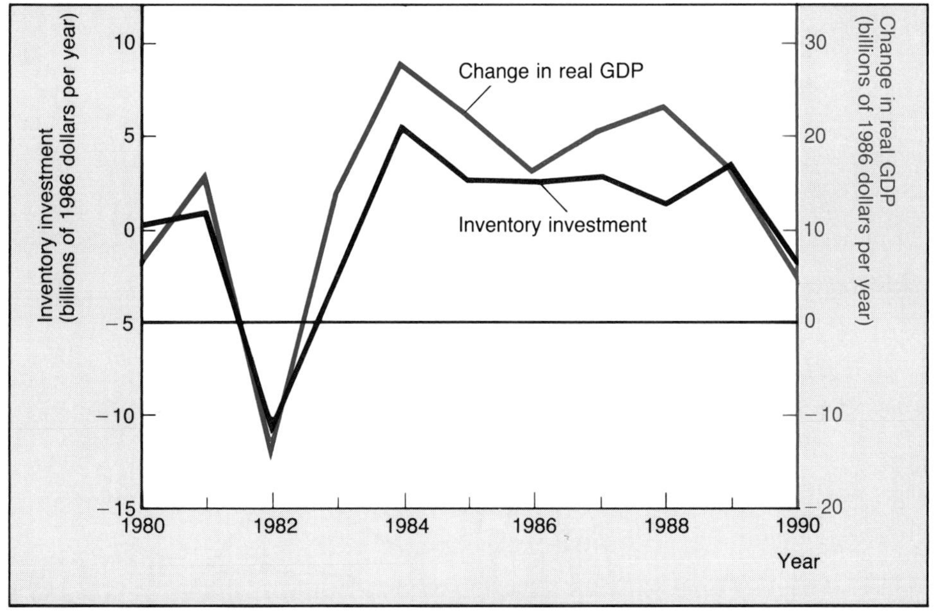

(b) Inventory investment

FIGURE 18.5
The Accelerator in Canada in the 1980s

The accelerator mechanism operates on the Canadian economy. The relationship between net fixed investment and the change in real GDP is closer in down-turns such as 1982 and 1990 than in recoveries such as 1983-1984 (part a). The inventory investment accelerator (part b) is strong and has no time lag.

Source: National Income and Expenditure Accounts, Statistics Canada, Catalogue 13-201.

The time lags The time lag associated with the change in net fixed investment is easy to explain. Inventory investment can be undertaken quickly. But fixed investment includes such megaprojects as electric power generation, transportation and communication systems, and custom-built factories for producing an incredible array of goods and services. Many of these items take years to design and build. For this reason, this type of investment responds to changes in real GDP with a time lag.

It appears that in the Canadian economy the accelerator mechanism is powerful. Is it as powerful everywhere? Let's take a look at another important economy, the United States.

The U.S. accelerator mechanism

The accelerator mechanism is even more powerful in the United States than in Canada. Figure 18.6 illustrates this fact. Every single peak and trough in inventory investment lines up with a peak and trough in real GDP growth and fixed investment lag exactly one year behind real GDP growth.

Although the accelerator mechanism is powerful and seems to account for a large amount of the variation in net investment, it's clear that other factors are also at work. The accelerator mechanism does not fit the data exactly. Let's now look at these other mechanisms.

FIGURE 18.6
The Accelerator in the United States in the 1980s

The accelerator mechanism in the U.S. economy is stronger than in Canada. The relationship between net fixed investment and the change in real GDP is very close (part a) but with a one-year time lag. For inventory investment (part b), the accelerator mechanism is strong and there is no time lag.

Source: Economic Report of the President, United States Government Printing Office, Washington, 1991.

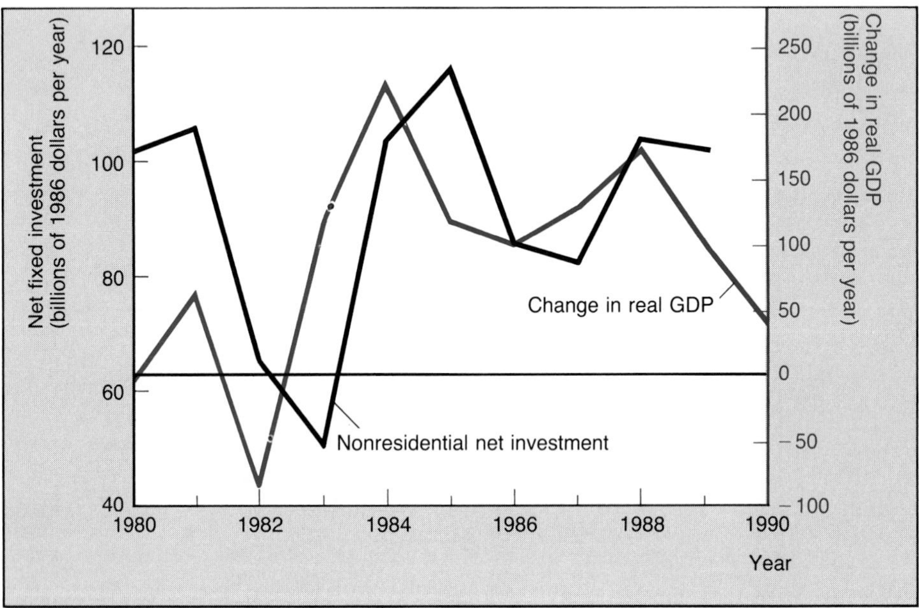

(a) Nonresidential net investment

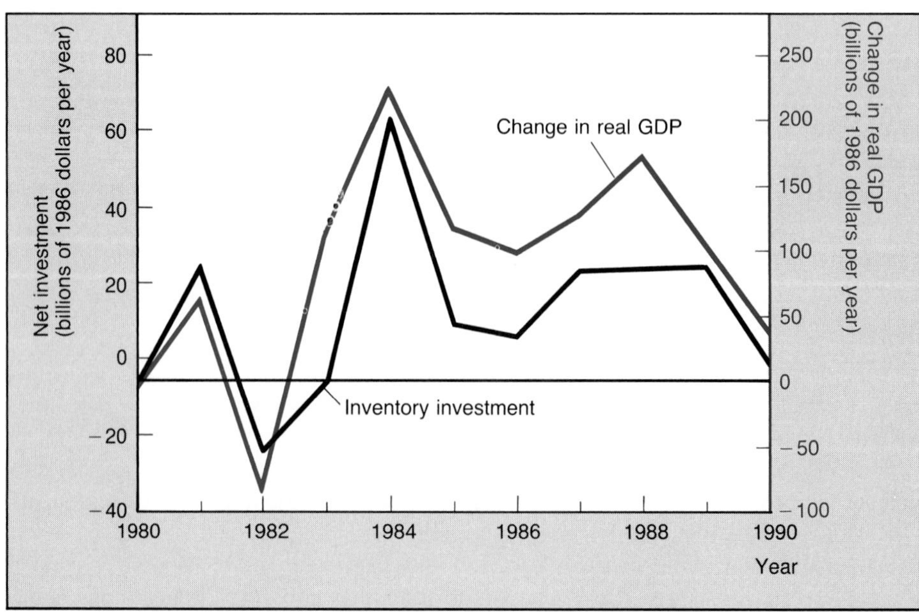

(b) Inventory investment

18.4 *Investment and the Rental Rate of Capital*

Almost any imaginable task can be performed using different combinations of capital and labor. For most tasks, the choice of technique ranges from one that uses a lot of capital and a very small amount of labor to one that uses a lot of labor and a very small amount of capital. For example, a dam could be built using massive earthmoving machines and a small amount of labor or masses of labor working by hand or using small wooden shovels, themselves made by hand. The Greening of Saskatchewan Water Company could operate desalting plants that use sophisticated and expensive computers to control the process or a large amount of skilled labor doing calculations and keeping records with paper and pencil.

A technique that uses a large amount of capital and a small amount of labor is called a **capital-intensive technique**. A technique that uses a large amount of labor and very little capital is called a **labor-intensive technique**. What determines whether a capital-intensive technique will be used rather than a labor-intensive technique? The answer determines the desired capital-output ratio—a ratio that we took as given when studying the accelerator mechanism. The choice depends on the relative costs of the alternative techniques. These relative costs, in turn, depend on the relative price of capital and labor. If capital is cheap relative to labor, then a capital-intensive technology will be used. But if labor is cheap relative to capital, then a labor-intensive technique will be employed.

But how can we calculate whether capital is cheap relative to labor? After all, buying a piece of equipment is buying something durable that can be used over a long period of time, while hiring labor is like buying a consumer good that can be used only once. How can we compare the price of capital and the price of labor in order to know whether capital is relatively cheap? The answer lies in a concept called the rental rate of capital. By comparing the rental rate of capital with the wage rate of labor we can establish the relative price of capital and labor.

Rental rate of capital

The **rental rate of capital** is the cost of *using* a piece of capital equipment, expressed in terms of dollars per hour. An alternative name is the **user cost of capital**. Most capital equipment is not rented, it is bought and used by its owners. Economists think of the owner of a piece of capital equipment as wearing two hats: one hat is that of the "owner" and the other is the hat of the "user." The owner rents the equipment to the user—implicitly. Thus the rental rate is sometimes called the implicit rent rate.

Some capital is explicitly rented—the owner and the user of the capital are different people. Travelers often rent cars at airports and students rent apartments or houses. Firms often rent equipment, for example, heavy earth-moving equipment and other specialized equipment used by civil engineering contractors. Whether capital equipment is implicitly or explicitly rented makes no difference to the general concept of the rental rate of capital.

The rental rate of an apartment Imagine that you are trying to decide whether to buy an apartment or rent one. The price of the apartment you are looking at is $100,000 and the mortgage interest rate is 10 percent a year. Suppose that apartment prices are expected to increase by 5 percent a year and that apartments depreciate by 2 percent a year. What is the maximum rent you will pay for such an apartment?

To answer this question you need to work out the implicit rental rate of the apartment. First you need to calculate the cost per year of owning the apartment: the depreciation cost, the interest you have to pay on the $100,000 needed to buy the apartment, and the capital gain you expect to make because apartment prices are expected to increase (a negative cost). The depreciation cost of a $100,000 apartment that depreciates at 2 percent a year is $2,000 a year. The interest on $100,000 at 10 percent a year is $10,000 a year. The total cost so far is $12,000 a year. But offset against this is the expected increase in the value of the apartment — the expected capital gain. Apartment prices are expected to increase at 5 percent a year, so the expected capital gain is $5,000. The cost of owning the apartment is $7,000 a year. Ignoring taxes and the costs of searching for an apartment and completing the purchase, $7,000 a year is the maximum rent you will pay for the apartment. The implicit rental rate of the apartment is $7,000 a year.

If apartments actually rent for less than $7,000 a year, it will pay you to rent rather than buy. If apartments rent for more than $7,000 a year, it will pay you to buy rather than rent. Since everyone is capable of doing the calculation you just performed, market forces will ensure that the actual rental rates on apartments do not stray too far away from their implicit rental rates. If the implicit rental rate is less than the actual rental rate, the demand for apartments for purchase will increase and the demand for apartments for rent will decrease. The purchase price of apartments will tend to rise and their rental rates fall. The process will continue until people are indifferent between owning and renting. Alternatively, if the implicit rental rate is greater than the actual rental rate, then the demand for apartments for purchase will decrease and the demand for apartments for rent will increase. The actual rental rate will rise and the purchase price will fall, bringing about equality between the actual and implicit rental rates. Thus the actual rental rate of a capital good (the apartment in this example) is the same as the implicit rental rate.

Rental rate formula We have just derived a formula for the rental rate, which we can now state in general terms: the rental rate of a piece of capital equipment is equal to the price of the capital (P_k) multiplied by the sum of its depreciation rate (δ) and the interest rate (r_m) minus the expected rate of increase of the price of the piece of capital equipment (P_k^e/P_k). That is,

$$\text{Rental rate} = P_k\left(\delta + r_m - \frac{\Delta P_k^e}{P_k}\right). \tag{18.3}$$

Let's check that this formula gives us the correct answer for the rental rate of the apartment we consider above. P_k equals $100,000; δ is 2 percent a year, which in proportionate terms is 0.02; r_m is 10 percent a year, which in proportionate terms is 0.1; and the expected rate of increase of apartment prices, $\Delta P_k^e/P_k$, is 5 percent a year, which as a proportion, is 0.05. Putting these numbers into the formula, we have

$$\begin{aligned}\text{Rental rate} &= \$100{,}000\,(0.02 + 0.10 - 0.05)\\ &= \$100{,}000 \times 0.07\\ &= \$7{,}000 \text{ a year.}\end{aligned}$$

Evidently the formula works.

Rental rate and the desired capital stock

Firms are in business to make as much profit as possible. One implication of this fact is that they produce a quantity of output such that its marginal cost is equal to its marginal revenue. To produce the profit maximizing level of output, the quantity of each factor of production hired is the amount that makes the factor's marginal product equal to its real marginal cost. We saw an example of this in our study of the labor market in Chapter 8. There we discovered that firms hire the quantity of labor such that the marginal product of labor equals the real wage rate. The same principle applies to capital. Firms employ the quantity of capital such that the marginal product of capital (*MPK*) equals the real rental rate (*RR*). That is,

$$MPK = RR. \tag{18.4}$$

The real rental rate (*RR*) is the rental rate divided by the price level. That is,

$$RR = \frac{P_k}{P}\left(\delta + r_m - \frac{\Delta P_k^e}{P_k}\right). \tag{18.5}$$

Since we're trying to explain *aggregate* investment, we're interested in the economy's average real rental rate. Let's simplify things a little bit by setting the value of the indexes that measure the price of capital, P_k, and the price level, P, such that the ratio P_k/P is equal to 1. Also, let's assume that capital goods prices inflate at the same pace as the prices of goods and services in general. Then the expected increase in the price of capital ($\Delta P_k^e//P_k$) is equal to the expected inflation rate (π^e). These assumptions make it possible to express the real rental rate as

$$RR = (\delta + r_m - \pi^e). \tag{18.6}$$

You've met the term $r_m - \pi^e$ before; it's the real interest rate. If we call the real interest rate r, the real rental rate is

$$RR = \delta + r. \tag{18.7}$$

The depreciation rate is determined by technological factors, so the only *variable* that affects the real rental rate is the real interest rate. The higher the real interest rate, the higher is the real rental rate of capital.

Tobin's *q*

Another way of looking at the determinants of a firm's desired capital stock uses **Tobin's *q***, the ratio of the stock market value of a firm to the price of the firm's capital assets. The price of capital is P_k. If we call the stock market value of the firm *SMV*, Tobin's q is

$$q = SMV/P_k. \tag{18.8}$$

There's a relationship between Tobin's q and the rental rate and marginal product of capital, which is summarized in Table 18.3. The table also provides a numerical example. Let's work through the table.

The first three rows define the marginal product of capital, the interest rate, and the stock market value of the firm, and provide some numerical values. There is no numerical value for the stock market value of a firm because that's something we have to calculate.

Row 4 tells us about **portfolio equilibrium**, a situation in which there is no reallocation of assets that would increase the return on a portfolio (for a given amount of risk). Investors can buy bonds yielding an interest rate r or they can buy stock in the firm we're considering. The firm's income is the marginal product of its capital, *MPK*. This income, expressed as a percentage of the value of the firm, must equal the interest rate on bonds. That is,

$$r = MPK/SMV. \tag{18.9}$$

TABLE 18.3
Tobin's q

ITEM	SYMBOLS AND EQUATIONS	NUMERICAL EXAMPLE
1. Marginal product of firm's capital	MFK	\$90,000
2. Interest rate on bonds	r	0.1 (10%)
3. Stock market value of firm	SMV	
4. Portfolio equilibrium	$r = \frac{MPK}{SMW}$	$0.1 = \frac{\$90{,}000}{SMV}$
5. Stock market value of firm	$SMV = MPK/r$	$SMV = \$90{,}000/0.1 = \$900{,}000$
6. Price of firm's capital	P_k	\$1,000,000
7. Rental rate of firm's capital	$R = rP_k$	$R = 0.1 \times \$1{,}000{,}000 = \$100{,}000$
8. Tobin's q	$q = \frac{SMV}{P_k}$	$q = \frac{\$900{,}000}{\$1{,}000{,}000} = 0.9$
9. Equivalently	$q = \frac{MPK}{R}$	$q = \frac{\$90{,}000}{100{,}000} = 0.9$

If the interest rate on bonds (r) exceeds the return from investing in the firm (MPK/SMV), it pays to buy bonds and sell stock in the firm. The stock market value of the firm will fall and continue to fall until the rate of return on holding stock in the firm equals the return on bonds. That is why portfolio equilibrium determines this equality. We can use this portfolio equilibrium condition to determine the stock market value of the firm. It is the firm's marginal product of capital divided by the interest rate on bonds. In the numerical example, with a marginal product of capital of \$90,000 and an interest rate of 10 percent (0.1), the stock market value of the firm is \$900,000.

Rows 6 and 7 define the price of the firm's capital and its rental rate. (This formula ignores depreciation and changes in capital prices for simplicity.) Tobin's q, by definition, is the stock market value of the firm divided by the price of buying the firm's capital assets. In the numerical example, Tobin's q is 0.9. The firm can be bought on the stock market for \$900,000 but it would cost \$1 million to buy the firm's capital assets in the capital market. Row 9 shows that Tobin's q is equivalently equal to the marginal product of capital divided by the rental rate of capital.

Long-run equilibrium In the long run, forces are at work moving the value of Tobin's q to 1. This means that in the long run the stock market value of the firm equals the cost of buying the firm's assets and also that the marginal product of capital equals the rental rate. In such a situation, the firm's capital stock is equal to its desired level. The firm is maximizing profit and its stock market value equals the cost of buying its capital assets.

When Tobin's q is less than 1, the firm's stock market value is less than the cost of buying its capital assets. Equivalently, the marginal product of capital is less than the rental rate. Such a firm is too big. It will pay the firm to sell some of its capital assets, decreasing its capital stock until the marginal product of capital equals the rental rate and the stock market value of the firm equals the cost of replacing the firm's assets.

If Tobin's q is greater than 1, the stock market value of the firm exceeds the cost of buying the firm's assets, and the marginal product of capital exceeds the rental rate. In such a situation, it will pay the firm to buy more capital assets and continue doing so until the marginal product of capital equals the rental rate and its stock market value equals the price of its capital assets.

Desired capital stock

When we studied the accelerator, we emphasized the fact that the desired capital stock is proportional to expected sales. For the economy as whole, sales are equal to GDP. Thus the desired capital stock is proportional to expected GDP. That is,

$$K_t^* = vY_t^e.$$

But the desired capital-sales ratio, v, is not a constant. It depends on the real rental rate of capital and, therefore, on the real interest rate. Other things being equal, the higher the real interest rate, the higher is the rental rate of capital and the lower is the desired capital-sales ratio. Figure 18.7 illustrates this relationship. In this example, a decrease in the real interest rate from 10 percent to 5 percent increases the desired capital-sales ratio from 3 to 4.

The flexible accelerator

Because the desired capital-sales ratio depends on the real interest rate, we have to modify the accelerator mechanism to take account of this additional source of variation in the desired capital stock. What drives investment and what makes investment fluctuations large is the fact that a change in the desired capital stock produces a temporary burst of net investment. The simple accelerator emphasizes the effect of a change in expected sales on the desired capital stock. But a change in the real interest rate also affects the desired capital stock. A decrease in the real interest rate brings an increase in the desired capital stock and a temporary increase in net investment.

It's important to note that no stable relationship exists between investment and the real interest rate. Instead, the stable relationship is between the desired capital-sales ratio and the real interest rate. This relationship is determined by technological factors. Any given change in the interest rate, other things being equal, brings a given change

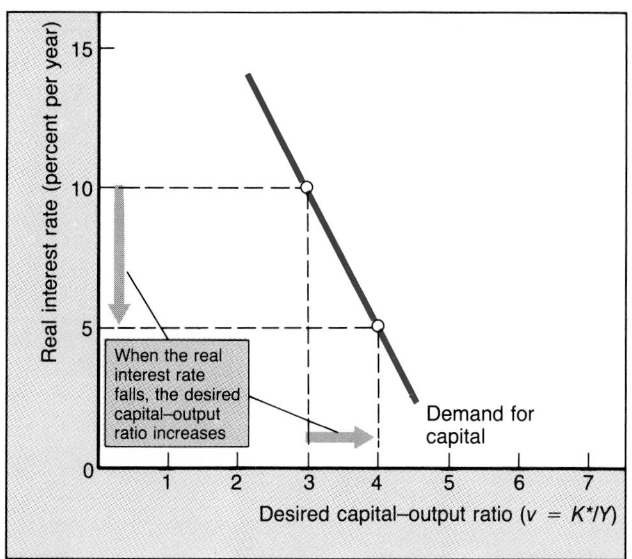

FIGURE 18.7
Interest Rates and the Desired Capital-Output Ratio

The desired capital-output ratio depends on the real rental rate. The real rental rate changes when the real interest rate changes. Hence there is a downward sloping relationship between the desired capital-output ratio and the real interest rate.

in the desired capital-sales ratio. As the firms move toward their new desired capital-sales ratio, there is a *temporary* change in investment. Once they're at the new desired capital-sales ratio, net investment returns to zero.

But gross investment increases, because the higher capital stock generates a higher steady-state amount of depreciation and replacement investment. Thus, other things being equal, the lower the real interest rate, the higher is the level of gross investment.

How important is the effect of fluctuations in the real interest rate on investment? Let's now answer this question.

TESTCASE

18.5 *Another Look at Canada in the 1980s*

To examine the importance of changes in the real interest rate, let's look again, but more closely, at net investment in Canada during the 1980s. We've already seen that net investment is influenced by the accelerator. If we are to examine the way in which the real interest rate influences net investment, we need to take these two separate influences into account simultaneously.

Real interest rate effect

In 1980 net investment was $28 billion and the real interest rate was 2.7 percent. These values are at a point on the Canadian investment curve for 1980. This curve is shown in Figure 18.8. With all other influences held constant, a change in the real interest rate results in a movement along that investment demand curve.

But as you know, other things are *not* constant, and one factor that has an important influence on net investment is the change in real GDP. Let's see how this influence interacts with the interest rate effect.

FIGURE 18.8
The Canadian Investment Demand Curve in 1980

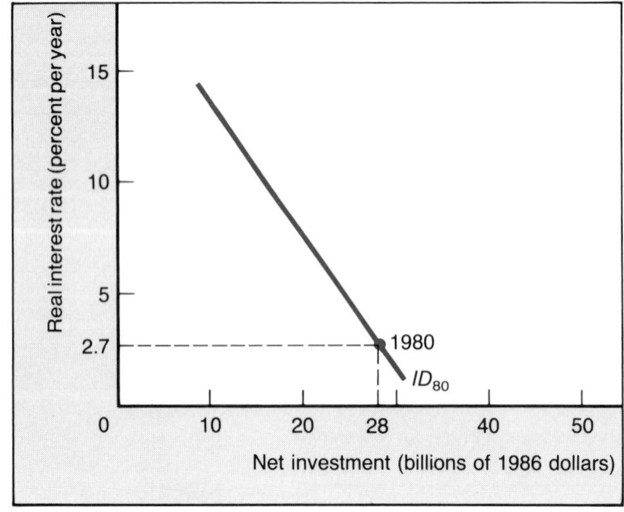

In 1980, the real interest rate was 2.7 percent a year and net investment was a little over $28 billion. The investment demand curve in Canada in that year was ID_{80}.

Accelerator mechanism and interest rates

Because of the accelerator, the investment demand curve is constantly shifting. The amount by which it shifts depends to a large degree on the change in the strength of the accelerator effect. When we studied the accelerator, we discovered that the *level* of investment is influenced by the *change* in GDP. We're now interested in understanding how investment itself *changes*. If the level of investment depends on the change in GDP, then the *change* in investment depends on the *change in the change* in GDP. If the growth rate of GDP increases, the investment demand curve shifts to the right. If the growth rate of GDP decreases, the investment demand curve shifts to the left.

You can see these effects in Figure 18.9. Part (a) shows the investment demand curve for each year of the 1980s. The blue arrows show the magnitudes of the shifts of the investment demand curve to the right when the growth rate of real GDP increases. The grey arrows show the magnitude of the shifts of the investment demand curve to the left when the growth rate of real GDP decreases.

If the only influences on net investment are the change in real GDP and the real interest rate, the magnitude of the shift in the investment demand curve will be closely

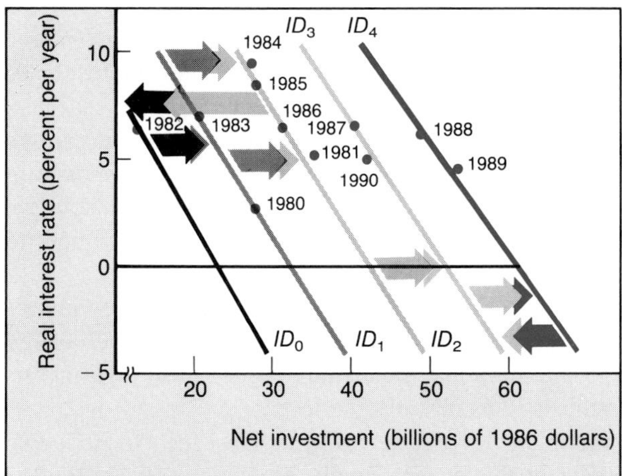

(a) Interest rate influence

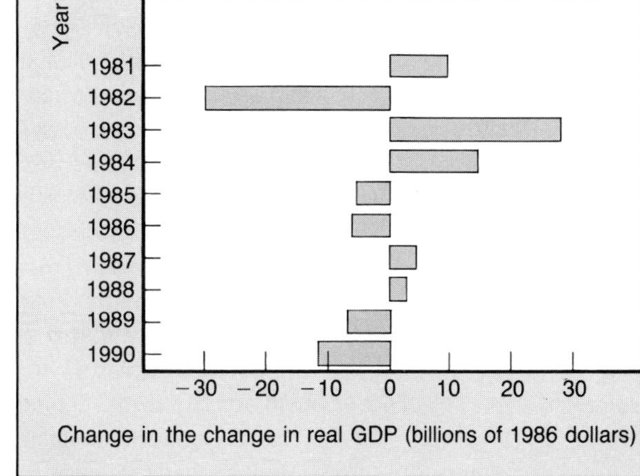

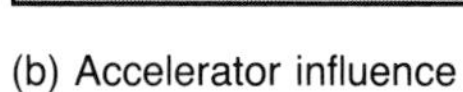

(b) Accelerator influence

FIGURE 18.9
The Shifting Investment Demand Curve

The investment demand curve shifts because of the accelerator. For a given change in real GDP, there is a given investment demand curve. When the change in real GDP itself changes, the investment demand curve shifts. The shifting investment demand curve is shown in part (a) and the change in the change in real GDP in part (b). The blue bars show the magnitude of the accelerator effect on the investment demand curve. The blue and grey arrows show the actual shifts in the investment demand curve. In most years, the shift in the investment demand curve is close to that predicted by the accelerator. The main exception is 1989 when the investment demand curve shifts to the right when the accelerator is shifting it to the left.

Source: National Income and Expenditure Accounts, Statistics Canada, Catalogue 13-201, *Bank of Canada Review*, various issues, and our calculations.

related to the magnitude of the change in the change in real GDP. Figure 18.9(b) shows whether this relationship holds. The blue bars show the magnitude of the *changes in the changes* in real GDP. As you can see, in most years the shift in the investment demand curve and the predicted accelerator mechanism line up quite closely. But there are one or two years in which the investment demand curve shifts, either by more or less than the shift predicted by the accelerator. Only in one year, 1989, does the investment demand curve shift in the wrong direction—the accelerator is decreasing investment but the investment demand curve shifts to the right. Aside from this year, the fluctuations in investment in the rest of the 1980s are well accounted for by these two main variables—the real interest rate and the change in the change in real GDP.

The fact that investment is significantly influenced by real interest rates has important implications for monetary and fiscal policy. Let's now explore those implications.

18.6 *Monetary Policy and Investment*

Monetary policy can influence investment through three channels:

- The interest rate effect
- The exchange rate effect
- The real balance effect

Interest rate effect

When the Bank of Canada slows down the money supply growth rate, interest rates increase and, since inflation expectations change much more slowly than interest rates, the real interest rate also increases. As a result, the desired capital-sales ratio decreases and so does the desired capital stock. Investment falls. It takes time for investment to respond, but once the response gets under way, the fall in investment can become large. Once the capital stock adjustment process is complete, the response of investment to interest rates becomes modest. The fall in investment was temporary.

A speedup in the growth rate of the money supply has the reverse effects on investment. It lowers interest rates and lowers the real interest rate, increasing the desired capital stock. Investment picks up, and there may be a temporary burst of high investment activity as the capital stock adjusts to its new desired level.

Only temporary changes in the money supply growth rate have the effects we've just described. A permanent change in the money supply growth rate that brings a permanent change in the inflation rate leaves the real interest rate unaffected and, in the long run, has no effect on the desired capital stock or investment.

Exchange rate effect

The exchange rate effect is indirect. An increase in the money supply growth rate lowers the exchange rate and stimulates net exports. As a result, firms' expected sales change and so does the desired capital stock. An accelerator effect (with gradual capital stock adjustment) takes place. A slowdown in the money supply growth rate has the opposite effects.

Just like the interest rate effect, the exchange rate effect arises only when there are temporary changes in the money supply growth rate. A permanent change in the money supply growth rate brings a continuous change in the exchange rate that matches the change in the inflation rate. The real exchange rate is left undisturbed. With no change in the real exchange rate, there is no change in net exports and therefore no induced effect on the desired capital stock and investment.

Real balance effect

A change in the money supply disturbs the portfolio equilibrium of households and firms. Excess real balances are reduced by acquiring other financial assets or real assets. Shortages of real balances are replenished by selling financial assets or real assets. To the extent that a portfolio adjustment involves a change in the desired stock of real assets, it has a temporary effect on the rate of investment.

Unlike the other two channels, it is possible that the real balance effect operates even in the long run. A permanent increase in the money supply growth rate leads to a permanent increase in the inflation rate and nominal interest rates and a permanent decrease in the desired ratio of money to income. With a given stock of wealth, the quantities of other assets held must be increased to accommodate the change in real balances. If real assets are substituted for real balances, there will be a permanent effect of a change in the inflation rate on the capital stock and on replacement investment.

Monetary policy in practice

Sorting out the separate influences of monetary policy on investment is a complicated matter and one that has not yet been done satisfactorily. But it is clear that changes in the money supply growth rate, operating through the three channels, have a powerful effect on investment. You can see these effects in some of the investment data we've looked at earlier in this chapter. The severe monetary contraction and interest rate hikes of the early 1980s brought a collapse of investment. The easing of monetary policy and the gradual reduction of interest rates through the mid-1980s brought a strong investment recovery. The (milder) investment downturn of 1990-1991 can also be seen, in part, as a consequence of the high real interest rates of the late 1980s.

18.7 *Taxes and Investment*

Taxes influence investment through two main channels:

- Aggregate demand effects
- Rental rate effects

Aggregate demand effects

We've seen that tax changes can either dampen or stimulate aggregate demand. Tax-induced changes in aggregate demand bring a change in the desired capital stock. Such changes operate in exactly the same way as the accelerator mechanism. That is, a tax *change* that *changes* aggregate expenditure changes firms' sales and brings a *temporary* change in investment. Once GDP and firms' sales have reached their new level, net investment returns to its original level.

Because of this accelerator mechanism, the fiscal policy multiplier effect on aggregate demand follows a cyclical path. For example, a tax cut increases expenditure and, as a result, investment increases, making the multiplier effect large. Later, as expenditure approaches its new equilibrium, investment declines. Thus any tax change tends to set up an adjustment path for aggregate demand that overshoots its long-run equilibrium.

Rental rate effect

Fiscal policy can have an important effect on the desired capital stock and investment by influencing the *after-tax* rental rate. The three main sources of tax effects on the after-tax rental rate are

- Corporate income taxes
- Depreciation deductions
- Investment tax credits

Corporate income taxes Stockholders, the ultimate owners of firms, are concerned with the after-tax return they make on their equity. Firms that maximize the after-tax returns of stockholders will have the best stock market performances. To maximize after-tax profit (and their stock market value), firms equate the marginal product of capital with the after-tax rental rate. Other things being equal, the higher the corporate income tax rate, the higher is the before-tax rental rate and the lower is the desired capital stock.

Depreciation deductions In calculating their profits, firms deduct depreciation costs. But the amounts deducted depend on rules determined by the tax laws. These rules are occasionally changed and, when they change, they bring a *temporary* change in the level of investment.

Investment tax credits An investment tax credit is a decrease in a firm's taxable profit, determined by the scale of the firm's investment in the current year. Investment tax credits are used to encourage investment, especially in small businesses.

Taxes and the rental rate formula

When we studied the rental rate formula and the relationship between the marginal product of capital and the real rental rate, we ignored taxes, but now we want to take taxes into account to see how they affect that formula.

If we ignore changes in the price of capital (ΔP_k), the rental rate formula is

$$R = P_k(\delta + r). \tag{18.10}$$

You can think of R, the firm's rental rate, as its return from employing its capital. It is equal to the value of the marginal product of the capital. This return is taxed at the corporate income tax rate, which we'll call u. Thus the firm makes not R but $(1 - u)R$. If this is the only feature of the tax system, the firm will want to set the value of the marginal product of capital equal to $(1 - u)R$. But the firm still has to buy its machines for P_k and bear the depreciation rate, δ, and the interest rate, r. Thus the firm will pick a capital stock such that

$$(1 - u)R = P_k(\delta + r). \tag{18.11}$$

We've seen there are two further features of the tax system: depreciation deductions and investment tax credits. Suppose that the depreciation deductions are equal to the actual depreciation, δP_k; then the firm's after-tax return is not $(1 - u)R$ but $(1 - u)R + u\delta P_k$. The amount $u\delta P_k$ is the decrease in taxes because of depreciation deductions. Thus the firm would choose a capital stock such that

$$(1 - u)R + u\delta P_k = P_k(\delta + r). \tag{18.12}$$

Investment tax credits lower the cost of capital to firms. When they buy their equipment, firms get a tax credit on that purchase. We'll designate the tax credit rate z. Thus the amount actually paid for a piece of capital is not P_k but $(1 - z)P_k$. Taking this final factor into account, firms will choose a capital stock that makes the marginal product of capital equal to the after-tax rental rate on capital and satisfy the equation

$$(1 - u)R = (1 - z)P_k[(1 - u)\delta + r]. \tag{18.13}$$

Dividing both sides by $(1 - u)$ gives

$$R = (1 - z)P_k\delta + \frac{(1 - z)}{(1 - u)}P_k r. \tag{18.14}$$

By manipulating the investment tax credit rate, z, and the corporate income tax rate, u, fiscal policy can influence investment. An increase in the investment tax credit lowers the rental rate and increases the demand for capital. An increase in the corporate income tax rate increases the rental rate and decreases the demand for capital.

Although there is disagreement about the effects of fiscal policy on investment, no one denies that the effects are present. The arguments centre on the precise magnitude of the effects. The consensus is that the effects are not large.

Sorting out the effects

Working out the effects of tax changes on investment is complicated by the fact that investment is influenced by expectations about the change in future sales, real interest rates, expectations about future prices of capital goods, and the general state of business confidence. Studies that attempt to disentangle these separate influences suggest that net investment as a percentage of GDP does respond to tax changes and in exactly the same way as it responds to changes in the real rental rate arising from other sources, such as the real interest rate.

Despite the fact that tax changes appear to affect investment, they are not regarded as a reliable tool for stabilizing fluctuations in investment and aggregate demand. Too many other factors more dominant than taxes influence this component of aggregate expenditure.

18.8 *Moods, Animal Spirits, and Sunspots*

All investment decisions are based on taking a view of the future. Often, they are decisions to use a technology that has never been tried before. Always, even when they use tried and trusted technologies, investment decisions involve a leap in the dark.

Those who undertake investment decisions make the best forecasts they can and assess the likely rate of return on an investment project as thoroughly as possible. But in the safest of safe investments, there is an enormous range of possible outcomes. Every investment project could possibly be a spectacular success or an equally spectacular disaster. Because of the inherent uncertainty involved in taking investment decisions, people tend to check their own hunches against the hunches of other people. There is a kind of safety in numbers. If most people believe the economy is about to embark on a period of rapid expansion and prosperity and if they're going to act on that expectation, the chances are they'll be right. If most people are filled with gloom and believe the economy is on the brink of recession, and if they act on that expectation, again they'll likely be right.

For although expectations about the change in sales affect the level of investment—the accelerator mechanism—*changes in investment* have a magnified effect on real GDP—the multiplier effect. Thus if there is a widespread expectation that real GDP is going to increase and if, based on this expectation, investment increases, then a multiplier effect will indeed increase real GDP.

Keynes coined the term ''animal spirits'' to describe the forces at work generating swings in mood and changes in expectations. The name conjures up the idea of instinctive reactions to collective swings of mood rather than rational responses to changes in the objective environment. The modern name for this set of ideas is ''sunspot theory.'' In the nineteenth century, British economist William Stanley Jevons thought that actual sunspots might cause fluctuations in the economy. An eleven-year cycle in sunspot activity had been discovered and Jevons thought that the business cycle was too similar in its duration to the sunspot cycle to be a coincidence. His research and subsequent research suggest that if there is a sunspot effect, it's a weak one.

But modern theorists have used the term ''sunspot'' to denote any variable that in fact has no effect but that people believe has an effect on the economy. The belief alone is enough to generate a sunspot effect. Whether ''sunspot'' effects operate in reality is not yet known and is the subject of a great deal of current research. Most of that research, at the present time, is theoretical.

Earlier in this chapter, we saw that changes in investment are very well accounted for by changes in the real interest rate and changes in the change in real GDP. To the extent that investment can be explained by these factors, it appears that invoking ''animal spirits,'' ''sunspots,'' and swings of mood is not required. But admittedly, there are other influences on investment. The accelerator and the real interest rate do not account for every last small change in investment. Also, there is, to some degree, a kind of two-way causation arising from the interaction of the multiplier effect and the accelerator. Thus isolating the underlying force moving both real GDP and investment could leave room for ''animal spirits'' and ''sunspots.''

Sorting out the possible influences of animal spirits and changes of mood remains an area of active research.

18.9 *Fluctuations in Investment, Output, and Interest Rates*

To close our study of investment, let's return to the *IS-LM* model of aggregate demand that we studied in Chapter 5 and see how the theory of investment that we have examined in this chapter enables us to understand fluctuations in real GDP and interest rates.

We've seen that investment fluctuates mainly because of the accelerator mechanism. A given expected change in sales generates a particular level of investment. The higher the expected change in sales, the higher the level of investment. As sales expectations fluctuate, so the level of investment fluctuates and the investment demand curve shifts.

The position of the investment demand curve determines the position of the *IS* curve in the *IS-LM* model. This model is illustrated in Figure 18.10. Suppose that there is a given quantity of money and a given demand for money. This gives rise to an *LM* curve that is fixed. But changes in expected sales bring swings in the investment demand curve and swings in the *IS* curve. Suppose that at times of extreme optimism, the *IS* curve is IS_1. At times of extreme pessimism, it is IS_0. Fluctuations in the *IS* curve between these two limits bring fluctuations in real GDP between Y_0 and Y_1 and in the interest rate between r_0 and r_1.

If fluctuations in investment are one of the most important sources of fluctuations in the economy, then we will see positive correlation between fluctuations in real GDP and fluctuations in interest rates. Interest rates will tend to be high when the economy is in boom and low in recession.

In fact, such a correlation tends to show up between interest rates and GDP. The correlation is not perfect, however, because not all the fluctuations arise from instability in investment. Changes in the money supply or in the demand for money that shift the *LM* curve bring changes in the opposite direction. Such shifts also occur, complicating the pattern of the relationship between interest rates and GDP.

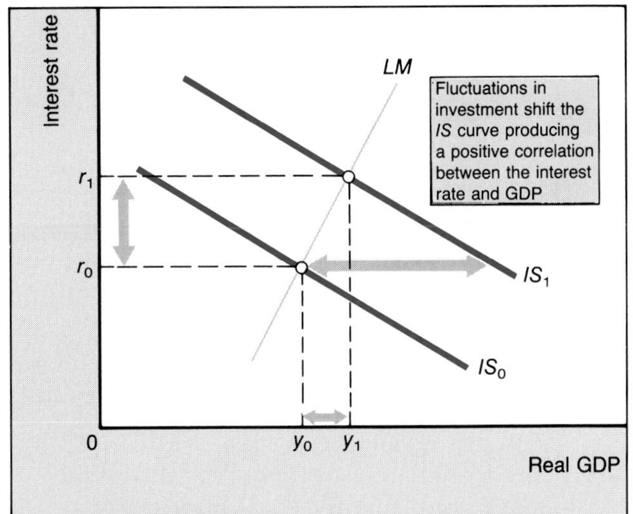

FIGURE 18.10
Fluctuations in Investment, GDP, and Interest Rates

Fluctuations in investment shift the *IS* curve between IS_0 and IS_1. With no change in the *LM* curve, the result is fluctuations in real GDP between Y_0 and Y_1 and the interest rate between r_0 and r_1. There is a positive correlation between interest rates and income. There is also a positive correlation between interest rates and investment.

Not only is there a positive correlation between interest rates and GDP, there is also a positive correlation between interest rates and investment. This fact does not mean that *other things being equal*, the higher the interest rate, the lower the level of investment. It means that most of the fluctuations in the economy result from shifts in the investment demand curve rather than movements along that curve.

■ We've now completed our study of the microeconomic foundations of investment decisions. We've seen why investment is a volatile element of aggregate expenditure. We've also seen how fluctuations in investment bring fluctuations in real GDP and interest rates. But we noted that they're not the only source of fluctuations in the economy. Another important source arises from fluctuations in the monetary sector. We examine these factors in the next chapter.

CHAPTER REVIEW

Summary

VOLATILITY OF INVESTMENT

Investment is the most volatile component of aggregate expenditure. All elements of investment—inventory investment, residential investment, and nonresidential investment—undergo large swings. Furthermore, fluctuations in investment in Canada are very similar to fluctuations in global investment. The component of investment that fluctuates most is net investment. Replacement investment grows steadily as the capital stock grows.

DEMAND FOR CAPITAL AND INVESTMENT

Capital is a stock and investment is a flow. Other things being equal, the higher the level of sales (and output), the higher the desired stock of capital. This relationship gives rise to the accelerator mechanism—a change in expected sales (and output) determines the level of investment. *Changes* in the level of investment result from *changes in the change* in expected sales. For the economy as a whole, sales are equal to GDP, so expected sales equal expected GDP. Changes in expected GDP determine the level of aggregate investment.

The accelerator is a powerful mechanism. In practice, it accounts for a large amount of the variation in investment.

THE RENTAL RATE OF CAPITAL

The rental rate of capital is the cost of *using* capital. It takes into account the interest on funds used to buy the capital (r_m), the depreciation of the capital (δ), the price of the capital (P_k), and the rate of change of its price ($\Delta P_k^e/P_k$). The formula for the rental rate is

$$R = P_k\left(r_m + \delta - \frac{\Delta P_k^e}{P_k}\right).$$

The rental rate of capital influences the desired capital stock. Firms employ capital up to the point at which its marginal product equals the real rental rate.

Tobin's q is another way of looking at the demand for capital. Tobin's q is the ratio of the stock market value of a firm to the current market price of its capital. If Tobin's q is less than 1, the firm is not worth as much on the stock market as the cost of its assets and the firm's capital stock is too large. If Tobin's q is greater than 1, the firm is worth more than the cost of its assets and its capital stock is too small.

Combining the interest rate with the accelerator produces the flexible accelerator—the theory of investment based on the proposition that investment adjusts the actual capital stock to its desired level and the desired capital stock depends on the rental rate of capital.

The accelerator—changes in real GDP—and the rental rate effect explain a large part of the fluctuation in aggregate investment in Canada.

HOW MONETARY POLICY AFFECTS INVESTMENT

Monetary policy can influence investment through interest rates, the exchange rate, and real balances. The first two are only short-run effects. A change in the anticipated inflation rate leaves the real interest rate and the real exchange rate undisturbed and has no effect on investment. But a temporary increase in the money supply or its growth rate lowers the real interest rate, depreciates the currency, and stimulates investment.

Changes in the inflation rate change the allocation of assets between financial and real so the real balance effect can influence the desired capital stock, even in the long run.

HOW TAXES AFFECT INVESTMENT

Taxes affect investment either by changing aggregate demand, operating through the accelerator mechanism, or by changing the effective after-tax real interest rate.

WAVES OF OPTIMISM AND PESSIMISM

Although fluctuations in investment are almost entirely explained by changes in real GDP (the accelerator effect) and changes in the real interest rate (the rental rate effect), it is possible that a deeper source of fluctuations in both investment and changes in real GDP are swings in business sentiment, swings from optimism to pessimism and back. The idea that investment and economic activity respond purely to ''animal spirits'' is controversial and subject to ongoing research.

FLUCTUATIONS IN INVESTMENT, OUTPUT, AND INTEREST RATES

Fluctuations in interest rates and fluctuations in real GDP are positively correlated. A major part of the explanation for this correlation is the behavior of investment and the accelerator mechanism. Shifts in the investment demand curve shift the *IS* curve. With the *LM* curve in place, the economy experiences fluctuations in interest rates and real GDP, with a positive correlation between the two.

Key Terms and Concepts

Accelerator mechanism The mechanism linking the *level* of net investment to the *change* in output.

Capital-intensive technique A technique that uses a large amount of capital and a small amount of labor.

Labor-intensive technique A technique that uses a large amount of labor and a small amount of capital.

Nonresidential fixed investment The expenditure by firms on new plant, buildings, and equipment.

Portfolio equilibrium A situation in which no reallocation of assets will increase the return on a portfolio for a given amount of risk.

Rental rate of capital The cost of using capital equipment, expressed in terms of dollars per hour. Alternative name to *user cost of capital*.

Residential fixed investment The expenditure by households and firms on new houses and apartments.

Tobin's *q* The ratio of the stock market value of a firm to the price of the firm's capital assets.

User cost of capital The cost of using capital equipment, expressed in terms of dollars per hour. Alternative name to *rental rate of capital*.

Review Questions

1. What are the three components of real gross private investment? Describe how each has grown in Canada since 1960. Also, describe the relationship between fluctuations in real gross private investment and fluctuations in its components.
2. Describe the pattern of investment in the world, in developing countries, in the industrial countries, and in the United States. Compare the volatility of investment in these groups of countries with that in Canada.
3. Investment is a "flow." What "stock" does investment change? What type of investment maintains the stock at a constant level? What type of investment increases the stock?
4. Compare the fluctuations in net investment and replacement investment in Canada since 1960.
5. What are the main determinants of the desired stock of capital? Explain their influences.
6. What is the accelerator mechanism? Explain how it works.
7. Describe how well the accelerator mechanism accounts for fluctuations in Canadian investment and in its components. Does the U.S. accelerator work as well as the Canadian accelerator? Explain your answer.
8. What is a capital-intensive technique of production? Under what circumstances would a firm adopt a capital-intensive technique?
9. What is the rental rate of capital? Explain how it is measured.
10. What is the desired capital stock? What determines its value?
11. Explain the relationship between the rental rate of capital and the desired capital stock.
12. What is Tobin's q? Explain how Tobin's q is related to the desired capital stock.
13. Explain the connection between the stock market value of a firm and the rental rate of capital.
14. Describe the relationship between investment and the real interest rate.
15. Describe the main influences on investment in Canada in the 1980s.
16. Explain how monetary policy affects investment.
17. Describe how taxes affect investment.
18. Explain the change in the rental rate of capital resulting from
    (a) An increase in corporate income tax rates
    (b) A decrease in depreciation deductions
    (c) A decrease in investment credits
19. What are "sunspots" and "animal spirits" and how are they thought to influence investment?

Problems

1. The Juicy Orange Company has a desired capital-sales ratio of 10 bottling plants per $1 billion of sales. Currently its sales are $5 billion and it owns 50 plants. If the rate of depreciation of bottling plants is 10 percent a year, for the Juicy Orange Company what are
    (a) Gross investment?
    (b) Replacement investment?
    (c) Net investment?

2. In problem 1, if sales increase to $8 billion what now are your answers to problem 1 if there is no investment lag?
3. Every year the Juicy Orange Company adjusts its capital stock in response to its expected permanent sales in the year, which is the previous year's actual sales plus half the error in the previous year's expected sales. If sales increase to $8 billion, draw a time-series graph of actual sales, expected sales, replacement investment, net investment, and gross investment for 5 years.
4. You need a computer for a year, and the one you're thinking of buying costs $2,000. The price of such computers is expected to fall 20 percent a year and the computer depreciates at 10 percent a year. To buy the computer you'd have to take a loan at 10 percent a year. Your friend owns one of these computers and is willing to rent it to you for the year at $240.
   (a) Calculate the implicit rental rate if you buy the computer.
   (b) Will you buy the computer or rent it?
5. Mario's Pizza took a loan at 10 percent a year to buy a van rather than lease one from AB Rentals for $3,000 a year. Mario expects the price of such vans to increase 7 percent a year. The depreciation rate on vans is 10 percent a year.
   (a) What is the highest price Mario would be willing to pay for the van?
   (b) What real interest rate would make Mario indifferent between buying and renting?
   (c) If inflation and the interest rate both increased by 2 percentage points, what now is your answer to (b)?
6. College Pro Copiers owns capital valued at $250,000. The marginal product of its capital is $16,000. If the market interest rate is 8 percent a year, calculate the following for College Pro Copiers:
   (a) Stock market value
   (b) Tobin's q
   (c) Rental rate of capital

CHAPTER

19 Money and Asset Holding

HEADING FOR THE CASHLESS SOCIETY?

HAVE YOU NOTICED HOW EASY IT IS to get along without cash — without Bank of Canada banknotes and coins? Just about every place you do business accepts credit cards, and some businesses — car rental agencies, for example — accept credit cards only. If you do need cash, there's always a handy automatic teller machine right around the corner ready to satisfy your instant requirement.

Getting along without cash isn't new. Ever since the invention of the cheque, most large transactions (the legal ones at least) have been done by that method. And since the advent of electronic records and transmission methods, most large transactions don't even leave a paper trail.

Are these technological developments actually reducing the amount of cash we use? And what about our demand for money, more broadly defined to include bank deposits? Are we getting along with fewer banks deposits too? These are two questions we'll study in this chapter.

But the chapter does more. It probes the microeconomic foundations of the demand for money and other financial assets. By doing so, it sheds light on the reasons why the demand for some components of money has shifted in recent years. It also provides a richer account of some of the issues surrounding the use of money for stabilization policy.

After studying this chapter, you will be able to

- Describe the trends in the velocity of circulation of various monetary aggregates
- Explain the inventory theory of the demand for money
- Explain the precautionary theory of the demand for money
- Explain the speculative theory of the demand for money
- Explain the modern quantity theory of money
- Explain the main influences on the amount of money held in Canada during the 1970s and 1980s
- Explain the effect of the demand for money on aggregate economic fluctuations
- Explain the implications of the demand for money for stabilization policy

MACROFACTS

19.1 The Velocity of Circulation of Money in the 1970s and 1980s

There are several different definitions of money. The most common ones are known as M1, M2, and M3.

M1, the narrowest definition of money, consists of currency (Bank of Canada notes and coins) in circulation and demand deposit balances at chartered banks.

M2 consists of M1 plus personal savings deposits and non-personal notice deposits at chartered banks

M3, the broadest definition, consists of M2 plus non-personal fixed-term deposits of residents booked in Canada at chartered banks

The **velocity of circulation** of money is the average number of times one dollar of money finances transactions in a given time period. The velocity of circulation is calculated as the flow of expenditure in a given time period divided by the stock of money.

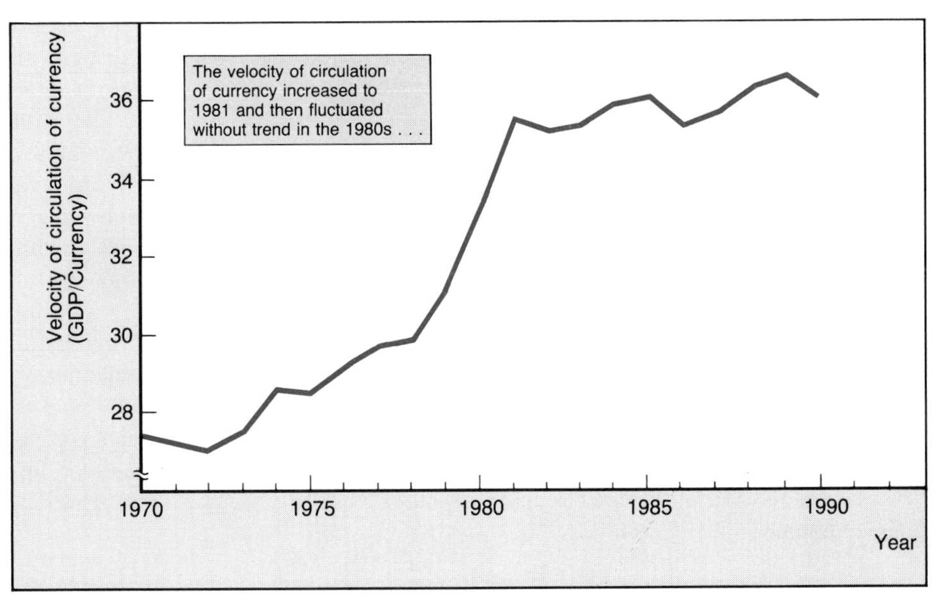

(a) Currency

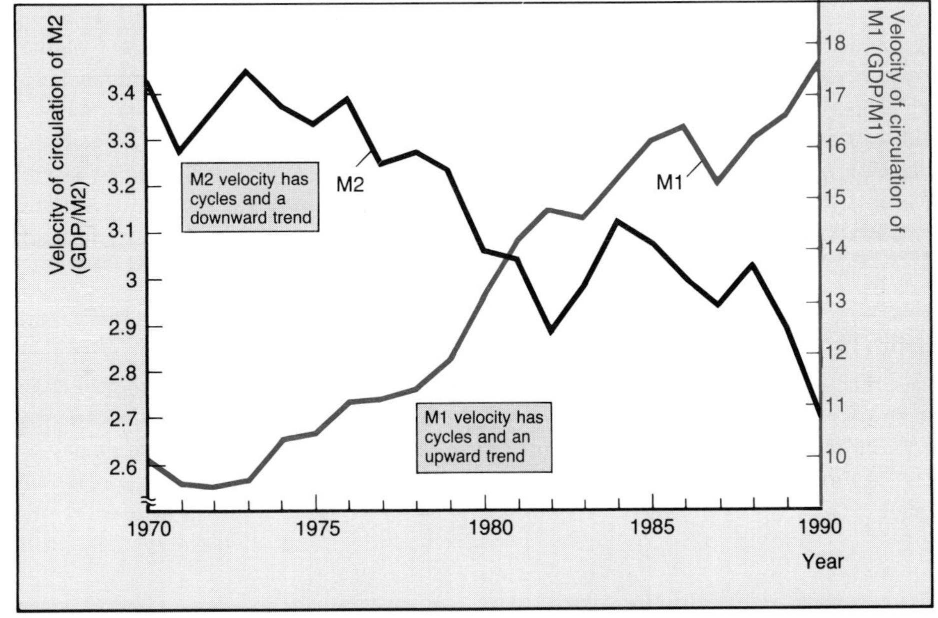

(b) M1 and M2

FIGURE 19.1
Velocities of Circulation

The velocity of circulation of currency (part a) followed an upward trend between 1970 and 1981 and had virtually no trend through the rest of the 1980s. The velocity of circulation of M1 (part b) has cycled around a rising trend and the velocity of circulation of M2 has cycled around a falling trend.

Source: Bank of Canada Review, February 1991, and *National Income and Expenditure Accounts*, Statistics Canada, Catalogue 13-201.

The most commonly calculated velocity is the GDP velocity of circulation, also known as the income velocity of circulation. The **income velocity of circulation** of money is GDP divided by the quantity of money.

Since money can be defined in several different ways, there are several different velocities of circulation. We've calculated three velocities of circulation, and Figure 19.1 plots them for the period 1970 to 1990. Part (a) shows the velocity of circulation of currency. This figure helps us answer one of the questions we posed in the chapter opener: is the amount of cash we're using really declining? Throughout the 1970s, the velocity of circulation of currency trended upward — and very strongly so toward the end of the decade. In 1970, each dollar of currency held was used to buy $27 of GDP. That is, it changed hands 27 times in making purchases of final goods and services. By 1981, this number had increased to 35. Throughout the 1980s the velocity of circulation of currency has fluctuated but its rapid growth has stopped. This means that, despite the continued growth of credit cards and automatic teller machines, the total amount of currency in circulation per dollar of GDP only fell slightly after 1982 . So we're not, at least not yet, heading for the cashless society.

Figure 19.1(b) shows the velocities of circulation of M1 and M2. The velocity of circulation of M1, ranging between 9 and 18, is much larger than that of M2 and is scaled separately on the right vertical axis. Notice that through the entire twenty years shown, the velocity of circulation of M1 trended steadily upward, with cycles around the trend. The velocity of circulation of M2 follows a downward trend and it too cycles around its trend.

Why have the velocities of circulation of currency and the two monetary aggregates behaved in the way shown in Figure 19.1? Why have the velocities of circulation of currency and M1 trended upward? Why has the velocity of circulation of M2 trended downward? And why are there cycles in the velocities of circulation? By the time you've finished studying this chapter, you'll be able to answer these questions. The answer lies in the microeconomics of the choices made by households and firms about the quantities of money to hold in their portfolios.

19.2 *Money, Interest Rates, and Opportunity Costs*

We studied the demand for money in Chapter 5 and introduced the concept of the *propensity to hold money*. The propensity to hold money is the amount of money held as a proportion of total income. For the economy as a whole, it is the amount of money held as a proportion of GDP. There is a close relationship between the propensity to hold money and the velocity of circulation. In fact, the velocity of circulation is the inverse of the propensity to hold money. Thus the explanation for fluctuations in the velocity of circulation is exactly the same as for fluctuations in the propensity to hold money and in the demand for money.

Opportunity cost of holding money

One of the most fundamental principles of economics is opportunity cost — the value of the best foregone alternative. Holding money in its various forms incurs an opportunity cost. But the particular opportunity cost borne depends on the way in which money is held. Let's consider the opportunity costs of holding each of the main components of money.

Money can be held as

1. Currency
2. Demand deposits
3. Savings deposits
4. Notice deposits
5. Fixed-term deposits

The first two components comprise M1; M1 plus the third and fourth is M2; and M2 plus the fifth is M3.

What is the opportunity cost of holding each of these various kinds of money? Let's start with the forms of money that bear the highest interest, fixed-term deposits, and call the interest rate on such deposits *rt*. The interest rate on fixed-term deposits is not as high as that on bonds and stocks. Thus in deciding to hold fixed-term deposits, a household or firm gives up the higher interest it could earn on such securities. The opportunity cost of holding fixed-term deposits is the interest rate on bonds and stocks minus the interest rate on fixed-term deposits. If we call the interest rate on bonds and stocks *r*, then the opportunity cost of holding fixed-term deposits is $r - rt$.

The next highest yielding component of money is saving deposits and notice deposits. A variety of different types of deposits fall into this category and each bears its own interest rate. But saving deposits come in two types: those that are chequable and those that are not. Let us consider for the moment those that are not chequable. For simplicity we'll suppose that these saving deposits earn the same interest rate as notice deposits and call this interest rate *rs*. These saving deposits and notice deposits are more convenient than fixed-term deposits, and because of this greater convenience they bear a lower interest rate. The opportunity cost of holding saving deposits and notice deposits is the interest rate on fixed-term deposits minus the interest rate on the saving deposits or notice deposits. Thus this opportunity cost is $rt - rs$.

Next, chequable deposits come in two main varieties: saving deposits that bear interest and demand deposits that bear no interest. Usually demand deposits bring other advantages, such as free foreign exchange services or free overdraft protection. People hold demand deposits, so it makes sense to suppose that they value these services at least as much as the interest rate they can earn on a chequable saving deposit. Let's suppose that, in effect, demand deposits bear an implicit interest rate in the form of these other benefits equal to the interest rate received on chequable saving deposits. Thus all chequable deposits earn a return that we'll call *rc*. But the interest rate on a demand deposit is less than that on a non-chequable savings and notice deposit. Thus the opportunity cost of holding money as a demand deposit rather than as a slightly less convenient non-chequable savings deposit or notice deposit is the interest rate on such savings or notice deposit minus that on the demand deposit, or $rs - rc$.

Finally, currency earns no interest. Its opportunity cost is the interest rate on the next most convenient form of money, demand deposits. Thus the opportunity cost of holding currency is *rc*.

Table 19.1 summarizes the above discussion.

Opportunity cost is a fundamental idea in economics because of its universal implication: the higher the opportunity cost of any action, the more people try to economize on that action. Holding money is no exception. The higher the opportunity cost of holding a particular type of money, the more people attempt to economize on their holding of that type of money. But how do people economize on holding money? How do people hold less money? The answers to these questions lie in the inventory theory of the demand for money.

TABLE 19.1

MONETARY AGGREGATE	COMPONENT	INTEREST RATE EARNED	OPPORTUNITY COST OF HOLDING
M1	Currency	0	rc
	demand deposits	rc	$rs - rc$
M2	Savings and notice deposits	rs	$rt - rs$
M3	Term deposits	rt	$r - rt$
The interest rate on bonds and stocks is		r	

19.3 *The Inventory Theory of the Demand for Money*

The **inventory theory of the demand for money** is based on the idea that people minimize the cost of managing their inventories of money.

The basic idea

The supermarket controls its inventory of canned soup by determining the number of cans of soup to buy and the frequency with which to buy them. For example, suppose a supermarket sells 1,000 cans of soup a week. If it buys one shipment of 1,000 cans of soup each week, its average inventory is 500 cans. It has 1,000 cans at the beginning of the week, sells them at an even pace throughout the week, and has a zero inventory when the new delivery arrives at the beginning of the next week. But suppose the supermarket took deliveries only at intervals of two weeks. In this case, it would buy 2,000 cans and have an average inventory of 1,000 cans. For the supermarket, holding inventory is costly because it has to borrow the money to finance its inventory holding. But taking delivery is also costly because it has to pay a transportation and handling charge. The inventory theory of the demand for money, suggested by John Hicks[1] in the 1930s, was worked out by William Baumol using exactly these same ideas.[2]

Managing an inventory of cash

To make the explanation of the inventory theory as clear and concrete as possible, we'll use a particular example. We'll consider a household's cash inventory management problem. Table 19.2 sets out the problem. Let's work out how a household solves its cash inventory management problem, using the table to keep track of the story.

The household gets paid once a month and immediately writes cheques to pay all its bills. It has \$1,600 left in its chequable deposit, which pays an interest rate r. The household uses this \$1,600 to make cash expenditures (Table 19.2, row 1). We'll suppose the interest rate to be 1 percent a month (row 2 of table).

The key decision for the household is the number of trips to make to the bank each month (n) and the amount of cash to withdraw on each trip (Y/n)—rows 3 and 4 of the table.

[1] J.R. Hicks, "A Suggestion for Simplifying the Theory of Money," *Economica*, Vol. 2 (February 1935), pp. 1-19.

[2] William J. Baumol, "The Transactions Demand for Cash: an Inventory-Theoretic Approach," *Quarterly Journal of Economics* (November 1952), pp. 545-556.

TABLE 19.2
The Inventory Theory of the Demand for Money

ITEM	SYMBOLS AND EQUATIONS	NUMERICAL EXAMPLE
1. Monthly cash expenditure	Y	\$1600
2. Interest rate on chequable deposits (percent per month)	r	0.01(1 percent)
3. Number of trips to the bank	n	to be chosen
4. Amount of cash withdrawn on each trip	$\frac{Y}{n}$	$\frac{\$1600}{n}$
5. Average cash holding	$\frac{Y}{2n}$	$\frac{\$1600}{2n}$
6. Cost of one trip to the bank	b	\$0.50
7. Cost of n trips to the bank	bn	\$0.50n
8. Opportunity cost of average cash holding	$\frac{rY}{2n}$	$\frac{0.01(\$1600)}{2n} = \frac{\$8}{n}$
9. Total cost of cash inventory	$TC = bn + \frac{rY}{2n}$	$TC = \$0.5n + \frac{\$8}{n}$
10. Number of trips to the bank that minimizes total cost	$n = \sqrt{\frac{rY}{2b}}$	$n = \sqrt{\frac{0.01(\$1600)}{2(\$0.50)}} = 4$

The connection between the number of trips to the bank and the amount of cash withdrawn is illustrated in Figure 19.2. The figure also illustrates the connection between the number of trips to the bank and the *average* cash holding. In part (a), the household withdraws \$400 on payday and \$400 on three subsequent occasions. (Let's suppose there are exactly four weeks in a month.) If the household spends its cash in equal amounts each day, its day-by-day currency holdings are illustrated by the sawtooth line in the figure. Its average cash holding is \$200. Part (b) shows a second possibility. Here the household makes just two trips to the bank to withdraw cash, one on payday and one two weeks later. It withdraws \$800 on each occasion and has an average cash holding of \$400. A third possibility, not illustrated in the figure, would have the household withdraw the entire \$1,600 on payday, holding nothing in its chequable deposit and an average of \$800 in cash over the month. Notice that the average currency holding depends on how frequently the household goes to the bank: the greater the number of trips to the bank, the smaller is average currency holding. Average currency holding (AC) is equal to

$$AC = \frac{Y}{2n} \tag{19.1}$$

where Y is income spent in the form of currency and n is the number of trips to the bank.

Each time the household goes to the bank, it costs b dollars. This cost includes the time it takes to go to the bank and the transportation costs. We'll suppose that b is equal to 50¢. Since the household makes n trips to the bank in the month, the total cost of its trips per month will be \$$bn$. The more frequently the household goes to the bank (the larger n), the higher this total cost.

But we've seen that the average cash holding by the household varies inversely with the number of trips to the bank. The greater the number of trips to the bank, the smaller is the amount withdrawn on each trip and the smaller is the average cash holding. The smaller the average cash holding, the larger is the average holding of interest-bearing

FIGURE 19.2
Trips to the Bank and Average Money Holdings

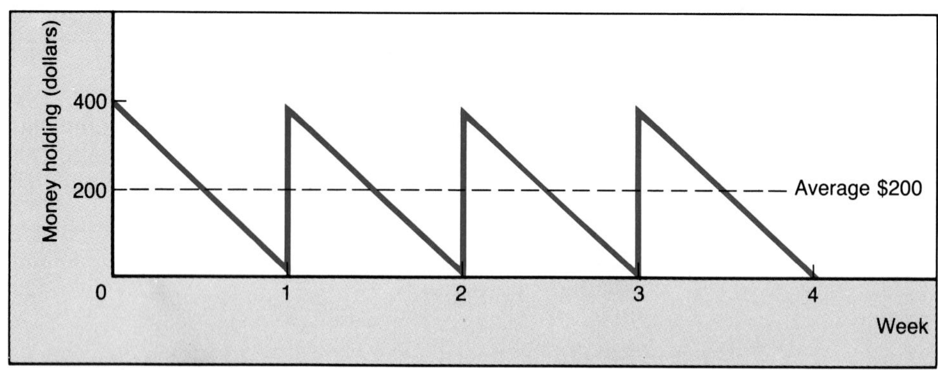

(a) A weekly trip to the bank

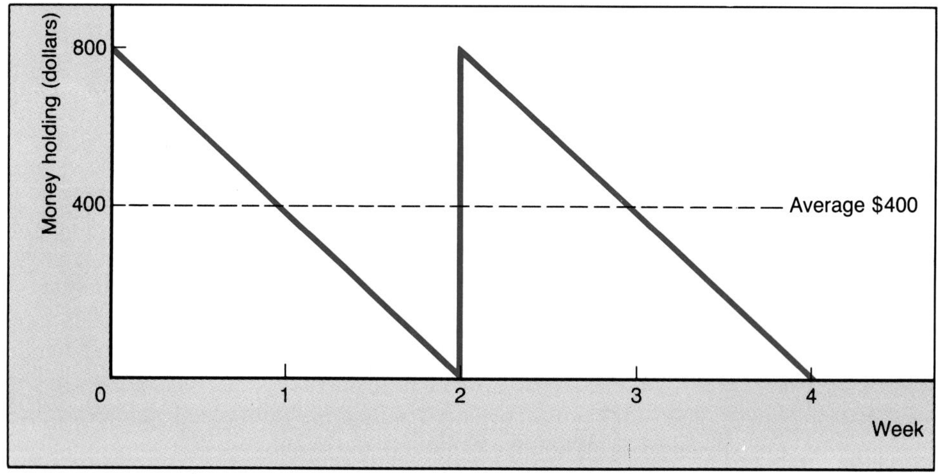

(b) Twice monthly trip to the bank

With a trip to the bank each week (part a) the amount withdrawn is one quarter of the month's expenditure and average money holdings of \$200 equals one eighth of a month's expenditure. With a trip to the bank twice a month (part b) the amount withdrawn is one half of a month's expenditure and average money holdings of \$400 are equal to one quarter of a month's expenditure.

chequable deposits. Thus less frequent trips have a cost—the opportunity cost of holding currency. This cost is equal to the interest rate foregone (r) on deposits multiplied by the average cash holding ($Y/2n$).

The total cost of managing the household's cash inventory is the sum of the cost of trips to the bank and the opportunity cost of holding cash. That total cost is

$$TC = bn + \frac{rY}{2n}. \tag{19.2}$$

Figure 19.3 illustrates these costs. The cost of trips to the bank (bn) increases with the number of trips to the bank (n). In our example, one trip costs 50¢, so two trips cost \$1 and eight trips \$4. The opportunity cost of currency holding, ($rY/2n$), decreases with the number of trips to the bank. In our example, if one trip is taken, the cost is \$8; if two trips are taken, the cost is \$4. The total cost curve (TC) is U-shaped and has a

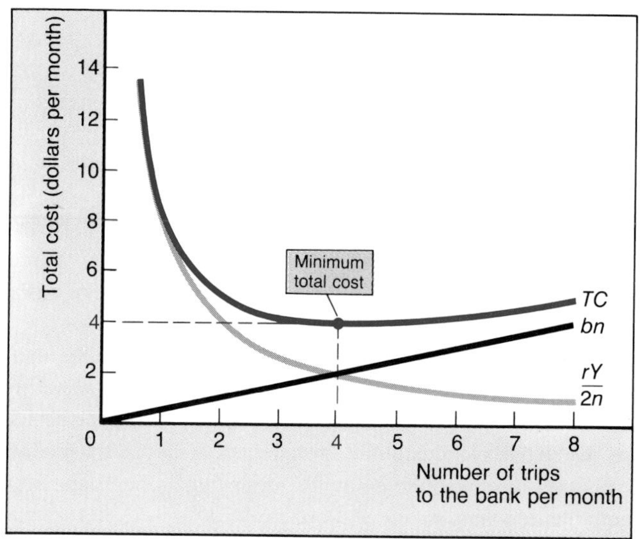

FIGURE 19.3
Inventory Management Costs

There are two components to inventory management costs. One is the interest foregone on money holding. This component equals the interest rate (r) multiplied by average money holdings ($Y/2n$). The other is a transaction cost that equals the cost per transaction (b) multiplied by the number of transactions (n). Total cost of the sum of these two and the total cost curve is U-shaped. Total cost is minimized, in this example, at four trips to the bank each month.

minimum at four trips to the bank per month. These four trips cost $2 to undertake and result in an average money holding of $200 that has an opportunity cost of $2.

The formula that determines the cost-minimizing number of trips to the bank is[3]

$$n = \sqrt{\frac{rY}{2b}} \tag{19.3}$$

[3]This result can be derived in a variety of ways. If you're familiar with calculus, you can obtain it very quickly as follows: differentiate the total cost equation,

$$TC = bn + \frac{rY}{2n}$$

and set the derivative to zero for a turning point

$$\frac{dTC}{dn} = b - \frac{rY}{2n^2} = 0.$$

Solve the resulting equation for n^2:

$$n^2 = \frac{rY}{2b}$$

and take the square root to give

$$n = \sqrt{\frac{rY}{2b}}.$$

Equivalently (and as you can see from Figure 19.3), total cost is minimized when the cost of trips to the bank (bn) is balanced against the opportunity cost of holding money $\frac{rY}{2n}$. That is, total cost is minimized when

$$bn = \frac{rY}{2n}.$$

Multiply both sides by n and divide by b to give

$$n^2 = \frac{rY}{2b}$$

and, taking the square root

$$n = \sqrt{\frac{rY}{2b}}.$$

The importance of the square root formula

This formula is important for two reasons. First, it makes a very precise prediction about the demand for cash. It predicts that as the amount of expenditure undertaken using cash increases, the amount of cash held increases, but only by the square root of the increase in expenditure. In other words, there is an *economy of scale* in holding cash. If spending increases fourfold, cash holdings increase only twofold. It also predicts that the higher the interest rate on the next convenient asset, the smaller is the amount of currency held. Again, the responsiveness is very precise. A 1 percent increase in interest rates brings a one-half-of-one percent decrease in the amount of currency held. For example, if the interest rate increases from 10 percent points to 11 percent — a 10 percent increase in the interest rate — the amount of cash held decreases by 5 percent according to this theory.

Second, the formula easily generalizes to deal with other components of money. In the example we've worked out, we studied the management of a cash inventory and the number of times a month to convert a chequable deposit into cash. Exactly the same principles apply to the management of the chequable deposit itself and decisions to convert assets such as non-chequable savings deposits, notice deposits and bonds and stocks into chequable deposits.

One trip to the bank

In the example we've just studied, it paid the household to make several trips to the bank each month. But it is possible that it will never pay the household to make more than one trip to the bank. In this case, the household goes to the bank on payday and withdraws the entire month's pay. The square root formula does not apply to such a household. That household's average money holding is simply one-half of its monthly cash expenditure, an amount not influenced by the interest rate. Thus there are two kinds of households, those to whom the square root formula applies and those who make just one trip to the bank. Since in general the economy consists of both kinds of households, the aggregate demand for currency — and for other types of money to which the same basic analysis applies — is a combination of the demands of these two types of households. Thus the aggregate demand for money is determined by a weighted average of

$$\sqrt{\frac{rY}{2b}} \text{ and } \frac{Y}{2}.$$

This means that the responsiveness of the demand for money to a change in income or interest rates will be less than indicated by the square root formula. A 1 percent increase in income will not increase the demand for money by 1 percent but only by between one-half a percent and 1 percent. Similarly, a 1 percent increase in the interest rate will not decrease the demand for money by one-half a percent but by between one-half a percent and zero.

Evidence

The evidence on the demand for money agrees with the inventory theory in some respects but not in others. The responsiveness of the amount of the money demanded to changes in income and the interest rate fall in the range predicted by the theory. But the theory fails to account for the absolute amount of currency, time deposits, and other types of money held.

According to the inventory theory, people will hold no more than one half their income per pay period in *all* the various types of money. The typical pay period is one month. If everyone were paid monthly, and if everyone used only saving and notice deposits, demand deposits, and currency (M2), average M2 holdings would be one half of one month's income, or 1/24 of the year's income. The velocity of circulation of M2 would be 24. In fact that velocity of circulation has ranged between 2.7 and 3.6 during the last 20 years. In 1990, on the average, we were holding currency, demand deposits, saving, and notice deposits equal to 19 weeks income.

The inventory theory seems to be a good theory insofar as it accounts for the *variations* in the amount of money held as income and interest rates vary, but it does not account for the absolute level of money holding. Some modification to the theory is required to deal with this fact.

19.4 *The Precautionary Theory of the Demand for Money*

The **precautionary theory of the demand for money** is based on the idea that money is held, in part, as a kind of general insurance against an uncertain future. If you take a trip to a place you're not familiar with, chances are that you'll take with you more cash than you're planning to spend. The extra cash is being taken "just in case." Many things could happen that would cause you to make some unplanned expenditure. For example, your car breaks down; you see a jacket that's exactly what you've been looking for but couldn't find; you run into an old friend (who happens to be penniless) and go out for a meal.

Carrying money as a precaution against possible future contingencies results in people holding more cash than predicted by the inventory theory. But it only modifies the inventory theory. Instead of waiting until your cash balances are zero before going to the bank to restore them, you restore them when your cash holdings fall to some critical level that you regard as the safe minimum. That safe minimum depends, in part, on your average level of expenditure. It also depends on how uncertain you are about the future. If you're very uncertain—if you believe that the range of possibilities is very wide — you'll plan to hold a larger precautionary cash balance than in a situation in which you're fairly sure about the future.

The precautionary theory of the demand for money is really just an extension of the inventory theory — allowing for periodic expenditures to be uncertain and resulting in extra money being held in response to that uncertainty. But another consequence of uncertainty modifies the demand for money yet further. This is uncertainty about future interest rates and asset prices.

19.5 *The Speculative Theory of the Demand for Money*

The **speculative theory of the demand for money** is based on the idea that people hold the mixture of money and other assets that gives the best available combination of risk and return. Like the inventory theory, the speculative theory was suggested by John Hicks in the 1930s but was worked out much later by James Tobin.[4] Tobin's idea can best be understood if you think of a household with a given amount of wealth that can be held in two types of assets—a savings deposit and a bond. If the household puts all

[4]James Tobin, "Liquidity Preferences Behavior Towards Risk," *Review of Economic Studies*, Vol. 25 (February 1958), pp. 65-86.

its wealth into its savings deposit, it will earn an interest rate of *rs*. This return is certain. (There is a slight chance that the bank will fail, but because deposit insurance takes care of that problem, the return is effectively guaranteed.) Alternatively, the household can put all its wealth into bonds. The current interest rate on bonds is *r*. The household's yield from investing in bonds depends not only on the interest income but also on the price for which the bonds are ultimately sold. This price is uncertain. If interest rates increase, bond prices fall and the household makes a capital loss. If interest rates decrease, bond prices increase and the household makes a capital gain. The expected return from putting the entire amount of wealth into bonds usually exceeds the return from putting the wealth into a savings deposit. Indeed, if the expected return on the bond did not exceed the return on the savings deposit there'd be no point in considering anything other than the savings deposit. It's safer *and* has a higher return. But when bonds are expected to yield a higher return than savings deposits, the household has a choice to make. It can put all its wealth in the lower yielding but safe savings deposit or in the higher yielding but risky bond or some combination of the two.

In general, each household chooses its preferred allocation of wealth between money and bonds based on their expected returns and the household's assessment of the riskiness of bonds. But, and this is the key point, other things being equal, the higher the expected return on bonds relative to the return on savings deposits, the larger is the proportion of the household's wealth placed in bonds and the smaller is the amount held in savings deposits. Thus the quantity of savings deposits — and the quantity of money demanded — varies inversely with the interest rate on bonds.

We've now studied three theories of the demand for money:

- Inventory theory
- Precautionary theory
- Speculative theory

All three theories yield the same prediction about the effect of interest rates on the quantity of money demanded. Other things equal, the higher the interest rate on non-money assets, the smaller is the quantity of money demanded. Two theories — the inventory theory and the precautionary theory — also emphasize the importance of income (or expenditure) in determining the quantity of money demanded. An increase in income or expenditure increases the quantity of money demanded, but the increase is less than proportionate.

The speculative theory implies that the quantity of money demanded depends not only on the interest rate but also on the total amount of wealth to be allocated between money and other assets.

19.6 *The Modern Quantity Theory of the Demand for Money*

The modern quantity theory of the demand for money, in effect, systematically combines the elements of the inventory, precautionary, and speculative theories into a single unified theory of asset allocation. The modern quantity theory was given its first statement by Milton Friedman.[5]

[5] Milton Friedman, "The Quantity Theory of Money, A Restatement," in Milton Friedman (ed.), *Studies in the Quantity Theory of Money* (Chicago: University of Chicago Press), 1956.

The theory

The modern quantity theory states that households allocate their given stock of wealth across four main types of assets:

1. Money
2. Bonds
3. Real capital
4. Human capital

In general, households substitute one form of capital for another based on expected relative rates of return. However, substitution into and out of human capital is more difficult and takes longer. Thus the demand for money depends on the part of total wealth that is nonhuman—money plus bonds plus real capital.

The relative rates of return on money, bonds, and real capital are calculated by first working out the real rates of return on the three assets. The real rate of return on money is equal to minus the inflation rate. The real rate of return on bonds is the nominal rate of return minus the inflation rate. The real rate of return on real capital is the real interest rate. The difference between the real rates of return on money and on bonds and real capital is the nominal interest rate—the real interest minus the inflation rate. Thus the opportunity cost of holding money relative to bonds and real capital is the nominal interest rate. Other things being equal, the higher the nominal interest rate, the lower is the quantity of money demanded and the larger is the quantity of bonds and real capital demanded.

The proportion of wealth allocated to money varies inversely with the nominal interest rate, but the total amount of wealth to be allocated also influences the demand for money. The demand for money depends on two things: the nominal interest rate and wealth.

In his formulation of the modern quantity theory of money, Friedman suggested that wealth could be measured as permanent income. This is the very same concept of permanent income Friedman used in the permanent income theory of the consumption function. The attractiveness of this approach is that it places the theory of the demand for money on the same theoretical basis as the theory of the consumption function and increases the degree of unity among the theories of household behavior. The key proposition in the modern quantity theory of money is that the quantity of money demanded depends inversely on the nominal interest rate and positively on permanent income.

Lags and buffer stocks

The proposition that the quantity of money demanded depends on permanent income immediately implies that there will be time lags in the relationship between the quantity of money demanded and current income. Because permanent income responds gradually to changes in current actual income, the quantity of money demanded will respond only gradually to changes in current income. Thus there will be a time lag between a change in income and the change in the quantity of money demanded.

Another potential source of time lags arises from the notion that money is a kind of buffer stock. A buffer stock is an inventory that is the first-line defence against random fluctuations. This idea ties in directly with the notion of a precautionary demand for money. The initial effect of random or unpredicted fluctuations in income and expenditure will be on the amount of money held, leading to potentially important random fluctuations in the amount of money held relative to income.

We've now reviewed the inventory, precautionary, and speculative theories of the demand for money and the broader unified modern quantity theory. All these theories of the demand for money point to the same general form of the demand for money function: the quantity of money demanded varies inversely with the interest rate and directly with income, and it is subject to time lags in the relationship and to random fluctuations. How does the actual demand for money correspond to the predictions of these theories?

TESTCASE

19.7 *Financial Innovation and the Demand for Money in the 1970s and 1980s*

We'll study the influences on the demand for money by looking again at the velocity of circulation of the monetary aggregates we examined at the beginning of this chapter. We've seen that according to the theory of the demand for money, the quantity of money demanded varies inversely with the interest rate and positively with income (or wealth or permanent income). Since the velocity of circulation is defined as GDP divided by the quantity of money, we would expect that the velocity of circulation is positively correlated with interest rates. That is, when an increase in the interest rate decreases the quantity of money demanded, the velocity of circulation of money increases. What are the facts?

M1 velocity and interest rates

Let's look first at the relationship between the velocity of circulation of M1 and the interest rate. Recall from Figure 19.1 that M1 velocity has had an upward trend. Interest rates have fluctuated and also had an upward trend, but the trend in interest rates is mild compared with that in M1 velocity. To *see* the relationship between M1 velocity and the interest rate, we need to remove the trend in velocity and examine its *fluctuations around trend*. This is done in Figure 19.4, which shows the relationship between deviations in M1 velocity from trend (left-hand scale) plotted against the interest rate (right-hand scale) from 1970 to 1990.

FIGURE 19.4
M1 Velocity and Interest Rates

The fluctuations around trend in the velocity of circulation of M1 follow a similar cycle to that in interest rates. The trend in M1 velocity (not visible in this figure) resulted from financial innovation.

Source: See Figure 19.1.

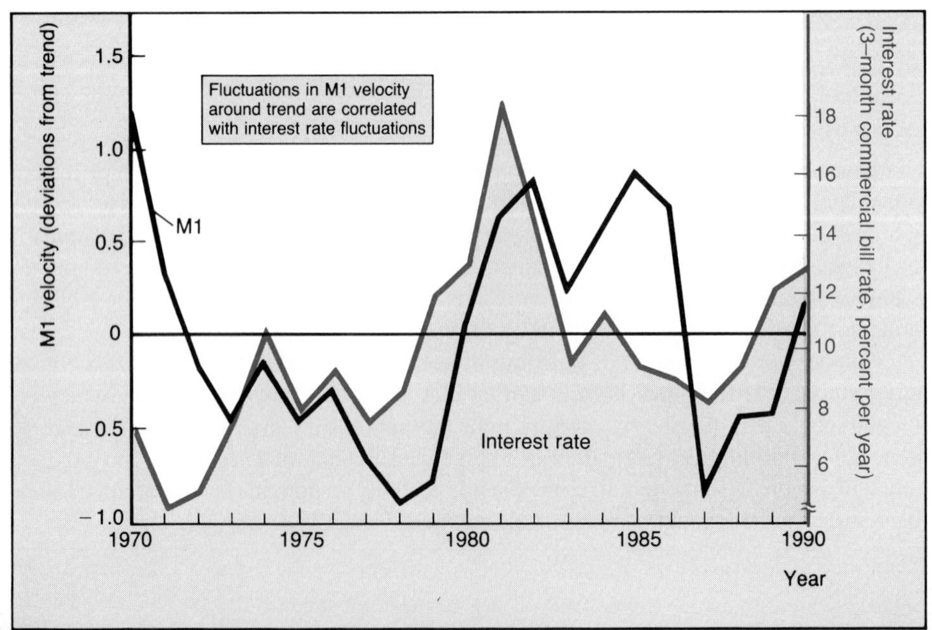

The main conclusion we reach from examining Figure 19.4 is that the velocity of circulation of M1 and the interest rate follow the same cycle. There are some differences in the extent of the fluctuations in the two variables but they generally move up and down together as predicted by the theories of the demand for money that we've studied.

M2 velocity and interest rates

The velocity of circulation of M2 and the interest rate are shown in Figure 19.5. Again, we have removed the trend (this time the downward trend) from M2 velocity and calculated its deviation from trend, plotted on the left-hand scale. And again, as predicted by the theory of the demand for money, there is a positive correlation between M2 velocity (deviation from trend) and the interest rate. But that relationship is not as clear as that for M1. In fact, in the late 1970s and early 1980s, the relationship temporarily breaks down and for a few years, the two variables move in *opposite* directions.

Some questions about velocity

Why are there strong trends in the velocities of circulation of M1 and M2 that need to be removed to reveal the relationship between velocity and the interest rate? Why does the velocity of M2 fluctuate in the opposite way to that predicted by the theory of the demand for money in the late 1970s and early 1980s?

Financial innovation, the demand for money, and velocity

The answers to the questions just posed almost certainly involve financial innovation. *Financial innovation* is the development of new financial products, items such as credit cards and types of bank deposits and other securities. Innovation in the financial sector occurs just as it does in other sectors of the economy because financial institutions are constantly seeking new ways of increasing business and making larger profits. The most important financial innovations that have influenced the demand for money and velocity of circulation since the late 1960s are summarized in Table 19.3. Innovations that

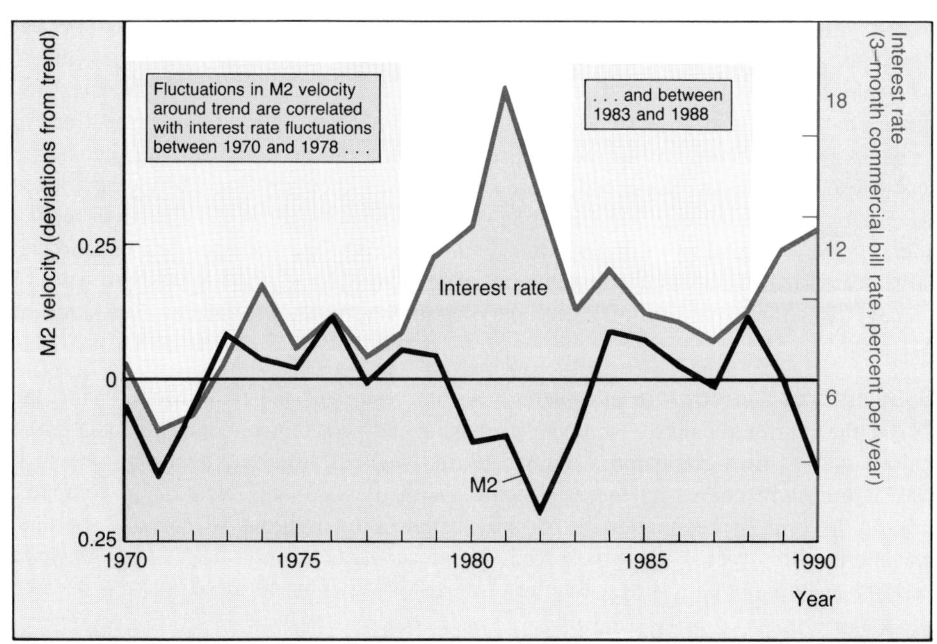

FIGURE 19.5
M2 Velocity and Interest Rates

The fluctuations around trend in the velocity of circulation of M2 follow a similar cycle to that in interest rates before 1978 and after 1982. But the velocity of M2 fell (the demand for M2 increased) when interest rates were rising to their peak in the early 1980s. This movement resulted from increased substitution of savings accounts for demand deposits.

Source: See Figure 19.1.

TABLE 19.3
A Thumbnail Sketch of Financial Innovation affecting the Demand for Money

PERIOD	INNOVATION	EFFECT ON VELOCITY OF CIRCULATION OF: M1	M2
Late 1960s and 1970s	Credit cards for everyone Eurodollars	+	+
Late 1970s and early 1980s	Daily interest chequing accounts Cash management accounts Money market mutual funds	+ + +	− − +

decrease the demand for a particular monetary aggregate increase its velocity of circulation. The table indicates the direction of the effect on the velocity of circulation of the two main aggregates, M1 and M2. A plus sign means that the velocity of circulation increases as a result of the innovation and a minus sign implies that it decreases. Let's briefly review these innovations and see why they have these predicted effects on velocity.

Credit cards Credit cards were introduced immediately after World War II, first by Diners' Club and later by American Express and Carte Blanche. But these cards were issued only to people and institutions with very high levels of spending. By the late 1960s, the cost of computing was low enough to make it feasible to issue credit cards on a large scale. VISA and Mastercard expanded in popularity, and by the end of the 1980s some 20 million of these cards were in use. Credit cards are not money. They are identification cards that enable people to create a loan at the moment they make a purchase. They pay the loan off at the end of the month (or at some later date) when they make payments to the credit card company. By reducing the proportion of transactions undertaken with currency or cheques, credit cards decrease the demand for currency and chequable deposits and therefore decrease the demand for all the monetary aggregates. Equivalently, they increase the velocity of circulation of money.

Eurodollars Eurodollars are bank deposits (originally denominated in U.S. dollars but now available in all the major currencies) held in Europe. Eurodollars were "invented" when the Soviet Union wanted to hold the proceeds of its international trade in U.S. dollars but didn't want to put the money in the United States. Eurodollars are attractive to banks because there are no required reserves on these deposits. Instead, banks can lend the entire amount deposited, thereby increasing their profits. Eurodollars, even when they are denominated in Canadian dollars, are not part of the Canadian money supply. The availability of Eurodollars with attractive interest rates has encouraged large-scale fund managers to substitute out of M1 and M2 and into the offshore types of money. Thus the expansion of Eurodollars has increased the velocity of circulation of M1 and M2.

Daily interest chequing accounts As interest rates edged upward during the 1970s, the chartered banks were under increasing competition from other financial institutions such as trust companies, and had to find ways of attracting deposits. One such way is the daily interest chequing account. With the dramatic decrease in computer prices, the cost of keeping track of daily balances on millions of accounts became feasible and this type of deposit spread. These accounts are not classified as *demand deposits* and are not part of M1. But they are part of M2. Thus as these accounts became ever more popular, the demand for M1 declined and the demand for M2 increased. The velocities of circulation moved in the opposite directions—M1 up and M2 down.

Cash management accounts Banks not only offered better deals for their personal customers. They were also innovative in pursuing the corporate client. To keep their big customers accounts, the banks offered an increasing array of sophisticated cash management services. One such service is a "sweep account," an arrangement whereby at the end of the business day, the bank "sweeps" the balances from chequable deposits and places them in overnight investments. This has the effect of decreasing the demand for money and increasing the velocity of circulation of all types of money.

Money market mutual funds Money market mutual funds are financial institutions that issue shares redeemable at a fixed price against which cheques can be written. But money market mutual funds are not really chequable deposits. There is a minimum size to the cheque, so they cannot be used for ordinary transactions. Nonetheless, money market mutual funds pay a relatively high rate of return and became extremely attractive during the 1980s. Since they are not part of the money supply, their growth has decreased the demand for money and increased the velocity of circulation.

Explaining velocity behavior

All the financial innovations we've just reviewed have increased the velocity of circulation of M1. It is likely that these innovations are responsible for the general tendency for the velocity of currency and M1 to trend upward through the 1970s rather than only following the cycles that interest rate movements would have generated. In other words, financial innovations rather than interest rates were likely the dominant influences on M1 velocity.

Financial innovation has had mixed effects on the velocity of M2. Some of the innovations, such as credit cards, Eurodollars, sweep accounts, and money market mutual funds have tended to decrease the demand for M2 and increase its velocity, while daily interest chequing accounts have tended to increase the demand for M2, decreasing its velocity. Although this is an after-the-fact rationalization, it seems that the influence of daily interest chequing and similar innovations making saving deposits at chartered banks more attractive types of deposits have been the dominant influence on the velocity of M2. They were especially powerful influences during the late 1970s and early 1980s at the time when M2 velocity was falling in the face of rising interest rates.

19.8 *The Demand for Money and Aggregate Fluctuations*

Do fluctuations in aggregate economic activity arise from the behavior of the demand for money? Equivalently, do fluctuations in aggregate economic activity arise from fluctuations in the velocity of circulation of money? The answer is, sometimes they do and sometimes they don't.

Velocity fluctuations that do not cause aggregate fluctuations

Fluctuations in the velocity of circulation induced by changes in interest rates do not cause fluctuations in aggregate economic activity. These fluctuations in velocity are a consequence of a *movement along* the demand curve for money. Fluctuations in the interest rate and in the velocity of circulation are each caused by fluctuations in the supply of money, investment or some other component of aggregate expenditure, and aggregate supply. But they are not caused by fluctuations in the demand for money itself. The *quantity of money demanded* fluctuates when the interest rate changes, but changes in the interest rate caused by some other factor do not change the demand for money.

Policy measures that stabilize interest rates also stabilize the quantity of money demanded and the velocity of circulation.

Demand for money changes that do bring aggregate fluctuations

Changes in the demand for money that also change the velocity of circulation independently of interest rates can cause fluctuations in aggregate economic activity. Such changes in the velocity of circulation result from shifts in the demand for money function. To see how such shifts influence the economy, we need to use the *IS-LM* model of Chapter 5. Figure 19.6 illustrates the effects. Suppose the *IS* curve is fixed at IS_0. Initially the demand and supply of money are such that the *LM* curve is LM_0. Real GDP is y_0, and the interest rate is r_0.

Now suppose that a financial innovation occurs that decreases the demand for money. This has the same effect on the *LM* curve as an increase in the supply of money —the *LM* curve shifts to the right. In this case, suppose that the *LM* curve shifts to LM_1, with real GDP increasing to y_1 and the interest rate falling to r_1.

A financial innovation that increases the demand for money has the effect opposite to that shown here. Financial innovations that occur at a random pace, bringing fluctuations in the demand for money that sometimes increase and sometimes decrease it, can lead to fluctuations in income and the interest rate. However, such fluctuations result in a negative correlation between real GDP and interest rates. But observing a negative correlation between real GDP and interest rates does not guarantee that the source of the correlation is fluctuations in the demand for money. Fluctuations in the *supply of money* have the same effect.

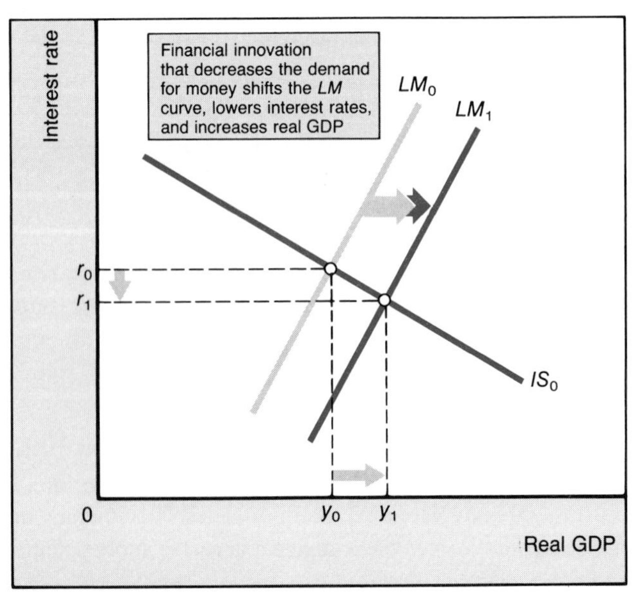

FIGURE 19.6
Financial Innovation and Aggregate Fluctuations

The financial innovation that decreases the demand for money shifts the *LM* curve to the right from LM_0 to LM_1. With a fixed *IS* curve, IS_0, the result is an increase in real GDP, from y_0 to y_1 and a decrease in the interest rate, from r_0 to r_1. Thus aggregate instability resulting from shifts in the demand for money produce countercyclical movements in interest rates.

■ We've now studied the microeconomic foundations of consumption, investment, and money and asset holdings. We've discovered that decisions in all three areas result in macroeconomic relationships — consumption function, investment function, and demand for money function—similar to those used in the basic *IS-LM* model. But we've also discovered important time lags and sources of independent variation in some of these functions. Permanent income produces time lags in the consumption function and the demand for money. The accelerator mechanism produces swings in the *IS* curve. These time lags and dynamic adjustments bring ever-changing aggregate demand conditions that are an important contributor to macroeconomic fluctuations. But the most important source of volatility in our economy is investment, not consumption or money holdings.

In the final part of this book we are going to look where macroeconomics is today and where it is heading in the future — the new classical and new Keynesian macroeconomics.

CHAPTER REVIEW

Summary

TRENDS IN THE VELOCITY OF CIRCULATION OF THE VARIOUS MONETARY AGGREGATES

The velocity of circulation of currency increased during the 1970s but stabilized during the 1980s. The velocity of circulation of M1 had an upward trend during the 1970s and 1980s and followed distinct cycles. The velocity of circulation of M2 had a downward trend during the 1970s and 1980s and it too cycled.

THE INVENTORY THEORY OF THE DEMAND FOR MONEY

The opportunity cost of holding money is the interest rate foregone on the best alternative asset. The inventory theory of the demand for money explains the amount of money held as the quantity that minimizes the total inventory management cost. That cost includes the opportunity cost of owning money but also the cost of transactions. The lower the average inventory, the more often transactions to replenish the inventory of money are necessary. Balancing transaction costs against opportunity costs of holding money produces the number of trips to the bank and average money holdings that minimize total cost.

All things being equal, the higher the level of income and expenditure and the lower the interest rate, the fewer is the number of trips to the bank and the higher is the average amount of money held. But there are economies of scale in money holding. An increase in income brings an increase in the quantity of money demanded, and the quantity of money is proportional to the square root of income.

THE PRECAUTIONARY THEORY OF THE DEMAND FOR MONEY

The precautionary theory of the demand for money is an extension of the inventory theory, which takes account of uncertainty about expenditure. People hold an inventory of money in excess of that needed for average expenditure as a kind of insurance policy against unforeseen future contingencies.

THE SPECULATIVE THEORY OF THE DEMAND FOR MONEY

The speculative theory of the demand for money is based on the idea that people hold their wealth in a variety of assets that give different combinations of risk and return. Money has a low return and low risk. Bonds and stocks have a higher return and a higher risk. By choosing the proportion of wealth to hold in the form of money and other assets, holders of wealth trade off risk against return in selecting their most preferred combination.

THE MODERN QUANTITY THEORY OF MONEY

The modern quantity theory of money in effect combines elements of the inventory, precautionary, and speculative theories systematically into a unified theory of asset allocation. Wealth can be allocated between money, bonds, real capital, and human capital. Other things being equal, the larger the opportunity cost of holding money, the less money is held. Also, other things being equal, the greater the amount of wealth, the larger is the quantity of money held.

By measuring wealth as permanent income, the modern quantity theory predicts a relationship between the quantity of money held and permanent income. Permanent income adjusts gradually to changes in current income, implying a time lag in the relationship between the quantity of money demanded and current income.

THE DEMAND FOR MONEY IN CANADA IN THE 1970s AND 1980s

The demand for money and the velocity of circulation are two different ways of looking at the same thing. During the 1970s and 1980s the velocity of circulation of M1 increased, so the demand for M1 decreased. This trend in the demand for M1 was most likely the result of financial innovation, making it possible for people to operate with smaller and smaller demand deposits and smaller currency holdings. These same innovations brought a decrease in the velocity of circulation of M2 and an increase in the demand for M2. Fluctuations in interest rates were responsible for the cycles around trend in M1 and M2 velocities.

THE DEMAND FOR MONEY AND AGGREGATE FLUCTUATIONS

Fluctuations in the velocity of circulation induced by interest rate changes do not cause fluctuations in aggregate economic activity. They are a consequence of fluctuations arising from some other source. The fluctuations in the velocity of circulation not caused by interest rate changes result from shifts in the demand for money function. Such shifts influence real GDP and interest rates. A decrease in the demand for money resulting from financial innovation shifts the *LM* curve, lowering interest rates and increasing real GDP.

Key Terms and Concepts

Eurodollars Bank deposits held in Europe denominated in a variety of currencies, including Canadian dollars.

Income velocity of circulation GDP divided by the quantity of money.

Inventory theory of demand for money A theory of the demand for money based on minimizing the cost of managing an inventory of money.

M1 Currency (Bank of Canada notes and coins) in circulation and demand deposit at chartered banks.

M2 M1 plus personal savings deposits and non-personal notice deposits at chartered banks.

M3 M2 plus non-personal fixed-term deposits at chartered banks.

Precautionary theory of the demand for money A theory of the demand for money based on the idea that money, in part, is held as a kind of general insurance against an uncertain future.

Speculative theory of demand for money A theory of the demand for money based on the idea that people hold the mixture of money and other assets that gives the best available combination of risk and return.

Velocity of circulation The average number of times one dollar of money finances transactions in a given time period.

Review Questions

1. Explain what is meant by the velocity of circulation. How is the income velocity of circulation calculated?
2. Explain why the velocity of circulation of money falls as the money aggregate gets broader.
3. Describe how the velocity of circulation of currency, M1, and M2 have evolved in Canada since 1970.
4. Explain how to calculate the opportunity cost of the main components of Canadian money.
5. Explain the inventory theory of the demand for money.
6. Using the inventory theory of the demand for money explain what determines the cost-minimizing number of trips to the bank.
7. Does the evidence on the demand for money agree with the inventory theory? If so, explain the agreement. If not, what modification is needed to make it agree?
8. Explain the precautionary theory of the demand for money.
9. Explain the speculative theory of the demand for money.
10. Explain the modern quantity theory of money.
11. Who first suggested each of the theories of the demand for money and who worked each theory out?
12. What are the main financial innovations that have taken place in Canada since 1970?
13. Use the theories of the demand for money to explain the changes in the demand for money in Canada in the 1970s and 1980s.
14. If the government banned credit cards, what would be the effect on the velocity of circulation of currency? And of M1?
15. What are Eurodollars? How did they get invented? Why do banks like them? What has been their effect on the demand for money in Canada?
16. Explain why the cycles in the deviations from trend of the velocity of circulation of M1 are similar to the cycles in interest rates.
17. Explain why the cycles in the deviations from trend of the velocity of circulation of M2 are correlated with the cycles in interest rates in the early 1970s but not correlated in the late 1970s and early 1980s.
18. Do fluctuations in the velocity of circulation induced by changes in interest rates cause fluctuations in real GDP? Explain why or why not.
19. Do fluctuations in investment produce fluctuations in interest rates, the velocity of circulation, and the demand for money? Explain why or why not.
20. Draw a diagram to show that changes in the demand for money change the velocity of circulation and cause aggregate economic fluctuations.

Problems

1. Joann earns $3,200 a month and she spends $600 on rent and other monthly expenses as soon as she's paid. She saves another $600, which she puts into a money market mutual fund. She spends the rest of her income at an even pace through the month. She keeps these funds in cash and in an interest-earning chequable bank deposit that yields 0.5 percent per month. It costs Joann $1.25 every time she goes to the bank to get cash.
   (a) How many times a month does Joann go to the bank?
   (b) How much does she withdraw on each occasion?
   (c) What is Joann's average currency holding?
   (d) What is Joann's average holding of chequable deposits?
   (e) What is Joann's average holding of M1?
   (f) How much does Joann add to her M2 holdings each month?
   (g) What does it cost Joann to manage her cash inventory?
   (h) How much of the cost of managing her cash inventory is the opportunity cost of holding cash and how much is the cost of transactions?
2. Suppose that Joann (in problem 1) is extremely uncertain about her monthly expenditure. How would that affect her decisions that you've just analyzed?
3. Suppose the interest rate on chequable bank deposits doubles. How does Joann (in problem 1) change her behavior?
4. Using the *IS-LM* model, explain the effects of the spread of credit cards on aggregate demand. Using the *AD-AS* model, explain the effect on real GDP and the price level.
5. Using the *Bank of Canada Review*, or a similarly handy source, get data on real GDP, the price level, the money supply, and interest rates for the most recent quarter.
   (a) What do you infer about the demand for money over this period?
   (b) Has the demand for money changed or has there been a movement along the demand for money curve?
6. What would happen to the demand for money if bonds and stocks became more risky? Which monetary aggregate would increase? M1, M2, or M3?

VII

The New Macroeconomics

CHAPTER

20 New Classical Macroeconomics

THE SURPRISING INVISIBLE HAND

IT WAS IN 1776, IN *THE WEALTH OF NATIONS*, that Adam Smith first introduced into economics the idea of the invisible hand. Said Smith, "as every individual . . . endeavors as much as he can . . . to employ his capital . . . so . . . that its produce may be of the greatest value . . . [intending] . . . only his own gain . . . he is . . . led by an invisible hand to promote an end which was no part of his intention. . . . By pursuing his own interest he frequently promotes that of the society more effectually than when he really intends to promote it."[1] Smith's idea of the invisible hand became one of the cornerstones of classical economics.

Another cornerstone was the idea that money is a veil—what really matters are the real quantities of goods and services produced and factors of production used to produce them, as well as the real or relative prices of the various goods and factors of production. Changes in the money supply merely change nominal prices, and money acts as a veil that covers the underlying reality. Despite this view of money, it is as long ago as 1741 that David Hume described what happens "when any quantity of money is imported into a nation." Said Hume, those who have received the money are able

> to employ more workmen than formerly, who never dream of demanding higher wages, but are glad of employment from such good paymasters. If workmen become scarce, the manufacturer gives higher wages, but at first requires an increase of labour; and this is willingly submitted to by the artisan, who can now eat and drink better, to compensate his additional toil and fatigue. He carries his money to market, where he finds everything at the same price as formerly, but returns with greater quantity, and of better kinds, for the use of his family. The farmer and gardener, finding that all their commodities are taken off, apply themselves with alacrity to raising more; and at the same time can afford to take better and more clothes from their tradesmen, whose price is the same as formerly, and their industry only whetted by so much new gain. It is easy to trace the money in its progress through the whole commonwealth; where we shall find, that it must

[1] Adam Smith, *The Wealth of Nations*, Vol. 1, (University of Chicago Press, 1976), pp. 477-8.

first quicken the diligence of every individual, before it increases the price of labour.[2]

Hume's observation—that when money increases the quantities of trade and production at first increase and eventually prices increase — did not feature as a formal part of classical macroeconomic theory. Instead, that theory emphasized the influence of money on the price level and not its influence on real economic activity.

During the Great Depression, classical macroeconomics seemed to be completely out of touch with reality and, with the intellectual revolution in the Keynes's *General Theory*, it seemed to be banished for all time. Following the publication of Keynes's *General Theory*, it was taken for granted by almost all economists for more than thirty years that classical economics and certainly classical macroeconomics was dead.

Then, to the surprise of everyone and the outrage of many, Robert E. Lucas Jr. revived classical macroeconomics. In a series of astounding papers in the early 1970s, Lucas suggested that classical macroeconomics was alive and well and, furthermore, it was capable of explaining such phenomena as business cycles, sticky prices and wages, and the response of real economic activity to monetary disturbances—"money is a veil, but when the veil flutters, real output sputters."[3]

Lucas's surprising revival of classical macroeconomics was based on formalizing the idea that people can be surprised by previously unexpected and currently unobserved changes in the money supply and nominal aggregate demand. We'll examine this revival of classical macroeconomics in this chapter.

An even greater surprise a decade or so later was the revival of the invisible hand. This was the birth of real business cycle theory developed by John Long and Charles Plosser at the University of Rochester and Finn Kydland and Edward C. Prescott then at the Carnegie Mellon University (Prescott is now at the University of Minnesota). These scholars defined a new research program for macroeconomics — a program designed to account for aggregate fluctuations using a dynamic version of classical macroeconomics. They suggested that Adam Smith's invisible hand is capable of generating cycles which are the best possible response to a changing technological environment. We also look at these contributions in this chapter.

After studying this chapter you will be able to

- Explain the new classical theory of the labor market
- Explain the Lucas aggregate supply curve
- Explain how surprise changes in aggregate demand produce an output-inflation tradeoff
- Explain the policy implications of Lucas's new classical macroeconomic model
- Describe the ability of the Lucas model to account for aggregate economic fluctuations
- Explain real business cycle theory
- Describe the ability of real business cycle theory to explain the business cycle in the post-war years
- Explain how new classical macroeconomics accounts for unemployment
- Describe the new classical account of unemployment over the business cycle in the post-war years
- Describe the research agenda of new classical macroeconomics

---

[2]David Hume, *Essays Moral, Political and Literary* (Oxford University Press, 1963), p. 294.

[3]Robert E. Lucas Jr., "Expectations and the Neutrality of Money," *Journal of Economic Theory*, Vol. 4 (April 1972), pp. 103-24.

MACROFACTS

20.1 *Output-Inflation Tradeoffs Around the World*

The **output-inflation tradeoff** is the relationship between deviations of real GDP from full employment and inflation from its expected level. The tradeoff tells us the cost of reducing inflation below its expected level in terms of the amount of real GDP foregone. This cost is measured by the slope at the output-inflation tradeoff. The slope of the output-inflation tradeoff varies enormously from country to country and from one time period to another. The facts about the output-inflation tradeoff that motivated the first work on new classical macroeconomics were based on a study of eighteen countries during the 1950s and 1960s. The output-inflation tradeoffs of four countries that illustrate the range of experience are shown in Figure 20.1. Notice the dramatic difference between Canada and the United States on the one hand and Argentina and Paraguay on the other. In Argentina and Paraguay, massive changes in the actual inflation rate relative to the expected inflation rate took place with almost no change in real GDP. In Canada and the United States the relationship is close to one for one.

These vastly different output-inflation tradeoffs are not just a phenomenon of this particular period. Such differences were also visible in the 1980s.

The idea of an output-inflation tradeoff suggests a stable relationship between deviations of GDP from its capacity level and the inflation rate. In fact, no such relationship exists. The evolution of inflation and deviations of GDP from capacity follow an unfolding loop-like pattern. You can see this by looking at Figure 20.2, which shows inflation and the ratio of GDP to capacity GDP in Canada between 1970 and 1990. There is no visible sign of a tradeoff here. To reveal the tradeoff shown in Figure 20.1 it is necessary to find a way of removing the influence of changes in inflation expectations because such changes shift the tradeoff. What you are seeing in Figure 20.2 is a sequence of points resulting from a combination of two forces — changes in inflation expectations and movements along an output-inflation tradeoff.

The initial goal of the new classical macroeconomics was to explain first why there is an output-inflation tradeoff and then to explain its existence in terms consistent with

FIGURE 20.1
Output-Inflation Tradeoffs

The output-inflation tradeoff is the loss of real GDP resulting from a given percentage decrease in inflation. The steeper the output-inflation tradeoff curve, the smaller is the cost of reducing inflation in terms of lost real GDP. Countries with high and variable inflation rates, such as Argentina and Paraguay, have a steep tradeoff. Countries with low and steady inflation rates, such as Canada and the United States, have a flat tradeoff.

Source: Based on calculations in Robert Lucas, Jr., "Some International Evidence on Output-Inflation Tradeoffs," *American Economic Review*, Vol. 63 (September 1973), pp. 326-334.

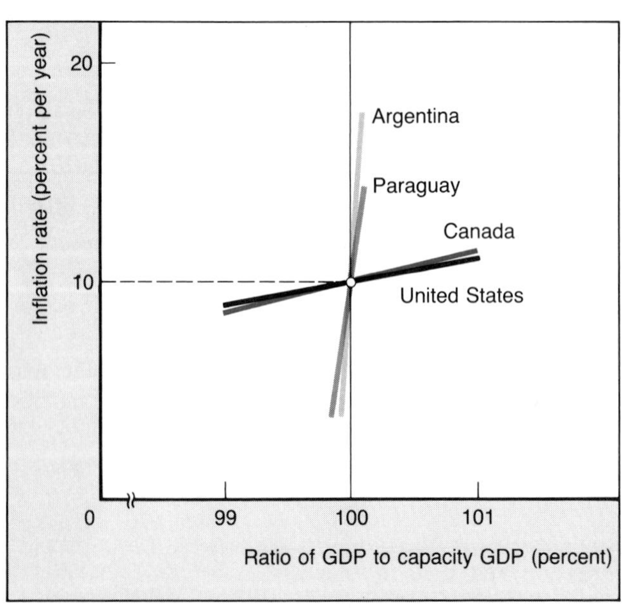

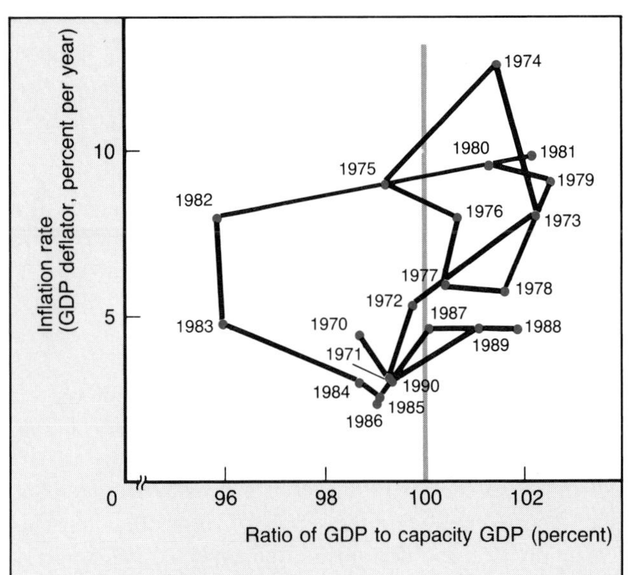

FIGURE 20.2
Output-Inflation Loops

The output-inflation tradeoff is not visible in the raw data showing the evolution of inflation and deviations of real GDP from capacity. Instead, the data unfold in a sequence of counterclockwise loop patterns. Changing inflation expectations are the main reason why the output-inflation tradeoff is not visible.

Source: National Income and Expenditure, Statistics Canada, Catalogue 13-201, and our calculations.

the precepts of classical economics. Another major challenge was to find a way of explaining inflation expectations and how they evolve. Let's examine those early attempts to rekindle classical economics to address these macroeconomic issues.

20.2 *The New Classical Theory of the Labor Market*

The new classical theory of the labor market is an extension of the labor market model presented in Chapter 8. Let's begin our review of the new classical theory by again asking the two basic questions: How do firms decide on the quantity of labor to hire, and how do households decide on the quantity of labor to supply? Recall that a firm maximizes its profit by hiring the quantity of labor that makes the marginal product of labor equal to the firm's real wage rate—the money wage rate divided by the price of its output. A household chooses the amount of labor to supply on the basis of the real wage rate it receives—the basket of goods and services it can buy with the money wage rate. This real wage rate is the money wage rate divided by the price level, such as measured by the Consumer Price Index.

Notice that the relevant price for calculating the real wage rate is not the same on both sides of the market: on the demand side, it's the price at which the firm can sell its output; on the supply side, it's the average price of all the goods and services households buy. Thus different information is needed by households and firms to calculate the relevant real wage rate. This information difference is the basis of the new classical theory of the labor market.

The new classical theory of the labor market assumes

1. The quantity of labor demanded depends on the *actual* real wage rate.
2. The quantity of labor supplied depends on the *expected* real wage rate.
3. The average money wage rate continually adjusts to achieve labor market equilibrium.

On the demand side

Each firm sells a small range of goods and services, and it and its workers know the prices of these goods and services. Each firm hires labor on the basis of the actual real wage it pays. If we sum the labor demands of all firms and take an average of the real wage rates faced by firms, we obtain the aggregate or economywide demand for labor. The aggregate quantity of labor demanded depends on the *actual* economy-average real wage rate. This may seem puzzling because firms do not know the actual price level. Each firm knows only the price of its own output but, in aggregate, firms behave as if they know the actual price level. That is, the aggregate quantity of labor demanded depends on the actual price level.

On the supply side

Households buy a large range of goods and services and cannot know all their prices. Households have to base their labor supply decisions on an expectation of the average price of the goods and services they buy. That is, the quantity of labor supplied by households is determined by their expectation of the real wage rate. The economywide aggregate supply of labor is the sum of the supply of labor of all households. Since each household's labor supply decision depends on the expected real wage rate, so does the aggregate quantity of labor supplied.

Thus, once households' incomplete information on prices is taken into account, a crucial difference exists between the aggregate demand and supply of labor: the quantity of labor demanded depends on the actual real wage rate, while the quantity of labor supplied depends on the expected real wage rate.

The labor market equilibrium

To study labor market equilibrium, let's see how the *money wage* is determined. To do so, we need to see how we can draw the demand and supply curves in the labor market against the money wage rate rather than the real wage rate.

The money wage rate Figure 20.3(a) shows the labor market as discussed in Chapter 8. Both suppliers and demanders of labor know the real wage rate and so the quantities of labor demanded and supplied depend on the real wage rate. The equilibrium real wage rate, measured in constant 1986 dollars, is $10 an hour and 225 million hours of labor services are employed. Suppose for a moment that the price level is equal to 100. That is, a current dollar buys the same quantity of goods and services as a 1986 dollar did. In this case, the vertical axis of Figure 20.3(a) measures both the real and the money wage rates, and the labor demand and supply curves plotted against the money wage rate are exactly the same as those plotted against the real wage rate. Figure 20.3(b) reproduces the labor demand and supply curves, LD and LS_0, and shows the same equilibrium — a price level of 100, a money wage rate of $10 an hour, and 225 million hours employed.

But an equilibrium real wage rate of $10 an hour can be attained at any money wage rate. All that is necessary is for the money wage rate and price level to stand in the appropriate relationship to each other: if the price level doubles, the money wage rate has to double; if the price level increases by 50 percent, the money wage rate has to increase by 50 percent. In part (a) where we plotted the labor demand and supply curves against the real wage rate, changes in the price level are not visible. The equilibrium shown there is a real equilibrium, independent of the price level.

But the equilibrium depicted in Figure 20.3(b) is not independent of the price level. The real equilibrium — real wage rate and employment — is independent of the price

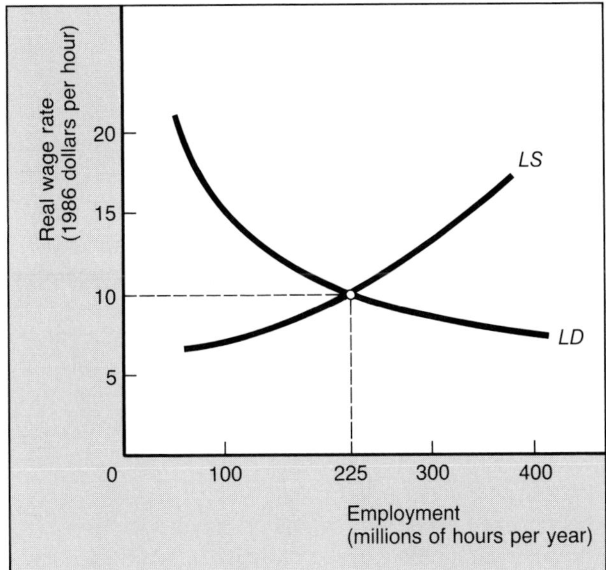

(a) Real wage rate

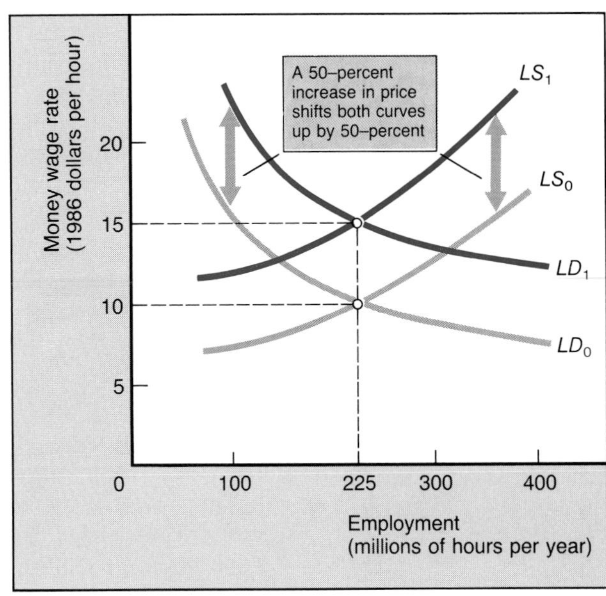

(b) Money wage rate

FIGURE 20.3
The Labor Market and the Money Wage

The supply and demand curves in the labor market, drawn against the real wage (part a), may equivalently be drawn against the money wage (part b). In that second case, there is a separate supply and demand curve for each price level. Both curves move vertically, one for one, as the price level varies.

level, but the equilibrium money wage rate is not. Since the money wage rate is measured on the vertical axis, the labor demand and supply curves can be drawn only for a given price level. The supply and demand curves, LD_0 and LS_0, are drawn for a price level equal to 100.

Suppose that the price level increases by 50 percent to 150. What money wage rate will firms now pay to hire 225 million hours of labor? The answer is, $15 an hour. We know from part (a) that firms hire 225 million hours if the real wage rate is $10 an hour. So at a price level of 150, firms will hire 225 million hours at a money wage rate of $15 an hour — a real wage of $10 an hour. Thus the labor demand curve shifts upward by the same percentage as the increase in the price level. Figure 20.3(b) shows the shift of the labor demand curve from LD_0 to LD_1 in response to an increase in the price level from 100 to 150.

What happens on the supply side? Precisely the same thing. Since the quantity of labor supplied depends on the real wage rate, the money wage rate will have to increase by 50 percent in response to the 50 percent increase in the price level for households to supply the same quantity of labor. Thus the curve LS_1 shows the supply of labor when the price level is 150. That is, the supply curve moves upward by 50 percent exactly as the demand curve does.

It is now easy to see that since a 50 percent increase in the price level shifts both the labor demand and the labor supply curves upward by 50 percent, the new equilibrium *money wage rate* increases by 50 percent to $15 an hour, and employment remains unchanged at 225 million hours. The equilibrium real wage rate also remains unchanged at $10 an hour.

Incomplete information and expectations Figure 20.4 shows how the new classical labor market works. The demand for labor curve depends on the actual price level. The demand curve LD_0 is the demand for labor when the price level equals 100. The supply of labor curve depends on the expected price level. The supply curve LS_0 is the supply of labor when the expected price level equals 100. Since these supply and demand curves are the same as the original curves in Figure 20.3, the equilibrium money wage rate is $10 an hour and 225 million hours are employed. At this equilibrium, the real wage is such that the quantity of labor demanded equals the quantity supplied, so unemployment is at its natural rate. That is, when the actual price level turns out to be the same as expected, unemployment is at its natural rate.

What happens to the labor market equilibrium if the actual price level turns out to be higher than expected? In particular, what happens if the actual price level turns out to be 50 percent higher, at 150? Each firm, knowing that the price of its output has increased by 50 percent, will now be willing to pay a higher money wage rate. That is, the demand for labor curve shifts upward by 50 percent, to LD_1. The supply of labor curve is not affected by the increase in the actual price level; it depends only on the expected price level and that has not changed. The supply of labor remains at *LS*.

Labor market equilibrium now occurs at a money wage rate of $12.50 an hour and 290 million hours of labor are employed. That is, with the actual price level higher than expected, the money wage rate increases, employment rises, and unemployment falls below its natural rate. The real wage rate falls. In Figure 20.4, the percentage increase in the price level is measured by the full vertical shift of the labor demand curve, the distance *AB*. You can see that the money wage rate increases by a smaller percentage, the distance *BC*. Since the price level increases by more than the money wage rate, the real wage rate falls. The fall in the real wage rate induces firms to hire more labor and increases employment from 225 million to 290 million hours. Households expect the

FIGURE 20.4
Expectations Equilibrium in the Labor Market

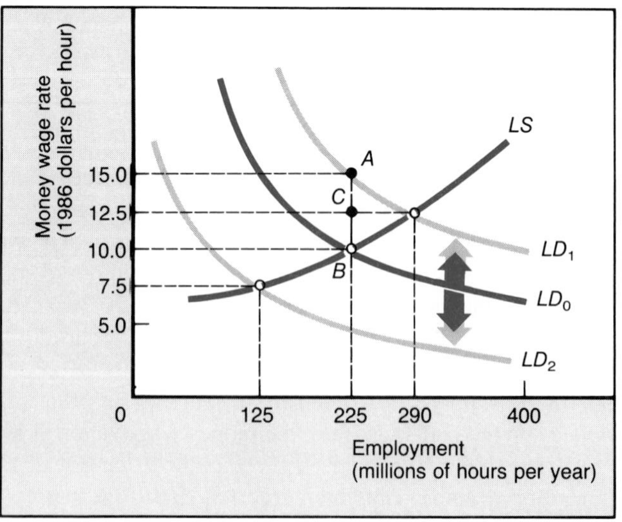

The demand for labor by each firm depends on the firm's own output price. As a consequence, the aggregate demand for labor depends on the actual price level. The supply of labor depends on the expected price level. For a given expected price level, the equilibrium wage and employment level is different at each different price level. If the price level is 100, the demand for labor curve is LD_0 and equilibrium occurs at *B*—full-employment equilibrium. If the price level increases by 50 percent, the demand for labor curve is LD_1 and equilibrium is above full employment. At a lower price level, the demand for labor curve is LD_2 and there is an unemployment equilibrium.

price level to be 100. As the money wage rate rises to $12.50, households expect that the real wage rate has increased to $12.50, so they increase the quantity of labor services supplied to 290 million hours.

In this situation, both households and firms are happy, and there is nothing that either can do to improve its situation. But as households become aware of the actual price level, they realize they've made a mistake—done too much work given the actual real wage rate. Of course, bygones are bygones. The only thing households can do is again use all the information available to them and make the best deal they can next time.

What happens if the price level turns out to be lower than expected? In particular, the price level turns out to be 50—50 percent lower than expected. The demand for labor curve shifts down to LD_2 and the labor market adjusts to an equilibrium in which unemployment is above its natural rate. The equilibrium money wage rate falls to $7.50 an hour and employment falls to 125 million hours. The fall in the money wage rate is less than the fall in the price level, so the real wage rate increases. The higher real wage rate induces firms to hire fewer workers and employment falls. Households do not expect the price level to fall and they read the fall in the money wage rate as a fall in the real wage rate. Households reduce the hours of labor services supplied to 125 million hours.

Both households and firms are happy — each is doing the best it can for itself. Households choose to reduce the hours supplied and their decision is correct in the light of the lower expected real wage rate. Each firm, on the other hand, knowing its own output price, regards the decrease in the money wage rate as insufficient to compensate for the decrease in its own price, and so the higher real wage rate induces firms to hire less labor.

Once we introduce incomplete information, equilibrium in the labor market depends on the price level relative to the expected price level. If the expected price level actually comes about, the labor market settles down at its natural rate of unemployment. If the price level is higher than expected, the labor market settles down with unemployment below its natural rate. If the price level turns out to be lower than expected, the labor market settles down with unemployment above its natural rate.

20.3 Lucas Aggregate Supply Curve

The **Lucas aggregate supply curve** shows the maximum real GDP supplied at each price level when the labor market is in equilibrium at a given expected price level. The Lucas aggregate supply curve is a particular case of the short-run aggregate supply curve. What's constant along the Lucas aggregate supply curve is the expected price level. The money wage is not fixed; it adjusts, given the expected price level, to keep the labor market in equilibrium.

Let's use the new classical labor market to derive the Lucas aggregate supply curve. Figure 20.5 illustrates the derivation. Part (a) simply reproduces Figure 20.4—it contains nothing new. If the price level is equal to 100, the demand for labor curve is LD_0; if the price level is equal to 150, the demand for labor curve is LD_1; and if the price level is equal to 50, the demand for labor curve is LD_2. The supply of labor curve is drawn for a fixed expected price level equal to 100. Part (b) shows the economy's short-run aggregate production function.

Let's begin by deriving the level of aggregate supply when the economy is at full employment. This occurs when the actual price level equals the expected price level—unemployment is at its natural rate. In Figure 20.5(a), the demand for labor curve is the

FIGURE 20.5
Derivation of the Lucas Aggregate Supply Curve

Part (a) is the same as Figure 20.4. At each different price level, there is a different labor market equilibrium. The employment levels associated with these equilibrium positions translate into different output levels, using the short-run production function (part b). The output levels associated with different price levels generate a short-run aggregate supply curve (the Lucas aggregate supply curve), *ASL* (part c). On that supply curve, at point *E* the economy is at full employment, at point *D* it is above full employment, and at point *F* there is unemployment.

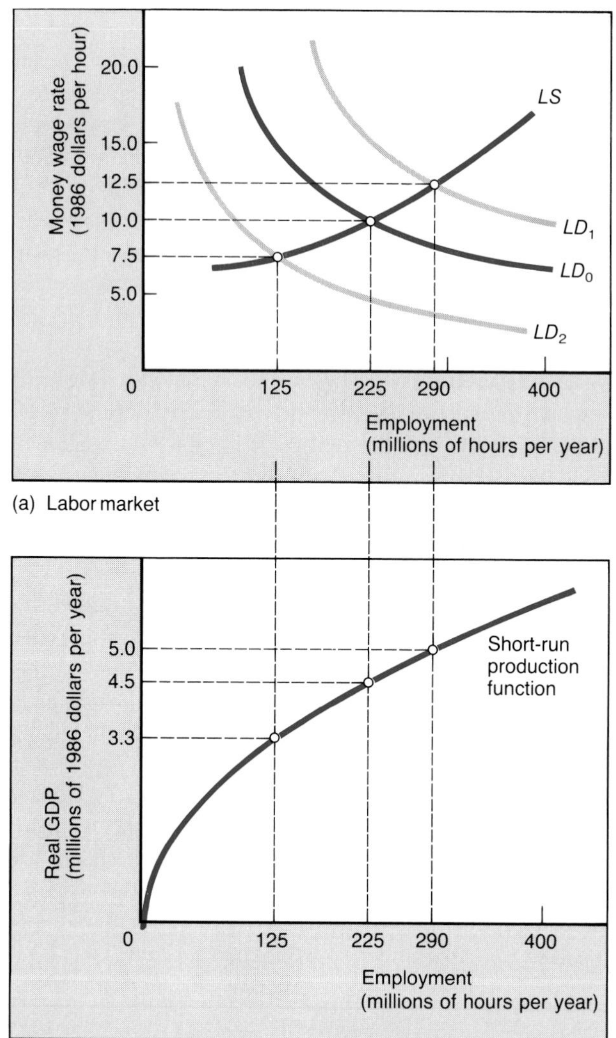

(a) Labor market

(b) Short-run production function

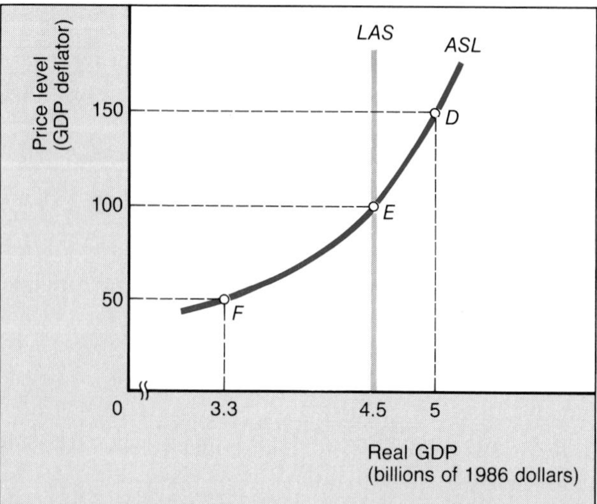

(c) Lucas aggregate supply curve

curve LD_0, and the employment level is 225 million hours. Transferring this employment level to part (b), you can see that maximum real GDP at full employment is $4.5 billion. That is, at an actual price level of 100, when the expected price level is also 100, real GDP is $4.5 billion. This combination of the actual price level and real GDP is plotted in part (c) as point *E*. Point *E* is one point on the Lucas aggregate supply curve, but it is also a point on the long-run aggregate supply curve, *LAS*.

Next consider what happens to real GDP supplied as the actual price level varies while the expected price level remains unchanged at 100. First, suppose the actual price level rises from 100 to 150. An increase in the actual price level shifts the demand for labor curve upward by the same percentage as the increase in the price level. That is, the demand for labor curve shifts up to LD_1. Since the expected price level is unchanged, the supply of labor curve remains stationary. The money wage rate increases to $12.50 an hour to restore labor market equilibrium. Employment increases to 290 million hours. At this higher level of employment, firms increase their output to $5 billion, as shown in part (b). That is, at an actual price level of 150 when the expected price level is 100, real GDP is $5 billion. The economy operates at point *D* in part (c). Point *D* is another point on the Lucas aggregate supply curve.

If the price level falls to 50 and the expected price level stays at 100, the demand for labor curve shifts downward to LD_2 and the money wage falls to $7.50 to restore labor market equilibrium. Employment falls to 125 million hours and firms cut their output to $3.3 billion, as shown in part (b). That is, at an actual price level of 50 and expected price level of 100, firms will supply $3.3 billion of output. The economy operates at point *F* in part (c). Point *F* is another point on the Lucas aggregate supply curve.

If we join together the points *D*, *E*, and *F* and all other points in between and beyond these, we will generate the Lucas aggregate supply curve, labeled *ASL*. The Lucas supply curve (*ASL*) cuts the long-run aggregate supply curve (*LAS*) at the point at which the actual price level equals the expected price level. In Figure 20.5(c), this price level is 100. This is not a coincidence. It happens because only when expectations turn out to be correct is unemployment at its natural rate and the economy at its full-employment level of real GDP.

Because the expected price level plays a critical role in Lucas's reformulation of classical macroeconomics, it is important to have a theory of the expected price level firmly grounded in classical economic principles. Let's see how Lucas proposed accomplishing this.

Rational expectation of the price level

The rational expectation of the price level is the price level that's expected on the basis of *all* relevant information available at the time the expectation is formed. Such relevant information includes the past history of the economic variables that influence the price level, along with the theory that determines the price level. We know that the price level that's expected to prevail in a *future* period influences the actual price level in that period. So for an expectation of the price level to be rational, the actual price level predicted by the theory must coincide with the expected price level.

The starting point is to form an expectation of aggregate demand. To do this we need to form an expectation of the money supply, government expenditure, and taxes next period. Suppose that the aggregate demand curve expected next period is AD^e, as shown in Figure 20.6. Let's also put in the diagram the long-run aggregate supply curve, the vertical line labeled *LAS*, at $4.5 billion of real GDP.

FIGURE 20.6
The Rational Expectation of the Price Level

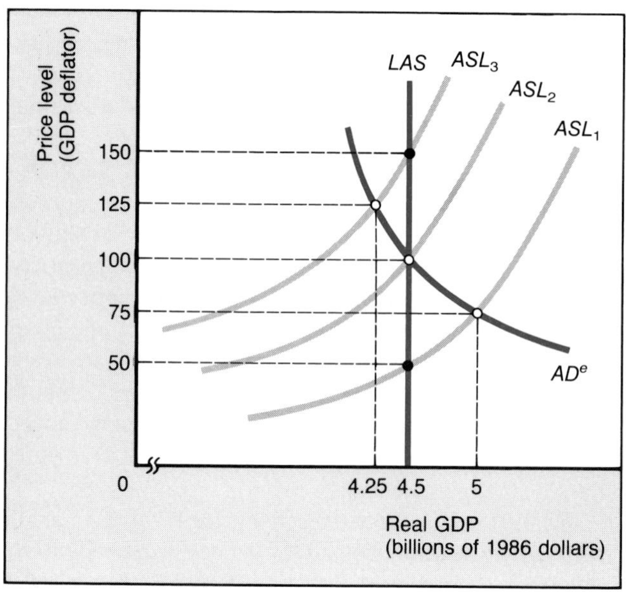

Expected aggregate demand is AD^e and the expected long-run aggregate supply is *LAS*. The position of the Lucas aggregate supply curve depends on the expected price level. To be a rational expectation, the expected price level must be consistent with the price level predicted by the model. If the expected price level is 50, the aggregate supply curve is ASL_1 and the model predicts a price level of 75. Thus 50 is not the rational expectation of the price level. If the expected price level is 150, the aggregate supply curve is ASL_3 and the model predicts a price level of 125. Thus 150 is not the rational expectation of the price level. If the expected price level is 100, the aggregate supply curve is ASL_2 and the predicted price level is 100. Thus 100 is the rational expectation of the price level.

Now let's perform a conceptual experiment. Suppose that we start out with an entirely arbitrary expectation of the price level next period equal to 50. The Lucas aggregate supply curve based on this expected price level is ASL_1. If the expected price level is 50, then the theory predicts an actual price level next period, given our expected aggregate demand, of 75. That is, the predicted actual price level exceeds the expected price level. We have a conflict: an expected price level of 50 does not coincide with the predicted actual price level of 75. Therefore the expectation is not rational.

Now try a different expected price level, say, 150. The Lucas aggregate supply curve becomes ASL_3, and the predicted actual price level is 125. Again, we have a conflict: the predicted actual price level doesn't equal the expected price level we arbitrarily assumed.

We've discovered that with the given expected aggregate demand, an expected price level of 50 leads to a predicted actual price level of 75 (higher than expected) and an expected price level of 150 leads to a predicted actual price level of 125 (lower than expected). The rational expectation of the price level lies somewhere between 50 and 150. What is it? It's 100 — the price level at intersection of the expected aggregate demand curve and the long-run aggregate supply curve *LAS*. Let's check it out.

With an expected price level of 100, the Lucas aggregate supply curve is ASL_2. The theory now predicts that, given the expected aggregate demand, the price level next period will also be 100. Notice that we are not saying that the price level next period will actually turn out to be 100. Rather, we are saying that the prediction of our theory is that the price level will be 100, given our expected aggregate demand AD^e.

20.4 *Explaining Output-Inflation Tradeoffs*

TESTCASE

Lucas's new classical model of aggregate supply combined with the standard model of aggregate demand enables us to understand the main facts about output-inflation tradeoffs we reviewed at the beginning of this chapter. Let's see how.

The existence of a tradeoff—the basic idea

Lucas's basic idea about why an output-inflation tradeoff exists is the presence of random (unforeseen) fluctuations in aggregate demand. Figure 20.7 illustrates the consequences of this fact. The long-run aggregate supply curve is *LAS*. The position of the Lucas aggregate supply curve depends on the expected price level, which in turn depends on expected aggregate demand and long-run aggregate supply. The *ASL* curve passes through the intersection point of the expected aggregate demand curve AD^e and the *LAS* curve.

Suppose that actual aggregate demand fluctuates around its expected level and the fluctuations cannot be predicted and that people are unaware of them until after they have occurred. Specifically, suppose that the actual aggregate demand curve fluctuates between AD_{high} and AD_{low}. Since the fluctuations in aggregate demand are not foreseen or expected, they have no effect on the expected aggregate demand curve, the expected price level, and the Lucas aggregate supply curve. Actual output and the price level are determined at the intersection of the actual aggregate demand curve and the Lucas aggregate supply curve. Thus real GDP fluctuates between y_2 (when aggregate demand is high) and y_1 (when aggregate demand is low). The price level fluctuates between P_2 (when aggregate demand is high) and P_1 (when aggregate demand is low).

If the only shocks to this economy are random aggregate demand fluctuations, the economy's price level and real GDP will trace out a set of points along the Lucas aggregate supply curve. If, in addition to the random fluctuations in aggregate demand, there are some fluctuations in long-run aggregate supply and these are very small relative to aggregate demand fluctuations, real GDP and the price level will still be positively correlated and will generate a sequence of points lying inside the ellipse shown in Figure 20.7.

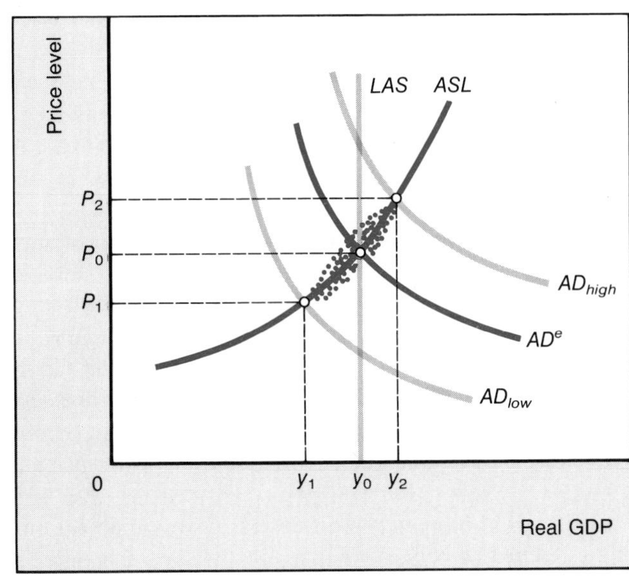

FIGURE 20.7
Procyclical Prices

For a given expected aggregate demand, AD^e, there is an expected price level P_0 and a Lucas aggregate supply curve *ASL*. Fluctuations in aggregate demand between AD_{high} and AD_{low} bring fluctuations in the price level and real GDP. These fluctuations generate points falling along the upward-sloping *ASL* curve and trace that curve. And if there are also small fluctuations in the expected level of aggregate demand, the points generated lie around *ASL*, as shown in the figure.

The tradeoff we've generated in Figure 20.7 is an output-price level tradeoff, not an output-inflation tradeoff. But it is easy to make the transition to an output-inflation tradeoff. Instead of the expected aggregate demand curve being fixed at AD^e, suppose that it shifts up at a constant rate. That is, a constant inflation rate is expected. If the actual aggregate demand curve shifts upward at exactly the same pace as the expected aggregate demand curve, the economy will remain at full-employment output (y_0) and inflation will equal its expected rate. Now, imagine that the actual aggregate demand curve shifts upward at a varying rate but at an average rate equal to the expected inflation rate. Sometimes it pulls ahead of its expected level by an amount indicated by the gap between AD^e and AD_{high} in Figure 20.7. At other times it falls below its expected level by an amount shown by the gap between AD^e and AD_{low} in Figure 20.7. The actual inflation rate will fluctuate around its expected rate. Sometimes, it will be $P_2 - P_0$ above the expected rate and sometimes $P_1 - P_0$ below its expected rate. Now we have an output-inflation tradeoff. The inflation rate varies around its expected rate as output varies around its capacity level.

The most important thing to bear in mind about the Lucas explanation for the output-inflation tradeoff is that the tradeoff exists even though the labor market is always in equilibrium—the quantity of labor demanded equals the quantity of labor supplied. You know this from the definition of the Lucas aggregate supply curve. It is the relationship between the price level and real GDP for a fixed expected price level that arises from a given production function when the labor market is in equilibrium.

Why slopes differ

We've seen that the Lucas model explains the existence of an output-inflation tradeoff. But how does it account for such vastly differing slopes as those described at the beginning of the chapter? Why in countries such as Argentina and Paraguay is the tradeoff extremely steep while in countries such as Canada and the United States the slope is much flatter?

The answer to this question lies in the inflation content in currently observed prices. Everyone knows *some* prices at the time they make their labor demand, labor supply, and production decisions. But in the Lucas setup they know only the prices of the things they are producing and selling. They do not know the prices of all the other goods and services they will buy later in the current period. What information does the price of the good they are producing provide? On its own it tells them the dollar price of that good. It does not tell them the dollar prices of the goods and services they will subsequently buy—it does not tell them anything about *relative prices*. To decide how much labor to hire, how much work to offer, and how much to produce, firms and households have to form an expectation of prices on the average against which to compare the price of the good in their own market. But they may use the price of the good in their own market to improve their inference about average prices in the economy as a whole.

In all economies two things happen to the prices of the output of an individual firm or sector. Prices change because the general price level changes—inflation. Prices also change because changes in technology and preferences produce changes in relative prices. Where the inflation rate is generally steady and does not vary much, firms and workers will infer from a change in the price in their own market that relative prices, not the price level, have changed. Thus they will not revise their expectations of inflation. Seeing the price change in their own market as a change in relative prices, they will respond by changing output. The output-inflation tradeoff in such an economy will be flat.

Contrast this with what happens in an economy in which the inflation rate is extremely variable—fluctuating between 50 percent and several hundred percent a year.

In such an economy, firms and their employees will infer from a large change in the price in their own sector that the price change is a reflection of changes in prices in general. They will assume that it is mainly inflation, with hardly any change in relative prices. Thus they will not respond by changing employment and output. The output-inflation tradeoff in such an economy will be steep.

The key prediction of the Lucas model, then, is that the slope of the output-inflation tradeoff depends on the variability of inflation. In economies where inflation hardly varies, the output-inflation tradeoff will have a gentle slope; but in economies with highly variable inflation, the output-inflation tradeoff will be steep.

Explaining the loops

Another feature of the relationship between inflation and real GDP fluctuations that we saw at the beginning of the chapter is a loop-like pattern in the time evolution of those variables. Why does this occur? The Lucas model explains the loops as the consequences of anticipated and unanticipated changes in aggregate demand. Anticipated changes in aggregate demand bring changes in the inflation rate with no change in real GDP. Unanticipated changes in aggregate demand bring a positive correlation between inflation and real GDP. In general, expected aggregate demand changes, but the changes will not be completely anticipated. They will be only partly anticipated. Since changes in actual and expected aggregate demand can be combined in many ways, their effects are capable, in principle, of generating the loop-like pattern in the evolution of inflation and real GDP fluctuations.

20.5 *The Policy Implications of New Classical Theory*

The policy implications of new classical theory were first worked out by Thomas Sargent (Hoover Institution and the University of Chicago) and Neil Wallace (the University of Minnesota). Their findings were startling. They discovered what came to be called the policy ineffectiveness proposition. The **policy ineffectiveness proposition** is that anticipated changes in monetary policy have no effect on employment, output, or any other real variable. They only affect the price level. Only unanticipated policy changes have real effects.

To understand the policy ineffectiveness proposition, imagine that the Bank of Canada uses an activist feedback rule to stabilize the economy. Whenever real GDP falls below capacity, the Bank of Canada increases the money supply and thus increases aggregate demand. Everyone in the economy understands this policy and the Bank of Canada never deviates from it. To see the consequences of pursuing such a policy in a model economy that behaves as described by Lucas, let's work out what happens following a random fall in aggregate demand. Figure 20.8 illustrates the analysis.

The long-run aggregate supply curve is *LAS*, initially expected aggregate demand is AD^e, and the Lucas aggregate supply curve is ASL_0. The expected price level is P_0. Now suppose aggregate demand decreases unexpectedly (such a decrease could arise from a fall in investment, a fall in world income that lowers net exports, or a variety of other sources). Real GDP falls to y_1 and the price level to P_1.

Now the Bank of Canada acts. Seeing the economy in a depressed state, it increases the money supply. If nothing else has changed, the increase in the money supply increases expected aggregate demand, from AD^e to AD^e_1, since everyone understands the

FIGURE 20.8
The Policy Ineffectiveness Proposition

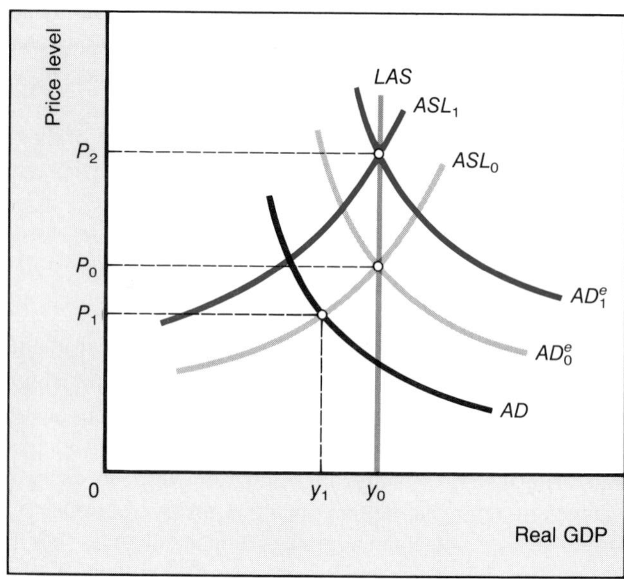

Expected aggregate demand is AD^e_0 and the initial aggregate supply curve ASL_0. The price level is P_0. If a temporary decrease in aggregate demand shifts the aggregate demand curve to AD_{low}, real GDP falls to y_1 and the price level to P_1. A policy feedback rule that injects additional money or fiscal stimulation to increase aggregate demand in a recession shifts the aggregate demand curve to the right. If the initial shock was temporary, the new aggregate demand curve is expected to be AD^e_1. The expected price level rises to P_2, and the aggregate supply curve shifts to ASL_1. If actual aggregate demand follows the expected path, real GDP returns to full employment and the price level rises to P_2. If policy had been passive—no policy feedback rule—expected and actual aggregate demand would have returned to AD^e_0 and real GDP to y_0. Real GDP is unaffected by the policy rule—hence the policy ineffectiveness proposition.

Bank's policy action. This new expected aggregate demand determines a new expected price level of P_2. Wages will increase and shift the Lucas aggregate supply curve to ASL_1. To isolate the effects of the policy, suppose that there are no further shocks in the next period. Actual aggregate demand turns out to be as expected. Real GDP returns to y_0 and the price level increases to P_2.

To see the policy effectiveness proposition we have to ask what would have happened if there had been no policy action—if, instead of an activist policy, the Bank of Canada pursued a fixed rule policy of keeping the money supply constant. In this case, the expected aggregate demand curve would have remained at AD^e, the price level would have returned to P_1, and real GDP to y_0. Thus the anticipated feedback policy action increased the price level in proportion to the Bank's increase in the money supply and left real GDP unchanged.

Unanticipated policy

The second part of the policy ineffectiveness proposition is that unanticipated policy has real effects. Suppose that the Bank of Canada makes the money supply fluctuate purely at random—in a completely unpredictable way. In this case the aggregate demand curve fluctuates unpredictably, generating fluctuations in real GDP and the price level that trace out an output-inflation tradeoff, as described in the previous section.

20.6 *Policy Surprises and the Business Cycle*

TESTCASE

New classical macroeconomics was initially a theory of aggregate supply. It had nothing new or special to say about aggregate demand. But most new classical economists came from the monetarist school of thought, and for them the money supply was the most important source of fluctuations in aggregate demand. They asked two important and related questions: Do *unanticipated* changes in the money supply generate fluctuations in aggregate economic activity? And do *anticipated* changes in the money supply produce changes only in the price level, leaving the real economy undisturbed?

For a brief period in the late 1970s it was believed that unexpected changes in the money supply indeed did generate aggregate fluctuations.[4] It was soon discovered, however, that the statistical basis for this proposition was not well-founded. Aggregate fluctuations could not, it seems, be explained by unanticipated fluctuations in the money supply.[5]

Statistical squabbles aside, it was widely agreed that unanticipated money could hardly affect the economy since the money supply itself is a well-publicized variable that is measured frequently and available for all to see. Having buried unanticipated money as a source of aggregate fluctuations, most economists (wrongly, in our view) concluded that the Lucas version of new classical economics was dead.

While this conclusion may turn out to be correct, it has not been established simply by showing that unanticipated *money* is not the key variable driving aggregate fluctuations. Any unanticipated component of aggregate demand, and there are many factors in addition to the money supply that influence the position of the aggregate demand curve, can produce the Lucas output-inflation tradeoff. It remains to be investigated whether such fluctuations have been important in generating the business cycle in the real-world economy.

But instead of pursuing such inquiries, new classical macroeconomics has taken a different turn, a turn toward an even more basic foundation of classical economics that strips the economy of the veil of money and studies the real forces operating beneath it. Let's now turn to an examination of this most recent development in new classical macroeconomics—real business cycle theory.

20.7 *Real Business Cycle Theory*

Real business cycle theory bases its explanation of aggregate fluctuations on exogenous, random technological change. In its extreme form, money plays no role in generating aggregate fluctuations. The business cycle is entirely a real phenomenon.[6]

The basic theory

The jumping-off point for real business cycle theory is the neoclassical growth model we studied in Chapter 10. But instead of emphasizing the ongoing expansion of the economy as growth theory does, real business cycle theory emphasizes the erratic nature of the process of economic expansion. We can best understand the essentials of the theory if we abstract from a growing population.

[4]This conclusion was based on Robert Barro's article, "Unanticipated Money Growth and Unemployment in the United States," *American Economic Review*, Vol. 67 (March 1977), pp. 101-115.

[5]The main paper reaching this conclusion is Frederic S. Mishkin, "Does Anticipated Monetary Policy Matter? An Econometric Investigation," *Journal of Political Economy*, Vol. 90 (February 1982), pp. 22-51.

[6]Two papers started real business cycle theory. They are Finn Kydland and Edward Prescott, "Time to Build and Aggregate Fluctuations," *Econometrica*, Vol. 50, 1982, pp. 1345-70, and John Long and Charles Plosser, "Real Business Cycles," *Journal of Political Economy*, Vol. 91, 1983, pp. 39-69.

Constraints Suppose that there is a given population and a fixed work force. Then the real GDP produced by this economy depends on technology and the capital stock. That is, with the *existing* technology, the maximum amount of real GDP that can be produced is determined by a production function, which links real GDP to the capital stock. Figure 20.9 illustrates such a production function, $zf(k)$, where z is the state of technology. Technology changes over time, but erratically. Sometimes z increases quickly and sometimes slowly; sometimes it might even decrease. With the production function $zf(k)$ and an initial capital stock k_0, real GDP is y_0.

The total resources available in the economy at the end of the period is the current period's output plus its capital stock. At the beginning of the period the capital stock is k_0, but capital depreciates at the rate δ. So the total resources available in the economy in the current period are determined by the curve $zf(k) + (1 - \delta)k$ in Figure 20.9. The production function and the undepreciated part of the capital stock determine the total resources available in the economy. These resources may either be consumed or kept in the form of capital for the next period.

Preferences Real business cycle theory assumes everyone has the same preferences. In effect, there is only one person in the economy who represents all people. The representative person's preferences depend only on consumption in each year over an infinite future planning period. Each year more consumption is preferred to less, and marginal utility from consumption diminishes. The best that the person can do is to smooth consumption over its lifetime.

Steady state In order to see how real business cycle theory generates cycles, it's best to begin with an economy that is in a *steady state* — not changing at all. Such a situation is illustrated in Figure 20.10. Let's orient ourselves before diving into this figure. The horizontal axis measures the capital stock (as in Figure 20.9). The vertical axis measures several variables — real GDP, consumption, the capital stock next period, and investment. The two blue curves are the production function and the total resources function that you first met in Figure 20.9. The maximum amount that can be consumed in the current period is equal to current income plus undepreciated capital. If this amount is consumed, there will be no capital stock next period. The constraint on consumption

FIGURE 20.9
Capital, Technology, and Production Possibilities

The amount of real GDP produced depends on the capital stock and on the state of technology. It is determined by the production function $zf(k)$. Total resources available at the end of a period include real GDP produced during the period plus the undepreciated capital stock $(1 - \delta)k$.

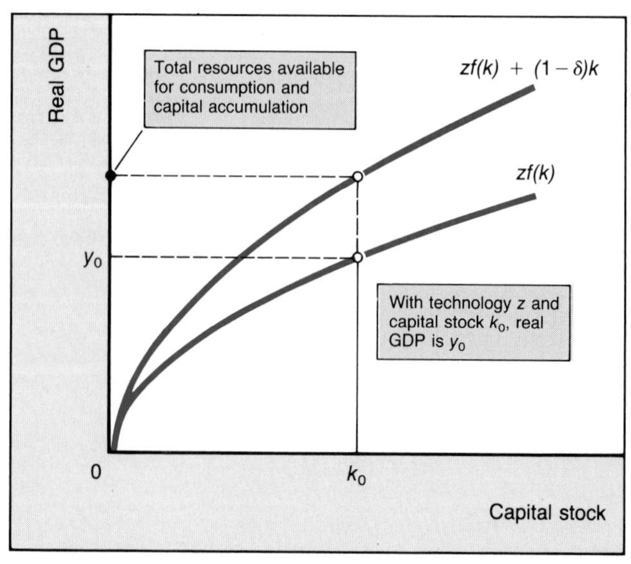

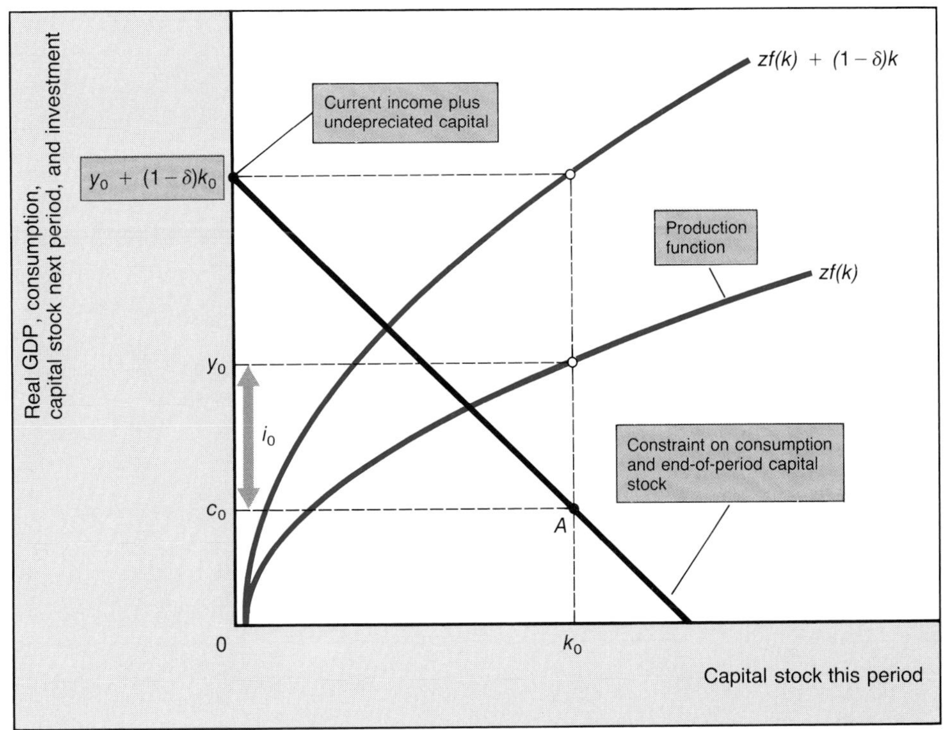

FIGURE 20.10
Constraint on Consumption and Capital Accumulation

With a capital stock k_0 and real GDP y_0, total resources available are $y_0 + (1 - \delta)k_0$. These total resources may be either consumed or accumulated as capital. Any point along the black constraint line can be chosen. Choosing point *A* gives us steady state: the capital stock next period equals k_0, and investment, i_0, exactly equals depreciation, δk_0. Points along the line above *A* decrease the capital stock and points below *A* increase the capital stock.

and next period's capital stock is given by the downward-sloping black line. Its slope is equal to -1 because one extra unit of capital stock next period requires one less unit of consumption this period. This economy is in a steady state at point *A*. Consumption is c_0, real GDP is y_0, and investment is i_0. (We're ignoring government purchases and net exports to keep the analysis as easy as possible.) Next period's capital stock is k_0 and so exactly the same values of all the variables repeat and continue to repeat as long as the production function and total resource curve stay in the positions shown in Figure 20.10.

Generating cycles

Technological change generates a business cycle. Here we will work out the effects of a single but permanent change in technology. Suppose technology improves so that the value of z increases from z_0 to z_1. The production function and the total resource curve shift upward (as shown in Figure 20.11). Real GDP immediately increases from y_0 to y_1 and total resources available increase. The constraint on consumption and capital stock next period shifts outward. With more resources available, both current consumption and capital accumulation increase. To determine the precise allocation of the additional resources between consumption and capital requires the solution of a more complicated problem than we are going to study here. Let's simply suppose that the economy moves to point *A*′. At *A*′, consumption increases from c_0 to c_1 and the capital stock increases from k_0 to k_1.

With a larger capital stock and no further change in technology, real GDP increases further next period, to y_2. Total resources also increase, and the constraint on consumption and capital stock next period shifts outward again. These further changes are not illustrated in the figure but you can easily visualize them. You can also imagine that with a yet further outward shift of the constraint on consumption and capital accumulation, even more consumption and capital accumulation takes place in the following

FIGURE 20.11
Technological Change

A technological advance increases z from z_0 to z_1. The production function and total resources function shift upward. Consumption and capital accumulation possibilities expand. With a capital stock k_0, output immediately increases from y_0 to y_1. Total resources increase to $y_1 + (1 - \delta)k_0$. Consumption and capital accumulation possibilities expand. In the next period, consumption increases and so does capital accumulation. If the point chosen is A', capital increases to k_1 and consumption rises to c_1. Real GDP increases further to y_2. The economy continues expanding until it reaches a new steady state with higher capital, consumption, and real GDP.

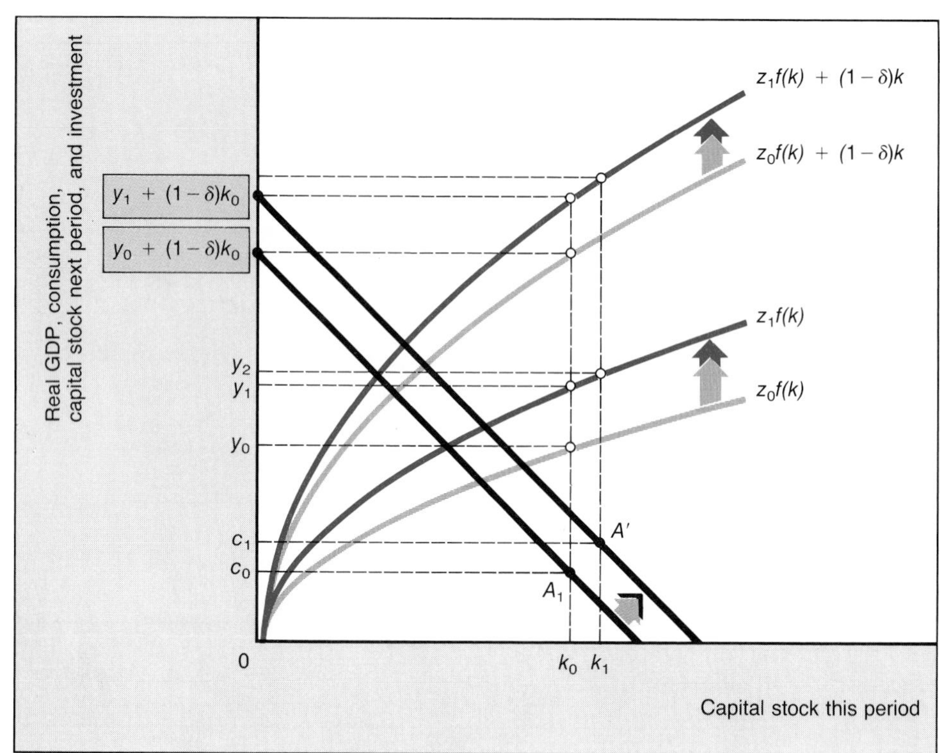

period. But the increase is smaller than in the initial period. The expanding economy is converging on the new steady state. Eventually the capital stock, real GDP, consumption, and investment will all have increased to their new steady-state levels.

Over time, this economy will generate paths illustrated in Figure 20.12. The change in technology at the end of period 1 increases z. At the same time there is a burst of capital accumulation—investment—and real GDP increases. Over time the amount of additional investment gradually falls off until it reaches a new higher steady-state level. Real GDP increases but its increments also gradually decline.

Accelerator mechanism? You've seen a picture like Figure 20.12 before. It looks almost exactly like the accelerator mechanism in Chapter 18. Indeed, it is an accelerator mechanism. The level of investment is connected with the change in real GDP (income). But the change in income does not cause a change in investment. Fluctuations in this economy arise from only one factor—technological change. The change in technology is the source of the change in both income and investment. They both respond to this deeper underlying cause.

Real interest rate The real interest rate in this economy also responds to a change in technology. The real interest rate is equal to the marginal product of capital. The marginal product of capital is the slope of the production function (as shown in Figure 20.10). When technological change takes place, the production function shifts upward and its slope increases. The marginal product of capital increases. As capital is accumulated along the adjustment path to the new steady state, the real interest rate falls and eventually returns to its original level.

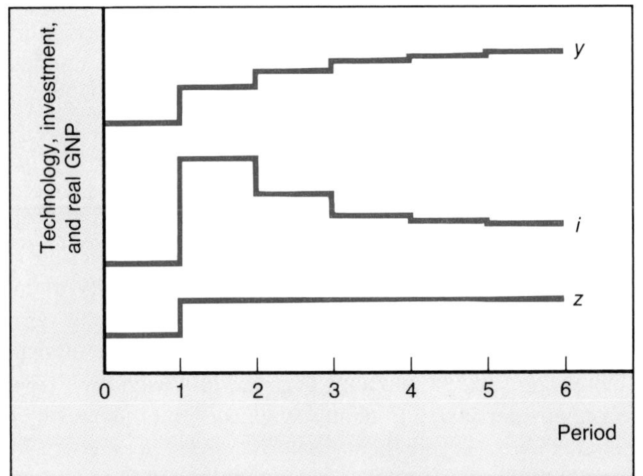

FIGURE 20.12
Technology Shock Amplifies Investment and Brings Real GDP Growth

At period 1, technology advances—z increases. There is an immediate rise in investment, i, and real GDP, y. As the economy approaches a new steady state, investment gradually falls but real GDP continues to increase. But the increases in real GDP and the decreases in investment get smaller and smaller.

Thus according to real business cycle theory, in an economic upturn such as that we've studied here, real GDP will grow, there'll be a burst of investment, and interest rates will be positively correlated with investment.

Extensions to labor market Real business cycle theory is easily extended to include an analysis of the labor market. When the technological change we've just described takes place, not only does the marginal product of capital increase but so does the marginal product of labor. As a result the demand curve for labor shifts to the right. The increase in demand for labor increases employment and the real wage rate. The extent of the increase in the real wage rate depends on the slope of the labor supply curve. If the quantity of labor supplied is highly responsive to a change in the real wage rate, the change in the real wage will be small and the change in employment will be large. Proponents of real business cycle theory generally reckon that the response of employment to a small change in the real wage rate is large. Thus real business cycle theory predicts that employment fluctuates with output over the business cycle. In other words, it predicts a relationship such as Okun's Law. It further predicts that real wages are procyclical—real wages increase when the economy moves into a boom.

Recessions and cycles To illustrate how the real business cycle theory works, we've looked at expansion. A contraction is just a reversal of that process. A decrease in z shifts the production function downward and decreases the available resources. It sets off a process of declining investment, capital stock, consumption, and real GDP that is the mirror image of the expansion process we've just studied.

Cycles occur because technology changes at an uneven pace. The value of z sometimes increases quickly, sometimes slowly, and occasionally declines.

Real business cycles, money, and prices

Money and the price level play no role in the real business cycle we've just studied. But there are some prices—the real interest rate and the real wage rate—and we've seen how they behave. But what about the price level and the money supply?

We've seen at several points in this book some interesting relationships between money and prices and economic activity. There is a generally positive correlation between changes in the money supply and the changes in economic activity. There is also a generally positive correlation between inflation and economic activity. In the mainstream economic models we've studied, these correlations arise from the fact that money is one of the variables influencing the economy. A change in the money supply changes aggregate demand and sets up some consequential changes in real GDP, employment, and the price level.

But according to real business cycle theory, no such effects take place. If money were grafted onto a real business cycle model it would be a veil. It would simply determine the price level. How then does real business cycle theory account for the correlations present in the data? The answer is, reverse causation—the proposition that the quantity of money is determined by economic conditions; it does not determine those conditions. According to real business cycle theory, the quantity of money increases more quickly when the economy is expanding because the banking system responds to the expanding economy by increasing loans and making more credit available. With the money supply increasing, prices increase. Thus the causation runs from technological change to real economic expansion to monetary expansion to increasing prices.

Whether the real business cycle theory is correct is not yet known. Most economists believe that it contains a germ of truth but is too simplistic. Other economists argue that indeed it is simplistic but that the germ of truth that it contains is, if not the whole truth, most of it. To justify that claim, they show how well the real business cycle theory accounts for aggregate fluctuations in the Canadian economy in the postwar years.

TESTCASE

20.8 *Calibrating the U.S. Economy*

To check whether real business cycle theory works, Kydland and Prescott compared the predictions of their artificial economy with a real economy, that of the United States. Let's see what they did and what they discovered.[7]

They set out a model economy that had a particular production function and a particular utility function to describe people's preferences for consumption, leisure, and the timing of consumption, and they chose specific values for the parameters of the model. They chose a Cobb-Douglas production function with constant returns to scale. A **Cobb-Douglas** production function is one in which a 1 percent increase in employment increases output by a percent and a 1 percent increase in the capital stock increases output by $(1 - a)$ percent. A production function has **constant returns to scale** if output increases by 1 percent when all inputs increase by 1 percent. The Cobb-Douglas production function may be written

$$y = zn^{a}k^{(1-a)}. \qquad \textbf{(20.1)}$$

To describe people's preferences for consumption, leisure, and the timing of consumption, Kydland and Prescott used a utility function in which total utility increases if consumption increases or leisure increases. But utility also depends on consumption and leisure each year from now through the indefinite future. The further in the future the consumption and leisure arise, the less present utility they create.

The final ingredient in the model economy is a process of technological change. According to real business cycle theory, the cycle itself is generated by such a process. In the model economy, Kydland and Prescott generated technological change by a series of random numbers—similar to drawing numbered balls from a bag.

[7]A similar exercise to that of Kydland and Prescott using Canadian data has been performed by Enrique Mendoza, ''Real Business Cycles in a Small Open Economy'' (September 1991), pp. 797-818. However the Canadian model is more complicated because it takes into account international trade and investment, aspects of the business cycle ignored in the work on the relatively less open U.S. economy. The findings of Mendoza are similar to those reviewed here.

Calibration

Making one set of measurements correspond to another is called **calibration**. For example, we calibrate the instruments that tell us how fast an automobile is going by timing a car over a measured mile. Kydland and Prescott calibrated their model economy to the real economy. To do so, they picked values for the model's parameters that correspond to known information about the real economy. One such parameter is a in the production function. The value chosen for a was the average share of labor income in U.S. GDP. (If markets are competitive, a is labor's share of GDP and $[1 - a]$ is capital's share.) Values for utility function parameters were also chosen to be consistent with known patterns in the allocation of time and consumption. The rate at which future utility is discounted (has a lower value than current consumption) was based on average real interest rates in the actual economy.

The final element in the calibration involved putting the right numbers on the balls that went into the bag to generate technological change. Depending on the average rate of technological change and its variability, different artificial economic time-series can be generated. Kydland and Prescott chose the process of technological change that made the model economy's growth rate of real GDP and its variability equal the actual economy's.

We've just described the calibration of a real business cycle model but not a test of it.

Testing the model

The Kydland-Prescott model was tested by checking its ability to produce growth and fluctuations in consumption, investment, the capital stock, and employment and then comparing the growth and variability produced in the model economy with their counterparts in the real economy. Kydland and Prescott concluded that their model economy behaved in a way very similar to the actual U.S. economy, although they did not present any statistical tests of the closeness of the fit with reality.

The behavior of the Solow residual

The key variable generating the business cycle according to real business cycle theory is technological change. One measure of technological change is the Solow residual. Using Kydland and Prescott's production function, Equation (20.1), and given data on output, employment, and the capital stock, it is possible to calculate z. We've done this calculation for the period 1955-1990 and the result is shown in Figure 20.13. Here, we plot the growth rate of the Solow residual—the growth rate of z in Equation (20.1). We also show the growth rate of real GDP in that figure. You can see immediately in Figure 20.13 a strong correlation between the growth rate of the Solow residual and the growth rate of real GDP. You can also see that in years with easily identified shocks, such as those inflicted by OPEC through the world price of oil, the Solow residual falls. But what does the correlation between the Solow residual and real GDP growth mean?

According to real business cycle theory, the Solow residual measures the exogenous rate of technological change. Fluctuations in the Solow residual drive everything else, producing fluctuations in real GDP and magnified fluctuations in investment. Many economists doubt this explanation for the correlation. Let's look at some of the main objections.

Technological regress Technological change usually takes the form of *progress*. That is, more can be produced with fewer inputs. If the Solow residual does measure technological change, there are times when technological change goes in the opposite direction—more inputs are needed to produce a given amount of output. Such periods

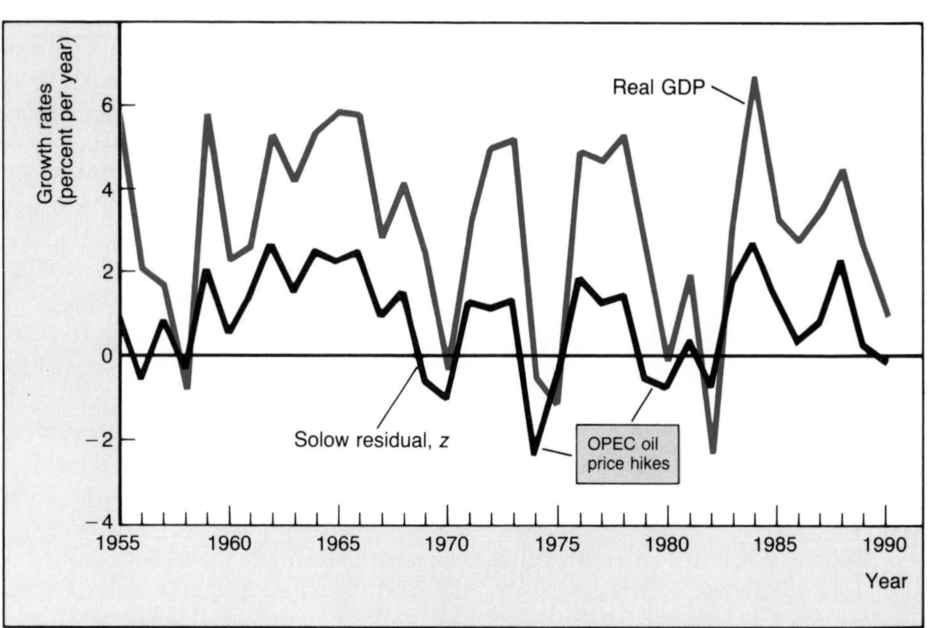

FIGURE 20.13
Real GDP Growth and the Solow Residual in the United States

The Solow residual measures the changes of real GDP resulting from changes other than the level of employment or the size of the capital stock. There is a high degree of correlation between the growth rates of this residual and of real GDP. Real business cycle theory assumes that fluctuations in the Solow residual bring fluctuations in real GDP. Other models interpret fluctuations in the Solow residual as arising from other sources that bring simultaneous fluctuations in real GDP.

Source: Economic Report of the President, 1991, and our calculations.

are not that rare. You can see them in Figure 20.13 in 1956, 1958, 1969, and 1970, 1974, 1979, 1980, 1982, and 1990. It seems incredible to most economists that these negative growth rates for the Solow residual could be interpreted as periods of technological amnesia.

Capacity utilization One clear fact about business cycles is that in recessions, the capital stock is not fully utilized. Often firms lay off workers and close down an entire shift, leaving their capital stock idle for a significant proportion of each work week. Thus fluctuations in output over the business cycle reflect fluctuations not in the size of the capital stock but in the degree to which it is utilized. These fluctuations in the capital stock utilization rate are reflected in the Solow residual. Thus the Solow residual measures at least two things—technological change and fluctuations in the degree of utilization of the capital stock. Does this observation rescue real business cycle theory? Possibly, but not necessarily. The key problem for real business cycle theory is to explain why the utilization rate of the capital stock varies. One such explanation—suggested by Jeremy Greenwood, Zvi Hercowitz, and Gregory Huffman and using a modified real business cycle model in which the rate of depreciation of capital depends on its utilization rate—is that firms pick the most efficient rate at which to use their capital stock and this rate fluctuates over the business cycle.[8] And these fluctuations are themselves generated by technological change.

But there is another interpretation of the data: fluctuations in real GDP growth and in the degree of capital utilization both respond to some other impulse, possibly arising on the aggregate demand side of the economy. In other words, a conventional aggregate demand–aggregate supply model with an upward sloping aggregate supply curve can account for these data. With sticky wages, the short-run aggregate supply curve slopes upward. A decrease in aggregate demand brings a decrease in output and employment

[8]Jeremy Greenwood, Zvi Hercowitz, and Gregory Huffman, "Investment, Capacity Utilization, and the Real Business Cycle," *American Economic Review*, Vol. 78 (June 1988), pp. 402-417.

and leads firms to lower the utilization rate of their capital stock, making the Solow residual turn down and possibly go negative. An increase in aggregate demand brings an increase in output and an increase in the utilization rate of the capital stock, making the Solow residual grow quickly.

This possible interpretation is strengthened by noticing that in periods when there was an undeniable decrease in aggregate demand, such as in 1981-1982, the Solow residual decreases.

There has been a lively debate about the relevance of the real business cycle theory to explaining aggregate fluctuations in the U.S. and world economies. This debate will continue.

20.9 *Unemployment and Real Business Cycles*

Kydland and Prescott's real business cycle theory does not explain the phenomenon of unemployment. But real business cycle theorists have addressed this problem and incorporated it into their models. There are three approaches to explaining unemployment that are consistent with real business cycle theory. They are

- Indivisible labor
- Sectoral reallocation
- Job creation and job destruction

Indivisible labor

You encountered the idea of indivisible labor in Chapter 9, when we studied the reasons for larger fluctuations in employment than in work hours. The idea is that each worker has an optimum number of work hours per week and that when the total demand for labor fluctuates, it pays firms to vary the number of people employed rather than the average hours per employed person.

We can make this idea precise by considering a particular example, and one that has been used by real business cycle theorists.

Suppose that Figure 20.14 shows the production function for a typical worker. With this production function, the first five hours of work produce nothing. You can think of these five hours as time spent setting up the job and cleaning up afterward—setup and shutdown effort. Work in excess of five hours produces output. For example, 40 hours a week produces an output of 50 units at point *A* on the production function. Instead of employing one person for 40 hours and producing 50 units of output, the firm could employ two people for 20 hours each. It still has 40 hours of labor a week. But in a 20-hour week, one worker produces only 10 units of output. Thus employing two workers for 20 hours a week produces only 20 units of output. Obviously, in these conditions it does not pay the firm to hire two workers for 20 hours a week. It is this fact that makes firms vary the number employed rather than the hours per employee when output fluctuates.

To see why firms vary the number employed, suppose the firm employs a hundred people, each for 40 hours a week, producing 5,000 units of output (50 times 100). If output decreases by 10 percent, the best response of the firm will be to decrease its labor force by 10 percent, employing 90 people for 40 hours a week to produce the 4,500 units of output. If, instead, the work hours of the entire 100 workers decrease by 10 percent, so that everyone works 36 hours a week, output will fall by more than 10 percent. Put the other way around, the firm can cut its output by 10 percent by employing the same work force for a smaller number of hours, but the hours per worker will decrease by less than 10 percent and the firm's wage bill will be higher.

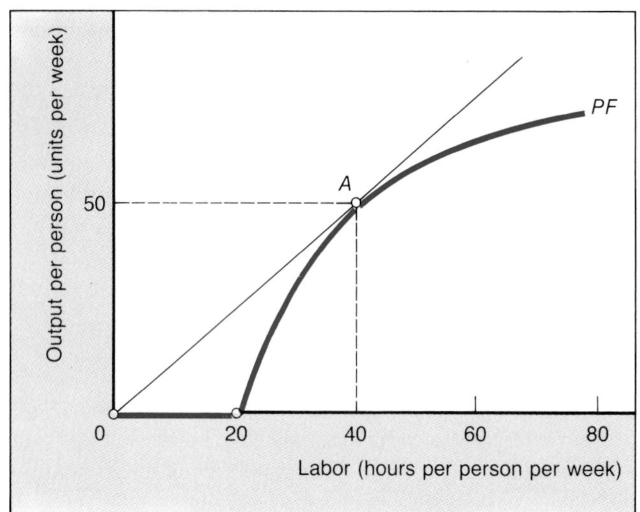

FIGURE 20.14
A Production Function with Startup Costs

The production function here shows that 20 hours of work are needed each week before any output can be produced. Work in excess of 20 hours produces positive amounts of output. For example, 40 hours produce 50 units of output. With such a production function, firms maximize profit by hiring workers for 40 hours a week or more and vary the output produced by varying the number of workers employed rather than the number of hours per employee.

Real business cycles again The heart of real business cycle theory is the idea that the production function shifts because of technological change. When such shifts occur, the equilibrium level of output and employment change. With indivisible labor, the changes in employment result from changes in the number of people employed rather than variations in hours of work. In this way, real business cycle theory explains unemployment.

Sectoral reallocation

You also met sectoral reallocation in Chapter 9. This phenomenon results from the continual creation and destruction of jobs in different parts of the economy. The more rapid the pace of job creation and destruction, the larger is the flow of workers from declining to expanding sectors of the economy. Since it takes time to find a new job, the more this type of reallocation goes on, the larger is the average unemployment rate.

Since technological change drives the real business cycle theory, and since, in principle at least, such change need not occur uniformly in all sectors of the economy, at times there will be a large amount of sectoral reallocation taking place. This topic is one being actively researched in the early 1990s.

Job creation and destruction

Technological change creates some jobs and destroys others not only across sectors but within sectors and even within individual firms. The **job creation rate** is the number of new jobs created in a given time period expressed as a percentage of the total number of jobs. The **job destruction rate** is the number of jobs that disappear in a given time period expressed as a percentage of the total number of jobs. A rapid pace of job creation and job destruction brings a large amount of labor turnover and a high unemployment rate. A slow pace of job creation and job destruction brings a small amount of labor turnover and a low unemployment rate. When the job destruction rate is greater than the job creation rate, unemployment increases, and when the job destruction rate is smaller than the job creation rate, unemployment falls.

There is no precise relationship between the rate of technological change and the job creation and destruction rates. That relationship depends on how particular technological changes alter the skills required to do particular jobs and on whether new technologies are labor saving or capital saving. A labor-saving technological change, by its very nature, destroys some jobs. But it also creates jobs for those who produce and maintain the new technology capital. Even technological change that replaces one kind of capital with another also destroys the jobs of the makers and operators of old technology capital and creates jobs building and learning how to operate new technology equipment.

Thus both the rate and the detailed nature of technological change influence job creation and destruction rates and the unemployment rate.

20.10 *Unemployment over the Business Cycle*

TESTCASE

Here we'll examine the effects of sectoral reallocation on unemployment and the relationship between job creation and job destruction rates and the business cycle.

Sectoral reallocation and unemployment

One attempt to measure the extent to which sectoral reallocation influences unemployment was undertaken by Lucy Samson of Laval University. Samson measured the flows of labor from one sector to another in the Canadian economy each year from 1957 to 1982. She then developed a measure of the natural rate of unemployment arising from this source. Her estimates of the natural rate of unemployment are graphed in Figure 20.15, alongside the actual unemployment rate.

Although Samson's estimate of the natural rate of unemployment is controversial, it is clear that fluctuations in her estimate are a reflection of fluctuations in the amount

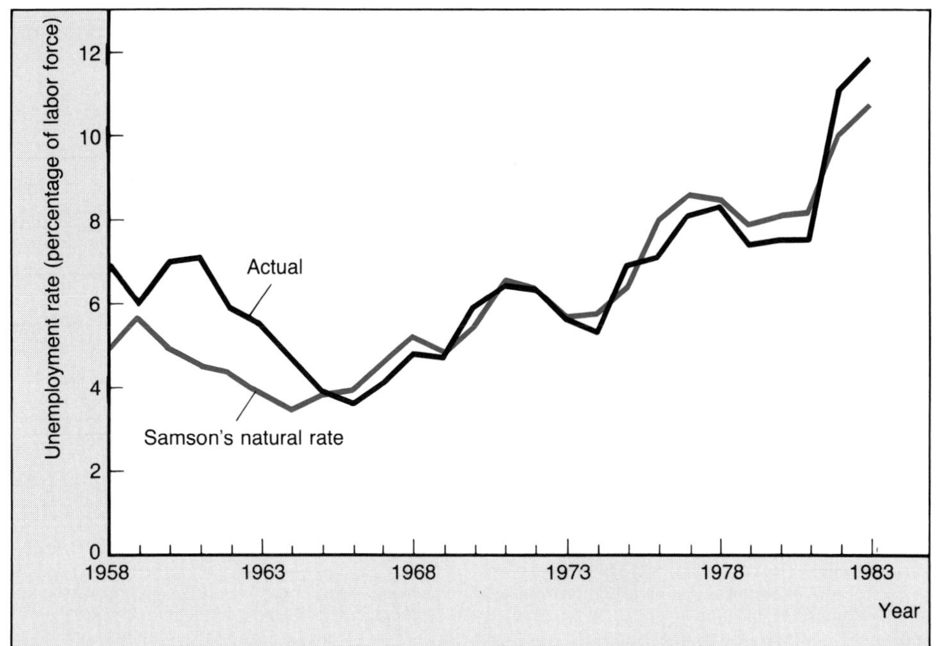

FIGURE 20.15
Sectoral Turnover and the Natural Rate of Unemployment

Measuring the amount of sectoral turnover of labor gives an estimate of the importance of technological change in generating fluctuations in unemployment. Fluctuations in actual unemployment are highly correlated with fluctuations in the amount of labor reallocated across the sectors of the economy.

Source: Lucy Samson, "A Study of the Impact of Sectoral Shifts on Aggregate Unemployment in Canada," *Canadian Journal of Economics*, XVIII, 3 (August 1985), p. 527.

of labor force reallocation from one sector to another. It's also clear, therefore, that there is indeed a high correlation between sectoral reallocation and unemployment.

However, interpreting this correlation is itself controversial. As with the Solow residual, causation may run not from the natural rate to the unemployment rate but the other way around. Again, a conventional aggregate demand–aggregate supply model can account for these observations. A decrease in aggregate demand with sticky wages brings lower output and lower employment. Job losses occur and the unemployment rate increases. More people are looking for work and more of these people will find work in other sectors of the economy, eventually. Thus the rate of sectoral reallocation increases. But notice that in this account, the direction of causation runs from aggregate demand to unemployment and the amount of sectoral reallocation, not the other way around.

Interpreting the correlations between unemployment and sectoral reallocation and between the Solow residual and real GDP growth is a good illustration of an important rule: correlation does not imply causation.

Job creation, job destruction, and the business cycle

Until recently, not much was known about job creation and job destruction rates. And we still lack good data for Canada. But some important work on the U.S. data by Steve Davis and John Haltiwanger has revealed the interesting information shown in Figure 20.16.[9] (Data from their study are available only for the years shown, 1972 to 1986.)

FIGURE 20.16
Job Creation, Job Destruction, and Technological Change

The job destruction rate and the total job creation and destruction rate (sum) are strongly countercyclical and the job creation rate and net job creation rate are procyclical. There is a correlation between the net rate of job creation and the rate of technological change as measured by the growth rate of the Solow residual, z.

Source: Job creation and destruction data provided by Steve Davis and John Haltiwanger. Solow residual, see Fig. 20.13.

[9]Steve Davis and John C. Haltiwanger, "Gross Job Creation and Destruction, Microeconomic Evidence and Macroeconomic Implications," in *NBER Macroeconomics Annual*, Vol. 5 (National Bureau of Economic Research, 1990), pp. 123-168. The data used in Figure 20.16 were kindly provided by Steve Davis and John Haltiwanger.

The figure shows that the job destruction rate fluctuates much more than the job creation rate. But both rates are correlated with the business cycle. Job destruction increases sharply in cyclical downturns, such as 1974 and 1982, and job creation decreases (but only slightly) in such years. Total job creation and destruction (measured as the sum of the job creation and destruction rates and marked "sum" in the figure) is strongly countercyclical. In contractions, such as 1974 and 1982, it increases, and in recoveries, such as in the mid-1980s, its rate declines. Net job creation (measured as the job creation rate minus the job destruction rate and marked "net" in the figure) is strongly procyclical.

Figure 20.16 also shows the growth rate of the Solow residual. By comparing the behavior of this variable with the net job creation rate, you can see that there is a general tendency for the two to fluctuate in sympathy with each other. But the caveat about correlation and causation applies to this relationship with the same force as that between sectoral reallocation and the Solow residual. Interpreting the correlation and uncovering causal links is an important item of unfinished research.

20.11 *An Assessment of New Classical Macroeconomics*

New classical macroeconomics is not a body of established empirical regularities with a classical interpretation for them. Rather, it is a research program—an attempt, using a particular theoretical approach, to explain all economic phenomena: the allocation of resources across different activities, space, and time, and fluctuations over time.

At the heart of new classical macroeconomics is the presumption that the essence of aggregate fluctuations is intertemporal substitution. Going with this is the presumption that coordination of decisions among individuals is not important — at least for explaining fluctuations in aggregates.

As a research agenda, classical macroeconomics is thriving. In fact, many economists believe it to be the main game in town for young researchers today. But as a tool for analyzing actual macroeconomic performance and for designing and conducting macroeconomic policy, new classical macroeconomics has not yet gotten off the ground. To do so will require a large number of notable empirical successes in accounting for phenomena that are difficult to explain. An exciting challenge lies ahead.

■ We've now reviewed the new classical macroeconomic research program and some of its main features. We've seen that its central proposition is that intertemporal substitution, rather than coordination problems, lies at the heart of aggregate fluctuations. This stands in marked contrast to the alternative new macroeconomics — the new Keynesian approach that places at centre stage the coordination of decisions and the difficulties markets have in achieving that coordination without generating fluctuations.

CHAPTER REVIEW

Summary

NEW CLASSICAL THEORY OF THE LABOR MARKET

The new classical theory of the labor market is based on an asymmetry between the demand and supply sides of the market. On the demand side, each firm chooses the quantity of labor to employ based on the actual real wage rate. On the supply side, each household decides how much work to do based on the expected real wage rate. For a given expected price level, fluctuations in the actual price level bring fluctuations in the level of employment, the money wage rate, and the real wage rate. Other things being equal, the higher the price level, the higher is the money wage rate and the expected real wage rate, and the lower is the actual real wage rate. And at a higher expected real wage rate, the larger is the quantity of labor supplied; at a lower actual real wage, the greater is the quantity of labor demanded. So at a higher price level, the equilibrium level of employment is greater.

THE LUCAS AGGREGATE SUPPLY CURVE

The Lucas aggregate supply curve is a short-run aggregate supply curve along which the expected price level is given. But the money wage changes along the Lucas aggregate supply curve. For a given expected price level, as the actual price level increases, the money wage increases and labor market equilibrium occurs at higher and higher levels of employment. With higher employment, there is a higher level of real GDP. The Lucas aggregate supply curve is steeper than the short-run aggregate supply curve, which has a fixed money wage rate.

The expected price level itself is the rational expectation of the price level. Since the expected price level determines the position of the Lucas short-run aggregate supply curve and since its position, together with the aggregate demand curve, determines the actual price level, the position of the Lucas short-run aggregate supply curve is determined by the expected aggregate demand curve and the long-run aggregate supply curve. The intersection of the expected aggregate demand curve and the long-run aggregate supply curve determines the expected price level, which in turn determines the position of the Lucas aggregate supply curve.

GENERATING AN OUTPUT-INFLATION TRADEOFF

For a given level of expected aggregate demand, there is a given Lucas aggregate supply curve. Fluctuations in actual aggregate demand around that expected level trace out a tradeoff along the Lucas aggregate supply curve. Fluctuations in expected aggregate demand that are small relative to those in actual aggregate demand create a looser relationship but do not disturb the positive correlation between price and output fluctuations.

The slope of the output-inflation tradeoff varies across economies because of the information content in the current price level. In an economy that experiences high and volatile inflation, fluctuations in prices are interpreted as fluctuations in the average level of prices rather than as relative price changes, and the output-inflation tradeoff is steeper. In an economy with a low and predictable inflation rate, fluctuations in the prices in individual sectors are interpreted as relative price changes, and the output-inflation tradeoff is flatter.

The output-inflation tradeoff is not directly visible in the raw data on inflation and real GDP fluctuations because of changes in the expected inflation rate.

POLICY IMPLICATIONS OF NEW CLASSICAL MODEL

The new classical model implies that anticipated policy changes have no effect on real GDP. Their ineffectiveness arises from the fact that although a policy change shifts the aggregate demand curve, anticipation of it also shifts the short-run aggregate supply curve. If policy is exactly anticipated, both curves shift by the same amount, changing the price level and leaving real GDP undisturbed.

NEW CLASSICAL MODEL AND AGGREGATE FLUCTUATIONS

In its narrowest form, the new classical model predicts that unexpected fluctuations in the money supply produce the business cycle. These predictions are not borne out by the facts. The money supply itself is a well-measured and frequently observed variable. It is possible that unanticipated fluctuations in aggregate demand arising from other sources create a business cycle. The full test of this idea has yet to be carried out.

REAL BUSINESS CYCLE THEORY

Real business cycle theory is an explanation of aggregate fluctuations based on a dynamic form of classical macroeconomics. According to real business cycle theory, the only source of aggregate fluctuations is the uneven pace of technological change. As technology advances, the economy responds to it. Technological advance shifts the production function and increases output, consumption, and investment. Higher investment adds to the capital stock and further increases output, consumption, and investment. A process of expansion continues at a pace determined by the size of the initial shock and the internal economic mechanism—the consumption and investment choices people make.

REAL BUSINESS CYCLE THEORY AND THE U.S. ECONOMY

Real business cycle theory has been used to explain cycles in the U.S. economy. There is a strong correspondence between the predictions of real business cycle theory and the Canadian business cycle. But a problem exists in determining the direction of causation. A correlation between technological shocks (measured as the Solow residual) and real GDP does not, on its own, tell us that technological change is causing changes in real GDP. Other theories suggest that real GDP and technological change are jointly determined by fluctuations in aggregate demand. Tests of these alternatives have still to be performed.

NEW CLASSICAL MACROECONOMICS AND UNEMPLOYMENT

New classical macroeconomics accounts for unemployment in two mains ways. First, indivisible labor arising from startup and shutdown costs make it inefficient for firms to vary average hours per worker, rather than the number of workers employed. Thus fluctuations in the economy bring the creation and destruction of jobs.
Second, ~~But~~ job creation and job destruction are not uniform phenomena. They vary enormously from industry to industry and even from firm to firm. As a result, technological change brings a need to reallocate labor between jobs. Such reallocations occur most often in recessions when the unemployment rate is highest.

RESEARCH AGENDA

The research agenda for new classical macroeconomists is to develop richer models of the economy based on the idea that rational individuals each do the best they can for themselves and interact in markets that achieve equilibrium. As time passes, more and more data on more and more variables will be accumulated; the challenge is to develop models that account for this rich diversity of economic experience.

Key Terms and Concepts

Calibration Making one set of measurements correspond to another.

Cobb-Douglas production function A production function in which a 1 percent increase in employment increases output by a percent and a 1 percent increase in the capital stock increases output by $(1 - a)$ percent.

Constant returns to scale When all inputs into production are increased by 1 percent, output also increases by 1 percent.

Lucas aggregate supply curve A curve showing the maximum real GDP supplied at each price level when the labor market is in equilibrium at a given expected price level.

Output-inflation tradeoff The relationship between deviations of real GDP from full employment and inflation from its expected level.

Policy ineffectiveness proposition The proposition that anticipated changes in monetary policy have no effect on employment, output, or any other real variable.

Real business cycle theory A theory that bases its explanation of aggregate fluctuations on exogenous, random technological change.

Review Questions

1. What is an output-inflation tradeoff? Is the Canadian output-inflation tradeoff constant over time? Is it identical to those in other countries? Explain.
2. Explain the new classical theory of the labor market.
3. Explain the effect of incomplete information on labor market equilibrium.
4. What is the Lucas aggregate supply curve? Draw a diagram to show its derivation.
5. Which markets are in equilibrium along a Lucas aggregate supply curve?
6. What is a rational expectation and the rational expectation of the price level? Draw a diagram to illustrate the rational expectation of the price level.
7. What is the new classical explanation of the output-inflation tradeoff? Draw a diagram to illustrate your answer. Explain what happens to this tradeoff if expected aggregate demand fluctuations are small relative to actual aggregate demand.
8. Compare the slopes of the short-run and the Lucas aggregate supply curves.
9. What is the new classical explanation of the loop-like patterns of the relationship between inflation and real GDP fluctuations? Draw a diagram to illustrate your answer.
10. What is the policy ineffectiveness proposition? Who first worked out the policy implications of new classical theory?
11. Draw a diagram to show the policy ineffectiveness of a feedback stabilization policy. What conditions make the feedback policy ineffective?
12. What is real business cycle theory? What is its explanation of the business cycle?
13. Explain how the real business cycle explains fluctuations in the real interest rate and investment.
14. Does the real business cycle theory predict that Okun's Law holds? Explain.
15. What is the role of money in real business cycle theory? Explain how inflation occurs.
16. How does real business cycle theory account for the accelerator mechanism?
17. How can the real business cycle theory be tested?
18. What does the Solow residual measure?
19. Why is the growth rate of the Solow residual correlated with the growth rate of real GDP?
20. How does indivisible labor cause unemployment?

Problems

1. Ecoland has the following labor market:
   Demand for labor

$$n^d = 250 - 2.5(W/P).$$

   Supply of labor

$$n^s = 100 + 2.5\,(W/P).$$

   The expected price level is 1.5 and the actual price level is 1. Calculate
   (a) The money wage rate
   (b) The number of people employed
   (c) The expected and actual real wage rates
2. In Ecoland, problem 1, if the actual price was 1.5, what are your answers?
3. In Ecoland, the short-run aggregate production function is

$$y^s = 100n - 0.2n^2.$$

   The expected price level is 1.5. Calculate real GDP supplied at an actual price level of
   (a) 1
   (b) 1.5
4. For an expected price level of 1.5, what is the equation to Ecoland's short-run aggregate supply curve in problem 3?
5. For an expected price level P^e, Leisureland has the following Lucas aggregate supply curve

$$y^s = 1000 - 250\,(P^e/P)^2$$

   and aggregate demand curve

$$y^d = M/P.$$

   Calculate the rational expectation of the price level if the expected money supply is 750 units.
6. In Leisureland, problem 5, the money supply turns out to be 1,000. Calculate the price level and real GDP. Is the fluctuation in the price level pro- or counter-cyclical?
7. What is Leisureland's output-inflation tradeoff in problem 5?
8. Ecoland has the following production function:

$$y_t = z_t k_t^{1/2} n_t^{1/2}$$

   where y is real GDP, k is the capital stock, and n is employment. The capital stock is 9 and employment is 16.
   (a) If, in year 1, z is 1, what is real GDP in that year?
   (b) Suppose that real GDP is 15 in year 2. What would you infer about z? What has been the rate of technological change?

C H A P T E R

21 New Keynesian Macroeconomics

COORDINATION COSTS AND FAILURES

THE TASK OF NEW KEYNESIAN MACROECONOMICS is the same as new classical macroeconomics — to explain aggregate fluctuations. But new Keynesians adopt a fundamentally different approach. They emphasize the idea that markets do not clear and that wages and prices fail to adjust quickly enough to keep the quantity of labor demanded equal to the quantity of labor supplied.

The notion that the quantity demanded does not equal the quantity supplied is sometimes called *disequilibrium*. But that is not how Keynes or the new Keynesians think about the economy. Like new classical economists, they are looking for an *equilibrium*, but an *unemployment equilibrium*. That is, they are seeking an explanation in terms of forces that balance — an equilibrium. But those forces don't balance the actual quantities supplied and demanded, they balance something else — the expected quantities of labor supplied and demanded.

Also, like the new classical economists, new Keynesians seek an explanation of aggregate fluctuations in terms of the microeconomic foundations. They want to understand the forces at work in terms of rational choices being made by households and firms. But in new Keynesian theories, households and firms cannot coordinate their choices and actions costlessly. Coordination costs lead to coordination failures.

Several strands have evolved in the new Keynesian literature but these can be summarized under three broad headings:

1. Sticky money wages
2. Sticky prices
3. Sticky real wages

We'll organize our study of new Keynesian macroeconomics around these three broad topics. We'll also examine the policy implications of new Keynesian explanations of aggregate fluctuations and contrast these with the policy implications of new classical theory. After completing your study of this chapter, you'll be able to

- Describe some key facts about wages and long-term wage contracts
- Explain the new Keynesian theory of the labor market
- Explain the new Keynesian interpretation of differences in performance in the North American and Japanese economies
- Explain the new Keynesian theory of price determination
- Explain the new Keynesian interpretation of price markups and cost changes
- Review and explain some models of real wage rigidity
- Explain how aggregate fluctuations arise according to new Keynesian theory
- Describe the policy implications of a new Keynesian theory

21.1 *High and Persistent Unemployment and Long-Term Wage Contracts*

MACROFACTS

Most wage contracts negotiated between unions and firms in the United States and many in Canada run for three years. Because it provides a better illustration of the main phenomenon that new Keynesian macroeconomics seeks to understand, we'll look at the U.S. case. In that country, contracts negotiated in one year influence wages, employment, and output three years hence. Thus wages set in 1991 influence the actual wages paid in 1991, 1992, and 1993. A consequence of three-year contracts is that wages in any one year contain elements of decisions made in that year and in the two preceding years. As a result, wages adjust in a series of waves, as illustrated by the blue arrows in Figure 21.1. This figure shows wage agreements in the year of settlement and in the subsequent two years throughout the 1980s and into the early 1990s. As you can see, wage increases gradually declined from 1981 through 1986. They increased in the second half of the 1980s.

Not all labor contracts are negotiated by unions. But unions set the tone, and many other wages respond in line with movements in union wages. As a result, average hourly earnings for the economy as whole (the black line in Figure 21.1) closely follow the trend set by the three-year contracts of the unions. Figure 21.1 shows the behavior of *money* wages — the rate of increase in the actual dollars paid. But firms make employment decisions based on the real cost of labor — the *real* wage rate. The behavior of the real wage rate depends partly on the behavior of the money wage rate and partly on prices. The U.S. real wage rate through the 1980s, measured in 1982 dollars an hour, is shown in Figure 21.2. That figure also shows the unemployment rate — an indicator of the cyclical position of the economy.

During the early 1980s, real wages actually fell, and at a time when the unemployment rate was increasing. That is, through the recession years of 1981 and 1982, real wages were falling. But their rate of fall was moderate. (Pay special attention to the scale on the left axis of Figure 21.2. It runs from \$7.50 to \$7.85 an hour — just 35¢ an hour.) The decrease in real wages between 1980 and 1982 was only 10¢ an hour, or

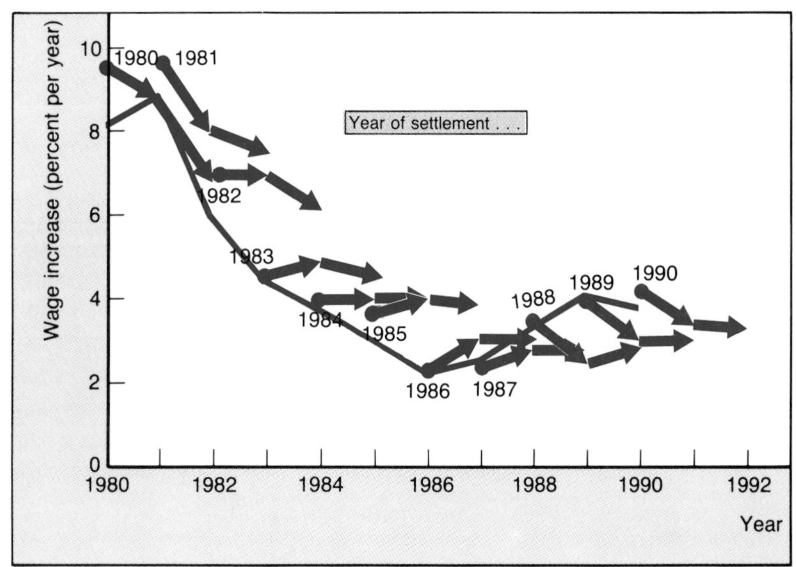

FIGURE 21.1
U.S. Wage Changes in the 1980s

Most union labor contracts in the United States run for three years and specify the agreed wage change for the year of contract plus the two subsequent years. The rate of wage change responds slowly, following a wavelike pattern shown by the blue arrows. For the economy as a whole, average hourly earnings (the black line) closely follow union contract wages.

Source: Median wage increases, all industries, including lump sum components: The Bureau of National Affairs, Inc., Washington, D.C. Average hourly earnings: *Economic Report of the President*, 1991.

FIGURE 21.2
U.S. Real Wages and Unemployment

Real wages fell as the U.S. economy went into recession in 1981 and 1982. They increased in 1983 while unemployment remained high. Real wages stayed fairly constant as unemployment declined through 1986 but then fell through 1990.

Source: Economic Report of the President, 1991.

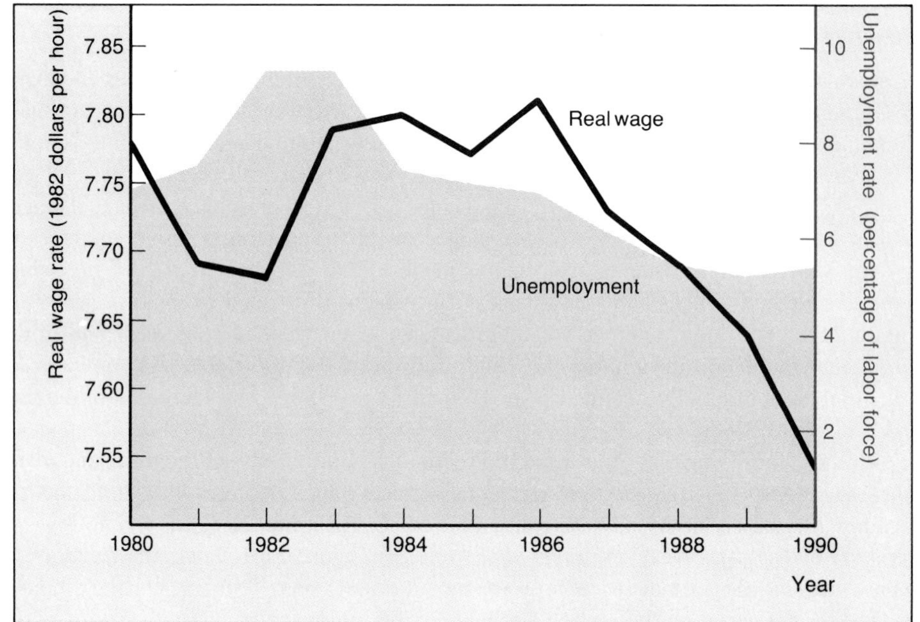

approximately 1.25 percent. At the same time, the unemployment rate climbed quickly. In 1983, with the unemployment rate remaining high at 9.5 percent of the labor force, real wages increased again. They stayed around $7.80 an hour through 1986. Then, real wages declined steadily as unemployment flattened off.

These facts about money wage increases, real wages, and unemployment raise most of the questions new Keynesian macroeconomics tries to answer. The facts are plainer to see in the United States but they are present in Canada and most European economies as well. Some of the questions the new Keynesians ask are; What are the effects of three-year wage contracts on real wages, employment, and real GDP? Why are real wages relatively sticky in the face of a massive increase in unemployment? Indeed, why do real wages seem to not adjust in order to keep employment and unemployment steady? These questions do not exhaust the list that new Keynesian economists try to answer, but they are the central ones and the questions with which we'll begin our study of this approach to macroeconomics.

21.2 *Sticky Wages and Overlapping Contracts*

The new Keynesian theory of the labor market was developed by Stanley Fisher of MIT, Edmund Phelps of Columbia University, John Taylor of Stanford University, and Jo Anna Gray of the Washington State University.[1]

[1]The main contributions to the new Keynesian theory of aggregate supply are Stanley Fischer, "Long-Term Contracts, Rational Expectations and the Optimal Money Supply Rule," *Journal of Political Economy*, Vol. 85 (February 1977), pp. 191-206; Edmund S. Phelps, John B. Taylor, "Stabilizing Powers of Monetary Policy under Rational Expectations," *Journal of Political Economy*, Vol. 85 (February 1977), pp. 213-90; John B. Taylor, "Staggered Wage Setting in a Macro Model," *American Economic Review*, Papers and Proceedings, Vol. 69 (May 1979), pp. 108-13; and Jo Anna Gray, "Wage Indexation: A Macroeconomic Approach," *Journal of Monetary Economics*, Vol. 2, No. 2 (April 1976), pp. 221-35.

The point of departure of the new Keynesian theory is the general prevalence in labor markets of contracts that specify, for a predetermined period, an agreed money wage rate. New Keynesian theory regards the fixed contractual money wages as such a crucial feature of the labor market that it must figure prominently in any theory of the labor market. According to the new Keynesian theory, labor markets do not act like continuous auction markets, with wages being frequently adjusted to achieve an ongoing equality between the quantities of labor supplied and demanded. Rather, the quantity of labor supplied equals the quantity demanded only on the average. At any particular moment in time, the quantity demanded may exceed or fall short of the quantity supplied. Taking explicit account of the institutional arrangement of contractually fixed money wages has important implications for the specification of the aggregate supply curve.

Assumptions of new Keynesian theory

There are three key assumptions in the new Keynesian theory of the labor market:

- Money wages are set for a fixed contract period.
- Money wages are set to make the *expected* quantity of labor demanded equal the *expected* quantity of labor supplied.
- The level of employment is determined by the *actual* demand for labor.

Fixed money wages Money wages are set in a contract for an agreed period *before* the quantity of labor supplied and demanded is known. New Keynesians rationalize the existence of such contracts by arguing that there are high costs of collecting information and negotiating wage agreements. These costs make it inefficient to adjust wages continuously to achieve continuous market clearing.

Wages set to achieve *expected* market clearing When unions and firms sit down together to agree on a money wage rate for each of the upcoming three years, they have to take a view of how the demand for and supply of labor will evolve over that period. New Keynesian theories assume that unions and firms form a rational expectation of future demand and supply and then agree on a wage that makes the expected quantity of labor demanded equal to the expected quantity supplied on the average over the contract period. This assumption is consistent with the idea that unions and employers are rational—they attempt to achieve the best outcome available. Firms and unions know that setting wages too high will result in too low an employment level on the average and too much unemployment. They also each know that setting wages too low will result in a shortage of labor. Thus it is not in the unions' interest to press for too high a wage and it's not in the firms' interest to press for too low a wage. They each can do better by agreeing on a wage that makes the expected quantity of labor demanded equal to the expected quantity supplied.

Employment equals quantity of labor demanded The actual supply and demand conditions in the labor market become known only when both suppliers and demanders of labor are tied into a labor contract. In these circumstances, there has to be a rule for determining the quantity of labor employed. The assumption of new Keynesian theory is that firms determine the level of employment. Workers are assumed to stand ready to supply whatever quantity of labor is demanded in exchange for the certainty of a fixed money wage over the duration of the contract.

Staggered contracts

In some countries, there is a distinct annual round of wage negotiations. One of the most spectacular of these occurs each spring in Japan, when a process called ***shunto*** takes place. *Shunto* translates into English as "spring wage offensive." In a period of about six weeks, labor contracts covering a very large proportion of the Japanese work force are negotiated and signed. These contracts run for a year—until the next spring offensive. Some Scandinavian countries also have an annual wage round with all contracts negotiated at the same time.

In Canada and the United States, there is no such synchronization in the timing of labor contracts. Contracts come up for renewal at various times so that the dates on which new contracts start are staggered and the contracts themselves overlap.

We're going to study the implications of staggered contracts. But doing so is more complicated than studying contracts that are not staggered. Consequently, the next step we'll take is to examine how new Keynesian theory operates in the Japanese and Scandinavian settings, where contracts are all signed on the same date and run for a common, fixed period. Then we'll look at staggered contracts such as those prevailing in the labor markets of Canada and the United States.

Determination of money wages

Figure 21.3 illustrates how money wages are determined according to new Keynesian theory. The expected supply of labor is based on the expected price level and expectations about the number of people available for work at different real wage rates. The curve *ELS* represents the expected supply of labor. The expected demand for labor is based on the expected price level and on forecasts about the marginal productivity of labor, which in turn determines the quantity of labor firms will hire at each possible real wage rate. The curve *ELD* represents the expected demand for labor.

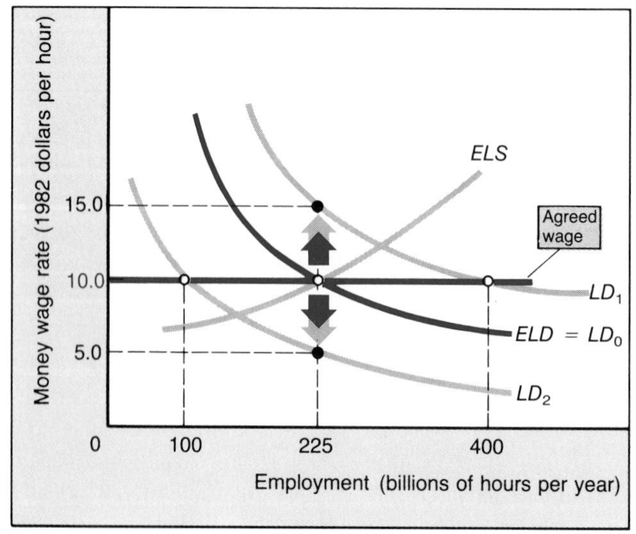

FIGURE 21.3
The New Keynesian Labor Market

Labor market participants meet to agree on a wage rate. They form a rational expectation of the supply of labor (*ELS*) and demand for labor (*ELD*) that will prevail over the contract period. They set the wage at a level that achieves expected labor market clearing. Here the agreed wage is $10 an hour and expected employment 225 million hours a year. If the demand for labor turns out to be higher than expected at LD_1, the quantity of labor employed increases to 400 million hours a year; if demand turns out to be LD_2, employment falls to 100 million hours a year.

Given the expected supply of labor, *ELS*, and the expected demand for labor, *ELD*, the expected quantity of labor demanded equals the expected quantity supplied at a money wage rate of $10 an hour. This wage rate is the one agreed by unions and firms as a result of their negotiations, and the expected employment level is 225 million hours a year. The contracted money wage does not change until the next contract is negotiated.

Fluctuations in employment

During the life of the contract, the effective supply curve of labor is the horizontal line at the agreed wage of $10 an hour. Workers, in agreeing to the contracted wage rate, also agree to supply whatever quantity of labor firms demand at that wage rate. The quantity of labor employed is determined by the demand for labor. Many forces influence the demand for labor and they can be summarized under two broad headings:

1. The price level
2. The marginal product of labor

An increase in the price level or an increase in the marginal product of labor shifts the demand for labor curve to the right. Equivalently, these increases increase the money wage rate that firms are willing to pay for a given level of employment. Figure 21.3 illustrates that a 50 percent higher price level shifts the demand for labor curve upwards by 50 percent. That is, with the price level 50 percent higher than was anticipated when the contract was signed, firms are willing to pay a 50 percent higher money wage ($15 an hour) to employ the same amount of labor (255 million hours of labor a year). In other words, the labor demand curve shifts from LD_0 to LD_1, and the quantity of labor employed increases to 400 million hours a year. The money wage rate remains at $10 an hour, but the real wage rate declines because the price level has increased.

The opposite result arises if the price level falls or the marginal product of labor decreases, shifting the demand for labor curve to the left. Suppose that the price level falls 50 percent below that expected at the time the wage contract was signed. In such a situation, firms will hire 225 million hours of labor only if they can cut the money wage to $5 an hour. Thus the demand curve shifts down to LD_2. With this lower price level and an agreed money wage of $10 an hour, firms will employ 100 million hours a year.

Notice that only if the demand for labor turns out to be the same as that expected (LD_0) is the level of employment equal to its expected level of 225 million a year.

New Keynesian short-run aggregate supply curve

The new Keynesian theory of money wages implies a new Keynesian theory of aggregate supply. Figure 21.4 shows the derivation of the new Keynesian aggregate supply curve.

Start with the labor market, in part (a), which reproduces the results we've established in Figure 21.3. The agreed wage rate is $10 an hour, and as the demand for labor fluctuates between LD_1 and LD_2 the level of employment fluctuates between 400 million and 100 million hours a year.

The short-run production function *PF*, in part (b), shows how employment fluctuations translate into fluctuations in real GDP. Part (c) shows the new Keynesian short-run aggregate supply curve. To see how the three parts of the figure are related, begin in part (c) with a price level of 100. Suppose that the expected price level on which the expected labor supply curve *ELS* and the expected labor demand curve *ELD* are based is also 100. This expected price level underlies the agreement to set the money wage rate at $10 an hour. If this expectation is fulfilled, the actual demand for labor curve is LD_0, the level of employment is 225 million hours a year, and real GDP is $4.5 billion.

FIGURE 21.4
The New Keynesian Aggregate Supply Curve

In the labor market (part a), the money wage rate is set at $10 an hour. If the quantity of labor demanded turns out to be the same as that expected (LD_0), employment is 225 million hours. The production function *PF* (part b) determines the level of real GDP. With 225 million hours employed, real GDP is $4.5 billion. This is the full-employment level of real GDP and determines the position of the long-run aggregate supply curve (*LAS*) in part (c). If the expected price level lying behind the expected demand for labor curve (*ELD*) is 100, a point on the new Keynesian aggregate supply curve is *E* in part (c). If the price level turns out to 150, the demand for labor is farther to the right, LD_1. Employment is 400 million hours a year and real GDP $6 billion. This gives point *D′* on the new Keynesian supply curve. If the price level turns out to be 50, the demand for labor is less and the demand curve lies to the left, LD_2. Employment is 100 million hours and real GDP $3 billion. This gives point *F′* on the new Keynesian aggregate supply curve. The new Keynesian aggregate supply curve (*ASK*) is generated by joining points *F′*; *E*, and *D′*.

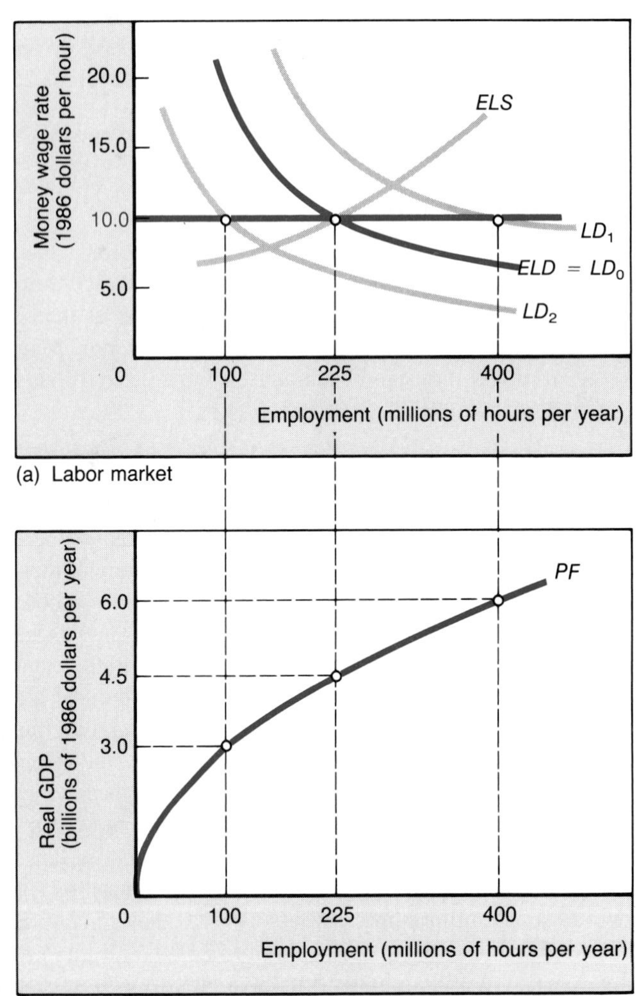

(a) Labor market

(b) Short-run production function

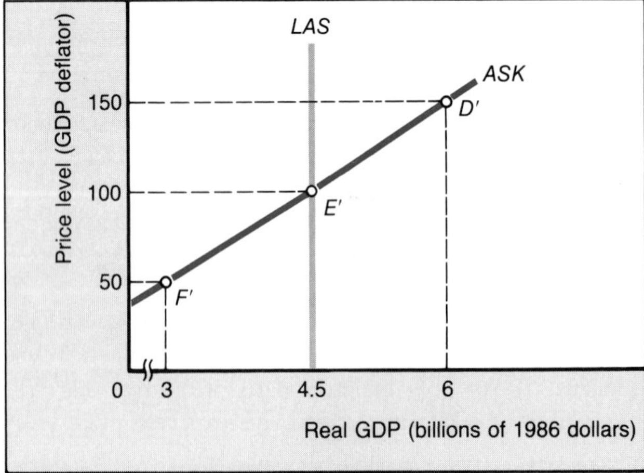

(c) New Keynesian aggregate supply curve

This combination of a price level of 100 and real GDP of $4.5 billion is point *E* in part (c). Since the actual price level equals the expected price level, the economy is at full employment and point *E* lies on the long-run aggregate supply curve (*LAS*).

Now suppose that the price level turns out to be 150 — 50 percent higher than expected. The actual demand for labor curve is LD_1 and employment is 400 million hours a year. Real GDP is $6 billion (part b) and the economy is at point *D′* in part (c).

Conversely, suppose that the price level turns out to be 50 percent lower than expected. The actual demand for labor curve is LD_2 and employment is 100 million hours a year. Real GDP is $3 billion and the economy is at point *F′* in part (c). Joining points *F′*, *E*, and *D′* together traces out the new Keynesian aggregate supply curve (*ASK*).

This aggregate supply curve, in fact, is exactly the same as the one we derived in Chapter 8. How does this new Keynesian aggregate supply curve compare with the Lucas aggregate supply curve in the new classical model?

New Keynesian and Lucas aggregate supply compared

The new Keynesian and Lucas aggregate supply curves are compared in Figure 21.5. You can see in part (c) the new Keynesian aggregate supply curve (*ASK*) we've just derived. You can also see, superimposed in part (c), the Lucas aggregate supply curve (*ASL*).

The Lucas aggregate supply curve is steeper than the new Keynesian. Why? The answer is, in the new classical model a change in the price level shifts the demand for labor curve and the money wage rate adjusts to restore equilibrium in the labor market. In the new classical model, the money wage rate is determined at the point of intersection of the demand for labor and supply of labor curves. The position of the labor supply curve depends on the expected price level, while the position of the demand for labor curve depends on the actual price level. Figure 21.5 is drawn for an expected price level of 100. If the actual price level increases from 100 to 150, the demand for labor curve shifts from LD_0 to LD_1, the wage rate increases to $12.50 an hour, and unemployment increases to 290 million hours a year. The economy moves to point *D* in parts (a) and (c). If the price level falls from 100 to 50, the demand for labor curve shifts from LD_0 to LD_2, the wage rate falls to $7.50 an hour, and employment falls to 125 million hours a year. The economy moves to point *F* in parts (a) and (c). Joining points *F*, *E*, and *D* traces out the Lucas aggregate supply curve.

The Lucas curve is steeper than the Keynesian curve simply because in the new classical model money wages adjust to clear the labor market, while in the new Keynesian model money wages are fixed by contracts.

Overlapping wage contracts

The new Keynesian theory of aggregate supply developed above is based on the idea that at the beginning of each time period, workers and employers form an expectation of the price level for the contract period, agree on the money wage rate that will achieve an expected equilibrium in the labor market, and then agree to trade labor at that wage rate for the contract period. The amount of labor traded is determined by the actual demand for labor.

The assumption that all contracts start and end at the same time is obviously a fiction used to simplify the diagrammatic analysis. Let's now get rid of that assumption. Suppose that at the beginning of January each year half the labor force sits down and negotiates a wage that is to prevail for two years. The analysis contained in Figures 21.3 and 21.4 still applies, but now it applies to only half the labor force. The other half has

FIGURE 21.5
Comparison of New Keynesian and New Classical Aggregate Supply Curves

The key difference between the new Keynesian and new classical theories of aggregate supply is the behavior of money wages. In the new Keynesian theory, the money wage rate is fixed at $10 an hour in this example, and as demand fluctuates between LD_2 and LD_1, employment varies between 100 and 400 million hours a year. In the new classical theory, demand fluctuations bring changes in wages. When demand is LD_2, wages fall to $7.50 an hour, limiting the decrease in employment to 125 million hours a year. When demand increases, wages increase to $12.50 an hour, limiting the increase in employment to 290 million hours a year. Because wages fluctuate more and employment fluctuates less in the new Keynesian model, so real GDP fluctuates less in response to price level changes. The Lucas aggregate supply curve (*ASL*) is steeper than the new Keynesian curve.

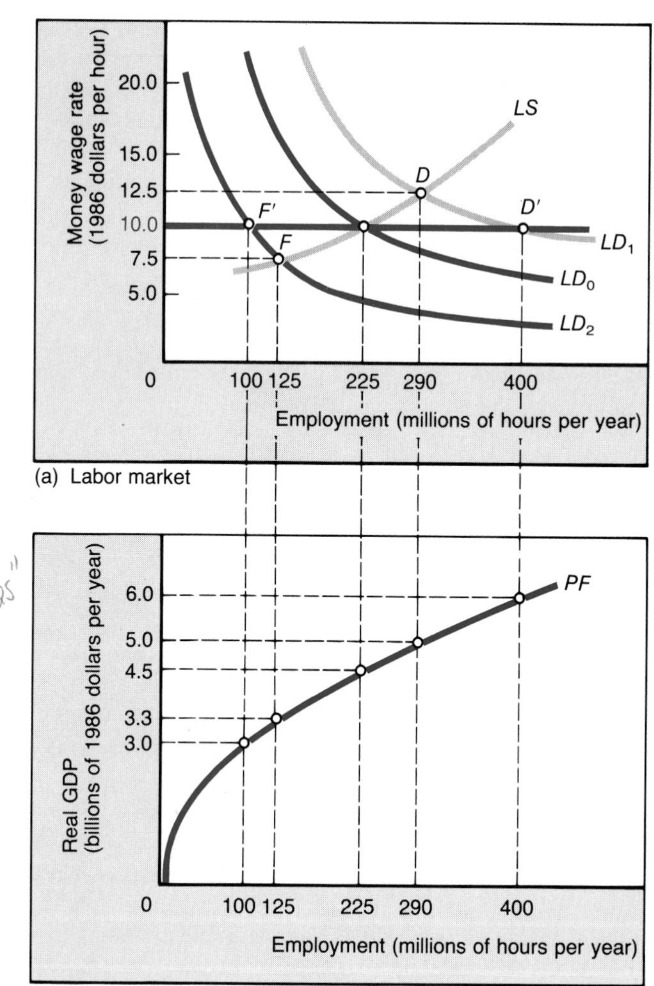

(a) Labor market

(b) Short-run production function

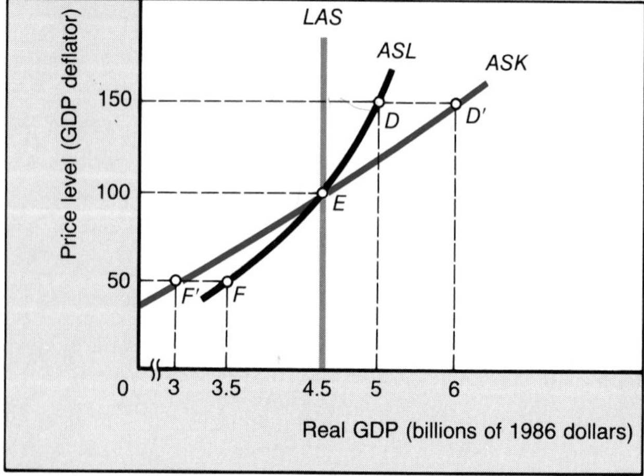

(c) Short-run aggregate supply curves

already gone through the same exercise one year earlier and will go through it again one year later. Thus the actual wage rate observed at any point in time will be the average of the wages that have been set at various dates in the past on contracts that are still current. In the example, half the labor force sets its wages in January of one year and the other half in January of the next year. Then the wage that prevails in any one year will be equal to one half the wage determined in January of the year in question plus one half the wage determined in the preceding January. This wage will be based on expectations of the price level that were formed at two different dates in the past.

This being so, the position of the short-run aggregate supply curve depends not only on current expectations of the current price level but also on older (and perhaps by now known to be wrong) expectations of the current price level. Once firms and workers are locked into a contract based on an old, and perhaps now wrong, expectation of the price level, there is (by the assumptions of the new Keynesian model) nothing they can do about it until the contract runs out.

The fact that labor market contracts run for a number of years and overlap has very important implications for the analysis of economic policy, as you will see later in this chapter.

There has been a lively debate concerning the efficiency of the labor contracts that new Keynesian economists use in their theory of aggregate supply. New classical economists such as Robert Barro insist that such contracts are inefficient and cannot be rationalized as the kinds of contracts that rational profit-maximizing and utility-maximizing agents would enter into.[2] New Keynesians agree that it is hard to think of convincing reasons why people would enter into contracts such as these. However, they insist that we do observe such contracts as commonplace, and in the absence of a firm understanding as to why, they argue that we have no alternative but to incorporate them into our macroeconomic models.

21.3 *Employment and Real Wages in North America and Japan*

TESTCASE

With three-year wage contracts making money wages relatively inflexible, fluctuations in the price level are predicted to generate countercyclical fluctuations in real wages. In other words, if wage contracts do make money wages rigid, we would expect to see a negative correlation between the growth of real wages and the employment rate. When real wages are growing quickly, the employment rate would be growing slowly, and vice versa.

The longer the term of the labor contracts, the more pronounced this effect would be, if labor contracts are an important source of employment fluctuations. Let's see whether these predictions of new Keynesian theory agree with the facts by looking at the growth of real wages and the employment rate in the United States and in Japan.

United States

Figure 21.6(a) shows the growth rate of real wages and of employment in the United States between 1980 and 1990. The prediction of new Keynesian theory that real wage growth is countercyclical is not strongly visible in these data. On the contrary, there is a tendency for real wage growth to be *procyclical*. That is, faster real wage growth, on the average, is associated with faster growth of the employment rate, not the reverse.

[2] Robert J. Barro, "Long-Term Contracting, Sticky Prices, and Monetary Policy," *Journal of Monetary Economics*, Vol. 3 (July 1977), pp. 305-16.

FIGURE 21.6
Real Wages and Employment in the United States and Japan

With long-term labor market contracts in the United States and one-year contracts in Japan, employment fluctuations should be larger in the United States. They are. These fluctuations are graphed measured against the right axis with the same scale for the United States (part a) and Japan (part b). Note the small amplitude of employment fluctuations in Japan relative to the United States.

New Keynesian theory predicts that employment and real wages fluctuate in opposite directions. They do in Japan, and there is some evidence that they do in the United States; but there are periods of procyclical movements in real wages in the United States as well, especially during the recession of 1981-1982.

Sources: Economic Report of the President, 1991, and *Economic Statistics Annual*, Research and Statistics Department, Bank of Japan, Tokyo, 1987 and 1989.

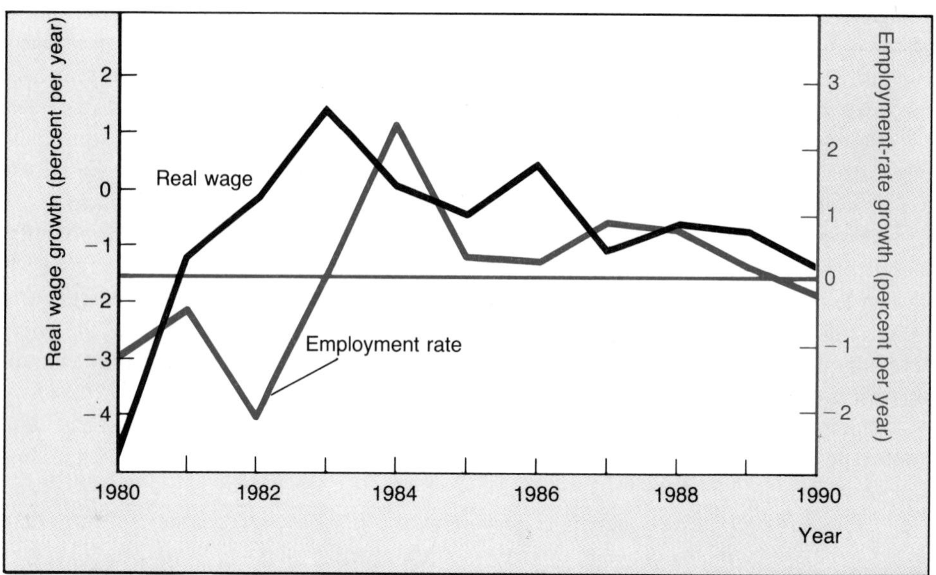

(a) United States

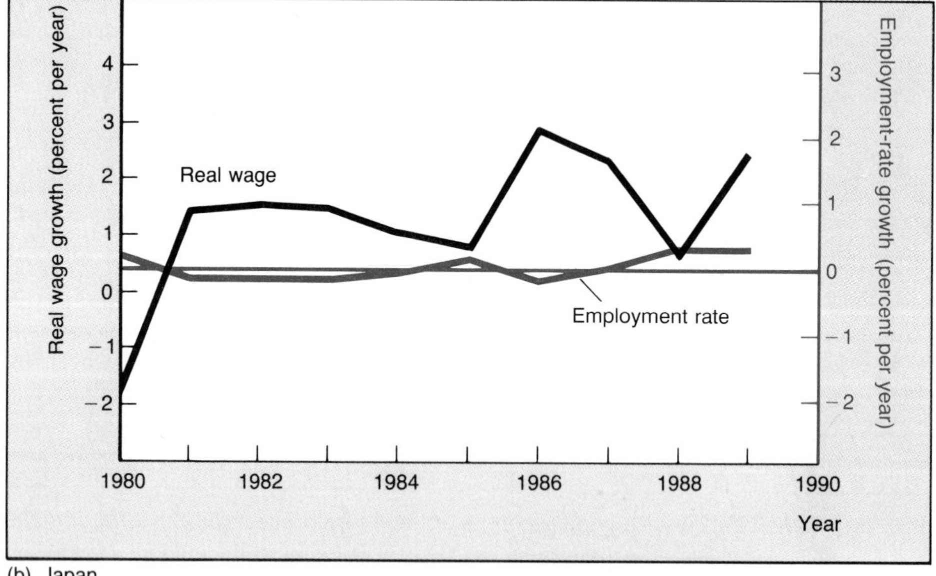

(b) Japan

Japan

In the case of Japan, shown in Figure 21.6(b), we do see a clear tendency for real wage growth to be countercyclical. That is, real wage growth fluctuates in a way that mirrors the fluctuations in the growth of the employment rate.

Similarities, differences, and lessons

The key difference in the behavior of the growth rate of real wages and the employment rate in the United States and Japan is that in the United States, real wage growth has been procyclical and in Japan, countercyclical. Another important difference is the range of variation in the growth rate of the employment rate. In the United States, the percentage of the work force employed (the employment rate) decreased by 2 percentage points in 1982 and increased by 2.5 percentage points in 1984. The growth of Japanese employment has not seen swings of this magnitude. Notice that the vertical axis on the right in each part of the figure has the same scale. In Japan the percentage of the labor force employed has been fairly constant. At its fastest the growth rate reached 0.3 percent a year in 1988 and 1989; and its slowest, occurring in 1981 through 1983, and in 1986, was only −0.2 percent.

Although U.S. real wages appear to be procyclical, this appearance is dominated by the increase in the growth rate of real wages in 1982-1983 and the strong increase in the employment rate in 1982-1984. If we abstract from the large movements in the early 1980s, it is possible to detect some tendency for the growth rates of real wages and the employment rate to move in opposite directions in the United States. Specific years that can be identified in the figure are 1981-1982, 1983-1984, and 1985 to 1988. In each of these years the growth of real wages moved in the direction opposite to the growth of the employment rate.

Sources of flexibility in wages

Although U.S. and Canadian wage contracts often last for three years, these contracts are not completely rigid. One source of flexibility in wage contracts is cost of living adjustments or COLAs. A **COLA** is an agreement that makes the rate of wage change over the term of a contract depend on the actual inflation rate. By agreeing to adjust wages in line with prices, labor contracts, in effect, commit to an agreed *real* wage. The importance of COLA clauses can be seen by looking at Figure 21.7. Here, we show the percentage change in wages in the given year, divided into three components. The first component, *Prior*, is the change in wages occurring in a given year as a result of commitments made in previous years. The second component, *COLA*, reflects changes

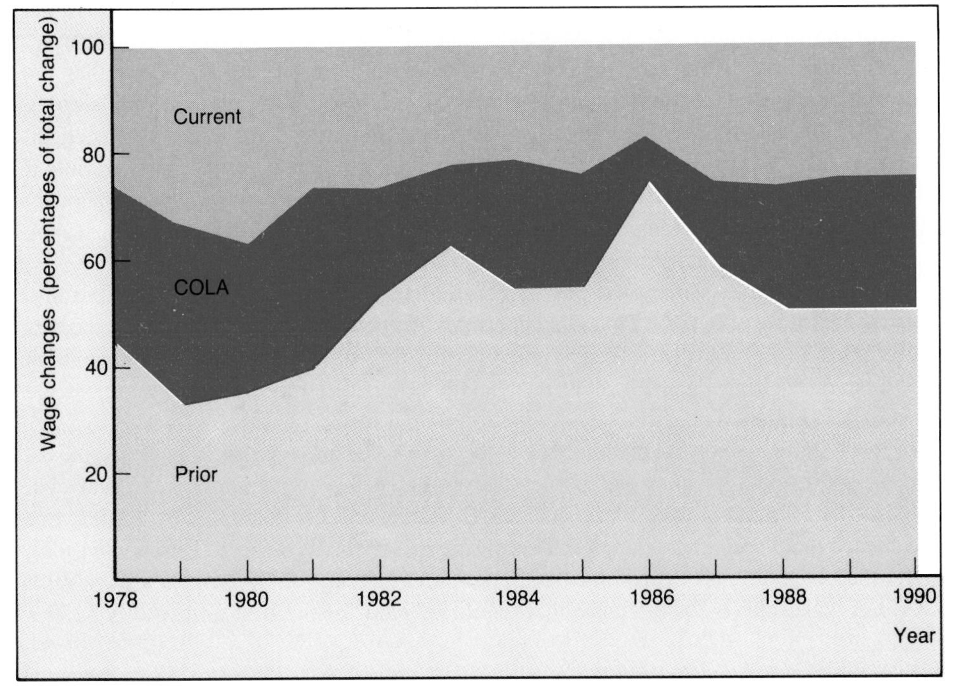

FIGURE 21.7
The Rigid and Flexible Components of Wages in the United States

On the average, about half of wage changes in any one year are the result of prior agreements. The other half represent COLAs and adjustments based on contracts being renewed in the current year. Current adjustments and COLAs are particularly important when inflation is high, and the economy is in recession. In a recovery with low inflation, COLAs become less important, as they did in 1986.

Source: U.S. Bureau of the Census, *Statistical Abstract of the United States: 1991* (111 edition), Washington, D.C., 1991.

in wages in the current year resulting from COLAs entered into in previous years. The third component, *Current*, is the change in the current year resulting from contracts being renewed in the current year.

As you can see, approximately half the wage change in any year is the result of prior commitments, but an important other half responds to the current state of the economy. In the late 1970s and early 1980s, years of slow growth and recession, COLAs and current adjustments were particularly important. At times when the economy is expanding steadily and inflation appears to be under control, as in the mid-1980s, COLAs become less important.

Let's now turn to another component of new Keynesian theory—a theory of sticky product prices.

21.4 Price Setting and Menu Costs

Real wages are determined by money wages and the price level. The new Keynesian theory of the labor market gives a theory of the determination of the money wage rate. There is also a new Keynesian theory of the price level.

Price setting in monopolistic competition

New Keynesians view the economy as consisting of a large number of monopolistically competitive firms. Each firm has to figure out how much to produce and the price at which to try to sell its output. Each firm faces a downward-sloping demand curve for its product. Other things being equal, the lower the price it charges, the larger is the quantity it sells.

Firms are in business to make the biggest profit possible. To maximize profit, a monopolistically competitive firm produces an output such that its marginal cost of production equals marginal revenue. **Marginal cost** is the increase in total cost resulting from producing the last unit of output. **Marginal revenue** is the increase in total revenue resulting from selling the last unit of output.

The firm's profit maximizing output and price is illustrated in Figure 21.8(a).[3] Think of the firm illustrated here as a food retailer that produces baskets of groceries. The demand curve facing it is the downward-sloping curve labeled D. The higher the price of a basket of groceries, the smaller is the quantity sold. The more steeply sloping curve, MR, is the firm's marginal revenue curve. For any given quantity, marginal revenue is less than price. If the firm lowers its price, it sells a larger quantity of output and gets more revenue. But it gets a lower price for all the units that it was previously selling at a higher price, and this amount has to be subtracted from the total revenue when calculating marginal revenue.

Suppose the firm's marginal cost is constant regardless of its level of output and illustrated by the curve MC. Thus the supermarket illustrated here can produce baskets of groceries at $50 a basket. To maximize profit, this supermarket prices its goods at $100 a basket, selling 10,000 baskets a day. This brings the store the maximum possible profit of $500,000 a day.

Figure 21.8(b) shows what happens if the firm faces an increase in its costs and an increase in demand of an equal percentage amount. In this example, marginal cost increases by 50 percent to $75 (the curve MC_1). Demand also increases by 50 percent. This means that the demand curve shifts upward and becomes steeper. To see why, look at what is happening at a zero quantity bought and also at 10,000 baskets a day. With the old demand curve D_1, the price that would be paid for the first unit sold is $150 a

[3] In Figures 21.8-21.10, and the others in this section, we ignore fixed costs.

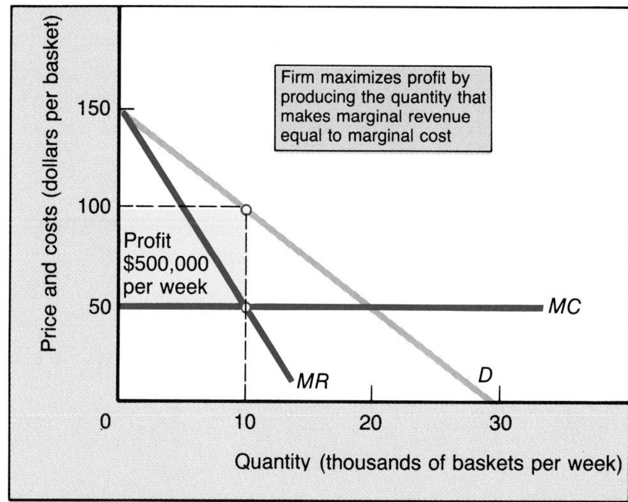

(a) Initial equilibrium

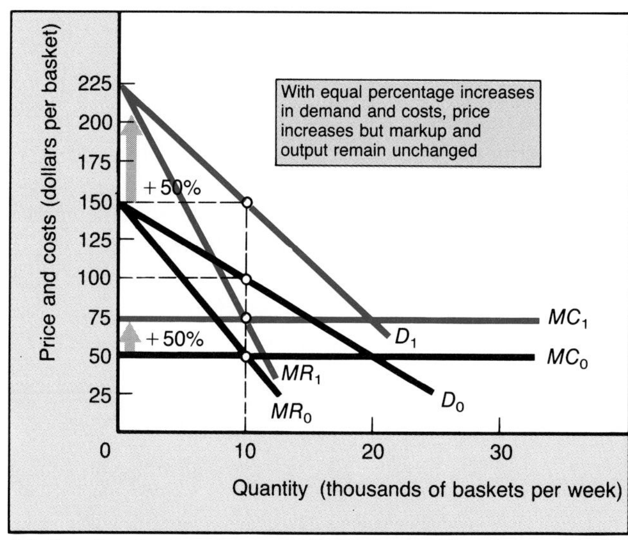

(b) Equal percentage increases in demand and costs

FIGURE 21.8
Monopolistic Price Setting

A monopolistically competitive firm faces a demand curve *D* (part a) and has marginal cost *MC*. It maximizes profit by producing the quantity at which marginal cost, *MC*, equals marginal revenue, *MR*. The firm produces 10,000 baskets a week and sells them for $100 a basket. In an inflationary situation, prices and costs increase by the same percentage amount. Marginal cost increases to MC_1 and demand to D_1 (part b). Marginal revenue also increases to MR_1. The profit-maximizing quantity and the profit-maximizing percentage markup remain the same. Price increases by the same percentage as the increase in cost.

basket. With a 50 percent increase in all prices and all costs, this amount increases to $225 a basket. At 10,000 baskets a day, people were willing to pay $100 before and now they're willing to pay $150. Just as the demand curve shifts upward to D_1 and becomes steeper than D_2, the marginal revenue curve also shifts upward, to MR_1, and becomes steeper than MR_0.

In this example, marginal cost and all other prices have increased by 50 percent and so the marginal cost and demand curves have shifted upward by 50 percent. The firm's profit maximizing point remains at the same 10,000 baskets a day but at a higher price —$150 a basket.

Notice that the relationship between price and cost is the same in these two examples. When cost increases by 50 percent, so does price. The difference between price and cost, expressed as a percentage of cost, is called the **markup**. In this example, the markup is 100 percent and remains constant as costs and other prices increase.

If all firms were monopolistically competitive (or were monopolies) and if, whenever their demand or cost conditions changed, they changed their prices to maximize profit, there would be nothing special about the economy being populated by monopolistically competitive firms. Prices would be flexible and outputs of individual firms would fluctuate in response to different rates of change of demand and costs, but the economy would not experience any particular macroeconomic disturbances resulting from the presence of monopoly.

There would be some social welfare costs resulting from the fact that firms restrict output below the competitive level to make a monopoly profit, but these costs would not fluctuate and generate phenomena such as the business cycle. They would be more or less constant.

Sticky prices

Sticky prices with macroeconomic consequences have two possible sources:

- Poor knowledge of demand curve
- Menu costs

Knowledge of demand curve A firm knows the price at which it is doing business and knows how much it's selling at that price. This knowledge gives the firm some information about its demand curve. To be precise, it tells it one point on its demand curve. But it does not give the firm information about the slope of its demand curve. It needs to know that slope in order to calculate the profit-maximizing price.

By having observed prices and quantities over some previous period, and also by having observed all the other potential influences on demand that can cause the demand curve to shift, the firm can arrive at a statistical estimate of its demand curve. But even so, its knowledge of the slope of its demand curve is imprecise.

Without knowledge of the slope of its demand curve, the firm is also ignorant about the position of its marginal revenue curve. As a practical matter, therefore, a firm cannot simply compute marginal cost and marginal revenue, set one equal to the other, and produce the appropriate profit-maximizing output. It has to use some other rule for deciding how much to produce and what price to charge.

In effect, firms operate by trial and error, and as a result firms in each sector of the economy arrive at rules of thumb about the percentage markup that gives maximum profit on the average.

Figure 21.9 illustrates the consequence of using such a rule of thumb. The firm knows its marginal cost curve MC and applies the conventional markup—in this example, 100 percent—to its marginal cost in order to arrive at a price. The firm then posts that price as the price at which it is willing to sell any quantity demanded. In effect, the horizontal line P becomes the firm's supply curve until it decides to change its price again. Fluctuations in demand will occur, shifting the demand and marginal revenue curves around. The firm will be aware of demand fluctuations because it will observe fluctuations in the quantity sold. It will presume, however, that it can do no better than apply the conventional markup over cost and, in the absence of cost changes, will stick to its price, absorbing the fluctuations in demand as fluctuations in output. Since the firm's output fluctuates when demand for its produce fluctuates, its own demand for factors of production, and especially labor, fluctuates.

Menu costs As the firm's costs increase, shifting its marginal cost curve upward, the firm will increase its price but perhaps not immediately. The reason? Menu costs.

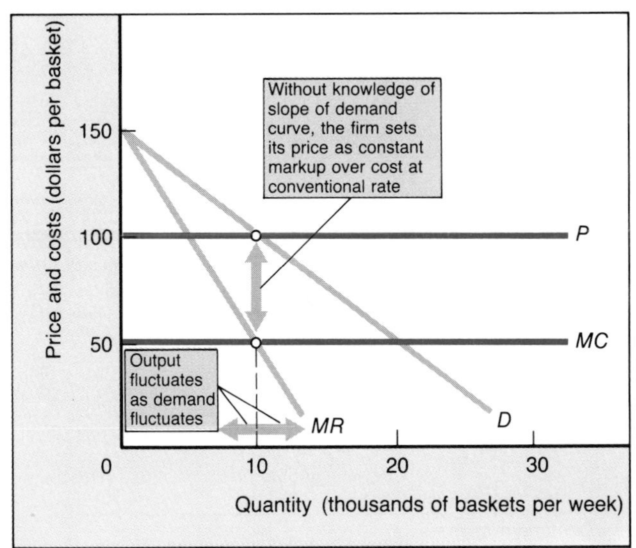

FIGURE 21.9
Markup Pricing

To produce a quantity at which price equals marginal cost, a firm has to know the slope of its demand curve. Without knowledge of the slope of the demand curve, the profit-maximizing calculation cannot be performed. Instead, firms operate by trial and error, and over time they converge on a conventional markup of price over cost that on the average achieves maximum profit. Fluctuations in demand bring fluctuations in output and price change only when costs change.

Changing prices requires the use of resources. Supermarkets have to relabel all the shelves with the new prices. Sears, Eddie Bauer, and Consumers Distributing have to print new catalogues. Restaurants have to rewrite their menus with new prices on them. The cost of changing a price is called the **menu cost**.

Because of menu costs, firms do not change their prices every time there is a change in cost or demand conditions. Since the menu cost has to be paid each time a price is changed, the frequency of price change is chosen optimally to balance menu costs against profits foregone from having the wrong price.

Figure 21.10 illustrates the role of menu costs for the same firm as illustrated before. Part (a) shows its demand and cost curves. A firm sets its price at *P*, 100 percent above its marginal cost. Initially, this is its profit-maximizing price. The firm is making a profit of $500,000 a day, shown by point *A* in part (b).

To illustrate how menu costs work, let's suppose that the firm's marginal cost and demand are steadily increasing. As they do so, the firm sells more, but because its price is fixed at *P* and because its marginal cost is increasing, its profit declines. Suppose that it tracks along with the blue curve in part (b) toward *B*. The firm is now making less than maximum profit. But does it pay the firm to change its price?

Suppose the firm's menu cost is $25,000. (This is a high menu cost, but the firm may have to print catalogues and fliers, and do a lot of advertising at the time of its price change.) The firm will not want to incur this menu cost unless it's sure that the cost and demand increases are going to persist long enough. During such a period, the firm will accept a profit below the maximum profit in the absence of menu costs. If it eventually changes the price and restores the conventional markup and if that markup is the appropriate one, it will make maximum profit again.

The two sources of sticky prices we've just considered imply that firms' prices will be a relatively stable percentage markup over cost but that the markup itself will fluctuate because firms will respond to cost changes when they've accumulated long enough and have become large enough to make incurring the menu cost worthwhile. Thus the new Keynesian theory of pricing implies that price markups will be relatively stable, though not precisely stable.

FIGURE 21.10
Menu Costs and Sticky Prices

A firm sets its price as a conventional markup over marginal cost (part a). As marginal cost increases, the firm charges the same price and makes a smaller profit. It slides down its profit curve (part b) from *A* toward *B*. Eventually, profit falls so far that the firm incurs the menu cost—the cost of changing its price—and increases its price. Menu costs lead to an optimum frequency of price change.

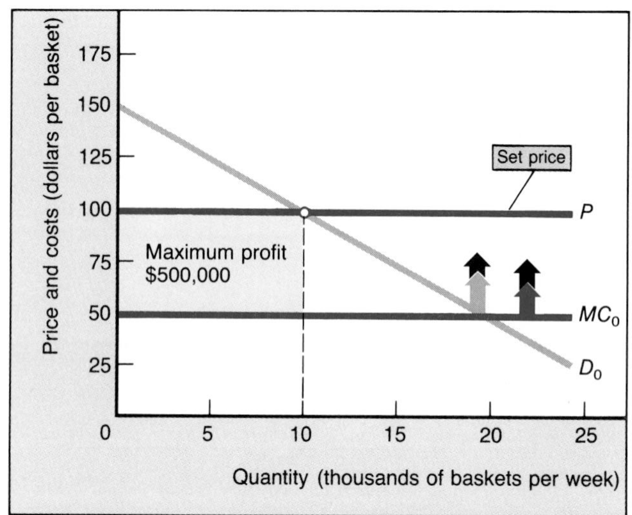

(a) Demand and costs

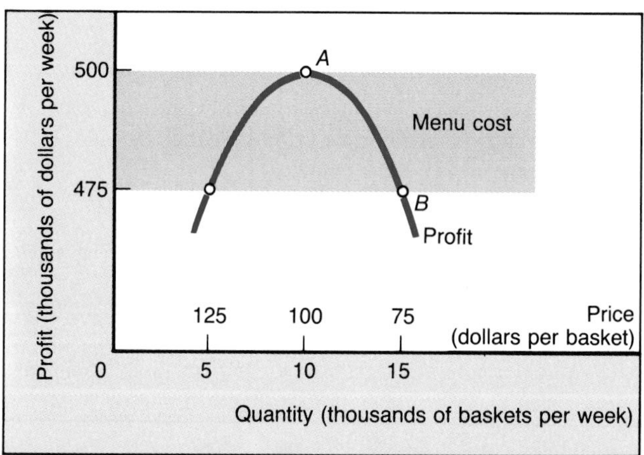

(b) Profit and menu cost

TESTCASE

21.5 *Price Markups and Cost Changes*

The new Keynesian theory of price determination implies that price changes and cost changes will be similar to each other and that markups will change very little. How does this prediction line up with the facts? It depends which country and which time period we look at, but again, the U.S. experience is closest to the new Keynesian prediction. In that country, the markups are relatively stable as you can see in Figure 21.11. In this figure, we show the rates of change of costs, prices, and markups for the nonfinancial sector of the U.S. economy through the 1980s and into 1990. As you can see by inspecting this figure, cost and price changes are indeed remarkably similar to each other and markups change very little.

There appears to be no systematic relationship between markups and the business cycle. When the economy was in recession in 1981 and 1982, markups increased at first

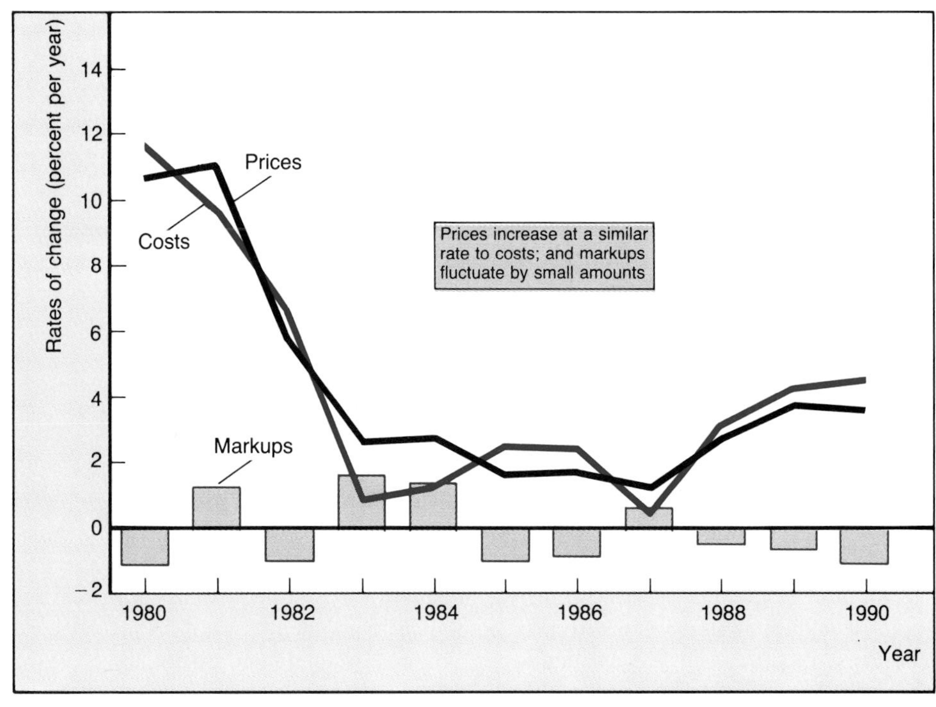

FIGURE 21.11
U.S. Prices, Costs, and Markups in the 1980s

Price and cost increases in the United States fluctuate in similar ways and markups are remarkably stable. The systematic cycle in the markups does not appear to be related to the business cycle.

Source: Economic Report of the President, 1991.

(1981) but then decreased (in 1982). Markups increased as the economy came out of the recession in 1983 and 1984, but they decreased slightly while the recovery continued through 1986. Markups again began to decline slightly while the economy continued to recover through 1990.

The data shown in Figure 21.11 are consistent with the new Keynesian theory of price determination. But they are not inconsistent with other classical theories. Even a competitive classical model such as that used in real business cycle theory implies a stable relationship between costs and prices. Stability of that relationship in the classical model stems from the fact that in equilibrium the shares of labor and capital income in GDP are technologically determined by the relative marginal products of labor and capital. With the share of labor and capital income in GDP being relatively stable, there is stability in the relationship between cost and price changes. This is just another example of more than one theory being consistent with the facts and of the limited power of correlation to determine direction of causation.

Although sticky prices are one possible element in the generation of aggregate fluctuations, most economists, including new Keynesians, do not regard price rigidities arising from the sources we've just considered as being strong enough to create the massive swings of real economic activity that sometimes occur. Although there are indeed menu costs, these do not appear to be so large as to prevent supermarkets and other retail establishments from moving their prices up and down a great deal as demand conditions fluctuate. We see price variations occurring within a space of a few weeks, and certainly months — due to seasonal factors — that make it hard to rationalize long-term recessions and depressions as consequences of this type of price stickiness.

Because of this general presumption that price stickiness cannot account for the major swings in economic activity, new Keynesian economists have developed a range of other models based on *real* wage rigidity.

21.6 *Other Models of Real Wage Rigidity*

We've just seen that one explanation of real wage rigidity comes from the theory of markup pricing. If prices are marked up a constant percentage of cost and if wages are the main component of cost, then a constant markup goes with relatively constant real wages. Another approach to explaining real wages and their rigidity attacks the problem directly from the labor market itself. There are four main approaches to explaining real wage rigidities as consequences of efficient labor market arrangements. They are

- Implicit contracts
- Asymmetric information
- Insider-outsider interests
- Efficiency wages

Implicit contracts

Most employment contracts are explicit agreements between workers and firms. They often have additional dimensions not written into the actual contract itself. These dimensions are called **implicit contracts**. Martin Neil Bailey of the Brookings Institution and Costas Azariades of the University of Pennsylvania suggested that firms and workers enter into implicit contracts concerning income and job insurance. Their idea was that workers dislike the risk arising from income and employment variability much more than firms do. As a result, firms could offer workers an implicit contract that is in part an employment contract and in part an income and job insurance contract. Bailey and Azariades worked out conditions under which such contracts would result in real wages that were insensitive to business conditions and employment levels that fluctuated over the business cycle.

In principle, however, this type of model can produce wage variability but with job security.

Asymmetric information

A pervasive fact of life is that we each have special knowledge about some things and are relatively ignorant about most things. This situation is known as one of **asymmetric information**. Each person is asymmetrically informed relative to everyone else.

This idea was put to work in explaining labor market arrangements by Sanford Grossman of the University of Chicago and Oliver Hart of Cambridge University in England. They developed a labor market model based on the assumption that managers know more about the interests of the firm than do workers. Given this better knowledge, it would be possible and profitable for managers to attempt to deceive workers about the true state of the firm. Such contracts could involve rigid real wages and employment commitments. However, such models usually imply an employment commitment that increases the amount of employment in firms with these characteristics.

Insiders' and outsiders' interests

A labor market model has been suggested by Assar Lindbeck of the University of Stockholm in Sweden and Dennis Snower of the University of London in England based on the idea that wages are determined by unions representing those who already have jobs — what Lindbeck and Snower call *insiders*. But the labor market also consists of those who don't have jobs — the unemployed — who, according to this model, are the *outsiders*.

Insiders represented by the union set wages at a level that is too high for the outsiders to get in. As a result, high and persistent unemployment can occur even in the face of increases in aggregate demand.

Efficiency wages

The presence of asymmetric information in labor markets often means that workers are better informed about how hard they, individually, are working than are their managers. One way of coping with this situation is to pay workers a wage above the market wage but hold over them the threat of being fired if they're found to be shirking. Such a higher wage is called an **efficiency wage**. The name stems from the idea that the higher wage is paid to induce a more efficient effort on the part of the worker. It was first suggested by George Akerlof of the University of California at Berkeley.

Fallacies of composition

All the theories of rigid real wages we've just reviewed are developed in a partial equilibrium setting. A **partial equilibrium analysis** is an economic analysis of one part of the economy, taking the rest of the economy as given. But macroeconomics is concerned with the economy as a whole. It is concerned with a *general* equilibrium analysis. So far, there are no truly general equilibrium macroeconomic models incorporating these four ideas about real wage rigidity. Some attempts have been made, but none is as thorough and comprehensive as the general equilibrium macroeconomic model of real business cycle theory discussed in Chapter 20. Therefore a challenge remains for macroeconomists seeking to provide a new Keynesian foundation for aggregate fluctuations to explore the implications of their ideas in a general equilibrium setting.

21.7 *Staggered Wage and Price Setting, Aggregate Fluctuations, and Policy*

Let's now see how a new Keynesian model with sticky wages and overlapping contracts generates a business cycle.[4] Let's also see how policy could be used to make the recession phase of the cycle less severe.

Overlapping contracts and aggregate fluctuations

To see how a new Keynesian model with sticky wages and overlapping contracts generates aggregate fluctuations, we'll use the version of the sticky *money* wage model developed earlier in the chapter. Let's use this model to generate a recession; Figure 21.12 illustrates.

Starting point The economy starts out on aggregate demand curve AD_0 and a new Keynesian aggregate supply curve ASK_0. The economy is at full employment — on the long-run aggregate supply curve LAS — at the price level P_0 and real GDP of y_0.

Being a full-employment equilibrium, the price level P_0 is the expected price level and it was the price level expected when all current labor contracts were agreed to.

[4] A more comprehensive analysis of overlapping is developed by T. Windsor Fields and William R. Hart, "An Exposition of Fischer's Model of Overlapping Contracts," *Journal of Economic Education*, 1991, forthcoming.

FIGURE 21.12
Overlapping Contracts

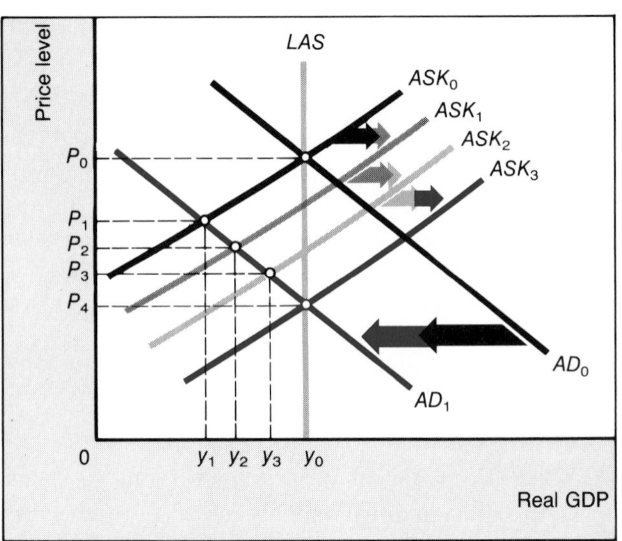

The economy starts out at full employment on aggregate demand curve AD_0 and short-run aggregate supply curve ASK_0 at the price level P_0 and real GDP y_0. An aggregate demand shock shifts the aggregate demand curve to AD_1. Real GDP falls to y_1 and the price level to P_1. The economy remains in this position until the first labor market contracts are renegotiated. When these contracts are negotiated, a lower wage is agreed to, to achieve an expected equality of demand and supply in that part of the labor market. With a lower wage, the short-run aggregate supply curve shifts, to ASK_1. The price level falls to P_2 and real GDP increases to y_2. After a further year, when more wages are renegotiated, they too come in at a lower wage rate and the aggregate supply curve shifts again, this time to ASK_2. The price level falls to P_3 and real GDP increases to y_3. In the last year, when all wages have been reset since the demand shock, the aggregate supply curve shifts to ASK_3, the price level falls to P_4, and full employment is restored at y_0.

Demand disturbance Suppose that aggregate demand decreases because of a decrease in investment demand resulting from a change in expectations about future rates of return; a contraction in the world economy decreasing net export demand; a tax increase; a government spending cut; or a decrease in the money supply. The aggregate demand disturbance shifts the aggregate demand curve to the left, to AD_1.

To keep the analysis as clear as possible, let's suppose that this demand shock is permanent. Aggregate demand remains at AD_1 for a long time. We're going to trace out the adjustment of the economy.

Adjustment process The first step in the adjustment process is that real GDP and the price level fall. The initial resting point for the economy is a level of real GDP of y_1 and a price level of P_1. This situation prevails until the first group of labor market contracts comes up for renewal. Let's suppose that all the labor market contracts run for three years. Further, assume that one third of all contracts come up each year. How do the unions and firms figure out the wages for the forthcoming contract?

According to the new Keynesian theory, the agreed wage for each year will be such that the expected demand for labor equals the expected supply. Let's suppose that the part of the labor market that negotiates its labor contract in the same year can be treated as an individual labor market. Thus the group of workers negotiating in the first year after the shock has to form a rational expectation about the wage in each of the succeeding three years that will keep the expected quantity of labor demanded equal to the expected quantity supplied in their part of the labor market. They will reason as follows.

By the time year 3 comes around, and the third group of contracts has been renegotiated, the new information about the lower level of aggregate demand will have been incorporated into all wage contracts. Thus in the third year of their contract, all the wages in the economy will have adjusted to a level consistent with the new lower level of aggregate demand. This wage level will be based on an expectation that the price level will have fallen to P_4. For only when the price level has fallen to P_4 has the economy returned to full employment and is there equality between the quantities of labor demanded and supplied in all parts of the labor market. They will agree to a wage rate for year 3, therefore, based on an expected price level of P_4.

For the second year of their contract, they will recognize that one third of the labor market still has to renegotiate its contract. They will therefore recognize that the wage rate in that one third of the market is higher than it is ultimately going to be. This higher wage rate, with firms marking up their prices above cost, will give rise to a new Keynesian aggregate supply curve that lies above ASK_3. Let's suppose that they work out that this curve is going to be ASK_2. Thus they'll be predicting a price level of P_3 and they will base their wage for the second period on this expectation. But a second group of workers is renegotiating its contract in that second year and it too will base its calculations on the same information as the firms renegotiating after year 1.

For the first year of the new wage contract, the workers negotiating in year 1 will recognize that they and only they are adjusting their wages in the current year and that two thirds of the labor market is stuck with the original wage rate based on a price level expectation of P_0. They will therefore expect the new Keynesian aggregate supply curve to move downward only to the extent that they lower their wages in the second period. Suppose that ASK_1 is the supply curve that they anticipate from this adjustment. They will therefore predict a price level of P_2 for the second year.

So far we've talked only about conjectures in the minds of the unions and firms in the third of the economy that's going to negotiate wages in the first year. But it's these conjectures that determine the path of wages for that first contract. Thus wages are determined for years 1, 2, and 3 of a contract based on expected prices P_2, P_3, and P_4. If those wages are put in place and if no further shocks occur, the economy will move to the price level P_2 and the output level y_2 in the year following the shock.

In the second year following the shock, a second group of workers renegotiates its contract. If the information remains exactly the same as before and if no further changes in aggregate demand or aggregate supply take place, these workers will expect the price level to be P_3 in the coming year and then P_4 thereafter. They will set their wages accordingly. The new Keynesian aggregate supply curve will shift to ASK_2, real GDP will increase to y_3, and the price level will fall to P_3.

By the third year after the shock, the final group of workers will negotiate its wage change. It will recognize that once its wages have been adjusted, all wages will have been adjusted to accommodate the new level of aggregate demand, and so the price level will have moved to P_4. This is the expected price level built into the wages determined by the group negotiating in the third year. The economy will now experience a further decrease in the price level to P_4 and an increase in real GDP to y_0, its full employment level.

This economy has gone through a three-year recession that could have been quite deep. How deep and how much the price level would have to fall depend on the slopes of the aggregate demand and aggregate supply curves. Furthermore, in a situation in which aggregate demand is increasing over time, such a recession could occur without a fall in the price level—with a decrease in the inflation rate instead.

The pattern of wage changes implied by the adjustment we've just described is very similar to the waves of wage adjustment illustrated in Figure 21.1. You can see how, starting in 1981, there was a shock to aggregate demand and the 1981 contracts provided for a wage increase that fell in 1982 and again in 1983. When the 1982 contracts were signed, they built in a wage increase for 1983 similar to that for 1982 but then a yet lower increase for 1983. By the time the 1983 contracts were signed, the depth of the recession had become even more clear and so the wage negotiated in that year was for a much lower increase than had occurred in the preceding years. By the time the economy had returned to full employment in 1984, wage contracts were calling for a constant annual increase in wages.

21.8 Stabilization Policy

The policy ineffectiveness proposition does not apply to a new Keynesian model. The reason is that a change in aggregate demand occurring after wage contracts have been signed but before all contracts in place come up for renewal can be reacted to with a policy change in aggregate demand that will move the economy back toward full employment. The simplest case to analyze is where all contracts run for a year; Figure 21.13 illustrates. Imagine that initially the economy is at full employment, at the point of intersection of *ASK* and AD_0. The day after the contracts are signed aggregate demand decreases, shifting the aggregate demand curve left, to AD_1. The policy authorities in this economy now have two choices. They can leave the economy in its depressed state with real GDP of y_1 and a price level of P_1. Alternatively, they can increase aggregate demand, using either fiscal or monetary stimulation. Such a policy would shift the aggregate demand curve back to AD_0 and return the economy to full employment, y_0, and the price level to P_0. Since no labor contracts are up for renewal until the end of the year, there will be no consequential change in the *ASK* curve. The stabilization policy is effective.

FIGURE 21.13
New Keynesian Stabilization Policy

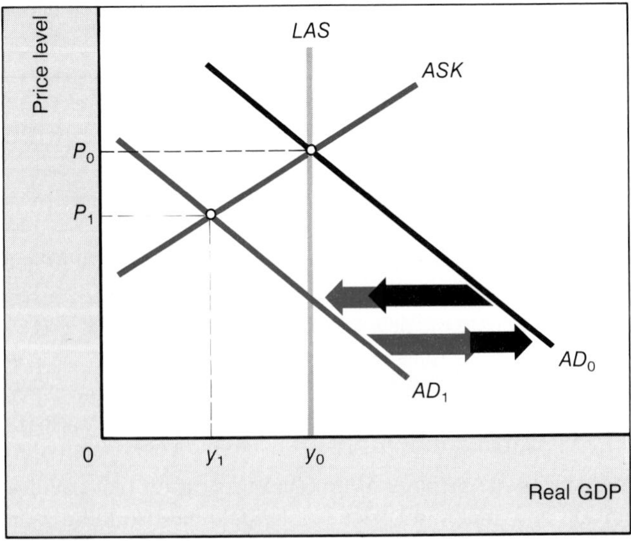

Starting at full employment with real GDP y_0 and the price level P_0, a shock to aggregate demand shifts the aggregate demand curve to AD_1. Real GDP falls to y_1 and the price level falls to P_1. If the monetary and fiscal policymakers increase aggregate demand to AD_0, the economy returns to P_0 and y_0. It does so even though workers and employers have rational expectations. The aggregate demand shock occurred after wage contracts based on those expectations were signed, so neither the aggregate demand shock nor the policy response can be reacted to until the next contract renewal date.

■ We've now reviewed the new Keynesian research program and its attempt to find a microeconomic foundation for price and wage stickiness. If prices and wages are indeed sticky in the sense that they change less frequently than policy can act, then we've seen that there is a role for stabilization policy even if people form their expectations about that policy in a rational way.

Both new classical and new Keynesian economists agree that wages are sticky. That is not what separates them. It is whether wages are sticky in the face of perceived and anticipated changes in policy and in other sources of change to aggregate demand and aggregate supply.

The coming years will see a refinement and sharpening of new Keynesian and new classical models of the economy, a sharpening of discriminating tests between the competing views, and an increasing degree of convergence on a mainstream explanation for aggregate fluctuations.

CHAPTER REVIEW

Summary

SOME KEY FACTS ABOUT WAGES AND LONG-TERM WAGE CONTRACTS

Many union wage contracts run for three years. As a result, wages respond to demand changes with a time lag. The rate of wage increase does not fall quickly in recession. In fact, in the United States, the economy with the longest wage contracts, the growth rate of *real wages* increased while unemployment was at a peak in the recession of 1981-1982.

New Keynesian macroeconomics studies the consequences of wage rigidities for unemployment and the business cycle.

THE NEW KEYNESIAN THEORY OF THE LABOR MARKET

The main feature of new Keynesian theory is an explanation of how money wages are determined in labor market contracts. According to the new Keynesian model, money wages are set at a level that is *expected* to achieve equality between the quantities of labor demanded and supplied over the period of the contract. Expectations about prices and other conditions are rational expectations. The actual level of employment is determined by the quantity of labor demanded at the prevailing real wage rate. The real wage rate is determined by the contractually agreed money wage rate and the price level. The new Keynesian theory of the labor market implies a short-run aggregate supply curve identical to the one derived in Chapter 8. This short-run aggregate supply curve is less steep than the new classical Lucas aggregate supply curve of Chapter 20. The reason is that in the new classical theory, wages adjust whenever the price level changes to keep the quantity of labor demanded equal to the quantity of labor supplied. The resulting change in the money wage rate limits the fluctuations in real GDP that result from a change in the price level. In the new Keynesian theory, no such wage adjustment takes place, so the economy slides up and down a short-run aggregate supply curve based on a fixed money wage rate.

A further important component of new Keynesian theory is overlapping wage contracts. In any given year, new contracts are being negotiated that cover only a part of the labor force. Thus the economy partly responds to current conditions but partly is locked into arrangements based on previous expectations of current conditions.

A NEW KEYNESIAN INTERPRETATION OF DIFFERENCES IN PERFORMANCE IN NORTH AMERICAN AND JAPANESE ECONOMIES

Japanese labor market contracts typically run for one year. New Keynesian theory predicts smaller fluctuations in employment in Japan than in Canada and the United States, where three-year contracts are the rule. This prediction is borne out by the data —employment fluctuates less in Japan than in the labor markets of Canada and the United States.

New Keynesian theory also predicts that real wage movements will be countercyclical—real wages increase in a recession and decrease in a boom. This response pattern is clearly visible in the Japanese data. It is less obvious in the North American data, where there are some important procyclical fluctuations in real wages.

NEW KEYNESIAN THEORY OF PRICE DETERMINATION

New Keynesian theory emphasizes monopoly elements in markets for goods and services. It assumes that firms set their prices to maximize profit. In practice, with limited knowledge of the slope of their demand curves, firms set prices as a conventional markup over cost. With prices set this way, fluctuations in demand bring fluctuations in the quantities produced and sold rather than in price.

A further source of price stickiness is the cost of price changing—menu costs. The presence of menu costs means that even if cost conditions change, bringing a need for a change in price, firms may wait until cost has changed by enough or in an apparently permanent fashion before adjusting price.

NEW KEYNESIAN INTERPRETATION OF PRICE MARKUPS AND COST CHANGES

New Keynesian theory predicts that price changes and cost changes will be similar to each other and that markups will be relatively constant. This prediction in fact accords with the facts. The new Keynesian interpretation of this relationship is based on sticky prices and conventional markups. But other competitive models imply constant markups as well, so this does not constitute a clear-cut test of new Keynesian theory.

OTHER MODELS OF REAL WAGE RIGIDITY

Several new Keynesian models seek to explain sticky *real* wages. Implicit contracts models suggest that wages may be sticky as firms offer implicit income insurance contracts to their workers. Asymmetric information models explain wage stickiness as the consequence of contracts that protect workers from being deceived by managers about the true state of the firm's profits and market conditions. Insider-outsider theories explain real wage stickiness on the basis of unionized insiders setting wages at levels that best serve their interests, with no concern for the interests of the unemployed outsiders. Efficiency wage theories explain high wages and unemployment as the consequence of firms' being able to generate a credible threat of firing workers found to be shirking.

NEW KEYNESIAN THEORY OF AGGREGATE FLUCTUATIONS

The major source of aggregate fluctuations, according to new Keynesian theory, is fluctuations in aggregate demand. Because of sticky wages and overlapping contracts, such demand fluctuations bring movements along a relatively slow-moving short-run aggregate supply curve. An increase in aggregate demand brings an increase in output and the price level. Eventually, wages adjust to reflect the new demand level and real GDP returns to its full-employment level, but such a process takes at least as long as the term of the longest contracts in place. A decrease in aggregate demand takes real GDP below its full employment level and lowers the price level. Eventually, wages adjust to the new level of aggregate demand, but again the process takes as many years as the longest labor market contract has to run, and through that period the economy remains below full employment.

POLICY IMPLICATIONS OF NEW KEYNESIAN THEORY

New Keynesian theory implies that active stabilization policy can be used to keep the economy at full employment. A shock to aggregate demand that was not foreseen when existing labor contracts were written can be offset by the appropriate policy response. Firms and workers may have rational expectations about the policy but, having agreed to a particular wage rate, they do not change it when policy changes.

Key Terms and Concepts

Asymmetric information A state in which one economic agent knows something of interest to but unknown by a second economic agent (and possibly, though not necessarily, the second knows something of interest to but unknown by the first).

COLA *C*ost *O*f *L*iving *A*djustment: A component of a wage agreement to change wage payments by amounts determined by the change in the Consumer Price Index —by changes in the cost of living.

Efficiency wage The wage above the market wage paid to workers while the firm holds a threat of being fired over them if they're found shirking.

Implicit contracts Dimensions of employment contracts that are not written into the actual contract itself.

Marginal cost The increase in total cost resulting from producing the last unit of output.

Marginal revenue The increase in total revenue resulting from selling the last unit of output.

Markup The difference between price and cost, expressed as a percentage of cost.

Menu cost The cost of the resources used to change a price.

Partial equilibrium analysis An economic analysis of one part of the economy, taking the rest of the economy as given.

Review Questions

1. Describe the path of average money wages in the United States since 1980. What is the most common wage contract length in the United States? Do these contracts overlap?
2. Describe the relationship between the average real wage rate and the unemployment rate in the United States since 1980.
3. What are the three key assumptions of the new Keynesian theory of the labor market?
4. If the actual price level turns out to be higher than expected, explain why employment rises in the new Keynesian labor market.
5. If the actual price level turns out to be lower than expected, explain why employment falls in the new Keynesian labor market.

6. In questions 4 and 5, explain the relationship between the actual and expected real wage rate.
7. Draw a diagram to show the derivation of the new Keynesian aggregate supply curve.
8. Why is the new Keynesian aggregate supply curve flatter than the Lucas aggregate supply curve?
9. The new Keynesian theory of the labor market assumes that households can be off their labor supply curve. How might firms induce households to behave in such a way? Can households be induced to be permanently off their labor supply curve?
10. What is *shunto* and what are its main macroeconomic implications?
11. What are staggered wages? Give two examples of countries in which wages are staggered and two in which they are not.
12. What are the implications of overlapping labor market contracts?
13. What is the nature of the debate about the labor contracts assumed by new Keynesian economists?
14. Explain the new Keynesian theory of price determination.
15. Explain the four main approaches to accounting for real wage rigidities.
16. Explain how the new Keynesian model of the labor market with sticky wages and overlapping contracts generates a business cycle.
17. Is stabilization policy effective in the new Keynesian model? Explain your answer.

Problems

1. An economy has the following labor market:
   The demand for labor is

   $$n^d = 250 - 2.5(W/P).$$

   The supply of labor is

   $$n^s = 100 + 2.5(W/P).$$

   If the expected price level is 1.5, calculate
   (a) The money wage set in a labor contract
   (b) The expected employment level
   (c) The expected real wage rate
2. In question 1, the price level turns out to be 1. Calculate
   (a) The employment level
   (b) The actual real wage rate
3. In question 1, the price level turns out to be 2. Calculate
   (a) The employment level
   (b) The actual real wage rate
4. The production function in the economy in problem 1 is

   $$y = 100n - 0.2n^2.$$

   What is the equation to the new Keynesian aggregate supply curve?
5. In problem 4, if the labor market had been new classical, what is the equation to the Lucas aggregate supply curve?
6. Show that the Lucas aggregate supply curve in problem 5 is steeper than the new Keynesian aggregate supply curve in problem 4.

7. A monopolistically competitive firm has the following demand, revenue, and cost curves:

Demand	$Q^d = 50{,}000 - 500P$
Marginal revenue	$MR = 100 - (1/250)Q$
Marginal cost	$MC = \$20$

Calculate the firm's
(a) Profit-maximizing output
(b) Profit-maximizing price
(c) Maximum profit

8. In problem 7, the firm's demand curve shifts *upward* by 10 percent; at the same time, its marginal cost increases 10 percent. Calculate the increase in the price the firm charges for its output.

9. In problem 7, the markup is constant and demand fluctuates. Draw a diagram to show the effect on the firm's output, price, and profit.

10. In problem 8, the menu cost is \$15,000; by how much do costs have to increase before it is optimal for the firm to change its price?

APPENDIX A

Data for Canada: 1926 to 1990

	CANADA									
	(1)	(2)	(3)	(4)	(5)	(6)	(7)	(8)	(9)	(10)
YEAR	GROWTH RATE	INFLATION RATE	UNEMPLOY-MENT RATE	LONG-TERM INTEREST RATE	REAL EXCHANGE RATE	NOMINAL EXCHANGE RATE	M1 GROWTH RATE	M2 GROWTH RATE	NET EXPORTS	GOVERN-MENT BUDGET BALANCE
1926			2.9	4.9	..	..	..	4.1	3.0	0.8
1927	9.5	−1.5	1.8	4.6	..	..	..	6.3	0.4	0.9
1928	9.1	−0.4	1.7	4.5	..	..	..	3.3	0.0	1.1
1929	0.4	1.5	2.9	4.9	..	..	..	−2.1	−4.3	0.8
1930	−4.3	−2.0	9.1	4.7	..	..	..	−5.4	−5.1	−1.4
1931	−12.7	−5.4	11.6	4.6	..	..	..	−5.1	−3.2	−2.3
1932	−10.4	−9.3	17.6	5.1	..	..	..	−4.2	−2.1	−5.4
1933	−6.7	−2.3	19.3	4.6	..	..	..	1.5	0.1	−3.6
1934	12.1	0.3	14.5	4.0	..	..	..	5.7	1.8	−2.8
1935	7.8	0.0	14.2	3.6	..	..	..	7.9	2.9	−3.5
1936	4.4	3.4	12.8	3.3	..	..	..	5.5	5.1	−1.6
1937	10.0	2.0	9.1	3.2	..	..	..	4.1	3.4	−0.3
1938	0.8	0.0	11.4	3.1	..	..	..	2.8	2.0	−0.9
1939	7.4	−0.9	11.4	3.2	..	..	..	13.7	2.2	−2.0
1940	14.1	4.0	9.0	3.3	..	..	..	6.1	2.7	−5.4
1941	14.4	6.3	4.1	3.1	..	..	..	13.4	5.7	−4.6
1942	18.6	3.5	2.7	3.1	..	..	..	16.4	0.4	−20.4
1943	4.0	3.4	1.4	3.0	..	..	..	17.2	4.6	−22.7
1944	4.0	2.8	1.2	3.0	..	..	..	18.5	−0.2	−21.2
1945	−2.2	2.2	1.4	2.9	..	..	..	12.3	5.4	−17.6
1946	−2.7	3.5	3.4	2.6	..	..	..	13.3	3.5	3.1
1947	4.3	9.0	2.2	2.6	..	..	..	3.6	0.4	4.8
1948	2.5	10.5	2.3	2.9	..	..	..	8.8	2.7	3.7
1949	3.8	4.4	2.8	2.8	..	..	..	4.3	0.9	0.8
1950	7.6	2.4	3.6	2.8	..	..	..	5.3	−1.7	1.1
1951	5.0	9.9	2.4	3.2	..	..	..	2.3	−2.4	1.1
1952	8.9	3.6	2.9	3.6	..	..	..	6.9	0.8	−0.2
1953	5.1	−0.3	3.0	3.7	..	..	1.0	1.0	−1.6	−0.1
1954	−1.2	1.7	4.6	3.1	..	..	5.9	7.9	−1.5	−0.9
1955	9.4	0.7	4.4	3.1	..	..	7.2	7.2	−2.2	−0.2
1956	8.4	3.6	3.4	3.6	..	..	−0.4	3.0	−4.0	0.8

Cont...

CANADA

YEAR	(1) GROWTH RATE	(2) INFLATION RATE	(3) UNEMPLOY-MENT RATE	(4) LONG-TERM INTEREST RATE	(5) REAL EXCHANGE RATE	(6) NOMINAL EXCHANGE RATE	(7) M1 GROWTH RATE	(8) M2 GROWTH RATE	(9) NET EXPORTS	(10) GOVERN-MENT BUDGET BALANCE
1957	2.4	2.3	4.6	4.2	..	..	0.3	2.9	−4.0	−0.2
1958	2.3	1.2	7.0	4.5	..	..	13.0	11.7	−2.8	−2.3
1959	3.8	2.2	6.0	5.0	..	..	−3.7	−0.6	−3.6	−1.2
1960	2.9	1.2	7.0	5.1	..	..	5.0	4.5	−2.8	−0.6
1961	2.8	0.8	7.1	5.0	..	..	6.3	8.2	−2.1	−2.4
1962	6.8	1.7	5.9	5.1	..	..	3.8	3.5	−1.8	−1.7
1963	5.2	2.1	5.5	5.1	..	..	3.6	6.6	−1.0	−1.4
1964	6.7	2.5	4.7	5.1	..	..	6.4	7.5	−0.8	0.1
1965	6.7	3.2	3.9	5.3	..	..	6.6	11.0	−2.0	0.4
1966	6.9	4.5	3.6	5.7	..	..	7.8	6.4	−1.9	−0.3
1967	3.3	3.7	4.1	6.0	..	..	7.5	14.4	−0.8	−1.0
1968	5.9	3.0	4.8	6.7	..	..	7.1	14.1	−0.4	−0.7
1969	5.4	4.3	4.7	7.6	..	..	3.0	3.3	−1.3	1.2
1970	2.6	4.4	5.9	8.0	..	..	5.5	11.1	1.1	0.3
1971	5.8	3.1	6.4	7.0	..	..	17.5	12.3	1.7	−0.1
1972	5.7	5.3	6.3	7.2	..	..	14.1	10.5	0.9	−0.5
1973	7.7	8.1	5.6	7.6	..	..	11.3	14.2	1.4	0.3
1974	4.4	12.6	5.3	8.9	..	..	6.2	20.1	0.3	0.8
1975	2.6	9.0	6.9	9.0	123.8	105.0	21.8	15.0	−1.4	−2.2
1976	6.2	8.0	7.1	9.2	130.4	116.5	1.6	12.6	−0.5	−1.7
1977	3.6	5.9	8.1	8.7	119.9	109.1	12.0	14.0	0.0	−3.4
1978	4.6	5.7	8.3	9.2	107.8	97.3	8.0	10.7	0.5	−4.5
1979	3.9	9.1	7.4	10.2	103.8	93.9	3.7	15.8	0.6	−3.4
1980	1.5	9.6	7.5	12.3	103.8	93.6	10.1	18.7	1.8	−3.4
1981	3.7	9.8	7.5	15.0	104.9	99.7	0.8	15.1	1.1	−2.1
1982	−3.2	8.0	11.0	14.4	105.5	102.4	2.8	9.4	3.8	−5.4
1983	3.2	4.8	11.8	11.8	107.6	106.9	8.7	5.8	3.4	−6.2
1984	6.3	3.0	11.2	12.7	104.7	104.9	0.5	4.4	3.5	−6.8
1985	4.8	2.5	10.5	11.1	100.0	100.0	9.9	9.5	2.4	−6.6
1986	3.3	2.3	9.5	9.5	91.7	93.7	5.2	8.7	0.9	−4.7
1987	4.0	4.6	8.8	10.0	92.4	99.8	8.5	10.1	0.9	−3.9
1988	4.4	4.6	7.8	10.2	98.1	112.5	7.1	7.6	0.7	−3.5
1989	3.0	4.6	7.5	9.9	103.8	130.2	2.3	13.1	0.1	−3.5
1990	0.9	3.0	8.1	10.8	103.2	139.4	−1.9	10.6	0.4	−3.7

Definitions:

(1) *Growth rate* is the annual percentage rate of change of real Gross Domestic Product.
(2) *Inflation rate* is the annual percentage rate of change of the Gross Domestic Product deflator.
(3) *Unemployment rate* is the annual average unemployment rate.
(4) *Long-term interest rate* is the rate on long-term Government of Canada bonds (10 years and over).
(5) *Real effective exchange rate* as calculated by the International Monetary Fund.
(6) *Nominal effective exchange rate* as calculated by the International Monetary Fund.
(7) *M1 growth rate* is the growth rate of the narrow money supply.
(8) *M2 growth rate* is the growth rate of the broad money supply.
(9) *Net exports* is exports minus imports (national accounts basis) as a percentage of its Gross Domestic Product.
(10) *Government budget balance* is the federal budget balance as a percentage of its Gross Domestic Product.

Sources:

(1) CANSIM series D20463, Statistics Canada and F. H. Leacy (Ed.), *Historical Statistics of Canada (HSC)*, Second Edition, Statistics Canada, Ottawa, 1983, series F-55, linked.
(2) CANSIM series D20556, Statistics Canada and *HSC*, ratio of series F-13 to F-55, linked.
(3) CANSIM series D768478, Statistics Canada and *HSC*, series D-132 as percentage of series D-127.
(4) *Bank of Canada Review*, Bank of Canada, Ottawa, (various issues) and *HSC*, series J-475.
(5) *International Financial Statistics*, International Monetary Fund, Washington, D.C.
(6) *International Financial Statistics*, International Monetary Fund, Washington, D.C.
(7) CANSIM series B1627, Statistics Canada and Bank of Canada.
(8) CANSIM series B1630, Statistics Canada and Bank of Canada and *HSC*, sum of series J-3 and J-9.
(9) CANSIM series D20476 minus D20480 as a percentage of D20000.
(10) CANSIM series D20193 as a percentage of D20000 and *HSC*, series H-18 minus H-34 as a percentage of F-13.

APPENDIX B

Data for France, Germany, Italy, Japan, the United Kingdom, and the United States: 1960 to 1990

FRANCE

YEAR	(1) GROWTH RATE	(2) INFLATION RATE	(3) UNEMPLOYMENT RATE	(4) LONG-TERM INTEREST RATE	(5) REAL EXCHANGE RATE	(6) NOMINAL EXCHANGE RATE	(7) M1 GROWTH RATE	(8) M2 GROWTH RATE	(9) CURRENT ACCOUNT BALANCE	(10) GOVERNMENT BUDGET BALANCE
1960	7.2	3.5	1.4	5.2	..	..	12.3	16.0	..	−1.4
1961	5.5	3.4	1.2	5.1	..	..	16.5	20.2	..	−1.4
1962	6.7	4.6	1.4	5.0	..	..	16.9	18.1	..	−1.7
1963	5.3	6.4	1.5	5.0	..	..	16.7	16.6	..	−2.0
1964	6.5	4.2	1.4	5.1	..	..	10.3	11.4	..	−0.4
1965	5.3	2.2	1.5	5.3	..	..	8.9	11.2	..	0.0
1966	5.2	2.9	1.8	5.4	..	..	8.9	12.3	..	−0.4
1967	4.7	3.2	1.9	5.7	..	..	6.2	13.5	0.2	−1.1
1968	4.3	4.3	2.6	5.9	..	..	5.5	16.8	−0.9	−1.5
1969	7.0	6.5	2.3	7.6	..	..	6.1	11.2	−1.2	−0.5
1970	5.7	7.1	2.4	8.1	..	..	−1.3	9.2	−0.1	0.5
1971	5.4	5.7	2.6	7.7	..	..	13.8	19.9	0.1	−0.4
1972	5.9	5.5	2.7	7.4	..	..	13.1	21.0	−0.1	0.7
1973	5.4	8.5	2.6	8.3	..	..	9.9	16.1	0.6	0.4
1974	3.2	11.7	2.8	10.5	..	..	12.6	18.7	−1.4	0.5
1975	0.2	12.6	4.0	9.5	112.2	143.0	9.9	15.9	0.8	−2.6
1976	5.2	10.0	4.4	9.2	110.9	138.6	14.9	17.5	−0.9	−1.0
1977	3.0	9.4	4.9	9.6	105.0	131.5	7.3	13.0	−0.1	−1.2
1978	3.3	10.1	5.2	9.0	104.5	129.3	12.2	13.5	1.5	−1.4
1979	3.2	10.1	5.9	9.5	106.0	129.5	14.4	14.3	0.9	−1.5
1980	1.6	11.4	6.3	13.0	109.5	129.9	7.7	10.8	−0.6	−0.1
1981	1.2	11.4	7.4	15.8	105.5	120.5	11.6	11.2	−0.8	−2.3
1982	2.5	11.7	8.1	15.7	105.8	111.1	11.0	11.0	−2.2	−3.4
1983	0.7	9.7	8.3	13.6	100.8	103.3	9.9	9.8	−1.0	−3.5
1984	1.3	7.5	9.7	12.5	99.8	99.1	10.9	9.9	−0.2	−2.7
1985	1.9	5.8	10.2	10.9	100.0	100.0	8.8	7.7	0.0	−2.7
1986	2.3	5.1	10.4	8.4	99.4	102.8	8.7	8.4	0.3	−3.3
1987	2.4	2.8	10.5	9.4	97.2	103.0	4.4	6.0	−0.5	−1.4
1988	3.9	3.0	10.0	9.1	95.0	100.9	1.8	5.6	−0.4	−2.3
1989	3.7	3.4	9.4	8.8	92.7	99.7	7.3	5.7	−0.4	−2.4
1990	2.8	2.0	8.9	10.0	96.6	104.8	3.4	0.6	−0.8	..

GERMANY

YEAR	(1) GROWTH RATE	(2) INFLATION RATE	(3) UNEMPLOY-MENT RATE	(4) LONG-TERM INTEREST RATE	(5) REAL EXCHANGE RATE	(6) NOMINAL EXCHANGE RATE	(7) M1 GROWTH RATE	(8) M2 GROWTH RATE	(9) CURRENT ACCOUNT BALANCE	(10) GOVERN-MENT BUDGET BALANCE
1960	16.1	4.2	1.3	6.4	..	..	8.8	13.6	1.5	−0.6
1961	5.1	4.3	0.8	5.9	..	..	9.4	11.5	0.9	0.3
1962	4.4	4.2	0.7	5.9	..	..	10.6	11.5	−0.6	−0.4
1963	3.0	2.9	0.8	6.1	..	..	6.9	11.3	0.2	−0.7
1964	6.7	3.0	0.4	6.2	..	..	8.6	12.6	0.0	−0.2
1965	5.6	3.5	0.3	7.1	..	..	9.5	13.5	−1.5	−0.4
1966	2.5	3.7	0.2	8.1	..	..	4.5	11.7	0.1	−0.5
1967	−0.2	1.5	1.3	7.0	..	..	3.2	11.5	2.0	−1.7
1968	6.3	1.5	1.5	6.5	..	..	8.3	12.3	2.2	−0.8
1969	7.5	4.2	0.9	6.8	..	..	8.6	13.4	1.3	0.3
1970	5.1	7.6	0.8	8.3	..	..	6.8	8.3	0.5	1.0
1971	2.9	8.0	0.9	8.0	..	..	12.3	11.9	0.4	0.8
1972	4.2	5.3	0.8	7.9	..	..	13.7	13.5	0.4	0.7
1973	4.7	6.4	0.8	9.3	..	..	5.0	10.8	1.5	1.4
1974	0.3	7.1	1.6	10.4	..	..	6.1	7.4	2.8	−0.7
1975	−1.6	6.0	3.6	8.5	103.3	76.9	14.1	9.0	1.1	−3.6
1976	5.4	3.6	3.7	7.8	104.8	81.8	10.0	10.6	0.8	−2.8
1977	3.0	3.7	3.6	6.2	111.3	88.1	8.1	8.5	0.8	−2.1
1978	2.9	4.3	3.5	5.8	114.2	92.6	13.5	10.0	1.4	−2.1
1979	4.1	4.0	3.2	7.4	115.2	96.8	7.2	8.2	−0.7	−2.0
1980	1.4	4.8	3.0	8.5	111.4	97.1	2.4	3.5	−1.7	−1.8
1981	0.2	4.0	4.4	10.4	101.6	92.4	9.0	4.8	−0.5	−2.4
1982	−0.6	4.4	6.1	9.0	101.9	97.4	3.2	6.1	0.8	−2.0
1983	1.5	3.3	8.0	7.9	103.7	101.1	10.3	6.7	0.8	−2.0
1984	2.8	2.0	7.0	7.8	98.3	100.0	3.4	4.8	1.6	−1.8
1985	2.0	2.2	7.2	6.9	100.0	100.0	4.1	5.3	2.7	−1.1
1986	2.3	3.1	6.5	5.9	111.3	108.8	8.7	6.1	4.5	−0.9
1987	1.8	2.0	6.2	5.8	121.3	115.4	9.4	7.0	4.1	−1.1
1988	3.7	1.5	6.1	6.1	122.3	114.6	10.1	5.8	4.2	−1.5
1989	3.8	2.1	5.6	7.1	121.4	113.6	6.5	4.5	4.7	−0.1
1990	4.5	3.6	5.2	8.9	129.1	119.1	13.4	18.6	3.0	..

ITALY

YEAR	(1) GROWTH RATE	(2) INFLATION RATE	(3) UNEMPLOY-MENT RATE	(4) LONG-TERM INTEREST RATE	(5) REAL EXCHANGE RATE	(6) NOMINAL EXCHANGE RATE	(7) M1 GROWTH RATE	(8) M2 GROWTH RATE	(9) CURRENT ACCOUNT BALANCE	(10) GOVERN-MENT BUDGET BALANCE
1960	..	−3.3	5.6	5.0	..	..	13.0	13.8	0.8	−1.6
1961	8.2	2.8	5.1	5.2	..	..	14.1	14.8	1.1	−1.4
1962	6.2	5.8	4.6	5.8	..	..	45.6	32.9	4.5	−2.0
1963	5.6	8.5	3.9	6.1	..	..	10.5	13.8	−1.3	−2.4
1964	2.8	6.5	4.3	7.4	..	..	−21.4	4.5	1.1	−2.3
1965	3.3	4.2	5.3	6.9	..	..	16.9	14.5	3.5	−4.0
1966	6.0	2.2	5.7	6.5	..	..	14.4	14.7	3.1	−4.3
1967	7.2	2.8	5.3	6.6	..	..	14.0	13.4	2.1	−2.7
1968	6.5	1.7	5.6	6.7	..	..	15.8	13.4	3.2	−4.0
1969	6.1	4.1	5.6	6.9	..	..	17.9	13.2	3.1	−3.1
1970	5.3	6.9	5.3	9.0	..	..	26.4	13.8	0.8	−5.1
1971	0.0	16.0	5.3	8.3	..	..	24.3	15.7	1.4	−6.5
1972	4.3	3.6	5.3	7.5	..	..	18.4	18.7	1.5	−7.4
1973	7.1	14.4	6.3	7.4	..	..	21.9	20.6	−1.5	−8.7
1974	5.4	19.8	6.2	9.9	..	..	18.3	20.7	−4.3	−9.9
1975	−2.7	16.5	5.3	11.5	100.8	208.2	7.7	18.9	−0.2	−15.5
1976	6.3	18.7	5.8	13.1	93.2	173.8	20.5	22.6	−1.4	−11.3
1977	3.7	18.2	6.6	14.6	91.2	159.3	19.7	20.4	1.0	−11.4
1978	3.7	14.1	7.0	13.7	88.6	148.4	23.6	22.3	2.1	−8.3
1979	6.0	15.3	7.6	14.1	93.1	142.4	24.2	21.0	1.5	−8.9
1980	4.2	20.0	7.5	16.1	94.0	137.0	16.1	14.4	−2.2	−10.7
1981	1.0	19.8	8.3	20.6	91.8	122.9	10.9	10.7	−2.4	−11.1
1982	0.3	15.9	9.0	20.9	92.4	115.0	11.8	12.3	−1.6	−9.9
1983	1.1	14.9	9.8	18.0	97.6	111.2	15.1	16.5	0.3	−11.3
1984	3.0	11.4	10.2	15.0	100.8	105.8	12.3	12.3	−0.6	−13.1
1985	2.6	8.9	10.1	13.0	100.0	100.0	13.6	13.9	−0.8	−13.3
1986	2.6	7.5	10.5	10.5	100.6	101.4	10.0	8.8	0.5	−14.3
1987	3.0	6.1	10.9	9.7	102.9	101.2	10.1	10.7	−0.2	−15.0
1988	4.2	5.7	11.0	10.2	101.9	97.8	7.2	7.9	−0.7	−14.1
1989	3.2	5.9	10.9	10.7	110.2	98.5	8.4	9.7	−1.2	−11.2
1990	1.6	7.9	9.9	11.5	117.0	100.6	7.9	9.9	..	−11.2

JAPAN

YEAR	(1) GROWTH RATE	(2) INFLATION RATE	(3) UNEMPLOYMENT RATE	(4) LONG-TERM INTEREST RATE	(5) REAL EXCHANGE RATE	(6) NOMINAL EXCHANGE RATE	(7) M1 GROWTH RATE	(8) M2 GROWTH RATE	(9) CURRENT ACCOUNT BALANCE	(10) GOVERNMENT BUDGET BALANCE
1960	13.3	5.7	1.6	..	..	..	18.1	20.0	−2.2	0.3
1961	14.5	7.9	1.4	..	..	..	22.6	21.0	−0.1	0.3
1962	7.0	3.6	1.3	..	..	..	13.0	17.3	−1.3	−0.3
1963	10.5	4.5	1.3	..	..	..	30.9	25.3	−0.7	−0.8
1964	13.1	4.4	1.1	..	..	..	38.2	26.4	1.1	−1.1
1965	5.1	5.1	1.2	..	..	..	16.8	16.7	1.4	−1.6
1966	10.5	5.1	1.3	6.9	..	..	16.3	17.4	−0.2	−2.4
1967	10.4	6.2	1.3	6.9	..	..	13.4	15.7	0.8	−1.6
1968	12.5	5.3	1.2	7.0	..	..	14.6	15.3	1.4	−1.3
1969	12.1	5.0	1.1	7.1	..	..	18.4	17.3	1.2	−1.0
1970	9.5	7.7	1.1	7.2	..	..	18.3	17.7	2.9	−0.4
1971	4.3	5.6	1.2	7.3	..	..	25.5	21.1	2.9	−0.2
1972	8.5	5.6	1.4	6.7	..	..	22.1	23.1	0.0	−1.6
1973	7.9	12.9	1.3	7.3	..	..	26.1	23.0	0.0	−1.6
1974	−1.4	20.8	1.4	9.3	..	..	13.1	12.9	−1.0	−1.3
1975	2.7	7.7	1.9	9.2	104.2	61.4	10.3	12.7	−0.1	−4.8
1976	4.8	7.2	2.0	8.7	102.9	64.6	14.2	15.2	0.7	−2.0
1977	5.3	5.8	2.0	7.3	110.8	71.2	7.0	11.4	1.6	−6.2
1978	5.2	4.8	2.2	6.1	127.9	86.5	10.8	11.9	1.7	−6.5
1979	5.3	3.0	2.1	7.7	110.9	79.7	9.9	11.1	−0.9	−5.3
1980	4.3	3.8	2.0	9.2	100.1	76.3	8.0	7.9	−1.0	..
1981	3.7	3.2	2.2	8.7	109.0	87.5	3.7	8.8	0.4	..
1982	3.1	1.9	2.4	8.1	97.1	83.0	7.1	9.1	0.6	..
1983	3.2	0.8	2.6	7.4	101.7	91.8	3.0	6.6	1.8	..
1984	5.1	1.2	2.7	6.8	100.7	97.9	2.9	6.8	2.8	..
1985	4.7	1.5	2.6	6.3	100.0	100.0	4.6	7.8	3.7	..
1986	2.7	1.7	2.8	4.9	122.9	124.4	7.4	9.1	4.4	..
1987	4.6	−0.3	2.8	4.2	128.4	133.2	9.0	10.2	3.6	..
1988	5.7	0.6	2.5	4.3	137.8	147.4	7.7	11.2	2.8	..
1989	4.8	1.6	2.2	5.1	131.1	142.0	4.6	10.0	2.0	..
1990	7.1	1.7	2.1	7.4	115.5	126.0	4.5	8.2	1.2	..

UNITED KINGDOM

YEAR	(1) GROWTH RATE	(2) INFLATION RATE	(3) UNEMPLOY-MENT RATE	(4) LONG-TERM INTEREST RATE	(5) REAL EXCHANGE RATE	(6) NOMINAL EXCHANGE RATE	(7) M1 GROWTH RATE	(8) M2 GROWTH RATE	(9) CURRENT ACCOUNT BALANCE	(10) GOVERN-MENT BUDGET BALANCE
1960	5.0	0.9	1.5	5.8	..	..	3.1	..	−7.9	−1.2
1961	3.0	3.6	1.5	6.3	..	..	0.7	2.7	−0.1	−0.8
1962	0.8	4.0	1.8	5.9	..	..	0.8	−2.0	3.1	0.3
1963	4.5	1.9	2.2	5.4	..	..	5.9	8.7	2.8	−0.5
1964	5.3	3.5	2.5	6.0	..	..	5.4	5.5	−8.9	−1.2
1965	2.2	5.1	2.2	6.6	..	..	3.1	7.6	−1.7	−1.6
1966	2.0	4.6	2.2	6.9	..	..	3.1	3.5	1.6	−1.4
1967	2.7	3.0	3.3	6.8	..	..	3.9	10.8	−7.5	−2.8
1968	4.2	4.2	3.1	7.6	..	..	4.5	7.1	−6.4	−1.7
1969	1.3	5.4	2.9	9.0	..	..	−0.5	3.1	6.2	1.9
1970	2.8	7.0	3.0	9.2	..	..	7.1	9.5	9.2	1.8
1971	2.8	9.4	3.6	8.9	..	..	13.3	13.2	11.4	−0.7
1972	2.4	8.2	4.0	8.9	..	..	16.7	27.9	2.0	−2.7
1973	7.7	7.1	3.0	10.7	..	..	10.0	27.5	−1.3	−3.4
1974	−1.0	15.0	2.9	14.8	..	..	3.5	12.9	−3.8	−4.6
1975	−0.7	27.2	4.3	14.4	81.9	125.0	15.1	..	−1.4	−7.3
1976	3.7	15.1	5.6	14.4	73.6	107.1	14.6	..	−0.7	−5.7
1977	1.0	14.0	6.0	12.7	71.4	101.2	13.5	9.5	−0.1	−3.4
1978	3.9	11.1	5.9	12.5	76.4	101.1	20.3	14.6	0.6	−5.2
1979	2.3	14.4	5.0	13.0	87.7	107.0	12.2	12.5	−0.2	−5.7
1980	−1.9	19.5	6.4	13.8	105.0	117.7	4.4	18.5	1.4	−4.7
1981	−1.1	11.4	9.8	14.7	112.4	119.1	10.2	..	2.8	−4.8
1982	1.3	7.6	11.3	12.9	107.9	113.7	11.8	..	1.7	−3.4
1983	3.7	5.3	12.5	10.8	101.9	105.3	16.0	..	1.3	−4.4
1984	1.8	4.6	11.7	10.7	101.0	100.6	14.2	..	0.6	−3.2
1985	3.8	5.6	11.2	10.6	100.0	100.0	15.7	11.2	1.0	−3.2
1986	3.5	3.6	11.2	9.9	94.2	91.6	22.2	..	0.0	−1.9
1987	4.4	5.3	10.3	9.5	94.0	90.1	25.0	..	−1.1	−0.8
1988	3.9	6.6	8.4	9.4	100.0	95.5	13.6	17.4	−3.2	1.4
1989	..	..	6.9	9.6	98.7	92.7	11.3	19.5	−4.1	1.0
1990	..	..	6.2	11.1	99.2	91.3	10.0	11.0	−7.7	0.8

UNITED STATES

YEAR	(1) GROWTH RATE	(2) INFLATION RATE	(3) UNEMPLOY-MENT RATE	(4) LONG-TERM INTEREST RATE	(5) REAL EXCHANGE RATE	(6) NOMINAL EXCHANGE RATE	(7) M1 GROWTH RATE	(8) M2 GROWTH RATE	(9) CURRENT ACCOUNT BALANCE	(10) GOVERN-MENT BUDGET BALANCE
1960	1.0	1.6	5.5	4.4	..	..	0.5	4.9	1.1	0.6
1961	1.1	1.0	6.7	4.4	..	..	3.2	7.4	1.4	−0.7
1962	2.2	2.2	5.5	4.3	..	..	1.9	8.1	1.2	−0.7
1963	1.7	1.6	5.7	4.3	..	..	3.7	8.4	1.4	0.0
1964	2.3	1.5	5.2	4.4	..	..	4.6	8.0	1.7	−0.5
1965	2.4	2.7	4.5	4.5	..	..	4.7	8.1	1.4	0.1
1966	2.4	3.6	3.8	5.1	..	..	2.5	4.5	1.0	−0.2
1967	1.2	2.6	3.8	5.5	..	..	6.5	9.3	0.9	−1.6
1968	1.8	5.0	3.6	6.2	..	..	7.7	8.0	0.6	−0.7
1969	1.0	5.6	3.5	7.0	..	..	3.3	4.1	0.6	0.9
1970	−0.1	5.5	4.9	8.0	..	..	5.1	6.5	0.8	−1.2
1971	1.2	5.7	5.9	7.4	..	..	6.5	13.5	0.6	−2.0
1972	2.1	4.7	5.6	7.2	..	..	9.2	13.0	0.3	−1.4
1973	2.2	6.5	4.9	7.4	..	..	5.5	6.9	1.2	−0.4
1974	−0.2	9.1	5.6	8.6	..	..	4.4	5.5	1.1	−0.8
1975	−0.5	9.8	8.5	8.8	76.4	75.8	4.8	12.6	1.9	−4.3
1976	2.1	6.4	7.7	8.4	79.0	79.8	6.5	13.7	1.1	−3.0
1977	2.0	6.7	7.1	8.0	76.9	78.5	8.1	10.6	0.1	−2.3
1978	2.2	7.3	6.1	8.7	69.2	70.4	8.2	8.0	0.2	−1.3
1979	1.1	8.9	5.8	9.6	68.1	68.5	6.8	7.8	0.7	−0.6
1980	−0.1	9.0	7.1	11.9	69.1	68.4	6.8	8.9	1.2	−2.2
1981	0.8	9.7	7.6	14.2	77.1	76.6	6.7	10.0	1.1	−2.1
1982	−1.1	6.4	9.7	13.8	87.2	85.5	8.7	8.9	0.8	−4.6
1983	1.5	3.9	9.6	12.0	93.2	89.7	9.8	12.0	−0.2	−5.2
1984	2.8	3.7	7.5	12.7	98.2	96.8	5.9	8.5	−1.6	−4.5
1985	1.4	3.0	7.2	11.4	100.0	100.0	12.3	8.4	−1.9	−4.9
1986	1.2	2.6	7.0	9.0	79.8	80.2	16.9	9.5	−2.3	−4.9
1987	1.5	3.1	6.2	9.4	68.9	70.2	3.5	3.5	−2.5	−3.5
1988	1.9	3.3	5.5	9.7	64.0	65.9	4.9	5.5	−1.5	−2.9
1989	1.1	4.1	5.3	9.3	65.4	69.3	0.9	4.9	−0.9	−2.6
1990	0.4	4.1	5.5	9.3	60.0	65.4	3.9	3.2	−0.7	−3.0

Definitions:

(1) *Growth rate* is the annual percentage rate of change of real Gross Domestic Product.

(2) *Inflation rate* is the annual percentage rate of change of the Gross Domestic Product deflator.

(3) *Unemployment rate* is the annual average unemployment rate calculated by the Organization for Economic Cooperation and Development using the same definition for all countries
(4) *Long-term interest rate* is the rate on long-term government bonds.
(5) *Real effective exchange rate* as calculated by the International Monetary Fund.
(6) *Nominal effective exchange rate* as calculated by the International Monetary Fund.
(7) *M1 growth rate* is the growth rate of the money supply as calculated by the International Monetary Fund.
(8) *M2 growth rate* is the growth rate of money plus quasi-money as calculated by the International Monetary Fund.
(9) *Current account balance* is the country's current account as a percentage of its Gross Domestic Product.
(10) *Government budget balance* is the country's central government budget balance as a percentage of its Gross Domestic Product.

Sources for France, Germany, Italy, Japan, and the United Kingdom

(1) *International Financial Statistics*, International Monetary Fund, Washington, D.C.
(2) *International Financial Statistics*, International Monetary Fund, Washington, D.C.
(3) *Main Economic Indicators*, OECD, Paris (monthly).
(4) *International Financial Statistics*, International Monetary Fund, Washington, D.C., country pages, line 61.
(5) *International Financial Statistics*, International Monetary Fund, Washington, D.C.
(6) *International Financial Statistics*, International Monetary Fund, Washington, D.C.
(7) *International Financial Statistics*, International Monetary Fund, Washington, D.C.
(8) *International Financial Statistics*, International Monetary Fund, Washington, D.C.
(9) *International Financial Statistics*, International Monetary Fund, Washington, D.C.
(10) *International Financial Statistics*, International Monetary Fund, Washington, D.C.

Sources for the United States:

(1) *Economic Report of the President, 1990* (Washington D.C.: U.S. Government Printing Office, 1990).
(2) *Economic Report of the President, 1990* (Washington D.C.: U.S. Government Printing Office, 1990).
(3) *Economic Report of the President, 1990* (Washington D.C.: U.S. Government Printing Office, 1990).
(4) *Economic Report of the President, 1990* (Washington D.C.: U.S. Government Printing Office, 1990), (Moody's Aaa).
(5) *International Financial Statistics*, International Monetary Fund, Washington, D.C.
(6) *International Financial Statistics*, International Monetary Fund, Washington, D.C.
(7) *Economic Report of the President, 1990* (Washington D.C.: U.S. Government Printing Office, 1990).
(8) *Economic Report of the President, 1990* (Washington D.C.: U.S. Government Printing Office, 1990).
(9) *Economic Report of the President, 1990* (Washington D.C.: U.S. Government Printing Office, 1990).
(10) *Economic Report of the President, 1990* (Washington D.C.: U.S. Government Printing Office, 1990).

Index